Green type indicates global example. 🍁 indicates Canadian feature.

SECOND CANADIAN EDITION

MICROECONOMICS

Paul Krugman
PRINCETON UNIVERSITY

Robin Wells

Iris Au
UNIVERSITY OF TORONTO

Jack Parkinson
UNIVERSITY OF TORONTO

WORTH PUBLISHERS
A Macmillan Higher Education Company

Vice President, Editorial: Charles Linsmeier

Associate Publisher: Steven Rigolosi

Executive Development Editor: Sharon Balbos

Marketing Manager: Thomas Digiano

Media Editor: Lukia Kliossis

Editorial Assistant: Carlos Marin

Director of Editing: Tracey Kuehn

Production Manager: Barbara Seixas

Associate Managing Editor: Lisa Kinne

Coordinating Editor: Debbie Smith of First Folio Resource Group Inc.

Managing Editor: Julie Kretchman of First Folio Resource Group Inc.

Developmental Editor: Bradley T. Smith of First Folio Resource Group Inc.

Art Director: Babs Reingold

Interior Designer: Babs Reingold

Cover Designer: Kevin Kall

Copy Editor: Arleane Ralph

Photo Editor: Cecilia Varas and Maria DeCambra

Photo Researcher: Elyse Rieder and Maria DeCambra

Composition: Kim Hutchinson of First Folio Resource Group Inc.

Printing and Binding: RR Donnelley

ISBN-13: 978-1-4292-4005-5

ISBN-10: 1-4292-4005-9

Library of Congress Control Number: 2012930398

Printed in the United States of America

Second printing 2015

Worth Publishers
41 Madison Avenue
New York, NY 10010

www.worthpublishers.com

Text Credits

Chapter 6, Source information for "Economics in Action" on page 181: Department of Finance Canada, Air Travel Demand Elasticities: Concepts, Issues and Measurement, www.fin.gc.ca/consultresp/Airtravel/airtravStdy_-eng.asp. **Chapter 11, Source information for "Economics in Action" on pages 352–353:** www.ercb.com, Dr. Dobb's Electronic Review of Computer Books. **Chapter 16, Source article for "Economics in Action" on page 495:** M. Gross, J. L. Sindelar, J. Mullahy, and R. Anderson, Policy Watch: Alcohol and Cigarette Taxes, *Journal of Economic Perspectives*, 7, 211–222, 1993. **Chapter 19, Source information for "For Inquiring Minds" box on page 573:** Nancy Stokey, A Quantitative Model of the British Industrial Revolution, 1780–1850. *Carnegie-Rochester Conference Series on Public Policy*, 55, 55–109, 2001. **Chapter 20, Source article for "For Inquiring Minds" box on page 620:** Joe Nocera, "Can We Turn Off Our Emotions When Investing?" *New York Times*, September 29, 2007. Retrieved from: http://www. nytimes.com/2007/09/29/business/29nocera.html?r=1&scp=1&sq=nocera%20 Zweig&st=cse&oref=slogin.

To beginning students everywhere,
which we all were at one time.

And, to Sophia & Jon and
Dora, Alena, & Hanna

Iris & Jack

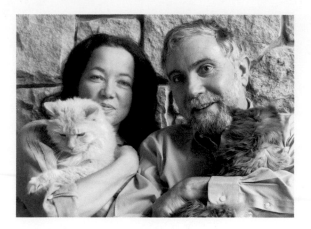

Paul Krugman, recipient of the 2008 Nobel Memorial Prize in Economic Sciences, is Professor of Economics at Princeton University, where he regularly teaches the principles course. He received his BA from Yale and his PhD from MIT. Prior to his current position, he taught at Yale, Stanford, and MIT. He also spent a year on the staff of the Council of Economic Advisers in 1982–1983. His research is mainly in the area of international trade, where he is one of the founders of the "new trade theory," which focuses on increasing returns and imperfect competition. He also works in international finance, with a concentration in currency crises. In 1991, Krugman received the American Economic Association's John Bates Clark medal. In addition to his teaching and academic research, Krugman writes extensively for nontechnical audiences. He is a regular op-ed columnist for the *New York Times*. His latest trade books, both bestsellers, are *End this Depression Now!*, a look at the recent global financial crisis and recovery, and *The Return of Depression Economics and the Crisis of 2008,* a history of recent economic troubles and their implications for economic policy. His earlier books, *The Conscience of a Liberal, Peddling Prosperity,* and *The Age of Diminished Expectations,* have become modern classics.

Robin Wells was a Lecturer and Researcher in Economics at Princeton University. She received her BA from the University of Chicago and her PhD from the University of California at Berkeley; she then did postdoctoral work at MIT. She has taught at the University of Michigan, the University of Southampton (United Kingdom), Stanford, and MIT. The subject of her teaching and research is the theory of organizations and incentives.

Iris Au is a Senior Lecturer in Economics at the University of Toronto Scarborough (UTSC). She received her BA, MA, and PhD from Simon Fraser University, British Columbia. She taught at Simon Fraser University and Kwantlen University College (now known as Kwantlen Polytechnic University) before joining UTSC. Currently, she teaches introductory and intermediate macroeconomics, international finance, economics of public policy, and topics on financial crises on a regular basis.

Jack Parkinson is a Senior Lecturer in Economics at the University of Toronto Scarborough (UTSC). He received his Hons. BA from Western University and his MA and PhD from the University of Toronto. He has worked as a corporate tax policy analyst for the Ontario Ministry of Finance while teaching during his lunchtime or evenings. Over the past twenty years he has taught on all three campuses of the University of Toronto. Currently, he teaches introductory microeconomics, intermediate and advanced macroeconomics, money and banking, economics of organization, and applied economic statistics.

BRIEF CONTENTS

CONTENTS

> *"Stories are good for us, whether we hear them, read them, write them, or simply imagine them. But stories that we read are particularly good for us. In fact I believe they are essential."*
> Frank Smith, *Reading: FAQ*

FROM PAUL AND ROBIN

More than a decade ago, when we began writing the first edition of this textbook, we had many small ideas: particular aspects of economics that we believed weren't covered the right way in existing textbooks. But we also had one big idea: the belief that an economics textbook could and should be built around narratives, that it should never lose sight of the fact that economics is, in the end, a set of stories about what people do.

Many of the stories economists tell take the form of models—for whatever else they are, economic models are stories about how the world works. But we believed that students' understanding of and appreciation for models would be greatly enhanced if they were presented, as much as possible, in the context of stories about the real world, stories that both illustrate economic concepts and touch on the concerns we all face as individuals living in a world shaped by economic forces.

Those stories have been integrated into every edition, including this one, which contains more stories than our earlier editions. Once again, you'll find them in the chapter opening stories, in boxed features like Economics in Action, For Inquiring Minds, and Global Comparisons, but now in our new Business Cases as well.

As in the previous edition, we've made extensive changes and updates in coverage to reflect current events—events that have come thick and fast in a turbulent, troubled world economy, which is affecting the lives and prospects of students everywhere. Currency is very important to us.

We have also expanded our coverage of business issues, both because business experience is a key source of economic lessons and because most students will eventually find themselves working in the business world. We are especially pleased with how the new Business Cases have turned out and how they augment the overall number and richness of our stories.

As you'll see, there's a great deal of new material, and there are some significant changes (and, we hope, improvements) in pedagogy. But we've tried to keep the spirit the same. This is a book about economics as the study of what people do and how they interact, a study very much informed by real-world experience.

FROM IRIS AND JACK

When we were approached about the possibility of adapting the latest edition of Paul and Robin's wonderful book for the Canadian market we were incredibly excited. The U.S. edition of the text, which started out as a top-tier product, has only improved with each new edition.

We believe the narratives approach adopted by Paul and Robin is an excellent way to expose students to the beauty of economics and its power to explain and understand the world we all live in.

Many of the narratives contained in the chapter opening stories, Economics in Action, For Inquiring Minds, Global Comparisons, and Business Cases have been altered, sometimes significantly, so as to infuse them with content relevant to Canadians. Of course Canadians, living in an open economy that is quite dependent on trade, are used to thinking about global economic issues and linkages. With that in mind a few of the narratives have not changed much from what appeared in the third U.S. edition. Throughout we have taken great care whenever altering the text so as to maintain the quality of the underlying narratives.

Chapter 7 was revised to deal specifically with the major types of taxes collected by different levels of government in Canada. Chapter 18, which provides a discussion of the welfare state, was almost entirely rewritten so as to properly cover the material from a Canadian perspective. The chapter also covers our health care system, comparing it to other systems around the world. Of course the coverage of many other concepts and theories have been given a Canadian treatment as well.

We are extremely pleased to be able to do our part to bring these narratives to a Canadian audience. If, after reading this text, some students decide that economics is really interesting and go on to take additional economics courses, we would be happy. But most importantly, we hope that all students feel this text greatly enhances and assists their study of economics.

What's New

Although the second U.S. edition was a resounding success, further establishing *Microeconomics* as one of the best-selling microeconomics textbooks in the United States, we learn with each new edition that there is always room for improvement. So, for the second Canadian edition, we undertook each revision with four goals in mind:

1. To make the book more relevant to Canadians
2. To expand the book's appeal to business students
3. To be as current and cutting edge as possible in the topics covered and the examples included
4. To make the book more teachable and accessible

We hope that the following revisions lead to a more successful teaching experience for you.

Selected Canadian Examples

- Introduction: Any Given Sunday (p. 1): Halifax's Spring Garden Road as an example of the market economy in action.

- Chapter 2: Economics in Action: Economists, Beyond the Ivory Tower (p. 43): Looking at jobs for Canadian economist outside academia.

- Chapter 3: Global Comparison: Pay More, Pump Less (p. 70): Comparing European fuel costs and consumption with those of Canada and the United States.

- Chapter 5: Economics in Action: The Lobsters of Atlantic Canada (p. 161): How quotas control the supply of lobster in Atlantic Canada.

- Chapter 6: Opener: More Precious Than a Flu Shot (p. 169): The impact on Canadians of the rush for H1N1 flu shots in 2009.

- Chapter 7: Economics in Action: Who Pays Canada's Payroll Taxes? (p. 205): Explaining how CPP (or QPP in Quebec) and EI affect Canadian paycheques.

- Chapter 7: Table 7-1: Results of Increases in Cigarette Taxes (p. 215): Calculating how increasing provincial and federal taxes on cigarettes can reduce sales but increase tax revenue.

- Chapter 8: For Inquiring Minds: Softwood Lumber Dispute (p. 257): A history of the contentious softwood lumber trade between Canada and the United States.

- Chapter 9: Business Case: Banks Help Cardholders Be CreditSmart and inControl (p. 289): Discussing new credit management systems offered by CIBC and Bank of Montreal.

- Chapter 11: Economics in Action: Don't Put Out the Welcome Mat (p. 361): How Canadian cities generate revenue from real estate through property tax and development charges.

- Chapter 13: Economics in Action: Change was Brewing (p. 425): Analyzing the end of the Canadian Wheat Board's monopoly.

- Chapter 14: Opener: Caught in the Act (p. 441): The 2013 price-fixing scandal involving chocolate producers Nestlé Canada, Mars Canada, and Hershey Canada Inc.

- Chapter 16: Positive Externalities in the Modern Economy (p. 506): The Technology Triangle of Kitchener, Waterloo, and Cambridge as an example of technology spillover.

- Chapter 17: Economics in Action: The St. Lawrence Seaway (p. 524): Analyzing the economic benefits of undertaking a major Canadian infrastructure project.

- Chapter 18: Table 18-1: Trends in the Canadian Poverty Rate, 1976–2011 (p. 541): Examining trends in the overall poverty rate by age group and by poverty measure.

- Chapter 18: Table 18-8: Health Care Expenditure Shares (p. 561): Breaking down how Canadian health care cost increased from 1983 to 2013.

- Chapter 20: Opener: A Tough Time for Insurers (p. 607): Examples of insured and uninsured disasters from around the world. Includes data on Canada's 2013 insurance claims: flooding in Alberta, the Lac-Mégantic explosion, and ice storms in eastern Canada.

New Business Case Studies

Now, more than ever, students entering the business community need a strong understanding of economic principles and their applications to business decisions. To meet this demand, every chapter now concludes with a real-world Business Case, showing how the economic issues discussed in the chapter play out in the world of entrepreneurs and bottom lines.

The cases range from the story of the trading firm Li & Fung, which is in the business of making money from comparative advantage, to a look at how smartphones are making the retail market for electronics much more competitive, to an examination of how lean production techniques at Boeing and Toyota have impacted comparative advantage in the airline and auto industries. The cases provide insight into business decision making in both Canadian and international companies and at recognizable firms like Air Canada, Amazon, and Priceline. Lesser-known firms are also used to illustrate economic concepts behind the supply costs of labour during seasonal work (Kiva Systems and the debate on human versus robotic order fulfillment), the role of incentives in the preservation of endangered species (Mauricedale Game Ranch), and the willingness of consumers to pay a premium for fair trade clothing (Knights Apparel's Alta Gracia factory in the Dominican Republic).

Each case is followed by critical thinking questions that prompt students to apply the economics they learned in the chapter to the real-life business situations. A full list of the Business Cases can be found on the inside front cover of this book.

New Coverage of Behavioural Economics

We have added a completely new section on behavioural economics to Chapter 9, "Decision Making by Individuals and Firms," because more and more principles instructors are including this groundbreaking perspective on "irrational" decision making in their courses. Originating in the research of Amos Tversky and Nobel laureate Daniel Kahneman, and further developed by a new generation of economists, this exciting subdiscipline probes multiple fallacies of the human mind.

Our coverage in the second Canadian edition includes such topics as how fairness intercedes in decision making, the effect of decisions made under risk and uncertainty, misperceptions of opportunity costs, and the dangers of overconfidence. We firmly believe that by learning how people make persistently irrational choices, students gain a deeper understanding of what constitutes rational economic decision making.

An Emphasis on Currency

The second Canadian edition is updated to remain the most current textbook on the market in its data, examples, and the opening stories—a currency that drives student interest in each chapter.

Economics in Action: A Richer Story to Be Told
Students and instructors alike have always championed *Microeconomics* for its applications of economic principles, especially our Economics in Action feature. In the second Canadian edition, we have revised or replaced a significant number of Economics in Action applications in every single chapter. We believe this provides the richness of content that drives student and instructor interest. All Economics in Action features are listed on the inside cover.

Opening Stories
We have always taken great care to ensure that each chapter's opening story illustrates the key concepts of that chapter in a compelling and accessible way. To continue to do so, almost every story in the second Canadian edition was updated and nearly half were replaced in an effort to bridge the gap between economic concepts and student interest in the world around them. New openers include the story of the Bombardier CSeries jets and their genesis in the wind tunnels that the Wright brothers built at Kitty Hawk; the story behind the 2013 scandal of price fixing in the chocolate industry; and the story of Maria, who in 2009 lost her job after 24 years and decided to return to school to become a social worker, as it reflects the decisions some mid-life workers must make in a depressed economy.

Coverage of Public Policy
The new edition continues to offer a significant examination of real-world policy that helps students see how the nation engages in public policy. We've included up-to-date coverage of both the sustainability of Canadian health care and the recent U.S. health care reform in Chapter 18, "The Economics of the Welfare State," plus much more.

A More Accessible and Visual Presentation

Streamlined Chapters Because less is often more, we've streamlined the exposition in a number of places where our desire for thoroughness got a little ahead of our pedagogy. The chapters on oligopoly and externalities, in particular, are now shorter and smoother in this edition.

A More Visual Exposition The research tells us that students read more online, in shorter bursts, and respond better to visual representations of information than ever before. In the second Canadian edition, we've worked hard to present information in the format that best teaches students.

We've shortened our paragraphs for easier reading and included numbered and bulleted lists whenever content would allow. You will find helpful new summary tables in this edition. And, most helpful, are the new visual displays in the book, including the dynamic representations of the factors that shift demand (p. 77) and the factors that shift supply (p. 84), among others.

Advantages of This Book

Our basic approach to textbook writing remains unchanged:

- **Chapters build intuition through realistic examples.** In every chapter, we use real-world examples, stories, applications, and case studies to teach the core concepts and motivate student learning. The best way to introduce concepts and reinforce them is through real-world examples; students simply relate more easily to them.

- **Pedagogical features reinforce learning.** We've crafted a genuinely helpful set of features that are described in the next section, "Tools for Learning."

- **Chapters are accessible and entertaining.** We use a fluid and friendly writing style to make concepts accessible and, whenever possible, we use examples that are familiar to students.

- **Although easy to understand, the book also prepares students for further coursework.** There's no need to choose between two unappealing alternatives: a textbook that is "easy to teach" but leaves major gaps in students' understanding, or a textbook that is "hard to teach" but adequately prepares students for future coursework. We offer the best of both worlds.

18

The Economics of the Welfare State

FEEDING MORE THAN 800 000

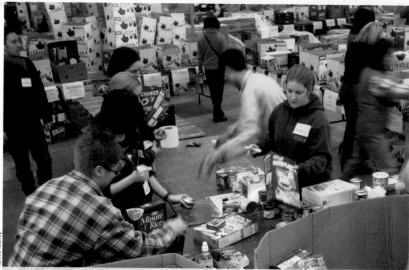

More than 800 000 Canadians turn to food banks every month.

Tannis Toohey

EVERY ONCE IN A WHILE, ESPEcially around holidays, you have probably heard Food Banks Canada asking for donations and organizing food drive campaigns. Why are food banks calling for such help? Each month, more than 800 000 Canadians seek help from food banks across the country because they face difficulty feeding themselves and their families.

The problem of hunger is not new. It has been around for centuries. The stunning fact is that the number of Canadians getting help from food banks has been rising. According to Food Banks Canada, the average number of people who turned to a food bank rose from 675 735 per month in 2008 to 833 098 in 2013. Unfortunately, in 2013 this rising demand for food bank services forced half of all food banks to cut back on the amount of food provided to each household

by Food Banks Canada, the people who turned to a food bank came from several different backgrounds including single-parent families, the working poor, individuals on welfare, and Canadians living on fixed income. The following provides a snapshot of those who got help from food banks in 2013:

- 36.4% of those turning to food banks are children and youth
- 4.3% of adults helped are over age 65
- 11.3% of people assisted are Aboriginal
- 50% of households helped receive social assistance (welfare)
- 11.5% have income from current or recent employment
  Source: Food Banks Canada.

All levels of government in Canada provide assistance to the less fortunate, either funding charitable organizations

providing support to financially troubled families.

It's the same around the world. Modern governments, especially in wealthy countries, devote a large chunk of their budgets to health care, income support for the elderly, aid to the poor, and other programs that reduce economic insecurity and, to some degree, income inequality. The collection of government programs devoted to these tasks is known as the *welfare state*.

We start this chapter by discussing the underlying rationale for welfare state programs. Then we describe and analyze the two main kinds of programs operating in Canada: income support programs, such as support for seniors via Canada/Quebec Pension Plan, Old Age Security, and Guaranteed Income Supplement payments, and health care programs—Canada's largest area of social spending by far. ◼

Economics in Action cases conclude every major text section. This much-lauded feature lets students immediately apply concepts they've read about to real phenomena.

Global Stamps identify which boxes, cases, and applications are global in focus.

ECONOMICS › IN ACTION

FREEING CANADA'S TRADE WITH THE WORLD

On December 5, 1996, government officials from Canada and Chile signed the Canada–Chile Free Trade Agreement (CCFTA). This bilateral trade agreement covering trade in both goods and services significantly liberalized trade between Canada and Chile. It was Canada's first free trade agreement with a South American country and was Chile's first comprehensive free trade agreement. The agreement, which was implemented on July 5, 1997, eliminated tariffs on 75% of the trade between the two countries and contained commitments to reduce non-tariff barriers.

Between 1997 and 2012, bilateral trade increased 350% and Canadian direct investment in Chile grew by over 300%. According to the Chilean government, Canada is the third largest investor overall in Chile—first in the mining sector—and the largest source of new direct investment in Chile in the past decade.

On April 16, 2012, Prime Minister Stephen Harper and Chilean president Sebastian Pinera signed an expanded CCFTA document. This amended agreement contains a section that will ensures Canadian financial services firms, such as banks and insurance companies, will enjoy preferential access to the Chilean market. It also contains new dispute settlement procedures and provisions on government procurement and customs procedures.

The government of Canada continues to negotiate other potential important trade agreements. For example, after years of negotiation, an agreement in principle on a CETA between Canada and the European Union (EU) was reached in late 2013. The EU is home to more than 500 million people and the world's largest economy, producing more than $16 trillion worth of output in 2012. In the joint press conference with EU president Jose Manuel Barroso, Prime Minister Harper said that the CETA "is the biggest deal our country has ever made. This is a historic win for Cana...   ...ership (TPP), which consists of ...   Chile, Japan, Malaysia, Mexico, ...   nd Vietnam. The TPP represen...   ombined output of $27.5 trillic...   ountries have held 18 rounds of...   ve free trade agreement among ...

Prime Minister Stephen Harper and Chilean president Sebastian Pinera at the signing of the expanded CCFTA.

Ivan Alvarado/Reuters/Landov

Check Your Understanding questions allow students to immediately test their understanding of a section. Solutions appear at the back of the book.

CHECK YOUR UNDERSTANDING 5-4

1. In Canada, over half of the steel consumed domestically is imported and steel is an input in many Canadian industries. The federal government has imposed import controls on steel and a variety of consumer goods. Explain why political lobbying to eliminate import controls on steel is more likely to be effective than lobbying to eliminate import controls on consumer goods such as clothing and eggs.

2. Over the years, the WTO has increasingly found itself adjudicating trade disputes that involve not just tariffs or quota restrictions but also restrictions based on quality, health, and environmental considerations. Why do you think this has occurred? What method would you, as a WTO official, use to decide whether a quality, health, or environmental restriction is in violation of a free trade agreement?

Solutions appe...

▼ Quick Review

- The three major justifications for trade protection are national security, job creation, and protection of infant industries.

- Despite the deadweight losses, import protections are often imposed because groups representing import-competing industries are more influential than groups of consumers.

- To further trade liberalization, countries engage in **international trade agreements.** Some agreements are among a small number of countries, such as the **North American Free Trade Agreement (NAFTA)** and the European Union (EU). The **World Trade Organization (WTO)** seeks to negotiate global trade agreements and referee trade disputes between members.

- Resistance to globalization has emerged in response to a surge in imports from relatively poor countries and the **ffshore outsourcing** of many jo... t had been considered safe... eign competition.

Quick Reviews offer students a short, bulleted summary of key concepts in the section to aid understanding.

GLOBAL COMPARISON

PAY MORE, PUMP LESS

For a real-world illustration of the law of demand, consider how gasoline consumption varies according to the prices consumers pay at the pump. Because of high taxes, gasoline and diesel fuel are more expensive in most European countries than in Canada and the United States. According to the law of demand, this should lead Europeans to buy less gasoline than Canadians and Americans—and they do. As you can see from the figure, Europeans consume less than half as much fuel per person as their counterparts in North America, mainly because they drive smaller cars with better fuel economy.

Prices aren't the only factor affecting fuel consumption, but they're a significant cause of the difference between European and North American fuel consumption per person.

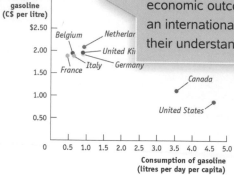

Sources: U.S. Energy Information Administra[tion]

Global Comparison boxes use real data from several countries and colourful graphs to illustrate how and why countries reach different economic outcomes. The boxes give students an international perspective that will expand their understanding of economics.

FOR INQUIRING MINDS

OCCUPY WALL STREET

In the fall of 2011, Zuccotti Park, a small open space in Manhattan's financial dis[trict] was taken over by protestors, part [of a] movement known as "Occupy Wall [Stre]et." The protestors had a number [of gri]evances, but the most pressing [of] their complaints about Wall Street [and] its perceived contribution to grow[ing in]equality. The Occupy Wall Street [take]over and protests inspired similar [prote]sts in hundreds of cities in dozens [of cou]ntries around the entire world, [in e]very province in Canada. "We [are the 99] percent!" became the move[ment's fa]vourite slogan, a reference to [the la]rge increase in share of income [goin]g to the top 1 percent of the popu[lation]. Wall Street, they charged, con[tribut]ed to growing inequality by paying [ba]nkers huge salaries and bonuses, [for] engaging in overly risky behaviour [lin]ked to the U.S. housing boom and [bust] of 2007–2009 that decimated the [emplo]yment…

Street, and the American finance industry in general, have made to the U.S. economy. Compared to other countries, the United States is a leader in financial services and innovation, generating billions annually in revenues, and attracting trillions of dollars of investment from abroad. High salaries on Wall Street, they contend, are simply the rewards to skill and hard work in the competitive market for talent on Wall Street.

What is incontrovertible, however, are the data that show that incomes in the finance industry have contributed to growing inequality in the United States. This is especially clear when you look not at the top percentile…

Many Occupy protests—like this one in Vancouver—began on October 15, 2011, which was called the global Day of Action.

Although financial industry people are a minority (18%), within this income elite—consisting also of executives, managers, lawyers, and others—they are greatly overrepresented since only about 6 percent of American workers are…

For Inquiring Minds boxes apply economic concepts to real-world events in unexpected and sometimes surprising ways, generating a sense of the power and breadth of economics. The feature furthers the book's goal of helping students build intuition with real-world examples.

PITFALLS

DEMAND VERSUS QUANTITY DEMANDED

When economists say "an increase in demand," they mean a rightward shift of the demand curve, and when they say "a decrease in demand," they mean a leftward shift of the demand curve—that is, when they're being careful. In ordinary speech, most people, including professional economists, use the word *demand* casually. For example, an economist might say "the

demand for air travel has doubl[ed in the] past 15 years, partly because of fall[ing] fares" when he or she really means that the *quantity demanded has doubled.*

It's [...] conv[...] ecor[...] make[...] in th[...] move[...] and [...]

Pitfalls boxes clarify concepts that are easily misunderstood by students new to economics.

TABLE 3-1	Factors That Shift Demand		
When this happens …	**… demand increases**	**But when this happens …**	**… demand decreases**
When the price of a substitute rises …		When the price of a substitute falls …	… demand for the original good decreases.
	… demand for the original good increases.		
When the price of a complement falls …	… demand for the original good increases.	When the price of a complement rises …	… demand for the original good decreases.

New! Summary Tables serve as a helpful study aid for readers. Many incorporate visuals to help students grasp important economic concepts.

BUSINESS CASE : Welfare State Entrepreneurs

"Wiggo Dalmo is a classic entrepreneurial type: the Working Class Kid Made Good." So began a profile in the January 2011 issue of *Inc.* magazine. Dalmo began as an industrial mechanic who worked for a large company, repairing mining equipment. Eventually, however, he decided to strike out on his own and start his own business. Momek, the company he founded, eventually grew into a $44 million, 150-employee operation that does a variety of contract work on oil rigs and in mines.

You can read stories like this all the time in business magazines. What was unusual about this particular article is that Dalmo and his company are Norwegian—and Norway, like other Scandinavian countries, has a very generous welfare state, supported by high levels of taxation. So what does Dalmo think of that system? He approves, saying that Norway's tax system is "good and fair," and he thinks the system is good for business. In fact, the *Inc.* article was titled, "In Norway, Start-Ups Say Ja to Socialism."

Why? After all, the financial rewards for being a successful entrepreneur are more limited in a country like Norway, with its high taxes. But there are other considerations. For example, a Canadian thinking of leaving a large company to start a new business needs to worry about whether he or she will be able to get supplementary health insurance, whereas a Norwegian in the same position is assured of health care regardless of employment. And the downside of failure is larger in North America, where minimal aid is offered to the unemployed.

Still, is Wiggo Dalmo an exceptional case? Table 18-10 shows the nations with the highest level of entrepreneurial activity, according to a study financed by the U.S. Small Business Administration, which tried to quantify the level of entrepreneurial activity in different nations. Canada and the United States made it into the top 10, but so did Norway. And the list also includes Denmark, New Zealand, Sweden, and Australia—all nations with high taxes and extensive social insurance programs.

The moral is that when comparing how business friendly different welfare state systems really are, you have to think a bit past the obvious question of the level of taxes.

TABLE 18-10 The Top 10 Entrepreneurial Countries

Rank	Country
1	Denmark
2	New Zealand
3	Ireland
4	Puerto Rico
5	Sweden
6	Canada
7	Australia
8	United States
9	Norway
10	Belgium

Source: Zoltan Acs and Laszlo Serb (2011) *The Global Entrepreneurship and Development Index 2010.*

QUESTIONS FOR THOUGHT

1. Why does Norway have to have higher taxes overall than the Canada?

2. This case suggests that government-paid health care helps entrepreneurs. How does this relate to the arguments we made for social insurance in the text?

3. How would the inc___ of people like Wiggo Dalmo be affected if Norwegian health

---

**New!
Business Cases**
close each chapter, applying key economic principles to real-life business situations in both American and international companies. Each case concludes with critical thinking questions.

SUMMARY

1. The **supply and demand model** illustrates how a **competitive market,** one with many buyers and ___llers, none of whom can influence the market pr___ works.

2. ___ __d schedule shows the **quantity** ___ epresented graphi- ___ __w of demand says ___ rd; that is, a higher ___ eople to demand a ___ l.

ing supply, they mean **shifts of the supply curve**—a change in the quantity supplied at any given price. An increase in supply causes a rightward shift of the supply curve. A decrease in supply causes a leftward shift.

8. There are six main factors that shift the supply curve:
   - A change in **input** prices
   - A change in the prices of related goods and services
   - A change in technology
   - A change in weather
   - A change in expectations

End-of-Chapter Reviews include a brief but complete summary of key concepts, a list of key terms, and a comprehensive, high-quality set of end-of-chapter Problems.

PROBLEMS

1. A survey indicated that chocolate is Canadians' favourite ice-cream flavour. For each of the following, indicate the possible effects on demand, supply, or both as well as equilibrium price and quantity of chocolate ice cream.

   a. A severe drought in Ontario causes dairy farmers to reduce the number of milk-producing cattle in their herds by a third. These dairy farmers supply cream that is used to manufacture chocolate ice cream.

   b. A new report by the Canadian Medical Association reveals that chocolate does, in fact, have significant ___

Case 2: There ___ which is repo___

   b. The market fc___
   Case 1: The C___
   Case 2: The p___

   c. The market fc___
   Case 1: People___
   Case 2: People___
   cooked break___

   d. The market fc___

KEY TERMS

Competitive market, p. 68
Supply and demand model, p. 68
Demand schedule, p. 69
Quantity demanded, p. 69
Demand curve, p. 70
Law of demand, p. 70
Shift of the demand curve, p. 71
Movement along the demand curve, p. 71

Substitutes, p. 73
Complements, p. 73
Normal good, p. 74
Inferior good, p. 74
Individual demand curve, p. 75
Quantity supplied, p. 78
Supply schedule, p. 78
Supply curve, p. 78
Shift of the supply curve, p. 79

Organization of This Book: What's Core, What's Optional

We realize that some of our chapters will be considered optional. Below and on the facing page is a list of what we view as core chapters and those that could be considered optional. We've annotated the list of chapters to indicate what they cover should you wish to consider incorporating them into your course.

Core	Optional
	Introduction: The Ordinary Business of Life Initiates students into the study of economics with basic terms and explains the difference between microeconomics and macroeconomics.
1. First Principles Outlines 12 principles underlying the study of economics: principles of individual choice, interaction between individuals, and economy-wide interaction.	
2. Economic Models: Trade-offs and Trade Employs two economic models—the production possibilities frontier and comparative advantage—as an introduction to gains from trade and international comparisons.	**Appendix 2A: Graphs in Economics** Offers a comprehensive review of graphing and math skills for students who would find a refresher helpful and to prepare them for better economic literacy.
3. Supply and Demand Covers the essentials of supply, demand, market equilibrium, surplus, and shortage.	**Appendix 3A: The Algebra of Demand, Supply, and Equilibrium** Offers a mathematical approach to the concepts of demand and supply, using algebra to determine the equilibrium price and quantity.
4. Consumer and Producer Surplus Introduces students to market efficiency, the ways markets fail, the role of prices as signals, and property rights.	
5. Price Controls and Quotas: Meddling with Markets Covers market interventions and their consequences: price and quantity controls, inefficiency, and deadweight loss.	
6. Elasticity Introduces the various elasticity measures and explains how to calculate and interpret them, including price, cross-price and income elasticity of demand, and price elasticity of supply.	**Appendix 6A: The Algebra of Elasticity** Offers a mathematical approach to the various elasticity measures.
7. Taxes Covers basic tax analysis along with a review of the burden of taxation and considerations of equity versus efficiency. The structure of taxation, tax policy, and public spending are also introduced.	
	8. International Trade Here we trace the sources of comparative advantage, consider tariffs and quotas, and explore the politics of trade protection. The chapter includes coverage on the controversy over imports from low-wage countries.
9. Decision Making by Individuals and Firms Microeconomics is a science of how to make decisions. The chapter focuses on marginal analysis ("either–or" and "how much" decisions) and the concept of sunk cost; it also includes a new section on behavioural economics, showing the limitations of rational thought.	
10. The Rational Consumer Provides a complete treatment of consumer behaviour for instructors who don't cover indifference curves, including the budget line, optimal consumption choice, diminishing marginal utility, and substitution effects.	**Appendix 10A: Consumer Preferences and Consumer Choice** Offers more detailed treatment for those who wish to cover indifference curves.

Core	Optional

Core

11. Behind the Supply Curve: Inputs and Costs
Develops the production function and the various cost measures of the firm, including discussion of the difference between average cost and marginal cost.

12. Perfect Competition and the Supply Curve
Explains the output decision of the perfectly competitive firm, its entry/exit decision, the industry supply curve, and the equilibrium of a perfectly competitive market.

13. Monopoly
A complete treatment of monopoly, including topics such as price discrimination and the welfare effects of monopoly.

14. Oligopoly
Streamlined for the new edition, the chapter focuses on defining the concept of oligopoly along with basic game theory in both a one-shot and repeated game context. Coverage of the kinked demand curve has moved online.

15. Monopolistic Competition and Product Differentiation
The chapter emphasizes instances in which students encounter monopolistic competition, covering the entry/exit decision, efficiency considerations, and advertising.

16. Externalities
Streamlined in the new edition, the chapter covers negative externalities and solutions to them, such as Coasian private trades, emissions taxes, and a system of tradable permits. Also examined are positive externalities (in a new section), technological spillovers, and network externalities.

17. Public Goods and Common Resources
Explains how to classify goods into four categories (private goods, common resources, public goods, and artificially scarce goods) based on excludability and rivalry in consumption, in the process clarifying why some goods but not others can be efficiently managed by markets.

Optional

Appendix 11A: Inverse Relationships Between Productivity and Cost
A derivation of the relationships between (1) the marginal product of labour and marginal cost and (2) the average product of labour and average cost.

18. The Economics of the Welfare State
Provides a comprehensive overview of the welfare state as well as its philosophical foundations. Examined in the chapter are health care economics (including new sections on the sustainability of Canada's health care spending and the 2010 U.S. health care reform), the problem of poverty, and the issue of income inequality.

19. Factor Markets and the Distribution of Income
Appendix 19A: Indifference Curve Analysis of Labour Supply
Covers the efficiency-wage model of the labour market as well as influence of education, discrimination, and market power. The appendix examines the labour-leisure trade-off and the backward bending labour supply curve.

20. Uncertainty, Risk, and Private Information
This unique, applied chapter explains attitudes toward risk, examines the benefits and limits of diversification, and considers private information, adverse selection, and moral hazard.

Supplements and Media

Worth Publishers is pleased to offer an enhanced and completely revised supplements and media package to accompany this textbook. The package has been crafted to help instructors teach their principles course and to give students the tools to develop their skills in economics.

For Instructors

Instructor's Resource Manual with Solutions Manual The Instructor's Resource Manual, is a resource meant to provide materials and tips to enhance the classroom experience. The Instructor's Resource Manual provides the following:

- Chapter-by-chapter learning objectives
- Chapter outlines
- Teaching tips and ideas that include:
  - Hints on how to create student interest
  - Tips on presenting the material in class
- Discussion of the examples used in the text, including points to emphasize with your students
- Activities that can be conducted in or out of the classroom
- Hints for dealing with common misunderstandings that are typical among students
- Web resources
- Solutions manual with detailed solutions to all of the end-of-chapter Problems from the textbook

Computerized Printed Test Bank *Coordinator and Consultant:* Doris Bennett, Jacksonville State University. The Test Bank is available in CD-ROM format for both Windows and Macintosh users. With this program, instructors can easily create and print tests and write and edit questions. Tests can be printed in a wide range of formats. The software's unique synthesis of flexible word-processing and database features creates a program that is extremely intuitive and capable. Totalling over 4500 questions, the Test Bank offers multiple-choice, true/false, and short-answer questions designed for comprehensive coverage of the text concepts. Questions have been checked for continuity with the text content, overall usability, and accuracy.

The Test Bank features include the following:

- To aid instructors in building tests, each question has been categorized according to its general *degree of difficulty.* The three levels are: *easy, moderate,* and *difficult.*

- *Easy* questions require students to recognize concepts and definitions. These are questions that can be answered by direct reference to the textbook.
- *Moderate* questions require some analysis on the student's part.
- *Difficult* questions usually require more detailed analysis by the student.
- Each question has also been categorized according to a *skill descriptor.* These include: *Fact-Based, Definitional, Concept-Based, Critical Thinking,* and *Analytical Thinking.*
  - *Fact-Based Questions* require students to identify facts presented in the text.
  - *Definitional Questions* require students to define an economic term or concept.
  - *Concept-Based Questions* require a straightforward knowledge of basic concepts.
  - *Critical Thinking Questions* require the student to apply a concept to a particular situation.
  - *Analytical Thinking Questions* require another level of analysis to answer the question. Students must be able to apply a concept and use this knowledge for further analysis of a situation or scenario.
- To further aid instructors in building tests, each question is conveniently cross-referenced to the appropriate topic heading in the textbook. Questions are presented in the order in which concepts are presented in the text.
- The Test Bank includes questions with tables that students must analyze to solve for numerical answers. It also contains questions based on the graphs that appear in the book. These questions ask students to use the graphical models developed in the textbook and to interpret the information presented in the graph. Selected questions are paired with scenarios to reinforce comprehension.

Lecture PowerPoint Presentation The enhanced PowerPoint presentation slides are designed to assist you with lecture preparation and presentations. The slides are organized by topic and contain graphs, data tables, and bulleted lists of key concepts suitable for lecture presentation. Key figures from the text are replicated and animated to demonstrate how they build. The slides have been designed to allow for easy editing of graphs and text. These slides can be customized to suit your individual needs by adding your own data, questions, and lecture notes.

Online Offering

CoursePacks Plug our content into your course management system. Whatever you teach, or whether you use Blackboard, WebCT, Desire2Learn, Angel, Sakai, or Moodle to manage your course, we have free content and support available. Registered instructors can download cartridges with no hassle, no strings attached. Content includes our most popular free resources and book-specific content. For more information, go to http://worthpublishers.com/catalog/Other/Coursepack.

Further Resources Offered

sapling learning

www.saplinglearning.com

Sapling Learning provides the most effective interactive homework and instruction that improves student-learning outcomes for the problem-solving disciplines.

Sapling Learning offers an enjoyable teaching and effective learning experience that is distinctive in three important ways:

- **Ease of Use:** Sapling Learning's easy-to-use interface keeps students engaged in problem solving, not struggling with the software.

- **Targeted Instructional Content:** Sapling Learning increases student engagement and comprehension by delivering immediate feedback and targeted instructional content.

- **Unsurpassed Service and Support:** Sapling Learning makes teaching more enjoyable by providing a dedicated Masters- or PhD-level colleague to service instructors' unique needs throughout the course, including content customization.

CourseSmart eBooks

http://www.coursesmart.com/ourproducts

CourseSmart eBooks offer the complete book in PDF format. Students can save money, up to 60% off the price of print textbooks. With the CourseSmart eBook, students have the ability to take notes, highlight, print pages, and more. A great alternative to renting print textbooks!

Worth Noting Worth Noting keeps you connected to your textbook authors in real time. Whether they were just on CNBC or published in the *New York Times*, this is the place to find out about it. Visit Worth Noting at http://blogs.worthpublishers.com/econblog/.

i>clicker Developed by a team of University of Illinois physicists, i>clicker is the most flexible and reliable classroom response system available. It is the only solution created *for* educators, *by* educators—with continuous product improvements made through direct classroom testing and faculty feedback. You'll love i>clicker, no matter your level of technical expertise, because the focus is on *your* teaching, *not the technology*. To learn more about packaging i>clicker with this textbook, please contact your local sales rep or visit www.iclicker.com.

Acknowledgments

Our deep appreciation and heartfelt thanks to the following reviewers, class-testers, and contributors whose input helped us shape this third U.S. edition.

Carlos Aguilar, *El Paso Community College*
Seemi Ahmad, *Dutchess Community College*
Farhad Ameen, *Westchester Community College*
Dean Baim, *Pepperdine University*
David Barber, *Quinnipiac College*
Janis Barry-Figuero, *Fordham University at Lincoln Center*
Hamid Bastin, *Shippensburg University*
Michael Bonnal, *University of Tennessee, Chattanooga*
Milicia Bookman, *Saint Joseph's University*
Anne Bresnock, *California State Polytechnic University, Pomona*
Colleen Callahan, *American University*
Giuliana Campanelli Andreopoulos, *William Patterson University*
Charles Campbell, *Mississippi State University*
Randall Campbell, *Mississippi State University*
Joel Carton, *Florida International University*
Andrew Cassey, *Washington State University*
Sanjukta Chaudhuri, *University of Wisconsin, Eau Claire*
Eric Chiang, *Florida Atlantic University*
Abdur Chowdhury, *Marquette University*
Chad Cotti, *University of Wisconsin, Oshkosh*
Maria DaCosta, *University of Wisconsin, Eau Claire*
James P. D'Angelo, *University of Cincinnati*
Orgul Demet Ozturk, *University of South Carolina*
Harold Elder, *University of Alabama*
Rudy Fichenbaum, *Wright State University*
Sherman Folland, *Oakland University*
Amanda Freeman, *Kansas State University*
Shelby Frost, *Georgia State University*
Sarah Ghosh, *University of Scranton*
Satyajit Ghosh, *University of Scranton*
Fidel Gonzalez, *Sam Houston State University*
Michael G. Goode, *Central Piedmont Community College*
Alan Gummerson, *Florida International University*
Eran Guse, *West Virginia University*
Don Holley, *Boise State University*
Scott Houser, *Colorado School of Mines*

Russell A. Janis, *University of Massachusetts, Amherst*
Jonatan Jelen, *The City College of New York*
Miles Kimball, *University of Michigan*
Colin Knapp, *University of Florida*
Stephan Kroll, *Colorado State University*
Vicky Langston, *Columbus State University*
Richard B. Le, *Cosumnes River College*
Yu-Feng Lee, *New Mexico State University*
Mary Lesser, *Iona College*
Solina Lindahl, *California Polytechnic State University*
Volodymyr Lugovskyy, *Indiana University*
Mark E. McBride, *Miami University*
Michael Mogavero, *University of Notre Dame*
Gary Murphy, *Case Western Reserve University*
Anna Musatti, *Columbia University*
Christopher Mushrush, *Illinois State University*
ABM Nasir, *North Carolina Central University*
Gerardo Nebbia, *El Camino College*
Pattabiraman Neelakantan, *East Stroudsburg University*
Pamela Nickless, *University of North Carolina, Asheville*
Nick Noble, *Miami University (Ohio)*
Walter Park, *American University*
Brian Peterson, *Central College*
Michael Polcen, *Northern Virginia Community College*
Reza Ramazani, *Saint Michael's College*
Ryan Ratcliff, *University of San Diego*
Robert Rebelein, *Vassar College*
Ken Roberts, *Southwestern University*
Greg Rose, *Sacramento City College*
Jeff Rubin, *Rutgers University, New Brunswick*
Jason C. Rudbeck, *University of Georgia*
Michael Sattinger, *State University of New York, Albany*
Elizabeth Sawyer Kelly, *University of Wisconsin, Madison*
Arzu Sen, *West Virginia University*
Marcia Snyder, *College of Charleston*
Liliana V. Stern, *Auburn University*
Adam Stevenson, *University of Michigan*
Eric Stuen, *University of Idaho*
Christine Tarasevich, *Del Mar College*
Henry S. Terrell, *George Washington University*
Mickey Wu, *Coe College*

We are indebted to the following reviewers for their suggestions and advice on improving the second Canadian edition.

Worku Aberra, *Dawson College*
Phil Curry, *University of Waterloo*
Philippe Ghayad, *Dawson College*

Susan Kamp, *University of Alberta*
Trien Nguyen, *University of Waterloo*
Shadab Qaiser, *York University*
Terri Rizzo, *Lakehead University*
John Richards, *Simon Fraser University*
Jonathan Rosborough, *St. Francis Xavier University*
Scott Skjei, *Acadia University*
C. Michael Wernerheim, *Memorial University of Newfoundland*
Andrew Wong, *University of Alberta*

We owe a huge debt of gratitude to Paul Krugman and Robin Wells who, with the assistance of many of the people named above, have created a wonderful text that is both a pleasure to read and a great tool for learning. We also benefitted from the extensive work undertaken by Anthony Myatt for the first Canadian edition.

We would like to thank all the fine people at Worth Publishers. In particular we are indebted to Chris Spavins who was the Worth sales representative that first recommended us for this project. Charles Linsmeier, publisher, skillfully guided the project along, providing us lots of freedom, but carefully nudging us or others whenever he sensed an improvement could be reached. Julia Jevmenova, field manager in the Canadian market, has provided plenty of support and marketing advice. We would also like to thank Tracey Kuehn, Barbara Seixas, Sharon Balbos, Craig Bleyer, and, of course, Elizabeth Widdicombe for making this project possible.

We have also benefitted greatly from all the hard work of the fantastic team at First Folio. Brad Smith patiently edited the drafts and acted as a sounding board for new ideas and refinements. Kim Hutchinson ensured the formatting and illustrating remained clear and concise. Arleane Ralph efficiently copy-edited and proofread the entire manuscript. Julie Kretchman acted as the project manager and helped make sure everyone had what they needed to stay on schedule.

We can honestly say that until you work on a project like this you truly don't understand the impact of the vast array of experts and professionals who are assembled to bring such an undertaking to completion. We are indebted to them all. Their assistance has not only made this text possible, it has made it much better.

Lastly, we would like to thank our families for all the love, support, and understanding they have provided us over the years. We hope that this book can help them, and the next generation of students, understand why we think economics is so cool.

Iris Au   *Jack Parkinson*

We must also thank the many people at Worth Publishers for their contributions. Elizabeth Widdicombe, president of Freeman and Worth, and Catherine Woods, senior vice president, played an important role in planning for this revision. We have Liz to thank for the idea that became the Business Case in each chapter. Charles Linsmeier, publisher, ably oversaw the revision and contributed throughout. A special thanks to Craig Bleyer, our original publisher at Worth and now national sales director, who put so much of his effort into making each edition a success. His keen instincts showed again in the revision plan for this edition.

Once again, we have had an incredible production and design team on the third U.S. edition, people whose hard work, creativity, and dedication paid off as we developed the second Canadian edition. Once again, you have outdone yourselves. Thank you all: Tracey Kuehn, Lisa Kinne, and Anthony Calcara for producing this book; Babs Reingold and Lyndall Culbertson for their beautiful interior design which is the basis for this second Canadian edition; Barbara Seixas, who worked her magic yet again despite the vagaries of the project schedule; Cecilia Varas and Elyse Rieder for photo research; Stacey Alexander for coordinating all the production of the supplemental materials.

Many thanks to Marie McHale for devising and coordinating the impressive collection of media and supplements that accompany our book. Thanks to the incredible team of supplements writers and coordinators who worked with Marie on the supplements and media package; we are forever grateful for your tireless efforts.

And most of all, special thanks to Sharon Balbos, executive development editor on each of our editions. Much of the success of this book is owed to Sharon's dedication and professionalism. As always, she kept her cool through rough spots. Sharon, we're not sure we deserved an editor as good as you, but we're sure that everyone involved as well as our adopters and their students have been made better off by your presence.

Paul Krugman   *Robin Wells*

Introduction: The Ordinary Business of Life

ANY GIVEN SUNDAY

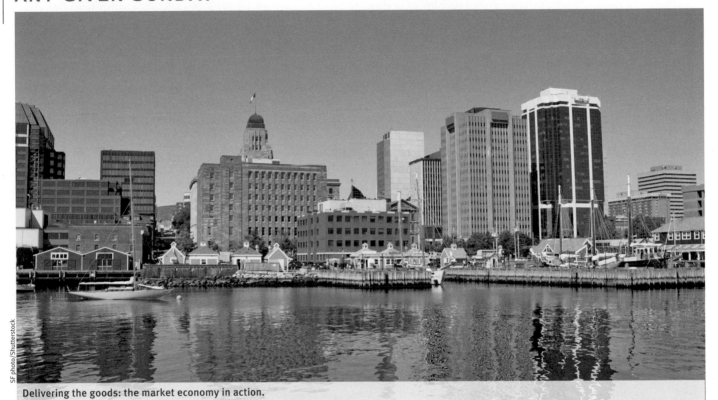

SF photo/Shutterstock

Delivering the goods: the market economy in action.

IT'S SUNDAY AFTERNOON IN MAY of 2013, and Spring Garden Road in downtown Halifax, Nova Scotia, is a busy place. Thousands of people crowd the more than 200 stores as well as the restaurants and coffee shops that line the road, while many more shop in the surrounding nine city blocks that make up the Spring Garden Road area. Most of the shoppers are cheerful—and why not? The stores in this area offer an extraordinary range of choice; you can buy everything from sophisticated electronic equipment to fashionable clothes to organic carrots. There are probably 100 000 distinct items available along that stretch of road and in the surrounding area. And most of these items are not luxury goods that only the rich can afford; they are products that

millions of Canadians can and do purchase every day.

The scene along Spring Garden Road on this day is, of course, perfectly ordinary—very much like the scene along hundreds of other stretches of road, all across Canada, that same afternoon. And the discipline of economics is mainly concerned with ordinary things. As the great nineteenth-century economist Alfred Marshall put it, economics is "a study of mankind in the ordinary business of life."

What can economics say about this "ordinary business"? Quite a lot, it turns out. What we'll see in this book is that even familiar scenes of economic life pose some very important questions—questions that economics can help answer. Among these questions are:

- How does our economic system work? That is, how does it manage to deliver the goods?

- When and why does our economic system go astray, leading people into counterproductive behaviour?

- Why are there ups and downs in the economy? That is, why does the economy sometimes have a "bad year"?

- Finally, why is the long run mainly a story of ups rather than downs? That is, why has Canada, along with other advanced nations, become so much richer over time?

Let's take a look at these questions and offer a brief preview of what you will learn in this book. ∎

1

The Invisible Hand

That ordinary scene in downtown Halifax would not have looked at all ordinary several centuries ago—say, to the people who General Cornwallis brought to the area in 1749 to establish a British community. Halifax has the second largest natural harbour in the world, but at that time the area was mostly unoccupied, and known mainly to the Mi'kmaq First Nations people.

Imagine that you could transport a Nova Scotian from 1749, or even from the time of the Halifax Explosion of 1917, forward in time to our own era. (Isn't that the plot of a movie? Several, actually.) What would this time traveller find amazing?

Surely the most amazing thing would be the sheer prosperity of modern Canada—the range of goods and services that ordinary families can afford. Looking at all that wealth, our transplanted traveller would wonder, "How can I get some of that?" Or perhaps she would ask herself, "How can my society get some of that?"

The answer is that to get this kind of prosperity, you need a well-functioning system for coordinating productive activities—the activities that create the goods and services people want and a means to get them to the people who want them. That kind of system is what we mean when we talk about the **economy.** And **economics** is the social science that studies the production, distribution, and consumption of goods and services.

An economy succeeds to the extent that it, literally, delivers the goods. A time traveller from the eighteenth century—or even from 1950—would be amazed at how many goods and services the modern Canadian economy delivers and at how many people can afford them. Compared with any past economy and with all but a few other countries today, Canada has an incredibly high standard of living.

So our economy must be doing something right, and the time traveller might want to compliment the person in charge. But guess what? There isn't anyone in charge. Canada has a **market economy,** in which production and consumption are the result of decentralized decisions by many firms and individuals. There is no central authority telling people what to produce or where to ship it. Each individual producer makes what he or she thinks will be most profitable; each consumer buys what he or she chooses.

[handwritten: uses the hand]

The alternative to a market economy is a *command economy,* in which there *is* a central authority making decisions about production and consumption. Command economies have been tried, most notably in the Soviet Union between 1917 and 1991. But they didn't work very well. Producers in the Soviet Union routinely found themselves unable to produce because they did not have crucial raw materials, or they succeeded in producing but then found that nobody wanted their products. Consumers were often unable to find necessary items—command economies are famous for long lines at shops.

Market economies, however, are able to coordinate even highly complex activities and to reliably provide consumers with the goods and services they want. Indeed, people quite casually trust their lives to the market system: residents of any major city would starve in days if the unplanned yet somehow orderly actions of thousands of businesses did not deliver a steady supply of food. Surprisingly, the unplanned "chaos" of a market economy turns out to be far more orderly than the "planning" of a command economy.

In 1776, in a famous passage in his book *The Wealth of Nations*, the pioneering Scottish economist Adam Smith wrote about how individuals, in pursuing their own interests, often end up serving the interests of society as a whole. Of a businessman whose pursuit of profit makes the nation wealthier, Smith wrote: "[H]e intends only his own gain, and he is in this, as in many other cases, led by an invisible hand to promote an end which was no part of his intention." Ever since, economists have used the term **invisible hand** to refer to the way a market

An **economy** is a system for coordinating society's productive activities.

Economics is the social science that studies the production, distribution, and consumption of goods and services.

A **market economy** is an economy in which decisions about production and consumption are made by individual producers and consumers.

The **invisible hand** refers to the way in which the individual pursuit of self-interest can lead to good results for society as a whole.

economy manages to harness the power of self-interest for the good of society.

The study of how individuals make decisions and how these decisions interact is called **microeconomics.** One of the key themes in microeconomics is the validity of Adam Smith's insight: individuals pursuing their own interests often do promote the interests of society as a whole.

So part of the answer to our time traveller's question—"How can my society achieve the kind of prosperity you take for granted?"—is that her society should learn to appreciate the virtues of a market economy and the power of the invisible hand.

But the invisible hand isn't always our friend. It's also important to understand when and why the individual pursuit of self-interest can lead to counterproductive behaviour.

ECONOMICS THROUGH THE AGES

My Benefit, Your Cost

One thing that our time traveller would not admire about the modern Spring Garden Road area is the traffic. In fact, although most things have gotten better in Canada over time, traffic congestion has gotten a lot worse.

When traffic is congested, each driver is imposing a cost on all the other drivers on the road—he is literally getting in their way (and they are getting in his way). This cost can be substantial: in major metropolitan areas, each time someone drives to work instead of taking public transportation or working at home, he can easily impose $15 or more in hidden costs on other drivers. Yet when deciding whether or not to drive, commuters have no incentive to take the costs they impose on others into account.

Traffic congestion is a familiar example of a much broader problem: sometimes the individual pursuit of one's own interest, instead of promoting the interests of society as a whole, can actually make society worse off. When this happens, it is known as **market failure.** Other important examples of market failure involve air and water pollution as well as the overexploitation of natural resources such as fish and forests.

The good news, as you will learn as you use this book to study microeconomics, is that economic analysis can be used to diagnose cases of market failure. And often, economic analysis can also be used to devise solutions for the problem.

Good Times, Bad Times

Spring Garden Road was bustling on that day in 2013. But if you'd visited the stores in 2009, the scene wouldn't have been quite as cheerful. That's because Nova Scotia's economy, along with that of Canada as a whole, was depressed in 2009: in late 2008, businesses began laying off workers in large numbers, and employment didn't start bouncing back until the fall of 2009.

Such troubled periods are a regular feature of modern economies. The fact is that the economy does not always run smoothly: it experiences fluctuations, a series of ups and downs. By middle age, a typical Canadian will have experienced two or three downs, known as *recessions.* (The Canadian economy experienced serious recessions beginning in 1982, 1990, and 2008.) During a severe recession, hundreds of thousands of workers may be laid off.

Microeconomics is the branch of economics that studies how people make decisions and how these decisions interact.

When the individual pursuit of self-interest leads to bad results for society as a whole, there is **market failure.**

Macroeconomics is the branch of economics that is concerned with overall ups and downs in the economy.

Economic growth is the growing ability of the economy to produce goods and services.

Like market failure, recessions are a fact of life; but also like market failure, they are a problem for which economic analysis offers some solutions. Recessions are one of the main concerns of the branch of economics known as **macroeconomics,** which is concerned with the overall ups and downs of the economy. If you study macroeconomics, you will learn how economists explain recessions and how government policies can be used to minimize the damage from economic fluctuations.

Despite the occasional recession, however, over the long run the story of the Canadian economy contains many more ups than downs. And that long-run ascent is the subject of our final question.

Onward and Upward

At the beginning of the twentieth century, most Canadians lived under conditions that we would now think of as extreme poverty. Less than 10% of homes had flush toilets or central heating; even fewer had electricity, and almost nobody had a car, let alone a washing machine or modern electrical air conditioning, which did not arrive in homes until the 1920s.

Such comparisons are a stark reminder of how much our lives have been changed by **economic growth,** the growing ability of the economy to produce goods and services. Why does the economy grow over time? And why does economic growth occur faster in some times and places than in others? These are key questions for economics because economic growth is a good thing, as those shoppers on Spring Garden Road can attest, and most of us want more of it.

An Engine for Discovery

We hope we have convinced you that the "ordinary business of life" is really quite extraordinary, if you stop to think about it, and that it can lead us to ask some very interesting and important questions.

In this book, we will describe the answers economists have given to these questions. But this book, like economics as a whole, isn't a list of answers: it's an introduction to a discipline, a way to address questions like those we have just asked. Or as Alfred Marshall, who described economics as a study of the "ordinary business of life," put it: "Economics ... is not a body of concrete truth, but an engine for the discovery of concrete truth."

So let's turn the key and start the ignition.

KEY TERMS

Economy, p. 2
Economics, p. 2
Market economy, p. 2

Invisible hand, p. 2
Microeconomics, p. 3
Market failure, p. 3

Macroeconomics, p. 4
Economic growth, p. 4

First Principles

COMMON GROUND

❯ A set of principles for understanding the economics of how individuals make choices

❯ A set of principles for understanding how economies work through the interaction of individual choices

❯ A set of principles for understanding economy-wide interactions

Brent Lewin/Bloomberg via Getty Images

One must choose.

THE ANNUAL MEETING OF THE Canadian Economic Association draws hundreds of economists, young and old, famous and obscure. There are booksellers, business meetings, and sometimes even a few job interviews. But mainly the economists gather to talk and listen. During the busiest times, 30 or more presentations may be taking place simultaneously on questions that range from financial market crises to who does the cooking in two-earner families.

What do these people have in common? An expert on financial markets probably knows very little about the economics of housework, and vice versa. Yet an economist who wanders into the wrong seminar and ends up listening to presentations on some unfamiliar topic is nonetheless likely to hear much that is familiar. The reason is that all economic analysis is based on a set of common principles that apply to many different issues.

Some of these principles involve *individual choice*—for economics is, first of all, about the choices that individuals make. Do you save your money and take the bus or do you buy a car? Do you keep your old smart phone or upgrade to a new one? These decisions involve *making a choice* from among a limited number of alternatives—limited because no one can have everything that he or she wants. Every question in economics at its most basic level involves individuals making choices.

But to understand how an economy works, you need to understand more than how individuals make choices. None of us is Robinson Crusoe, alone on an island. We must make decisions in an environment that is shaped by the decisions of others. Indeed, in a modern economy even the simplest decisions you make—say, what to have for breakfast—are shaped by the decisions of thousands of other people, from the banana grower in Costa Rica who decided to grow the fruit you eat to the farmer in Ontario who provided the corn in your cornflakes.

Because each of us in a market economy depends on so many others—and they, in turn, depend on us—our choices interact. So although all economics at a basic level is about individual choice, in order to understand how market economies behave we must also understand *economic interaction*—how my choices affect your choices, and vice versa.

Many important economic interactions can be understood by looking at the markets for individual goods, like the market for corn. But an economy as a whole has ups and downs, and we therefore need to understand economy-wide interactions as well as the more limited interactions that occur in individual markets.

In this chapter, we will look at twelve basic principles of economics—four principles involving individual choice, five involving the way individual choices interact, and three more involving economy-wide interactions. ■

Principles That Underlie Individual Choice: The Core of Economics

Every economic issue involves, at its most basic level, **individual choice**—decisions by an individual about what to do and what not to do. In fact, you might say that it isn't economics if it isn't about choice.

Step into a big store like Walmart or Hudson's Bay. There are thousands of different products available, and it is extremely unlikely that you—or anyone else—could afford to buy everything you might want to have. And anyway, there's only so much space in your dorm room or apartment. So will you buy another bookcase or a mini-refrigerator? Given limitations on your budget and your living space, you must choose which products to buy and which to leave on the shelf.

The fact that those products are on the shelf in the first place involves choice—the store manager chose to put them there, and the manufacturers of the products chose to produce them. All economic activities involve individual choice.

Four economic principles underlie the economics of individual choice, as shown in Table 1-1. We'll now examine each of these principles in more detail.

TABLE 1-1	The Principles of Individual Choice
1. People must make choices because resources are scarce.	
2. The opportunity cost of an item—what you must give up in order to get it—is its true cost.	
3. "How much" decisions require making trade-offs at the margin: comparing the costs and benefits of doing a little bit more of an activity versus doing a little bit less.	
4. People usually respond to incentives, exploiting opportunities to make themselves better off.	

Principle #1: Choices Are Necessary Because Resources Are Scarce

You can't always get what you want. Everyone would like to have a beautiful house in a great location (and have help with the housecleaning), a new car or two, and a nice vacation in a fancy hotel. But even in a rich country like Canada, not many families can afford all that. So they must make choices—whether to travel by train through the Rockies this year or buy a better car, whether to make do with a small backyard or accept a longer commute in order to live where land is cheaper.

Limited income isn't the only thing that keeps people from having everything they want. Time is also in limited supply: there are only 24 hours in a day. And because the time we have is limited, choosing to spend time on one activity also means choosing not to spend time on a different activity—spending time studying for an exam means forgoing a night spent watching a movie. Indeed, many people are so limited by the number of hours in the day that they are willing to trade money for time. For example, convenience stores normally charge higher prices than a regular supermarket. But they fulfill a valuable role by catering to time-pressured customers who would rather pay more than travel farther to the supermarket.

This leads us to our first principle of individual choice:

People must make choices because resources are scarce.

A **resource** is anything that can be used to produce something else. Lists of the economy's resources usually begin with land, labour (the time of workers), capital (machinery, buildings, and other manufactured productive assets), and human capital (the educational achievements and skills of workers). A resource is **scarce** when there's not enough of the resource available to satisfy all the ways a society wants to use it. There are many scarce resources. These include natural resources—resources that come from the physical environment, such as minerals, lumber, and petroleum. There is also a limited quantity of human resources—labour, skill, and intelligence. And in a growing world economy with a rapidly increasing human population, even clean air and water have become scarce resources.

Individual choice is the decision by an individual of what to do, which necessarily involves a decision of what not to do.

A **resource** is anything that can be used to produce something else.

Resources are **scarce**—not enough of the resources are available to satisfy all the various ways a society wants to use them.

Just as individuals must make choices, the scarcity of resources means that society as a whole must make choices. One way a society makes choices is by allowing them to emerge as the result of many individual choices, which is what usually happens in a market economy. For example, Canadians as a group have only so many hours in a week: how many of those hours will they spend going to supermarkets to get lower prices, rather than saving time by shopping at convenience stores? The answer is the sum of individual decisions: each of the millions of individuals in the economy makes his or her own choice about where to shop, and the overall choice is simply the sum of those individual decisions.

But for various reasons, there are some decisions that a society decides are best not left to individual choice. For example, the authors live in areas that until recently were mainly farmland but are now being rapidly built up. Most local residents feel that the community would be a more pleasant place to live if some of the land was left undeveloped. But no individual has an incentive to keep his or her land as open space, rather than sell it to a developer. So, a trend has emerged in many communities across Canada of governments either purchasing undeveloped land, or putting restrictions on its use, to preserve it as open space. For example, the federal government created Rouge Park, Canada's first urban national park, in the Greater Toronto area, to protect about 40 square kilometres of wilderness. The Agricultural Land Reserve was created by the provincial government of British Columbia to protect about 47 000 square kilometres of agricultural land. The Ontario government established the 7300 square kilometre greenbelt surrounding the Golden Horseshoe region to protect farmland and natural space from urban development. Similar greenbelts are proposed for Montreal and Quebec City.

We'll see in later chapters why decisions about how to use scarce resources are often best left to individuals but sometimes should be made at a higher, community-wide, level.

Principle #2: The True Cost of Something Is Its Opportunity Cost

It is the last term before you graduate, and your class schedule allows you to take only one elective. There are two, however, that you would really like to take: Intro to Computer Graphics and History of Jazz.

Suppose you decide to take the History of Jazz course. What's the cost of that decision? It is the fact that you can't take the computer graphics class, your next best alternative choice. Economists call that kind of cost—what you must give up in order to get an item you want—the **opportunity cost** of that item. This leads us to our second principle of individual choice:

> *The opportunity cost of an item—what you must give up in order to get it—is its true cost.*

So the opportunity cost of taking the History of Jazz class is the benefit you would have derived from the Intro to Computer Graphics class.

The concept of opportunity cost is crucial to understanding individual choice because, in the end, all decisions dealing with scarcity involve opportunity costs. That's because every choice you make means forgoing some other alternative and these costs can be both monetary and non-monetary.

Let's consider two cases for our elective course example. First, suppose that taking any elective class involves a tuition fee of $750. In this case, you would have to spend that $750 no matter which class you take. So what you give up to take the History of Jazz class is still only the benefit derived from the computer graphics class, period—you would have to spend that $750 either way. But suppose there isn't any fee for the computer graphics class. In that case, what you give up to take the jazz class is the benefit from the computer graphics class *plus* the benefit you could have gained from spending the $750 on other things.

So the opportunity costs of taking the History of Jazz class are both monetary (any additional tuition you paid over the computer graphics class) and

The real cost of an item is its **opportunity cost**: what you must give up in order to get it.

By the time he was eighteen years old, Sidney Crosby was playing in the NHL. He understood the concept of opportunity cost.

non-monetary (the benefits derived from taking the computer graphics class). In other words, the real cost of taking your preferred class is everything you must give up (by not choosing your next best alternative) to get it. As you expand the set of decisions that underlie each choice—whether to take an elective or not, whether to finish this term or not, whether to drop out or not—you'll realize that all costs are ultimately opportunity costs.

Sometimes the money you have to pay for something is a good indication of its opportunity cost. But many times it is not. One very important example of how poorly monetary cost alone can indicate opportunity cost is the cost of attending college or university. Tuition and housing are major monetary expenses for most post-secondary students; but even if these things were free, attending school would still be an expensive proposition because most college and university students, if they were not in school, would have a job. That is, by going to college or university, students *forgo* the income they could have earned if they had worked instead. This means that the opportunity cost of attending a post-secondary institution is what you pay for tuition and housing plus the forgone income you would have earned in a job.

It's easy to see that the opportunity cost of going to a post-secondary institution is especially high for people who could be earning a lot during what would otherwise have been their university or college years. That is why star athletes like Sidney Crosby, entertainers like Celine Dion, and entrepreneurs like Mike Lazardis, founder of BlackBerry, often skip or drop out of college. Other famous people who left school early include Mark Zuckerberg, Bill Gates, Steve Jobs, and Mick Jagger.

Principle #3: "How Much" Is a Decision at the Margin

Some important decisions involve an "either–or" choice—for example, you decide either to go to college or university or to begin working; you decide either to take economics or to take something else. But other important decisions involve "how much" choices—for example, if you are taking both economics and chemistry this semester, you must decide how much time to spend studying for each. When it comes to understanding "how much" decisions, economics has an important insight to offer: "how much" is a decision made at the margin.

Suppose you are taking both economics and chemistry. And suppose you are a pre-med student, so your grade in chemistry matters more to you than your grade in economics. Does that therefore imply that you should spend *all* your study time on chemistry and wing it on the economics exam? Probably not; even if you think your chemistry grade is more important, you should put some effort into studying economics.

Spending more time studying chemistry involves a benefit (a higher expected grade in that course) and a cost (you could have spent that time doing something else, such as studying to get a higher grade in economics). That is, your decision involves a **trade-off**—a comparison of costs and benefits.

How do you decide this kind of "how much" question? The typical answer is that you make the decision a bit at a time, by asking how you should spend the next hour. Say both exams are on the same day, and the night before you spend time reviewing your notes for both courses. At 6:00 P.M., you decide that it's a good idea to spend at least an hour on each course. At 8:00 P.M., you decide you'd better spend another hour on each course. At 10:00 P.M., you are getting tired and figure you have one more hour to study before bed—chemistry or economics? If you are pre-med, it's likely to be chemistry; if you are pre-MBA, it's likely to be economics.

Note how you've made the decision to allocate your time: at each point the question is whether or not to spend *one more hour* on either course. And in deciding whether to spend another hour studying for chemistry, you weigh the costs (an hour forgone of studying for economics or an hour forgone of sleeping) versus

You make a **trade-off** when you compare the costs with the benefits of doing something.

the benefits (a likely increase in your chemistry grade). As long as the benefit of studying chemistry for one more hour outweighs the cost, you should choose to study for that additional hour.

Decisions of this type—whether to do a bit more or a bit less of an activity, like what to do with your next hour, your next dollar, and so on—are **marginal decisions.** This brings us to our third principle of individual choice:

> *"How much" decisions require making trade-offs at the margin: comparing the costs and benefits of doing a little bit more of an activity versus doing a little bit less.*

The study of such decisions is known as **marginal analysis.** Many of the questions that we face in economics—as well as in real life—involve marginal analysis: How many workers should I hire in my shop? After how many kilometres of driving should I change the oil in my car? What is an acceptable rate of negative side effects from a new medicine? Marginal analysis plays a central role in economics because it is the key to deciding "how much" of an activity to do.

> Decisions about whether to do a bit more or a bit less of an activity are **marginal decisions**. The study of such decisions is known as **marginal analysis**.
>
> An **incentive** is anything that offers rewards to people who change their behaviour.

Principle #4: People Usually Respond to Incentives, Exploiting Opportunities to Make Themselves Better Off

One day, while listening to the morning financial news, one of the American-based authors of this textbook heard a great tip about how to park cheaply in Manhattan. Garages in the Wall Street area charge as much as $30 per day. But according to the newscaster, some people had found a better way: instead of parking in a garage, they had their oil changed at the Manhattan Jiffy Lube, where it costs $19.95 to change your oil—and they keep your car all day!

It's a great story, but unfortunately it turned out not to be true—in fact, there is no Jiffy Lube in Manhattan. But if there were, you can be sure there would be a lot of oil changes there. Why? Because when people are offered opportunities to make themselves better off, they normally take them—and if they could find a way to park their car all day for $19.95 rather than $30, they would.

In this example economists say that people are responding to an **incentive**— an opportunity to make themselves better off. We can now state our fourth principle of individual choice:

> *People usually respond to incentives, exploiting opportunities to make themselves better off.*

When you try to predict how individuals will behave in an economic situation, it is a very good bet that they will respond to incentives—that is, exploit opportunities to make themselves better off. Furthermore, individuals will *continue* to exploit these opportunities until they have been fully exhausted. If there really were a Manhattan Jiffy Lube and an oil change really were a cheap way to park your car, we can safely predict that before long the waiting list for oil changes would be weeks, if not months, long.

In fact, the principle that people will exploit opportunities to make themselves better off is the basis of *all* predictions by economists about individual behaviour. If the earnings of those who get MBAs soar while the earnings of those who get law degrees decline, we can expect more students to go to business school and fewer to go to law school. If the price of gasoline rises and stays high for an extended period of time, we can expect people to buy smaller cars with better fuel efficiency—making themselves better off in the presence of higher gas prices by driving more fuel-efficient cars.

One last point: economists tend to be skeptical of any attempt to change people's behaviour that *doesn't* change their incentives. For example, a plan that calls on manufacturers to reduce pollution voluntarily probably won't be effective

FOR INQUIRING MINDS

CASHING IN AT SCHOOL

The true reward for learning is, of course, the learning itself. Many students, however, struggle with their motivation to study and work hard. Teachers and policy-makers have been particularly challenged to help students from disadvantaged backgrounds, who often have poor school attendance, high dropout rates, and low standardized test scores. In a 2007–2008 study, Harvard economist Roland Fryer Jr. found that monetary incentives—cash rewards—could improve students' academic performance in schools in economically disadvantaged areas. How cash incentives work, however, is both surprising and predictable.

Fryer conducted his research in four different school districts, employing a different set of incentives and a different measure of performance in each. In New York City, students were paid according to their scores on standardized tests; in Chicago, they were paid according to their grades; in Washington, D.C., they were paid according to attendance and good behaviour as well as their grades; in Dallas, Grade Two students were paid each time they read a book. Fryer evaluated the results by comparing the performance of students who were in the program to other students in the same school who were not.

In New York, the program had no perceptible effect on test scores. In Chicago, students in the program got better grades and attended class more. In Washington, the program boosted the outcomes of the kids who are normally the hardest to reach, those with serious behavioural problems, raising their test

scores by an amount equivalent to attending five extra months of school. The most dramatic results occurred in Dallas, where students significantly boosted their reading-comprehension test scores; results continued into the next year, after the cash rewards had ended.

So what explains the various results?

To motivate students with cash rewards, Fryer found that students had to believe that they could have a significant effect on the performance measure. So in Chicago, Washington, and Dallas—where students had a significant amount of control over outcomes such as grades, attendance, behaviour, and the number of books read—the program produced significant results. But because New York students had little idea how to affect their score on a standardized test, the prospect of a reward had little influence on their behaviour. Also, the timing of the reward matters: a $1 reward has more effect on behaviour if performance is measured at shorter intervals and the reward is delivered soon after.

Fryer's experiment revealed some critical insights about how to motivate behaviour with incentives. How incentives are designed is very important: the relationship between effort and outcome, as well as the speed of reward, matters a lot. Moreover, the design of incentives may depend quite a lot on the characteristics of the people you are trying to motivate: what motivates a student from an economically privileged background may not motivate a student

Cash incentives have been shown to improve student performance.

from an economically disadvantaged one. Fryer's insights give teachers and policy-makers an important new tool for helping disadvantaged students succeed in school.

In Canada, using publicly funded cash incentives to motivate at-risk students is a controversial topic. Some educators claim that financial incentives do work, and are needed, citing the success of such a program in Portage la Prairie, Manitoba. Aboriginal students at Portage Collegiate Institute receive $50 per month to attend school regularly and complete their homework. Students who graduate from Grade 12 receive $1000. This program is funded by the Long Plains First Nations. The result? More students are attending and graduating from Portage Collegiate. Similar programs are operating elsewhere in Canada. But many people think that other solutions should be found to encourage students. When, in 2010, the Toronto District School Board suggested paying students from disadvantaged communities, provincial politicians firmly rejected the plan.

---

because it hasn't changed manufacturers' incentives. In contrast, a plan that gives them a financial reward to reduce pollution or a penalty for not doing so is a lot more likely to work because it has changed their incentives.

So are we ready to do economics? Not yet—because most of the interesting things that happen in the economy are the result not merely of individual choices but of the way in which individual choices interact.

ECONOMICS ▸ IN ACTION

BOY OR GIRL? IT DEPENDS ON THE COST

One fact about China is indisputable: it's a big country with lots of people. As of 2013, the population of China was about 1 349 586 000. That's right: over *one billion three hundred million.*

In 1978, the government of China introduced the "one-child policy" to address the economic and demographic challenges presented by China's large population. China was very, very poor in 1978, and its leaders worried that the country could not afford to adequately educate and care for its growing population. The average Chinese woman in the 1970s was giving birth to more than five children during her lifetime. So the government restricted most couples, particularly those in urban areas, to one child, imposing penalties on those who defied the mandate. As a result, by 2013 the average number of births for a woman in China was only 1.6.

But the one-child policy had an unfortunate unintended consequence. Because China is an overwhelmingly rural country and sons can perform the manual labour of farming, families had a strong preference for sons over daughters. In addition, tradition dictates that brides become part of their husbands' families and that sons take care of their elderly parents. As a result of the one-child policy, China soon had too many "unwanted girls." Some were given up for adoption abroad, but all too many simply "disappeared" during the first year of life, the victims of neglect and mistreatment.

India, another highly rural poor country with high demographic pressures, also has a significant problem with "disappearing girls." In 1990, Amartya Sen, an Indian-born British economist who would go on to win the Nobel Prize in 1998, estimated that there were up to 100 million "missing women" in Asia. (The exact figure is in dispute, but it is clear that Sen identified a real and pervasive problem.)

Demographers have recently noted a distinct turn of events in China, which is quickly urbanizing. In all but one of the provinces with urban centres, the gender imbalance between boys and girls peaked in 1995 and has steadily fallen toward the biologically natural ratio since then. Many believe that the source of the change is China's strong economic growth and increasing urbanization. As people move to cities to take advantage of job growth there, they don't need sons to work the fields. Moreover, land prices in Chinese cities are skyrocketing, making the custom of parents buying an apartment for a son before he can marry unaffordable for many. To be sure, sons are still preferred in the rural areas. But as a sure mark of how times have changed, Internet websites have recently popped up that advise couples on how to have a girl rather than a boy.

The cost of China's "one-child policy" was a generation of "disappeared" daughters—a phenomenon that has itself begun to disappear as economic conditions have changed.

CHECK YOUR UNDERSTANDING   1-1

1. Explain how each of the following situations illustrates one of the four principles of individual choice.
   a. You are on your third trip to a restaurant's all-you-can-eat dessert buffet and are feeling very full. Although it would cost you no additional money, you forgo a slice of coconut cream pie but have a slice of chocolate cake.
   b. Even if there were more resources in the world, there would still be scarcity.
   c. Different teaching assistants teach several Economics 101 tutorials. Those taught by the teaching assistants with the best reputations fill up quickly, with spaces left unfilled in the ones taught by assistants with poor reputations.
   d. To decide how many hours per week to exercise, you compare the health benefits of one more hour of exercise to the effect on your grades of one fewer hour spent studying.

2. You make $45 000 per year at your current job with Whiz Kids Consultants. You are considering a job offer from Brainiacs, Inc., that will pay you $50 000 per year. Which of the following are elements of the opportunity cost of accepting the new job at Brainiacs, Inc.?
   a. The increased time spent commuting to your new job
   b. The $45 000 salary from your old job
   c. The more spacious office at your new job

Solutions appear at back of book.

Interaction: How Economies Work

As we learned in the Introduction, an economy is a system for coordinating the productive activities of many people. In a market economy like we live in, coordination takes place without any coordinator: each individual makes his or her own choices. Yet those choices are by no means independent of one another: each individual's opportunities, and hence choices, depend to a large extent on the choices made by other people. So to understand how a market economy behaves, we have to examine this **interaction** in which my choices affect your choices, and vice versa.

When studying economic interaction, we quickly learn that the end result of individual choices may be quite different from what any one individual intends. For example, over the past century North American farmers have eagerly adopted new farming techniques and crop strains that have reduced their costs and increased their yields. Clearly, it's in the interest of each farmer to keep up with the latest farming techniques.

But the end result of each farmer trying to increase his or her own income has actually been to drive many farmers out of business. Because Canadian farmers have been so successful at producing larger yields, agricultural prices have steadily fallen. These falling prices have reduced the incomes of many farmers, and as a result fewer and fewer people find farming worth doing. That is, an individual farmer who plants a better variety of corn is better off; but when many farmers plant a better variety of corn, the result may be to make farmers as a group worse off.

A farmer who plants a new, more productive corn variety doesn't just grow more corn. Such a farmer also affects the market for corn through the increased yields attained, with consequences that will be felt by other farmers, consumers, and beyond.

Just as there are four economic principles that underlie individual choice, there are five principles that underlie the economics of interaction. These five principles are summarized in Table 1-2. We will now examine each of these principles more closely.

TABLE 1-2	The Principles of the Interaction of Individual Choices
5.	There are gains from trade.
6.	Because people respond to incentives, markets move toward equilibrium.
7.	Resources should be used as efficiently as possible to achieve society's goals.
8.	Because people usually exploit gains from trade, markets usually lead to efficiency.
9.	When markets don't achieve efficiency, government intervention can improve society's welfare.

Interaction of choices—my choices affect your choices, and vice versa—is a feature of most economic situations. The results of this interaction are often quite different from what the individuals intend.

In a market economy, individuals engage in **trade**: they provide goods and services to others and receive goods and services in return.

There are **gains from trade**: people can get more of what they want through trade than they could if they tried to be self-sufficient. This increase in output is due to **specialization**: each person specializes in the task that he or she is good at performing.

Principle #5: There Are Gains from Trade

Why do the choices I make interact with the choices you make? A family could try to take care of all its own needs—growing its own food, sewing its own clothing, providing itself with entertainment, writing its own economics textbooks. But trying to live that way would be very hard. The key to a much better standard of living for everyone is **trade,** in which people divide tasks among themselves and each person provides a good or service that other people want in return for different goods and services that he or she wants.

The reason we have an economy, not many self-sufficient individuals, is that there are **gains from trade:** by dividing tasks and trading, two people (or 7 billion people) can each get more of what they want than they could get by being self-sufficient. This leads us to our fifth principle:

There are gains from trade.

Gains from trade arise from this division of tasks, which economists call **specialization**—a situation in which different people each engage in a different task, specializing in those tasks that they are good at performing. The advantages of specialization, and the resulting gains from trade, were the starting point for Adam Smith's 1776 book *The Wealth of Nations*, which many regard as the beginning of economics as a discipline. Smith's book begins with a description of an eighteenth-century pin factory where, rather than each of the 10 workers making a pin from start to finish, each worker specialized in one of the many steps in pin-making:

> One man draws out the wire, another straights it, a third cuts it, a fourth points it, a fifth grinds it at the top for receiving the head; to make the head requires two or three distinct operations; to put it on, is a particular business, to whiten the pins is another; it is even a trade by itself to put them into the paper; and the important business of making a pin is, in this manner, divided into about eighteen distinct operations ... . Those ten persons, therefore, could make among them upwards of forty-eight thousand pins in a day. But if they had all wrought separately and independently, and without any of them having been educated to this particular business, they certainly could not each of them have made twenty, perhaps not one pin a day ... .

The same principle applies when we look at how people divide tasks among themselves and trade in an economy. *The economy, as a whole, can produce more when each person specializes in a task and trades with others.*

The benefits of specialization are the reason a person typically chooses only one career. It takes many years of study and experience to become a doctor; it also takes many years of study and experience to become a commercial airline pilot. Many doctors might well have had the potential to become excellent pilots, and vice versa; but it is very unlikely that anyone who decided to pursue both careers would be as good a pilot or as good a doctor as someone who decided at the beginning to specialize in that field. So it is to everyone's advantage that individuals specialize in their career choices.

"I hunt and she gathers—otherwise we couldn't make ends meet."

Markets are what allow a doctor and a pilot to specialize in their own fields. Because markets for commercial flights and for doctors' services exist, a doctor is assured that she can find a flight and a pilot is assured that he can find a doctor. As long as individuals know that they can find the goods and services they want in the market, they are willing to forgo self-sufficiency and to specialize. But what assures people that markets will deliver what they want? The answer to that question leads us to our second principle of how individual choices interact.

Principle #6: Markets Move Toward Equilibrium

It's a busy afternoon at the supermarket; there are long lines at the checkout counters. Then one of the previously closed cash registers opens. What happens? The first thing, of course, is a rush to that register. After a couple of minutes, however, things will have settled down; shoppers will have rearranged themselves so that the line at the newly opened register is about the same length as the lines at all the other registers.

How do we know that? We know from our fourth principle that people will exploit opportunities to make themselves better off. This means that people will rush to the newly opened register in order to save time standing in line. And things will settle down when shoppers can no longer improve their position by switching lines—that is, when the opportunities to make themselves better off have all been exploited.

A story about supermarket checkout lines may seem to have little to do with how individual choices interact, but in fact it illustrates an important principle. A situation in which individuals cannot make themselves better off by doing something different—the situation in which all the checkout lines are the same length—is what economists call an **equilibrium.** An economic situation is in equilibrium when no individual would be better off doing something different.

Recall the story about the mythical Jiffy Lube, where it was supposedly cheaper to leave your car for an oil change than to pay for parking. If the opportunity had really existed and people were still paying $30 to park in garages, the situation

An economic situation is in **equilibrium** when no individual would be better off doing something different.

FOR INQUIRING MINDS

CHOOSING SIDES

Why do people in North America drive on the right side of the road? Of course, it's the law. But long before it was the law, it was an equilibrium.

Before there were formal traffic laws, there were informal "rules of the road," practices that everyone expected everyone else to follow. These rules included an understanding that people would normally keep to one side of the road. In some places, such as England, the rule was to keep to the left; in others, such as France, it was to keep to the right.

Why would some places choose the right and others, the left? That's not completely clear, although it may have depended on the dominant form of traffic. Men riding horses and carrying swords on their left hip preferred to ride on the left (think about getting on or off the horse, and you'll see why). On the other hand, right-handed people walking but leading horses apparently preferred to walk on the right.

In any case, once a rule of the road was established, there were strong incentives for each individual to stay on the "usual" side of the road: those who didn't would keep colliding with oncoming traffic. So once established, the rule of the road would be self-enforcing—that is, it would be an equilibrium. Nowadays, of course, which side you drive on is determined by law; some jurisdictions have even changed sides. British Columbia, New Brunswick, Nova Scotia, and Prince Edward Island all switched from the left to the right in the 1920s, and Newfoundland switched in 1947, two years before it joined Canada. In Europe, Sweden and Iceland went from left to right in the 1960s.

But what about pedestrians? There are no laws—but there are informal rules. In Canada, urban pedestrians normally keep to the right. But if you should happen to visit a country where people drive on the left, watch out: people who drive on the left also typically walk on the left. So when in a foreign country, do as the locals do. You won't be arrested if you walk on the right, but you will be worse off than if you accept the equilibrium and walk on the left.

---

would *not* have been an equilibrium. And that should have been a giveaway that the story couldn't be true. In reality, people would have seized an opportunity to park cheaply, just as they seize opportunities to save time at the checkout line. And in so doing they would have eliminated the opportunity! Either it would have become very hard to get an appointment for an oil change or the price of a lube job would have increased to the point that it was no longer an attractive option (unless you really needed a lube job). This brings us to our sixth principle:

Because people respond to incentives, markets move toward equilibrium.

As we will see, markets usually reach equilibrium via changes in prices, which rise or fall until no opportunities for individuals to make themselves better off remain.

The concept of equilibrium is extremely helpful in understanding economic interactions because it provides a way of cutting through the sometimes complex details of those interactions. To understand what happens when a new line is opened at a supermarket, you don't need to worry about exactly how shoppers rearrange themselves, who moves ahead of whom, which register just opened, and so on. What you need to know is that any time there is a change, the situation will move to an equilibrium.

The fact that markets move toward equilibrium is why we can depend on them to work in a predictable way. In fact, we can trust markets to supply us with the essentials of life. For example, people who live in big cities can be sure that the supermarket shelves will always be fully stocked. Why? Because if some merchants who distribute food *didn't* make deliveries, a big profit opportunity would be created for any merchant who did—and there would be a rush to supply food, just like the rush to a newly opened cash register. So the market ensures that food will always be available for city dwellers. And, returning to our fifth principle, this allows city dwellers to be city dwellers—to specialize in doing city jobs rather than living on farms and growing their own food.

A market economy, as we have seen, allows people to achieve gains from trade. But how do we know how well such an economy is doing? The next principle gives us a standard to use in evaluating an economy's performance.

Principle #7: Resources Should Be Used Efficiently to Achieve Society's Goals

Suppose you are taking a course in which the classroom is too small for the number of students—many people are forced to stand or sit on the floor—despite the fact that large, empty classrooms are available nearby. You would say, correctly, that this is no way to run a college or university. Economists would call this an *inefficient* use of resources. But if an inefficient use of resources is undesirable, just what does it mean to use resources *efficiently*? You might imagine that the efficient use of resources has something to do with money, maybe that it is measured in dollars-and-cents terms. But in economics, as in life, money is only a means to other ends. The measure that economists really care about is not money but people's happiness or welfare. Economists say that *an economy's resources are used efficiently when they are used in a way that has fully exploited all opportunities to make everyone better off.* To put it another way, an economy is **efficient** if it takes all opportunities to make some people better off without making other people worse off.

In our classroom example, there clearly was a way to make everyone better off—moving the class to a larger room would make people in the class better off without hurting anyone else in the school. Assigning the course to the smaller classroom was an inefficient use of the school's resources, whereas assigning the course to the larger classroom would have been an efficient use of the school's resources.

When an economy is efficient, it is producing the maximum gains from trade possible given the resources available. Why? Because there is no way to rearrange how resources are used in a way that can make everyone better off. When an economy is efficient, one person can be made better off by rearranging how resources are used *only* by making someone else worse off. In our classroom example, if all larger classrooms were already occupied by large classes, the school would have been run in an efficient way: your class could be made better off by moving to a larger classroom only by making people in the larger classroom worse off by making them move to a smaller classroom.

We can now state our seventh principle:

> *Resources should be used as efficiently as possible to achieve society's goals.*

Should economic policy-makers always strive to achieve economic efficiency? Well, not quite, because efficiency is only a means to achieving society's goals. Sometimes efficiency may conflict with a goal that society has deemed worthwhile to achieve. For example, in most societies, people also care about issues of fairness, or **equity.** And there is typically a trade-off between equity and efficiency: policies that promote equity often come at a cost of decreased efficiency in the economy, and vice versa.

To see this, consider the case of disabled-designated parking spaces in public parking lots. Many people have difficulty walking due to age or disability, so it seems only fair to assign closer parking spaces specifically for their use. You may have noticed, however, that a certain amount of inefficiency is involved. To make sure that there is always a parking space available should a person with disabilities want one, there are typically more such spaces available than there are people with disabilities who want one. As a result, desirable parking spaces are unused. (And the temptation for people without disabilities to use them is so great that we must be dissuaded by fear of getting a ticket.) So, short of hiring parking valets to allocate spaces, there is a conflict between *equity*, making life "fairer" for people with disabilities, and *efficiency*, making sure that all opportunities to make people better off have been fully exploited by never letting close-in parking spaces go unused.

An economy is **efficient** if it takes all opportunities to make some people better off without making other people worse off.

Equity means that everyone gets his or her fair share. Since people can disagree about what's "fair," equity isn't as well defined a concept as efficiency.

Sometimes equity trumps efficiency.

Exactly how far policy-makers should go in promoting equity over efficiency is a difficult question that goes to the heart of the political process. As such, it is not a question that economists can answer. What is important for economists, however, is always to seek to use the economy's resources as efficiently as possible in the pursuit of society's goals, whatever those goals may be.

Principle #8: Markets Usually Lead to Efficiency

No branch of the Canadian government is entrusted with ensuring the general economic efficiency of our market economy—we don't have agents who go around making sure that brain surgeons aren't plowing fields or that Manitoba farmers aren't trying to grow oranges. The government doesn't need to enforce the efficient use of resources, because in most cases the invisible hand does the job.

The incentives built into a market economy ensure that resources are usually put to good use and that opportunities to make people better off are not wasted. If a university or college were known for its habit of crowding students into small classrooms while large classrooms went unused, it would soon find its enrollment dropping, putting the jobs of its administrators at risk. The "market" for post-secondary students would respond in a way that induced administrators to run the school efficiently.

A detailed explanation of why markets are usually very good at making sure that resources are used well will have to wait until we have studied how markets actually work. But the most basic reason is that in a market economy, in which individuals are free to choose what to consume and what to produce, people normally exploit opportunities for mutual gain—that is, gains from trade. If there is a way in which some people can be made better off, people will usually be able to take advantage of that opportunity. And that is exactly what defines efficiency: all the opportunities to make some people better off without making other people worse off have been exploited. This gives rise to our eighth principle:

> *Because people usually exploit gains from trade, markets usually lead to efficiency.*

As we learned in the Introduction, however, there are exceptions to this principle that markets are generally efficient. In cases of *market failure*, the individual pursuit of self-interest found in markets makes society worse off—that is, the market outcome is inefficient. And, as we will see in examining the next principle, when markets fail, government intervention can help. But short of instances of market failure, the general rule is that markets are a remarkably good way of organizing an economy.

Principle #9: When Markets Don't Achieve Efficiency, Government Intervention Can Improve Society's Welfare

Let's recall from the Introduction the nature of the market failure caused by traffic congestion—a commuter driving to work has no incentive to take into account the cost that his or her action inflicts on other drivers in the form of increased traffic congestion. There are several possible remedies to this situation; examples include charging road tolls, subsidizing the cost of public transportation, and taxing sales of gasoline to individual drivers. All these remedies work by changing the incentives of would-be drivers, motivating them to drive less and use alternative transportation. But they also share another feature: each relies on government intervention in the market. This brings us to our ninth principle:

> *When markets don't achieve efficiency, government intervention can improve society's welfare.*

That is, when markets go wrong, an appropriately designed government policy can sometimes move society closer to an efficient outcome by changing how society's resources are used.

A very important branch of economics is devoted to studying why markets fail and what policies should be adopted to improve social welfare. We will study these problems and their remedies in depth in later chapters; but, briefly, there are three principal ways in which they fail:

- Individual actions have side effects that are not properly taken into account by the market. An example is an action that causes pollution.

- One party prevents mutually beneficial trades from occurring in an attempt to capture a greater share of resources for itself. An example is a drug company that prices a drug higher than the cost of producing it, making it unaffordable for some people who would benefit from it.

- Some goods, by their very nature, are unsuited for efficient management by markets. An example of such a good is air traffic control.

An important part of your education in economics is learning to identify not just when markets work but also when they don't work, and to judge what government policies are appropriate in each situation.

ECONOMICS ▶ IN ACTION

RESTORING EQUILIBRIUM ON THE FREEWAYS

Back in 1994 a powerful earthquake struck the Los Angeles area, causing several freeway bridges to collapse and thereby disrupting the normal commuting routes of hundreds of thousands of drivers. The events that followed offer a particularly clear example of interdependent decision-making—in this case, the decisions of commuters about how to get to work.

In the immediate aftermath of the earthquake, there was great concern about the impact on traffic, since motorists would now have to crowd onto alternative routes or detour around the blockages by using city streets. Public officials and news programs warned commuters to expect massive delays and urged them to avoid unnecessary travel, reschedule their work to commute before or after the rush, or use mass transit. These warnings were unexpectedly effective. In fact, so many people heeded them that in the first few days following the quake, those who maintained their regular commuting routine actually found the drive to and from work faster than before.

Witness equilibrium in action on a Los Angeles freeway.

Of course, this situation could not last. As word spread that traffic was relatively light, people abandoned their less convenient new commuting methods and reverted to their cars—and traffic got steadily worse. Within a few weeks after the quake, serious traffic jams had appeared. After a few more weeks, however, the situation stabilized: the reality of worse-than-usual congestion discouraged enough drivers to prevent the nightmare of citywide gridlock from materializing. Los Angeles traffic, in short, had settled into a new equilibrium, in which each commuter was making the best choice he or she could, given what everyone else was doing.

This was not, by the way, the end of the story: fears that the city would strangle on traffic led local authorities to repair the roads with record speed. A mere 18 months after the quake, all the freeways were back to normal.

CHECK YOUR UNDERSTANDING   1-2

1. Explain how each of the following situations illustrates one of the five principles of interaction.
   a. Using a university website, any student who wants to sell a used textbook for at least $30 is able to sell it to someone who is willing to pay $30.
   b. At a college tutoring co-op, students can arrange to provide tutoring in subjects they are good in (like economics) in return for receiving tutoring in subjects they are poor in (like philosophy).
   c. The local municipality imposes a law that requires bars and nightclubs near residential areas to keep their noise levels below a certain threshold.
   d. To provide better care for low-income patients, the province has decided to close some underutilized neighbourhood clinics and shift funds to nearby hospitals.
   e. On a university website, books of a given title with approximately the same level of wear and tear sell for about the same price.

2. Which of the following describes an equilibrium situation? Which does not? Explain your answer.
   a. The restaurants across the street from the university dining hall serve better-tasting and cheaper meals than those served at the university dining hall. The vast majority of students continue to eat at the dining hall.
   b. You currently take the bus to work. Although riding your bicycle is cheaper, the ride takes longer. So you are willing to pay the higher transit fare in order to save time.

Solutions appear at back of book.

Economy-Wide Interactions

TABLE 1-3	The Principles of Economy-Wide Interactions
10.	One person's spending is another person's income.
11.	Overall spending sometimes gets out of line with the economy's productive capacity.
12.	Government policies can change overall spending.

As we mentioned in the Introduction, the economy as a whole has its ups and downs. For example, business for Canada's auto dealers and shopping malls was depressed in 2009, because the economy was in a recession. By 2013, the economy had somewhat recovered. To understand recessions and recoveries, we need to understand economy-wide interactions, and understanding the big picture of the economy requires understanding three more important economic principles. Those three economy-wide principles are summarized in Table 1-3.

Principle #10: One Person's Spending Is Another Person's Income

In late 2008, home construction in Canada began a rapid decline because builders found it increasingly hard to make sales. At first the damage was mainly limited to the construction industry. But over time the slump spread into just about every part of the economy, with consumer spending falling across the board.

But why should a fall in home construction mean empty stores in the shopping malls? After all, malls are places where families, not builders, do their shopping. The answer is that lower spending on construction led to lower incomes throughout the economy; people who had been employed either directly in construction, producing goods and services builders need (like drywall), or in producing goods and services new homeowners need (like new furniture), either lost their jobs or were forced to take pay cuts—or expected that these steps might be imminent. And as incomes fell, so did spending by consumers. This example illustrates our tenth principle:

One person's spending is another person's income.

In a market economy, people make a living selling things—including their labour—to other people. If some group in the economy decides, for whatever reason, to spend more, the income of other groups will rise. If some group decides to spend less, the income of other groups will fall.

Because one person's spending is another person's income, a chain reaction of changes in spending behaviour tends to have repercussions that spread through the economy. For example, a cut in business investment spending, like the one that happened in 2009, leads to reduced family incomes; families respond by reducing consumer spending; this leads to another round of income cuts; and so on. These repercussions play an important role in our understanding of recessions and recoveries.

Principle #11: Overall Spending Sometimes Gets Out of Line with the Economy's Productive Capacity

Macroeconomics emerged as a separate branch of economics in the 1930s, when a collapse of consumer and business spending, a crisis in the U.S. banking industry, and other factors led to a plunge in overall spending. This plunge in spending, in turn, led to a period of very high unemployment worldwide known as the Great Depression.

The lesson economists learned from the troubles of the 1930s is that overall spending—the amount of goods and services that consumers and businesses want to buy—sometimes doesn't match the amount of goods and services the economy is capable of producing. In the 1930s, spending fell far short of what was needed to keep Canadian workers employed, and the result was a severe economic slump. In fact, shortfalls in spending are responsible for most, though not all, recessions.

It's also possible for overall spending to be too high. In that case, the economy experiences *inflation*, a rise in prices throughout the economy. This rise in prices occurs because when the amount that people want to buy outstrips the supply, producers can raise their prices and still find willing customers. Taking account of both shortfalls in spending and excesses in spending brings us to our eleventh principle:

> ***Overall spending sometimes gets out of line with the economy's productive capacity.***

Principle #12: Government Policies Can Change Overall Spending

Overall spending sometimes gets out of line with the economy's productive capacity. But can anything be done about that? Yes—which leads to our twelfth and last principle:

> ***Government policies can change overall spending.***

In fact, government policies can dramatically affect overall spending (sometimes referred to as aggregate expenditure).

For one thing, the government itself does a lot of spending on everything from military equipment to employment insurance benefits—and it can choose to do more or less. The government can also vary how much it collects from the public in taxes, which in turn affects how much income consumers and businesses have left to spend. And the government's control of the quantity of money in circulation, it turns out, gives it another powerful tool with which to affect total spending. Government spending, taxes, and control of the money supply are the tools of *macroeconomic policy*.

Modern governments deploy these macroeconomic policy tools in an effort to manage overall spending in the economy, trying to steer it between the perils of recession and inflation. These efforts aren't always successful—recessions still happen, and so do periods of inflation. But it's widely believed that aggressive efforts to sustain spending in 2009 and 2010, such as Canada's Economic Action Plan, helped prevent the financial crisis of 2008 from turning into a full-blown depression.

As participants in a babysitting co-op soon discovered, fewer nights out made everyone worse off.

ECONOMICS > IN ACTION

ADVENTURES IN BABYSITTING

The website sittingaround.com, which offers advice to families on locating babysitting services, suggests that parents consider joining a babysitting co-operative—an arrangement that is common in many walks of life. In a babysitting co-operative, a number of parents exchange babysitting services rather than hire someone to babysit. But how do these organizations make sure that all members do their fair share of the work? As sittingaround.com explains, "Instead of exchanging cash, members simply exchange sitting for sitting. Coops make sure everything nets out equitably by tracking points. You get points when you sit for someone else, and you spend points when others are sitting for you. The Johnsons can sit for the Browns, the Browns can sit for the Smiths, and the Smiths can sit for the Johnsons. Because you are part of a group, you never have to worry about reciprocating directly with those sitting for you—eventually, it all gets around."

In other words, a babysitting co-op is a miniature economy in which people buy and sell babysitting services. And it happens to be a type of economy that can have macroeconomic problems. A famous article titled "Monetary Theory and the Great Capitol Hill Babysitting Co-Op Crisis," published in 1977, described the troubles of a babysitting co-operative that issued too few tickets (its medium for tracking points). Bear in mind that, on average, people in a babysitting co-op want to have a reserve of tickets or points in case they need to go out several times before they can replenish their reserve by doing some more babysitting.

In this case, because there weren't that many tickets out there to begin with, most parents were anxious to add to their reserves by babysitting but reluctant to run them down by going out. But one parent's decision to go out was another's chance to babysit, so it became difficult to earn tickets. Knowing this, parents became even more reluctant to use their reserves except on special occasions.

In short, the co-op had fallen into a recession. Recessions in the larger, non-babysitting economy are a bit more complicated than this, but the troubles of the Capitol Hill babysitting co-op demonstrate two of our three principles of economy-wide interactions. One person's spending is another person's income: opportunities to babysit arose only to the extent that other people went out. And an economy can suffer from too little spending: when not enough people were willing to go out, everyone was frustrated at the lack of babysitting opportunities.

And what about government policies to change spending? Actually, the Capitol Hill co-op did that, too. Eventually, it solved its problem by handing out more tickets, and with increased reserves, people were willing to go out more.

▼ Quick Review

- In a market economy, one person's spending is another person's income. As a result, changes in spending behaviour have repercussions that spread through the economy.

- Overall spending sometimes gets out of line with the economy's capacity to produce goods and services. When spending is too low, the result is a recession. When spending is too high, it causes inflation.

- Modern governments use macroeconomic policy tools to affect the overall level of spending in an effort to steer the economy between recession and inflation.

CHECK YOUR UNDERSTANDING   1-3

1. Explain how each of the following examples illustrates one of the three principles of economy-wide interactions.
   a. The prime minister urged Parliament to pass a package of temporary spending increases and tax cuts in early 2009, a time when employment was plunging and unemployment soaring.
   b. Oil companies are investing heavily in projects that will extract oil from the "oil sands" in Alberta. In Edmonton, near the projects, restaurants and other consumer businesses are booming.
   c. In the mid-2000s, Spain, which was experiencing a big housing boom, also had the highest inflation rate in Europe.

Solutions appear at back of book.

BUSINESS CASE • How Priceline.com Revolutionized the Travel Industry

In 2001 and 2002, the travel industry was in deep trouble. After the terrorist attacks of September 11, 2001, many people simply stopped flying. As the economy went into a deep slump, airplanes sat empty on the tarmac and airlines around the world lost billions of dollars. When several major U.S. airlines spiralled toward bankruptcy and laid off more than 100 000 workers, the U.S. Congress passed a US$15 billion aid package that was critical in stabilizing the American airline industry. At the same time, Air Canada, sought a government bailout of $2 to $4 billion. In the end, the Canadian government compensated all Canadian air carriers with a bailout package worth $160 million.

This was also a particularly difficult time for Priceline.com, the online travel service. Just four years after its founding, Priceline.com was in danger of going under. The change in the company's fortunes had been dramatic. In 1999, one year after Priceline.com was formed, investors were so impressed by its potential for revolutionizing the travel industry that they valued the company at US$9 billion dollars. But by 2002 investors had taken a decidedly dimmer view of the company, reducing its valuation by 95% to only US$425 million.

To make matters worse, Priceline.com was losing several million dollars a year. Yet the company managed to survive; as of the time of writing in 2013, it was valued by investors at US$40.3 billion. Not only has it survived, it has thrived.

So exactly how did Priceline.com bring such dramatic change to the travel industry? And what has allowed it to survive and prosper as a company in the face of dire economic conditions?

Priceline.com's success lies in its ability to spot exploitable opportunities for itself and its customers. The company understood that when a plane departs with empty seats or a hotel has empty beds, it bears a cost—the revenue that would have been earned if that seat or bed had been filled. And although some travellers like the security of booking their flights and hotels well in advance and are willing to pay for that, others are quite happy to wait until the last minute, risking not getting the flight or hotel they want but enjoying a lower price.

Customers specify the price they are willing to pay for a given trip or hotel location, and then Priceline.com presents them with a list of options from airlines or hotels that are willing to accept that price, with the price typically declining as the date of the trip nears. By bringing airlines and hotels with unsold capacity together with travellers who are willing to sacrifice some of their preferences for a lower price, Priceline.com made everyone better off—including itself, since it charged a small commission for each trade it facilitated.

Priceline.com was also quick on its feet when it saw its market challenged by newcomers Expedia and Orbitz. In response, it began aggressively moving more of its business toward hotel bookings and into Europe, where the online travel industry was still quite small. Its network was particularly valuable in the European hotel market, which is comprised of many more small hotels in comparison to the North American market, which is dominated by nationwide chains. The efforts paid off, and by 2003 Priceline.com had turned its first profit.

Priceline.com now operates within a network of more than 295 000 hotels in over 190 countries and territories globally. As of 2013, its revenues had grown at least 21% over each of the previous three years, even growing during the recession by 24% in 2009 and 32% in 2010.

QUESTION FOR THOUGHT

1. Explain how each of the twelve principles of economics is illustrated in this story.

SUMMARY

1. All economic analysis is based on a set of basic principles that apply to three levels of economic activity. First, we study how individuals make choices; second, we study how these choices interact; and third, we study how the economy functions overall.

2. Everyone has to make choices about what to do and what *not* to do. **Individual choice** is the basis of economics—if it doesn't involve choice, it isn't economics.

3. The reason choices must be made is that **resources**—anything that can be used to produce something else—are **scarce.** Individuals are limited in their choices by money and time; economies are limited by their supplies of human and natural resources.

4. Because you must choose among limited alternatives, the true cost of anything is what you must give up to get it—all costs are **opportunity costs.**

5. Many economic decisions involve questions not of "whether" but of "how much"—how much to spend on some good, how much to produce, and so on. Such decisions must be made by performing a **trade-off** *at the margin*—by comparing the costs and benefits of doing a bit more or a bit less. Decisions of this type are called **marginal decisions,** and the study of them, **marginal analysis,** plays a central role in economics.

6. The study of how people *should* make decisions is also a good way to understand actual behaviour. Individuals usually respond to **incentives**—exploiting opportunities to make themselves better off.

7. The next level of economic analysis is the study of **interaction**—how my choices depend on your choices, and vice versa. When individuals interact, the end result may be different from what anyone intends.

8. Individuals interact because there are **gains from trade:** by engaging in the **trade** of goods and services

with one another, the members of an economy can all be made better off. **Specialization**—each person specializes in the task he or she is good at—is the source of gains from trade.

9. Because individuals usually respond to incentives, markets normally move toward **equilibrium**—a situation in which no individual can make himself or herself better off by taking a different action.

10. An economy is **efficient** if all opportunities to make some people better off without making other people worse off are taken. Resources should be used as efficiently as possible to achieve society's goals. But efficiency is not the sole way to evaluate an economy: **equity,** or fairness, is also desirable, and there is often a trade-off between equity and efficiency.

11. Markets usually lead to efficiency, with some well-defined exceptions.

12. When markets fail and do not achieve efficiency, government intervention can improve society's welfare.

13. Because people in a market economy earn income by selling things, including their own labour, one person's spending is another person's income. As a result, changes in spending behaviour can spread throughout the economy.

14. Overall spending in the economy can get out of line with the economy's productive capacity. Spending below the economy's productive capacity leads to a recession; spending in excess of the economy's productive capacity leads to inflation.

15. Governments have the ability to strongly affect overall spending, an ability they use in an effort to steer the economy between recession and inflation.

KEY TERMS

Individual choice, p. 6
Resource, p. 6
Scarce, p. 6
Opportunity cost, p. 7
Trade-off, p. 8

Marginal decisions, p. 9
Marginal analysis, p. 9
Incentive, p. 9
Interaction, p. 12
Trade, p. 12

Gains from trade, p. 12
Specialization, p. 12
Equilibrium, p. 13
Efficient, p. 15
Equity, p. 15

PROBLEMS

1. In each of the following situations, identify which of the twelve principles is at work.

   a. You choose to shop at the local discount store rather than paying a higher price for the same merchandise at the local department store.

   b. On your spring break trip, your budget is limited to $35 a day.

   c. The student union provides a website on which departing students can sell items such as used books, appliances, and furniture rather than give them away to their roommates as they formerly did.

   d. After a hurricane did extensive damage to homes on the island of St. Crispin, homeowners wanted to purchase many more building materials and hire many more workers than were available on the island. As a result, prices for goods and services rose dramatically across the board.

   e. You buy a used textbook from your roommate. Your roommate uses the money to buy songs from iTunes.

   f. You decide how many cups of coffee to have when studying the night before an exam by considering how much more work you can do by having another cup versus how jittery it will make you feel.

   g. There is limited lab space available to do the project required in Chemistry 101. The lab supervisor assigns lab time to each student based on when that student is able to come.

   h. You realize that you can graduate a semester early by forgoing a semester of study abroad.

   i. At the student union, there is a bulletin board on which people advertise used items for sale, such as bicycles. Once you have adjusted for differences in quality, all the bikes sell for about the same price.

   j. You are better at performing lab experiments, and your lab partner is better at writing lab reports. So the two of you agree that you will do all the experiments and she will write up all the reports.

   k. Provincial and territorial governments mandate that it is illegal to drive without passing a driving exam.

   l. Your parents' after-tax income has increased because of a tax cut passed by Parliament. They therefore increase your allowance, which you spend on a spring break vacation.

2. Describe some of the opportunity costs when you decide to do the following.

   a. Attend college or university instead of taking a job

   b. Watch a movie instead of studying for an exam

   c. Ride the bus instead of driving your car

3. Liza needs to buy a textbook for the next economics class. The price at the university bookstore is $65. One online site offers it for $55 and another site, for $57. All prices include sales tax. The accompanying table indicates the typical shipping and handling charges for the textbook ordered online.

Shipping method	Delivery time	Charge
Standard shipping	3–7 days	$3.99
Second-day air	2 business days	8.98
Next-day air	1 business day	13.98

   a. What is the opportunity cost of buying online instead of at the bookstore? Note that if you buy the book online, you must wait to get it.

   b. Show the relevant choices for this student. What determines which of these options the student will choose?

4. Use the concept of opportunity cost to explain the following.

   a. More people choose to get graduate degrees when the job market is poor.

   b. More people choose to do their own home repairs when the economy is slow and hourly wages are down.

   c. There are more parks in suburban than in urban areas.

   d. Convenience stores, which have higher prices than supermarkets, cater to busy people.

   e. Fewer students enroll in classes that meet before 10:00 A.M.

5. In the following examples, state how you would use the principle of marginal analysis to make a decision.

   a. Deciding how many days to wait before doing your laundry

   b. Deciding how much library research to do before writing your term paper

   c. Deciding how many bags of chips to eat

   d. Deciding how many lectures of a class to skip

6. This morning you made the following individual choices: you bought a bagel and coffee at the local café, you drove to school in your car during rush hour, and you typed your roommate's term paper because you are a fast typist—in return for which she will do your laundry for a month. For each of these actions, describe how your individual choices interacted with the individual choices made by others. Were other people left better off or worse off by your choices in each case?

7. The Duguay family lives on the east side of Shediac Bay, and the Legault family lives on the west side. Each family's diet consists of lobster and potatoes, and each is self-sufficient, trapping their own lobsters and growing

their own potatoes. Explain the conditions under which each of the following would be true.

a. The two families are made better off when the Duguays specialize in trapping lobsters, the Legaults specialize in growing potatoes, and the two families trade.

b. The two families are made better off when the Legaults specialize in trapping lobsters, the Duguays specialize in growing potatoes, and the two families trade.

8. Which of the following situations describes an equilibrium? Which does not? If the situation does not describe an equilibrium, what would an equilibrium look like?

a. Many people regularly commute from the suburbs to downtown Pleasantville. Due to traffic congestion, the trip takes 30 minutes when you travel by highway but only 15 minutes when you go by side streets.

b. At the intersection of Victoria and Main are two gas stations. One station charges 135.5¢ per litre for regular gas and the other charges 131.9¢ per litre. Customers can get service immediately at the first station but must wait in a long line at the second.

c. Every student enrolled in Economics 101 must also attend a weekly tutorial. This year there are two sections offered: section A and section B, which meet at the same time in adjoining classrooms and are taught by equally competent instructors. Section A is overcrowded, with people sitting on the floor and often unable to see the board. Section B has many empty seats.

9. In each of the following cases, explain whether you think the situation is efficient or not. If it is not efficient, why not? What actions would make the situation efficient?

a. Electricity is included in the rent at your dorm. Some residents in your dorm leave lights, computers, and appliances on when they are not in their rooms.

b. Although they cost the same amount to prepare, the cafeteria in your dorm consistently provides too many dishes that diners don't like, such as tofu casserole, and too few dishes that diners do like, such as roast turkey with dressing.

c. The enrollment for a particular course exceeds the spaces available. Some students who need to take this course to complete their major are unable to get a space even though others who are taking it as an elective do get a space.

10. Discuss the efficiency and equity implications of each of the following policies. How would you go about balancing the concerns of equity and efficiency in these areas?

a. The government pays the full tuition for every post-secondary student to study whatever subject he or she wishes.

b. When people lose their jobs, the government provides employment insurance (EI) until they find new ones.

11. Governments often adopt certain policies in order to promote desired behaviour among their citizens. For each of the following policies, determine what the incentive is and what behaviour the government wishes to promote. In each case, why do you think that the

government might wish to change people's behaviour, rather than allow their actions to be solely determined by individual choice?

a. A tax of $5 per pack is imposed on cigarettes.

b. The government pays parents $100 when their child is vaccinated for measles.

c. The government pays college and university students to tutor children from low-income families.

d. The government imposes a tax on the amount of air pollution that a company discharges.

12. In each of the following situations, explain how government intervention could improve society's welfare by changing people's incentives. In what sense is the market going wrong?

a. Pollution from auto emissions has reached unhealthy levels.

b. Everyone in Woodville would be better off if streetlights were installed in the town. But no individual resident is willing to pay for installation of a streetlight in front of his or her house because it is impossible to recoup the cost by charging other residents for the benefit they receive from it.

13. On June 6, 2013, Stephen Poloz, the newly appointed governor of the Bank of Canada, addressed the House of Commons Standing Committee on Finance. In this speech he said, "In the immediate aftermath of the crisis (the Great Recession of 2008), stimulative monetary and fiscal policies proved highly effective in supporting robust growth in domestic demand, particularly household expenditures, which grew to record levels. Yet, as effective as it has been, with domestic demand now slowing, the limits of this growth model are clear." Which two of the three principles of economy-wide interaction are at work in this statement?

14. In 2007, a sharp downturn in the U.S. housing market reduced the income of many who worked in the American home construction industry. In October of that year, a *Conference Board of Canada* report stated falling house prices in parts of the United States, combined with low savings and rising energy costs, would result in weak U.S. consumer spending. Furthermore, U.S. imports of wood and autos would decline because of the slower U.S. economic growth. With this information, use one of the principles of economy-wide interaction to trace a chain of links that explains how reduced spending for U.S. home purchases is likely to affect the performance of the Canadian economy.

15. In 2005, Hurricane Katrina caused massive destruction to the U.S. Gulf Coast. Tens of thousands of people lost their homes and possessions. Even those who weren't directly affected by the destruction were hurt because businesses failed or contracted and jobs dried up. Using one of the principles of economy-wide interaction, explain how government intervention can help in this situation.

16. During the Great Depression, food was left to rot in the fields or fields that had once been actively cultivated were left fallow. Use one of the principles of economy-wide interaction to explain how this could have occurred.

Economic Models: Trade-offs and Trade

FROM KITTY HAWK TO CSERIES

The Wright Brothers' model made modern airplanes, including the CSeries jets, possible.

Paul Chiasson/CP Images

AP Photo

> ❯ Why **models**—simplified representations of reality—play a crucial role in economics
>
> ❯ Two simple but important models: the **production possibility frontier** and **comparative advantage**
>
> ❯ The **circular-flow diagram,** a schematic representation of the economy
>
> ❯ The difference between **positive economics,** which analyzes how the economy works, and **normative economics,** which prescribes economic policy based on how the world should work
>
> ❯ When economists agree and why they sometimes disagree

ON SEPTEMBER 16, 2013, THE CS100, the newest jet in Bombardier's cutting-edge CSeries of aircraft, took its first test flight. It was a game-changing moment: the CS100 is part of a new aerodynamic revolution—an ultra-efficient airplane designed to cut airline operating costs and one of the first to use super-lightweight composite materials. To ensure that the CS100 was sufficiently lightweight and aerodynamic, it underwent more than 4500 hours of wind tunnel tests—tests that resulted in subtle design changes that improved its performance, reducing fuel consumption and CO_2 emissions each by 20% compared to existing passenger jets.

The CSeries is a spectacular advance from the 1903 maiden voyage of the Wright *Flyer,* the first successful powered airplane flight, in Kitty Hawk, North Carolina. Yet the Bombardier engineers—and all aeronautic engineers—owe an enormous debt to the Wright *Flyer's* inventors, Wilbur and

Orville Wright. What made the Wrights truly visionary was their wind tunnel, an apparatus that let them experiment with many different designs for wings and control surfaces. Doing experiments with a miniature airplane inside a wind tunnel the size of a shipping crate gave the Wright Brothers the knowledge that would make heavier-than-air flight possible.

Some 110 years later, Bombardier tested the design of its CSeries aircraft using more than 20 sophisticated miniature scale models inside state-of-the-art wind tunnel facilities in six countries. It also augmented its wind tunnel testing with leading-edge computational fluid dynamics testing, made possible through the use of supercomputers that are 100 000 times faster than the computers in use when the aircraft currently serving this market were designed. Thus, while a miniature airplane—whether inside a packing crate, an ultramodern wind tunnel, or a complex simulation scenario—is not

the same thing as an actual aircraft in flight, it is clearly a very useful *model* of a flying plane—a simplified representation of the real thing that can be used to answer crucial questions, such as how much lift a given wing shape will generate at a given airspeed.

Needless to say, testing an airplane design in a wind tunnel or with computer simulations is cheaper and safer than building a full-scale version and hoping it will fly. Likewise, models play a crucial role in almost all scientific research—economics very much included.

In fact, you could say that economic theory consists mainly of a collection of models, a series of simplified representations of economic reality that allow us to understand a variety of economic issues. In this chapter, we'll look at two economic models that are crucially important in their own right and also illustrate why such models are so useful. We'll conclude with a look at how economists actually use models in their work. ■

A **model** is a simplified representation of a real situation that is used to better understand real-life situations.

The **other things equal assumption** (or ceteris paribus) means that all other relevant factors remain unchanged.

Models in Economics: Some Important Examples

A **model** is any simplified representation of reality that is used to better understand real-life situations. But how do we create a simplified representation of an economic situation?

One possibility—an economist's equivalent of a wind tunnel—is to find or create a real but simplified economy. For example, economists interested in the economic role of money have studied the system of exchange that developed in World War II prison camps, in which cigarettes became a universally accepted form of payment even among prisoners who didn't smoke.

Another possibility is to simulate the workings of the economy on a computer. For example, when changes in tax law are proposed, government officials use *tax models*—large mathematical computer programs—to assess how the proposed changes would affect different types of people.

Models are important because their simplicity allows economists to focus on the effects of only one change at a time. That is, they allow us to hold everything else constant and study how one change affects the overall economic outcome. So an important assumption when building economic models is the **other things equal assumption,** which means that all other relevant factors remain unchanged. In economics, the phrase *ceteris paribus*—Latin for "other things remain the same (or held constant)"—is also often used.

But you can't always find or create a small-scale version of the whole economy, and a computer program is only as good as the data it uses. (Programmers have a saying: "garbage in, garbage out.") For many purposes, the most effective form of economic modelling is the construction of "thought experiments": simplified, hypothetical versions of real-life situations.

In Chapter 1 we illustrated the concept of equilibrium with the example of how customers at a supermarket would rearrange themselves when a new cash register opens. Though we didn't say it, this was an example of a simple model—an imaginary supermarket, in which many details were ignored. (What were customers buying? Never mind.) This simple model can be used to answer a "what if" question: what if another cash register were opened?

As the cash register story showed, it is often possible to describe and analyze a useful economic model in plain English. However, because much of economics involves changes in quantities—in the price of a product, the number of units produced, or the number of workers employed in its production—economists often find that using some mathematics helps clarify an issue. In particular, a numerical example, a simple equation, or—especially—a graph can be key to understanding an economic concept.

Whatever form it takes, a good economic model can be a tremendous aid to understanding. The best way to grasp this point is to consider some simple but important economic models and what they tell us. First, we will look at the *production possibility frontier*, a model that helps economists think about the trade-offs every economy faces. Then we will turn to *comparative advantage*, a model that clarifies the principle of gains from trade— trade both between individuals and between countries. In addition, we'll examine the *circular-flow diagram*, a schematic representation that helps us understand how flows of money, goods, and services are channelled through the economy.

In discussing these models, we make considerable use of graphs to represent mathematical relationships. Graphs play an important role throughout this book. If you are already familiar with the use of graphs, you may feel free to skip the appendix to this chapter, which provides a brief introduction to the use of graphs in economics. If not, this would be a good time to turn to it.

FOR INQUIRING MINDS

THE MODEL THAT ATE THE ECONOMY

A model is just a model, right? So how much damage can it do? Economists probably would have answered that question quite differently before the financial meltdown of 2008–2009 than after it. The financial crisis continues to reverberate today—a testament to why economic models are so important. The fact is an economic model—a *bad* economic model, it turned out—played a significant role in the origins of the crisis.

"The model that ate the economy" originated in finance theory, the branch of economics that seeks to understand what assets like stocks and bonds are worth. Financial theorists often get hired (at very high salaries, mind you) to devise complex mathematical models to help investment companies decide what assets to buy and sell and at what price.

Finance theory has become increasingly important as major investment companies have shifted from trading simple assets like stocks and bonds to more complex assets—notably, mortgage-backed securities (or MBS's for short). An MBS is an asset that entitles its owner to a stream of earnings based on the payments made by thousands of people on their home loans. Investors wanted to know how risky these complex assets were. That is, how likely was it that an investor would lose money on an MBS?

Although we won't go into the details, estimating the likelihood of losing money on an MBS is a complicated problem. It involves calculating the probability that a significant number of the thousands of homeowners backing your security will stop paying their mortgages. Until that probability could be calculated, investors didn't want to buy MBS's. In order to generate sales, investment firms needed to provide potential MBS buyers with some estimate of their risk.

In 2000, on Wall Street (the district in New York City where nearly all major American investment companies have their headquarters), one financial theorist announced that he had solved the problem by employing a huge statistical abstraction—assuming that current homeowners were no more likely to stop paying their mortgages than in previous decades. With this assumption, he devised a simple model for estimating the risk of buying an MBS. Financial traders loved the model as it opened up a huge and extraordinarily profitable market for them. Using this simple model, Wall Street was able to create and sell billions of MBS's, generating billions in profits for itself.

Or investors *thought* they had calculated the risk of losing money on an MBS. Some financial experts—particularly Darrell Duffie, a Stanford University finance professor—warned from the sidelines that the estimates of risk calculated by this simple model were just plain wrong. He, and other critics, said that in the search for simplicity, the model seriously underestimated the likelihood that many homeowners would stop paying their mortgages at the same time, leaving MBS investors in danger of incurring huge losses.

The warnings fell on deaf ears—no doubt because Wall Street was making so much money. Billions of dollars worth of MBS's were sold to investors both in the United States and abroad. In 2008–2009, the problems critics warned about exploded in catastrophic fashion. Over the previous decade, American home prices had risen too high, and mortgages had been extended to many who were unable to pay. As home prices fell to earth, millions of American homeowners didn't pay their mortgages. With losses mounting for MBS investors all around the world, it became all too clear that the model had indeed underestimated the risks. When investors and financial institutions around the world realized the extent of their losses, the worldwide economy ground to an abrupt halt. To this day, it has not fully recovered.

Trade-offs: The Production Possibility Frontier

The first principle of economics we introduced in Chapter 1 was that resources are scarce and that, as a result, any economy—whether it's an isolated group of a few dozen hunter–gatherers or the 7 billion people making up the twenty-first-century global economy—faces trade-offs. No matter how lightweight the CS100 jet is, no matter how efficient Bombardier's assembly line, producing CSeries

The **production possibility frontier** illustrates the trade-offs facing an economy that produces only two goods. It shows the maximum quantity of one good that can be produced for any given quantity produced of the other.

aircrafts means using resources (labour, land, and capital) that therefore can't be used to produce something else.

To think about the trade-offs that face any economy, economists often use the model known as the **production possibility frontier.** The idea behind this model is to improve our understanding of trade-offs by considering a simplified economy that produces only two goods. This simplification enables us to show the trade-off graphically.

Suppose, for a moment, that Canada was a one-company economy, with Bombardier its sole employer and trains and commercial aircraft its only products. So there is a choice of what kinds of transportation vehicles to produce—say, Toronto Rocket subway trains versus CSeries commercial passenger jets. Figure 2-1 shows a hypothetical production possibility frontier (*PPF*) representing the trade-off this one-company economy would face. The frontier—the line in the diagram—shows the maximum quantity of jets that Bombardier can produce per year *given* the quantity of subway trains it produces per year, and vice versa. That is, it answers questions of the form, "What is the maximum quantity of jets that Bombardier can produce in a year if it also produces 21 (or 35, or 70) subway trains that year?"

There is a crucial distinction between points *inside* or *on* the production possibility frontier (the shaded area) and *outside* the frontier. If a production point lies inside or on the frontier—like point *C*, at which Bombardier produces 10 jets and 21 subway trains in a year—it is feasible. After all, the frontier tells us that if Bombardier produces 10 jets, it could also produce a maximum of 35 subway trains that year, so it could certainly make 21 subway trains. However, a production point that lies outside the frontier—such as the hypothetical production point *D*, where Bombardier produces 20 jets and 70 subway trains—isn't feasible. Bombardier can produce 20 jets and no subway trains, *or* it can produce 70 subway trains and no jets, but it can't do both.

In Figure 2-1 the production possibility frontier intersects the horizontal axis at 20 jets. This means that if Bombardier dedicated all its production capacity[1] to making jets, it could produce 20 jets per year but could produce no subway trains. The production possibility frontier intersects the vertical axis at 70 subway trains. This means that if Bombardier dedicated all its production capacity to making subway trains, it could produce 70 subway trains per year but no jets.

FIGURE **2-1** The Production Possibility Frontier

The production possibility frontier illustrates the trade-offs Bombardier faces in producing subway trains and jets. It shows the maximum quantity of one good that can be produced given the quantity of the other good produced. Here, the maximum quantity of subway trains manufactured per year depends on the quantity of jets manufactured that year, and vice versa. Bombardier's feasible production is shown by the area *inside* or *on* the curve. Production at point *C* is feasible but not efficient. Points *A* and *B* are feasible and efficient in production, but point *D* is not feasible.

[1]The amount of production capacity is determined by the production technology used and amount of productive resources (labour, land, and capital) available.

The figure also shows less extreme trade-offs. For example, if Bombardier's managers decide to make 10 jets this year, they can produce at most 35 subway trains; this production choice is illustrated by point *A*. And if Bombardier's managers decide to produce 14 jets, they can make at most 21 subway trains, as shown by point *B*.

Thinking in terms of a production possibility frontier simplifies the complexities of reality. The real-world Canadian economy produces millions of different goods. Even Bombardier can produce more than two different types of planes and trains. Yet it's important to realize that even in its simplicity, this stripped-down model gives us important insights about the real world.

By simplifying reality, the production possibility frontier helps us understand some aspects of the real economy better than we could without the model: efficiency, opportunity cost, and economic growth.

Efficiency First of all, the production possibility frontier is a good way to illustrate the general economic concept of *efficiency*. Recall from Chapter 1 that an economy is efficient if there are no missed opportunities—there is no way to →on the line make some people better off without making other people worse off.

One key element of efficiency is that there are no missed opportunities in production—there is no way to produce more of one good without producing less of other goods. As long as Bombardier operates on its production possibility frontier, its production is efficient. At point *A*, 35 subway trains is the maximum quantity feasible given that Bombardier has also committed to producing 10 jets; at point *B*, 21 subway trains is the maximum number that can be made given the choice to produce 14 jets; and so on. But suppose for some reason that Bombardier was operating at point *C*, making 10 jets and 21 subway trains. In this case, it would not be operating efficiently and would therefore be *inefficient*: using the same resources, it could be producing more of both transportation vehicles.

Although we have used an example of the production choices of a one-firm, two-good economy to illustrate efficiency and inefficiency, these concepts also carry over to the real economy, which contains many firms and produces many goods. If the economy as a whole could not produce more of any one good without producing less of something else—that is, if it is on its production possibility frontier—then we say that the economy is *efficient in production*. If, however, the economy could produce more of some things without producing less of others—which typically means that it could produce more of everything—then it is inefficient in production. For example, an economy in which large numbers of workers are involuntarily unemployed is clearly inefficient in production. And that's a bad thing, because the economy could be producing more useful goods and services.

Although the production possibility frontier helps clarify what it means for an economy to be efficient in production, it's important to understand that efficiency in production is only *part* of what's required for the economy as a whole to be efficient. Efficiency also requires that the economy allocate its resources so that consumers are as well off as possible. If an economy does this, we say that it is *efficient in consumption* (an efficient consumption allocation). To see why efficiency in the consumption allocation is as important as efficiency in production, notice that points *A* and *B* in Figure 2-1 both represent situations in which the economy is efficient in production, because in each case it can't produce more of one good without producing less of the other. But these two situations may not be equally desirable from society's point of view. Suppose that society prefers to have more jets and fewer subway trains than at point *A*; say, it prefers to have 14 jets and 21 subway trains, corresponding to point *B*. In this case, point *A* is an inefficient consumption allocation from the point of view of the economy as a whole because it would rather have Bombardier produce at point *B* than at point *A*.

This example shows that efficiency for the economy as a whole requires *both* efficiency in production and efficiency in consumption: to be efficient, an economy must produce as much of each good as it can given the production of other goods, and it must also produce the mix of goods that people want to consume. (And it must also deliver those goods to the right people: an economy that gives subway trains to airports and commercial passenger jets to intercity transit authorities is inefficient, too.)

In the real world, command economies, such as the former Soviet Union, are notorious for inefficiency in the consumption allocation. For example, it was common in the U.S.S.R. for consumers to find stores well stocked with items few people wanted but lacking such basics as soap and toilet paper.

Opportunity Cost The production possibility frontier is also useful as a reminder of the fundamental point that the true cost of any good isn't the money it costs to buy it, but what must be given up in order to get that good—the *opportunity cost*. If, for example, Bombardier decides to change its production from point A to point B, it will produce 4 more jets but 14 fewer subway trains. So the opportunity cost of 4 jets is 14 subway trains—the 14 subway trains that must be forgone to produce 4 more jets. This means that each jet has an opportunity cost of $^{14}/_4 = ^7/_2$, or, put another way, 3½ subway trains do not get made for each jet that is produced.

Is the opportunity cost of an extra jet in terms of subway trains always the same, no matter how many jets and subway trains are currently produced? In the example illustrated by Figure 2-1, the answer is yes. If Bombardier increases its production of jets from 14 to 20, the number of subway trains it produces falls from 21 to zero. So Bombardier's opportunity cost per additional jet is $^{21}/_6$ or 3½ subway trains, the same as it was when Bombardier went from 10 jets produced to 14. However, the fact that in this example the opportunity cost of a jet in terms of a subway train is always the same is a result of an assumption we've made, an assumption that's reflected in how Figure 2-1 is drawn. Specifically, whenever we assume that the opportunity cost of an additional unit of a good doesn't change regardless of the output mix, the production possibility frontier is a straight line. Note that a linear production possibility frontier implies constant marginal productivity of production for both trains and planes.

Moreover, as you might have already guessed, the absolute value of the slope of a straight-line production possibility frontier is equal to the opportunity cost—specifically, the opportunity cost for the good measured on the horizontal axis in terms of the good measured on the vertical axis.[2] In Figure 2-1, the production possibility frontier has a *constant slope* of $-^7/_2$, implying that Bombardier faces a *constant opportunity cost* for 1 jet equal to 3½ subway trains. (A review of how to calculate the slope of a straight line is found in this chapter's appendix.) This is the simplest case, but the production possibility frontier model can also be used to examine situations in which opportunity costs change as the mix of output changes.[3]

Figure 2-2 illustrates a different assumption, a case in which Bombardier faces *increasing opportunity cost*. Here, the more jets it produces, the more costly it is to produce yet another jet in terms of forgone production of subway trains. And the same holds true in reverse: the more subway trains Bombardier produces, the more costly it is to produce yet another subway train in terms of forgone production of jets. For example, to go from producing zero jets to producing 10, Bombardier has to forgo producing 10 subway trains. That is, the opportunity cost of those 10 jets is 10 subway trains. But to increase its production of jets to

---

[2]To show this algebraically, suppose we have a production possibility frontier drawn with X on the horizontal axis and Y on the vertical axis. The *opportunity cost of X (OC_X)* is equal to the number of units of Y production we must give up in order to produce 1 more unit of X. So, $OC_X = -(\text{slope of the PPF}) = -\left(\dfrac{\Delta Y}{\Delta X}\right)$.

Also, the *opportunity cost of Y (OC_Y)* is the inverse of the opportunity cost of X, so $OC_Y = -\left(\dfrac{\Delta X}{\Delta Y}\right) = \left(\dfrac{1}{OC_X}\right)$, which is the number of units of X production we must give up to produce 1 more unit of Y.

[3]If the production possibilities frontier is not linear, the opportunity cost at a point continues to be equal to the absolute value of the slope of the production possibilities frontier (at that point). But the slope varies as we move along the production possibility frontier.

FIGURE   **2-2**   **Increasing Opportunity Cost**

The bowed-out shape of the production possibility frontier reflects increasing opportunity cost. In this example, to produce the first 10 jets, Bombardier must forgo producing 10 subway trains. But to produce an additional 10 jets, Bombardier must forgo manufacturing 60 more subway trains.

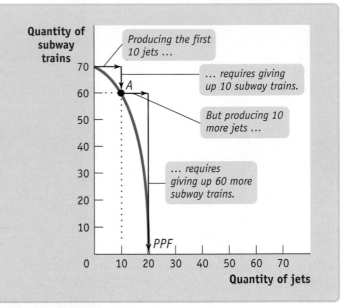

20—that is, to produce an additional 10 jets—it must forgo producing 60 more subway trains, a much higher opportunity cost. As you can see in Figure 2-2, when opportunity costs are increasing rather than constant, the production possibility frontier is a (strictly concave) bowed-out curve rather than a straight line.

Although it's often useful to work with the simple assumption that the production possibility frontier is a straight line, economists believe that in reality opportunity costs are typically increasing. When only a small amount of a good is produced, the opportunity cost of producing that good is relatively low because the economy needs to use only those resources that are especially well suited for its production. For example, if an economy grows only a small amount of corn, that corn can be grown in places where the soil and climate are perfect for corn growing but less suitable for growing anything else, like wheat. So growing that corn involves giving up only a small amount of potential wheat output. Once the economy grows a lot of corn, however, land that is well suited for wheat but isn't so great for corn must be used to produce corn anyway. As a result, the additional corn production involves sacrificing considerably more wheat production. In other words, as more of a good is produced, its opportunity cost typically rises because well-suited inputs are already used up and less adaptable inputs must be used instead.

Economic Growth   Finally, the production possibility frontier helps us understand what it means to talk about *economic growth*. We introduced the concept of economic growth in the Introduction, defining it as *the growing ability of the economy to produce goods and services*. As we saw, economic growth is one of the fundamental features of the real economy. But are we really justified in saying that the economy has grown over time? After all, although the Canadian economy produces more of many things than it did a century ago, it produces less of other things—for example, horse-drawn carriages. Production of many goods, in other words, is actually down. So how can we say for sure that the economy as a whole has grown?

The answer is illustrated in Figure 2-3, where we have drawn two hypothetical production possibility frontiers for the economy. In them we have assumed once again that everyone in the economy works for Bombardier and, consequently, the economy produces only two goods, subway trains and jets. Notice how the two curves are nested, with the one labelled "Original *PPF*" lying completely inside the

FIGURE **2-3** Economic Growth

Economic growth results in an *outward shift* of the production possibility frontier because production possibilities are expanded. The economy can now produce more of everything. For example, if production is initially at point *A* (60 subway trains and 10 jets), economic growth means that the economy could move to point *E* (70 subway trains and 12 jets).

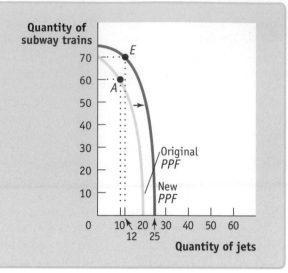

one labelled "New *PPF*." Now we can see graphically what we mean by economic growth of the economy: economic growth means an *expansion of the economy's production possibilities; that is, the economy can produce more of everything.* For example, if the economy initially produces at point *A* (60 subway trains and 10 jets), economic growth means that the economy could move to point *E* (70 subway trains and 12 jets). Point *E* lies outside the original frontier; so in the production possibility frontier model, growth is shown as an outward shift of the frontier.

What can lead the production possibility frontier to shift outward? There are basically two sources of economic growth. One is an increase in the economy's **factors of production,** the resources used to produce goods and services. Economists usually use the term *factor of production* to refer to a resource that is not used up in production. For example, in traditional airplane manufacture, workers used riveting machines to connect metal sheets when constructing a plane's fuselage; the workers and the riveters are factors of production, but the rivets and the sheet metal are not. Once a fuselage is made, a worker and riveter can be used to make another fuselage, but the sheet metal and rivets used to make one fuselage cannot be used to make another.

Broadly speaking, the main factors of production are the resources of land, labour, physical capital, and human capital. Land is a resource supplied by nature; labour is the economy's pool of workers; physical capital refers to created resources such as machines and buildings; and human capital refers to the educational achievements and skills of the labour force, which enhance its productivity. Of course, each of these is really a category rather than a single factor: land in Labrador is quite different from land in southern Ontario.

To see how adding to an economy's factors of production leads to economic growth, suppose that Bombardier builds another construction facility that allows it to increase the number of transportation vehicles—subway trains or CSeries jets or both—it can produce in a year. The new construction facility is a factor of production, a resource Bombardier can use to increase its yearly output. We can't say how many more planes or subway trains Bombardier will produce; that's a management decision that will depend on, among other things, customer demand. But we can say that Bombardier's production possibility frontier has shifted outward because it can now produce more subway trains without reducing the number of CSeries jets it makes, or it can make more CSeries jets without reducing the number of subway trains produced.

The other source of economic growth is progress in **technology,** the technical means for the production of goods and services. Composite and advanced

Factors of production are resources (labour, land, and capital) used to produce goods and services.

Technology is the technical means for producing goods and services.

aluminum materials had been used in some parts of aircraft before the Bombardier CSeries was developed. But Bombardier engineers realized that there were large additional advantages to building a whole plane out of composites and advanced aluminum. The plane would be lighter, stronger, and have better aerodynamics than a plane built in the traditional way. It would therefore have longer range, be able to carry more people, and use less fuel, in addition to being able to maintain higher cabin pressure. So in a real sense Bombardier's innovation—a whole plane built out of advanced materials—was a way to do more with any given amount of resources, pushing out the production possibility frontier.

Because improved jet technology has pushed out the production possibility frontier, it has made it possible for the economy to produce more of everything, not just jets and air travel. Over the past 30 years, the biggest technological advances have taken place in information technology, not in construction or food services. Yet Canadians have chosen to buy bigger houses and eat out more than they used to because the economy's growth has made it possible to do so.

The production possibility frontier is a very simplified model of an economy. Yet it teaches us important lessons about real-life economies. It gives us our first clear sense of what constitutes economic efficiency, it illustrates the concept of opportunity cost, and it makes clear what economic growth is all about.

Comparative Advantage and Gains from Trade

Among the twelve principles of economics described in Chapter 1 was the principle of *gains from trade*—the mutual gains that individuals or countries can achieve by specializing in doing different things and trading with one another. *→ more production* Our next illustration of an economic model is a particularly useful model of gains from trade—trade based on *comparative advantage*.

One of the most important insights in all of economics is that there are gains from trade—that it makes sense to produce the things you're especially good at producing and to buy from other people the things you aren't as good at producing. This would be true even if you could produce everything for yourself: even if a brilliant brain surgeon *could* repair her own dripping faucet, it's probably a better idea for her to call in a professional plumber.

How can we model the gains from trade? Let's stay with our mass transportation vehicle example and once again imagine that Canada is a one-company economy in which everyone works for Bombardier, producing airplanes and subway trains. Let's now assume, however, that Canada has the ability to trade with Brazil—another one-company economy in which everyone works for a company that manufactures aircraft and subway trains. (In the real world, the Brazilian company Embraer is an internationally successful producer of small commuter jets. If you fly from one Canadian city to another, your plane is likely to be made by Bombardier; but if you fly within other countries, the odds are equally good that your plane will have been made by Embraer.)

In our example, the only two goods produced are subway trains and jets. Both countries could produce both kinds of mass transportation vehicles. But as we'll see in a moment, they can gain by producing different things and trading with each other. For the purposes of this example, let's return to the simpler case of straight-line production possibility frontiers. Canada's production possibilities are represented by the production possibility frontier in panel (a) of Figure 2-4, which is similar to the production possibility frontier in Figure 2-1. According to this diagram, Canada can produce 70 subway trains if it makes no jets and can manufacture 20 jets if it produces no subway trains. Recall that this means that the slope of the Canadian production possibility frontier is $-7/2$: its opportunity cost of 1 jet is $7/2$ of a subway train (i.e., to make 1 more jet, Canada has to give up making 3.5 subway trains).

Panel (b) of Figure 2-4 shows Brazil's production possibilities. Like Canada, Brazil's production possibility frontier is a straight line, implying a constant opportunity cost of jets in terms of subway trains. Brazil's production possibility

FIGURE **2-4** Production Possibilities for Two Countries

Here, both Canada and Brazil have a constant opportunity cost of jets, illustrated by a straight-line production possibility frontier. For Canada, each jet has an opportunity cost of ½ of a subway train (i.e., 3.5 subway trains). Brazil has an opportunity cost of a jet equal to 6 subway trains.

frontier has a constant slope of −6. Brazil can't produce as much of anything as Canada can: at most it can produce 60 subway trains or 10 jets. But it is relatively better at manufacturing subway trains than Canada is; whereas Canada sacrifices 2/7 of a jet per subway train produced, for Brazil the opportunity cost of a subway train is only 1/6 of a jet. Table 2-1 summarizes the two countries' opportunity costs of subway trains and jets.

Now, Canada and Brazil could each choose to make their own subway trains and jets, not trading any airplanes or trains and consuming only what each produced within its own country. (A country "consumes" an airplane or train when it is owned by a domestic resident.) Let's suppose that the two countries start out this way and make the consumption choices shown in Figure 2-4: in the absence of trade, Canada produces and consumes 28 subway trains and 12 jets per year, while Brazil produces and consumes 30 subway trains and 5 jets per year.

But is this the best the two countries can do? No, it isn't. Given that the two producers—and therefore the two countries—have different opportunity costs, Canada and Brazil can strike a deal that makes both of them better off.

TABLE **2-1** Canadian and Brazilian Opportunity Costs of Subway Trains and Jets

	Canadian Opportunity Cost		Brazilian Opportunity Cost
One subway train	2/7 jet	>	1/6 jet
One jet	7/2 subway trains	<	6 subway trains

TABLE **2-2** How Canada and Brazil Gain from Trade

		Without Trade		With Trade		Gains from Trade
		Production	Consumption	Production	Consumption	
Canada	Subway trains	28	28	0	29	+1
	Jets	12	12	20	14	+2
Brazil	Subway trains	30	30	60	31	+1
	Jets	5	5	0	6	+1

FIGURE **2-5** **Comparative Advantage and Gains from Trade**

By specializing and trading, Canada and Brazil can produce and consume more of both jets and subway trains. Canada specializes in manufacturing jets, where its comparative advantage exists, and Brazil—which has an *absolute* disadvantage in both goods but a *comparative* advantage in subway trains—specializes in manufacturing subway trains. With trade, both countries can consume more of both goods than either could without trade.

Table 2-2 shows how such a deal works: Canada specializes in the production of jets, manufacturing 20 per year, and sells 6 to Brazil. Meanwhile, Brazil specializes in the production of subway trains, producing 60 per year, and sells 29 to Canada. The result is shown in Figure 2-5. Canada now consumes more of both subway trains and jets than before: instead of 28 subway trains and 12 jets, it now consumes 29 subway trains and 14 jets. Brazil also consumes more, going from 30 subway trains and 5 jets to 31 subway trains and 6 jets. As Table 2-2 also shows, both Canada and Brazil reap gains from trade, consuming more of both types of transportation vehicle than they would have without trade.

Both countries are better off when they each specialize in what they are relatively good at producing and then trade their products. It's a good idea for Canada to specialize in the production of jets because its opportunity cost of a jet is smaller than Brazil's: $^7/_2 < 6$. Correspondingly, Brazil should specialize in the production of subway trains because its opportunity cost of a subway train is smaller than Canada's: $^1/_6 < ^2/_7$.

What we would say in this case is that Canada has a comparative advantage in the production of jets and Brazil has a comparative advantage in the production of subway trains. A country has a **comparative advantage** in producing something if the opportunity cost of that production is lower for that country than for other countries. The same concept applies to firms and people: a firm or an individual has a comparative advantage in producing something if its, his, or her opportunity cost of production is lower than for others.

One point of clarification before we proceed further. You may have wondered why Canada traded 6 jets to Brazil in return for 29 subway trains. Why not some other deal, like trading 6 jets for 20 subway trains? The answer to that question has two parts. First, there may indeed be other trades that Canada and Brazil might agree to. Second, there are some deals that we can safely rule out—one like 6 jets for 20 subway trains.

A country has a **comparative advantage** in producing a good or service if its opportunity cost of producing the good or service is lower than that of other countries. Likewise, an individual has a comparative advantage in producing a good or service if his or her opportunity cost of producing the good or service is lower than for other people.

A country has an **absolute advantage** in producing a good or service if the country can produce more output per worker than other countries. Likewise, an individual has an absolute advantage in producing a good or service if he or she is better at producing it than other people. Having an absolute advantage is not the same thing as having a comparative advantage.

To understand why, re-examine Table 2-1 and consider Canada first. Without trading with Brazil, the Canadian opportunity cost of a subway train is $2/7$ of a jet. So it's clear that Canada will not accept any trade that requires it to give up more than $2/7$ of a jet for a subway train — as doing so would make it worse off. Trading 6 jets in return for 20 subway trains would require Canada to pay an opportunity cost of $6/20 = 3/10$ of a jet for a subway train. Because $3/10$ is *greater than* $2/7$, this is a deal that Canada would reject. Similarly, Brazil won't accept a trade that gives it less than 6 subway trains for a jet.

The point to remember is that Canada and Brazil will be willing to trade only if the "price" of the good each country obtains in the trade is less than its own opportunity cost of producing the good domestically. Moreover, this is a general statement that is true whenever two parties—countries, firms, or individuals—trade voluntarily.

While our story clearly simplifies reality, it teaches us some very important lessons that apply to the real economy, too.

First, the model provides a clear illustration of the gains from trade: through specialization and trade, both countries produce more and consume more than if they were self-sufficient.

Second, the model demonstrates a very important point that is often overlooked in real-world arguments: each country has a comparative advantage in producing something. This applies to firms and people as well: *everyone has a comparative advantage in something, and everyone has a comparative disadvantage in something.*

Crucially, in our example it doesn't matter if, as is probably the case in real life, Canadian workers are just as good as or even better than Brazilian workers at producing subway trains and jets. Suppose that Canada is actually better than Brazil at production of both types of transportation vehicles. In that case, we would say that Canada has an **absolute advantage** in both subway train and jet production: in an hour, a Canadian worker can produce more of either a subway train or jet than a Brazilian worker could. You might be tempted to think that in that case Canada has nothing to gain from trading with the less productive Brazil.

But we've just seen that Canada can indeed benefit from trading with Brazil because *comparative, not absolute, advantage is the basis for mutual gains from trade.*[4] It doesn't matter whether it takes Brazil more resources than Canada to make a subway train; what matters for trade is that for Brazil the opportunity cost of a subway train is lower than the Canadian opportunity cost. So Brazil, despite its absolute disadvantage, even

 PITFALLS

MISUNDERSTANDING COMPARATIVE ADVANTAGE

Students do it, pundits do it, and politicians do it all the time: they confuse *comparative* advantage with *absolute* advantage. For example, back in the 1980s, when the North American economy seemed to be lagging behind that of Japan, one often heard commentators warn that if we didn't improve our productivity, we would soon have no comparative advantage in anything.

What those commentators meant was that we would have no *absolute* advantage in anything—that there might come a time

when the Japanese were better at everything than we were. (It didn't turn out that way, but that's another story.) And they had the idea that in that case we would no longer be able to benefit from trade with Japan.

But just as Brazil, in our example, was able to benefit from trade with Canada (and vice versa) despite the fact that Canada was absolutely better at manufacturing both jets and subway trains, in real life nations can still gain from trade even if they are less productive in all industries than the countries they trade with.

---

[4]In 1817, David Ricardo formulated the idea that comparative advantage was the basis of mutually beneficial trade between individuals and nations. It is a very powerful idea that comparative advantage and specialization in production are all that is needed for trade to be beneficial. Before this time, many people mistakenly believed that a nation with an absolute advantage in the production of all goods could not benefit from trade.

GLOBAL COMPARISON

PYJAMA REPUBLICS

Poor countries tend to have low productivity in clothing manufacture, but even lower productivity in other industries (see the upcoming Economics in Action), giving them a comparative advantage in clothing manufacture. As a result, the clothing industry tends to dominate their economies. An official from one such country once joked, "We are not a banana republic—we are a pyjama republic."

The figure to the right plots per capita income (the total income of the country divided by the size of the population) against the share of manufacturing employment devoted to clothing production for several countries. The graph shows just how strongly negative the relationship is between a country's per capita income level and the size of its clothing industry: poor countries have relatively large clothing industries, while rich countries have relatively small ones.

According to the U.S. Department of Commerce, Bangladesh's clothing industry has "low productivity, largely low literacy levels, frequent labour unrest, and outdated technology." Yet Bangladesh devotes most of its manufacturing workforce to clothing, the sector in which it nonetheless has a comparative advantage because its productivity in non-clothing industries is even lower. In

contrast, Costa Rica has "relatively high productivity" in clothing. Yet, a much smaller and declining fraction of Costa Rica's workforce is employed in clothing production. That's because productivity in non-clothing industries is somewhat higher in Costa Rica than in Bangladesh.

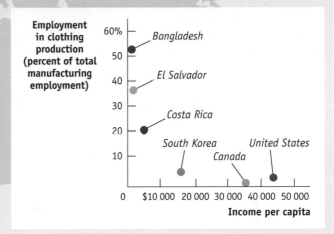

Source: World Bank, World Development Indicators; Nicita A. and M. Olarreaga, "Trade, Production and Protection 1976–2004," *World Bank Economic Review* 21, no. 1 (2007): 165–171.

in subway trains, has a comparative advantage in the manufacture of subway trains. Meanwhile Canada, which can use its resources most productively by manufacturing jets, has a comparative *dis*advantage in manufacturing subway trains.

Comparative Advantage and International Trade, in Reality

Look at the label on a manufactured good sold in Canada, and there's a good chance you will find that it was produced in some other country, such as China or Japan. On the other side, many Canadian industries sell a large fraction of their output overseas. (This is particularly true of agriculture, high technology, and entertainment.)

Should all this international exchange of goods and services be celebrated, or is it cause for concern? Politicians and the public often question the desirability of international trade, arguing that the nation should produce goods for itself rather than buying them from foreigners. Industries around the world demand protection from foreign competition: Japanese farmers want to keep out North American rice, Canadian steelworkers want to keep out European steel. And these demands are often supported by public opinion.

Economists, however, have a very positive view of international trade. Why? Because they view it in terms of comparative advantage. As we learned from our hypothetical example of Canadian jets and Brazilian subway trains, international trade benefits both countries. Each country can consume more than if it didn't trade and remained self-sufficient. Moreover, these mutual gains don't depend on each country being absolutely better than other countries at producing one kind of good. Even if one country has, say, higher output per worker in both industries— that is, even if one country has an absolute advantage in both industries—there are still gains from trade. The above Global Comparison, which explains the pattern of clothing production throughout the global economy, illustrates just this point.

Trade takes the form of **barter** when people directly exchange goods or services that they have for goods or services that they want.

The **circular-flow diagram** represents the transactions in an economy by flows around a circle.

A **household** is a person or a group of people that share their income.

A **firm** is an organization that produces goods and services for sale.

Firms sell goods and services that they produce to households in **markets for goods and services.**

Transactions: The Circular-Flow Diagram

The model economies that we've studied so far—each containing only one firm—are a huge simplification. We've also greatly simplified trade between Canada and Brazil, assuming that they engage only in the simplest of economic transactions, **barter**, in which one party directly trades a good or service for another good or service without using money. In a modern economy, simple barter is rare: usually people trade goods or services for money—pieces of coloured paper with no inherent value—and then trade those pieces of coloured paper for the goods or services they want. That is, they sell goods or services and buy other goods or services.

And they both sell and buy a lot of different things. The Canadian economy is a vastly complex entity, with almost 18 million workers employed by hundreds of thousands of companies, producing thousands of different goods and services. Yet you can learn some very important things about the economy by considering the simple graphic shown in Figure 2-6, the **circular-flow diagram.** This diagram represents the transactions that take place in an economy by two kinds of flows around a circle: flows of things such as goods, services, labour, or raw materials in one direction, and flows of money that pay for these things in the opposite direction. In this case the physical and intangible flows are shown in yellow, the money flows in green.

The simplest circular-flow diagram illustrates an economy that contains only two kinds of inhabitants: **households** and **firms.** A household consists of either an individual or a group of people (usually, but not necessarily, a family) that share their income. A firm is an organization that produces goods and services for sale—and that employs members of households.

As you can see in Figure 2-6, there are two kinds of markets in this simple economy. On one side (here the left side) there are **markets for goods and services** in which households buy the goods and services they want from firms. This produces a flow of goods and services to households and a return flow of money to firms.

FIGURE **2-6** The Circular-Flow Diagram

This diagram represents the flows of money and of goods and services in the economy. In the markets for goods and services, households purchase goods and services from firms, generating a flow of money to the firms and a flow of goods and services to the households. The money flows back to households as firms rent the factors of production (labour, land, and capital) from the households in factor markets.

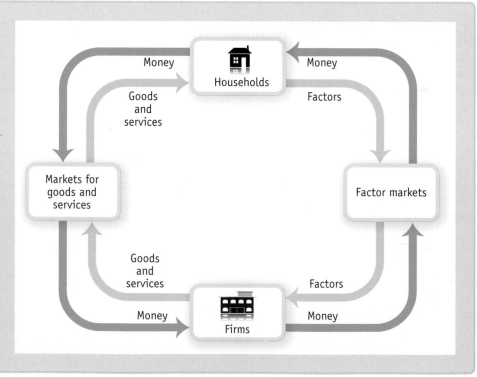

On the other side, there are **factor markets** in which firms buy or rent the resources they need to produce goods and services. Recall from earlier in the chapter that the main factors of production are land, labour, and capital.

The factor market most of us know best is the labour market, in which workers sell their services. In addition, we can think of households as owning, selling, and renting the other factors of production to firms. For example, when a firm buys physical capital in the form of machines, the payment ultimately goes to the households that own the machine-making firm. In this case, the transactions are occurring in the capital market, the market in which capital is bought and sold. As we'll examine in detail later, factor markets ultimately determine an economy's **income distribution,** how the total income created in an economy is allocated between less skilled workers, highly skilled workers, and the owners of capital and land.

The circular-flow diagram ignores a number of real-world complications in the interests of simplicity. A few examples:

- In the real world, the distinction between firms and households isn't always that clear-cut. Consider a small, family-run business—a farm, a shop, a small hotel. Is this a firm or a household? A more complete picture would include a separate box for family businesses.

- Many of the sales firms make are not to households but to other firms; for example, steel companies sell mainly to other companies such as auto manufacturers, not to households. A more complete picture would include these flows of goods, services, and money within the business sector.

- The figure doesn't show the government, which in the real world diverts quite a lot of money out of the circular flow in the form of taxes but also injects a lot of money back into the flow in the form of spending.

Figure 2-6, in other words, is by no means a complete picture either of all the types of inhabitants of the real economy or of all the flows of money and physical items and intangible services that take place among these inhabitants.

Despite its simplicity, the circular-flow diagram is a very useful aid to thinking about the economy.

Firms buy or rent the resources they need to produce goods and services in **factor markets.**

An economy's **income distribution** is the way in which total income is divided among the owners of the various factors of production.

ECONOMICS ▸ *IN ACTION*

RICH NATION, POOR NATION

Try taking off your clothes—at a suitable time and in a suitable place, of course—and taking a look at the labels inside that say where they were made. It's a very good bet that much, if not most, of your clothing was manufactured overseas, in a country that is much poorer than Canada—say, in El Salvador, Sri Lanka, or Bangladesh.

Why are these countries so much poorer than we are? The immediate reason is that their economies are much less *productive*—firms in these countries are just not able to produce as much from a given quantity of resources as comparable firms in Canada or other wealthy countries. Why countries differ so much in productivity is a deep question—indeed, one of the main questions that preoccupy economists. But in any case, the difference in productivity is a fact.

Although less productive than Canadian workers, Bangladeshi workers have a comparative advantage in clothing production.

But if the economies of these countries are so much less productive than ours, how is it that they make so much of our clothing? Why don't we do it for ourselves?

The answer is "comparative advantage." Just about every industry in Bangladesh is much less productive than the corresponding industry in Canada. But the productivity difference between rich and poor countries varies across goods; it is very large in the production of sophisticated goods like aircraft but not that large in the production of simpler goods like clothing. So Bangladesh's position with regard to clothing production is like Brazil's position with respect to producing subway trains in our example: it's not as good (absolutely) at it as Canada is, but it's the thing Brazil does comparatively (relatively) well.

Bangladesh, though it is at an absolute disadvantage compared with Canada in almost everything, has a comparative advantage in clothing production. This means that both Canada and Bangladesh are able to consume more because they specialize in producing different things, with Bangladesh supplying our clothing and Canada supplying Bangladesh with more sophisticated goods.

CHECK YOUR UNDERSTANDING   2-1

1. True or false? Explain your answer.
   a. An increase in the amount of resources available to Bombardier for use in producing CSeries jets and subway trains does not change its production possibility frontier.
   b. A technological change that allows Bombardier to build more subway trains for any amount of CSeries jets built results in a change in its production possibility frontier.
   c. The production possibility frontier is useful because it illustrates how much of one good an economy must give up to get more of another good regardless of whether resources are being used efficiently.

2. In Italy, an automobile can be produced by 8 workers in one day and a washing machine by 3 workers in one day. In Canada, an automobile can be produced by 6 workers in one day and a washing machine by 2 workers in one day.
   a. Which country has an absolute advantage in the production of automobiles? In washing machines?
   b. Which country has a comparative advantage in the production of washing machines? In automobiles?
   c. What pattern of specialization results in the greatest gains from trade between the two countries?

3. Using the numbers from Table 2-1, explain why Canada and Brazil are willing to engage in a trade of 7 jets for 29 subway trains.

4. Use the circular-flow diagram to explain how an increase in the amount of money spent by households results in an increase in the number of jobs in the economy. Describe in words what the circular-flow diagram predicts.

Solutions appear at back of book.

Using Models

Economics, we have now learned, is mainly a matter of creating models that draw on a set of basic principles but add some more specific assumptions that allow the modeller to apply those principles to a particular situation. But what do economists actually *do* with their models?

Positive versus Normative Economics

Imagine that you are an economic adviser to the premier of your province. What kinds of questions might the premier ask you to answer?

Well, here are three possible questions:

1. How much revenue will the provincial gasoline tax yield next year?

2. How much would that revenue increase if the tax were raised by 5 percentage points?

3. Should the government increase the tax, bearing in mind that the tax increase will raise much-needed revenue and reduce traffic and air pollution, but will impose some financial hardship on frequent commuters and the trucking industry?

There is a big difference between the first two questions and the third one. The first two are questions about facts. Your forecast of next year's gasoline tax will be proved right or wrong when the numbers actually come in. Your estimate of the impact of a change in the tax is a little harder to check—revenue depends on other factors besides the tax, and it may be hard to disentangle the causes of any change in revenue. Still, in principle there is only one right answer.

But the question of whether the tax on gasoline should be raised may not have a "right" answer—two people who agree on the effects of a higher gasoline tax could still disagree about whether raising this tax is a good idea. For example, someone who takes public transit or walks to work probably won't care about the increased gasoline tax but may care about the reduced traffic and pollution. However, a regular car commuter may have the opposite priorities.

This example highlights a key distinction between two roles of economic analysis. Analysis that tries to answer questions about the way the world works, which have definite right and wrong answers, is known as **positive economics.** In contrast, analysis that involves saying how the world *should* work is known as **normative economics.** To put it another way, positive economics is about objective description; normative economics is about subjective prescription.

Positive economics occupies most of the time and effort of the economics profession. And models play a crucial role in almost all positive economics. As we mentioned earlier, the Canadian government uses computer models to assess proposed changes in federal tax policy, and many provincial and territorial governments have similar models to assess the effects of their own tax policies.

It's worth noting that there is a subtle but important difference between the first and second questions we imagined the premier asking. Question 1 asked for a simple prediction about next year's revenue—a **forecast.** Question 2 was a "what if" question, asking how revenue would change if the tax law were changed. Economists are often called upon to answer both types of questions, but models are especially useful for answering "what if" questions.

The answers to such questions often serve as a guide to policy, but they are still predictions, not prescriptions. That is, they tell you what will happen if a policy is changed; they don't tell you whether or not that result is good. Suppose your economic model tells you that the premier's proposed increase in gasoline taxes will raise inner city property values but will hurt people who must use their cars to get to work. Does that make this proposed tax increase a good idea or a bad one? It depends on whom you ask. As we've just seen, someone who is very concerned about pollution will support the increase, but someone who is very concerned with the welfare of drivers will feel differently. That's a value judgment—it's not a question of economic analysis.

Still, economists often do engage in normative economics and give policy advice. How can they do this when there may be no "right" answer?

One answer is that economists are also citizens, and we all have our opinions. But economic analysis can often be used to show that some policies are clearly better than others, regardless of anyone's opinions.

Suppose that policies A and B achieve the same goal, but policy A makes everyone better off than policy B—or at least makes some people better off without making other people worse off. Then A is clearly more efficient than B. That's not a value judgment: we're talking about how best to achieve a goal, not about the goal itself.

For example, two different policies have been used to help low-income families obtain housing: rent control, which limits the rents landlords are allowed to charge, and rent subsidies, which provide families with additional money to pay rent. Almost all economists agree that subsidies are the more efficient policy. And so the great majority of economists, whatever their personal politics, favour subsidies over rent control.

When policies can be clearly ranked in this way, then economists generally agree. But it is no secret that economists sometimes disagree.

Positive economics is the branch of economic analysis that describes the way the economy actually works.

Normative economics makes prescriptions about the way the economy should work.

A **forecast** is a simple prediction of the future.

FOR INQUIRING MINDS

WHEN ECONOMISTS AGREE

"If all the economists in the world were laid end to end, they still couldn't reach a conclusion." So goes one popular economist joke. But do economists really disagree that much?

Not according to a classic survey of members of the American Economic Association, reported in the May 1992 issue of the *American Economic Review*. The authors asked respondents to agree or disagree with a number of statements about the economy; what they found was a high level of agreement among professional economists on many of the statements. At the top, with more than 90 percent of the economists agreeing, were "Tariffs and import quotas usually reduce general economic welfare" and "A ceiling on rents reduces the quantity and quality of housing available." What's striking about these two statements is that many non-economists disagree:

tariffs and import quotas to keep out foreign-produced goods are favoured by many voters, and proposals to do away with rent control in cities like New York and San Francisco have met fierce political opposition.

So is the stereotype of quarrelling economists a myth? Not entirely: economists do disagree quite a lot on some issues, especially in macroeconomics. But there is a large area of common ground.

When and Why Economists Disagree

Economists have a reputation for arguing with each other. Where does this reputation come from, and is it justified?

One important answer is that media coverage tends to exaggerate the real differences in views among economists. If nearly all economists agree on an issue—for example, the proposition that rent controls lead to housing shortages—reporters and editors are likely to conclude that it's not a story worth covering, meaning that professional consensus tends to go unreported. But an issue on which prominent economists take opposing sides—for example, whether cutting taxes right now would help the economy—makes a news story worth reporting. So you hear much more about the areas of disagreement within economics than you do about the large areas of agreement.

It is also worth remembering that economics is, unavoidably, often tied up in politics. On a number of issues powerful interest groups know what opinions they want to hear; they therefore have an incentive to find and promote economists who profess those opinions, giving these economists a prominence and visibility out of proportion to their support among their colleagues.

While the appearance of disagreement among economists exceeds the reality, it remains true that economists often do disagree about important things. For example, some well-respected economists argue vehemently that the Canadian government should replace the income tax with a *consumption tax*. Other equally respected economists disagree. Why this difference of opinion?

One important source of differences lies in values: as in any diverse group of individuals, reasonable people can differ. In comparison to an income tax, a consumption tax typically falls more heavily on people of modest means. So an economist who values a society with more social and income equality for its own sake will tend to oppose a consumption tax. An economist with different values will be less likely to oppose it.

A second important source of differences arises from economic modelling. Because economists base their conclusions on models, which are simplified representations of reality, two economists can legitimately disagree about which simplifications are appropriate—and therefore arrive at different conclusions.

In 2009, British Columbia decided to harmonize its provincial sales tax with the federal Goods and Services Tax (GST) starting in 2010, only to return to the original system after the harmonized sales tax (HST) was defeated in a 2011 referendum. Suppose that two economists were asked for their opinion on the situation. Economist A may focus on the loss of provincial control over the design and collection of sales taxes or the additional sales tax now imposed on certain purchases.[5] But economist B may think that the right way to approach the question is to ignore sovereignty and broadening of the sales tax base and focus on the ways in which the proposed law would change consumption behaviour and the ways in which firms conduct their businesses. This economist might point to studies suggesting that a harmonized sales tax lowers the cost of operating a business, lowers some prices, and promotes more business investment and job creation, all desirable results.

Because the economists have used different models—that is, made different simplifying assumptions about what is most important—they arrive at different conclusions. And so the two economists may find themselves on different sides of the issue.

Behavioural economics, a relatively new approach to modelling that combines concepts from psychology and economics, also leads to different models, which can cause disagreement among economists. Traditional economic models assume that decision-makers are rational, unemotional, and capable of processing large amounts of information in order to make an optimal choice. Meanwhile, behavioural economics acknowledges that economic decision-makers are human beings who can be irrational, emotional, and may not learn from their mistakes. Some might say the traditional approach describes how the world should be (normative economics) while behavioural economics attempts to describe the world as it really is (positive economics).

Both methods of creating models help us better understand economic decision-making, but their differing assumptions can lead to very different results. In finance, for example, the traditional assumptions imply that agents learn from past mistakes and thus do not repeatedly make the same mistakes, resulting in very efficient financial markets, while in behavioural economic models irrational agents can make systematic errors, which can help explain the existence of stock market anomalies.

In most cases such disputes are eventually resolved by the accumulation of evidence showing which of the various models proposed by economists does a better job of fitting the facts. However, in economics, as in any science, it can take a long time before research settles important disputes—decades, in some cases. And since the economy is always changing, in ways that make old models invalid or raise new policy questions, there are always new issues on which economists disagree. The policy-maker must then decide which economist to believe.

The important point is that economic analysis is a method, not a set of conclusions.

ECONOMICS > IN ACTION

ECONOMISTS, BEYOND THE IVORY TOWER

Many economists are mainly engaged in teaching and research. But quite a few economists have a more direct hand in events.

As described earlier in this chapter (For Inquiring Minds, "The Model That Ate the Economy"), one specific branch of economics, finance theory, plays an important role on Bay Street, Wall Street, and other financial centres around the world—not always to good effect. But pricing assets is by no means the only useful function economists serve in the business world. Businesses need forecasts of the future demand for their products, predictions of future raw-material prices, assessments of their future financing needs, and more; for all of these purposes, economic analysis is essential.

Stephen Poloz, the Governor of the Bank of Canada, discusses interest rates as Deputy Governor Tiff Macklem watches. Both men have multiple degrees in economics.

Adrian Wyld/CP Images

---

[5]Prior to the implementation of BC's HST, newly-constructed homes, restaurant meals, and several services only faced the 5% federal GST. The rate rose to 12% with the HST. A complicated rebate system for new homes meant that purchasers of homes costing less than $525 000 paid no more sales taxes than before, while purchasers of homes costing more than $525 000 paid more sales tax under the HST.

Some of the economists employed in the business world work directly for the institutions that need their input. Top financial institutions like Royal Bank and National Bank maintain high-quality economics groups, which produce analyses of forces and events likely to affect financial markets. Other economists are employed by consulting firms, which sell analysis and advice to a wide range of other businesses.

Last but not least, economists participate extensively in government. Indeed, government agencies at both federal and provincial levels are major employers of economists. This shouldn't be surprising: one of the most important functions of government is to make economic policy, and almost every government policy decision must take economic effects into consideration. So governments around the world employ economists in a variety of roles.

You are likely to find economists working in almost every branch of the Canadian government. Consider the mandates of the departments dealing with Aboriginal affairs, agriculture, environment, immigration, interprovincial relations, natural resources, transportation, or science and technology! No matter what department comes to mind, there is a strong economic dimension involved. However, the strongest concentration of economists is likely to be found in the Department of Finance, which plans and prepares the federal government's budget, and analyzes and designs tax policies. This department also develops policies on international finance and helps design Canada's tariff policies. The Bank of Canada employs economists who help design monetary policy, implement that policy, and regulate chartered banks. And economists play an especially important role in two international organizations headquartered in Washington, D.C.: the International Monetary Fund, which provides advice and loans to countries experiencing economic difficulties, and the World Bank, which provides advice and loans to promote long-term economic development.

In the past, it wasn't that easy to track what all these economists working on practical affairs were up to. These days, however, there is a very lively online discussion of economic prospects and policy, on websites that range from the home page of the International Monetary Fund (www.imf.org), to business-oriented sites like economy.com, to the blogs of individual economists, like that of Mark Thoma (economistsview.typepad.com) or, yes, our own blog, which is among the Technorati top 100 blogs, at krugman.blogs.nytimes.com.

▼ Quick Review

- **Positive economics**—the focus of most economic research—is the analysis of the way the world works, in which there are definite right and wrong answers. If often involves making **forecasts.** But in **normative economics,** which makes prescriptions about how things ought to be, there are often no right answers and only value judgments.

- Economists do disagree—though not as much as legend has it—for two main reasons. One, they may disagree about which simplifications to make in a model. Two, economists may disagree—like everyone else—about values.

CHECK YOUR UNDERSTANDING   2-2

1. Which of the following statements is a positive statement? Which is a normative statement?
   a. Society should take measures to prevent people from engaging in dangerous personal behaviour.
   b. People who engage in dangerous personal behaviour impose higher costs on society through higher medical costs.

2. True or false? Explain your answer.
   a. Policy choice A and policy choice B attempt to achieve the same social goal. Policy choice A, however, results in a much less efficient use of resources than policy choice B. Therefore, economists are more likely to agree on choosing policy choice B.
   b. When two economists disagree on the desirability of a policy, it's typically because one of them has made a mistake.
   c. Policy-makers can always use economics to figure out which goals a society should try to achieve.

Solutions appear at back of book.

BUSINESS CASE • Efficiency, Opportunity Cost, and the Logic of Lean Production

Corbis/Photolibrary

In the summer and fall of 2010, workers were rearranging the furniture in Boeing's final assembly plant in Everett, Washington, in preparation for the production of the Boeing 767. It was a difficult and time-consuming process, however, because the items of "furniture"—Boeing's assembly equipment—weighed on the order of 180 tonnes each. It was a necessary part of setting up a production system based on "lean manufacturing," also called "just-in-time" production. Lean manufacturing, pioneered by Toyota Motors of Japan, is based on the practice of having parts arrive on the factory floor just as they are needed for production. This reduces the amount of parts Boeing holds in inventory as well as the amount of the factory floor needed for production—in this case, reducing the space required for manufacture of the 767 by 40%.

Boeing had adopted lean manufacturing in 1999 in the manufacture of the 737, the most popular commercial airplane. By 2005, after constant refinement, Boeing had achieved a 50% reduction in the time it takes to produce a plane and a nearly 60% reduction in parts inventory. An important feature is a continuously moving assembly line, moving products from one assembly team to the next at a steady pace and eliminating the need for workers to wander across the factory floor from task to task or in search of tools and parts.

Toyota's lean production techniques have been the most widely adopted of all manufacturing techniques and have revolutionized manufacturing worldwide. In simple terms, lean production is focused on organization and communication. Workers and parts are organized so as to ensure a smooth and consistent workflow that minimizes wasted effort and materials. Lean production is also designed to be highly responsive to changes in the desired mix of output—for example, quickly producing more sedans and fewer minivans according to changes in customers' demands.

Toyota's lean production methods were so successful that they transformed the global auto industry and severely threatened once-dominant North American automakers. Until the 1980s, the "Big Three"—Chrysler, Ford, and General Motors—dominated the North American auto industry. In the 1980s, however, Toyotas became increasingly popular in North America due to their high quality and relatively low price—so popular that the Big Three eventually prevailed upon the U.S. government to protect them by restricting the sale of Japanese autos in the United States. A few months later, the Canadian government set a limit on the number of cars Toyota could export to Canada. Over time, Toyota responded by building assembly plants in the United States and in Canada, bringing along its lean production techniques, which then spread throughout North American manufacturing. Toyota's growth continued, and by 2008 it had eclipsed General Motors as the largest automaker in the world.

QUESTIONS FOR THOUGHT

1. What is the opportunity cost associated with having a worker wander across the factory floor from task to task or in search of tools and parts?

2. Explain how lean manufacturing improves the economy's efficiency in production and consumption.

3. Before lean manufacturing innovations, Japan mostly sold consumer electronics to Canada and the United States. How did lean manufacturing innovations alter Japan's comparative advantage vis-à-vis North America?

4. Predict how the shift in the location of Toyota's production from Japan to North America is likely to alter the pattern of comparative advantage in automaking between the two regions.

SUMMARY

1. Almost all economics is based on **models,** "thought experiments" or simplified versions of reality, many of which use mathematical tools such as graphs. An important assumption in economic models is the **other things equal assumption,** which allows analysis of the effect of a change in one factor by holding all other relevant factors unchanged.

2. One important economic model is the **production possibility frontier.** It illustrates *opportunity cost* (showing how much less of one good can be produced if more of the other good is produced); *efficiency* (an economy is efficient in production if it produces on the production possibility frontier and efficient in consumption if it produces the mix of goods and services that people want to consume); and *economic growth* (an outward shift of the production possibility frontier). There are two basic sources of growth: an increase in **factors of production**—resources such as land, labour, and capital, inputs that are not used up in production—and improved **technology.**

3. Another important model is **comparative advantage,** which explains the source of gains from trade between individuals and countries. Everyone has a comparative advantage in something—some good or service in which that person has a lower opportunity cost than everyone else. But it is often confused with **absolute advantage,** an ability to produce a particular good or service better than anyone else. This confusion leads some to erroneously conclude that there are no gains from trade between people or countries.

4. In the simplest economies people **barter**—trade goods and services for one another—rather than trade them for money, as in a modern economy. The **circular-flow diagram** represents transactions within the economy as flows of goods, services, and money between **households** and **firms.** These transactions occur in **markets for goods and services** and **factor markets,** markets for factors of production—land, labour, and capital. It is useful in understanding how spending, production, employment, income, and growth are related in the economy. Ultimately, factor markets determine the economy's **income distribution,** how an economy's total income is allocated to the owners of the factors of production.

5. Economists use economic models for both **positive economics,** which objectively describes how the economy works, and for **normative economics,** which prescribes how the economy *should* work. Positive economics often involves making **forecasts.** Economists can determine correct answers for positive questions but typically not for normative questions, which involve value judgments. The exceptions are when policies designed to achieve a certain objective can be clearly ranked in terms of efficiency.

6. There are two main reasons economists disagree. One, they may disagree about which simplifications to make in a model. Two, economists may disagree—like everyone else—about values.

KEY TERMS

Model, p. 26
Other things equal assumption, p. 26
Production possibility frontier, p. 28
Factors of production, p. 32
Technology, p. 32
Comparative advantage, p. 35

Absolute advantage, p. 36
Barter, p. 38
Circular-flow diagram, p. 38
Household, p. 38
Firm, p. 38
Markets for goods and services, p. 38

Factor markets, p. 39
Income distribution, p. 39
Positive economics, p. 41
Normative economics, p. 41
Forecast, p. 41

PROBLEMS

1. Two important industries on the island of Bermuda are fishing and tourism. According to data from the Food and Agriculture Organization of the United Nations and the Bermuda Department of Statistics, in the year 2009 the 306 registered fishers in Bermuda caught 387 tonnes of marine fish. And the 2719 people employed by hotels produced 554 400 hotel stays (measured by the number of visitor arrivals). Suppose that this production point is efficient in production. Assume also that the opportunity cost of 1 additional tonne of fish is 2000 hotel stays and that this opportunity cost is constant (the opportunity cost does not change).

   a. If all 306 registered fishers were to be employed by hotels (in addition to the 2719 people already working in hotels), how many hotel stays could Bermuda produce?

   b. If all 2719 hotel employees were to become fishers (in addition to the 306 fishers already working in the fishing industry), how many tonnes of fish could Bermuda produce?

c. Draw a production possibility frontier for Bermuda, with fish on the horizontal axis and hotel stays on the vertical axis, and label Bermuda's actual production point for the year 2009.

2. Atlantis is a small, isolated island in the South Atlantic. The inhabitants grow potatoes and catch fish. The accompanying table shows the maximum annual output combinations of potatoes and fish that can be produced. Obviously, given their limited resources and available technology, as they use more of their resources for potato production, there are fewer resources available for catching fish.

Maximum annual output options	Quantity of potatoes (kilograms)	Quantity of fish (kilograms)
A	1000	0
B	800	300
C	600	500
D	400	600
E	200	650
F	0	675

a. Draw a production possibility frontier with potatoes on the horizontal axis and fish on the vertical axis illustrating these options, showing points *A–F*.

b. Can Atlantis produce 500 kg of fish and 800 kg of potatoes? Explain. Where would this point lie relative to the production possibility frontier?

c. What is the opportunity cost of increasing the annual output of potatoes from 600 to 800 kg?

d. What is the opportunity cost of increasing the annual output of potatoes from 200 to 400 kg?

e. Can you explain why the answers to parts (c) and (d) are not the same? What does this imply about the slope of the production possibility frontier?

3. According to Statistics Canada, 11.0 million hectares of land in Canada were used for wheat or corn farming in 2012. Of those 11.0 million hectares, farmers used 9.6 million hectares to grow 999.62 million bushels of wheat and 1.4 million hectares of land to grow 514.15 million bushels of corn. Suppose that Canada's wheat farming and corn farming are efficient in production. At that production point, the opportunity cost of producing 1 additional bushel of wheat is 1.7 fewer bushels of corn. However, because farmers have increasing opportunity costs at higher levels of wheat production, additional bushels of wheat have an opportunity cost greater than 1.7 bushels of corn. For each of the following production points, decide whether that production point is (i) feasible and efficient in production, (ii) feasible but not efficient in production, (iii) not feasible, or (iv) unclear as to whether or not it is feasible.

a. Farmers use 1.6 million hectares of land to produce 180 million bushels of wheat, and they use 2.4 million hectares of land to produce 900 million bushels of corn. The remaining 7.0 million hectares are left unused.

b. From their original production point, farmers transfer 1.6 million hectares of land from corn to wheat production. They now produce 1009.62 million of bushels of wheat and 497.15 million bushels of corn.

c. Farmers reduce their production of wheat to 950 million bushels and increase their production of corn to 588.58 million bushels. Along the production possibility frontier, the opportunity cost of going from 514.15 million bushels of corn to 588.58 million bushels of corn is 0.666 bushels of wheat per bushel of corn.

4. In the ancient country of Roma, only two goods, spaghetti and meatballs, are produced. There are two tribes in Roma, the Tivoli and the Frivoli. By themselves, the Tivoli each month can produce either 30 kg of spaghetti and no meatballs, or 50 kg of meatballs and no spaghetti, or any combination in between. The Frivoli, by themselves, each month can produce 40 kg of spaghetti and no meatballs, or 30 kg of meatballs and no spaghetti, or any combination in between.

a. Assume that all production possibility frontiers are straight lines. Draw one diagram showing the monthly production possibility frontier for the Tivoli and another showing the monthly production possibility frontier for the Frivoli. Show how you calculated them.

b. Which tribe has the comparative advantage in spaghetti production? In meatball production?

In 100 A.D. the Frivoli discover a new technique for making meatballs that doubles the quantity of meatballs they can produce each month.

c. Draw the new monthly production possibility frontier for the Frivoli.

d. After the innovation, which tribe now has an absolute advantage in producing meatballs? In producing spaghetti? Which has the comparative advantage in meatball production? In spaghetti production?

5. According to the Canadian International Merchandise Trade Database from Statistics Canada, in December 2012, Canada sold aircraft and spacecraft worth $27.23 million to China and bought aircraft and spacecraft worth only $8.1 million from China. During the same month, however, Canada bought $255.1 million worth of apparel and clothing accessories from China but sold only $56 253 worth of apparel and clothing accessories to China. Using what you have learned about how trade is determined by comparative advantage, answer the following questions.

a. Which country has the comparative advantage in aircraft production? In production of apparel and clothing accessories?

b. Can you determine which country has the absolute advantage in aircraft production? In apparel and clothing accessories?

6. Peter Pundit, an economics reporter, states that the European Union (EU) is increasing its productivity very rapidly in all industries. He claims that this productivity advance is so rapid that output from the EU in these industries will soon exceed that of Canada and, as a result, Canada will no longer benefit from trade with the EU.

   a. Do you think Peter Pundit is correct or not? If not, what do you think is the source of his mistake?

   b. If the EU and Canada continue to trade, what do you think will characterize the goods that the EU sells to Canada and the goods that Canada sells to the EU?

7. You are in charge of allocating residents to your dormitory's baseball and basketball teams. You are down to the last four people, two of whom must be allocated to baseball and two to basketball. The accompanying table gives each person's batting average and free-throw average.

Name	Batting average	Free-throw average
Kelley	70%	60%
Nina	50%	50%
Curt	10%	30%
Yul	80%	70%

   a. Explain how you would use the concept of comparative advantage to allocate the players. Begin by establishing each player's opportunity cost of free throws in terms of batting average.

   b. Why is it likely that the other basketball players will be unhappy about this arrangement but the other baseball players will be satisfied? Nonetheless, why would an economist say that this is an efficient way to allocate players for your dormitory's sports teams?

8. The inhabitants of the fictional economy of Atlantis use money in the form of cowrie shells. Draw a circular-flow diagram showing households and firms. Firms produce potatoes and fish, and households buy potatoes and fish. Households also provide the land and labour to firms. Identify where in the flows of cowrie shells or physical things (goods and services, or resources) each of the following impacts would occur. Describe how this impact spreads around the circle.

   a. A devastating hurricane floods many of the potato fields.

   b. A very productive fishing season yields a very large number of fish caught.

   c. The inhabitants of Atlantis discover Shakira and spend several days a month at dancing festivals.

9. An economist might say that colleges and universities "produce" education, using faculty members and students as inputs. According to this line of reasoning, education is then "consumed" by households. Construct a circular-flow diagram to represent the sector of the economy devoted to post-secondary education: colleges and universities represent firms, and households both consume education and provide faculty and students to colleges and universities. What are the relevant markets in this diagram? What is being bought and sold in each direction? What would happen in the diagram if the government decided to subsidize 50% of all college and university students' tuition?

10. Your dormitory roommate plays loud music most of the time; you, however, would prefer more peace and quiet. You suggest that she buy some earphones. She responds that although she would be happy to use earphones, she has many other things that she would prefer to spend her money on right now. You discuss this situation with a friend who is an economics major. The following exchange takes place:

He: How much would it cost to buy earphones?

You: $15.

He: How much do you value having some peace and quiet for the rest of the semester?

You: $30.

He: It is efficient for you to buy the earphones and give them to your roommate. You gain more than you lose; the benefit exceeds the cost. You should do that.

You: It just isn't fair that I have to pay for the earphones when I'm not the one making the noise.

   a. Which parts of this conversation contain positive statements and which parts contain normative statements?

   b. Construct an argument supporting your viewpoint that your roommate should be the one to change her behaviour. Similarly, construct an argument from the viewpoint of your roommate that you should be the one to buy the earphones. If your dormitory has a policy that gives residents the unlimited right to play music, whose argument is likely to win? If your dormitory has a rule that a person must stop playing music whenever a roommate complains, whose argument is likely to win?

11. A representative of the Canadian clothing industry recently made the following statement: "Workers in Asia often work in sweatshop conditions earning only pennies an hour. Canadian workers are more productive and as a result earn higher wages. In order to preserve the dignity of the Canadian workplace, the government should enact legislation banning imports of low-wage Asian clothing."

   a. Which parts of this quote are positive statements? Which parts are normative statements?

   b. Is the policy that is being advocated consistent with the preceding statements about the wages and productivities of Canadian and Asian workers?

   c. Would such a policy make some Canadians better off without making any other Canadians worse off? That is, would this policy be efficient from the viewpoint of all Canadians?

   d. Would low-wage Asian workers benefit from or be hurt by such a policy?

12. Are the following statements true or false? Explain your answers.

   a. "When people must pay higher taxes on their wage earnings, it reduces their incentive to work" is a positive statement.

b. "We should lower taxes to encourage more work" is a positive statement.

c. Economics cannot always be used to completely decide what society ought to do.

d. "The system of public education in this country generates greater benefits to society than the cost of running the system" is a normative statement.

e. All disagreements among economists are generated by the media.

13. Evaluate the following statement: "It is easier to build an economic model that accurately reflects events that have already occurred than to build an economic model to forecast future events." Do you think this is true or not? Why? What does this imply about the difficulties of building good economic models?

14. Economists who work for the government are often called on to make policy recommendations. Why do you think it is important for the public to be able to differentiate normative statements from positive statements in these recommendations?

15. The mayor of Gotham City, worried about a potential epidemic of deadly influenza this winter, asks an economic adviser the following series of questions. Determine whether a question requires the economic adviser to make a positive assessment or a normative assessment.

a. How much vaccine will be in stock in the city by the end of November?

b. If we offer to pay 10% more per dose to the pharmaceutical companies providing the vaccines, will they provide additional doses?

c. If there is a shortage of vaccine in the city, whom should we vaccinate first—the elderly or the very young? (Assume that a person from one group has an equal likelihood of dying from influenza as a person from the other group.)

d. If the city charges $25 per shot, how many people will pay?

e. If the city charges $25 per shot, it will make a profit of $10 per shot, money that can go to providing poor people with free flu shots. Should the city engage in such a scheme?

16. Assess the following statement: "If economists just had enough data, they could solve all policy questions in a way that maximizes the social good. There would be no need for divisive political debates, such as whether the government should provide free medical care for all."

Graphs in Economics

Getting the Picture

Whether you're reading about economics in the *Globe and Mail* or in your economics textbook, you will see many graphs. Visual images can make it much easier to understand verbal descriptions, numerical information, or ideas. In economics, graphs are the type of visual image used to facilitate understanding. To fully understand the ideas and information being discussed, you need to be familiar with how to interpret these visual aids. This appendix explains how graphs are constructed and interpreted and how they are used in economics.

Graphs, Variables, and Economic Models

One reason to attend university is that a bachelor's degree provides access to higherpaying jobs. Additional degrees, such as MBAs or law degrees, increase earnings even more. If you were to read an article about the relationship between educational attainment and income, you would probably see a graph showing the income levels for workers with different amounts of education. And this graph would depict the idea that, in general, more education increases income. This graph, like most of those in economics, would depict the relationship between two economic variables. A **variable** is a quantity that can take on more than one value, such as the number of years of education a person has, the price of a can of pop, or a household's income.

As you learned in this chapter, economic analysis relies heavily on *models*, simplified descriptions of real situations. Most economic models describe the relationship between two variables, simplified by holding constant other variables that may affect the relationship. For example, an economic model might describe the relationship between the price of a can of pop and the number of cans of pop that consumers will buy, assuming that everything else that affects consumers' purchases of pop stays constant. This type of model can be described mathematically or verbally, but illustrating the relationship in a graph makes it easier to understand. Next we show how graphs that depict economic models are constructed and interpreted.

How Graphs Work

Most graphs in economics are based on a grid built around two perpendicular lines that show the values of two variables, helping you visualize the relationship between them. So a first step in understanding the use of such graphs is to see how this system works.

Two-Variable Graphs

Figure 2A-1 shows a typical two-variable graph. It illustrates the data in the accompanying table on outside temperature and the number of cans of pop a typical vendor can expect to sell at a baseball stadium during one game. The first column shows the values of outside temperature (the first variable) and the second column shows the values of the number of cans of pop sold (the second variable). Five combinations or pairs of the two variables are shown, each denoted by *A* through *E* in the third column.

Now let's turn to graphing the data in this table. In any two-variable graph, one variable is called the *x*-variable and the other is called the *y*-variable.

A quantity that can take on more than one value is called a **variable**.

FIGURE **2A-1**   Plotting Points on a Two-Variable Graph

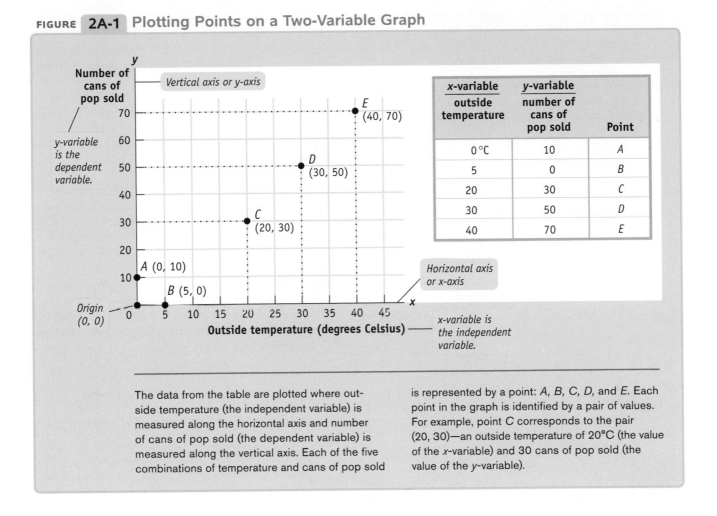

The data from the table are plotted where outside temperature (the independent variable) is measured along the horizontal axis and number of cans of pop sold (the dependent variable) is measured along the vertical axis. Each of the five combinations of temperature and cans of pop sold is represented by a point: *A*, *B*, *C*, *D*, and *E*. Each point in the graph is identified by a pair of values. For example, point *C* corresponds to the pair (20, 30)—an outside temperature of 20°C (the value of the *x*-variable) and 30 cans of pop sold (the value of the *y*-variable).

Here we have made outside temperature the *x*-variable and number of cans of pop sold the *y*-variable. The solid horizontal line in the graph is called the **horizontal axis or x-axis,** and values of the *x*-variable—outside temperature—are measured along it. Similarly, the solid vertical line in the graph is called the **vertical axis or y-axis,** and values of the *y*-variable—number of cans of pop sold—are measured along it. At the **origin,** the point where the two axes meet, each variable is equal to zero. As you move rightward from the origin along the *x*-axis, values of the *x*-variable are positive and increasing. As you move up from the origin along the *y*-axis, values of the *y*-variable are positive and increasing.

You can plot each of the five points *A* through *E* on this graph by using a pair of numbers—the values that the *x*-variable and the *y*-variable take on for a given point. In Figure 2A-1, at point *C*, the *x*-variable takes on the value 20 and the *y*-variable takes on the value 30. You plot point *C* by drawing a line straight up from 20 on the *x*-axis and a horizontal line across from 30 on the *y*-axis. We write point *C* as (20, 30). We write the origin as (0, 0).

Looking at point *A* and point *B* in Figure 2A-1, you can see that when one of the variables for a point has a value of zero, it will lie on one of the axes. If the value of the *x*-variable is zero, the point will lie on the vertical axis, like point *A*. If the value of the *y*-variable is zero, the point will lie on the horizontal axis, like point *B*.

Most graphs that depict relationships between two economic variables represent a **causal relationship,** a relationship in which the value taken by one variable directly influences or determines the value taken by the other variable. In a causal relationship, the determining variable is called the **independent variable;** the variable it determines is called the **dependent variable.** In our example of pop

The line along which values of the *x*-variable are measured is called the **horizontal axis** or **x-axis.** The line along which values of the *y*-variable are measured is called the **vertical axis** or **y-axis.** The point where the axes of a two-variable graph meet is the **origin.**

A **causal relationship** exists between two variables when the value taken by one variable directly influences or determines the value taken by the other variable. In a causal relationship, the determining variable is called the **independent variable;** the variable it determines is called the **dependent variable.**

A **curve** is a line on a graph that depicts a relationship between two variables. It may be either a straight line or a curved line. If the curve is a straight line, the variables have a **linear relationship.** If the curve is not a straight line, the variables have a **non-linear relationship.**

sales, the outside temperature is the independent variable. It directly influences the number of cans of pop that are sold, the dependent variable in this case.

By convention, we put the independent variable on the horizontal axis and the dependent variable on the vertical axis. Figure 2A-1 is constructed consistent with this convention; the independent variable (outside temperature) is on the horizontal axis and the dependent variable (number of cans of pop sold) is on the vertical axis. An important exception to this convention is in graphs showing the economic relationship between the price of a product and quantity of the product: although price is generally the independent variable that determines quantity, it is always measured on the vertical axis.

Curves on a Graph

Panel (a) of Figure 2A-2 contains some of the same information as Figure 2A-1, with a line drawn through the points *B, C, D,* and *E.* Such a line on a graph is called a **curve,** regardless of whether it is a straight line or a curved line. If the curve that shows the relationship between two variables is a straight line, or linear, the variables have a **linear relationship.** When the curve is not a straight line, or non-linear, the variables have a **non-linear relationship.**

A point on a curve indicates the value of the *y*-variable for a specific value of the *x*-variable. For example, point *D* indicates that at a temperature of 30°C, a vendor can expect to sell 50 cans of pop. The shape and orientation of a curve reveal

FIGURE 2A-2 Drawing Curves

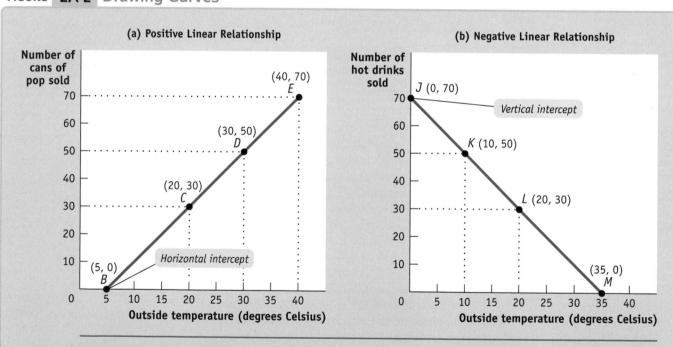

The curve in panel (a) illustrates the relationship between the two variables, outside temperature and number of cans of pop sold. The two variables have a positive linear relationship: positive because the curve has an upward tilt or slope, and linear because it is a straight line. It implies that an increase in the *x*-variable (outside temperature) leads to an increase in the *y*-variable (number of cans of pop sold). The curve in panel (b) is also a straight line, but it slopes (tilts)

downward. The two variables here, outside temperature and number of hot drinks sold, have a negative linear relationship: an increase in the *x*-variable (outside temperature) leads to a decrease in the *y*-variable (number of hot drinks sold). The curve in panel (a) has a horizontal intercept at point *B,* where it hits the horizontal axis. The curve in panel (b) has a vertical intercept at point *J,* where it hits the vertical axis, and a horizontal intercept at point *M,* where it hits the horizontal axis.

the general nature of the relationship between the two variables. The upward tilt of the curve in panel (a) of Figure 2A-2 means that vendors can expect to sell more cans of pop at higher outside temperatures.

When variables are related this way—that is, when an increase in one variable is associated with an increase in the other variable—the variables are said to have a **positive relationship.** It is illustrated by a curve that slopes upward from left to right. Because this curve is also linear, the relationship between outside temperature and number of cans of pop sold illustrated by the curve in panel (a) of Figure 2A-2 is a positive linear relationship.

When an increase in one variable is associated with a decrease in the other variable, the two variables are said to have a **negative relationship.** It is illustrated by a curve that slopes downward from left to right, like the curve in panel (b) of Figure 2A-2. Because this curve is also linear, the relationship it depicts is a negative linear relationship. Two variables that might have such a relationship are the outside temperature and the number of hot drinks a vendor can expect to sell at a baseball stadium.

Return for a moment to the curve in panel (a) of Figure 2A-2 and you can see that it hits the horizontal axis at point *B*. This point, known as the **horizontal intercept,** shows the value of the *x*-variable when the value of the *y*-variable is zero. In panel (b) of Figure 2A-2, the curve hits the vertical axis at point *J*. This point, called the **vertical intercept,** indicates the value of the *y*-variable when the value of the *x*-variable is zero.

A Key Concept: The Slope of a Curve

The **slope** of a curve is a measure of how steep or flat it is and indicates how sensitive the *y*-variable is to a change in the *x*-variable. In our example of outside temperature and the number of cans of pop a vendor can expect to sell, the slope of the curve would indicate how many more cans of pop the vendor could expect to sell with each 1 degree increase in temperature. Interpreted this way, the slope gives meaningful information. Even without numbers for *x* and *y*, it is possible to arrive at important conclusions about the relationship between the two variables by examining the slope of a curve at various points.

The Slope of a Linear Curve

Along a linear curve the slope, or steepness, is measured by dividing the "rise" between two points on the curve by the "run" between those same two points. The rise is the amount that *y* changes, and the run is the amount that *x* changes. Here is the formula:

(2A-1) $\dfrac{\text{Change in } y}{\text{Change in } x} = \dfrac{\Delta y}{\Delta x} = \text{Slope}$

In the formula, the symbol Δ (the Greek uppercase delta) stands for "change in." When a variable increases, the change in that variable is positive; when a variable decreases, the change in that variable is negative.

The slope of a curve is positive when the rise (the change in the *y*-variable) has the same sign as the run (the change in the *x*-variable). That's because when two numbers have the same sign, the ratio of those two numbers is positive. The curve in panel (a) of Figure 2A-2 has a positive slope: along the curve, both the *y*-variable and the *x*-variable increase. The slope of a curve is negative when the rise and the run have different signs. That's because when two numbers have different signs, the ratio of those two numbers is negative. The curve in panel (b) of Figure 2A-2 has a negative slope: along the curve, an increase in the *x*-variable is associated with a decrease in the *y*-variable.

Figure 2A-3 illustrates how to calculate the slope of a linear curve. Let's focus first on panel (a). From point *A* to point *B* the value of the *y*-variable changes from

Two variables have a **positive relationship** when an increase in the value of one variable is associated with an increase in the value of the other variable. It is illustrated by a curve that slopes upward from left to right.

Two variables have a **negative relationship** when an increase in the value of one variable is associated with a decrease in the value of the other variable. It is illustrated by a curve that slopes downward from left to right.

The **horizontal intercept** of a curve is the point at which it hits the horizontal axis; it indicates the value of the *x*-variable when the value of the *y*-variable is zero.

The **vertical intercept** of a curve is the point at which it hits the vertical axis; it shows the value of the *y*-variable when the value of the *x*-variable is zero.

The **slope** of a line or curve is a measure of how steep or flat it is. The slope of a line is measured by "rise over run"—the change in the *y*-variable between two points on the line divided by the change in the *x*-variable between those same two points.

FIGURE **2A-3** Calculating the Slope

Panels (a) and (b) show two linear curves. Between points A and B on the curve in panel (a), the change in y (the rise) is -5 and the change in x (the run) is 10. So the slope from A to B is $\frac{\Delta y}{\Delta x} = \frac{-5}{10} = -\frac{1}{2} = -0.5$, where the negative sign indicates that the curve is downward sloping. In panel (b), the curve has a slope from A to B of $\frac{\Delta y}{\Delta x} = \frac{10}{2} = 5$. The slope from C to

D is $\frac{\Delta y}{\Delta x} = \frac{20}{4} = 5$. The slope is positive, indicating that the curve is upward sloping. Furthermore, the slope between A and B is the same as the slope between C and D, making this a linear curve. The slope of a linear curve is constant: it is the same regardless of where it is measured along the curve.

25 to 20 and the value of the x-variable changes from 10 to 20. So the slope of the line between these two points is:

$$\frac{\text{Change in } y}{\text{Change in } x} = \frac{\Delta y}{\Delta x} = \frac{-5}{10} = -\frac{1}{2} = -0.5$$

Because a straight line is equally steep at all points, the slope of a straight line is the same at all points. In other words, a straight line has a constant slope. You can check this by calculating the slope of the linear curve between points A and B and between points C and D in panel (b) of Figure 2A-3.

Between A and B: $\qquad\qquad \frac{\Delta y}{\Delta x} = \frac{10}{2} = 5$

Between C and D: $\qquad\qquad \frac{\Delta y}{\Delta x} = \frac{20}{4} = 5$

Horizontal and Vertical Curves and Their Slopes

When a curve is horizontal, the value of the y-variable along that curve never changes—it is constant. Everywhere along the curve, the change in y is zero. Now, zero divided by any non-zero number is zero. So, regardless of the value of the change in x, the slope of a horizontal curve is always zero.

If a curve is vertical, the value of the x-variable along the curve never changes—it is constant. Everywhere along the curve, the change in x is zero. This means that the slope of a vertical curve is a ratio with zero in the denominator. A ratio with zero in the denominator is equal to infinity—that is, an infinitely large number. So the slope of a vertical curve is equal to infinity.

A vertical or a horizontal curve has a special implication: it means that the x-variable and the y-variable are unrelated. Two variables are unrelated when a change in one variable (the independent variable) has no effect on the other variable (the dependent variable). Or to put it a slightly different way, two variables are unrelated when the dependent variable is constant regardless of the value of the independent variable. If, as is usual, the y-variable is the dependent variable, the curve is horizontal. If the dependent variable is the x-variable, the curve is vertical.

A **non-linear curve** is one in which the slope is not the same between every pair of points.

The **absolute value** of a negative number is the value of the negative number without the minus sign.

The Slope of a Non-linear Curve

A **non-linear curve** is one in which the slope changes as you move along it. Panels (a), (b), (c), and (d) of Figure 2A-4 show various non-linear curves. Panels (a) and (b) show non-linear curves whose slopes change as you move along them, but the slopes always remain positive. Although both curves tilt upward, the curve in panel (a) gets steeper as you move from left to right in contrast to the curve in panel (b), which gets flatter. A curve that is upward sloping and gets steeper, as in panel (a), is said to have *positive increasing* slope. A curve that is upward sloping but gets flatter, as in panel (b), is said to have *positive decreasing* slope.

When we calculate the slope along these non-linear curves, we obtain different values for the slope at different points. How the slope changes along the curve determines the curve's shape. For example, in panel (a) of Figure 2A-4, the slope of the curve is a positive number that steadily increases as you move from left to right, whereas in panel (b), the slope is a positive number that steadily decreases.

The slopes of the curves in panels (c) and (d) are negative numbers. Economists often prefer to express a negative number as its **absolute value,** which is the value of the negative number without the minus sign. In general, we denote the absolute value of a number by two parallel bars around the number; for example, the absolute value of -4 is written as $|-4| = 4$. In panel (c), the absolute value of the slope steadily increases as you move from left to right. The curve therefore has *negative increasing* slope (i.e., the absolute value of the slope is increasing, so the curve is getting steeper). And in panel (d), the absolute value of the slope of the curve steadily decreases along the curve. This curve therefore has *negative decreasing* slope.

Calculating the Slope Along a Non-linear Curve

We've just seen that along a non-linear curve, the value of the slope depends on where you are on that curve. So how do you calculate the slope of a non-linear curve? We will focus on two methods: the *arc method* and the *point method*.

The Arc Method of Calculating the Slope

An arc of a curve is some piece or segment of that curve. For example, panel (a) of Figure 2A-4 shows an arc consisting of the segment of the curve between points A and B. To calculate the slope along a non-linear curve using the arc method, you draw a straight line between the two end-points of the arc. The slope of that straight line is a measure of the average slope of the curve between those two end-points. You can see from panel (a) of Figure 2A-4 that the straight line drawn between points A and B increases along the x-axis from 6 to 10 (so that $\Delta x = 4$) as it increases along the y-axis from 10 to 20 (so that $\Delta y = 10$). Therefore the slope of the straight line connecting points A and B is:

$$\frac{\Delta y}{\Delta x} = \frac{10}{4} = 2.5$$

This means that the average slope of the curve between points A and B is 2.5.

FIGURE 2A-4 Non-linear Curves

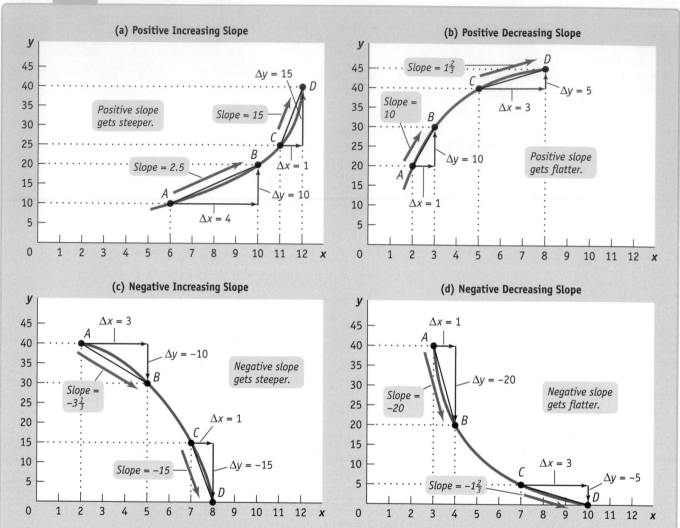

In panel (a) the slope of the curve from A to B is $\frac{\Delta y}{\Delta x} = \frac{10}{4} = 2.5$, and from C to D it is $\frac{\Delta y}{\Delta x} = \frac{15}{1} = 15$. The slope is positive and increasing; the curve gets steeper as you move to the right. In panel (b) the slope of the curve from A to B is $\frac{\Delta y}{\Delta x} = \frac{10}{1} = 10$, and from C to D it is $\frac{\Delta y}{\Delta x} = \frac{5}{3} = 1\frac{2}{3}$. The slope is positive and decreasing; the curve gets flatter as you move to the right. In panel (c) the slope from A to B is $\frac{\Delta y}{\Delta x} = \frac{-10}{3} = -3\frac{1}{3}$, and from C to D it is $\frac{\Delta y}{\Delta x} = \frac{-15}{1} = -15$. The slope is negative and increasing;

the curve gets steeper as you move to the right. And in panel (d) the slope from A to B is $\frac{\Delta y}{\Delta x} = \frac{-20}{1} = -20$, and from C to D it is $\frac{\Delta y}{\Delta x} = \frac{-5}{3} = -1\frac{2}{3}$. The slope is negative and decreasing; the curve gets flatter as you move to the right. The slope in each case has been calculated by using the arc method—that is, by drawing a straight line connecting two points along a curve. The average slope between those two points is equal to the slope of the straight line between those two points.

Now consider the arc on the same curve between points C and D. A straight line drawn through these two points increases along the x-axis from 11 to 12 ($\Delta x = 1$) as it increases along the y-axis from 25 to 40 ($\Delta y = 15$). So the average slope between points C and D is:

$$\frac{\Delta y}{\Delta x} = \frac{15}{1} = 15$$

Therefore the average slope between points C and D is larger than the average slope between points A and B. These calculations verify what we have already observed—that this upward-tilted curve gets steeper as you move from left to right and therefore has positive increasing slope.

The Point Method of Calculating the Slope The point method calculates the slope of a non-linear curve at a specific point on that curve. Figure 2A-5 illustrates how to calculate the slope at point B on the curve. First, we draw a straight line that just touches the curve at point B. Such a line is called a **tangent line:** the fact that it just touches the curve at point B and does not touch the curve at any other point on the curve means that the straight line is *tangent* to the curve at point B. The slope of this tangent line is equal to the slope of the non-linear curve at point B.

You can see from Figure 2A-5 how the slope of the tangent line is calculated: from point A to point C, the change in y is 15 and the change in x is 5, generating a slope of:

$$\frac{\Delta y}{\Delta x} = \frac{15}{5} = 3$$

By the point method, the slope of the curve at point B is equal to 3.

A natural question to ask at this stage is how to determine which method to use—the arc method or the point method—in calculating the slope of a non-linear curve. The answer depends on the curve itself and the data used to construct it. You use the arc method when you don't have enough information to be able to draw a smooth curve. For example, suppose that in panel (a) of Figure 2A-4 you have only the data represented by points A, C, and D and don't have the data represented by point B or any of the rest of the curve. Clearly, then, you can't use the point method to calculate the slope at point B; you would have to use the arc method to approximate the slope of the curve in this area by drawing a straight line between points A and C. But if you have sufficient data to draw the smooth curve shown in panel (a) of Figure 2A-4, then you could use the point method to calculate the slope at point B—and at every other point along the curve as well.

A **tangent line** is a straight line that just touches, or is tangent to, a non-linear curve at a particular point. The slope of the tangent line is equal to the slope of the non-linear curve at that point.

FIGURE 2A-5 Calculating the Slope Using the Point Method

Here a tangent line has been drawn, a line that just touches the curve at point B. The slope of this line is equal to the slope of the curve at point B. The slope of the tangent line, measuring from A to C, is $\frac{\Delta y}{\Delta x} = \frac{15}{5} = 3$.

A non-linear curve may have a **maximum** point, the highest point along the curve. At the maximum, the slope of the curve changes from positive to negative.

A non-linear curve may have a **minimum** point, the lowest point along the curve. At the minimum, the slope of the curve changes from negative to positive.

Maximum and Minimum Points

The slope of a non-linear curve can change from positive to negative or vice versa. When the slope of a curve changes from positive to negative, it creates what is called a *maximum* point of the curve. When the slope of a curve changes from negative to positive, it creates a *minimum* point.

Panel (a) of Figure 2A-6 illustrates a curve in which the slope changes from positive to negative as you move from left to right. When *x* is between 0 and 50, the slope of the curve is positive. At *x* equal to 50, the curve attains its highest point—the largest value of *y* along the curve. This point is called the **maximum** of the curve. When *x* exceeds 50, the slope becomes negative as the curve turns downward. Many important curves in economics, such as the curve that represents how the profit of a firm changes as it produces more output, are hill-shaped like this.

FIGURE **2A-6** Maximum and Minimum Points

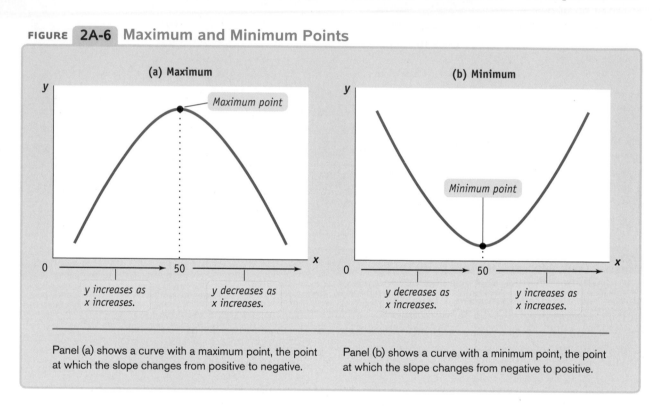

Panel (a) shows a curve with a maximum point, the point at which the slope changes from positive to negative.

Panel (b) shows a curve with a minimum point, the point at which the slope changes from negative to positive.

In contrast, the curve shown in panel (b) of Figure 2A-6 is U-shaped: it has a slope that changes from negative to positive. At *x* equal to 50, the curve reaches its lowest point—the smallest value of *y* along the curve. This point is called the **minimum** of the curve. Various important curves in economics, such as the curve that represents how the per-unit costs of some firms change as output increases, are U–shaped like this.

Calculating the Area Below or Above a Curve

Sometimes it is useful to be able to measure the size of the area below or above a curve. We will encounter one such case in an upcoming chapter. To keep things simple, we'll only calculate the area below or above a linear curve.

How large is the shaded area below the linear curve in panel (a) of Figure 2A-7? First note that this area has the shape of a right triangle. A right triangle is a triangle that has two sides that make a right angle with each other. We will refer to one of these sides as the *height* of the triangle and the other side as the *base* of the triangle. For our purposes, it doesn't matter which of these two

FIGURE **2A-7** Calculating the Area Below and Above a Linear Curve

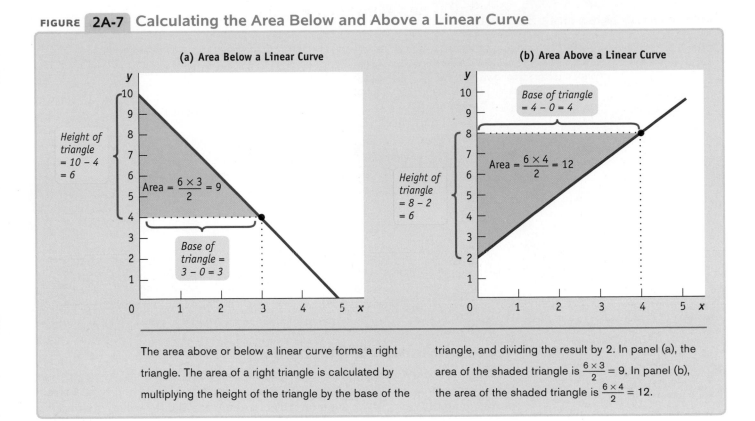

The area above or below a linear curve forms a right triangle. The area of a right triangle is calculated by multiplying the height of the triangle by the base of the triangle, and dividing the result by 2. In panel (a), the area of the shaded triangle is $\frac{6 \times 3}{2} = 9$. In panel (b), the area of the shaded triangle is $\frac{6 \times 4}{2} = 12$.

sides we refer to as the base and which as the height. Calculating the area of a right triangle is straightforward: multiply the height of the triangle by the base of the triangle, and divide the result by 2. The height of the triangle in panel (a) of Figure 2A-7 is $10 - 4 = 6$. And the base of the triangle is $3 - 0 = 3$. So the area of that triangle is:

$$\frac{6 \times 3}{2} = 9$$

How about the shaded area above the linear curve in panel (b) of Figure 2A-7? We can use the same formula to calculate the area of this right triangle. The height of the triangle is $8 - 2 = 6$. And the base of the triangle is $4 - 0 = 4$. So the area of that triangle is:

$$\frac{6 \times 4}{2} = 12$$

Graphs That Depict Numerical Information

Graphs can also be used as a convenient way to summarize and display data without assuming some underlying causal relationship. Graphs that simply display numerical information are called *numerical graphs*. Here we will consider four types of numerical graphs: *time-series graphs, scatter diagrams, pie charts*, and *bar graphs*. These are widely used to display real, empirical data about different economic variables because they often help economists and policy-makers identify patterns or trends in the economy. But as we will also see, you must be careful not to misinterpret or draw unwarranted conclusions from numerical graphs. That is, you must be aware of both the usefulness and the limitations of numerical graphs.

FIGURE **2A-8** Time-Series Graph

Time-series graphs show successive dates on the x-axis and values for a variable on the y-axis. This time-series graph shows real gross domestic product per capita, a measure of a country's standard of living, in Canada from 1980 to late 2011.
Source: Statistics Canada.

Standard of Living in Canada, 1980–2011

Types of Numerical Graphs

You have probably seen graphs in newspapers that show what has happened over time to economic variables such as the unemployment rate or stock prices. A **time-series graph** has successive dates on the horizontal axis and the values of a variable that occurred on those dates on the vertical axis. For example, Figure 2A-8 shows real gross domestic product (GDP) per capita—a rough measure of a country's standard of living—in Canada from 1980 to 2011. A line connecting the points that correspond to real GDP per capita for each calendar quarter during those years gives a clear idea of the overall trend in the standard of living over these years.

Figure 2A-9 is an example of a different kind of numerical graph. It represents information from a sample of 34 countries in a single year on the standard of living,

A **time-series graph** has dates on the horizontal axis and values of a variable that occurred on those dates on the vertical axis.

FIGURE **2A-9** Scatter Diagram

In a scatter diagram, each point represents the corresponding values of the x- and y-variables for a given observation. Here, each point indicates the GDP per capita and the amount of carbon emissions per capita for a given country for a sample of 34 countries in a single year. The upward-sloping fitted line here is the best linear approximation of the general relationship between the two variables.
Source: OECD Factbook, 2012.

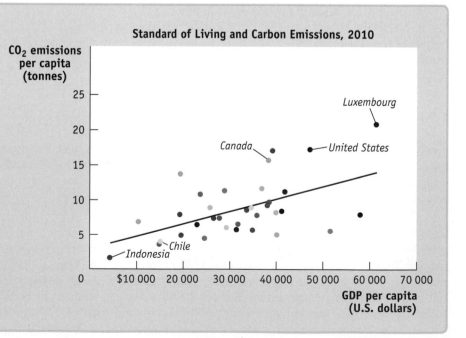

Standard of Living and Carbon Emissions, 2010

again measured by GDP per capita, and the amount of carbon emissions per capita, a measure of environmental pollution. Each point here indicates an average resident's standard of living and his or her annual carbon emissions for a given country. The points lying in the upper right of the graph, which show combinations of a high standard of living and high carbon emissions, represent economically advanced countries such as Canada. Points lying in the bottom left of the graph, which show combinations of a low standard of living and low carbon emissions, represent economically less developed countries such as Indonesia and Chile. The pattern of points indicates that there is generally a positive relationship between living standard and carbon emissions per capita: on the whole, people create more pollution in countries with a higher standard of living. This type of graph is called a **scatter diagram,** a diagram in which each point corresponds to an actual observation of the *x*-variable and the *y*-variable. In scatter diagrams, a curve is typically fitted to the scatter of points; that is, a curve is drawn that approximates as closely as possible the general relationship between the variables. As you can see, the fitted line in Figure 2A-9 is upward sloping, indicating the underlying positive relationship between the two variables. Scatter diagrams are often used to show how a general relationship can be inferred from a set of data.

A **pie chart** shows the share of a total amount that is accounted for by various components, usually expressed in percentages. For example, Figure 2A-10 is a pie chart that depicts what percentage of all unemployed in Canada in 2012 came from different age groups. The fraction of unemployed is the highest among people in the 15 to 24 years age group; about 30% of the unemployed in 2012 fell into this age group.

Bar graphs use bars of various heights or lengths to indicate values of a variable. In the bar graph in Figure 2A-11, the bars show the percent change in the number of unemployed workers in Canada between 2010 and 2011 by different immigrant status—those born in Canada, immigrants

FIGURE 2A-10 Pie Chart

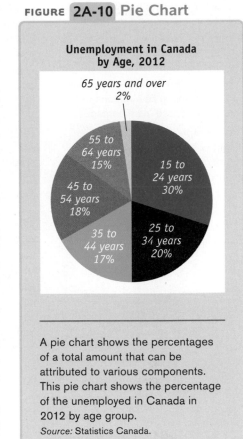

Unemployment in Canada by Age, 2012

65 years and over 2%
55 to 64 years 15%
15 to 24 years 30%
45 to 54 years 18%
25 to 34 years 20%
35 to 44 years 17%

A pie chart shows the percentages of a total amount that can be attributed to various components. This pie chart shows the percentage of the unemployed in Canada in 2012 by age group.
Source: Statistics Canada.

FIGURE 2A-11 Bar Graph

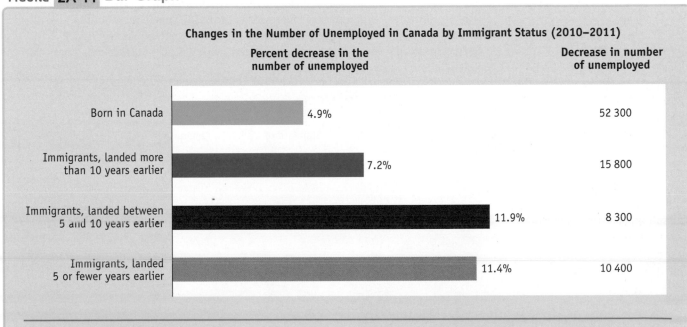

Changes in the Number of Unemployed in Canada by Immigrant Status (2010–2011)

	Percent decrease in the number of unemployed	Decrease in number of unemployed
Born in Canada	4.9%	52 300
Immigrants, landed more than 10 years earlier	7.2%	15 800
Immigrants, landed between 5 and 10 years earlier	11.9%	8 300
Immigrants, landed 5 or fewer years earlier	11.4%	10 400

A bar graph measures a variable by using bars of various heights or lengths. This bar graph shows the percent decrease in the number of unemployed workers in Canada between 2010 and 2011 by different immigrant status.
Source: Statistics Canada.

A **scatter diagram** shows points that correspond to actual observations of the *x*- and *y*-variables. A curve is usually fitted to the scatter of points.

A **pie chart** shows how some total is divided among its components, usually expressed in percentages.

A **bar graph** uses bars of varying height or length to show the comparative sizes of different observations of a variable.

An axis is **truncated** when some of the values on the axis are omitted, usually to save space or to make changes to a variable appear larger.

landed in Canada more than 10 years earlier, immigrants landed in Canada between 5 and 10 years earlier, and immigrants landed in Canada fewer than 5 years earlier. Exact values of the variable that is being measured may be written at the end of the bar, as in this figure. For instance, the number of unemployed workers who were born in Canada fell by 4.9% between 2010 and 2011.

Problems in Interpreting Numerical Graphs

Although the beginning of this appendix emphasized that graphs are visual images that make ideas or information easier to understand, graphs can be constructed (intentionally or unintentionally) in ways that are misleading and can lead to inaccurate conclusions. This section raises some issues that you should be aware of when you interpret graphs.

Features of Construction Before drawing any conclusions about what a numerical graph implies, you should pay attention to the scale, or size of increments, shown on the axes. Small increments tend to visually exaggerate changes in the variables, whereas large increments tend to visually diminish them. So the scale used in construction of a graph can influence your interpretation of the significance of the changes it illustrates—perhaps in an unwarranted way.

Take, for example, Figure 2A-12, which shows real GDP per capita in Canada from 1980 to 1984 using increments of $500. You can see that real GDP per capita fell from $26 081 in 1981 to $25 035 in 1982. A decrease, sure, but is it as enormous as the scale chosen for the vertical axis makes it seem? If you go back and re-examine Figure 2A-8, which shows real GDP per capita in Canada from 1980 to 2011, you can see that this would be a misguided conclusion. Figure 2A-8 includes the same data shown in Figure 2A-12, but it is constructed with a scale having increments of $5000 rather than $500. From it, you can see that the fall in real GDP per capita from 1981 to 1982 was, in fact, relatively insignificant. In fact, the story of real GDP per capita—a measure of the standard of living—in Canada is mostly a story of ups, not downs. This comparison shows that if you are not careful to factor in the choice of scale in interpreting a graph, you can arrive at very different, and possibly mistaken, conclusions.

Related to the choice of scale is the use of *truncation* in constructing a graph. An axis is **truncated** when part of the range is omitted. This is indicated by two slashes (//) in the axis near the origin. You can see that the vertical axis of Figure 2A-12 has been truncated—some of the range of values from 0 to $24 000 has been omitted and

FIGURE 2A-12 Interpreting Graphs: The Effect of Scale

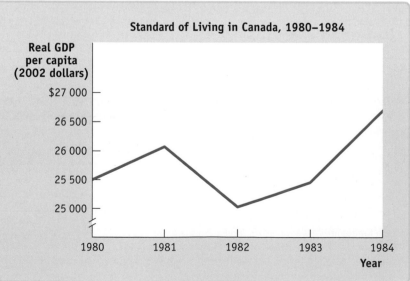

Some of the same data for the years 1980 and 1984 used in Figure 2A-8 are represented here, except that here they are shown using increments of $500 rather than increments of $5000. As a result of this change in scale, changes in the standard of living look much larger in this figure compared to Figure 2A-8.
Source: Statistics Canada.

a // appears in the axis. Truncation saves space in the presentation of a graph and allows smaller increments to be used in constructing it. As a result, changes in the variable depicted on a graph that has been truncated appear larger compared to a graph that has not been truncated and that uses larger increments.

You must also pay close attention to exactly what a graph is illustrating. For example, in Figure 2A-11, you should recognize that what is being shown here are percentage changes in the number of unemployed, not numerical changes. The percentage change in the number of unemployed immigrants landed between 5 and 10 years earlier decreased by the highest percentage, 11.9% in this example. If you were to confuse numerical changes with percentage changes, you would erroneously conclude that the largest absolute reduction of unemployed workers were immigrants landed between 5 and 10 years earlier. But, in fact, Figure 2A-11 shows that the greatest reduction of unemployed workers were those who were born in Canada: the total number of Canadian-born unemployed workers fell by 52 300 workers, which is greater than the decrease in the number of unemployed immigrants landed between 5 and 10 years earlier, which is 8300 in this example.

Omitted Variables From a scatter diagram that shows two variables moving either positively or negatively in relation to each other, it is easy to conclude that there is a causal relationship. But relationships between two variables are not always due to direct cause and effect. Quite possibly an observed relationship between two variables is due to the *unobserved* effect of a third variable on each of the other two variables. An unobserved variable that, through its influence on other variables, creates the erroneous appearance of a direct causal relationship among those variables is called an **omitted variable.** For example, in Manitoba, a greater amount of snowfall during a given week will typically cause people to buy more snow shovels. It will also cause people to buy more lock de-icer. But if you omitted the influence of the snowfall and simply plotted the number of snow shovels sold versus the number of bottles of lock de-icer sold, you would produce a scatter diagram that showed an upward tilt in the pattern of points, indicating a positive relationship between snow shovels sold and lock de-icer sold. To attribute a causal relationship between these two variables, however, is misguided; more snow shovels sold does not cause more lock de-icer to be sold, or vice versa. They move together because they are both influenced by a third, determining, variable—the weekly snowfall, which is the omitted variable in this case. So before assuming that a pattern in a scatter diagram implies a cause-and-effect relationship, it is important to consider whether the pattern is instead the result of an omitted variable. Or to put it succinctly: correlation does not imply causation.

Reverse Causality Even when you are confident that there is no omitted variable and that there is a causal relationship between two variables shown in a numerical graph, you must also be careful that you don't make the mistake of **reverse causality**—coming to an erroneous conclusion about which is the dependent and which is the independent variable by reversing the true direction of causality between the two variables. For example, imagine a scatter diagram that depicts the grade point averages (GPAs) of 20 of your classmates on one axis and the number of hours that each of them spends studying on the other. A line fitted between the points will probably have a positive slope, showing a positive relationship between GPA and hours of studying. We could reasonably infer that hours spent studying is the independent variable and that GPA is the dependent variable. But you could make the error of reverse causality: you could infer that a high GPA causes a student to study more, whereas a low GPA causes a student to study less.

The significance of understanding how graphs can mislead or be incorrectly interpreted is not purely academic. Policy decisions, business decisions, and political arguments are often based on interpretation of the types of numerical graphs that we've just discussed. Problems of misleading features of construction, omitted variables, and reverse causality can lead to very important and undesirable consequences.

An **omitted variable** is an unobserved variable that, through its influence on other variables, may create the erroneous appearance of a direct causal relationship among those variables.

The error of **reverse causality** is committed when the true direction of causality between two variables is reversed.

PROBLEMS

1. Study the four accompanying diagrams. Consider the following statements and indicate which diagram matches each statement. Which variable would appear on the horizontal and which on the vertical axis? In each of these statements, is the slope positive, negative, zero, or infinity?

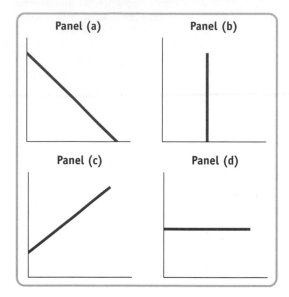

a. If the price of movies increases, fewer consumers go to see movies.

b. More experienced workers typically have higher incomes than less experienced workers.

c. Whatever the temperature outside, Canadians consume the same number of hot dogs per day.

d. Consumers buy more frozen yogourt when the price of ice cream goes up.

e. Research finds no relationship between the number of diet books purchased and the number of kilograms lost by the average dieter.

f. Regardless of its price, Canadians buy the same quantity of salt.

2. In the early 1980s, economist Arthur Laffer argued in favour of lowering income tax rates in order to increase tax revenues. Like most economists, he believed that at tax rates above a certain level, tax revenue would fall because high taxes would discourage some people from working and that people would refuse to work at all if they received no income after paying taxes. This relationship between tax rates and tax revenue is graphically summarized in what is widely known as the Laffer curve. Plot the Laffer curve relationship assuming that it has the shape of a non-linear curve. The following questions will help you construct the graph.

a. Which is the independent variable? Which is the dependent variable? On which axis do you therefore measure the income tax rate? On which axis do you measure income tax revenue?

b. What would tax revenue be at a 0% income tax rate?

c. The maximum possible income tax rate is 100%. What would tax revenue be at a 100% income tax rate?

d. Estimates now show that the maximum point on the Laffer curve is (approximately) at a tax rate of 80%. For tax rates less than 80%, how would you describe the relationship between the tax rate and tax revenue, and how is this relationship reflected in the slope? For tax rates higher than 80%, how would you describe the relationship between the tax rate and tax revenue, and how is this relationship reflected in the slope?

3. In the accompanying figures, the numbers on the axes have been lost. All you know is that the units shown on the vertical axis are the same as the units on the horizontal axis.

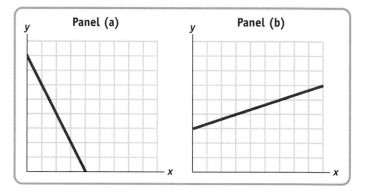

a. In panel (a), what is the slope of the line? Show that the slope is constant along the line.

b. In panel (b), what is the slope of the line? Show that the slope is constant along the line.

4. Answer each of the following questions by drawing a schematic diagram.

a. Taking measurements of the slope of a curve at three points farther and farther to the right along the horizontal axis, the slope of the curve changes from −0.3, to −0.8, to −2.5, measured by the point method. Draw a schematic diagram of this curve. How would you describe the relationship illustrated in your diagram?

b. Taking measurements of the slope of a curve at five points farther and farther to the right along the horizontal axis, the slope of the curve changes from 1.5, to 0.5, to 0, to −0.5, to −1.5, measured by the point method. Draw a schematic diagram of this curve. Does it have a maximum or a minimum?

5. For each of the accompanying diagrams, calculate the area of the shaded right triangle.

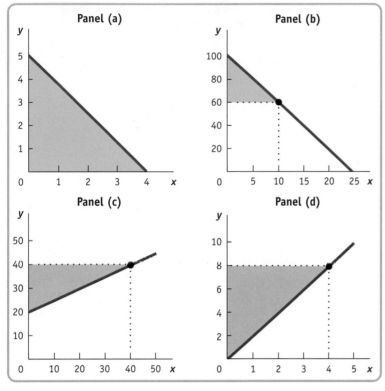

Panel (a)

Panel (b)

Panel (c)

Panel (d)

6. The base of a right triangle is 10, and its area is 20. What is the height of this right triangle?

7. The accompanying table shows the relationship between workers' hours of work per week and their hourly wage rate. Apart from the fact that they receive a different hourly wage rate and work different hours, these five workers are otherwise identical.

Name	Quantity of labour (hours per week)	Wage rate (per hour)
Athena	30	$15
Boris	35	30
Chinedu	37	45
Diego	36	60
Emily	32	75

a. Which variable is the independent variable? Which is the dependent variable?

b. Draw a scatter diagram illustrating this relationship. Draw a (non-linear) curve that connects the points. Put the hourly wage rate on the vertical axis.

c. As the wage rate increases from $15 to $30, how does the number of hours worked respond according to the relationship depicted here? What is the average slope of the curve between Athena's and Boris's data points using the arc method?

d. As the wage rate increases from $60 to $75, how does the number of hours worked respond according to the relationship depicted here? What is the average slope of the curve between Diego's and Emily's data points using the arc method?

8. Studies have found a relationship between a country's yearly rate of economic growth and the yearly rate of increase in airborne pollutants. It is believed that a higher rate of economic growth allows a country's residents to have more cars and travel more, thereby releasing more airborne pollutants.

a. Which variable is the independent variable? Which is the dependent variable?

b. Suppose that in the country of Sudland, when the yearly rate of economic growth fell from 3.0% to 1.5%, the yearly rate of increase in airborne pollutants fell from 6% to 5%. What is the average slope of a non-linear curve between these points using the arc method?

c. Now suppose that when the yearly rate of economic growth rose from 3.5% to 4.5%, the yearly rate of increase in airborne pollutants rose from 5.5% to 7.5%. What is the average slope of a non-linear curve between these two points using the arc method?

d. How would you describe the relationship between the two variables here?

9. An insurance company has found that the severity of property damage in a fire is positively related to the number of firefighters arriving at the scene.

a. Draw a diagram that depicts this finding with number of firefighters on the horizontal axis and amount of property damage on the vertical axis. What is the argument made by this diagram? Suppose you reverse what is measured on the two axes. What is the argument made then?

b. In order to reduce its payouts to policyholders, should the insurance company therefore ask the city to send fewer firefighters to any fire?

10. The accompanying table illustrates annual salaries and income tax owed by five individuals. Apart from the fact that they receive different salaries and owe different amounts of income tax, these five individuals are otherwise identical.

Name	Annual salary	Annual income tax owed
Susan	$22 000	$3 304
Eduardo	63 000	14 317
John	3 000	454
Sheeza	94 000	23 927
Ling	37 000	7 020

a. If you were to plot these points on a graph, what would be the average slope of the curve between the points for Eduardo's and Sheeza's salaries and taxes using the arc method? How would you interpret this value for slope?

b. What is the average slope of the curve between the points for John's and Susan's salaries and taxes using the arc method? How would you interpret that value for slope?

c. What happens to the slope as salary increases? What does this relationship imply about how the level of income taxes affects a person's incentive to earn a higher salary?

CHAPTER 3

Supply and Demand

BLUE JEAN BLUES

How did flood-ravaged cotton crops in Pakistan lead to higher-priced blue jeans and more polyester in T-shirts?

Matt Nager Photography

WHAT YOU WILL LEARN IN THIS CHAPTER

❭ What a **competitive market** is and how it is described by the **supply and demand model**

❭ What the **demand curve** and the **supply curve** are

❭ The factors that determine the demand for, and supply of, a good

❭ The difference between **movements along a curve** and **shifts of a curve**

❭ How the supply and demand curves together determine a market's **equilibrium price** and **equilibrium quantity**

❭ In the case of a **shortage** or **surplus**, how price moves the market back to equilibrium

IF YOU BOUGHT A PAIR OF BLUE jeans in 2011, you may have been shocked at the price. Or maybe not: fashions change, and maybe you thought you were paying the price for being fashionable. But you weren't—you were paying for cotton. Jeans are made of denim, which is a particular weave of cotton, and by late 2010, when jeans manufacturers were buying supplies for the coming year, cotton prices were more than triple their level just two years earlier. The price of cotton continued to rise in early 2011, peaking in March of that year at a price of US$2.30 per pound. (Cotton is traded internationally in U.S. dollars per pound, the equivalent of 0.454 kg). It was the highest level since records began in 1870. The price of cotton softened subsequently but remained relatively high compared to historical standards.

And why were cotton prices so high?

On one side, demand for clothing of all kinds was surging. In 2008–2009, as the world struggled with the effects of a financial crisis, nervous consumers cut back on clothing purchases. But by 2010, with the worst apparently over, buyers were back in force. On the supply side, severe weather events hit world cotton production. Most notably, Pakistan, the world's fourth-largest cotton producer, was hit by devastating floods that put one-fifth of the country under water and virtually destroyed its cotton crop.

Fearing that consumers had limited tolerance for large increases in the price of cotton clothing, apparel makers began scrambling to find ways to reduce costs without offending consumers' fashion sense. They adopted changes like smaller buttons, cheaper linings, and—yes—polyester, doubting that consumers would be willing to pay more for cotton goods. In fact, some experts on the cotton market warned that the sky-high prices of cotton in 2010–2011 might lead to a permanent shift in tastes, with consumers becoming more willing to wear synthetics even when cotton prices came down.

At the same time, it was not all bad news for everyone connected with the cotton trade. In North America, cotton producers had not been hit by bad weather and were relishing the higher prices. Farmers responded to sky-high cotton prices by sharply increasing the farmland devoted to the crop. None of this was enough, however, to produce immediate price relief.

Wait a minute: how, exactly, does flooding in Pakistan translate into higher jeans prices and more polyester in your T-shirts? It's a matter of supply and demand—but what does that mean? Many people use "supply and demand" as a sort of catchphrase to mean "the laws of the marketplace at work." To economists, however, the concept of supply and demand has a precise meaning: it is a *model of how a competitive market behaves*.

In this chapter, we lay out the pieces that make up the *supply and demand model*, put them together, and show how this simple model can be used to understand how many—but not all—markets behave. ■

A **competitive market** is a market in which there are many buyers and sellers of the same good or service, none of whom can influence the price at which the good or service is sold.

The **supply and demand model** is a model of how a competitive market behaves.

Supply and Demand: A Model of a Competitive Market

Cotton sellers and cotton buyers constitute a market—a group of producers and consumers who exchange a good or service for payment. In this chapter, we'll focus on a particular type of market known as a *competitive market*. Roughly, a **competitive market** is a market in which there are many buyers and sellers of the same good or service. More precisely, the key feature of a competitive market is that no individual's actions have a noticeable effect on the price at which the good or service is sold. It's important to understand, however, that this is not an accurate description of every market.

For example, it's not an accurate description of the market for cola beverages. That's because in the market for cola beverages, Coca-Cola and Pepsi account for such a large proportion of total sales that they are able to influence the price at which cola beverages are bought and sold. But it is an accurate description of the market for cotton. The global marketplace for cotton is so huge that even a jeans maker as large as Levi Strauss & Co. accounts for only a tiny fraction of transactions, making it unable to influence the price at which cotton is bought and sold.

It's a little hard to explain why competitive markets are different from other markets until we've seen how a competitive market works. So let's take a rain check—we'll return to that issue at the end of this chapter. For now, let's just say that it's easier to model competitive markets than other markets. When taking an exam, it's always a good strategy to begin by answering the easier questions. In this book, we're going to do the same thing. So we will start with competitive markets.

When a market is competitive, its behaviour is well described by the **supply and demand model.** Because many markets are competitive, the supply and demand model is a very useful one indeed.

There are five key elements in this model:

- The *demand curve*
- The *supply curve*
- The set of factors that cause the demand curve to shift and the set of factors that cause the supply curve to shift
- The *market equilibrium*, which includes the *equilibrium price* and *equilibrium quantity*
- The way the market equilibrium changes when the supply curve or demand curve shifts

To understand the supply and demand model, we will examine each of these elements.

The Demand Curve

How many pounds of cotton, packaged in the form of blue jeans, do consumers around the world want to buy in a given year? You might at first think that we can answer this question by looking at the total number of pairs of blue jeans purchased around the world each day, multiply that number by the amount of cotton it takes to make a pair of jeans, and then multiply by 365. But that's not enough to answer the question, because how many pairs of jeans—in other words, how many pounds of cotton—consumers want to buy depends on the price of a pound of cotton.

When the price of cotton rises, as it did in 2010–2011, some people will respond to the higher price of cotton clothing by buying fewer cotton garments or, perhaps, by switching completely to garments made from other materials, such as synthetics or linen. In general, the quantity of cotton clothing, or of any good or service that people want to buy, depends on the price. The higher the price, the less of the good or service people want to purchase; alternatively, the lower the price, the more they want to purchase.

So the answer to the question "How many pounds of cotton do consumers want to buy?" depends on the price of a pound of cotton. If you don't yet know what the price will be, you can start by making a table of how many pounds of cotton people would want to buy at a number of different prices. Such a table is known as a *demand schedule*. This, in turn, can be used to draw a *demand curve*, which is one of the key elements of the supply and demand model.

The Demand Schedule and the Demand Curve

A **demand schedule** is a table showing how much of a good or service consumers will want to buy at different prices. At the right of Figure 3-1, we show a hypothetical demand schedule for cotton. It's hypothetical in that it doesn't use actual data on the world demand for cotton and it assumes that all cotton is of equal quality.

According to the table, if a pound of cotton costs $1, consumers around the world will want to purchase 10 billion pounds of cotton over the course of a year. If the price is $1.25 a pound, they will want to buy only 8.9 billion pounds; if the price is only $0.75 a pound, they will want to buy 11.5 billion pounds; and so on. The higher the price, the fewer pounds of cotton consumers will want to purchase. So, as the price rises, the **quantity demanded** of cotton—the actual amount consumers are willing to buy at some specific price—falls.

The graph in Figure 3-1 is a visual representation of the information in the table. (You might want to review the discussion of graphs in economics in Appendix 2A.) The vertical axis shows the price of cotton and the horizontal axis shows the quantity of cotton. Each point on the graph corresponds to one of the entries in the

A **demand schedule** shows how much of a good or service consumers will want to buy at different prices.

The **quantity demanded** is the actual amount of a good or service consumers are willing and able to buy at some specific price.

FIGURE 3-1   The Demand Schedule and the Demand Curve

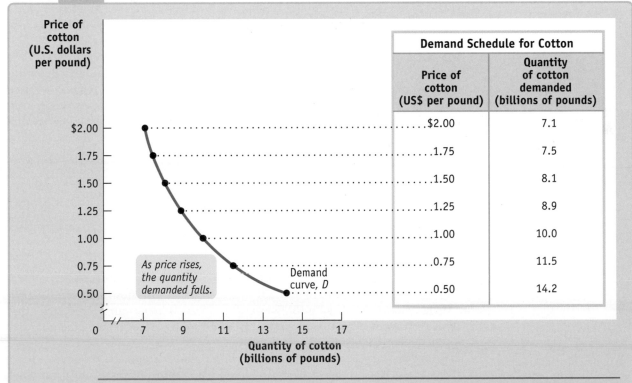

Demand Schedule for Cotton	
Price of cotton (US$ per pound)	Quantity of cotton demanded (billions of pounds)
$2.00	7.1
1.75	7.5
1.50	8.1
1.25	8.9
1.00	10.0
0.75	11.5
0.50	14.2

The demand schedule for cotton yields the corresponding demand curve, which shows how much of a good or service consumers want to buy at any given price. The demand curve and the demand schedule reflect the law of demand: all other things equal, as price rises, the quantity demanded falls. Similarly, all other things equal, a fall in price raises the quantity demanded. As a result, the demand curve is downward sloping.

PAY MORE, PUMP LESS

For a real-world illustration of the law of demand, consider how gasoline consumption varies according to the prices consumers pay at the pump. Because of high taxes, gasoline and diesel fuel are more expensive in most European countries than in Canada and the United States. According to the law of demand, this should lead Europeans to buy less gasoline than Canadians and Americans—and they do. As you can see from the figure, Europeans consume less than half as much fuel per person as their counterparts in North America, mainly because they drive smaller cars with better fuel economy.

Prices aren't the only factor affecting fuel consumption, but they're a significant cause of the difference between European and North American fuel consumption per person.

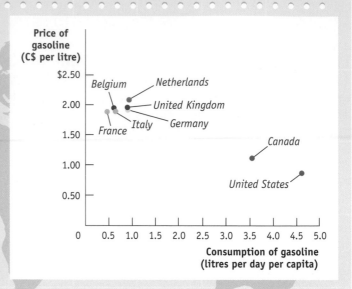

Sources: U.S. Energy Information Administration; Natural Resources Canada, 2010.

table. The curve that connects these points is a **demand curve.** A demand curve is a graphical representation of the demand schedule, another way of showing the relationship between the quantity demanded and price.

Note that the demand curve shown in Figure 3-1 slopes downward. This reflects the general proposition that a higher price reduces the quantity demanded. For example, jeans makers know that they will sell fewer pairs when the price of a pair of jeans is higher, reflecting a $2 price for a pound of cotton, compared to the number they will sell when the price of a pair is lower, reflecting a price of only $1 for a pound of cotton. Similarly, someone who buys a pair of cotton jeans when its price is relatively low will switch to synthetic or linen when the price of cotton jeans is relatively high. So in the real world, demand curves almost always *do* slope downward. (The exceptions are so rare that for practical purposes we can ignore them.) Generally, the proposition that a higher price for a good, *other things equal,* leads people to demand a smaller quantity of that good is so reliable that economists are willing to call it a "law"—the **law of demand.**

Shifts of the Demand Curve

Although cotton prices in 2010 and 2011 were higher than they had been in 2007, total world consumption of cotton was higher in 2010. How can we reconcile this fact with the law of demand, which says that a higher price reduces the quantity demanded, other things equal?

The answer lies in the crucial phrase *other things equal*. In this case, other things weren't equal: the world had changed between 2007 and 2010, in ways that increased the quantity of cotton demanded at any given price. For one thing, the world's population, and therefore the number of potential cotton clothing wearers, increased. In addition, the growing popularity of cotton clothing, as well as higher incomes in countries like China that allowed people to buy more clothing than before, led to an increase in the quantity of cotton demanded at any given price. Figure 3-2 illustrates this phenomenon using the

A **demand curve** is a graphical representation of the demand schedule. It shows the relationship between quantity demanded and price.

The **law of demand** says that a higher price for a good or service, other things equal, leads people to demand a smaller quantity of that good or service.

FIGURE **3-2**   An Increase in Demand

Demand Schedules for Cotton		
Price of cotton (US$ per pound)	Quantity of cotton demanded (billions of pounds)	
	in 2007	in 2010
$2.00	7.1	8.5
1.75	7.5	9.0
1.50	8.1	9.7
1.25	8.9	10.7
1.00	10.0	12.0
0.75	11.5	13.8
0.50	14.2	17.0

An increase in the population is one factor that generates an increase in demand—a rise in the quantity demanded at any given price. This is represented by the two demand schedules—one showing demand in 2007, before the rise in population, the other showing demand in 2010, after the rise in population—and their corresponding demand curves. The increase in demand shifts the demand curve to the right.

demand schedule and demand curve for cotton. (As before, the numbers in Figure 3-2 are hypothetical.)

The table in Figure 3-2 shows two demand schedules. The first is the demand schedule for 2007, the same as shown in Figure 3-1. The second is the demand schedule for 2010. It differs from the 2007 demand schedule due to factors such as a larger population and the increased popularity of cotton clothing, factors that led to an increase in the quantity of cotton demanded at any given price. So at each price the 2010 schedule shows a larger quantity demanded than the 2007 schedule. For example, the quantity of cotton consumers wanted to buy at a price of $1 per pound increased from 10 billion to 12 billion pounds per year, the quantity demanded at $1.25 per pound went from 8.9 billion to 10.7 billion, and so on.

What is clear from this example is that the changes that occurred between 2007 and 2010 generated a *new* demand schedule, one in which the quantity demanded was greater at any given price than in the original demand schedule. The two curves in Figure 3-2 show the same information graphically. As you can see, the demand schedule for 2010 corresponds to a new demand curve, D_2, that is to the right of the demand schedule for 2007, D_1. This **shift of the demand curve** shows the change in the quantity demanded at any given price, represented by the change in position of the original demand curve D_1 to its new location at D_2.

It's crucial to make the distinction between such shifts of the demand curve and **movements along the demand curve,** changes in the quantity demanded of a good arising from a change in that good's price. Figure 3-3 on the next page illustrates the difference.

The movement from point A to point B is a movement along the demand curve: the quantity demanded rises due to a fall in price as you move down D_1. Here, a fall in the price of cotton from $1.50 to $1 per pound generates a rise in the quantity demanded from 8.1 billion to 10 billion pounds per year. But the quantity demanded can also rise

A **shift of the demand curve** is a change in the quantity demanded at any given price, represented by the change (shift) of the original demand curve to a new position, denoted by a new demand curve.

A **movement along the demand curve** is a change in the quantity demanded of a good arising from a change in the good's price.

The rise in quantity demanded when going from point A to point B reflects a movement along the demand curve: it is the result of a fall in the price of the good. The rise in quantity demanded when going from point A to point C reflects a shift of the demand curve (called an increase in demand): it is the result of a rise in the quantity demanded at any given price.

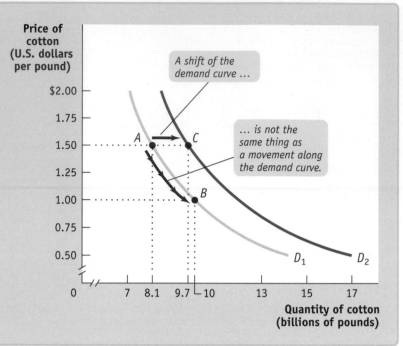

when the price is unchanged if there is an *increase in demand*—a rightward shift of the demand curve. This is illustrated in Figure 3-3 by the shift of the demand curve from D_1 to D_2. Holding the price constant at $1.50 a pound, the quantity demanded rises from 8.1 billion pounds at point A on D_1 to 9.7 billion pounds at point C on D_2.

When economists say "the demand for X increased" or "the demand for Y decreased," they mean that the demand curve for X or Y shifted—not that the quantity demanded rose or fell because of a change in the price.

 PITFALLS

DEMAND VERSUS QUANTITY DEMANDED

When economists say "an increase in demand," they mean a rightward shift of the demand curve, and when they say "a decrease in demand," they mean a leftward shift of the demand curve—that is, when they're being careful. In ordinary speech, most people, including professional economists, use the word *demand* casually. For example, an economist might say "the

demand for air travel has doubled over the past 15 years, partly because of falling air-fares" when he or she really means that the *quantity demanded* has doubled.

It's okay to be a bit sloppy in ordinary conversation. But when you're doing economic analysis, it's important to make the distinction between changes in the quantity demanded, which involve movements along a demand curve, and shifts of the demand curve (see

Figure 3-3 for an illustration). Sometimes students end up writing something like this: "If demand increases, the price will go up, but that will lead to a fall in demand, which pushes the price down …" and then go around in circles. If you make a clear distinction between changes in *demand*, which mean shifts of the demand curve, and changes in *quantity demanded*, you can avoid a lot of confusion.

Understanding Shifts of the Demand Curve

Figure 3-4 illustrates the two basic ways in which demand curves can shift. When economists talk about an "increase in demand," they mean a *rightward* shift of the demand curve: at any given price, consumers demand a larger quantity of the good or service than before. This is shown by the rightward shift of the original demand curve D_1 to D_2. And when economists talk about a "decrease in demand," they mean a *leftward* shift of the demand curve: at any given price, consumers demand a smaller quantity of the good or service than before. This is shown by the leftward shift of the original demand curve D_1 to D_3.

FIGURE **3-4** Shifts of the Demand Curve

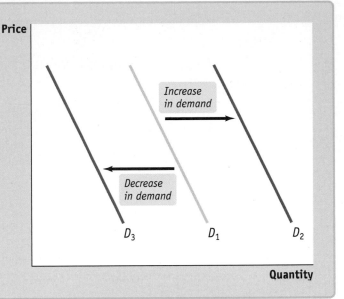

Any event that increases demand shifts the demand curve to the right, reflecting a rise in the quantity demanded at any given price. Any event that decreases demand shifts the demand curve to the left, reflecting a fall in the quantity demanded at any given price.

What caused the demand curve for cotton to shift? We have already mentioned two reasons: changes in population and a change in the popularity of cotton clothing. If you think about it, you can come up with other things that would be likely to shift the demand curve for cotton. For example, suppose that the price of polyester rises. This will induce some people who previously bought polyester clothing to buy cotton clothing instead, increasing the demand for cotton.

Economists believe that there are five principal factors that shift the demand curve for a good or service:

- Changes in the prices of related goods or services
- Changes in income
- Changes in tastes
- Changes in expectations
- Changes in the number of consumers

Although this is not an exhaustive list, it contains the five most important factors that can shift demand curves. So when we say that the quantity of a good or service demanded falls as its price rises, *other things equal*, we are in fact stating that the factors that shift demand are remaining unchanged. Let's now explore, in more detail, how those factors shift the demand curve.

Changes in the Prices of Related Goods or Services Although there's nothing quite like a comfortable pair of all-cotton blue jeans, for some purposes khakis—generally made from polyester blends—aren't a bad alternative. Khakis are what economists call a *substitute* for jeans. Two goods are **substitutes** if a rise in the price of one good (jeans) makes consumers more willing to buy the other good (khakis). Substitutes are usually goods that in some way serve a similar function: coffee and tea, muffins and doughnuts, train rides and air flights. A rise in the price of the alternative good induces some consumers to purchase the original good *instead* of it, shifting demand for the original good to the right.

But sometimes a rise in the price of one good makes consumers *less* willing to buy another good. Such pairs of goods are known as **complements.** Complements are usually goods that in some sense are consumed together: computers and software, cappuccinos and cookies, cars and gasoline. Because consumers like to consume a good and its complement together, a change in the price

Two goods are **substitutes** if a rise in the price of one of the goods leads to an increase in the demand for the other good.

Two goods are **complements** if a rise in the price of one good leads to a decrease in the demand for the other good.

When a rise in income increases the demand for a good—the normal case—it is a **normal good.**

When a rise in income decreases the demand for a good, it is an **inferior good.**

of one of the goods will affect the demand for its complement. In particular, when the price of one good rises, the demand for its complement decreases, shifting the demand curve for the complement to the left. So, for example, when the price of gasoline rose in 2007–2008, the demand for gas-guzzling cars fell.

Changes in Income When individuals have more income, they are normally more likely to purchase a good at any given price. For example, if a family's income rises, it is more likely to take that long-anticipated summer trip to Disney World—and therefore also more likely to buy plane tickets. So a rise in consumer incomes will cause the demand curves for most goods to shift to the right.

Why do we say "most goods," not "all goods"? Most goods are **normal goods**—the demand for them increases when consumer income rises. However, the demand for some products falls when income rises. Goods for which demand decreases when income rises are known as **inferior goods.** Usually an inferior good is one that is considered less desirable than more expensive alternatives—such as a bus ride versus a taxi ride. When they can afford to, people stop buying an inferior good and switch their consumption to the preferred, more expensive alternative. So when a good is inferior, a rise in income shifts the demand curve to the left. And, not surprisingly, a fall in income shifts the demand curve to the right.

One example of the distinction between normal and inferior goods that has drawn considerable attention in the business press is the difference between so-called casual-dining restaurants such as Swiss Chalet or White Spot and fast-food chains such as Harvey's and McDonald's. When Canadians' incomes rise, they tend to eat out more at casual-dining restaurants. However, some of this increased dining out comes at the expense of fast-food venues—to some extent, people visit Harvey's or McDonald's less once they can afford to move upscale. So casual dining is a normal good, whereas fast-food consumption appears to be an inferior good.

Changes in Tastes Why do people want what they want? Fortunately, we don't need to answer that question—we just need to acknowledge that people have certain preferences, or tastes, that determine what they choose to consume and that these tastes can change. Economists usually lump together changes in demand due to fads, beliefs, cultural shifts, and so on under the heading of changes in tastes or preferences.

For example, once upon a time men routinely wore undershirts (or vests). But then came a dramatic moment—American actor Clark Gable removed his shirt in Frank Capra's classic film *It Happened One Night* (1934)—revealing bare skin rather than an undershirt! Reportedly, the sales of vests immediately plummeted. Fashion had changed overnight, and the demand for men's undershirts never recovered.

Economists have relatively little to say about the forces that influence consumers' tastes. (Although marketers and advertisers have plenty to say about them!) However, a change in tastes has a predictable impact on demand. When tastes change in favour of a good, more people want to buy it at any given price, so the demand curve shifts to the right. When tastes change against a good, fewer people want to buy it at any given price, so the demand curve shifts to the left.

Changes in Expectations When consumers have some choice about when to make a purchase, current demand for a good is often affected by expectations about its future price. For example, savvy shoppers often wait for seasonal sales—say, buying next year's holiday gifts during the post-holiday markdowns. In this case, expectations of a future drop in price lead to a decrease in demand today. Alternatively, expectations of a future rise in price are likely to cause an increase in demand today. For example, as cotton prices began to rise in 2010, many textile mills began purchasing more cotton and stockpiling it in anticipation of further price increases.

Expected changes in future income can also lead to changes in demand. If you expect your income to rise in the future, you will typically borrow today and increase your demand for certain goods; if you expect your income to fall in the future, you are likely to save today and reduce your demand for some goods.

Changes in the Number of Consumers
As we've already noted, one of the reasons for rising cotton demand between 2007 and 2010 was a growing world population. Because of population growth, overall demand for cotton would have risen even if the demand of each individual wearer of cotton clothing had remained unchanged.

Let's introduce a new concept: the **individual demand curve,** which shows the relationship between quantity demanded and price for an individual consumer. For example, suppose that Darla is a consumer of cotton blue jeans; also suppose that all pairs of jeans are the same, so they sell for the same price. Panel (a) of Figure 3-5 shows how many pairs of jeans she will buy per year at any given price. Then D_{Darla} is Darla's individual demand curve.

The *market demand curve* shows how the combined quantity demanded by all consumers depends on the market price of that good. (Most of the time, when economists refer to the demand curve, they mean the market demand curve.) The market demand curve is the *horizontal sum* of the individual demand curves of all consumers in that market. To see what we mean by the term *horizontal sum,* assume for a moment that there are only two consumers of blue jeans, Darla and Dino. Dino's individual demand curve, D_{Dino}, is shown in panel (b). Panel (c) shows the market demand curve. At any given price, the quantity demanded by the market is the sum of the quantities demanded by Darla and Dino. For example, at a price of $30 per pair, Darla demands 3 pairs of jeans per year and Dino demands 2 pairs per year. So the quantity demanded by the market is 5 pairs per year.

Clearly, the quantity demanded by the market at any given price is larger with Dino present than it would be if Darla were the only consumer. The quantity

An **individual demand curve** illustrates the relationship between quantity demanded and price for an individual consumer.

FIGURE 3-5   Individual Demand Curves and the Market Demand Curve

Darla and Dino are the only two consumers of blue jeans in the market. Panel (a) shows Darla's individual demand curve: the number of pairs of blue jeans she will buy per year at any given price. Panel (b) shows Dino's individual demand curve. Given that Darla and Dino are the only two consumers, the *market demand curve*, which shows the quantity of blue jeans demanded by all consumers at any given price, is shown in panel (c). The market demand curve is the *horizontal sum* of the individual demand curves of all consumers. In this case, at any given price, the quantity demanded by the market is the sum of the quantities demanded by Darla and Dino.

demanded at any given price would be even larger if we added a third consumer, then a fourth, and so on. So an increase in the number of consumers leads to an increase in demand.

There are several ways the number of consumers can change on a large scale. For example, demographic trends have seen senior citizens represent a growing percentage of Canada's population, increasing the overall demand for the goods and services seniors tend to demand more than younger people (for example, prescription medicine and assisted care residences). Changes to access to international markets also affect the number of consumers. The demand for Canadian softwood lumber increased after the United States made it easier for Canadians to export lumber to U.S. markets. Conversely, an embargo would reduce the number of consumers.

For a review of the factors that shift demand, see Table 3-1.

ECONOMICS ▸ *IN ACTION*

BEATING THE TRAFFIC

Cities can reduce traffic congestion by raising the price of driving. This sign tells drivers they are approaching the centre of London.

All big cities have traffic problems, and many local authorities try to discourage driving in the crowded city centre. If we think of a car trip to the city centre as a good that people consume, we can use the economics of demand to analyze anti-traffic policies.

One common strategy is to reduce the demand for car trips by lowering the prices of substitutes. Many Canadian municipalities subsidize bus and rail service, hoping to lure commuters out of their cars. An alternative is to raise the price of complements: several Canadian municipalities impose high taxes on commercial parking garages and impose short time limits on parking meters, both to raise revenue and to discourage people from driving into the city.

A few major cities—including Singapore, London, Oslo, Stockholm, and Milan—have been willing to adopt a direct and politically controversial approach: reducing congestion by raising the price of driving. Under "congestion pricing" (or "congestion charging" in the United Kingdom), a charge is imposed on cars entering the city centre during business hours. Drivers buy passes, which are then debited electronically as they drive by monitoring stations. Compliance is monitored with automatic cameras that photograph licence plates. Moscow is currently contemplating a congestion charge scheme to tackle the worst traffic jams of all major cities, with 40% of drivers reporting traffic jams exceeding three hours.

The current daily cost of driving in London ranges from £9 to £12 (about $14 to $19). And drivers who don't pay and are caught pay a fine of £120 (about $189) for each transgression.

Not surprisingly, studies have shown that after the implementation of congestion pricing, traffic does indeed decrease. In the 1990s, London had some of the worst traffic in Europe. The introduction of its congestion charge in 2003 immediately reduced traffic in the city centre by about 15%, with overall traffic falling by 21% between 2002 and 2006. And there was increased use of substitutes, such as public transportation, bicycles, motorbikes, and ridesharing.

In Canada, some cities have contemplated imposing similar charges. In Vancouver, commuters pay a toll to cross the new Port Mann Bridge. Officials believed the toll would help reduce congestion there, one of the worst traffic bottlenecks in British Columbia. In Toronto, city council has debated the use of tolls and congestion charges. The most common proposal was for the imposition of a road toll on some of the city's busiest roads, such as the Gardiner Expressway and the Don Valley Parkway. At the time of writing, no such charges have been imposed within Toronto.

TABLE **3-1** Factors That Shift Demand

When this happens ...	... demand increases	But when this happens ...	... demand decreases
When the price of a substitute rises ...		When the price of a substitute falls ...	
	... demand for the original good increases.		... demand for the original good decreases.
When the price of a complement falls ...		When the price of a complement rises ...	
	... demand for the original good increases.		... demand for the original good decreases.
When income rises ...		When income falls ...	
	... demand for a normal good increases.		... demand for a normal good decreases.
When income falls ...		When income rises ...	
	... demand for an inferior good increases.		... demand for an inferior good decreases.
When tastes change in favour of a good ...		When tastes change against a good ...	
	... demand for the good increases.		... demand for the good decreases.
When the price is expected to rise in the future ...		When the price is expected to fall in the future ...	
	... demand for the good increases today.		... demand for the good decreases today.
When the number of consumers rises ...		When the number of consumers falls ...	
	... market demand for the good increases.		... market demand for the good decreases.

The **quantity supplied** is the actual amount of a good or service people are willing and able to sell at some specific price.

A **supply schedule** shows how much of a good or service would be supplied at different prices.

A **supply curve** shows the relationship between quantity supplied and price.

The Supply Curve

Some parts of the world are especially well-suited to growing cotton, and the United States is one of those. But even in the United States, some land is better suited to growing cotton than other land. Whether American farmers restrict their cotton-growing to only the most ideal locations or expand it to less suitable land depends on the price they expect to get for their cotton. Moreover, there are many other areas in the world where cotton could be grown—such as Pakistan, India, Brazil, Turkey, and China. Whether farmers there actually grow cotton depends, again, on the price.

So just as the quantity of cotton that consumers want to buy depends on the price they have to pay, the quantity that producers are willing and able to produce and sell—the **quantity supplied**—depends on the price they are offered.

The Supply Schedule and the Supply Curve

The table in Figure 3-6 shows how the quantity of cotton made available varies with the price—that is, it shows a hypothetical **supply schedule** for cotton.

A supply schedule works the same way as the demand schedule shown in Figure 3-1: in this case, the table shows the number of pounds of cotton farmers are willing to sell at different prices. At a price of $0.50 per pound, farmers are willing to sell only 8 billion pounds of cotton per year. At $0.75 per pound, they're willing to sell 9.1 billion pounds. At $1, they're willing to sell 10 billion pounds, and so on.

In the same way that a demand schedule can be represented graphically by a demand curve, a supply schedule can be represented by a **supply curve,** as shown in Figure 3-6. Each point on the curve represents an entry from the table.

Suppose that the price of cotton rises from $1 to $1.25; we can see that the quantity of cotton farmers are willing to sell rises from 10 billion to 10.7 billion pounds. This is the normal situation for a supply curve, that a higher price leads to a higher quantity supplied. So just as demand curves normally slope downward, supply curves normally slope upward: the higher the price being offered, the more of any good or service producers will be willing to sell (and vice versa).

Shifts of the Supply Curve

Until recently, cotton remained relatively cheap over the past several decades. One reason is that the amount of land cultivated for cotton worldwide expanded more than 35% from 1945 to 2007. However, the major factor accounting for cotton's

FIGURE **3-6** The Supply Schedule and the Supply Curve

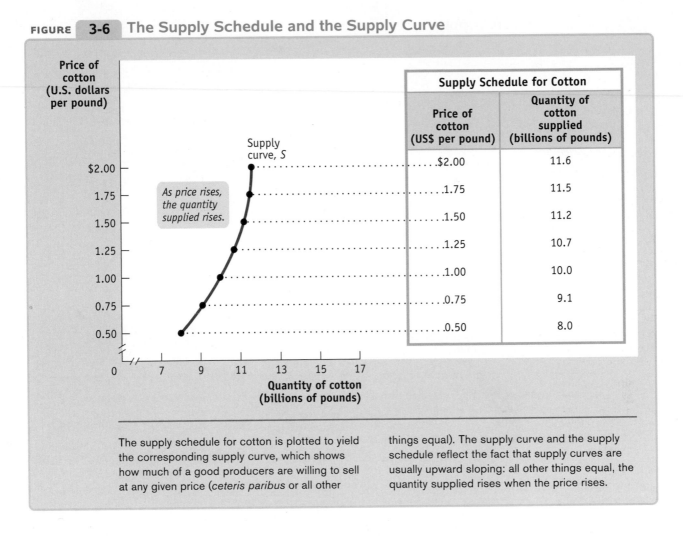

The supply schedule for cotton is plotted to yield the corresponding supply curve, which shows how much of a good producers are willing to sell at any given price (*ceteris paribus* or all other things equal). The supply curve and the supply schedule reflect the fact that supply curves are usually upward sloping: all other things equal, the quantity supplied rises when the price rises.

relative cheapness was advances in the production technology, with output per hectare more than quadrupling from 1945 to 2007. Figure 3-7 illustrates these events in terms of the supply schedule and the supply curve for cotton.

The table in Figure 3-7 shows two supply schedules. The schedule before improved cotton-growing technology was adopted is the same one as in Figure 3-6. The second schedule shows the supply of cotton *after* the improved technology was adopted. Just as a change in demand schedules leads to a shift of the demand curve, a change in supply schedules leads to a **shift of the supply curve**—a change in the quantity supplied at any given price. This is shown in Figure 3-7 by the shift of the supply curve before the adoption of new cotton-growing technology, S_1, to its new position after the adoption of new cotton-growing technology, S_2. Notice that S_2 lies to the right of S_1, a reflection of the fact that quantity supplied has risen at any given price.

As in the analysis of demand, it's crucial to draw a distinction between such shifts of the supply curve and **movements along the supply curve**—changes in the quantity supplied arising from a change in price (all other things equal). We can see this difference in Figure 3-8. The movement from point A to point B is a movement along the supply curve: the quantity supplied rises along S_1 due to a rise in price. Here, a rise in price from $1 to $1.50 leads to a rise in the quantity supplied from 10 billion to 11.2 billion pounds of cotton. But the quantity supplied can also rise when the price is unchanged if there is an increase in supply—a rightward shift of the supply curve. This is shown by the rightward shift of the supply curve from S_1 to S_2. Holding the price constant at $1, the quantity supplied rises from 10 billion pounds at point A on S_1 to 12 billion pounds at point C on S_2.

A **shift of the supply curve** is a change in the quantity supplied of a good or service at any given price. It is represented by the change (shift) of the original supply curve to a new position, denoted by a new supply curve.

A **movement along the supply curve** is a change in the quantity supplied of a good arising from a change in the good's price.

FIGURE **3-7** An Increase in Supply

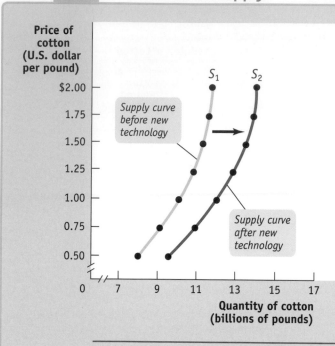

The adoption of improved cotton-growing technology generated an increase in supply—a rise in the quantity supplied at any given price. This event is represented by the two supply schedules—one showing supply before the new technology was adopted, the other showing supply after the new technology was adopted—and their corresponding supply curves. The increase in supply shifts the supply curve to the right.

FIGURE **3-8** Movement Along the Supply Curve versus Shift of the Supply Curve

The increase in quantity supplied when going from point *A* to point *B* reflects a movement along the supply curve: it is the result of a rise in the price of the good. The increase in quantity supplied when going from point *A* to point *C* reflects a shift of the supply curve: it is the result of an increase in the quantity supplied at any given price.

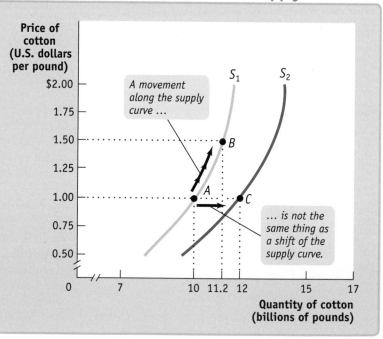

Understanding Shifts of the Supply Curve

Figure 3-9 illustrates the two basic ways in which supply curves can shift. When economists talk about an "increase in supply," they mean a *rightward* shift of the supply curve: at any given price, producers supply a larger quantity of the good than before. This is shown in Figure 3-9 by the rightward shift of the original supply curve S_1 to S_2. And when economists talk about a "decrease in supply," they mean a *leftward* shift of the supply curve: at any given price, producers supply a smaller quantity of the good than before. This is represented by the leftward shift of S_1 to S_3.

FIGURE   **3-9**   Shifts of the Supply Curve

Any event that increases supply shifts the supply curve to the right, reflecting a rise in the quantity supplied at any given price. Any event that decreases supply shifts the supply curve to the left, reflecting a fall in the quantity supplied at any given price.

Economists believe that shifts of the supply curve for a good or service are mainly the result of six factors (though, as in the case of demand, there are other possible causes):

- Changes in input prices
- Changes in the prices of related goods or services
- Changes in technology
- Changes in weather
- Changes in expectations
- Changes in the number of producers

Changes in Input Prices To produce output, you need inputs. For example, to make vanilla ice cream, you need vanilla beans, cream, sugar, and so on. An **input** is any good or service that is used to produce another good or service. Inputs, like outputs, have prices. And an increase in the price of an input makes the production of the final good more costly for those who produce and sell it. So producers are less willing to supply the final good at any given price, and the supply curve shifts to the left. For example, fuel is a major cost for airlines. When oil prices surged in 2007–2008, airlines began cutting back on their flight schedules and some, like Canada's Zoom Airlines, went out of business. Similarly, a fall in the price of an input makes the production of the final good less costly for sellers. They are more willing to supply the good at any given price because they are making more profit than before, and the supply curve shifts to the right.

Changes in the Prices of Related Goods or Services A single producer often produces a mix of goods rather than a single product. For example, an oil refinery produces gasoline from crude oil, but it also produces heating oil

An **input** is a good or service that is used to produce another good or service.

and other products from the same raw material. When a producer sells several products, the quantity of any one good it is willing to supply at any given price depends on the prices of its other co-produced goods.

This effect can run in either direction. An oil refiner will supply less gasoline at any given price when the price of heating oil rises, shifting the supply curve for gasoline to the left. But it will supply more gasoline at any given price when the price of heating oil falls, shifting the supply curve for gasoline to the right. This means that gasoline and other co-produced oil products are *substitutes in production* for refiners.

In contrast, due to the nature of the production process, other goods can be *complements in production*. For example, producers of crude oil—oil-well drillers—often find that oil wells also produce natural gas as a by-product of oil extraction. The higher the price at which a driller can sell its natural gas, the more oil wells it will drill and the more oil it will supply at any given price for oil. As a result, natural gas is a complement in production for crude oil.

Changes in Technology
When economists talk about "technology," they don't necessarily mean high technology—they mean all the methods people can use to turn inputs into useful goods and services. In that sense, the whole complex sequence of activities that turn cotton from Pakistan into the pair of jeans hanging in your closet is technology.

Improvements in technology enable producers to spend less on inputs yet still produce the same output. When a better technology becomes available, reducing the cost of production, supply increases, and the supply curve shifts to the right. As we have already mentioned, improved technology enabled farmers worldwide to more than quadruple cotton output per hectare planted over the past several decades. Improved technology is the main reason that, until recently, cotton remained relatively cheap even as worldwide demand grew.

Changes in Weather
A change in growing conditions or weather can also affect the supply of a good. For example, when a drought hits the Prairies, the growing conditions for wheat and other grain products becomes unfavourable. As a result, the supply of grain products decreases. Similarly, flooding in Alberta may result in a reduction in supply of grain or other goods due to the disruptions it causes.

Changes in Expectations
Just as changes in expectations can shift the demand curve, they can also shift the supply curve. When suppliers have some choice about when they put their good up for sale, changes in the expected future price of the good can lead a supplier to supply less or more of the good today.

For example, consider the fact that gasoline and other oil products are often stored for significant periods of time at oil refineries before being sold to consumers. In fact, storage is normally part of producers' business strategy. Knowing that the demand for gasoline peaks in the summer, oil refiners normally store some of their gasoline produced during the spring for summer sale. Similarly, knowing that the demand for heating oil peaks in the winter, they normally store some of their heating oil produced during the fall for winter sale. In each case, there's a decision to be made between selling the product now versus storing it for later sale. Which choice a producer makes depends on a comparison of the current price versus the expected future price. This example illustrates how changes in expectations can alter supply. An increase in the anticipated future price of a good or service reduces supply today, a leftward shift of the supply curve. But a fall in the anticipated future price increases supply today, a rightward shift of the supply curve.

Changes in the Number of Producers Just as changes in the number of consumers affect the (market) demand curve, changes in the number of producers affect the (market) supply curve. Let's examine the **individual supply curve,** by looking at panel (a) in Figure 3-10. The individual supply curve shows the relationship between quantity supplied and price for an individual producer. For example, suppose that Mr. Silva is a Brazilian cotton farmer and that panel (a) of Figure 3-10 shows how many pounds of cotton he will supply per year at any given price. Then S_{Silva} is his individual supply curve.

> An **individual supply curve** illustrates the relationship between quantity supplied and price for an individual producer.

The *market supply curve* shows how the combined total quantity supplied by all individual producers in the market depends on the market price of that good. Just as the market demand curve is the horizontal sum of the individual demand curves of all consumers, the market supply curve is the horizontal sum of the individual supply curves of all producers. Assume for a moment that there are only two producers of cotton, Mr. Silva and Mr. Liu, a Chinese cotton farmer. Mr. Liu's individual supply curve is shown in panel (b). Panel (c) shows the market supply curve. At any given price, the quantity supplied to the market is the sum of the quantities supplied by Mr. Silva and Mr. Liu. For example, at a price of $2 per pound, Mr. Silva supplies 3000 pounds of cotton per year and Mr. Liu supplies 2000 pounds per year, making the quantity supplied to the market 5000 pounds.

Clearly, the quantity supplied to the market at any given price is larger with Mr. Liu present than it would be if Mr. Silva were the only supplier. The quantity supplied at a given price would be even larger if we added a third producer, then a fourth, and so on. So an increase in the number of producers leads to an increase in supply and a rightward shift of the supply curve.

For a review of the factors that shift supply, see Table 3-2.

FIGURE 3-10 The Individual Supply Curve and the Market Supply Curve

Panel (a) shows the individual supply curve for Mr. Silva, S_{Silva}, the quantity of cotton he will sell at any given price. Panel (b) shows the individual supply curve for Mr. Liu, S_{Liu}. The market supply curve, which shows the quantity of cotton supplied by all producers at any given price, is shown in panel (c). The market supply curve is the horizontal sum of the individual supply curves of all producers.

TABLE **3-2** Factors That Shift Supply

When this happens ...	... supply increases	But when this happens ...	... supply decreases
When the price of an input falls ...	... supply of the good increases.	When the price of an input rises ...	... supply of the good decreases.
When the price of a substitute in production falls ...	... supply of the original good increases.	When the price of a substitute in production rises ...	... supply of the original good decreases.
When the price of a complement in production rises ...	... supply of the original good increases.	When the price of a complement in production falls ...	... supply of the original good decreases.
When the technology used to produce the good improves ...	... supply of the good increases.	When the best technology used to produce the good is no longer available ...	... supply of the good decreases.
When the weather helps production ...	... supply of the good increases.	When the weather disrupts production ...	... supply of the good decreases today.
When the price is expected to fall in the future ...	... supply of the good increases today.	When the price is expected to rise in the future ...	... supply of the good decreases today.
When the number of producers rises ...	... market supply of the good increases.	When the number of producers falls ...	... market supply of the good decreases.

ECONOMICS ▸ IN ACTION

ONLY CREATURES SMALL AND PAMPERED

During the 1970s, British television featured a popular show titled *All Creatures Great and Small*. It chronicled the real life of James Herriot, a country veterinarian who tended to cows, pigs, sheep, horses, and the occasional house pet, often under arduous conditions, in rural England during the 1930s. The show made it clear that in those days the local vet was a critical member of farming communities, saving valuable farm animals and helping farmers survive financially. And it was also clear that Mr. Herriot considered his life's work well spent.

Higher spending on pets means fewer veterinarians are available to tend to farm animals.

But that was then and this is now. Canada and the United States have experienced a severe decline in the number of farm vets over the past two decades. The source of the problem is competition. As the number of household pets has increased and the incomes of pet owners have grown, the demand for pet vets has increased sharply. As a result, vets are being drawn away from the business of caring for farm animals into the more lucrative business of caring for pets. As one American vet stated, she began her career caring for farm animals but changed her mind after "doing a C-section on a cow and it's 50 bucks. Do a C-section on a Chihuahua and you get $300. It's the money. I hate to say that." Add to this the relatively long hours and greater need for travel required of farm vets and it's easy to see why this choice less appealing than being a pet vet in an urban centre.

How can we translate this into supply and demand curves? Farm veterinary services and pet veterinary services are like gasoline and fuel oil: they're related goods that are substitutes in production. A vet typically specializes in one type of practice or the other, and that decision often depends on the going price for the service. The growing pet population in North America, combined with the increased willingness of doting owners to spend on their companions' care, has driven up the price of pet veterinary services. As a result, fewer and fewer vets have gone into farm animal practice. So the supply curve of farm vets has shifted leftward—fewer farm vets are offering their services at any given price.

In the end, farmers understand that it is all a matter of dollars and cents; they get fewer vets because they are unwilling or unable to pay more. As one farmer, who had recently lost an expensive cow due to the unavailability of a vet, stated, "The fact that there's nothing you can do, you accept it as a business expense now. You didn't used to. If you have livestock, sooner or later you're going to have deadstock."

CHECK YOUR UNDERSTANDING 3-2

1. Explain whether each of the following events represents (i) a *shift of* the supply curve or (ii) a *movement along* the supply curve.
   a. More homeowners put their houses up for sale during a real estate boom that causes house prices to rise.
   b. Many strawberry farmers open temporary roadside stands during harvest season, even though prices are usually low at that time.
   c. Immediately after the school year begins, fast-food chains must raise wages, which represent the price of labour, to attract workers.
   d. Due to favourable growing conditions, wheat farmers in the Prairie provinces experience bumper crops.
   e. Since new technologies have made it possible to build larger cruise ships (which are cheaper to run per passenger), Caribbean cruise lines offer more cabins, at lower prices, than before.

Solutions appear at back of book.

A competitive market is in equilibrium when price has moved to a level at which the quantity of a good or service demanded equals the quantity of that good or service supplied. The price at which this takes place is the **equilibrium price**, also referred to as the **market-clearing price.** The quantity of the good or service bought and sold at that price is the **equilibrium quantity.**

Supply, Demand, and Equilibrium

We have now covered the first three key elements in the supply and demand model: the demand curve, the supply curve, and the set of factors that shift each curve. The next step is to put these elements together to show how they can be used to predict the actual price at which the good is bought and sold, as well as the actual quantity transacted.

In the basic model of a competitive market we normally assume that all buyers and sellers have full information about the product and its price. In addition, it is usually assumed that the good being sold is standardized (i.e., all units are identical).

What determines the price at which a good or service is bought and sold? What determines the quantity transacted of the good or service? In Chapter 1 we learned the general principle that *markets move toward equilibrium*, a situation in which no individual would be better off taking a different action. In the case of a competitive market, we can be more specific: a competitive market is in equilibrium when the price has moved to a level at which the quantity of a good demanded equals the quantity of that good supplied. At that price, no individual seller could make herself better off by offering to sell either more or less of the good and no individual buyer could make himself better off by offering to buy more or less of the good. In other words, at the competitive market equilibrium, price has moved to a level that exactly matches the quantity demanded by consumers to the quantity supplied by sellers.

The price that matches the quantity supplied and the quantity demanded is the **equilibrium price;** the quantity bought and sold at that price is the **equilibrium quantity.** The equilibrium price is also known as the **market-clearing price:** it is the price that "clears the market" by ensuring that every buyer willing to pay that price finds a seller willing to sell at that price, and vice versa. So how do we find the equilibrium price and quantity?

Finding the Equilibrium Price and Quantity

The easiest way to determine the equilibrium price and quantity in a market is by putting the supply curve and the demand curve on the same diagram. Since the supply curve shows the quantity supplied at any given price and the demand curve shows the quantity demanded at any given price, the price at which the two curves cross is the equilibrium price: the price at which quantity supplied equals quantity demanded.

Figure 3-11 combines the demand curve from Figure 3-1 and the supply curve from Figure 3-6. They *intersect* at point *E,* which is the equilibrium of this market; $1 is the equilibrium price and 10 billion pounds is the equilibrium quantity.

⚠ **PITFALLS**

BOUGHT AND SOLD?
We have been talking about the price at which a good or service is bought *and* sold, as if the two were the same. But shouldn't we make a distinction between the price received by sellers and the price paid by buyers? In principle, yes; but it is helpful at this point to sacrifice a bit of realism in the interest of simplicity—by assuming away the difference between the

prices received by sellers and those paid by buyers.

In reality, there is often an intermediary—someone who brings buyers and sellers together. The intermediary buys from suppliers, then sells to consumers at a markup—for example, cotton brokers who buy from cotton farmers and sell to textile mills—which turn the cotton into clothing for you and me. The farmers generally receive less than the

mills, who eventually buy their bales of cotton, pay. No mystery there: that difference is how cotton brokers or any other intermediaries make a living. In many markets, however, the difference between the buying and selling price is quite small. So it's not a bad approximation to think of the price paid by buyers as being the *same* as the price received by sellers. And that is what we assume in this chapter.

FIGURE **3-11** Market Equilibrium

Market equilibrium occurs at point *E*, where the supply curve and the demand curve intersect. In equilibrium, the quantity demanded is equal to the quantity supplied. In this market, the equilibrium price is $1 per pound and the equilibrium quantity is 10 billion pounds per year.

Let's confirm that point *E* fits our definition of equilibrium. At a price of $1 per pound, cotton farmers are willing to sell 10 billion pounds a year and cotton consumers want to buy 10 billion pounds a year. So at the price of $1 a pound, the quantity of cotton supplied equals the quantity demanded. Notice that at any other price the market would not clear: every willing buyer would not be able to find a willing seller, or vice versa. More specifically, if the price were more than $1, the quantity supplied would exceed the quantity demanded; if the price were less than $1, the quantity demanded would exceed the quantity supplied.

The model of supply and demand, then, predicts that given the demand and supply curves shown in Figure 3-11, 10 billion pounds of cotton would change hands at a price of $1 per pound. But how can we be sure that the market will arrive at the equilibrium price? We begin by answering three simple questions:

1. Why do all sales and purchases in a market take place at the same price?

2. Why does the market price fall if it is above the equilibrium price?

3. Why does the market price rise if it is below the equilibrium price?

Why Do All Sales and Purchases in a Market Take Place at the Same Price?

There are some markets where the same good can sell for many different prices, depending on who is selling or who is buying. For example, have you ever bought a souvenir in a "tourist trap" and then seen the same item on sale somewhere else (perhaps even in the shop next door) for a lower price? Because tourists don't know which shops offer the best deals and don't have time for comparison shopping, sellers in tourist areas can charge different prices for the same good.

There is a **surplus** of a good or service when the quantity supplied exceeds the quantity demanded. Surpluses occur when the price is above its equilibrium level.

But in any market where the buyers and sellers have both been around for some time, sales and purchases tend to converge at a generally uniform price, so we can safely talk about *the* market price. It's easy to see why. Suppose a seller offered a potential buyer a price noticeably above what the buyer knew other people to be paying. The buyer would clearly be better off shopping elsewhere—unless the seller were prepared to offer a better deal. Conversely, a seller would not be willing to sell for significantly less than the amount he knew most buyers were paying; he would be better off waiting to get a more reasonable customer. So in any well-established, ongoing market, all sellers receive and all buyers pay approximately the same price. This is what we call the *market price*.

Why Does the Market Price Fall if It Is Above the Equilibrium Price?

Suppose the supply and demand curves are as shown in Figure 3-11 but the market price is above the equilibrium level of $1—say, $1.50. This situation is illustrated in Figure 3-12. Why can't the price stay there?

As the figure shows, at a price of $1.50 there would be more pounds of cotton available than consumers wanted to buy: 11.2 billion pounds versus 8.1 billion pounds. The difference of 3.1 billion pounds is the **surplus**—also known as the *excess supply*—of cotton at $1.50.

This surplus means that some cotton farmers are frustrated: at the current price, they cannot find consumers who want to buy their cotton. The surplus offers an incentive for those frustrated would-be sellers to offer a lower price in order to poach business from other producers and entice more consumers to buy. Similarly, in this situation, as buyers become aware of the surplus, they will offer less than the prevailing price in order to buy this output. Either way, the result of this price cutting will be to push the prevailing price down until it reaches the equilibrium price. So the price of a good will fall whenever there is a surplus— that is, whenever the market price is above its equilibrium level.

FIGURE **3-12** Price Above Its Equilibrium Level Creates a Surplus

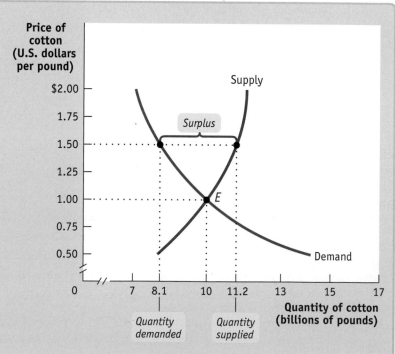

The market price of $1.50 is above the equilibrium price of $1. This creates a surplus: at a price of $1.50, producers would like to sell 11.2 billion pounds but consumers want to buy only 8.1 billion pounds, so there is a surplus of 3.1 billion pounds. This surplus will push the price down until it reaches the equilibrium price of $1 (at which point the excess supply has been eliminated).

Why Does the Market Price Rise if It Is Below the Equilibrium Price?

Now suppose the market price is below its equilibrium level—say, at $0.75 per pound, as shown in Figure 3-13. In this case, the quantity demanded, 11.5 billion pounds, exceeds the quantity supplied, 9.1 billion pounds, implying that there are would-be buyers who cannot find cotton: there is a **shortage,** also known as an *excess demand,* of 2.4 billion pounds.

When there is a shortage, there are frustrated would-be buyers—people who want to purchase cotton but cannot find willing sellers at the current price. In this situation, either buyers will offer more than the prevailing price or sellers will realize that they can charge higher prices. Either way, the result is to drive up the prevailing price. This bidding up of prices happens whenever there are shortages—and there will be shortages whenever the price is below its equilibrium level. So the market price will always rise if it is below the equilibrium level.

> There is a **shortage** of a good or service when the quantity demanded exceeds the quantity supplied. Shortages occur when the price is below its equilibrium level.

FIGURE 3-13 Price Below Its Equilibrium Level Creates a Shortage

The market price of $0.75 is below the equilibrium price of $1. This creates a shortage: consumers want to buy 11.5 billion pounds, but only 9.1 billion pounds are for sale, so there is a shortage of 2.4 billion pounds. This shortage will push the price up until it reaches the equilibrium price of $1 (at which point the excess demand has been eliminated).

Using Equilibrium to Describe Markets

We have now seen that a market tends to have a single price, the equilibrium price. If the market price is above the equilibrium level, the ensuing surplus leads buyers and sellers to take actions that lower the price. And if the market price is below the equilibrium level, the ensuing shortage leads buyers and sellers to take actions that raise the price. So the market price always *moves toward* the equilibrium price, the price at which there is neither surplus nor shortage.

ECONOMICS ➤ IN ACTION

THE PRICE OF ADMISSION

The market equilibrium, so the theory goes, is pretty egalitarian because the equilibrium price applies to everyone. That is, all buyers pay the same price—the equilibrium price—and all sellers receive that same price. But is this realistic?

The competitive market model determines the price you pay for concert tickets.

The market for concert tickets is an example that seems to contradict the theory—there's one price at the box office, and there's another price (typically much higher) for the same event on Internet sites where people who already have tickets resell them, such as StubHub.com or eBay. For example, compare the box office price for a recent Drake concert in Vancouver, British Columbia, to the StubHub.com price for seats in the same seating area: $75.80 versus $167.15.

Puzzling as this may seem, there is no contradiction once we take opportunity costs and tastes into account. For major events, buying tickets from the box office means waiting in very long lines. Ticket buyers who use Internet resellers have decided that the opportunity cost of their time is too high to spend waiting in line. And tickets for major events being sold at face value by online box offices often sell out within minutes. In this case, some people who want to go to the concert badly but have missed out on the opportunity to buy cheaper tickets from the online box office are willing to pay the higher Internet reseller price.

Not only that—perusing the StubHub.com website, you can see that markets really do move to equilibrium. You'll notice that the prices quoted by different sellers for seats close to one another are also very close: $235.50 versus $240.75 for seats in the same row on the main floor of the Drake concert. As the competitive market model predicts, units of the same good end up selling for the same price. And prices move in response to demand and supply. According to an article in *Canadian Business,* tickets on StubHub.com can sell for less than the face value for events with little appeal, but prices can skyrocket for events that are in high demand. (The article quotes a price of $0.01 for a ticket to a New Jersey Nets game three months before the team moved to Brooklyn, while an article in the *Edmonton Journal* quotes asking prices as high as $2000 for tickets to a local concert by Pink.) Even StubHub.com's chief executive says his site is "the embodiment of supply-and-demand economics."

So the theory of competitive markets isn't just speculation. If you want to experience it for yourself, try buying tickets to a concert.

CHECK YOUR UNDERSTANDING   3-3

1. In the following three situations, the market is initially in equilibrium. Explain the changes in either supply or demand that result from each event. After each event described below, does a surplus or shortage exist at the original equilibrium price? What will happen to the equilibrium price as a result?
   a. 2012 was a very good year for Ontario wine-grape growers, who produced a bumper crop.
   b. After a large snowstorm, Ottawa hoteliers often find that many people cancel their upcoming vacations, leaving them with empty hotel rooms.
   c. After a heavy snowfall, many people want to buy second-hand snow blowers at the local hardware store.

Solutions appear at back of book.

Changes in Supply and Demand

The 2010 floods in Pakistan came as a surprise, but the subsequent increase in the price of cotton was no surprise at all. Suddenly there was a decrease in supply: the quantity of cotton available at any given price fell. Predictably, a decrease in supply raises the equilibrium price.

The flooding in Pakistan is an example of an event that shifted the supply curve for a good without having much effect on the demand curve. There are many such events. There are also events that shift the demand curve without shifting the supply curve. For example, a medical report that chocolate is good for you increases the demand for chocolate but does not affect the supply. Events often shift either the supply curve or the demand curve, but not both; it is therefore useful to ask what happens in each case.

We have seen that when a curve shifts, the equilibrium price and quantity change. We will now concentrate on exactly how the shift of a curve alters the equilibrium price and quantity.

What Happens When the Demand Curve Shifts

Cotton and polyester are substitutes: if the price of polyester rises, the demand for cotton will increase, and if the price of polyester falls, the demand for cotton will decrease. But how does the price of polyester affect the *market equilibrium* for cotton?

Figure 3-14 shows the effect of a rise in the price of polyester on the market for cotton. The rise in the price of polyester increases the demand for cotton. Point E_1 shows the equilibrium corresponding to the original demand curve, with P_1 the equilibrium price and Q_1 the equilibrium quantity bought and sold.

An increase in demand is indicated by a *rightward* shift of the demand curve from D_1 to D_2. At the original market price P_1, this market is no longer in equilibrium: a shortage occurs because the quantity demanded exceeds the quantity supplied. So the price of cotton rises and generates an increase in the quantity supplied, an upward *movement along the supply curve*. A new equilibrium is established at point E_2, with a higher equilibrium price, P_2, and higher equilibrium quantity, Q_2. This sequence of events reflects a general principle: *When demand for a good or service increases, the equilibrium price and the equilibrium quantity of the good or service both rise.*

What would happen in the reverse case, a fall in the price of polyester? A fall in the price of polyester reduces the demand for cotton, shifting the demand

FIGURE **3-14** **Equilibrium and Shifts of the Demand Curve**

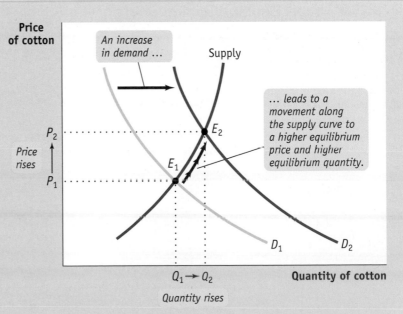

The original equilibrium in the market for cotton is at E_1, at the intersection of the supply curve and the original demand curve, D_1. A rise in the price of polyester, a substitute, shifts the demand curve rightward to D_2. A shortage exists at the original price, P_1, causing both the price and quantity supplied to rise, a movement along the supply curve. A new equilibrium is reached at E_2, with a higher equilibrium price, P_2, and a higher equilibrium quantity, Q_2. When demand for a good or service increases, the equilibrium price and the equilibrium quantity of the good or service both rise.

curve to the *left*. At the original price, a surplus occurs as quantity supplied exceeds quantity demanded. The price falls and leads to a decrease in the quantity supplied, resulting in a lower equilibrium price and a lower equilibrium quantity. This illustrates another general principle: *When demand for a good or service decreases, the equilibrium price and the equilibrium quantity of the good or service both fall.*

To summarize how a market responds to a change in demand: *An increase in demand leads to a rise in both the equilibrium price and the equilibrium quantity. A decrease in demand leads to a fall in both the equilibrium price and the equilibrium quantity.*

What Happens When the Supply Curve Shifts

In the real world, it is a bit easier to predict changes in supply than changes in demand. Physical factors that affect supply, like weather or the availability of inputs, are easier to get a handle on than the fickle tastes that affect demand. Still, with supply as with demand, what we can best predict are the *effects* of shifts of the supply curve.

As we mentioned in this chapter's opening story, devastating floods in Pakistan sharply reduced the supply of cotton in 2010. Figure 3-15 shows how this shift affected the market equilibrium. The original equilibrium is at E_1, the point of intersection of the original supply curve, S_1, and the demand curve, with an equilibrium price P_1 and equilibrium quantity Q_1. As a result of the bad weather, supply falls and S_1 shifts *leftward* to S_2. At the original price P_1, a shortage of cotton now exists and the market is no longer in equilibrium. The shortage causes a rise in price and a fall in quantity demanded, an upward movement along the demand curve. The new equilibrium is at E_2, with an equilibrium price P_2 and an equilibrium quantity Q_2. In the new equilibrium, E_2, the price is higher and the equilibrium quantity lower than before. This can be stated as a general principle: *When supply of a good or service decreases, the equilibrium price of the good or service rises and the equilibrium quantity of the good or service falls.*

FIGURE **3-15** **Equilibrium and Shifts of the Supply Curve**

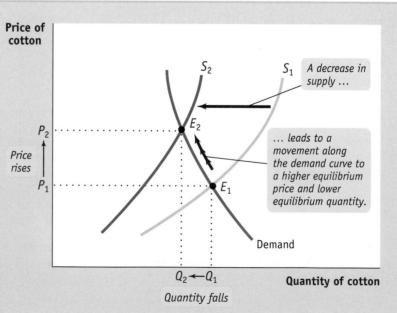

The original equilibrium in the market for cotton is at E_1. Bad weather in cotton-growing areas causes a fall in the supply of cotton and shifts the supply curve leftward from S_1 to S_2. A new equilibrium is established at E_2, with a higher equilibrium price, P_2, and a lower equilibrium quantity, Q_2.

What happens to the market when supply increases? An increase in supply leads to a *rightward* shift of the supply curve. At the original price, a surplus now exists; as a result, the equilibrium price falls and the quantity demanded rises. This describes what happened to the market for cotton as the use of new technology increased cotton yields. We can formulate a general principle: *When supply of a good or service increases, the equilibrium price of the good or service falls and the equilibrium quantity of the good or service rises.*

To summarize how a market responds to a change in supply: *An increase in supply leads to a fall in the equilibrium price and a rise in the equilibrium quantity. A decrease in supply leads to a rise in the equilibrium price and a fall in the equilibrium quantity.*

Simultaneous Shifts of Supply and Demand Curves

Finally, it sometimes happens that events shift *both* the demand and supply curves at the same time. This is not unusual; in real life, supply curves and demand curves for many goods and services shift quite often because the economic environment continually changes. Figure 3-16 illustrates two examples of simultaneous shifts. In both panels there is an increase in demand—that is, a rightward shift of the demand curve, from D_1 to D_2—say, for example, representing an increase in the demand for cotton due to changing tastes. Notice that the rightward shift in panel (a) is larger than the one in panel (b): we can suppose that panel (a) represents a year in which many more people than usual choose to buy jeans and cotton T-shirts and panel (b) represents a normal year. Both panels also show a decrease in supply—that

⚠ PITFALLS

WHICH CURVE IS IT, ANYWAY?
When the price of some good or service changes, in general, we can say that this reflects a change in either supply or demand. But it is easy to get confused about which one. A helpful clue is the direction of change in the quantity. If the quantity sold changes in the *same* direction as the price—for example, if both the price and the quantity rise—this suggests that the demand curve has shifted. If the price and the quantity move in *opposite* directions, the likely cause is a shift of the supply curve.

FIGURE **3-16** Simultaneous Shifts of the Demand and Supply Curves

In panel (a) there is a simultaneous rightward shift of the demand curve and leftward shift of the supply curve. Here the increase in demand is relatively larger than the decrease in supply, so the equilibrium price and equilibrium quantity both rise. In panel (b) there is also a simultaneous rightward shift of the demand curve and leftward shift of the supply curve. Here the decrease in supply is relatively larger than the increase in demand, so the equilibrium price rises and the equilibrium quantity falls.

FOR INQUIRING MINDS

TRIBULATIONS ON THE RUNWAY

You probably don't spend much time worrying about the trials and tribulations of fashion models. Most of them don't lead glamorous lives; in fact, except for a lucky few, life as a fashion model today can be very trying and not very lucrative. And it's all because of supply and demand.

Consider the case of Bianca Gomez, a willowy 18-year-old from Los Angeles, with green eyes, honey-coloured hair, and flawless skin, whose experience was detailed in a *Wall Street Journal* article. Bianca began modelling while still in high school, earning about $30 000 in modelling fees during her senior year. Having attracted the interest of some top designers in New York, she moved there after graduation, hoping to land jobs in leading fashion houses and photo-shoots for leading fashion magazines.

But once in New York, Bianca entered the global market for fashion models. And it wasn't very pretty. Due to the ease of transmitting photos over the Internet and the relatively low cost of international travel, top fashion centres such as New York and Milan are now deluged with beautiful young women from all over the world, eagerly trying to make it as models. Although Russians, other Eastern Europeans,

Photo by Carlo Buscemi/WireImage/Getty Images

Bianca Gomez on the runway before intense global competition got her thinking about switching careers.

and Brazilians are particularly numerous, some hail from places such as Kazakhstan and Mozambique. As one designer said, "There are so many models now … . There are just thousands every year."

Returning to our (less glamorous) economic model of supply and demand, the influx of aspiring fashion models from around the world can be represented

by a rightward shift of the supply curve in the market for fashion models, which would by itself tend to lower the price paid to models. And that wasn't the only change in the market. Unfortunately for Bianca and others like her, the tastes of many of those who hire models have changed as well. Over the past few years, fashion magazines have come to prefer using celebrities such as Angelina Jolie on their pages rather than anonymous models, believing that their readers connect better with a familiar face. This amounts to a leftward shift of the demand curve for models—again reducing the equilibrium price paid to them.

This was borne out in Bianca's experiences. After paying her rent, her transportation, all her modelling expenses, and 20% of her earnings to her modelling agency (which markets her to prospective clients and books her jobs), Bianca found that she was barely breaking even. Sometimes she even had to dip into savings from her high school years. To save money, she ate macaroni and hot dogs; she travelled to auditions, often four or five in one day, by subway. As the *Wall Street Journal* reported, Bianca was seriously considering quitting modelling altogether.

is, a leftward shift of the supply curve from S_1 to S_2. Also notice that the leftward shift in panel (b) is relatively larger than the one in panel (a): we can suppose that panel (b) represents the effect of particularly bad weather in Pakistan and panel (a) represents the effect of a much less severe weather event.

In both cases, the equilibrium price rises from P_1 to P_2, as the equilibrium moves from E_1 to E_2. But what happens to the equilibrium quantity, the quantity of cotton bought and sold? In panel (a) the increase in demand is large relative to the decrease in supply, and the equilibrium quantity rises as a result. In panel (b), the decrease in supply is large relative to the increase in demand, and the equilibrium quantity falls as a result. That is, when demand increases and supply decreases, the actual quantity bought and sold in equilibrium can rise, fall, or remain the same, depending on *how much* the demand and supply curves have shifted.

In general, when supply and demand shift in opposite directions, we can't predict what the ultimate effect will be on the quantity bought and sold. What we can say is that a curve that shifts a disproportionately greater distance than the other curve will have a disproportionately greater effect on the equilibrium quantity bought and sold. That said, we can make the following prediction about the outcome when the supply and demand curves shift in opposite directions:

- When demand increases and supply decreases, the equilibrium price rises but the change in the equilibrium quantity is ambiguous.

- When demand decreases and supply increases, the equilibrium price falls but the change in the equilibrium quantity is ambiguous.

But suppose that the demand and supply curves shift in the same direction. Before 2010, this was the case in the global market for cotton, where both supply and demand had increased over the past decade. Can we safely make any predictions about the changes in price and quantity? In this situation, the change in quantity bought and sold can be predicted, but the change in price is ambiguous. The two possible outcomes when the supply and demand curves shift in the same direction (which you should check for yourself) are as follows:

- When both demand and supply increase, the equilibrium quantity rises but the change in equilibrium price is ambiguous.

- When both demand and supply decrease, the equilibrium quantity falls but the change in equilibrium price is ambiguous.

ECONOMICS ▸ IN ACTION

THE RICE RUN OF 2008

In April 2008, the price of rice exported from Thailand—a global benchmark for the price of rice traded in international markets—reached $1029 per tonne, up from $398 per tonne at the beginning of 2008. Within hours, prices for rice at major rice-trading exchanges around the world were breaking record levels. The factors that lay behind the surge in rice prices were both demand-related and supply-related: growing incomes in China and India, traditionally large consumers of rice; drought in Australia; and pest infestation in Vietnam. But it was also hoarding by farmers, panic buying by consumers, and an export ban by India, one of the largest exporters of rice, that explained the breathtaking speed of the rise in price.

In much of Asia, governments are major buyers of rice. They buy rice from their rice farmers, who are paid a government-set price, and then sell it to the poor at subsidized prices (prices lower than the market equilibrium price). In the past, the government-set price was better than anything farmers could get in the private market.

Now, even farmers in rural areas of Asia have access to the Internet and can see the price quotes on global rice exchanges. And as rice prices rose in response to changes in demand and supply, farmers grew dissatisfied with the government price and instead hoarded their rice in the belief that they would eventually get higher prices. This was a self-fulfilling belief, as the hoarding shifted the supply curve leftward and raised the price of rice even further.

At the same time, India, one of the largest growers of rice, banned Indian exports of rice in order to protect its domestic consumers, causing yet another leftward shift of the supply curve and pushing the price of rice even higher.

As shown in Figure 3-17, the effects even spilled over to North America, which had not suffered any fall in its rice production. North American rice consumers grew alarmed when large retailers limited some bulk rice purchases by consumers in response to the turmoil in the global rice market.

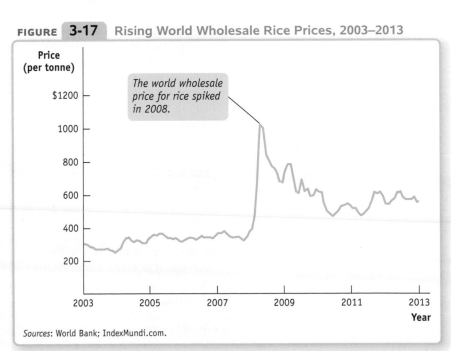

FIGURE **3-17**   Rising World Wholesale Rice Prices, 2003–2013

The world wholesale price for rice spiked in 2008.

Sources: World Bank; IndexMundi.com.

Fearful of paying even higher prices in the future, panic buying set in. As one woman who was in the process of buying 30 pounds of rice said, "We don't even eat that much rice. But I read about it in the newspaper and decided to buy some." According to Canwest, Bruce Cran, president of the Consumers Association of Canada, said he was getting calls in British Columbia that store shelves were being emptied of rice by panicked buyers: "I was in one of the national chains and there was one packet of rice left on the shelf." And, predictably, this panic buying led to even higher prices as it shifted the demand curve rightward, further feeding the buying frenzy. As one market owner said, "People are afraid. We tell them, 'There's no shortage yet' but it was crazy in here."

CHECK YOUR UNDERSTANDING 3-4

1. In each of the following examples, determine (i) the market in question; (ii) whether a shift in demand or supply occurred, the direction of the shift, and what induced the shift; and (iii) the effect of the shift on the equilibrium price and the equilibrium quantity.
   a. As the price of gasoline fell in Canada during the 1990s, more people bought large cars.
   b. As technological innovation has lowered the cost of recycling used paper, fresh paper made from recycled stock is used more frequently.
   c. When a local cable company offers cheaper on-demand films, local movie theatres have more unfilled seats.

2. When a new, faster computer chip is introduced, demand for computers using the older, slower chips decreases. Simultaneously, computer makers increase their production of computers containing the old chips in order to clear out their stocks of old chips.
   Draw two diagrams of the market for computers containing the old chips:
   a. one in which the equilibrium quantity falls in response to these events and
   b. one in which the equilibrium quantity rises.
   What happens to the equilibrium price in each diagram?

Solutions appear at back of book.

Competitive Markets—And Others

Early in this chapter, we defined a competitive market and explained that the supply and demand framework is a model of competitive markets. But we took a rain check on the question of why it matters whether or not a market is competitive. Now that we've seen how the supply and demand model works, we can offer some explanation.

To understand why competitive markets are different from other markets, compare the problems facing two individuals: a wheat farmer who must decide whether to grow more wheat and the president of a giant aluminum company—say, Rio Tinto Alcan—who must decide whether to produce more aluminum.

For the wheat farmer, the question is simply whether the extra wheat can be sold at a price high enough to justify the extra production cost. The farmer need not worry about whether producing more wheat will affect the price of the wheat he or she was already planning to grow. That's because the wheat market is competitive. There are thousands of wheat farmers, and no one farmer's decision will have any impact on the market price.

For the Rio Tinto Alcan executive, things are not that simple because the aluminum market is *not* competitive. There are only a few big producers, including Rio Tinto Alcan, and each of them is well aware that its actions *do* have a noticeable impact on the market price. This adds a whole new level of complexity to the decisions producers have to make. Rio Tinto Alcan can't decide whether or not to produce more aluminum just by asking whether the additional product will sell for more than it costs to make. The company also has to ask whether producing more aluminum will drive down the market price and reduce its *profit,* its net gain from producing and selling all its output.

When a market is competitive, individuals can base decisions on less complicated analyses than those used in a non-competitive market. This in turn means that it's easier for economists to build a model of a competitive market than of a non-competitive market.

Don't take this to mean that economic analysis has nothing to say about non-competitive markets. On the contrary, economists can offer some very important insights into how other kinds of markets work. But those insights require other models, which are studied in microeconomics.

BUSINESS CASE : Good Exchanges Make Great Cities

Chuck Eckert/Alamy

Around the world, commodities are bought and sold on "exchanges," markets organized in a specific location, where buyers and sellers meet to trade. But it wasn't always like this.

The first modern commodity exchange was the Chicago Board of Trade, founded in 1848. At the time, the United States was already a major wheat producer. And St. Louis, not Chicago, was the leading city of the American West and the dominant location for wheat trading. But the St. Louis wheat market suffered from a major flaw: there was no central marketplace, no specific location where everyone met to buy and sell wheat. Instead, sellers would sell their grain from various warehouses or from stacked sacks of grain on the river levee. Buyers would wander around town, looking for the best price.

In Chicago, however, sellers had a better idea. The Chicago Board of Trade, an association of the city's leading grain dealers, created a much more efficient method for trading wheat. There, traders gathered in one place—the "pit"—where they called out offers to sell and accepted offers to buy. The Board guaranteed that these contracts would be fulfilled, removing the need for the wheat to be physically in place when a trade was agreed upon.

This system meant that buyers could very quickly find sellers and vice-versa, reducing the cost of doing business. It also ensured that everyone could see the latest price, leading the price to rise or fall quickly in response to market conditions. For example, news of bad weather in a wheat-growing area hundreds of miles away would send the price in the Chicago pit soaring in a matter of minutes.

The Winnipeg Grain Exchange, later called the Winnipeg Commodity Exchange, opened in 1887 and operated in much the same manner as the Chicago Board of Trade. It helped make Winnipeg one of the fastest growing cities in North America in the early 1900s, earning it the nickname "The Chicago of the North." Its head office building, opened in 1907, was one of the largest office buildings in the British Empire for more than twenty years. By 1911, assisted by the thriving business of selling and shipping commodities, Winnipeg had grown to become the third largest city in Canada. Just as the Chicago Board of Trade was integral to the rise of Chicago, so also did the Grain Exchange have a central role in Winnipeg's rapid growth. Establishing a successful market, it turns out, is very good for business indeed.

QUESTIONS FOR THOUGHT

1. In the chapter we mention how prices can vary in a tourist trap. Which market, St. Louis or Chicago, was more likely to behave like a tourist trap? Explain.

2. What was the advantage to buyers from buying their wheat in the Chicago pit instead of in St. Louis? What was the advantage to sellers?

3. Based on what you have learned from this case, explain why eBay is like a commodity exchange. Why has it been so successful as a marketplace for second-hand items compared to a market composed of various flea markets and dealers?

SUMMARY

1. The **supply and demand model** illustrates how a **competitive market,** one with many buyers and sellers, none of whom can influence the market price, works.

2. The **demand schedule** shows the **quantity demanded** at each price and is represented graphically by a **demand curve.** The **law of demand** says that demand curves slope downward; that is, a higher price for a good or service leads people to demand a smaller quantity, other things equal.

3. A **movement along the demand curve** occurs when a price change leads to a change in the quantity demanded. When economists talk of increasing or decreasing demand, they mean **shifts of the demand curve**—a change in the quantity demanded at any given price. An increase in demand causes a rightward shift of the demand curve. A decrease in demand causes a leftward shift.

4. There are five main factors that shift the demand curve:
   - A change in the prices of related goods or services, such as **substitutes** or **complements**
   - A change in income: when income rises, the demand for **normal goods** increases and the demand for **inferior goods** decreases.
   - A change in tastes
   - A change in expectations
   - A change in the number of consumers

5. The market demand curve for a good or service is the horizontal sum of the **individual demand curves** of all consumers in the market.

6. The **supply schedule** shows the **quantity supplied** at each price and is represented graphically by a **supply curve.** Supply curves usually slope upward.

7. A **movement along the supply curve** occurs when a price change leads to a change in the quantity supplied. When economists talk of increasing or decreas-

ing supply, they mean **shifts of the supply curve**—a change in the quantity supplied at any given price. An increase in supply causes a rightward shift of the supply curve. A decrease in supply causes a leftward shift.

8. There are six main factors that shift the supply curve:
   - A change in **input** prices
   - A change in the prices of related goods and services
   - A change in technology
   - A change in weather
   - A change in expectations
   - A change in the number of producers

9. The market supply curve for a good or service is the horizontal sum of the **individual supply curves** of all producers in the market.

10. The supply and demand model is based on the principle that the price in a competitive market moves to its **equilibrium price,** or **market-clearing price,** the price at which the quantity demanded is equal to the quantity supplied. This quantity is the **equilibrium quantity.** When the price is above its market-clearing level, there is a **surplus** that pushes the price down. When the price is below its market-clearing level, there is a **shortage** that pushes the price up.

11. An increase in demand increases both the equilibrium price and the equilibrium quantity; a decrease in demand has the opposite effect. An increase in supply reduces the equilibrium price and increases the equilibrium quantity; a decrease in supply has the opposite effect.

12. Shifts of the demand curve and the supply curve can happen simultaneously. When they shift in opposite directions, the change in equilibrium price is predictable but the change in equilibrium quantity is not. When they shift in the same direction, the change in equilibrium quantity is predictable but the change in equilibrium price is not. In general, the curve that shifts the greater distance has a greater effect on the changes in equilibrium price and quantity.

KEY TERMS

PROBLEMS

1. A survey indicated that chocolate is Canadians' favourite ice-cream flavour. For each of the following, indicate the possible effects on demand, supply, or both as well as equilibrium price and quantity of chocolate ice cream.

   a. A severe drought in Ontario causes dairy farmers to reduce the number of milk-producing cattle in their herds by a third. These dairy farmers supply cream that is used to manufacture chocolate ice cream.

   b. A new report by the Canadian Medical Association reveals that chocolate does, in fact, have significant health benefits.

   c. The discovery of cheaper synthetic vanilla flavouring lowers the price of vanilla ice cream.

   d. New technology for mixing and freezing ice cream lowers manufacturers' costs of producing chocolate ice cream.

2. In a supply and demand diagram, draw the shift of the demand curve for hamburgers in your hometown due to the following events. In each case, show the effect on equilibrium price and quantity.

   a. The price of tacos increases.

   b. All hamburger sellers raise the price of their french fries.

   c. Income falls in town. Assume that hamburgers are a normal good for most people.

   d. Income falls in town. Assume that hamburgers are an inferior good for most people.

   e. Hot dog stands cut the price of hot dogs.

3. The market for many goods changes in predictable ways according to the time of year, in response to events such as holidays, vacation times, seasonal changes in production, and so on. Using the supply and demand model, explain the change in price in each of the following cases. Note that supply and demand may shift simultaneously.

   a. Lobster prices usually fall during the summer peak lobster harvest season, despite the fact that people like to eat lobster during the summer more than at any other time of year.

   b. The price of a Christmas tree is lower after Christmas than before but fewer trees are sold.

   c. The price of a round-trip ticket to Paris on Air France falls by more than $200 in September, after summer vacation. This happens despite the fact that generally worsening weather increases the cost of operating flights to Paris, and Air France therefore reduces the number of flights to Paris at any given price.

4. Show in a diagram the effect on the demand curve, the supply curve, the equilibrium price, and the equilibrium quantity of each of the following events.

   a. The market for newspapers in your town
   Case 1: The salaries of journalists go up.

   Case 2: There is a big news event in your town, which is reported in the newspapers.

   b. The market for Montreal Canadiens cotton T-shirts
   Case 1: The Canadiens win the Stanley Cup.
   Case 2: The price of cotton increases.

   c. The market for bagels
   Case 1: People realize how fattening bagels are.
   Case 2: People have less time to make themselves a cooked breakfast.

   d. The market for the Krugman, Wells, Au, and Parkinson economics textbook
   Case 1: Your professor makes it required reading for all of his or her students.
   Case 2: Printing costs for textbooks are lowered by the use of synthetic paper.

5. Statistics Canada reported that in 2009 each person in Canada consumed an average of 85 L of soft drinks at an average price of $0.72 per litre. Assume that, at a price of $0.55 per litre, each individual consumer would demand 102 L of soft drinks. The Canadian population in 2009 was 33.7 million. From this information about the individual demand schedule, calculate the market demand schedule for soft drinks for the prices of $0.55 and $0.72 per litre.

6. Suppose that the supply schedule of Nova Scotia lobsters is as follows:

Price of lobster (per pound)*	Quantity of lobster supplied (pounds)
$25	800
20	700
15	600
10	500
5	400

*Commercially, lobsters are priced in dollars per pound.

Suppose that Nova Scotia lobsters can be sold only in Canada. The Canadian demand schedule for Nova Scotia lobsters is as follows:

Price of lobster (per pound)	Quantity of lobster demanded (pounds)
$25	200
20	400
15	600
10	800
5	1000

   a. Draw the demand curve and the supply curve for Nova Scotia lobsters. What are the equilibrium price and quantity of lobsters?

Now suppose that Nova Scotia lobsters can be sold in France. The demand schedule for Nova Scotia lobsters in France is as follows:

Price of lobster (per pound)	Quantity of lobster supplied (pounds)
$25	100
20	300
15	500
10	700
5	900

b. What is the new demand schedule for Nova Scotia lobsters? Draw a supply and demand diagram that illustrates the new equilibrium price and quantity of lobsters. What will happen to the price at which fishers can sell lobster? What will happen to the price paid by Canadian consumers? What will happen to the quantity consumed by Canadian consumers?

7. Find the flaws in reasoning in the following statements, paying particular attention to the distinction between shifts of and movements along the supply and demand curves. Draw a diagram to illustrate what actually happens in each situation.

a. "A technological innovation that lowers the cost of producing a good might seem at first to result in a reduction in the price of the good to consumers. But a fall in price will increase demand for the good, and higher demand will send the price up again. It is not certain, therefore, that an innovation will really reduce price in the end."

b. "A study shows that eating a clove of garlic a day can help prevent heart disease, causing many consumers to demand more garlic. This increase in demand results in a rise in the price of garlic. Consumers, seeing that the price of garlic has gone up, reduce their demand for garlic. This causes the demand for garlic to decrease and the price of garlic to fall. Therefore, the ultimate effect of the study on the price of garlic is uncertain."

8. The following demand schedule is for a normal good.

Price	Quantity demanded
$23	70
21	90
19	110
17	130

a. Do you think that the increase in quantity demanded (say, from 90 to 110 in the table) when price decreases (from $21 to $19) is due to a rise in consumers' income? Explain clearly (and briefly) why or why not.

b. Would the demand schedule still be valid if it was for an inferior good?

c. Lastly, assume you do not know whether the good is normal or inferior. Devise an experiment that would allow you to determine which one it was. Explain.

9. According to the *New York Times* (November 18, 2006), the number of car producers in China is increasing rapidly. The newspaper reports that "China has more car brands now than the United States. ... But while car sales have climbed 38 percent in the first three quarters of this year, automakers have increased their output even faster, causing fierce competition and a slow erosion in prices." At the same time, Chinese consumers' incomes have risen. Assume that cars are a normal good. Use a diagram of the supply and demand curves for cars in China to explain what has happened in the Chinese car market.

10. Aaron Hank is a star hitter for his baseball team. It is widely anticipated that in the next game he will break the major league record for home runs hit during one season. As a result, tickets for the team's next game have been a hot commodity. But today it is announced that, due to a knee injury, he will not in fact play in the team's next game. Assume that season ticket-holders are able to resell their tickets if they wish. Use supply and demand diagrams to explain the following.

a. Show the case in which this announcement results in a lower equilibrium price and a lower equilibrium quantity than before the announcement.

b. Show the case in which this announcement results in a lower equilibrium price and a higher equilibrium quantity than before the announcement.

c. What accounts for whether case a or case b occurs?

d. Suppose that a scalper had secretly learned before the announcement that Aaron Hank would not play in the next game. What actions do you think he would take?

11. In *Rolling Stone* magazine, several fans and rock stars, including Pearl Jam, were bemoaning the high price of concert tickets. One superstar argued, "It just isn't worth $75 to see me play. No one should have to pay that much to go to a concert." Assume this star sold out arenas around the country at an average ticket price of $75.

a. How would you evaluate the argument that ticket prices are too high?

b. Suppose that due to this star's protests, ticket prices were lowered to $50. In what sense is this price too low? Draw a diagram using supply and demand curves to support your argument.

c. Suppose Pearl Jam really wanted to bring down ticket prices. Since the band controls the supply of its services, what do you recommend they do? Explain using a supply and demand diagram.

d. Suppose the band's next album was a total dud. Do you think they would still have to worry about ticket prices being too high? Why or why not? Draw a supply and demand diagram to support your argument.

e. Suppose the group announced their next tour was going to be their last. What effect would this likely have on the demand for and price of tickets? Illustrate with a supply and demand diagram.

12. The accompanying table gives the annual Canadian demand and supply schedules for pickup trucks.

Price of truck	Quantity of trucks demanded (millions)	Quantity of trucks supplied (millions)
$20 000	2.0	1.4
25 000	1.8	1.5
30 000	1.6	1.6
35 000	1.4	1.7
40 000	1.2	1.8

a. Plot the demand and supply curves using these schedules. Indicate the equilibrium price and quantity on your diagram.

b. Suppose the tires used on pickup trucks are found to be defective. What would you expect to happen in the market for pickup trucks? Show this on your diagram.

c. Suppose that Environment Canada imposes costly regulations on manufacturers that cause them to reduce supply by one-third at any given price. Calculate and plot the new supply schedule. Indicate the new equilibrium price and quantity on your diagram.

13. After several years of decline, the market for handmade acoustic guitars is making a comeback. These guitars are usually made in small workshops employing relatively few highly skilled luthiers. Assess the impact on the equilibrium price and quantity of handmade acoustic guitars as a result of each of the following events. In your answers indicate which curve(s) shift(s) and in which direction.

a. Environmentalists succeed in having the use of Brazilian rosewood banned in Canada, forcing luthiers to seek out alternative, more costly woods.

b. A foreign producer re-engineers the guitar-making process and floods the market with identical guitars.

c. Music featuring handmade acoustic guitars makes a comeback as audiences tire of heavy metal and alternative rock music.

d. The country goes into a deep recession and the income of the average Canadian falls sharply.

14. *Demand twisters:* Sketch and explain the demand relationship in each of the following statements.

a. I would never buy a Justin Bieber CD! You couldn't even give me one for nothing.

b. I generally buy a bit more coffee as the price falls. But once the price falls to $10 per kilogram, I'll buy out the entire stock of the supermarket.

c. I spend more on orange juice even as the price rises. (Does this mean that I'm violating the law of demand?)

d. Due to a tuition rise, most students at a college find themselves with less disposable income. Almost all of them eat more frequently at the school cafeteria and less often at restaurants, even though prices at the cafeteria have risen, too. (This one requires that you draw both the demand and the supply curves for school cafeteria meals.)

15. The small town of Middling experiences a sudden doubling of the birth rate. After three years, the birth rate returns to normal. Use a diagram to illustrate the effect of these events on the following.

a. The market for an hour of babysitting services in Middling today

b. The market for an hour of babysitting services 14 years into the future, after the birth rate has returned to normal, by which time children born today are old enough to work as babysitters

c. The market for an hour of babysitting services 30 years into the future, when children born today are likely to be having children of their own

16. Use a diagram to illustrate how each of the following events affects the equilibrium price and quantity of pizza. Assume that pizza is an inferior good.

a. The price of mozzarella cheese rises.

b. A new study reveals hamburgers are unhealthy.

c. The price of tomato sauce falls.

d. The incomes of consumers rise.

e. Consumers expect the price of pizza to fall next week.

17. Although he was a prolific artist, Pablo Picasso painted only 1000 canvases during his "Blue Period." Picasso is now dead, and all of his Blue Period works are currently on display in museums and private galleries throughout Europe, Asia, and North America.

a. Draw a supply curve for Picasso Blue Period works. Why is this supply curve different from ones you have seen?

b. Given the supply curve from part (a), the price of a Picasso Blue Period work will be entirely dependent on what factor(s)? Draw a diagram showing how the equilibrium price of such a work is determined.

c. Suppose rich art collectors decide that it is essential to acquire Picasso Blue Period art for their collections. Show the impact of this on the market for these paintings.

18. Draw the appropriate curve in each of the following cases. Is it like or unlike the curves you have seen so far? Explain.

a. The demand for cardiac bypass surgery, given that the government pays the full cost for any patient

b. The demand for elective cosmetic plastic surgery, given that the patient pays the full cost

c. The supply of reproductions of Rembrandt paintings

The Algebra of Demand, Supply, and Equilibrium

Often algebraic models are employed in economics to convey the essence of what is being investigated. In particular these models often assume that the curves being studied are nice, linear expressions so that our analysis is easier and we don't get bogged down with less important details and end up getting nowhere.

The Demand Curve

The law of demand says that, other things equal, a higher price for a good or service leads people to demand a smaller quantity of that good or service. On a graph, this means the demand curve is a downward sloping function of the price of the good or service being studied. For each quantity, the demand curve reveals the maximum price consumers are willing (and able) to pay. Similarly, at each level of the price, the demand curve reveals the maximum quantity that consumers are willing (and able) to purchase. In the case of a linear expression, a demand curve in its simplest form would be:

(3A-1) $P = a - b \times Q^d$

where P is the price, Q^d is the quantity, and a and b are positive constants.[1] That $b \times Q^d$ is *subtracted* from a constant tells us the law of demand holds here—as price rises, all else constant, a lower level of quantity is demanded and vice versa (the demand curve slopes downward). The b term describes how sensitive the price is to changes in the quantity demanded (i.e., the slope of the demand curve). If b takes on a larger value, then the demand curve becomes relatively steeper—the same change in quantity results in a larger change in the maximum price consumers are willing to pay. If b takes on a smaller value, the effect is opposite—the demand curve becomes relatively flatter and the same change in quantity results in a smaller change in the maximum price consumers are willing to pay.

Although Equation 3A-1 looks straightforward, there is a lot more going on beneath the surface. The constant a contains information on the factors that shift the demand curve: changes in the price(s) of related goods and services, changes in income, changes in tastes, changes in expectations, and changes in the number of consumers. For example, the annual demand for maple syrup, with the price in dollars per litre and the quantity in millions of litres, may be given by a linear demand curve such as:

$$P = a_0 + a_1 \times P_{corn\ syrup} - a_2 \times P_{pancake\ mix} + a_3 \times Y + a_4 \times Tastes + a_5 \times P^e_{future} + a_6 \times Pop - b \times Q^d$$

with a expanded to include several factors multiplied by constants that are summarized in Table 3A-1. These factors are all multiplied by positive constants that, like b, describe how sensitive the demand curve is to changes in those factors. The constant a_0 picks up the impact of all other determinants of the demand for maple syrup that have been left out of the equation of the demand curve.

---

[1] The price term P should be interpreted as the maximum price consumers are willing to pay (this is sometimes called the *demand price*). Naturally, they would be happy to pay less than this price.

TABLE **3A-1** Variable Factors That Shift Maple Syrup Demand

Factor	Denoted by	Change to the demand curve
Price of corn syrup	$P_{corn\ syrup}$	As the price of a substitute increases (decreases), the demand for maple syrup increases (decreases).
Price of pancake mix	$P_{pancake\ mix}$	As the price of a complement increases (decreases), the demand for maple syrup decreases (increases).
Average consumer income	Y	As the income of consumers increases (decreases), the demand for normal goods increases (decreases) and the demand for inferior goods decreases (increases).[2]
Consumer preference index	$Tastes$	As consumer preference for maple syrup increases (decreases), the demand for maple syrup increases (decreases).
Expected future price	P^e_{future}	As the expected future price of maple syrup increases (decreases), the demand for maple syrup increases (decreases).
Population of potential consumers	Pop	As the population of potential consumers increases (decreases), the demand for maple syrup increases (decreases).

Note that the "other things equal" assumption means that everything in the demand curve equation, except P and Q^d, are being held constant. So, other things equal, when we move along the demand curve as P and Q^d change—the *quantity demanded* either increases or decreases. If one of these other factors does change, then the *entire* demand curve shifts either to the right (up) or left (down)—*demand* either increases or decreases. Figure 3A-1 examines a shift in the demand curve using algebra.

FIGURE **3A-1** Shifts of the Demand Curve

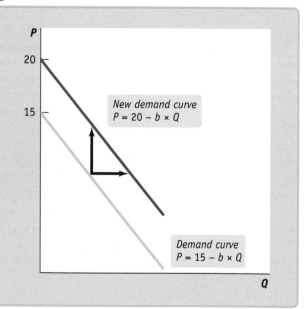

According to geometry, if the value of *a* increases, then the demand curve should shift up. But in economics, an increase in the value of *a* leads to an increase in demand, which shifts the demand curve to the right. Both interpretations are correct because the new demand curve is shifted to the right and shifted up. In this diagram, the value of *a* changes from 15 to 20.

Note that if demand decreases (i.e., *a* decreases), the demand curve shifts down (or to the left).

New demand curve $P = 20 - b \times Q$

Demand curve $P = 15 - b \times Q$

Let us simplify the expanded equation. Suppose the following values apply for factors that affect the demand curve for maple syrup: $P_{corn\ syrup} = \$10$, $P_{pancake\ mix} = \$5$, $Y = \$40$, which represents the average income of a Canadian (in thousands of dollars), $Tastes = 9$, $P^e_{future} = \$20$ (per litre), and $Pop = 34$, which is the population of Canada (in millions of people). Suppose also the values for the constants are $a_0 = \$5$, $a_1 = 0.25$, $a_2 = 2$, $a_3 = 0.5$, $a_4 = \$0.45$, $a_5 = 1.5$, $a_6 = \$0.05$, and $b = 1.25$.

Given these assumed values, the demand curve for maple syrup becomes:

$$P = 5 + 0.25(10) - 2(5) + 0.5(40) + 0.45(9) + 1.5(20) + 0.05(34) - 1.25Q^d$$
$$P = 53.25 - 1.25Q^d$$

[2]Here we have assumed that maple syrup is a normal good.

The Supply Curve

Usually, in the short run, other things equal, the supply curve is an upward sloping function of the price of the good or service being studied. For each level of output, the supply curve reveals the minimum price at which suppliers are willing to sell. Similarly, at each level of the price the supply curve reveals the maximum quantity that suppliers are willing to sell. In the case of linear expressions, a supply curve in its simplest form would be:

(3A-2) $P = c + d \times Q^S$

where P is the price, Q^S is the quantity, and c and d are positive constants.[3] That $d \times Q^S$ is *added* to a constant tells us that as price rises, all else constant, a higher level of quantity is supplied and vice versa (the supply curve slopes upward). The d term describes how sensitive the price is to changes in the quantity supplied (i.e., the slope of the supply curve). If d takes on a larger value then the supply curve becomes relatively steeper—the same change in quantity results in a larger change in the minimum price at which suppliers are willing to sell. If d takes on a smaller value, the effect is opposite—the demand curve becomes relatively flatter and the same change in quantity results in a smaller change in the minimum price at which suppliers are willing to sell.

Again, the simple appearance of Equation 3A-2 hides enormous amounts of information. The constant c contains information on the factors that shift the supply curve: changes in the prices of inputs, changes in the prices of related goods and services, changes in technology, changes in weather, changes in expectations, and changes in the number of producers. For example, the supply of maple syrup, again with the price in dollars per litre and the quantity in millions of litres, might be represented by a linear supply curve such as:

$$P = c_0 + c_1 \times P_{input} + c_2 \times P_{lumber} - c_3 \times P_{tourism} - c_4 \times Tech - c_5 \times Weather$$
$$+ c_6 \times P^e_{future} - c_7 \times N - d \times Q^S$$

with c expanded to include several factors multiplied by constants that are summarized in Table 3A-2. These factors are all multiplied by positive constants that, like d, describe how sensitive the supply curve is to change in those factors. The constant c_0 picks up the impact of all other determinants of the supply of maple syrup that have been left out of the equation of the supply curve. Like the demand curve, if any of these values change, then the supply curve changes too. Figure 3A-2 examines a shift in the supply curve using algebra.

TABLE **3A-2** **Variable Factors That Shift Maple Syrup Supply**

Factor	Denoted by	Change to the supply curve
Input costs	P_{input}	As the price of an input increases (decreases), the supply of maple syrup decreases (increases).
Price of maple lumber	P_{lumber}	As the price of a substitute in production increases (decreases), the supply of maple syrup decreases (increases).
Income from maple farm tourism	$P_{tourism}$	As the income from a complement in production increases (decreases), the supply of maple syrup increases (decreases).
Technology index	$Tech$	As technology improves, the supply of maple syrup increases.
Weather-impact index	$Weather$	As the benefits from the weather increases (decreases), the supply of maple syrup increases (decreases).
Expected future price	P^e_{future}	As the expected future price of maple syrup increases (decreases), the supply of maple syrup decreases (increases).
Number of producers	N	As the number of producers increases (decreases), the supply of maple syrup increases (decreases).

[3]The price term P should be interpreted as the minimum price suppliers are willing to charge (this is sometimes called the *supply price*). Naturally, they would be happy to charge more than this price.

FIGURE **3A-2** Shifts of the Supply Curve

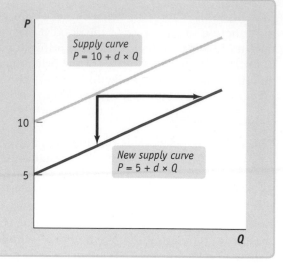

As with the demand curve in Figure 3A-1, there are two ways to interpret a shift in the supply curve. In economics, a decrease in the value of c represents an increase in supply, which shifts the supply curve to the right. The shift right can also be seen as a shift down because the constant term decreased. In this diagram, the value of c changes from 10 to 5.

Note that if supply decreases (i.e., c increases), the supply curve shifts up (or to the left).

Suppose that, given a set of values for all the factors and constants, we get the following supply curve for maple syrup:

$$P = 12.75 + 0.25Q^S$$

Before we use the demand and supply curves for maple syrup to find the equilibrium price and quantity, let's look at Figure 3A-3, which provides a visual summary of the demand and supply curves. For a summary of how to interpret points along these curves, see Table 3A-3.

FIGURE **3A-3** Demand and Supply Curves

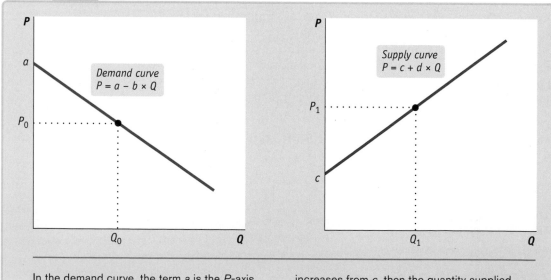

In the demand curve, the term a is the P-axis intercept. This is the lowest price with zero demand. If the price falls below a, then the quantity demanded rises above zero. Similarly, in the supply curve, the term c is the P-axis intercept. This is the price that is so low, the quantity supplied falls to zero. If the price increases from c, then the quantity supplied rises above zero. The slope of the demand curve is equal to −b and the slope of the supply curve is equal to d. Table 3A-3 provides a summary of alternative interpretations of the points along the demand and supply curves.

TABLE **3A-3**   Interpreting Points along Demand and Supply Curves

Curve	Along the Q-axis	Along the P-axis
Demand Curve	At each given price level, the demand curve reveals the maximum quantity that consumers are willing (and able) to buy.	For each given level of output, the demand curve reveals the maximum price consumers are willing (and able) to pay.
	So at the price $P = P_0$, the quantity demanded is equal to $Q^d = Q_0$.	Thus at the output level $Q = Q_0$, the maximum price consumers are willing to pay is $P = P_0$.
Supply Curve	At each level of the price, the supply curve reveals the maximum quantity that suppliers are willing (and able) to sell.	For each level of output, the supply curve reveals the minimum price at which suppliers are willing to sell.
	So at the price $P = P_1$, the quantity supplied is equal to $Q^S = Q_1$.	So at the output level $Q = Q_1$, the minimum price at which suppliers are willing to sell is $P = P_1$.

Market Equilibrium

Along the demand curve, all consumers have voluntarily chosen how much to buy at each specific price to maximize their level of utility or satisfaction. Similarly, along the supply curve all suppliers have voluntarily chosen the quantity they are willing to sell at each specific price to maximize their level of profit. Recall that the market equilibrium occurs where the demand and supply curves intersect. At this intersection, the market outcome is efficient—nobody can be made better off. Figure 3A-4 shows the point of intersection for our maple syrup example.

FIGURE **3A-4** Market Equilibrium for Maple Syrup

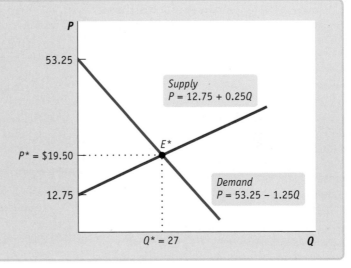

By graphing the pair of lines, we can see that they intersect at E^*, the equilibrium. At this point, $Q^* = 27$ (millions of litres) and $P^* = \$19.50$ per litre. We can use these values to check our answer when we solve for the equilibrium price and quantity algebraically.

Supply
$P = 12.75 + 0.25Q$

Demand
$P = 53.25 - 1.25Q$

In the same way we find the intersection of two lines in geometry, we can determine the equilibrium quantity by equating the supply and demand curves. At equilibrium, P^S and P^d should both be equal to the equilibrium price, P^*. Likewise, Q^S and Q^d should both be equal to the equilibrium quantity, Q^*. So in our maple syrup example, we can say:

$$12.75 + 0.25Q^* = 53.25 - 1.25Q^*$$

and solve for Q^*:

$$1.50Q^* = 40.50$$
$$Q^* = 27$$

Knowing that the equilibrium quantity is 27 million litres per year, we can now determine the equilibrium price using either the demand curve or the supply curve:

$$P^* = 53.25 - 1.25Q^* \qquad P^* = 12.75 + 0.25Q^*$$
$$= 53.25 - 1.25(27) \qquad = 12.75 + 0.25(27)$$
$$= \$19.50 \qquad = \$19.50$$

The equilibrium price is $19.50 per litre of maple syrup.

Since the market is based on voluntary exchanges at the equilibrium point (Q^*, P^*), it is not possible to make either consumers (buyers) or suppliers (sellers) better off without making the other group worse off. For example, consumers would like to buy more maple syrup at a lower price per litre, as this would raise their level of utility or satisfaction. The problem with this is that such a move would result in a reduction in the profits of suppliers, which makes them worse off. Neither group would voluntarily do something that would harm themselves. Thus once we have arrived at the equilibrium intersection, this outcome is a stable situation—stable until such a time that there is a shift in one or both of the curves. Such shifts drive the market to a new equilibrium.

PROBLEMS

1. Suppose that the demand and supply for maple syrup are given by the following equations:

$$P = 53.25 - 1.25Q^d \qquad \text{Demand Curve}$$
$$P = 12.75 + 0.25Q^S \qquad \text{Supply Curve}$$

In each case below, compute the new equilibrium price and quantity exchanged. Has there been an increase/decrease in demand or supply? An increase/decrease in the quantity supplied or demanded? Show in a diagram the initial and new equilibrium locations.

a. Improved weather conditions shift the supply curve to $P = 5.25 + 0.25Q^S$.

b. Increased use of corn to make gasoline additives causes the price of corn syrup to increase, and as a result, the demand curve shifts to $P = 60 - 1.25Q^d$.

c. A new labour contract results in a significant increase in the wages of workers in the maple syrup industry, causing the supply curve to shift to $P = 15.45 + 0.25Q^S$.

d. The income of consumers rises, which shifts the demand curve to $P = 55.50 - 1.25Q^d$; and at the same time an improvement in technology shifts the supply curve to $P = 7.50 + 0.25Q^S$.

2. Suppose the monthly demand and supply for iPods are given by the following equations:

$$P = 500 - 0.001Q^d \qquad \text{Demand Curve}$$
$$P = 200 + 0.0005Q^S \qquad \text{Supply Curve}$$

a. Use the demand and supply curves to solve for the equilibrium price and quantity. Create a diagram to depict this equilibrium.

b. Rewrite the demand curve as an expression that shows quantity demanded (Q^d) in terms of the price.

c. Rewrite the supply curve as an expression that shows quantity supplied (Q^S) in terms of the price.

d. Use the demand and supply curves you derived in parts (b) and (c) to solve for the equilibrium levels of price and quantity. How does this result differ from part (a)? Briefly explain why this is so.

e. Suppose the introduction of new low cost smart phones that also play music causes the demand curve for iPods to shift to $P = 425 - 0.001Q^d$. Derive the resulting new equilibrium levels of price and quantity. Show in a diagram this new equilibrium along with the initial equilibrium location. Are Apple shareholders pleased by this outcome? Briefly explain why or why not.

f. Suppose instead that the offshoring of the production of iPods to a lower cost country causes the supply curve to shift to $P = 140 + 0.0005Q^S$. Derive the resulting new equilibrium levels of price and quantity. Show in a diagram this new equilibrium along with the initial equilibrium location. Are Apple shareholders pleased by this outcome? Briefly explain why or why not.

CHAPTER 4

Consumer and Producer Surplus

WHAT YOU
WILL LEARN
IN THIS
CHAPTER

MAKING GAINS BY THE BOOK

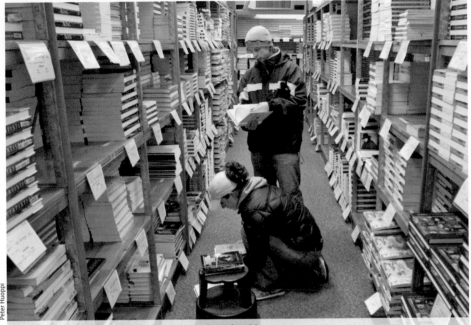

Peter Huoppi

How much am I willing to pay for that used textbook?

> ❭ What **consumer surplus** is and its relationship to the demand curve
>
> ❭ What **producer surplus** is and its relationship to the supply curve
>
> ❭ What **total surplus** is and how it can be used both to measure the gains from trade and to illustrate why markets work so well
>
> ❭ Why **property rights** and prices as **economic signals** are critical to smooth functioning of a market
>
> ❭ Why markets typically lead to efficient outcomes despite the fact that they sometimes fail

THERE IS A LIVELY MARKET IN second-hand college and university textbooks. At the end of each term, some students who took a course decide that the money they can make by selling their used books is worth more to them than keeping the books. And some students who are taking the course next term prefer to buy a somewhat battered but less expensive used textbook rather than a new textbook at full price.

Textbook publishers and authors are not happy about these transactions because they cut into sales of new books. But both the students who sell used books and those who buy them clearly benefit from the existence of second-hand textbook markets. That is why many campus bookstores create them, buying used textbooks and selling them alongside the new books. And it is why there are several websites devoted exclusively to the buying and selling of second-hand textbooks.

So can we put a number on the benefit that used textbook buyers and sellers gain from these transactions? Can we answer the question "How much do the buyers and sellers of textbooks gain from the existence of the used-book market?"

Yes, we can. In this chapter we will see how to measure benefits, such as those to buyers of used textbooks, from being able to purchase a good—known as *consumer surplus*. And we will see that there is a corresponding measure, *producer surplus,* of the benefits sellers receive from being able to sell a good.

The concepts of consumer surplus and producer surplus are extremely useful for analyzing a wide variety of economic issues. They let us calculate how much benefit producers and consumers receive from the existence of a market. They also allow us to calculate how the welfare of consumers and producers is affected by changes in market prices. Such calculations play a crucial role in evaluating many economic policies.

What information do we need to calculate consumer and producer surplus? Surprisingly, all we need are the demand and supply curves for a good. That is, the supply and demand model isn't just a model of how a competitive market works—it's also a model of how much consumers and producers gain from participating in that market.

So our first step will be to learn how consumer and producer surplus can be derived from the demand and supply curves. We will then see how these concepts can be applied to actual economic issues. ■

Consumer Surplus and the Demand Curve

The market in used textbooks is a big business in terms of dollars and cents—at least 10% of the $1.4 billion market for textbooks in 2013. More importantly for us, it is a convenient starting point for developing the concepts of consumer and producer surplus. We'll use the concepts of consumer and producer surplus to understand exactly how buyers and sellers benefit from a competitive market and how big those benefits are. In addition, these concepts play important roles in analyzing what happens when competitive markets don't work well or there is interference in the market.

So let's begin by looking at the market for used textbooks, starting with the buyers. The key point, as we'll see in a minute, is that the demand curve is derived from buyers' tastes or preferences—and that those same preferences also determine how much they gain from the opportunity to buy used books.

Willingness to Pay and the Demand Curve

A used book is not as good as a new book—it will be scuffed up and coffee-stained, may include someone else's highlighting, and may not be completely up to date. How much this bothers you depends on your preferences. Some potential buyers would prefer to buy the used book even if it is only slightly cheaper than a new one; others would buy the used book only if it is considerably cheaper. Let's define a potential buyer's **willingness to pay** as the maximum price at which he or she would buy a good, in this case a used textbook. An individual won't buy the good if it costs more than this amount but will be eager to do so if it costs less. If the price is just equal to an individual's willingness to pay, he or she is indifferent to buying or not buying. For the sake of simplicity, we'll assume that the individual buys the good in this case.

The table in Figure 4-1 shows five potential buyers of a used book that costs $100 new, listed in order of their willingness to pay. At one extreme is Aleisha, who will buy a second-hand book even if the price is as high as $59. Brad is less willing to have a used book and will buy one only if the price is $45 or less. Claudia is willing to pay only $35 and Darren, only $25. And Emiko, who really doesn't like the idea of a used book, will buy one only if it costs no more than $10.

How many of these five students will actually buy a used book? It depends on the price. If the price of a used book is $55, only Aleisha will buy one; if the price is $40, both Aleisha and Brad will buy used books, and so on. So the information in the table can be used to construct the *demand schedule* for used textbooks.

As we saw in Chapter 3, we can use this demand schedule to derive the market demand curve shown in Figure 4-1. Because we are considering only a small number of consumers, this curve doesn't look like the smooth demand curves of Chapter 3, where markets contained hundreds or thousands of consumers. Instead, this demand curve is step-shaped, with alternating horizontal and vertical segments. Each horizontal segment—each step—corresponds to one potential buyer's willingness to pay. However, we'll see shortly that for the analysis of consumer surplus it doesn't matter whether the demand curve is step-shaped, as in this figure, or whether there are many consumers, making the curve smooth.

Willingness to Pay and Consumer Surplus

Suppose that the campus bookstore makes used textbooks available at a price of $30. In that case Aleisha, Brad, and Claudia will buy used books. Do they gain from their purchases, and if so, how much?

FIGURE **4-1**   The Demand Curve for Used Textbooks

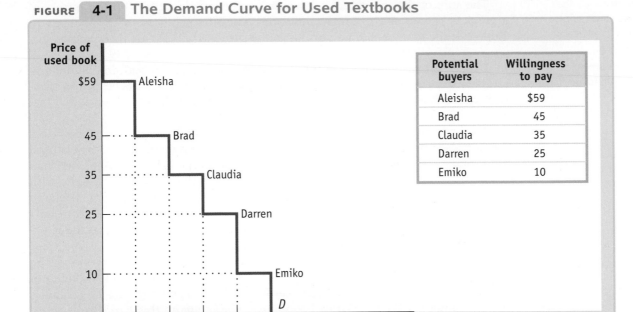

Potential buyers	Willingness to pay
Aleisha	$59
Brad	45
Claudia	35
Darren	25
Emiko	10

With only five potential consumers in this market, the demand curve is step-shaped. Each step represents one consumer, and its height indicates that consumer's willingness to pay—the maximum price at which he or she will buy a used textbook—as indicated in the table. Aleisha has the highest willingness to pay at $59, Brad has the next highest at $45, and so on down to Emiko with the lowest willingness to pay at $10. At a price of $59, the quantity demanded is one (Aleisha); at a price of $45, the quantity demanded is two (Aleisha and Brad); and so on until you reach a price of $10, at which all five students are willing to purchase a used textbook.

The answer, shown in Table 4-1, is that each student who purchases a used book does achieve a net gain but that the amount of the gain differs among students.

Aleisha would have been willing to pay $59, so her net gain is $59 – $30 = $29. Brad would have been willing to pay $45, so his net gain is $45 – $30 = $15. Claudia would have been willing to pay $35, so her net gain is $35 – $30 = $5. Darren and Emiko, however, wouldn't be willing to buy a used book at a price of $30, so they would neither gain nor lose.

The net gain that a buyer achieves from the purchase of a good is called that buyer's **individual consumer surplus.** What we learn from this example is that whenever a buyer pays a price less than his or her willingness to pay, the buyer achieves some individual consumer surplus.

Individual consumer surplus is the net gain to an individual buyer from the purchase of a good. It is equal to the difference between the buyer's willingness to pay and the price paid.

TABLE **4-1**   Consumer Surplus If Price of Used Textbook = $30

Potential buyer	Willingness to pay	Price paid	Individual consumer surplus = Willingness to pay – Price paid
Aleisha	$59	$30	$29
Brad	45	30	15
Claudia	35	30	5
Darren	25	—	—
Emiko	10	—	—
All buyers			**Total consumer surplus = $49**

Total consumer surplus is the sum of the individual consumer surpluses of all the buyers of a good in a market.

The term **consumer surplus** is often used to refer both to individual and to total consumer surplus.

The sum of the individual consumer surpluses achieved by all the buyers of a good is known as the **total consumer surplus** achieved in the market. In Table 4-1, the total consumer surplus is the sum of the individual consumer surpluses achieved by Aleisha, Brad, and Claudia: $29 + $15 + $5 = $49.

Economists use the term **consumer surplus** to refer to both individual and total consumer surplus. We will follow this practice; it will always be clear in context whether we are referring to the consumer surplus achieved by an individual or by all buyers.

Total consumer surplus can be represented graphically. Figure 4-2 reproduces the demand curve from Figure 4-1. Each step in that demand curve is one used book wide and represents one consumer. For example, the height of Aleisha's step is $59, her willingness to pay. This step forms the top of a rectangle, with $30—the price she actually pays for a used book—forming the bottom. The area of Aleisha's rectangle, ($59 − $30) × 1 = $29, is her consumer surplus from purchasing one used book at $30. So the individual consumer surplus Aleisha gains is the *area of the dark blue rectangle* shown in Figure 4-2.

In addition to Aleisha, Brad and Claudia will also each buy a used book when the price is $30. Like Aleisha, they will benefit from their purchases, though not as much, because they each have a lower willingness to pay. Figure 4-2 also shows the consumer surplus gained by Brad and Claudia; again, this can be measured by the areas of the appropriate rectangles. Darren and Emiko, because they do not buy used books at a price of $30, receive no consumer surplus.

The total consumer surplus achieved in this market is the sum of the individual consumer surpluses received by Aleisha, Brad, and Claudia. So total consumer surplus is equal to the combined area of the three rectangles—the entire shaded area in Figure 4-2. Another way to say this is that total consumer surplus is equal to the area below the demand curve but above the price.

Figure 4-2 illustrates the following general principle: *The total consumer surplus generated by purchases of a good at a given price is equal to the area below the demand curve but above that price.* The same principle applies regardless of the number of consumers.

FIGURE   4-2   Consumer Surplus in the Used-Textbook Market

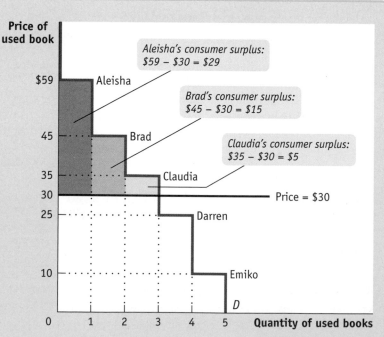

At a price of $30, Aleisha, Brad, and Claudia each buy a used book but Darren and Emiko do not. Aleisha, Brad, and Claudia receive individual consumer surpluses equal to the difference between their willingness to pay and the price, illustrated by the areas of the shaded rectangles. Both Darren and Emiko have a willingness to pay less than $30, so they are unwilling to buy a used book in this market; they receive zero consumer surplus. The total consumer surplus is given by the entire shaded area—the sum of the individual consumer surpluses of Aleisha, Brad, and Claudia, which is equal to $29 + $15 + $5 = $49.

FIGURE **4-3** Consumer Surplus

The demand curve for tablets is smooth because there are many potential buyers. At a price of $500, 1 million tablets are demanded. The consumer surplus at this price is equal to the shaded area: the area below the demand curve but above the price. This is the total net gain to consumers generated from buying and consuming tablets when the price is $500.

All other things equal, a shift in the demand curve will lead to a change in the consumer surplus. For example, an increase in the demand for tablets increases the consumer surplus for any given price level, as the maximum willingness to pay rises. In the graph, as the demand curve shifts right, the shaded area gets larger.

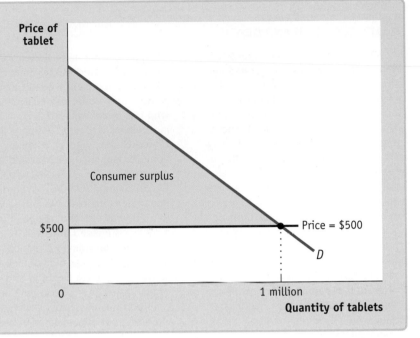

When we consider large markets, this graphical representation of consumer surplus becomes extremely helpful. Consider, for example, the sales of tablet computers to millions of potential buyers. Each potential buyer has a maximum price that he or she is willing to pay. With so many potential buyers, the demand curve will be smooth, like the one shown in Figure 4-3.

Suppose that at a price of $500, a total of 1 million tablets are purchased. How much do consumers gain from being able to buy those 1 million tablets? We could answer that question by calculating the individual consumer surplus of each buyer and then adding these numbers up to arrive at a total. But it is much easier just to look at Figure 4-3 and use the fact that total consumer surplus is equal to the shaded area. As in our original example, consumer surplus is equal to the area below the demand curve but above the price. (You can refresh your memory on how to calculate the area of a right triangle by reviewing Appendix 2A.)

How Changing Prices Affect Consumer Surplus

It is often important to know how much consumer surplus *changes* when the price changes. For example, we may want to know how much consumers are hurt if a flood in Pakistan drives up cotton prices or how much consumers gain if the introduction of fish farming makes salmon steaks less expensive. The same approach we have used to derive consumer surplus can be used to answer questions about how changes in prices affect consumers.

Let's return to the example of the market for used textbooks. Suppose that the bookstore decided to sell used textbooks for $20 instead of $30. How much would this fall in price increase consumer surplus?

The answer is illustrated in Figure 4-4. As shown in the figure, there are two parts to the increase in consumer surplus. The first part, shaded dark blue, is the gain of those who would have bought used books even at the higher price of $30. Each of the students who would have bought used books at $30—Aleisha, Brad, and Claudia—now pays $10 less, and therefore each gains $10 in consumer surplus from the fall in price to $20. So the dark blue area represents the $10 × 3 = $30 increase in consumer surplus to those three buyers.

FOR INQUIRING MINDS

A MATTER OF LIFE AND DEATH

In 2011, while slightly more than 2100 organ transplants were performed in Canada, 265 people died while waiting for a transplant and almost 4600 Canadians were wait-listed. Of those waiting for an organ transplant, about three-quarters are waiting for a kidney transplant. Since the number of those in need of an organ far exceeds availability, what is the best way to allocate available organs? A market isn't feasible. For understandable reasons, the sale of human body parts is illegal in this country. In the case of the sickest individuals needing a kidney, Canadian transplant hospitals have set up a national wait-list that gives these patients priority. For other organs, and patients needing a kidney who are not extremely ill, there is no single national wait-list. Each province is free to set its own mechanism to allocate donated organs. But a national, coordinated system (excluding Quebec) for handling the donation and transplantation of organs (and tissues) is being developed by Canadian Blood Services.

Under current kidney transplant guidelines, if a donated kidney does not go to a critically ill patient who will die in days without this organ, it goes to the person who has been waiting the longest. This is very similar to what happens in the United States, where the kidney allocation protocol has been devised by the non-profit group United Network for Organ Sharing (UNOS). According to this system, an available kidney would go to a 75-year-old who has been waiting for 2 years instead of to a 25-year-old who has been waiting 6 months, even though the 25-year-old will likely live longer and benefit from the transplanted organ for a longer period of time.

To address this issue, UNOS is devising a new set of guidelines based on a concept it calls "net benefit." According to these new guidelines, kidneys would be allocated on the basis of who will receive the greatest net benefit, where net benefit is measured as the expected increase in lifespan from the transplant. And age is by far the biggest predictor of

how long someone will live after a transplant. For example, a typical 25-year-old diabetic will gain an extra 8.7 years of life from a transplant, but a typical 55-year-old diabetic will gain only 3.6 extra years.

Under the current UNOS system, based on waiting times, transplants lead to about 44 000 extra years of life for recipients; under the new system, that number would jump to 55 000 extra years. The share of kidneys going to those in their 20s would triple; the share going to those 60 and older would be halved.

What does this have to do with consumer surplus? As you may have guessed, the UNOS concept of "net benefit" is a lot like individual consumer surplus—the individual consumer surplus generated from getting a new kidney. In essence, UNOS has devised a system that allocates donated kidneys according to who gets the greatest individual consumer surplus. In terms of results, then, its proposed "net benefit" system operates a lot like a competitive market.[1]

The second part, shaded light blue, is the gain to those who would not have bought a used book at $30 but are willing to pay more than $20. In this case that gain goes to Darren, who would not have bought a used book at $30 but will buy one at $20. He gains $5—the difference between his willingness to pay of $25 and the new price of $20. So the light blue area represents a further $5 gain in consumer surplus.

The total increase in consumer surplus is the sum of the shaded areas, $35. Likewise, a rise in price from $20 to $30 would decrease consumer surplus by an amount equal to the sum of the shaded areas.

Figure 4-4 illustrates that when the price of a good falls, the area under the demand curve but above the price—which we have seen is equal to total consumer surplus—increases. Figure 4-5 shows the same result for the case of a smooth demand curve, the demand for tablets. Here we assume that the price of tablets falls from $2000 to $500, leading to an increase in the quantity demanded from 200 000 to 1 million units.

As in the used-textbook example, we divide the gain in consumer surplus into two parts. The dark blue rectangle in Figure 4-5 corresponds to the dark blue area in Figure 4-4: it is the gain to the 200 000 people who would

[1]This situation is similar to a properly functioning competitive market, which is efficient but not necessarily equitable. In fact, these two goals, efficiency and equity, might be in conflict. Advocates of equity, sometimes called fairness or justice, might argue that the sickest people should have a higher priority for receiving donated kidneys, as without transplant they will most certainly die. This objective could conflict with the view of others who feel the limited supply of donated kidneys should be allocated in a way that maximizes net benefit (efficiency), as this might instead direct a kidney away from the sickest individuals.

FIGURE   4-4   Consumer Surplus and a Fall in the Price of Used Textbooks

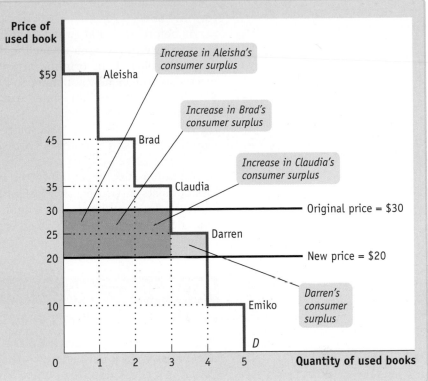

There are two parts to the increase in consumer surplus generated by a fall in price from $30 to $20. The first is given by the dark blue rectangle: each person who would have bought at the original price of $30—Aleisha, Brad, and Claudia—receives an increase in consumer surplus equal to the total reduction in price, $10. So the area of the dark blue rectangle corresponds to an amount equal to 3 × $10 = $30. The second part is given by the light blue area: the increase in consumer surplus for those who would not have bought at the original price of $30 but who buy at the new price of $20—namely, Darren. Darren's willingness to pay is $25, so he now receives consumer surplus of $5. The total increase in consumer surplus is (3 × $10) + $5 = $35, represented by the sum of the shaded areas. Likewise, a rise in price from $20 to $30 would decrease consumer surplus by $35, the amount corresponding to the sum of the shaded areas.

have bought tablets even at the higher price of $2000. As a result of the price reduction, each receives additional surplus of $1500. The light blue triangle in Figure 4-5 corresponds to the light blue area in Figure 4-4: it is the gain to people who would not have bought the good at the higher price but are willing to do so at a price of $500. For example, the light blue triangle includes the

FIGURE   4-5   A Fall in the Price Increases Consumer Surplus

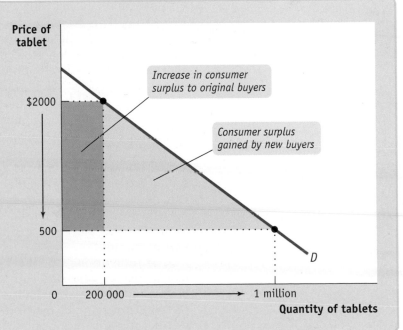

All other things equal, a fall in the price of a tablet from $2000 to $500 leads to an increase in the quantity demanded and an increase in consumer surplus. The change in total consumer surplus is given by the sum of the shaded areas: the total area below the demand curve and between the old and new prices. Here, the dark blue area represents the increase in consumer surplus for the 200 000 consumers who would have bought a tablet at the original price of $2000; they each receive an increase in consumer surplus of $1500. The light blue area represents the increase in consumer surplus for those willing to buy at a price equal to or greater than $500 but less than $2000. Similarly, a rise in the price of a tablet from $500 to $2000 generates a decrease in consumer surplus equal to the sum of the two shaded areas.

gain to someone who would have been willing to pay $1000 for a tablet and therefore gains $500 in consumer surplus when it is possible to buy a tablet for only $500.

As before, the total gain in consumer surplus is the sum of the shaded areas: the increase in the area under the demand curve but above the price. The consumer surplus of the original buyers increases by $300 million. The new lower price encourages new consumers to buy a tablet, and these new consumers gain $600 million of new consumer surplus. The total gain in consumer surplus is $900 million.

What would happen if the price of a good were to rise instead of fall? We would do the same analysis in reverse. Suppose, for example, that for some reason the price of tablets rises from $500 to $2000. This would lead to a fall in consumer surplus, equal to the sum of the shaded areas in Figure 4-5. This loss consists of two parts. The dark blue rectangle represents the loss to consumers who would still buy a tablet, even at a price of $2000. The light blue triangle represents the loss to consumers who would decide not to buy a tablet at the higher price.

ECONOMICS ▸ IN ACTION

WHEN MONEY ISN'T ENOUGH

The key insight we get from the concept of consumer surplus is that purchases yield a net benefit to the consumer because the consumer typically pays a price less than his or her willingness to pay for the good. Another way to say this is that the right to buy a good at the going price is a valuable thing in itself.

Most of the time we don't think about the value associated with the right to buy a good. In a market economy, we take it for granted that we can buy whatever we want, as long as we are willing to pay the market price.

But that hasn't always been true. For example, during World War II the demands of wartime production created shortages of consumer goods when these goods were sold at pre-war prices. Rather than

For those who purchased World War II ration coupons illegally, the right to consumer surplus had a steep price.

allow prices to rise, government officials in many countries created a system of rationing. To buy sugar, meat, coffee, gasoline, and many other goods, you not only had to pay cash; you also had to present stamps or coupons from books issued to each family by the government. These pieces of paper, which represented the right to buy goods at the government-regulated price, quickly became valuable commodities in themselves.

As a result, illegal markets in meat stamps and gasoline coupons sprang into existence. Moreover, criminals began stealing coupons and even counterfeiting stamps.

The funny thing was that even if you had bought a gasoline coupon on the illegal market, you still had to pay to purchase gasoline. So what you were buying on the illegal market was not the good but the right to buy the good at the government-regulated price. That is, people who bought ration coupons on the illegal market were paying for the right to get some consumer surplus.

1. Consider the market for cheese-stuffed jalapeno peppers. There are two consumers, Casey and Josey, and their willingness to pay for each pepper is given in the accompanying table. (Neither is willing to consume more than 4 peppers at any price.) Use the table (i) to construct the demand schedule for peppers for prices of $0.00, $0.10, and so on, up to $0.90, and (ii) to calculate the total consumer surplus when the price of a pepper is $0.40.

Quantity of peppers	Casey's willingness to pay	Josey's willingness to pay
1st pepper	$0.90	$0.80
2nd pepper	0.70	0.60
3rd pepper	0.50	0.40
4th pepper	0.30	0.30

Solutions appear at back of book.

▼ **Quick Review**

● The demand curve for a good is determined by each potential consumer's **willingness to pay.**

● **Individual consumer surplus** is the net gain an individual consumer gets from buying a good.

● The **total consumer surplus** in a given market is equal to the area below the market demand curve but above the price.

● All other things equal, a fall in the price of a good increases **consumer surplus** through two channels: a gain to consumers who would have bought at the original price and a gain to consumers who are persuaded by the lower price to buy. A rise in the price of a good reduces consumer surplus in a similar fashion.

Producer Surplus and the Supply Curve

Just as some buyers of a good would be willing to pay more for their purchase than the price they actually pay, some sellers of a good would be willing to sell it for less than the price they actually receive. So just as there are consumers who receive consumer surplus from buying in a market, there are producers who receive producer surplus from selling in a market.

Cost and Producer Surplus

Consider a group of students who are potential sellers of used textbooks. Because they have different preferences, the various potential sellers differ in the price at which they are willing to sell their second-hand books. The table in Figure 4-6 shows the prices at which several different students would be willing to sell. Andrew is willing to sell his book as long as he can get at least $5; Bahira won't sell unless she can get at least $15; Carlos, unless he can get $25; Donna, unless she can get $35; Etienne, unless he can get $45.

The lowest price at which a potential seller is willing to sell has a special name in economics: it is called the seller's **cost.** So Andrew's cost is $5, Bahira's is $15, and so on.

Using the term *cost*, which people normally associate with the monetary cost of producing a good, may sound a little strange when applied to sellers of used textbooks. The students don't have to manufacture the books, so it doesn't cost the student who sells a used textbook anything to make that book available for sale, does it?

Yes, it does. A student who sells a book won't have it later, as part of his or her personal collection. So there is an *opportunity* cost to selling a used textbook, even if the owner has completed the course for which it was required. And remember that one of the basic principles of economics is that the true measure of the cost of doing something is always its opportunity cost. That is, the real cost of something is what you must give up to get it.

So it is good economics to talk of the minimum price at which someone will sell a good as the "cost" of selling that good, even if he or she doesn't spend any money to make the good available for sale. Of course, in most real-world markets the sellers are also those who produce the good and therefore *do* spend money to make it available for sale. In this case, the cost of making the good available for sale includes monetary costs, but it may also include other opportunity costs.

Getting back to the example, suppose that Andrew sells his used book for $30. Clearly he has gained from the transaction: he was willing to sell for only $5, so

An individual seller's **cost** is the lowest price at which he or she is willing to sell a good.

FIGURE **4-6** The Supply Curve for Used Textbooks

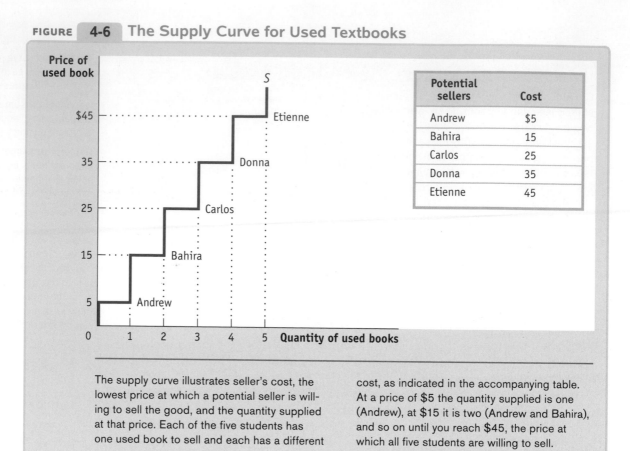

The supply curve illustrates seller's cost, the lowest price at which a potential seller is willing to sell the good, and the quantity supplied at that price. Each of the five students has one used book to sell and each has a different cost, as indicated in the accompanying table. At a price of $5 the quantity supplied is one (Andrew), at $15 it is two (Andrew and Bahira), and so on until you reach $45, the price at which all five students are willing to sell.

he has gained $25. This net gain, the difference between the price he actually gets and his cost—the minimum price at which he would have been willing to sell—is known as his **individual producer surplus.**

Just as we derived the demand curve from the willingness of different consumers to pay, we can derive the supply curve from the cost of different producers. The step-shaped curve in Figure 4-6 shows the supply curve implied by the costs shown in the accompanying table. At a price less than $5, none of the students are willing to sell; at a price between $5 and $15, only Andrew is willing to sell, and so on.

As in the case of consumer surplus, we can add the individual producer surpluses of sellers to calculate the **total producer surplus,** the total net gain to all sellers in the market. Economists use the term **producer surplus** to refer to either individual or total producer surplus. Table 4-2 shows the net

Individual producer surplus is the net gain to an individual seller from selling a good. It is equal to the difference between the price received and the seller's cost.

Total producer surplus is the sum of the individual producer surpluses of all the sellers of a good in a market.

Economists use the term **producer surplus** to refer both to individual and to total producer surplus.

TABLE **4-2** Producer Surplus When the Price of a Used Textbook = $30

Potential seller	Cost	Price received	Individual producer surplus = Price received – Cost
Andrew	$5	$30	$25
Bahira	15	30	15
Carlos	25	30	5
Donna	35	—	—
Etienne	45	—	—
All sellers			**Total producer surplus = $45**

FIGURE 4-7   Producer Surplus in the Used-Textbook Market

At a price of $30, Andrew, Bahira, and Carlos each sell a used book but Donna and Etienne do not. Andrew, Bahira, and Carlos get individual producer surpluses equal to the difference between the price and their cost, illustrated here by the shaded rectangles. Donna and Etienne each have a cost that is greater than the price of $30, so they are unwilling to sell a used book and so receive zero producer surplus. The total producer surplus is given by the entire shaded area—the sum of the individual producer surpluses of Andrew, Bahira, and Carlos, which is equal to $25 + $15 + $5 = $45.

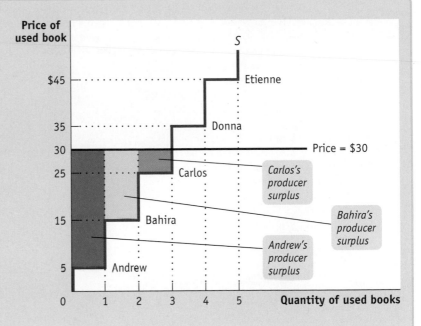

gain to each of the students who would sell a used book at a price of $30: $25 for Andrew, $15 for Bahira, and $5 for Carlos. The total producer surplus is $25 + $15 + $5 = $45.

As with consumer surplus, the producer surplus gained by those who sell used books can be represented graphically. Figure 4-7 reproduces the supply curve from Figure 4-6. Each step in that supply curve is one used book wide and represents one seller. The height of Andrew's step is $5, his cost. This forms the bottom of a rectangle, with $30, the price he actually receives for his book, forming the top. The area of this rectangle, ($30 − $5) × 1 = $25, is his producer surplus. So the producer surplus Andrew gains from selling his book is the *area of the dark red rectangle* shown in the figure.

Let's assume that the campus bookstore is willing to buy all the used copies of this book that students are willing to sell at a price of $30. Then, in addition to Andrew, Bahira and Carlos will also sell their books. They will also benefit from their sales, though not as much as Andrew, because they have higher costs. Andrew, as we have seen, gains $25. Bahira gains a smaller amount: since her cost is $15, she gains only $15. Carlos gains even less, only $5.

Again, as with consumer surplus, we have a general rule for determining the total producer surplus from sales of a good: *The total producer surplus from sales of a good at a given price is the area above the supply curve but below that price.*

This rule applies both to examples like the one shown in Figure 4-7, where there are a small number of producers and a step-shaped supply curve, and to more realistic examples, where there are many producers and the supply curve is smooth.

Consider, for example, the supply of wheat. Figure 4-8 shows how producer surplus depends on the price per bushel. Suppose that, as shown in the figure, the price is $5 per bushel and farmers supply 1 million bushels. What is the benefit to the farmers from selling their wheat at a price of $5? Their producer surplus is equal to the shaded area in the figure—the area above the supply curve but below the price of $5 per bushel.

FIGURE **4-8** Producer Surplus

Here is the supply curve for wheat. At a price of $5 per bushel, farmers supply 1 million bushels. The producer surplus at this price is equal to the shaded area: the area above the supply curve but below the price. This is the total gain to producers—farmers in this case—from supplying their product when the price is $5.

All other things equal, a shift in the supply curve will lead to a change in the producer surplus. For example, after an increase in the supply of wheat (i.e., a rightward shift of the supply curve), the producer surplus increases.

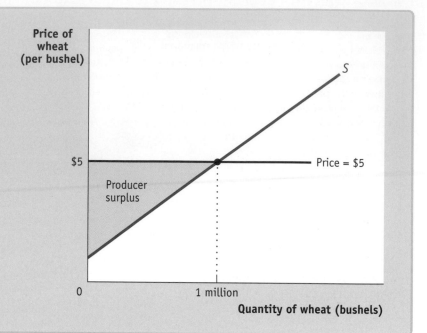

How Changing Prices Affect Producer Surplus

As with the case of consumer surplus, a change in price alters producer surplus. But the effects are opposite. While a fall in price increases consumer surplus, it reduces producer surplus. And a rise in price reduces consumer surplus but increases producer surplus.

To see this, let's first consider a rise in the price of the good. Producers of the good will experience an increase in producer surplus, though not all producers gain the same amount. Some producers would have produced the good even at the original price; they will gain the entire price increase on every unit they pro-

FIGURE **4-9** A Rise in the Price Increases Producer Surplus

All other things equal, a rise in the price of wheat from $5 to $7 leads to an increase in the quantity supplied and an increase in producer surplus. The change in total producer surplus is given by the sum of the shaded areas: the total area above the supply curve but between the old and new prices. The dark red area represents the gain to the farmers who would have supplied 1 million bushels at the original price of $5; they each receive an increase in producer surplus of $2 for each of those bushels. The triangular light red area represents the increase in producer surplus achieved by the farmers who supply the additional 500 000 bushels because of the higher price. Similarly, a fall in the price of wheat from $7 to $5 generates a reduction in producer surplus equal to the sum of the shaded areas.

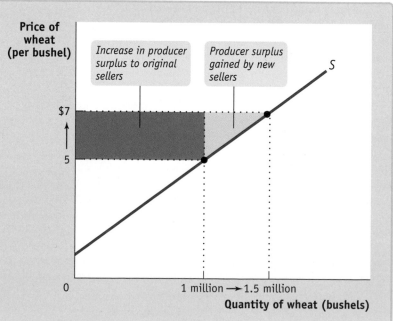

duce. Other producers will enter the market because of the higher price; they will gain only the difference between the new price and their cost.

Figure 4-9 is the supply counterpart of Figure 4-5. It shows the effect on producer surplus of a rise in the price of wheat from $5 to $7 per bushel. The increase in producer surplus is the $2.5 million sum of the shaded areas, which consists of two parts. First, there is a dark red rectangle corresponding to the $2 million in gains to those farmers who would have supplied wheat even at the original $5 price. Second, there is an additional light red triangle that corresponds to the $500 000 in gains to those farmers who would not have supplied wheat at the original price but are drawn into the market by the higher price.

If the price were to fall from $7 to $5 per bushel, the story would run in reverse. The sum of the shaded areas would now be the decline in producer surplus, the decrease in the area above the supply curve but below the price. The loss would consist of two parts, the loss to farmers who would still grow wheat at a price of $5 (the dark red rectangle) and the loss to farmers who cease to grow wheat because of the lower price (the light red triangle).

ECONOMICS ▸ IN ACTION

HIGH TIMES DOWN ON THE FARM

According to Statistics Canada, the average value of farmland in Ontario hit a record high in 2012, surging by 19.6% for the year. Figure 4-10 shows the significant increase in the price of Ontario farmland from 1950 to 2012. The average price of a hectare of Ontario farmland doubled from 2002 to 2012. The recessions in the early 1980s and in the early 1990s caused average prices to fall for a few years, but remarkably the Great Recession, that began in 2008, did not have the same effect. It only temporarily slowed the upward trend. And there was no mystery as to why: it was all about the high prices being paid for wheat, corn, and soybeans. In 2010, the price of corn jumped by 52%; soybeans, by 34%; and wheat, by 47%.

Why were Ontario farm products commanding such high prices? There are three main reasons: ethanol, rising incomes in countries like China, and poor weather in other foodstuff-producing countries like Australia and Ukraine.

Ethanol—a product made from corn and the same kind of alcohol that's in beer and other alcoholic drinks—can also fuel automobiles. And in recent years U.S. government policy, at both the federal and state levels, has encouraged the use of gasoline that contains a percentage of ethanol. There are a couple of reasons for this policy, including some benefits in fighting air pollution and the hope that using more ethanol will reduce U.S. dependence on imported oil. Since ethanol comes from corn, the shift to ethanol fuel has led to an increase in the demand for corn.

FIGURE **4-10**   The Price of Ontario and Canadian Farmland, 1950–2012

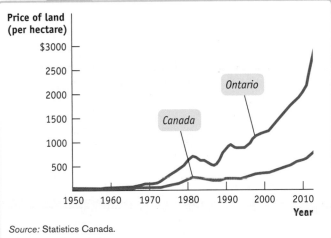

Source: Statistics Canada.

But Ontario farmers have also benefitted greatly from events beyond North America. As in the case of cotton, which we studied in Chapter 3, changes in the demand for and supply of foodstuffs in world markets have led to rising prices for Canadian corn, soybeans, and wheat. Rising incomes in countries like China have led to increased food consumption and increased demand for foodstuffs. Simultaneously, very bad weather in Australia and Ukraine has led to a fall in supply. Predictably, increased demand coupled with reduced supply has led to a surge in foodstuff prices and a windfall for Ontario farmers.

What does this have to do with the price of land? A person who buys a farm in Ontario buys the producer surplus generated by that farm. And higher prices for corn, soybeans, and wheat, which raise the producer surplus of Ontario farmers, make Ontario farmland more valuable. According to the RE/MAX Market Trends Report: Farm Edition, between 2010 and late 2013, the average price of a hectare of prime farmland in southern Ontario increased by as much as 140% depending on location, well above the national average. Land prices continued to climb in 2013, even though the price of corn decreased by 38%, soybeans by 19%, and wheat by 22% in that year. Land buyers clearly expected these price decreases to be either smaller or temporary.

CHECK YOUR UNDERSTANDING   4-2

1. Consider again the market for cheese-stuffed jalapeno peppers. There are two producers, Cara and Jamie, and their marginal (or incremental) costs of producing each pepper are given in the accompanying table. (Neither is willing to produce more than 4 peppers at any

Quantity of peppers	Cara's cost	Jamie's cost
1st pepper	$0.10	$0.30
2nd pepper	0.10	0.50
3rd pepper	0.40	0.70
4th pepper	0.60	0.90

price.) Use the table (i) to construct the supply schedule for peppers for prices of $0.00, $0.10, and so on, up to $0.90, and (ii) to calculate the total producer surplus when the price of a pepper is $0.70.

Solutions appear at back of book.

Consumer Surplus, Producer Surplus, and the Gains from Trade

One of the 12 core principles of economics we introduced in Chapter 1 is that markets are a remarkably effective way to organize economic activity: they generally make society as well off as possible given the available resources. The concepts of consumer surplus and producer surplus can help us deepen our understanding of why this is so.

The Gains from Trade

Let's return to the market in used textbooks but now consider a much bigger market—say, one at a large university like the University of British Columbia (UBC). There are many potential buyers and sellers, so the market is quite competitive. Let's line up incoming students who are potential buyers of a used book in order of their willingness to pay, so that the entering student with the highest willingness to pay is potential buyer number 1, then the student with the next highest willingness to pay is number 2, and so on. Then we can use their willingness to pay to derive a demand curve like the one in Figure 4-11.

Similarly, we can line up outgoing students, who are potential sellers of the used book, in order of their (opportunity) cost—starting with the student with the lowest cost, then the student with the next lowest cost, and so on—to derive a supply curve like the one shown in the same figure.

As we have drawn the curves, the market reaches equilibrium at a price of $30 per book, and 1000 used books are bought and sold at that price. The two shaded triangles show the consumer surplus (blue) and the producer surplus (red) generated by this market. The sum of consumer and producer surpluses is known as the **total surplus** generated in a market.

The **total surplus** generated in a market is the total net gain to consumers and producers from trading in the market. It is the sum of the producer and the consumer surpluses.

FIGURE **4-11** Total Surplus

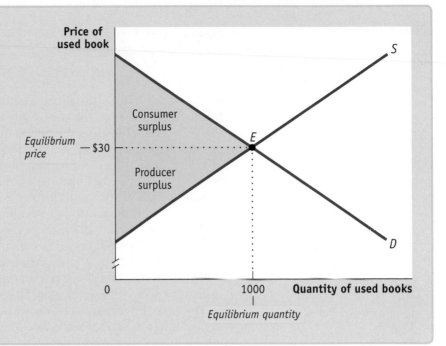

In the market for used textbooks, the equilibrium price is $30 and the equilibrium quantity is 1000 used books. Consumer surplus is given by the blue area, the area below the demand curve but above the price. Producer surplus is given by the red area, the area above the supply curve but below the price. The sum of the blue and the red areas is total surplus, the total benefit to society from the production and consumption of the good.

The striking thing about this picture is that both consumers and producers gain—that is, both consumers and producers are better off because there is a market for this good. But this should come as no surprise—it illustrates another core principle of economics: *There are gains from trade.* These gains from trade are the reason everyone is better off participating in a market economy than they would be if each individual tried to be self-sufficient.

But are we as well off as we could be? This brings us to the question of the efficiency of markets.

The Efficiency of Markets

Markets produce gains from trade, but in Chapter 1 we made an even bigger claim: that markets are usually *efficient*. That is, we claimed that once the market has produced its gains from trade, there is no way to make some people better off without making other people worse off, except under some well-defined special conditions.

The analysis of consumer and producer surplus helps us understand why markets are usually efficient. To gain more intuition into why this is so, consider the fact that market equilibrium is just *one* way of deciding who consumes the good and who sells the good. There are other possible ways of making that decision.

Consider, for example, the case of kidney transplants, discussed earlier in For Inquiring Minds. There you learned that, in Canada and the United States, available kidneys currently go to the people who have been waiting the longest, rather than to those most likely to benefit from the organ for a longer time. In the United States, to address this inefficiency, a new set of guidelines is being devised to determine eligibility for a kidney transplant based on "net benefit," a concept an awful lot like consumer surplus: kidneys would be allocated largely on the basis of who will benefit from them the most.

To further our understanding of why markets usually work so well, imagine a committee charged with improving on the market equilibrium by deciding who gets and who gives up a used textbook. The committee's ultimate goal: to bypass the market outcome and devise another arrangement, one that would produce higher total surplus.

Let's consider the three ways in which the committee might try to increase the total surplus:

1. Reallocate consumption among consumers
2. Reallocate sales among sellers
3. Change the quantity traded

Reallocate Consumption Among Consumers The committee might try to increase total surplus by selling used books to different consumers. Figure 4-12 shows why this will result in lower surplus compared to the market equilibrium outcome. Points *A* and *B* show the positions on the demand curve of two potential buyers of used books, Ana and Bob. As we can see from the figure, Ana is willing to pay $35 for a used book, but Bob is willing to pay only $25. Since the market equilibrium price is $30, under the market outcome Ana buys a used book and Bob does not.

Now suppose the committee reallocates consumption. This would mean taking the used book away from Ana and giving it to Bob. Since the used book is worth $35 to Ana but only $25 to Bob, this change *reduces total consumer surplus* by $35 – $25 = $10. Moreover, this result doesn't depend on which two students we pick. Every student who buys a used book at the market equilibrium has a willingness to pay of $30 or more, and every student who doesn't buy a used book has a willingness to pay of less than $30. So reallocating the good among consumers always means taking a used book away from a student who values it more and giving it to one who values it less. This necessarily reduces total consumer surplus.

Reallocate Sales Among Sellers The committee might try to increase total surplus by altering who sells their used books, taking sales away from sellers who would have sold their used books at the market equilibrium and instead compelling those who would not have sold their used books at the market equilibrium to sell them.

Figure 4-13 shows why this will result in lower surplus. Here points *X* and *Y* show the positions on the supply curve of Xavier, who has a cost of $25, and Yvonne, who has a cost of $35. At the equilibrium market price of $30, Xavier

FIGURE **4-12** **Reallocating Consumption Lowers Consumer Surplus**

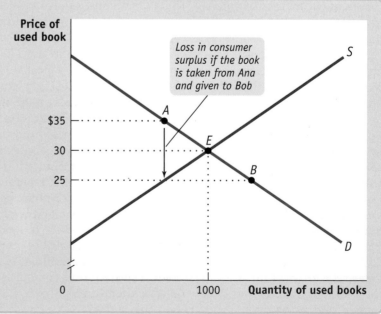

Ana (point *A*) has a willingness to pay of $35. Bob (point *B*) has a willingness to pay of only $25. At the market equilibrium price of $30, Ana purchases a used book but Bob does not. If we rearrange consumption by taking a used book from Ana and giving it to Bob, consumer surplus declines by $10 and, as a result, total surplus declines by $10.

FIGURE **4-13** **Reallocating Sales Lowers Producer Surplus**

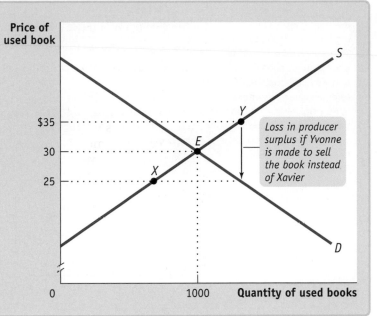

Yvonne (point *Y*) has a cost of $35, $10 more than Xavier (point *X*), who has a cost of $25. At the market equilibrium price of $30, Xavier sells a used book but Yvonne does not. If we rearrange sales by preventing Xavier from selling his used book and compelling Yvonne to sell hers, producer surplus declines by $10 and, as a result, total surplus declines by $10.

Loss in producer surplus if Yvonne is made to sell the book instead of Xavier

would sell his used book but Yvonne would not sell hers. If the committee reallocated sales, forcing Xavier to keep his used book and Yvonne to sell hers, total producer surplus would be reduced by $35 − $25 = $10.

Again, it doesn't matter which two students we choose. Any student who sells a used book at the market equilibrium has a lower cost than any student who keeps a used book. So reallocating sales among sellers necessarily increases total cost and reduces total producer surplus.

Change the Quantity Traded The committee might try to increase total surplus by compelling students to trade either more used books or fewer used books than the market equilibrium quantity.

Figure 4-14 shows why this will result in lower surplus. It shows all four students: potential buyers Ana and Bob, and potential sellers Xavier and Yvonne. To reduce sales, the committee will have to prevent one or more transactions that would have occurred in the market equilibrium—for example, they might prevent Xavier from selling to Ana. Since Ana is willing to pay $35 and Xavier's cost is $25, preventing this transaction reduces total surplus by $35 − $25 = $10.

Once again, this result doesn't depend on which two students we pick: any student who would have sold the used book at the market equilibrium has a cost of $30 or less, and any student who would have purchased the used book at the market equilibrium has a willingness to pay of $30 or more. So preventing any sale that would have occurred in the market equilibrium necessarily reduces total surplus.

Finally, the committee might try to increase sales by forcing Yvonne, who would not have sold her used book at the market equilibrium, to sell it to someone like Bob, who would not have bought a used book at the market equilibrium. Because Yvonne's cost is $35, but Bob is only willing to pay $25, this transaction reduces total surplus by $10. And once again it doesn't matter which two students we pick—anyone who wouldn't have bought the used book has a willingness to pay of less than $30, and anyone who wouldn't have sold has a cost of more than $30.

The key point to remember is that once this market is in equilibrium, there is no way to increase the gains from trade. Any other outcome reduces total surplus. (This is why the United Network for Organ Sharing, or UNOS, is trying, with its new guidelines based on "net benefit," to reproduce the allocation

FIGURE **4-14** **Changing the Quantity Lowers Total Surplus**

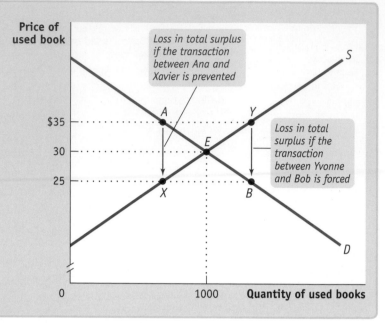

If Xavier (point *X*) were prevented from selling his used book to someone like Ana (point *A*), total surplus would fall by $10, the difference between Ana's willingness to pay ($35) and Xavier's cost ($25). This means that total surplus falls whenever fewer than 1000 used books—the equilibrium quantity—are transacted. Likewise, if Yvonne (point *Y*) were compelled to sell her book to someone like Bob (point *B*), total surplus would also fall by $10, the difference between Yvonne's cost ($35) and Bob's willingness to pay ($25). This means that total surplus falls whenever more than 1000 used books are transacted. These two examples show that at market equilibrium, all mutually beneficial transactions—and only mutually beneficial transactions—occur.

of donated kidneys that would occur if there were a market for the organs.) We can summarize our results by stating that an efficient market performs four important functions:

1. It allocates consumption of the good to the potential buyers who most value it, as indicated by the fact that they have the highest willingness to pay.

2. It allocates sales to the potential sellers who most value the right to sell the good, as indicated by the fact that they have the lowest cost.

3. It ensures that every consumer who makes a purchase values the good more than every seller who makes a sale, so that all transactions are mutually beneficial.

4. It ensures that every potential buyer who doesn't make a purchase values the good less than every potential seller who doesn't make a sale, so that no mutually beneficial transactions are missed.

As a result of these four functions, *any way of allocating the good other than the market equilibrium outcome lowers total surplus.*

There are three caveats, however. First, although a market may be efficient, it isn't necessarily *fair*. In fact, fairness, or *equity*, is often in conflict with efficiency. We'll discuss this next.

The second caveat is that markets sometimes *fail*. As we mentioned in Chapter 1, under some well-defined conditions, markets can fail to deliver efficiency. When this occurs, markets no longer maximize total surplus. We provide a brief overview of why markets fail at the end of this chapter, reserving a more detailed analysis for later chapters.

Third, even when the market equilibrium maximizes total surplus, this does not mean that it results in the best outcome for every *individual* consumer and producer. All other things equal, each buyer would like to pay a lower price and each seller would like to receive a higher price. So if the government were to intervene in the market—say, by lowering the price below the equilibrium price to make consumers happy or by raising the price to make producers happy—the outcome would no longer be efficient. Although some people would be happier, total surplus would be lower.

Equity and Efficiency

For many patients who need kidney transplants, the proposed UNOS guidelines, covered earlier, will be unwelcome news. Those who have waited years for a transplant will no doubt find these guidelines, which give precedence to younger patients, unfair. And the guidelines raise other questions about fairness: Why limit potential transplant recipients to citizens? Why include younger patients with other chronic diseases? Why not give precedence to those who have made recognized contributions to society? And so on.

The point is that efficiency is about *how to achieve goals, not what those goals should be*. For example, UNOS decided that its goal is to maximize the lifespan of kidney recipients. Some might have argued for a different goal, and efficiency does not address which goal is the best. *What efficiency does address is the best way to achieve a goal once that goal has been determined*—in this case, using the UNOS concept of "net benefit."

It's easy to get carried away with the idea that markets are always right and that economic policies that interfere with efficiency are bad. But that would be misguided because there is another factor to consider: society cares about equity, or what's "fair."

As we discussed in Chapter 1, there is often a trade-off between equity and efficiency: policies that promote equity often come at the cost of decreased efficiency, and policies that promote efficiency often result in decreased equity. So it's important to realize that a society's choice to sacrifice some efficiency for the sake of equity, however it defines equity, is a valid one. And it's important to understand that fairness, unlike efficiency, can be very hard to define. Fairness is a concept about which well-intentioned people often disagree.

ECONOMICS ▸ *IN ACTION*

TAKE THE KEYS, PLEASE

Without doubt, history books (or digital readers) will one day cite eBay, the online auction service, as one of the great innovations of the twentieth century. Founded in 1995, the company says that its mission is "to help practically anyone trade practically anything on earth." It provides a way for would-be buyers and would-be sellers—sometimes of unique or used items—to find one another. And the gains from trade accruing to eBay users were evidently large: in 2012, eBay enabled $175 billion in commerce on its websites. In Canada, the most popular online classified services website is the eBay-owned Kijiji. At the time of writing, there were about 6 million classified listings. The kinds of listings range from used products such as books, video games, and electronics to specialized services such as child care and housekeeping.

eBay has been connecting buyers and sellers since 1995.

And the online matching hasn't stopped there. Websites are now popping up that allow people to rent out their personal possessions—items like cars, power tools, personal electronics, and spare bedrooms. Similar to what eBay did for buyers and sellers, these new websites provide a platform for renters and owners to find one another.

A recent article in *The Globe and Mail* describes how cottage owners in Ontario use websites such as Cottage Country Vacation Rentals (CottageCountry.com) to list their properties for holiday rentals. Mara Sofferin, vice-president of marketing at CottageCountry.com, said that the site helps to match cottage owners with the right cottage renters. Depending on the location and condition of a cottage, the site can fetch more than $1000 per week for participating cottage owners.

Judith Chevalier, a Yale School of Management economist says, "These companies let you wring a little bit of value out of … goods that are just sitting there."

Cottage Country Vacation Rentals and companies like it are hoping that they can earn a nice return by helping you generate a little bit more surplus from your possessions.

CHECK YOUR UNDERSTANDING   4-3

1. Using the tables in Check Your Understanding 4-1 and 4-2, find the equilibrium price and quantity in the market for cheese-stuffed jalapeno peppers. What is total surplus in the equilibrium in this market, and who receives it?

2. Show how each of the following three actions reduces total surplus:
   a. Having Josey consume one fewer pepper, and Casey one more pepper, than in the market equilibrium
   b. Having Cara produce one fewer pepper, and Jamie one more pepper, than in the market equilibrium
   c. Having Josey consume one fewer pepper, and Cara produce one fewer pepper, than in the market equilibrium

3. Suppose UNOS alters its guidelines for the allocation of donated kidneys, no longer relying solely on the concept of "net benefit" but also giving preference to patients with small children. If "total surplus" in this case is defined to be the total lifespan of kidney recipients, is this new guideline likely to reduce, increase, or leave total surplus unchanged? How might you justify this new guideline?

Solutions appear at back of book.

A Market Economy

As we learned earlier in the book, in a market economy decisions about production and consumption are made via markets. In fact, the economy as a whole is made up of many *interrelated markets*. Up until now, to learn how markets work, we've been examining a single market—the market for used textbooks. But in reality, consumers and producers do not make decisions in isolated markets. For example, a student's decision in the market for used textbooks might be affected by how much interest must be paid on a student loan; thus, the decision in the used-textbook market would be influenced by what is going on in the market for money.

We know that an efficient market equilibrium maximizes total surplus—the gains to buyers and sellers in that market. Is there a comparable result for an economy as a whole, an economy composed of a vast number of individual markets? The answer is yes, but with qualifications.

When each and every market in the economy maximizes total surplus, then the economy as a whole is efficient. This is a very important result: just as it is impossible to make someone better off without making other people worse off in a single market when it is efficient, the same is true when each and every market in that economy is efficient. However, it is important to realize that this is a *theoretical* result: it is virtually impossible to find an economy in which every market is efficient.

For now, let's examine why markets and market economies typically work so well. Once we understand why, we can then briefly address why markets sometimes get it wrong.

Why Markets Typically Work So Well

Economists have written volumes about why markets are an effective way to organize an economy. In the end, well-functioning markets owe their effectiveness to two powerful features: *property rights* and the role of prices as *economic signals*.

By **property rights** we mean a system in which valuable items in the economy have specific owners who can use, rent, or dispose of them as they choose. In a system of property rights, by purchasing a good you receive "ownership rights": the right to use and dispose of the good as you see fit. Property rights are what make the mutually beneficial transactions in the used-textbook market, or any market, possible.

To see why property rights are crucial, imagine that students do not have full property rights in their textbooks and are prohibited from reselling them when the semester ends.[2] This restriction on property rights would prevent many mutually beneficial transactions. Some students would be stuck with textbooks they will never reread when they would be much happier receiving some cash instead. Other students would be forced to pay full price for brand-new books when they would be happier getting slightly battered copies at a lower price.

Once a system of well-defined property rights is in place, the second necessary feature of well-functioning markets—prices as economic signals—can operate. An **economic signal** is any piece of information that helps people make better economic decisions. There are thousands of signals that businesses watch in the real world. For example, business forecasters say that sales of cardboard boxes are a good early indicator of changes in industrial production: if businesses are buying lots of cardboard boxes, you can be sure that they will soon increase their production.

But prices are far and away the most important signals in a market economy, because they convey essential information about other people's costs and their willingness to pay. If the equilibrium price of used books is $30, this in effect tells everyone both that there are consumers willing to pay $30 and up and that there are potential sellers with a cost of $30 or less. The signal given by the market price ensures that total surplus is maximized by telling people whether to buy used books, sell used books, or do nothing at all.

Each potential seller with a cost of $30 or less learns from the market price that it's a good idea to sell her used book; if she has a higher cost, it's a good idea to keep it. Likewise, each consumer willing to pay $30 or more learns from the market price that it's a good idea to buy a used book; if he is unwilling to pay $30, then it's a good idea not to buy a used book.

This example shows that the market price "signals" to consumers with a willingness to pay equal to or more than the market price that they should buy the good, just as it signals to producers with a cost equal to or less than the market price that they should sell the good. And since, in equilibrium, the quantity demanded equals the quantity supplied, all willing consumers will find willing sellers and vice versa.

Prices can sometimes fail as economic signals. Sometimes a price is not an accurate indicator of how desirable a good is. When there is uncertainty about the quality of a good, price alone may not be an accurate indicator of the value of the good. For example, you can't infer from the price alone whether a used car is good or a "lemon." In fact, a well-known problem in economics is "the market for lemons," a market in which prices don't work well as economic signals. (We'll learn about the market for lemons in Chapter 20.)

A Few Words of Caution

As we've seen, markets are an amazingly effective way to organize economic activity. But as we've noted, markets can sometimes get it wrong. We first learned about this in Chapter 1 in our fifth principle of interaction: *When markets don't achieve efficiency, government intervention can improve society's welfare.* When markets are **inefficient,** there are missed opportunities—ways in which production or consumption can be rearranged (reallocated) that would make some people better off without making other people worse off. In other

Property rights are the rights of owners of valuable items, whether resources or goods, to use, rent, or dispose of those items as they choose.

An **economic signal** is any piece of information that helps people make better economic decisions.

A market or an economy is **inefficient** if there are missed opportunities: some people could be made better off without making other people worse off.

---

[2]This is similar to the rights consumers have in relation to their ebooks. Although Apple and Amazon have patented the technology to resell ebooks they, like other sellers of ebooks, currently do not allow resales.

Market failure occurs when a market fails to be efficient.

words, there are gains from trade that go unrealized: total surplus could be increased. And when a market or markets are inefficient, the economy in which they are embedded is also inefficient.

Markets can be rendered inefficient for a number of reasons. Two of the most important are a lack of property rights and inaccuracy of prices as economic signals. When a market is inefficient, we have what is known as **market failure.** We will examine various types of market failure in later chapters. For now, let's review the three main ways in which markets sometimes fall short of efficiency.

First, markets can fail when, in an attempt to capture more surplus, one party prevents mutually beneficial trades from occurring. This situation arises, for instance, when a market contains only a single seller of a good, known as a *monopolist*. In this case, the assumption we have relied on in supply and demand analysis—that no individual buyer or seller can have a noticeable effect on the market price—is no longer valid; the monopolist can determine the market price. As we'll see in Chapter 13, this gives rise to inefficiency as a monopolist manipulates the market price in order to increase profits, driving the price higher, which thereby prevents mutually beneficial trades from occurring.

Second, actions of individuals sometimes have side effects on the welfare of others that markets don't take into account. In economics, these side effects are known as *externalities*, and the best-known example is pollution. We can think of the problem of pollution as a problem of incomplete property rights; for example, existing property rights don't guarantee a right to ownership of clean air. We'll see in Chapter 16 that pollution and other externalities also give rise to inefficiency since with spillovers, market prices do not fully account for the social cost of the good.

Third, markets for some goods fail because these goods, by their very nature, are unsuited for efficient management by markets. In Chapter 20, we will analyze goods that fall into this category because of problems of *private information*—information about a good that some people possess but others don't. For example, the seller of a used car that is a "lemon" may have information that is unknown to potential buyers. With private information, a high price need not signal good quality. In the used car market, asking for a higher price than a car is worth hides the fact that it is secretly worth less!

In Chapter 17, we will encounter other types of goods that fall into the category of being unsuited for efficient management by markets—*public goods, common resources,* and *artificially scarce goods.* Markets for these goods fail because of problems in limiting people's access to and consumption of the good; examples are fish in the sea and trees in the Amazon rainforest. In these instances, markets generally fail due to incomplete property rights.

But even with these caveats, it's remarkable how well markets work at maximizing the gains from trade.

ECONOMICS ▸ IN ACTION

A GREAT LEAP—BACKWARD

Economies in which a central planner, rather than markets, makes consumption and production decisions are known as *planned economies*. Russia (formerly part of the U.S.S.R.), many Eastern European countries, and several Southeast Asian countries once had planned economies, and countries such as India and Brazil once had significant parts of their economies under central planning. China still does today.

Planned economies are notorious for their inefficiency. Probably the most compelling example of that is the so-called Great Leap Forward, an ambitious economic plan instituted in China during the late 1950s by its leader Mao Zedong. Its intention was to speed up the country's industrialization.

Although some aspects of central planning remain, China's economy has moved closer to a free-market system, allowing for higher economic growth, increased wealth, and the emergence of a middle class.

Key to this plan was a shift from urban to rural manufacturing: farming villages were supposed to start producing heavy industrial goods such as steel.

Unfortunately, the plan backfired. Diverting farmers from their usual work led to a sharp fall in food production. Meanwhile, because raw materials for steel, such as coal and iron ore, were sent to ill-equipped and inexperienced rural producers rather than to urban factories, industrial output declined as well. The plan, in short, led to a fall in the production of everything in China.

Because China started off as a very poor country, the results were catastrophic. The famine that followed is estimated to have reduced China's population by as much as 30 million.[3]

China has recently moved closer to a free-market system, allowing for greater economic growth, increased wealth, and the emergence of a middle class. But some aspects of central planning remain, largely in the allocation of financial capital and other inputs to politically connected businesses. As a result, significant inefficiencies persist. Many economists have commented that these inefficiencies must be addressed if China is to sustain its rapid growth and Chinese consumers are to enjoy the efficient level of consumer surplus.

▼ Quick Review

- In a market economy, markets are interrelated. When each and every market in an economy is efficient, the economy as a whole is efficient. But in the real world, some markets in a market economy will almost certainly fail to be efficient.

- A system of **property rights** and the proper operation of prices as **economic signals** are two key factors that enable a market to be efficient. But under conditions in which property rights are incomplete or prices give inaccurate economic signals, markets can fail.

- Under certain conditions, **market failure** occurs and the market is **inefficient:** some gains from trade are unrealized. The three principal ways in which markets fail are the prevention of mutually beneficial transactions caused by one party's attempt to capture more surplus, side effects that aren't properly accounted for, and problems in the nature of the goods themselves.

CHECK YOUR UNDERSTANDING   4-4

1. In some jurisdictions that are rich in natural resources, such as oil, the law separates the right to above ground use of the land from the right to drill below ground (called "mineral rights"). Someone who owns both the above ground rights and the mineral rights can sell the two rights separately. Explain how this division of the property rights enhances efficiency compared to a situation in which the two rights must always be sold together.

2. Suppose that in the market for used textbooks the equilibrium price is $30, but it is mistakenly reported that the equilibrium price is $300. How does this affect the efficiency of the market? Be specific.

3. What is wrong with the following statement? "Markets are always the best way to organize economic activity. Any policies that interfere with markets reduce society's welfare."

Solutions appear at back of book.

---

[3]The Great Chinese Famine between 1958 and 1961 was partly caused by the Great Leap Forward and partly caused by drought and poor weather in China.

BUSINESS CASE : StubHub Shows Up Springsteen

AP Photo/Chris Pizzello

Back in 1965, long before Ticketmaster, StubHub, and TicketsNow, legendary rock music promoter Bill Graham noticed that mass parties erupted wherever local rock groups played. Graham realized that fans placed a high value on the experience of the concert, in addition to paying for a recording of the music. He went on to revolutionize the business of rock concert promoting—booking and managing multi-city tours for bands and selling lots of tickets. Those tickets were carefully rationed, with a single purchaser allowed to buy only a limited number. Fans would line up at box offices, sometimes camping out the night before for popular bands.

Wanting to maintain the aura of the 1960s that made rock concerts accessible to all their fans, many top bands choose to price their tickets below the market equilibrium level. (Some bands, such as Montreal's Arcade Fire and Toronto's Broken Social Scene, have even played free shows when they have returned to their home towns after a tour.) In 2009 Bruce Springsteen sold tickets at his concerts in New Jersey (his home state and home to his most ardent fans) for between $65 and $95. Tickets for Springsteen concerts could have sold for far more: economists Alan Krueger and Marie Connolly analyzed a 2002 Springsteen concert for which every ticket sold for $75 and concluded that Springsteen forfeited about $4 million by not charging the market price, about $280.

So what was Springsteen thinking? Cheap tickets can ensure that a concert sells out, making it a better experience for both band and audience. But it is believed that other factors are at work—that cheap tickets are a way for a band to reward fans' loyalty as well as a means to seem more "authentic" and less commercial. As Bruce Springsteen has said, "In some fashion, I help people hold on to their own humanity—if I'm doing my job right."

But the rise of the Internet has made things vastly more complicated. Now, rather than queue for tickets at the venue, fans buy tickets online, either from a direct seller like Ticketmaster (which obtains tickets directly from the concert producer) or a reseller like StubHub or TicketsNow (which is owned by Ticketmaster). Resellers (otherwise known as scalpers) can—and do—make lots of money by scooping up large numbers of tickets at the box office price and reselling them at the market price. StubHub, for example, made $1 billion in the resale market for tickets in 2010. Even in provincial and territorial markets where scalping is illegal, the enforcement of the law is relatively weak and the potential for profit offsets the penalty.

This practice has infuriated fans as well as the bands. But resellers have cast the issue as one of the freedom to dispose of one's ticket as one chooses. In 2013, both sides—bands and their fans versus ticket resellers—are busily lobbying government officials to shape ticket-reselling laws to their advantage.

QUESTIONS FOR THOUGHT

1. Use the concepts of consumer surplus and producer surplus to analyze the exchange between Bruce Springsteen and his fans. Draw a diagram to illustrate.

2. Explain how the rise of the Internet has disrupted this exchange.

3. Draw a diagram to show the effect of resellers on the allocation of consumer surplus and producer surplus in the market for concert tickets. What are the implications of the Internet for all such exchanges?

SUMMARY

1. The **willingness to pay** of each individual consumer determines the demand curve. When price is less than or equal to the willingness to pay, the potential consumer purchases the good. The difference between willingness to pay and price is the net gain to the consumer, the **individual consumer surplus.**

2. **Total consumer surplus** in a market, the sum of all individual consumer surpluses in a market, is equal to the area below the market demand curve but above the price. All other things equal, a rise in the price of a good reduces consumer surplus; a fall in the price increases consumer surplus. The term **consumer surplus** is often used to refer to both individual and total consumer surplus.

3. Each potential seller's **cost,** the lowest price at which he or she is willing to supply a unit of a particular good, determines the supply curve. If the price of a good is above a seller's cost, a sale generates a net gain to the producer, known as the **individual producer surplus.**

4. **Total producer surplus** in a market, the sum of the individual producer surpluses in a market, is equal to the area above the market supply curve but below the price. All other things equal, a rise in the price of a good increases producer surplus; a fall in the price reduces producer surplus. The term **producer surplus** is often used to refer to both individual and total producer surplus.

5. **Total surplus,** the total gain to society from the production and consumption of a good, is the sum of consumer and producer surpluses.

6. Usually markets are efficient and achieve the maximum total surplus. Any possible reallocation of consumption or sales, or a change in the quantity bought and sold, reduces total surplus. However, society also cares about equity. So government intervention in a market that reduces efficiency but increases equity can be a valid choice by society.

7. An economy composed of efficient markets is also efficient, although this is virtually impossible to achieve in reality. The keys to the efficiency of a market economy are **property rights** and the proper operation of prices as **economic signals.** Under certain conditions, **market failure** occurs, making a market **inefficient.** Three principal sources of market failure are one party's attempts to capture more surplus, creating inefficiencies; side effects of some transactions; and problems in the nature of the good.

KEY TERMS

PROBLEMS

1. Determine the amount of consumer surplus generated in each of the following situations.

   a. Leon is willing to pay up to $10 for a new T-shirt. He picks out one he likes with a price tag of exactly $10. When he is paying for it, he learns that the T-shirt has been discounted by 50%.

   b. Alberto goes to a store hoping to find a used copy of The Tragically Hip's *Yer Favourites* for up to $10. The store has one copy selling for $10, which he buys.

   c. After soccer practice, Stacey is willing to pay $2 for a bottle of mineral water. The 7-Eleven sells mineral water for $2.25 per bottle, so she declines to purchase it.

2. Determine the amount of producer surplus generated in each of the following situations.

   a. Gordon lists his old Lionel electric trains on eBay. He sets a minimum acceptable price, known as his reserve price, of $75. After five days of bidding, the final high bid is exactly $75. He accepts the bid.

   b. So-Hee advertises her car for sale in the used-car section of the student newspaper for $2000, but she is willing to sell the car for any price higher than $1500. The best offer she gets is $1200, which she declines.

   c. Sanjay likes his job so much that he would be willing to do it for free. However, his annual salary is $80 000.

3. There are six potential consumers of computer games, each willing to buy only one game. Consumer 1 is willing to pay $40 for a computer game, consumer 2 is willing to pay $35, consumer 3 is willing to pay $30, consumer 4 is willing to pay $25, consumer 5 is willing to pay $20, and consumer 6 is willing to pay $15.

   a. Suppose the market price is $29. What is the total consumer surplus?

b. The market price decreases to $19. What is the total consumer surplus now?

c. When the price falls from $29 to $19, how much does each consumer's individual consumer surplus change? How does total consumer surplus change?

4. a. In an auction, potential buyers compete for a good by submitting bids. Adam Galinsky, a social psychologist at Northwestern University, compared eBay auctions in which the same good was sold. He found that, on average, the larger the number of bidders, the higher the sales price. For example, in two auctions of identical iPods, the one with the larger number of bidders brought a higher selling price. According to Galinsky, this explains why smart sellers on eBay set absurdly low opening prices (the lowest price that the seller will accept), such as 1 cent for a new iPod. Use the concepts of consumer and producer surplus to explain Galinsky's reasoning.

b. You are considering selling your vintage 1969 convertible Volkswagen Beetle. If the car is in good condition, it is worth a lot; if it is in poor condition, it is useful only as scrap. Assume that your car is in excellent condition but that it costs a potential buyer $500 for an inspection to learn the car's condition. Use what you learned in part (a) to explain whether or not you should pay for an inspection and share the results with all interested buyers.

5. According to Statistics Canada, due to an increase in demand, the average domestic airline fare increased from $182.18 in 2010 to $190.92 in 2011, an increase of $8.74. The number of passenger tickets sold in 2010 was 65.8 million. Assume that over the same period, the airlines' costs remained roughly the same (in reality they did not: the price of jet fuel rose from $0.57 per litre in January 2010 to $0.78 per litre in December 2011, and airline pilots' salaries rose 2%).

Can you determine precisely by how much producer surplus increased as a result of the $8.74 increase in the average fare? If you cannot be precise, can you determine whether it was less than, or more than, a specific amount?

6. Hollywood screenwriters negotiate a new agreement with movie producers stipulating that they will receive 10% of the revenue from every video rental of a movie they authored. They have no such agreement for movies shown on on-demand television.

a. When the new writers' agreement comes into effect, what will happen in the market for video rentals— that is, will supply or demand shift, and how? As a result, how will consumer surplus in the market for video rentals change? Illustrate with a diagram. Do you think the writers' agreement will be popular with consumers who rent videos?

b. Consumers consider video rentals and on-demand movies substitutable to some extent. When the new writers' agreement comes into effect, what will happen in the market for on-demand movies—that is, will supply or demand shift, and how? As a

result, how will producer surplus in the market for on-demand movies change? Illustrate with a diagram. Do you think the writers' agreement will be popular with cable television companies that show on-demand movies?

7. The accompanying table shows the supply and demand schedules for used copies of the first edition of this textbook. The supply schedule is derived from offers at Amazon.com. The demand schedule is hypothetical.

Price of used book	Quantity of used books demanded	Quantity of used books supplied
$55	50	0
60	35	1
65	25	3
70	17	3
75	14	6
80	12	9
85	10	10
90	8	18
95	6	22
100	4	31
105	2	37
110	0	42

a. Calculate consumer and producer surplus at the equilibrium in this market.

b. Now the second edition of this textbook becomes available. As a result, the willingness to pay of each potential buyer for a second-hand copy of the first edition falls by $20. In a table, show the new demand schedule and again calculate consumer and producer surplus at the new equilibrium.

8. On Thursday nights, a local restaurant has a pasta special. Ari likes the restaurant's pasta, and his willingness to pay for each serving is shown in the accompanying table.

Quantity of pasta (servings)	Willingness to pay for pasta (per serving)
1	$10
2	8
3	6
4	4
5	2
6	0

a. If the price of a serving of pasta is $4, how many servings will Ari buy? How much consumer surplus does he receive?

b. The following week, Ari is back at the restaurant again, but now the price of a serving of pasta is $6. By how much does his consumer surplus decrease compared to the previous week?

c. One week later, he goes to the restaurant again. He discovers that the restaurant is offering an "all-you-can-eat" special for $25. How much pasta will Ari eat, and how much consumer surplus does he receive now?

d. Suppose you own the restaurant and Ari is a typical customer. What is the highest price you can charge for the "all-you-can-eat" special and still attract customers?

9. You are the manager of Fun World, a small amusement park. The accompanying diagram shows the demand curve of a typical customer at Fun World.

a. Suppose that the price of each ride is $5. At that price, how much consumer surplus does an individual consumer get? (Recall that the area of a right triangle is 1/2 × the height of the triangle × the base of the triangle.)

b. Suppose that Fun World considers charging an admission fee, even though it maintains the price of each ride at $5. What is the maximum admission fee consumers would be willing to pay? (Assume that all potential customers have enough money to pay the fee.)

c. Suppose that Fun World lowered the price of each ride to zero. How much consumer surplus does an individual consumer get? What is the maximum admission fee consumers would be willing to pay?

10. The accompanying diagram illustrates a taxi driver's individual supply curve (assume that each taxi ride is the same distance).

a. Suppose the city sets the price of taxi rides at $4 per ride, and at $4 the taxi driver is able to sell as many taxi rides as he desires. What is this taxi driver's producer surplus? (Recall that the area of a right triangle is 1/2 × the height of the triangle × the base of the triangle.)

b. Suppose that the city keeps the price of a taxi ride set at $4, but it decides to charge taxi drivers a "licensing fee." What is the maximum licensing fee the city could extract from this taxi driver?

c. Suppose that the city allowed the price of taxi rides to increase to $8 per ride. Again assume that, at this price, the taxi driver sells as many rides as he is willing to offer. How much producer surplus does an individual taxi driver now get? What is the maximum licensing fee the city could charge this taxi driver?

11. On May 10, 2010, a judge ruled in a copyright infringement lawsuit against the popular file-sharing website LimeWire and in favour of the 13 major record companies that had brought the lawsuit. The companies, including Sony, Virgin, and Warner Brothers, had alleged that the file-sharing service encourages users to make illegal copies of copyrighted material. Allowing Internet users to obtain music for free limits the record companies' right to dispose of the music as they choose; in particular, it limits their right to give access to their music only to those who have paid for it. In other words, it limits the record companies' property rights.

a. If everyone obtained music and video content for free from websites such as LimeWire, instead of paying the record companies, what would the record companies' producer surplus be from music sales? What are the implications for record companies' incentive to produce music content in the future?

b. If the record companies had lost the lawsuit and music could be freely downloaded from the Internet, what do you think would happen to mutually beneficial transactions (the producing and buying of music) in the future?

CHAPTER 5

Price Controls and Quotas: Meddling with Markets

BIG CITY, NOT-SO-BRIGHT IDEAS

New York City: an empty taxi is hard to find.

> ❭ The meaning of **price controls** and **quantity controls,** two kinds of government intervention in markets
>
> ❭ How price and quantity controls create problems and can make a market inefficient
>
> ❭ What deadweight loss is
>
> ❭ Why the predictable side effects of intervention in markets often lead economists to be skeptical of its usefulness
>
> ❭ Who benefits and who loses from market interventions, and why they are used despite their well-known problems

IMAGINE YOURSELF IN DOWNTOWN Calgary or Montreal, eager to get a taxi to avoid being late for an important appointment—it is difficult to find an empty cab, especially during peak hours. Or think about the challenges in finding a rental apartment in an urban area—in major Canadian cities, the percentage of apartments that are available to rent is declining. But if you think the conditions are bad in Canada, then you definitely don't want to try to travel by taxicab or to get a decent, affordable rental apartment in New York City because it is almost impossible to do so. Why does this happen in the Big Apple? You might think that New York's notorious shortages of cabs and apartments are the inevitable price of big-city living. However, they are largely the product of government policies—specifically, of government policies that have, one way or another, tried to prevail over the market forces of supply and demand.

In Chapter 3, we learned the principle that a market moves to equilibrium—that the market price rises or falls to the level at which the quantity of a good that people are willing to supply is equal to the quantity that other people demand.

But sometimes governments try to defy that principle. Whenever a government tries to dictate either a market price or a market quantity that's different from the equilibrium price or quantity, the market strikes back in predictable ways. Our ability to predict what will happen when governments try to defy the forces of supply and demand shows the power and usefulness of supply and demand analysis itself.

The shortages of apartments and taxicabs in New York are particular examples that illuminate what happens when the logic of the market is defied. New York's housing shortage is the result of *rent control,* a law that prevents landlords from raising rents except when specifically given permission. Rent control in New York was introduced during World War II to protect the interests of tenants, and it still remains in force. Many other North American cities have had rent control at one time or another, but with the notable exceptions of New York and San Francisco, these controls have largely been done away with. In much of Canada rent controls have been eliminated or, in fact, never existed in

the first place. Where they still exist, in British Columbia, Manitoba, Ontario, Quebec, and Prince Edward Island, rent controls are significantly weaker than they were several decades ago.

Similarly, New York's limited supply of taxis is the result of a licensing system introduced in the 1930s. New York taxi licences are known as "medallions," and only taxis with medallions are allowed to pick up passengers. Although this system was originally intended to protect the interests of both drivers and customers, it has generated a shortage of taxis in the city. The number of medallions remained fixed for nearly 60 years, with no significant increase until 2004.

In this chapter, we begin by examining what happens when governments try to control prices in a competitive market, keeping the price in a market either below its equilibrium level—a *price ceiling* such as rent control—or above it—a *price floor* such as the minimum wage paid to workers in many countries. We then turn to schemes such as agricultural quotas and taxi medallions that attempt to dictate the quantity of a good bought and sold. ■

Price controls are legal restrictions on how high or low a market price may go. They can take two forms: a **price ceiling,** a maximum price sellers are allowed to charge for a good or service, or a **price floor,** a minimum price buyers are required to pay for a good or service.

Why Governments Control Prices

You learned in Chapter 3 that a market moves to equilibrium—that is, the market price moves to the level at which the quantity supplied equals the quantity demanded. But this equilibrium price does not necessarily please either buyers or sellers.

After all, buyers would always like to pay less if they could, and sometimes they can make a strong moral or political case that they should pay lower prices. For example, what if the equilibrium between supply and demand for apartments in a major city leads to rental rates that an average working person can't afford? In that case, a government might well be under pressure to impose limits on the rents landlords can charge.

Sellers, however, would always like to get more money for what they sell, and sometimes they can make a strong moral or political case that they should receive higher prices. For example, consider the labour market: the price to rent an hour of a worker's time is the wage rate. What if the equilibrium between supply and demand for less skilled workers leads to wage rates that yield an income below the poverty level? In that case, a government might well be pressured to require employers to pay a rate no lower than some specified minimum wage.

In other words, there is often a strong political demand for governments to intervene in markets. And powerful interests can make a compelling case that a market intervention favouring them is "fair." When a government intervenes to regulate prices, we say that it imposes **price controls.** These controls typically take the form either of an upper limit, a **price ceiling,** or a lower limit, a **price floor.**

Unfortunately, it's not that easy to tell a market what to do. As we will now see, when a government tries to legislate prices—whether it legislates them *down* by imposing a price ceiling or *up* by imposing a price floor—there are certain predictable and unpleasant side effects.

We make an important assumption in this chapter: the markets in question are efficient before price controls are imposed. As we noted in chapter 4, markets can sometimes be inefficient—for example, a market dominated by a monopolist, a single seller that has the power to influence the market price. When markets are inefficient, price controls don't necessarily cause problems and can potentially move the market closer to efficiency. In practice, however, price controls are often imposed on efficient markets—like the New York apartment market. And so the analysis in this chapter applies to many important real-world situations.

Price Ceilings

Rent control continues to exist to some degree in Ontario, Quebec, British Columbia, Manitoba, and Prince Edward Island. In Ontario, units that were built, or came onto the rental market, after November 1, 1991 are exempt from rent controls. Units on the market prior to that date tend to have rent increases tied to the growth rate of the consumer price index (CPI), but when a tenant moves out rents can be raised to whatever the market will bear. (The Ontario New Democratic Party (NDP) has recently proposed extending rent controls to all Ontario rental apartments.) In Quebec, rent increases are tied to landlord cost increases, but can be lower than these cost increases and, as in Ontario, once a unit is vacated the landlord has some ability to raise the rent. In British Columbia, provincial government guidelines cap rent increases at the growth rate of the CPI plus 2%. In Manitoba, the government mandated maximum rent increase is usually set below the growth rate of the CPI. In Prince Edward Island, maximum percent rent increases are set annually based on the type of dwelling.

Aside from rent control, there are other price ceilings in Canada today. Currently some form of price controls exists in Canadian markets for pharmaceutical drugs, electricity, basic residential phone services, and agricultural commodities (such as eggs, chicken, turkey, and dairy). In the case of patented prescription drug prices, there are two stages of control. The federal government grants monopoly rights to the patent holder to be the sole supplier of a particular drug formulation, but in return the government imposes a price ceiling that the supplier can't exceed. The provincial and territorial governments, which are responsible for delivering health care services within their borders, use their market power as purchasers of large volumes of drugs to negotiate prices that can be well below the ceiling price.

At times, price ceilings have been widespread. They are typically imposed during crises—wars, harvest failures, natural disasters—because these events often lead to sudden price increases that hurt many people but produce big gains for a lucky few. The Canadian government imposed ceilings on many prices during World War II: the war sharply increased demand for raw materials (such as aluminum and steel) and necessities (such as home rentals, sugar, milk, and coal), and price controls prevented those who supplied these goods and services from earning huge profits. World oil prices spiked in 1979–1980 due to uncertainty caused by the Iranian revolution in 1979 and the 1980 outbreak of war between Iran and Iraq (both large oil producing nations). Price controls on oil were imposed in 1980, when Prime Minister Pierre Trudeau's government introduced the National Energy Program to help Canada achieve energy self-sufficiency, redistribute the wealth from non-renewable energy production to all parts of the country, and increase Canadian ownership of the oil industry.

Rent control in New York City is a legacy of World War II: it was imposed because wartime production produced an economic boom, which increased demand for apartments at a time when the labour and raw materials that might have been used to build them were being used to fight the war instead. Although most price controls were removed soon after the war ended, New York's rent limits were retained and gradually extended to buildings not previously covered, leading to some very strange situations.

You can rent a one-bedroom apartment in Manhattan on fairly short notice—if you are able and willing to pay several thousand dollars a month and live in a less-than-desirable area. Yet some people pay only a small fraction of this for comparable apartments, and others pay hardly more for bigger apartments in better locations.[1]

Aside from producing great deals for some renters, however, what are the broader consequences of New York's rent-control system? To answer this question, we turn to the model we developed in Chapter 3: the supply and demand model.

Modelling a Price Ceiling

To see what can go wrong when a government imposes a price ceiling on an efficient market, consider Figure 5-1, which shows a simplified model of the market for apartments in a large city. For the sake of simplicity, we imagine that all apartments are exactly the same and so would rent for the same price in an

---

[1]Being a tenant in a rent-controlled apartment is very desirable since the tenant could have the right to live in the unit until he or she dies. Landlords have been known to pay tens of thousands of dollars in order to get tenants to move out and abandon their claim to a unit. The landlord is then able to rent out the apartment at a much higher market rent. In fact, the value of removing a rent-controlled tenant is so high that some truly exceptional landlords have hired thugs to attack or even murder tenants to free up units.

FIGURE **5-1**   The Market for Apartments in the Absence of Price Controls

Monthly rent (per apartment)	Quantity of apartments (millions)	
	Quantity demanded	Quantity supplied
$1400	1.6	2.4
1300	1.7	2.3
1200	1.8	2.2
1100	1.9	2.1
1000	2.0	2.0
900	2.1	1.9
800	2.2	1.8
700	2.3	1.7
600	2.4	1.6

Without government intervention, the market for apartments reaches equilibrium at point *E* with a market rent of $1000 per month and 2 million apartments rented.

unregulated market. The table in the figure shows the demand and supply schedules; the demand and supply curves are shown on the left. We show the quantity of apartments on the horizontal axis and the monthly rent per apartment on the vertical axis. You can see that in an unregulated market the equilibrium would be at point *E:* two million apartments would be rented for $1000 each per month.

Now suppose that the government imposes a price ceiling, limiting rents to a price below the equilibrium price—say, no more than $800.

Figure 5-2 shows the effect of the price ceiling, represented by the line at $800. At the enforced rental rate of $800, landlords have less incentive to offer apartments, so they won't be willing to supply as many as they would at the equilibrium rate of $1000. They will choose point *A* on the supply curve, offering only 1.8 million apartments for rent, 200 000 fewer than in the unregulated market. At the same time, more people will want to rent apartments at a price of $800 than at the equilibrium price of $1000; as shown at point *B* on the demand curve, at a monthly rent of $800 the quantity of apartments demanded rises to 2.2 million, 200 000 more than in the unregulated market and 400 000 more than are actually available at the price of $800. So there is now a persistent shortage of rental housing: at that price, 400 000 more people want to rent than are able to find apartments.

Do price ceilings always cause shortages? No. If a price ceiling is set at or above the equilibrium price, it won't have any effect. Suppose that the equilibrium rental rate on apartments is $1000 per month and the city government sets a ceiling of $1200. Who cares? In this case, the price ceiling won't be *binding*—it won't actually constrain market behaviour—and it will have no effect.

Over time, a binding price ceiling can become non-binding if the demand and/or supply curves shift enough to make the equilibrium price less than or equal to the price ceiling. In our rental apartment example, a decrease in demand due to falling house prices, making owning a home more attractive than renting, would shift the demand curve to the left. Similarly, if more apartment buildings are constructed,

FIGURE **5-2** The Effects of a Price Ceiling

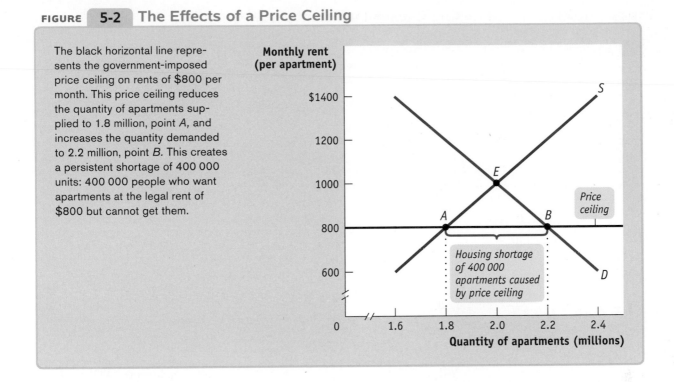

The black horizontal line represents the government-imposed price ceiling on rents of $800 per month. This price ceiling reduces the quantity of apartments supplied to 1.8 million, point *A*, and increases the quantity demanded to 2.2 million, point *B*. This creates a persistent shortage of 400 000 units: 400 000 people who want apartments at the legal rent of $800 but cannot get them.

then the supply of rental apartments increases, shifting the supply curve to the right. In Figure 5-2, if these shifts move the intersection of the demand and supply curves to $800 or less, then the rent control is a non-binding price ceiling.

How a Price Ceiling Causes Inefficiency

The housing shortage shown in Figure 5-2 is not merely annoying: like any shortage induced by price controls, it can be seriously harmful because it leads to inefficiency. In other words, there are gains from trade that go unrealized. Rent control, like all price ceilings, creates inefficiency in at least four distinct ways. It reduces the quantity of apartments rented below the efficient level; it typically leads to misallocation of apartments among would-be renters; it leads to wasted time and effort as people search for apartments; and it leads landlords to maintain apartments in inefficiently low quality or condition. In addition to inefficiency, price ceilings give rise to illegal behaviour as people try to circumvent them.

Inefficiently Low Quantity In Chapter 4 we learned that the market equilibrium of an efficient market leads to the "right" quantity of a good or service being bought and sold—that is, the quantity that maximizes the sum of producer and consumer surplus. Because rent controls reduce the number of apartments supplied, they reduce the number of apartments rented, too.

Figure 5-3 shows the implications for total surplus. Recall that total surplus is the sum of the area above the supply curve and below the demand curve. If the only effect of rent control was to reduce the number of apartments available, it would cause a loss of surplus equal to the area of the shaded triangle in the figure. The area represented by that triangle has a special name in economics, **deadweight loss:** the lost surplus associated with the transactions that no longer occur due to the market intervention. In this example, the deadweight loss is the lost surplus associated with the apartment rentals that no longer occur due to the price ceiling, a loss that is experienced by both disappointed renters and frustrated landlords. Economists often call triangles like the one in Figure 5-3 a *deadweight-loss triangle*.

Deadweight loss is the loss in total surplus that occurs whenever an action or a policy reduces the quantity transacted below the efficient market equilibrium quantity.

FIGURE **5-3** A Price Ceiling Causes Inefficiently Low Quantity

A price ceiling reduces the quantity supplied below the market equilibrium quantity, leading to a deadweight loss. The area of the shaded triangle corresponds to the amount of total surplus lost due to the inefficiently low quantity transacted.

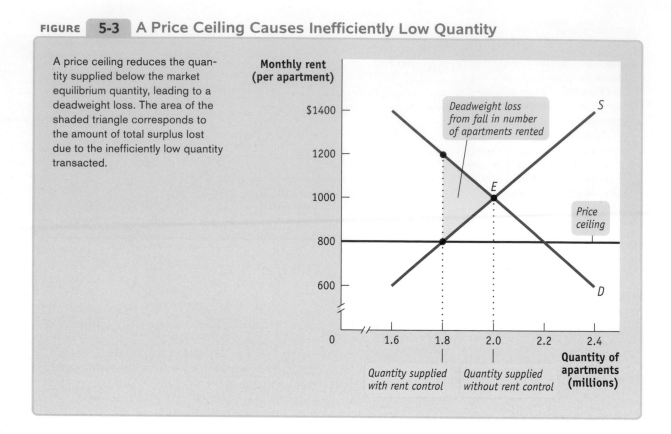

Deadweight loss is a key concept in economics, one that we will encounter whenever an action or a policy leads to a reduction in the quantity transacted below the efficient market equilibrium quantity. It is important to realize that deadweight loss is a *loss to society*—it is a reduction in total surplus, a loss in surplus that accrues to no one as a gain. It is not the same as a loss in surplus to one person that then accrues as a gain to someone else, what an economist would call a *transfer* of surplus from one person to another. For an example of how a price ceiling can create deadweight loss as well as a transfer of surplus between renters and landlords, see the upcoming For Inquiring Minds.

Deadweight loss is not the only type of inefficiency that arises from a price ceiling. The types of inefficiency created by rent control go beyond reducing the quantity of apartments available. These additional inefficiencies—inefficient allocation to consumers, wasted resources, and inefficiently low quality—lead to a loss of surplus over and above the deadweight loss.

Inefficient Allocation to Consumers Rent control doesn't just lead to too few apartments being available. It can also lead to misallocation of the apartments that are available: people who badly need a place to live may not be able to find an apartment, but some apartments may be occupied by people with much less urgent needs.

In the case shown in Figure 5-2, 2.2 million people would like to rent an apartment at $800 per month, but only 1.8 million apartments are available. Of those 2.2 million who are seeking an apartment, some want an apartment badly and are willing to pay a high price to get one. Others have a less urgent need and are only willing to pay a low price, perhaps because they have alternative housing. An efficient allocation of apartments would reflect these differences: people who really want an apartment will get one and people who aren't all that anxious to find an apartment won't. In an inefficient distribution of apartments, the opposite

FOR INQUIRING MINDS

WINNERS, LOSERS, AND RENT CONTROL

Price controls create winners and losers: some people benefit from the policy but others are made worse off.

In New York City, some of the biggest beneficiaries of rent control are affluent tenants who have lived for decades in choice apartments that would now command very high rents. These winners include celebrities like actor Al Pacino and the pop singer Cyndi Lauper; Lauper pays only $989 a month for an apartment that would be worth $3750 if unregulated. There is also the classic case of the actress Mia Farrow's apartment, which, when it lost its rent control status, rose from the bargain rate of $2900 per month to $8000. Ironically, in cases like these, the losers are the working-class renters the system was intended to help.

We can use the concepts of consumer and producer surplus, which you learned about in Chapter 4, to graphically evaluate the winners and the losers from rent control. Panel (a) of Figure 5-4

shows the consumer surplus and producer surplus in the equilibrium of the unregulated market for apartments—before rent control. Recall that the consumer surplus, represented by the area below the demand curve and above the price, is the total net gain to consumers in the market equilibrium. Likewise, producer surplus, represented by the area above the supply curve and below the price, is the total net gain to producers in the market equilibrium.

Panel (b) of this figure shows the consumer and producer surplus in the market after the price ceiling of $800 has been imposed. As you can see, for consumers who can still obtain apartments under rent control, consumer surplus has increased. These renters are clearly winners: they obtain an apartment at $800, paying $200 less than the unregulated market price. These people receive a direct transfer of surplus from landlords in the form of lower rent. But not all renters win: there are fewer apart-

ments to rent now than if the market had remained unregulated, making it hard, if not impossible, for some to find a place to call home.

Without direct calculation of the surpluses gained and lost, it is generally unclear whether renters as a whole are made better or worse off by rent control. What we can say is that the greater the deadweight loss—the larger the reduction in the quantity of apartments rented—the more likely it is that renters as a whole lose.

However, we can say unambiguously that landlords are worse off: producer surplus has clearly decreased. Landlords who continue to rent out their apartments get $200 a month less in rent, and others withdraw their apartments from the market altogether. The deadweight-loss triangle, shaded yellow in panel (b), represents the value lost to both renters and landlords from rentals that essentially vanish thanks to rent control.

FIGURE   5-4   Winners and Losers from Rent Control

Panel (a) shows the consumer surplus and producer surplus in the equilibrium of the unregulated market for apartments—before rent control. Panel (b) shows the consumer and producer surplus in the market after a

price ceiling of $800 has been imposed. As you can see, for those consumers who can still obtain apartments under rent control, consumer surplus has increased but producer surplus and total surplus have decreased.

will happen: some people who are not especially anxious to find an apartment will get one and others who are very anxious to find an apartment won't.

Because people usually get apartments through luck or personal connections under rent control, it generally results in an **inefficient allocation to consumers** of the few apartments available.

To see the inefficiency involved, consider the plight of the Lees, a family with young children who have no alternative housing and would be willing to pay up to $1500 for an apartment—but are unable to find one. Also consider George, a retiree who lives most of the year in Florida but still has a lease on the New York City apartment he moved into 40 years ago. George pays $800 per month for this apartment, but if the rent were even slightly more—say, $850—he would give it up and stay with his children when he is in the city.

This allocation of apartments—George has one and the Lees do not—is a missed opportunity: there is a way to make the Lees and George both better off at no additional cost. The Lees would be happy to pay George, say, $1200 a month to sublet his apartment, which he would happily accept since the apartment is worth no more than $849 a month to him. George would prefer the money he gets from the Lees to keeping his apartment; the Lees would prefer to have the apartment rather than the money. So both would be made better off by this transaction—and nobody else would be made worse off.

Generally, if people who really want apartments could sublet them from people who are less eager to live there, both those who gain apartments and those who trade their occupancy for money would be better off. However, subletting is illegal under rent control because it would occur at prices above the price ceiling.

The fact that subletting is illegal doesn't mean it never happens. In fact, chasing down illegal subletting is a major business for New York City private investigators. An article in the *New York Times* described how private investigators use hidden cameras and other tricks to prove that the legal tenants in rent-controlled apartments actually live in the suburbs, or even in other states, and have sublet their apartments at two or three times the controlled rent. This subletting is a kind of illegal activity, which we will discuss shortly. For now, just note that landlords and legal agencies actively discourage the practice of illegal subletting. As a result, the problem of inefficient allocation of apartments remains.

Wasted Resources Another reason a price ceiling causes inefficiency is that it leads to **wasted resources:** people expend money, effort, and time to cope with the shortages caused by the price ceiling. Back in 1979, U.S. price controls on gasoline led to shortages that forced millions of Americans to spend hours each week waiting in lines at gas stations. The opportunity cost of the time spent in gas lines—the wages not earned, the leisure time not enjoyed—constituted wasted resources from the point of view of consumers and of the economy as a whole.

Because of rent control, the Lees will spend all their spare time for several months searching for an apartment, time they would rather spend working or in family activities. That is, there is an opportunity cost to the Lee's prolonged search for an apartment—the leisure or income they would have to forgo. If the market for apartments worked freely, the Lees would quickly find an apartment at the equilibrium rent of $1000, leaving them time to earn more or to enjoy themselves—an outcome that would make them better off without making anyone else worse off. Again, rent control creates missed opportunities.

Indeed, in the long run, the time and resources that families like the Lees spend searching for a rental apartment might increase as the city population rises. All other things equal, a larger population increases the demand for rental apartments. Following an increase in demand, the shortage of units grows and renters find it more difficult to locate a rental unit. Also, it is often the case that the demand and supply curves become flatter over time (i.e., for a given price change, the quantity supplied or demanded changes more in

Price ceilings often lead to inefficiency in the form of **inefficient allocation to consumers:** some people who want the good badly and are willing to pay a high price don't get it, and some who care relatively little about the good and are only willing to pay a low price do get it.

Price ceilings typically lead to inefficiency in the form of **wasted resources:** people expend money, effort, and time to cope with the shortages caused by the price ceiling.

FOR INQUIRING MINDS

RENT CONTROL, MUMBAI STYLE

How far would you go to keep a rent-controlled apartment? Some tenants in the city of Mumbai, India, went very far indeed. According to a *Wall Street Journal* article, three people were killed when four floors in a rent-controlled apartment building in Mumbai collapsed. Despite demands by the city government to vacate the deteriorated building, 58 other tenants refused to leave. They stayed put even after having their electricity and water shut off, being locked out of their apartments, and surviving a police raid. Tenants camped out on the building's veranda, vowing not to give up.

Not all of these tenants were desperately poor and lacking other options. One rent-controlled tenant, the owner of a thriving textile business, paid a total of $8.50 a month for a spacious two-bedroom apartment. (Luxury apartments in Mumbai can go for thousands of dollars a month.)

Although it's a world away, the dynamics of rent control in Mumbai are a lot like those in North America (although Mumbai has clearly had a much more extreme experience). Rent control began in Mumbai in 1947, to address a critical shortage of housing caused by a flood of refugees fleeing conflict between Hindus

and Muslims. Clearly intended to be a temporary measure, it was so popular politically that it has been extended 20 times and now applies to about 60% of the buildings in the city's centre. Tenants pass apartments on to their heirs or sell the right to occupy to other tenants.

Despite the fact that home prices in Mumbai surged more than 60% between 2007 and 2010, landlords of rent-controlled buildings have suffered financially, with the result that across the city prime buildings have been abandoned to decay, even though half of the city's 12 million residents live in slums because of a lack of new housing.

---

the long run than it does in the short run). So in the long run, the size of a shortage caused by a price ceiling tends to grow—with or without an increase in demand.

Inefficiently Low Quality   Yet another way a price ceiling creates inefficiency is by causing goods to be of inefficiently low quality. **Inefficiently low quality** means that sellers offer low-quality goods at a low price even though some buyers would rather have higher quality and would be willing to pay a higher price for it.

Again, consider rent control. Landlords have no incentive to provide better conditions because they cannot raise rents to cover their repair costs but are able to find tenants easily. In many cases, tenants would be willing to pay much more for improved conditions than it would cost for the landlord to provide them—for example, the upgrade of an antiquated electrical system that cannot safely run air conditioners or computers. But any additional payment for such improvements would be legally considered a rent increase, which is prohibited. Indeed, rent-controlled apartments are notoriously badly maintained, rarely painted, subject to frequent electrical and plumbing problems, and sometimes even hazardous to inhabit. As one former manager of Manhattan buildings described the situation: "At unregulated apartments we'd do most things that the tenants requested. But on the rent-regulated units, we did absolutely only what the law required. ... We had a perverse incentive to make those tenants unhappy."

This whole situation is a missed opportunity—some tenants would be happy to pay for better conditions, and landlords would be happy to provide them for payment. But such an exchange would occur only if the market were allowed to operate freely.

Black Markets   And that leads us to a last aspect of price ceilings: the incentive they provide for illegal activities, specifically the emergence of **black markets.** We have already described one kind of black market activity—illegal subletting by tenants. But it does not stop there. Clearly, there is a temptation for a landlord to say to a potential tenant, "Look, you can have the place if you slip me an extra few hundred in cash each month"—and for the tenant to agree if he or she is one of those people who would be willing to pay much more than the maximum legal rent. Let's look again at Figure 5-3. If there is subletting, then the monthly rent for a sublet apartment would be $1200—the so-called demand price given

Price ceilings often lead to inefficiency in that the goods being offered are of **inefficiently low quality:** sellers offer low-quality goods at a low price even though some buyers would prefer a higher quality at a higher price.

A **black market** is a market in which goods or services are bought and sold illegally—either because it is illegal to sell them at all or because the prices charged are legally prohibited by a price control (either a price ceiling or floor).

the number of units available. Alternatively, the landlord could demand an extra cash payment of $400 each month as a "bribe" to rent out the apartment—thereby making the total rental payment actually $1200 per month.

What's wrong with black markets? In general, it's a bad thing if people break any law, because it encourages disrespect for the law in general. Worse yet, in this case illegal activity worsens the position of those who are honest. If the Lees are scrupulous about upholding the rent-control law, but other people—who may need an apartment less than the Lees—are willing to bribe landlords, the Lees may never find an apartment.

So Why Are There Price Ceilings?

We have seen three common results of price ceilings:

- A persistent shortage of the good

- Inefficiency arising from this persistent shortage in the form of inefficiently low quantity transacted, inefficient allocation of the good to consumers, resources wasted in searching for the good, and the inefficiently low quality of the good offered for sale

- The emergence of illegal, black market activity

Given these unpleasant consequences, why do governments still sometimes impose price ceilings? Why does rent control, in particular, persist in New York City?

One answer is that although price ceilings may have adverse effects, they do benefit some people. In practice, New York's rent-control rules—which are more complex than our simple model—hurt most residents but give a small minority of renters much cheaper housing than they would get in an unregulated market. And those who benefit from the controls are typically better organized and more vocal than those who are harmed by them.

Also, when price ceilings have been in effect for a long time, buyers may not have a realistic idea of what would happen without them. In our previous example, the rental rate in an unregulated market (Figure 5-1) would be only 25% higher than in the regulated market (Figure 5-2): $1000 instead of $800. But how would renters know that? Indeed, they might have heard about black market transactions at much higher prices—the Lees or some other family paying George $1200 or more—and would not realize that these black market prices are much higher than the price that would prevail in a fully unregulated market.

A last answer is that government officials often do not understand supply and demand analysis! It is a great mistake to suppose that economic policies in the real world are always sensible or well informed.

ECONOMICS ▸ *IN ACTION*

HUNGER AND PRICE CONTROLS IN VENEZUELA

Something was rotten in the state of Venezuela—specifically, more than 25 000 tonnes of decomposing food in Puerto Cabello in June 2010. The discovery was particularly embarrassing for the then president Hugo Chávez. He was elected in 1998 on a platform denouncing the country's economic elite and promising policies favouring the poor and working classes. Among those policies were price controls on basic foodstuffs, which led to shortages that began in 2003 and had become severe by 2006.

Generous government policies led to higher spending by consumers and sharply rising prices for goods that weren't subject to price controls or which were bought on the black market. The result was a big increase in the demand for price-controlled goods. But a sharp decline in the value of Venezuela's currency led to a fall in imports of foreign food, and the result was empty shelves in the nation's food stores.

As the shortages persisted and inflation of food prices worsened (in the first five months of 2010, the prices of food and drink rose by 21%), Chávez declared "economic war" on the private sector, berating it for "hoarding and smuggling." The government expropriated farms, food manufacturers, and grocery stores, creating in their place government-owned ones, which were corrupt and inefficient—it was the government-owned food-distribution company, PDVAL, that left tens of thousands of tonnes of food to rot in Venezuelan ports. Food production also fell; Venezuela must now import 70% of its food.

Not surprisingly, the shelves have been far more bare in government-run grocery stores than in those still in private hands. The food shortages were so severe that they greatly diminished Chávez's popularity among working-class Venezuelans and halted his expropriation plans. As an old Venezuelan saying has it, "Love with hunger doesn't last."

After the death of President Chávez in March 2013, Vice President Nicolás Maduro took over before a special presidential election was held in April to pick a new president. Maduro promised to continue Chávez's socialist revolution while the opposition candidate, Henrique Capriles, argued that this regime had put the country on the road to ruin. During the campaign, shortages of food and basic household items hit a five-year high, and partly as a result, Maduro barely won the election. In May 2013, monthly inflation peaked at 6.1%, the highest monthly rate in 17 years, contributing to an annual rate of inflation of 35.1%. However, according to the central bank, in May shortages were becoming less severe, as the "shortage indicator," which measures the difficulties to obtain a basket of basic goods, declined from 21.3% to 20.5%. Regrettably, some of the decline in shortages may actually be due to the widespread existence and use of black markets. The inefficiency of the price ceilings continues.

Venezuela's food shortages offer a lesson in why price ceilings, however well intentioned, are usually not a good idea.

CHECK YOUR UNDERSTANDING   5-1

1. On game nights, homeowners near Middletown Arena used to rent parking spaces in their driveways to fans at a going rate of $11. A new town ordinance now sets a maximum parking fee of $7. Use the accompanying supply and demand diagram to explain how each of the following corresponds to a price-ceiling concept.
   a. Some homeowners now think it's not worth the hassle to rent out spaces.
   b. Some fans who used to carpool to the game now drive alone.
   c. Some fans can't find parking and leave without seeing the game.

   Explain how each of the following adverse effects arises from the price ceiling.
   d. Some fans now arrive several hours early to find parking.
   e. Friends of homeowners near the stadium regularly attend games, even if they aren't big fans. But some serious fans have given up because of the parking situation.
   f. Some homeowners rent spaces for more than $7 but pretend that the buyers are non-paying friends or family.

2. True or false? Explain your answer. A price ceiling below the equilibrium price of an otherwise efficient market does the following:
   a. Increases quantity supplied
   b. Makes some people who want to consume the good worse off
   c. Makes all producers worse off

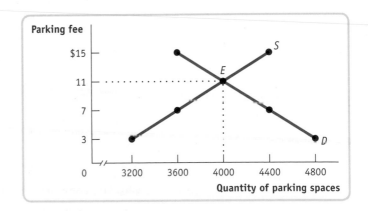

3. Which of the following create deadweight loss? Which do not and are simply a transfer of surplus from one person to another? Explain your answer.

   a. You have been evicted from your rent-controlled apartment after the landlord discovered your pet boa constrictor. The apartment is quickly rented to someone else at the same price. You and the new renter do not necessarily have the same willingness to pay for the apartment.

   b. In a contest, you won a ticket to a jazz concert. But you can't go to the concert because of an exam, and the terms of the contest do not allow you to sell the ticket or give it to someone else. Would your answer to this question change if you could not sell the ticket but could give it to someone else?

   c. Your school's dean of students, who is a proponent of a low-fat diet, decrees that ice cream can no longer be served on campus.

   d. Your ice-cream cone falls on the ground and your dog eats it. (Take the liberty of counting your dog as a member of society, and assume that, if he could, your dog would be willing to pay the same amount for the ice-cream cone as you.)

Solutions appear at back of book.

Price Floors

Sometimes governments intervene to push market prices up instead of down. *Price floors* have been widely legislated for agricultural products, such as wheat and milk, as a way to support the incomes of farmers. (In 2012, the federal government ended the monopoly position of the Canadian Wheat Board (CWB), which used government subsidies to guarantee farmers a minimum price for wheat and barley.[2]) Historically, there were also price floors on such services as trucking and air travel, although these were phased out by the government of Canada in the 1970s and 1980s. If you have ever worked in a fast-food restaurant, you are likely to have encountered a price floor: governments in Canada, the United States, and many other countries maintain a lower limit on the hourly wage rate of a worker's labour; that is, a floor on the price of labour—called the **minimum wage.**

Just like price ceilings, price floors are intended to help some people but generate predictable and undesirable side effects. Figure 5-5 shows hypothetical supply and demand curves for butter. Left to itself, the market would move to equilibrium at point *E*, with 10 million kilograms of butter bought and sold at a price of $1 per kilogram.

Now suppose that the government, in order to help dairy farmers, imposes a price floor on butter of $1.20 per kilogram. Its effects are shown in Figure 5-6, where the line at $1.20 represents the price floor. At a price of $1.20 per kilogram, producers would want to supply 12 million kilograms (point *B* on the supply curve) but consumers would want to buy only 9 million kilograms (point *A* on the demand curve). So the price floor leads to a persistent surplus of 3 million kilograms of butter.

Does a price floor always lead to an unwanted surplus? No. Just as in the case of a price ceiling, the floor may not be binding—that is, it may be irrelevant. If the equilibrium price of butter is $1 per kilogram but the floor is set at only $0.80, the floor has no effect. And sometimes, a surplus can be saved in order to maintain the price floor in later years. For example, the Federation of Quebec Maple Syrup Producers regulates the production and marketing of maple syrup in Quebec, the

The **minimum wage** is a legal floor on the wage rate, which is the market price of labour.

---

[2]The CWB generally paid farmers in two parts. A first payment (or initial payment) equal to a portion of the expected grain price was made when farmers delivered their grain to the board. A second payment (or the final payment) could occur at the end of a crop year if prices were high enough—that is, higher than the initial payment. If the grain was actually sold at a lower price than the initial payment, the farmers received no final payment. In such cases, the federal government covered any CWB deficit so that farmers did not have to pay back a portion of their earlier payment, so the first payment acted as a price floor.

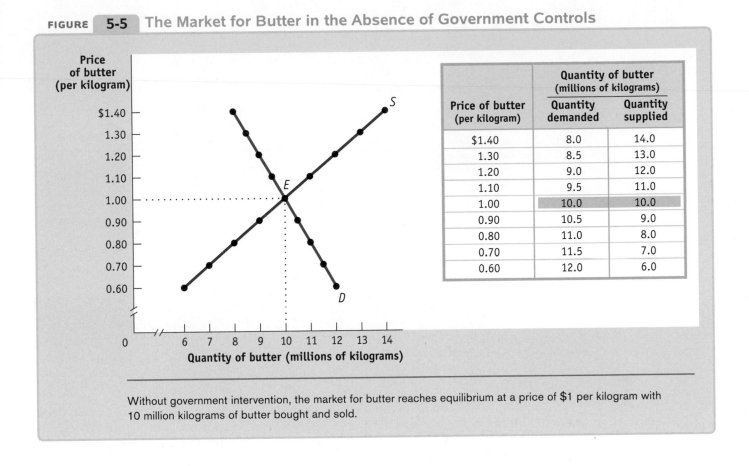

Price of butter (per kilogram)	Quantity of butter (millions of kilograms)	
	Quantity demanded	Quantity supplied
$1.40	8.0	14.0
1.30	8.5	13.0
1.20	9.0	12.0
1.10	9.5	11.0
1.00	10.0	10.0
0.90	10.5	9.0
0.80	11.0	8.0
0.70	11.5	7.0
0.60	12.0	6.0

Without government intervention, the market for butter reaches equilibrium at a price of $1 per kilogram with 10 million kilograms of butter bought and sold.

source of more than 75% of the world's supply. Besides setting production limits and quality, it holds a strategic reserve of maple syrup equal to about 42% of the world's 2011 production. During high production years the reserve grows in order to limit sales and maintain higher prices, and during years of lower production reserves are sold off at higher prices.

But suppose that a price floor is binding and the surplus is unwanted: what happens to it? The answer depends on government policy. In the case of agricultural price floors, governments buy up unwanted surplus. (The European Commission, which administers price floors for a number of European countries, once found itself the owner of a so-called butter mountain, equal in weight to the entire population of Austria.) The government then has to find a way to dispose of these unwanted goods.

Some countries pay exporters to sell products at a loss overseas; this is standard procedure for the European Union. Sometimes Canada gives surplus food away as foreign aid to less developed countries. In some cases, governments have actually destroyed the surplus production. For example, in 1975 about 90 million surplus eggs were destroyed in Canada. To avoid the problem of dealing with the unwanted surplus, the Canadian government typically either pays farmers not to produce the products at all or limits their ability to produce more output.

When the government is not prepared to purchase the unwanted surplus, a price floor means that would-be sellers cannot find buyers. This is what happens when there is a price floor on the wage rate paid for an hour of labour, the minimum wage: when the minimum wage is above the equilibrium wage rate, some people who are willing to work—that is, sell labour—cannot find buyers—that is, employers—willing to give them jobs. These people are unemployed thanks in part to the binding minimum wage constraint.

FIGURE   **5-6**   The Effects of a Price Floor

The black horizontal line represents the government-imposed price floor of $1.20 per kilogram of butter. The quantity of butter demanded falls to 9 million kilograms, and the quantity supplied rises to 12 million kilograms, generating a persistent surplus of 3 million kilograms of butter.

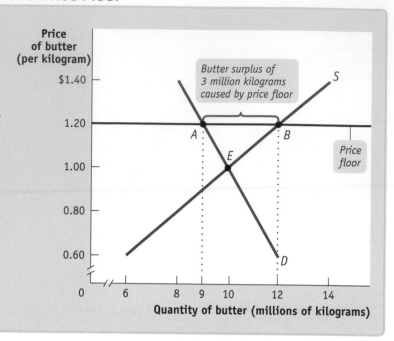

As we said earlier, price floors don't always create a surplus: if a price floor is set below the equilibrium price, it is non-binding and won't have any effect. However, a binding price floor can become non-binding if shifts in the demand and/or supply curves cause the equilibrium price to be greater than or equal to the price floor. In our butter example, the price floor of $1.20 per kilogram may no longer be a binding price floor if there is an increase in the demand for butter due to a change in consumers' preferences. If the demand curve in Figure 5-6 shifts far enough to the right to raise the equilibrium price to $1.20 per kilogram or more, then the price floor is no longer binding. Similarly, if the supply of butter decreases, causing the equilibrium price to increase to $1.20 per kilogram or more, then the price floor will be non-binding.

Figure 5-7 (on the next page) shows the effect of a binding minimum wage in the labour market. At a minimum wage of $10 per hour, there will be involuntary unemployment in the labour market as the number of workers seeking jobs (the quantity supplied) exceeds the number of jobs available (the quantity demanded), and so there is an excess supply of labour. This surplus of labour supplied represents the level of (involuntary) unemployment. In Canada, each province and territory sets its own minimum wage. Table 5-1 summarizes the minimum wages across Canada at the end of 2013. As you can see, most provinces and territories have set the minimum wage in their jurisdiction at about $10 per hour.

TABLE   **5-1**   Minimum Wage by Province/Territory, July 1, 2014

Province/Territory	Minimum Wage
Alberta	$9.95
British Columbia	$10.25
Manitoba	$10.45
New Brunswick	$10.00
Northwest Territories	$10.00
Newfoundland and Labrador	$10.00
Nova Scotia	$10.40
Nunavut	$11.00
Ontario	$11.00
Prince Edward Island	$10.00
Quebec	$10.35
Saskatchewan	$10.00
Yukon	$10.72

FIGURE **5-7** Minimum Wage as a Price Floor Quantity

The black horizontal line represents the government-imposed price floor (minimum wage) of $10 per hour worked. The quantity of workers demanded falls to 900 thousand, and the quantity of workers supplied rises to 1200 thousand, generating a persistent surplus of 300 thousand workers. These 300 thousand workers also represent the level of (involuntary) unemployment.

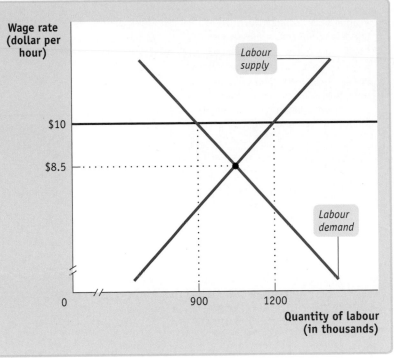

How a Price Floor Causes Inefficiency

The persistent surplus that results from a price floor creates missed opportunities—inefficiencies—that resemble those created by the shortage that results from a price ceiling. These include a deadweight loss from an inefficiently low quantity transacted, inefficient allocation of sales among sellers, wasted resources, inefficiently high quality, and the temptation to break the law by selling below the legal price.

Inefficiently Low Quantity Because a price floor raises the price of a good to consumers, it reduces the quantity of that good demanded; because sellers can't sell more units of a good than buyers are willing to buy, a price floor reduces the quantity of a good bought and sold below the market equilibrium quantity and leads to a deadweight loss. Notice that this is the *same* effect as a price ceiling. You might be tempted to think that a price floor and a price ceiling have opposite effects, but both have the effect of reducing the quantity of a good bought and sold (see Pitfalls at right).

As in the case of a price ceiling, the low quantity sold is an inefficiency due to missed opportunities: price floors prevent mutually beneficial transactions from occurring, transactions that would benefit both buyers and sellers. Figure 5-8 shows the inefficiently low quantity of butter sold with a price floor on the price of butter. Total surplus is the sum of the area above the supply curve and below the demand curve. By reducing the quantity of butter sold, a price floor causes a deadweight loss equal to the area of the shaded triangle in the figure. As in the case of a price ceiling, however, deadweight loss is only one of the forms of inefficiency that the price control creates.

Inefficient Allocation of Sales Among Sellers Like a price ceiling, a price floor can lead to *inefficient allocation*—but in this

 PITFALLS

CEILINGS, FLOORS, AND QUANTITIES
A price ceiling pushes the price of a good *down*. A price floor pushes the price of a good *up*. So it's easy to assume that the effects of a price floor are the opposite of the effects of a price ceiling. In particular, if a price ceiling reduces the quantity of a good bought and sold, doesn't a price floor increase the quantity?

No, it doesn't. In fact, both floors and ceilings reduce the quantity bought and sold. Why? When the quantity of a good supplied isn't equal to the quantity demanded, the actual quantity sold is determined by the "short side" of the market—whichever quantity is less. If sellers don't want to sell as much as buyers want to buy, it's the sellers who determine the actual quantity sold, because buyers can't force unwilling sellers to sell. If buyers don't want to buy as much as sellers want to sell, it's the buyers who determine the actual quantity sold, because sellers can't force unwilling buyers to buy.

FIGURE **5-8**   A Price Floor Causes Inefficiently Low Quantity

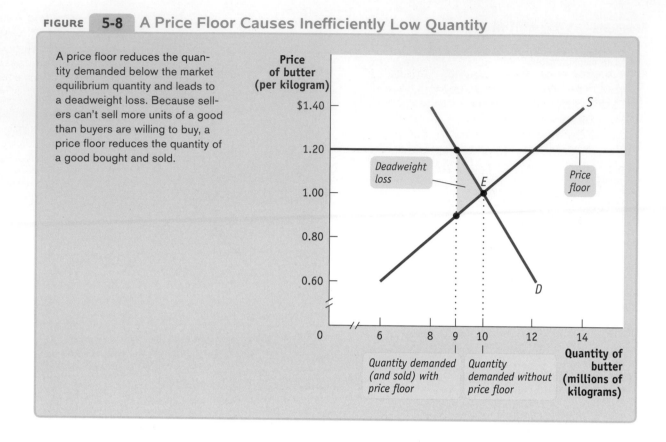

A price floor reduces the quantity demanded below the market equilibrium quantity and leads to a deadweight loss. Because sellers can't sell more units of a good than buyers are willing to buy, a price floor reduces the quantity of a good bought and sold.

Price floors lead to inefficient allocation of sales among sellers: those who would be willing to sell the good at the lowest price are not always those who actually manage to sell it.

case **inefficient allocation of sales among sellers** rather than inefficient allocation to consumers.

An episode from the Belgian movie *Rosetta,* a realistic fictional story, illustrates the problem of inefficient allocation of selling opportunities quite well. Like many European countries, Belgium has a high minimum wage, and jobs for young people are scarce. At one point Rosetta, a young woman who is very anxious to work, loses her job at a fast-food stand because the owner of the stand replaces her with his son—a very reluctant worker. Rosetta would be willing to work for less money, and with the money he would save, the owner could give his son an allowance and let him do something else. But to hire Rosetta for less than the minimum wage would be illegal.

Wasted Resources   Also like a price ceiling, a price floor generates inefficiency by *wasting resources.* The most graphic examples involve government purchases of the unwanted surpluses of agricultural products caused by price floors. The surplus production is sometimes destroyed, which is pure waste; in other cases the stored produce goes, as officials euphemistically put it, "out of condition" and must be thrown away.

Price floors also lead to wasted time and effort. Consider the minimum wage. Would-be workers who spend many hours searching for jobs, or waiting in line in the hope of getting jobs, play the same role in the case of price floors as hapless families searching for apartments in the case of price ceilings.

Inefficiently High Quality   Again like price ceilings, price floors lead to inefficiency in the quality of goods produced.

We saw that when there is a price ceiling, suppliers produce products that are of inefficiently low quality: some buyers prefer higher-quality products and are willing to pay for them, but sellers refuse to improve the quality of their products because the price ceiling prevents their being compensated for doing so. Of course, a binding price ceiling means excess demand is created, so some sellers are able to sell all their low-quality units. This same logic applies to price floors, but in reverse: suppliers offer goods of **inefficiently high quality.** A binding price floor creates excess supply, so some sellers must offer higher quality to avoid being shut out of the market.

How can this be? Isn't high quality a good thing? Yes, but only if it is worth the cost. Suppose that some suppliers spend a lot to make goods of very high quality but that this quality isn't worth much to some consumers, who would rather receive the money spent on that quality in the form of a lower price. This represents a missed opportunity: suppliers and buyers could make a mutually beneficial deal in which buyers got goods of lower quality for a much lower price.

A good example of the inefficiency of excessive quality comes from the days when transatlantic airfares were set artificially high by international treaty. Forbidden to compete for customers by offering lower ticket prices, airlines instead offered expensive services, like lavish in-flight meals that went largely uneaten. At one point the regulators tried to restrict this practice by defining maximum service standards—for example, that snack service should consist of no more than a sandwich. One airline then introduced what it called a "Scandinavian Sandwich," a towering affair that forced the convening of another

> Price floors often lead to inefficiency in that goods of **inefficiently high quality** are offered: some sellers offer high-quality goods at a high price, even though some buyers would prefer a lower quality at a lower price.

CHECK OUT THESE LOW WAGES!

As you can see in the graph below, the minimum wage rate in Canada is actually quite reasonable compared with that of other rich countries. Since minimum wages are set in national currency—the British minimum wage is set in British pounds, the French minimum wage is set in euros, and so on—the comparison depends on the exchange rate on any given day. As of July 16, 2013, Australia had a minimum wage over twice as high as the U.S. rate, with France, Ireland, and Canada not far behind. You can see one effect of this difference in the supermarket checkout line. In Canada and Europe, shoppers usually bag their own groceries. In the United States, where hiring a bagger is a lot less expensive, there is usually someone to bag the groceries for you.

The accompanying data reveals that of these countries, the United States had the greatest percentage of workers employed in low-paying jobs. In 2009, about one in four American workers earned the minimum wage. Also, according to the Organisation for Economic Co-operation and Development (OECD), in 2011 the U.S. minimum wage was only 38% of the median wage of American workers. Unfortunately, Canadian workers did not fare much better in respect to either measure, implying a relatively high degree of income inequality in Canada compared to France where many fewer workers are paid the minimum wage and this minimum wage is a much larger percentage of the median wage.

	Minimum wage (per hour)	Workers in minimum wage jobs (in 2009)	Minimum wage as a percent of median wage (in 2011)
Australia	A$15.96 = C$15.29	14.4%	54%
France	€9.43 = C$12.87	11.1	60
Ireland	€8.65 = C$11.81	20.2	48
Canada*	$10.25*	20.5	40
United Kingdom	£6.19 = C$9.72	20.6	47
United States	US$7.25 = C$7.53	24.8	38

Sources: OECD; Bank of Canada.

*The Canadian minimum wage varied by province and territory in 2013, ranging from $9.50 to $11.00.

conference to define *sandwich*. All of this was wasteful, especially considering that what passengers really wanted was less food and lower airfares.

Since the deregulation of North American airlines in the 1970s and 1980s, Canadian passengers have experienced a large decrease in ticket prices accompanied by a decrease in the quality of in-flight service—smaller seats, lower quality food, and so on. Everyone complains about the service—but thanks to lower fares, the number of people flying on Canadian carriers has grown several hundred percent since airline deregulation.

Illegal Activity Finally, like price ceilings, price floors provide incentives for illegal activity. For example, in countries where the minimum wage is far above the equilibrium wage rate, workers desperate for jobs sometimes agree to work off the books for employers who conceal their employment from the government—or bribe the government inspectors. This practice, known in Europe as "black labour," is especially common in southern European countries such as Italy and Spain (see the upcoming Economics in Action).

So Why Are There Price Floors?

To sum up, a price floor creates various negative side effects:

- A persistent surplus of the good
- Inefficiency arising from the persistent surplus in the form of inefficiently low quantity transacted (which creates a deadweight loss), inefficient allocation of sales among sellers, wasted resources, and an inefficiently high level of quality offered by some suppliers
- The temptation to engage in illegal activity, particularly bribery and corruption of government officials

So why do governments impose price floors when they have so many negative side effects? The reasons are similar to those for imposing price ceilings. Government officials often disregard warnings about the consequences of price floors either because they believe that the relevant market is poorly described by the supply and demand model or, more often, because they do not understand the model. Above all, just as price ceilings are often imposed because they benefit some influential buyers of a good, price floors are often imposed because they benefit some influential sellers.

The generous minimum wage in many European countries has contributed to a high rate of unemployment and the flourishing of an illegal labour market.

ECONOMICS › *IN ACTION*

"BLACK LABOUR" IN SOUTHERN EUROPE

The best-known example of a price floor is the minimum wage. Most economists believe, however, that the minimum wage has relatively little effect on the job market if the floor is relatively low. For example, in the United States, the minimum wage was 53% of the average wage of blue-collar production workers in 1964; by 2010, despite several recent increases, it had fallen to about 44%.

The situation is different, however, in many European countries, where minimum wages have been set much higher than in Canada and the United States. This has happened despite the fact that workers in most European countries are somewhat less productive than their North American counterparts, which means that the equilibrium wage in Europe—the wage that would clear the labour market—is probably lower in Europe than in North America. Moreover, European countries often require employers to pay for health and retirement benefits, which are more extensive and so more costly than comparable American and even

Canadian benefits. These mandated benefits make the actual cost of employing a European worker considerably more than the worker's paycheque.

The result is that in Europe the price floor on labour is definitely binding: the minimum wage is well above the wage rate that would make the quantity of labour supplied by workers equal to the quantity of labour demanded by employers.

The persistent surplus that results from this price floor appears in the form of high unemployment—millions of workers, especially young workers, seek jobs but cannot find them.

In countries where the enforcement of labour laws is lax, however, there is a second, entirely predictable result: widespread evasion of the law. In both Italy and Spain, officials believe there are hundreds of thousands, if not millions, of workers who are employed by companies that pay them less than the legal minimum, fail to provide the required health and retirement benefits, or both. In many cases the jobs are simply unreported: Spanish economists estimate that about a third of the country's reported unemployed are in the black labour market—working at unreported jobs. In fact, Spaniards waiting to collect cheques from the unemployment office have been known to complain about the long lines that keep them from getting back to work!

Employers in these countries have also found legal ways to evade the wage floor. For example, Italy's labour regulations apply only to companies with 15 or more workers. This gives a big cost advantage to small Italian firms, many of which remain small in order to avoid paying higher wages and benefits. And sure enough, in some Italian industries there is an astonishing proliferation of tiny companies. For example, one of Italy's most successful industries is the manufacture of fine woollen cloth, centred in the Prato region. The average textile firm in that region employs only four workers!

▼ **Quick Review**

● The most familiar price floor is the **minimum wage.** Price floors are also commonly imposed on agricultural goods.

● A price floor above the equilibrium price benefits successful sellers but causes predictable adverse effects such as a persistent surplus, which leads to four kinds of inefficiencies: deadweight loss from inefficiently low quantity transacted, **inefficient allocation of sales among sellers,** wasted resources, and **inefficiently high quality.**

● Price floors encourage illegal activity, such as workers who work off the books, often leading to official corruption.

CHECK YOUR UNDERSTANDING   5-2

1. A provincial legislature mandates a price floor for gasoline of P_F per litre. Assess the following statements and illustrate your answer using the figure provided.

   a. Proponents of the law claim it will increase the income of gas station owners. Opponents claim it will hurt gas station owners because they will lose customers.

   b. Proponents claim consumers will be better off because gas stations will provide better service. Opponents claim consumers will be generally worse off because they prefer to buy gas at cheaper prices.

   c. Proponents claim that they are helping gas station owners without hurting anyone else. Opponents claim that consumers are hurt and will end up doing things like buying gas across the border or on the black market.

   Solutions appear at back of book.

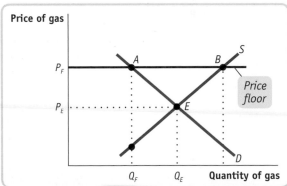

Controlling Quantities

n the 1930s, New York City instituted a system of licensing for taxicabs: only taxis with a special **licence** called a "medallion" were allowed to pick up passengers. Because this system was intended to ensure quality, medallion owners were supposed to maintain certain standards, including safety and cleanliness. A total of 11 787 medallions were issued, with taxi owners paying $10 for each medallion.

A **licence** gives its owner the right to supply a good.

In 1995, there were still only 11 787 licensed taxicabs in New York, even though the city had meanwhile become the financial capital of the world, a place where hundreds of thousands of people in a hurry tried to hail a cab every day. (An additional 400 medallions were issued in 1995, and after several rounds of sales of additional medallions, today there are 13 128 medallions.)

The result of this restriction on the number of taxis was that a New York City taxi medallion became very valuable: if you wanted to operate a taxi in New York, you had to lease a medallion from someone else or buy one for a going price of several hundred thousand dollars.

It turns out that this story is not unique; other cities introduced similar medallion systems in the 1930s and, like New York, have issued few new medallions since. In San Francisco and Boston, as in New York, taxi medallions trade for six-figure prices.

In Toronto, standard taxi licences come in the form of a special numbered plate that, like a New York City taxi medallion, must be affixed to the cab. Fifteen hundred of these standard taxi licences were issued in 1953 and no new plates were issued until 1961. New licensing rules in 1963 allowed these licences to be sold on the open market—making them a capital asset for the licence holder, rather than the issuer. By 1973, the number of licences had risen to about 2100 and the following year the leasing of taxi licences was allowed. The limited supply of licences coupled with the transferability and leasing options resulted in the market price of a taxi plate rising significantly while encouraging the decline in taxicab quality. Many plate owners leased out their licences, rather than drive their own cabs. These owners sought to maximize their leasing revenues by setting lease fees as a high percentage of the driver's revenue, which encouraged drivers to keep operating costs as low as possible. Of course, low operating costs meant that cab maintenance was minimized and replacement of the cars was usually delayed as long as legally permitted. Many customers complained about cars in bad or unsafe condition operated by overworked, stressed-out drivers.

In 1998, Toronto decided to introduce a new class of licence with the sale of 1400 new Ambassador taxi licences, and going forward, no new standard licences would ever be issued. Unlike a standard licence, Ambassador licences can't be sold, leased, or otherwise transferred— a licence holder is the owner and operator of the taxi—and the licence remains the property of the city. The aim was to allow these drivers to be entrepreneurs who cared about the quality of their car since they couldn't lease from some other party—so if everything worked as intended, quality in the market would rise.

By 2013, there were about 4850 taxi licences in Toronto of both types. Standard licences sold for about $300 000 and most owners of Ambassador licences wished they too could sell or lease their plates to someone else. Interestingly, a 2013 report to the city licensing commission recommended moving to a single "harmonized" licence that could not be sold or leased for long periods of time. If adopted, this proposal could improve customer service by ensuring that owner-operators are driving full time.

In Vancouver, the city issues taxi licences to only four companies, charging them $522 for each licence. These companies then sell shares in the licence, dividing them into two shares: one for the day shift and one for the night shift. Each share comes with the right to drive a car, but also pays dividends from real estate the taxi company owns. These shares cost about $300 000 to $400 000, making the cost of acquiring rights to an entire car (two shares) about as costly as obtaining a taxi medallion in New York.

A **quantity control, or quota,** is an upper limit on the quantity of some good that can be bought or sold. The total amount of the good that can be legally transacted is the **quota limit.**

A taxi licensing or medallion system is a form of **quantity control, or quota,** by which the government regulates the quantity of a good that can be bought and sold rather than the price at which it is transacted. The total amount of the good that can be transacted under the quantity control is called the **quota limit.** Typically, the government limits quantity in a market by issuing licences; only people with a licence can legally supply the good.

There are many other cases of quantity controls, ranging from limits on how much foreign currency (for instance, British pounds or Mexican pesos) people are allowed to buy to the quantity of snow crabs Newfoundland and Labrador fishing boats are allowed to catch. Notice, by the way, that although there are price controls on both sides of the equilibrium price—price ceilings and price floors—in the real world, quantity controls always set an upper, not a lower, limit on quantities. After all, nobody can be forced to buy or sell more than they want to!

Some attempts to control quantities are undertaken for good economic reasons, some for bad ones. In many cases, as we will see, quantity controls introduced to address a temporary problem become politically hard to remove later because the beneficiaries don't want them abolished, even after the original reason for their existence is long gone. But whatever the reasons for such controls, they have certain predictable—and usually undesirable—economic consequences.

The Anatomy of Quantity Controls

To understand why a New York City taxi medallion is worth so much money, we consider a simplified version of the market for taxi rides, shown in Figure 5-9. Just as we assumed in the analysis of rent control that all apartments are the same, we now suppose that all taxi rides are the same—ignoring the real-world complication that some taxi rides are longer, and so more expensive, than others. The table in the figure shows supply and demand schedules. The equilibrium— indicated by point *E* in the figure and by the shaded entries in the table—is a fare of $5 per ride, with 10 million rides taken per year. (You'll see in a minute why we present the equilibrium this way.)

The New York medallion system limits the number of taxis, but each taxi driver can offer as many rides as he or she can manage. (Now you know why New York taxi drivers are so aggressive!) To simplify our analysis, however, we will assume that a medallion system limits the number of taxi rides that can legally be given to 8 million per year.

FIGURE 5-9 The Market for Taxi Rides in the Absence of Government Controls

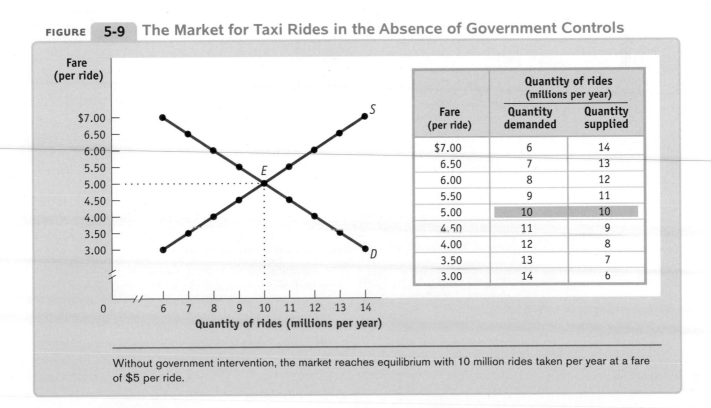

Fare (per ride)	Quantity of rides (millions per year)	
	Quantity demanded	Quantity supplied
$7.00	6	14
6.50	7	13
6.00	8	12
5.50	9	11
5.00	10	10
4.50	11	9
4.00	12	8
3.50	13	7
3.00	14	6

Without government intervention, the market reaches equilibrium with 10 million rides taken per year at a fare of $5 per ride.

The **demand price** of a given quantity is the price at which consumers will demand that quantity.

The **supply price** of a given quantity is the price at which producers will supply that quantity.

Until now, we have derived the demand curve by answering questions of the form: "What is the maximum number of taxi rides passengers will want to take if the price is $5 per ride?" But it is possible to reverse the question and ask instead: "What is the maximum price per ride consumers will pay to buy 10 million rides per year?" The price at which consumers want to buy a given quantity—in this case, 10 million rides at $5 per ride—is the **demand price** of that quantity. You can see from the demand schedule in Figure 5-9 that the demand price of 6 million rides is $7 per ride, the demand price of 7 million rides is $6.50 per ride, and so on.

Similarly, the supply curve represents the answer to questions of the form: "What is the maximum number of taxi rides drivers are willing to supply at a price of $5 each?" But we can also reverse this question to ask: "What is the minimum price at which suppliers would be willing to supply 10 million rides per year?" The price at which suppliers will supply a given quantity—in this case, 10 million rides at $5 per ride—is the **supply price** of that quantity. We can see from the supply schedule in Figure 5-9 that the supply price of 6 million rides is $3 per ride, the supply price of 7 million rides is $3.50 per ride, and so on.

Now we are ready to analyze a quota. We have assumed that the city government limits the quantity of taxi rides to 8 million per year. Medallions, each of which carries the right to provide a certain number of taxi rides per year, are made available to selected people in such a way that a total of 8 million rides will be provided. Medallion-holders may then either drive their own taxis or rent their medallions to others for a fee.

Figure 5-10 shows the resulting market for taxi rides, with the black vertical line at 8 million rides per year representing the quota limit. Because the

FIGURE **5-10** Effect of a Quota on the Market for Taxi Rides

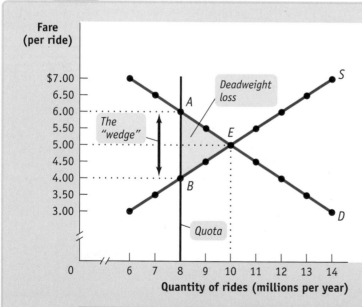

Fare (per ride)	Quantity of rides (millions per year)	
	Quantity demanded	Quantity supplied
$7.00	6	14
6.50	7	13
6.00	8	12
5.50	9	11
5.00	10	10
4.50	11	9
4.00	12	8
3.50	13	7
3.00	14	6

The table shows the demand price and the supply price corresponding to each quantity: the price at which that quantity would be demanded and supplied, respectively. The city government imposes a quota of 8 million rides by selling licences for only 8 million rides, represented by the black vertical line. The price paid by consumers rises to $6 per ride, the demand price of 8 million rides, shown by point *A*. The supply price of 8 million rides is only $4 per ride, shown by point *B*. The difference between these two prices is the quota rent per ride, the earnings that accrue to the owner of a licence. The quota rent drives a wedge between the demand price and the supply price, and the quota discourages mutually beneficial transactions, it creates a deadweight loss equal to the shaded triangle.

quantity of rides is limited to 8 million, consumers must be at point *A* on the demand curve, corresponding to the shaded entry in the demand schedule: the demand price of 8 million rides is $6 per ride. Meanwhile, taxi drivers must be at point *B* on the supply curve, corresponding to the shaded entry in the supply schedule: the supply price of 8 million rides is $4 per ride.

But how can the price received by taxi drivers be $4 when the price paid by taxi riders is $6? The answer is that in addition to the market in taxi rides, there is also a market in medallions. Medallion-holders may not always want to drive their taxis: they may be ill or on vacation. Those who do not want to drive their own taxis will sell the right to use the medallion to someone else. So we need to consider two sets of transactions here, and so two prices: (1) the transactions in taxi rides and the price at which these will occur, and (2) the transactions in medallions and the price at which these will occur. It turns out that since we are looking at two markets, the $4 and $6 prices will both be right.

To see how this all works, consider two imaginary taxi drivers, Sunil and Harriet. Sunil has a medallion but can't use it because he's recovering from a severely sprained wrist. So he's looking to rent his medallion out to someone else. Harriet doesn't have a medallion but would like to rent one. Furthermore, at any point in time, there are many other people like Harriet who would like to rent a medallion. Suppose Sunil agrees to rent his medallion to Harriet. To make things simple, assume that any driver can give only one ride per day and that Sunil is renting his medallion to Harriet for one day. What rental price will they agree on?

To answer this question, we need to look at the transactions from the viewpoints of both drivers. Once she has the medallion, Harriet knows she can make $6 per day—the demand price of a ride under the quota. And she is willing to rent the medallion only if she makes at least $4 per day—the supply price of a ride under the quota. So Sunil cannot demand a rent of more than $2—the difference between $6 and $4. And if Harriet offered Sunil less than $2—say, $1.50—there would be other eager drivers willing to offer him more, up to $2. So, in order to get the medallion, Harriet must offer Sunil at least $2. Since the rent can be no more than $2 and no less than $2, it must be exactly $2.

It is no coincidence that $2 is exactly the difference between $6, the demand price of 8 million rides, and $4, the supply price of 8 million rides. In every case in which the supply of a good is legally restricted, there is a **wedge** between the demand price of the quantity transacted and the supply price of the quantity transacted. This wedge, illustrated by the double-headed arrow in Figure 5-10, has a special name: the **quota rent.** It is the earnings that accrue to the licence-holder from ownership of a valuable commodity, the licence. In the case of Sunil and Harriet, the quota rent of $2 goes to Sunil because he owns the licence, and the remaining $4 from the total fare of $6 goes to Harriet.

So Figure 5-10 also illustrates the quota rent in the market for taxi rides. The quota limits the quantity of rides to 8 million per year, a quantity at which the demand price of $6 exceeds the supply price of $4. The wedge between these two prices, $2, is the quota rent that results from the restrictions placed on the quantity of taxi rides in this market.

But wait a second. What if Sunil doesn't rent out his medallion? What if he uses it himself? Doesn't this mean that he gets a price of $6? No, not really. Even if Sunil doesn't rent out his medallion, he could have rented it out, which means that the medallion has an *opportunity cost* of $2: if Sunil decides to use his own medallion and drive his own taxi rather than renting his medallion to Harriet, the $2 represents his opportunity cost of not renting out his medallion. That is, the $2 quota rent is now the rental income he forgoes by driving his own taxi.

In effect, Sunil is in two businesses—the taxi-driving business and the medallion-renting business. He makes $4 per ride from driving his taxi and $2 per ride from renting out his medallion. It doesn't make any difference that in this particular case he has rented his medallion to himself! So regardless of whether the medallion

A quantity control, or quota, drives a **wedge** between the demand price and the supply price of a good; that is, the price paid by buyers ends up being higher than that received by sellers.

The difference between the demand and supply price at the quota limit is the **quota rent,** the earnings that accrue to the licence-holder from ownership of the right to sell the good. It is equal to the rental market price of the licence when the licences are traded (rented).

owner uses the medallion himself or herself, or rents it to others, it is a valuable asset. And this is represented in the going price for a New York City taxi medallion: in June 2013, some traded for more than $1 million. Since 1980, medallion prices are up more than 2200%, much more than the Dow Jones Industrial Average (1750%), the Toronto Stock Exchange S&P/TSX index (565%), and gold (150%). Plus leasing out a medallion can bring the owner more than $1000 per week.

Notice, by the way, that quotas—like price ceilings and price floors—don't always have a real effect. If the quota were set at 12 million rides—that is, above the equilibrium quantity in an unregulated market—it would have no effect because it would not be binding.

The Costs of Quantity Controls

Like price controls, quantity controls can have some predictable and undesirable side effects. The first is the by-now-familiar problem of inefficiency due to missed opportunities: quantity controls create deadweight loss by preventing mutually beneficial transactions from occurring, transactions that would benefit both buyers and sellers. Looking back at Figure 5-10, you can see that starting at the quota limit of 8 million rides, New Yorkers would be willing to pay at least $5.50 per ride for an additional 1 million rides and that taxi drivers would be willing to provide those rides as long as they got at least $4.50 per ride. These are rides that would have taken place if there were no quota limit.

The same is true for the next 1 million rides: New Yorkers would be willing to pay at least $5 per ride when the quantity of rides is increased from 9 to 10 million, and taxi drivers would be willing to provide those rides as long as they got at least $5 per ride. Again, these rides would have occurred without the quota limit.

Only when the market has reached the unregulated market equilibrium quantity of 10 million rides are there no "missed-opportunity rides"—the quota limit of 8 million rides has caused 2 million "missed-opportunity rides."

Generally, *as long as the demand price of a given quantity exceeds the supply price, there is a missed opportunity which creates a deadweight loss.* A buyer would be willing to buy the good at a price that the seller would be willing to accept, but such a transaction does not occur because it is forbidden by the quota. The deadweight loss arising from the 2 million in missed-opportunity rides is represented by the shaded triangle in Figure 5-8.

And because there are transactions that people would like to make but are not allowed to, quantity controls generate an incentive to evade them or even to break the law. New York's taxi industry again provides clear examples. Taxi regulation applies only to those drivers who are hailed by passengers on the street. A car service that makes prearranged pickups does not need a medallion. As a result, such hired cars provide much of the service that might otherwise be provided by taxis, as in other cities. In addition, there are substantial numbers of unlicensed cabs that simply defy the law by picking up passengers without a medallion. Because these cabs are illegal, their drivers are completely unregulated, and they generate a disproportionately large share of traffic accidents in New York City.[3]

In fact, in 2004 the hardships caused by the limited number of New York taxis led city leaders to authorize an increase in the number of licensed taxis.

---

[3]In Toronto, there are a significant number of unlicensed cabs for hire, especially for trips to Pearson International Airport, Canada's busiest airport, which is situated mostly outside of Toronto in Mississauga, Ontario. Legally, taxis with a licence from Toronto can drop off fares at the airport but are not allowed to pick up another fare there unless prearranged. In order to pick up fares both in the city and at the airport, a driver with a municipal taxi licence must also have a second licence issued by the Greater Toronto Airport Authority (the body that runs the airport). So we have a complex collection of rules coupled with the high volume of demand for taxi rides that are often quite profitable, easily running $50 or more for one trip. This has resulted in not only some Toronto cabs breaking these rules, but the rise of a large fleet of unlabelled taxicabs servicing this large and lucrative market to and from the airport.

In a series of sales, the city sold 900 new medallions, to bring the total number up to the current 13 128 medallions—a move that certainly cheered New York riders.

But those who already owned medallions were less happy with the increase; they understood that the 900 new taxis would reduce or eliminate the shortage of taxis. As a result, taxi drivers anticipated a decline in their revenues because they would no longer always be assured of finding willing customers. And, in turn, the value of a medallion would fall. So to placate the medallion owners, city officials also raised taxi fares: by 25% in 2004, by 11% in 2006, and again by 17% in 2012. Although taxis are now easier to find, a ride now costs more—and that price increase slightly diminished the newfound cheer of New York taxi riders.

Dangerous, unlicensed cabs are one cost of quantity controls.

In sum, quantity controls typically create the following undesirable side effects:

- Deadweight loss because some mutually beneficial transactions that don't occur
- Incentives for illegal activities

ECONOMICS ➤ IN ACTION

THE LOBSTERS OF ATLANTIC CANADA

Forget the various finned species of fish. When it comes to Canada's fisheries, lobster truly is the "King of Seafood." This industry employs thousands of people in New Brunswick, Newfoundland and Labrador, Nova Scotia, Prince Edward Island, and Quebec, and contributed more than $1 billion in export sales in 2012. According to the federal government, lobsters are exported to more than 50 countries worldwide and are one of the exports most closely associated with Canada.

But all is not well in this fishery, which has been hit by several negative shocks in recent years. First, usually about 80% of Canadian lobster exports go to the United States, but demand there has softened since the start of the 2008–2009 recession. This situation is worsened by the appreciation of the Canadian dollar against the U.S. dollar, which put additional downward pressure on the value of Canadian exports. At the same time, landings of lobster in Atlantic Canada and the United States (mostly in the state of Maine) have risen almost 50% in the past 12 years. Catches in 2012 and 2013 have been described as the best seen in years. And while the number of lobster fishing licences is limited and, under current rules, licensed Canadian fishers are restricted in the number of traps they can operate, there is no quota on the number of lobsters they can bring in from those traps.

So demand is down and supply is up, and together these have resulted in prices plummeting from about $9–14/kg in 2005 to about $7.15/kg (or $3.25/lb) in 2013. Nova Scotian fisher Leonard LeBlanc told the CBC that he couldn't remember prices this low in 30 years. "At $3.25 [per pound], we're not covering our costs; we're just trying to mitigate the expenses—at least pay some of them—not all of them and we're praying we don't have any major repairs."

The low prices hurt more than just fishers according to Merill MacInnis, also of Nova Scotia, who told the CBC, "at one time, Nova Scotia boat builders, for example, were going flat out building new boats, because money was good

Fishers sort the lobster haul on the warf in Pointe-Sapin, New Brunswick.

and fishers were investing in the industry. Well now, when you're just making enough to make your payments, people are not going to do that; they're going to keep going with what they have, and it'll have an effect on everybody, whether it be car dealers, boat builders, restaurant owners, whatever. It all has an effect; it all trickles down."

Of course, limiting the number of lobster fishing licences is a form of a quota, but unfortunately, with low demand and high supply (due to the high volume caught per trap), this quota had become a non-binding constraint. As a result, the price of lobster is not supported above the current low level at the intersection of the supply and demand curves.

The continuation of such low prices has led to calls for the introduction of either new rules that would effectively lower the quota or measures geared toward finding additional demand in other markets at home or abroad, so as to help raise the price of lobster. One way the government has reacted to this situation is via the Atlantic Lobster Sustainability Measures program, which is buying back and retiring about 600 lobster fishing licences. This measure will remove more than 200 000 traps from the water by March 2014.

In 2013, some processing plants, overwhelmed by large catches and hoping to help deal with low prices, imposed their own daily quotas on the volume of lobster per boat they would accept. In other cases, fishers either voluntarily stayed home to reduce supply or agreed to limit catches. Many have called upon the government to buy back even more licences and to impose new rules limiting the daily catch of every licensed boat, a much stronger and clearer quota system.

Notice, by the way, that this is an example of a proposed quota that is probably justified by broader economic and environmental considerations—unlike the New York taxicab quota, which has long since lost any economic rationale. Still, whatever its rationale, the proposed Atlantic Canada lobster quota would work the same way as any other quota.

Once the quota system is established, many boat owners will stop fishing for lobsters. They will realize that rather than operating a boat, it is more profitable to sell or rent their licences to someone else. The value of a licence required to fish for lobsters will easily be worth more than the boat itself.

▼ Quick Review

- **Quantity controls,** or **quotas,** are government-imposed limits on how much of a good may be bought or sold. The quantity allowed for sale is the **quota limit.** The government then issues a **licence**—the right to sell a given quantity of a good under the quota.

- When the quota limit is smaller than the equilibrium quantity in an unregulated market, the **demand price** is higher than the **supply price**—there is a **wedge** between them at the quota limit.

- This wedge is the **quota rent,** the earnings that accrue to the licence-holder from ownership of the right to sell the good—whether by actually supplying the good or by renting the licence to someone else. The market rental price of a licence equals the quota rent.

- Like price controls, quantity controls create deadweight loss and encourage illegal activity.

CHECK YOUR UNDERSTANDING   5-3

1. Suppose that the supply and demand for taxi rides is given by Figure 5-9 but the quota is set at 6 million rides instead of 8 million. Find the following and indicate them on Figure 5-9.
   a. The price of a ride
   b. The quota rent
   c. deadweight loss

2. Suppose the quota limit on taxi rides is increased to 9 million. What happens to the quota rent?

3. Assume that the quota limit is 8 million rides. Suppose demand decreases due to a decline in tourism. What is the smallest parallel leftward shift in demand that would result in the quota no longer having an effect on the market? Illustrate your answer using Figure 5-9.

Solutions appear at back of book.

BUSINESS CASE : Medallion Financial: Cruising Right Along

Owaki/Kulla/Corbis

Back in 1937, before New York City froze its number of taxi medallions, Andrew Murstein's immigrant grandfather bought his first one for $10. Over time, the grandfather accumulated 500 medallions, which he rented to other drivers. Those 500 taxi medallions became the foundation for Medallion Financial: the company that would eventually pass to Andrew, its current president.

With a market value of over $300 million in mid-2013, Medallion Financial has shifted its major line of business from renting out medallions to financing the purchase of new ones, lending money to those who want to buy a medallion but don't have the sizable amount of cash required to do so. Murstein believes that he is helping people who, like his Polish immigrant grandfather, want to buy a piece of the American dream.

Andrew Murstein carefully watches the value of a New York City taxi medallion: the more one costs, the more demand there is for loans from Medallion Financial, and the more interest the company makes on the loan. A loan from Medallion Financial is secured by the value of the medallion itself. If the borrower is unable to repay the loan, Medallion Financial takes possession of his or her medallion and resells it to offset the cost of the loan default. As of 2013, the value of a medallion had risen faster than stocks, oil, and gold. Over the past three decades, from 1980 through mid-2013, the value of a medallion rose an average of 6.8% per year, faster than U.S. and Canadian stock market indexes.

But medallion prices can fluctuate dramatically, threatening profits. During periods of a very strong economy, such as 1999 and 2001, the price of New York taxi medallions fell as drivers found jobs in other sectors. When the New York economy tanked in the aftermath of 9/11, the price of a medallion fell to $180 000, its lowest level in 12 years. In 2004, medallion owners were concerned about the impending sale by the New York City Taxi and Limousine Commission of an additional 900 medallions. As Peter Hernandez, a worried New York cabdriver who financed his medallion with a loan from Medallion Financial, said at the time: "If they pump new taxis into the industry, it devalues my medallion. It devalues my daily income, too."

Yet Murstein has always been optimistic that medallions would hold their value. He believed that a 25% fare increase would offset potential losses in their value caused by the sale of new medallions. In addition, more medallions would mean more loans for his company. As of 2013, Murstein's optimism had been justified. Because of the financial crisis of 2007–2009, many New York companies cut back the limousine services they ordinarily provided to their employees, forcing them to take taxis instead. As a result, the price of a medallion rose to an astonishing $1 million in early 2013. And investors have noticed the value in Medallion Financial's line of business: from July 2012 to July 2013, shares of Medallion Financial rose 31%.

QUESTIONS FOR THOUGHT

1. How does Medallion Financial benefit from the restriction on the number of New York taxi medallions?

2. What will be the effect on Medallion Financial if New York companies resume widespread use of limousine services for their employees? What is the economic motivation that prompts companies to offer this perk to their employees? (Note that it is very difficult and expensive to own a personal car in New York City.)

3. Predict the effect on Medallion Financial's business if New York City eliminates restrictions on the number of taxis.

SUMMARY

1. Even when a market is efficient, governments often intervene to pursue greater fairness or to please a powerful interest group. Interventions can take the form of **price controls** or **quantity controls,** both of which generate predictable and undesirable side effects consisting of various forms of inefficiency and illegal activity.

2. A **price ceiling,** a maximum market price below the equilibrium price, benefits successful buyers but creates persistent shortages. Because the price is maintained below the equilibrium price, the quantity demanded is increased and the quantity supplied is decreased compared to the equilibrium quantity. This leads to predictable problems: inefficiencies in the form of **deadweight loss, inefficient allocation to consumers, wasted resources,** and **inefficiently low quality.** It also encourages illegal activity as people turn to **black markets** to get the good. Because of these problems, price ceilings have generally lost favour as an economic policy tool. But some governments continue to impose them either because they don't understand the effects or because the price ceilings benefit some influential group.

3. A **price floor,** a minimum market price above the equilibrium price, benefits successful sellers but creates persistent surplus. Because the price is maintained above the equilibrium price, the quantity demanded is decreased and the quantity supplied is increased compared to the equilibrium quantity. This leads to predictable problems: inefficiencies in the form of inefficiently low quantity transacted, **inefficient allocation of sales among sellers,** wasted resources, and **inefficiently high quality.** It also encourages illegal activity and black markets. The most well known kind of price floor is the **minimum wage,** but price floors are also commonly applied to agricultural products.

4. Quantity controls, or **quotas,** limit the quantity of a good that can be bought or sold. The quantity allowed for sale is the **quota limit.** The government issues **licences** to individuals, the right to sell a given quantity of the good. The owner of a licence earns a **quota rent,** earnings that accrue from ownership of the right to sell the good. It is equal to the difference between the **demand price** at the quota limit, what consumers are willing to pay for that quantity, and the **supply price** at the quota limit, what suppliers are willing to accept for that quantity. Economists say that a quota drives a **wedge** between the demand price and the supply price; this wedge is equal to the quota rent. Quantity controls lead to inefficiencies in the form of mutually beneficial transactions that do not occur, in addition to encouraging illegal activity.

KEY TERMS

Price controls, p. 138
Price ceiling, p. 138
Price floor, p. 138
Deadweight loss, p. 141
Inefficient allocation to consumers, p. 144
Wasted resources, p. 144

Inefficiently low quality, p. 145
Black markets, p. 145
Minimum wage, p. 148
Inefficient allocation of sales among sellers, p. 152
Inefficiently high quality, p. 153
Licence, p. 155

Quantity control, p. 156
Quota, p. 156
Quota limit, p. 156
Demand price, p. 158
Supply price, p. 158
Wedge, p. 159
Quota rent, p. 159

PROBLEMS

1. Suppose it is decided that rent control in a city will be abolished and that market rents will now prevail. Assume that all rental units are identical and so are offered at the same rent. To address the plight of residents who may be unable to pay the market rent, an income supplement will be paid to all low-income households equal to the difference between the old controlled rent and the new market rent.

   a. Use a diagram to show the effect on the rental market of the elimination of rent control. What will happen to the quality and quantity of rental housing supplied?

   b. Use a second diagram to show the additional effect of the income-supplement policy on the market.

   What effect does it have on the market rent and quantity of rental housing supplied in comparison to your answers to part (a)?

   c. Are tenants better or worse off as a result of these policies? Are landlords better or worse off?

   d. From a political standpoint, why do you think cities have been more likely to resort to rent control rather than a policy of income supplements to help low-income people pay for housing?

2. In order to ingratiate himself with voters, the mayor of Gotham City decides to lower the price of taxi rides. Assume, for simplicity, that all taxi rides are the same

distance and therefore cost the same. The accompanying table shows the demand and supply schedules for taxi rides.

	Quantity of rides (millions per year)	
Fare (per ride)	Quantity demanded	Quantity supplied
$7.00	10	12
6.50	11	11
6.00	12	10
5.50	13	9
5.00	14	8
4.50	15	7

a. Assume that there are no restrictions on the number of taxi rides that can be supplied (there is no licensing system). Find the equilibrium price and quantity.

b. Suppose that the mayor sets a price ceiling at $5.50. How large is the shortage of rides? Illustrate with a diagram. Who loses and who benefits from this policy?

c. Suppose that the stock market crashes and, as a result, people in Gotham City are poorer. This reduces the quantity of taxi rides demanded by 6 million rides per year at any given price. What effect will the mayor's new policy have now? Illustrate with a diagram.

d. Suppose that the stock market rises and the demand for taxi rides returns to normal (that is, returns to the demand schedule given in the table). The mayor now decides to ingratiate himself with taxi drivers. He announces a policy in which operating licences are given to existing taxi drivers; the number of licences is restricted such that only 10 million rides per year can be given. Illustrate the effect of this policy on the market, and indicate the resulting price and quantity transacted. What is the quota rent per ride?

3. In the mid-eighteenth century, the government of New France (modern-day Quebec) controlled the price of bread, which was set at a predetermined price below the free market price.

a. Draw a diagram showing the effect of the policy. Did the policy act as a price ceiling or a price floor?

b. What kinds of inefficiencies were likely to have arisen when the controlled price of bread was below the market price? Explain in detail.

Suppose that one year during this period, a large wheat harvest caused a rightward shift in the supply of bread and therefore a decrease in its free market price. Bakers found that, as a result, the controlled price of bread was above the free market price.

c. Draw a diagram showing the effect of the price control on the market for bread during this one-year

period. Did the policy act as a price ceiling or a price floor?

d. What kinds of inefficiencies do you think occurred during this period? Explain in detail.

4. The Canadian Dairy Commission (CDC) administers the price floor for butter, which was set at $7.28 per kilogram in 2012. At that price, according to data from the CDC, the quantity of butter supplied in 2012 was 114.3 million kilograms, and the quantity demanded was 97.5 million kilograms. To support the price of butter at the price floor, the CDC therefore had to buy up 16.8 million kilograms of butter. The accompanying diagram shows supply and demand curves illustrating the market for butter.

a. In the absence of a price floor, how much consumer surplus is created? How much producer surplus? What is the total surplus?

b. With the price floor at $7.28/kg of butter, consumers buy 97.5 million kilograms of butter. How much consumer surplus is created now?

c. With the price floor at $7.28/kg of butter, producers sell 114.3 million kilograms of butter (some to consumers and some to the CDC). How much producer surplus is created now?

d. How much money does the CDC spend on buying up surplus butter?

e. Suppose the federal government covers the cost of surplus butter using tax revenue, as they do in the United States.[4] As a result, total surplus (producer plus consumer) is reduced by the amount the CDC spent on buying surplus butter. Using your answers for parts (b)–(d), what is the total surplus when there is a price floor? How does this compare to the total surplus without a price floor from part (a)?

---

[4]In reality, with the help of provincial marketing boards, the CDC uses a number of supply management techniques to help ensure that it is not buying butter and ultimately destroying it. The CDC and the marketing boards set the price floor based on supplier costs so that suppliers can earn a fair rate of return and use production quotas to attempt to limit supply. The CDC buys and sells butter at the support price so as to eliminate seasonal price fluctuations; any surplus butter bought one year is sold in the following year when demand is firmer. This eliminates the need for the CDC to use government tax revenue to subsidize its buying activities. Part (e) of this question asks you to imagine that this is not how the CDC actually operates.

5. The accompanying table shows hypothetical demand and supply schedules for milk per year. The Canadian government decides that the incomes of dairy farmers should be maintained at a level that allows the traditional family dairy farm to survive. So it implements a price floor of $1 per litre by buying surplus milk until the market price is $1 per litre.

Price of milk (per litre)	Quantity of milk (millions of litres per year)	
	Quantity demanded	Quantity supplied
$1.20	550	850
1.10	600	800
1.00	650	750
0.90	700	700
0.80	750	650

a. In a diagram, show the deadweight loss from the inefficiently low quantity bought and sold.

b. How much surplus milk will be produced as a result of this policy?

c. What will be the cost to the government of this policy?

d. Since milk is an important source of protein and calcium, the government decides to provide the surplus milk it purchases to elementary schools at a price of only $0.60 per litre. Assume that schools will buy any amount of milk available at this low price. But parents now reduce their purchases of milk at any price by 50 million litres per year because they know their children are getting milk at school. How much will the dairy program now cost the government?

e. Explain how inefficiencies in the form of inefficient allocation of sales among sellers and wasted resources arise from this policy.

6. European governments tend to make greater use of price controls than does the Canadian government. For example, the French government sets minimum starting yearly wages for new hires who have completed *le bac*, certification roughly equivalent to a high school diploma. The demand schedule for new hires with *le bac* and the supply schedule for similarly credentialed new jobseekers are given in the accompanying table. The price here—given in euros, the currency used in France—is the same as the yearly wage.

Wage (per year)	Quantity demanded (new job offers per year)	Quantity supplied (new jobseekers per year)
€45 000	200 000	325 000
40 000	220 000	320 000
35 000	250 000	310 000
30 000	290 000	290 000
25 000	370 000	200 000

a. In the absence of government interference, what are the equilibrium wage and number of graduates hired per year? Illustrate with a diagram. Will there be anyone seeking a job at the equilibrium wage who is unable to find one—that is, will there be anyone who is involuntarily unemployed?

b. Suppose the French government sets a minimum yearly wage of €35 000. Is there any involuntary unemployment at this wage? If so, how much? Illustrate with a diagram. What if the minimum wage is set at €40 000? Also illustrate with a diagram.

c. Given your answer to part (b) and the information in the table, what do you think is the relationship between the level of involuntary unemployment and the level of the minimum wage? Who benefits from such a policy? Who loses? What is the missed opportunity here?

7. Until recently, the standard number of hours worked per week for a full-time job in France was 39, just as in Canada. But in response to social unrest over high levels of involuntary unemployment, the French government instituted a 35-hour workweek—a worker could not work more than 35 hours per week even if both the worker and employer wanted it. The motivation behind this policy was that if current employees worked fewer hours, employers would be forced to hire more new workers. Assume that it is costly for employers to train new workers. French employers were greatly opposed to this policy and threatened to move their operations to neighbouring countries that did not have such employment restrictions. Can you explain their attitude? Give an example of both an inefficiency and an illegal activity that are likely to arise from this policy.

8. For the last 70 years the Canadian government has used price supports to provide income assistance to Canadian farmers. To implement these price supports, at times the government has used price floors, which it maintains by buying up the surplus farm products. At other times, it has used target prices, a policy by which the government gives the farmer an amount equal to the difference between the market price and the target price for each unit sold. Consider the market for corn depicted in the accompanying diagram.

a. If the government sets a price floor of $5 per bushel, how many bushels of corn are produced? How many are purchased by consumers? By the government? How much does the program cost the government? How much revenue do corn farmers receive?

b. Suppose the government sets a target price of $5 per bushel for any quantity supplied up to 1000 bushels. How many bushels of corn are purchased by consumers and at what price? By the government? How much does the program cost the government? How much revenue do corn farmers receive?

c. Which of these programs (in parts (a) and (b)) costs corn consumers more? Which program costs the government more? Explain.

d. Is one of these policies less inefficient than the other? Explain.

9. The waters off the North Atlantic coast were once teeming with fish, but because of overfishing by the commercial fishing industry, the stocks of fish became seriously depleted. In 1991, the International Commission for the Conservation of Atlantic Tunas (ICCAT) implemented an international set of quotas to allow Atlantic tuna and swordfish stocks to recover. The quota limited the amount of swordfish caught per year by all Canadian-licensed fishing boats to 2 million kilograms. As soon as the Canadian fishing fleet had met the quota limit, the swordfish catch was closed down for the rest of the year. The accompanying table gives the hypothetical demand and supply schedules for swordfish caught in Canada per year.

Price of swordfish (per kilogram)	Quantity of swordfish (millions of kilogram per year)	
	Quantity demanded	Quantity supplied
$40	1	10
36	2	8
32	3	6
28	4	4
26	5	2

a. Use a diagram to show the effect of the quota on the market for swordfish in 1991. In your diagram, illustrate the deadweight loss from inefficiently low quantity transacted.

b. How do you think fishers changed how they fished in response to this policy?

10. In the Atlantic provinces and Quebec, you must have a licence to harvest lobster commercially; these licences are issued yearly. Suppose the federal Department of Fisheries and Oceans is concerned about the dwindling supplies of lobsters. This department decides to place a yearly quota of 80 000 kg of lobsters harvested in all Canadian waters. It also decides to give licences this year only to those fishers who had licences last year. The accompanying diagram shows the demand and supply curves for Canadian lobsters.

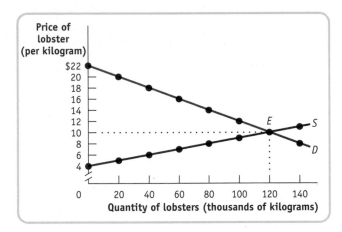

a. In the absence of government restrictions, what are the equilibrium price and quantity?

b. What is the *demand price* at which consumers wish to purchase 80 000 kg of lobsters?

c. What is the *supply price* at which suppliers are willing to supply 80 000 kg of lobsters?

d. What is the *quota rent* per kilogram of lobster when 80 000 kg are sold? Illustrate the quota rent and the deadweight loss on the diagram.

e. Explain a transaction that benefits both buyer and seller but is prevented by the quota restriction.

11. The accompanying diagram shows data from the U.S. Bureau of Labor Statistics on the average price of an airline ticket in the United States from 1975 until 1985, adjusted to eliminate the effect of *inflation* (the general increase in the prices of all goods over time). In 1978, the United States Airline Deregulation Act removed the price floor on airline fares, and it also allowed the airlines greater flexibility to offer new routes. (*Note:* Canada experienced similar airline deregulation in 1978.)

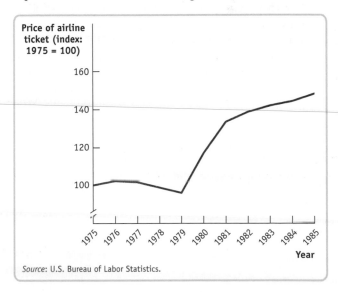

Source: U.S. Bureau of Labor Statistics.

a. Looking at the data on airline ticket prices in the diagram, do you think the price floor that existed before 1978 was binding or non-binding? That is, do you think it was set above or below the equilibrium price? Draw a supply and demand diagram, showing where the price floor that existed before 1978 was in relation to the equilibrium price.

b. Most economists agree that the average airline ticket price per mile travelled actually *fell* as a result of the Airline Deregulation Act. How might you reconcile that view with what you see in the diagram?

12. In Canada, all provinces except Alberta have a minimum legal retail price for beer (a price floor). Part of the rationale for this policy is to discourage immoderate consumption of alcohol.

Suppose the fictitious province of Beerlandia has the following annual demand and supply schedule for beer (sold in cases of 24 bottles).

Price (per case)	Quantity demanded (thousands of cases)	Quantity supplied (thousands of cases)
$16	1040	800
18	1000	1000
20	960	1200
22	920	1400
24	880	1600

a. Find the equilibrium price and quantity of cases of beer in Beerlandia. Draw a diagram representing the market for beer in the province of Beerlandia. Clearly label the price paid by consumers, the quantity of beer exchanged, and the price received by suppliers in equilibrium.

b. Suppose the provincial government of Beerlandia decides to impose a legal minimum price of $28.00 per case of 24 bottles of beer. Briefly describe the winners and losers of this minimum price law.

c. Suppose the majority of the residents of Beerlandia live close to the border and have access to beer at a lower price either in another province or in the United States. What do you expect to occur? What does this imply about the ability of the provincial government of Beerlandia to independently set their tax and alcohol/beer pricing policy? Which jurisdiction is likely to be more problematic, other Canadian provinces or U.S. states?

13. This question uses the algebraic method of determining equilibrium from Appendix 3A. In Canada, producers of milk, poultry, and eggs are protected by government-imposed supply management rules. This supply management system is made up of a combination of import controls, production planning quotas, and minimum prices for these products.

Suppose, for simplicity, the Canadian market for turkeys is described by the following demand and supply curves.

$$P = 30 - 0.125Q^d \qquad \text{Demand Curve}$$
$$P = 1.48 + 0.03Q^S \qquad \text{Supply Curve}$$

where Q represents the monthly quantity of turkey in thousands of kilograms and the price P is the price per kilogram.

a. Suppose Canada does not have any supply management for turkey farmers. Derive the equilibrium price and quantity of turkey. Draw a diagram representing the market for turkey. Clearly label the equilibium price and quantity.

b. Suppose, to support the incomes of farmers who raise turkeys, the government imposes a price floor for turkeys at $9.00 per kilogram. Determine the resulting price paid by consumers, quantity of turkeys exchanged, and the price received by suppliers in equilibrium. Sketch this into your diagram from part (a).

c. Briefly explain how this price floor supports the income of farmers.

d. Why might the government need to also impose limitations on the quantity of turkeys imported? Explain.

e. Show that the imposition of a production quota of 168 000 kg of turkey per month results in the same price paid by consumers as the price floor in part (b). What are the resulting demand price, supply price, and quota rent?

f. Would the government (or a supply management authority) need to have the means to impose penalties for violating the price floor and/or the supply quota? Explain why or why not.

g. Would farmers who were unable to get a turkey production quota licence be pleased by this supply management system? Explain why or why not. Suppose, if they wish, these farmers could rent a production quota licence from another farmer who was awarded one. Would this make these other farmers extremely happy? Explain why or why not.

Elasticity

MORE PRECIOUS THAN A FLU SHOT

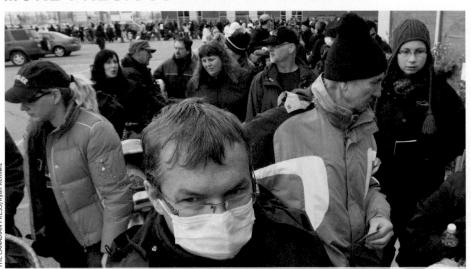

THE CANADIAN PRESS/Ryan Remiorz

Because consumers of flu shots are relatively unresponsive to the price of flu vaccine, availability of the vaccine will determine its price.

PANIC WAS THE ONLY WORD TO describe the situation in the fall of 2009 when Canadians across the country attempted to get the H1N1 (swine) flu vaccination. Scenes of extremely long lineups and other frustrations were common from coast to coast. In some cities, such as Calgary and Toronto, lineups of people outside flu shot clinics would start to form at 3 or 4 A.M. What in the world was happening?

The long lines were partly caused by a supply shortage of the H1N1 flu vaccine as the manufacturer, GlaxoSmithKline Inc., experienced difficulties growing the vaccine, a bottleneck filling vials quickly, and delays obtaining government approval for the version of the vaccine intended for the general population. Health Canada ordered 50.4 million doses, but GlaxoSmithKline could only supply about 440 000 doses to the federal government by early November as the company tried to meet international demand.

The H1N1 vaccine delays and shortage were worsened by the significant demand for H1N1 flu shots by Canadians. In the summer of 2009 the World Health

Organization declared the outbreak to be a pandemic (a worldwide epidemic). So for many months, the Canadian public was repeatedly warned by health officials that the H1N1 flu would soon arrive and that all Canadians should get a flu shot—creating significant demand. In October, Canadian demand spiked when two relatively healthy children in Ontario were killed by the virus. Many Canadians, even those who were not considered to be high risk, scrambled to get a shot.

A big controversy during the 2009 H1N1 flu pandemic was that some private for-profit health clinics in Toronto and Vancouver, which charge thousands of dollars in membership fees and/or for checkups, had received vaccines from the government and that their patients could jump the line for the shot. This news sparked another round of debate about the perils of two-tier health care in the country. Although most people either refused to or couldn't go to these clinics, some Canadians were willing to pay more to get the shot.

Clearly, the demand for flu vaccine is unusual in this respect because getting

vaccinated could mean the difference between life and death: in 2009, 428 Canadians died as a result of the H1N1 flu pandemic. Let's consider a very different and less urgent scenario. Suppose, for example, that the supply of a particular type of breakfast cereal was halved due to manufacturing problems. It would be extremely unlikely, if not impossible, to find a consumer willing to pay 10 times the original price for a box of this particular cereal. In other words, consumers of breakfast cereal are much more responsive to price changes than consumers of flu vaccine.

But how do we define *responsiveness*? Economists measure responsiveness of consumers to price changes with a particular number, called the *price elasticity of demand*. In this chapter we will show how the price elasticity of demand is calculated and why it is the best measure of how the quantity demanded responds to changes in price. We will then see that the price elasticity of demand is only one of a family of related concepts, including the *income elasticity of demand, cross-price elasticity of demand,* and *price elasticity of supply.* ■

The **price elasticity of demand** is the ratio of the percentage change in the quantity demanded to the percentage change in the price as we move along the demand curve. (Given the demand is normally downward sloping, when interpreting the price elasticity of demand, we only look at the absolute value.)

Defining and Measuring Elasticity

Most Canadians don't have to pay for a flu shot, although we do pay for some other types of vaccinations, such as the Hepatitis B vaccine. However, it is not uncommon for residents of other countries, such as the United States, to have to pay for their flu shots. So, what if individual Canadians did have to pay for flu vaccines? In order for Flunomics, a hypothetical flu vaccine distributor, to know whether it could raise its revenue by significantly raising the price of its flu vaccine when it was most needed, it would have to know the *price elasticity of demand* for flu vaccinations.

Calculating the Price Elasticity of Demand

Figure 6-1 shows a hypothetical demand curve for flu vaccinations. At a price of $20 per vaccination, consumers would demand 10 million vaccinations per year (point *A*); at a price of $21, the quantity demanded would fall to 9.9 million vaccinations per year (point *B*).

Figure 6-1, then, tells us the change in the quantity demanded for a particular change in the price. But how can we turn this into a measure of price responsiveness? The answer is to calculate the *price elasticity of demand*, also known as the *own price elasticity of demand* because it relates the change in the quantity demanded of a product to a change in its *own* price (as opposed to the prices of other products).

The **price elasticity of demand** is the ratio of the *percentage change in quantity demanded* to the *percentage change in price* as we move along the demand curve. As we'll see later in this chapter, the reason economists use percentage changes is to obtain a measure that doesn't depend on the units in which a good is measured (say, a child-size dose versus an adult-size dose of vaccine). But before we get to that, let's look at how elasticity is calculated.

To calculate the price elasticity of demand, we first calculate the *percentage change in the quantity demanded* and the corresponding *percentage change in the price* as we move along the demand curve. These are defined as follows:

(6-1) % change in quantity demanded $= \dfrac{\text{Change in quantity demanded}}{\text{Initial quantity demanded}} \times 100$

and

(6-2) % change in price $= \dfrac{\text{Change in price}}{\text{Initial price}} \times 100$

$$\frac{b-a}{a}$$

In Figure 6-1, we see that when the price rises from $20 to $21, the quantity demanded falls from 10 million to 9.9 million vaccinations, yielding a change in the quantity demanded of 0.1 million vaccinations. So the percentage change in the quantity demanded is

$$\text{\% change in quantity demanded} = \frac{9.9 \text{ mil vaccinations} - 10 \text{ mil vaccinations}}{10 \text{ million vaccinations}} \times 100$$

$$= \frac{-0.1 \text{ mil vaccinations}}{10 \text{ mil vaccinations}} \times 100 = -1\%$$

The initial price is $20 and the change in the price is $1, so the percentage change in price is

$$\text{\% change in price} = \frac{\$21 - \$20}{\$20} \times 100$$

$$= \frac{\$1}{\$20} \times 100 = 5\%$$

FIGURE **6-1** **The Demand for Vaccinations**

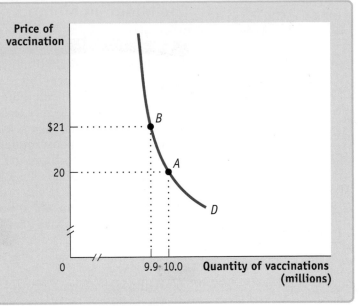

At a price of $20 per vaccination, the quantity of vaccinations demanded is 10 million per year (point *A*). When price rises to $21 per vaccination, the quantity demanded falls to 9.9 million vaccinations per year (point *B*).

To calculate the price elasticity of demand, we find the ratio of the percentage change in the quantity demanded to the percentage change in the price:

(6-3) Price elasticity of demand $= \dfrac{\% \text{ change in quantity demanded}}{\% \text{ change in price}}$

In Figure 6-1, the price elasticity of demand[1] is therefore

$$\text{Price elasticity of demand} = \frac{1\%}{5\%} = 0.2$$

The *law of demand* says that demand curves are downward sloping, so price and quantity demanded always move in opposite directions. In other words, a positive percentage change in price (a rise in price) leads to a negative percentage change in the quantity demanded; a negative percentage change in price (a fall in price) leads to a positive percentage change in the quantity demanded. This means that the price elasticity of demand is, in strictly mathematical terms, a negative number. However, it is inconvenient to repeatedly write a minus sign. So when economists talk about the price elasticity of demand, they usually drop the minus sign and report the absolute value of the price elasticity of demand. In this case, for example, economists would usually say "the price elasticity of demand is 0.2," taking it for granted that you understand they mean *minus* 0.2. We follow this convention here.

The larger the price elasticity of demand, the more responsive the quantity demanded is to the price. When the price elasticity of demand is large—when consumers change their quantity demanded by a large percentage compared with the percentage change in the price—economists say that demand is highly elastic.

As we'll see shortly, a price elasticity of 0.2 indicates a small response of quantity demanded to price. That is, the quantity demanded will fall by a relatively small amount when price rises. This is what economists call *inelastic* demand. And inelastic demand is exactly what Flunomics needed for its strategy to increase revenue by raising the price of its flu vaccines.

---

[1]In practice, a price elasticity of demand of 0.2 means that, other things equal, a 1% increase in price would lead to a 0.2% reduction in quantity demanded and a 10% price reduction would result in a 2% increase in demand.

The **midpoint method** is a technique for calculating the percentage change. In this approach, we calculate changes in a variable compared with the average, or midpoint, of the starting and final values.

An Alternative Way to Calculate Elasticities: The Midpoint Method

Price elasticity of demand compares the *percentage change in quantity demanded* with the *percentage change in price*. When we look at some other elasticities, which we will do shortly, we'll learn why it is important to focus on percentage changes. But at this point we need to discuss a technical issue that arises when you calculate percentage changes in variables.

The best way to understand the issue is with a real example. Suppose you were trying to estimate the price elasticity of demand for gasoline by comparing gasoline prices and consumption in different countries. Because of higher taxes, gasoline usually costs more in Canada than in the United States (approximately thirty cents more per litre in 2013). So what is the percentage difference between Canadian and American gas prices?

Well, it depends on which way you measure it. In 2013, the average price of a litre of gas in Canada was about $1.23 while the average price of a litre of gas in the United States was closer to $0.91. Because the price of a litre of gas in Canada was $0.32 higher than in the United States, it was 35% ($0.32/$0.91 × 100%) higher. Because the price of gasoline in the United States was $0.32 lower, it was 26% ($0.32/$1.23 × 100%) lower.

This is a nuisance: we'd like to have a percentage measure of the difference in prices that doesn't depend on which way you measure it. To avoid computing different elasticities for rising and falling prices we use the *midpoint method*.

The **midpoint method** replaces the usual definition of the percentage change in a variable, X, with a slightly different definition:

$$\textbf{(6-4)} \quad \%\text{ change in } X = \frac{\text{Change in } X}{\text{Average value of } X} \times 100$$

where the average value of X is defined as

$$\text{Average value of } X = \frac{\text{Starting value of } X + \text{Final value of } X}{2}$$

When calculating the price elasticity of demand using the midpoint method, both the percentage change in the price and the percentage change in the quantity demanded are found using this method. To see how this method works, suppose you have the following data for some good:

	Price	Quantity demanded
Situation A	$0.90	1100
Situation B	$1.10	900

To calculate the percentage change in quantity going from situation A to situation B, we compare the change in the quantity demanded—a fall of 200 units—with the *average* of the quantity demanded in the two situations. So we calculate

$$\%\text{ change in quantity demanded} = \frac{900 - 1100}{(1100 + 900)/2} \times 100 = \frac{-200}{1000} \times 100 = -20\%$$

In the same way, we calculate

$$\%\text{ change in price} = \frac{\$1.10 - \$0.90}{(\$0.90 + \$1.10)/2} \times 100 = \frac{\$0.20}{\$1.00} \times 100 = 20\%$$

So in this case we would calculate the price elasticity of demand to be

$$\text{Price elasticity of demand} = \frac{\%\text{ change in quantity demanded}}{\%\text{ change in price}} = \frac{20\%}{20\%} = 1$$

again dropping the minus sign.

The important point is that we would get the same result, a price elasticity of demand of 1, whether we go up the demand curve from situation A to situation B or down from situation B to situation A.

To arrive at a more general formula for price elasticity of demand, suppose that we have data for two points on a demand curve. At point 1 the quantity demanded and price are (Q_1, P_1); at point 2 they are (Q_2, P_2). Then the formula for calculating the price elasticity of demand is:

(6-5) Price elasticity of demand $= \dfrac{\dfrac{Q_2 - Q_1}{(Q_1 + Q_2)/2}}{\dfrac{P_2 - P_1}{(P_1 + P_2)/2}}$

As before, when finding a price elasticity of demand calculated by the midpoint method, we drop the minus sign and use the absolute value.

ECONOMICS ▸ IN ACTION

ESTIMATING ELASTICITIES

You might think it's easy to estimate price elasticities of demand from real-world data: just compare percentage changes in prices with percentage changes in quantities demanded. Unfortunately, it's rarely that simple because changes in price aren't the only thing affecting changes in the quantity demanded: other factors—such as changes in income, changes in tastes, and changes in the prices of other goods—shift the demand curve, thereby changing the quantity demanded at any given price. To estimate price elasticities of demand, economists must use careful statistical analysis to separate the influence of these different factors, holding other things equal.

In 2007, Agriculture and Agri-Food Canada released a report on the estimated demand elasticities for food in Canada. The study aggregated 246 food categories in the Food Expenditure Survey (FOODEX) into 14 food groups. The price elasticities of some of the selected food groups are ranked in ascending order in Table 6-1.

You may notice that the price elasticity of demand varies across food groups. With the exception of non-alcoholic beverages, the price elasticities of demand in Table 6-1 are less than 1. In economics, we say that these goods have inelastic demand. The price elasticity of non-alcoholic beverages is greater than 1; we say that the demand for non-alcoholic beverages is elastic. We'll explain in the next section the difference between inelastic demand and elastic demand.

Price Elasticities of Selected Food Groups

TABLE **6-1**

Food group	Price elasticity of demand
Fish	0.11
Eggs	0.35
Bakery	0.43
Beef	0.46
Vegetables	0.65
Pork	0.68
Poultry	0.82
Fruit	0.85
Dairy	0.88
Non-alcoholic beverages	1.14

Source: Ruth Pomboza and Msafiri Mbaga, *The Estimation of Food Demand Elasticities in Canada*, (Agriculture and Agri-Food Canada, 2007), ageconsearch.umn.edu/bitstream/52705/2/estimation_e.pdf

▼ Quick Review

- The **price elasticity of demand** is equal to the percentage change in the quantity demanded divided by the percentage change in the price as you move along the demand curve, dropping any minus sign.

- In practice, percentage changes are best measured using the **midpoint method,** in which the percentage change in each variable is calculated using the average of starting and final values.

CHECK YOUR UNDERSTANDING 6-1

1. The price of strawberries falls from $1.50 to $1.00 per carton and the quantity demanded goes from 100 000 to 200 000 cartons. Use the midpoint method to find the price elasticity of demand.

2. At the present level of consumption, 4000 movie tickets, and at the current price, $5 per ticket, the price elasticity of demand for movie tickets is 1. Using the midpoint method, calculate the percentage by which the owners of movie theatres must reduce price in order to sell 5000 tickets.

3. The price elasticity of demand for ice cream sandwiches is 1.2 at the current price of $0.50 per sandwich and the current consumption level of 100 000 sandwiches. Calculate the change in the quantity demanded when price rises by $0.05. Use Equations 6-1 and 6-2 to calculate percentage changes and Equation 6-3 to relate price elasticity of demand to the percentage changes.

Solutions appear at back of book.

Interpreting the Price Elasticity of Demand

During a 2004 flu vaccine shortage in the United States, some pharmaceutical distributors believed they could sharply drive up flu vaccine prices because the price elasticity of vaccine demand was small. But what does that mean? How low does a price elasticity have to be for us to classify it as low? How big does it have to be for us to consider it high? And what determines whether the price elasticity of demand is high or low, anyway?

To answer these questions, we need to look more deeply at the price elasticity of demand.

How Elastic Is Elastic?

As a first step toward classifying price elasticities of demand, let's look at the extreme cases.

First, consider the demand for a good when people pay no attention to the price—say, snake antivenom. Suppose that consumers will buy 1000 doses of antivenom per year regardless of the price. In this case, the demand curve for antivenom would look like the curve shown in panel (a) of Figure 6-2: it would be a vertical line at 1000 doses of antivenom. Since the percentage change in the quantity demanded is zero for *any* change in the price, the price elasticity of demand in this case is zero. The case of a zero price elasticity of demand is known as **perfectly inelastic demand.**

The opposite extreme occurs when even a tiny rise in the price will cause the quantity demanded to drop to zero or even a tiny fall in the price will cause the quantity demanded to get extremely large.

Panel (b) of Figure 6-2 shows the case of pink tennis balls; we suppose that tennis players really don't care what colour their balls are and that other colours, such as neon green and vivid yellow, are available at $5 per dozen balls. In this case, consumers will buy no pink balls if they cost more than $5 per dozen but will buy only pink balls if they cost less than $5. The demand curve will therefore be a horizontal line at a price of $5 per dozen balls. As you move back and forth along this line, there is a change in the quantity demanded but no change in the price. Roughly speaking, when you divide a number by zero, you get infinity, denoted by the symbol ∞. So a horizontal demand curve implies an infinite price elasticity of demand. When the price elasticity of demand is infinite, economists say that demand is **perfectly elastic.**

The price elasticity of demand for the vast majority of goods is somewhere between these two extreme cases. Economists use one main criterion for classifying these intermediate cases: they ask whether the price elasticity of demand is greater or less than 1. When the price elasticity of demand is greater than 1, economists say that demand is **elastic.** When the price elasticity of demand is less than 1, they say that demand is **inelastic.** The borderline case is **unit-elastic demand,** where the price elasticity of demand is—surprise—exactly 1.

To see why a price elasticity of demand equal to 1 is a useful dividing line, let's consider a hypothetical example: a toll bridge operated by the provincial ministry of transportation. Other things equal, the number of drivers who use the bridge depends on the toll, the price for crossing the bridge: the higher the toll, the fewer the drivers who use the bridge.

Figure 6-3 shows three hypothetical demand curves—one in which demand is unit-elastic, one in which it is inelastic, and one in which it is elastic. In each case, point A shows the quantity demanded if the toll is $0.90 and point B shows the quantity demanded if the toll is $1.10. An increase in the toll from $0.90 to $1.10 is an increase of 20% if we use the midpoint method to calculate percentage changes.

Panel (a) shows what happens when the toll is raised from $0.90 to $1.10 and the demand curve is unit-elastic. Here the 20% price rise leads to a fall in the quantity

---

Demand is **perfectly inelastic** when the quantity demanded does not respond at all to changes in the price. When demand is perfectly inelastic, the demand curve is a vertical line.

Demand is **perfectly elastic** when any price increase will cause the quantity demanded to drop to zero. When demand is perfectly elastic, the demand curve is a horizontal line.

Demand is **elastic** if the price elasticity of demand is greater than 1, **inelastic** if the price elasticity of demand is less than 1, and **unit-elastic** if the price elasticity of demand is exactly 1.

FIGURE 6-2 Two Extreme Cases of Price Elasticity of Demand

Panel (a) shows a perfectly inelastic demand curve, which is a vertical line. The quantity of snake antivenom demanded is always 1000 doses, regardless of price. As a result, the price elasticity of demand is zero—the quantity demanded is unaffected by the price. Panel (b) shows a

perfectly elastic demand curve, which is a horizontal line. At a price of $5, consumers will buy any quantity of pink tennis balls, but they will buy none at a price above $5. If the price falls below $5, they will buy an extremely large number of pink tennis balls and none of any other colour.

of cars using the bridge each day from 1100 to 900, which is a 20% decline (again using the midpoint method). So the price elasticity of demand is 20%/20% = 1.[2]

Panel (b) shows a case of inelastic demand when the toll is raised from $0.90 to $1.10. The same 20% price rise reduces the quantity demanded from 1050 to 950. That's only a 10% decline, so in this case the price elasticity of demand is 10%/20% = 0.5.

Panel (c) shows a case of elastic demand when the toll is raised from $0.90 to $1.10. The 20% price increase causes the quantity demanded to fall from 1200 to 800—a 40% decline, so the price elasticity of demand is 40%/20% = 2.

Why does it matter whether demand is unit-elastic, inelastic, or elastic? Because this classification predicts how changes in the price of a good will affect the *total revenue* earned by producers from the sale of that good. In many real-life situations, such as the one faced by GlaxoSmithKline, it is crucial to know how price changes affect total revenue. **Total revenue** is defined as the total value of sales of a good or service, equal to the price multiplied by the quantity sold:

(6-6) Total revenue = Price × Quantity sold

Total revenue has a useful graphical representation that can help us understand why knowing the price elasticity of demand is crucial when we ask whether a price rise will increase or reduce total revenue. Panel (a) of Figure 6-4 shows the same demand curve as panel (a) of Figure 6-3. We see that 1100 drivers will use the bridge if the toll is $0.90. So the total revenue at a price of $0.90 is $0.90 × 1100 = $990.

---

[2]Using the midpoint method, the price elasticity of demand $= \dfrac{\dfrac{900 - 1000}{(900 + 1100)/2} \times 100}{\dfrac{\$1.10 - \$0.90}{(\$0.90 + \$1.10)/2} \times 100} = \dfrac{20\%}{20\%} = 1$

The **total revenue** is the total value of sales of a good or service. It is equal to the price multiplied by the quantity sold.

FIGURE **6-3** Unit-Elastic Demand, Inelastic Demand, and Elastic Demand

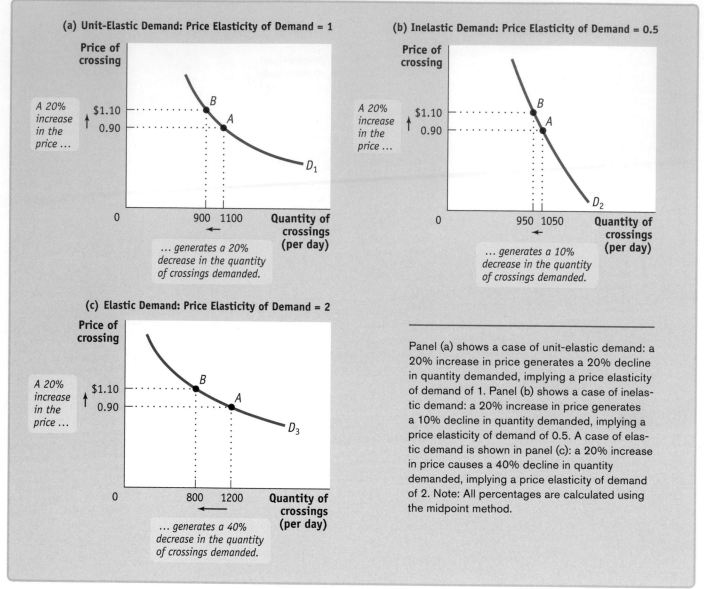

(a) Unit-Elastic Demand: Price Elasticity of Demand = 1

A 20% increase in the price ...

... generates a 20% decrease in the quantity of crossings demanded.

(b) Inelastic Demand: Price Elasticity of Demand = 0.5

A 20% increase in the price ...

... generates a 10% decrease in the quantity of crossings demanded.

(c) Elastic Demand: Price Elasticity of Demand = 2

A 20% increase in the price ...

... generates a 40% decrease in the quantity of crossings demanded.

Panel (a) shows a case of unit-elastic demand: a 20% increase in price generates a 20% decline in quantity demanded, implying a price elasticity of demand of 1. Panel (b) shows a case of inelastic demand: a 20% increase in price generates a 10% decline in quantity demanded, implying a price elasticity of demand of 0.5. A case of elastic demand is shown in panel (c): a 20% increase in price causes a 40% decline in quantity demanded, implying a price elasticity of demand of 2. Note: All percentages are calculated using the midpoint method.

This value is equal to the area of the green rectangle, which is drawn with the bottom left corner at the point (0, 0) and the top right corner at (1100, 0.90). In general, the total revenue at any given price is equal to the area of a rectangle whose height is the price and whose width is the quantity demanded at that price.

To get an idea of why total revenue is important, consider the following scenario. Suppose that the toll on the bridge is currently $0.90 but that the ministry of transportation must raise extra money for road repairs. One way to do this is to raise the toll on the bridge. But this plan might backfire, since a higher toll will reduce the number of drivers who use the bridge. And if traffic on the bridge dropped a lot, a higher toll would actually reduce total revenue instead of increasing it. So it's important for the ministry of transportation to know how drivers will respond to a toll increase.

We can see graphically how the toll increase affects total bridge revenue by examining panel (b) of Figure 6-4. At a toll of $0.90, total revenue is given by the sum of the areas *A* and *B*. After the toll is raised to $1.10, total revenue is given by the sum of areas *B* and *C*. So when the toll is raised, revenue represented by area *A* is lost but revenue represented by area *C* is gained.

FIGURE **6-4** Total Revenue

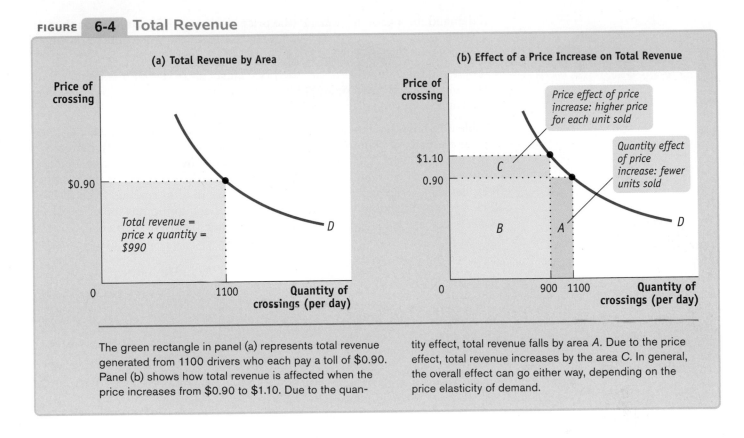

(a) Total Revenue by Area

(b) Effect of a Price Increase on Total Revenue

The green rectangle in panel (a) represents total revenue generated from 1100 drivers who each pay a toll of $0.90. Panel (b) shows how total revenue is affected when the price increases from $0.90 to $1.10. Due to the quan-

tity effect, total revenue falls by area *A*. Due to the price effect, total revenue increases by the area *C*. In general, the overall effect can go either way, depending on the price elasticity of demand.

These two areas have important interpretations. Area *C* represents the revenue gain that comes from the additional $0.20 paid by drivers who continue to use the bridge. That is, the 900 who continue to use the bridge contribute an additional $0.20 × 900 = $180 per day to total revenue, represented by area *C*. But 200 drivers who would have used the bridge at a price of $0.90 no longer do so, generating a loss to total revenue of $0.90 × 200 = $180 per day, represented by area *A*. (In this particular example, because demand is unit-elastic—the same as in panel (a) of Figure 6-3—the rise in the toll has no effect on total revenue; areas *A* and *C* are the same size.)

Except in the rare case of a good with perfectly elastic or perfectly inelastic demand, when a seller raises the price of a good, two countervailing effects are present:

- *A price effect:* After a price increase, each unit sold sells at a higher price, which tends to raise revenue.

- *A quantity effect:* After a price increase, fewer units are sold, which tends to lower revenue.

But then, you may ask, what is the ultimate net effect on total revenue: does it go up or down? The answer is that, in general, the effect on total revenue can go either way—a price rise may either increase total revenue or lower it. If the price effect, which tends to raise total revenue, is the stronger of the two effects, then total revenue goes up. If the quantity effect, which tends to reduce total revenue, is the stronger, then total revenue goes down. And if the strengths of the two effects are exactly equal—as in our toll bridge example, where a $180 gain offsets a $180 loss—total revenue is unchanged by the price increase.

The price elasticity of demand tells us what happens to total revenue when price changes: its size determines which effect—the price effect or the quantity effect—is stronger. Specifically:

- If demand for a good is *unit-elastic* (the price elasticity of demand is 1), an increase in price does not change total revenue. In this case, the quantity effect and the price effect exactly offset each other.

- If demand for a good is *inelastic* (the price elasticity of demand is less than 1), a higher price increases total revenue. In this case, the price effect is stronger than the quantity effect.
- If demand for a good is *elastic* (the price elasticity of demand is greater than 1), an increase in price reduces total revenue. In this case, the quantity effect is stronger than the price effect.

Table 6-2 shows how the effect of a price increase on total revenue depends on the price elasticity of demand, using the same data as in Figure 6-3. An increase in the price from $0.90 to $1.10 leaves total revenue unchanged at $990 when demand is unit-elastic. When demand is inelastic, the price effect dominates the quantity effect; the same price increase leads to an increase in total revenue from $945 to $1045. And when demand is elastic, the quantity effect dominates the price effect; the price increase leads to a decline in total revenue from $1080 to $880.

TABLE 6-2 Price Elasticity of Demand and Total Revenue

	Price of crossing = $0.90	Price of crossing = $1.10
Unit-elastic demand (price elasticity of demand = 1)		
Quantity demanded	1100	900
Total revenue	$990	$990
Inelastic demand (price elasticity of demand = 0.5)		
Quantity demanded	1050	950
Total revenue	$945	$1045
Elastic demand (price elasticity of demand = 2)		
Quantity demanded	1200	800
Total revenue	$1080	$880

The price elasticity of demand also predicts the effect of a *fall* in price on total revenue. When the price falls, the same two countervailing effects are present, but they work in the opposite directions as compared to the case of a price rise. There is the price effect of a lower price per unit sold, which tends to lower revenue. This is countered by the quantity effect of more units sold, which tends to raise revenue. Which effect dominates depends on the price elasticity. Here is a quick summary:

- When demand is *unit-elastic,* the two effects exactly balance; so a fall in price has no effect on total revenue.
- When demand is *inelastic,* the price effect dominates the quantity effect; so a fall in price reduces total revenue.
- When demand is *elastic,* the quantity effect dominates the price effect; so a fall in price increases total revenue.

Price Elasticity Along the Demand Curve

Suppose an economist says that "the price elasticity of demand for coffee is 0.25." What he or she means is that *at the current price* the elasticity is 0.25. In the previous discussion of the toll bridge, what we were really describing was the elasticity *at the price* of $0.90. Why this qualification? Because for the vast majority of demand curves, the price elasticity of demand at one point along the curve is different from the price elasticity of demand at other points along the same curve.

To see this, consider the table in Figure 6-5, which shows a hypothetical demand schedule. It also shows in the last column the total revenue generated at each price and quantity combination in the demand schedule. The upper panel of the graph in Figure 6-5 shows the corresponding demand curve. The lower panel illustrates the same data on total revenue: the height of a bar at each quantity demanded—which corresponds to a particular price—measures the total revenue generated at that price.

In Figure 6-5, you can see that when the price is low, raising the price increases total revenue: starting at a price of $1, raising the price to $2 increases total revenue from $9 to $16. This means that when the price is low, demand is inelastic. Moreover, you can see that demand is inelastic on the entire section of the demand curve from a price of $0 to a price of $5.

When the price is high, however, raising it further reduces total revenue: starting at a price of $8, raising the price to $9 reduces total revenue, from $16 to $9. This means that when the price is high, demand is elastic. Furthermore, you can see that demand is elastic over the section of the demand curve from a price of $5 to $10.

For the vast majority of goods, the price elasticity of demand changes along the demand curve. So whenever you measure a good's elasticity, you are really measuring it at a *particular point or section* of the good's demand curve.

FIGURE 6-5 The Price Elasticity of Demand Changes Along the Demand Curve

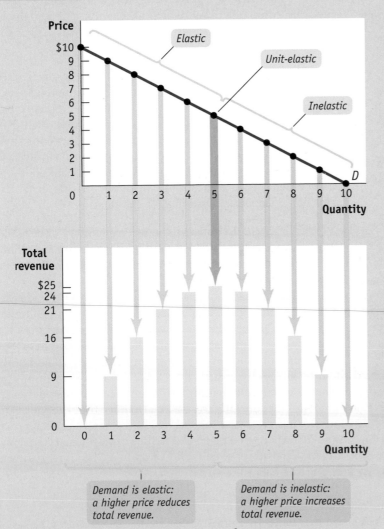

Demand Schedule and Total Revenue for a Linear Demand Curve		
Price	Quantity demanded	Total revenue
$0	10	$0
1	9	9
2	8	16
3	7	21
4	6	24
5	5	25
6	4	24
7	3	21
8	2	16
9	1	9
10	0	0

The upper panel shows a demand curve corresponding to the demand schedule in the table. The lower panel shows how total revenue changes along that demand curve: at each price and quantity combination, the height of the bar represents the total revenue generated. You can see that at a low price, raising the price increases total revenue. So demand is inelastic at low prices. At a high price, however, a rise in price reduces total revenue. So demand is elastic at high prices.

What Factors Determine the Price Elasticity of Demand?

During a shortage of flu vaccines, vaccine distributors could significantly raise their prices for two important reasons: substitutes are very difficult to obtain, and the vaccine is seen as a medical necessity.

People are left with a few options. Some will pay high prices to become patients of the expensive private clinics that have access to the vaccine, and some will travel long distances to wait in lines for the chance to get vaccinated. Others will simply do without (and over time may change their habits to avoid catching the flu, such as eating out less often and avoiding mass transit). This illustrates the four main factors that determine elasticity: the availability of close substitutes, whether the good is a necessity or a luxury, the share of income a consumer spends on the good, and how much time has elapsed since the price change. We'll briefly examine each of these factors.

The Availability of Close Substitutes The price elasticity of demand tends to be high (or elastic) if there are other readily available goods that consumers regard as similar and would be willing to consume instead. The price elasticity of demand tends to be low (or inelastic) if there are no close substitutes or they are very difficult to obtain.

"Three hundred dollars' of regular."

David Sipress/The New Yorker Collection/www.cartoonbank.com

Whether the Good Is a Necessity or a Luxury The price elasticity of demand tends to be low (or inelastic) if a good is something you must have, like a life-saving medicine. The price elasticity of demand tends to be high (or elastic) if the good is a luxury—something you can easily live without.

Share of Income Spent on the Good The price elasticity of demand tends to be low (or inelastic) when spending on a good accounts for a small share of a consumer's income. In that case, a significant change in the price of the good has little impact on how much the consumer spends. In contrast, when a good accounts for a significant share of a consumer's spending, the consumer is likely to be very responsive to a change in price. In this case, the price elasticity of demand is high (or elastic).

Time Elapsed Since Price Change In general, the price elasticity of demand tends to increase (or become more elastic) as consumers have more time to adjust to a price change. This means that the long-run price elasticity of demand is often higher (or more elastic) than the short-run elasticity.

A good illustration of the effect of time on the elasticity of demand is drawn from the 1970s, the first time gasoline prices increased dramatically in Canada. Initially, consumption fell very little because there were no close substitutes for gasoline and because driving their cars was necessary for people to carry out the ordinary tasks of life. Over time, however, Canadians changed their habits in ways that enabled them to gradually reduce their gasoline consumption. The result was a steady decline in gasoline consumption over the next decade, even though the price of gasoline did not continue to rise, confirming that the long-run price elasticity of demand for gasoline was indeed much greater than the short-run elasticity. According to a study on the price elasticities of gasoline from 1960 to 1980, the price elasticity of demand for gasoline in Canada in the short run was 0.25, while in the long run it was 1.07.[3]

---

[3]*Source:* Daniel J. Graham and Stephen Glaister, "The Demand for Automobile Fuel: a Survey of Elasticities," *Journal of Transport Economics and Policy* 36, no. 1 (2007): 1-25.

ECONOMICS ▶ IN ACTION

FLIGHT FLEXIBILITY

It is a well-known fact that airfares between any pair of destinations and the responsiveness of demand to changes in airfares vary significantly. Do they depend on the nature of air travel and the travel distance? Not surprisingly, the answer is yes.

In 2008, the Department of Finance Canada released a summary report on the empirical studies of the price elasticities of demand for air travel in Canada and other major countries. The report found that the price elasticity of air travel varies by the nature of the travel (business or leisure) and the travel distance (short-haul or long-haul). The report summarized the range and median price elasticities of demand for air travel for 6 distinct markets based on 21 Canadian and international studies. The results of the report are summarized in the table.

	Business travel	Leisure travel
Long-haul international	0.265	1.04
Long-haul domestic	1.15	1.104
Short-haul	0.7	1.520

You probably noticed that the demand for long-haul international flights is more inelastic compared to domestic flights. What causes these differences? Basically, they are driven by the availability of close substitutes. Long-haul international flights are more inelastic for both groups of travellers because of the lack of close substitutes. If you are going abroad, from Toronto to Beijing for example, your travel options are rather limited. With time constraints, travel by air is likely to be the only option; thus, you are less responsive to changes in airfares (prices). The same applies to long-haul domestic flight for both business and leisure travel. The flight may take several hours, but the same trip will take days by car or train. There are better options for short-haul international travel than for long-haul as travellers can reach their destinations by cars, trains, and planes within a reasonable time frame. For example, you can drive from Vancouver to Seattle in roughly the same amount of time as flying.

The report also shows that the demand for air travel for business travel tends to be more inelastic than for leisure travel. For business people, the travel is usually a necessity, so they will be less responsive to a change in airfares. On the other hand, air travel can be a luxury for some vacationers, so they are more responsive to price changes (as they can easily change their vacation destinations). For example, if airfares rise significantly, vacationers have the option to spend their vacation at home or at much closer attractions.

Both these reasons help explain why business people tend to pay more, sometimes a lot more, for what is largely the same service. (Source note on copyright page.)

▶●●

CHECK YOUR UNDERSTANDING 6-2

1. For each case, choose the condition that characterizes demand: elastic demand, inelastic demand, or unit-elastic demand.
   a. Total revenue decreases when price increases.
   b. The additional revenue generated by an increase in quantity sold is exactly offset by revenue lost from the fall in price received per unit.
   c. Total revenue falls when output increases.
   d. Producers in an industry find they can increase their total revenues by coordinating a reduction in industry output.

▼ **Quick Review**

- Demand is **perfectly inelastic** if it is completely unresponsive to price. It is **perfectly elastic** if it is infinitely responsive to price.

- Demand is **elastic** if the price elasticity of demand is greater than 1. It is **inelastic** if the price elasticity of demand is less than 1. It is **unit-elastic** if the price elasticity of demand is exactly 1.

- When demand is elastic, the quantity effect of a price increase dominates the price effect and **total revenue** falls. When demand is inelastic, the price effect of a price increase dominates the quantity effect and total revenue rises.

- Because the price elasticity of demand can change along the demand curve, economists refer to a particular point on the demand curve when speaking of "the" price elasticity of demand.

- Ready availability of close substitutes makes demand for a good more elastic, as does the length of time elapsed since the price change. Demand for a necessity is less elastic, and demand for a luxury good is more elastic. Demand tends to be inelastic for goods that absorb a small share of a consumer's income and elastic for goods that absorb a large share of income.

2. For the following goods, what is the elasticity of demand? Explain. What is the shape of the demand curve?

a. Demand for a blood transfusion by an accident victim

b. Demand by students for green erasers

Solutions appear at back of book.

Other Demand Elasticities

The quantity of a good demanded depends not only on the price of that good but also on other variables. In particular, demand curves shift because of changes in the prices of related goods and changes in consumers' incomes. It is often important to have a measure of these other effects, and the best measures are—you guessed it—elasticities. Specifically, we can best measure how the demand for a good is affected by prices of other goods using a measure called the *cross-price elasticity of demand,* and we can best measure how demand is affected by changes in income using the *income elasticity of demand.*

The Cross-Price Elasticity of Demand

In Chapter 3 you learned that the demand for a good is often affected by the prices of other, related goods—goods that are substitutes or complements. There you saw that a change in the price of a related good shifts the demand curve of the original good, reflecting a change in the quantity demanded at any given price. The strength of such a "cross" effect on demand can be measured by the **cross-price elasticity of demand,** defined as the ratio of the percentage change in the quantity demanded of one good to the percentage change in the price of the other:

(6-7) Cross-price elasticity of demand between goods A and B

$$= \frac{\% \text{ change in quantity of A demanded}}{\% \text{ change in price of B}}$$

When two goods are substitutes, like hot dogs and hamburgers, the cross-price elasticity of demand is positive: a rise in the price of hot dogs increases the demand for hamburgers—that is, it causes a rightward shift of the demand curve for hamburgers. If the goods are close substitutes, the cross-price elasticity will be positive and large; if they are not close substitutes, the cross-price elasticity will be positive and small. So when the cross-price elasticity of demand is positive, its size is a measure of how closely substitutable the two goods are.

When two goods are complements, like hot dogs and hot dog buns, the cross-price elasticity is negative: a rise in the price of hot dogs decreases the demand for hot dog buns—that is, it causes a leftward shift of the demand curve for hot dog buns. As with substitutes, the size of the cross-price elasticity of demand between two complements tells us how strongly complementary they are: if the cross-price elasticity is only slightly below zero, they are weak complements; if it is very negative, they are strong complements.

Note that in the case of the cross-price elasticity of demand, the sign (plus or minus) is very important: it tells us whether the two goods are complements or substitutes. So we cannot drop the minus sign as we did for the price elasticity of demand.

Our discussion of the cross-price elasticity of demand is a useful place to return to a point we made earlier: elasticity is a *unit-free* measure—that is, it doesn't depend on the units in which goods are measured.

To see the potential problem, suppose someone told you that "if the price of hot dog buns rises by $0.30, Canadians will buy 1 million fewer hot dogs this year." If you've ever bought hot dog buns, you'll immediately wonder: is that a $0.30 increase in the price *per bun,* or is it a $0.30 increase in the price *per package of eight?* It makes a big difference what units we are talking about! However,

> The **cross-price elasticity of demand** between two goods measures the effect of the change in one good's price on the quantity demanded of the other good. It is equal to the percentage change in the quantity demanded of one good divided by the percentage change in the other good's price.

if someone says that the cross-price elasticity of demand between buns and hot dogs is −0.3, it doesn't matter whether buns are sold individually or by the package. So elasticity is defined as a ratio of percentage changes, as a way of making sure that confusion over units doesn't arise.

The Income Elasticity of Demand

The **income elasticity of demand** is a measure of how much the demand for a good is affected by changes in consumers' incomes. It allows us to determine whether a good is a normal or inferior good as well as to measure how intensely the demand for the good responds to changes in income:

$$\textbf{(6-8)} \text{ Income elasticity of demand} = \frac{\% \text{ change in quantity demanded}}{\% \text{ change in income}}$$

Just as the cross-price elasticity of demand between two goods can be either positive or negative, depending on whether the goods are substitutes or complements, the income elasticity of demand for a good can also be either positive or negative. Recall from Chapter 3 that goods can be either *normal goods,* for which demand increases when income rises, or *inferior goods,* for which demand decreases when income rises. These definitions relate directly to the sign of the income elasticity of demand:

- When the income elasticity of demand is positive, the good is a normal good. In this case, the quantity demanded at any given price increases as income increases.

- When the income elasticity of demand is negative, the good is an inferior good. In this case, the quantity demanded at any given price decreases as income increases.

Economists often use estimates of the income elasticity of demand to predict which industries will grow most rapidly as the incomes of consumers grow over time. In doing this, they often find it useful to make a further distinction among normal goods, identifying which are *income-elastic* and which are *income-inelastic.*

> The **income elasticity of demand** is the percentage change in the quantity of a good demanded when a consumer's income changes divided by the percentage change in the consumer's income.

FOR INQUIRING MINDS

WILL CHINA SAVE THE CANADIAN FARMING SECTOR?

In the early days of this country, the great majority of Canadians lived on farms. However, over the last hundred years the percentage of our population living on farms has plunged. According to the 2011 Census of Agriculture, the farm population had declined to about 2.2% of the total population. Why do so few people now live and work on farms in Canada? There are two main reasons, both involving elasticities.

First, the income elasticity of demand for food is much less than 1—it is income-inelastic. As consumers grow richer, other things equal, spending on food rises less than income. As a result, as the Canadian economy has grown, the share of income spent on food—and therefore the share of total Canadian

income earned by farmers—has fallen.

Second, the demand for food is price inelastic. This is important because technological advances in Canadian agriculture have steadily raised yields over time and led to a long-term trend of lower Canadian food prices for most of the past century and a half. The combination of price inelasticity and falling prices led to falling total revenue for farmers. That's right: progress in farming has been good for Canadian consumers but bad for Canadian farmers.

The combination of these effects explains the long-term relative decline of farming in Canada. The low income elasticity of demand for food ensures that the income of farmers grows more slowly than the economy as a whole. And the combi-

nation of rapid technological progress in farming with price-inelastic demand for foodstuffs reinforces this effect, further reducing the growth of farm income.

That is, up until now. Starting in the mid-2000s, increased demand for foodstuffs from rapidly growing developing countries like China has pushed up the prices of agricultural products around the world. And Canadian farmers have benefitted; the net operating income of farmers increased by 22% from 2010 to 2011. Eventually, as the growth in developing countries tapers off and agricultural innovation continues to progress, it's likely that the agricultural sector will resume its downward trend. But for now and for the foreseeable future, Canadian farmers are enjoying the sector's revival.

FOOD'S BITE IN WORLD BUDGETS

In 2011, the United States Department of Agriculture (USDA) released a report on the food consumption patterns for 114 countries. In the report, the USDA estimated the income elasticities for food eaten at home for these 114 countries. The estimates ranged from 0.346 (in the United States) to 0.854 (in the Democratic Republic of Congo). In Canada, the income elasticity of food was 0.477. These results indicate that food is income-inelastic, even for low-income countries. If this were the case, we would expect to find that people in low-income countries spend a larger share of their income on food than people in rich countries do. Does the data agree with this prediction? The answer is yes. In this graph, we show the share of income that is spent on food for selected countries. In low-income countries such as Pakistan and Kenya, people spend a large fraction of their income on food. In middle-income countries such as Mexico and South Africa, the share of spending that goes to food is much lower. And, it's even lower in high-income countries like Canada and the United States.

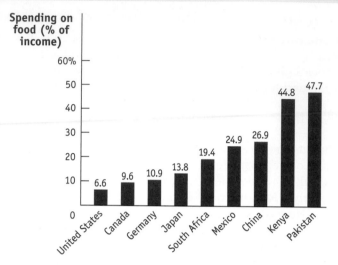

Source: The U.S. Department of Agriculture.

Source: Andrew Muhammad, James L. Seale, Jr., Birgit Meade, and Anita Regmi, "International Evidence on Food Consumption Patterns: An Update Using 2005 International Comparison Program Data," United States Department of Agriculture Technical Bulletin No. 1929 (March 2011).

The demand for a good is **income-elastic** if the income elasticity of demand for that good is greater than 1.

The demand for a good is **income-inelastic** if the income elasticity of demand for that good is positive but less than 1.

The demand for a good is **income-elastic** if the income elasticity of demand for that good is greater than 1. When income rises, the demand for income-elastic goods rises *faster* than income. Luxury goods such as second homes and international travel tend to be income-elastic. The demand for a good is **income-inelastic** if the income elasticity of demand for that good is positive but less than 1. When income rises, the demand for income-inelastic goods rises, but more slowly than income. Necessities such as food and clothing tend to be income-inelastic.

ECONOMICS ▸ *IN ACTION*

SPENDING IT

Statistics Canada carries out extensive surveys of how families spend their incomes. This is not just a matter of intellectual curiosity. Quite a few government benefit programs involve some adjustment for changes in the cost of living; to estimate those changes, the government must know how people spend their money. But an additional payoff to these surveys is data on the income elasticity of demand for various goods.

What stands out from these studies? As expected, the income elasticity of demand for "food eaten at home" is considerably less than 1: as a family's income rises, the share of its income spent on food consumed at home falls, which is consistent with *Engel's law*. (Ernst Engel, a German statistician and economist, observed that, all other things equal, a household's spending on food as a percentage of income falls as income increases.) Correspondingly, the lower a family's income, the higher the share of income spent on food consumed at home.

In poor countries, many families spend more than half their income on food consumed at home. Although the income elasticity of demand for "food eaten at home" is estimated at less than 0.5 in Canada, the income elasticity of demand for restaurant meals ("food eaten away from home") is estimated to be much higher. Using data from the Survey of Household Spending (SHS) and Survey of Employment, Payrolls and Hours (SEPH), from 2010 to 2011, the income elasticities of food eaten away from home for employees paid hourly and for salaried employees are estimated to be 0.92 and 1.82, respectively—much higher than the income elasticity of food eaten at home.

Families with higher incomes eat out more often and at fancier places. In 1981, about 14% of Canadian income was spent on food consumed at home, a number that has dropped to about 9% in 2011. But over the same time period, the share of Canadian income spent on food consumed away from home has stayed constant at 5%. In fact, a sure sign of rising income levels in developing countries is the arrival of fast-food restaurants that cater to newly affluent customers. For example, McDonald's can now be found in Jakarta, Shanghai, and Mumbai.

There is one clear example of an inferior good found in the surveys: rental housing. Families with higher income actually spend a smaller fraction of their income on rent than families with lower income, because they are much more likely to own their own homes. And the category identified as "other housing"—which basically means second homes—is highly income-elastic. Only higher-income families can afford a luxury like a vacation home, so "other housing" has an income elasticity of demand greater than 1.

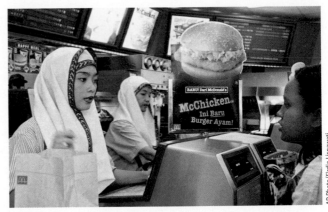

Judging from the activity at this busy McDonald's, incomes are rising in Jakarta, Indonesia.

CHECK YOUR UNDERSTANDING 6-3

1. After Chelsea's income increased from $12 000 to $18 000 a year, her purchases of CDs increased from 10 to 40 CDs a year. Calculate Chelsea's income elasticity of demand for CDs using the midpoint method.

2. Expensive restaurant meals are income-elastic goods for most people, including Sanjay. Suppose his income falls by 10% this year. What can you predict about the change in Sanjay's consumption of expensive restaurant meals?

3. As the price of margarine rises by 20%, a manufacturer of baked goods increases its quantity of butter demanded by 5%. Calculate the cross-price elasticity of demand between butter and margarine. Are butter and margarine substitutes or complements for this manufacturer?

Solutions appear at back of book.

▼ Quick Review

- Goods are substitutes when the **cross-price elasticity of demand** is positive. Goods are complements when the cross-price elasticity of demand is negative.

- Inferior goods have a negative **income elasticity of demand.** Most goods are normal goods, which have a positive income elasticity of demand.

- Normal goods may be either **income-elastic,** with an income elasticity of demand greater than 1, or **income-inelastic,** with an income elasticity of demand that is positive but less than 1.

The Price Elasticity of Supply

In the wake of a flu vaccine shortfall, attempts by vaccine distributors to drive up the price of vaccines would have been much less effective if the higher price had induced a large increase in the output of flu vaccines by other manufacturers. In fact, if a rise in price precipitated a significant increase in flu vaccine production, the price would be pushed back down. But that wouldn't happen because, as we mentioned earlier, it is far too costly and technically difficult to produce more vaccine for the flu season in a short period of time. (In reality, the production of flu vaccine begins a year before distribution.)

The **price elasticity of supply** is a measure of the responsiveness of the quantity of a good supplied to the price of that good. It is the ratio of the percentage change in the quantity supplied to the percentage change in the price as we move along the supply curve.

This is another critical element in the ability of some flu vaccine distributors, like our hypothetical company Flunomics, to get significantly higher prices by restricting supply of their product: a low responsiveness in the quantity of output supplied to the higher price of flu vaccine by flu vaccine producers. To measure the response of producers to price changes, we need a measure parallel to the price elasticity of demand—the *price elasticity of supply*.

Measuring the Price Elasticity of Supply

The **price elasticity of supply** is defined the same way as the price elasticity of demand (although there is no minus sign to be eliminated here):

(6-9) Price elasticity of supply $= \dfrac{\% \text{ change in quantity supplied}}{\% \text{ change in price}}$

The only difference is that here we consider movements along the supply curve rather than movements along the demand curve.

Suppose that the price of tomatoes rises by 10%. If the quantity of tomatoes supplied also increases by 10% in response, the price elasticity of supply of tomatoes is 1 (10%/10%) and supply is unit-elastic. If the quantity supplied increases by 5%, the price elasticity of supply is 0.5 and supply is inelastic; if the quantity increases by 20%, the price elasticity of supply is 2 and supply is elastic.

As in the case of demand, the extreme values of the price elasticity of supply have a simple graphical representation. Panel (a) of Figure 6-6 shows the supply of cellphone frequencies, the portion of the radio spectrum that is suitable for sending and receiving cellphone signals. Governments own the right to sell the use of this part of the radio spectrum to cellphone operators inside their borders. But governments can't increase or decrease the number of cellphone frequencies

FIGURE **6-6** **Two Extreme Cases of Price Elasticity of Supply**

Panel (a) shows a perfectly inelastic supply curve, which is a vertical line. The price elasticity of supply is zero: the quantity supplied is always the same, regardless of price. Panel (b) shows a perfectly elastic supply curve, which is a horizontal line. At a price of $12, producers will supply any quantity, but they will supply none at a price below $12. If the price rises above $12, they will supply an extremely large quantity.

that they have to offer—for technical reasons, the quantity of frequencies suitable for cellphone operation is a fixed quantity.

So the supply curve for cellphone frequencies is a vertical line, which we have assumed is set at the quantity of 100 frequencies. As you move up and down that curve, the change in the quantity supplied by the government is zero, whatever the change in price. So panel (a) illustrates a case in which the price elasticity of supply is zero. This is a case of **perfectly inelastic supply.**

Panel (b) shows the supply curve for pizza. We suppose that it costs $12 to produce a pizza, including all opportunity costs. At any price below $12, it would be unprofitable to produce pizza and all the pizza parlours in Canada would go out of business. Alternatively, there are many producers who could operate pizza parlours if they were profitable. The ingredients—flour, tomatoes, cheese—are plentiful. And if necessary, more tomatoes could be grown, more milk could be produced to make mozzarella, and so on. So any price above $12 would elicit an extremely large quantity of pizzas supplied. The implied supply curve is therefore a horizontal line at $12.

Since even a tiny increase in the price would lead to a huge increase in the quantity supplied, the price elasticity of supply would be more or less infinite. This is a case of **perfectly elastic supply.**

As our cellphone frequencies and pizza examples suggest, real-world instances of both perfectly inelastic and perfectly elastic supply are easy to find—much easier than their counterparts in demand.

What Factors Determine the Price Elasticity of Supply?

Our examples tell us the main determinant of the price elasticity of supply: the availability of inputs. In addition, as with the price elasticity of demand, time may also play a role in the price elasticity of supply. Here we briefly summarize the two factors.

The Availability of Inputs The price elasticity of supply tends to be large when inputs are readily available and can be shifted into and out of production at a relatively low cost. It tends to be small when inputs are difficult to obtain—and can be shifted into and out of production only at a relatively high cost.

Time The price elasticity of supply tends to grow larger as producers have more time to respond to a price change. This means that the long-run price elasticity of supply is often higher than the short-run elasticity. (In the case of a flu vaccine shortfall, time is the crucial element because flu vaccine must be grown in cultures over many months.)

The price elasticity of pizza supply is very high because the inputs needed to expand the industry are readily available. The price elasticity of cellphone frequencies is zero because an essential input—the radio spectrum—cannot be increased at all.

Many industries are like pizza production and have large price elasticities of supply: they can be readily expanded because they don't require any special or unique resources. In contrast, the price elasticity of supply is usually substantially less than perfectly elastic for goods that involve limited natural resources: minerals like gold or copper, agricultural products like coffee that flourish only on certain types of land, and renewable resources like ocean fish that can only be exploited up to a point without destroying the resource.

But given enough time, producers are often able to significantly change the amount they produce in response to a price change, even when production involves a limited natural resource. For example, consider again the effects of a surge in flu vaccine prices, but this time focus on the supply response. If the price were to rise to $90 per vaccination and stay there for a number of years,

There is **perfectly inelastic supply** when the price elasticity of supply is zero, so that changes in the price of the good have no effect on the quantity supplied. A perfectly inelastic supply curve is a vertical line.

There is **perfectly elastic supply** when even a tiny increase or reduction in the price will lead to very large changes in the quantity supplied, so that the price elasticity of supply is infinite. A perfectly elastic supply curve is a horizontal line.

there would almost certainly be a substantial increase in flu vaccine production. Producers such as GlaxoSmithKline would eventually respond by increasing the size of their manufacturing plants, hiring more lab technicians, and so on. But significantly enlarging the capacity of a biotech manufacturing lab takes several years, not weeks or months or even a single year.

For this reason, economists often make a distinction between the short-run elasticity of supply, usually referring to a few weeks or months, and the long-run elasticity of supply, usually referring to several years. In most industries, the long-run elasticity of supply is larger than the short-run elasticity.

ECONOMICS > IN ACTION

EUROPEAN FARM SURPLUSES

One of the policies we analyzed in Chapter 5 was the imposition of a *price floor*, a lower limit below which price of a good could not fall. We saw that price floors are often used by governments to support the incomes of farmers but create large unwanted surpluses of farm products. The most dramatic example of this is found in the European Union, where price floors have created a "butter mountain," a "wine lake," and so on.

Were European politicians unaware that their price floors would create huge surpluses? They probably knew that surpluses would arise but underestimated the price elasticity of agricultural supply. In fact, when the agricultural price supports were put in place, many analysts thought they were unlikely to lead to big increases in production. After all, European countries are densely populated and there is little new land available for cultivation.

What the analysts failed to realize, however, was how much farm production could expand by adding other resources, especially fertilizer and pesticides, which were readily available. So although European farm acreage didn't increase much in response to the imposition of price floors, European farm production did!

CHECK YOUR UNDERSTANDING   6-4

1. Using the midpoint method, calculate the price elasticity of supply for web-design services when the price per hour rises from $100 to $150 and the number of hours transacted increases from 300 000 to 500 000. Is supply elastic, inelastic, or unit-elastic?

2. True or false? If the demand for milk rose, then, in the long run, milk drinkers would be better off if supply were elastic rather than inelastic.

3. True or false? Long-run price elasticities of supply are generally larger than short-run price elasticities of supply. As a result, the short-run supply curves are generally flatter than the long-run supply curves.

4. True or false? When supply is perfectly elastic, changes in demand have no effect on price.

Solutions appear at back of book.

An Elasticity Menagerie

We've just run through quite a few different elasticities. Keeping them all straight can be a challenge. So in Table 6-3 we provide a summary of all the elasticities we have discussed and their implications. Appendix 6A covers the use of algebra to compute different types of elasticities in greater detail.

TABLE **6-3**   An Elasticity Menagerie

Price elasticity of demand = $\dfrac{\text{\% change in quantity demanded}}{\text{\% change in price}}$ (dropping the minus sign)	
0	**Perfectly inelastic:** price has no effect on quantity demanded (vertical demand curve).
Between 0 and 1	**Inelastic:** a rise in price increases total revenue.
Exactly 1	**Unit-elastic:** changes in price have no effect on total revenue.
Greater than 1, less than ∞	**Elastic:** a rise in price reduces total revenue.
∞	**Perfectly elastic:** any rise in price causes quantity demanded to fall to 0. Any fall in price leads to an infinite quantity demanded (horizontal demand curve).
Cross-price elasticity of demand = $\dfrac{\text{\% change in quantity } \textit{of one good } \text{demanded}}{\text{\% change in price } \textit{of another good}}$	
Negative	**Complements:** quantity demanded of one good falls when the price of another rises.
Positive	**Substitutes:** quantity demanded of one good rises when the price of another rises.
Income elasticity of demand = $\dfrac{\text{\% change in quantity demanded}}{\text{\% change in income}}$	
Negative	**Inferior good:** quantity demanded falls when income rises.
Positive, less than 1	**Normal good, income-inelastic:** quantity demanded rises when income rises, but not as rapidly as income.
Greater than 1	**Normal good, income-elastic:** quantity demanded rises when income rises, and more rapidly than income.
Price elasticity of supply = $\dfrac{\text{\% change in quantity supplied}}{\text{\% change in price}}$	
0	**Perfectly inelastic:** price has no effect on quantity supplied (vertical supply curve).
Greater than 0, less than ∞	ordinary upward-sloping supply curve.
∞	**Perfectly elastic:** any fall in price causes quantity supplied to fall to 0. Any rise in price elicits an infinite quantity supplied (horizontal supply curve).

BUSINESS CASE • The Airline Industry: Fly Less, Charge More

Aaron Harris/Bloomberg via Getty Images

The recession that began in 2008 hit the airline industry very hard as both businesses and households cut back their travel plans. According to the International Air Transport Association, the industry lost more than $10 billion in 2008. However, by 2009, despite the fact that the economy was still extremely weak and airline traffic was still well below normal, the industry's profitability began to rebound. And by 2010, even in the midst of continued economic weakness, the airline industry's prospects had definitely recovered, with the industry achieving a $9 billion profit that year. As Calin Rovinescu, President and CEO of Air Canada, mentioned in the company's 2010 Annual Report, "We made significant progress in 2010 toward the goal of achieving long-term, sustained profitability. Although we benefitted from the general upturn in the global airline industry, our strong performance in 2010 was also due to deliberate actions taken to transform and strengthen the company." His statement was supported by a turnaround in Air Canada's operating income from an operating loss of $316 million in 2009 to an operating income of $278 million in 2010, and the operating income improved to $437 million in 2012.

How did the airline industry achieve such a dramatic turnaround? Simple: fly less and charge more. In 2011, fares were 14% higher than they had been the previous year, and flights were more crowded than they had been in decades.

In addition to cutting back on the number of flights—particularly money losing ones—airlines implemented more extreme variations in ticket prices based on when a flight departed and when the ticket was purchased. For example, the cheapest day to fly is Wednesday, with Friday and Saturday the most expensive days to travel. The first flight of the morning (the one that requires you to get up at 4 A.M.) is cheaper than flights departing the rest of the day. And some claim the cheapest time to buy a ticket is Tuesday at 3 P.M. Eastern Standard Time, with tickets purchased over the weekend carrying the highest prices.

And it doesn't stop there. As every beleaguered traveller knows, airlines have tacked on a wide variety of new fees and increased old ones—fees for food, for a blanket, for headphones, for checked bags, for carry-on bags, for the right to board a flight first, for the right to choose your seat in advance, and so on. Airlines have also gotten more inventive in imposing fees that are hard for travellers to track in advance—such as claiming that fares have not risen during the holidays while imposing a "holiday surcharge." In 2010, airlines collected more than $4.3 billion from fees for checking baggage and changing tickets, up 13.5% from 2009.

But the question in the minds of industry analysts is whether airlines can manage to maintain their currently high levels of profitability. In the past, as travel demand picked up, airlines increased capacity—added seats—too quickly, leading to falling airfares. "The wild card is always capacity discipline," says William Swelbar, an airline industry researcher. "All it takes is one carrier to begin to add capacity aggressively, and then we follow and we undo all the good work that's been done."

QUESTIONS FOR THOUGHT

1. How would you describe the price elasticity of demand for airline flights given the information in this case? Explain.

2. Using the concept of elasticity, explain why airlines would create such great variations in the price of a ticket depending on when it is purchased and the day and time the flight departs. Assume that some people are willing to spend time shopping for deals as well as fly at inconvenient times, but others are not.

3. Using the concept of elasticity, explain why airlines have imposed fees on things such as checked bags. Why might they try to hide or disguise fees?

4. Use an elasticity concept to explain under what conditions the airline industry will be able to maintain its high profitability in the future. Explain.

SUMMARY

1. Many economic questions depend on the size of consumer or producer responses to changes in prices or other variables. *Elasticity* is a general measure of responsiveness that can be used to answer such questions.

2. The **price elasticity of demand**—the percentage change in the quantity demanded divided by the percentage change in the price (given the demand is normally downward slowing, when interpreting the price elasticity of demand, we only look at the absolute value)—is a measure of the responsiveness of the quantity demanded to changes in the price. In practical calculations, it is usually best to use the **midpoint method,** which calculates percentage changes in prices and quantities based on the average of starting and final values.

3. The responsiveness of the quantity demanded to price can range from **perfectly inelastic demand,** where the quantity demanded is unaffected by the price, to **perfectly elastic demand,** where there is a unique price at which consumers will buy as much or as little as they are offered. When demand is perfectly inelastic, the demand curve is a vertical line; when it is perfectly elastic, the demand curve is a horizontal line.

4. The price elasticity of demand is classified according to whether it is more or less than 1. If it is greater than 1, demand is **elastic;** if it is less than 1, demand is **inelastic;** if it is exactly 1, demand is **unit-elastic.** This classification determines how **total revenue,** the total value of sales, changes when the price changes. If demand is elastic, total revenue falls when the price increases and rises when the price decreases. If demand is inelastic, total revenue rises when the price increases and falls when the price decreases.

5. The price elasticity of demand depends on whether there are close substitutes for the good in question, whether the good is a necessity or a luxury, the share of income spent on the good, and the length of time that has elapsed since the price change.

6. The **cross-price elasticity of demand** measures the effect of a change in one good's price on the quantity of another good demanded. The cross-price elasticity of demand can be positive, in which case the goods are substitutes, or negative, in which case they are complements.

7. The **income elasticity of demand** is the percentage change in the quantity of a good demanded when a consumer's income changes divided by the percentage change in income. The income elasticity of demand indicates how intensely the demand for a good responds to changes in income. It can be negative; in that case the good is an inferior good. Goods with positive income elasticities of demand are normal goods. If the income elasticity is greater than 1, a good is **income-elastic;** if it is positive and less than 1, the good is **income-inelastic.**

8. The **price elasticity of supply** is the percentage change in the quantity of a good supplied divided by the percentage change in the price. If the quantity supplied does not change at all, we have an instance of **perfectly inelastic supply;** the supply curve is a vertical line. If the quantity supplied is zero below some price but infinite above that price, we have an instance of **perfectly elastic supply;** the supply curve is a horizontal line.

9. The price elasticity of supply depends on the availability of resources to expand production and on time. It is higher when inputs are available at relatively low cost and the longer the time elapsed since the price change.

KEY TERMS

Price elasticity of demand, p. 170
Midpoint method, p. 172
Perfectly inelastic demand, p. 174
Perfectly elastic demand, p. 174
Elastic demand, p. 174

Inelastic demand, p. 174
Unit-elastic demand, p. 174
Total revenue, p. 175
Cross-price elasticity of demand, p. 182
Income elasticity of demand, p. 183

Income-elastic demand, p. 184
Income-inelastic demand, p. 184
Price elasticity of supply, p. 186
Perfectly inelastic supply, p. 187
Perfectly elastic supply, p. 187

PROBLEMS

1. Nile.ca, the online bookseller, wants to increase its total revenue. One strategy is to offer a 10% discount on every book it sells. Nile.ca knows that its customers can be divided into two distinct groups according to their likely responses to the discount. The accompanying table shows how the two groups respond to the discount.

	Group A (sales per week)	Group B (sales per week)
Volume of sales before the 10% discount	1.55 million	1.50 million
Volume of sales after the 10% discount	1.65 million	1.70 million

a. Using the midpoint method, calculate the price elasticities of demand for group A and group B.

b. Explain how the discount will affect total revenue from each group.

c. Suppose Nile.ca knows which group each customer belongs to when he or she logs in and can choose whether or not to offer the 10% discount. If Nile.ca wants to increase its total revenue, should discounts be offered to group A or to group B, to neither group, or to both groups?

2. Do you think the price elasticity of demand for Ford sport-utility vehicles (SUVs) will increase, decrease, or remain the same when each of the following events occurs? Explain your answer.

a. Other car manufacturers, such as General Motors, decide to make and sell SUVs.

b. SUVs produced in foreign countries are banned from the Canadian market.

c. Due to ad campaigns, Canadians believe that SUVs are much safer than ordinary passenger cars.

d. The time period over which you measure the elasticity lengthens. During that longer time, new models such as four-wheel-drive cargo vans appear.

3. The following table shows the quantity of wheat flour demanded and the average price in Canada between 2011 and 2012.

	2011	2012
Quantity demanded (1000 kg)	2 377 600	2 304 620
Average price (per kg)	$1.98	$2.07

Source: Statistics Canada.

a. Using the midpoint method, calculate the price elasticity of demand for wheat flour.

b. What is the total revenue for Canadian flour suppliers in 2011 and 2012?

c. Did the price change increase or decrease the total revenue of Canadian flour suppliers? How could you have predicted this from your answer to part (a)?

4. The accompanying table gives part of the supply schedule for personal computers in Canada.

Price of computer	Quantity of computers supplied
$1100	12 000
900	8 000

a. Calculate the price elasticity of supply when the price increases from $900 to $1100 using the midpoint method.

b. Suppose firms produce 1000 more computers at any given price due to improved technology. As price increases from $900 to $1100, is the price elasticity of supply now greater than, less than, or the same as it was in part (a)?

c. Suppose a longer time period under consideration means that the quantity supplied at any given price is 20% higher than the figures given in the table. As price increases from $900 to $1100, is the price elasticity of supply now greater than, less than, or the same as it was in part (a)?

5. The accompanying table lists the cross-price elasticities of demand for several goods, where the percentage quantity change is measured for the first good of the pair, and the percentage price change is measured for the second good.

Good	Cross-price elasticities of demand
Air-conditioning units and kilowatts of electricity	−0.34
Coke and Pepsi	+0.63
High-fuel-consuming sport-utility vehicles (SUVs) and gasoline	−0.28
McDonald's burgers and Harvey's burgers	+0.82
Butter and margarine	+1.54

a. Explain the sign of each of the cross-price elasticities. What does it imply about the relationship between the two goods in question?

b. Compare the absolute values of the cross-price elasticities and explain their magnitudes. For example, why is the cross-price elasticity of McDonald's burgers and Harvey's burgers less than the cross-price elasticity of butter and margarine?

c. Use the information in the table to calculate how a 5% increase in the price of Pepsi affects the quantity of Coke demanded.

d. Use the information in the table to calculate how a 10% decrease in the price of gasoline affects the quantity of SUVs demanded.

6. What can you conclude about the price elasticity of demand in each of the following statements?

a. "The pizza delivery business in this town is very competitive. I'd lose half my customers if I raised the price by as little as 10%."

b. "I owned both of the two Jerry Garcia autographed lithographs in existence. I sold one on eBay for a high price. But when I sold the second one, the price dropped by 80%."

c. "My economics professor has chosen to use the Krugman, Wells, Au, and Parkinson textbook for this class. I have no choice but to buy this book."

d. "I always spend a total of exactly $10 per week on coffee."

7. Take a linear demand curve like the one shown in Figure 6-5, where the range of prices for which demand is elastic and inelastic is labelled. In each of the following scenarios, the supply curve shifts. Show along which portion of the demand curve (that is, the elastic or the inelastic portion) the supply curve must

have shifted in order to generate the event described. In each case, show on the diagram the quantity effect and the price effect.

a. Recent attempts by the Mexican army to stop the flow of illegal drugs into Canada have actually benefitted drug dealers.

b. New construction increased the number of seats in the football stadium and resulted in greater total revenue from box-office ticket sales.

c. A fall in input prices has led to higher output of Porsches. But total revenue for the Porsche Company has declined as a result.

8. The accompanying table shows the price and yearly quantity sold of souvenir T-shirts in the town of Saint John according to the average income of the tourists visiting.

Price of T-shirt	Quantity of T-shirts demanded when average tourist income is $20 000	Quantity of T-shirts demanded when average tourist income is $30 000
$4	3000	5000
5	2400	4200
6	1600	3000
7	800	1800

a. Using the midpoint method, calculate the price elasticity of demand when the price of a T-shirt rises from $5 to $6 and the average tourist income is $20 000. Also calculate it when the average tourist income is $30 000.

b. Using the midpoint method, calculate the income elasticity of demand when the price of a T-shirt is $4 and the average tourist income increases from $20 000 to $30 000. Also calculate it when the price is $7.

9. A recent study determined the following elasticities for Volkswagen Beetles:

Price elasticity of demand = 2
Income elasticity of demand = 1.5

The supply of Beetles is elastic. Based on this information, are the following statements true or false? Explain your reasoning.

a. A 10% increase in the price of a Beetle will reduce the quantity demanded by 20%.

b. An increase in consumer income will increase the price and quantity of Beetles sold. Since price elasticity of demand is greater than 1, total revenue will go down.

10. In each of the following cases, do you think the price elasticity of supply is (i) perfectly elastic; (ii) perfectly inelastic; (iii) elastic, but not perfectly elastic; or (iv) inelastic, but not perfectly inelastic? Explain using a diagram.

a. An increase in demand this summer for luxury cruises leads to a huge jump in the sales price of a cabin on the *Carnival Splendor*.

b. The price of a kilowatt of electricity is the same during periods of high electricity demand as during periods of low electricity demand.

c. Fewer people want to fly during February than during any other month. The airlines cancel about 10% of their flights as ticket prices fall about 20% during this month.

d. Owners of cottages on Prince Edward Island rent them out during the summer. Due to the soft economy this year, a 30% decline in the price of a vacation rental leads more than half of homeowners to occupy their vacation homes themselves during the summer.

11. Use an elasticity concept to explain each of the following observations.

a. During economic booms, the number of new personal care businesses, such as gyms and salons, is proportionately greater than the number of other new businesses, such as grocery stores.

b. Cement is the primary building material in Mexico. After new technology makes cement cheaper to produce, the supply curve for the Mexican cement industry becomes relatively flatter.

c. Some goods that were once considered luxuries, like a telephone, are now considered virtual necessities. As a result, the demand curve for telephone services has become steeper over time.

d. Consumers in a less developed country like Guatemala spend proportionately more of their income on equipment for producing things at home, like sewing machines, than consumers in a more developed country like Canada.

12. Taiwan is a major world supplier of semiconductor chips. A recent earthquake severely damaged the production facilities of Taiwanese chip-producing companies, sharply reducing the amount of chips they could produce.

a. Assume that the total revenue of a typical non-Taiwanese chip manufacturer rises due to these events. In terms of an elasticity, what must be true for this to happen? Illustrate the change in total revenue with a diagram, indicating the price effect and the quantity effect of the Taiwan earthquake on this company's total revenue.

b. Now assume that the total revenue of a typical non-Taiwanese chip manufacturer falls due to these events. In terms of an elasticity, what must be true for this to happen? Illustrate the change in total revenue with a diagram, indicating the price effect and the quantity effect of the Taiwan earthquake on this company's total revenue.

13. There is a debate about whether sterile hypodermic needles should be passed out free of charge in cities with high drug use. Proponents argue that doing so will reduce the incidence of diseases, such as HIV/AIDS, that are often spread by needle sharing among drug users. Opponents believe that doing so will encourage more drug use by reducing the risks of this behaviour. As an economist asked to assess the policy, you must know the following: (i) how responsive the spread of diseases like HIV/AIDS is to the price of sterile needles and (ii) how responsive drug use is to the price of sterile needles. Assuming that you know these two things, use the concepts of price elasticity of demand for sterile needles and the cross-price elasticity between drugs and sterile needles to answer the following questions.

a. In what circumstances do you believe this is a beneficial policy?

b. In what circumstances do you believe this is a bad policy?

14. Worldwide, the average coffee grower has increased the amount of land under cultivation over the past few years. The result has been that the average coffee plantation produces significantly more coffee than it did 10 to 20 years ago. Unfortunately for the growers, however, this has also been a period in which their total revenues have plunged. In terms of an elasticity, what must be true for these events to have occurred? Illustrate these events with a diagram, indicating the quantity effect and the price effect that gave rise to these events.

15. Anindya Sen and May Luong studied the relationship between the price of beer and rates of sexually transmitted infections (STIs) in Canada. Their result indicated that there is a significant relationship between beer price and STI rates. Their findings suggest that "higher beer prices do result in lower STI rates and price elas-

ticities within a range of –0.6 to –1.4."[4] According to this estimate of the cross-price elasticity of demand by Sen and Leong, are beer and STIs complements or substitutes? Explain.

16. The U.S. government is considering reducing the amount of carbon dioxide that firms are allowed to produce by issuing a limited number of tradable allowances for carbon dioxide (CO_2) emissions. In an April 25, 2007, report, the U.S. Congressional Budget Office (CBO) argues that "most of the cost of meeting a cap on CO_2 emissions would be borne by consumers, who would face persistently higher prices for products such as electricity and gasoline ... poorer households would bear a larger burden relative to their income than wealthier households would." What assumption about one of the elasticities you learned about in this chapter has to be true for poorer households to be disproportionately affected?

17. According to data from auto sales data website, Good Car Bad Car (www.goodcarbadcar.net), Canadian sales of the fuel-efficient Toyota Prius hybrid rose from 1581 vehicles sold in 2011 to 3371 in 2012. Over the same period, according to data from Natural Resources Canada, the average price of regular gasoline rose from $1.24 to $1.27 per litre. Using the midpoint method, calculate the cross-price elasticity of demand between Toyota Prii (the official plural of "Prius" is "Prii") and regular gasoline. According to your estimate of the cross-price elasticity, are the two goods complements or substitutes? Does your answer make sense?

---

[4]Anindya Sen and May Luong, "Estimating the impact of beer prices on the incidence of sexually transmitted diseases: cross-province and time series evidence from Canada," *Contemporary Economic Policy*, 26, no. 4 (2008): 505–517.

The Algebra of Elasticity

As we have noted our simple algebraic models often use nice linear expressions so that our analysis is easy, yet still contains the essence of supply and demand.

Price Elasticity of Demand

Let's return to our example from Appendix 3A, the demand for maple syrup, to look at the algebra of elasticity. There, we started with a very simple linear demand curve in its simplest form:

(3A-1) $P = a - b \times Q^d$

where P denotes the price (in dollars per litre), Q^d denotes the quantity (in millions of litres), and a and b are positive constants.

If we isolate Q^d as a function of the other terms, we get:

(6A-1) $Q^d = \dfrac{a}{b} - \dfrac{1}{b} \times P$

According to this equation, if the price of maple syrup increases by \$1 per litre (i.e., $\Delta P = 1$), then the quantity of maple syrup demanded decreases by $\dfrac{1}{b}$ (i.e., $\Delta Q^d = -\dfrac{1}{b}$). Therefore, the ratio $\dfrac{\Delta Q^d}{\Delta P}$ is equal to $-\dfrac{1}{b}$, a fact we will need to use later.

Now we can look more closely at the price elasticity of demand, which was expressed in Equation 6-5 as:

(6-5) Price elasticity of demand $= \dfrac{\dfrac{Q_2 - Q_1}{(Q_1 + Q_2)/2}}{\dfrac{P_2 - P_1}{(P_1 + P_2)/2}}$

This equation can be simplified after rewriting it using algebraic terms such as ΔQ^d for the change in $Q^d = Q_2 - Q_1$, ΔP for the change in $P = P_2 - P_1$, and using the values P and Q^d instead of the midpoint values:

(6A-2) Price elasticity of demand $= \dfrac{\dfrac{Q_2 - Q_1}{(Q_1 + Q_2)/2}}{\dfrac{P_2 - P_1}{(P_1 + P_2)/2}} = \dfrac{\left(\dfrac{\Delta Q^d}{Q^d}\right)}{\left(\dfrac{\Delta P}{P}\right)} = \left(\dfrac{\Delta Q^d}{\Delta P}\right) \times \left(\dfrac{P}{Q^d}\right)$

When interpreting the price elasticity of demand, we only look at the absolute value, so we can redefine the price elasticity of demand, E_d, as:

(6A-3) $E_d = \left|\left(\dfrac{\Delta Q^d}{\Delta P}\right) \times \left(\dfrac{P}{Q^d}\right)\right| = \left|\left(-\dfrac{1}{b}\right) \times \left(\dfrac{P}{Q^d}\right)\right| = \left(\dfrac{1}{b}\right) \times \left(\dfrac{P}{Q^d}\right)$

This formula for the price elasticity of demand comes in handy when analyzing a graph of the demand curve. As we move along the demand curve in Figure 6A-1, b remains constant but the ratio of P divided by Q^d varies. Therefore the price elasticity of demand varies as we move along a linear demand curve. The ratio P/Q^d is the slope of the line passing through the origin and the point (Q^d, P) on

Price Elasticity along a Linear Demand Curve

FIGURE 6A-1

Price elasticity varies along the demand curve. A line with a slope b that passes through the origin will intersect the demand curve. At the point of intersection, price elasticity is 1 (the unit-elastic point). To the left of the point, price elasticity is greater than 1. To the right, price elasticity is less than 1.

the demand curve (because the rise of the line is P and the run is Q^d). When the slope of the line is equal to b, the point at which this line intersects the demand curve has a price elasticity of demand of one—the unit-elastic point. All lines steeper than this one intersect at points on the demand curve with a price elasticity of demand greater than one—the region of elastic demand points. Similarly, the points on the demand curve that lie below the unit-elastic point have price elasticity of demand less than one—the inelastic points.

These regions can be determined algebraically by first substituting $P = a - b \times Q^d$ into Equation 6A-2 to express E_d in terms of a, b, and Q^d:

$$\textbf{(6A-4)} \; E_d = \left(\frac{1}{b}\right) \times \left(\frac{P}{Q^d}\right) = \left(\frac{1}{b}\right) \times \left(\frac{a - b \times Q^d}{Q^d}\right)$$

$$= \left(\frac{a - b \times Q^d}{b \times Q^d}\right) = \left(\frac{a}{b \times Q^d}\right) - 1$$

Notice that by carefully selecting values of Q^d, we can generate values of E_d that are less than, greater than, or equal to 1.

$$\text{If} \quad Q^d = \left(\frac{a}{2 \times b}\right), \quad \text{then } E_d = \left(\frac{a}{b \times Q^d}\right) - 1 = 2 - 1 = 1$$

$$\text{If} \quad Q^d < \left(\frac{a}{2 \times b}\right), \quad \text{then } E_d = \left(\frac{a}{b \times Q^d}\right) - 1 > 1$$

$$\text{If} \quad Q^d > \left(\frac{a}{2 \times b}\right), \quad \text{then } E_d = \left(\frac{a}{b \times Q^d}\right) - 1 < 1$$

Income Elasticity of Demand

The income elasticity of demand measures how sensitive the demand curve is to changes in consumers' incomes by measuring how far the demand curve parallel shifts along the quantity axis as consumers' incomes change. More precisely, it measures the percentage change in quantity demand per percentage change in income. To examine income algebraically, we need to revisit the expanded version of Equation 3A-1 from Appendix 3A:

$$P = a_0 + a_1 \times P_{corn\;syrup} - a_2 \times P_{pancake\;mix} + a_3 \times Y + a_4 \times Tastes +$$

$$a_5 \times P^e_{future} + a_6 \times Pop - b \times Q^d$$

where P denotes the price, Q^d denotes the quantity, and the other terms are positive constants. Table 6A-1 summarizes the factors in this equation. For the income elasticity of demand, we are dealing with the Y term, average consumer income.

If we isolate Q^d as a function of the other terms, we get:

$$\textbf{(6A-5)} \; Q^d = \left(\frac{a_0}{b}\right) + \left(\frac{a_1}{b}\right) \times P_{corn\;syrup} - \left(\frac{a_2}{b}\right) \times P_{pancake\;mix} + \left(\frac{a_3}{b}\right) \times Y +$$

$$\left(\frac{a_4}{b}\right) \times Tastes + \left(\frac{a_5}{b}\right) \times P^e_{future} + \left(\frac{a_6}{b}\right) \times Pop - \left(\frac{1}{b}\right) \times P$$

Variable Factors That Shift Maple Syrup Demand

TABLE 6A-1

Factor	Denoted by
Price of corn syrup	$P_{corn\;syrup}$
Price of pancake mix	$P_{pancake\;mix}$
Average consumer income	Y
Consumer preference index	$Tastes$
Expected future price	P^e_{future}
Population of potential consumers	Pop

As we noticed in Equation 6A-1, according to Equation 6A-5, if the average consumer income increases by \$1 (i.e., $\Delta Y = 1$), then the quantity demanded for maple syrup will increase by $\frac{a_3}{b}$ (i.e., $\Delta Q^d = \frac{a_3}{b}$). Therefore, the ratio $\frac{\Delta Q^d}{\Delta Y}$ is equal to $\frac{a_3}{b}$. So, using the general demand curve given above, we get:

(6A-6) Income elasticity of demand $= E_{Inc} = \left(\dfrac{\Delta Q^d}{\Delta Y}\right) \times \left(\dfrac{Y}{Q^d}\right) = \left(\dfrac{a_3}{b}\right) \times \left(\dfrac{Y}{Q^d}\right)$

We know that b, Y, and Q^d are all positive, so a_3 determines whether the income elasticity of demand is positive or negative:

If $a_3 > 0$,   then $E_{Inc} = \left(\dfrac{a_3}{b}\right) \times \left(\dfrac{Y}{Q}\right) > 0$

If $a_3 < 0$,   then $E_{Inc} = \left(\dfrac{a_3}{b}\right) \times \left(\dfrac{Y}{Q}\right) < 0$

So if $a_3 > 0$, this good is a normal good (like maple syrup) because an increase in income results in an increase in demand. Similarly, if $a_3 < 0$, this good is an inferior good because an increase in income results in a decrease in demand.

Cross-Price Elasticity of Demand

The cross-price elasticity of demand measures how sensitive the demand curve is to changes in the price of some other good or service by measuring how far the demand curve shifts along the quantity axis as the other price changes. More precisely it measures the percentage change in quantity demand per percentage change in the other goods price. Using the general demand curve given above in Equation (6A-5) we get:

(6A-7) Cross-price elasticity of demand $= E_{cross\text{-}price} = \left(\dfrac{\Delta Q^d}{\Delta P_{corn\ syrup}}\right) \times \left(\dfrac{P_{corn\ syrup}}{Q^d}\right)$

$$= \left(\dfrac{a_1}{b}\right) \times \left(\dfrac{P_{corn\ syrup}}{Q^d}\right)$$

Again, analyzing Equation 6A-5 reveals that when the price of corn syrup increases by \$1 (i.e., $\Delta P_{corn\ syrup} = 1$), then the quantity of maple syrup demanded increases by $\frac{a_1}{b}$ (i.e., $\Delta Q^d = \frac{a_1}{b}$). Therefore, the ratio $\frac{\Delta Q^d}{\Delta P_{corn\ syrup}}$ is equal to $\frac{a_1}{b}$.

Since b, $P_{corn\ syrup}$, and Q^d are all positive, a_1 determines whether the cross-price elasticity of demand is positive or negative:

If $a_1 > 0$,   then $E_{cross\text{-}price} = \left(\dfrac{a_1}{b}\right) \times \left(\dfrac{P_{corn\ syrup}}{Q^d}\right) > 0$

If $a_1 < 0$,   then $E_{cross\text{-}price} = \left(\dfrac{a_1}{b}\right) \times \left(\dfrac{P_{corn\ syrup}}{Q^d}\right) < 0$

So if $a_1 > 0$, the other good is a substitute (as corn syrup is for maple syrup) and an increase in the price of the second good causes an increase in demand for the first good. Similarly, if $a_1 < 0$, the other good is a complement (as pancake mix is for maple syrup) and an increase in the price of the second good causes a decrease in demand for the first good.

Elasticity of Supply

In the case of linear expressions, a supply curve in its simplest form would be:

(6A-8) $P = c + d \times Q^S$

or

(6A-9) $Q^S = \left(\dfrac{c}{d}\right) + \left(\dfrac{1}{d}\right) \times P$

where P denotes the price, Q^S denotes the quantity, and c and d are positive constants. Continuing with the maple syrup example, if the price of maple syrup increases by \$1 per litre (i.e., $\Delta P = 1$), then the quantity supplied will increase by $\dfrac{1}{d}$ (i.e., $\Delta Q^S = -\dfrac{1}{d}$). Therefore, the ratio $\dfrac{\Delta Q^S}{\Delta P}$ is equal to $\dfrac{1}{d}$.

Now we can look more closely at the price elasticity of supply:

(6A-10) $E_S = \text{Elasticity of supply} = \left(\dfrac{\Delta Q^S}{\Delta P}\right) \times \left(\dfrac{P}{Q^S}\right)$

$$= \left(\dfrac{1}{d}\right) \times \left(\dfrac{P}{Q^S}\right) = \left(\dfrac{1}{d}\right) \times \left(\dfrac{c + d \times Q^S}{Q^S}\right) = \left(\dfrac{c + d \times Q^S}{d \times Q^S}\right) = \left(\dfrac{c}{d \times Q^S}\right) + 1$$

Notice:

- If $c = 0$, then the supply curve goes through the origin and the price elasticity of supply is equal to one.
- If $c > 0$, then the supply curve intersects along the P-axis and the price elasticity of supply is greater than one (elastic supply).
- If $c < 0$, then the supply curve intersects along the Q^S-axis and the price elasticity of supply is less than one (inelastic supply).
- If $c \neq 0$, as we move along the supply curve c and d remain constant but Q^S varies. Therefore the price elasticity of supply varies as we move along a linear supply curve that does not pass through the origin.

PROBLEMS

1. This question uses the algebraic method of determining equilibrium from Appendix 3A. Suppose that the demand and supply for maple syrup is given by the following equations:

$P = 53.25 - 1.25Q^d$ Demand Curve
$P = 12.75 + 0.25Q^S$ Supply Curve

a. Solve for the equilibrium price and quantity. Determine the price elasticity of demand and supply in equilibrium.

b. Determine the unit-elastic point for this demand curve.

c. Given $P_{pancake\ mix} = 12$ and $a_2 = -1.8$ (the coefficient of the price of pancake mix in the expanded demand curve), determine the cross-price elasticity of demand at the equilibrium point.

d. The incomes of consumers rises, which shifts the demand curve to $P = 55.50 - 1.25Q^d$ and at the same time an improvement in technology shifts the supply curve to $P = 7.50 + 0.25Q^S$. Solve for the new equilibrium price and quantity. Determine the price elasticity of demand and supply at this new equilibrium.

2. This question uses the algebraic method of determining equilibrium from Appendix 3A. Suppose the monthly demand and supply for iPods are given by the following equations:

$P = 500 - 0.001Q^d$ Demand Curve
$P = 200 + 0.0005Q^S$ Supply Curve

a. Use the supply and demand curves given above to solve for the equilibrium levels of price and quantity. Determine the price elasticity of demand and supply in equilibrium.

b. Given $Y = 40\ 000$ and $a_3 = 0.004$ (the coefficient of the average consumer index from the expanded demand curve), determine the income elasticity of demand at the equilibrium point.

c. Suppose instead that the offshoring of the production of iPods to a lower-cost country causes the supply curve to shift to $P = 140 + 0.0005Q^S$. Derive the resulting new equilibrium levels of price and quantity. Determine the price elasticity of demand and supply at this new equilibrium.

CHAPTER 7

Taxes

AN ABORIGINAL TAX CONFLICT

Taxation was one of the issues behind the 1990 Oka conflict in Quebec.

CP Photo/Tom Hanson

WHAT YOU WILL LEARN IN THIS CHAPTER

❭ The effects of taxes on supply and demand

❭ What determines who really bears the burden of a tax

❭ The costs and benefits of taxes, and why taxes impose a cost that is larger than the tax revenue they raise

❭ The difference between progressive and regressive taxes and the trade-off between tax equity and tax efficiency

❭ The structure of the Canadian tax system

In the summer of 1990, Mohawks from the Kanesatake reserve near Montreal held marches and erected a peaceful blockade to protest the planned expansion of a golf course in Oka, Quebec. The Mohawks claimed the golf course expansion would further encroach on their land. Early in the 78-day standoff, after the arrival of supporters from the Akwesasne reserve, police attacked the barricade with tear gas and flash grenades. Gunfire soon erupted and officer Corporal Marcel Lemay was killed.

What was the fighting about? Land claims, certainly, but also taxes. Most bands of Aboriginal Canadians have signed treaties with the federal government recognizing them as distinct nations within Canada, exempt from taxation. The government has a bad record of not fully honouring treaties, which has led to frequent disputes over territory. For some Mohawk reserves, issues related to taxation were never far away.

You could say the Oka conflict started with the Akwesasne reserve, which overlaps parts of Ontario, Quebec, and New York State. This was the centre of "tax-based" conflicts related to gambling and smuggling, starting in the 1980s. According to one source, by the spring of 1990, Akwesasne had become the fourth largest gambling centre in North America. More than a dozen casinos were bringing in millions of dollars, paying no taxes, and were not accountable to anyone, including Mohawk band leaders. The smuggling business and sale of tax-free cigarettes were similarly large-scale, very profitable, and depriving governments of many millions in tax revenue.

In early 1990, divisions within the Akwesasne reserve led to anti-casino blockades erected by Mohawks, violence, several killings, and the eventual intervention from Canadian and U.S. police forces. The casinos and alleged smuggling operations were shut down. A few months later, those on the losing side, eager to repair their image and regain strength within the Mohawk reserves, happily sent weapons and manpower to Oka.

And tax and land disputes continue. The sale of tax-free cigarettes remains a thriving business, providing impoverished people with income, but possibly dodging tax laws. In 1994, a Revenue Canada building in downtown Toronto was occupied for over a month by protesters reacting to a government plan to tax Aboriginal people and businesses for any income earned for work off-reserve (even if the employer was on a reserve).

There are two main (tax) morals to these stories. One, taxes are necessary: all governments need money to function. Without taxes, governments could not provide the services we want, from national defence to public parks. But taxes have a cost that normally exceeds the money actually paid to the government. That's because taxes distort incentives to engage in mutually beneficial transactions.

And that leads us to the second moral: making tax policy isn't easy—in fact, if you are a politician, it can be dangerous to your professional health. But these stories also illustrate some crucial issues in tax policy—issues that economic models help clarify.

One principle used for guiding tax policy is efficiency: taxes should be designed to distort incentives as little as possible. But efficiency is not the only concern when designing tax rates. As the government learned from the Revenue Canada occupation and the on-reserve gambling, it's also important that a tax be seen as fair. Tax policy always involves striking a balance between the pursuit of efficiency and the pursuit of perceived fairness.

In this chapter, we will look at how taxes affect efficiency and fairness as well as raise revenue for the government. ■

An **excise tax** is a per unit tax on sales of a good or service.

The Economics of Taxes: A Preliminary View

To understand the economics of taxes, it's helpful to look at a simple type of tax known as an **excise tax**—a tax charged on each unit of a good or service that is sold. Most tax revenue in Canada comes from other kinds of taxes, which we'll describe later in this chapter. But excise taxes are common. For example, there are excise taxes on gasoline, cigarettes, and fuel-inefficient vehicles or ones with air conditioning. Many local governments impose excise taxes on services such as hotel room rentals. The lessons we'll learn from studying excise taxes apply to other, more complex taxes as well.

The Effect of an Excise Tax on Quantities and Prices

Suppose that the supply and demand for hotel rooms in the city of Potterville are as shown in Figure 7-1. We'll make the simplifying assumption that all hotel rooms are the same. In the absence of taxes, the equilibrium price of a room is $80 per night and the equilibrium quantity of hotel rooms rented is 10 000 per night.

Now suppose that Potterville's government imposes an excise tax of $40 per night on hotel rooms—that is, every time a room is rented for the night, the owner of the hotel must pay the city $40. For example, if a customer pays $80, $40 is collected as a tax, leaving the hotel owner with only $40. As a result, hotel owners are less willing to supply rooms at any given price.

What does this imply about the supply curve for hotel rooms in Potterville? To answer this question, we must compare the incentives of hotel owners *pre-tax* (before the tax is levied) to their incentives *post-tax* (after the tax is levied).

From Figure 7-1 we know that pre-tax, hotel owners are willing to supply 5000 rooms per night at a price of $60 per room. But after the $40 tax per room is levied,

FIGURE   7-1   **The Supply and Demand for Hotel Rooms in Potterville**

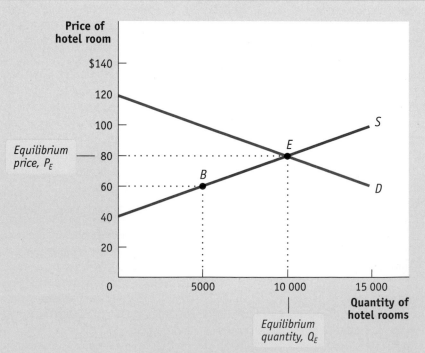

In the absence of taxes, the equilibrium price (P_E) of hotel rooms is $80 a night, and the equilibrium number (Q_E) of rooms rented is 10 000 per night, as shown by point E. The supply curve, S, shows the quantity supplied at any given price, pre-tax. At a price of $60 a night, hotel owners are willing to supply 5000 rooms, point B. But post-tax, hotel owners are willing to supply the same quantity only at a price of $100: $60 for themselves plus $40 paid to the city as tax.

they are willing to supply the same amount, 5000 rooms, only if they receive $100 per room—$60 for themselves plus $40 paid to the city as tax. In other words, in order for hotel owners to be willing to supply the same quantity post-tax as they would have pre-tax, they must receive an additional $40 per room, the amount of the tax. This implies that the post-tax supply curve shifts up by the amount of the tax compared to the pre-tax supply curve. At every quantity supplied, the supply price—the price that producers must receive to produce a given quantity—has increased by $40.

The upward shift of the supply curve caused by the tax is shown in Figure 7-2, where T is the amount of tax, S_1 is the pre-tax supply curve, and $S_2 = S_1 + T$ is the post-tax supply curve. As you can see, the market equilibrium moves from E, at the equilibrium price of $P_E = \$80$ per room and 10 000 rooms rented each night, to A, at a market price of $P_C = \$100$ per room and only 5000 rooms rented each night. A is, of course, on both the demand curve D and the new supply curve S_2. In this case, $100 is the demand price (P_C) of 5000 rooms—but in effect hotel owners receive only $60 ($P_P$), when you account for the fact that they have to collect and remit the $40 tax. From the point of view of hotel owners, it is as if they were on *→ they still earn same* their original supply curve at point B.

Let's check this again. How do we know that 5000 rooms will be supplied at a price of $100? Because the price net of tax ($P_P = P_C - T$) is $60, and according to the original supply curve, 5000 rooms will be supplied at a price of $60, as shown by point B in Figure 7-2.

Does this look familiar? It should. In Chapter 5 we described the effects of a quota on sales: a quota *drives a wedge* between the price paid by consumers and the price received by producers. An excise tax does the same thing. As a result of this wedge, consumers pay more (P_C) and producers receive less (P_P), with the gap being the tax wedge (T), so that $P_C = P_P + T$. *→ consumers pay more so producers earn same*

In our example, consumers—people who rent hotel rooms—end up paying $100 a night, $20 more than the pre-tax price of $80. At the same time, producers—the hotel owners—receive a price net of tax of $60 per room, $20 less than the pre-tax price. In addition, the tax creates missed opportunities: 5000 potential consumers who would have rented hotel rooms—those willing to pay $80 but not $100 per night—are discouraged from doing so.

FIGURE 7-2 An Excise Tax Imposed on Hotel Owners

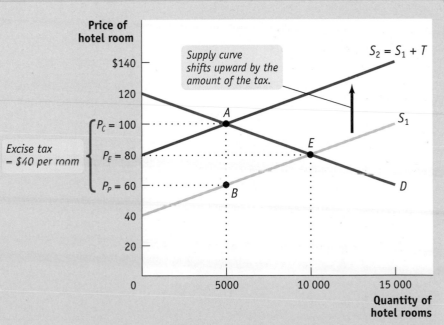

A $40 per room tax imposed on hotel owners shifts the supply curve from S_1 to S_2, an upward shift of $T = \$40$. The equilibrium price of hotel rooms rises from $80 to $100 a night, and the equilibrium quantity of rooms rented falls from 10 000 to 5000. Although hotel owners pay the tax, they actually bear only half the burden: the price they receive net of tax falls only $20, from $80 to $60. Guests who rent rooms bear the other half of the burden, because the price they pay rises by $20, from $80 to $100.

The **incidence** of a tax is a measure of who really pays it.

Correspondingly, 5000 rooms that would have been made available by hotel owners when they receive $80 are not offered when they receive only $60. Like a quota, this tax leads to inefficiency by distorting incentives and creating missed opportunities for mutually beneficial transactions.

It's important to recognize that as we've described it, Potterville's hotel tax is a tax on the hotel owners, not their guests—it's a tax on the producers, not the consumers. Yet the price received by producers, net of tax (P_P), is down by only $20, half the amount of the tax, and the price paid by consumers (P_C) is up by $20. In effect, half the tax is actually being paid by consumers—the burden of the tax is shared between the suppliers and demanders.

What would happen if the city levied a tax on consumers instead of producers? That is, suppose that instead of requiring hotel owners to pay $40 a night for each room they rent, the city required hotel *guests* to pay $40 for each night they stayed in a hotel. The answer is shown in Figure 7-3. If a hotel guest must pay a tax of $40 per night, then the pre-tax price for a room paid by that guest must be reduced by $40 in order for the quantity of hotel rooms demanded post-tax to be the same as that demanded pre-tax. So the demand curve shifts *downward* by the amount of the tax from D_1 to $D_2 = D_1 - T$.

At every quantity demanded, the demand price—the price that consumers must be offered to demand a given quantity—has fallen by $40. This shifts the equilibrium from E to B, where the market price of hotel rooms is $60 and 5000 hotel rooms are bought and sold. In effect, hotel guests pay $100 when you include the tax. So from the point of view of guests, it is as if they were on their original demand curve at point A.

If you compare Figures 7-2 and 7-3, you will immediately notice that they show the same price effect. In each case, consumers pay an effective price of $100 ($P_C$), producers receive an effective price of $60 ($P_P$), and 5000 hotel rooms are bought and sold. *In fact, it doesn't matter who the government officially asks to pay the tax—whether it's levied on suppliers or consumers—the equilibrium outcome is the same.*

This insight illustrates a general principle of the economics of taxation: the **incidence** of a tax—who really bears the burden of the tax—is typically not a question you can answer by asking who writes the cheque to the government. In

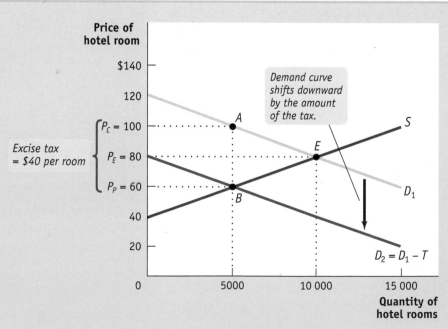

FIGURE 7-3 An Excise Tax Imposed on Hotel Guests

A $40 per room tax imposed on hotel guests shifts the demand curve from D_1 to D_2, a downward shift of $40. The equilibrium price of hotel rooms falls from $80 to $60 a night, and the quantity of rooms rented falls from 10 000 to 5000. Although in this case the tax is officially paid by (levied on, or collected from) consumers, while in Figure 7-2 the tax was paid by (collected from) producers, the outcome is the same: after taxes, hotel owners receive $60 per room but guests pay $100. This illustrates a general principle: *The incidence of an excise tax doesn't depend on whether the government levies the tax on consumers or producers.*

this particular case, a $40 tax on hotel rooms is reflected in a $20 increase in the price paid by consumers and a $20 decrease in the price received by producers. Here, regardless of whether the tax is levied on consumers or producers, the incidence of the tax is evenly split between them.[1]

Price Elasticities and Tax Incidence

We've just learned that the economic incidence of an excise tax doesn't depend on whom the government rules require to officially pay it. In the example shown in Figures 7-1 through 7-3, a tax on hotel rooms falls equally on consumers and producers, no matter who the tax is levied on. But it's important to note that this 50–50 split between consumers and producers is a result of our assumptions in this example. In the real world, the incidence of an excise tax usually falls unevenly between consumers and producers, as one group bears more of the burden than the other.

What determines how the burden of an excise tax is allocated between consumers and producers? The answer depends on the shapes of the supply and the demand curves. *More specifically, the incidence of an excise tax depends on the price elasticity of supply and the price elasticity of demand.* We can see this by looking first at a case in which consumers pay most of an excise tax, then at a case in which producers pay most of the tax.

When an Excise Tax Is Paid Mainly by Consumers Figure 7-4 shows an excise tax that falls mainly on consumers: an excise tax on gasoline, which we set at $0.25 per litre. (There really is a federal excise tax on gasoline, though it is actually only $0.10 per litre in Canada. In addition, provinces, territories, and even several cities impose excise taxes between $0.09 and $0.24 per litre. Finally, the GST/HST and, if applicable, provincial sales taxes also apply to gasoline sales.) According to Figure 7-4, in the absence of the tax, gasoline would sell for $1.05 per litre.

Two key assumptions are reflected in the shapes of the supply and demand curves in Figure 7-4. First, the price elasticity of demand for gasoline is assumed

FIGURE **7-4** **An Excise Tax Paid Mainly by Consumers**

The relatively steep demand curve here reflects a low price elasticity of demand for gasoline. The relatively flat supply curve reflects a high price elasticity of supply. The pre-tax price of a litre of gasoline is $1.05, and a tax of $0.25 per litre is imposed. The price paid by consumers rises by $0.20 to $1.25, reflecting the fact that most of the burden of the tax falls on consumers. Only a small portion of the tax is borne by producers: the price they receive falls by only $0.05 to $1.00.

[1]In both cases, the new level of output (Q_T), the price paid by consumers (P_C), the price received by suppliers (P_P), the tax revenue collected by the government ($Q_T \times T$), and the deadweight loss created by the tax are all the same.

to be very low, so the demand curve is relatively steep. Recall that a low price elasticity of demand means that the quantity demanded changes little in response to a change in price—a feature of a steep demand curve. Second, the price elasticity of supply of gasoline is assumed to be very high, so the supply curve is relatively flat. A high price elasticity of supply means that the quantity supplied changes a lot in response to a change in price—a feature of a relatively flat supply curve.

We have just learned that an excise tax drives a wedge, equal to the size of the tax, between the price paid by consumers and the price received by producers. This wedge drives the price paid by consumers up and the price received by producers down. But as we can see from Figure 7-4, in this case those two effects are very unequal in size. The price received by producers falls only slightly, from $1.05 to $1.00, but the price paid by consumers rises by a lot, from $1.05 to $1.25. In this case consumers bear the greater share of the tax burden.

This example illustrates another general principle of taxation: *When the price elasticity of demand is low and the price elasticity of supply is high, the burden of an excise tax falls mainly on consumers.* Why? A low price elasticity of demand means that consumers have few substitutes and so little alternative to buying higher-priced gasoline. In contrast, a high price elasticity of supply results from the fact that producers have many production substitutes for their gasoline (that is, other uses for the crude oil from which gasoline is refined). This gives producers much greater flexibility in refusing to accept lower prices for their gasoline. And, not surprisingly, the party with the least flexibility—in this case, consumers—gets stuck paying most of the tax. This is a good description of how the burden of the main excise taxes actually collected in Canada today, such as those on cigarettes and alcoholic beverages, is allocated between consumers and producers.

When an Excise Tax Is Paid Mainly by Producers Figure 7-5 shows an example of an excise tax paid mainly by producers, a $5.00 per day tax on downtown parking in a small city. In the absence of the tax, the market equilibrium price of parking is $6.00 per day.

We've assumed in this case that the price elasticity of supply is very low because the lots used for parking have very few alternative uses. This makes the supply curve for parking spaces relatively steep. The price elasticity of demand, however, is assumed to be high: consumers can easily switch from the downtown spaces to other parking spaces a few minutes' walk from downtown, spaces that are not subject to the tax. This makes the demand curve relatively flat.

FIGURE **7-5** An Excise Tax Paid Mainly by Producers

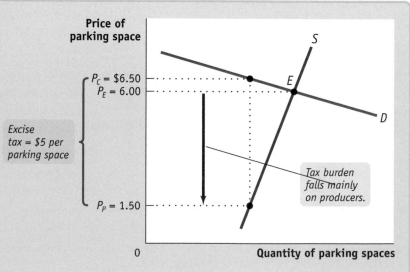

The relatively flat demand curve here reflects a high price elasticity of demand for downtown parking, and the relatively steep supply curve results from a low price elasticity of supply. The pre-tax price of a daily parking space is $6.00 and a tax of $5.00 is imposed. The price received by producers falls a lot, to $1.50, reflecting the fact that they bear most of the tax burden. The price paid by consumers rises a small amount, $0.50, to $6.50, so they bear very little of the burden.

The tax drives a wedge between the price paid by consumers and the price received by producers. In this example, however, the tax causes the price paid by consumers to rise only slightly, from $6.00 to $6.50, but the price received by producers falls a lot, from $6.00 to $1.50. In the end, consumers bear only $0.50 of the $5.00 tax burden, with producers bearing the remaining $4.50.

Again, this example illustrates a general principle: *When the price elasticity of demand is high and the price elasticity of supply is low, the burden of an excise tax falls mainly on producers.* A real-world example is a tax on purchases of existing houses. Just before the recession hit Canada in 2008, the cash-strapped city of Toronto implemented a municipal land transfer tax to raise revenue. A land transfer tax is collected as a percentage of the price at which a residential or commercial property sells. To politicians, the idea was simple: homes sales were strong and in the preceding years prices had steadily risen. The tax rate was designed to rise somewhat as the price increased, so to some degree the higher the price paid the more tax paid in both relative and absolute terms. So besides helping the city meet its budgetary needs, the tax was intended to be paid mostly by well-off outsiders moving into desirable locations and purchasing homes from the less well-off original occupants. But this ignores the fact that the price elasticity of demand for houses in Toronto is often high, because potential buyers can choose to move to other towns. Furthermore, the price elasticity of supply is often low because most sellers must sell their houses due to job transfers or to provide funds for their retirement. So taxes on home purchases are actually paid mainly by the less well-off sellers—not, as Toronto officials may have imagined, by wealthy buyers.[2]

Putting It All Together We've just seen that when the price elasticity of supply is high and the price elasticity of demand is low, an excise tax falls mainly on consumers. And when the price elasticity of supply is low and the price elasticity of demand is high, an excise tax falls mainly on producers. This leads us to the general rule: *When the price elasticity of demand is higher than the price elasticity of supply, an excise tax falls mainly on producers. When the price elasticity of supply is higher than the price elasticity of demand, an excise tax falls mainly on consumers.* So it is elasticity—not the tax legislation—that determines the incidence of an excise tax.

ECONOMICS ▸ IN ACTION

WHO PAYS CANADA'S PAYROLL TAXES?

Anyone who works for an employer receives a paycheque that itemizes not only the wages paid but also the money deducted from the paycheque for various taxes. For most people, one of the big deductions is for Canada's various payroll taxes. Nationally these payroll taxes fund the Canada Pension Plan (CPP), a national pension plan for Canada's workers (workers in Quebec contribute to the Quebec Pension Plan (QPP)), and Employment Insurance (EI), an insurance program that provides assistance to many of Canada's workers during spells of unemployment. At the provincial level, payroll taxes exist to fund worker compensation systems for injured workers and, in some cases, to help fund provincial health and education spending.

In 2013, most Canadian workers paid 6.83% of about the first $50 000 of their earnings in CPP (4.95%) and EI (1.88%) contributions. But this isn't even the half of it: each employer is required to pay an amount equal to the CPP contributions and 1.4 times the EI contributions of its employees. And when it comes to the various other provincial payroll taxes, which range from 1.12% to as much as 6.34%, the employer is expected to pay the entire amount.

Contrary to widely held beliefs, for many Canadians it's payroll taxes, not the income tax, that takes the biggest bite from their paycheques.

[2]In fact, if you know the price elasticities of demand and supply, you can determine the incidence of the tax, as follows: $\frac{\text{(Price elasticity of supply)}}{\text{(Price elasticity of demand)}} = \frac{\text{(Consumer's share of tax)}}{\text{(Producer's share of tax)}}$.

How should we think about Canada's payroll taxes? Are they really shared by workers and employers? We can use our previous analysis to answer that question because payroll taxes are like an excise tax—a tax on the sale and purchase of labour. A portion of it is a tax levied on the sellers—that is, workers. The rest is a tax levied on the buyers—that is, employers.

But we already know that the incidence of a tax does not really depend on who actually makes out the cheque. Almost all economists agree that payroll taxes are more costly for workers than for their employers. The reason for this conclusion lies in a comparison of the price elasticities of the supply of labour by households and the demand for labour by firms. Evidence indicates that the price elasticity of demand for labour is quite high, at least 3. That is, an increase in average wages of 1% would lead to at least a 3% decline in the number of hours of work demanded by employers. Labour economists believe, however, that the price elasticity of supply of labour is very low. The reason is that although a fall in the wage rate reduces the incentive to work more hours, it also makes people poorer and less able to afford leisure time. The strength of this second effect is shown in the data: the number of hours people are willing to work falls very little—if at all—when the wage per hour goes down.

Our general rule of tax incidence says that when the price elasticity of demand is much higher than the price elasticity of supply, the burden of an excise tax falls mainly on the suppliers. So the burden of Canada's payroll taxes falls mainly on the suppliers of labour, that is, workers—even though on paper most of these taxes are paid by employers. Payroll taxes are largely borne by workers in the form of lower wages, rather than by employers in the form of lower profits.

This conclusion tells us something important about the Canadian tax system: payroll taxes, rather than the much-maligned income tax, are the main tax burden on families in the lower half of the income distribution. For most workers, payroll taxes amount to more than 15.5% of all wages and salaries up to about $50 000 per year (note that $6.83\% + 4.95\% + 1.4 \times 1.88\% + 1.12\% = 15.532\%$). Thus, the great majority of workers in Canada pay at least 15.5% of their wages in payroll taxes. Meanwhile, only middle- and high-income Canadian families pay more than 15% of their income in income tax. In fact, according to the Fraser Institute, the average Canadian household earned an income of $74 113 in 2012 and paid $9195 in income taxes and $6769 in payroll taxes, which represented 29.1% and 21.4% of the total taxes paid by such a family. So for the average family, payroll taxes represent their second largest tax burden.

▼ **Quick Review**

- An **excise tax** drives a wedge between the price paid by consumers and that received by producers, leading to a fall in the quantity transacted. It creates inefficiency by distorting incentives and creating missed opportunities.

- The **incidence** of an excise tax doesn't depend on whom the tax is officially levied on. Rather, it depends on the price elasticities of demand and of supply.

- The higher the price elasticity of supply and the lower the price elasticity of demand, the heavier the burden of an excise tax on consumers. The lower the price elasticity of supply and the higher the price elasticity of demand, the heavier the burden on producers.

CHECK YOUR UNDERSTANDING   7-1

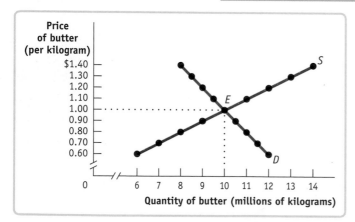

1. Consider the market for butter, shown in the accompanying figure. The government imposes an excise tax of $0.30 per kilogram of butter. What is the price paid by consumers post-tax? What is the price received by producers post-tax? What is the quantity of butter transacted? How is the incidence of the tax allocated between consumers and producers? Show this on the figure.

2. The demand for economics textbooks is very inelastic, but the supply is somewhat elastic. What does this imply about the incidence of an excise tax? Illustrate with a diagram.

3. True or false? When a substitute for a good is readily available to consumers, but it is difficult for producers to adjust the quantity of the good produced, then the burden of a tax on the good falls more heavily on producers.

4. The supply of bottled spring water is very inelastic, but the demand for it is somewhat elastic. What does this imply about the incidence of a tax? Illustrate with a diagram.

5. True or false? Other things equal, consumers would prefer to face a less elastic supply curve for a good or service when an excise tax is imposed.

Solutions appear at back of book.

The Benefits and Costs of Taxation

When a government is considering whether to impose a tax or how to design a tax system, it has to weigh the benefits of a tax against its costs. We don't usually think of a tax as something that provides benefits, but governments need money to provide things people want, such as building roads and providing health care. The benefit of a tax is the revenue it raises for the government to pay for these services. Unfortunately, this benefit comes at a cost—a cost that is normally larger than the amount consumers and producers pay. Let's look first at what determines how much money a tax raises, then at the costs a tax imposes.

"What taxes would you like to see imposed on other people?"

The Revenue from an Excise Tax

How much revenue does the government collect from an excise tax? In our hotel tax example, the revenue is equal to the area of the shaded rectangle in Figure 7-6.

To see why this area represents the revenue collected by a $40 tax on hotel rooms, notice that the height of the rectangle is $40, equal to the tax per room. It is also, as we've seen, the size of the wedge that the tax drives between the supply price (the price received by producers) and the demand price (the price paid by consumers). Meanwhile, the width of the rectangle is 5000 rooms, equal to the equilibrium quantity of rooms given the $40 tax. With that information, we can make the following calculations.

The tax revenue collected is:

[handwritten: tax per room × # of rooms]

Tax revenue = $40 per room × 5000 rooms = $200 000

FIGURE 7-6 The Revenue from an Excise Tax

The revenue from a $40 excise tax on hotel rooms is $200 000, equal to the tax rate, $40—the size of the wedge that the tax drives between the supply price and the demand price—multiplied by the number of rooms rented, 5000. This is equal to the area of the shaded rectangle.

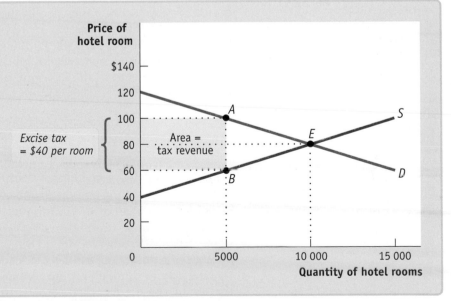

The area of the shaded rectangle is:

$$\text{Area} = \text{Height} \times \text{Width} = \$40 \text{ per room} \times 5000 \text{ rooms} = \$200\,000$$

or

$$\text{Tax revenue} = \text{Area of shaded rectangle}$$

This is a general principle: *The revenue collected by an excise tax is equal to the area of the rectangle whose height is the tax wedge between the supply and demand curves and whose width is the quantity transacted under the tax.*

Tax Rates and Revenue

In Figure 7-6, $40 per room is the *tax rate* on hotel rooms. A *tax rate* is the amount of tax levied per unit of whatever is being taxed. Sometimes tax rates are defined in terms of dollar amounts per unit of a good or service; for example, $6.75 per pack of cigarettes sold. In other cases, they are defined as a percentage of the price; for example, the payroll tax is 15.5% of a worker's earnings up to $50 000.

There's obviously a relationship between tax rates and revenue. That relationship is not, however, one-for-one. In general, doubling the excise tax rate on a good or service won't double the amount of revenue collected, because the tax increase will reduce the quantity of the good or service transacted. And the relationship between the level of the tax and the amount of revenue collected may not even be positive: in some cases raising the tax rate actually *reduces* the amount of revenue the government collects.

We can illustrate these points using our hotel room example. Figure 7-6 showed the revenue the government collects from a $40 tax on hotel rooms. Figure 7-7 shows the revenue the government would collect from two alternative tax rates—a lower tax of only $20 per room and a higher tax of $60 per room.

Figure 7-7 shows the case of a $20 tax, equal to half the tax rate illustrated in Figure 7-6. At this lower tax rate, 7500 rooms are rented, generating tax revenue of:

$$\text{Tax revenue} = \$20 \text{ per room} \times 7500 \text{ rooms} = \$150\,000$$

Recall that the tax revenue collected from a $40 tax rate is $200 000. So the revenue collected from a $20 tax rate, $150 000, is only 75% of the amount collected when the tax rate is twice as high ($150 000/$200 000 × 100 = 75%). To put it another way, a 100% increase in the tax rate from $20 to $40 per room leads to only a one-third, or 33.3%, increase in revenue, from $150 000 to $200 000 (($200 000 – $150 000)/$150 000 × 100 = 33.3%).

Figure 7-7 also depicts what happens if the tax rate is raised from $40 to $60 per room, leading to a fall in the number of rooms rented from 5000 to 2500. The revenue collected at a $60 per room tax rate is:

$$\text{Tax revenue} = \$60 \text{ per room} \times 2500 \text{ rooms} = \$150\,000$$

This is also *less* than the revenue collected by a $40 per room tax. So raising the tax rate from $40 to $60 actually reduces revenue. More precisely, in this case raising the tax rate by 50% (($60 – $40)/$40 × 100 = 50%) lowers the tax revenue by 25% (($150 000 – $200 000)/$200 000 × 100 = –25%). Why did this happen? It happened because the fall in tax revenue caused by the reduction in the number of rooms rented more than offset the increase in the tax revenue caused by the rise in the tax rate. In other words, setting a tax rate so high that it deters a significant number of transactions is likely to lead to a fall in tax revenue.

One way to think about the revenue effect of increasing an excise tax is that the tax increase affects tax revenue in two ways. On one side, the tax increase means that the government raises more revenue for each unit of the good sold, which other things equal would lead to a rise in tax revenue. On the other side, the

A **tax rate** is the amount of tax people are required to pay per unit of whatever is being taxed.

FIGURE **7-7** Tax Rates and Revenue

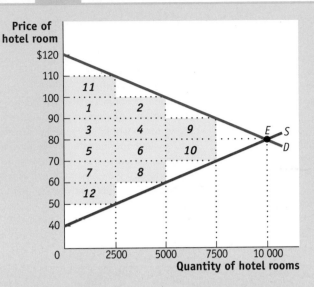

	Initial excise tax of $40	New excise tax of $20	Change
Quantity traded	5000 rooms	7500 rooms	↑ by 2500 rooms
Price paid by consumers	$100 per room	$90 per room	↓ by $10 per room
Price received by suppliers	$60 per room	$70 per room	↑ by $10 per room
Tax wedge	$40 per room	$20 per room	↓ by $20 per room
Tax revenue	areas *1 + 2 + 3 + 4 + 5 + 6 + 7 + 8*	areas *3 + 4 + 5 + 6 + 9 + 10*	areas (*9 + 10*) − (*1 + 2 + 7 + 8*)
Tax revenue (dollars)	$200 000	$150 000	↓ by $50 000

	Initial excise tax of $40	New excise tax of $60	Change
Quantity traded	5000 rooms	2500 rooms	↓ by 2500 rooms
Price paid by consumers	$100 per room	$110 per room	↑ by $10 per room
Price received by suppliers	$60 per room	$50 per room	↓ by $10 per room
Tax wedge	$40 per room	$60 per room	↑ by $20 per room
Tax revenue	areas *1 + 2 + 3 + 4 + 5 + 6 + 7 + 8*	areas *1 + 3 + 5 + 7 + 11 + 12*	areas (*11 + 12*) − (*2 + 4 + 6 + 8*)
Tax revenue (dollars)	$200 000	$150 000	↓ by $50 000

The tables above compare the effect of a change to an excise tax on the market. When the excise tax falls from $40 per room to $20 per room, tax revenue falls by $50 000 because the tax revenue gained from the higher quantity traded (areas *9 + 10*) doesn't offset the revenue lost as a result of the lower tax rate (areas *1 + 2 + 7 + 8*). When the excise tax rises from $40 per room to $60 per room, tax revenue falls by $50 000 because the tax revenue gained from the higher tax rate (areas *11 + 12*) doesn't offset the revenue lost as a result of the lower quantity traded (areas *2 + 4 + 6 + 8*). In general, doubling an excise tax rate doesn't double the amount of revenue collected because the tax increase reduces the quantity of the good or service sold. And the relationship between the level of the tax and the amount of revenue collected may not even be positive.

→ more cost less demand

tax increase reduces the quantity of sales, which other things equal would lead to a fall in tax revenue. The end result depends both on the price elasticities of supply and demand and on the initial level of the tax. If the price elasticities of both supply and demand are low, the tax increase won't reduce the quantity of the good sold very much, so tax revenue will definitely rise. If the price elasticities are high, the result is less certain; if they are high enough, the tax reduces the quantity sold so much that tax revenue falls. Also, if the initial tax rate is low, the government doesn't lose much revenue from the decline in the quantity of the good sold, so the tax increase will definitely increase tax revenue. If the initial tax rate is high, the result is again less certain. Tax revenue is likely to fall or rise very little from a tax increase only in cases where the price elasticities are high and there is already a high tax rate.

The possibility that a higher tax rate can reduce tax revenue, and the corresponding possibility that cutting taxes can increase tax revenue, is a basic principle of taxation that policy-makers take into account when setting tax rates. That is, when considering a tax created for the purpose of raising revenue

becaus more of little > less of more

FOR INQUIRING MINDS

THE LAFFER CURVE

One afternoon in 1974, the economist Arthur Laffer got together in a cocktail lounge with Jude Wanniski, a writer for the *Wall Street Journal*, and Dick Cheney, who would later become vice president of the United States but at the time was the deputy White House chief of staff. During the course of their conversation, Laffer drew a diagram on a napkin that was intended to explain how tax cuts could sometimes lead to higher tax revenue. According to Laffer's diagram, raising tax rates initially increases tax revenue, but beyond a certain level revenue falls instead as tax rates continue to rise. That is, at some point tax rates are so high and reduce the number of transactions so greatly that tax revenues fall.

There was nothing new about this idea, but in later years that napkin became the stuff of legend. The editors of the *Wall Street Journal* began promoting the "Laffer curve" as a justification for tax cuts. And when Ronald Reagan became president of the United States in 1981, he used the Laffer curve to argue that his proposed cuts in income tax rates would not reduce the federal government's revenue.

So is there a Laffer curve? Yes—as a theoretical proposition it's definitely possible that tax rates could be so high that cutting taxes would increase tax revenue. But very few economists now believe that Reagan's tax cuts actually increased revenue, and real-world examples in which revenue and tax rates move in opposite directions are very hard to find. That's because it's rare to find an existing tax rate so high that reducing it leads to an increase in tax revenue.

(in contrast to taxes created to discourage undesirable behaviour, known as "sin taxes"), a well-informed policy-maker won't impose a tax rate so high that cutting the tax would increase revenue. In the real world, policy-makers aren't always well informed, but they usually aren't complete fools either. That's why it's very hard to find real-world examples in which raising a tax reduced revenue or cutting a tax increased revenue. Nonetheless, the theoretical possibility that a tax reduction increases tax revenue has played an important role in the folklore of North American politics.[3] As explained in For Inquiring Minds, an economist who, in the 1970s, sketched on a napkin the figure of a revenue-increasing income tax reduction had a significant impact on the economic policies adopted in the United States in the 1980s.

The Costs of Taxation

What is the cost of a tax? You might be inclined to answer that it is the money taxpayers pay to the government. In other words, you might believe that the cost of a tax is the tax revenue collected. But suppose the government uses the tax revenue to provide services that taxpayers want. Or suppose that the government simply hands the tax revenue back to taxpayers. Would we say in those cases that the tax didn't actually cost anything?

No—because a tax, like a quota, prevents mutually beneficial transactions from occurring. Consider Figure 7-6 once more. Here, with a $40 tax on hotel rooms, guests pay $100 per room but hotel owners receive only $60 per room. Because of the wedge created by the tax, we know that some transactions don't occur that would have occurred without the tax. More specifically, we know from the supply and demand curves that there are some potential guests who would be

---

[3]Kevin Milligan from the University of British Columbia estimates that if Canada's personal income tax rate were to hit 57% (don't worry, we aren't there yet) then an increase in the tax rate would lower tax revenue. On the other hand, Jack Mintz from the University of Calgary estimates that the revenue maximizing corporate tax rate is 28%. This exceeds Canada's top combined corporate tax rate applied to the income of large companies. The reason why the revenue maximizing tax rate for corporations is lower is simple: corporations have much higher income mobility than individuals do. Like the case of having a more elastic demand (i.e., more responsive), if corporate tax rates are increased too much, then companies will shift economic activities (and the income they create) offshore to avoid the tax. If Mintz's estimate is correct, then a reduction in the corporate tax rate from 28% would result in an increase in corporate tax revenue.

FIGURE **7-8** A Tax Reduces Consumer and Producer Surplus

Before the tax, the equilibrium price and quantity are P_E and Q_E, respectively. After an excise tax of T per unit is imposed, the price to consumers rises to P_C and consumer surplus falls by the sum of the dark blue rectangle, labelled A, and the light blue triangle, labelled B. The tax also causes the price to producers to fall to P_P; producer surplus falls by the sum of the dark red rectangle, labelled C, and the light red triangle, labelled F. The government receives revenue from the tax, $Q_T \times T$, which is given by the sum of the areas A and C. Areas B and F represent the losses to consumer and producer surplus that are not collected by the government as revenue; they are the deadweight loss to society due to the tax.

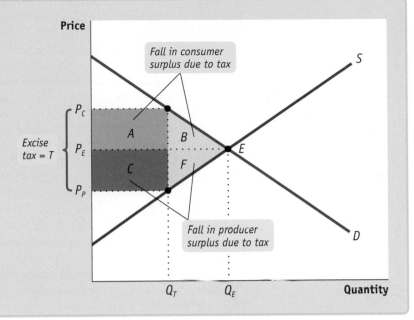

willing to pay up to $90 per night and some hotel owners who would be willing to supply rooms if they received at least $70 per night. If these two sets of people were allowed to trade with each other without the tax, they would engage in mutually beneficial transactions—more hotel rooms would be rented. But such deals would be illegal, because the $40 tax would not be paid. In our example, 5000 potential hotel room rentals that would have occurred in the absence of the tax, to the mutual benefit of guests and hotel owners, do not take place because of the tax.

So an excise tax imposes costs over and above the tax revenue collected in the form of inefficiency, which occurs because the tax discourages mutually beneficial transactions. As we learned in Chapter 5, the cost to society of this kind of inefficiency—the value of the forgone mutually beneficial transactions—is called the deadweight loss. While all real-world taxes impose some deadweight loss, a badly designed tax imposes a larger deadweight loss than a well-designed one.

To measure the deadweight loss from a tax, we turn to the concepts of producer and consumer surplus. Figure 7-8 shows the effects of an excise tax on consumer and producer surplus. In the absence of the tax, the equilibrium is at E and the equilibrium price and quantity are P_E and Q_E, respectively. An excise tax drives a wedge equal to the amount of the tax between the price received by producers and the price paid by consumers, reducing the quantity sold. In this case, where the tax is T dollars per unit, the quantity sold falls to Q_T. The price paid by consumers rises to P_C, the demand price of the reduced quantity, Q_T, and the price received by producers falls to P_P, the supply price of that quantity. The difference between these prices, $P_C - P_P$, is equal to the excise tax, T.

Using the concepts of producer and consumer surplus, we can show exactly how much surplus producers and consumers lose as a result of the tax. From Figure 4-5 we learned that, other things equal, a fall in the price of a good generates a gain in consumer surplus that is equal to the sum of the areas of a rectangle and a triangle. Similarly, other things equal, a price increase causes a loss to consumers that is represented by the sum of the areas of a rectangle and a triangle. So it's not surprising that in the case of an excise tax, the rise in the price paid by consumers causes a loss equal to the sum of the areas of a rectangle and a triangle: the area of the dark blue rectangle labelled A and the area of the light blue triangle labelled B in Figure 7-8.

Meanwhile, the fall in the price received by producers leads to a fall in producer surplus. This, too, is equal to the sum of the areas of a rectangle and a triangle. The loss in producer surplus is the sum of the areas of the dark red rectangle labelled *C* and the light red triangle labelled *F* in Figure 7-8.

Of course, although consumers and producers are hurt by the tax, the government gains revenue. The revenue the government collects is equal to the tax per unit sold, *T*, multiplied by the quantity sold, Q_T. This revenue is equal to the area of a rectangle Q_T wide and *T* high. And we already have that rectangle in the figure: it is the sum of rectangles *A* and *C*. So the government gains part of what consumers and producers lose from an excise tax.

But a portion of the loss to producers and consumers from the tax is not offset by a gain to the government—specifically, the two triangles *B* and *F*. The deadweight loss caused by the tax is equal to the combined area of these two triangles. It represents the total surplus lost to society because of the tax—that is, the amount of surplus that would have been generated by transactions that now do not take place because of the tax.

Figure 7-9 is a version of Figure 7-8 that leaves out rectangles *A* (the surplus shifted from consumers to the government) and *C* (the surplus shifted from producers to the government) and shows only the deadweight loss, drawn here as a shaded triangle. The base of that triangle is equal to the tax wedge, *T*; the height of the triangle is equal to the reduction in the quantity transacted due to the tax, $Q_E - Q_T$. Clearly, the larger the tax wedge and the larger the reduction in the quantity transacted, the greater the inefficiency from the tax. But also note an important, contrasting point: if the excise tax somehow *didn't* reduce the quantity bought and sold in this market—if Q_T remained equal to Q_E after the tax was levied—the shaded triangle would disappear and the deadweight loss from the tax would be zero. This observation is simply the flip-side of the principle found earlier in the chapter: a tax causes inefficiency because it discourages mutually beneficial transactions between buyers and sellers. So if a tax does not discourage transactions, it causes no deadweight loss. In this case, the tax simply shifts surplus straight from consumers and producers to the government.

Using a triangle to measure deadweight loss is a technique used in many economic applications. For example, triangles are used to measure the deadweight loss produced by types of taxes other than excise taxes. They are also used to measure the deadweight

FIGURE   **7-9**   **The Deadweight Loss of a Tax**

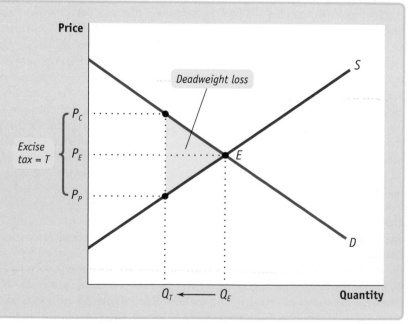

A tax leads to a deadweight loss because it creates inefficiency: some mutually beneficial transactions never take place because of the tax—namely, the transactions $Q_E - Q_T$. The shaded area here represents the value of the deadweight loss: it is the total surplus that would have been gained from the $Q_E - Q_T$ transactions. If the tax had not discouraged transactions—had the number of transactions remained at Q_E—no deadweight loss would have been incurred.

loss produced by monopoly, another kind of market distortion. And deadweight-loss triangles are often used to evaluate the benefits and costs of public policies besides taxation—such as whether to impose stricter safety standards on a product.

In considering the total amount of inefficiency caused by a tax, we must also take into account something not shown in Figure 7-9: the resources actually used by the government to collect the tax, and by taxpayers to pay it, over and above the amount of the tax. These lost resources are called the **administrative costs** of the tax. The most familiar administrative cost of the Canadian tax system is the time individuals spend filling out their income tax forms or the money they spend on accountants to prepare their tax forms for them. (The latter is considered an inefficiency from the point of view of society because accountants could instead be performing other, non-tax-related services.) Included in the administrative costs that taxpayers incur are resources used to evade the tax, both legally and illegally. The costs of operating the Canada Revenue Agency, the arm of the federal government tasked with collecting the federal and most provincial income taxes are actually quite small in comparison to the administrative costs paid by taxpayers.

So the total inefficiency caused by a tax is the sum of its deadweight loss and its administrative costs. The general rule for economic policy is that, other things equal, a tax system should be designed to minimize the total inefficiency it imposes on society. In practice, other considerations also apply (as the federal government learned in 1990), but this principle nonetheless gives valuable guidance. Administrative costs are usually well known, and are more or less determined by the current technology of collecting taxes (for example, filing paper returns versus filing electronically). But how can we predict the size of the deadweight loss associated with a given tax? Not surprisingly, as in our analysis of the incidence of a tax, the price elasticities of supply and demand play crucial roles in making such a prediction.

Elasticities and the Deadweight Loss of a Tax

We know that the deadweight loss from an excise tax arises because it prevents some mutually beneficial transactions from occurring. In particular, the producer and consumer surplus that is forgone because of these missing transactions is equal to the size of the deadweight loss itself. This means that the larger the number of transactions that are prevented by the tax, the larger the deadweight loss.

This fact gives us an important clue in understanding the relationship between elasticity and the size of the deadweight loss from a tax. Recall that when demand or supply is elastic, the quantity demanded or the quantity supplied is relatively responsive to changes in the price. So a tax imposed on a good for which either demand or supply, or both, is elastic will cause a relatively large decrease in the quantity transacted and a relatively large deadweight loss. And when we say that demand or supply is inelastic, we mean that the quantity demanded or the quantity supplied is relatively unresponsive to changes in the price. As a result, a tax imposed when demand or supply, or both, is inelastic will cause a relatively small decrease in the quantity transacted and a relatively small deadweight loss.

The four panels of Figure 7-10 illustrate the positive relationship between a good's price elasticity of either demand or supply and the deadweight loss from taxing that good. Each panel represents the same amount of tax imposed but on a different good; the size of the deadweight loss is given by the area of the shaded triangle. In panel (a), the deadweight-loss triangle is large because demand for this good is relatively elastic—a large number of transactions fail to occur because of the tax. In panel (b), the same supply curve is drawn as in panel (a), but demand for this good is relatively inelastic; as a result, the triangle is small because only a small number of transactions are forgone. Likewise, panels (c) and (d) contain the same demand curve but different supply curves. In panel (c), an elastic supply curve gives rise to a large deadweight-loss triangle, but in panel (d) an inelastic supply curve gives rise to a small deadweight-loss triangle.

The **administrative costs** of a tax are the resources used by government to collect the tax, and by taxpayers to pay it, over and above the amount of the tax, as well as to evade it.

FIGURE 7-10 Deadweight Loss and Elasticities

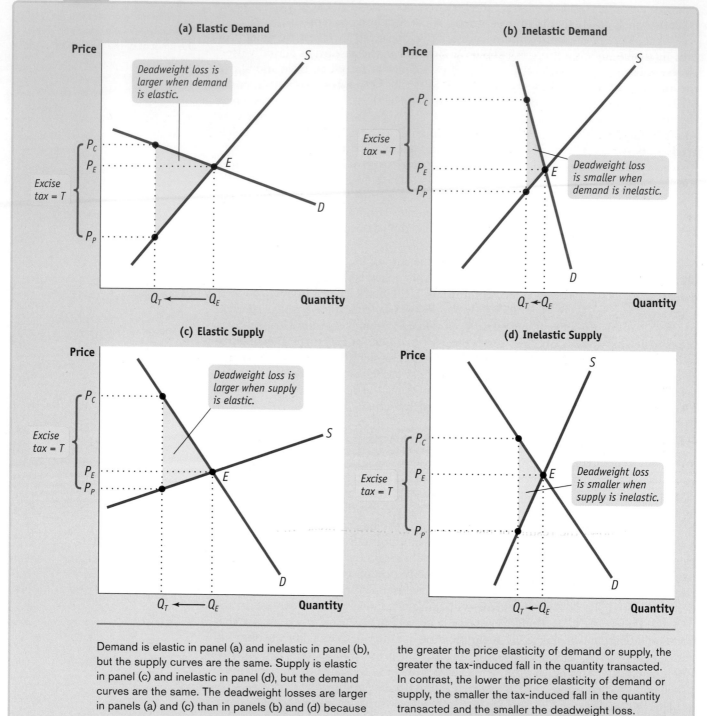

Demand is elastic in panel (a) and inelastic in panel (b), but the supply curves are the same. Supply is elastic in panel (c) and inelastic in panel (d), but the demand curves are the same. The deadweight losses are larger in panels (a) and (c) than in panels (b) and (d) because the greater the price elasticity of demand or supply, the greater the tax-induced fall in the quantity transacted. In contrast, the lower the price elasticity of demand or supply, the smaller the tax-induced fall in the quantity transacted and the smaller the deadweight loss.

The implication of this result is clear: if you want to minimize the efficiency costs of taxation, you should choose to tax only those goods for which demand or supply, or both, is relatively inelastic. For such goods, a tax has little effect on behaviour because behaviour is relatively unresponsive to changes in the price. In the extreme case in which demand is perfectly inelastic (a vertical demand curve), the quantity demanded is unchanged by the imposition of the tax. As a result, the tax imposes no deadweight loss. Similarly, if supply is perfectly inelastic (a vertical supply curve), the quantity supplied is unchanged by the tax and there is also no deadweight loss. So if the goal in choosing whom to tax is to minimize deadweight loss, then taxes should be imposed on goods and services that have the most inelastic response—that is, goods and services for which consumers or producers will change their behaviour the least in response to the tax. (Unless they have a tendency to revolt, of course.) And this lesson carries a flip side: using a tax to purposely decrease the amount of a harmful activity, such as underage drinking, will have the most impact when that activity is elastically demanded or supplied.

ECONOMICS ➤ IN ACTION

TAXING SMOKES

One of the most important excise taxes in Canada is the tax on cigarettes. The federal government imposes a tax of $1.70 a pack; provincial and territorial governments impose taxes that range from $2.47 a pack in Ontario to $5.80 a pack in Manitoba; and throughout the country the GST/HST applies on top of these excise taxes (in Manitoba and Saskatchewan, the PST also applies on top of the excise tax). The combined tax on a pack of cigarettes varies from $4.65 per pack in Quebec to $8.79 a pack in Manitoba. In general, tax rates on cigarettes have increased over time, because more and more governments have seen them not just as a source of revenue but as a way to discourage smoking. But the rise in cigarette taxes has not been gradual. Once a government decides to raise cigarette taxes, it usually raises them a lot—which provides economists with useful data on what happens when there is a big tax increase.

The time span for the data was chosen to reflect the significant tax increases that followed the 2001 introduction of the Federal Tobacco Control Strategy that, among other things, sought to protect Canadians from the harms of tobacco consumption via higher federal taxes. The federal government raised the excise tax per pack of cigarettes from $0.94 in 2000 to $1.70 by 2008—an 80.7% increase. Many of the provinces followed the federal lead. The largest provincial increase occurred in Ontario, where the excise tax per pack rose from $0.89 in 2000 to $2.45 by 2008—a 175.1% increase. The smallest provincial increase was in New Brunswick, where the excise tax per pack rose from $1.43 in 2000 to $2.29 by 2008—a 59.7% increase.

Table 7-1 shows the results of big increases in cigarette taxes. In each case, sales fell, just as our analysis predicts. Although it's theoretically possible for tax revenue to fall after such a large tax increase, in reality, tax revenue rose in each case. That's because cigarettes have a low price elasticity of demand.

TABLE **7-1**   **Results of Increases in Cigarette Taxes**

Jurisdiction	Year span	Increase in tax (per pack)	New jurisdiction tax (per pack)	Change in quantity transacted	Change in tax revenue
Canada (federal)	2001-08	$0.76	$1.70	−33.2%	+19.5%
Ontario[4]	2001-08	1.56	2.45	−16.9	+123.6
New Brunswick[4]	2001-08	0.86	2.29	−34.5	+68.0

Sources: Nachum Gabler and Diane Katz, Contraband Tobacco in Canada: Tax Policies and Black Market Incentives, (Fraser Institute, 2010); Statistics Canada; Health Canada; Department of Finance.

[4]These rows only show the provincial excise tax. It has not been combined with the federal excise tax. The quantity transacted is only within the province. The change in tax revenue represents the change in provincial government excise tax revenue only—no estimate of the change of federal excise tax revenue collected within the boundaries of this province has been made. From 2000 to 2008 the combined federal and provincial excise tax per pack of cigarettes rose 126.6% in Ontario and 68% in New Brunswick.

CHECK YOUR UNDERSTANDING 7-2

1. The accompanying table shows five consumers' willingness to pay for one can of diet cola each as well as five producers' costs of selling one can of diet cola each. Each consumer buys at most one can of cola; each producer sells at most one can of cola. The government asks your advice about the effects of an excise tax of $0.40 per can of diet cola. Assume that there are no administrative costs from the tax.

Consumer	Willingness to pay	Producer	Cost
Ana	$0.70	Zhang	$0.10
Bernice	0.60	Yves	0.20
Chizuko	0.50	Xavier	0.30
Dagmar	0.40	Walter	0.40
Ella	0.30	Vern	0.50

   a. Without the excise tax, what is the equilibrium price and the equilibrium quantity of cola transacted?

   b. The excise tax raises the price paid by consumers post-tax to $0.60 and lowers the price received by producers post-tax to $0.20. With the excise tax, what is the quantity of cola transacted?

   c. Without the excise tax, how much individual consumer surplus does each of the consumers gain? How much with the tax? How much total consumer surplus is lost as a result of the tax?

   d. Without the excise tax, how much individual producer surplus does each of the producers gain? How much with the tax? How much total producer surplus is lost as a result of the tax?

   e. How much government revenue does the excise tax create?

   f. What is the deadweight loss from the imposition of this excise tax?

2. In each of the following cases, focus on the price elasticity of demand and use a diagram to illustrate the likely size—small or large—of the deadweight loss resulting from a tax. Explain your reasoning.

   a. Gasoline

   b. Milk chocolate bars

Solutions appear at back of book.

Tax Fairness and Tax Efficiency

We've just seen how economic analysis can be used to determine the inefficiency caused by a tax. It's clear that, other things equal, policy-makers should choose a tax that creates less inefficiency over a tax that creates more. But that guideline still leaves policy-makers with wide discretion in choosing what to tax and, consequently, who bears the burden of the tax. How should they exercise this discretion?

One answer is that policy-makers should make the tax system fair. But what exactly does fairness mean? Moreover, however you define fairness, how should policy-makers balance considerations of fairness versus considerations of efficiency?

Two Principles of Tax Fairness

According to the **benefits principle** of tax fairness, those who benefit from public spending should bear the burden of the tax that pays for that spending.

Fairness, like beauty, is often in the eyes of the beholder. When it comes to taxes, however, most debates about fairness rely on one of two principles of tax fairness: the *benefits principle* and the *ability-to-pay principle*.

According to the **benefits principle** of tax fairness, those who benefit from public spending should bear the burden of the tax that pays for that spending. For example, those who benefit from a road should pay for that road's upkeep, those who fly on airplanes should pay for air traffic control, and so on. The benefits principle is the basis for some parts of the Canadian tax system. For example, the federal Gas Tax Fund specifically reserves a portion of federal taxes collected on the sale of gasoline and diesel fuel for the maintenance and improvement of municipal infrastructure projects. In this way motorists who benefit from the use of public roads also pay for it. Another example is the Air Travellers Security Charge (ATSC) that channels all ATSC payments collected from air travellers to pay for enhancements to and the operation of the air security system at 89 airports in Canada.

The benefits principle is attractive from an economic point of view because it matches well with one of the major justifications for public spending—the theory of *public goods,* which will be covered in Chapter 17. This theory explains why government action is sometimes needed to provide people with goods that markets alone would not provide, goods like national defense. If that's the role of government, it seems natural to charge each person in proportion to the benefits he or she gets from those goods.

Practical considerations, however, make it impossible to base the entire tax system on the benefits principle. It would be too cumbersome to have a specific tax for each of the many distinct programs that the government offers. Also, attempts to base taxes on the benefits principle often conflict with the other major principle of tax fairness: the **ability-to-pay principle,** according to which those with greater ability to pay a tax should pay more.

The ability-to-pay principle is usually interpreted to mean that high-income individuals should pay more in taxes than low-income individuals. Often the ability-to-pay principle is used to argue not only that high-income individuals should pay more taxes but also that they should pay a higher *percentage* of their income in taxes. We'll consider the issue of how taxes vary as a percentage of income later.

Discussions on government policy issues often use the ability-to-pay principle as a means to argue either for change or in support of the status quo. For example, during debates about Canadian municipal property taxes complaints are commonly made that the residential property tax system is "unfair" because the tax is a percentage of the value of a property. The fact that one house is worth $500 000 while another is worth $250 000 does not imply that the former creates a burden on municipal services that is twice as large. The tax violates the benefits principle of tax fairness. But that is not the end of it. During such debates, one often also hears that just because a senior citizen owns a home worth $500 000 does not imply they have the ability-to-pay a large property tax amount. So this tax also violates the ability-to-pay principle, which may force "lucky" seniors, who have had the good fortune to see their home value rise significantly over time, to sell their homes so as to live within their income.

According to the **ability-to-pay principle** of tax fairness, those with greater ability to pay a tax should pay more tax.

A **lump-sum tax** is the same for everyone, regardless of any actions people take.

Equity versus Efficiency

Canadian taxes on the manufacture and retail sale of alcohol are complex. In general, most provinces require makers to have a special manufacturer licence, the cost of which is a flat fee or tax paid by both large and small producers. This is an example of a **lump-sum tax,** a tax that is the same regardless of any actions people take. In this case, the large producers pay the same amount of tax regardless of how many litres they produce. Lump-sum taxes are widely perceived to be much less fair than a tax that is proportional to the amount of the transaction. Small producers may feel that they should pay less tax than much larger producers pay. If the fixed licensing fee is set quite high then some smaller producers may find their profit maximizing response is to shut down their firm.

But provincial and territorial alcohol taxes applied on retail sales are usually levied on what is essentially a per-litre basis, which definitely distorts incen-

In a well-designed tax system, there is a **trade-off between equity and efficiency:** the system can be made more efficient only by making it less fair, and vice versa.

tives to engage in mutually beneficial transactions and creates deadweight loss. Because of these alcohol sales taxes, some producers will reduce how much alcohol they make, with some forgoing production altogether. The result, surely, is a lower production of alcohol and less income earned by manufacturers and employees in the alcohol sector because of these sales taxes.

In contrast, a lump-sum tax does not distort incentives. Because under a lump-sum tax people have to pay the same amount of tax regardless of their actions, it does not lead them to change their actions and therefore causes no deadweight loss. So lump-sum taxes, although unfair, are better than other taxes at promoting economic efficiency.

A tax system can be made fairer by moving it in the direction of the benefits principle or the ability-to-pay principle. But this will come at a cost because the tax system will now tax people more heavily based on their actions, increasing the amount of deadweight loss. This observation reflects a general principle that we learned in Chapter 1: There is often a trade-off between equity and efficiency. Here, unless a tax system is badly designed, it can be made fairer only by sacrificing efficiency. Conversely, it can be made more efficient only by making it less fair. This means that there is normally a **trade-off between equity and efficiency** in the design of a tax system.

It's important to understand that economic analysis cannot say how much weight a tax system should give to equity and how much to efficiency. That choice is a value judgment, one we make through the political process.

ECONOMICS ► IN ACTION

FEDERAL TAX PHILOSOPHY

What is the principle underlying the federal tax system? (By federal, we mean taxes collected by the federal government, as opposed to the taxes collected by provincial, territorial, and local governments.) The answer is that it depends on the tax.

The best-known federal tax, accounting for about half of all federal revenue, is the personal income tax. The structure of the income tax reflects the ability-to-pay principle: families with low incomes pay little or no income tax. In fact, some families pay negative income tax: a program known as the Working Income Tax Benefit "tops up," or adds to, the earnings of low-wage workers. Meanwhile, those with high incomes not only pay a lot of income tax but also must pay a larger share of their income in income taxes than the average family.

Alongside the personal income tax system that generally flows money from individuals to governments in the form of tax payments is a system of government personal transfer payments that flow money in the other direction. Since transfers flow from governments at all levels to individuals, they are like a tax but with a negative (tax) rate. Major transfer programs exist for old age security benefits and for children's benefits payments. The Old Age Security (OAS) is Canada's first public pension plan established in 1927. Today the OAS is a taxable monthly pension entitlement available to most Canadians 65 years of age or older.

THE CANADIAN PRESS/Chris Young

Every year, Canadians use the T1 Schedule 1 form to calculate the amount of federal taxes that they owe.

Canadian seniors living with low income or who are widowed may qualify for further supplemental payments to help raise their standard of living. In 2013, about $40 billion in regular and supplemental OAS payments were paid to Canadian seniors. This far eclipsed the $13 billion in government transfers in the form of children's benefits payments made to assist people with the cost of raising a young family.

These transfer payments are financed out of general government revenues and have built-in reductions. In order to qualify either for a larger amount or even a payment at all, the potential recipient must have an income below some set threshold. This ensures that larger payments are directed to those who need them the most, while keeping transfer program expenses down, which helps keep the program affordable.

Table 7-2 illustrates the difference in which families bear the burden of income taxes (to the federal and provincial/territorial governments) and which families receive government transfers. The table divides Canadian families into quintiles, based on after-tax income: the bottom quintile is the poorest 20% of families after income taxes have been paid; the second quintile is the next poorest 20%, and so on. The second column shows the share of total Canadian pre-tax and pre-transfer income received by each quintile. The third column shows the share of personal income tax collected that is paid by each quintile.

TABLE 7-2	Share of Pre-Tax Income, Income Tax, and Government Transfers, by Quintile in 2011		
Income group	Percent of total income received before tax and transfer	Percent of total personal income tax paid	Percent of total government transfers received
Bottom quintile	2.1%	0.9%	19.0%
Second quintile	7.4	4.6	25.6
Third quintile	14.4	10.8	22.7
Fourth quintile	24.4	22.1	19.4
Top quintile	51.8	61.6	13.4

Source: Statistics Canada.

As you can see, low-income families earn little income and pay even less income tax. Even middle-income families paid a substantially smaller share of total income tax collected than their share of total income. In contrast, the fifth or top quintile, the richest 20% of families, paid a much higher share of total federal income tax collected compared with its share of total income. The fourth column shows the share of total government transfers that is received by each quintile, and the results are very different: the share of total transfer payments received by the bottom two quintiles is well above their share of income received and slightly above their share of the population. Plus the share of transfers received by the top quintile is substantially less than its share of total income. It is the only quintile that really falls short of a 20% share.

Generally transfer payments are financed out of general government revenues. But the burden of personal income taxes falls more on higher-income earners. At the same time, high-income families do not get an equal share of the transfer payments distributed, despite providing most of the funds needed for these programs. So the beneficiaries of government transfers in the form of OAS and children's benefits (i.e., seniors and low-income families with young children) do not bear the tax burden necessary to support this spending. Thus the design of these transfer programs does not adhere to the benefits principle. Instead the funding, and distribution of transfers, adheres to the ability-to-pay principle. As a society, we have decided to spread the costs of these government transfer programs unequally across all taxpayers.

▼ Quick Review

- Other things equal, government tax policy aims for tax efficiency. But it also tries to achieve tax fairness, or tax equity.

- There are two important principles of tax fairness: the **benefits principle** and the **ability to-pay principle.**

- A **lump-sum tax** is efficient because it does not distort incentives, but it is generally considered unfair. In any well-designed tax system, there is a **trade-off between equity and efficiency.** How the tax system should weight equity and efficiency is a value judgment to be decided by the political process.

CHECK YOUR UNDERSTANDING 7-3

1. Assess each of the following taxes in terms of the benefits principle versus the ability-to-pay principle. What, if any, actions are distorted by the tax? Assume for simplicity in each case that the purchaser of the good bears 100% of the burden of the tax.
   a. A federal tax of $500 for each new car purchased that finances highway safety programs
   b. A local tax of 20% on hotel rooms that finances local government expenditures
   c. A local tax of 1% on the assessed value of homes that finances local schools
   d. A 1% sales tax on food that pays for government food safety regulation and inspection programs

Solutions appear at back of book.

Understanding the Tax System

An excise tax is the easiest tax to analyze, making it a good vehicle for understanding the general principles of tax analysis. However, in Canada today, excise taxes are actually a relatively minor source of government revenue. In this section, we develop a framework for understanding more general forms of taxation and look at some of the major taxes used in Canada.

Tax Bases and Tax Structure

Every tax consists of two pieces: a *base* and a *structure*. The **tax base** is the measure or value that determines how much tax an individual or firm pays. It is usually a monetary measure, like income or property value. The **tax structure** specifies how the tax depends on the tax base. It is usually expressed in percentage terms; for example, homeowners in some areas might pay yearly property taxes equal to 2% of the value of their homes.

Some important taxes and their tax bases are as follows:

- **Income tax:** a tax that depends on the income of an individual or family from wages and investments (also known as the personal income tax)
- **Payroll tax:** a tax that depends on the earnings an employer pays to an employee
- **Sales tax:** a tax that depends on the value of goods sold (also known as an excise tax)
- **Profits tax:** a tax on an incorporated firm's profits (also known as the corporate income tax)
- **Property tax:** a tax that depends on the value of property, such as the value of a home
- **Wealth tax:** a tax on an individual's wealth

Once the tax base has been defined, the next question is how the tax depends on the base. The simplest tax structure is a **proportional tax,** also sometimes called a *flat tax*, which is the same percentage of the base regardless of the taxpayer's income or wealth. For example, a property tax that is set at 2% of the value of the property, whether the property is worth $10 000 or $10 000 000, is a proportional tax. Many taxes, however, are not proportional. Instead, different people pay different percentages, usually because the tax law tries to take account of either the benefits principle or the ability-to-pay principle.

Because taxes are ultimately paid out of income, economists classify taxes according to how they vary with the income of individuals. A tax that rises *more* than in proportion to income, so that high-income taxpayers pay a larger percentage of their income than low-income taxpayers, is a **progressive tax.** A tax that rises *less* than in proportion to income, so that higher-income taxpayers pay a smaller percentage of their income than low-income taxpayers, is a **regressive tax.** A proportional tax on income would be neither progressive nor regressive.

The Canadian tax system contains a mixture of progressive and regressive taxes, though it is somewhat progressive overall.

Equity, Efficiency, and Progressive Taxation

Most, though not all, people view a progressive tax system as fairer than a regressive system. The reason is the ability-to-pay principle: a high-income family that pays 29% of its income in taxes is still left with a lot more money than a low-income family that pays only 15% in taxes. But attempts to make taxes strongly progressive run up against the trade-off between equity and efficiency.

To see why, consider a hypothetical example, illustrated in Table 7-3. We assume that there are two kinds of people in the nation of Taxmania: half of the population earns $40 000 a year and half earns $80 000, so the average income is

---

The **tax base** is the measure or value, such as income or property value, that determines how much tax an individual or firm pays.

The **tax structure** specifies how the tax depends on the tax base.

An **income tax** is a tax on an individual's or family's income.

A **payroll tax** is a tax on the earnings an employer pays to an employee.

A **sales tax** is a tax on the value of goods sold.

A **profits tax** is a tax on a firm's profits.

A **property tax** is a tax on the value of property, such as the value of a home.

A **wealth tax** is a tax on an individual's wealth.

A **proportional tax** is the same percentage of the tax base regardless of the taxpayer's income or wealth.

A **progressive tax** takes a larger share of the income of high-income taxpayers than of low-income taxpayers.

A **regressive tax** takes a smaller share of the income of high-income taxpayers than of low-income taxpayers.

$60 000 a year. We also assume that the Taxmanian government needs to collect one-fourth of that income—$15 000 a year per person—in taxes.

One way to raise this revenue would be through a proportional tax that takes one-fourth of everyone's income. The results of this proportional tax are shown in the second column of Table 7-3: after taxes, lower-income Taxmanians would be left with an income of $30 000 a year and higher-income Taxmanians, $60 000.

Even this system might have some negative effects on incentives. Suppose, for example, that finishing college improves a Taxmanian's chance of getting a higher-paying job. Some people who would invest time and effort in going to college in hopes of raising their income from $40 000 to $80 000, a $40 000 gain, might not bother if the potential gain is only $30 000, the after-tax difference in pay between a lower-paying and higher-paying job.

But a strongly progressive tax system could create a much bigger incentive problem. Suppose that the Taxmanian government decided to exempt the poorer half of the population from all taxes but still wanted to raise the same amount of revenue. To do this, it would have to collect $30 000 from each individual earning $80 000 a year. As the third column of Table 7-3 shows, people earning $80 000 would then be left with income after taxes of $50 000—only $10 000 more than the after-tax income of people earning half as much before taxes. This would greatly reduce the incentive for people to invest time and effort to raise their earnings.

The point here is that any income tax system will tax away part of the gain an individual gets by moving up the income scale, reducing the incentive to earn more. But a progressive tax takes away a larger share of the gain than a proportional tax, creating a more adverse effect on incentives. In comparing the incentive effects of tax systems, economists often focus on the **marginal tax rate:** the percentage of an increase in income that is taxed away. In this example, the marginal tax rate on income above $40 000 is 25% with proportional taxation but 75% with progressive taxation.

Our hypothetical example is much more extreme than the reality of progressive taxation in Canada today—although, as the Economics in Action explains, in previous years the marginal tax rates paid by high earners were very high. However, these have moderated over time as concerns arose about the severe incentive effects of extremely progressive taxes. In short, the ability-to-pay principle pushes governments toward a highly progressive tax system, but efficiency considerations push them the other way.

The **marginal tax rate** is the percentage of an increase in income that is taxed away.

TABLE 7-3 Proportional versus Progressive Taxes in Taxmania

Pre-tax income	After-tax income with proportional taxation	After-tax income with progressive taxation
$40 000	$30 000	$40 000
$80 000	$60 000	$50 000

Taxes in Canada

Table 7-4 shows the revenue raised by major taxes in Canada in 2012. Some of the taxes are collected by the federal government and the others by provincial, territorial, and local governments.

There is a major tax corresponding to five of the six tax bases we identified earlier. There are income taxes, payroll taxes, sales taxes, profits taxes, and property taxes, all of which play an important role in the overall tax system. The only item missing is a wealth tax. In fact, most Canadian provinces and territories do have a wealth tax, called *probate fees,* which depends on the value of someone's estate at the time of his or her death.

Probate fees are charged by the provincial court to recognize the validity of a deceased person's will and the appointment of the executor. When the court grants letters of probate this notifies the public that the will is adequate and that it was not being challenged. Thus probate protects the executor and all parties who received an inheritance payment under the will from future legal challenges or claims. These fees vary significantly from province to province, in Quebec probate costs about $100 while in Ontario probate fees depend on

TABLE 7-4 Major Taxes in Canada, 2012

Federal taxes (billions)		Provincial, territorial, and local taxes (billions)	
Income	$125.1	Income	$81.5
Payroll	60.4	Payroll	24.9
Sales	47.4	Sales	106.2
Profits	34.4	Profits	22.5
		Property	48.5

Source: Statistics Canada.

the size of the estate rising to 15% of the value of the estate above $50 000. The deceased's assets are deemed to have been sold on the day of the death, and any tax owing from this sale is payable through the regular income tax system on a final tax return. There is one important exception when someone dies: the assets can be passed, tax free, to a spouse.

In addition to the taxes shown in Table 7-4, provincial and local governments collect substantial revenue from other sources as varied as driver's licence fees and sewer charges. These fees and charges are an important part of the tax burden but very difficult to summarize or analyze.

Are the taxes in Table 7-4 progressive or regressive? It depends on the tax. The personal income tax is strongly progressive. Payroll taxes, except for the CPP and EI portions paid only on earnings up to about $50 000, are somewhat regressive. Sales taxes are generally regressive, because higher-income families save more of their income and thus spend a smaller share of it on taxable goods than do lower-income families.

Property taxes, which together with sales taxes represent the largest source of revenue for provincial, territorial, and local governments, are somewhat regressive. In addition, those other taxes principally levied at the provincial and local level are typically quite regressive: it costs the same amount to renew a driver's licence or pay your vehicle licensing fee no matter what your income is.

Overall, the federal income tax is quite progressive. The second column of Table 7-5 shows the share of all income earned by different percentiles of income earners. The third column of this table shows that as we move higher up the income distribution the share of federal income tax paid declines more slowly than the share of income earned does. In 2011, the people in the top half of the income distribution earned 83% of all income earned but paid 96% of federal income tax. The table shows that the federal tax income is indeed progressive, with low-income families paying a relatively small share of their income in federal income taxes and high-income families paying a greater share of their income.

TABLE 7-5 Estimated Distribution of Income Earned and Income Tax Paid, 2011

Income group	Total Income Earned	Federal Personal Income Tax Paid
Top 1% of earners	12%	24%
Top 5% of earners	25	42
Top 10% of earners	36	56
Top 25% of earners	59	79
Top 50% of earners	83	96

Source: Brett Stuckey and Adriane Yong, *A Primer on Federal Personal Income Taxes*, (Library of Parliament, 2011).

Since the mid- to late-1990s, the federal government and most provincial governments have cut income taxes for most families. The largest cuts, both as a share of income and as a share of taxes collected, have gone to families with high incomes. As a result, the personal income tax system is less progressive (at the time of writing) than it was in 1995 because the share of income paid by high-income families has fallen relative to the share paid by middle- and low-income families.

And the overall tax system is likely even less progressive than in the past. The reduction of the GST from 7% to 5% helped make the tax system less regressive (or more progressive). But, increases in payroll tax rates and other fees charged by governments make the tax system more regressive. Also, corporate tax rates have fallen very significantly since the mid-1990s. Of course people with higher incomes are more likely to own a greater fraction of Canada's corporations than lower income people. So you could argue that corporate tax cuts also make the tax system more regressive.

In summary, the Canadian tax system is somewhat progressive, with the richest tenth of the population paying a somewhat higher share of income in taxes than families in the middle, and the poorest Canadians paying considerably less. Although our tax system is progressive, the degree of progressiveness varies with the nature of the taxes. The federal income tax is more progressive than payroll taxes. And personal income taxation is more progressive than sales and property taxes.

GLOBAL COMPARISON

YOU THINK YOU PAY HIGH TAXES?

Everyone, everywhere complains about taxes. But citizens of Canada actually have less to complain about than citizens of most other wealthy countries.

To assess the overall level of taxes, economists usually calculate taxes as a share of *gross domestic product*—the total value of goods and services produced in a country. By this measure, as you can see in the accompanying figure, in 2009, Canadian taxes were near the middle of the scale. Our neighbour the United States has a significantly lower overall tax burden. But tax rates in Europe, where governments need a lot of revenue to pay for extensive benefits such as guaranteed health care and generous unemployment benefits, are up to 50% higher than in Canada.

Source: OECD.

FOR INQUIRING MINDS

TAXING INCOME VERSUS TAXING CONSUMPTION

The Canadian government taxes people mainly on the money they *make,* and less so on the money they spend on consumption. Yet most tax experts argue that this policy badly distorts incentives. Someone who earns income and then invests that income for the future gets taxed twice: once on the original sum and again on any earnings made from the investment. So a system that taxes income rather than consumption discourages people from saving and investing, instead it provides an incentive to spend their income today. And encouraging saving and investing is an important policy goal, both because empirical data show that Canadians tend to save too little for retirement and health expenses in their later years and because saving and investing contribute to economic growth.

Moving from a system that taxes income to one that taxes consumption could solve this problem. In fact, the governments of many countries get much of their revenue from a value-added tax, or VAT, which acts like a national sales tax. In some countries VAT rates are very high; in the United Kingdom, for example, the rate is 20%.

Canada has taken mixed steps towards taxing consumption instead of income. The introduction of tax-free saving accounts (TFSA) helps to reduce the double taxation issue. In 2013–2014 Canadian adults were allowed to contribute $5500 per year to a TFSA, and any income earned on assets held in a TFSA is exempted from taxation. Also, the federal government does have a VAT in the Goods and Services Tax (GST). Several provinces integrated this national VAT with a provincial VAT to form a single Harmonized Sales Tax (HST) that, like the GST, applies on the sale

of most goods and services. Alberta and the three territories only have the GST. Other provinces have the GST along with a provincial retail sales tax that does not function like a value-added tax, but does tax the consumption of many goods. Between 2006 and 2008 the Conservative Party of Canada delivered on promises they made during the 2006 federal election campaign to lower the GST from 7% to 5%, moving the federal government away from taxing consumption as much.

Value-added taxes have two main negative qualities. One is that it is difficult, though not impossible, to make a consumption tax progressive. The other is that a VAT typically has very high administrative costs. So with the federal cuts to GST, Canadians are left with all of the bad parts of a VAT and fewer of the benefits.

Different Taxes, Different Principles

Why are some taxes progressive but others regressive? Can't the government make up its mind?

There are two main reasons for the mixture of regressive and progressive taxes in the Canadian system: the difference between levels of government and the fact that different taxes are based on different principles.

Provincial and especially local governments generally do not make as much effort to apply the ability-to-pay principle. This is largely because they are subject to *tax competition:* a province or local government that imposes high taxes on people with high incomes faces the prospect that those people may move to other locations where taxes are lower. This is much less of a concern at the national level, although a handful of very rich people have given up their Canadian citizenship to avoid paying Canadian taxes.

Although the federal government is in a better position than provincial or local governments to apply principles of fairness, it applies different principles to different taxes. We saw an example of this in the preceding Economics in Action. The most important tax, the federal income tax, is strongly progressive, reflecting the ability-to-pay principle. But the federal payroll taxes, the second most important tax, are somewhat regressive, because most of this tax revenue is linked to specific programs—Canada Pension Plan and Employment Insurance—and, reflecting the benefits principle, payroll taxes are levied more or less in proportion to the benefits received from these programs.

ECONOMICS ▸ *IN ACTION*

THE TOP MARGINAL INCOME TAX RATE

The amount of money a Canadian owes in federal income taxes is found by applying marginal tax rates on successively higher "brackets" of income. For example, in 2013 a single person would have paid 15% on the first $43 561 of taxable income (i.e., income after subtracting exemptions and deductions); 22% on the next $43 562; 26% on the next $47 931; and a top rate of 29% on his or her income, if any, over $135 054. Relatively few people (less than 5% of taxpayers) have incomes high enough to pay the top marginal rate. In fact, about 90% of Canadians pay no income tax or they fall into one of the first two bracket. But the top marginal income tax rate is often viewed as a useful indicator of the progressivity of the tax system, because it shows just how high a tax rate the Canadian government is willing to impose on the affluent.

While the top marginal tax rate is interesting, almost equally important is the taxable income cut-off where this rate begins to apply. Figure 7-11 shows the level of taxable income where the top federal tax bracket starts from 1985 to 2013. In each of these years any taxable income earned above this limit faced the highest marginal income tax rate. According to the Canadian Tax Foundation, the top combined federal and provincial marginal income tax rate in 1949 was 84%, and in 1971 it was 80% (both on taxable income above $400 000); in 1972 it was 59.93% (on taxable income above $60 000); in 1986 it was 53.38%; in 1987 it was 51.07%; in 1994 it was 46.4%. This is where it has pretty much stayed since. But the tax rate is only part of the story, the tax base matters, too. For example, the 1981 federal budget lowered personal tax rates and broadened the tax base. The 1987 budget lowered rates and broadened the base further, including converting tax deductions into tax credits. So Canada moved from a country with high rates and a narrow base to one with lower rates and a much broader tax base.

FIGURE 7-11   The Top Income Tax Bracket Threshold (1985–2013)

Source: Canada Revenue Agency.

CHECK YOUR UNDERSTANDING   7-4

1. An income tax taxes 1% of the first $10 000 of income and 2% on all income above $10 000.
   a. What is the marginal tax rate for someone with income of $5000? How much total tax does this person pay? How much is this as a percentage of his or her income?
   b. What is the marginal tax rate for someone with income of $20 000? How much total tax does this person pay? How much is this as a percentage of his or her income?
   c. Is this income tax proportional, progressive, or regressive?

2. When comparing households at different income levels, economists find that consumption spending grows more slowly than income. Assume that when income grows by 50%, from $10 000 to $15 000, consumption grows by 25%, from $8000 to $10 000. Compare the percent of income paid in taxes by a family with $15 000 in income to that paid by a family with $10 000 in income under a 1% tax on consumption purchases. Is this a proportional, progressive, or regressive tax?

3. True or false? Explain your answers.
   a. Payroll taxes do not affect a person's incentive to take a job because they are paid by employers.
   b. A lump-sum tax is a proportional tax because it is the same amount for each person.

Solutions appear at back of book.

BUSINESS CASE : Cross-Border Taxing

The rules for collecting taxes in Canada are relatively straightforward. When you buy something online from a Canadian retailer, you are charged the sales tax for your province or territory. It does not matter where in Canada the item is coming from, the shipping address determines the taxes. Similarly, you are expected to pay sales tax on major purchases from outside of Canada. The company shipping the item is in charge of collecting the proper sales tax, and generally charges their own brokerage fee for doing it.

Online shoppers in the United States have a different experience. According to the law, online retailers that don't have a physical presence in a given state can sell products in that state without collecting sales tax. (The tax is still due, but residents are supposed to report the transaction and pay the tax themselves—a fact overlooked by online customers.) Sales tax is levied on transactions of most non-essential goods and services in 45 U.S. states (the exceptions are Alaska, Delaware, Montana, New Hampshire, and Oregon), with the average sales tax bite being about 8% of the purchase price.

So, for example, if you compare the final price of *An Astronaut's Guide to Life on Earth* by Chris Hadfield, shipped to Florida, the Amazon.com price is lower than the BarnesandNoble.com price. The difference between the two prices is the 6% Florida sales tax added to the final price by BarnesandNoble.com; Amazon doesn't collect the tax on its orders to Florida.

In fact, Amazon collects sales tax only in states where it has a retail or corporate presence, and the advantage for Amazon in the United States is that it has a physical presence in very few states—only Kansas, Kentucky, New York, North Dakota, and Washington. Amazon has also adopted a strategy of tax minimization, often taking extreme measures, such as forbidding employees to work or even send emails while in certain states to avoid the possibility of triggering state tax levies. In response to a tough new tax law in California, in 2011 Amazon terminated its joint advertising program with 25 000 California affiliates.

In contrast, the brick-and-mortar retailer Barnes and Noble, the parent company of BarnesandNoble.com, has bookstores in every state. (A brick-and-mortar retailer is one that has a physical store.) As a result, BarnesandNoble.com is compelled to collect sales tax on its online orders.

As reported in the *Wall Street Journal*, interviews and company documents have shown that Amazon believes that its tax policy is crucial to its success. It has been estimated that Amazon would have lost as much as $653 million in sales in 2011, or 1.4% of its annual revenue, if forced to collect sales tax. But its ability to avoid collecting sales tax is coming under assault by state tax authorities, hungry for new revenue during tough economic times. For example, Texas, where Amazon has a warehouse but no retail store, has only recently been able to force it to begin collecting state sales tax. And authorities in California have been arguing that Amazon should have to collect state sales tax there because it has affiliated vendors located in the state. In these and other cases, Amazon is fighting vigorously to retain its right not to collect U.S. sales tax. Now this may finally be coming to an end as a group of U.S. Members of Congress have proposed a new bill called the Marketplace Fairness Act, which is meant to level the playing field between online businesses that do not currently have to charge sales taxes and local brick-and-mortar stores that do. This bill, if enacted into law, would let individual U.S. states decide whether or not to have the (out-of-state) businesses collect and report sales taxes for Internet purchases, or to continue to leave it up to the consumers to report their purchases. And it's not hard to guess which side BarnesandNoble.com is on.

QUESTIONS FOR THOUGHT

1. What effect do you think the difference in state sales tax collection has on Amazon's sales versus BarnesandNoble.com's sales?

2. Suppose, as proposed by the Marketplace Fairness Act, sales tax is collected on all online books sales in the United States. From the evidence in this case, what do you think is the incidence of the tax between seller and buyer? What does this imply about the elasticity of supply of books by book retailers? (*Hint:* Compare the pre-tax prices of the book.)

3. How do you think Amazon's tax strategy has distorted its business behaviour? What tax policy would eliminate those distortions?

SUMMARY

1. **Excise taxes**—taxes on the purchase or sale of a good—raise the price paid by consumers and reduce the price received by producers, driving a wedge between the two. The **incidence** of the tax—how the burden of the tax is divided between consumers and producers—does not depend on whom the government requires to pay the tax.

2. The incidence of an excise tax depends on the price elasticities of supply and demand. If the price elasticity of demand is higher than the price elasticity of supply, the tax falls mainly on producers; if the price elasticity of supply is higher than the price elasticity of demand, the tax falls mainly on consumers.

3. The tax revenue generated by a tax depends on the **tax rate** and on the number of taxed units transacted. Excise taxes cause inefficiency in the form of deadweight loss because they discourage some mutually beneficial transactions. Taxes also impose **administrative costs:** resources used to collect the tax, to pay it (over and above the amount of the tax), and to evade it.

4. An excise tax generates revenue for the government but lowers total surplus. The loss in total surplus exceeds the tax revenue, resulting in a deadweight loss to society. This deadweight loss is represented by a triangle, the area of which equals the value of the transactions discouraged by the tax. The greater the elasticity of demand or supply, or both, the larger the deadweight loss from a tax. If either demand or supply is perfectly inelastic, there is no deadweight loss from a tax.

5. An efficient tax minimizes both the sum of the deadweight loss due to distorted incentives and the administrative costs of the tax. However, tax fairness, or tax equity, is also a goal of tax policy.

6. There are two major principles of tax fairness, the **benefits principle** and the **ability-to-pay principle.** The most efficient tax, a **lump-sum tax,** does not distort incentives but performs badly in terms of fairness. The fairest taxes in terms of the ability-to-pay principle, however, distort incentives the most and perform badly on efficiency grounds. So in a well-designed tax system, there is a **trade-off between equity and efficiency.**

7. Every tax consists of a **tax base,** which defines what is taxed, and a **tax structure,** which specifies how the tax depends on the tax base. Different tax bases give rise to different taxes—**income tax, payroll tax, sales tax, profits tax, property tax,** and **wealth tax.** A **proportional tax** is the same percentage of the tax base for all taxpayers.

8. A tax is **progressive** if higher-income people pay a higher percentage of their income in taxes than lower-income people and **regressive** if they pay a lower percentage. Progressive taxes are often justified by the ability-to-pay principle. However, a highly progressive tax system significantly distorts incentives because it leads to a high **marginal tax rate,** the percentage of an increase in income that is taxed away, on high earners. The Canadian tax system is progressive overall, although it contains a mixture of progressive and regressive taxes.

KEY TERMS

Excise tax, p. 200
Incidence, p. 202
Tax rate, p. 208
Administrative costs, p. 213
Benefits principle, p. 216
Ability-to-pay principle, p. 217
Lump-sum tax, p. 217

Trade-off between equity and efficiency, p. 218
Tax base, p. 220
Tax structure, p. 220
Income tax, p. 220
Payroll tax, p. 220
Sales tax, p. 220

Profits tax, p. 220
Property tax, p. 220
Wealth tax, p. 220
Proportional tax, p. 220
Progressive tax, p. 220
Regressive tax, p. 220
Marginal tax rate, p. 221

PROBLEMS

1. To help fund airport security, Canada imposes the Air Travellers Security Charge (ATSC), an excise tax on the sale of domestic airline tickets. In 2011 the total excise tax was $14.96 per round-trip domestic airline ticket. According to Statistics Canada, 67.8 million passengers travelled on domestic airline trips that year at an average price of $248.60 per trip. The accompanying table shows the supply and demand schedules for airline trips. The quantity demanded at the average price of $248.60 is actual data; the rest is hypothetical.

Price of a trip	Quantity of trips demanded (millions)	Quantity of trips supplied (millions)
$250.00	66.0	82.4
248.60	67.8	77.6
241.60	73.8	73.8
233.64	80.8	67.8
233.00	85.3	66.0

a. What is the revenue in 2011 from this excise tax?

b. Suppose that on January 1, 2017, the total excise tax increases to $17.00 per ticket. Assume the supply and demand schedules have not changed. What is the quantity of tickets transacted now? What is the average ticket price now? What will be the 2017 revenue of the ATSC?

c. Does this increase in the excise tax increase or decrease the revenue of the ATSC?

2. The Canadian government would like to help the North American auto industry compete against overseas automakers that sell trucks in Canada. It can do this by imposing an excise tax on each foreign truck sold in Canada. The hypothetical pre-tax demand and supply schedules for imported trucks are given in the accompanying table.

Price of imported truck	Quantity of imported trucks (thousands)	
	Quantity demanded	Quantity supplied
$32 000	100	400
31 000	200	350
30 000	300	300
29 000	400	250
28 000	500	200
27 000	600	150

a. In the absence of government interference, what is the equilibrium price of an imported truck? The equilibrium quantity? Illustrate with a diagram.

b. Assume that the government imposes an excise tax of $3000 per imported truck. Illustrate the effect of this excise tax in your diagram from part (a). How many imported trucks are now purchased and at what price? How much does the foreign automaker receive per truck?

c. Calculate the government revenue raised by the excise tax in part (b). Illustrate it on your diagram.

d. How does the excise tax on imported trucks benefit North American automakers? Whom does it hurt? How does inefficiency arise from this government policy?

3. Suppose, in order to raise additional revenue and hopefully make sales taxes more progressive, the federal government imposes a tax on sales of new luxury cars. For simplicity, assume that the tax is an excise tax of $6000 per car. The accompanying figure shows hypothetical demand and supply curves for luxury cars.

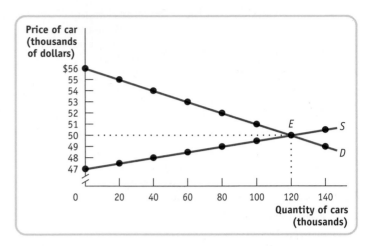

a. Under the tax, what is the price paid by consumers? What is the price received by producers? What is the government tax revenue from the excise tax?

Suppose a new prime minister is elected who promises to reduce the excise tax on luxury cars. As a result the excise tax falls from $6000 per car to $4500 per car.

b. After the reduction in the excise tax from $6000 to $4500 per car, what is the price paid by consumers? What is the price received by producers? What is tax revenue now?

c. Compare the tax revenue created by the taxes in parts (a) and (b). What accounts for the change in tax revenue from the reduction in the excise tax?

4. All provinces impose excise taxes on gasoline. According to the Alberta Treasury Board and Finance, Alberta imposes an excise tax of $0.09 per litre of gasoline. In 2012, gasoline sales in Alberta totalled 6 billion litres. What was Alberta's tax revenue from the gasoline excise tax? If Alberta doubled the excise tax, would tax revenue double? Why or why not?

5. In Canada, each provincial and territorial government can impose its own excise tax on the sale of cigarettes. Suppose that in the province of Upper Canada, the provincial government imposes a tax of $2.00 per pack sold within the province. In contrast, the neighbouring province of Lower Canada imposes no excise tax on cigarettes. The pre-tax price of a pack of cigarettes is $1.00 in both provinces. A person bringing cigarettes from Lower Canada to Upper Canada is expected to pay $2.00 per pack at the border. Assume that the total cost to a resident of Upper Canada to smuggle a pack of cigarettes from Lower Canada is $1.85 per pack (the cost of time, gasoline, etc.). Assume that the supply curve for cigarettes is neither perfectly elastic nor perfectly inelastic.

a. Draw a diagram of the supply and demand curves for cigarettes in Upper Canada showing a situation in which it makes economic sense for a person to smuggle a pack of cigarettes from Lower Canada to Upper Canada. Explain your diagram.

b. Draw a corresponding diagram showing a situation in which it does not make economic sense for a person to smuggle a pack of cigarettes from Lower Canada to Upper Canada. Explain your diagram.

c. Suppose the demand for cigarettes in Upper Canada is perfectly inelastic. How high could the cost of smuggling a pack of cigarettes go until a person no longer found it profitable to smuggle?

d. Still assume that demand for cigarettes in Upper Canada is perfectly inelastic and that all smokers in Upper Canada are smuggling their cigarettes at a cost of $1.85 per pack, so no tax is paid. Is there any inefficiency in this situation? If so, how much per pack? Suppose chip-embedded cigarette packaging makes it impossible to smuggle cigarettes across the provincial border. Is there any inefficiency in this situation? If so, how much per pack?

6. In each of the following cases involving taxes, explain: (i) whether the incidence of the tax falls more heavily on consumers or producers, (ii) why government revenue raised from the tax is not a good indicator of the true cost of the tax, and (iii) how deadweight loss arises as a result of the tax.

a. The government imposes an excise tax on the sale of all university and college textbooks. Before the tax was imposed, 1 million textbooks were sold every year at a price of $50. After the tax is imposed, 600 000 books are sold yearly; students pay $55 per book, $30 of which publishers receive.

b. The government imposes an excise tax on the sale of all airline tickets. Before the tax was imposed, 3 million airline tickets were sold every year at a price of $500. After the tax is imposed, 1.5 million tickets are sold yearly; travellers pay $550 per ticket, $450 of which the airlines receive.

c. The government imposes an excise tax on the sale of all toothbrushes. Before the tax, 2 million toothbrushes were sold every year at a price of $1.50. After the tax is imposed, 800 000 toothbrushes are sold every year; consumers pay $2 per toothbrush, $1.25 of which producers receive.

7. The accompanying diagram shows the market for cigarettes. The current equilibrium price per pack is $4, and every day 40 million packs of cigarettes are sold. In order to recover some of the health care costs associated with smoking, the government imposes a tax of $2 per pack. This will raise the equilibrium price to $5 per pack and reduce the equilibrium quantity to 30 million packs.

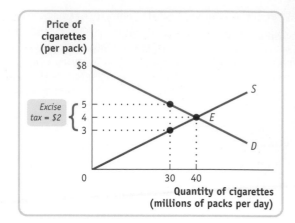

The economist working for the tobacco lobby claims that this tax will reduce consumer surplus for smokers by $40 million per day, since 40 million packs now cost $1 more per pack. The economist working for the lobby for sufferers of second-hand smoke argues that this is an enormous overestimate and that the reduction in consumer surplus will be only $30 million per day, since after the imposition of the tax only 30 million packs of cigarettes will be bought and each of these packs will now cost $1 more. They are both wrong. Why?

8. Consider the original market for pizza in Lafacville, illustrated in the accompanying table. Lafacville officials decide to impose an excise tax on pizza of $4 per pizza.

Price of pizza	Quantity of pizza demanded	Quantity of pizza supplied
$10	0	6
9	1	5
8	2	4
7	3	3
6	4	2
5	5	1
4	6	0
3	7	0
2	8	0
1	9	0

a. What is the quantity of pizza bought and sold after the imposition of the tax? What is the price paid by consumers? What is the price received by producers?

b. Calculate the consumer surplus and the producer surplus after the imposition of the tax. By how much has the imposition of the tax reduced consumer surplus? By how much has it reduced producer surplus?

c. How much tax revenue does Lafacville earn from this tax?

d. Calculate the deadweight loss from this tax.

9. A province needs to raise money, and the finance minister has a choice of imposing an excise tax of the same amount on one of two previously untaxed goods: the province can tax sales of either restaurant meals or gasoline. Both the demand for and the supply of restaurant meals are more elastic than the demand for and the supply of gasoline. If the finance minister wants to minimize the deadweight loss caused by the tax, which good should be taxed? For each good, draw a diagram that illustrates the deadweight loss from taxation.

10. Assume that the demand for gasoline is inelastic and supply is relatively elastic. The government imposes a sales tax on gasoline. The tax revenue is used to fund research into clean fuel alternatives to gasoline, which will improve the air we all breathe.

   a. Who bears more of the burden of this tax, consumers or producers? Show in a diagram who bears how much of the excess burden.

   b. Is this tax based on the benefits principle or the ability-to-pay principle? Explain.

11. Assess the following four tax policies in terms of the benefits principle versus the ability-to-pay principle.

   a. A tax on gasoline that finances maintenance of provincial roads

   b. An 8% tax on imported goods valued in excess of $800 per household brought in on passenger flights

   c. Airline-flight landing fees that pay for air traffic control

   d. A reduction in the amount of income tax paid based on the number of dependent children in the household

12. You are advising the government on how to pay for national defense. There are two proposals for a tax system to fund national defense. Under both proposals, the tax base is an individual's income. Under proposal A, all citizens pay exactly the same lump-sum tax, regardless of income. Under proposal B, individuals with higher incomes pay a greater proportion of their income in taxes.

   a. Is the tax in proposal A progressive, proportional, or regressive? What about the tax in proposal B?

   b. Is the tax in proposal A based on the ability-to-pay principle or on the benefits principle? What about the tax in proposal B?

   c. In terms of efficiency, which tax is better? Explain.

13. Each of the following tax proposals has income as the tax base. In each case, calculate the marginal tax rate for each level of income. Then calculate the percentage of income paid in taxes for an individual with a pre-tax income of $5000 and for an individual with a pre-tax income of $40 000. Classify the tax as being proportional, progressive, or regressive. (*Hint:* You can calculate the marginal tax rate as the percentage of an additional $1 in income that is taxed away.)

   a. All income is taxed at 20%.

   b. All income up to $10 000 is tax-free. All income above $10 000 is taxed at a constant rate of 20%.

   c. All income between $0 and $10 000 is taxed at 10%. All income between $10 000 and $20 000 is taxed at 20%. All income higher than $20 000 is taxed at 30%.

   d. Each individual who earns more than $10 000 pays a lump-sum tax of $10 000. If the individual's income is less than $10 000, that individual pays in taxes exactly what his or her income is.

   e. Of the four tax policies, which is likely to cause the worst incentive problems? Explain.

14. In Transylvania the basic income tax system is fairly simple. The first 40 000 sylvers (the official currency of Transylvania) earned each year are free of income tax. Any additional income is taxed at a rate of 25%. In addition, every individual pays a social security tax, which is calculated as follows: all income up to 80 000 sylvers is taxed at an additional 20%, but there is no additional social security tax on income above 80 000 sylvers.

   a. Calculate the marginal tax rates (including income tax and social security tax) for Transylvanians with the following levels of income: 20 000 sylvers, 40 000 sylvers, and 80 000 sylvers. (*Hint:* You can calculate the marginal tax rate as the percentage of an additional 1 sylver in income that is taxed away.)

   b. Is the income tax in Transylvania progressive, regressive, or proportional? Is the social security tax progressive, regressive, or proportional?

   c. Which income group's incentives are most adversely affected by the combined income and social security tax systems?

15. You work for the Saskatoba Treasury Board and Finance, providing economic advice to the finance minister. The premier wants to overhaul the personal income tax system and asks your advice. The current income tax system in Saskatoba consists of a proportional tax of 10% on all income. Suppose there is one person in the province who earns $110 million; everyone else earns less than $100 million. The premier proposes a tax cut targeted at the very rich so that the new tax system would consist of a proportional tax of 10% on all income up to $100 million and a marginal tax rate of 0% (no tax) on income above $100 million. You are asked to evaluate this tax proposal.

   a. For incomes of $100 million or less, is this tax system progressive, regressive, or proportional? For incomes of more than $100 million? Explain.

   b. Would this tax system create more or less tax revenue, other things equal? Is this tax system more or less efficient than the current tax system? Explain.

16. Suppose the government decides to levy a small excise tax on consumers in a perfectly competitive market in which the elasticity of demand is greater than the elasticity of supply. Who will bear more of the tax burden: the suppliers or the consumers? Explain why.

17. In extreme cases the supply or demand curve can be either vertical (perfectly inelastic) or horizontal (perfectly elastic). In such extreme situations the burden of a per-unit excise tax falls entirely on one side of the market. Using a diagram in each case, explain why each of the following scenarios occurs.

    a. A horizontal demand curve results in the suppliers bearing the entire burden of an excise tax.

    b. A horizontal supply curve results in the consumers bearing the entire burden of an excise tax

    c. A vertical demand curve results in the consumers bearing the entire burden of an excise tax.

    d. A vertical supply curve results in the suppliers bearing the entire burden of an excise tax.

    e. A vertical supply or demand curve results no deadweight loss when an excise tax is imposed.

18. This question uses the algebraic method to solve problems from Appendix 3A and Appendix 6A. Suppose that the demand and supply for maple syrup are given by the following equations:

$$P = 53.25 - 1.25Q^d \qquad \text{Demand Curve}$$
$$P = 12.75 + 0.25Q^S \qquad \text{Supply Curve}$$

where Q is the quantity in millions of litres and P is the price per litre. The federal government is considering imposing an excise tax equal to $1.50 a litre.

    a. Determine the price and quantity in the initial equilibrium where no tax is charged.

    b. Solve for the new equilibrium quantity, the price paid by consumers, the price received by producers (excluding the tax), the tax revenue collected, and the buyer's and seller's shares of the tax burden.

    c. How do your answers to parts (a) and (b) change after the income of consumers rises, shifting the demand curve to $P = 55.50 - 1.25Q^d$?

    d. How do your answers to parts (a) and (b) change if instead an improvement in technology shifts the supply curve to $P = 7.50 + 0.25Q^S$?

    e. How do your answers to parts (a) and (b) change if instead an improvement in technology shifts the supply curve to $P = 11.25 + 0.15Q^S$? (*Hint:* Round your price and quantity figures to 2 decimal places.)

19. This question uses the algebraic method to solve problems from Appendix 3A and Appendix 6A. Suppose the monthly demand and supply for iPods are given by the following equations:

$$P = 500 - 0.001Q^d \qquad \text{Demand Curve}$$
$$P = 200 + 0.0005Q^S \qquad \text{Supply Curve}$$

    a. Use the demand and supply curves to solve for the equilibrium price and quantity. Create a diagram to depict this equilibrium.

    b. Suppose the government is considering introducing a tax on electronics that would add $50 to the cost of an iPod. Solve for the new equilibrium quantity, the price paid by consumers, the price received by producers (excluding the tax), the tax revenue collected, and the buyer's and seller's shares of the tax burden.

    c. How did the consumer surplus, producer surplus, and total economic surplus change?

    d. What is the deadweight loss created by the tax? How much comes from consumers? How much from producers?

CHAPTER 8

International Trade

CAR PARTS AND SUCKING SOUNDS

International trade improves the welfare of Mexican producers of auto parts as well as Canadian and American car buyers and sellers.

❱ How comparative advantage leads to mutually beneficial international trade

❱ The sources of international comparative advantage

❱ Who gains and who loses from international trade, and why the gains exceed the losses

❱ How **tariffs** and **import quotas** cause inefficiency and reduce total surplus

❱ Why governments often engage in **trade protection** and how **international trade agreements** counteract this

STOP IN AN AUTO SHOWROOM, and odds are that the majority of cars on display were produced in either Canada or the United States. Even if they're foreign brands like Toyotas, Hondas, or Volkswagens, most cars sold in Canada were made here either by the Big Three U.S. auto firms or by subsidiaries of foreign firms. Canadian-made cars are assembled mostly in southern Ontario, within the corridor from Windsor to Oshawa.[1]

Although that car you're looking at may have been made in Canada or the United States, a significant part of what's inside was probably made elsewhere, very likely in Mexico. Since the 1980s, auto production in North America has increasingly relied on factories in Mexico to produce *labour-intensive* auto parts, such as seat parts—products that use a relatively high amount of labour in their production.

Changes in economic policy over the years have contributed greatly to the emergence of large-scale Canadian and U.S. imports of auto parts from Mexico. Until the 1980s, Mexico had a system of *trade protection*—taxes and regulations limiting imports—that both kept out foreign manufactured goods and

encouraged Mexican industry to focus on selling to Mexican consumers rather than to a wider market. In 1985, however, the Mexican government began dismantling much of its trade protection, boosting trade with its trading partners. A further boost came in 1993, when Canada, the United States, and Mexico signed the North American Free Trade Agreement (NAFTA), which eliminated most taxes on trade among the three nations and provided guarantees that business investments in Mexico would be protected from arbitrary changes in government policy.

NAFTA was deeply controversial when it went into effect: Mexican workers were paid only a fraction of what their Canadian and American counterparts were paid, and many workers, especially in the United States, expressed concern that jobs would be lost to low-wage competition. Ross Perot, a U.S. presidential candidate in 1992, warned that there would be a "giant sucking sound" as U.S. manufacturing moved south of the border. And although apocalyptic predictions about NAFTA's impact haven't come to pass, the agreement remains controversial even now.

Most economists disagreed with those who saw NAFTA as a threat to the Canadian economy. We saw in Chapter 2 how international trade can lead to mutual *gains from trade*. Economists, for the most part, believed that the same logic applied to NAFTA, that the treaty would make both Canada and Mexico richer. But making a nation as a whole richer isn't the same thing as improving the welfare of everyone living in a country, and there were and are reasons to believe that NAFTA hurts some Canadian citizens.

Until now, we have analyzed the economy as if it were self-sufficient, as if the economy produces all the goods and services it consumes, and vice versa. This is, of course, true for the world economy as a whole. But it's not true for any individual country. Assuming self-sufficiency would have been far more accurate 50 years ago, when Canada exported only a small fraction of what it produced and imported only a small fraction of what it consumed. Since then, however, Canadian imports and exports have grown much faster than the Canadian economy as a whole. Nowadays, to have a full picture of

---

[1] Industry Canada provides a list of vehicles made in Canada. For the list of cars made in 2012, see www.ic.gc.ca/eic/site/auto-auto.nsf/eng/am02365.html and for a list of the Canadian assembly plants in 2012, see www.ic.gc.ca/eic/site/auto-auto.nsf/eng/am00767.html.

how national economies work, we must understand international trade.

This chapter examines the economics of international trade. We start from the model of comparative advantage, which, as we saw in Chapter 2, explains why there are gains from international trade. We will briefly recap that model here, and then extend our study to address deeper questions about international trade, such as why some individuals can be hurt by international trade while the country, as a whole, gains. At the conclusion of the chapter, we'll examine the effects of policies that countries use to limit imports or promote exports as well as how governments work together to overcome barriers to trade. ■

Goods and services purchased from other countries are **imports;** goods and services sold to other countries are **exports.**

Globalization is the phenomenon of growing economic linkages among countries.

Comparative Advantage and International Trade

C anada buys auto parts—and many other goods and services—from other countries. At the same time, it sells many goods and services to other countries. Goods and services purchased from abroad are **imports;** goods and services sold abroad are **exports.**

As illustrated by the opening story, imports and exports have taken on an increasingly important role in the Canadian economy. Over the last 50 years, both imports into and exports from Canada have grown faster than the Canadian economy. Panel (a) of Figure 8-1 shows how the values of Canadian imports and exports have grown as a percentage of gross domestic product (GDP). Panel (b) shows imports and exports as a percentage of GDP for a number of countries. It shows that foreign trade is more important for some countries than it is for Canada.

Foreign trade isn't the only way countries interact economically. In the modern world, investors from one country often invest funds in another nation; many companies are multinational, with subsidiaries operating in several countries; and a growing number of individuals work in a country different from the one in which they were born. The growth of all these forms of economic linkages among countries is often called **globalization.**

FIGURE 8-1 The Growing Importance of International Trade

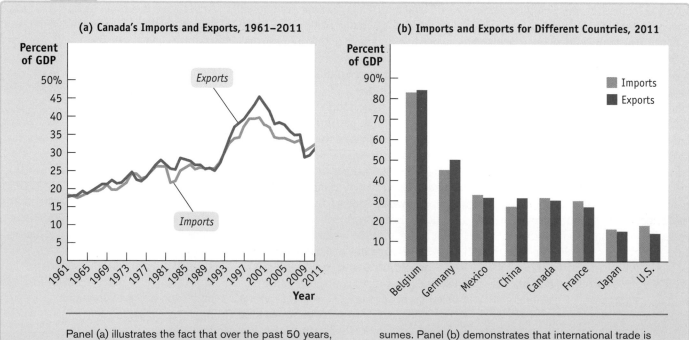

Panel (a) illustrates the fact that over the past 50 years, Canada has exported a growing share of its GDP to other countries and imported a growing share of what it consumes. Panel (b) demonstrates that international trade is more important to some countries than it is to Canada.
Sources: Statistics Canada [panel (a)] and World Bank [panel (b)].

In this chapter, however, we'll focus mainly on international trade. To understand why international trade occurs and why economists believe it is beneficial to the economy, we will first review the concept of comparative advantage.

Production Possibilities and Comparative Advantage, Revisited

To produce auto parts, any country must use resources—land, labour, capital, and so on—that could have been used to produce other things. The potential production of other goods a country must forgo to produce an auto part is the opportunity cost of that part.

In some cases, it's easy to see why the opportunity cost of producing a good is especially low in a given country. Consider, for example, shrimp—much of which now comes from seafood farms in Vietnam and Thailand. It's a lot easier to produce shrimp in Vietnam, where the climate is nearly ideal and there's plenty of coastal land suitable for shellfish farming, than it is in Canada. Conversely, other goods are not produced as easily in Vietnam as in Canada. For example, Vietnam doesn't have the base of skilled workers and technological know-how that makes Canada so good at producing high-technology goods. So the opportunity cost of a tonne of shrimp, in terms of other goods such as aircraft, is much less in Vietnam than it is in Canada.

In other cases, matters are a bit less obvious. It's as easy to produce auto parts in Canada as it is in Mexico, and Mexican auto parts workers are, if anything, less efficient than their Canadian counterparts. But Mexican workers are a *lot* less productive than Canadian workers in other areas, such as aircraft and chemical production. This means that diverting a Mexican worker into auto parts production reduces output of other goods less than diverting a Canadian worker into auto parts production. That is, the opportunity cost of producing auto parts in Mexico is less than it is in Canada.

So we say that Mexico has a comparative advantage in producing auto parts. Let's repeat the definition of comparative advantage from Chapter 2: *A country has a comparative advantage in producing a good or service if the opportunity cost of producing the good or service is lower for that country than for other countries.*

Figure 8-2 provides a hypothetical numerical example of comparative advantage in international trade. We assume that only two goods are produced and consumed, auto parts and airplanes, and that there are only two countries in the world, Canada and Mexico. (In real life, auto parts aren't worth much without auto bodies to put them in, but let's set that issue aside). The figure shows hypothetical production possibility frontiers for Canada and Mexico.

As in Chapter 2, we simplify the model by assuming that the production possibility frontiers are straight lines, as shown in Figure 2-1, rather than the more realistic bowed-out shape shown in Figure 2-2. The straight-line shape implies that the opportunity cost of an auto part in terms of airplanes in each country is constant—it does not depend on how many units of each good the country produces. The analysis of international trade under the assumption that opportunity costs are constant, which makes production possibility frontiers straight lines, is known as the **Ricardian model of international trade,** named after the English economist David Ricardo, who introduced this analysis in the early nineteenth century.

In Figure 8-2 we have grouped auto parts into bundles of 10 000, so, for example, a country that produces 500 bundles of auto parts is producing 5 million individual auto parts. You can see in the figure that Canada can produce 2000 airplanes if it produces no auto parts, or 1000 bundles of auto parts if it produces no airplanes. Thus, the slope of Canada's production possibility frontier, or PPF, is −2000/1000 = −2. That is, to produce an additional bundle of auto parts, Canada must forgo the production of 2 airplanes.

Similarly, Mexico can produce 1000 airplanes if it produces no auto parts or 2000 bundles of auto parts if it produces no airplanes. Thus, the slope of Mexico's

The **Ricardian model of international trade** analyzes international trade under the assumption that opportunity costs are constant.

FIGURE **8-2** Comparative Advantage and the Production Possibility Frontier

Canada's opportunity cost of 1 bundle of auto parts in terms of airplanes is 2: for every additional bundle of auto parts, 2 airplanes must be forgone. The Mexican opportunity cost of 1 bundle of auto parts in terms of airplanes is ½: for every additional bundle of auto parts, only ½ of an airplane must be forgone. As a result,

Canada has a comparative advantage in airplane production, and Mexico has a comparative advantage in auto parts production. In autarky, each country is forced to consume only what it produces: 1000 airplanes and 500 bundles of auto parts for Canada; 500 airplanes and 1000 bundles of auto parts for Mexico.

Autarky is a situation in which a country does not trade with other countries.

PPF is −1000/2000 = −1/2. That is, to produce an additional bundle of auto parts, Mexico must forgo the production of 1/2 an airplane.

Economists use the term **autarky** to refer to a situation in which a country does not trade with other countries—it is self-sufficient. We assume that in autarky Canada chooses to produce and consume 500 bundles of auto parts and 1000 airplanes. We also assume that in autarky Mexico produces 1000 bundles of auto parts and 500 airplanes.

The trade-offs facing the two countries when they don't trade are summarized in Table 8-1. As you can see, Canada has a comparative advantage in the production of airplanes because it has a lower opportunity cost in terms of auto parts than Mexico has: producing an airplane costs Canada only ½ a bundle of auto parts, while it costs Mexico 2 bundles of auto parts. Correspondingly, Mexico has a comparative advantage in auto parts production: 1 bundle costs it only ½ an airplane, while it costs Canada 2 airplanes.

TABLE **8-1** Canadian and Mexican Opportunity Costs of Auto Parts and Airplanes

	Canadian Opportunity Cost		Mexican Opportunity Cost
1 bundle of auto parts	2 airplanes	>	1/2 airplane
1 airplane	1/2 bundle of auto parts	<	2 bundles of auto parts

As we learned in Chapter 2, each country can do better by engaging in trade than it could by not trading. A country can accomplish this by specializing in the production of the good in which it has a comparative advantage and exporting that good, while importing the good in which it has a comparative *dis*advantage. Let's see how this works.

The Gains from International Trade

Figure 8-3 illustrates how both countries can gain from specialization and trade, by showing a hypothetical rearrangement of production and consumption that allows *each* country to consume more of *both* goods. Again, panel (a) represents Canada and panel (b) represents Mexico. In each panel we indicate again the

FIGURE **8-3** The Gains from International Trade

Trade increases world production of both goods, allowing both countries to consume more. Here, each country specializes its production as a result of trade: Canada concentrates on producing airplanes, and

Mexico concentrates on producing auto parts. Total world production of both goods rises, which means that it is possible for both countries to consume more of both goods.

autarky production and consumption assumed in Figure 8-2. Once trade becomes possible, however, everything changes. With trade, each country can move to producing only the good in which it has a comparative advantage—airplanes for Canada and auto parts for Mexico. Because the world production of both goods is now higher than in autarky, trade makes it possible for each country to consume more of both goods.

Table 8-2 sums up the changes as a result of trade and shows why both countries can gain. The left part of the table shows the autarky situation, before trade, in which each country must produce the goods it consumes. The right part of the table shows what happens as a result of trade. After trade, Canada specializes in the production of airplanes, producing 2000 airplanes and no auto parts; Mexico specializes in the production of auto parts, producing 2000 bundles of auto parts and no airplanes.

TABLE **8-2** How Canada and Mexico Gain from Trade

		In Autarky		With Trade		
		Production	Consumption	Production	Consumption	Gains from trade
Canada	**Bundles of auto parts**	500	500	0	750	+250
	Airplanes	1000	1000	2000	1250	+250
Mexico	**Bundles of auto parts**	1000	1000	2000	1250	+250
	Airplanes	500	500	0	750	+250

The result is a rise in total world production of both goods. As you can see in Table 8-2, with trade, Canada is able to consume both more airplanes and more auto parts than before, even though it no longer produces auto parts, because it can import parts from Mexico. Mexico can also consume more of both goods, even though it no longer produces airplanes, because it can import airplanes from Canada.

The key to this mutual gain is the fact that trade liberates both countries from self-sufficiency—from the need to produce the same mixes of goods they consume. Because each country can concentrate on producing the good in which it has a comparative advantage, total world production rises, making a higher standard of living possible in both nations.

Now, in this example we have simply assumed the post-trade consumption bundles of the two countries. In fact, the consumption choices of a country reflect both the preferences of its residents and the *relative prices*—the prices of one good in terms of another in international markets. Although we have not explicitly given the price of airplanes in terms of auto parts, that price is implicit in our example: Mexico sells Canada the 750 bundles of auto parts Canada consumes in return for the 750 airplanes Mexico consumes, so 1 bundle of parts is traded for 1 airplane. This tells us that the price of an airplane on world markets must be equal to the price of one bundle of 10 000 auto parts in our example.

One requirement that the relative price must satisfy is that no country pays a relative price greater than its opportunity cost of obtaining the good in autarky. That is, Canada won't pay more than 2 airplanes for each 1 bundle of 10 000 auto parts from Mexico, and Mexico won't pay more than 2 bundles of 10 000 auto parts for each 1 airplane from Canada. Once this requirement is satisfied, the actual relative price in international trade is determined by supply and demand—and we'll turn to supply and demand in international trade in the next section. However, first let's look more deeply into the nature of the gains from trade.

Comparative Advantage versus Absolute Advantage

It's easy to accept the idea that Vietnam and Thailand have a comparative advantage in shrimp production: they have a tropical climate that's better suited to shrimp farming than that of Canada, and they have a lot of usable coastal area. So Canada imports shrimp from Vietnam and Thailand. In other cases, however, it may be harder to understand why we import certain goods from abroad.

Canadian imports of auto parts from Mexico is a case in point. There's nothing about Mexico's climate or resources that makes it especially good at manufacturing auto parts. In fact, it almost surely takes *fewer* hours of labour to produce an auto seat or wiring harness in Canada than in Mexico.

With their tropical climate, Vietnam and Thailand have a comparative advantage in shrimp production.

Why, then, do we buy Mexican auto parts? Because the gains from trade depend on *comparative advantage*, not *absolute advantage*. Yes, it takes less labour to produce a wiring harness in Canada than in Mexico. That is, the productivity of Mexican auto parts workers is less than that of their Canadian counterparts. But what determines comparative advantage is not the amount of resources used to produce a good but the opportunity cost of that good— here, the quantity of other goods forgone in order to produce an auto seat. And the opportunity cost of auto parts is lower in Mexico than in Canada.

Here's how it works: Mexican workers have low productivity compared with Canadian workers in the auto parts industry. But Mexican workers have even lower productivity compared with Canadian workers in other industries. Because Mexican labour productivity in industries other than auto parts is relatively very low, producing a wiring harness in Mexico, even though it takes a lot of labour, does not require forgoing the production of large quantities of other goods.

In Canada, the opposite is true: very high productivity in other industries (such as high-technology goods) means that producing an auto seat in Canada, even though it doesn't require much labour, requires sacrificing lots of other goods. So the opportunity cost of producing auto parts is less in Mexico than in Canada. Despite its lower labour productivity, Mexico has a comparative advantage in the production of many auto parts, although Canada has an absolute advantage.

Mexico's comparative advantage in auto parts is reflected in global markets by the wages Mexican workers are paid. That's because a country's wage rates, in general, reflect its labour productivity. In countries where labour is highly productive in many industries, employers are willing to pay high wages to attract workers, so competition among employers leads to an overall high wage rate. In countries where labour is less productive, competition for workers is less intense and wage rates are correspondingly lower.

As the accompanying Global Comparison shows, there is indeed a strong relationship between overall levels of productivity and wage rates around the world. Because Mexico has generally low productivity, it has a relatively low wage rate. Low wages, in turn, give Mexico a cost advantage in producing goods where its productivity is only moderately low, like auto parts. As a result, it's cheaper to produce these parts in Mexico than in Canada.

The kind of trade that takes place between low-wage, low-productivity economies like Mexico and high-wage, high-productivity economies like Canada and the United States gives rise to two common misperceptions. One, the *pauper labour fallacy*, is the belief that when a country with high wages imports goods produced by workers who are paid low wages, this must hurt the standard of living of workers in the importing country. The other, the *sweatshop labour fallacy*, is the belief that trade must be bad for workers in poor exporting countries because those workers are paid very low wages by our standards.

Both fallacies miss the nature of gains from trade: it's to the advantage of *both* countries if the poorer, lower-wage country exports goods in which it has

GLOBAL COMPARISON   PRODUCTIVITY AND WAGES AROUND THE WORLD

Is it true that both the pauper labour argument and the sweatshop labour argument are fallacies? Yes, it is. The real explanation for low wages in poor countries is low overall productivity.

The graph shows estimates of labour productivity, measured by the value of output (GDP) per worker, and wages, measured by the monthly compensation of the average worker, for several countries in 2009. Both productivity and wages are expressed as percentages of U.S. productivity and wages; for example, productivity and wages in Japan were 79% and 91%, respectively, of their U.S. levels. You can see the strong positive relationship between productivity and wages. The relationship isn't perfect. For example, Germany has higher wages than its productivity might lead you to expect. But simple comparisons of wages give a misleading sense of labour costs in poor countries: their low-wage advantage is mostly offset by low productivity.

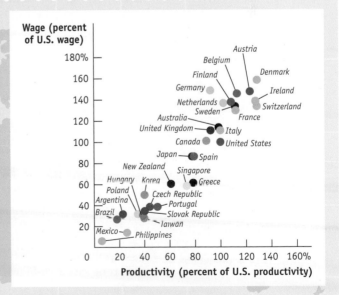

Sources: Bureau of Labor Statistics; International Monetary Fund.

a comparative advantage, even if its cost advantage in these goods depends on low wages. That is, both countries are able to achieve a higher standard of living through trade.

It's particularly important to understand that buying a good made by someone who is paid much lower wages than most Canadian workers doesn't necessarily imply that you're taking advantage of that person. It depends on the alternatives. Because workers in poor countries have low productivity across the board, they are offered low wages whether they produce goods exported to Canada or goods sold in local markets. A job that looks terrible by rich-country standards can be a step up for someone in a poor country.

International trade that depends on low-wage exports can nonetheless raise a country's standard of living. This is especially true of very-low-wage nations. For example, Bangladesh and similar countries would be much poorer than they are—their citizens might even be starving—if they weren't able to export goods such as clothing based on their low wage rates.

Sources of Comparative Advantage

International trade is driven by comparative advantage, but where does comparative advantage come from? Economists who study international trade have found three main sources of comparative advantage: international differences in *climate*, international differences in *factor endowments*, and international differences in *technology*.

Differences in Climate
One key reason the opportunity cost of producing shrimp in Vietnam and Thailand is less than in Canada is that shrimp need warm water—Vietnam has plenty of that, but Canada doesn't. In general, differences in climate play a significant role in international trade. Tropical countries export tropical products like coffee, sugar, bananas, and shrimp. Countries in the temperate zones export crops like wheat and corn. Some trade is even driven by the difference in seasons between the northern and southern hemispheres: winter deliveries of Chilean grapes and New Zealand apples have become commonplace in North American and European supermarkets.

Differences in Factor Endowments
Canada is a major exporter of forest products—lumber and products derived from lumber, like pulp and paper—to the United States. These exports don't reflect the special skill of Canadian lumberjacks. Canada has a comparative advantage in forest products because its forested area is much greater compared to the size of its labour force than the ratio of forestland to the labour force in the United States.

Forestland, like labour and capital, is a *factor of production:* an input used to produce goods and services. (Recall from Chapter 2 that the factors of production are land, labour, and capital.) Due to history and geography, the mix of available factors of production differs among countries, providing an important source of comparative advantage. The relationship between comparative advantage and factor availability is found in an influential model of international trade, the *Heckscher–Ohlin model,* developed by two Swedish economists in the first half of the twentieth century.

Two key concepts in the model are *factor abundance* and *factor intensity.* Factor abundance refers to how large a country's supply of a factor is relative to its supply of other factors. Factor intensity refers to the fact that producers use different ratios of factors of production in the production of different goods. For example, oil refineries use much more capital per worker than clothing factories. Economists use the term **factor intensity** to describe this difference among goods: oil refining is capital-intensive, because it tends to use a high ratio of capital

The **factor intensity** of production of a good is a measure of which factor is used in relatively greater quantities than other factors in production.

to labour, but auto seats production is labour-intensive, because it tends to use a high ratio of labour to capital.

According to the **Heckscher–Ohlin model,** *a country that has an abundant supply of a factor of production will have a comparative advantage in goods whose production is intensive in that factor.* So a country that has a relative abundance of capital will have a comparative advantage in capital-intensive industries such as oil refining, but a country that has a relative abundance of labour will have a comparative advantage in labour-intensive industries such as auto seats production.

The basic intuition behind this result is simple and based on opportunity cost. The opportunity cost of a given factor—the value that the factor would generate in alternative uses—is low for a country when it is relatively abundant in that factor. Relative to Canada, Mexico has an abundance of low-skilled labour. As a result, the opportunity cost of the production of low-skilled, labour-intensive goods is lower in Mexico than in Canada.

The most dramatic example of the validity of the Heckscher–Ohlin model is world trade in clothing. Clothing production is a labour-intensive activity: it doesn't take much physical capital, nor does it require a lot of human capital in the form of highly educated workers. So you would expect labour-abundant countries such as China and Bangladesh to have a comparative advantage in clothing production. And they do.

That much international trade is the result of differences in factor endowments helps explain another fact: international specialization of production is often *incomplete*. That is, a country often maintains some domestic production of a good that it imports. A good example of this is Canada and oil. Saudi Arabia exports oil to Canada because Saudi Arabia has an abundant supply of oil relative to its other factors of production; Canada exports medical devices to Saudi Arabia because it has an abundant supply of expertise in medical technology relative to its other factors of production. But Canada also produces some oil domestically because the size of its domestic oil reserves in Alberta makes it economical to do so.

In our supply and demand analysis in the next section, we'll consider incomplete specialization by a country to be the norm. We should emphasize, however, that the fact that countries often incompletely specialize does not in any way change the conclusion that there are gains from trade.

Differences in Technology In the 1970s and 1980s, Japan became by far the world's largest exporter of automobiles, selling large numbers to North America and the rest of the world. Japan's comparative advantage in automobiles wasn't the result of climate. Nor can it easily be attributed to differences in factor endowments: aside from a scarcity of land, Japan's mix of available factors is quite similar to that in other developed countries. Instead, as we discussed in the Chapter 2 Business Case on lean production at Toyota and Boeing, Japan's comparative advantage in automobiles was based on the superior production techniques developed by its manufacturers, which allowed them to produce more cars with a given amount of labour and capital than their North American or European counterparts.

Japan's comparative advantage in automobiles was a case of comparative advantage caused by differences in technology—the techniques used in production.

The causes of differences in technology are somewhat mysterious. Sometimes they seem to be based on knowledge accumulated through experience—for example, Switzerland's comparative advantage in watches reflects a long tradition of watchmaking. Sometimes they are the result of a set of innovations that for some reason occur in one country but not in others. Technological advantage,

According to the **Heckscher–Ohlin model,** a country has a comparative advantage in a good whose production is intensive in the factors that are abundantly available in that country.

INCREASING RETURNS TO SCALE AND INTERNATIONAL TRADE

Most analysis of international trade focuses on how differences between countries—differences in climate, factor endowments, and technology—create national comparative advantage. However, economists have also pointed out another reason for international trade: the role of *increasing returns to scale*.

Production of a good is characterized by increasing returns to scale if the average productivity of labour and other resources used in production rise with the quantity of output. For example, in an industry characterized by increasing returns to scale, increasing output by 10% might require only 8% more labour

and 9% more raw materials. Examples of industries with increasing returns to scale include auto manufacturing, oil refining, and the production of jumbo jets, all of which require large outlays of capital. Increasing returns to scale (sometimes also called economies of scale) can give rise to monopoly, a situation in which an industry is composed of only one producer, because it gives large firms a cost advantage over small ones.

But increasing returns to scale can also give rise to international trade. The logic runs as follows: If production of a good is characterized by increasing returns to scale, it makes sense to

concentrate production in only a few locations, so each location has a high level of output. But that also means production occurs in only a few countries that export the good to other countries. A commonly cited example is the North American auto industry: although both Canada and the United States produce automobiles and their components, each particular model or component tends to be produced in only one of the two countries and exported to the other.

Increasing returns to scale probably play a large role in the trade in manufactured goods between advanced countries, which is about 25% of the total value of world trade.

---

however, is often transitory. As we also discussed in the Chapter 2 Business Case, by adopting lean production, auto manufacturers in North America have now closed much of the gap in productivity with their Japanese competitors. In addition, a technological advantage can be acquired or supported by government funding for research and development. For instance, government support for nuclear and aerospace industries has helped Canada occupy a niche in the world markets for these products. At any given point in time, however, differences in technology are a major source of comparative advantage.

ECONOMICS > IN ACTION

SKILL AND COMPARATIVE ADVANTAGE

In 1953 U.S. workers were clearly better equipped with machinery than their counterparts in other countries. Most economists at the time thought that America's comparative advantage lay in capital-intensive goods. But economist Wassily Leontief made a surprising discovery: America's comparative advantage was in something other than capital-intensive goods. In fact, goods that the United States exported were slightly less capital-intensive than goods the country imported. This discovery came to be known as the Leontief paradox, and it led to a sustained effort to make sense of U.S. trade patterns.

The main resolution of this paradox, it turns out, depends on the definition of *capital*. U.S. exports aren't intensive in *physical* capital—machines and buildings. Instead, they are *skill-intensive*—that is, they are intensive in *human* capital. U.S. exporting industries use a substantially higher ratio of highly educated workers to other workers than is found in U.S. industries that compete against imports. For example, one of America's biggest export sectors is aircraft; the aircraft industry employs large numbers of engineers and other people with graduate degrees relative to the number of manual labourers. Conversely, the United States imports a lot of clothing, which is often produced by workers with little formal education.

In general, countries with highly educated workforces tend to export skill-intensive goods, while countries with less educated workforces tend to export goods whose production requires little skilled labour. Figure 8-4 illustrates this point by comparing the goods the United States imports from Germany, a country with a highly educated labour force, with the goods the United States imports from Bangladesh, where about half of the adult population is still illiterate. In each country industries are ranked, first, according to how skill-intensive they are. Next, for each industry, we calculate its share of exports to the United States. This allows us to plot, for each country, various industries according to their skill intensity and their share of exports to the United States.

In Figure 8-4, the horizontal axis shows a measure of the skill intensity of different industries, and the vertical axes show the share of U.S. imports in each industry coming from Germany (on the left) and Bangladesh (on the right). As you can see, each country's exports to the United States reflect its skill level. The curve representing Germany slopes upward: the more skill-intensive a German industry is, the higher its share of exports to the United States. In contrast, the curve representing Bangladesh slopes downward: the less skill-intensive a Bangladeshi industry is, the higher its share of exports to the United States.

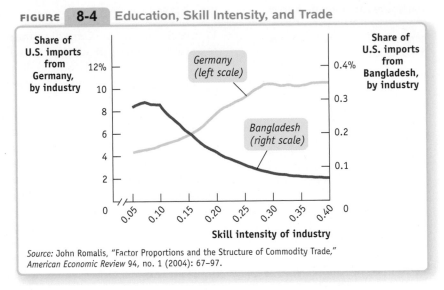

FIGURE 8-4 Education, Skill Intensity, and Trade

Source: John Romalis, "Factor Proportions and the Structure of Commodity Trade," *American Economic Review* 94, no. 1 (2004): 67–97.

CHECK YOUR UNDERSTANDING 5-1

1. In Canada, the opportunity cost of 1 tonne of wheat is 50 bicycles. In China, the opportunity cost of 1 bicycle is 0.01 tonne of wheat.
   a. Determine the pattern of comparative advantage.
   b. In autarky, Canada can produce 200 000 bicycles if no wheat is produced, and China can produce 3000 tonnes of wheat if no bicycles are produced. Draw each country's production possibility frontier assuming constant opportunity cost, with tonnes of wheat on the vertical axis and bicycles on the horizontal axis.
   c. With trade, each country specializes its production. Canada consumes 1000 tonnes of wheat and 200 000 bicycles; China consumes 3000 tonnes of wheat and 100 000 bicycles. Indicate the production and consumption points on your diagrams, and use them to explain the gains from trade.

2. Explain the following patterns of trade using the Heckscher–Ohlin model.
   a. France exports wine to Canada, and Canada exports lumber to France.
   b. Brazil exports shoes to Canada, and Canada exports shoe-making machinery to Brazil.

Solutions appear at back of book.

Supply, Demand, and International Trade

Simple models of comparative advantage are helpful for understanding the fundamental causes of international trade. However, to analyze the effects of international trade at a more detailed level and to understand trade policy, it helps to return to the supply and demand model. We'll start by looking at the effects of imports on domestic producers and consumers, then turn to the effects of exports.

The **domestic demand curve** shows how the quantity of a good demanded by domestic consumers depends on the price of that good.

The **domestic supply curve** shows how the quantity of a good supplied by domestic producers depends on the price of that good.

The **world price** of a good is the price at which that good can be bought or sold abroad.

The Effects of Imports

Figure 8-5 shows the Canadian market for auto seats, ignoring international trade for a moment. It introduces a few new concepts: the *domestic demand curve*, the *domestic supply curve*, and the domestic or autarky price.

The **domestic demand curve** shows how the quantity of a good demanded by residents of a country depends on the price of that good. Why "domestic"? Because people living in other countries may demand the good, too. Once we introduce international trade, we need to distinguish between purchases of a good by domestic consumers and purchases by foreign consumers. So the domestic demand curve reflects only the demand of residents of our own country. Similarly, the **domestic supply curve** shows how the quantity of a good supplied by producers inside our own country depends on the price of that good. Once we introduce international trade, we need to distinguish between the supply of domestic producers and foreign supply—supply brought in from abroad.

In autarky, with no international trade in auto seats, the equilibrium in this market would be determined by the intersection of the domestic demand and domestic supply curves, point A. The equilibrium price of auto seats would be P_A, and the equilibrium quantity of auto seats produced and consumed would be Q_A. As always, both consumers and producers gain from the existence of the domestic market. Economists refer to the net gain that buyers receive from the purchase of a good as *consumer surplus*. Likewise, *producer surplus* is the net gain to sellers from selling a good. *Total surplus* is the sum of consumer and producer surplus. We analyzed these three concepts in detail in Chapter 4. In autarky, consumer surplus would be equal to the area of the blue-shaded triangle in Figure 8-5. Producer surplus would be equal to the area of the red-shaded triangle. And total surplus would be equal to the sum of these two shaded triangles.

Now let's imagine opening up this market to imports. To do this, we must make an assumption about the supply of imports. The simplest assumption, which we will adopt here, is that unlimited quantities of auto seats can be purchased from abroad at a fixed price, known as the **world price** of auto seats. Figure 8-6 shows a situation in which the world price of an auto seat, P_W, is lower than the price of an auto seat that would prevail in the domestic market in autarky, P_A.

FIGURE **8-5** Consumer and Producer Surplus in Autarky

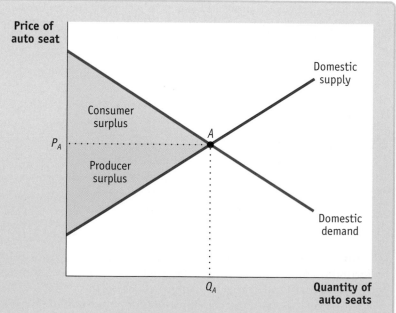

In the absence of trade, the domestic price is P_A, the autarky price at which the domestic supply curve and the domestic demand curve intersect. The quantity produced and consumed domestically is Q_A. Consumer surplus is represented by the blue-shaded area, and producer surplus is represented by the red-shaded area.

FIGURE   **8-6**   The Domestic Market with Imports

Here the world price of auto parts, P_W, is below the autarky price, P_A. When the economy is opened to international trade, imports enter the domestic market, and the domestic price falls from the autarky price, P_A, to the world price, P_W. As the price falls, the domestic quantity demanded rises from Q_A to Q_D and the domestic quantity supplied falls from Q_A to Q_S. The difference between domestic quantity demanded and domestic quantity supplied at P_W, the quantity $Q_D - Q_S$, is filled by imports.

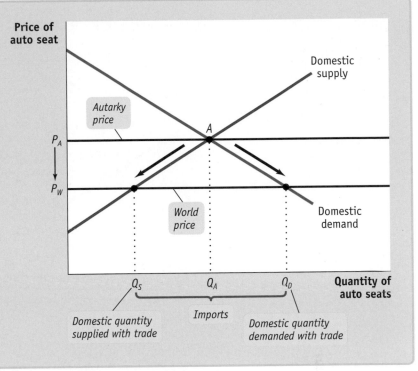

Given that the world price is below the domestic price of an auto seat, it is profitable for importers to buy auto seats abroad and resell them domestically. The imported auto seats increase the supply of auto seats in the domestic market, driving down the domestic market price. Auto seats will continue to be imported until the domestic price falls to a level equal to the world price.

The result is shown in Figure 8-6. Because of imports, the domestic price of an auto seat falls from P_A to P_W. The quantity of auto seats demanded by domestic consumers rises from Q_A to Q_D, and the quantity supplied by domestic producers falls from Q_A to Q_S. The difference between the domestic quantity demanded and the domestic quantity supplied, $Q_D - Q_S$, is filled by imports.

Now let's turn to the effects of imports on consumer surplus and producer surplus. Because imports of auto seats lead to a fall in their domestic price, consumer surplus rises and producer surplus falls. Figure 8-7 shows how this works. We label four areas: W, X, Y, and Z. The autarky consumer surplus we identified in Figure 8-5 corresponds to W, and the autarky producer surplus corresponds to the sum of X and Y. The fall in the domestic price to the world price leads to an increase in consumer surplus; it increases by X and Z, so consumer surplus now equals the sum of W, X, and Z. At the same time, producers lose X in surplus, so producer surplus now equals only Y.

The table in Figure 8-7 summarizes the changes in consumer and producer surplus when the auto seats market is opened to imports. Consumers gain surplus equal to the areas $X + Z$. Producers lose surplus equal to X. So the sum of producer and consumer surplus—the total surplus generated in the auto seats market—increases by Z. As a result of trade, consumers gain and producers lose, but the gain to consumers exceeds the loss to producers.

This is an important result. We have just shown that opening up a market to imports leads to a net gain in total surplus, which is what we should have

FIGURE **8-7** **The Effects of Imports on Surplus**

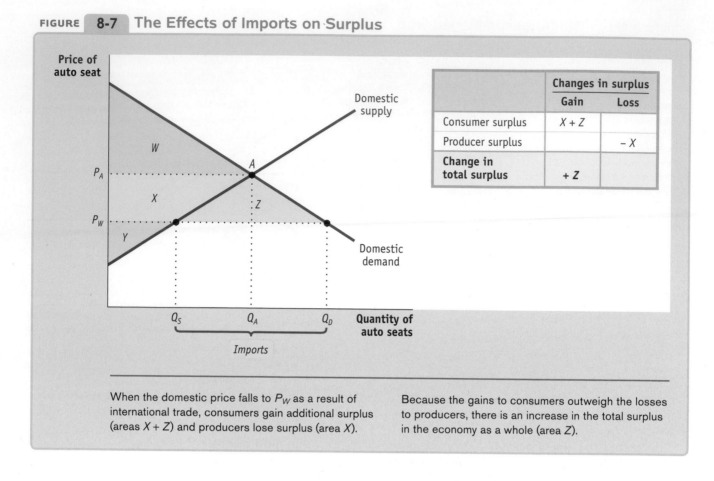

When the domestic price falls to P_W as a result of international trade, consumers gain additional surplus (areas $X + Z$) and producers lose surplus (area X).

Because the gains to consumers outweigh the losses to producers, there is an increase in the total surplus in the economy as a whole (area Z).

expected given the proposition that there are gains from international trade. However, we have also learned that although the country as a whole gains, some groups—in this case, domestic producers of auto parts—lose as a result of international trade. As we'll see shortly, the fact that international trade typically creates losers as well as winners is crucial for understanding the politics of trade policy.

We turn next to the case in which a country exports a good.

The Effects of Exports

Figure 8-8 shows the effects on a country when it exports a good, in this case airplanes. For this example, we assume that unlimited quantities of airplanes can be sold abroad at a given world price, P_W, which is higher than the price that would prevail in the domestic market in autarky, P_A.

The higher world price makes it profitable for exporters to buy airplanes domestically and sell them overseas. The purchases of domestic airplanes drive the domestic price up until it is equal to the world price. As a result, the quantity demanded by domestic consumers falls from Q_A to Q_D and the quantity supplied by domestic producers rises from Q_A to Q_S. This difference between domestic production and domestic consumption, $Q_S - Q_D$, is exported.

Like imports, exports lead to an overall gain in total surplus for the exporting country but also create losers as well as winners. Figure 8-9 shows the effects of airplane exports on producer and consumer surplus. In the absence of trade, the price of each airplane would be P_A. Consumer surplus in the absence of trade is the sum of areas W and X, and producer surplus is area Y. As a result of trade, price rises from P_A to P_W, consumer surplus falls to W, and producer surplus rises to $Y + X + Z$. So producers gain $X + Z$, consumers lose X, and, as shown in the

FIGURE   **8-8**   **The Domestic Market with Exports**

Here the world price, P_W, is greater than the autarky price, P_A. When the economy is opened to international trade, some of the domestic supply is now exported. The domestic price rises from the autarky price, P_A, to the world price, P_W. As the price rises, the domestic quantity demanded falls from Q_A to Q_D and the domestic quantity supplied rises from Q_A to Q_S. The portion of domestic production that is not consumed domestically, $Q_S - Q_D$, is exported.

table accompanying the figure, the economy as a whole gains total surplus in the amount of Z.

We have learned, then, that imports of a particular good hurt domestic producers of that good but help domestic consumers, whereas exports of a particular good hurt domestic consumers of that good but help domestic producers. In each case, the gains are larger than the losses.

FIGURE   **8-9**   **The Effects of Exports on Surplus**

	Changes in surplus	
	Gain	Loss
Consumer surplus		– X
Producer surplus	X + Z	
Change in total surplus	**+ Z**	

When the domestic price rises to P_W as a result of trade, producers gain additional surplus (areas X + Z) but consumers lose surplus (area X). Because the gains to producers outweigh the losses to consumers, there is an increase in the total surplus in the economy as a whole (area Z).

International Trade and Wages

So far we have focused on the effects of international trade on producers and consumers in a particular industry. For many purposes this is a very helpful approach. However, producers and consumers are not the only parts of society affected by trade—so are the owners of factors of production. In particular, the owners of labour, land, and capital employed in producing goods that are exported, or goods that compete with imported goods, can be deeply affected by trade.

Moreover, the effects of trade aren't limited to just those industries that export or compete with imports because *factors of production can often move between industries.* So now we turn our attention to the long-run effects of international trade on income distribution—how a country's total income is allocated among its various factors of production.

To begin our analysis, consider the position of Maria, an accountant at Ontario Auto Parts, Inc. If the economy is opened up to imports of auto parts from Mexico, the domestic auto parts industry will contract, and it will hire fewer accountants. But accounting is a profession with employment opportunities in many industries, and Maria might well find a better job in the aircraft industry, which expands as a result of international trade. So it may not be appropriate to think of her as a producer of auto parts who is hurt by competition from imported parts. Rather, we should think of her as an accountant who is affected by auto part imports only to the extent that these imports change the wages of accountants in the economy as a whole.

The wage rate of accountants is a *factor price*—the price employers have to pay for the services of a factor of production. One key question about international trade is how it affects factor prices—not just narrowly defined factors of production like accountants, but broadly defined factors such as capital, unskilled labour, and post-secondary-educated or skilled labour.

Earlier in this chapter we described the Heckscher–Ohlin model of trade, which states that comparative advantage is determined by a country's factor endowment. This model also suggests how international trade affects factor prices in a country: compared to autarky, international trade tends to raise the prices of factors that are abundantly available and reduce the prices of factors that are scarce.

We won't work this out in detail, but the idea is simple. The prices of factors of production, like the prices of goods and services, are determined by supply and demand. If international trade increases the demand for a factor of production, that factor's price will rise; if international trade reduces the demand for a factor of production, that factor's price will fall.

Now think of a country's industries as consisting of two kinds: **exporting industries,** which produce goods and services that are sold abroad, and **import-competing industries,** which produce goods and services that are also imported from abroad. Compared with autarky, international trade leads to higher production in exporting industries and lower production in import-competing industries. This indirectly increases the demand for the factors used by exporting industries and decreases the demand for factors used by import-competing industries.

In addition, the Heckscher–Ohlin model says that a country tends to export goods that are intensive in its abundant factors and to import goods that are intensive in its scarce factors. So *international trade tends to increase the demand for factors that are abundant in our country compared with other countries, and to decrease the demand for factors that are scarce in our country compared with other countries.* As a result, *the prices of abundant factors tend to rise, and the prices of scarce factors tend to fall as international trade grows.* In other words, international

Exporting industries produce goods and services that are sold abroad.

Import-competing industries produce goods and services that are also imported.

trade tends to redistribute income toward a country's abundant factors and away from its less abundant factors.

The Economics in Action at the end of the preceding section pointed out that U.S. exports tend to be human-capital-intensive and U.S. imports tend to be unskilled-labour-intensive. This suggests that the effect of international trade on U.S. factor markets is to raise the wage rate of highly educated American workers and reduce the wage rate of unskilled American workers.

This effect has been a source of much concern in recent years. Wage inequality— the gap between the wages of high-paid and low-paid workers—has increased substantially over the last 30 years. Some economists believe that growing international trade is an important factor in that trend. If international trade has the effects predicted by the Heckscher–Ohlin model, its growth raises the wages of highly educated North American workers, who already have relatively high wages, and lowers the wages of less educated North American workers, who already have relatively low wages. But keep in mind another phenomenon: trade reduces the income inequality *between* countries as poor countries improve their standard of living by exporting to rich countries.

How important are these effects? In some historical episodes, the impacts of international trade on factor prices have been very large. As we explain in the following Economics in Action, the opening of transatlantic trade in the late nineteenth century had a large negative impact on land rents in Europe, hurting landowners but helping workers and owners of capital.

The effects of trade on wages in Canada and the United States have generated considerable controversy in recent years. Most economists who have studied the issue agree that growing imports of labour-intensive products from newly indus-trializing economies, and the export of high-technology goods in return, have helped cause a widening wage gap between highly educated and less educated workers in developed nations like Canada and the United States. However, most economists believe that it is only one of several forces explaining the growth in North American wage inequality.

ECONOMICS ▸ IN ACTION

TRADE, WAGES, AND LAND PRICES IN THE NINETEENTH CENTURY

Beginning around 1870, there was an explosive growth of world trade in agricultural products, based largely on the steam engine. Steam-powered ships could cross the ocean much more quickly and reliably than sailing ships. Until about 1860, steamships had higher costs than sailing ships, but after that costs dropped sharply. At the same time, steam-powered rail transport made it possible to bring grain and other bulk goods cheaply from the interior to ports. The result was that land-abundant countries—Canada, the United States, Argentina, and Australia—began shipping large quantities of agricultural goods to the densely populated, land-scarce countries of Europe.

This opening up of international trade led to higher prices of agricultural products, such as wheat, in exporting countries and a decline in

International trade redistributes income toward a country's abundant factors and away from its less abundant factors.

their prices in importing countries. Notably, the difference between wheat prices in western Canada and England plunged.

The change in agricultural prices created winners and losers on both sides of the Atlantic as factor prices adjusted. In England, land prices fell by half compared with average wages; landowners found their purchasing power sharply reduced, but workers benefitted from cheaper food. In Canada, the reverse happened: land prices doubled compared with wages. Landowners did very well, but workers found the purchasing power of their wages dented by rising food prices.

CHECK YOUR UNDERSTANDING 5-2

1. Due to a strike by truckers, trade in food between Canada and Mexico is halted. In autarky, the price of Mexican grapes is lower than that of Canadian grapes. Using a diagram of the Canadian domestic demand curve and the Canadian domestic supply curve for grapes, explain the effect of these events on the following.
   a. Canadian grape consumers' surplus
   b. Canadian grape producers' surplus
   c. Canadian total surplus

2. What effect do you think this event will have on Mexican grape producers? Mexican grape pickers? Mexican grape consumers? Canadian grape pickers?

Solutions appear at back of book.

The Effects of Trade Protection

Ever since David Ricardo laid out the principle of comparative advantage in the early nineteenth century, most economists have advocated **free trade.** That is, they have argued that government policy should not attempt either to reduce or to increase the levels of exports and imports that occur naturally as a result of supply and demand. Despite the free-trade arguments of economists, however, many governments use taxes and other restrictions to limit imports. Less frequently, governments offer subsidies to encourage exports. Policies that limit imports, usually with the goal of protecting domestic producers in import-competing industries from foreign competition, are known as **trade protection** or simply as **protection.**

Let's look at the two most common protectionist policies, tariffs and import quotas, then turn to the reasons governments follow these policies.

The Effects of a Tariff

A **tariff** is a form of excise tax, one that is levied only on sales of imported goods. For example, the Canadian government could declare that anyone bringing in auto seats must pay a tariff of $100 per unit. In the distant past, tariffs were an important source of government revenue because they were relatively easy to collect. But in the modern world, tariffs are usually intended to discourage imports and protect import-competing domestic producers rather than as a source of government revenue.

The tariff raises both the price received by domestic producers and the price paid by domestic consumers. Suppose, for example, that our country imports auto seats, and an auto seat costs $200 on the world market. As we saw earlier, under free trade the domestic price would also be $200. But if a tariff of $100 per

An economy has **free trade** when the government does not attempt either to reduce or to increase the levels of exports and imports that occur naturally as a result of supply and demand.

Policies that limit imports are known as **trade protection** or simply as **protection.**

A **tariff** is a tax levied on imports.

FIGURE   **8-10**   The Effect of a Tariff

A tariff raises the domestic price of the good from P_W to P_T. The domestic quantity demanded shrinks from Q_D to Q_{DT}, and the domestic quantity supplied increases from Q_S to Q_{ST}. As a result, imports—which had been $Q_D - Q_S$ before the tariff was imposed—shrink to $Q_{DT} - Q_{ST}$ after the tariff is imposed.

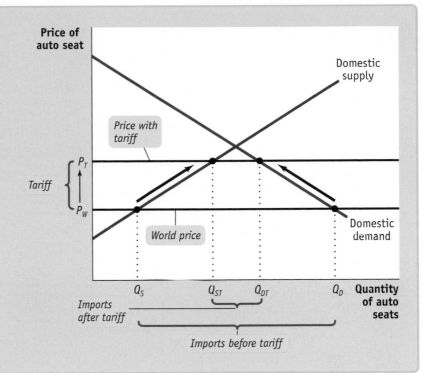

unit is imposed, the domestic price will rise to $300, because it won't be profitable to import auto seats unless the price in the domestic market is high enough to compensate importers for the cost of paying the tariff.

Figure 8-10 illustrates the effects of a tariff on imports of auto seats. As before, we assume that P_W is the world price of an auto seat. Before the tariff is imposed, imports have driven the domestic price down to P_W, so that pre-tariff domestic production is Q_S, pre-tariff domestic consumption is Q_D, and pre-tariff imports are $Q_D - Q_S$.

Now suppose that the government imposes a tariff on each auto seat imported. As a consequence, it is no longer profitable to import auto seats unless the domestic price received by the importer is greater than or equal to the world price *plus* the tariff. So the domestic price rises to P_T, which is equal to the world price, P_W, plus the tariff. Domestic production rises to Q_{ST}, domestic consumption falls to Q_{DT}, and imports fall to $Q_{DT} - Q_{ST}$.

A tariff, then, raises domestic prices, leading to increased domestic production and reduced domestic consumption compared to the situation under free trade. Figure 8-11 shows the effects on surplus. There are three effects:

1. The higher domestic price increases producer surplus, a gain equal to area A.

2. The higher domestic price reduces consumer surplus, a reduction equal to the sum of areas A, B, C, and D.

3. The tariff yields revenue to the government. How much revenue? The government collects the tariff—which, remember, is equal to the difference between P_T and P_W on each of the $Q_{DT} - Q_{ST}$ units imported. So total revenue is $(P_T - P_W) \times (Q_{DT} - Q_{ST})$. This is equal to area C.

The welfare effects of a tariff are summarized in the table in Figure 8-11. Producers gain, consumers lose, and the government gains. But consumer losses are greater than the sum of producer and government gains, leading to a net reduction in total surplus equal to areas $B + D$.

FIGURE **8-11** A Tariff Reduces Total Surplus

		Changes in surplus	
		Gain	**Loss**
Consumer surplus			$-(A + B + C + D)$
Producer surplus		A	
Government revenue		C	
Change in total surplus			$-(B + D)$

When the domestic price rises as a result of a tariff, producers gain additional surplus (area A), the government gains revenue (area C), and consumers lose surplus (areas $A + B + C + D$). Because the losses to consumers outweigh the gains to producers and the government, the economy as a whole loses surplus (areas $B + D$).

An excise tax creates inefficiency, or deadweight loss, because it prevents mutually beneficial trades from occurring. The same is true of a tariff, where the deadweight loss imposed on society is equal to the loss in total surplus represented by areas $B + D$.

Tariffs generate deadweight losses because they create inefficiencies in two ways:

1. Some mutually beneficial trades go unexploited: some consumers who are willing to pay more than the world price, P_W, do not purchase the good, even though P_W is the true cost of a unit of the good to the economy. The cost of this inefficiency is represented in Figure 8-11 by area D.

2. The economy's resources are wasted on inefficient production: some producers whose cost exceeds P_W produce the good, even though an additional unit of the good can be purchased abroad for P_W. The cost of this inefficiency is represented in Figure 8-11 by area B.

The Effects of an Import Quota

An **import quota,** another form of trade protection, is a legal limit on the quantity of a good that can be imported. For example, a Canadian import quota on Mexican auto seats might limit the quantity imported each year to 50 000 units. Import quotas are usually administered through licences: a number of licences are issued, each giving the licence-holder the right to import a limited quantity of the good each year.

An **import quota** is a legal limit on the quantity of a good that can be imported.

A quota on sales has the same effect as an excise tax, with one difference: the money that would otherwise have accrued to the government as tax revenue under an excise tax becomes licence-holders' revenue under a quota—also known as quota rents. ("Quota rent" was defined in Chapter 5.) Similarly, an import quota has the same effect as a tariff, with one difference: the money that would otherwise have been government revenue becomes quota rents to licence-holders. Look again at Figure 8-11. An import quota that limits imports to $Q_{DT} - Q_{ST}$ will raise the domestic price of auto parts by the same amount as the tariff we considered previously. That is, it will raise the domestic price from P_W to P_T. However, area C will now represent quota rents rather than government revenue.

Who receives import licences and so collects the quota rents? In the case of Canadian import protection, the answer may surprise you: the most important import licences—mainly for textiles and clothing—are granted to foreign governments.

Because the quota rents for most Canadian import quotas go to foreigners, the cost to Canada of such quotas is larger than that of a comparable tariff (a tariff that leads to the same level of imports). In Figure 8-11, the net loss to Canada from such an import quota would be equal to areas $B + C + D$, the difference between consumer losses and producer gains.

When a country imposes trade barriers (import tariffs or import quotas), it has economic impacts on foreign countries. Both types of barriers, in effect, raise the price of foreign products in the importing country and lower the domestic demand for foreign goods. This reduction of domestic demand for foreign goods could lead to job losses and reduced export revenues in foreign countries. In the case of poor or developing countries, the impact of such barriers on their exports may have profound negative effects on their economies.

ECONOMICS ▸ IN ACTION

TRADE PROTECTION IN CANADA

Canada was created as a nation by the British North America Act of 1867. At that time, Canada's western provinces were barely settled, most of the country's trading links were north–south, there was no transcontinental railway, and Canada's fledgling manufacturing industry faced stiff competition from the United States and Britain.

In an attempt to forge Canada's small, diverse, and far-flung people into a single nation, the government of Sir John A. Macdonald implemented a "National Policy" in 1879. This policy had several pillars. It involved encouraging western settlement with homestead grants of free land. It involved building a transcontinental railway to transport manufactured goods from the East and to route food from the West. And, most significantly, it involved a system of high tariffs designed to protect and promote Canadian manufacturing. The aim of the National Policy was to replace existing north–south trading relationships with newly created east–west ones, to create a national market, and to achieve a truly east–west transcontinental union. The tariffs were part of this nation-building enterprise.

Since then, Canada and its infant industries have grown up. In 1947, Canada and 22 other countries signed the General Agreement on Tariffs and Trade (GATT) with the aim of reducing trade barriers. Successive waves of negotiations resulted in additional rounds of GATT, the most notable being the Uruguay Round, completed in 1994. This round had success on four broad fronts. First, it succeeded in reducing world tariffs by about 40%. Second, while Canada and the European Union (EU) prevented an agreement on liberalizing trade in agricultural goods, both were forced to replace agricultural quotas with "tariff equivalents." Those countries pushing for free trade in agricultural goods hoped that pressure would build for reduction of the high tariffs over subsequent decades. Third, quotas restricting trade in textiles and garments had to be phased out over a 10-year period ending January 1, 2005. Fourth, and perhaps most significant, the Uruguay Round eliminated the GATT structure and replaced it with the World Trade Organization (WTO), which has a formal dispute settlement mechanism and whose rulings are binding on member governments.

Besides these multilateral agreements toward trade liberalization, Canada has also negotiated separately with the United States. In 1989 Canada and the United States signed a Free Trade Agreement (FTA), and in 1994 the North American Free Trade Agreement (NAFTA) extended the original agreement to include Mexico.

In recent years, Canada has negotiated with the EU toward a comprehensive economic and trade agreement (CETA), a very ambitious trade initiative because of the size of the EU. These trade negotiations covered many sectors, from agricultural to manufacturing, from the lumber industry to the information technology industry. Even though it is not easy to enter into such an agreement (since it is very difficult for countries to reach consensus on the various issues), Canada and the EU finally signed a free trade agreement in principle on October 18, 2013. For the deal to start in 2015, it requires ratification by all Canadian provinces and territories and all EU member countries. Once the CETA is implemented, most tariffs between Canada and the EU will be eliminated.

Canada today generally follows a policy of free trade, at least in comparison with other countries and in comparison with its own past. Most manufactured goods are subject to either no tariff or a low tariff. However, Canada does still limit imports of many agricultural goods, textiles, and clothing, and has export controls on some agricultural products and strategic goods. According to the Department of Foreign Affairs, Trade, and Development, the federal department that is responsible for issues related to Canada's international trade, import and export controls are justified for the following reasons:

- To protect national security
- To protect domestic industries that are deemed strategic or vulnerable
- To fulfill other international obligations
- To implement United Nations Security Council trade sanctions

CHECK YOUR UNDERSTANDING   **5-3**

1. Suppose the world price of butter is $2.00 per kilogram and the domestic price in autarky is $4.00 per kilogram. Use a diagram similar to Figure 8-10 to show the following.
   a. If there is free trade, domestic butter producers want the government to impose a tariff of no less than $2.00 per kilogram.
   b. A tariff greater than $2.00 per kilogram is imposed.
2. Suppose the government imposes an import quota rather than a tariff on butter. What quota limit would generate the same quantity of imports as a tariff of $2.00 per kilogram?

Solutions appear at back of book.

The Political Economy of Trade Protection

We have seen that international trade produces mutual benefits to the countries that engage in it. We have also seen that tariffs and import quotas, although they produce winners as well as losers, reduce total surplus. Yet many countries continue to impose tariffs and import quotas as well as to enact other protectionist measures.

To understand why trade protection takes place, we will first look at some common justifications for protection. Then we will look at the politics of trade protection. Finally, we will look at an important feature of trade protection in today's world: tariffs and import quotas are the subject of international negotiation and are policed by international organizations.

Arguments for Trade Protection

Advocates for tariffs and import quotas offer a variety of arguments. Three common arguments are *national security, job creation,* and the *infant industry argument.*

The national security argument is based on the proposition that overseas sources of goods are vulnerable to disruption in times of international conflict; therefore, a country should protect domestic suppliers of crucial goods, with the aim to be self-sufficient in those goods. In the 1960s, the United States—which had begun to import oil as domestic oil reserves ran low—had an import quota on oil, justified on national security grounds. Currently, Canada imposes import restrictions on agricultural products to protect Canadian farmers, ensure a stable domestic supply of food, and prevent price fluctuations.

The job creation argument points to the additional jobs created in import-competing industries as a result of trade protection.[2] Economists argue that these jobs are offset by the jobs lost elsewhere, such as industries that use imported inputs and now face higher input costs. But non-economists don't always find this argument persuasive.

Finally, the infant industry argument, often raised in newly industrializing countries, holds that new industries require a temporary period of trade protection to get established. For example, in the 1950s many countries in Latin America imposed tariffs and import quotas on manufactured goods, in an effort to switch from their traditional role as exporters of raw materials to a new status as industrial countries.

In theory, the argument for infant industry protection can be compelling, particularly in high-tech industries that increase a country's overall skill level. Reality, however, is more complicated: it is most often industries that are politically influential that gain protection. In addition, governments tend to be poor predictors of the best emerging technologies. Finally, it is often very difficult to wean an industry from protection when it should be mature enough to stand on its own.

The Politics of Trade Protection

In reality, much trade protection has little to do with the arguments just described. Instead, it reflects the political influence of import-competing producers.

We've seen that a tariff or import quota leads to gains for import-competing producers and losses for consumers. Producers, however, usually have much more influence over trade policy decisions. The producers who compete with imports of a particular good are usually a smaller, more cohesive group than the consumers of that good.

An example is trade protection for eggs: Canada has a limit on how many eggs can be imported, which on average causes our domestic price to be higher than the world price, so Canadian families pay more for the eggs they consume. For example, according to the *National Post,* a carton of eggs cost about $3.19 in Vancouver but only $2.09 in Washington State in 2012 (the higher price was mostly caused by an import quota and supply management policies). This quota is difficult to rationalize in terms of any economic argument. However, consumers rarely complain about the quota because they are unaware that it exists. According to Agriculture and Agri-Food Canada, Canadian egg consumption was 16.1 dozen per person in 2009. At that rate, the average Canadian would pay about $18 more a year for eggs

---

[2]Advocates of "buy local" policies encourage domestic households, firms, and governments to buy from domestic producers rather than foreign producers. To support their position, they sometimes appeal to the job-creation angle, in addition to citing the benefits from less pollution and greater environmental sustainabiity that buying local will bring.

International trade agreements are treaties in which a country promises to engage in less trade protection against the exports of other countries in return for a promise by other countries to do the same for its own exports.

The **North American Free Trade Agreement,** or **NAFTA,** is a trade agreement between Canada, the United States, and Mexico.

The **World Trade Organization,** or **WTO,** oversees international trade agreements and rules on disputes between countries over those agreements.

than an American with similar egg consumption would, a difference small enough to not attract notice. But, according to Egg Farmers of Canada, although there are only a few thousand egg farmers in Canada, the Canadian egg industry employs 16 800 people across the country and contributes $1.4 billion to Canada's output. They are very aware of the benefits they receive from the quota and they make sure that their interest in the matter is heard in Parliament.

Given these political realities, it may seem surprising that trade is as free as it is. For example, Canada has low tariffs, and its import quotas are mainly confined to clothing and a few agricultural products. It would be nice to say that the main reason trade protection is so limited is that economists have convinced governments of the virtues of free trade. A more important reason, however, is the role of *international trade agreements*.

International Trade Agreements and the World Trade Organization

When a country engages in trade protection, it hurts two groups. We've already emphasized the adverse effect on domestic consumers, but protection also hurts foreign export industries. This means that countries care about one anothers' trade policies: the Canadian lumber industry, for example, has a strong interest in keeping U.S. tariffs on forest products low.

Because countries care about one anothers' trade policies, they enter into **international trade agreements:** treaties in which a country promises to engage in less trade protection against the exports of another country in return for a promise by the other country to do the same for its own exports. Most world trade is now governed by such agreements.

Some international trade agreements involve just two countries or a small group of countries. As we mentioned in the opening story, Canada, the United States, and Mexico are joined together by the **North American Free Trade Agreement,** or **NAFTA.** This agreement, signed in 1993, will eventually remove all barriers to trade among the three nations. In Europe, as of July 1, 2013, 28 nations are part of an even more comprehensive agreement, the European Union, or EU. In NAFTA, the member countries set their own tariff rates against imports from other non-member countries. The EU, however, is a *customs union:* tariffs are levied at the same rate on goods from outside the EU entering the union.

There are also global trade agreements covering most of the world. Such global agreements are overseen by the **World Trade Organization,** or **WTO,** an international organization composed of 151 member countries, accounting for the bulk of world trade. The WTO plays two roles. First, it provides the framework for the massively complex negotiations involved in a major international trade agreement (the full text of the last major agreement, approved in 1994, was 24 000 pages long). Second, the WTO resolves disputes between its members. These disputes typically arise when one country claims that another country's policies violate its previous agreements.

The WTO is sometimes, with great exaggeration, described as a world government. In fact, it has no army, no police, and no direct enforcement power. The grain of truth in that description is that when a country joins the WTO, it agrees to accept the organization's judgments—and these judgments apply not only to tariffs and import quotas but also to domestic policies that the organization considers trade protection disguised under another name. So in joining the WTO a country does give up some of its sovereignty.

Trade disputes among countries usually take a long time to get resolved. By the time a settlement or a resolution has been reached, a significant amount of costs or hardships may have been incurred. As seen in the For Inquiring Minds on the next page, countries may not follow the intent of the agreements. Having an agreement and abiding by that agreement are not necessarily the same thing.

FOR INQUIRING MINDS

SOFTWOOD LUMBER DISPUTE

The softwood lumber dispute between Canada and the United States has a long history. Since 1982, there have been several points of contention between the two nations, but at the core of the dispute have been American claims regarding Canada's system of stumpage, a fee that provincial governments set and charge logging companies for the right to harvest lumber from public land (the logging right). The United States has argued that the fee is too low and has viewed it as a subsidy to Canadian-based lumber producers. According to this view, Canadian lumber producers could sell lumber at a price lower than the American lumber producers, constituting unfair trade and hurting the American lumber industry.

In response to these complaints from the U.S. lumber industry, the U.S. Department of Commerce imposed countervailing duties on Canadian softwood lumber.[3] At the Canadian government's request, a dispute-resolution panel of five experts was selected according to the Canada–U.S. Free Trade Agreement. Rulings were in Canada's favour. However, the U.S. government challenged the rulings and delayed the removal of the countervailing duties. On May 29, 1996, Canada and the United States finalized the Softwood Lumber Agreement 1996, covering the five-year period to March 31, 2001. The essence of this agreement was a tariff rate quota administered by Canada whereby 14.7 billion board feet of lumber could be shipped duty-free to the United States annually. Amounts over 14.7 billion board feet were subject to increasingly prohibitive tariff rates. Also, exports from Atlantic Canada were unrestricted.

As the agreement approached its end in 2001, the U.S. lumber industry lobbied to the U.S. Department of Commerce again for the imposition of countervailing duties. This time the United States imposed a 27% duty on Canadian softwood lumber based on the claims that Canada unfairly subsidized lumber producers and that Canadian lumber was sold at a lower price in the United States than in Canada (referred to as *dumping* in international trade). Once again, Canada appealed this 27% duty to NAFTA and WTO panels, and again, many of the rulings were in favour of Canada. The settlement breakthrough came in 2006, when Canada and the United States reached an agreement to provide a resolution to the softwood lumber dispute. In the 2006 Softwood Lumber Agreement, the United States was to remove the countervailing and antidumping duties, and to return over US$4 billion in duties collected from Canadian importers since 2002. The agreement had a seven-year term, with a possible two-year extension.

The signing of the 2006 Softwood Lumber Agreement did not really end the softwood lumber dispute. In recent years, the United States has filed several cases to the London Court of International Arbitration regarding the implementation of the agreement by Canada. Some of the rulings from the London Court of International Arbitration favoured Canada and some did not, so the future of Canada's softwood lumber industry remains uncertain.

New Challenges to Globalization

The forward march of globalization over the past century is generally considered a major political and economic success. Economists and policymakers alike have viewed growing world trade, in particular, as a good thing. We would be remiss, however, if we failed to acknowledge that many people are having second thoughts about globalization. To a large extent, these second thoughts reflect two concerns shared by many economists: worries about the effects of globalization on inequality and worries that new developments, in particular the growth in *offshore outsourcing,* are increasing economic insecurity.

Globalization and Inequality We've already mentioned the implications of international trade for factor prices, such as wages: when wealthy countries like Canada export skill-intensive products like aircraft while importing labour-intensive products like clothing, they can expect to see the wage gap between more educated and less educated domestic workers widen. Thirty years ago, this wasn't a significant concern, because most of the goods wealthy countries imported from poorer countries were raw materials or goods where comparative advantage depended on climate. Today, however, many manufactured goods are imported from relatively poor countries, with a potentially much larger effect on the distribution of income.

---

[3]A government imposes countervailing duties on imported goods that it feels are unfairly subsidized by the exporting nation; the reason for imposing countervailing duties is to minimize the negative effects of a subsidized imported good on the domestic industry.

Offshore outsourcing takes place when businesses hire people in another country to perform various tasks.

Trade with China, in particular, raises concerns among labour groups trying to maintain wage levels in rich countries. Although China has experienced spectacular economic growth since the economic reforms that began in the late 1970s, it remains a relatively poor, low-wage country. In 2012, wages of Chinese manufacturing workers were only about 14% of their Canadian counterparts' wages. Meanwhile, imports from China have soared. In 1992, only 1.67% of Canada's imports came from China; by 2012, the figure had risen to 11%. There's not much question that these surging imports from China put at least some downward pressure on the wages of less educated Canadian workers.

Outsourcing Chinese exports to Canada overwhelmingly consist of labour-intensive manufactured goods. However, some Canadian workers have recently found themselves facing a new form of international competition. *Outsourcing*, in which a company hires another company to perform some task, such as running the corporate computer system, is a long-standing business practice. Until recently, however, outsourcing was normally done locally, with a company hiring another company in the same city or country.

Now, modern telecommunications increasingly makes it possible to engage in **offshore outsourcing,** in which businesses hire people in another country to perform various tasks. The classic example is call centres: the person answering the phone when you call a company's 1-800 help line may well be in India, which has taken the lead in attracting offshore outsourcing. Offshore outsourcing has also spread to fields such as software design/programming and the financial sector. In April 2013, the Royal Bank of Canada (RBC) came under fire when the public found out the bank had outsourced 45 of its information technology (IT) jobs to foreign workers. Although the number of positions being outsourced seems small, it was sufficient to cause concerns among Canadians. According to International Data Corporation (IDC) Canada, this recent outsourcing of 45 IT jobs by RBC is just the tip of an iceberg. An IDC Canada survey found that 6 out of 10 Canadian firms would use outsourcing as a means to cut costs. It is not surprising then that some economists have warned that millions or even tens of millions of North American workers who have never thought they could face foreign competition for their jobs may face unpleasant surprises in the not-too-distant future.

Concerns about income distribution and outsourcing, as we've said, are shared by many economists. There is also, however, widespread opposition to globalization. In 1999, an attempt to start a major round of trade negotiations failed in part because the WTO meeting, in Seattle, was disrupted by antiglobalization demonstrators. However, the more important reason for its failure was disagreement among the countries represented. Another round of negotiations that began in 2001 in Doha, Qatar, known as the "Doha development round," stalled in 2008, mainly because of disagreements over agricultural trade rules. No significant progress has been made since then.

What motivates the antiglobalization movement? To some extent it's the sweatshop labour fallacy: it's easy to get outraged about the low wages paid to the person who made your shirt, and harder to appreciate how much worse off that person would be if denied the opportunity to sell goods in rich countries' markets. It's also true, however, that the movement represents a backlash against supporters of globalization who have oversold its benefits. Countries in Latin America, in particular, were promised that reducing their tariff rates would produce an economic takeoff; instead, they have experienced disappointing results. Some groups, such as poor farmers facing new competition from imported food, ended up worse off.

Do these new challenges to globalization undermine the argument that international trade is a good thing? The great

To some extent, the antiglobalization movement is motivated by the sweatshop labour fallacy.

majority of economists would argue that the gains from reducing trade protection still exceed the losses. However, it has become more important than before to make sure that the gains from international trade are widely spread. And the politics of international trade is becoming increasingly difficult as the extent of trade has grown.

ECONOMICS > IN ACTION

FREEING CANADA'S TRADE WITH THE WORLD

On December 5, 1996, government officials from Canada and Chile signed the Canada–Chile Free Trade Agreement (CCFTA). This bilateral trade agreement covering trade in both goods and services significantly liberalized trade between Canada and Chile. It was Canada's first free trade agreement with a South American country and was Chile's first comprehensive free trade agreement. The agreement, which was implemented on July 5, 1997, eliminated tariffs on 75% of the trade between the two countries and contained commitments to reduce non-tariff barriers.

Between 1997 and 2012, bilateral trade increased 350% and Canadian direct investment in Chile grew by over 300%. According to the Chilean government, Canada is the third largest investor overall in Chile—first in the mining sector—and the largest source of new direct investment in Chile in the past decade.

On April 16, 2012, Prime Minister Stephen Harper and Chilean president Sebastian Pinera signed an expanded CCFTA document. This amended agreement contains a section that will ensures Canadian financial services firms, such as banks and insurance companies, will enjoy preferential access to the Chilean market. It also contains new dispute settlement procedures and provisions on government procurement and customs procedures.

The government of Canada continues to negotiate other potential important trade agreements. For example, after years of negotiation, an agreement in principle on a CETA between Canada and the European Union (EU) was reached in late 2013. The EU is home to more than 500 million people and the world's largest economy, producing more than $16 trillion worth of output in 2012. In the joint press conference with EU president Jose Manuel Barroso, Prime Minister Harper said that the CETA "is the biggest deal our country has ever made. This is a historic win for Canada." Canada has also joined the Trans-Pacific Partnership (TPP), which consists of twelve Pacific nations: Australia, Brunei, Canada, Chile, Japan, Malaysia, Mexico, New Zealand, Peru, Singapore, the United States, and Vietnam. The TPP represents a population of almost 800 million people and a combined output of $27.5 trillion, more than 38% of the world's economy. These countries have held 18 rounds of talks on the possibility of reaching a comprehensive free trade agreement among all 12 member countries.

Prime Minister Stephen Harper and Chilean president Sebastian Pinera at the signing of the expanded CCFTA.

Ivan Alvarado/Reuters/Landov

CHECK YOUR UNDERSTANDING   5-4

1. In Canada, over half of the steel consumed domestically is imported and steel is an input in many Canadian industries. The federal government has imposed import controls on steel and a variety of consumer goods. Explain why political lobbying to eliminate import controls on steel is more likely to be effective than lobbying to eliminate import controls on consumer goods such as clothing and eggs.

2. Over the years, the WTO has increasingly found itself adjudicating trade disputes that involve not just tariffs or quota restrictions but also restrictions based on quality, health, and environmental considerations. Why do you think this has occurred? What method would you, as a WTO official, use to decide whether a quality, health, or environmental restriction is in violation of a free trade agreement?

Solutions appear at back of book.

BUSINESS CASE : Li & Fung: From Guangzhou to You

Daniel J. Groshong/Bloomberg via Getty Images

It's a very good bet that as you read this, you're wearing something manufactured in Asia. And if you are, it's also a good bet that the Hong Kong company Li & Fung was involved in getting your garment designed, produced, and shipped to your local store. From Levi's to Aéropostale to Walmart, Li & Fung is a critical conduit from factories around the world to the shopping mall nearest you.

The company was founded in 1906 in Guangzhou, China. According to Victor Fung, the company's chairman, his grandfather's "value added" was that he spoke English, allowing him to serve as an interpreter in business deals between Chinese and foreigners. When Mao's Communist Party seized control in mainland China, the company moved to Hong Kong. There, as Hong Kong's market economy took off during the 1960s and 1970s, Li & Fung grew as an export broker, bringing together Hong Kong manufacturers and foreign buyers.

The real transformation of the company came, however, as Asian economies grew and changed. Hong Kong's rapid growth led to rising wages, making Li & Fung increasingly uncompetitive in garments, its main business. So the company reinvented itself: rather than being a simple broker, it became a "supply chain manager." Not only would it allocate production of a good to a manufacturer, it would also break production down, allocate production of the inputs, and then allocate final assembly of the good among its 12 000+ suppliers around the globe. Sometimes production would be done in sophisticated economies like those of Hong Kong or even Japan, where wages are high but so is quality and productivity; sometimes it would be done in less advanced locations like mainland China or Thailand, where labour is less productive but cheaper.

For example, suppose you own a Canadian retail chain and want to sell garment-washed blue jeans. Rather than simply arrange for production of the jeans, Li & Fung will work with you on their design, providing you with the latest production and style information, like what materials and colours are hot. After the design has been finalized, Li & Fung will arrange for the creation of a prototype, find the most cost-effective way to manufacture it, and then place an order on your behalf. Through Li & Fung, the yarn might be made in Korea and dyed in Taiwan, and the jeans sewn in Thailand or mainland China. And because production is taking place in so many locations, Li & Fung provides transport logistics as well as quality control.

Li & Fung has been enormously successful. In 2012 the company had a market capitalization of approximately US$14.8 billion and business turnover of US$20.2 billion, with offices and distribution centres in more than 40 countries. Li & Fung employs more than 28 000 people worldwide and has access to a sourcing network of over 15 000 suppliers.

QUESTIONS FOR THOUGHT

1. Why do you think it was profitable for Li & Fung to go beyond brokering exports to becoming a supply chain manager, breaking down the production process and sourcing the inputs from various suppliers across many countries?

2. What principle do you think underlies Li & Fung's decisions on how to allocate production of a good's inputs and its final assembly among various countries?

3. Why do you think a retailer prefers to have Li & Fung arrange international production of its jeans rather than purchase them directly from a jeans manufacturer in mainland China?

4. What is the source of Li & Fung's success? Is it based on human capital, on ownership of a natural resource, or on ownership of capital?

SUMMARY

1. International trade is of growing importance to Canada and of even greater importance to most other countries. International trade, like trade among individuals, arises from comparative advantage: the opportunity cost of producing an additional unit of a good is lower in some countries than in others. Goods and services purchased abroad are **imports;** those sold abroad are **exports.** Foreign trade, like other economic linkages between countries, has been growing rapidly, a phenomenon called **globalization.**

2. The **Ricardian model of international trade** assumes that opportunity costs are constant. It shows that there are gains from trade: two countries are better off with trade than in **autarky.**

3. In practice, comparative advantage reflects differences between countries in climate, factor endowments, and technology. The **Heckscher–Ohlin model** shows how differences in factor endowments determine comparative advantage: goods differ in **factor intensity,** and countries tend to export goods that are intensive in the factors they have in abundance.

4. The **domestic demand curve** and the **domestic supply curve** determine the price of a good in autarky. When international trade occurs, the domestic price is driven to equality with the **world price,** the price at which the good is bought and sold abroad.

5. If the world price is below the autarky price, a good is imported. This leads to an increase in consumer surplus, a fall in producer surplus, and a gain in total surplus. If the world price is above the autarky price, a good is exported. This leads to an increase in producer surplus, a fall in consumer surplus, and a gain in total surplus.

6. International trade leads to expansion in **exporting industries** and contraction in **import-competing industries.** This raises the domestic demand for abundant factors of production, reduces the demand for scarce factors, and so affects factor prices, such as wages.

7. Most economists advocate **free trade,** but in practice many governments engage in **trade protection.** The two most common forms of **protection** are tariffs and quotas. In rare occasions, export industries are subsidized.

8. A **tariff** is a tax levied on imports. It raises the domestic price above the world price, hurting consumers, benefitting domestic producers, and generating government revenue. As a result, total surplus falls (this loss of surplus is called deadweight loss). An **import quota** is a legal limit on the quantity of a good that can be imported. It has the same effects as a tariff, except that the revenue goes not to the government but to those who receive import licences.

9. Although several popular arguments have been made in favour of trade protection, in practice the main reason for protection is probably political: import-competing industries are well organized and well informed about how they gain from trade protection, while consumers are unaware of the costs they pay. Still, Canadian trade is fairly free, mainly because of the role of **international trade agreements,** in which countries agree to reduce trade protection against one anothers' exports. The **North American Free Trade Agreement (NAFTA)** and the European Union (EU) cover a small number of countries. In contrast, the **World Trade Organization (WTO)** covers a much larger number of countries, accounting for the bulk of world trade. It oversees trade negotiations and adjudicates disputes among its members.

10. In the past few years, many concerns have been raised about the effects of globalization. One issue is the increase in income inequality due to the surge in imports from relatively poor countries over the past 20 years. Another concern is the increase in **offshore outsourcing,** as many jobs that were once considered safe from foreign competition have been moved abroad.

KEY TERMS

Imports, p. 234
Exports, p. 234
Globalization, p. 234
Ricardian model of international trade, p. 235
Autarky, p. 236
Factor intensity, p. 240
Heckscher–Ohlin model, p. 241

Domestic demand curve, p. 244
Domestic supply curve, p. 244
World price, p. 244
Exporting industries, p. 248
Import-competing industries, p. 248
Free trade, p. 250
Trade protection, p. 250
Protection, p. 250

Tariff, p. 250
Import quota, p. 252
International trade agreements, p. 256
North American Free Trade Agreement (NAFTA), p. 256
World Trade Organization (WTO), p. 256
Offshore outsourcing, p. 258

PROBLEMS

1. Assume Saudi Arabia and Canada face the production possibilities for oil and cars shown in the accompanying table.

Saudi Arabia		Canada	
Quantity of oil (millions of barrels)	Quantity of cars (millions)	Quantity of oil (millions of barrels)	Quantity of cars (millions)
0	4	0	10.0
200	3	100	7.5
400	2	200	5.0
600	1	300	2.5
800	0	400	0

   a. What is the opportunity cost of producing a car in Saudi Arabia? In Canada? What is the opportunity cost of producing a barrel of oil in Saudi Arabia? In Canada?

   b. Which country has the comparative advantage in producing oil? In producing cars?

   c. Suppose that in autarky, Saudi Arabia produces 200 million barrels of oil and 3 million cars; similarly, Canada produces 300 million barrels of oil and 2.5 million cars. Without trade, can Saudi Arabia produce more oil *and* more cars? Without trade, can Canada produce more oil *and* more cars?

2. The production possibilities for Canada and Saudi Arabia are given in Problem 1. Suppose now that each country specializes in the good in which it has the comparative advantage, and the two countries trade. Also assume that for each country the value of imports must equal the value of exports.

   a. What is the total quantity of oil produced? What is the total quantity of cars produced?

   b. Is it possible for Saudi Arabia to consume 400 million barrels of oil and 5 million cars and for Canada to consume 400 million barrels of oil and 5 million cars?

   c. Suppose that, in fact, Saudi Arabia consumes 300 million barrels of oil and 4 million cars and Canada consumes 500 million barrels of oil and 6 million cars. How many barrels of oil does Canada import? How many cars does Canada export? Suppose a car costs $10 000 on the world market. How much, then, does a barrel of oil cost on the world market?

3. Both Canada and the United States produce lumber and music CDs with constant opportunity costs. The United States can produce either 10 tonnes of lumber and no CDs, or 1000 CDs and no lumber, or any combination in between. Canada can produce either 8 tonnes of lumber and no CDs, or 400 CDs and no lumber, or any combination in between.

   a. Draw the U.S. and Canadian production possibility frontiers in two separate diagrams, with CDs on the horizontal axis and lumber on the vertical axis.

   b. In autarky, if the United States wants to consume 500 CDs, how much lumber can it consume at most? Label this point A in your diagram. Similarly, if Canada wants to consume 1 tonne of lumber, how many CDs can it consume in autarky? Label this point C in your diagram.

   c. Which country has the absolute advantage in lumber production?

   d. Which country has the comparative advantage in lumber production?

   Suppose each country specializes in the good in which it has the comparative advantage, and there is trade.

   e. How many CDs does the United States produce? How much lumber does Canada produce?

   f. Is it possible for the United States to consume 500 CDs and 7 tonnes of lumber? Label this point B in your diagram. Is it possible for Canada at the same time to consume 500 CDs and 1 tonne of lumber? Label this point D in your diagram.

4. For each of the following trade relationships, explain the likely source of the comparative advantage of each of the exporting countries.

   a. Canada exports BlackBerry smart phones to Venezuela, and Venezuela exports oil to Canada.

   b. Canada exports airplanes to China, and China exports clothing to Canada.

   c. Canada exports wheat to Colombia, and Colombia exports coffee to Canada.

5. Industry Canada provides statistics on Canada's imports and exports on its website. The following steps will take you to the foreign trade statistics. Use them to answer the questions below.

   i. Go to Industry Canada's website at www.ic.gc.ca

   ii. At the top of the page, under All topics, look for the subheading "Import, export and investment," and then select "Find import/export statistics"

   iii. Once you reach the Trade Data Online page, click on "Search by industry"

   iv. In the drop-down menu "Trade Type," select "Total Exports" if you are looking for data on exports or "Total Imports" if you are looking for data on imports

   v. In the drop-down menu "Trading Partner," select "TOP 10 countries"

   vi. In the drop-down menu "Time Period," select "Specific Year(s)" and choose the year(s) you want. Try 2012 and any other year you desire.

   vii. In the drop-down menu "Industry Options," select "Browse List of Industries"

   viii. In the drop-down menu "Browse for an industry," select the good or service you are interested in, or use the North American Industry Classification System (NAICS) code, then hit "View Industries"

ix. In the "Industry List," choose the industry you are interested in and hit "Add to Selected Industries"

x. Click on "Run Report"

a. Look up recent data for Canadian imports of clothing accessories and other clothing manufacturing (NAICS code 3159). From which country do we import the most clothing accessories? Which of the three sources of comparative advantage (climate, factor endowments, and technology) accounts for that country's comparative advantage in clothing accessories?

b. Look up recent data for Canadian imports of fruits (NAICS code 1113). From which country do we import the most fruit? Which of the three sources of comparative advantage (climate, factor endowments, and technology) accounts for that country's comparative advantage in fruit?

c. Look up recent data for Canadian imports of industrial machinery (NAICS code 3332). From which country do we import the most industrial machinery? Which of the three sources of comparative advantage (climate, factor endowments, and technology) accounts for that country's comparative advantage in industrial machinery?

6. Compare the data for Canadian imports of clothing accessories from China in 2012 that you found in Problem 5 with the same data for the year 2002.

a. What happened to the value of Canadian imports of clothing accessories from China in this 10-year period?

b. What prediction does the Heckscher–Ohlin model make about the wages received by labour in China?

7. Shoes are labour-intensive and satellites are capital-intensive to produce. Canada has abundant capital. China has abundant labour. According to the Heckscher–Ohlin model, which good will China export? Which good will Canada export? In Canada, what will happen to the price of labour (the wage) and to the price of capital?

8. Before the North American Free Trade Agreement (NAFTA) gradually eliminated import tariffs on goods, the autarky price of tomatoes in Mexico was below the world price and in Canada was above the world price. Similarly, the autarky price of poultry in Mexico was above the world price and in Canada was below the world price. Draw diagrams with domestic supply and demand curves for each country and each of the two goods. As a result of NAFTA, Canada now imports tomatoes from Mexico and Canada now exports poultry to Mexico. How would you expect the following groups to be affected?

a. Mexican and Canadian consumers of tomatoes. Illustrate the effect on consumer surplus in your diagram.

b. Mexican and Canadian producers of tomatoes. Illustrate the effect on producer surplus in your diagram.

c. Mexican and Canadian tomato workers.

d. Mexican and Canadian consumers of poultry. Illustrate the effect on consumer surplus in your diagram.

e. Mexican and Canadian producers of poultry. Illustrate the effect on producer surplus in your diagram.

f. Mexican and Canadian poultry workers.

9. The accompanying table indicates the Canadian domestic demand schedule and domestic supply schedule for commercial jet airplanes. Suppose that the world price of a commercial jet airplane is $100 million.

Price of jet (millions)	Quantity of jets demanded	Quantity of jets supplied
$120	100	1000
110	150	900
100	200	800
90	250	700
80	300	600
70	350	500
60	400	400
50	450	300
40	500	200

a. In autarky, how many commercial jet airplanes does Canada produce, and at what price are they bought and sold?

b. With trade, what will the price for commercial jet airplanes be? Will Canada import or export airplanes? How many?

10. The accompanying table shows the Canadian domestic demand schedule and domestic supply schedule for apples. Suppose that the world price of apples is $0.30 per apple.

Price of apples	Quantity of apples demanded (thousands)	Quantity of apples supplied (thousands)
$1.00	2	11
0.90	4	10
0.80	6	9
0.70	8	8
0.60	10	7
0.50	12	6
0.40	14	5
0.30	16	4
0.20	18	3

a. Draw the Canadian domestic supply curve and domestic demand curve.

b. With free trade, how many apples will Canada import or export?

Suppose that the Canadian government imposes a tariff on apples of $0.20 per apple.

c. How many apples will Canada import or export after introduction of the tariff?

d. In your diagram, shade the gain or loss to the economy as a whole from the introduction of this tariff.

11. The Canadian domestic demand schedule and domestic supply schedule for apples was given in Problem 10. Suppose that the world price of apples is $0.30. Canada introduces an import quota of 3000 apples and assigns the quota rents to foreign apple exporters.

a. Draw the domestic demand and supply curves.

b. What will the domestic price of apples be after introduction of the quota?

c. What is the value of the quota rents that foreign exporters of apples receive?

12. The accompanying diagram illustrates the Canadian domestic demand curve and domestic supply curve for textiles.

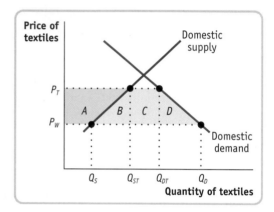

The world price of textiles is P_W. Canada currently imposes an import tariff on textiles, so the price of textiles is P_T. The Canadian government decides to eliminate the tariff. In terms of the areas marked in the diagram, answer the following questions.

a. What is the gain/loss in consumer surplus?

b. What is the gain/loss in producer surplus?

c. What is the gain/loss to the government?

d. What is the gain/loss to the economy as a whole?

13. As Canada has opened up to trade, it has lost many of its low-skill manufacturing jobs, but it has gained jobs in high-skill industries, such as the software industry. Explain whether Canada as a whole has been made better off by trade.

14. Canada is highly protective of its agricultural industry, imposing import tariffs and import quotas on imports of agricultural goods. This chapter presented three arguments for trade protection. For each argument, discuss whether it is a valid justification for trade protection of Canadian agricultural products.

15. In World Trade Organization (WTO) negotiations, if a country agrees to reduce trade barriers (tariffs or quotas), it usually refers to this as a *concession* to other countries. Do you think that this terminology is appropriate?

16. Producers in import-competing industries often make the following argument: "Other countries have an advantage in production of certain goods purely because workers abroad are paid lower wages. In fact, Canadian workers are much more productive than foreign workers. So import-competing industries need to be protected." Is this a valid argument? Explain your answer.

17. In Canada, producers of milk, poultry, and eggs are protected by government imposed supply management rules. This supply management system is made up of a combination of import controls, production planning quotas, and minimum prices for these products.

a. Suppose the goal of the government is to design a supply management system for agricultural products that works to support the incomes of farmers. Explain how the use of production quotas and/or price floors would help to achieve this goal. Briefly explain who benefits and who loses under such a system and why this is so.

b. Why might the supply management system use a combination of a price floor and a production quota?

c. One important facet of this supply management system are restrictions limiting the import of agricultural products. Explain why such import limits are necessary.

d. These Canadian import restrictions are generally not welcomed by foreign suppliers (i.e., farmers in the rest of the world). In fact, this is one of the main reasons that talks between Canada and the European Union (EU) on a trade pact were so slow (a free trade agreement in principle was reached in 2013). Explain why the imposition of Canadian import restrictions on many agricultural products is viewed negatively by some of our trading partners.

e. Suppose European and American farmers are subsidized by their governments in a way that reduces the farmers' costs. Would the existence of such subsidies strengthen or weaken the need for Canadian import restrictions (to protect the incomes of Canadian farmers)? Explain why or why not.

CHAPTER 9

Decision Making by Individuals and Firms

GOING BACK TO SCHOOL

Additional schooling or a job? Each year millions have to make that choice.

HOW WOULD YOU HANDLE losing your job after 24 years? For its August 2009 article "Recession refugees go back to school," the *Financial Post* interviewed "Maria" (her real name was withheld) on how she managed in such a situation. After more than two decades at a large Canadian bank, Maria was laid off in February 2009 during the depth of the recession. As the article noted, "She knew opportunities in financial services were scarce, so after talking to a friend who had switched careers mid-life, Maria decided to return to school to become a social worker."

Maria was far from alone in her decision. In the spring of 2009 and again in 2010, colleges and universities across the country were reporting a record number of applications. Applications soared not just for bachelor and community college programs; they also soared for graduate and continuing education programs of all sorts.

Why did so many people make a similar choice in the spring of 2009 and again in 2010? We'll answer that question shortly. Before we do, note that every year millions of people—just like

you—face a choice about work versus continued schooling: should I continue another year (or semester) in school, or should I get a job? That is, they are making a decision.

This chapter is about the economics of making decisions: how to make a decision that results in the best possible economic outcome. Economists have formulated principles of decision making that lead to the best possible—often called "optimal"—outcome, regardless of whether the decision maker is a consumer or a producer.

We'll start by examining three different types of economic decisions. For each of these types, there is a corresponding principle, or method, of decision making that leads to the best possible economic outcome. In this chapter, we'll see why economists consider decision making to be the very essence of microeconomics.

Despite the fact that people *should* use the principles of economic decision making to achieve the best possible economic outcome, they sometimes fail to do so. In other words, people are not always rational when making decisions. For example, a shopper driving around

❭ Why good decision making begins with accurately defining costs and benefits

❭ The importance of **implicit** as well as **explicit costs** in decision making

❭ The difference between **accounting profit** and **economic profit,** and why economic profit is the correct basis for decisions

❭ Why there are three different types of economic decisions: "either–or" decisions, "how much" decisions, and decisions involving **sunk costs**

❭ The principles of decision making that correspond to each type of economic decision

❭ Why people sometimes behave irrationally in predictable ways

in pursuit of a bargain may knowingly spend more on gasoline than he or she saves on the discounted item. Yet economists have also discovered that people are frequently *irrational in predictable ways.* In this chapter, we'll learn about these tendencies when we discuss *behavioural economics,* the branch of economics that studies predictably irrational economic behaviour. ▪

An **explicit cost** is a cost that requires an outlay of money.

An **implicit cost** does not require an outlay of money; it is measured by the value, in dollar terms, of benefits that are forgone.

Costs, Benefits, and Profits

In making any type of decision, it's critical to define the costs and benefits of that decision accurately. If you don't know the costs and benefits, it is nearly impossible to make a good decision. So that is where we begin.

An important first step is to recognize the role of *opportunity cost*, a concept we first encountered in Chapter 1, where we learned that opportunity costs arise because *resources are scarce*. Because resources are scarce, the true cost of anything is what you must give up to get it—its opportunity cost.

Whether you decide to continue in school for another year or leave to find a job, each choice has costs and benefits. Because your time—a resource—is scarce, you cannot be both a full-time student and a full-time worker. If you choose to be a full-time student, the opportunity cost of that choice is the income you would have earned at a full-time job. And there may be additional opportunity costs, such as the value of the experience you would have gained by working.

When making decisions, it is crucial to think in terms of opportunity cost, because the opportunity cost of an action is often considerably more than the cost of any outlays of money. Economists use the concepts of *explicit costs* and *implicit costs* to compare the relationship between opportunity costs and monetary outlays. We'll discuss these two concepts first. Then we'll define the concepts of *accounting profit* and *economic profit*, which are *ways of measuring whether the benefit of an action is greater than the cost*. Armed with these concepts for assessing costs and benefits, we will be in a position to consider our first principle of economic decision making: how to make "either–or" decisions.

Explicit versus Implicit Costs

Suppose that, after graduating from college or university, you have two options: to go to school for an additional year to get an advanced degree or to take a job immediately. You would like to enrol in the extra year in school but are concerned about the cost.

What exactly is the cost of that additional year of school? Here is where it is important to remember the concept of opportunity cost: the cost of the year spent getting an advanced degree includes what you forgo by not taking a job for that year. The opportunity cost of an additional year of school, like any cost, can be broken into two parts: the *explicit* cost of the year's schooling and the *implicit* cost.

An **explicit cost** is a cost that requires an outlay of money. For example, the explicit cost of the additional year of schooling includes tuition. An **implicit cost,** though, does not involve an outlay of money; instead, it is measured by the value, in dollar terms, of the benefits that are forgone. For example, the implicit cost of the year spent in school includes the income you would have earned if you had taken a job instead:

(9-1) Opportunity cost = Explicit cost(s) + Implicit cost(s)

A common mistake, both in economic analysis and in life—whether individual or business—is to ignore implicit costs and focus exclusively on explicit costs. But often the implicit cost of an activity is quite substantial—indeed, sometimes it is much larger than the explicit cost.

Table 9-1 gives a breakdown of hypothetical explicit and implicit costs associated with spending an additional year in school instead of taking a job. The explicit cost consists of tuition, books, supplies, and a computer for doing assignments—all of which require you to spend money. The implicit cost is the salary you would have earned if you had taken

TABLE 9-1 Opportunity Cost of an Additional Year of School

Explicit cost		Implicit cost	
Tuition	$7000	Forgone salary	$35 000
Books and supplies	1000		
Computer	1500		
Total explicit cost	**9500**	**Total implicit cost**	**35 000**
Total opportunity cost = Total explicit cost + Total implicit cost = $44 500			

a job instead. As you can see, the total cost of attending an additional year of schooling is $44 500, the sum of the total implicit cost—$35 000 in forgone salary, and the total explicit cost—$9500 in outlays on tuition, supplies, and computer. Because the implicit cost is more than three times as much as the explicit cost, ignoring the implicit cost would lead to a seriously misguided decision.

A slightly different way of looking at the implicit cost in this example can deepen our understanding of opportunity cost. The forgone salary is the cost of using your own resources—your time (labour)—in going to school rather than working. The use of your time for more schooling, despite the fact that you don't have to spend any money on it, is still costly to you. This illustrates an important aspect of opportunity cost: in considering the cost of an activity, you should include the cost of using any of your own resources for that activity. You can calculate the cost of using your own resources by determining what they would have earned in their next best use.

Understanding the role of opportunity costs makes clear the reason for the surge in school applications in 2009 and 2010: a rotten job market. Starting in the fall of 2008, the Canadian job market deteriorated sharply as the economy entered a severe recession. By 2010, the job market was still quite weak; although job openings had begun to reappear, a relatively high proportion of those openings were for jobs with low wages and no benefits. As a result, the opportunity cost of another year of schooling had declined significantly, making spending another year at school a much more attractive choice than when the job market was strong.

> **Accounting profit** is equal to revenue minus explicit cost.
>
> **Economic profit** is equal to revenue minus the opportunity cost of resources used. It is usually less than the accounting profit.

Accounting Profit versus Economic Profit

Let's return to Maria from this chapter's opening story. Assume, hypothetically, that Maria is offered a two-year job in the financial services sector. Also, since she took some university courses in the 1990s, in order to be certified as a social worker, she must complete two years of full-time studies. So she faces the choice of either completing two years of full-time undergraduate studies in social work or spending those two years working in her original field. Which choice should she make?

First, let's consider what Maria gains by getting the social work degree—what we might call her *revenue* from the social work degree. Once she has completed her social work degree two years from now, she will receive earnings from her social work degree valued at $600 000 over the rest of her lifetime. In contrast, if she doesn't get the social work degree and stays in financial services, two years from now her future lifetime earnings will be valued at $500 000. The cost of the tuition for her social work degree program is $40 000, which she pays for with a student loan that costs her $4000 in interest.

At this point, what she should do might seem obvious: if she chooses the social work degree, she gets a lifetime increase in the value of her earnings of $600 000 − $500 000 = $100 000, and she pays $40 000 in tuition plus $4000 in interest. Doesn't that mean she makes a profit of $100 000 − $40 000 − $4000 = $56 000 by getting her social work degree? This $56 000 is Maria's **accounting profit** from obtaining her social work degree: her revenue minus her explicit cost. In this example her explicit cost of getting the degree is $44 000, the amount of her tuition plus student loan interest:

(9-2) Accounting profit = Revenue − Explicit cost(s)

Although accounting profit is a useful measure, it would be misleading for Maria to use it alone in making her decision. To make the right decision, the one that leads to the best possible economic outcome for her, she needs to calculate her **economic profit**—the revenue she receives from the social work degree minus her opportunity cost of staying in school (which is equal

"I've done the numbers, and I will marry you."

to her explicit cost *plus* her implicit cost). In general, the economic profit of a given project will be less than the accounting profit because there are almost always implicit costs in addition to explicit costs:

(9-3) Economic profit = Revenue − Opportunity cost(s)
= Revenue − (Explicit costs + Implicit costs)
= Accounting profit − Implicit cost(s)

When economists use the term *profit*, they are referring to *economic* profit, not *accounting* profit. This will be our convention in the remainder of the book: when we use the term *profit*, we mean economic profit.

How does Maria's economic profit of staying in school differ from her accounting profit? We've already encountered one source of the difference: her two years of forgone job earnings. This is an implicit cost of going to school full time for two years. We assume that Maria's total forgone earnings for the two years is $57 000.

Once we factor in Maria's implicit costs and calculate her economic profit, we see that she is better off not getting a social work degree. You can see this in Table 9-2: her economic profit from getting the social work degree is −$1000. In other words, she incurs an *economic loss* of $1000 if she gets the degree. Clearly, she is better off sticking to financial services and going to work now.

TABLE **9-2** **Maria's Economic Profit from Acquiring Social Work Degree**

Value of increase in lifetime earnings	$100 000
Explicit cost:	
Tuition	−40 000
Interest paid on student loan	− 4 000
Accounting Profit	**56 000**
Implicit cost:	
Income forgone during 2 years spent in school	−57 000
Economic Profit	**−1 000**

To make sure that the concepts of opportunity costs and economic profit are well understood, let's consider a slightly different scenario. Let's suppose that Maria does not have to take out $40 000 in student loans to pay her tuition. Instead, she can pay for it with an inheritance from her grandmother. As a result, she doesn't have to pay $4000 in interest. In this case, her accounting profit is $60 000 rather than $56 000. Would the right decision now be for her to get the social work degree? Wouldn't the economic profit of the degree now be $60 000 − $57 000 = $3000?

The answer is no, because Maria is using her own *capital* to finance her education, and the use of that capital has an opportunity cost even when she owns it. **Capital** is the total value of the assets of an individual or a firm. An individual's capital usually consists of cash in the bank, stocks, bonds, and the ownership value of real estate such as a house. In the case of a business, capital also includes its equipment, its tools, and its inventory of unsold goods and used parts. (Economists like to distinguish between *financial assets*, also known as *financial capital*, such as cash, stocks, and bonds, and *physical assets*, also known as *physical capital*, such as buildings, equipment, tools, and inventory.)

The point is that even if Maria owns the $40 000, using it to pay tuition incurs an opportunity cost—what she forgoes in the next best use of that $40 000. If she hadn't used the money to pay her tuition, her next best use of the money would have been to deposit it in a bank to earn interest. To keep things simple, let's assume that she earns $4000 on that $40 000 once it is deposited in a bank. Now, rather than pay $4000 in explicit costs in the form of student loan interest, Maria pays $4000 in implicit costs from the forgone interest she could have earned.

Capital is the total value of assets owned by an individual or firm— physical assets (physical capital) plus financial assets (financial capital).

This $4000 in forgone interest earnings is what economists call the **implicit cost of capital**—the income the owner of the capital could have earned if the capital had been employed in its next best alternative use. The net effect is that it makes no difference whether Maria finances her tuition with a student loan or by using her own funds. This comparison reinforces how carefully you must keep track of opportunity costs when making a decision.

Making "Either–Or" Decisions

An "either–or" decision is one in which you must choose between two activities. Since doing one precludes you from doing the other, the choice is really between alternative A or alternative B. That's in contrast to a "how much" decision, which requires you to choose how much of a given activity to undertake. For example, Maria faced an "either–or" decision: to spend two years obtaining a social work degree, or to work. In contrast, a "how much" decision would be deciding how many hours to study or how many hours to work at a job. Table 9-3 contrasts a variety of "either–or" and "how much" decisions.

TABLE 9-3 "Either–Or" versus "How Much" Decisions

"Either–or" decisions	"How much" decisions
Tide or Cheer?	How many days before you do your laundry?
Buy a car or not?	How many kilometres do you go before an oil change in your car?
An order of nachos or a sandwich?	How many jalapenos on your nachos?
Run your own business or work for someone else?	How many workers should you hire in your company?
Prescribe drug A or drug B for your patients?	How much should a patient take of a drug that generates side effects?
Graduate school or not?	How many hours to study?

The **implicit cost of capital** is the opportunity cost of the use of one's own capital—the income earned if the capital had been employed in its next best alternative use.

According to the **principle of "either–or" decision making,** when faced with an "either–or" choice between two activities, choose the one with the positive economic profit.

In making economic decisions, as we have already emphasized, it is vitally important to calculate opportunity costs correctly. The best way to make an "either–or" decision, the method that leads to the best possible economic outcome, is the straightforward **principle of "either–or" decision making.** According to this

PITFALLS

WHY ARE THERE ONLY TWO CHOICES?

In "either–or" decision making, we have assumed that there are only two activities to choose from. But, what if, instead of just two alternatives, there are three or more? Does the principle of "either–or" decision making still apply?

Yes, it does. That's because any choice between three (or more) alternatives can always be boiled down to a series of choices between two alternatives. Here's an illustration using three alternative activities: A, B, or C. (Remember that this is an "either–or" decision: you can choose only one of the three alternatives.) Let's

say you begin by considering A versus B: in this comparison, A has a positive economic profit but B yields an economic loss. At this point, you should discard B as a viable choice because A will always be superior to B. The next step is to compare A to C: in this comparison, C has a positive economic profit but A yields an economic loss. You can now discard A because C will always be superior to A. You are now done: since A is better than B, and C is better than A, C is the correct choice.

But what is the opportunity cost of C? It looks like there are two possible answers: the opportunity cost of C compared to A and the opportunity cost of C compared to

B. In general though, most economists like to quote only one opportunity cost. How do they do that? They quote the opportunity cost relative to the next best alternative. In our example, since A is better than B, this implies that "the opportunity cost of C" is the opportunity cost of C compared to A.

So if we are choosing among ten different options, the opportunity cost of the optimal option is a single answer rather than nine different opportunity costs. Of the nine inferior options, we ignore the eight least viable options. The economic profit of the optimal choice is equal to the revenue this choice brings minus the opportunity cost(s) of the next best option.

principle, *when making an "either–or" choice between two activities, choose the one with the positive economic profit.* In other words, we should do an activity only if its benefit outweighs its opportunity cost.

Let's examine Maria's dilemma from a different angle to understand how this principle works. First, recall Equation 9-3: the economic profit of an alternative is the revenue that choice brings minus the opportunity cost(s) of its alternative (the opportunity costs consist of both explicit and implicit costs). If Maria continues with financial services and goes to work immediately, the total value of her lifetime earnings (her revenue) is $57 000 (her earnings over the next two years) + $500 000 (the value of her lifetime earnings thereafter) = $557 000. Going to work immediately involves no explicit costs, but she does incur implicit costs. Let's consider those implicit costs.

If she gets her social work degree instead and works in that field, the total value of her lifetime earnings (net of explicit costs) is $600 000 (value of her lifetime earnings after two years in school) – $40 000 (tuition) – $4000 (interest payments) = $556 000. So by going to work immediately, rather than school, her implicit cost is the forgone $556 000. Therefore the economic profit from continuing in financial services versus becoming a social worker is $557 000 – $556 000 = $1000.

So the right choice for Maria is to begin work in financial services immediately, since this gives her an economic profit of $1000, rather than become a social worker, which would give her an economic profit of –$1000.[1] In other words, by becoming a social worker she loses the $1000 economic profit she would have gained by working in financial services immediately.

When choosing between a pair of alternatives, notice that the economic profit of one alternative is always the opposite of the economic profit of the other. This is a general principle, so having calculated the economic profit of one alternative we immediately know the economic profit of the other alternative by using symmetry:

(9-4) Economic profit of doing action A (instead of B)
     = –Economic profit of doing action B (instead of A)

In making "either–or" decisions, mistakes most commonly arise when people or businesses use their own assets in projects rather than rent or borrow assets. That's because they fail to account for the implicit cost of using self-owned capital. In contrast, when they rent or borrow assets, these rental or borrowing costs show up as explicit costs. If, for example, a restaurant owns its equipment and tools, it would have to compute its implicit cost of capital by calculating how much the equipment could be sold for and how much could be earned by using those funds in the next best alternative project. In addition, businesses run by the owner (an *entrepreneur)* often fail to calculate the opportunity cost of the owner's time in running the business. In that way, small businesses often underestimate their opportunity costs and overestimate their economic profit of staying in business.

Are we implying that the hundreds of thousands who have chosen to go back to school rather than find work in recent years are misguided? Not necessarily. As we mentioned before, the poor job market had greatly diminished the opportunity cost of forgone wages for many students, making continuing their education the optimal choice for them.

The following Economics in Action illustrates just how important it is in real life to understand the difference between accounting profit and economic profit.

---

[1]Let's confirm that number. If Maria decides to go back to school rather than working, the lifetime revenue this brings is $600 000. Her explicit costs of schooling are $40 000 (for tuition) + $4000 (for interest payments) = $44 000. Her implicit costs are $57 000 (for the two years of income she forgoes by not working in financial services while in school) + $500 000 (for the income lost by not working in financial services for all the years following her two-year program) = $557 000. Don't forget to include the $500 000 as she can't work both full-time jobs. This makes her economic profit equal to $600 000 – ($40 000 + $4000) – ($57 000 + $500 000) = –$1000. This amount is exactly her economic profit from working in financial services multiplied by –1.

ECONOMICS ▶ IN ACTION

FARMING IN THE SHADOW OF SUBURBIA

Beyond the sprawling suburbs of the Golden Horseshoe region, much of southern Ontario is covered by a mix of farms and forests. This region is home to more than a quarter of Canada's population. According to Statistics Canada, about half of Canada's urbanized land is located on the country's most productive farmland.

Many Ontario farms are located close to large metropolitan areas. These farmers can get high prices for their produce from city dwellers willing to pay a premium for locally grown, extremely fresh fruits and vegetables.

But now even these farms are under economic pressure caused by a rise in the implicit cost of farming close to a metropolitan area. As metropolitan areas have expanded during the last two decades, farmers increasingly ask themselves whether they could do better by selling their land to property developers.

Working the land instead of selling it incurs a large implicit cost of capital.

In 2012, the average value of a hectare of farmland and buildings in Canada as a whole was $4443; in Ontario, home to half of Canada's highest quality farmland, the average was $16 045. Since 2006, farmland prices in Canada have risen by 9% per year and triple the return of the Toronto Stock Exchange index over the past decade. The U.S. Federal Reserve Bank of Boston has noted that "high land prices put intense pressure on the region's farms to generate incomes that are substantial enough to justify keeping the land in agriculture."

The important point is that the pressure is intense even if the farmer owns the land because the land is a form of capital used to run the business. As Ron Bonnett, president of the Canadian Federation of Agriculture, has noted, development eats up land surrounding farms, driving land values up and with them property taxes. "This has an effect on the decision-making of any farmer who has to factor in the cost of purchasing additional land and debt servicing related to land ownership, and the increased rental costs as well." So maintaining the land as a farm instead of selling it to a developer constitutes a large implicit cost of capital. A fact that two of the authors saw firsthand in 2009, when the 83-hectare Beckett Farm located just outside of Toronto was sold to developers for $100 million.

Less than 10% of Canada's land can be farmed, only 0.5% of Canada's land is class 1 (meaning it has no significant limitations for farming), and less than 1% of this class 1 land is suitable for growing tender fruit. The David Suzuki Foundation notes that "southern Ontario has some of the best remaining agricultural lands in Canada in terms of soil fertility, crop productivity, and economic value. While there is currently no effort to inventory or track the loss of agricultural land in Ontario, the most recent analysis found that between 1996 and 2001, 16% of the farmland in the Greater Toronto Area was lost to urban encroachment." In the past four decades, urbanization in Canada has consumed an area of farmland about three times the size of Prince Edward Island. In the next 30 years Ontario's population is expected to grow by another 2 million people, which could consume more than 40 000 acres of prime farmland.

▶●●

CHECK YOUR UNDERSTANDING   9-1

1. Karma and Don run a furniture-refinishing business from their home. Which of the following represent an explicit cost of the business and which represent an implicit cost?
   a. Supplies such as paint stripper, varnish, polish, sandpaper, and so on
   b. Basement space that has been converted into a workroom

▼ Quick Review

- All costs are opportunity costs. They can be divided into **explicit costs** and **implicit costs**.

- An activity's **accounting profit** is not necessarily equal to its **economic profit**.

- Due to the **implicit cost of capital**—the opportunity cost of using self-owned **capital**—and the opportunity cost of one's own time (labour), economic profit is often substantially less than accounting profit.

- The **principle of "either–or" decision making** says that when making an "either–or" choice between two activities, choose the one with the positive economic profit.

    c. Wages paid to a part-time helper

    d. A van that they inherited and use only for transporting furniture

    e. The job at a larger furniture restorer that Karma gave up in order to run the business

2. Assume that Maria has a third alternative to consider: entering a two-year apprenticeship program for skilled machinists that would, upon completion, make her a licensed machinist. During the apprenticeship, she earns a reduced salary of $15 000 per year. At the end of the apprenticeship, the value of her lifetime earnings is $725 000. What is Maria's best career choice?

3. Suppose you have three alternatives—A, B, and C—and you can undertake only one of them. In comparing A versus B, you find that B has an economic profit and A yields an economic loss. But in comparing A versus C, you find that C has an economic profit and A yields an economic loss. How do you decide what to do?

Solutions appear at back of book.

Making "How Much" Decisions: The Role of Marginal Analysis

Although many decisions in economics are "either–or," many others are "how much." Not many people will give up their cars if the price of gasoline goes up, but many people will drive less. How much less? A rise in corn prices won't necessarily persuade a lot of people to take up farming for the first time, but it will persuade farmers who were already growing corn to plant more. How much more?

Recall from our principles of microeconomics that "how much" is a decision at the margin. So to understand "how much" decisions, we will use an approach known as *marginal analysis*. Marginal analysis involves comparing the benefit of doing a little bit more of some activity with the cost of doing a little bit more of that activity. The benefit of doing a little bit more of something is what economists call its *marginal benefit*, and the cost of doing a little bit more of something is what they call its *marginal cost*.

Why is this called "marginal" analysis? A margin is an edge; what you do in marginal analysis is push out the edge a bit and see whether that is a good move. We will study marginal analysis by considering a hypothetical decision of how many years of school to complete. We'll consider the case of Alex, who studies computer programming and design. Since there are many computer languages, app design methods, and graphics programs that can be learned one year at a time, each year Alex can decide whether to continue his studies or not. Unlike Maria, who faced an "either–or" decision of whether to get a social work degree, Alex faces a "how much" decision of how many years to study computer programming and design. For example, he could study one more year, or five more years, or any number of years in between. We'll begin our analysis of Alex's decision problem by defining Alex's *marginal cost* of another year of study.

Marginal Cost

We'll assume that each additional year of schooling costs Alex $10 000 in explicit costs—tuition, interest on a student loan, and so on. In addition to the explicit costs, he also has implicit costs—the income forgone by spending one more year in school. Unlike Alex's explicit costs, which are constant (that is, the same each year), Alex's implicit cost changes each year. That's because each year he spends in school leaves him better trained than the year before; and the better trained he is, the higher the salary he can command. Consequently, the income he forgoes by not working rises each additional year he stays in school. In other words, the greater the number of years Alex has already spent in school, the higher his implicit cost of another year of school.

Table 9-4 contains the data on how Alex's cost of an additional year of schooling changes as he completes more years. The second column shows how his total cost of schooling changes as the number of years he has completed increases. For example, Alex's first year has a total cost of $30 000: $10 000 in explicit costs of tuition and the like as well as $20 000 in forgone salary.

The second column also shows that the total cost of attending two years is $70 000: $30 000 for his first year plus $40 000 for his second year. During his second year in school, his explicit costs have stayed the same ($10 000) but his implicit cost of forgone salary has gone up to $30 000. That's because he's a more valuable worker with one year of schooling under his belt than with no schooling. Likewise, the total cost of three years of schooling is $130 000: $30 000 in explicit cost for three years of tuition plus $100 000 in implicit cost of three years of forgone salary. The total cost of attending four years is $220 000, and $350 000 for five years.

TABLE 9-4	Alex's Marginal Cost of Additional Years in School	
Quantity of schooling (years)	Total cost	Marginal cost
0	$0	
		$30 000
1	30 000	
		40 000
2	70 000	
		60 000
3	130 000	
		90 000
4	220 000	
		130 000
5	350 000	

The change in Alex's total cost of schooling when he goes to school an additional year is his *marginal cost* of the one-year increase in years of schooling. In general, the **marginal cost** of producing a good or service (in this case, producing one's own education) is the additional cost incurred by producing one more unit of that good or service. The arrows, which zigzag between the total costs in the second column and the marginal costs in the third column, are there to help you to see how marginal cost is calculated from total cost, and vice versa. As a formula, marginal cost, or *MC*, is:

(9-5) $MC = \frac{\Delta TC}{\Delta q}$

where ΔTC is the change in total cost and Δq is the change in quantity. For each step in Table 9-4, $\Delta q = 1$, so the marginal cost is simply the change in total cost.

As already mentioned, the third column of Table 9-4 shows Alex's marginal costs of more years of schooling, which have a clear pattern: they are increasing. They go from $30 000, to $40 000, to $60 000, to $90 000, and finally to $130 000 for the fifth year of schooling. That's because each year of schooling would make Alex a more valuable and highly paid employee if he were to work. As a result, forgoing a job becomes more and more costly as he becomes better educated. This is an example of what economists call **increasing marginal cost,** which occurs when each unit of a good costs more to produce than the previous unit.

Figure 9-1 shows a **marginal cost curve,** a graphic representation of Alex's marginal costs. The height of each shaded bar corresponds to the marginal cost of a given year of schooling. The red line connecting the dots at the midpoint of the top of each bar is Alex's marginal cost curve. Alex has an upward-sloping marginal cost curve because he has increasing marginal cost of additional years of schooling.

Although increasing marginal cost is a frequent phenomenon in real life, it's not the only possibility. **Constant marginal cost** occurs when the cost of producing an additional unit is the same as the cost of producing the previous unit. Plant nurseries, for example, typically have constant marginal cost—the cost of growing one more plant is the same, regardless of how many plants have already been produced. With constant marginal cost, the marginal cost curve is a horizontal line.

There can also be **decreasing marginal cost,** which occurs when marginal cost falls as the number of units produced increases. With decreasing marginal cost, the marginal cost line is downward sloping. Decreasing marginal cost is often due to *learning effects* in production: for complicated tasks, such as assembling a new model of a car, workers are often slow and mistake-prone when assembling the earliest units, making for higher marginal cost on those units. But as workers gain experi-

The **marginal cost** of producing a good or service is the additional cost incurred by producing one more unit of that good or service.

Production of a good or service has **increasing marginal cost** when each additional unit costs more to produce than the previous one.

The **marginal cost curve** shows how the cost of producing one more unit depends on the quantity that has already been produced.

Production of a good or service has **constant marginal cost** when each additional unit costs the same to produce as the previous one.

Production of a good or service has **decreasing marginal cost** when each additional unit costs less to produce than the previous one.

FIGURE **9-1** Marginal Cost

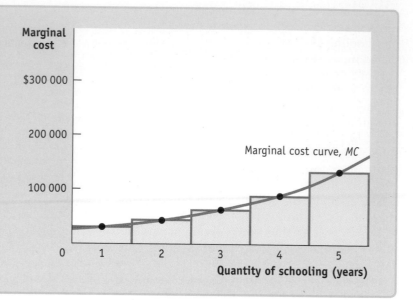

The height of each shaded bar corresponds to Alex's marginal cost of an additional year of schooling. The height of each bar is higher than the preceding one because each year of schooling costs more than the previous year. As a result, Alex has increasing marginal cost and the marginal cost curve, the line connecting the midpoints at the top of each bar, is upward sloping.

ence, assembly time and the rate of mistakes fall, resulting in lower marginal cost for later units. As a result, overall production has decreasing marginal cost.

Finally, for the production of some goods and services the shape of the marginal cost curve changes as the number of units produced increases. For example, auto production is likely to have decreasing marginal costs for the first batch of cars produced as workers iron out kinks and mistakes in production. Then production has constant marginal costs for the next batch of cars as workers settle into a predictable pace. But at some point, as workers produce more and more cars, marginal cost begins to increase as they run out of factory floor space and the auto company incurs costly overtime wages. This gives rise to what we call a "swoosh"-shaped marginal cost curve—a topic we will discuss in more detail in Chapter 11. For now, we'll stick to the simpler example of an increasing marginal cost curve.

⚠ PITFALLS

TOTAL COST VERSUS MARGINAL COST

It can be easy to conclude that marginal cost and total cost must always move in the same direction. That is, if total cost is rising, then marginal cost must also be rising. Or if marginal cost is falling, then total cost must be falling as well. But the following example shows that this conclusion is wrong.

Let's consider the example of auto production, which, as we mentioned earlier, is likely to involve learning effects. Suppose that for the first batch of cars of a new model, each car costs $10 000 to assemble. As workers gain experience with the new model, they become better at production. As a result,

the per-car cost of assembly falls to $8000 for the second batch. For the third batch, the per-car assembly cost falls again to $6500 as workers continue to gain expertise. For the fourth batch, the per-car cost of assembly falls to $5000 and remains constant for the rest of the production run.

In this example, marginal cost is *decreasing* over batches one through four, falling from $10 000 to $5000. However, it's important to note that total cost is still *increasing* over the entire production run because marginal cost is greater than zero. To see this point, assume that each batch consists of 100 cars. Then the total cost of producing the first batch is 100 × $10 000 = $1 000 000. The total cost of

producing the first and second batch of cars is $1 000 000 + (100 × $8000) = $1 800 000. Likewise, the total cost of producing the first, second, and third batch is $1 800 000 + (100 × $6500) = $2 450 000, and so on. As you can see, although marginal cost is decreasing over the first few batches of cars, total cost is increasing over the same batches.

This shows us that totals and marginals can sometimes move in opposite directions. So it is wrong to assert that they always move in the same direction. What we can assert is that *total cost increases whenever marginal cost is positive*, regardless of whether marginal cost is increasing or decreasing.

Marginal Benefit

Alex benefits from higher lifetime earnings as he completes more years of school. Exactly how much he benefits is shown in Table 9-5. Column 2 shows Alex's total benefit according to the number of years of school completed, expressed as the value of the increase in lifetime earnings. The third column shows Alex's *marginal benefit* from an additional year of schooling. In general, the **marginal benefit** of producing a good or service is the additional benefit earned from producing one more unit.

As in Table 9-4, the data in the third column of Table 9-5 show a clear pattern. However, this time the numbers are decreasing rather than increasing. The first year of schooling gives Alex a $300 000 increase in the value of his lifetime earnings. The second year also gives him a positive return, but the size of that return has fallen to $150 000; the third year's return is also positive, but its size has fallen yet again to $90 000; and so on. In other words, the more years of school that Alex has already completed, the smaller the increase in the value of his lifetime earnings from attending one more year. Alex's schooling decision has what economists call **decreasing marginal benefit:** each additional year of school yields a smaller benefit than the previous year. Or, to put it slightly differently, with decreasing marginal benefit, the benefit from producing one more unit of the good or service falls as the quantity already produced rises.

Just as marginal cost can be represented by a marginal cost curve, marginal benefit can be represented by a **marginal benefit curve,** shown in blue in Figure 9-2. Alex's marginal benefit curve slopes downward because he faces decreasing marginal benefit from additional years of schooling.

Not all goods or activities exhibit decreasing marginal benefit. In fact, there are many goods for which the marginal benefit of production is constant—that is, the additional benefit from producing one more unit is the same regardless of the number of units already produced. In later chapters where we study firms, we

TABLE 9-5 Alex's Marginal Benefit of Additional Years in School

Quantity of schooling (years)	Total benefit	Marginal benefit
0	$0	
		$300 000
1	300 000	
		150 000
2	450 000	
		90 000
3	540 000	
		60 000
4	600 000	
		50 000
5	650 000	

The **marginal benefit** of a good or service is the additional benefit derived from producing one more unit of that good or service.

There is **decreasing marginal benefit** from an activity when each additional unit of the activity yields less benefit than the previous unit.

The **marginal benefit curve** shows how the benefit from producing one more unit depends on the quantity that has already been produced.

FIGURE 9-2 Marginal Benefit

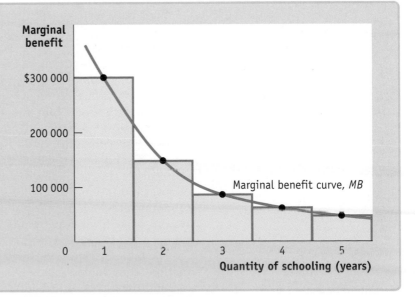

The height of each shaded bar corresponds to Alex's marginal benefit of an additional year of schooling. The height of each bar is lower than the one preceding it because an additional year of schooling has decreasing marginal benefit. As a result, Alex's marginal benefit curve, the curve connecting the midpoints at the top of each bar, is downward sloping.

will see that the shape of a firm's marginal benefit curve from producing output has important implications for how that firm behaves within its industry. We'll also see in Chapters 11 and 12 why constant marginal benefit is considered the norm for many important industries.

Now we are ready to see how the concepts of marginal benefit and marginal cost are brought together to answer the question of how many years of additional schooling Alex should undertake.

Marginal Analysis

Table 9-6 shows the marginal cost and marginal benefit numbers from Tables 9-4 and 9-5. It also adds an additional column: the additional profit to Alex from staying in school one more year, equal to the difference between the marginal benefit and the marginal cost of that additional year in school. (Remember that it is Alex's economic profit that we care about, not his accounting profit.) We can now use Table 9-6 to determine how many additional years of schooling Alex should undertake in order to maximize his total profit.

TABLE **9-6** **Alex's Profit from Additional Years of Schooling**

Quantity of schooling (years)	Marginal benefit	Marginal cost	Additional profit
0			
	$300 000	$30 000	$270 000
1			
	150 000	40 000	110 000
2			
	90 000	60 000	30 000
3			
	60 000	90 000	–30 000
4			
	50 000	130 000	–80 000
5			

First, imagine that Alex chooses not to attend any additional years of school. We can see from column 4 that this is a mistake if Alex wants to achieve the highest total profit from his schooling—the sum of the additional profits generated by another year of schooling. If he attends one additional year of school, he increases the value of his lifetime earnings by $270 000, the profit from the first additional year attended.

Now, let's consider whether Alex should attend the second year of school. The additional profit from the second year is $110 000, so Alex should attend the second year as well. What about the third year? The additional profit from that year is $30 000; so, yes, Alex should attend the third year as well. What about a fourth year? In this case, the additional profit is negative: it is –$30 000. Alex loses $30 000 of the value of his lifetime earnings if he attends the fourth year. Clearly, Alex is worse off by attending the fourth additional year rather than taking a job. And the same is true for the fifth year as well: it has a negative additional profit of –$80 000.

What have we learned? That Alex should attend three additional years of school and stop at that point. Although the first, second, and third years of additional schooling increase the value of his lifetime earnings, the fourth and fifth years diminish it. So three years of additional schooling lead to the quantity that generates the maximum possible total profit. It is what economists call the **optimal quantity**—the quantity that generates the maximum possible total profit.

Figure 9-3 shows how the optimal quantity can be determined graphically. Alex's marginal benefit and marginal cost curves are shown together. If Alex chooses fewer than three additional years (that is, 0, 1, or 2 years), he will choose a level of schooling at which his marginal benefit curve lies *above* his marginal cost curve. He can make himself better off by staying in school. If instead he chooses more than three additional years (4 or 5 years), he will choose a level of schooling at which his marginal benefit curve lies *below* his marginal cost curve. He can make himself better off by not attending the additional year of school and taking a job instead.

The table in Figure 9-3 confirms our result. The second column repeats information from Table 9-6, showing Alex's marginal benefit minus marginal cost—the additional profit per additional year of schooling. The third column shows Alex's total profit for different years of schooling. The total profit for each possible year of schooling is simply the sum of numbers in the second column up to and

The **optimal quantity** is the quantity that generates the highest possible total profit.

FIGURE   9-3   Alex's Optimal Quantity of Years of Schooling

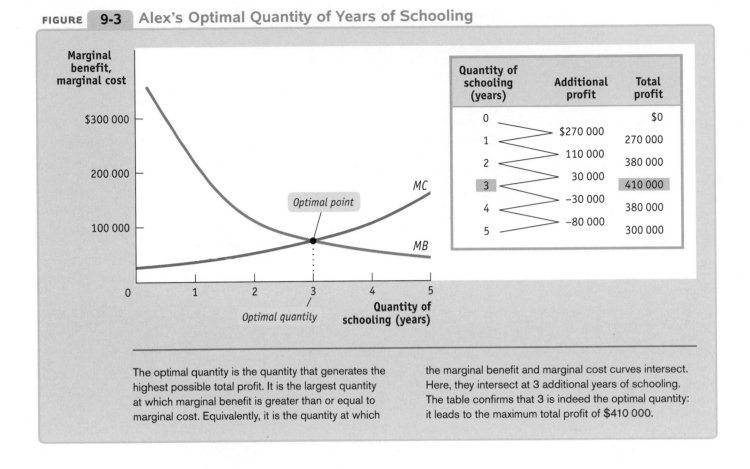

The optimal quantity is the quantity that generates the highest possible total profit. It is the largest quantity at which marginal benefit is greater than or equal to marginal cost. Equivalently, it is the quantity at which the marginal benefit and marginal cost curves intersect. Here, they intersect at 3 additional years of schooling. The table confirms that 3 is indeed the optimal quantity: it leads to the maximum total profit of $410 000.

including that year. For example, Alex's profit from additional years of schooling is $270 000 for the first year and $110 000 for the second year. So the total profit for two additional years of schooling is $270 000 + $110 000 = $380 000. Similarly, the total profit for three additional years is $270 000 + $110 000 + $30 000 = $410 000. Our claim that three years is the optimal quantity for Alex is confirmed by the data in the table in Figure 9-3: at three years of additional schooling, Alex reaps the greatest total profit, $410 000.

Alex's decision problem illustrates how you go about finding the optimal quantity when the choice involves a small number of quantities (in this example, one through five years). With small quantities, the rule for choosing the optimal quantity is: *Increase the quantity as long as the marginal benefit from one more unit is greater than the marginal cost, but stop before the marginal benefit becomes less than the marginal cost.*

In contrast, when a "how much" decision involves relatively large quantities, the rule for choosing the optimal quantity simplifies to this: *The optimal quantity is the quantity at which marginal benefit is equal to marginal cost.*

To see why this is so, consider the example of a farmer who finds that her optimal quantity of wheat produced is 5000 bushels. Typically, she will find that in going from 4999 to 5000 bushels, her marginal benefit is only very slightly greater than her marginal cost—that is, the difference between marginal benefit and marginal cost is close to zero. Similarly, in going from 5000 to 5001 bushels, her marginal cost is only very slightly greater than her marginal benefit—again, the difference between marginal cost and marginal benefit is very close to zero. So a simple rule for her in choosing the optimal quantity of wheat is to produce the quantity at which the difference between marginal benefit and marginal cost is approximately zero—that is, the quantity at which marginal benefit equals marginal cost.

Now we are ready to state the general rule for choosing the optimal quantity—one that applies for decisions involving either small quantities or large quantities. This

GLOBAL COMPARISON PORTION SIZES

Health experts call it the "French Paradox." If you think French food is fattening, you're right: the French diet is, on average, higher in fat than the North American diet. Yet the French themselves are considerably thinner than we are: in 2011, between 9% and 11% of French adults were classified as obese, compared with 24.2% of Canadians, 30% of Mexicans, and 33.8% of Americans.

What's the secret? It seems that the French simply eat less, largely because they eat smaller portions. This chart compares average portion sizes at food establishments in Paris, France and Philadelphia, USA. In four cases, researchers looked at portions served by the same chain; in the other cases, they looked at comparable establishments, such as local pizza parlours. In every case but one, U.S. portions were bigger, in most cases much bigger. It should be noted that while serving sizes at fast-food restaurants in Canada and Mexico are largely the same as in the United States, this is not the case for other restaurants. Even though restaurant serving sizes are largest on average in the United States, serving sizes in Canada and Mexico are still much larger than in France.

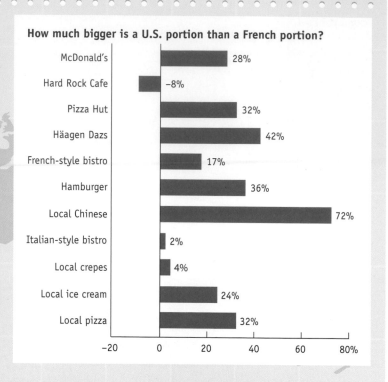

How much bigger is a U.S. portion than a French portion?

Why are North American portions so big? Because food is cheaper here! At the margin, it makes sense for restaurants to offer big portions, since the additional cost of enlarging a portion is relatively small. As a recent newspaper article states: "So while it may cost a restaurant a few pennies to offer 25% more French fries, it can raise its prices much more than a few cents. The result is that larger portions are a reliable way to bolster the average [price at North American] restaurants." So if you have ever wondered why dieting seems to be a uniquely North American obsession, the principle of marginal analysis can help provide the answer: it's to counteract the effects of our larger portion sizes.

Source: Paul Rozin, Kimberly Kabnick, Erin Pete, Claude Fischler, and Christy Shields, "The Ecology of Eating," *Psychological Science* 14 (September 2003): 450–454.

---

general rule is known as the **profit-maximizing principle of marginal analysis:** *When making a profit-maximizing "how much" decision, the optimal quantity is the largest quantity at which marginal benefit is greater than or equal to marginal cost.*

Graphically, the optimal quantity is the quantity of an activity at which the marginal benefit curve intersects the marginal cost curve. For example, in Figure 9-3 the marginal benefit and marginal cost curves cross each other at three years—that is, marginal benefit equals marginal cost at the choice of three additional years of schooling, which we have already seen is Alex's optimal quantity.

A straightforward application of marginal analysis explains why so many people went back to school in 2009 through 2012: in the depressed job market, the marginal cost of another year of school fell because the opportunity cost of forgone wages had fallen.

Simple applications of marginal analysis can explain many facts, such as why restaurant portion sizes in the United States and, to some extent, Canada are typically larger than those in other countries (as was just discussed in the Global Comparison).

A Principle with Many Uses

The profit-maximizing principle of marginal analysis can be applied to just about any "how much" decision in which you want to maximize the total profit for an activity. It is equally applicable to production decisions, consumption decisions, and

According to the **profit-maximizing principle of marginal analysis,** when faced with a profit-maximizing "how much" decision, the optimal quantity is the largest quantity at which the marginal benefit is greater than or equal to marginal cost.

policy decisions. Furthermore, decisions where the benefits and costs are not expressed in dollars and cents can also be made using marginal analysis (as long as benefits and costs can be measured in some type of common units). Here are a few examples of decisions that are suitable for marginal analysis:

- A producer, the retailer PalMart, must decide on the size of the new store it is constructing in Beijing. It makes this decision by comparing the marginal benefit of enlarging the store by one square metre (the value of the additional sales it makes from that additional square metre of floor space) to the marginal cost (the cost of constructing and maintaining the additional square metre). The optimal store size for PalMart is the largest size at which marginal benefit is greater than or equal to marginal cost.

- Many useful drugs have side effects that depend on the dosage. So a physician must consider the marginal cost, in terms of side effects, of increasing the dosage of a drug versus the marginal benefit of improving health by increasing the dosage. The optimal dosage level is the largest level at which the marginal benefit of disease amelioration is greater than or equal to the marginal cost of side effects.

- A farmer must decide how much fertilizer to apply. More fertilizer increases crop yield but also costs more. The optimal amount of fertilizer is the largest quantity at which the marginal benefit of higher crop yield is greater than or equal to the marginal cost of purchasing and applying more fertilizer.

- A jewellery maker must decide on how many sets of earrings to make. Assuming they can all be sold, making more earrings increases revenue but may also drive up the marginal cost of production. The optimal level of production is the largest quantity at which the marginal benefit of production (the revenue) is greater or equal to the marginal cost of production.

A Preview: How Consumption Decisions Are Different We've established that marginal analysis is an extraordinarily useful tool. It is used in "how much" decisions that are applied to both consumption choices and to profit maximization. Producers use it to make optimal production decisions at the margin and individuals use it to make optimal consumption decisions at the margin. But consumption decisions differ in form from production decisions. Why the difference? Because when individuals make choices, they face a limited amount of income. As a result, when they choose more of one good to consume (say, new clothes), they must choose less of another good (say, restaurant dinners). In contrast, decisions that involve maximizing profit by producing a good or service —such as years of education or tonnes of wheat—are not affected by income limitations. For example, in Alex's case, we assume he is not limited by income because he can always borrow to pay for another year of school. In Chapter 10 we will see in greater detail how consumption decisions differ from production decisions—but also how they are similar.

⚠ PITFALLS

MUDDLED AT THE MARGIN

The idea of setting marginal benefit equal to marginal cost sometimes confuses people. Aren't we trying to maximize the *difference* between benefits and costs? Yes. And don't we wipe out our gains by setting benefits and costs equal to each other? Yes. But that is not what we are doing. Rather, what we are doing is setting *marginal*, not *total*, benefit and cost equal to each other.

Once again, the point is to maximize the total profit from an activity. If the marginal benefit from the activity is greater than the marginal cost, doing a bit more will increase that gain. If the marginal benefit is less than the marginal cost, doing a bit less will increase the total profit. So only when the *marginal* benefit and *marginal* cost are equal is the difference between *total* benefit and *total* cost at a maximum.

ECONOMICS ▶ IN ACTION

THE COST OF A LIFE

What's the marginal benefit to society of saving a human life? You might be tempted to answer that human life is infinitely precious. If in the real world, resources are scarce, so we must decide how much to spend on saving lives since we cannot spend infinite amounts. After all, we could surely reduce highway deaths by dropping the speed limit on highways to 60 kilometres per hour, but the cost of such a lower speed limit—in time and money—is more than most people are willing to pay.

Generally, people are reluctant to talk in a straightforward way about comparing the marginal cost of a life saved with the marginal benefit—it sounds too callous. Sometimes, however, the question becomes unavoidable.

For example, the cost of saving a life became an object of intense discussion in the United Kingdom in 1999 after a horrible train crash near London's Paddington station killed 31 people. There were accusations that the British government was spending too little on rail safety. However, the government estimated that improving rail safety would cost more than $6 million per life saved. But if that amount was worth spending—that is, if the estimated marginal benefit of saving a life exceeded $6 million—then the implication was that the British government was spending far too little on traffic safety. In contrast, the estimated marginal cost per life saved through highway improvements was only $1.5 million, making it a much better deal than saving lives through greater rail safety.

More recently, a 2013 train derailment in Lac-Mégantic, Quebec caused explosions and fire that killed 47 people. According to reports, one possible contributing factor in this disaster was the exemption the rail company had received that allowed it to use a one-person crew rather than the usual minimum two-person crew. This exemption allowed the rail company to park an unattended train loaded with highly flammable crude oil several kilometres uphill from the town. This exemption, used to save a few hundred dollars per train shipment, resulted in 47 deaths, the destruction of most of the town's downtown, and the release of about 7.6 million litres of crude oil. The exemption is no longer permitted on trains carrying dangerous materials in Canada.

CHECK YOUR UNDERSTANDING 9-2

1. For each of the "how much" decisions listed in Table 9-3, describe the nature of the marginal cost and of the marginal benefit.

2. Suppose that Alex's school charges a fixed fee of $70 000 for four years of schooling. If Alex drops out before he finishes those four years, he still has to pay the $70 000. Alex's total cost for different years of schooling is now given by the data in the accompanying table. Assume that Alex's total benefit and marginal benefit remain as reported in Table 9–5.

    Use this information to calculate (i) Alex's new marginal cost, (ii) his new profit, and (iii) his new optimal years of schooling. What kind of marginal cost does Alex now have—constant, increasing, or decreasing?

Quantity of schooling (years)	Total cost
0	$0
1	90 000
2	120 000
3	170 000
4	250 000
5	370 000

Solutions appear at back of book.

The $250 you already spent on brake pads is irrelevant because it is a sunk cost.

Daniel Grill/Getty Images

Sunk Costs

When making decisions, knowing what to ignore can be as important as what to include. Although we have devoted much attention in this chapter to costs that are important to take into account when making a decision, some costs should be ignored when doing so. In this section we will focus on the kinds of costs that people should ignore when making decisions—what economists call *sunk costs*—and why they should be ignored.

To gain some intuition, consider the following scenario. You own a car that is a few years old, and you have just replaced the brake pads at a cost of $250. But then you find out that the entire brake system is defective and also must be replaced. This will cost you an additional $1500. Alternatively, you could sell the car and buy another of comparable quality, but with no brake defects, by spending an additional $1600. What should you do: fix your old car, or sell it and buy another?

Some might say that you should take the latter option. After all, this line of reasoning goes, if you repair your car, you will end up having spent $1750: $1500 for the brake system and $250 for the brake pads. If instead you sell your old car and buy another, you would spend only $1600.

But this reasoning, although it sounds plausible, is wrong. It is wrong because it ignores the fact that you have *already* spent $250 on brake pads, and that $250 is *nonrecoverable*. That is, having already been spent, the $250 cannot be recouped. Therefore, it should be ignored and should have no effect on your decision whether or not to repair your car and keep it. From a rational viewpoint, the real cost at this time of repairing and keeping your car is $1500, not $1750. So the correct decision is to repair your car and keep it rather than spend $1600 on a new car.

In this example, the $250 that has already been spent and cannot be recovered is what economists call a **sunk cost.** Sunk costs should be ignored in making decisions about future actions because they have no influence on their actual costs and benefits. It's like the old saying, "There's no use crying over spilled milk": once something can't be recovered, it is irrelevant in making decisions about what to do in the future.

Another example of sunk cost is the time spent waiting. Imagine getting all your textbooks from the bookstore at the beginning of a term. You have already waited in the line for 30 minutes. Should you continue waiting or come back earlier tomorrow? In making your decision, you should not factor in the 30 minutes you already spent in the line because you cannot recoup the time: that half hour is a sunk cost. If you expect it will take another 20 minutes to check out, but your total wait time tomorrow will be less than 20 minutes, then you should leave the line and abandon the sunk cost.

It is often psychologically hard to ignore sunk costs. And if, in fact, you haven't yet incurred the costs, then you should take them into consideration. That is, if you had known at the beginning that it would cost $1750 to repair your car, then the right choice at that time would have been to buy a new car for $1600. But once you have already paid the $250 for brake pads, you should no longer include it in your decision making about your next actions. It may be hard to accept that "bygones are bygones," but it is the right way to make a decision.

> A **sunk cost** is a cost that has already been incurred and is nonrecoverable. A sunk cost should be ignored in decisions about future actions.

ECONOMICS › IN ACTION

A BILLION HERE, A BILLION THERE ...

If there is any industry that exemplifies the principle that sunk costs don't matter, it has to be the biotech industry. Biotech firms use cutting-edge bioengineering techniques to combat disease. But according to Arthur Levinson, chief executive of Genentech, one of the largest and most successful biotech firms, biotechnology has been "one of the biggest money-losing industries in the history of mankind." He estimates that the industry has lost nearly $100 billion since 1976 (yes, that's "billion"). Of 286 publicly held American biotech firms, only 28 were profitable in 2012, and Canadian biotech firms do not fair any better. The industry proudly speaks about the amount of capital raised, revenue earned, research and development expenditures, new patents filed, and their great potential in the future, but is generally silent about the lack of profitability of many of its members.

The biotech industry has been built on the premise that sunk costs don't matter.

However, this is not a tale of incompetence because the problem lies in the nature of the science. It takes about seven to eight years, on average, to develop and bring a new drug to the market. Moreover, there is a huge failure rate along the way, as only one in five drugs tested on humans ever makes it to market.

The company Xoma is a case in point: it has suffered setbacks on several drugs addressing diseases as varied as acne and complications from organ transplants. Since 1981, it has never earned a profit on one of its own drugs and has burned through more than $780 million dollars. Why does Xoma keep going? And, more importantly, why are investors willing to keep providing it with more money? It's because Xoma possesses a very promising technology and because shrewd investors understand the principle of sunk costs.

CHECK YOUR UNDERSTANDING 9-3

1. You have decided to go into the ice-cream business and have bought a used ice-cream truck for $8000. Now you are reconsidering. What is your sunk cost in each of the following scenarios?
   a. The truck cannot be resold.
   b. The truck can be resold, but only at a 50% discount.
   c. An ice-cream vendor who wants to expand his business is willing to purchase the truck from you at full price.

2. You have gone through two years of medical school but are suddenly wondering whether you wouldn't be happier as a musician. Which of the following statements are potentially valid arguments and which are not?
   a. "I can't give up now, after all the time and money I've put in."
   b. "If I had thought about it from the beginning, I never would have gone to med school, so I should give it up now."
   c. "I wasted two years, but never mind—let's start from here."
   d. "My parents would kill me if I stopped now." (*Hint:* We're discussing your decision-making ability, not your parents'.)

Solutions appear at back of book.

Behavioural Economics

Most economic models assume that people make choices based on achieving the best possible economic outcome for themselves. Human behaviour, however, is often not so simple. Rather than acting like economic computing machines, people often make choices that fall short—sometimes far short—of the greatest possible economic outcome, or payoff. Why people sometimes make less-than-perfect choices is the subject of behavioural economics, a branch of economics that combines economic modelling with insights from human psychology. Behavioural economics grew out of economists' and psychologists' attempts to understand how people actually make—instead of theoretically make—economic choices.

It's well documented that people consistently engage in *irrational* behaviour, choosing an option that leaves them worse off than other available options. Yet, as we'll soon learn, sometimes it's entirely *rational* for people to make a choice that is different from the one that generates the highest possible profit for themselves. For example, Maria may decide to earn a social work degree because she enjoys social work more than financial services, even though the profit from the social work degree is less than that from continuing with financial services.

The study of irrational economic behaviour was largely pioneered by Daniel Kahneman and Amos Tversky. Kahneman won the 2002 Nobel Prize in economics for his work integrating insights from the psychology of human judgment and decision making into economics. Their work and the insights of others into why people often behave irrationally are having a significant influence on how economists analyze financial markets, labour markets, and other economic concerns.

Rational, but Human, Too

If you are **rational,** you will choose the available option that leads to the outcome you most prefer. But is the outcome you most prefer always the same as the one that gives you the best possible economic payoff? No. It can be entirely rational to choose an option that gives you a worse economic payoff because you care about something other than the size of the economic payoff. There are three principal rational reasons why people might prefer a worse economic payoff: concerns about fairness, bounded rationality, and risk aversion.

Concerns About Fairness
In social situations, people often care about fairness as well as about the economic payoff to themselves. For example, no law requires you to tip a waiter or waitress. But concern for fairness leads most people to leave a tip (unless they've had outrageously bad service) because a tip is seen as fair compensation for good service according to society's norms. Tippers are reducing their own economic payoff in order to be fair to waiters and waitresses. A related behaviour is gift-giving: if you care about another person's welfare, it's rational for you to lower your own economic payoff in order to give that person a gift.

Bounded Rationality
Being an economic computing machine—choosing the option that gives you the best economic payoff—can require a fair amount of work: sizing up the options, computing the opportunity costs, calculating the marginal amounts, and so on. The mental effort required has its own opportunity cost. This realization led economists to the concept of **bounded rationality**—making a choice that is close to but not exactly the one that leads to the highest possible payoff because the effort of finding the best payoff is too costly. In other words, bounded rationality is the "good enough" method of decision making. When someone needs to replace an appliance like a broken washing machine, it is too time-consuming to research each available model. Some people might read magazines such as *Consumer Reports* or check online for reviewer comments before making a choice. The washing machine might not maximize their payoff in terms of features based on the price paid, but the new machine is good enough.

Retailers are particularly good at exploiting their customers' tendency to engage in bounded rationality. For example, pricing items in units ending in 99¢ takes advantage of shoppers' tendency to interpret an item that costs, say, $2.99 as significantly cheaper than one that costs $3.00. Bounded rationality leads them to give more weight to the $2 part of the price (the first number they see) than the 99¢ part.

Risk Aversion
Because life is uncertain and the future unknown, sometimes a choice comes with significant risk. Although you may receive a high payoff if things turn out well, the possibility also exists that things may turn out badly and leave you worse off. So even if you think a choice will give you the best payoff of all your available options, you may forgo it because you find the possibility that things could turn out badly too, well, risky. This is called **risk aversion**—the willingness to sacrifice some potential economic payoff in order to avoid a potential loss. (We'll discuss risk aversion in more detail in Chapter 20.) Because risk makes most people uncomfortable, it's rational for them to give up some potential economic gain in order to avoid it. In fact, if it weren't for risk aversion, there would be no such thing as insurance.

A **rational** decision maker chooses the available option that leads to the outcome he or she most prefers.

A decision maker operating with **bounded rationality** makes a choice that is close to but not exactly the one that leads to the best possible economic outcome.

Risk aversion is the willingness to sacrifice some economic payoff in order to avoid a potential loss.

Irrationality: An Economist's View

Sometimes, though, instead of being rational, people are **irrational**—they make choices that leave them worse off in terms of economic payoff *and* other considerations like fairness than if they had chosen another available option. Is there anything systematic that economists and psychologists can say about economically irrational behaviour? Yes, because most people are irrational in predictable ways. People's irrational behaviour *typically* stems from six mistakes they make when thinking about economic decisions. The mistakes are listed in Table 9-7, and we will discuss each in turn.

TABLE 9-7	The Six Common Mistakes in Economic Decision Making
1. Misperceiving opportunity costs	
2. Being overconfident	
3. Having unrealistic expectations about future behaviour	
4. Counting dollars unequally	
5. Being loss-averse	
6. Having a bias toward the status quo	

Misperceptions of Opportunity Costs   As we discussed at the beginning of this chapter, people tend to ignore non-monetary opportunity costs—opportunity costs that don't involve an outlay of cash. Likewise, a misperception of what exactly constitutes an opportunity cost (and what does not) is at the root of the tendency to count sunk costs in one's decision making. In this case, someone takes an opportunity cost into account when none actually exists.

For example, shortly after a firm spends thousands of dollars in upgrading their equipment, newer more efficient equipment becomes available. This newer equipment would allow the firm to produce its products at lower cost (and with higher expected future profit). However, it will cost the firm thousands of dollar to acquire the equipment. Focusing on the short-run profit and thinking of the sunk costs, the firm may be reluctant to pay additional money to purchase the new equipment. However, that choice is irrational. By giving up the opportunity to use more efficient equipment, the firm forgoes higher long-run profits.

Overconfidence   It's a function of ego: we tend to think we know more than we actually do. And even if alerted to how widespread overconfidence is, people tend to think that it's someone else's problem, not theirs. (Certainly not yours or mine!) For example, a 1994 study asked students to estimate how long it would take them to complete their thesis "if everything went as well as it possibly could" and "if everything went as poorly as it possibly could." The results: the typical student thought it would take him or her 33.9 days to finish, with an average estimate of 27.4 days if everything went well and 48.6 days if everything went poorly. In fact, the average time it took to complete a thesis was much longer, 55.5 days. Students were, on average, from 14% to 102% more confident than they should have been about the time it would take to complete their thesis.

As you can see in the nearby For Inquiring Minds, overconfidence can cause problems with meeting deadlines. But it can cause far more trouble by having a strong adverse effect on people's financial health. Overconfidence often persuades people that they are in better financial shape than they actually are. It can also lead to bad investment and spending decisions. For example, non-professional investors who engage in a lot of speculative investing—such as quickly buying and selling stocks—on average have significantly worse results than professional brokers because of their misguided faith in their ability to spot a winner. Similarly, overconfidence can lead people to make a large spending decision, such as buying a car, without doing research on the pros and cons, relying instead on anecdotal evidence. Even worse, people tend to remain overconfident because they remember their successes, and explain away or forget their failures.

Unrealistic Expectations About Future Behaviour   Another form of overconfidence is being overly optimistic about your future behaviour: tomorrow you'll study, tomorrow you'll give up ice cream, tomorrow you'll spend less and save more, and so on. Of course, as we all know, when tomorrow arrives, it's still just as hard to study or give up something that you like as it is right now.

An **irrational** decision maker chooses an option that leaves him or her worse off than choosing another available option.

FOR INQUIRING MINDS

IN PRAISE OF HARD DEADLINES

Dan Ariely, a professor of psychology and behavioural economics, likes to do experiments with his students that help him explore the nature of irrationality. In his book *Predictably Irrational,* Ariely describes an experiment that gets to the heart of procrastination and ways to address it.

At the time, Ariely was teaching the same subject matter to three different classes, but he gave each class different assignment schedules. The grade in all three classes was based on three equally weighted papers.

Students in the first class were required to choose their own personal deadlines for submitting each paper. Once set, the deadlines could not be changed. Late papers would be penalized at the rate of 1% of the grade for each day late. Papers could be turned in early without penalty but also without any advantage, since Ariely would not grade papers until the end of the semester.

Students in the second class could turn in the three papers whenever they wanted, with no preset deadlines, as long as it was before the end of the term. Again, there would be no benefit for early submission.

Students in the third class faced what Ariely called the "dictatorial treatment." He established three hard deadlines at the fourth, eighth, and twelfth weeks.

So which classes do you think achieved the best and the worst grades? As it turned out, the class with the least flexible deadlines—the one that received the dictatorial treatment—got the best grades. The class with complete flexibility got the worst grades. And the class that got to choose its deadlines performed in the middle.

Ariely learned two simple things about overconfidence from these results. First—no surprise—students tend to procrastinate. Second, hard, equally spaced deadlines are the best cure for procrastination.

But the biggest revelation came from the class that set its own deadlines. The majority of those students spaced their deadlines far apart and got grades as good as those of the students under the dictatorial treatment. Some, however, did not space their deadlines far enough apart, and a few did not space them out at all. These last two groups did less well, putting the average of the entire class below the average of the class with the least flexibility. As Ariely notes, without well-spaced deadlines, students procrastinate and the quality of their work suffers.

This experiment provides two important insights:

1. People who acknowledge their tendency to procrastinate are more likely to use tools for committing to a path of action.

2. Providing those tools allows people to make themselves better off.

If you have a problem with procrastination, hard deadlines, as irksome as they may be, are truly for your own good.

Strategies that keep a person on the straight-and-narrow over time are often, at their root, ways to deal with the problem of unrealistic expectations about one's future behaviour. Examples are automatic payroll deduction savings plans, diet plans with prepackaged foods, and mandatory attendance at study groups. By providing a way for someone to commit today to an action tomorrow, such plans counteract the habit of pushing difficult actions off into the future.

Counting Dollars Unequally If you tend to spend more when you pay with a credit card than when you pay with cash, particularly if you tend to splurge, then you are very likely engaging in **mental accounting.** This is the habit of mentally assigning dollars to different accounts, making some dollars worth more than others. By spending more with a credit card, you are in effect treating dollars in your wallet as more valuable than dollars on your credit card balance, although in reality they count equally in your budget.

Credit card overuse is the most recognizable form of mental accounting. However, there are other forms as well, such as splurging after receiving a windfall, like an unexpected inheritance, or overspending at sales, buying something that seemed like a great bargain at the time whose purchase you later regretted. It's the failure to understand that, regardless of the form it comes in, a dollar is a dollar.

Loss Aversion **Loss aversion** is an oversensitivity to loss, leading to an unwillingness to recognize a loss and move on. In fact, in the lingo of the financial markets, "selling discipline"—being able and willing to quickly acknowledge when a stock you've bought is a loser and sell it—is a highly desirable trait to have. Many investors, though, are reluctant to acknowledge that they've lost money on a stock and won't make it back. Although it's rational

Mental accounting is the habit of mentally assigning dollars to different accounts so that some dollars are worth more than others.

Loss aversion is an oversensitivity to loss, leading to unwillingness to recognize a loss and move on.

The **status quo bias** is the tendency to avoid making a decision and sticking with the status quo.

to sell the stock at that point and redeploy the remaining funds, most people find it so painful to admit a loss that they avoid selling for much longer than they should. According to Daniel Kahneman and Amos Tversky, most people feel the misery of losing $100 about twice as keenly as they feel the pleasure of gaining $100.

Loss aversion can help explain why sunk costs are so hard to ignore: ignoring a sunk cost means recognizing that the money you spent is unrecoverable and therefore lost.

Status Quo Bias Another irrational behaviour is **status quo bias,** the tendency to avoid making a decision altogether. A well-known example is the way that employees make decisions about investing in their employer-directed pension plan or group registered retirement saving plan (RRSP). With a pension plan, employees can, through payroll deductions, set aside part of their salary tax-free, a practice that saves a significant amount of money every year in taxes. Some companies operate on an opt-in basis: employees have to actively choose to participate in the pension plan. Other companies operate on an opt-out basis: employees are automatically enrolled in the pension plan unless they choose to opt out.

If everyone behaved rationally, then the proportion of employees enrolled in the company pension plan at opt-in companies would be roughly equal to the proportion enrolled at opt-out companies. In other words, your decision about whether to participate in a company pension plan should be independent of the default choice at your company. But, in reality, when companies switch to automatic enrolment and an opt-out system, employee enrolment rises dramatically. Clearly, people tend to just go with the status quo.

Why do people exhibit status quo bias? Some claim it's a form of "decision paralysis": when given many options, people find it harder to make a decision. Others claim it's due to loss aversion and the fear of regret, to thinking that "if I do nothing, then I won't have to regret my choice." Irrational, yes. But not altogether surprising. However, rational people know that, in the end, the act of not making a choice is still a choice.

Rational Models for Irrational People?

So why do economists still use models based on rational behaviour when people are at times manifestly irrational? For one thing, models based on rational behaviour still provide robust predictions about how people behave in most markets. For example, the great majority of farmers will use less fertilizer when it becomes more expensive—a result consistent with rational behaviour.

Another explanation is that sometimes market forces can compel people to behave more rationally over time. For example, if you are a small-business owner who persistently exaggerates your abilities or refuses to acknowledge that your favourite line of items is a loser, then sooner or later you will be out of business unless you learn to correct your mistakes. As a result, it is reasonable to assume that when people are disciplined for their mistakes, as happens in most markets, rationality will win out over time.

Finally, economists depend on the assumption of rationality for the simple but fundamental reason that it makes modelling so much simpler. Remember that models are built on generalizations, and it's much harder to extrapolate from messy, irrational behaviour. Even behavioural economists, in their research, search for *predictably* irrational behaviour in an attempt to build better models of how people behave. Clearly, there is an ongoing dialogue between behavioural economists and the rest of the economics profession, and economics itself has been irrevocably changed by it.

ECONOMICS ▶ IN ACTION

"THE JINGLE MAIL BLUES"

It's called jingle mail—when a U.S. homeowner seals the keys to his or her house in an envelope and leaves them with the bank that holds the mortgage on the house. (A mortgage is a loan taken out to buy a house.) By leaving the keys with the bank, the homeowner is walking away not only from the house but also from the obligation to continue paying the mortgage. And to their great consternation, U.S. banks have been flooded with jingle mail in the last decade.

To default on a mortgage—that is, to walk away from one's obligation to repay the loan and lose the house to the bank in the process—used to be a fairly rare phenomenon in the United States. For decades, continually rising U.S. home values made homeownership a good investment for the typical U.S. household. In recent years, though, an entirely different phenomenon—called "strategic default"—has appeared. In a strategic default, a homeowner who is financially capable of paying the mortgage instead chooses not to, voluntarily walking away. Strategic defaults account for a significant proportion of U.S. jingle mail; in March 2010, they accounted for 31% of all foreclosures, up from 22% in 2009. And unfortunately that number will likely be slow to change. In the spring of 2011, strategic defaults still accounted for 30% of all defaults. By 2013, rising home prices had lifted an additional 2.5 million homes into positive equity territory in the second quar-

"Officer, that couple is walking away from their mortgage!"

ter, and foreclosures in August were down 34% year over year. Although this news was positive, home price gains were slowing, household incomes were declining, and interest rates were expected to climb. According to CoreLogic, as of August 2013, about 7.1 million homes in the United States (14.5% of all homes with a mortgage), were in negative equity; these homeowners owed more than their homes were worth, making them prime candidates for strategic default. A further 10.3 million homes (21.2% of all homes with a mortgage), are "under-equitied," meaning they have less than 20% equity. This later group is essentially locked into their homes as selling and moving would cost so much that they would come out behind.

What happened? The Great American Housing Bust happened. After decades of huge increases, house prices began a precipitous fall in 2008. Prices dropped so much that a significant proportion of homeowners found their homes "underwater"—they owed more on their homes than the homes were worth. And with house prices projected to stay depressed for several years, possibly a decade, there appeared to be little chance that an underwater house would recover its value enough in the foreseeable future to move "abovewater."

Many homeowners suffered a major loss. They lost their down payment, money spent on repairs and renovation, moving expenses, and so on. And because they were paying a mortgage that was greater than the house was now worth, they found they could rent a comparable dwelling for less than their monthly mortgage payments. In the words of Benjamin Koellmann, who paid $215 000 for an apartment in Miami where similar units were now selling for $90 000, "There is no financial sense in staying."

Realizing their losses were sunk costs, underwater homeowners walked away. Perhaps they hadn't made the best economic decision when purchasing their houses, but in leaving them showed impeccable economic logic.

▼ **Quick Review**

- Behavioural economics combines economic modelling with insights from human psychology.

- **Rational** behaviour leads to the outcome a person most prefers. **Bounded rationality, risk aversion,** and concerns about fairness are reasons why people might prefer outcomes with worse economic payoffs.

- **Irrational** behaviour occurs because of misperceptions of opportunity costs, overconfidence, **mental accounting,** and unrealistic expectations about the future. **Loss aversion** and **status quo bias** can also lead to choices that leave people worse off than they would be if they chose another available option.

CHECK YOUR UNDERSTANDING   9-4

1. Which of the types of irrational behaviour are suggested by the following events?
   a. Although the housing market has fallen and Jenny wants to move, she refuses to sell her house for any amount less than what she paid for it.
   b. Dan worked more overtime hours last week than he had expected. Although he is strapped for cash, he spends his unexpected overtime earnings on a weekend getaway rather than trying to pay down his student loan.
   c. Carol has just started her first job and deliberately decided to opt out of the company's savings plan. Her reasoning is that she is very young and there is plenty of time in the future to start saving. Why not enjoy life now?
   d. Jeremy's company requires employees to download and fill out a form if they want to participate in the company-sponsored savings plan. One year after starting the job, Jeremy had still not submitted the form needed to participate in the plan.

2. How would you determine whether a decision you made was rational or irrational?

3. Suppose you are approached by a corporation that asks you to go over Niagara Falls in their newly designed Barrel-o-Death. Your chance of survival is one in a million, but the corporation has guaranteed to pay you $10 million if you survive. If you are not successful you will be paid nothing and the corporation is not liable for your death. Are you rational, irrational, risk averse, or a risk lover if you decline the offer?

Solutions appear at back of book.

BUSINESS CASE

Banks Help Cardholders Be CreditSmart and inControl

In 2007, CIBC, Canada's fifth largest bank with about 11 million customers, served by 1100 bank branches throughout Canada, and a market capitalization of more than $35 billion, became the first Canadian company to introduce a free and unique suite of information and credit management tools, which they named *CreditSmart*. Available to all CIBC credit card holders, this suite contains enhanced monthly statements, plus budgeting and alert features that help cardholders stay within their spending limits and prevent credit card fraud. With CreditSmart, cardholders can do the following:

- Use enhanced statements to better track and manage spending in 10 common categories
- Set up budgets for particular types of spending
- Set up and manage a budget spending limit on each spending category—including personalized custom categories
- Monitor changes to their Equifax credit reports, be aware of fraudulent uses of their cards, and deal with identity theft
- Receive alerts via phone, email, or through CIBC's Online Banking Message Centre to safeguard against overspending (related to personal budget or credit limit) and fraud

According to CIBC, "Canadians planning to use a credit card to pay for their holiday (or other) expenses should ensure they have a plan to pay off their balance to avoid incurring interest charges. With a plan in place, you can earn rewards for your purchases that may save you money on other items, such as discounts on gas purchases or cash back." And CreditSmart gives them the tools to do so. Cheryl Longo from CIBC explained that "you can set your budget and we will send you alerts, so you can be your own money manager, your own smart money manager. If you say, 'I don't want to spend more than x amount,' we will send you an alert when you hit that amount. But consumers have a choice, and they need to take accountability for the choices they make."

Following suit, the Bank of Montreal, Canada's fourth largest bank, introduced a special set of features known as *inControl* to their MasterCard. Previously introduced in the United Kingdom by Barclays Bank, inControl cards, like the CreditSmart suite, contain budgeting and alert features that help credit card holders stay within their spending limits and prevent credit card fraud. inControl contains one major feature not found in the CreditSmart suite: the ability of cardholders to manage where, when, how, and for what types of purchases their credit cards can be used.[2]

Users of inControl can customize their cards, choosing to either receive alerts or have a card declined when they are exceeding their limits. So, for example, if you choose the latter and have set a monthly limit on restaurant meals, your card will be rejected for restaurant bills above your preset cap. Cardholders can also arrange to have their credit cards shut off once a limit that corresponds to monthly disposable income is reached.

Until inControl was introduced, no other product allowed you to completely cut off certain types of spending. "The personalization of consumer products has

---

[2]Early in 2011, the Bank of Montreal also launched BMO MoneyLogic, an online personal financial management tool, which gives customers the ability to view, track, and manage both spending and savings accounts, as well as prepare budgets and set and track financial goals. Unlike inControl, however, the MoneyLogic suite does not allow users to limit where, when, how, and for what types of purchases their credit cards can be used.

reached far deeper than it ever has before," says Ed McLaughlin, chief payments officer of MasterCard.

But what about the obvious question of whether credit card companies are hurting or helping themselves by introducing this product? After all, if consumers get serious about budgeting and place caps on their credit card spending, won't that reduce the interest that credit card companies profit from? In answer to this question, McLaughlin replied, "I think anyone knows that having a superior offering wins out in the long run."

The service, though, is not ironclad—having hit the self-imposed limit, a customer can turn the card back on with a phone call or text message. The thinking goes, however, that having your card rejected will make a significant enough impression to put a damper on your urge to splurge.

In the end, how well inControl does, and whether something like it is adopted by competitors like VISA, depends on whether customers actually use the service *and* how much customers' newfound discipline hurts credit card companies' bottom lines.

QUESTIONS FOR THOUGHT

1. What aspects of decision making does the CreditSmart suite and inControl card address? Be specific.

2. Consider credit scores, the scores assigned to individuals by credit-rating agencies, based on whether you pay your bills on time, how many credit cards you have (too many is a bad sign), whether you have ever declared bankruptcy, and so on. Now consider people who choose inControl cards and those who don't. Which group do you think has better credit scores *before* they adopt the inControl cards? After adopting the inControl cards? Explain.

3. What do you think explains Ed McLaughlin's optimism that his company will profit from the introduction of inControl?

SUMMARY

1. All economic decisions involve the allocation of scarce resources. Some decisions are "either–or" decisions, in which the question is whether to do one action or another. Other decisions are "how much" decisions, in which the question is how much of a resource to put into a given activity.

2. The cost of using a resource for a particular activity is the opportunity cost of that resource. Some opportunity costs are **explicit costs;** they involve a direct outlay of money. Other opportunity costs, however, are **implicit costs;** they involve no outlay of money but are measured by the dollar value of the benefits that are forgone. Both explicit and implicit costs should be taken into account in making decisions. Many decisions involve the use of **capital** and time, for both individuals and firms. So they should base decisions on **economic profit,** which takes into account implicit costs such as the opportunity cost of your own time and the **implicit cost of capital.** Making decisions based on **accounting profit** can be misleading. It is often considerably larger than the economic profit because it includes only explicit costs and not implicit costs.

3. According to the **principle of "either–or" decision making,** when faced with an "either–or" choice between two activities, one should choose the activity with the positive economic profit.

4. A "how much" decision is made using marginal analysis, which involves comparing the benefit to the cost of doing an additional unit of an activity. The **marginal cost** of producing a good or service is the additional cost incurred by producing one more unit of that good or service. The **marginal benefit** of producing a good or service is the additional benefit earned by producing one more unit. The **marginal cost curve** is the graphical illustration of marginal cost, and the **marginal benefit curve** is the graphical illustration of marginal benefit.

5. In the case of **constant marginal cost,** each additional unit costs the same amount to produce as the previous unit. However, marginal cost and marginal benefit typically depend on how much of the activity has already been done. With **increasing marginal cost,** each unit costs more to produce than the previous unit and is represented by an upward-sloping marginal cost curve. With **decreasing marginal cost,** each unit costs less to produce than the previous unit, leading to a downward-sloping marginal cost curve. In the case of **decreasing marginal benefit,** each additional unit produces a smaller benefit than the unit before.

6. The **optimal quantity** is the quantity that generates the highest possible total profit. According to the **profit-maximizing principle of marginal analysis,** the optimal quantity is the largest quantity at which marginal benefit is greater than or equal to marginal cost. It is the quantity at which the marginal cost curve and the marginal benefit curve intersect.

7. A cost that has already been incurred and that is nonrecoverable is a **sunk cost.** Sunk costs should be ignored in decisions about future actions because they have no effect on future benefits and costs.

8. With **rational** behaviour, individuals will choose the available option that leads to the outcome they most prefer. **Bounded rationality** occurs because the effort needed to find the best economic payoff is costly. **Risk aversion** causes individuals to sacrifice some economic payoff in order to avoid a potential loss. People might also prefer outcomes with worse economic payoffs because they are concerned about fairness.

9. An **irrational** choice leaves someone worse off than if they had chosen another available option. It takes the form of misperceptions of opportunity cost; overconfidence; unrealistic expectations about future behaviour; **mental accounting,** in which dollars are valued unequally; **loss aversion,** an oversensitivity to loss; and **status quo bias,** avoiding a decision by sticking with the status quo.

KEY TERMS

Explicit cost, p. 266
Implicit cost, p. 266
Accounting profit, p. 267
Economic profit, p. 267
Capital, p. 268
Implicit cost of capital, p. 269
Principle of "either–or" decision making, p. 269
Marginal cost, p. 273

Increasing marginal cost, p. 273
Marginal cost curve, p. 273
Constant marginal cost, p. 273
Decreasing marginal cost, p. 273
Marginal benefit, p. 275
Decreasing marginal benefit, p. 275
Marginal benefit curve, p. 275
Optimal quantity, p. 276
Profit-maximizing principle of marginal analysis, p. 278

Sunk cost, p. 281
Rational, p. 283
Bounded rationality, p. 283
Risk aversion, p. 283
Irrational, p. 284
Mental accounting, p. 285
Loss aversion, p. 285
Status quo bias, p. 286

PROBLEMS

1. Hiro owns and operates a small business that provides economic consulting services. During the year he spends $57 000 on travel to clients and other expenses. In addition, he owns a computer that he uses for business. If he didn't use the computer, he could sell it and earn yearly interest of $100 on the money created through this sale. Hiro's total revenue for the year is $100 000. Instead of working as a consultant for the year, he could teach economics at a small local college and make a salary of $50 000.

   a. What is Hiro's accounting profit?

   b. What is Hiro's economic profit?

   c. Should Hiro continue working as a consultant, or should he teach economics instead?

2. Jackie owns and operates a web-design business. To keep up with new technology, she spends $5000 per year upgrading her computer equipment. She runs the business out of a room in her home. If she didn't use the room as her business office, she could rent it out for $2000 per year. Jackie knows that if she didn't run her own business, she could return to her previous job at a large software company that would pay her a salary of $60 000 per year. Jackie has no other expenses.

   a. How much total revenue does Jackie need to make in order to break even in the eyes of her accountant? That is, how much total revenue would give Jackie an accounting profit of just zero?

   b. How much total revenue does Jackie need to make in order for her to want to remain self-employed? That is, how much total revenue would give Jackie an economic profit of just zero?

   c. If Jackie earns a negative economic profit but decides to remain self-employed, is her behaviour irrational? Explain why or why not.

3. You own and operate a bike store. Each year, you receive revenue of $200 000 from your bike sales, and it costs you $100 000 to obtain the bikes. In addition, you pay $20 000 for electricity, taxes, and other expenses per year. Instead of running the bike store, you could become an accountant and receive a yearly salary of $40 000. A large clothing retail chain wants to expand and offers to rent the store from you for $50 000 per year. How do you explain to your friends that despite making a profit, it is too costly for you to continue running your store?

4. Suppose you have just paid a nonrefundable fee of $1000 for your meal plan for this academic term. This allows you to eat dinner in the cafeteria every evening.

   a. You are offered a part-time job in a restaurant where you can eat for free each evening. Your parents say that you should eat dinner in the cafeteria anyway, since you have already paid for those meals. Are your parents right? Explain why or why not.

   b. You are offered a part-time job in a different restaurant where, rather than being able to eat for free, you receive only a large discount on your meals. Each meal there will cost you $2; if you eat there each evening this semester, it will add up to $200. Your roommate says that you should eat in the restaurant since it costs less than the $1000 that you paid for the meal plan. Is your roommate right? Explain why or why not.

5. New Brunswick, Ontario, and Quebec are the only provinces that have nuclear power plants. Recently, the nuclear plant at Darlington, Ontario, which was completed in 1993 at a price of $14.4 billion, was due for repairs to extend its useful life. According to estimates by Ontario's Ministry of Energy, the repair cost of the plant could run from $6 billion to $10 billion. At the same time, the cost of building a new nuclear plant in Ontario could range from $10 billion to $20 billion, depending on its size. Is repairing the Darlington plant the right economic decision? Explain.

6. You have bought a $10 ticket in advance for a lacrosse game, a ticket that cannot be resold. You know that going to the lacrosse game will give you a benefit equal to $20. After you have bought the ticket, you hear that there will be a CFL football game at the same time. Tickets to the football game cost $20, and you know that going to the football game will give you a benefit equal to $35. You tell your friends the following: "If I had known about the football game before buying the ticket to the lacrosse game, I would have gone to the football game instead. But now that I already have the ticket to the lacrosse game, it's better for me to just go to the lacrosse game." Are you making the correct decision? Justify your answer by calculating the benefits and costs of your decision.

7. Amy, Bill, and Carla all mow lawns for money. Each of them operates a different lawn mower. The accompanying table shows the total cost to Amy, Bill, and Carla of mowing lawns.

Quantity of lawns mowed	Amy's total cost	Bill's total cost	Carla's total cost
0	$0	$0	$0
1	20	10	2
2	35	20	7
3	45	30	17
4	50	40	32
5	52	50	52
6	53	60	82

   a. Calculate Amy's, Bill's, and Carla's marginal costs, and draw each of their marginal cost curves.

b. Who has increasing marginal cost, who has decreasing marginal cost, and who has constant marginal cost?

8. You are the manager of a gym, and you have to decide how many customers to admit each hour. Assume that each customer stays exactly one hour. Customers are costly to admit because they inflict wear and tear on the exercise equipment. Moreover, each additional customer generates more wear and tear than the customer before. As a result, the gym faces increasing marginal cost. The accompanying table shows the marginal costs associated with each number of customers per hour.

Quantity of customers per hour	Marginal cost of customer
0	
	$14.00
1	
	14.50
2	
	15.00
3	
	15.50
4	
	16.00
5	
	16.50
6	
	17.00
7	

a. Suppose that each customer pays $15.25 for a one-hour workout. Use the profit-maximizing principle of marginal analysis to find the optimal number of customers that you should admit per hour.

b. You increase the price of a one-hour workout to $16.25. What is the optimal number of customers per hour that you should admit now?

9. Georgia and Lauren are economics students who go to a karate class together. Both have to choose how many classes to go to per week. Each class costs $20. The accompanying table shows Georgia's and Lauren's estimates of the marginal benefit that each of them gets from each class per week.

Quantity of classes	Lauren's marginal benefit of each class	Georgia's marginal benefit of each class
0		
	$23	$28
1		
	19	22
2		
	14	15
3		
	8	7
4		

a. Use marginal analysis to find Lauren's optimal number of karate classes per week. Explain your answer.

b. Use marginal analysis to find Georgia's optimal number of karate classes per week. Explain your answer.

10. The Canadian National Advisory Committee on Immunization (NACI) has recommended against vaccinating the whole population against the smallpox virus because the vaccination has undesirable, and sometimes fatal, side effects. Suppose the accompanying table gives the data that are available about the effects of a smallpox vaccination program.

Percent of population vaccinated	Deaths due to smallpox	Deaths due to vaccination side effects
0%	200	0
10	180	4
20	160	10
30	140	18
40	120	33
50	100	50
60	80	74

a. Calculate the marginal benefit (in terms of lives saved) and the marginal cost (in terms of lives lost) of each 10% increment of smallpox vaccination. Calculate the net increase in human lives for each 10% increment in population vaccinated.

b. Using marginal analysis, determine the optimal percentage of the population that should be vaccinated.

11. Patty delivers pizza using her own car, and she is paid according to the number of pizzas she delivers. The accompanying table shows Patty's total benefit and total cost when she works a specific number of hours.

Quantity of hours worked	Total benefit	Total cost
0	$0	$0
1	30	10
2	55	21
3	75	34
4	90	50
5	100	70

a. Use marginal analysis to determine Patty's optimal number of hours worked.

b. Calculate the total profit to Patty from working 0 hours, 1 hour, 2 hours, and so on. Now suppose Patty chooses to work for 1 hour. Compare her total profit from working for 1 hour with her total profit from working the optimal number of hours. How much would she lose by working for only 1 hour?

12. Assume De Beers is the sole producer of diamonds. When it wants to sell more diamonds, it must lower its price in order to induce shoppers to buy more. Furthermore, each additional diamond that is produced costs more than the previous one due to the difficulty of mining for diamonds. De Beers's total benefit schedule is given in the accompanying table, along with its total cost schedule.

Quantity of diamonds	Total benefit	Total cost
0	$0	$0
1	1000	50
2	1900	100
3	2700	200
4	3400	400
5	4000	800
6	4500	1500
7	4900	2500
8	5200	3800

a. Draw the marginal cost curve and the marginal benefit curve and, from your diagram, graphically derive the optimal quantity of diamonds to produce.

b. Calculate the total profit to De Beers from producing each quantity of diamonds. Which quantity gives De Beers the highest total profit?

13. In each of the following examples, explain whether the decision is rational or irrational. Describe the type of behaviour exhibited.

a. Kookie's best friend likes to give her gift cards that Kookie can use at her favourite stores. Kookie, however, often forgets to use the cards or loses them. Kookie, though, is careful with her own cash.

b. The Western Canada Theatre, in Kamloops, British Columbia, offers Pay-What-You-Can mati-nees to ensure everyone can experience live theatre. This payment system allows patrons to pay any amount they like for a seat, instead of the fixed price, although the usual seat prices are publicized as a point of comparison.

c. Rick has just gotten his teaching degree and has two job offers. One job, replacing a teacher who has gone on leave, will last only two years. It is at a private high school, and he will be paid $35 000 per year. He thinks he will probably be able to find another good job in the area after the two years are up but isn't sure. The other job, also at a high school, pays $25 000 per year and is virtually guaranteed for five years; after those five years, he will be evaluated for a permanent teaching position at the school. About 75% of the teachers who start at the school are hired for permanent positions. Rick takes the five-year position at $25 000 per year.

d. Kimora has planned a trip to Florida during reading week in February. She has several school projects due after her return. Rather than do them in February, she figures she can take her books with her to Florida and complete her projects there.

e. Sahir overpaid when buying a used car that has turned out to be a lemon. He could sell it for parts, but instead he lets it sit in his garage and deteriorate.

f. Barry considers himself an excellent investor in stocks. He selects new stocks by finding ones with characteristics similar to those of his previous winning stocks. He chalks up losing trades to ups and downs in the macroeconomy.

14. You have been hired as a consultant by a company to develop the company's retirement plan, taking into account different types of predictably irrational behaviour commonly displayed by employees. State at least two types of irrational behaviour employees might display with regard to the retirement plan and the steps you would take to forestall such behaviour.

CHAPTER 10

The Rational Consumer

A WING TOO FAR

Darryl Brooks/Alamy

When is more of a good thing too much?

RESTAURANTS OCCASIONALLY offer "all-you-can-eat" specials to entice customers: all-you-can-eat salad bars, all-you-can-eat breakfast buffets, and all-you-can-eat chicken wing dinners.

But how can a restaurant owner who offers such a special be sure he or she won't be eaten out of business? If the restaurant charges $12.99 for an all-you-can-eat wing dinner, what prevents the average customer from wolfing down $30 worth of wings?

The answer is that even though every once in a while you see someone really take advantage of the offer—heaping a plate high with 30 or 40 chicken wings—it's a rare occurrence. And even those of us who like chicken wings shudder a bit at the sight. Five or even 10 chicken wings can be a treat, but 50 is ridiculous. Anyone who pays for an all-you-can-eat

meal wants to make the most of it, but a sensible person knows when one more wing would be one wing too many.

Notice that last sentence. We said that customers in a restaurant want to "make the most" of their meal; that sounds as if they are trying to *maximize* something. And we also said that they will stop when consuming one more wing would be a mistake; that sounds as if they are making a *marginal decision.*

The answer is yes, it is a matter of taste—and economists can't say much about where tastes come from. But economists *can* say a lot about how a rational individual goes about satisfying his or her tastes. And that is in fact the way that economists think about consumer choice. They work with a model of a *rational consumer*—a consumer who knows what he or she

wants and makes the most of the available opportunities.

In this chapter, we will show how to analyze the decisions of a rational consumer. We will begin by showing how the concept of *utility*—a measure of consumer satisfaction—allows us to begin thinking about rational consumer choice. We will then look at how *budget constraints* determine what a consumer can buy and how marginal analysis can be used to determine the consumption choice that maximizes utility. Finally, we will see how this analysis can be used to understand the law of demand and why the demand curve slopes downward.

For those interested in a more detailed treatment of consumer behaviour and coverage of indifference curves, see the appendix that follows this chapter. ■

Utility: Getting Satisfaction

The **utility** of a consumer is a measure of the satisfaction the consumer derives from consumption of goods and services.

An individual's **consumption bundle** is the collection of all the goods and services consumed by that individual.

An individual's **utility function** gives the total utility generated by his or her consumption bundle.

A **util** is a unit of utility.

When analyzing consumer behaviour, we're talking about people trying to get satisfaction—that is, about subjective feelings. Yet there is no simple way to measure subjective feelings. How much satisfaction do I get from my third chicken wing? Is it less or more than yours? Does it even make sense to ask the question?

Luckily, we don't need to make comparisons between your feelings and mine. All that is required to analyze consumer behaviour is to suppose that each individual is trying to maximize some personal measure of the satisfaction gained from consumption of goods and services. That measure is known as the consumer's **utility,** a concept we use to understand behaviour but don't expect to measure in practice. Nonetheless, we'll see that the assumption that rational consumers maximize utility helps us think clearly about consumer choice.

Utility and Consumption

An individual's utility depends on everything that individual consumes, from apples to Ziploc bags. The set of all the goods and services an individual consumes is known as the individual's **consumption bundle.** The relationship between an individual's consumption bundle and the total amount of utility it generates for that individual is known as the **utility function.** The utility function is a personal matter; two people with different tastes will have different utility functions. Someone who actually likes to consume 40 chicken wings at a sitting must have a utility function that looks different from that of someone who would rather stop at 5 wings.

So we can think of consumers as using consumption to "produce" utility, much in the same way as in later chapters we will think of producers as using inputs to produce output. However, it's obvious that people do not have a little computer in their heads that calculates the utility generated by their consumption choices. Nonetheless, people must make choices, and they usually base them on at least a rough attempt to decide which choice will give them greater satisfaction. I can have either soup or salad with my dinner. Which will I enjoy more? I can go on a big vacation this year or save the money toward buying a new car. Which will make me happier?

The concept of a utility function is just a way of representing the fact that when people consume, they take into account their preferences and tastes in a more or less rational way.

How do we measure utility? For the sake of simplicity, it is useful to suppose that we can measure utility in hypothetical units called—what else?—**utils.**

Figure 10-1 illustrates a utility function. It shows the total utility that Cassie, who likes chicken wings, gets from an all-you-can-eat wing dinner. We suppose that her consumption bundle consists of a side of salad, which comes with the meal, plus a number of wings to be determined. The table that accompanies the figure shows how Cassie's total utility depends on the number of wings; the curve in panel (a) of the figure shows that same information graphically.

Cassie's utility function slopes upward over most of the range shown, but it gets flatter as the number of wings consumed increases. And in this example it eventually turns downward. According to the information in the table in Figure 10-1, nine wings is a wing too far. Adding that additional wing actually makes Cassie worse off: it would lower her total utility. If she's rational, of course, Cassie will realize that and not consume the ninth wing.

So when Cassie chooses how many wings to consume, she will make this decision by considering the *change* in her total utility from consuming one more wing. This illustrates the general point: to maximize *total* utility, consumers must focus on *marginal* utility.

FIGURE **10-1**   Cassie's Total Utility and Marginal Utility

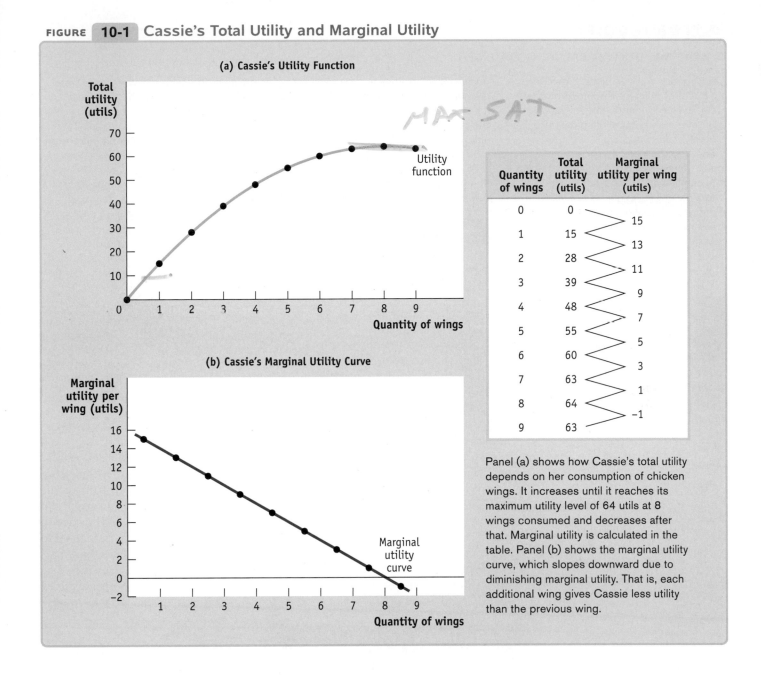

(a) Cassie's Utility Function

(b) Cassie's Marginal Utility Curve

Quantity of wings	Total utility (utils)	Marginal utility per wing (utils)
0	0	
		15
1	15	
		13
2	28	
		11
3	39	
		9
4	48	
		7
5	55	
		5
6	60	
		3
7	63	
		1
8	64	
		−1
9	63	

Panel (a) shows how Cassie's total utility depends on her consumption of chicken wings. It increases until it reaches its maximum utility level of 64 utils at 8 wings consumed and decreases after that. Marginal utility is calculated in the table. Panel (b) shows the marginal utility curve, which slopes downward due to diminishing marginal utility. That is, each additional wing gives Cassie less utility than the previous wing.

The Principle of Diminishing Marginal Utility

In addition to showing how Cassie's total utility depends on the number of wings she consumes, the table in Figure 10-1 also shows the **marginal utility** generated by consuming each additional wing—that is, the *change* in total utility from consuming one additional wing. Panel (b) shows the implied **marginal utility curve.** Following our practice in Chapter 9 with the marginal benefit curve, the marginal utility curve is constructed by plotting points at the midpoint of the unit intervals.[1]

The marginal utility curve slopes downward: each successive wing adds less to total utility than the previous wing. This is reflected in the table: marginal utility falls from a high of 15 utils for the first wing consumed to −1 for the ninth wing consumed. The fact that the ninth wing has negative marginal utility means that

The **marginal utility** of a good or service is the change in total utility generated by consuming one additional unit of that good or service.

The **marginal utility curve** shows how marginal utility depends on the quantity of a good or service consumed.

---

[1]Students familiar with calculus techniques will realize that the marginal utility is simply the derivative of the total utility function, in which case, the marginal utility curve simply plots the slope of the total utility curve at each quantity.

FOR INQUIRING MINDS

IS MARGINAL UTILITY REALLY DIMINISHING?

Are all goods really subject to diminishing marginal utility? Of course not; there are a number of goods for which, at least over some range, marginal utility is surely *increasing*.

For example, there are goods that require some experience to enjoy. The first time one of the Canadian authors tried indoor rock climbing, the fear of falling kept her close to the ground. Once she overcame her fear, a few sessions later, climbing became very enjoyable. It only becomes a pleasurable activity if you do it enough to become reasonably competent. And even some less strenuous forms of

consumption take practice; people who are not accustomed to drinking coffee say it has a bitter taste and can't understand its appeal. (On the other hand, two of the authors regard coffee as one of the basic food groups.)

Another example would be goods that only deliver positive utility if you buy enough. The great Victorian economist Alfred Marshall, who more or less invented the supply and demand model, gave the example of wallpaper: buying only enough to do half a room is worse than useless. If you need two rolls of wallpaper to finish a room, the marginal

utility of the second roll is larger than the marginal utility of the first roll.

So why does it make sense to assume diminishing marginal utility? For one thing, most goods don't suffer from these qualifications: nobody needs to learn to like ice cream. Also, although most people don't rock climb and some people don't drink coffee, those who do rock climb or drink coffee do enough of it that the marginal utility of one more climbing session or one more cup is less than that of the last. So *in the relevant range* of consumption, marginal utility is still diminishing.

According to the **principle of diminishing marginal utility,** each successive unit of a good or service consumed adds less to total utility than the previous unit.

consuming it actually reduces total utility. (Restaurants that offer all-you-can-eat meals depend on the proposition that you can have too much of a good thing.) Not all marginal utility curves eventually become negative. But it is generally accepted that marginal utility curves do slope downward—that consumption of most goods and services is subject to *diminishing marginal utility*.

The basic idea behind the **principle of diminishing marginal utility** is that the additional satisfaction a consumer gets from one more unit of a good or service declines as the amount of that good or service consumed rises.[2] Or, to put it slightly differently, the more of a good or service you consume, the closer you are to being satiated—reaching a point at which an additional unit of the good adds nothing to your satisfaction. For someone who almost never gets to eat a banana, the occasional banana is a marvellous treat. (This was the case in Eastern Europe before the fall of communism, when bananas were very hard to find.) For someone who eats them all the time, a banana is just, well, a banana.

The principle of diminishing marginal utility isn't always true. But it is true in the great majority of cases, enough to serve as a foundation for our analysis of consumer behaviour.

ECONOMICS ▶ IN ACTION

OYSTERS VERSUS CHICKEN

How much utility would you get from eating one more oyster?

Is a particular food a special treat, something you consume on special occasions? Or is it an ordinary, take-it-or-leave-it dish? The answer depends a lot on how much of that food people normally consume, which determines how much utility they get *at the margin* from having a bit more.

Consider chicken. Modern North Americans eat a lot of chicken, so much that they regard it as nothing special. Yet this was not always the case. Traditionally chicken was a luxury dish because chickens were expensive to raise. Restaurant menus from two centuries ago show chicken dishes as the most expensive items listed. In 1928, Herbert Hoover ran for president of the United States on the slogan "A chicken in every pot," a promise to voters of great prosperity if he was elected.

---

[2]In calculus terms, diminishing marginal utility implies that the derivative of marginal utility with respect to quantity consumed is negative. Since marginal utility is itself a derivative, diminishing marginal utility implies that the second derivative of the utility function is negative.

What changed the status of chicken was the emergence of new, technologically advanced methods for raising and processing the birds. (You don't want to know.) These methods made chicken abundant, cheap, and also—thanks to the principle of diminishing marginal utility—nothing to get excited about.

The reverse evolution took place for oysters. Not everyone likes oysters or, for that matter, has ever tried them—they are definitely not ordinary food. But they are regarded as a delicacy by some; at restaurants that serve them, an oyster appetizer often costs more than the main course.

Yet oysters were once very cheap and abundant—and were regarded as poverty food. In *The Pickwick Papers* by Charles Dickens, published in the 1830s, the author remarks that "poverty and oysters always seem to go together."

What changed? Pollution, which destroyed many oyster beds, greatly reduced the supply, while human population growth greatly increased the demand. As a result, thanks to the principle of diminishing marginal utility, oysters went from being a common food, regarded as nothing special, to being a highly prized luxury good.

CHECK YOUR UNDERSTANDING   10-1

1. Explain why a rational consumer who has diminishing marginal utility for a good would not consume an additional unit when it generates negative marginal utility, even when that unit is free.

2. Marta drinks three cups of coffee a day, for which she has diminishing marginal utility. Which of her three cups generates the greatest increase in total utility? Which generates the least?

3. In each of the following cases, does the consumer have diminishing, constant, or increasing marginal utility? Explain your answers.
   a. The more Mabel exercises, the more she enjoys each additional visit to the gym.
   b. Although Mei's classical CD collection is huge, her enjoyment from buying another CD has not changed as her collection has grown.
   c. When Dexter was a struggling student, his enjoyment from a good restaurant meal was greater than now, when he has them more frequently.

Solutions appear at back of book.

Budgets and Optimal Consumption

The principle of diminishing marginal utility explains why most people eventually reach a limit, even at an all-you-can-eat buffet where the cost of another wing is measured only in future indigestion. Under ordinary circumstances, however, it costs some additional resources to consume more of a good, and consumers must take that cost into account when making choices.

What do we mean by cost? As always, the fundamental measure of cost is *opportunity cost*. Because the amount of money a consumer can spend is limited, a decision to consume more of one good is also a decision to consume less of some other good.

Budget Constraints and Budget Lines

Consider Sammy, whose appetite is exclusively for wings and potatoes (there's no accounting for tastes). He has a weekly income of $20 and he spends all of it on wings and potatoes. We will assume that wings cost $4 per kilogram and potatoes cost $2 per kilogram. What are his possible choices?

Whatever Sammy chooses, we know that the cost of his consumption bundle cannot exceed his income, the amount of money he has to spend. That is:

(10-1) Expenditure on wings + Expenditure on potatoes ≤ Total income

A **budget constraint** requires that the cost of a consumer's consumption bundle be no more than the consumer's income.

A consumer's **consumption possibilities** is the set of all consumption bundles that can be consumed given the consumer's income and prevailing prices.

Consumers always have limited income, which constrains how much they can consume. So the requirement illustrated by Equation 10-1—that a consumer must choose a consumption bundle that costs no more than his or her income—is known as the consumer's **budget constraint.** It's a simple way of saying that a consumer can't spend more than the total amount of income available to him or her. In other words, consumption bundles are affordable when they obey the budget constraint. We call the set of all of Sammy's affordable consumption bundles his **consumption possibilities.** In general, whether or not a particular consumption bundle is included in a consumer's consumption possibilities depends on the consumer's income and the prices of goods and services.

Figure 10-2 shows Sammy's consumption possibilities. The quantity of wings in his consumption bundle is measured on the horizontal axis and the quantity of potatoes on the vertical axis. The downward-sloping line connecting points *A* through *F* shows which consumption bundles are affordable and which are not. Every bundle on or inside this line (the shaded area) is affordable; every bundle outside this line is unaffordable.

As an example of one of the points, let's look at point *C*, representing 2 kilograms of wings and 6 kilograms of potatoes, and check whether it satisfies Sammy's budget constraint. The cost of bundle *C* is 6 kilograms of potatoes × $2 per kilogram + 2 kilograms of wings × $4 per kilogram = $12 + $8 = $20. So bundle *C* does indeed satisfy Sammy's budget constraint: it costs no more than his weekly income of $20. In fact, bundle *C* costs exactly as much as Sammy's income. By doing the arithmetic, you can check that all the other points lying on the downward-sloping line are also bundles at which Sammy spends all of his income.

FIGURE **10-2** **The Budget Line**

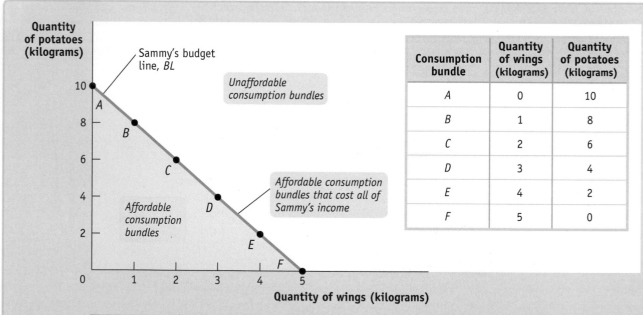

Consumption bundle	Quantity of wings (kilograms)	Quantity of potatoes (kilograms)
A	0	10
B	1	8
C	2	6
D	3	4
E	4	2
F	5	0

The *budget line* represents all the possible combinations of quantities of potatoes and wings that Sammy can purchase if he spends all of his income. Also, it is the boundary between the set of affordable consumption bundles (the *consumption possibilities*) and unaffordable ones. Given that wings cost $4 per kilogram and potatoes cost $2 per kilogram, if Sammy spends all of his income on wings (bundle *F*), he can purchase 5 kilograms of wings; if he spends all of his income on potatoes (bundle *A*), he can purchase 10 kilograms of potatoes.

The downward-sloping line has a special name, the **budget line.** It shows all the consumption bundles available to Sammy when he spends all of his income. It's downward sloping because when Sammy is consuming all of his income, say consuming at point A on the budget line, then in order to consume more wings he must consume fewer potatoes—that is, he must move to a point like *B*. In other words, when Sammy chooses a consumption bundle that is on his budget line, the opportunity cost of consuming more wings is consuming fewer potatoes, and vice versa. As Figure 10-2 indicates, any consumption bundle that lies above the budget line is unaffordable.

Do we need to consider the other bundles in Sammy's consumption possibilities, the ones that lie *within* the shaded region in Figure 10-2 bounded by the budget line? The answer is, for all practical situations, no: as long as Sammy continues to get positive marginal utility from consuming either good (in other words, Sammy doesn't get *satiated*)—and he doesn't get any utility from saving income rather than spending it, then he will always choose to consume a bundle that lies on his budget line and not within the shaded area. This assumption is sometimes simply stated as "more is preferred to less" or "more is better than less."

Given his $20 per week budget, which point on his budget line will Sammy choose?

Optimal Consumption Choice

Because Sammy has a budget constraint, which means that he will consume a consumption bundle on the budget line, a choice to consume a given quantity of wings also determines his potato consumption, and vice versa. We want to find the consumption bundle—the point on the budget line—that maximizes Sammy's total utility. This bundle is Sammy's **optimal consumption bundle,** the consumption bundle that maximizes his total utility given the budget constraint.

Table 10-1 shows how much utility Sammy gets from different levels of consumption of wings and potatoes, respectively. According to the table, Sammy has a healthy appetite; the more of either good he consumes, the higher his utility.

But because he has a limited budget, he must make a trade-off: the more kilograms of wings he consumes, the fewer kilograms of potatoes, and vice versa. That is, he must choose a point on his budget line.

Table 10-2 shows how his total utility varies for the different consumption bundles along his budget line. Each of six possible consumption bundles, *A* through *F* from Figure 10-2, is given in the first column. The second column shows the level of wing consumption corresponding to each choice. The third column shows the

A consumer's **budget line** shows the consumption bundles available to a consumer who spends all of his or her income.

A consumer's **optimal consumption bundle** is the consumption bundle that maximizes the consumer's total utility given his or her budget constraint.

TABLE 10-1   Sammy's Utility from Wing and Potato Consumption

Utility from wing consumption		Utility from potato consumption	
Quantity of wings (kilograms)	Utility from wings (utils)	Quantity of potatoes (kilograms)	Utility from potatoes (utils)
0	0	0	0
1	15	1	11.5
2	25	2	21.4
3	31	3	29.8
4	34	4	36.8
5	36	5	42.5
		6	47.0
		7	50.5
		8	53.2
		9	55.2
		10	56.7

TABLE **10-2** Sammy's Budget and Total Utility

Consumption bundle	Quantity of wings (kilograms)	Utility from wings (utils)	Quantity of potatoes (kilograms)	Utility from potatoes (utils)	Total utility (utils)
A	0	0	10	56.7	56.7
B	1	15	8	53.2	68.2
C	2	25	6	47.0	72.0
D	3	31	4	36.8	67.8
E	4	34	2	21.4	55.4
F	5	36	0	0	36.0

utility Sammy gets from consuming those wings. The fourth column shows the quantity of potatoes Sammy can afford *given* the level of wing consumption; this quantity goes down as his wing consumption goes up, because he is sliding down the budget line. The fifth column shows the utility he gets from consuming those potatoes. And the final column shows his *total utility*. In this example, Sammy's total utility is the sum of the utility he gets from wings and the utility he gets from potatoes.

Figure 10-3 gives a visual representation of the data shown in Table 10-2. Panel (a) shows Sammy's budget line, to remind us that when he decides to consume more wings he is also deciding to consume fewer potatoes. Panel (b) then shows how his total utility depends on that choice. The horizontal axis in panel (b) has two sets of labels: it shows both the quantity of wings, increasing from left to right, and the quantity of potatoes, increasing from right to left. The reason we can use the same axis to represent consumption of both goods is, of course, the budget line: the more kilograms of wings Sammy consumes, the fewer kilograms of potatoes he can afford, and vice versa.

Clearly, the consumption bundle that makes the best of the trade-off between wing consumption and potato consumption, the optimal consumption bundle, is the one that maximizes Sammy's total utility. That is, Sammy's optimal consumption bundle puts him at the highest point of the total utility curve.

As always, we can find the highest point of the curve by direct observation. We can see from Figure 10-3 that Sammy's total utility is maximized at point C—that his optimal consumption bundle contains 2 kilograms of wings and 6 kilograms of potatoes. But we know that we usually gain more insight into "how much" problems when we use marginal analysis. So in the next section we turn to representing and solving the optimal consumption choice problem with marginal analysis.

FOR INQUIRING MINDS

FOOD FOR THOUGHT ON BUDGET CONSTRAINTS

Budget constraints aren't just about money. In fact, there are many other budget constraints affecting our lives. You face a budget constraint if you have a limited amount of closet space for your clothes or limited storage on your phone. All of us face a budget constraint on time: there are only so many hours in the day.

And people trying to lose weight on the Weight Watchers plan face a budget constraint on the foods they eat.

The Weight Watchers plan assigns each food a certain number of "points." A 100-gram serving of ice cream gets 7 points, a slice of pizza 5 points, any serving of grapes zero points, a large fast-food hamburger 13 points.

You are allowed a maximum number of points each day but are free to choose which foods you eat. In other words, a dieter on the Weight Watchers plan is just like a consumer choosing a consumption bundle: points are the equivalent of prices, and the overall point limit is the equivalent of total income.

FIGURE **10-3** Optimal Consumption Bundle

Panel (a) shows Sammy's budget line and his six possible consumption bundles. If we assume that these goods, potatoes and wings, are perfectly divisible, then Sammy can buy fractions of kilograms. This implies that points in between the consumption bundles (*A* to *F*), but still on the budget line, are also attainable.

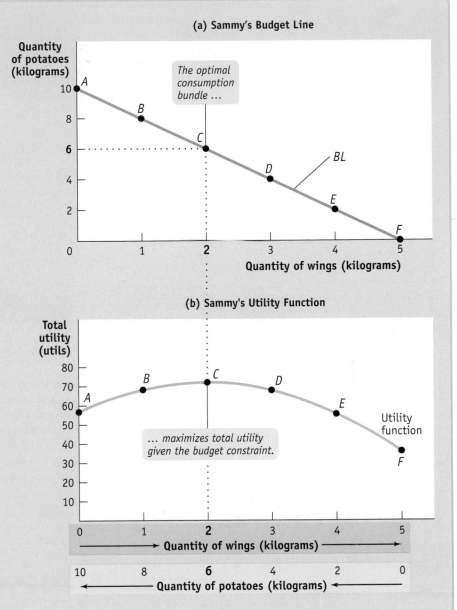

Panel (b) shows how Sammy's total utility is affected by his consumption bundle, which must lie on his budget line. The quantity of wings is measured from left to right on the horizontal axis, and the quantity of potatoes is measured from right to left. His total utility is maximized at bundle *C*, the highest point on his utility function, where he consumes 2 kilograms of wings and 6 kilograms of potatoes. This is Sammy's *optimal consumption bundle*.

ECONOMICS ＞ IN ACTION

THE GREAT CONDIMENT CRAZE

Those of us of a certain age remember when the only kind of mustard available in Canadian grocery stores was a runny, fluorescent yellow concoction packaged in plastic squeeze bottles. Ditto for ketchup and mayonnaise—what little selection there was, tasted the same. As for salsa—wasn't that some sort of dance step?

No longer. Lately, Canadians have developed an intense liking for condiments—in a dizzying array of varieties. Who wants plain mustard when you can get mustard flavoured with roasted garlic, apricot, or even maple and bacon? Likewise, would you like saffron and garlic mayonnaise or wasabi mayonnaise on your club sandwich?

Would you prefer the horseradish mayo or the smoky bacon mayo?

So what happened? Tastes changed and budgets changed. With budget-conscious consumers more likely to eat at home, but having been exposed to gourmet cooking and ethnic cuisine, specialty condiments have become an affordable way of spicing up home cooking. In 2012, the Canadian market for sauces, dressings, and condiments was valued at $2.9 billion and projected to grow to $3.1 billion by 2017, while stable overall demand is increasing for healthy options as well as for Asian, Indian, and spicy flavours.

The explosion of varieties stems from the fact that it's fairly easy to make bottled condiments. This enables smaller companies to experiment with exotic flavours, finding the ones that appeal to consumers' increasingly sophisticated tastes. Eventually, the flavours that attract a significant following are picked up by the larger companies such as Kraft. As one industry analyst put it, "People want cheaper, more specialized gourmet products. It's like fashion."

Although some analysts believe that the great condiment craze can continue indefinitely, others think that a limit will eventually be reached as food buyers' zest for experimentation wanes.

▼ Quick Review

- The **budget constraint** requires that a consumer's total expenditure be no more than his or her income. The set of consumption bundles that satisfy the budget constraint is the consumer's **consumption possibilities.**

- A consumer who spends all of his or her income chooses a point on his or her **budget line.** The budget line slopes downward because on the budget line a consumer must consume less of one good in order to consume more of another.

- The consumption choice that maximizes total utility given the consumer's budget constraint is the **optimal consumption bundle.** With economic goods, more is generally preferred to less, so the optimal consumption bundle must lie on the consumer's budget line.

CHECK YOUR UNDERSTANDING 10-2

1. In the following two examples, find all the consumption bundles that lie on the consumer's budget line. Illustrate these consumption possibilities in a diagram and draw the budget line through them.
    a. The consumption bundle consists of movie tickets and buckets of popcorn. The price of each ticket is $10.00, the price of each bucket of popcorn is $5.00, and the consumer's income is $20.00. In your diagram, put movie tickets on the vertical axis and buckets of popcorn on the horizontal axis.
    b. The consumption bundle consists of underwear and socks. The price of each pair of underwear is $4.00, the price of each pair of socks is $2.00, and the consumer's income is $12.00. In your diagram, put pairs of socks on the vertical axis and pairs of underwear on the horizontal axis.

Solutions appear at back of book.

Spending the Marginal Dollar

As we've just seen, we can find Sammy's optimal consumption choice by finding the total utility he receives from each consumption bundle on his budget line and then choosing the bundle at which total utility is maximized. But we can use marginal analysis instead, turning Sammy's problem of finding his optimal consumption choice into a "how much" problem.

How do we do this? By thinking about choosing an optimal consumption bundle as a problem of *how much to spend on each good.* That is, to find the optimal consumption bundle with marginal analysis, we ask whether Sammy can make himself better off by spending a little bit more of his income on wings and less on potatoes, or by doing the opposite—spending a little bit more on potatoes and less on wings. In other words, the marginal decision is a question of how to *spend the marginal dollar*—how to allocate an additional dollar between wings and potatoes in a way that maximizes utility.

Our first step in applying marginal analysis is to ask if Sammy is made better off by spending an additional dollar on either good; and if so, by how much is he better off. To answer this question we must calculate the **marginal utility per dollar** spent on either wings or potatoes—how much additional utility Sammy gets from spending an additional dollar on either good.

The **marginal utility per dollar** spent on a good or service is the additional utility gained from spending one more dollar on that good or service.

⚠ PITFALLS

THE RIGHT MARGINAL COMPARISON
Marginal analysis solves "how much" decisions by weighing costs and benefits at the margin: the *benefit* of doing a little bit more versus the *cost* of doing a little bit more. However, as we noted in Chapter 9, the form of the marginal analysis can differ, depending upon whether you are making a production decision that maximizes profits or a consumption decision that maximizes utility. Let's review that difference again to make sure that it's clearly understood.

In Chapter 9, Alex's decision was a production decision because the problem he faced was maximizing the profit from years of schooling. The optimal quantity of years that maximized his profit was

found using marginal analysis: at the optimal quantity, the marginal benefit of another year of schooling was equal to its marginal cost. Alex did not face a budget constraint because he could always borrow to finance another year of school.

But if you were to extend the way we solved Alex's production problem to Sammy's consumption problem without any change in form, you might be tempted to say that Sammy's optimal consumption bundle is the one at which the marginal utility of wings and the marginal utility of potatoes are equal, or that the marginal utility of wings was equal to the price of wings. But both those statements would be wrong because they don't properly

account for the budget constraint and the fact that consuming more of one good requires consuming less of another.

In a consumption decision, your objective is to maximize the utility that your limited budget can deliver. And the right way for finding the optimal consumption bundle is to set the *marginal utility per dollar* equal for each good in the consumption bundle. When this condition is satisfied and the consumption bundle is on the budget line, the "bang per buck" is the same across all the goods and services you consume. Only then is there no way to rearrange your consumption and get more utility from your budget.

Marginal Utility per Dollar

We've already introduced the concept of marginal utility, the additional utility a consumer gets from consuming one more unit of a good or service; now let's see how this concept can be used to derive the related measure of marginal utility per dollar.

Table 10-3 shows how to calculate the marginal utility per dollar spent on wings and potatoes, respectively.

In panel (a) of the table, the first column shows different possible amounts of wing consumption. The second column shows the utility Sammy derives from each amount of wing consumption; the third column then shows the marginal utility, the increase in utility Sammy gets from consuming an additional kilogram of wings. Panel (b) provides the same information for potatoes. The next

TABLE 10-3   Sammy's Marginal Utility per Dollar

(a) Wings (price of wings = $4 per kilogram)				(b) Potatoes (price of potatoes = $2 per kilogram)			
Quantity of wings (kilograms)	Utility from wings (utils)	Marginal utility per kilogram of wings (utils)	Marginal utility per dollar (utils)	Quantity of potatoes (kilograms)	Utility from potatoes (utils)	Marginal utility per kilogram of potatoes (utils)	Marginal utility per dollar (utils)
0	0			0	0		
		15	3.75			11.5	5.75
1	15			1	11.5		
		10	2.50			9.9	4.95
2	25			2	21.4		
		6	1.50			8.4	4.20
3	31			3	29.8		
		3	0.75			7.0	3.50
4	34			4	36.8		
		2	0.50			5.7	2.85
5	36			5	42.5		
						4.5	2.25
				6	47.0		
						3.5	1.75
				7	50.5		
						2.7	1.35
				8	53.2		
						2.0	1.00
				9	55.2		
						1.5	0.75
				10	56.7		

step is to derive marginal utility *per dollar* for each good. To do this, we must divide the marginal utility of the good by its price in dollars.

To see why we must divide by the price, compare the third and fourth columns of panel (a). Consider what happens if Sammy increases his wing consumption from 2 kilograms to 3 kilograms. As we can see, this increase in wing consumption raises his total utility by 6 utils. But he must spend $4 for that additional kilogram, so the increase in his utility per additional dollar spent on wings is 6 utils/$4 = 1.5 utils per dollar. Similarly, if he increases his wing consumption from 3 kilograms to 4 kilograms, his marginal utility is 3 utils but his marginal utility per dollar is 3 utils/$4 = 0.75 util per dollar. Notice that because of diminishing marginal utility, Sammy's marginal utility per kilogram of wings falls as the quantity of wings he consumes rises. As a result, his marginal utility per dollar spent on wings also falls as the quantity of wings he consumes rises.

So the last column of panel (a) shows how Sammy's marginal utility per dollar spent on wings depends on the quantity of wings he consumes. Similarly, the last column of panel (b) shows how his marginal utility per dollar spent on potatoes depends on the quantity of potatoes he consumes. Again, marginal utility per dollar spent on each good declines as the quantity of that good consumed rises, because of diminishing marginal utility.

We will use the symbols MU_W and MU_P to represent the marginal utility per kilogram of wings and potatoes, respectively. And we will use the symbols P_W and P_P to represent the price of wings (per kilogram) and the price of potatoes (per kilogram). Then the marginal utility per dollar spent on wings is MU_W/P_W and the marginal utility per dollar spent on potatoes is MU_P/P_P. In general, the additional utility generated from an additional dollar spent on a good is equal to:

(10-2) Marginal utility per dollar spent on a good
$\qquad$ = Marginal utility of one unit of the good/Price of one unit of the good
$\qquad$ = MU_{Good}/P_{Good}

Now let's see how this concept helps us derive a consumer's optimal consumption using marginal analysis.

Optimal Consumption

Let's consider Figure 10-4. As in Figure 10-3, we can measure both the quantity of wings and the quantity of potatoes on the horizontal axis due to the budget constraint. By construction, at each consumption bundle on the horizontal axis the budget constraint holds exactly. Along the horizontal axis of Figure 10-4— also as in Figure 10-3—the quantity of wings increases as you move from left to right, and the quantity of potatoes increases as you move from right to left. The curve labelled MU_W/P_W in Figure 10-4 shows Sammy's marginal utility per dollar spent on wings as derived in Table 10-3. Likewise, the curve labelled MU_P/P_P shows his marginal utility per dollar spent on potatoes. Notice that the two curves, MU_W/P_W and MU_P/P_P, cross at the optimal consumption bundle, point C, consisting of 2 kilograms of wings and 6 kilograms of potatoes. Moreover, Figure 10-4 illustrates an important feature of Sammy's optimal consumption bundle: when Sammy consumes 2 kilograms of wings and 6 kilograms of potatoes, his marginal utility per dollar spent is the same, 2, for both goods. That is, at the optimal consumption bundle $MU_W/P_W = MU_P/P_P = 2$.

This isn't an accident. Consider another one of Sammy's possible consumption bundles—say, B in Figure 10-3, at which he consumes 1 kilogram of wings and 8 kilograms of potatoes. The marginal utility per dollar spent on each good is shown by points B_W and B_P in Figure 10-4. At that consumption bundle, Sammy's marginal utility per dollar spent on wings would be approximately 3,

FIGURE 10-4 | Marginal Utility per Dollar

Sammy's optimal consumption bundle is at point *W*, where his marginal utility per dollar spent on wings, MU_W/P_W, is equal to his marginal utility per dollar spent on potatoes, MU_P/P_P. This illustrates the *utility-maximizing principle of marginal analysis*: at the optimal consumption bundle, the marginal utility per dollar spent on each good and service is the same. At any other consumption bundle on Sammy's budget line, such as bundle *B* in Figure 10-3, represented here by points B_W and B_P, consumption is not optimal: Sammy can increase his utility at no additional cost by reallocating his spending.

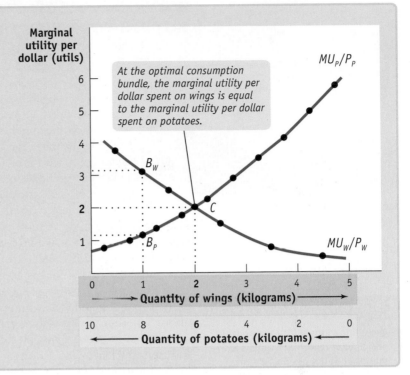

At the optimal consumption bundle, the marginal utility per dollar spent on wings is equal to the marginal utility per dollar spent on potatoes.

but his marginal utility per dollar spent on potatoes would be only approximately 1. This shows that he has made a mistake: he is consuming too many potatoes and not enough wings.

How do we know this? If Sammy's marginal utility per dollar spent on wings is higher than his marginal utility per dollar spent on potatoes, he has a simple way to make himself better off while staying within his budget: spend $1 less on potatoes and $1 more on wings. By spending an additional dollar on wings, he adds about 3 utils to his total utility; meanwhile, by spending $1 less on potatoes, he subtracts only about 1 util from his total utility.

Because his marginal utility per dollar spent is higher for wings than for potatoes, reallocating his spending toward wings and away from potatoes would increase his total utility. But if his marginal utility per dollar spent on potatoes is higher, he can increase his utility by spending less on wings and more on potatoes. So if Sammy has in fact chosen his optimal consumption bundle, his marginal utility per dollar spent on wings and potatoes must be equal.

This is a general principle, which we call the **utility-maximizing principle of marginal analysis:** when a consumer maximizes utility in the face of a budget constraint, the marginal utility per dollar spent on each good or service in the consumption bundle is the same. That is, for any two goods *W* and *P* the **optimal consumption rule** says that the optimal consumption bundle is on the budget line and:

$$(10\text{-}3) \quad \frac{MU_W}{P_W} = \frac{MU_P}{P_P}$$

It's easiest to understand this rule using examples in which the consumption bundle contains only two goods, but it applies no matter how many goods or services a consumer buys: in the optimal consumption bundle, the marginal utilities per dollar spent for each and every good or service in that bundle are equal.

According to the **utility-maximizing principle of marginal analysis,** the marginal utility per dollar spent must be the same for all goods and services in the optimal consumption bundle.

The **optimal consumption rule** says that (1) the optimal consumption bundle is on the budget line; and (2) the marginal utility per dollar spent on each good in the bundle is equal.

For many consumers, paying extra for smaller portions is worth it.

ECONOMICS > *IN ACTION*

BUYING YOUR WAY OUT OF TEMPTATION

It might seem odd to pay more to get less. But snack food companies have discovered that consumers are indeed willing to pay more for smaller portions, and exploiting this trend is a recipe for success. Over the last few years, North American sales of 100-calorie packs of crackers, chips, cookies, and candy have passed the $20 million-a-year mark, growing much more quickly than the rest of the snack industry. Individually packaged snacks are convenient for parents facing time constraints, who prefer spending more on convenient packages to dividing larger-size boxes into smaller servings for their little ones. A company executive offered another reason why small packages are popular—they help consumers eat less without having to count calories themselves. "The irony," said David Adelman, a food industry analyst, "is if you take Wheat Thins or Goldfish, buy a large-size box, count out the items and put them in a Ziploc bag, you'd have essentially the same product." He estimates that snack packs are about 20% more profitable for snack makers than larger packages.

It's clear that in this case consumers are making a calculation: the extra utility gained from having individual portions readily available and not having to worry about whether they've eaten too much is worth the extra cost. As one shopper said, "They're pretty expensive, but they're worth it. It's individually packaged for the amount I need, so I don't go overboard." So it's clear that consumers aren't being irrational here. Rather, they're being entirely rational: in addition to their snack, they're buying convenience and a little hand-to-mouth restraint.

●●◁

CHECK YOUR UNDERSTANDING   10-3

1. In Table 10-3 you can see that marginal utility per dollar spent on wings and marginal utility per dollar spent on potatoes are equal when Sammy increases his consumption of wings from 3 kilograms to 4 kilograms and his consumption of potatoes from 9 kilograms to 10 kilograms. Explain why this is not Sammy's optimal consumption bundle. Illustrate your answer using the budget line in Figure 10-3.

2. Explain what is faulty about the following statement, using data from Table 10-3: "In order to maximize utility, Sammy should consume the bundle that gives him the maximum marginal utility per dollar for each good."

Solutions appear at back of book.

From Utility to the Demand Curve

We have now analyzed the optimal consumption choice of a consumer with a given amount of income who faces one particular set of prices—in our Sammy example, $20 of income per week, $4 per kilogram of wings, and $2 per kilogram of potatoes.

But the main reason for studying consumer behaviour is to go behind the market demand curve—to explain how the utility-maximizing behaviour of individual consumers leads to the downward slope of the market demand curve.

Marginal Utility, the Substitution Effect, and the Law of Demand

Suppose that the price of chicken wings, P_W, rises. The price increase doesn't change the marginal utility a consumer gets from an additional kilogram of wings, MU_W, at any given level of wing consumption. However, it does reduce the marginal utility *per dollar spent* on chicken wings, MU_W/P_W. And the decrease in marginal utility per dollar spent on wings gives the consumer an incentive to consume fewer wings when the price of wings rises.

To see why, recall the utility-maximizing principle of marginal analysis: a utility-maximizing consumer chooses a consumption bundle for which the marginal utility per dollar spent on all goods is the same. If the marginal utility per dollar spent on wings falls because the price of wings rises, the consumer can increase his or her utility by purchasing fewer wings and more of other goods.

The opposite happens if the price of wings falls. In that case the marginal utility per dollar spent on wings, MU_W/P_W, increases at any given level of wing consumption. As a result, a consumer can increase his or her utility by purchasing more wings and less of other goods when the price of wings falls.

So when the price of a good increases, an individual will normally consume less of that good and more of other goods. Correspondingly, when the price of a good decreases, an individual will normally consume more of that good and less of other goods. This explains why the individual demand curve, which relates an individual's consumption of a good to the price of that good, normally slopes downward—that is, it obeys the law of demand. And since—as we learned in Chapter 3—the market demand curve is the horizontal sum of all the individual demand curves of consumers, it, too, will slope downward.

An alternative way to think about why demand curves slope downward is to focus on opportunity costs. When the price of wings decreases, an individual doesn't have to give up as many units of other goods in order to buy one more unit of wings. So consuming wings becomes more attractive. Conversely, when the price of a good increases, consuming that good becomes a less attractive use of resources, and the consumer buys less.

This effect of a price change on the quantity consumed is always present. It is known as the **substitution effect**—the change in the quantity consumed as the consumer substitutes other goods that are now relatively cheaper in place of the good that has become relatively more expensive. When a good absorbs only a small share of an individual consumer's spending, the substitution effect is essentially the complete explanation of why the individual demand curve of that consumer slopes downward. And, by implication, when a good absorbs only a small share of the typical consumer's spending, the substitution effect is essentially the sole explanation of why the market demand curve slopes downward. However, some goods, such as housing, absorb a large share of a typical consumer's spending. For such goods, the story behind the individual demand curve and the market demand curve becomes slightly more complicated.

The Income Effect

For the vast majority of goods, the substitution effect is pretty much the entire story behind the slopes of the individual and market demand curves. There are, however, some goods, like food or housing, that account for a substantial share of many consumers' spending. In such cases another effect, called the *income effect*, also comes into play.

Consider the case of a family that spends half its income on rental housing. Now suppose that the price of housing increases everywhere. This will have a substitution effect on the family's demand: other things equal, the family will have an incentive to consume less housing—say, by moving to a smaller apartment—and more of other goods. But the family will also, in a real sense, be made poorer by that higher housing price—its income will buy less housing than before. The amount of income adjusted to reflect its true purchasing power is often termed "real income," in contrast to "money income" or "nominal income," which has not been adjusted. And this reduction in a consumer's real income will have an additional effect, beyond the substitution effect, on the family's consumption bundle, including its consumption of housing.

The **substitution effect** of a change in the price of a good is the change in the quantity of that good consumed as the consumer substitutes other goods that are now relatively cheaper in place of the good that has become relatively more expensive.

The **income effect** of a change in the price of a good is the change in the quantity of that good consumed that results from a change in the consumer's purchasing power due to the change in the price of the good.

A **Giffen good** is a hypothetical inferior good for which the income effect outweighs the substitution effect and as a result, the demand curve slopes upward.

The change in the quantity of a good consumed that results from a change in the overall purchasing power of the consumer due to a change in the price of that good is known as the **income effect** of the price change. In this case, a change in the price of a good effectively changes a consumer's income because it alters the consumer's purchasing power. Along with the substitution effect, the income effect is another means by which changes in prices alter consumption choices.

It's possible to give more precise definitions of the substitution effect and the income effect of a price change, and we do this in Appendix 10A. For most purposes, however, there are only two things you need to know about the distinction between these two effects.

First, for the great majority of goods and services, the income effect is not important and has no significant effect on individual consumption. So most market demand curves slope downward solely because of the substitution effect—end of story.

Second, when it matters at all, the income effect usually reinforces the substitution effect. That is, when the price of a good that absorbs a substantial share of income rises, consumers of that good become a bit poorer because their purchasing power falls. As we learned in Chapter 3, the vast majority of goods are *normal goods*, goods for which demand decreases when income falls. So this effective reduction in income leads to a reduction in the quantity demanded and reinforces the substitution effect.

However, in the case of an *inferior good*, a good for which demand increases when income falls, the income and substitution effects work in opposite directions. Although the substitution effect tends to produce a decrease in the quantity of any good demanded as its price increases, in the case of an inferior good the income effect of a price increase tends to produce an *increase* in the quantity demanded.

As a result, there are hypothetical cases involving inferior goods in which the distinction between income and substitution effects is important. The most extreme example of this distinction is a **Giffen good,** a good that has an upward-sloping demand curve.

The classic story used to describe a Giffen good harks back to nineteenth-century Ireland, when it was a desperately poor country and a large portion of a typical household's diet consisted of potatoes. *Other things equal,* an increase in the price of potatoes would have led people to reduce their demand for potatoes. But other things were not equal: for the nineteenth-century Irish, a higher price of potatoes would have left them poorer and increased their demand for potatoes because potatoes were an inferior good. If the income effect of a price increase outweighs the substitution effect—as was conjectured for potatoes in nineteenth-century Ireland—a rise in price leads to an increase in the quantity demanded. As a result, the demand curve slopes upward and the law of demand does not hold.

In theory, Giffen goods can exist; but they have never been validated in any real situation, nineteenth-century Ireland included. So as a practical matter, it's not a subject we need to worry about when discussing the demand for most goods. Typically, income effects are important only for a very limited number of goods. Indeed, we will make the (usual) assumption that the substitution effect dominates the income effect. Therefore, the demand curve will be downward sloping even for inferior goods.

ECONOMICS > IN ACTION

MORTGAGE RATES AND CONSUMER DEMAND

Most people buy houses with mortgages—loans backed by the value of the house. The interest rates on such mortgages change over time; for example, they fell quite a lot over the period from 2000 to 2003. And in late 2012 and early 2013, mortgage interest rates reached their lowest levels in more than 50 years. When mortgage rates fall, the cost of housing falls for millions of people—even people who have mortgages at high interest rates are often able to "refinance" them at lower rates. The percentage of Canadian families who owned their homes increased from 65.8% in 2001 to a historical high of 69% in 2011. (It seems the financial crisis of 2008–2009 and the recession that followed only slowed the rise in the homeownership rate.)

It's not surprising that the demand for housing goes up when mortgage rates go down. Economists have noticed, however, that the demand for many other goods also rises when mortgage rates fall. Some of these goods are items connected with new or bigger houses, such as furniture. But people also buy new cars, eat more meals in restaurants, and take more vacations. Why?

The answer illustrates the distinction between substitution and income effects. When housing becomes cheaper, there is a *substitution effect:* people have an incentive to substitute housing in place of other goods in their consumption bundle. But housing also happens to be a good that absorbs a large part of consumer spending, with many families spending a quarter or more of their income on mortgage payments. So when the cost of housing falls, people are in effect richer—there is a significant *income effect.*

The increase in the quantity of housing demanded when mortgage rates fall is the result of both effects: housing becomes a better buy compared with other consumer goods, and people also buy more and bigger houses because they feel richer. And because they feel richer, they also buy more of all other normal goods, such as cars, restaurant meals, and vacations.

An unfortunate by-product of having mortgage interest rates so unusually low (and for so many years) is how many Canadians are getting themselves into financial difficulties. Low interest rates have encouraged more people to buy homes, perhaps more expensive homes than they can really afford, along with other purchases that can increase their level of consumer debt. It is not surprising to learn that, in the past decade, home prices have grown faster than incomes, and consumer debt (as a percent of after-tax income) has hit all-time highs.

Demand for housing goes up when mortgage rates go down. But so does the demand for exotic vacations.

CHECK YOUR UNDERSTANDING   10-4

1. In each of the following cases, state whether the income effect, the substitution effect, or both are significant. In which cases do they move in the same direction? In opposite directions? Why?
   a. Orange juice represents a small share of Clare's spending. She buys more lemonade and less orange juice when the price of orange juice goes up. She does not change her spending on other goods.
   b. Apartment rents have risen dramatically this year. Since rent absorbs a major part of her income, Delia moves to a smaller apartment. Assume that rental housing is a normal good.
   c. The cost of a semester-long meal ticket at the student cafeteria rises, representing a significant increase in living costs. Assume that cafeteria meals are an inferior good.

2. In the example described in Question 1c, how would you determine whether or not cafeteria meals are a Giffen good?

Solutions appear at back of book.

▼ Quick Review

- Most goods absorb only a small fraction of a consumer's spending. For such goods, the **substitution effect** of a price change is the only important effect of the price change on consumption. It causes individual demand curves and the market demand curve to slope downward.

- When a good absorbs a large fraction of a consumer's spending, the **income effect** of a price change is present in addition to the substitution effect.

- For normal goods, demand rises when a consumer becomes richer and falls when a consumer becomes poorer, so that the income effect reinforces the substitution effect. For inferior goods, demand rises when a consumer becomes poorer and falls when a consumer becomes richer, so that the income and substitution effects move in opposite directions. But we usually assume that the substitution effect dominates the income effect.

- The demand curve of a **Giffen good** slopes upward because it is an inferior good in which the income effect outweighs the substitution effect.

BUSINESS CASE : Having a Happy Meal at McDonald's

In July 2011, McDonald's announced that it would begin making its standard child's Happy Meal healthier. To be sure, healthier options were always available: a kid-size yogourt; juice or milk instead of a pop; a cup of apple slices instead of a small fries. But most people opted for the standard meal by default.

With healthier choices in a Happy Meal, McDonald's is aiming to lower the salt, sugar, fat, and calorie content. But it is still up to parents to choose the beverage (low-fat milk, apple juice, or a pop), and the snack (a serving of small fries or a cup of apple slices). According to restaurant analyst Peter Saleh, "This is good publicity, and if you sell more Happy Meals, you're selling more Big Macs to the parents."

In the fall of 2013, McDonald's announced that it would only list water, juice, and milk as the drink options for Happy Meals. They also promised to change advertising and packaging (so as to make healthier options more appealing to children) and to offer side salads, fruit, or vegetables as options in value meals that target teens and adults.

The changes are likely to help offset long-standing criticism of the company for the lack of nutritional balance in its menu and concerns over the growing epidemic of childhood obesity. In some U.S. cities, food advocates had proposed banning Happy Meals if they didn't meet certain nutritional standards. Critics say that the current changes are only a small first step in the right direction.

Long-time observers say that more than just countering its critics, McDonald's is trying to hold onto a loyal customer base: Happy Meals account for an estimated 10% of its annual sales, and a larger share of McDonald's profits. And the competition isn't standing still: Burger King, Pizza Pizza, Tim Hortons, White Spot, Swiss Chalet, Harvey's, the Pickle Barrel, and others have all made menu changes to address levels of trans fats and sodium in all of their meals, including popular kids' meals.

McDonald's has, in fact, been amazingly successful at keeping its customers happy even in a tough environment. In 2009, at the lowest point of the recession that began in 2008, sales at full-service restaurants fell about 1% but increased by more than 3% at fast-food outlets. These restaurants kept their sales up by offering discounts and promotions as well as $1 menus and cheap combination meals.

However, many fast-food chains, such as Burger King, KFC, Boston Pizza, Taco Bell, and Pizza Pizza, saw their sales fall during the recession. Some cut back their advertising spending as the much larger McDonald's increased its spending by 7% and increased its market share. And McDonald's has aggressively expanded its menus—from the healthier Happy Meals to the "McCafé" line of espresso drinks, smoothies, and exotically flavoured wraps.

Observers are divided as to whether McDonald's is earnestly attempting to get its customers to eat healthier food or is just engaging in advertising spin. One unknown is how customers will react: as one commenter said, "Salt may be bad for you, but it tastes great. … You can't demand that McDonald's or Burger King stop selling hamburgers and fries." In the same vein, one franchise owner noted, "Expect customers to try the apples and then revert to asking for fries."

QUESTIONS FOR THOUGHT

1. Give an example of a normal good and an inferior good mentioned in this case. Cite examples of substitution effects and income effects from the case.

2. To induce fast-food customers to eat more healthful meals, what alternatives are there to bans? Do you think these alternatives would work? Why or why not?

3. What do you think accounts for McDonald's success? Relate this to concepts discussed in the chapter.

SUMMARY

1. Consumers maximize a measure of satisfaction called **utility.** Each consumer has a **utility function** that determines the level of total utility generated by his or her **consumption bundle,** the goods and services that are consumed. We measure utility in hypothetical units called **utils.**

2. A good's or service's **marginal utility** is the additional utility generated by consuming one more unit of the good or service. We usually assume that the **principle of diminishing marginal utility** holds: consumption of another unit of a good or service yields less additional utility than the previous unit. As a result, the **marginal utility curve** slopes downward.

3. A **budget constraint** limits a consumer's spending to no more than his or her income. It defines the consumer's **consumption possibilities,** the set of all affordable consumption bundles. A consumer who spends all of his or her income will choose a consumption bundle on the **budget line.** An individual chooses the consumption bundle that maximizes total utility, the **optimal consumption bundle.**

4. We use marginal analysis to find the optimal consumption bundle by analyzing how to allocate the marginal dollar. According to the **utility-maximizing principle of marginal analysis,** at the optimal consumption bundle the **marginal utility per dollar** spent on each good and service—the marginal utility of a good divided by its price—is the same. The **optimal consumption rule** says (1) the optimal

consumption bundle is on the budget line; and (2) the marginal utility per dollar spent on each good in the bundle is equal.

5. Changes in the price of a good affect the quantity consumed in two possible ways: the **substitution effect** and the **income effect.** Most goods absorb only a small share of a consumer's spending; for these goods, only the substitution effect—buying less of the good that has become relatively more expensive and more of goods that are now relatively cheaper—is significant. It causes the individual and the market demand curves to slope downward. When a good absorbs a large fraction of spending, the income effect is also significant: an increase in a good's price makes a consumer poorer, but a decrease in price makes a consumer richer. This change in purchasing power makes consumers demand more or less of a good, depending on whether the good is normal or inferior. For normal goods, the substitution and income effects reinforce each other. For inferior goods, however, they work in opposite directions. The demand curve of a **Giffen good** slopes upward because it is an inferior good in which the income effect outweighs the substitution effect. However, data have never confirmed the existence of a Giffen good. Therefore, we usually assume the substitution effect dominates the income effect for inferior goods and thus the demand curve will slope downward.

KEY TERMS

Utility, p. 296
Consumption bundle, p. 296
Utility function, p. 296
Util, p. 296
Marginal utility, p. 297
Marginal utility curve, p. 297

Principle of diminishing marginal
 utility, p. 298
Budget constraint, p. 300
Consumption possibilities, p. 300
Budget line, p. 301
Optimal consumption bundle, p. 301
Marginal utility per dollar, p. 304

Utility-maximizing principle of
 marginal analysis, p. 307
Optimal consumption rule, p. 307
Substitution effect, p. 309
Income effect, p. 310
Giffen good, p. 310

PROBLEMS

1. For each of the following situations, decide whether Ali has increasing, constant, or diminishing marginal utility.

   a. The more economics classes Ali takes, the more he enjoys the subject. And the more classes he takes, the easier each one gets, making him enjoy each additional class even more than the one before.

   b. Ali likes loud music. In fact, according to him, "the louder, the better." Each time he turns the volume up a notch, he adds 5 utils to his total utility.

   c. Ali enjoys watching reruns of the old sitcom *Corner Gas*. He claims that these episodes are always funny, but he does admit that the more he sees an episode, the less funny it gets.

   d. Ali loves toasted marshmallows. The more he eats, however, the fuller he gets and the less he enjoys each additional marshmallow. And there is a point at which he becomes satiated: beyond that point, more marshmallows actually make him feel worse rather than better.

2. Use the concept of marginal utility to explain the following: Newspaper vending machines are designed so that once you have paid for one paper, you could take more than one paper at a time. But soft drink vending machines, once you have paid for one can of pop, dispense only one can of pop at a time.

3. Brenda likes to have bagels and coffee for breakfast. The accompanying table shows Brenda's total utility from various consumption bundles of bagels and coffee.

Consumption bundle		Total utility (utils)
Quantity of bagels	Quantity of coffee (cups)	
0	0	0
0	2	28
0	4	40
1	2	48
1	3	54
2	0	28
2	2	56
3	1	54
3	2	62
4	0	40
4	2	66

Suppose Brenda knows she will consume 2 cups of coffee for sure. However, she can choose to consume different quantities of bagels: she can choose either 0, 1, 2, 3, or 4 bagels.

a. Calculate Brenda's marginal utility from bagels as she goes from consuming 0 bagel to 1 bagel, from 1 bagel to 2 bagels, from 2 bagels to 3 bagels, and from 3 bagels to 4 bagels.

b. Draw Brenda's marginal utility curve of bagels. Does Brenda have increasing, diminishing, or constant marginal utility of bagels?

4. Brenda, the consumer in Problem 3, now has to make a decision about how many bagels and how much coffee to have for breakfast. She has $8 of income to spend on bagels and coffee. Use the information given in the table in Problem 3 to answer the following questions.

a. Bagels cost $2 each, and coffee costs $2 per cup. Which bundles are on Brenda's budget line? For each of these bundles, calculate the level of utility (in utils) that Brenda enjoys. Which bundle is her optimal bundle?

b. The price of bagels increases to $4, but the price of coffee remains at $2 per cup. Which bundles are now on Brenda's budget line? For each bundle, calculate Brenda's level of utility (in utils). Which bundle is her optimal bundle?

c. What do your answers to parts (a) and (b) imply about the slope of Brenda's demand curve for bagels? Describe the substitution effect and the income effect of this increase in the price of bagels, assuming that bagels are a normal good.

5. Bruno can spend his income on two different goods: Drake CDs and notebooks for his class notes. For each of the following three situations, decide if the given consumption bundle is within Bruno's consumption possibilities. Then decide if it lies on the budget line or not.

a. CDs cost $10 each, and notebooks cost $2 each. Bruno has income of $60. He is considering a consumption bundle containing 3 CDs and 15 notebooks.

b. CDs cost $10 each, and notebooks cost $5 each. Bruno has income of $110. He is considering a consumption bundle containing 3 CDs and 10 notebooks.

c. CDs cost $20 each, and notebooks cost $10 each. Bruno has income of $50. He is considering a consumption bundle containing 2 CDs and 2 notebooks.

6. Bruno, the consumer in Problem 5, is best friends with Bernie, who shares his love for notebooks and Drake CDs. The accompanying table shows Bernie's utilities from notebooks and Drake CDs.

Quantity of notebooks	Utility from notebooks (utils)	Quantity of CDs	Utility from CDs (utils)
0	0	0	0
2	70	1	80
4	130	2	150
6	180	3	210
8	220	4	260
10	250	5	300

The price of a notebook is $5, the price of a CD is $10, and Bernie has $50 of income to spend.

a. Which consumption bundles of notebooks and CDs can Bernie consume if he spends all his income? Illustrate Bernie's budget line with a diagram, putting notebooks on the horizontal axis and CDs on the vertical axis.

b. Calculate the marginal utility of each notebook and the marginal utility of each CD. Then calculate the marginal utility per dollar spent on notebooks and the marginal utility per dollar spent on CDs.

c. Draw a diagram like Figure 10-4 in which both the marginal utility per dollar spent on notebooks and the marginal utility per dollar spent on CDs are illustrated. Using this diagram and the utility-maximizing principle of marginal analysis, predict which bundle—from all the bundles on his budget line—Bernie will choose.

7. For each of the following situations, decide whether the bundle Lakshani is considering optimal or not. If it is not optimal, how could Lakshani improve her overall level of utility? That is, determine which good she should spend more on and which good should she spend less on.

a. Lakshani has $200 to spend on running shoes and sweaters. Running shoes cost $50 per pair, and sweaters cost $20 each. She is thinking about buying 2 pairs of running shoes and 5 sweaters. She tells her friend that the additional utility she would get from the second pair of running shoes is the same as the additional utility she would get from the fifth sweater.

b. Lakshani has $5 to spend on pens and pencils. Each pen costs $0.50 and each pencil costs $0.10. She is thinking about buying 6 pens and 20 pencils. The last pen would add five times as much to her total utility as the last pencil.

c. Lakshani has $50 per season to spend on tickets to football games and tickets to soccer games. Each football ticket costs $10 and each soccer ticket costs $5. She is thinking about buying 3 football tickets and 2 soccer tickets. Her marginal utility from the third football ticket is twice as much as her marginal utility from the second soccer ticket.

8. Cal "Cool" Cooper has $200 to spend on cellphones and sunglasses.

a. Each cellphone costs $100 and each pair of sunglasses costs $50. Which bundles lie on Cal's budget line? Draw a diagram like Figure 10-4 in which both the marginal utility per dollar spent on cellphones and the marginal utility per dollar spent on sunglasses are illustrated. Use this diagram and the optimal consumption rule to decide how Cal should allocate his money. That is, from all the bundles on his budget line, which bundle will Cal choose? The accompanying table gives his utility of cellphones and sunglasses.

Quantity of cellphones	Utility from cellphones (utils)	Quantity of sunglasses (pairs)	Utility from sunglasses (utils)
0	0	0	0
1	400	2	600
2	700	4	700

b. The price of cellphones falls to $50 each, but the price of sunglasses remains at $50 per pair. Which bundles lie on Cal's budget line? Draw a diagram like Figure 10-4 in which both the marginal utility per dollar spent on cellphones and the marginal utility per dollar spent on sunglasses are illustrated. Use this diagram and the utility-maximizing principle of marginal analysis to decide how Cal should allocate his money. That is, from all the bundles on his budget line, which bundle will Cal choose? The accompanying table gives his utility of cellphones and sunglasses.

Quantity of cellphones	Utility from cellphones (utils)	Quantity of sunglasses (pairs)	Utility from sunglasses (utils)
0	0	0	0
1	400	1	325
2	700	2	600
3	900	3	825
4	1000	4	700

c. How does Cal's consumption of cellphones change as the price of cellphones falls? In words, describe

the income effect and the substitution effect of this fall in the price of cellphones, assuming that cellphones are a normal good.

9. Damien Matthews is a busy actor. He allocates his free time to watching movies and working out at the gym. The accompanying table shows his utility from the number of times per week he watches a movie or goes to the gym.

Quantity of gym visits per week	Utility from gym visits (utils)	Quantity of movies per week	Utility from movies (utils)
1	100	1	60
2	180	2	110
3	240	3	150
4	280	4	180
5	310	5	190
6	330	6	195
7	340	7	197

Damien has 14 hours per week to spend on watching movies and going to the gym. Each movie takes 2 hours and each gym visit takes 2 hours. (*Hint:* Damien's free time is analogous to income he can spend. The hours needed for each activity are analogous to the price of that activity.)

a. Which bundles of gym visits and movies can Damien consume per week if he spends all his time either going to the gym or watching movies? Draw Damien's budget line in a diagram with gym visits on the horizontal axis and movies on the vertical axis.

b. Calculate the marginal utility of each gym visit and the marginal utility of each movie. Then calculate the marginal utility per hour spent at the gym and the marginal utility per hour spent watching movies.

c. Draw a diagram like Figure 10-4 in which both the marginal utility per hour spent at the gym and the marginal utility per hour spent watching movies are illustrated. Use this diagram and the utility-maximizing principle of marginal analysis to decide how Damien should allocate his time.

10. Anna Jenniferson is an actress who currently spends several hours each week watching movies and going to the gym. On the set of a new movie she meets Damien, the consumer in Problem 9. She tells him that she likes watching movies much more than going to the gym. In fact, she says that if she had to give up seeing 1 movie, she would need to go to the gym twice to make up for the loss in utility from not seeing the movie. A movie takes 2 hours, and a gym visit also lasts 2 hours. Damien tells Anna that she is not watching enough movies. Is he right?

11. Sven is a poor student who covers most of his dietary needs by eating cheap breakfast cereal, since it contains most of the important vitamins. As the price of cereal increases, he decides to buy even less of other foods and even more breakfast cereal to maintain his intake of important nutrients. This makes breakfast cereal a Giffen good for Sven. Describe in words the substitution effect and the income effect from this increase in the price of cereal. In which direction does each effect move, and why? What does this imply for the slope of Sven's demand curve for cereal?

12. In each of the following situations, describe the substitution effect and, if it is significant, the income effect. In which direction does each of these effects move? Why?

   a. Ed spends a large portion of his income on his children's education. Because tuition fees rise, one of his children has to withdraw from college.

   b. Homer spends much of his monthly income on home mortgage payments. The interest on his adjustable-rate mortgage falls, lowering his mortgage payments, and Homer decides to move to a larger house.

   c. Pam thinks that Spam is an inferior good. Yet as the price of Spam rises, she decides to buy less of it.

13. Restaurant meals and housing (measured in the number of rooms) are the only two goods that Neha buys. She has income of $1000. Initially, she buys a consumption bundle such that she spends exactly half her income on restaurant meals and the other half of her income on housing. Then her income increases by 50%, but the price of restaurant meals increases by 100% (it doubles). The price of housing remains the same. After these changes, if she wanted to, could Neha still buy the same consumption bundle as before?

14. Scott finds that the higher the price of orange juice, the more money he spends on orange juice. Does that mean that Scott has discovered a Giffen good?

15. Margo's marginal utility of one dance lesson is 100 utils per lesson. Her marginal utility of a new pair of dance shoes is 300 utils per pair. The price of a dance lesson is $50 per lesson. She currently spends all her income, and she buys her optimal consumption bundle. What is the price of a pair of dance shoes?

16. According to Statistics Canada, the average retail price of a litre of regular gasoline in Regina, Saskatchewan rose from $0.547 in 1990 to $1.217 in 2011, a 122% increase.

   a. Other things equal, describe the effect of this price increase on the quantity of gasoline demanded. In your explanation, make use of the utility-maximizing principle of marginal analysis and describe income and substitution effects.

In fact, however, other things were not equal. Over the same time period, the prices of other goods and services rose as well. According to Statistics Canada, the overall price of a bundle of goods and services consumed by an average consumer in Regina rose by 63% (from 1990 to 2011).

   b. Taking into account the rise in the price of gasoline and in overall prices, other things equal, describe the effect on the quantity of gasoline demanded.

However, this is not the end of the story. Between 1990 and 2011, the typical consumer's nominal income increased, too: Statistics Canada reports that in Saskatchewan, average household nominal after-tax and transfer income rose from $30 300 in 1990 to $47 100 in 2011, an increase of 55%.

   c. Taking into account the rise in the price of gasoline, in overall prices, and in consumers' incomes, describe the effect on the quantity of gasoline demanded.

17. Sometimes, consumers might purchase goods not because of their particular functionality but rather for the social status associated with owning these goods. In economics, we call these goods *positional goods* as they serve as status symbols. Luxury homes, cars, jewellery, designer clothing, and other luxury goods and services can be considered positional goods.

   a. Why would consumers purchase these goods? (*Hint:* Take luxury automobiles as an example. If you just want a means of transportation, then any car should do.)

   b. Are the consumers of positional goods acting rationally or irrationally? Why is that so?

Consumer Preferences and Consumer Choice

Different people have different preferences. But even given an individual's preferences, there may be different consumption bundles—different combinations of the goods and services an individual consumes—that yield the same total utility. This insight leads to the concept of *indifference curves*, a useful way to represent individual preferences. In this appendix, we will look closely at indifference curves.

In addition, the total level of utility an individual can obtain depends not only on income but also on prices—and that both income and prices affect consumer's feasible and optimal choices. We will apply this more complete analysis of consumer choice to the important distinction between *complements* and *substitutes*. Finally, we will use this insight to examine further the *income* and *substitution effects* we covered briefly in Chapter 10.

But, let's begin with indifference curves.

Mapping the Utility Function

In Chapter 10 we introduced the concept of a utility function, which determines a consumer's total utility given his or her consumption bundle. In Figure 10-1 we saw how Cassie's total utility changed as we changed the quantity of fried wings consumed, holding fixed the quantities of other items in her bundle. That is, in Figure 10-1 we showed how total utility changed as consumption of only *one* good changed. But we also learned in Chapter 10, from our example of Sammy, that finding the optimal consumption bundle involves the problem of how to allocate the last dollar spent between *two* goods, wings and potatoes. In this appendix we will extend the analysis by learning how to express total utility as a function of consumption of two goods. In this way we will deepen our understanding of the trade-off involved when choosing the optimal consumption bundle and of how the optimal consumption bundle itself changes in response to changes in the prices of goods. In order to do that, we now turn to a different way of representing a consumer's utility function, based on the concept of *indifference curves*.

Indifference Curves

Ingrid is a consumer who buys only two goods: housing, measured in the number of rooms, and restaurant meals. How can we represent her utility function in a way that takes account of her consumption of both goods?

One way is to draw a three-dimensional picture. Figure 10A-1 shows a three-dimensional "total utility hill." The distance along the horizontal axis measures the quantity of housing Ingrid consumes in terms of numbers of rooms; the distance along the vertical axis measures the number of restaurant meals she consumes. The altitude or height of the hill at each point is indicated by a contour line, along which the height of the hill is constant. For example, point *A*, which corresponds to a consumption bundle of 3 rooms and 30 restaurant meals, lies on the contour line labelled 450. So the total utility Ingrid receives from consuming 3 rooms and 30 restaurant meals is 450 utils.

A three-dimensional picture like Figure 10A-1 helps us think about the relationship between consumption bundles and total utility. But anyone who has ever

FIGURE **10A-1** Ingrid's Utility Function

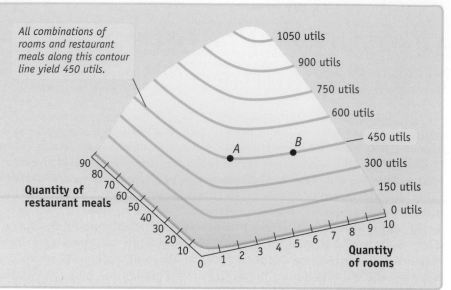

The three-dimensional hill shows how Ingrid's total utility depends on her consumption of housing and restaurant meals. Point A corresponds to consumption of 3 rooms and 30 restaurant meals. That consumption bundle yields Ingrid 450 utils, corresponding to the height of the hill at point A. The lines running around the hill are contour lines, along which the height is constant. So every point on a given contour line generates the same level of utility.

All combinations of rooms and restaurant meals along this contour line yield 450 utils.

used a topographical map to plan a hiking trip knows that it is possible to represent a three-dimensional surface in only two dimensions. A topographical map doesn't offer a three-dimensional view of the terrain; instead, it conveys information about altitude solely through the use of contour lines.

The same principle can be applied to representing the utility function. In Figure 10A-2, Ingrid's consumption of rooms is measured on the horizontal axis and her consumption of restaurant meals on the vertical axis. The curve here corresponds to the contour line in Figure 10A-1, drawn at a total utility of 450 utils. This curve shows all the consumption bundles that yield a total utility of 450 utils. One point on that contour line is A, a consumption bundle consisting of 3 rooms and 30 restaurant meals. Another point on that contour line is B, a consumption bundle

FIGURE **10A-2** An Indifference Curve

An indifference curve is a contour line along which total utility is constant. In this case, we show all the consumption bundles that yield Ingrid 450 utils. Consumption bundle A, consisting of 3 rooms and 30 restaurant meals, yields the same total utility as bundle B, consisting of 6 rooms and 15 restaurant meals. That is, Ingrid is indifferent between bundle A and bundle B.

consisting of 6 rooms but only 15 restaurant meals. Because *B* lies on the same contour line, it yields Ingrid the same total utility—450 utils—as *A*. We say that Ingrid is *indifferent* between *A* and *B:* because bundles *A* and *B* yield the same total utility level, Ingrid is equally well off with either bundle.

A contour line that maps all the consumption bundles yielding the same amount of total utility is known as an **indifference curve.** An individual is always indifferent between any two bundles that lie on the same indifference curve. For a given consumer, there is an indifference curve corresponding to each possible level of total utility. For example, the indifference curve in Figure 10A-2 shows consumption bundles that yield Ingrid 450 utils; different indifference curves would show consumption bundles that yield Ingrid 400 utils, 500 utils, and so on.

A collection of indifference curves that represents a given consumer's entire utility function, with each indifference curve corresponding to a different level of total utility, is known as an **indifference curve map.** Figure 10A-3 shows three indifference curves—*I*₁, *I*₂, and *I*₃—from Ingrid's indifference curve map, as well as several consumption bundles, *A*, *B*, *C*, and *D*. The accompanying table lists each bundle, its composition of rooms and restaurant meals, and the total utility it yields. Because bundles *A* and *B* generate the same number of utils, 450, they lie on the same indifference curve, *I*₂. Although Ingrid is indifferent between *A* and *B*, she is certainly not indifferent between *A* and *C:* as you can see from the table, *C* generates only 391 utils, a lower total utility than *A* or *B*. So Ingrid prefers consumption bundles *A* and *B* to bundle *C*. This is represented by the fact that *C* is on indifference curve *I*₁, and *I*₁ lies below *I*₂. Bundle *D*, though, generates 519 utils, a higher total utility than *A* and *B*. It is on *I*₃, an indifference curve that lies above *I*₂. Clearly, Ingrid prefers *D* to either *A* or *B*. And, even more strongly, she prefers *D* to *C*.

An **indifference curve** is a line that shows all the consumption bundles that yield the same amount of total utility for an individual.

The entire utility function of an individual can be represented by an **indifference curve map,** a collection of indifference curves in which each curve corresponds to a different total utility level.

FIGURE **10A-3** An Indifference Curve Map

The utility function can be represented in greater detail by increasing the number of indifference curves drawn, each corresponding to a different level of total utility. In this figure bundle *C* lies on an indifference curve corresponding to a total utility of 391 utils. As in Figure 10A-2, bundles *A* and *B* lie on an indifference curve corresponding to a total utility of 450 utils. Bundle *D* lies on an indifference curve corresponding to a total utility of 519 utils. Ingrid prefers any bundle on *I*₂ to any bundle on *I*₁, and she prefers any bundle on *I*₃ to any bundle on *I*₂.

Properties of Indifference Curves

No two individuals have the same indifference curve map because no two individuals have the same preferences. But economists believe that, regardless of the person, every indifference curve map has two general properties. These are illustrated in panel (a) of Figure 10A-4:

- *Indifference curves never cross.* Suppose that we tried to draw an indifference curve map like the one depicted in the left diagram in panel (a), in which two indifference curves cross at *A*. What is the total utility at *A*? Is it 100 utils or

FIGURE 10A-4 Properties of Indifference Curves

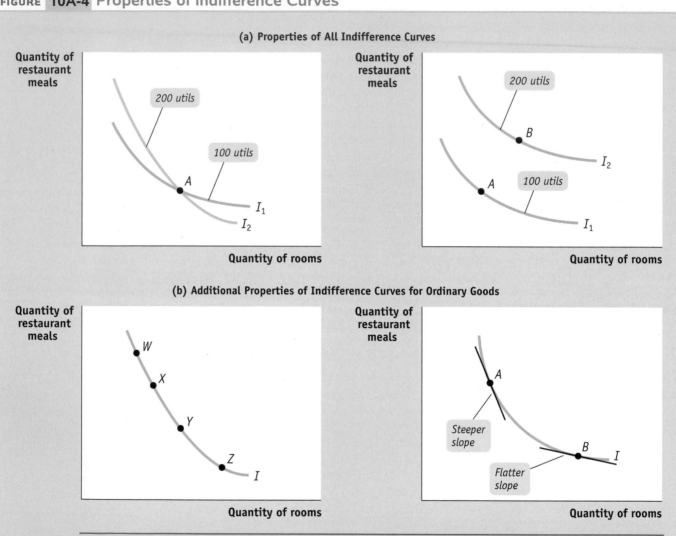

Panel (a) represents two general properties that all indifference curves share. The left diagram shows why indifference curves cannot cross: if they did, a consumption bundle such as *A* would yield both 100 and 200 utils, a contradiction. The right diagram of panel (a) shows that indifference curves that are farther out yield higher total utility: bundle *B*, which contains more of both goods than bundle *A*, yields higher total utility. Panel (b) depicts two additional properties of indifference curves for ordinary goods. The left diagram of

panel (b) shows that indifference curves slope downward: as you move down the curve from bundle *W* to bundle *Z*, consumption of rooms increases. To keep total utility constant, this must be offset by a reduction in quantity of restaurant meals. The right diagram of panel (b) shows a strictly convex-shaped indifference curve. The slope of the indifference curve gets flatter as you move down the curve to the right, a feature arising from diminishing marginal utility.

200 utils? Indifference curves cannot cross because each consumption bundle must correspond to a unique total utility level—not, as shown at *A*, two different total utility levels.

- *The farther out an indifference curve lies—the farther it is from the origin—the higher the level of total utility it indicates.* The reason, illustrated in the right diagram in panel (a), is that we assume that more is better than less—we consider only the consumption bundles for which the consumer is not satiated. Bundle *B*, on the outer indifference curve, contains more of both goods than bundle *A* on the inner indifference curve. So *B*, because it generates a higher total utility level (200 utils), lies on a higher indifference curve than *A*.

Furthermore, economists believe that, for most goods, consumers' indifference curve maps also have two additional properties. They are illustrated in panel (b) of Figure 10A-4:

- *Indifference curves slope downward.* Here, too, the reason is that more is better than less. The left diagram in panel (b) shows four consumption bundles on the same indifference curve: *W*, *X*, *Y*, and *Z*. By definition, these consumption bundles yield the same level of total utility. But as you move along the curve to the right, from *W* to *Z*, the quantity of rooms consumed increases. The only way a person can consume more rooms without gaining utility is by giving up some restaurant meals. So the indifference curve must slope downward.

- *Indifference curves have a convex shape.* The right diagram in panel (b) shows that the slope of each indifference curve changes as you move down the curve to the right: the curve gets flatter. If you move up an indifference curve to the left, the curve gets steeper. So the indifference curve is steeper at *A* than it is at *B*. When this occurs, we say that an indifference curve has a strictly *convex* shape—it is bowed-in toward the origin. This feature arises from diminishing marginal utility, a principle we discussed in Chapter 10. Recall that when a consumer has diminishing marginal utility, consumption of another unit of a good generates a smaller increase in total utility than the previous unit consumed. In the next section, we will examine in detail how diminishing marginal utility gives rise to strictly convex-shaped indifference curves.[1]

Goods that satisfy all four properties of indifference curve maps are called *ordinary goods*. The vast majority of goods in any consumer's utility function fall into this category. In the next section, we will define ordinary goods and see the key role that diminishing marginal utility plays for them.

Indifference Curves and Consumer Choice

At the beginning of the last section, we used indifference curves to represent the preferences of Ingrid, whose consumption bundles consist of rooms and restaurant meals. Our next step is to show how to use Ingrid's indifference curve map to find her utility-maximizing consumption bundle given her budget constraint, the fact that she must choose a consumption bundle that costs no more than her total income.

---

[1] Indifference curves do not have to be strictly convex (i.e., bowed toward the origin) or smooth. For example, a person's preferences could treat two goods as perfect substitutes, such as three sliders being equivalent to one hamburger, which makes linear indifference curves that are convex, but not strictly convex. Alternatively, if a person views two goods as perfect complements, always consuming them in fixed proportions, their indifference curves would be L-shaped and convex, but not smooth. We'll see examples of these indifference curves later in this appendix.

It's important to understand how our analysis here relates to what we did in Chapter 10. We are not offering a new theory of consumer behaviour in this appendix—just as in Chapter 10, consumers are assumed to maximize total utility. In particular, we know that consumers will follow the *optimal consumption rule* from Chapter 10: the optimal consumption bundle lies on the budget line, and the marginal utility per dollar is the same for every good in that bundle.

But as we'll see shortly, we can derive this optimal consumer behaviour in a somewhat different way—a way that yields deeper insights into consumer choice.

The Marginal Rate of Substitution

The first element of our approach is a new concept, the *marginal rate of substitution*. The essence of this concept is illustrated in Figure 10A-5.

Recall from the last section that for most goods, consumers' indifference curves are downward sloping and strictly convex. Figure 10A-5 shows such an indifference curve. The points labelled *V, W, X, Y,* and *Z* all lie on this indifference curve—that is, they represent consumption bundles that yield Ingrid the same level of total utility. The table accompanying the figure shows the components of each of the bundles. As we move along the indifference curve from *V* to *Z*, Ingrid's consumption of housing steadily increases from 2 rooms to 6 rooms, her consumption of restaurant meals steadily decreases from 30 meals to 10 meals, and her total utility is kept constant. As we move down such a strictly convex indifference curve, then, Ingrid is trading more of one good in place of less of the other, with the *terms* of that trade-off—the ratio of additional rooms consumed to restaurant meals sacrificed—chosen to keep her total utility constant.

FIGURE **10A-5** **The Changing Slope of an Indifference Curve**

This indifference curve is downward sloping and strictly convex, implying that restaurant meals and rooms are ordinary goods for Ingrid. As Ingrid moves down along her indifference curve from *V* to *Z*, she trades reduced consumption of restaurant meals for increased consumption of housing. However, the terms of that trade-off change. As she moves from *V* to *W*, she is willing to give up 10 restaurant meals in return for 1 more room. As her consumption of rooms rises and her consumption of restaurant meals falls, she is willing to give up fewer restaurant meals in return for each additional room. The flattening of the slope as you move from left to right arises from diminishing marginal utility.

Notice that the quantity of restaurant meals that Ingrid is willing to give up in return for an additional room changes along the indifference curve. As we move from V to W, housing consumption rises from 2 to 3 rooms and restaurant meal consumption falls from 30 to 20—a trade-off of 10 restaurant meals for 1 additional room. But as we move from Y to Z, housing consumption rises from 5 to 6 rooms and restaurant meal consumption falls from 12 to 10, a trade-off of only 2 restaurant meals for an additional room.

To put it in terms of slopes, the slope of the indifference curve between V and W is -10: the change in restaurant meal consumption, -10, divided by the change in housing consumption, 1. Similarly, the slope of the indifference curve between Y and Z is -2. So the indifference curve gets flatter as we move down it to the right—that is, it has a strictly convex shape, one of the four properties of an indifference curve for ordinary goods.

Why does the trade-off change in this way? Let's think about it intuitively, and then work through it more carefully. When Ingrid moves down along her indifference curve, whether from V to W or from Y to Z, she gains utility from her additional consumption of housing but loses an equal amount of utility from her reduced consumption of restaurant meals. But at each step, the initial position from which Ingrid begins is different. At V, Ingrid consumes only a small quantity of rooms; because of diminishing marginal utility, her marginal utility per room at that point is high. At V, then, an additional room adds a lot to Ingrid's total utility. But at V she already consumes a large quantity of restaurant meals, so her marginal utility of restaurant meals is low at that point. This means that, at V, it takes a large reduction in her quantity of restaurant meals consumed to offset the increased utility she gets from the extra room of housing.

At Y, in contrast, Ingrid consumes a much larger quantity of rooms and a much smaller quantity of restaurant meals than at V. This means that an additional room adds fewer utils, and a restaurant meal forgone costs more utils, than at V. So Ingrid is willing to give up fewer restaurant meals in return for another room of housing at Y (where she gives up 2 meals for 1 room) than she is at V (where she gives up 10 meals for 1 room).

Now let's express the same idea—that the trade-off Ingrid is willing to make depends on where she is starting from—by using a little math. We do this by examining how the slope of the indifference curve changes as we move down it. Moving down along the indifference curve—reducing restaurant meal consumption and increasing housing consumption—will produce two opposing effects on Ingrid's total utility: lower restaurant meal consumption will reduce her total utility, but higher housing consumption will raise her total utility. And since we are moving down along the indifference curve, these two effects must exactly cancel out:

Along the indifference curve:
(10A-1) (Change in total utility due to lower restaurant meal consumption) +
(Change in total utility due to higher housing consumption) = 0

or, rearranging terms,

Along the indifference curve:
(10A-2) −(Change in total utility due to lower restaurant meal consumption) =
(Change in total utility due to higher housing consumption)

Let's now focus on what happens as we move only a short distance down the indifference curve, trading off a small increase in housing consumption in place of a small decrease in restaurant meal consumption. Following our notation from Chapter 10, let's use MU_R and MU_M to represent the marginal utility of rooms and restaurant meals, respectively, and ΔQ_R and ΔQ_M to represent the changes in room and meal consumption, respectively. In general, the change in total utility caused by a small change in consumption of a good is equal to the change in consumption multiplied by the *marginal utility* of that good. This means that we can calculate the change in Ingrid's total utility generated by a change in her consumption bundle using the following equations:

(10A-3) Change in total utility due to a change in restaurant meal consumption = $MU_M \times \Delta Q_M$

and

(10A-4) Change in total utility due to a change in housing consumption = $MU_R \times \Delta Q_R$

So we can write Equation 10A-2 in symbols as:

Along the indifference curve:
(10A-5) $-MU_M \times \Delta Q_M = MU_R \times \Delta Q_R$

Note that the left-hand side of Equation 10A-5 has a minus sign; it represents the loss in total utility from decreased restaurant meal consumption. This must equal the gain in total utility from increased room consumption, represented by the right-hand side of the equation.

What we want to know is how this translates into the slope of the indifference curve. To find the slope, we divide both sides of Equation 10A-5 by ΔQ_R, and again by $-MU_M$, in order to get the ΔQ_M, ΔQ_R terms on one side and the MU_R, MU_M terms on the other. This results in:

Slope along the indifference curve:
(10A-6) $\dfrac{\Delta Q_M}{\Delta Q_R} = -\dfrac{MU_R}{MU_M}$

The left-hand side of Equation 10A-6 is the slope of the indifference curve; it is the rate at which Ingrid is willing to trade rooms (the good on the horizontal axis) in place of restaurant meals (the good on the vertical axis) without changing her total utility level. The right-hand side of Equation 10A-6 is minus the ratio of the marginal utility of rooms to the marginal utility of restaurant meals—that is, the ratio of what she gains from one more room to what she gains from one more meal.

Putting all this together, we see that Equation 10A-6 shows that, along the indifference curve, the quantity of restaurant meals Ingrid is willing to give up in return for a room, $\Delta Q_M/\Delta Q_R$, is exactly equal to minus the ratio of the marginal utility of a room to that of a meal, $-MU_R/MU_M$. Only when this condition is met will her total utility level remain constant as she consumes more rooms and fewer restaurant meals.

Economists have a special name for the ratio of the marginal utilities found in the right-hand side of Equation 10A-6: it is called the **marginal rate of substitution,** or **MRS,** of rooms (the good on the horizontal axis) in place of restaurant meals (the good on the vertical axis). That's because as we slide down Ingrid's indifference curve, we are substituting more rooms in place of fewer restaurant meals in her consumption bundle. As we'll see shortly, the marginal rate of substitution plays an important role in finding the optimal consumption bundle.

Recall that indifference curves get flatter as you move down them to the right. The reason, as we've just discussed, is diminishing marginal utility: as Ingrid consumes more housing and fewer restaurant meals, her marginal utility from housing falls and her marginal utility from restaurant meals rises. So her marginal rate of substitution, which is equal to minus the slope of her indifference curve, falls as she moves down along the indifference curve.

The flattening of indifference curves as you slide down them to the right—which reflects the same logic as the principle of diminishing marginal utility—is known

The **marginal rate of substitution,** or **MRS,** of good R in place of good M is equal to MU_R/MU_M, the ratio of the marginal utility of R to the marginal utility of M.

as the principle of **diminishing marginal rate of substitution.** It says that an individual who consumes only a little bit of good A and a lot of good B will be willing to trade off a lot of B in return for one more unit of A; an individual who already consumes a lot of A and not much B will be less willing to make that trade-off.

We can illustrate this point by referring back to Figure 10A-5. At point V, a bundle with a high proportion of restaurant meals to rooms, Ingrid is willing to forgo 10 restaurant meals in return for 1 room. But at point Y, a bundle with a low proportion of restaurant meals to rooms, she is willing to forgo only 2 restaurant meals in return for 1 room.

From this example we can see that, in Ingrid's utility function, rooms and restaurant meals possess the two additional properties that characterize ordinary goods. Ingrid requires additional rooms to compensate her for the loss of a meal, and vice versa; so her indifference strictly curves for these two goods slope downward. And her indifference curves are strictly convex: the slope of her indifference curve—*minus* the marginal rate of substitution—becomes flatter as we move down it. In fact, an indifference curve is strictly convex only when it has diminishing marginal rate of substitution—these two conditions are equivalent.

With this information, we can define **ordinary goods,** which account for the great majority of goods in any consumer's utility function. A pair of goods are ordinary goods in a consumer's utility function if they possess two properties: the consumer requires more of one good to compensate for less of the other, and the consumer experiences a diminishing marginal rate of substitution when substituting one good in place of the other.

Next we will see how to determine Ingrid's optimal consumption bundle using indifference curves.

> The principle of **diminishing marginal rate of substitution** states that the more of good R a person consumes in proportion to good M, the less M he or she is willing to substitute for another unit of R.
>
> Two goods, R and M, are **ordinary goods** in a consumer's utility function when (1) the consumer requires additional units of R to compensate for less M, and vice versa; and (2) the consumer experiences a diminishing marginal rate of substitution when substituting one good in place of another.

The Tangency Condition

Now let's put some of Ingrid's indifference curves on the same diagram as her budget line, to illustrate an alternative way of representing her optimal consumption choice. Figure 10A-6 shows Ingrid's budget line, BL, when her income is $2400 per month, housing costs $150 per room each month, and restaurant meals cost $30 each. What is her optimal consumption bundle?

FIGURE 10A-6 The Optimal Consumption Bundle

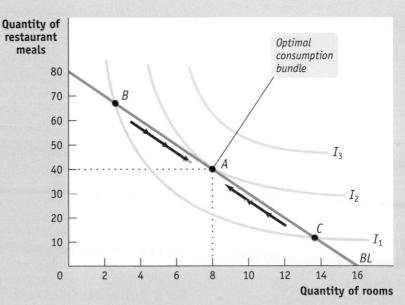

The budget line, BL, shows Ingrid's possible consumption bundles given an income of $2400 per month, when rooms cost $150 per month and restaurant meals cost $30 each. I_1, I_2, and I_3 are indifference curves. Consumption bundles such as B and C are not optimal because Ingrid can move to a higher indifference curve. The optimal (or utility-maximizing) consumption bundle is A, where the budget line is just tangent to the highest possible indifference curve.

The **tangency condition** between the indifference curve and the budget line holds when the indifference curve and the budget line just touch. This condition determines the optimal consumption bundle when the indifference curves have the typical strictly convex shape.

To answer this question, we show several of Ingrid's indifference curves: I_1, I_2, and I_3. Ingrid would like to achieve the total utility level represented by I_3, the highest of the three curves, but she cannot afford to because she is constrained by her income: no consumption bundle on her budget line yields that much total utility. But she shouldn't settle for the level of total utility generated by B, which lies on I_1: there are other bundles on her budget line, such as A, that clearly yield higher total utility than B.

In fact, A—a consumption bundle consisting of 8 rooms and 40 restaurant meals per month—is Ingrid's optimal consumption choice. The reason is that A lies on the highest indifference curve Ingrid can reach given her income.

At the optimal consumption bundle A, Ingrid's budget line *just touches* the relevant indifference curve—the budget line is *tangent* to the indifference curve. This **tangency condition** between the indifference curve and the budget line applies to the optimal consumption bundle when the indifference curves have the typical strictly convex shape: *at the optimal consumption bundle, the budget line just touches—is tangent to—the indifference curve.*

To see why, let's look more closely at how we know that a consumption bundle that *doesn't* satisfy the tangency condition can't be optimal. Re-examining Figure 10A-6, we can see that the consumption bundles B and C are both affordable because they lie on the budget line. However, neither is optimal. Both of them lie on the indifference curve I_1, which cuts through the budget line at both points. But because I_1 cuts through the budget line, Ingrid can do better: she can move down the budget line from B or up the budget line from C, as indicated by the arrows. In each case, this allows her to get onto a higher indifference curve, I_2, which increases her total utility.

Ingrid cannot, however, do any better than I_2: any other indifference curve either cuts through her budget line or doesn't touch it at all. And the bundle that allows her to achieve I_2 is, of course, her optimal consumption bundle.

The Slope of the Budget Line

Figure 10A-6 shows us how to use a graph of the budget line and the indifference curves to find the optimal consumption bundle, the bundle at which the budget line and the indifference curve are tangent. But rather than rely on drawing graphs, we can determine the optimal consumption bundle by using a bit of math. As you can see from Figure 10A-6, at A, the optimal consumption bundle, the budget line and the indifference curve have the same slope. Why? Because two curves can only touch each other if they have the same slope at their point of tangency. Otherwise, they would cross each other somewhere. And we know that if we are on an indifference curve that crosses the budget line (like I_1 in Figure 10A-6), we can't be on the indifference curve that contains the optimal consumption bundle (like I_2).

So we can use information about the slopes of the budget line and the indifference curve to find the optimal consumption bundle. To do that, we must first analyze the slope of the budget line, a fairly straightforward task. We know that Ingrid will get the highest possible utility by spending all of her income and consuming a bundle on her budget line. So we can represent Ingrid's budget line, the consumption bundles available to her when she spends all of her income, with the equation:

(10A-7) $(Q_R \times P_R) + (Q_M \times P_M) = N$

where N stands for Ingrid's income. To find the slope of the budget line, we divide its vertical intercept (where the budget line hits the vertical axis) by its horizontal intercept (where it hits the horizontal axis). The vertical intercept is the point at which Ingrid spends all her income on restaurant meals and none on housing (that is, $Q_R = 0$). In that case the number of restaurant meals she consumes is:

(10A-8) $Q_M = N/P_M = \$2400/(\$30 \text{ per meal}) = 80 \text{ meals}$
$= \text{Vertical intercept of budget line}$

At the other extreme, Ingrid spends all her income on housing and none on restaurant meals (so that $Q_M = 0$). This means that at the horizontal intercept of the budget line, the number of rooms she consumes is:

(10A-9) $Q_R = N/P_R = \$2400/(\$150 \text{ per room}) = 16 \text{ rooms}$
$\qquad\qquad = \text{Horizontal intercept of budget line}$

Now we have the information needed to find the slope of the budget line. It is:

(10A-10) Slope of budget line $= -(\text{Vertical intercept})/(\text{Horizontal intercept})$

$$= -\frac{\dfrac{N}{P_M}}{\dfrac{N}{P_R}} = -\frac{P_R}{P_M}$$

Notice the minus sign in Equation 10A-10; it's there because the budget line slopes downward. The quantity P_R/P_M is known as the **relative price** of rooms in terms of restaurant meals, to distinguish it from an ordinary price in terms of dollars. Because buying one more room requires Ingrid to give up P_R/P_M quantity of restaurant meals, or 5 meals, we can interpret the relative price P_R/P_M as the rate at which a room trades for restaurant meals in the market; it is the price—in terms of restaurant meals—Ingrid has to "pay" to get one more room.

Looking at this another way, the slope of the budget line—minus the relative price—tells us the opportunity cost of each good in terms of the other. The relative price illustrates the opportunity cost to an individual of consuming one more unit of one good in terms of how much of the other good in his or her consumption bundle must be forgone. This opportunity cost arises from the consumer's limited resources—his or her limited budget. It's useful to note that Equations 10A-8, 10A-9, and 10A-10 give us all the information we need about what happens to the budget line when relative price or income changes. From Equations 10A-8 and 10A-9 we can see that a change in income, N, leads to a parallel shift of the budget line: both the vertical and horizontal intercepts will shift. That is, how far out the budget line is from the origin depends on the consumer's income. If a consumer's income rises, the budget line moves outward. If the consumer's income shrinks, the budget line shifts inward. In each case, the slope of the budget line stays the same because the relative price of one good in terms of the other does not change.

In contrast, a change in the relative price P_R/P_M will lead to a change in the slope of the budget line. We'll analyze these changes in the budget line and how the optimal consumption bundle changes when the relative price changes or when income changes in greater detail later in the appendix.

Prices and the Marginal Rate of Substitution

Now we're ready to bring together the slope of the budget line and the slope of the indifference curve to find the optimal consumption bundle. From Equation 10A-6, we know that the slope of the indifference curve at any point is equal to minus the marginal rate of substitution:

(10A-11) Slope of indifference curve $= -\dfrac{MU_R}{MU_M}$

As we've already noted, at the optimal consumption bundle the slope of the budget line and the slope of the indifference curve are equal. We can write this formally by putting Equations 10A-10 and 10A-11 together, which gives us the **relative price rule** for finding the optimal consumption bundle:

The **relative price** of good R in terms of good M is equal to P_R/P_M, the rate at which R trades for M in the market. It equals the number of units of good M that must be traded in the market to obtain one more unit of good R.

The **relative price rule** says that at the optimal consumption bundle, the marginal rate of substitution between two goods is equal to their relative price.

At the optimal consumption bundle:

$$(10A\text{-}12) \quad -\frac{MU_R}{MU_M} = -\frac{P_R}{P_M} \quad \text{or} \quad \frac{MU_R}{MU_M} = \frac{P_R}{P_M}$$

That is, at the optimal consumption bundle, the marginal rate of substitution between any two goods is equal to the ratio of their prices. Or to put it in a more intuitive way, at Ingrid's optimal consumption bundle, the rate at which she would trade a room in exchange for having fewer restaurant meals along her indifference curve, MU_R/MU_M, is equal to the rate at which rooms are traded for restaurant meals in the market, P_R/P_M.

What would happen if this equality did not hold? We can see by examining Figure 10A-7. There, at point *B*, the slope of the indifference curve, $-MU_R/MU_M$, is greater in absolute value than the slope of the budget line, $-P_R/P_M$. This means that, at *B*, Ingrid values an additional room in place of meals *more* than it costs her to buy an additional room and forgo some meals. As a result, Ingrid would be better off moving down along her budget line toward *A*, consuming more rooms and fewer restaurant meals—and because of that, *B* could not have been her optimal bundle! Likewise, at *C*, the slope of Ingrid's indifference curve is less than the slope of the budget line. The implication is that, at *C*, Ingrid values additional meals in place of a room *more* than it costs her to buy additional meals and forgo a room. Again, Ingrid would be better off moving up along her budget line—consuming more restaurant meals and fewer rooms—until she reaches *A*, her optimal consumption bundle.

But suppose that we do the following transformation to the last term of Equation 10A-12: divide both sides by P_R and multiply both by MU_M. Then the relative price rule becomes (from Chapter 10, Equation 10-3):

Optimal consumption rule:

$$(10A\text{-}13) \quad \frac{MU_R}{P_R} = \frac{MU_M}{P_M}$$

So using either the optimal consumption rule (from Chapter 10) or the relative price rule (from this appendix), we find the same optimal consumption bundle. At the optimal consumption bundle, not only do Equations 10A-12 and 10A-13 hold, but also the budget constraint Equation 10A-7 must hold, since the bundle

---

FIGURE **10A-7** Understanding the Relative Price Rule

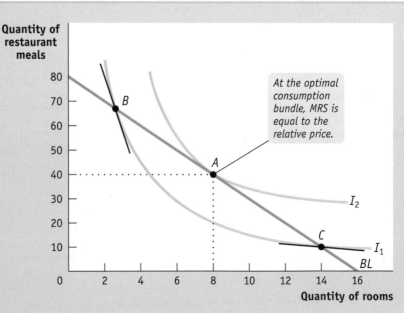

The *relative price* of rooms in terms of restaurant meals is equal to minus the slope of the budget line. The *marginal rate of substitution* of rooms in place of restaurant meals is equal to minus the slope of the indifference curve. The *relative price rule* says that at the optimal consumption bundle, the marginal rate of substitution must equal the relative price. This point can be demonstrated by considering what happens when the marginal rate of substitution is not equal to the relative price. At consumption bundle *B*, the marginal rate of substitution is larger than the relative price; Ingrid can increase her total utility by moving down along her budget line, *BL*. At *C*, the marginal rate of substitution is smaller than the relative price, and Ingrid can increase her total utility by moving up the budget line. Only at *A*, where the relative price rule holds, is her total utility maximized given her budget constraint.

is on the budget line. So the budget constraint and the indifference curves have the same slope at the optimal consumption bundle.

Preferences and Choices

Now that we have seen how to represent optimal consumption choice in an indifference curve diagram, we can turn briefly to the relationship between consumer preferences and consumer choices.

When we say that two consumers have different preferences, we mean that they have different utility functions. This in turn means that they will have indifference curve maps with different shapes. And those different maps will translate into different optimal consumption choices, even among consumers with the same income and who face the same prices.

To see this, suppose that Ingrid's friend Lars also consumes only housing and restaurant meals. However, Lars has a stronger preference for restaurant meals and a weaker preference for housing. This difference in preferences is shown in Figure 10A-8, which shows *two* sets of indifference curves: panel (a) shows Ingrid's preferences and panel (b) shows Lars's preferences. Note the difference in their shapes.

FIGURE 10A-8 Differences in Preferences

Ingrid and Lars have different preferences, reflected in the different shapes of their indifference curve maps. So they will choose different consumption bundles even when they have the same possible choices. Both of them have an income of $2400 per month and face prices of $30 per meal and $150 per room. Panel (a) shows Ingrid's consumption choice: 8 rooms and 40 restaurant meals. Panel (b) shows Lars's choice: even though he has the same budget line, he consumes fewer rooms and more restaurant meals.

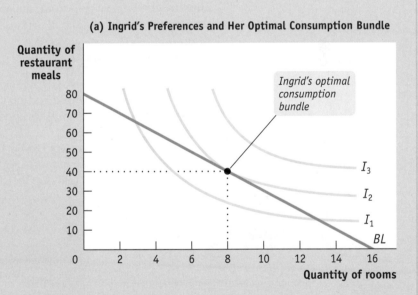

(a) Ingrid's Preferences and Her Optimal Consumption Bundle

(b) Lars's Preferences and His Optimal Consumption Bundle

Suppose, as before, that rooms cost $150 per month and restaurant meals cost $30. Let's also assume that both Ingrid and Lars have incomes of $2400 per month, giving them identical budget lines. Nonetheless, because they have different preferences, they will make different optimal consumption choices, as shown in Figure 10A-8. Ingrid will choose 8 rooms and 40 restaurant meals; Lars will choose 4 rooms and 60 restaurant meals.

Using Indifference Curves: Substitutes and Complements

Now that we've seen how to analyze consumer choice using indifference curves, we can get some payoffs from our new technique. First up is a new insight into the distinction between *substitutes* and *complements*.

Back in Chapter 3, we pointed out that the price of one good often affects the demand for another but that the direction of this effect can go either way: a rise in the price of tea increases the demand for coffee, but a rise in the price of cream reduces the demand for coffee. Tea and coffee are substitutes; cream and coffee are complements.

But how can we tell whether two goods are substitutes or complements? We can use the shape of a consumer's indifference curves. This relationship can be illustrated with two extreme cases: the cases of *perfect substitutes* and *perfect complements*.

Perfect Substitutes

Consider Cokie, who likes cookies. She isn't particular: it doesn't matter to her whether she has 3 peanut butter cookies and 7 chocolate chip cookies, or vice versa. What would her indifference curves between peanut butter and chocolate chip cookies look like?

The answer is that they would be straight lines like I_1 and I_2 in Figure 10A-9. For example, I_1 shows that any combination of peanut butter cookies and chocolate chip cookies that adds up to 10 cookies yields Cokie the same utility.

FIGURE 10A-9 Perfect Substitutes

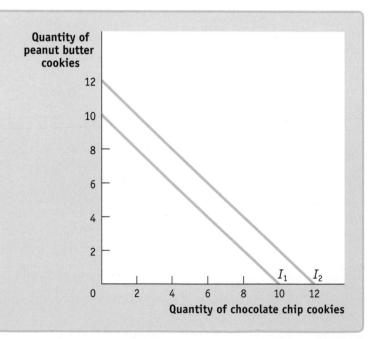

Two goods are perfect substitutes when the marginal rate of substitution does not depend on the quantities consumed. In that case, the indifference curves are straight lines.

A consumer whose indifference curves are straight lines is always willing to substitute the same amount of one good in place of one unit of the other, regardless of how much of either good he or she consumes. Cokie, for example, is always willing to accept one less peanut butter cookie in exchange for one more chocolate chip cookie, making her marginal rate of substitution *constant.*

When indifference curves are straight lines, we say that goods are **perfect substitutes.** When two goods are perfect substitutes, there is only one relative price at which consumers will be willing to purchase both goods; a slightly higher or lower relative price will cause consumers to buy only one of the two goods.

Figure 10A-10 illustrates this point. The indifference curves are the same as those in Figure 10A-9, but now we include Cokie's budget line, *BL.* In each panel we assume that Cokie has $12 to spend. In panel (a) we assume that chocolate chip cookies cost $1.20 and peanut butter cookies cost $1.00. Cokie's optimal consumption bundle is then at point *A*: she buys 12 peanut butter cookies and no chocolate chip cookies. In panel (b) the situation is reversed: chocolate chip cookies cost $1.00 and peanut butter cookies cost $1.20. In this case, her optimal consumption is at point *B,* where she consumes only chocolate chip cookies.

Why does such a small change in the price cause Cokie to switch all her consumption from one good to the other? Because her marginal rate of substitution is constant and therefore doesn't depend on the composition of her consumption bundle. If the relative price of chocolate chip cookies is more than the marginal rate of substitution of chocolate chip cookies in place of peanut butter cookies, she buys only peanut butter cookies; if it is less, she buys only chocolate chip.

Two goods are **perfect substitutes** if the marginal rate of substitution of one good in place of the other good is constant, regardless of how much of each an individual consumes.

FIGURE 10A-10 Consumer Choice Between Perfect Substitutes

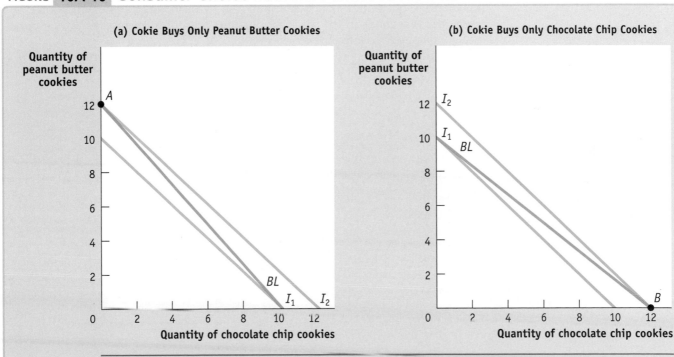

(a) Cokie Buys Only Peanut Butter Cookies

(b) Cokie Buys Only Chocolate Chip Cookies

When two goods are perfect substitutes, small price changes can lead to large changes in the consumption bundle. In panel (a), the relative price of chocolate chip cookies is slightly higher than the marginal rate of substitution of chocolate chip cookies in place of peanut butter cookies; this is enough to induce Cokie to choose consumption bundle *A*, which consists entirely of peanut butter cookies. In panel (b), the relative price of chocolate chip cookies is slightly lower than the marginal rate of substitution of chocolate chip cookies in place of peanut butter cookies; this induces Cokie to choose bundle *B*, consisting entirely of chocolate chip cookies.

Two goods are **perfect complements** when a consumer wants to consume the goods in the same ratio regardless of their relative price.

And if the relative price of chocolate chip cookies is equal to the marginal rate of substitution, Cokie can maximize her utility by buying any bundle on her budget line. That is, she will be equally happy with any combination of chocolate chip cookies and peanut butter cookies that she can afford. As a result, in this case we cannot predict which particular bundle she will choose among all the bundles that lie on her budget line.

Perfect Complements

The case of perfect substitutes represents one extreme form of consumer preferences; the case of perfect complements represents the other. Goods are **perfect complements** when a consumer wants to consume two goods in the same ratio, regardless of their relative price.

Suppose that Aaron likes cookies and milk—but only together. An extra cookie without an extra glass of milk yields no additional utility; neither does an extra glass of milk without another cookie. Aaron prefers to consume milk and cookies in the fixed ratio (sometimes called a fixed proportion) of one to one: one glass of milk with each cookie consumed. In this case, his indifference curves will form right angles, as shown in Figure 10A-11.

To see why, consider the three bundles labelled A, B, and C. At B, on I_4, Aaron consumes 4 cookies and 4 glasses of milk. At A, he consumes 4 cookies and 5 glasses of milk; but the extra glass of milk adds nothing to his utility. So A is on the same indifference curve as B, I_4. Similarly, at C he consumes 5 cookies and 4 glasses of milk, but this yields the same total utility as 4 cookies and 4 glasses of milk. So C is also on the same indifference curve, I_4.

Also shown in Figure 10A-11 is a budget line that would allow Aaron to choose bundle B. The important point is that the slope of the budget line has no effect on his relative consumption of cookies and milk. This means that he will always consume the two goods in the same proportions regardless of prices—which makes the goods perfect complements.

You may be wondering what happened to Aaron's marginal rate of substitution in Figure 10A-11, given that he insists on consuming cookies and milk in

FIGURE **10A-11** Perfect Complements

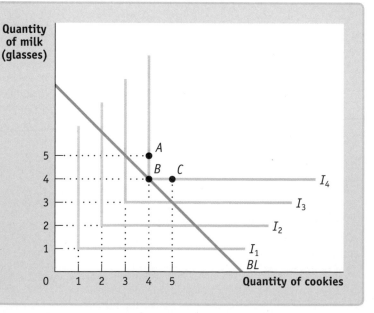

When two goods are perfect complements, indifference curves take the form of right angles. In this case, Aaron will choose to consume 4 glasses of milk and 4 cookies (bundle B) regardless of the slope of the budget line passing through B. The reason is that neither an additional glass of milk without an additional cookie (bundle A) nor an additional cookie without an additional glass of milk (bundle C) adds to his total utility.

the same ratio regardless of their relative price. The answer is that in the case of perfect complements, the marginal rate of substitution is *undefined*: an individual with this type of preferences is unwilling to allow *any* substitution between the two goods. Figure 10A-12 shows the optimal consumption bundle for Aaron with different relative prices of cookies as shown by different budget lines, BL_1, BL_2, and BL_3. It is obvious that for such a person, the relative prices of milk to cookies is irrelevant to his optimal consumption choice (4 glasses of milk and 4 cookies in this case), as he will always choose to consume at the highest affordable "kink" of his indifference curve.

FIGURE **10A-12** Perfect Complements and the Marginal Rate of Substitution

The marginal rate of substitution is undefined when two goods are perfect complements. This is because this kind of consumer always wants to consume the two goods in the same ratio regardless of their relative prices.

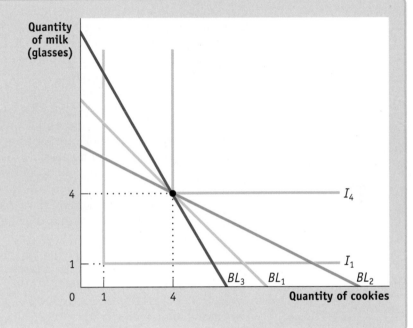

Less Extreme Cases

There are real-world examples of pairs of goods that are very close to being perfect substitutes. For example, the list of ingredients on a package of Bisquick pancake mix says that it contains "soybean and/or cottonseed oil": the producer uses whichever is cheaper, since consumers can't tell the difference. There are other pairs of goods that are very close to being perfect complements—for example, cars and tires.

In most cases, however, the possibilities for substitution lie somewhere between these extremes. In some cases it isn't easy to be sure whether goods are substitutes or complements.

Prices, Income, and Demand

Let's return now to Ingrid's consumption choices. In the situation we've considered, her income was $2400 per month, housing cost $150 per room, and restaurant meals cost $30 each. Her optimal consumption bundle, as seen in Figure 10A-7, contained 8 rooms and 40 restaurant meals.

Let's now ask how her consumption choice would change if either the rent per room or her income changed. As we'll see, we can put these pieces together to deepen our understanding of consumer demand.

The Effects of a Price Increase

Suppose that there is a sharp increase in housing prices. Ingrid must now pay $600 per room instead of $150, but the price of restaurant meals and her income remain unchanged. How does this change affect her consumption choices?

When the price of rooms rises, the relative price of rooms in terms of restaurant meals rises; as a result, Ingrid's budget line changes (for the worse—but we'll get to that). She responds to that change by choosing a new consumption bundle.

Figure 10A-13 shows Ingrid's original (BL_1) and new (BL_2) budget lines—again, under the assumption that her income remains constant at $2400 per month. With housing costing $150 per room and a restaurant meal costing $30, her budget line, BL_1, intersected the horizontal axis at 16 rooms and the vertical axis at 80 restaurant meals. After the price of a room rises to $600 per room, the budget line, BL_2, still hits the vertical axis at 80 restaurant meals, but it hits the horizontal axis at only 4 rooms. That's because we know from Equation 10A-9 that the new horizontal intercept of the budget line is now $2400/$600 = 4. Her budget line has rotated inward and become steeper, reflecting the new, higher relative price of a room in terms of restaurant meals.

Figure 10A-14 shows how Ingrid responds to her new circumstances. Her original optimal consumption bundle consists of 8 rooms and 40 meals. After her budget line rotates in response to the change in relative price, she finds her new optimal consumption bundle by choosing the point on BL_2 that brings her to as high an indifference curve as possible. At the new optimal consumption bundle, she consumes fewer rooms and more restaurant meals than before: 1 room and 60 restaurant meals.

Why does Ingrid's consumption of rooms fall? Part—but only part—of the reason is that the rise in the price of rooms reduces her purchasing power, making her poorer. That is, the higher relative price of rooms rotates her budget line inward toward the origin, reducing her consumption possibilities and putting her on a lower indifference curve. In a sense, when she faces a higher price of housing, it's as if her income declined.

To understand this effect, and to see why it isn't the whole story, let's consider a different change in Ingrid's circumstances: a change in her income.

FIGURE 10A-13 Effects of a Price Increase on the Budget Line

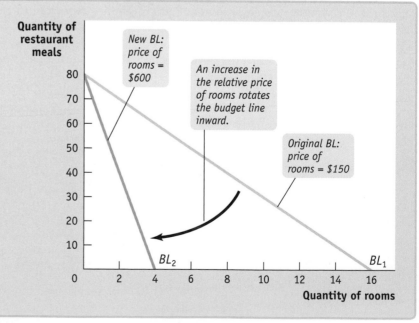

An increase in the price of rooms, holding income and the price of restaurant meals constant, increases the relative price of rooms in terms of restaurant meals. As a result, Ingrid's original budget line, BL_1, rotates inward to BL_2. Her maximum possible purchase of restaurant meals is unchanged, but her maximum possible purchase of rooms is reduced.

FIGURE **10A-14** Responding to a Price Increase

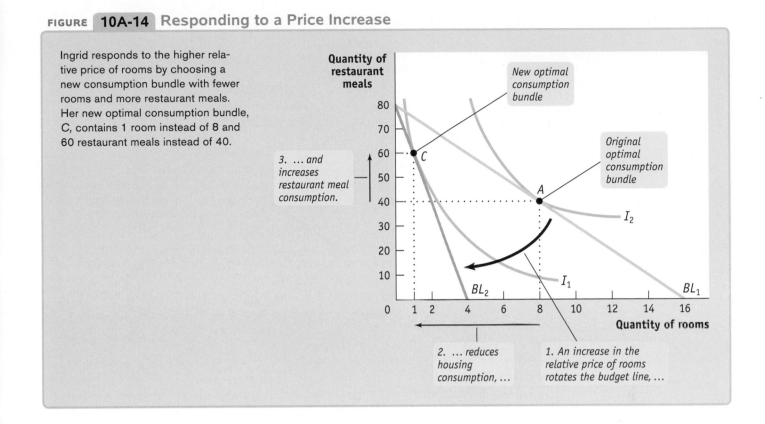

Ingrid responds to the higher relative price of rooms by choosing a new consumption bundle with fewer rooms and more restaurant meals. Her new optimal consumption bundle, *C*, contains 1 room instead of 8 and 60 restaurant meals instead of 40.

3. ... and increases restaurant meal consumption.

2. ... reduces housing consumption, ...

1. An increase in the relative price of rooms rotates the budget line, ...

Income and Consumption

In Chapter 3 we learned about the individual demand curve, which shows how a consumer's consumption choice will change as the price of one good changes, holding income and the prices of other goods constant. That is, movement along the individual demand curve primarily shows the substitution effect, as we learned in Chapter 10—how quantity consumed changes in response to changes in the *relative price* of the two goods. But we can also ask how the consumption choice will change if *income* changes, holding relative price constant.

Before we proceed, it's important to understand how a change in income, holding relative price constant, affects the budget line. Suppose that Ingrid's income fell from $2400 to $1200 and we hold prices constant at $150 per room and $30 per restaurant meal. As a result, the maximum number of rooms she can afford drops from 16 to 8, and the maximum number of restaurant meals drops from 80 to 40. In other words, Ingrid's consumption possibilities have shrunk, as shown by the parallel inward shift of the budget line in Figure 10A-15 from BL_1 to BL_2. It's a parallel shift because the slope of the budget line—the relative price—remains unchanged when income changes. Alternatively, suppose Ingrid's income rises from $2400 to $3000. She can now afford a maximum of 20 rooms or 100 meals, leading to a *parallel outward shift* of the budget line—the shift from BL_1 to BL_3 in Figure 10A-15. In this case, Ingrid's consumption possibilities have expanded.

Now we are ready to consider how Ingrid responds to a direct change in income—that is, a change in her income level holding relative price constant. Figure 10A-16 compares Ingrid's budget line and optimal consumption choice at an income of $2400 per month ($BL_1$) with her budget line and optimal consumption choice at an income of $1200 per month ($BL_2$), keeping prices constant at $150 per room and $30 per restaurant meal. Point *A* is Ingrid's optimal consumption bundle at an income of $2400, and point *B* is her optimal consumption bundle at an income of $1200. In each case, her optimal consumption bundle is given by the

When relative prices are held constant, the budget line shifts parallel in response to changes in income. For example, if Ingrid's income falls from $2400 to $1200, she is clearly worse off: her budget line shifts inward from BL_1 to its new position at BL_2. In contrast, if Ingrid's income rises from $2400 to $3000, she is clearly better off: her budget line shifts outward from BL_1 to its new position at BL_3.

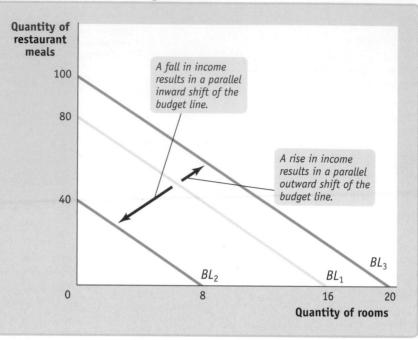

point at which the budget line is tangent to the indifference curve. As you can see, at the lower income her budget line shifts inward compared to her budget line at the higher income but maintains the same slope because relative price has not changed.

This means that she must reduce her consumption of either housing or restaurant meals, or both. As a result, she is at a lower level of total utility, represented by a lower indifference curve.

FIGURE **10A-16** Income and Consumption: Normal Goods

At a monthly income of $2400, Ingrid chooses bundle A, consisting of 8 rooms and 40 restaurant meals. When relative price remains unchanged, a fall in income shifts her budget line inward to BL_2. At a monthly income of $1200, she chooses bundle B, consisting of 4 rooms and 20 restaurant meals. Since Ingrid's consumption of both restaurant meals and rooms falls when her income falls, both goods are normal goods.

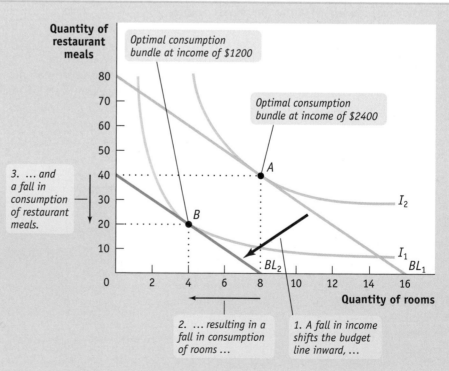

As it turns out, Ingrid chooses to consume less of both goods when her income falls: as her income goes from $2400 to $1200, her consumption of housing falls from 8 to 4 rooms and her consumption of restaurant meals falls from 40 to 20. This is because in her utility function both goods are *normal goods,* as defined in Chapter 3: goods for which demand increases when income rises and for which demand decreases when income falls.

Although most goods are normal goods, we also pointed out in Chapters 3 and 6 that some goods are *inferior goods,* goods for which demand moves in the opposite direction to the change in income: demand decreases when income rises, and demand increases when income falls. Examples might include second-hand furniture, public transit rides, economy cars, cheap cuts of meat, and laundry done at a laundromat. Whether a good is an inferior or normal good depends on the shape of the consumer's indifference curve map. Figure 10A-17 illustrates such a case, where second-hand furniture is measured on the horizontal axis and restaurant meals are measured on the vertical axis. Note that when Ingrid's income falls from $2400 ($BL_1$) to $1200 ($BL_2$), and her optimal consumption bundle goes from D to E, her consumption of second-hand furniture increases—implying that second-hand furniture is an inferior good. Simultaneously, her consumption of restaurant meals decreases—implying that restaurant meals are a normal good.

FIGURE **10A-17** Income and Consumption: An Inferior Good

When Ingrid's income falls from $2400 to $1200, her optimal consumption bundle changes from D to E. Her consumption of second-hand furniture increases, implying that second-hand furniture is an inferior good. In contrast, her consumption of restaurant meals falls, implying that restaurant meals are a normal good.

Income and Substitution Effects

Now that we have examined the effects of a change in income, we can return to the issue of a change in price—and show in a more specific way that the effect of a higher price on demand has an income component.

Figure 10A-18 shows, once again, Ingrid's original (BL_1) and new (BL_2) budget lines and consumption choices with a monthly income of $2400. At a housing price of $150 per room, Ingrid chooses the consumption bundle at A; at a housing price of $600 per room, she chooses the consumption bundle at C.

Let's notice again what happens to Ingrid's budget line after the increase in the price of housing. It continues to hit the vertical axis at 80 restaurant meals; that is, if Ingrid were to spend all her income on restaurant meals, the increase in the price of housing would not affect her. But the new budget line hits the horizontal axis at only 4 rooms. So the budget line has rotated, *shifting inward* and *becoming steeper,* as a consequence of the rise in the relative price of rooms.

We already know what happens: Ingrid's consumption of housing falls from 8 rooms to 1 room. But the figure suggests that there are *two* reasons for the fall in Ingrid's housing consumption. One reason she consumes fewer rooms is that,

FIGURE **10A-18** Income and Substitution Effects

The movement from Ingrid's original optimal consumption bundle when the price of rooms is $150, *A*, to her new optimal consumption bundle when the price of rooms is $600, *C*, can be decomposed into two parts. The movement from *A* to *B*—the movement along the original indifference curve, *I₂*, as relative price changes—is the pure substitution effect. It captures how her consumption would change if she were given a hypothetical increase in income that just compensates her for the increase in the price of rooms so that her total utility is unchanged. The movement from *B* to *C*, the change in consumption when we remove that hypothetical income compensation, is the income effect of the price increase—how her consumption changes as a result of the fall in her purchasing power.

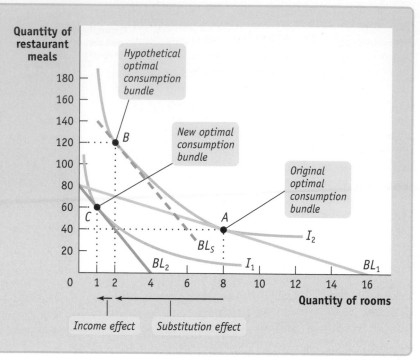

because of the higher relative price of rooms, the opportunity cost of a room measured in restaurant meals—the quantity of restaurant meals she must give up to consume an additional room—has increased. This change in opportunity cost, which is reflected in the steeper slope of the budget line, gives her an incentive to substitute toward relatively cheaper restaurant meals in place of rooms (which are now relatively more expensive) in her consumption bundle.

But the other reason Ingrid consumes fewer rooms after their price increases is that the rise in the price of rooms makes her *poorer*. True, her money income hasn't changed. But she must pay more for rooms, and as a result her budget line has rotated inward. So she cannot reach the same level of total utility as before, meaning that her real income has fallen. That is why she ends up on a lower indifference curve.

In the real world, these effects—an increase in the price of a good raises its opportunity cost and also makes consumers poorer—usually go together. But in our imagination we can separate them. In Chapter 10 we introduced the distinction between the *substitution effect* of a price change (the change in consumption that arises from the substitution of the good that is now relatively cheaper in place of the good that is now relatively more expensive) and the *income effect* (the change in consumption caused by the change in purchasing power arising from a price change). Now we can show these two effects more clearly.

To isolate the substitution effect, let's temporarily change the story about why Ingrid faces an increase in rent: it's not that housing has become more expensive, it's the fact that she has moved from Saskatoon to Vancouver, where rents are higher. But let's consider a hypothetical scenario—let's suppose momentarily that she earns more in Vancouver and that the higher income is just enough to *compensate* her for the higher price of housing, so that her total utility is exactly the same as before.

Figure 10A-18 shows her situation before and after the move. The bundle labelled *A* represents Ingrid's original consumption choice: 8 rooms and 40 restaurant meals. When she moves to Vancouver, she faces a higher price of housing, so her budget line becomes steeper. But we have just assumed that her move increases her income by just enough to compensate for the higher price of housing—that is, just enough to let her reach the original indifference curve.

So her new *hypothetical* optimal consumption bundle is at *B*, where the steeper dashed hypothetical budget line (*BL_S*) is just tangent to the original indifference curve (*I₂*). By assuming that we have compensated Ingrid for the loss in purchasing power due to the increase in the price of housing, we isolate the *pure substitution effect* of the change in relative price on her consumption.

At *B*, Ingrid's consumption bundle contains 2 rooms and 120 restaurant meals. This costs $4800 (2 rooms at $600 each, and 120 meals at $30 each). So if Ingrid faces an increase in the price of housing from $150 to $600 per room, but also experiences a rise in her income from $2400 to $4800 per month, she ends up with the same level of total utility.

The movement from *A* to *B* is the pure substitution effect of the price change. It is the effect on Ingrid's consumption choice when we change the relative price of housing while keeping her total utility constant.

Now that we have isolated the substitution effect, we can bring back the income effect of the price change. That's easy: we just go back to the original story, in which Ingrid faces an increase in the price of housing *without* any rise in income. We already know that this leads her to *C* in Figure 10A-18. But we can think of the move from *A* to *C* as taking place in two steps. First, Ingrid moves from *A* to *B*, the substitution effect of the change in relative price. Then we take away the extra income needed to keep her on the original indifference curve, causing her to move to *C*. The movement from *B* to *C* is the additional change in Ingrid's demand that results because the increase in housing prices actually reduces her utility. So this is the income effect of the price change.

We can use Figure 10A-18 to confirm that rooms are a normal good in Ingrid's preferences. For normal goods, the income effect and the substitution effect work in the same direction: a price increase induces a fall in quantity consumed by the substitution effect (the move from *A* to *B*) and a fall in quantity consumed by the income effect (the move from *B* to *C*). That's why demand curves for normal goods always slope downward.

What would have happened as a result of the increase in the price of housing if, instead of being a normal good, rooms had been an inferior good for Ingrid? First, the movement from *A* to *B* depicted in Figure 10A-18, the substitution effect, would remain unchanged. But because Ingrid's preferences will be different, the shape of her indifference curves will be different than the one drawn in Figure 10A-18. Recall that an income change causes quantity consumed to move in the opposite direction for an inferior good. So the movement from *B* to *C* shown in Figure 10A-18, the income effect for a normal good, would no longer hold. Instead, the income effect for an inferior good would cause Ingrid's quantity of rooms consumed to *increase* from *B*—say, to a bundle consisting of 3 rooms and 20 restaurant meals.

In the end, the demand curves for inferior goods normally slope downward: if Ingrid consumes 3 rooms after the increase in the price of housing, it is still 5 fewer rooms than she consumed before. So although the income effect moves in the opposite direction of the substitution effect in the case of an inferior good, in this example the substitution effect is stronger than the income effect.

But what if there existed a type of inferior good in which the income effect is so strong that it dominates the substitution effect? Would a demand curve for that good then slope upward—that is, would quantity demanded increase when price increases? The answer is yes: you have encountered such a good already—it is called a *Giffen good*, and it was described in Chapter 10. As we noted there, Giffen goods are rare creatures, but they cannot be ruled out.

Is the distinction between income and substitution effects important in practice? For analyzing the demand for goods, the answer is that it usually isn't that important. However, in Chapter 19 we'll discuss how individuals make decisions about how much of their labour to supply to employers. In that case income and substitution effects work in opposite directions, and the distinction between them becomes crucial.

PROBLEMS

1. For each of the following situations, draw a diagram containing three of Isabella's indifference curves.

   a. For Isabella, cars and tires are perfect complements, but in a ratio of 1:4; that is, for each car, Isabella wants exactly four tires. Be sure to label and number the axes of your diagram. Place tires on the horizontal axis and cars on the vertical axis.

   b. Isabella gets utility only from her caffeine intake. She can consume Valley Dew or cola, and Valley Dew contains twice as much caffeine as cola. Be sure to label and number the axes of your diagram. Place cola on the horizontal axis and Valley Dew on the vertical axis.

   c. Isabella gets utility from consuming two goods: leisure time and income. Both have diminishing marginal utility. Be sure to label the axes of your diagram. Place leisure on the horizontal axis and income on the vertical axis.

   d. Isabella can consume two goods: skis and bindings. For each ski she wants exactly one binding. Be sure to label and number the axes of your diagram. Place bindings on the horizontal axis and skis on the vertical axis.

   e. Isabella gets utility from consuming coffee. But she gets no utility from consuming water: any more, or any less, water leaves her total utility level unchanged. Be sure to label the axes of your diagram. Place water on the horizontal axis and coffee on the vertical axis.

2. Use the four properties of indifference curves for ordinary goods illustrated in Figure 10A-4 to answer the following:

   a. Can you rank the following two bundles? If so, which property of indifference curves helps you rank them?

   Bundle *A:* 2 movie tickets and 3 cafeteria meals

   Bundle *B:* 4 movie tickets and 8 cafeteria meals

   b. Can you rank the following two bundles? If so, which property of indifference curves helps you rank them?

   Bundle *A:* 2 movie tickets and 3 cafeteria meals

   Bundle *B:* 4 movie tickets and 3 cafeteria meals

   c. Can you rank the following two bundles? If so, which property of indifference curves helps you rank them?

   Bundle *A:* 12 videos and 4 bags of chips

   Bundle *B:* 5 videos and 10 bags of chips

   d. Suppose you are indifferent between the following two bundles:

   Bundle *A:* 10 breakfasts and 4 dinners

   Bundle *B:* 4 breakfasts and 10 dinners

   Now compare bundle *A* and the following bundle:

   Bundle *C:* 7 breakfasts and 7 dinners

Can you rank bundle *A* and bundle *C*? If so, which property of indifference curves helps you rank them? (*Hint:* It may help if you draw this, placing dinners on the horizontal axis and breakfasts on the vertical axis. And remember that breakfasts and dinners are ordinary goods.)

3. The four properties of indifference curves for ordinary goods illustrated in Figure 10A-4 rule out certain indifference curves. Determine whether those general properties allow each of the following indifference curves. If not, state which of the general principles rules out the curves.

a.

b.

c.

d.

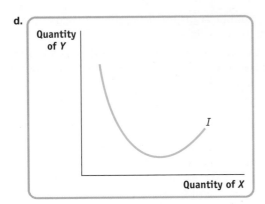

4. Restaurant meals and housing (measured by the number of rooms) are the only two goods that Neha can buy. She has an income of $1000, and the price of each room is $100. The relative price of 1 room in terms of restaurant meals is 5. How many restaurant meals can she buy if she spends all her money on them?

5. Answer the following questions based on two assumptions: (1) Inflation increases the prices of all goods by 20%. (2) Ina's income increases from $50 000 to $55 000.
   a. Has Ina's budget line become steeper, less steep, or equally as steep?
   b. Has Ina's budget line shifted outward, inward, or not at all?

6. Kory has an income of $50, which she can spend on two goods: CDs and cups of hot chocolate. Both are normal goods for her. Each CD costs $10, and each cup of hot chocolate costs $2. For each of the following situations, decide whether this is Kory's optimal consumption bundle. If not, what should Kory do to achieve her optimal consumption bundle?
   a. Kory is considering buying 4 CDs and 5 cups of hot chocolate. At that bundle, her marginal rate of substitution of CDs in place of hot chocolate is 1; that is, she would be willing to forgo only 1 cup of hot chocolate to acquire 1 CD.
   b. Kory is considering buying 2 CDs and 15 cups of hot chocolate. Kory's marginal utility of the second CD is 25, and her marginal utility of the fifteenth cup of hot chocolate is 5.
   c. Kory is considering buying 1 CD and 10 cups of hot chocolate. At that bundle, her marginal rate of substitution of CDs in place of hot chocolate is 5; that is, she would be just willing to exchange 5 cups of hot chocolate for 1 CD.

7. Siu Bo has 4 Wayne Gretzky and 2 Guy Lafleur hockey cards. The prices of these hockey cards are $24 for Gretzky and $12 for Lafleur. Siu Bo, however, would be willing to exchange 1 Gretzky card for 1 Lafleur card.
   a. What is Siu Bo's marginal rate of substitution of Wayne Gretzky in place of Guy Lafleur hockey cards?
   b. Can Siu Bo buy and sell hockey cards to make herself better off? How?

c. Suppose Siu Bo has traded hockey cards and after trading still has some of each kind of card. Also, she now no longer wants to make any more trades. What is her marginal rate of substitution of Wayne Gretzky in place of Guy Lafleur cards now?

8. Ralph and Lauren are talking about how much they like going to the gym and how much they like eating out at their favourite restaurant and they regularly do some of each. A session at the gym costs the same as a meal at the restaurant. Ralph says that, for his current consumption of gym sessions and restaurant meals, he values 1 more meal twice as much as he values 1 more session at the gym. Lauren is studying economics, and she tells him that his current consumption bundle cannot be optimal.
   a. Is Lauren right? Why or why not? Draw a diagram of Ralph's budget line and the indifference curve that he is on by making his current consumption choice. Place restaurant meals on the horizontal axis and gym sessions on the vertical axis.
   b. How should Ralph adjust his consumption so that it is optimal? Illustrate an optimal choice in your diagram.

9. Sabine can't tell the difference between Coke and Pepsi—the two taste exactly the same to her.
   a. What is Sabine's marginal rate of substitution of Coke in place of Pepsi?
   b. Draw a few of Sabine's indifference curves for Coke and Pepsi. Place Coke on the horizontal axis and Pepsi on the vertical axis.
   c. Sabine has $6 to spend on cola this week. Coke costs $1.50 per six-pack and Pepsi costs $1.00. Draw Sabine's budget line for Coke and Pepsi on the same diagram.
   d. What is Sabine's optimal consumption bundle? Show this on your diagram.
   e. If the price of Coke and Pepsi is the same, what combination of Coke and Pepsi will Sabine buy?

10. For Norma, both nachos and salsa are normal goods. They are also ordinary goods for Norma. The price of nachos rises, but the price of salsa remains unchanged.
    a. Can you determine definitively whether she consumes more or fewer nachos? Explain with a diagram, placing nachos on the horizontal axis and salsa on the vertical axis.
    b. Can you determine definitively whether she consumes more or less salsa? Explain with a diagram, placing nachos on the horizontal axis and salsa on the vertical axis.

11. Tyrone is a utility maximizer. His income is $100, which he can spend on cafeteria meals and on notepads. Each meal costs $5, and each notepad costs $2. At these prices Tyrone chooses to buy 16 cafeteria meals and 10 notepads.
    a. Draw a diagram that shows Tyrone's choice using an indifference curve and his budget line, placing notepads on the vertical axis and cafeteria meals on the horizontal axis. Label the indifference curve I_1 and the budget line BL_1.

b. The price of notepads falls to $1; the price of cafeteria meals remains the same. On the same diagram, draw Tyrone's budget line with the new prices and label it BL_H.

c. Lastly, Tyrone's income falls to $90. On the same diagram, draw his budget line with this income and the new prices and label it BL_2. Is he worse off, better off, or equally as well off with these new prices and lower income than compared to the original prices and higher income? (*Hint:* Determine whether Tyrone can afford to buy his original consumption bundle of 16 meals and 10 notepads with the lower income and new prices.) Illustrate your answer using an indifference curve and label it I_2.

d. Give an intuitive explanation of your answer to part (c).

12. Gus spends his income on gas for his car and food. The government raises the tax on gas, thereby raising the price of gas. But the government also lowers the income tax, thereby increasing Gus's income. And this rise in income is just enough to place Gus on the same indifference curve as the one he was on before the price of gas rose. Will Gus buy more, less, or the same amount of gas as before these changes? Illustrate your answer with a diagram, placing gas on the horizontal axis and food on the vertical axis.

13. Pam spends her money on bread and Spam, and her indifference curves obey the four properties of indifference curves for ordinary goods. Suppose that, for Pam, Spam is an inferior, but not a Giffen, good; bread is a normal good. Bread costs $2 per loaf, and Spam costs $2 per can. Pam has $20 to spend.

a. Draw a diagram of Pam's budget line, placing Spam on the horizontal axis and bread on the vertical axis. Suppose her optimal consumption bundle is 4 cans of Spam and 6 loaves of bread. Illustrate that bundle and draw the indifference curve on which it lies.

b. The price of Spam falls to $1; the price of bread remains the same. Pam now buys 7 loaves of bread and 6 cans of Spam. Illustrate her new budget line and new optimal consumption bundle in your diagram. Also draw the indifference curve on which this bundle lies.

c. In your diagram, show the income and substitution effects from this fall in the price of Spam. Remember that Spam is an inferior good for Pam.

14. Katya commutes to work. She can either use public transport or her own car. Her indifference curves obey the four properties of indifference curves for ordinary goods.

a. Draw Katya's budget line with car travel on the vertical axis and public transport on the horizontal axis. Suppose that Katya consumes some of both goods. Draw an indifference curve that helps you illustrate her optimal consumption bundle.

b. Now the price of public transport falls. Draw Katya's new budget line.

c. For Katya, public transport is an inferior, but not a Giffen, good. Draw an indifference curve that illustrates her optimal consumption bundle after the

price of public transport has fallen. Is Katya consuming more or less public transport?

d. Show the income and substitution effects from this fall in the price of public transport.

15. For Crandall, cheese cubes and crackers are perfect complements: he wants to consume exactly 1 cheese cube with each cracker. He has $2.40 to spend on cheese and crackers. One cheese cube costs 20 cents, and 1 cracker costs 10 cents. Draw a diagram, with crackers on the horizontal axis and cheese cubes on the vertical axis, to answer the following questions.

a. Which bundle will Crandall consume?

b. The price of crackers rises to 20 cents. How many cheese cubes and how many crackers will Crandall consume?

c. Show the income and substitution effects from this price rise.

16. Carmen consumes nothing but cafeteria meals and CDs. Her indifference curves exhibit the four general properties of indifference curves. Cafeteria meals cost $5 each, and CDs cost $10. Carmen has $50 to spend.

a. Draw Carmen's budget line and an indifference curve that illustrates her optimal consumption bundle. Place cafeteria meals on the horizontal axis and CDs on the vertical axis. You do not have enough information to know the specific tangency point, so choose one arbitrarily.

b. Now Carmen's income rises to $100. Draw her new budget line on the same diagram, as well as an indifference curve that illustrates her optimal consumption bundle. Assume that cafeteria meals are an inferior good.

c. Can you draw an indifference curve showing that cafeteria meals and CDs are both inferior goods?

17. The Japanese Ministry of Internal Affairs and Communications collects data on the prices of goods and services in the Ku-area of Tokyo, as well as data on the average Japanese household's monthly income. The accompanying table shows some of this data. (¥ denotes the Japanese currency the yen.)

Year	Price of eggs (per pack of 10)	Price of tuna (per 100-gram portion)	Average monthly income
2003	¥187	¥392	¥524 810
2005	231	390	524 585

a. For each of the two years for which you have data, what is the maximum number of packs of eggs that an average Japanese household could have consumed each month? The maximum number of 100-gram portions of tuna? In one diagram, draw the average Japanese household's budget line in 2003 and in 2005.

b. Calculate the relative price of eggs in terms of tuna for each year. Use the relative price rule to determine how the average household's consumption of eggs and tuna would have changed between 2003 and 2005.

Behind the Supply Curve: Inputs and Costs

THE FARMER'S MARGIN

How intensively a hectare of land is worked—a decision at the margin—depends on the price of wheat a farmer faces.

Terrance Klassen/AgeFotostock

❭ The importance of a firm's **production function,** the relationship between quantity of inputs and quantity of output

❭ Why production is often subject to **diminishing returns to inputs**

❭ The various types of costs a firm faces and how they generate the firm's **marginal and average cost curves**

❭ Why a firm's costs may differ in the **short run** versus the **long run**

❭ How a firm's technology of production can generate **increasing returns to scale**

ALTHOUGH LESS THAN 2% OF Canada's population lives on farms, our agricultural sector is immensely productive and feeds much of the world. If you look at agricultural statistics, however, something may seem a bit surprising: when it comes to yield per hectare, Canadian farmers are often nowhere near the top. For example, farmers in Western European countries grow about three times as much wheat per hectare as their Canadian counterparts. Are the Europeans better at growing wheat than we are?

No: European farmers are very skillful, but no more so than Canadians. They produce more wheat per hectare because they employ more inputs— more fertilizer and, especially, more labour—per hectare. Of course, this means that European farmers have

higher costs than their Canadian counterparts. But because of government policies, European farmers receive a much higher price for their wheat than Canadian farmers. This gives them an incentive to use more inputs and to expend more effort at the margin to increase the crop yield per hectare.

Notice our use of the phrase "at the margin." Like most decisions that involve a comparison of benefits and costs, decisions about inputs and production involve a comparison of marginal quantities—the marginal cost versus the marginal benefit of producing a bit more from each hectare.

In Chapter 9 we considered the case of Alex, who had to choose the number of years of schooling that maximized his profit from schooling. There we used the profit-maximizing principle of marginal

analysis to find the optimal quantity of years of schooling. In this chapter, we will encounter producers who have to make similar "how much" decisions: choosing the quantity of output produced to maximize profit.

In this chapter and in Chapter 12, we will show how marginal analysis can be used to understand these output decisions—decisions that lie behind the supply curve. The first step in this analysis is to show how the relationship between a firm's inputs and its output—its *production function*—determines its *cost curves,* the relationship between cost and quantity of output produced. That is what we do in this chapter. In Chapter 12, we will use our understanding of the firm's cost curves to derive the individual and the market supply curves. ■

A **production function** is the relationship between the quantity of inputs a firm uses and the quantity of output it produces, for a given state of the production technology.

A **fixed input** is an input whose quantity is fixed for a period of time and cannot be varied.

A **variable input** is an input whose quantity the firm can vary at any time.

The **long run** is the time period in which all inputs can be varied.

The **short run** is the time period in which at least one input is fixed.

The **total product curve** shows how the quantity of output depends on the quantity of the variable input employed, for a given quantity of the fixed input and production technology.

The Production Function

A *firm* is an organization that produces goods or services for sale. To do this, it must transform inputs into output. The quantity of output a firm produces depends on the quantity of inputs and the state or generosity of the production technology; this relationship is known as the firm's **production function.** As we'll see, a firm's production function underlies its *cost curves.* As a first step, let's look at the characteristics of a hypothetical production function.

Inputs and Output

To understand the concept of a production function, let's consider a farm that we assume, for the sake of simplicity, produces only one output, wheat, and uses only two inputs, land and labour. This particular farm is owned by a couple named Alec and Janet. They hire workers to do the actual physical labour on the farm. Moreover, we will assume that all potential workers are of the same quality—they are all equally knowledgeable and capable of performing farmwork.

Alec and Janet's farm sits on 1 hectare of land; no more land is available to them, and they are currently unable to either increase or decrease the size of their farm by selling, buying, or leasing land. Land here is what economists call a **fixed input**—an input whose quantity is fixed for a period of time and cannot be varied. Alec and Janet are, however, free to decide how many workers to hire. The labour provided by these workers is called a **variable input**—an input whose quantity the firm can vary at any time.

In reality, whether or not the quantity of an input is really fixed depends on the time horizon. In the **long run**—that is, given that a long enough period of time has elapsed—firms can adjust the quantity of any input. For example, in the long run, Alec and Janet can vary the amount of land they farm by buying or selling land. So there are no fixed inputs in the long run. In contrast, the **short run** is defined as the time period during which at least one input is fixed. Later in this chapter, we'll look more carefully at the distinction between the short run and the long run. But for now, we will restrict our attention to the short run and assume that at least one input is fixed.

Alec and Janet know that the quantity of wheat they produce depends on the number of workers they hire. Using modern farming techniques, one worker can cultivate the 1 hectare farm, albeit not very intensively. When an additional worker is added, the land is divided equally among all the workers: each worker has ½ of a hectare to cultivate when 2 workers are employed, each cultivates ⅓ of a hectare when 3 are employed, and so on. So as additional workers are employed, the land is cultivated more intensively and more bushels of wheat are produced. The relationship between the quantity of labour and the quantity of output, for a given amount of the fixed input and the given production technology (i.e., farming techniques used in this example), constitutes the farm's production function. The production function for Alec and Janet's farm, where land is the fixed input and labour is a variable input, is shown in the first two columns of the table in Figure 11-1; the diagram there shows the same information graphically. The curve in Figure 11-1 shows how the quantity of output depends on the quantity of the variable input, for a given quantity of the fixed input and the given production technology; it is called the farm's **total product curve.** The physical quantity of output, bushels of wheat, is measured on the vertical axis; the quantity of the variable input, labour (that is, the number of workers employed), is measured on the horizontal axis. The total product curve here slopes upward, reflecting the fact that more bushels of wheat are produced as more workers are employed.

Quantity of labour L (workers)	Quantity of wheat q (bushels)	Marginal product of labour $MPL = \Delta q/\Delta L$ (bushels per worker)
0	0	
		19
1	19	
		17
2	36	
		15
3	51	
		13
4	64	
		11
5	75	
		9
6	84	
		7
7	91	
		5
8	96	

Adding a 7th worker leads to an increase in output of only 7 bushels.

Adding a 2nd worker leads to an increase in output of 17 bushels.

Total product, *TP*

The table shows the production function, the relationship between the quantity of the variable input (labour, measured in number of workers) and the quantity of output (wheat, measured in bushels) for a given quantity of the fixed input and production technology. It also calculates the marginal product of labour on Alec and Janet's farm.

The total product curve shows the production function graphically. It slopes upward because more wheat is produced as more workers are employed. It also becomes flatter because the marginal product of labour declines as more and more workers are employed.

Although the total product curve in Figure 11-1 slopes upward along its entire length, the slope isn't constant: as you move up the curve to the right, it flattens out. To understand why the slope changes, look at the third column of the table in Figure 11-1, which shows the *change in the quantity of output* that is generated by adding one more worker. This is called the *marginal product* of labour, or *MPL:* the additional quantity of output from using one more unit of labour (where one unit of labour is equal to one worker), holding other inputs and the production technology fixed. In general, the **marginal product** of an input is the additional quantity of output that is produced by using one more unit of that input.   } *the rate of change*

In this example, we have data on changes in output at intervals of 1 worker. Sometimes data aren't available in increments of 1 unit—for example, you might have information only on the quantity of output when there are 40 workers and when there are 50 workers. In this case, we use the following equation to calculate the marginal product of labour:

(11-1) Marginal product of labour $=$ Change in quantity of output produced by one additional unit of labour $=$ $\dfrac{\text{Change in quantity of output}}{\text{Change in quantity of labour}}$

or

$$MPL = \frac{\Delta q}{\Delta L}$$ ← *Ideally over 1*

In this equation, Δ, the Greek uppercase delta, represents the change in a variable. Here, the lowercase q represents the quantity of output made by an individual

The **marginal product** of an input is the additional quantity of output that is produced by using one more unit of that input, holding other inputs and the production technology fixed.

WHEAT YIELDS AROUND THE WORLD

Wheat yields differ substantially around the world. The disparity between France and Canada that you see in this graph is particularly striking, given that they are both wealthy countries with comparable agricultural technology. Yet the reason for that disparity is straightforward: differing government policies. In Canada, farmers receive payments from the government to supplement their incomes, but European farmers benefit from price floors. Since European farmers get higher prices for their output than Canadian farmers, they employ more variable inputs, and produce significantly higher yields. Interestingly, in poor countries like Uganda and Ethiopia, foreign aid can lead to significantly depressed yields. Foreign aid from wealthy countries has often taken the form of surplus food, which depresses local market prices, severely hurting the local agriculture that poor countries normally depend on. Charitable organizations like OXFAM have asked wealthy food-producing countries to modify their aid policies—principally, to give aid in cash rather than in food products except in the case of acute food shortages—to avoid this problem.

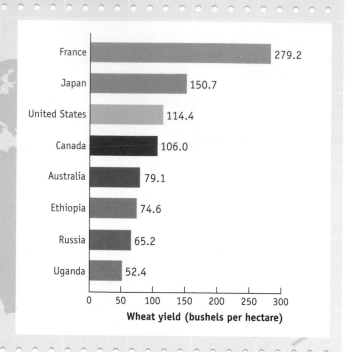

Source: Food and Agriculture Organization of the United Nations. Data are from 2012.

firm, as opposed to an uppercase Q, which represents the quantity of output in the market as a whole.

Now we can explain the significance of the slope of the total product curve: it is equal to the marginal product of labour. The slope of a line is equal to "rise" over "run" (see Appendix 2A). This implies that the slope of the total product curve is the change in the quantity of output (the "rise", Δq) divided by the change in the quantity of labour (the "run", ΔL). And this, as we can see from Equation 11-1, is simply the marginal product of labour. So in Figure 11-1, the fact that the marginal product of the first worker is 19 also means that the slope of the total product curve in going from 0 to 1 worker is 19. Similarly, the slope of the total product curve in going from 1 to 2 workers is the same as the marginal product of the second worker, 17, and so on.

In this example, the marginal product of labour declines as more workers are hired—that is, each successive worker adds less to output than the previous worker. So as employment increases, the total product curve gets flatter.

Figure 11-2 shows how the marginal product of labour depends on the number of workers employed on the farm. The marginal product of labour, *MPL*, is measured on the vertical axis in units of physical output—bushels of wheat—produced per additional worker, and the number of workers employed is measured on the horizontal axis. You can see from the table in Figure 11-1 that if 5 workers are employed instead of 4, output rises from 64 to 75 bushels; in this case the marginal product of labour is 11 bushels—the same number found in Figure 11-2. To indicate that 11 bushels is the marginal product when employment rises from 4 to 5, we place the point corresponding to that information halfway between 4 and 5 workers.

In this example the marginal product of labour falls as the number of workers increases. That is, there are *diminishing returns to labour* on Alec and Janet's farm. In general, there are **diminishing returns to an input** when an increase in the

There are **diminishing returns to an input** when an increase in the quantity of that input, holding the levels of all other inputs and the production technology fixed, leads to a decline in the marginal product of that input.

FIGURE 11-2 Marginal Product of Labour Curve for Alec and Janet's Farm

The marginal product of labour curve plots each worker's marginal product, the increase in the quantity of output generated by each additional worker, holding other inputs and the production technology fixed. The change in the quantity of output is measured on the vertical axis and the number of workers employed on the horizontal axis. The first worker employed generates an increase in output of 19 bushels, the second worker generates an increase of 17 bushels, and so on. The curve slopes downward due to diminishing returns to labour.

quantity of that input, holding the quantity of all other inputs and the production technology fixed, reduces that input's marginal product. Due to diminishing returns to labour, the *MPL* curve is negatively sloped.

To grasp why diminishing returns can occur, think about what happens as Alec and Janet add more and more workers without increasing the amount of land or improving their farming techniques. As the number of workers increases, the land is farmed more intensively and the number of bushels produced increases. But each additional worker is working with a smaller share of the 1 hectare—the fixed input—than the previous worker. As a result, the additional worker cannot produce as much output as the previous worker. So it's not surprising that the marginal product of the additional worker falls.

The crucial point to emphasize about diminishing returns is that, like many propositions in economics, it is an "other things equal" proposition: each successive unit of an input will raise production by less than the last *if the quantity of all other inputs is and the production technology are held fixed.*

What would happen if the levels of other inputs or production techniques were allowed to change? You can see the answer illustrated in Figure 11-3. Panel (a) shows two total product curves, *TP*₁ and *TP*₂. *TP*₁ is the farm's total product curve when its total area is 1 hectare (the same curve as in Figure 11-1). *TP*₂ is the total product curve when the farm has increased to 2 hectares, holding farming techniques fixed. Except when 0 workers are employed, *TP*₂ lies above *TP*₁ everywhere because with more land available, any given number of workers produces more output. Panel (b) shows the corresponding marginal product of labour curves. *MPL*₁ is the marginal product of labour curve given 1 hectare to cultivate (the same curve as in Figure 11-2), and *MPL*₂ is the marginal product of labour curve given 2 hectares. Both curves slope downward because, in each case, the amount of land is fixed, albeit at different levels. But *MPL*₂ lies above *MPL*₁ everywhere, reflecting the fact that the marginal product of the same worker is higher when he or she has more of the fixed input to work with.

Figure 11-3 demonstrates a general result: the position of the total product curve of a given input depends on the quantities of other inputs.

⚠ PITFALLS

WHAT'S A UNIT?
The marginal product of labour (or any other input) is defined as the increase in the quantity of output when you increase the quantity of that input by one unit, holding all other inputs and the production technology fixed. But what do we mean by a "unit" of labour? Is it an additional hour of labour, an additional week, or a person-year?

The answer is that it doesn't matter, *as long as you are consistent.* One common source of error in economics is getting units confused—say, comparing the output added by an additional *hour* of labour with the cost of employing a worker for a *week*. Whatever units you use, always be careful that you use the same units throughout your analysis of any problem.

FIGURE **11-3** Total Product, Marginal Product, and the Fixed Input

This figure shows how the quantity of output and the marginal product of labour depend on the level of the fixed input and a given state of technology. Panel (a) shows two total product curves for Alec and Janet's farm, TP_1 when their farm is 1 hectare and TP_2 when it is 2 hectares. With more land, each worker can produce more wheat. So an increase in the fixed input shifts the total product curve up from TP_1 to TP_2. This implies that the marginal product of each worker is higher when the farm is 2 hectares than when it is 1 hectare. Panel (b) shows the marginal product of labour curves. The increase in land also shifts the marginal product of labour curve up from MPL_1 to MPL_2. Note that both marginal product of labour curves still slope downward due to diminishing returns to labour. Likewise, if there is an improvement in production technique, both the total product curve and marginal product of labour curve will shift upwards.

If you change the quantity of the other inputs, both the total product curve and the marginal product curve of the remaining input will shift. Similarly, if there is an improvement in farming techniques (an example of an improvement in production technology), both the total product curve and the marginal product of labour curve would shift upward. With improved farming techniques, farmers can produce more bushels of wheat for any given amount of land.

The Average Product of Labour

Alec and Janet may also be interested in knowing how much wheat is harvested per worker. The *average product of labour*, or *APL*, is the amount of output produced per unit of labour. In general, the **average product** of an input is the amount of output produced per unit of that input employed in the production process:

(11-2) Average product of labour $= \dfrac{\text{Total quantity of output}}{\text{Total quantity of labour employed}}$

or

$$APL = \frac{q}{L}$$

The **average product** of an input is the amount of output produced per unit of that input.

The average product of labour is important because it tells the producer how many units of output the *average* or *typical* unit of labour can produce. Recall,

FIGURE   11-4   Average and Marginal Product of Labour Curve for Alec and Janet's Farm

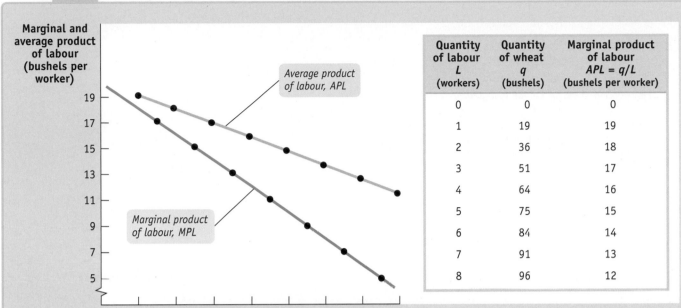

Quantity of labour L (workers)	Quantity of wheat q (bushels)	Marginal product of labour $APL = q/L$ (bushels per worker)
0	0	0
1	19	19
2	36	18
3	51	17
4	64	16
5	75	15
6	84	14
7	91	13
8	96	12

The table shows the production function, the relationship between the quantity of the variable input (labour, measured in number of workers) and the quantity of output (wheat, measured in bushels) for a given quantity of the fixed input and the productive technology. It also calculates the average product of labour on Alec and Janet's farm. The average product of labour curve shows the average amount of output produced per unit of labour, for a given amount of workers employed. When the farm has 1 worker, its average product is 19 (the same as the total product). When the farm employs 2 workers each worker, on average, produces 18 bushels, and so on. The curve slopes downward due to diminishing returns to labour.

the marginal product of labour shows the *change in the quantity of output* that is generated by adding one more worker. Although these quantities sound similar, they are typically not the same and confusion between them is a common source of errors in economics. Figure 11-4 shows the average product of labour curve for Alec and Janet's farm compared to the marginal product of labour.

As you can see from the table in Figure 11-4, all other things equal, as the number of workers employed increases, output rises but the average product of labour falls. For example, when the number of workers employed increases from 4 to 5, output increases from 64 bushels to 75 bushels. However, the average product of labour falls from 16 bushels to 15 bushels. Why does this happen? It is because the marginal product is less than the average product; thus, the average product is decreasing. When the number of workers rises from 4 to 5, the marginal product of the fifth worker is 11 bushels (the table in Figure 11-1 shows the marginal product labour). The marginal contribution of that additional worker is below the average productivity of the first 4 workers, so the fifth worker lowers the average product of the whole group. On the farm, the marginal product of labour is less than the average product of labour for all quantities of labour, so the entire average product curve slopes downward.

Our example shows that both marginal product and average product are downward sloping. In practice, however, economists believe that both the marginal product and average product curves often slope *upward* as a firm increases its variable input from some low level (such as zero), sloping downward only at

FIGURE **11-5** Common Marginal and Average Product of Labour Curves

More realistic marginal product and average product of labour curves look like inverted U-shapes. Starting from a very low input level, the marginal product often rises as the firm employs more of the variable input. That's because hiring additional workers allows greater specialization of their tasks and leads to increasing returns. Once specialization is exhausted, however, diminishing returns to additional workers set in and the marginal product falls. In addition, the average product of labour rises when marginal product exceeds average product, while the average product falls when marginal product is less than average product.

Marginal and average product of labour (bushels per worker)

A

MPL *APL*

Quantity of labour (workers)

higher levels of this input: so they look like inverted U-shape curves as shown in Figure 11-5.

At a low level of the variable input, the marginal product is increasing because when the firm starts with a low number of workers. Adding more workers in the production process allows these workers to specialize in various tasks. Specialization can allow workers to become more productive, which raises their marginal product. For example, one individual producing salsa would have to perform all the tasks involved: selecting and preparing the ingredients, mixing the salsa, bottling and labelling it, packing it into cases, and so on. As more workers are employed, they can divide the tasks, with each worker specializing in one or a few aspects of salsa-making. This specialization leads to *increasing returns* and the hiring of additional workers, resulting in a marginal product curve that initially slopes upward. But once there are enough workers to have exhausted the benefits of specialization, diminishing returns to labour set in and the marginal product curve starts sloping downward. Thus, a typical marginal product curve has an inverted U-shape as shown in Figure 11-5.

By looking at Figure 11-5, you can also observe the following key facts about the relationship between marginal product and average product:

- When marginal product is *greater than* average product, average product rises.
- When marginal product is *less than* average product, average product falls.
- When marginal product is the same as average product, average product remains unchanged. Indeed, the average product is maximized when the marginal product *is equal to* the average product.

As a result, when the marginal product curve has an inverted U-shape, the average product of labour curve also has an inverted U-shape.

From the Production Function to Cost Curves

Once Alec and Janet know their production function, they know the relationship between inputs of labour and land and output of wheat for a given level of farming technique (or technology). But if they want to maximize their profits, they need to translate this knowledge into information about the relationship between the quantity of output and cost. Let's see how they can do this.

To translate information about a firm's production function into information about its costs, we need to know how much the firm must pay for its inputs. We will assume that Alec and Janet face either an explicit or an implicit cost of $400 for the use of the land. As we learned in Chapter 9, it is irrelevant whether Alec and Janet must rent the land for $400 from someone else or whether they own the land themselves and forgo earning $400 from renting it to someone else. Either way, they pay an opportunity cost of $400 by using the land to grow wheat. Moreover, since the land is a fixed input, the $400 Alec and Janet pay for it is a **fixed cost,** denoted by *FC*—a cost that does not depend on the quantity of output produced (in the short run). In business, fixed cost is often referred to as "overhead cost."

We also assume that Alec and Janet must pay each worker $200. Using their production function, Alec and Janet know that the number of workers they must hire depends on the amount of wheat they intend to produce. So the cost of labour, which is equal to the number of workers multiplied by $200, is a **variable cost,** denoted by *VC*—a cost that depends on the quantity of output produced. Adding the fixed cost and the variable cost of a given quantity of output gives the **total cost,** or *TC*, of that quantity of output. We can express the relationship among fixed cost, variable cost, and total cost as an equation:

(11-3) Total cost = Fixed cost + Variable cost

or

$$TC = FC + VC$$

The table in Figure 11-6 shows how total cost is calculated for Alec and Janet's farm. The second column shows the number of workers employed, *L*. The third column shows the corresponding level of output, *q*, taken from the table in Figure 11-1. The fourth column shows the variable cost, *VC*, equal to the number of workers multiplied by $200. The fifth column shows the fixed cost, *FC*, which is $400 regardless of how many workers are employed. The sixth column shows the total cost of output, *TC*, which is the variable cost plus the fixed cost.

The first column labels each row of the table with a letter, from *A* to *I*. These labels will be helpful in understanding our next step: drawing the **total cost curve,** a curve that shows how total cost depends on the quantity of output.

Alec and Janet's total cost curve is shown in the diagram in Figure 11-6, where the horizontal axis measures the quantity of output in bushels of wheat and the vertical axis measures total cost in dollars. Each point on the curve corresponds to one row of the table in Figure 11-6. For example, point *A* shows the situation when 0 workers are employed: output is 0, and total cost is equal to fixed cost, $400. Similarly, point *B* shows the situation when 1 worker is employed: output is 19 bushels, and total cost is $600, equal to the sum of $400 in fixed cost and $200 in variable cost.

Like the total product curve, the total cost curve slopes upward: due to the variable cost, the more output produced, the higher the farm's total cost. But unlike the total product curve, which gets flatter as employment rises, the total cost curve gets *steeper*. That is, the slope of the total cost curve is greater as the amount of output produced increases. As we will soon see, the steepening of the total cost curve is also due to diminishing returns to the variable input. Before we can understand this, we must first look at the relationships among several useful measures of cost.

A **fixed cost** is a cost that does not depend on the quantity of output produced. It is the cost of the fixed input.

A **variable cost** is a cost that depends on the quantity of output produced. It is the cost of the least amount of the variable input needed to make the quantity of output.

The **total cost** of producing a given quantity of output is the sum of the fixed cost and the variable cost of producing that quantity of output.

The **total cost curve** shows how total cost depends on the quantity of output.

FIGURE **11-6** Total Cost Curve for Alec and Janet's Farm

The table shows the variable cost, fixed cost, and total cost for various output quantities on Alec and Janet's 1-hectare farm. The total cost curve shows how total cost (measured on the vertical axis) depends on the quantity of output (measured on the horizontal axis). The labelled points on the curve correspond to the rows of the table. The total cost curve slopes upward because the number of workers employed, and hence total cost, increases as the quantity of output increases. The curve gets steeper as output increases due to diminishing returns to labour.

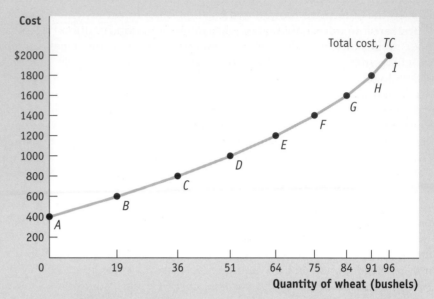

Point on graph	Quantity of labour *L* (workers)	Quantity of wheat *q* (bushels)	Variable cost *VC*	Fixed cost *FC*	Total cost *TC = FC + VC*
A	0	0	$0	$400	$400
B	1	19	200	400	600
C	2	36	400	400	800
D	3	51	600	400	1000
E	4	64	800	400	1200
F	5	75	1000	400	1400
G	6	84	1200	400	1600
H	7	91	1400	400	1800
I	8	96	1600	400	2000

ECONOMICS ▸ IN ACTION

THE MYTHICAL MAN-MONTH

The concept of diminishing returns to an input was first formulated by economists during the late eighteenth century. These economists, notably including Thomas Malthus, drew their inspiration from agricultural examples. Although still valid, examples drawn exclusively from agriculture can seem somewhat old-fashioned in our modern economy.

However, the idea of diminishing returns to an input applies with equal force to the most modern of economic activities—such as, say, the design of software. In 1975 Frederick P. Brooks Jr., a project manager at IBM during the days when it dominated the computer business, published a book titled *The Mythical Man-Month* that soon became a classic—so much so that a special anniversary edition was published 20 years later.

The chapter that gave its title to the book is basically about diminishing returns to labour in the writing of software. Brooks observed that multiplying the number of programmers assigned to a project did not produce a proportionate reduction in the time it took to get the program written. A project that could be done by 1 programmer in 12 months could *not* be done by 12 programmers in 1 month—

hence the "mythical man-month," the false notion that the number of lines of programming code produced was proportional to the number of code writers employed. In fact, above a certain number, adding another programmer on a project actually *increased* the time to completion.

The argument of *The Mythical Man-Month* is summarized in Figure 11-7. The upper part of the figure shows how the quantity of the project's output, as measured by the number of lines of code produced per month, varies with the number of programmers. Each additional programmer accomplishes less than the previous one, and beyond a certain point an additional programmer is actually counterproductive. The lower part of the figure shows the marginal product of each successive programmer, which falls as more programmers are employed and eventually becomes negative. In other words, programming is subject to diminishing returns so severe that at some point more programmers actually have negative marginal product. The source of the diminishing returns lies in the nature of the production function for a programming project: each programmer must coordinate his or her work with that of all the other programmers on the project, leading to each person spending more and more time communicating with others as the number of programmers increases. In other words, other things equal, there are diminishing returns to labour. It is likely, however, that if fixed inputs devoted to programming projects are increased—say, installing a faster Wiki system—the problem of diminishing returns for additional programmers can be mitigated.

A reviewer of the reissued edition of *The Mythical Man-Month* summarized the reasons for these diminishing returns: "There is an inescapable overhead to yoking up programmers in parallel. The members of the team must 'waste time' attending meetings, drafting project plans, exchanging e-mail, negotiating interfaces, enduring performance reviews, and so on. … At Microsoft, there will be at least one team member that just designs T-shirts for the rest of the team to wear." (See source note on copyright page.)

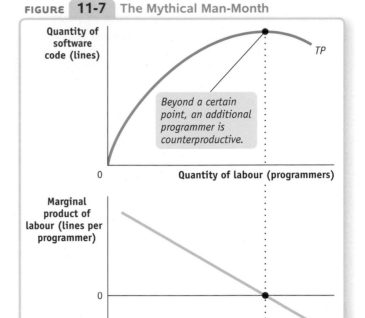

FIGURE **11-7** The Mythical Man-Month

Beyond a certain point, an additional programmer is counterproductive.

▼ Quick Review

- The firm's **production function** is the relationship between quantity of inputs and output for a given state of production technology. The **total product curve** shows how the quantity of output depends on the quantity of the **variable input** for a given quantity of the **fixed input** and production technique, and its slope is equal to the **marginal product** of the variable input. In the **short run,** the fixed input cannot be varied; in the **long run** all inputs are variable.

- When the levels of all other inputs and production technique are fixed, **diminishing returns to an input** may arise, yielding a downward-sloping marginal product curve and a total product curve that becomes flatter as more output is produced.

- The **average product** of an input is the amount of output produced per unit of that input.

- The **total cost** of a given quantity of output equals the **fixed cost** plus the **variable cost** of that output. The **total cost curve** becomes steeper as more output is produced due to diminishing returns to the variable input.

CHECK YOUR UNDERSTANDING 11-1

1. Bernie's ice-making company produces ice cubes using a 10-tonne machine and electricity. The quantity of output, measured in terms of kilograms of ice, is given in the accompanying table.

   a. What is the fixed input? What is the variable input?

   b. Construct a table showing the marginal product of the variable input. Does it show diminishing returns?

   c. Construct a table showing the average product of the variable input. What happens to the average product as the quantity of variable input used increases?

Quantity of electricity (kilowatt-hours)	Quantity of ice (kilograms)
0	0
1	1000
2	1800
3	2400
4	2800

   d. Suppose a 50% increase in the size of the fixed input increases output by 100% for any given amount of the variable input. What is the fixed input now? Construct a table showing the quantity of output, marginal product, and average product in this case.

Solutions appear at back of book.

Two Key Concepts: Marginal Cost and Average Cost

We've just learned how to derive a firm's total cost curve from its production function. Our next step is to take a deeper look at total cost by deriving two extremely useful measures: *marginal cost* and *average cost*. As we'll see, these two measures of the cost of production have a somewhat surprising relationship to each other. Moreover, they will prove to be vitally important in Chapter 12, where we will use them to analyze the firm's output decision and the market supply curve.

Marginal Cost

We defined marginal cost in Chapter 9: it is the change in total cost generated by producing one more unit of output. We've already seen that the marginal product of an input is easiest to calculate if data on output are available in increments of one unit of that input, all other things equal. Similarly, marginal cost is easiest to calculate if data on total cost are available in increments of one unit of output. When the data come in less convenient increments, it's still possible to calculate marginal cost. But for the sake of simplicity, let's work with an example in which the data come in convenient one-unit increments.

Selena's Gourmet Salsas produces bottled salsa and Table 11-1 shows how its costs per day depend on the number of cases of salsa it produces per day. The firm has fixed cost of $108 per day, shown in the second column, which represents the daily cost of its food-preparation equipment. The third column shows the variable cost, and the fourth column shows the total cost. Panel (a) of Figure 11-8 plots the total cost curve. Like the total cost curve for Alec and Janet's farm in Figure 11-6, this curve slopes upward, getting steeper as you move up it to the right.

FIGURE 11-8   Total Cost and Marginal Cost Curves for Selena's Gourmet Salsas

Panel (a) shows the total cost curve from Table 11-1. Like the total cost curve in Figure 11-6, it slopes upward and gets steeper as we move up it to the right. Panel (b) shows the marginal cost curve. It also slopes upward, reflecting diminishing returns to the variable input.

TABLE **11-1**   Costs at Selena's Gourmet Salsas

Quantity of salsa q (cases)	Fixed cost FC	Variable cost VC	Total cost TC = FC + VC	Marginal cost of case MC = ΔTC/Δq
0	$108	$0	$108	
				$12
1	108	12	120	
				36
2	108	48	156	
				60
3	108	108	216	
				84
4	108	192	300	
				108
5	108	300	408	
				132
6	108	432	540	
				156
7	108	588	696	
				180
8	108	768	876	
				204
9	108	972	1080	
				228
10	108	1200	1308	

The significance of the slope of the total cost curve is shown by the fifth column of Table 11-1, which calculates *marginal cost:* the additional cost of each additional unit, all other things equal. The general formula for marginal cost is:

(11-4) Marginal cost = $\dfrac{\text{Change in total cost generated by one additional unit of output}}{}$ = $\dfrac{\text{Change in total cost}}{\text{Change in quantity of output}}$

or

$$MC = \frac{\Delta TC}{\Delta q}$$

As in the case of marginal product, marginal cost is equal to "rise" (the increase in total cost) divided by "run" (the increase in the quantity of output). So just as marginal product is equal to the slope of the total product curve, marginal cost is equal to the slope of the total cost curve.

Now we can understand why the total cost curve gets steeper as we move up it to the right: as you can see in Table 11-1, marginal cost at Selena's Gourmet Salsas rises as output increases. Panel (b) of Figure 11-8 shows the marginal cost curve corresponding to the data in Table 11-1. Notice that, as in Figure 11-2, we plot the marginal cost for increasing output from 0 to 1 case of salsa halfway between 0 and 1, the marginal cost for increasing output from 1 to 2 cases of salsa halfway between 1 and 2, and so on.

Why does the marginal cost curve slope upward? Because there are diminishing returns to inputs in this example. All other things equal, as output increases, the marginal product of the variable input declines. This implies that more and more of the variable input must be used to produce each additional unit of output as the amount of output already produced rises. And since each unit of the variable input must be paid for, the additional cost per additional unit of output also rises.

In addition, recall that the flattening of the total product curve is also due to diminishing returns: the marginal product of an input falls as more of that input is used if the quantities of other inputs are fixed. The flattening of the total product curve as output increases and the steepening of the total cost curve as output increases are just flip-sides of the same phenomenon. That is, as output increases, the marginal cost of output also increases because the marginal product of the variable input decreases.

The inverse relationship between productivity and costs is discussed in greater detail in Appendix 11A. We will return to marginal cost in Chapter 12, when we consider the firm's profit-maximizing output decision. Our next step is to introduce another measure of cost: *average cost*.

Average Total Cost

In addition to total cost and marginal cost, it's useful to calculate another measure, **average total cost,** often simply called **average cost.** The average total cost is total cost divided by the quantity of output produced; that is, it is equal to total cost per unit of output. If we let *ATC* denote average total cost, the equation looks like this:

$$\textbf{(11-5)} \quad ATC = \frac{\text{Total cost}}{\text{Quantity of output}} = \frac{TC}{q}$$

Average total cost is important because it tells the producer how much the *average* or *typical* unit of output costs to produce. Marginal cost, meanwhile, tells the producer how much *one more* unit of output costs to produce. Although they may look very similar, these two measures of cost typically differ. And confusion between them is a major source of error in economics, both in the classroom and in real life, as illustrated by the upcoming Economics in Action.

Table 11-2 uses data from Selena's Gourmet Salsas to calculate average total cost. For example, the total cost of producing 4 cases of salsa is $300, consisting of $108 in fixed cost and $192 in variable cost (from Table 11-1). So the average total cost of producing 4 cases of salsa is $300/4 = $75. You can see from Table 11-2 that as quantity of output increases, average total cost first falls, then rises.

Figure 11-9 plots that data to yield the *average total cost curve*, which shows how average total cost depends on output. As before, cost in dollars is measured

TABLE 11-2 **Average Costs for Selena's Gourmet Salsas**

Quantity of salsa q (cases)	Total cost TC	Average total cost of case ATC = TC/q	Average fixed cost of case AFC = FC/q	Average variable cost of case AVC = VC/q
1	$120	$120.00	$108.00	$12.00
2	156	78.00	54.00	24.00
3	216	72.00	36.00	36.00
4	300	75.00	27.00	48.00
5	408	81.60	21.60	60.00
6	540	90.00	18.00	72.00
7	696	99.43	15.43	84.00
8	876	109.50	13.50	96.00
9	1080	120.00	12.00	108.00
10	1308	130.80	10.80	120.00

Average total cost, often referred to simply as **average cost,** is total cost divided by quantity of output produced.

A **U-shaped average total cost curve** falls at low levels of output, then rises at higher levels.

Average fixed cost is the fixed cost per unit of output.

on the vertical axis and quantity of output is measured on the horizontal axis. The average total cost curve has a distinctive U shape that corresponds to how average total cost first falls and then rises as output increases. Economists believe that such **U-shaped average total cost curves** are the norm for producers in many industries.

To help our understanding of why the average total cost curve is U-shaped, Table 11-2 breaks average total cost into its two underlying components, *average fixed cost* and *average variable cost*. **Average fixed cost,** or *AFC*, is fixed cost divided by the quantity of output, also known as the fixed cost per unit of output.

FIGURE **11-9** Average Total Cost Curve for Selena's Gourmet Salsas

The average total cost curve at Selena's Gourmet Salsas is U-shaped. At low levels of output, average total cost falls because the "spreading effect" of falling average fixed cost dominates the "diminishing returns effect" of rising average variable cost. At higher levels of output, the opposite is true and average total cost rises. At point *M*, corresponding to an output of three cases of salsa per day, average total cost is at its minimum level, the minimum average total cost.

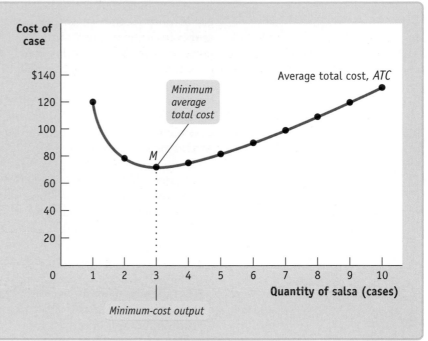

For example, if Selena's Gourmet Salsas produces 4 cases of salsa, average fixed cost is $108/4 = $27 per case. **Average variable cost,** or *AVC,* is variable cost divided by the quantity of output, also known as variable cost per unit of output. At an output of 4 cases, average variable cost is $192/4 = $48 per case. Writing these in the form of equations:

(11-6) $AFC = \dfrac{\text{Fixed cost}}{\text{Quantity of output}} = \dfrac{FC}{q}$

$AVC = \dfrac{\text{Variable cost}}{\text{Quantity of output}} = \dfrac{VC}{q}$

Average total cost is the sum of average fixed cost and average variable cost. It has a U shape because these components move in opposite directions as output rises.

Average fixed cost falls as more output is produced because the numerator (the fixed cost) is a fixed number but the denominator (the quantity of output) increases as more is produced. Another way to think about this relationship is that, as more output is produced, the fixed cost is spread over more units of output; the end result is that the fixed cost *per unit of output*—the average fixed cost—falls. You can see this effect in the fourth column of Table 11-2: average fixed cost drops continuously as output increases.

Average variable cost, however, rises as output increases. As we've seen, this reflects diminishing returns to the variable input: each additional unit of output incurs more variable cost to produce than the previous unit. So variable cost rises at a faster rate than the quantity of output increases.

So increasing output has two opposing effects on average total cost—the "spreading effect" and the "diminishing returns effect":

• *The spreading effect.* The larger the output, the greater the quantity of output over which fixed cost is spread, leading to lower average fixed cost.

• *The diminishing returns effect.* The larger the output, the greater the amount of variable input required to produce additional units, leading to higher average variable cost.

Average variable cost is the variable cost per unit of output.

At low levels of output, the spreading effect is very powerful because even small increases in output cause large reductions in average fixed cost. So at low levels of output, the spreading effect dominates the diminishing returns effect and causes the average total cost curve to slope downward. But when output is large, average fixed cost is already quite small, so increasing output further has only a very small spreading effect. Diminishing returns, however, usually grow increasingly important as output rises. As a result, when output is large, the diminishing returns effect dominates the spreading effect, causing the average total cost curve to slope upward. At the bottom of the U-shaped average total cost curve, point *M* in Figure 11-9, the two effects exactly balance each other. At this point average total cost is at its minimum level, the minimum average total cost.

Figure 11-10 brings together in a single picture four members of the family of cost curves that we have derived from the total cost curve for Selena's Gourmet Salsas: the marginal cost curve (*MC*), the average total cost curve (*ATC*), the average variable cost curve (*AVC*), and the average fixed cost curve (*AFC*). All are based on the information in Tables 11-1 and 11-2. As before, cost is measured on the vertical axis and the quantity of output is measured on the horizontal axis.

Let's take a moment to note some features of the various cost curves. First of all, marginal cost slopes upward—the result of diminishing returns that make an additional unit of output more costly to produce than the one before. Average variable cost also slopes upward—again, due to diminishing returns—but is flatter than the marginal cost curve. This is because the higher cost of an additional unit of output is averaged across all units, not just the additional units, in the average variable cost measure. Meanwhile, average fixed cost slopes downward because of the spreading effect.

Finally, notice that the marginal cost curve intersects the average total cost curve from below, crossing it at its lowest point, point *M* in Figure 11-10. This last feature is our next subject of study.

FIGURE **11-10** Marginal Cost and Average Cost Curves for Selena's Gourmet Salsas

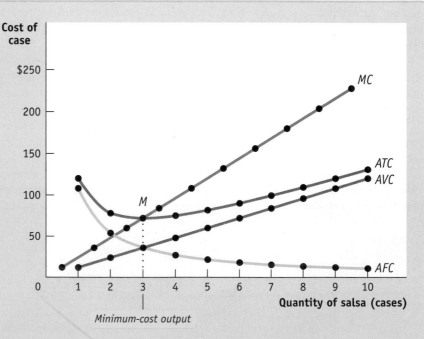

Here we have the family of cost curves for Selena's Gourmet Salsas: the marginal cost curve (*MC*), the average total cost curve (*ATC*), the average variable cost curve (*AVC*), and the average fixed cost curve (*AFC*). Note that the average total cost curve is U-shaped and the marginal cost curve crosses the average total cost curve at the bottom of the U, point *M*, corresponding to the minimum average total cost from Table 11-2 and Figure 11-9.

Minimum Average Total Cost

For a U-shaped average total cost curve, average total cost is at its minimum level at the bottom of the U. Economists call the quantity of output that corresponds to the minimum average total cost the **minimum-cost output.** In the case of Selena's Gourmet Salsas, the minimum-cost output is three cases of salsa per day.

In Figure 11-10, the bottom of the U is at the level of output at which the marginal cost curve crosses the average total cost curve from below. Is this an accident? No—it reflects general principles that are always true about a firm's marginal cost and average total cost curves:

- At the minimum-cost output, average total cost *is equal to* marginal cost.

- At output less than the minimum-cost output, marginal cost *is less than* average total cost and average total cost is falling.

- At output greater than the minimum-cost output, marginal cost *is greater than* average total cost and average total cost is rising.

To understand these principles, think about how your grade in one course—say, a 3.0 in physics—affects your overall grade point average. If your GPA before receiving that grade was more than 3.0, the new grade lowers your average.

Similarly, if marginal cost—the cost of producing one more unit—is less than average total cost, producing that extra unit lowers average total cost. This is shown in Figure 11-11 by the movement from A_1 to A_2. In this case, the marginal cost of producing an additional unit of output is low, as indicated by the point MC_L on the marginal cost curve. When the cost of producing the next unit of output is less than average total cost, increasing production reduces average total cost. So any quantity of output at which marginal cost is less than average total cost must be on the downward-sloping segment of the U.

But if your grade in physics is more than the average of your previous grades, this new grade raises your GPA. Similarly, if marginal cost is greater than average total cost, producing that extra unit raises average total cost. This is illustrated by the movement from B_1 to B_2 in Figure 11-11, where the marginal cost, MC_H, is higher than average total cost. So any quantity of output at which

> The **minimum-cost output** is the quantity of output at which average total cost is lowest—the bottom of the U-shaped average total cost curve.

FIGURE 11-11 The Relationship Between the Average Total Cost and the Marginal Cost Curves

To see why the marginal cost curve (*MC*) must cut through the average total cost curve at the minimum average total cost (point *M*), corresponding to the minimum-cost output, we look at what happens if marginal cost is different from average total cost. If marginal cost is *less* than average total cost, an increase in output must reduce average total cost, as in the movement from A_1 to A_2. If marginal cost is *greater* than average total cost, an increase in output must increase average total cost, as in the movement from B_1 to B_2.

marginal cost is greater than average total cost must be on the upward-sloping segment of the U.

Finally, if a new grade is exactly equal to your previous GPA, the additional grade neither raises nor lowers that average—it stays the same. This corresponds to point *M* in Figure 11-11: when marginal cost equals average total cost, we must be at the bottom of the U, because only at that point is average total cost neither falling nor rising.

Does the Marginal Cost Curve Always Slope Upward?

Up to this point, we have emphasized the importance of diminishing returns, which lead to a marginal product curve that always slopes downward and a marginal cost curve that always slopes upward. In practice, however, economists believe that marginal cost curves often slope *downward* as a firm increases its production from zero up to some low level, sloping upward only at higher levels of production: they look like the curve *MC* in Figure 11-12.

This initial downward slope occurs because a firm often finds that, when it starts with only a very small number of workers, employing more workers and expanding output allows specialization to take place. This specialization leads to *increasing returns* to the hiring of additional workers (i.e., the marginal product of labour curve begins by sloping upward) and results in a marginal cost curve that initially slopes downward. But once the benefits of specialization have been exhausted, diminishing returns to labour set in (i.e., the marginal product of labour curve begins sloping downward) and the marginal cost curve changes direction and slopes upward. So typical marginal cost curves actually have the "swoosh" shape shown by *MC* in Figure 11-12. For the same reason, average variable cost curves typically look like *AVC* in Figure 11-12: they are U-shaped rather than strictly upward sloping. The appendix of this chapter uses mathematics to investigate the relationship between marginal product and marginal cost, and between average product and average cost.

However, as Figure 11-12 also shows, the key features we saw from the example of Selena's Gourmet Salsas remain true: the average total cost curve is U-shaped, and the marginal cost curve passes through the point of minimum average total cost.

FIGURE **11-12** More Realistic Cost Curves

A realistic marginal cost curve has a "swoosh" shape. Starting from a very low output level, marginal cost often falls as the firm increases output. That's because hiring additional workers allows greater specialization of their tasks and leads to increasing returns. Once specialization is achieved, however, diminishing returns to additional workers set in and marginal cost rises. The corresponding average variable cost curve is now U-shaped, like the average total cost curve.

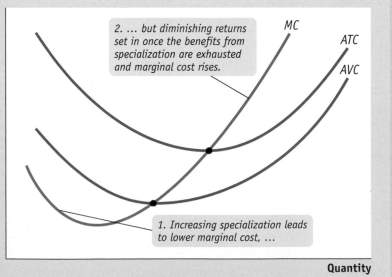

ECONOMICS ▸ IN ACTION

DON'T PUT OUT THE WELCOME MAT

Housing developments play an important role in the Canadian economy; directly and indirectly, such development provides thousands of jobs to Canadian workers. With our abundant supply of undeveloped land, real estate developers have long found it profitable to buy big parcels of land, build a large number of homes, and create entire new communities. But what is profitable for developers is not necessarily good for the existing residents.

In the past few years, real estate developers have encountered increasingly stiff resistance from local residents because of the additional costs—the marginal costs—imposed on existing homeowners from new developments. Let's look at why.

In Canada, a large percentage of the funding for local services such as roads, transit, water and sewer infrastructure, community centres, and fire and police facilities comes from taxes paid by local homeowners. For many cities, property taxes are the largest source of revenue: representing 39% of Toronto's revenues, 41% of Calgary's revenue, 54% of Edmonton's revenue, and 57% of Vancouver's revenue. In a sense, the municipal government uses those taxes to "produce" municipal services for the city. The overall level of property taxes is set to reflect the costs of providing those services.

The local tax rate that new homeowners pay on their new homes is the same as what existing homeowners pay on their older homes. That tax rate reflects the current total cost of services, and the taxes that an average homeowner pays reflect the average total cost of providing services to a household. The average total cost of providing services is based on the town's use of existing facilities, such as the existing school buildings, the existing number of teachers, the number of community centres and libraries, and so on.

But when a large development of homes is constructed, those facilities are no longer adequate: new schools must be built, new teachers hired, and so on. The quantity of output increases. So the *marginal cost* of providing municipal services per household associated with a new, large-scale development turns out to be much higher than the *average total cost* per household of existing homes. As a result, new developments and facilities cause everyone's local tax rate to go up, just as you would expect from Figure 11-12. To cover the cost of building this new infrastructure, cities in Ontario and in other provinces impose development charges on the construction of new homes. These development charges vary from city to city. For example, the average development charges for a similar unit vary significantly between Toronto and its surrounding municipalities. In early 2014, development charges for a large apartment unit ranged from about $13 000 in Toronto to $45 000 in nearby Brampton, Ontario. Although the development charges are lower in Toronto, the city government is considering a proposal to almost double them to cover the rising costs of providing services to residents. Toronto is not alone. As a result of the rising average cost of providing municipal services in many cities across Canada, potential new housing developments and newcomers are now facing a distinctly chilly reception.

New housing developments lead to higher taxes for everyone in the neighbourhood.

CP PHOTO/Larry MacDougal

▼ Quick Review

- Marginal cost is equal to the slope of the total cost curve. Diminishing returns cause the marginal cost curve to slope upward.

- **Average total cost** (or **average cost**) is equal to the sum of **average fixed cost** and **average variable cost.** When the **U-shaped average total cost curve** slopes downward, the spreading effect dominates: fixed cost is spread over more units of output. When it slopes upward, the diminishing returns effect dominates: an additional unit of output requires more variable inputs.

- Marginal cost is equal to average total cost at the **minimum-cost output.** At higher output levels, marginal cost is greater than average total cost and average total cost is rising. At lower output levels, marginal cost is lower than average total cost and average total cost is falling.

- At low levels of output there are often increasing returns to the variable input due to the benefits of specialization, making the marginal cost curve "swoosh"-shaped: initially sloping downward before sloping upward.

CHECK YOUR UNDERSTANDING 11-2

1. Alicia's Apple Pies is a roadside business. Alicia must pay $9.00 in rent each day. In addition, it costs her $1.00 to produce the first pie of the day, and each subsequent pie

costs 50% more to produce than the one before. For example, the second pie costs $1.00 × 1.5 = $1.50 to produce, and so on.

  a. Calculate Alicia's marginal cost, variable cost, average total cost, average variable cost, and average fixed cost as her daily pie output rises from 0 to 6. (*Hint:* The variable cost of two pies is just the marginal cost of the first pie, plus the marginal cost of the second, and so on.)

  b. Indicate the range of pies for which the spreading effect dominates and the range for which the diminishing returns effect dominates.

  c. What is Alicia's minimum-cost output? Explain why making one more pie lowers Alicia's average total cost when output is lower than the minimum-cost output. Similarly, explain why making one more pie raises Alicia's average total cost when output is greater than the minimum-cost output.

Solutions appear at back of book.

Short-Run versus Long-Run Costs

Up to this point, we have treated fixed cost as completely outside the control of a firm because we have focused on the short run. But as we noted earlier, all inputs are variable in the long run: this means that in the long run fixed cost may also be varied. *In the long run, in other words, a firm's fixed cost becomes a variable it can choose.* For example, given time, Selena's Gourmet Salsas can acquire additional food-preparation equipment or dispose of some of its existing equipment. In this section, we will examine how a firm's costs behave in the short run and in the long run. We will also see that the firm will choose its fixed cost in the long run based on the level of output it expects to produce.

Let's begin by supposing that Selena's Gourmet Salsas is considering whether to acquire additional food-preparation equipment. Acquiring additional machinery will affect its total cost in two ways. First, the firm will have to either rent or buy the additional equipment; either way, that will mean higher fixed cost in the short run. Second, if the workers have more equipment, they will be more productive: fewer workers will be needed to produce any given output, so variable cost for any given output level will be reduced.

The table in Figure 11-13 shows how acquiring an additional machine affects costs. In our original example, we assumed that Selena's Gourmet Salsas had a fixed cost of $108. The left half of the table shows variable cost as well as total cost and average total cost assuming a fixed cost of $108. The average total cost curve for this level of fixed cost is given by ATC_1 in Figure 11-13. Let's compare that to a situation in which the firm buys additional food-preparation equipment, doubling its fixed cost to $216 but reducing its variable cost at any given level of output. The right half of the table shows the firm's variable cost, total cost, and average total cost with this higher level of fixed cost. The average total cost curve corresponding to $216 in fixed cost is given by ATC_2 in Figure 11-13.

From the figure you can see that when output is small, 4 cases of salsa per day or fewer, average total cost is smaller when Selena forgoes the additional equipment and maintains the lower fixed cost of $108: ATC_1 lies below ATC_2. For example, at 3 cases per day, average total cost is $72 without the additional machinery and $90 with the additional machinery. But as output increases beyond 4 cases per day, the firm's average total cost is lower if it acquires the additional equipment, raising its fixed cost to $216. For example, at 9 cases of salsa per day, average total cost is $120 when fixed cost is $108 but only $78 when fixed cost is $216.

Why does average total cost change like this when fixed cost increases? When output is low, the increase in fixed cost from the additional equipment outweighs the reduction in variable cost from higher worker productivity—that is, there are too few units of output over which to spread the additional fixed cost. So if Selena plans to produce 4 or fewer cases per day, she would be better off choosing

FIGURE **11-13** Choosing the Level of Fixed Cost for Selena's Gourmet Salsas

There is a trade-off between higher fixed cost and lower variable cost for any given output level, and vice versa. ATC_1 is the average total cost curve corresponding to a fixed cost of $108; it leads to lower fixed cost and higher variable cost. ATC_2 is the average total cost curve corresponding to a higher fixed cost of $216 but lower variable cost. At low output levels, at 4 or fewer cases of salsa per day, ATC_1 lies below ATC_2: average total cost is lower with only $108 in fixed cost. But as output goes up, average total cost is lower with the higher amount of fixed cost, $216: at more than 4 cases of salsa per day, ATC_2 lies below ATC_1.

Quantity of salsa (cases)	Low fixed cost (FC = $108)			High fixed cost (FC = $216)		
	High variable cost	Total cost	Average total cost of case ATC_1	Low variable cost	Total cost	Average total cost of case ATC_2
1	$12	$120	$120.00	$6	$222	$222.00
2	48	156	78.00	24	240	120.00
3	108	216	72.00	54	270	90.00
4	192	300	75.00	96	312	78.00
5	300	408	81.60	150	366	73.20
6	432	540	90.00	216	432	72.00
7	588	696	99.43	294	510	72.86
8	768	876	109.50	384	600	75.00
9	972	1080	120.00	486	702	78.00
10	1200	1308	130.80	600	816	81.60

the lower level of fixed cost, $108, to achieve a lower average total cost of production. When planned output is high, however, she should acquire the additional machinery.

In general, for each output level there is some choice of fixed cost that minimizes the firm's average total cost for that output level. So when the firm has a desired output level that it expects to maintain over time, it should choose the level of fixed cost optimal for that level—that is, the level of fixed cost that minimizes its average total cost.

Now that we are studying a situation in which fixed cost can change, we need to take time into account when discussing average total cost. All of the average total cost curves we have considered until now are defined for a given level of fixed cost—that is, they are defined for the short run, the period of time over which fixed cost doesn't vary. To reinforce that distinction, for the rest of this chapter we will refer to these average total cost curves as "short-run average total cost curves."

For most firms, it is realistic to assume that there are many possible choices of fixed cost, not just two. The implication: for such a firm, many possible short-run average total cost curves will exist, each corresponding to a different choice

The **long-run average total cost curve** shows the relationship between output and average total cost when fixed cost has been chosen to minimize average total cost for each level of output.

of fixed cost and so giving rise to what is called a firm's "family" of short-run average total cost curves.

At any given point in time, a firm will find itself on one of its short-run cost curves, the one corresponding to its current level of fixed cost; a change in output will cause it to move along that curve. If the firm expects that change in output level to be long-standing, then it is likely that the firm's current level of fixed cost is no longer optimal. Given sufficient time, it will want to adjust its fixed cost to a new level that minimizes average total cost for its new output level. For example, if Selena had been producing 2 cases of salsa per day with a fixed cost of $108 but found herself increasing her output to 8 cases per day for the foreseeable future, then in the long run she should rent or purchase more equipment and increase her fixed cost to a level that minimizes average total cost at the 8-cases-per-day output level.

Suppose we do a thought experiment and calculate the lowest possible average total cost that can be achieved for each output level if the firm were to choose its fixed cost for each output level. Economists have given this thought experiment a name: the *long-run average total cost curve*. Specifically, the **long-run average total cost curve,** or *LRATC*, is the relationship between output and average total cost when fixed cost has been chosen to minimize average total cost *for each level of output*. This means that the long-run average total cost curve touches the lowest values of all the possible short-run average cost curves (for every possible fixed cost configuration).[1] In the long run, a firm generally has greater flexibility and thus can do at least as well as in the short run, and possibly much better. If there are many possible choices of fixed cost, the long-run average total cost curve will have the familiar, smooth U shape, as shown by *LRATC* in Figure 11-14.

We can now draw the distinction between the short run and the long run more fully. In the long run, when a producer has had time to choose the fixed cost appropriate for its desired level of output, that producer will be at some point on the long-run average total cost curve. But if the output level is altered, the firm will no longer be on its long-run average total cost curve and will instead be moving along its current short-run average total cost curve. It will not be on its long-run average total cost curve again until it readjusts its fixed cost for its new output level.

Figure 11-14 illustrates this point. The curve ATC_3 shows short-run average total cost if Selena has chosen the level of fixed cost that minimizes average total cost at an output of 3 cases of salsa per day. This is confirmed by the fact that at 3 cases per day, ATC_3 touches *LRATC*, the long-run average total cost curve. Similarly, ATC_6 shows short-run average total cost if Selena has chosen the level of fixed cost that minimizes average total cost if her output is 6 cases per day. It touches *LRATC* at 6 cases per day. And ATC_9 shows short-run average total cost if Selena has chosen the level of fixed cost that minimizes average total cost if her output is 9 cases per day. It touches *LRATC* at 9 cases per day.

Suppose that Selena initially chose to be on ATC_6. If she actually produces 6 cases of salsa per day, her firm will be at point *C* on both its short-run and long-run average total cost curves. Suppose, however, that Selena ends up producing only 3 cases of salsa per day. In the short run, her average total cost is indicated by point *B* on ATC_6; it is no longer on *LRATC*. If Selena had known that she would be producing only 3 cases per day, she would have been better off choosing a lower level of fixed cost, the one corresponding to ATC_3, thereby achieving a lower average total cost. Then her firm would have found itself at point *A* on the long-run average total cost curve, which lies below point *B*.

---

[1]This does not imply that the *LRATC* touches the minimum point of each short-run average cost curve. As Figure 11-14 demonstrates, at each level of output the *LRATC* is the lowest level of short-run average total cost possible to make that level of output (over all possible fixed cost configurations or over all possible short-run average total cost curves).

FIGURE **11-14** Short-Run and Long-Run Average Total Cost Curves

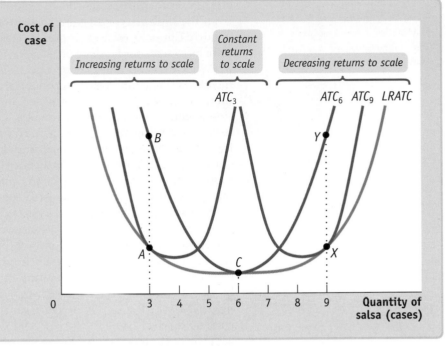

Short-run and long-run average total cost curves differ because a firm can choose its fixed cost in the long run. If Selena has chosen the level of fixed cost that minimizes short-run average total cost at an output of 6 cases, and actually produces 6 cases, then she will be at point C on *LRATC* and *ATC*₆. But if she produces only 3 cases, she will move to point B. If she expects to produce only 3 cases for a long time, in the long run she will reduce her fixed cost and move to point A on *ATC*₃. Likewise, if she produces 9 cases (putting her at point Y) and expects to continue this for a long time, she will increase her fixed cost in the long run and move to point X.

Suppose, conversely, that Selena ends up producing 9 cases per day even though she initially chose to be on ATC_6. In the short run her average total cost is indicated by point Y on ATC_6. But she would be better off acquiring more equipment and incurring a higher fixed cost in order to reduce her variable cost and move to ATC_9. This would allow her to reach point X on the long-run average total cost curve, which lies below Y.

The distinction between short-run and long-run average total costs is extremely important in making sense of how real firms operate over time. A company that has to increase output suddenly to meet a surge in demand will typically find that in the short run its average total cost rises sharply because it is hard to get extra production out of existing facilities. But given time to build new factories or add machinery, short-run average total cost falls.

Returns to Scale

What determines the shape of the long-run average total cost curve? The answer is that *scale,* the size of a firm's operations, is often an important determinant of its long-run average total cost of production. Firms that experience scale effects in production find that their long-run average total cost changes substantially depending on the quantity of output they produce. There are **increasing returns to scale** (also known as *economies of scale*) when long-run average total cost declines as output increases. As you can see in Figure 11-14, Selena's Gourmet Salsas experiences increasing returns to scale over output levels ranging from 0 up to 6 cases of salsa per day—the output levels over which *LRATC* is declining. In contrast, there are **decreasing returns to scale** (also known as *dis-economies of scale*) when long-run average total cost increases as output increases. For Selena's Gourmet Salsas, decreasing returns to scale occur at output levels greater than 6 cases, the output levels over which its long-run average total cost curve is rising. There is also a third possible relationship between long-run average total cost and scale: firms experience **constant returns to scale** when long-run average total cost is constant as output increases. In this case, the firm's long-run average total cost curve is horizontal over the output levels for which there are constant

There are **increasing returns to scale** when long-run average total cost declines as output increases.

There are **decreasing returns to scale** when long-run average total cost increases as output increases.

There are **constant returns to scale** when long-run average total cost is constant as output increases.

returns to scale. As you can see in Figure 11-14, Selena's Gourmet Salsas has constant returns to scale when it produces 6 cases of salsa per day. (You may notice from the high fixed cost table in Figure 11-13 that, since their average cost curve is fairly flat near 6 cases of output, Selena's Gourmet Salsas almost has constant returns to scale for levels of production anywhere from 5 to 7 cases of salsa per day.)

What explains these scale effects in production? The answer ultimately lies in the firm's technology of production. Increasing returns often arise from the increased *specialization* that larger output levels allow—a larger scale of operation means that individual workers can limit themselves to more specialized tasks, becoming more skilled and efficient at doing them. Another source of increasing returns is very large initial set-up cost; in some industries—such as auto manufacturing, electricity generating, or petroleum refining—incurring a high fixed cost in the form of plant and equipment is necessary to produce any output. A third source of increasing returns, found in certain high-tech industries such as software development, is *network externalities*, a topic covered in Chapter 16. As we'll see in Chapter 13, where we study monopoly, increasing returns have very important implications for how firms and industries interact and behave.

Decreasing returns—the opposite scenario—typically arise in large firms due to problems of coordination and communication: as the firm grows in size, it becomes ever more difficult and so more costly to communicate and to organize its activities. Although increasing returns induce firms to get larger, decreasing returns tend to limit their size. And when there are constant returns to scale, scale has no effect on a firm's long-run average total cost: it is the same regardless of whether the firm produces 1 unit or 100 000 units.

Summing Up Costs: The Short and Long of It

If a firm is to make the best decisions about how much to produce, it has to understand how its costs relate to the quantity of output it chooses to produce. Table 11-3 provides a quick summary of the concepts and measures of cost you have learned about.

TABLE 11-3 Concepts and Measures of Cost

	Measurement	Definition	Mathematical term
Short run	Fixed cost	Cost that does not depend on the quantity of output produced	FC
	Average fixed cost	Fixed cost per unit of output	$AFC = FC/q$
Short run and long run	Variable cost	Cost that depends on the quantity of output produced	VC
	Average variable cost	Variable cost per unit of output	$AVC = VC/q$
	Total cost	The sum of fixed cost (short run) and variable cost	$TC = FC$ (short run) $+ VC$
	Average total cost (average cost)	Total cost per unit of output	$ATC = TC/q$ $= (FC + VC)/q$ $= AFC + AVC$
	Marginal cost	The change in total cost generated by producing one more unit of output	$MC = \Delta TC/\Delta q$
Long run	Long-run average total cost	Average total cost when fixed cost has been chosen to minimize average total cost for each level of output	$LRATC$

ECONOMICS ▸ IN ACTION

THERE'S NO BUSINESS LIKE SNOW BUSINESS

Anyone who has lived both in a snowy city, like Montreal, and in a city that only occasionally experiences significant snowfall, like Victoria, is aware of the differences in total cost that arise from making different choices about fixed cost.

In Victoria, even a minor snowfall—say, 4 or 5 centimetres overnight—is enough to create chaos during the next morning's commute. The same snowfall in Montreal has hardly any effect at all. The reason is not that Victorians are wimps and Montrealers are made of sterner stuff; it is that Victoria, where it rarely snows, has only a fraction as many snowplows and other snowclearing equipment as cities where heavy snow is a fact of life.

In this sense Victoria and Montreal are like two producers who expect to produce different levels of output, where the "output" is snow removal. Victoria, which rarely has significant snow, has chosen a low level of fixed cost in the form of snow-clearing equipment. This makes sense under normal circumstances but leaves the city unprepared when major snow does fall. Montreal, which knows that it will face lots of snow, chooses to accept the higher fixed cost that leaves it in a position to respond effectively.

Cities with higher average annual snowfall maintain larger snowplow fleets.

▶●● CHECK YOUR UNDERSTANDING 11-3

1. The accompanying table shows three possible combinations of fixed cost and average variable cost. Average variable cost is constant in this example (it does not vary with the quantity of output produced).
   a. For each of the three choices, calculate the average total cost of producing 12 000, 22 000, and 30 000 units. For each of these quantities, which choice results in the lowest average total cost?
   b. Suppose that the firm, which has historically produced 12 000 units, experiences a sharp, permanent increase in demand that leads it to produce 22 000 units. Explain how its average total cost will change in the short run and in the long run.

Choice	Fixed cost	Average variable cost
1	$8 000	$1.00
2	12 000	0.75
3	24 000	0.25

   c. Explain what the firm should do instead if it believes the change in demand is temporary.

2. In each of the following cases, explain what kind of scale effects you think the firm will experience and why.
   a. A telemarketing firm in which employees make sales calls using computers and telephones
   b. An interior design firm in which design projects are based on the expertise of the firm's owner
   c. A diamond-mining company

3. Draw a graph like Figure 11-14 and insert a short-run average total cost curve corresponding to a long-run output choice of 5 cases of salsa per day. Use the graph to show why Selena should change her fixed cost if she expects to produce only 4 cases per day for a long period of time.

Solutions appear at back of book.

▾ Quick Review

- In the long run, firms choose fixed cost according to expected output. Higher fixed cost reduces average total cost when output is high. Lower fixed cost reduces average total cost when output is low.

- There are many possible short-run average total cost curves, each corresponding to a different level of fixed cost. The **long-run average total cost curve, *LRATC*,** shows average total cost over the long run, when the firm has chosen fixed cost to minimize average total cost for each level of output.

- A firm that has fully adjusted its fixed cost for its output level will operate at a point that lies on both its current short-run and long-run average total cost curves. A change in output moves the firm along its current short-run average total cost curve. Once it has readjusted its fixed cost, the firm will operate on a new short-run average total cost curve and on the long-run average total cost curve.

- Scale effects arise from the technology of production. **Increasing returns to scale** tend to make firms larger, **Decreasing returns to scale** tend to limit their size. With **constant returns to scale,** scale has no effect.

BUSINESS CASE : Kiva Systems' Robots versus Humans

Beth Hall/Bloomberg via Getty Images

When you order a product such as a book online, your order is likely packed and shipped by humans and robots working together as a team. E-commerce retailers can see their sales quadruple during the run-up to the Christmas holidays. So in North America, online retailers such as Amazon, Crate & Barrel, Toys "R" Us, Gap, and others have been increasingly using robots in their order fulfillment. According to the Business News Network (BNN), with the help of greater use of mobile robots, online sales in the United States rose by 17.3% on Thanksgiving and Black Friday in 2013, outpacing sales growth at brick-and-mortar stores.

The leader in these technological advances in warehouse automation is Kiva Systems. The Kiva robots receive orders via a computer system and deliver the products from the warehouse to human employees who pack the products for shipping. According to *Canadian Business,* the online shoe retailer Zappos.com found that its productivity doubled and its energy cost was cut in half less than a year after adopting the Kiva system. With the help of its Kiva robots, Zappos.com was still guaranteeing Christmas Eve delivery to U.S. customers on the morning of December 23rd.

Behind these technological advances in warehouse automation, however, lies a debate: people versus robots. The use of robots definitely boosts productivity and reduces labour requirements, but it might also reduce job security. Also, why don't we observe all online retailers using more robots to fulfill their orders? The answer is simple: it is not cheap to install a robotic system. According to Kiva, it can install a robotic system for as little as a few million dollars, but some installations have cost as much as $20 million. Yet hiring workers has a cost, too: during the 2013 holiday season, Amazon, the world's largest online retailer, hired about 70 000 temporary workers at its distribution centres around the globe.[2]

And as one industry analyst noted, an obstacle to the adoption of a robotic system for many e-commerce retailers is that it doesn't make economic sense: it's too expensive to buy sufficient robots for the busiest time of the year because they would be idle at other times. Kiva is now testing a program to rent out its robots seasonally so that retailers can "hire" enough robots to handle their holiday orders just like Amazon hires more humans.

Canadian retailers wishing to capture the benefits of Kiva without the costs of installing the system can choose to outsource their warehouse management to a logistic company. Based in Vaughan, Ontario, Think Logistics uses Kiva Systems robots to fill online orders for several companies. By serving multiple companies, Think Logistics can more fully utilize the benefits of their Kiva system all year round and is less prone to seasonal fluctuations in sales revenue.

QUESTIONS FOR THOUGHT

1. Assume that a firm can sell a robot, but that the sale takes time and the firm is likely to get less than what it paid. Other things equal, which system, human-based or robotic, will have a higher fixed cost? Which will have a higher variable cost? Explain.

2. Predict the pattern of off-holiday sales versus holiday sales that would induce a retailer to keep a human-based system. Predict the pattern that would induce a retailer to move to a robotic system. Explain how Kiva's "robot-for-hire" program would affect your answers.

3. Explain why the adoption of the Kiva robotic system could allow a company like Think Logistics to expand and hire additional workers.

---

[2]Although temporary workers may cost less than permanent workers in terms of wages and fringe benefits, it is still costly to hire and train them, especially during the holiday season when many other retailers are hiring additional workers to handle higher sales volumes.

SUMMARY

1. The relationship between inputs and output is a producer's **production function.** In the **short run,** the quantity of a **fixed input** cannot be varied but the quantity of a **variable input** can. In the **long run,** the quantities of all inputs can be varied. For a given amount of the fixed input, the **total product curve** shows how the quantity of output changes as the quantity of the variable input changes, holding the production technology fixed. We may also calculate the **marginal product** of an input, the increase in output from using one more unit of that input, or the **average product** of an input, the amount of output produced per unit of that input, holding the quantity of all other inputs and the production technology fixed.

2. There are **diminishing returns to an input** when its marginal product declines as more of the input is used, holding the quantity of all other inputs and the production technique fixed.

3. **Total cost,** represented by the **total cost curve,** is equal to the sum of **fixed cost,** which does not depend on output, and **variable cost,** which does depend on output. Due to diminishing returns, marginal cost, the increase in total cost generated by producing one more unit of output, normally increases as output increases.

4. **Average total cost** (also known as **average cost**), total cost divided by quantity of output, is the cost of the average unit of output, and marginal cost is the cost of one more unit produced. Economists believe that **U-shaped average total cost curves** are typical, because average total cost consists of two parts: **average fixed cost,** which falls when output increases (the spreading effect), and **average variable cost,** which rises with output (the diminishing returns effect).

5. When average total cost is U-shaped, the bottom of the U is the level of output at which average total cost is minimized, the point of **minimum-cost output.** This is also the point at which the marginal cost curve crosses the average total cost curve from below. Due to gains from specialization, the marginal cost curve may slope downward initially before sloping upward, giving it a "swoosh" shape.

6. In the long run, a producer can change its fixed input and its level of fixed cost. By accepting higher fixed cost, a firm can lower its variable cost for any given output level, and vice versa. The **long-run average total cost curve** shows the relationship between output and average total cost when fixed cost has been chosen to minimize average total cost at each level of output. A firm moves along its short-run average total cost curve as it changes the quantity of output, and in the long run it returns to a point on both its short-run and long-run average total cost curves once it has adjusted fixed cost to its new output level.

7. As output increases, there are **increasing returns to scale** if long-run average total cost declines; **decreasing returns to scale** if it increases; and **constant returns to scale** if it remains constant. Scale effects depend on the technology of production.

KEY TERMS

Production function, p. 344
Fixed input, p. 344
Variable input, p. 344
Long run, p. 344
Short run, p. 344
Total product curve, p. 344
Marginal product, p. 345
Diminishing returns to an input, p. 346

Average product, p. 348
Fixed cost, p. 351
Variable cost, p. 351
Total cost, p. 351
Total cost curve, p. 351
Average total cost, p. 356
Average cost, p. 356
U-shaped average total cost curve, p. 356

Average fixed cost, p. 356
Average variable cost, p. 357
Minimum-cost output, p. 359
Long-run average total cost curve, p. 364
Increasing returns to scale, p. 365
Decreasing returns to scale, p. 365
Constant returns to scale, p. 365

PROBLEMS

1. Changes in the prices of key commodities can have a significant impact on a company's bottom line. According to a September 27, 2007, article in the *Wall Street Journal*, "Now, with oil, gas and electricity prices soaring, companies are beginning to realize that saving energy can translate into dramatically lower costs." Another *Wall Street Journal* article, dated September 9, 2007, states, "Higher grain prices are taking an increasing financial toll." Energy is an input into virtually all types of production; corn is an input into the production of beef, chicken, high-fructose corn syrup, and ethanol (the gasoline substitute fuel).

   a. Explain how the cost of energy can be both a fixed cost and a variable cost for a company.

   b. Suppose energy is a fixed cost and energy prices rise. What happens to the company's average total cost curve? What happens to its marginal cost curve? Illustrate your answer with a diagram.

c. Explain why the cost of corn is a variable cost but not a fixed cost for an ethanol producer.

d. When the cost of corn goes up, what happens to the average total cost curve of an ethanol producer? What happens to its marginal cost curve? Illustrate your answer with a diagram.

2. Marty's Frozen Yogourt is a small shop that sells cups of frozen yogourt in a university town. Marty owns three frozen-yogourt machines. His other inputs are refrigerators, frozen-yogourt mix, cups, sprinkle toppings, and, of course, workers. He estimates that his daily production function when he varies the number of workers employed (and at the same time, of course, yogourt mix, cups, and so on) is as shown in the accompanying table.

Quantity of labour (workers)	Quantity of frozen yogourt (cups)
0	0
1	110
2	200
3	270
4	300
5	320
6	330

a. What are the fixed inputs and variable inputs in the production of cups of frozen yogourt?

b. Draw the total product curve. Put the quantity of labour on the horizontal axis and the quantity of frozen yogourt on the vertical axis.

c. What is the marginal product of the first worker? The second worker? The third worker? Why does marginal product decline as the number of workers increases?

d. What is the average product of labour when there are 2 workers? 3 workers? 4 workers? Why does average product decline as the number of workers increases?

3. The production function for Marty's Frozen Yogourt is given in Problem 2. Now suppose that, with experience, Marty's workers learn how to make frozen yogourt faster. As a result, their productivity increases by 20%.

a. Draw the initial and new total product curves. Put the quantity of labour on the horizontal axis and the quantity of frozen yogourt on the vertical axis. What happens to the total product curve?

b. What are the marginal product and average product for the workers in Marty's Frozen Yogourt after the productivity improvement?

c. Draw the initial and new marginal product and average product curves. Put the quantity of labour on the horizontal axis and the quantity of frozen yogourt on the vertical axis. What happens to the marginal product curve? What happens to the average product curve?

4. The production function for Marty's Frozen Yogourt is given in Problem 2. Marty pays each of his workers $80 per day. The cost of his other variable inputs is $0.50 per cup of yogourt. His fixed cost is $100 per day.

a. What is Marty's variable cost and total cost when he produces 110 cups of yogourt? 200 cups? Calculate variable and total cost for every level of output given in Problem 2.

b. Draw Marty's variable cost curve. On the same diagram, draw his total cost curve.

c. What is the marginal cost per cup for the first 110 cups of yogourt? For the next 90 cups? Calculate the marginal cost for all remaining levels of output.

5. The production function for Marty's Frozen Yogourt is given in Problem 2. The costs are given in Problem 4.

a. For each of the given levels of output, calculate the average fixed cost (AFC), average variable cost (AVC), and average total cost (ATC) per cup of frozen yogourt.

b. On one diagram, draw the AFC, AVC, and ATC curves.

c. What principle explains why the AFC declines as output increases? What principle explains why the AVC increases as output increases? Explain your answers.

d. How many cups of frozen yogourt are produced when average total cost is minimized?

6. The accompanying table shows a car manufacturer's total cost of producing cars.

Quantity of cars	TC
0	$500 000
1	540 000
2	560 000
3	570 000
4	590 000
5	620 000
6	660 000
7	720 000
8	800 000
9	920 000
10	1 100 000

a. What is this manufacturer's fixed cost?

b. For each level of output, calculate the variable cost (VC). For each level of output except zero output, calculate the average variable cost (AVC), average total cost (ATC), and average fixed cost (AFC). What is the minimum-cost output?

c. For each level of output, calculate this manufacturer's marginal cost (MC).

d. On one diagram, draw the manufacturer's AVC, ATC, and MC curves.

7. Labour costs represent a large percentage of total costs for many firms. According to Statistics Canada, Canada's labour costs were up by 2.98% from 2011 to 2012.

   a. When labour costs increase, what happens to average total cost and marginal cost? Consider a case in which labour costs are only variable costs and a case in which they represent a portion of both variable and fixed costs.

   An increase in labour productivity means each worker can produce more output. Recent data on productivity show that labour productivity in the Canadian business sector grew annually by 1.5% between 1991 and 1999, by 1.0% between 2000 and 2009, and by 0.85% between 2010 and 2012.

   b. When productivity growth is positive, what happens to the total product curve and the marginal product of labour curve? Illustrate your answer with a diagram.

   c. When productivity growth is positive, what happens to the marginal cost curve and the average total cost curve? Illustrate your answer with a diagram.

   d. If labour costs are rising over time on average, why would a company want to adopt equipment and methods that increase labour productivity?

8. Magnificent Blooms is a florist specializing in floral arrangements for weddings, graduations, and other events. Magnificent Blooms has a fixed cost associated with space and equipment of $100 per day. Each worker is paid $50 per day. The daily production function for Magnificent Blooms is shown in the accompanying table.

Quantity of labour (workers)	Quantity of floral arrangements
0	0
1	5
2	9
3	12
4	14
5	15

   a. Calculate the marginal product of each worker. What principle explains why the marginal product per worker declines as the number of workers employed increases?

   b. Calculate the marginal cost of each level of output. What principle explains why the marginal cost per floral arrangement increases as the number of arrangements increases?

9. You have the information shown in the accompanying table about a firm's costs. Complete the missing data.

Quantity	TC	MC	ATC	AVC
0	$20		—	—
		$20		
1	?		?	?
		10		
2	?		?	?
		16		
3	?		?	?
		20		
4	?		?	?
		24		
5	?		?	?

10. Evaluate each of the following statements. If a statement is true, explain why; if it is false, identify the mistake and try to correct it.

   a. A decreasing marginal product tells us that marginal cost must be rising.

   b. An increase in fixed cost increases the minimum-cost output.

   c. An increase in fixed cost increases marginal cost.

   d. When marginal cost is above average total cost, average total cost must be falling.

11. Husain and Sami operate a small company that produces souvenir footballs. Their fixed cost is $2000 per month. They can hire workers for $1000 per worker per month. Their monthly production function for footballs is as given in the accompanying table.

Quantity of labour (workers)	Quantity of footballs
0	0
1	300
2	800
3	1200
4	1400
5	1500

   a. For each quantity of labour, calculate average variable cost (AVC), average fixed cost (AFC), average total cost (ATC), and marginal cost (MC).

   b. On one diagram, draw the AVC, ATC, and MC curves.

   c. At what level of output is Husain and Sami's average total cost minimized?

12. You produce widgets. Currently you produce 4 widgets at a total cost of $40.

   a. What is your average total cost?

   b. Suppose you could produce one more (the fifth) widget at a marginal cost of $5. If you do produce that fifth widget, what will your average total cost be? Has your average total cost increased or decreased? Why?

c. Suppose instead that you could produce one more (the fifth) widget at a marginal cost of $20. If you do produce that fifth widget, what will your average total cost be? Has your average total cost increased or decreased? Why?

13. In your economics class, each homework problem set is graded on the basis of a maximum score of 100. You have completed 9 out of 10 of the problem sets for the term, and your current average grade is 88. What range of grades for your 10th problem set will raise your overall average? What range will lower your overall average? Explain your answer.

14. Don owns a small concrete-mixing company. His fixed cost is the cost of the concrete-batching machinery and his mixer trucks. His variable cost is the cost of the sand, gravel, and other inputs for producing concrete; the gas and maintenance for the machinery and trucks; and his workers. He is trying to decide how many mixer trucks to purchase. He has estimated the costs shown in the accompanying table based on estimates of the number of orders his company will receive per week.

Quantity of trucks	FC	VC		
		20 orders	40 orders	60 orders
2	$6000	$2000	$5000	$12 000
3	7000	1800	3800	10 800
4	8000	1200	3600	8 400

a. For each level of fixed cost, calculate Don's total cost for producing 20, 40, and 60 orders per week.

b. If Don is producing 20 orders per week, how many trucks should he purchase and what will his average total cost be? Answer the same questions for 40 and 60 orders per week.

15. Consider Don's concrete-mixing business, described in Problem 14. Assume that Don purchased 3 trucks, expecting to produce 40 orders per week.

a. Suppose that, in the short run, business declines to 20 orders per week. What is Don's average total cost per order in the short run? What will his average

total cost per order in the short run be if his business booms to 60 orders per week?

b. What is Don's long-run average total cost for 20 orders per week? Explain why his short-run average total cost of producing 20 orders per week when the number of trucks is fixed at 3 is greater than his long-run average total cost of producing 20 orders per week.

c. Draw Don's long-run average total cost curve. Draw his short-run average total cost curve if he owns 3 trucks.

16. True or false? Explain your reasoning.

a. The short-run average total cost can never be less than the long-run average total cost.

b. The short-run average variable cost can never be less than the long-run average total cost.

c. In the long run, choosing a higher level of fixed cost shifts the long-run average total cost curve upward.

17. Wolfsburg Wagon (WW) is a small automaker. The accompanying table shows WW's long-run average total cost.

Quantity of cars	LRATC of car
1	$30 000
2	20 000
3	15 000
4	12 000
5	12 000
6	12 000
7	14 000
8	18 000

a. For which levels of output does WW experience increasing returns to scale?

b. For which levels of output does WW experience decreasing returns to scale?

c. For which levels of output does WW experience constant returns to scale?

Inverse Relationships Between Productivity and Cost

In this chapter, we mentioned an inverse relationship between marginal product and marginal cost, and between average product and average variable cost. We noted that, all other things equal, when marginal product is rising, the marginal cost is falling. Similarly, we also noted that when the average product is rising, the average variable cost is falling. This appendix uses mathematics to explain these relationships.

Deriving the Inverse Relationships

In the chapter, we defined the marginal product of labour (*MPL*) and the average product of labour (*APL*):

(11-1) $MPL = \dfrac{\Delta q}{\Delta L}$

(11-2) $APL = \dfrac{q}{L}$

Now, let's turn to a firm's costs of production. For any firm, the amount of capital employed in the production process (such as property, machinery, and equipment) is assumed to be constant in the short run. We also assume that the state of production technology is fixed. In the short run, the firm can only adjust the amount of labour employed, the variable input. Since the firm must pay both fixed costs (*FC*) and the variable cost (*VC*) of labour to produce its output, its total cost (*TC*) can be expressed in terms of labour:

(11-3) $TC = FC + VC$
$ = FC + w \times L$

where w is the wage rate page for one unit of labour. For example, suppose the hourly wage at a bakery is $15 and the daily fixed costs total $2000. We can express the bakery's total cost in terms of the number of hours of labour as:

$$TC = 2000 + 15 \times L$$

A firm should be interested in minimizing its cost of production for a given level of output. Then, the problem becomes how to minimize *TC*, subject to q.

Recall, marginal cost, *MC*, is the additional cost incurred by producing an additional unit of output. We expressed it as the change in total cost divided by the change in output:

(11-4) $MC = \dfrac{\Delta TC}{\Delta q}$

$ = \dfrac{\Delta(FC + w \times L)}{\Delta q} = \dfrac{\Delta(FC)}{\Delta q} + \dfrac{\Delta(w \times L)}{\Delta q}$

Due to the inverse relationship between marginal product of labour and marginal cost, and between average product of labour and average variable cost, the marginal cost curve mirrors the marginal product curve while the average variable cost curve mirrors the average product curve. Marginal cost falls when marginal product of labour rises; while marginal cost rises when marginal product of labour falls. When marginal product of labour is maximized (point A), marginal cost reaches its minimum (point A′). Similarly, when average product of labour rises, average variable costs falls; when average product of labour falls, average variable costs rises. When average product of labour is maximized (point B), average variable cost reaches its minimum (point B′).

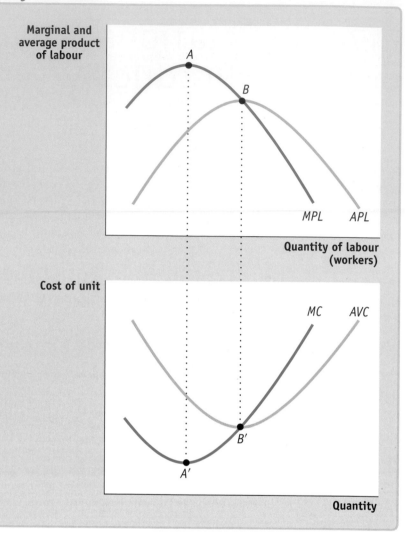

Since fixed costs do not change, ΔFC is zero. The wage is also constant, so the term w can be moved outside of the fraction:

(11A-1) $MC = w \times \dfrac{\Delta L}{\Delta q}$

An example may make this algebra clearer. For the bakery, the change in total cost ($TC = 2000 + 15 \times L$) can be separated into the change in the fixed cost ($2000) plus the change in the variable cost of $15 multiplied by the change in hours of labour. The fixed amount does not change by definition, and only the number of hours of labour changes. At the bakery, the marginal cost is:

$MC = 15 \times \dfrac{\Delta L}{\Delta q}$

Now go back and look at Equation 11-1. The fraction in the equations above is the inverse of Δq divided by ΔL, the marginal product of labour. Therefore, we can rewrite marginal cost as:

(11A-2) $MC = w \times \dfrac{1}{MPL}$

Now, it is clear that marginal cost falls when marginal product of labour rises; when the marginal product of labour falls, the marginal cost rises. Also, when marginal product is maximized, marginal cost reaches its minimum.

Discovering the inverse relationship between the average product of labour and average variable cost, AVC, is somewhat easier. In the chapter, we defined AVC as the variable cost per unit of output:

(11-6) $AVC = \dfrac{VC}{q}$

$$= \dfrac{w \times L}{q} = w \times \dfrac{L}{q}$$

Since Equation 11-2 describes APL as q divided by L, we have another inverse relationship. We can rewrite the average variable cost as:

(11A-3) $AVC = w \times \dfrac{1}{APL}$

Now, you can clearly see the inverse relationship between these two concepts. When average product of labour rises, average variable costs falls; when average product of labour falls, average variable costs rises. When average product is maximized, average variable cost reaches its minimum. Figure 11A-1 summarizes these relationships geometrically.

PROBLEMS

1. Magnificent Blooms is a florist specializing in floral arrangements for weddings, graduations, and other events. The daily marginal product of labour and average product of labour are:

   $MPL = 0.25 \times L^{-0.5}$
   $APL = 0.50 \times L^{-0.5}$

   where L is the number of workers used in a day. Each worker is paid $54 per day.

   a. If Magnificent Blooms employs 9 workers, what is the average product of labour? What is the marginal product of labour?

   b. If Magnificent Blooms increases the number of workers employed, what happens to the marginal product of labour and the average product of labour? Explain.

   c. Derive the marginal cost and the average variable cost functions in terms of labour.

   d. If Magnificent Blooms needs to make 18 floral arrangements per day, how many workers will it hire? (*Hint:* Use Equation 11-2 with $q = 18$ and solve for L.)

   e. Determine the marginal cost, the average cost, and average variable cost for 18 floral arrangements per day.

2. Suppose a firm's short-run total costs and marginal costs in dollars are given by:

   $TC = 0.5 \times q^2 + 2.5 \times q + 72$
   $MC = q + 2.5$

   where q is the output per day. The firm has a fixed cost of $40, which is included in the TC equation above.

   a. Determine this firm's average variable cost and average total cost in terms of q.

   b. Draw a rough sketch of this firm's average total cost, average variable cost, and marginal cost curves. Put the quantity of output on the horizontal axis and the cost on the vertical axis.

   c. Determine the level of output where average total cost is at a minimum. At this level of output, what do average total cost and marginal cost equal? Is this surprising? Explain why or why not.

   d. Determine the level of output where average variable cost is at a minimum. At this level of output, what do average variable cost and marginal equal?

Perfect Competition and the Supply Curve

DOING WHAT COMES NATURALLY

Thinkstock

Whether it's organic strawberries or satellites, how a good is produced determines its cost of production.

❭ What a **perfectly competitive market** is and the characteristics of a **perfectly competitive industry**

❭ How a **price-taking producer** determines its profit-maximizing quantity of output

❭ How to assess whether or not a producer is profitable and why an unprofitable producer may continue to operate in the short run

❭ Why industries behave differently in the short run and the long run

❭ What determines the **industry supply curve** in both the short run and the long run

FOOD CONSUMERS IN CANADA are concerned about health issues. Demand for natural foods and beverages, such as bottled water and organically grown fruits and vegetables, increased rapidly at an average growth rate of 21% per year since 2006. The small group of farmers who had pioneered organic farming techniques prospered thanks to higher prices.

But everyone knew that the high prices of organic produce were unlikely to persist even if the new, higher demand for naturally grown food continued: the supply of organic food, although relatively price-inelastic in the short run, was surely price-elastic in the long run. Over time, farms already producing organically would increase their capacity, and conventional farmers

would enter the organic food business. So the increase in the quantity supplied in response to the increase in price would be much larger in the long run than in the short run.

Where does the supply curve come from? Why is there a difference between the short-run and the long-run supply curves? In this chapter we will use our understanding of costs, developed in Chapter 11, as the basis for an analysis of the supply curve. As we'll see, this will require that we understand the behaviour both of individual firms and of an entire industry, composed of these many individual firms.

Our analysis in this chapter assumes that the industry in question is characterized by *perfect competition*. We begin by explaining the concept of perfect

competition, providing a brief introduction to the conditions that give rise to a perfectly competitive industry. We then show how a producer under perfect competition decides how much to produce. Finally, we use the cost curves of the individual producers to derive the *industry supply curve* under perfect competition. By analyzing the way a competitive industry evolves over time, we will come to understand the distinction between the short-run and long-run effects of changes in demand on a competitive industry—such as, for example, the effect of Canada's new taste for organic food on the organic farming industry. By the end of the chapter, we will have a better understanding of the conditions necessary for an industry to be perfectly competitive. ◼

A **price-taking producer** is a producer whose actions have no effect on the market price of the good or service it sells.

A **price-taking consumer** is a consumer whose actions have no effect on the market price of the good or service he or she buys.

A **perfectly competitive market** is a market in which all market participants are price-takers.

A **perfectly competitive industry** is an industry in which all producers are price-takers.

Perfect Competition

Suppose that Yves and Zoe are neighbouring farmers, both of whom grow organic tomatoes. Both sell their output to the same grocery store chains that carry organic foods; so, in a real sense, Yves and Zoe compete with each other.

Does this mean that Yves should try to stop Zoe from growing tomatoes or that Yves and Zoe should form an agreement to grow less? Almost certainly not: there are hundreds or thousands of organic tomato farmers, and Yves and Zoe are competing with all those other growers as well as with each other. Because so many farmers sell organic tomatoes, if any one of them produced more or less, there would be no measurable effect on market prices.

When people talk about business competition, the image they often have in mind is a situation in which two or three rival firms are intensely struggling for advantage. But economists know that when an industry consists of a few main competitors, it's actually a sign that competition is fairly limited. As the example of organic tomatoes suggests, when there is enough competition, it doesn't even make sense to identify your rivals: there are so many competitors that you cannot single out any one of them as a rival.

We can put it another way: Yves and Zoe are **price-taking producers.** A producer is a price-taker when it controls so little of the market that its actions will not have any influence on the market price of the good or service it sells. As a result, a price-taking producer considers the market price as given. When there is enough competition—when competition is what economists call "perfect"—then every producer is a price-taker. And there is a similar definition for consumers: a **price-taking consumer** is a consumer who cannot influence the market price of the good or service by his or her actions. That is, the market price is unaffected by how much or how little of the good the consumer buys.

Defining Perfect Competition

In a **perfectly competitive market,** all market participants, both consumers and producers, are price-takers. That is, neither consumption decisions by individual consumers nor production decisions by individual producers affect the market price of the good.

The supply and demand model, which we introduced in Chapter 3 and have used repeatedly since then, is a model of a perfectly competitive market. It depends fundamentally on the assumption that the actions of an individual buyer or seller of a good, such as coffee beans or organic tomatoes, cannot affect the price at which he or she can buy or sell the good.

As a general rule, consumers are indeed price-takers. Instances in which consumers are able to affect the prices they pay are rare. It is, however, quite common for producers to have a significant ability to affect the prices they receive, a phenomenon we'll address in Chapter 13. So the model of perfect competition is appropriate for some but not all markets. An industry in which all producers are price-takers is called a **perfectly competitive industry.** Clearly, some industries aren't perfectly competitive; in later chapters we'll learn how to analyze industries that don't fit the perfectly competitive model.

Under what circumstances will all producers be price-takers? In the next section we will find that there are two necessary conditions for a perfectly competitive industry and that a third condition is often present as well.

Two Necessary Conditions for Perfect Competition

The markets for major grains, like wheat and corn, are perfectly competitive: individual wheat and corn farmers, as well as individual buyers of wheat and corn, take market prices as given. In contrast, the markets for some of the food items made from these grains—in particular, breakfast cereals—are by no means perfectly competitive. There is intense competition among cereal brands, but not *perfect* competition. To understand the difference between the market for wheat and the market for shredded wheat cereal is to understand the importance of the two necessary conditions for perfect competition.

First, for an industry to be perfectly competitive, it must contain many producers, none of whom have a large **market share.** A producer's market share is the fraction of the total industry output accounted for by that producer's output. The distribution of market share constitutes a major difference between the grain industry and the breakfast cereal industry. There are thousands of wheat farmers, none of whom account for more than a tiny fraction of total wheat sales.

The breakfast cereal industry, however, is dominated by four producers: Kellogg's, General Mills, Post Foods, and the Quaker Oats Company. Kellogg's alone accounts for more than 40% of all cereal sales. Kellogg's executives know that if they try to sell more cornflakes, they are likely to drive down the market price of cornflakes. That is, they know that their actions influence market prices, simply because they are so large a part of the market that changes in their production will significantly affect the overall quantity supplied. It makes sense to assume that producers are price-takers only when an industry does *not* contain any large producers like Kellogg's.

Second, an industry can be perfectly competitive only if consumers regard the products of all producers as equivalent. This clearly isn't true in the breakfast cereal market: Cap'n Crunch isn't considered a good substitute for Multi Grain Cheerios. As a result, the maker of Multi Grain Cheerios has some ability to increase its price without fear that it will lose all its customers to the maker of Cap'n Crunch.

Contrast this with the case of a **standardized product,** which is a product that consumers regard as the same good even when it comes from different producers, sometimes known as a **commodity.** Because wheat is a standardized product,[1] consumers regard the output of one wheat producer as a perfect substitute for that of another producer. Consequently, one farmer cannot increase the price for his or her wheat without losing all sales to other wheat farmers. *So the second necessary condition for a competitive industry is that the industry output is a standardized product* (see the upcoming For Inquiring Minds).

Free Entry and Exit

All perfectly competitive industries have many producers with small market shares, producing a standardized product. Most perfectly competitive industries are also characterized by one more feature: it is easy for new firms to enter the industry or for firms that are currently in the industry to leave. That is, no obstacles in the form of government regulations or limited access to key resources prevent new producers from entering the market. And no additional costs are associated with shutting down a company and leaving the industry. Economists refer to the arrival of new firms into an industry as *entry;* they refer to the departure of firms from an industry as *exit.* When there are no obstacles to entry into or exit from an industry, we say that the industry has **free entry and exit.** For example, in the convenience store market, the set-up cost of a corner shop is relatively low, which allows owners to enter and leave the market easily.

Free entry and exit is not strictly necessary for perfect competition. In Chapter 5 we described the case of lobster fishing in Atlantic Canada, where regulations limit the number of licences and thus lobster traps, so entry into the industry is limited. Despite this, there are enough boats operating that the fishers are price-takers. But free entry and exit is a key factor in most competitive industries. It ensures that the number of producers in an industry can adjust to changing market conditions. And, in particular, it ensures that producers in an industry cannot act to keep new firms out.

A producer's **market share** is the fraction of the total industry output accounted for by that producer's output.

A good is a **standardized product,** also known as a **commodity,** when consumers regard the products of different producers as the same good.

An industry has **free entry and exit** when new producers can easily enter into an industry and existing producers can easily leave that industry.

---

[1]Wheat is actually classified into different grades. Depending on the quality, each grade of wheat will command a different price. In this chapter, we are assuming the wheat is of the same quality or grade.

FOR INQUIRING MINDS

WHAT'S A STANDARDIZED PRODUCT?

A perfectly competitive industry must produce a standardized product. But is it enough for the products of different firms actually to be the same? No: people must also *think* that they are the same. And producers often go to great lengths to convince consumers that they have a distinctive, or *differentiated*, product, even when they don't.

Consider, for example, champagne—not the super-expensive premium champagnes but the more ordinary stuff. Most people cannot tell the difference between champagne actually produced in the Champagne region of France, where the product originated, and similar products from Spain, British Columbia, or Ontario. But the French government has sought and obtained legal protection for the winemakers of Champagne, ensuring that around the world only bubbly wine from that region

In the end, only kimchi eaters can tell you if there is truly a difference between Korean-produced kimchi and the Japanese-produced variety.

AP/Wide World Photos

can be called champagne. If it's from someplace else, all the seller can do is say that it was produced using the *méthode Champenoise*. This creates a differentiation in the minds of consumers and lets the champagne producers of Champagne charge higher prices.

Similarly, Korean producers of *kimchi*, the spicy fermented cabbage that is the Korean national side dish, are doing their best to convince consumers that the same product packaged by Japanese firms is just not the real thing. The purpose is, of course, to ensure higher prices for Korean *kimchi*.

So is an industry perfectly competitive if it sells products that are indistinguishable except in name but that consumers, for whatever reason, don't think are standardized? No. When it comes to defining the nature of competition, the consumer is always right.

To sum up, then, perfect competition depends on two necessary conditions. First, the industry must contain many producers, each having a small market share. Second, the industry must produce a standardized product. In addition, perfectly competitive industries are normally characterized by free entry and exit.

How does an industry that meets these three criteria behave? As a first step toward answering that question, let's look at how an individual producer in a perfectly competitive industry maximizes profit.

ECONOMICS > *IN ACTION*

THE PAIN OF COMPETITION

Sometimes it is possible to see an industry become perfectly competitive. In fact, it happens frequently in the case of pharmaceuticals when the patent on a popular drug expires.

When a company develops a new drug, it is usually able to receive a patent, which gives it a *legal monopoly*—the exclusive right to sell the drug—for 20 years from the date of filing. Legally, no one else can sell that drug without the patent owner's permission. When the patent expires, the market is open for other companies to sell their own versions of the drug, known collectively as *generics*. Generics are standardized products, much like the painkillers ASA and ibuprofen, and are often sold by many producers.

The shift from a market with a single seller to perfect competition, not coincidentally, is accompanied by a sharp fall in the market price. For example, when the patent expired for the painkiller ibuprofen and generics were introduced, its price eventually fell by more than 60%; the price of the painkiller naproxen fell by about 80%. On average, drug prices are 40% lower after a generic enters the market.

Patents allow drug makers to have a legal monopoly on new medications for 20 years.

Jacky Chapman/Janine Wiedel Photolibrary/Alamy

Not surprisingly, the makers of patent-protected drugs are eager to forestall the entry of generic competitors and have tried a variety of strategies. A firm applying to Health Canada to market a generic version of a drug must show that it does not infringe on patents filed by brand-name firms. However, brand-name companies can challenge the application, resulting in an automatic 24-month delay. As a result, the original drug maker continues to charge high prices and reap high profits. In the United States, one especially successful tactic is for the original drug maker to make an agreement with a potential generic competitor, essentially paying the competitor to delay its entry into the market. These agreements have been fiercely contested by many government regulators, who view them as anti-competitive practices that hurt consumers. As of the time of writing, drug makers, consumers, and government officials were awaiting a decision by the courts on the legality of these agreements.

CHECK YOUR UNDERSTANDING   12-1

1. In each of the following situations, do you think the industry described will be perfectly competitive or not? Explain your answer.
   a. There are two producers of aluminum in the world, a good sold in many places.
   b. The price of natural gas is determined by global supply and demand. A small share of that global supply is produced by a handful of companies located in the North Sea.
   c. Dozens of designers sell high-fashion clothes. Each designer has a distinctive style and a loyal clientele.
   d. There are many NHL teams in North America, one or two in each major city and each selling tickets to its hometown events.

Solutions appear at back of book.

Production and Profits

Consider Jennifer and Jason, who run an organic tomato farm. Suppose that the market price of organic tomatoes is $18 per bushel and that Jennifer and Jason are price-takers—they can sell as much as they like at that price. Then we can use the data in Table 12-1 to find their profit-maximizing level of output by direct calculation.

The first column shows the quantity of output in bushels, and the second column shows Jennifer and Jason's total revenue from their output: the market value of their output. Total revenue, *TR*, is equal to the market price multiplied by the quantity of output:

(12-1) $TR = P \times q$

In this example, total revenue is equal to $18 per bushel times the quantity of output in bushels.

The third column of Table 12-1 shows Jennifer and Jason's total cost. The fourth column shows their profit, equal to total revenue minus total cost:

(12-2) $\text{Profit} = TR - TC$

TABLE **12-1**   Profit for Jennifer and Jason's Farm When Market Price Is $18

Quantity of tomatoes *q* (bushels)	Total revenue *TR*	Total cost *TC*	Profit *TR − TC*
0	$0	$14	−$14
1	18	30	−12
2	36	36	0
3	54	44	10
4	72	56	16
5	90	72	18
6	108	92	16
7	126	116	10

As indicated by the numbers in the table, profit is maximized at an output of 5 bushels, where profit is equal to $18. But we can gain more insight into the profit-maximizing choice of output by viewing it as a problem of marginal analysis, a task we'll do next.

Marginal revenue is the change in total revenue generated by an additional unit of output.

According to the **optimal output rule,** profit is maximized by producing the quantity of output at which the marginal revenue of the last unit produced is equal to its marginal cost.

According to the **price-taking firm's optimal output rule,** a price-taking firm's profit is maximized by producing the quantity of output at which the market price is equal to the marginal cost of the last unit produced.

Using Marginal Analysis to Choose the Profit-Maximizing Quantity of Output

Recall from Chapter 9 the *profit-maximizing principle of marginal analysis:* the optimal amount of an activity is the level at which marginal benefit is equal to marginal cost. To apply this principle, consider the effect on a producer's profit of increasing output by one unit. The marginal benefit of that unit is the additional revenue generated by selling it; this measure has a name—it is called the **marginal revenue** of that unit of output. The general formula for marginal revenue is:

(12-3) Marginal revenue = $\dfrac{\text{Change in total revenue generated by one additional unit of output}}{} = \dfrac{\text{Change in total revenue}}{\text{Change in quantity of output}}$

or

$$MR = \Delta TR/\Delta q$$

So Jennifer and Jason maximize their profit by producing bushels up to the point at which the marginal revenue is equal to marginal cost. We can summarize this as the producer's **optimal output rule:** profit is maximized by producing the quantity at which the marginal revenue of the last unit produced is equal to its marginal cost. That is, $MR = MC$ at the optimal quantity of output.

We can learn how to apply the optimal output rule with the help of Table 12-2, which provides various short-run cost measures for Jennifer and Jason's farm. The second column contains the farm's variable cost, and the third column shows its total cost of output based on the assumption that the farm incurs a fixed cost of $14. The fourth column shows their marginal cost. Notice that, in this example, the marginal cost initially falls as output rises but then begins to increase. This gives the marginal cost curve has the "swoosh" shape described in Figure 11-10 in Chapter 11. (Shortly it will become clear that this shape has important implications for short-run production decisions.)

The fifth column contains the farm's marginal revenue, which has an important feature: Jennifer and Jason's marginal revenue is constant at $18 for every output level. The sixth and final column shows the calculation of the net gain per bushel of tomatoes, which is equal to marginal revenue minus marginal cost—or, equivalently in this case, market price minus marginal cost. As you can see, it is positive for the 1st through 5th bushels; producing each of these bushels raises Jennifer and Jason's profit. For the 6th and 7th bushels, however, net gain is negative: producing them would decrease, not increase, profit. (You can verify this by examining Table 12-1.) So 5 bushels are Jennifer and Jason's profit-maximizing output; it is the level of output at which marginal cost is equal to the market price, $18.

This example, in fact, illustrates another general rule derived from marginal analysis—the **price-taking firm's optimal output rule,** which says that a price-taking firm's profit is maximized by producing the quantity of output at which the market price is equal to the marginal cost of the last unit produced. That is, $P = MC$ at the price-taking firm's optimal quantity of output. In fact, the

TABLE 12-2 **Short-Run Costs for Jennifer and Jason's Farm**

Quantity of tomatoes q (bushels)	Variable cost VC	Total cost TC	Marginal cost of bushel $MC = \Delta TC/\Delta q$	Marginal revenue of bushel MR	Net gain of bushel = MR − MC
0	$0	$14			
			$16	$18	$2
1	16	30			
			6	18	12
2	22	36			
			8	18	10
3	30	44			
			12	18	6
4	42	56			
			16	18	2
5	58	72			
			20	18	−2
6	78	92			
			24	18	−6
7	102	116			

price-taking firm's optimal output rule is just an application of the optimal output rule to the particular case of a price-taking firm. Why? Because *in the case of a price-taking firm, marginal revenue is equal to the market price.*

A price-taking firm cannot influence the market price by its actions. It always takes the market price as given because it cannot lower the market price by selling more or raise the market price by selling less. So, for a price-taking firm, the additional revenue generated by producing one more unit is always the market price. We will need to keep this fact in mind in future chapters, where we will learn that marginal revenue is not equal to the market price if the industry is not perfectly competitive. As a result, firms are not price-takers when an industry is not perfectly competitive.

For the remainder of this chapter, we will assume that the industry in question is like organic tomato farming, perfectly competitive. Figure 12-1 shows that Jennifer and Jason's profit-maximizing quantity of output is, indeed, the number of bushels at which the marginal cost of production is equal to price. The figure shows the marginal cost curve, *MC*, drawn from the data in the fourth column of Table 12-2. As in Chapter 9, we plot the marginal cost of increasing output from 1 to 2 bushels halfway between 1 and 2, and so on. The horizontal line at $18 is Jennifer and Jason's **marginal revenue curve.**

Note that whenever a firm is a price-taker, its marginal revenue curve is a horizontal line at the market price: it can sell as much as it likes at the market price. Regardless of whether it sells more or less, the market price is unaffected. *In effect, the individual firm faces a horizontal, perfectly elastic demand curve for its output—an individual demand curve for its output that is equivalent to its marginal revenue curve.* The marginal cost curve crosses the marginal revenue curve at point *E*. Sure enough, the quantity of output at *E* is 5 bushels.

Does this mean that the price-taking firm's production decision can be entirely summed up as "produce up to the point where the marginal cost of production is equal to the price"? No, not quite. Before applying the profit-maximizing principle of marginal analysis to determine how much to produce, a potential producer must as a first step answer an "either–or" question: should it produce at all? If the answer to that

The **marginal revenue curve** shows how marginal revenue varies as output varies.

 PITFALLS

WHAT IF MARGINAL REVENUE AND MARGINAL COST AREN'T EXACTLY EQUAL?
The optimal output rule says that to maximize profit, you should produce the quantity at which marginal revenue is equal to marginal cost. But what do you do if there is no output level at which marginal revenue equals marginal cost? In that case, you produce the largest quantity for which marginal revenue exceeds marginal cost. This is the case in Table 12-2 at an output of 5 bushels. The simpler version of the optimal output rule applies when production involves large numbers, such as hundreds or thousands of units. In such cases marginal cost comes in small increments, and there is always a level of output at which marginal cost almost exactly equals marginal revenue.

FIGURE 12-1 The Price-Taking Firm's Profit-Maximizing Quantity of Output

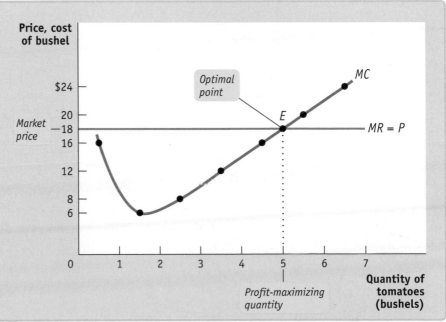

At the profit-maximizing quantity of output, the market price is equal to marginal cost. It is located at the point where the marginal cost curve crosses the marginal revenue curve, which is a horizontal line at the market price. Here, the profit-maximizing point is at an output of 5 bushels of tomatoes, the output quantity at point *E*.

question is yes, it then proceeds to the second step—a "how much" decision: maximizing profit by choosing the quantity of output at which marginal cost is equal to price.

To understand why the first step in the production decision involves an "either–or" question, we need to ask how we determine whether it is profitable or unprofitable to produce at all.

When Is Production Profitable?

Recall from Chapter 9 that a firm's decision whether or not to stay in a given business depends on its *economic profit*—the measure of profit based on the opportunity cost of resources used in the business. To put it a slightly different way: in the calculation of economic profit, a firm's total cost incorporates the implicit cost—the benefits forgone in the next best use of the firm's resources—as well as the explicit cost in the form of actual cash outlays.

In contrast, *accounting profit* is profit calculated using only the explicit costs incurred by the firm. This means that economic profit incorporates the opportunity cost of resources owned by the firm and used in the production of output, while accounting profit does not.

A firm may make positive accounting profit while making zero or even negative economic profit. It's important to understand clearly that a firm's decision to produce or not, to stay in business or to close down permanently, should be based on economic profit, not accounting profit.

So we will assume, as we always do, that the cost numbers given in Tables 12-1 and 12-2 include all costs, implicit as well as explicit, and that the profit numbers in Table 12-1 are therefore economic profit. So what determines whether Jennifer and Jason's farm earns a profit or generates a loss? The answer is that, *given the farm's cost curves, whether or not it is profitable depends on the market price of tomatoes—specifically, whether the market price is more or less than the farm's minimum average total cost.*

In Table 12-3 we calculate short-run average variable cost and short-run average total cost for Jennifer and Jason's farm. These are short-run values because we take fixed cost as given. (We'll turn to the long-run effects of changing fixed cost shortly.) The short-run average total cost curve, ATC, is shown in Figure 12-2, along with the marginal cost curve, MC, from Figure 12-1. As you can see, average total cost is minimized at point C, corresponding to an output of 4 bushels—the *minimum-cost output*—and an average total cost of $14 per bushel.

To see how these curves can be used to decide whether production is profitable or unprofitable, recall that profit is equal to total revenue minus total cost, $TR - TC$. This means:

TABLE 12-3 **Short-Run Average Costs for Jennifer and Jason's Farm**

Quantity of tomatoes q (bushels)	Variable cost VC	Total cost TC	Short-run average variable cost of bushel AVC = VC/q	Short-run average total cost of bushel ATC = TC/q
1	$16.00	$30.00	$16.00	$30.00
2	22.00	36.00	11.00	18.00
3	30.00	44.00	10.00	14.67
4	42.00	56.00	10.50	14.00
5	58.00	72.00	11.60	14.40
6	78.00	92.00	13.00	15.33
7	102.00	116.00	14.57	16.57

- If the firm produces a quantity at which $TR > TC$, the firm is profitable.
- If the firm produces a quantity at which $TR = TC$, the firm breaks even.
- If the firm produces a quantity at which $TR < TC$, the firm incurs a loss.

We can also express this idea in terms of revenue and cost per unit of output. If we divide profit by the number of units of output, q, we obtain the following expression for profit per unit of output:

(12-4) $\text{Profit}/q = TR/q - TC/q$

12-2 Costs and Production in the Short Run

This figure shows the marginal cost curve, *MC*, and the short-run average total cost curve, *ATC*. When the market price is $14, output will be 4 bushels of tomatoes (the minimum-cost output), represented by point *C*. The price of $14, equal to the firm's minimum average total cost, is the firm's *break-even price*.

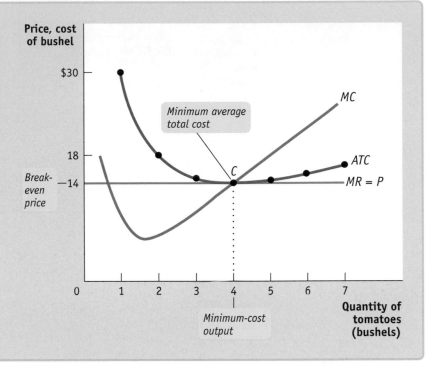

TR/q is average revenue, which is the market price. *TC/q* is average total cost. So a firm is profitable if the market price for its product is more than the average total cost of the quantity the firm produces; a firm loses money if the market price is less than average total cost of the quantity the firm produces. This means:

- If the firm produces a quantity at which $P > ATC$, the firm is profitable.
- If the firm produces a quantity at which $P = ATC$, the firm breaks even.
- If the firm produces a quantity at which $P < ATC$, the firm incurs a loss.

Figure 12-3 illustrates this result, showing how the market price determines whether a firm is profitable. It also shows how profits are depicted graphically. Each panel shows the marginal cost curve, *MC*, and the short-run average total cost curve, *ATC*. Average total cost is minimized at point *C*. Panel (a) shows the case we have already analyzed, in which the market price of tomatoes is $18 per bushel. Panel (b) shows the case in which the market price of tomatoes is lower, $10 per bushel.

In panel (a), we see that at a price of $18 per bushel the profit-maximizing quantity of output is 5 bushels, indicated by point *E*, where the marginal cost curve, *MC*, intersects the marginal revenue curve—which for a price-taking firm is a horizontal line at the market price. At that quantity of output, average total cost is $14.40 per bushel, indicated by point *Z*. Since the price per bushel exceeds average total cost per bushel, Jennifer and Jason's farm is profitable.

Jennifer and Jason's total profit when the market price is $18 is represented by the area of the shaded rectangle in panel (a). To see why, notice that total profit can be expressed in terms of profit per unit:

(12-5) $\text{Profit} = TR - TC = (TR/q - TC/q) \times q$

or, equivalently,

$$\text{Profit} = (P - ATC) \times q$$

FIGURE **12-3** Profitability and the Market Price

In panel (a) the market price is $18. The farm is profitable because price exceeds minimum average total cost, the break-even price, $14. The farm's optimal output choice is indicated by point *E*, corresponding to an output of 5 bushels. The average total cost of producing 5 bushels is indicated by point *Z* on the *ATC* curve, corresponding to an amount of $14.40. The vertical distance between *E* and *Z* corresponds to the farm's per-unit profit, $18.00 − $14.40 = $3.60. Total profit is given by the area of the shaded rectangle, 5 × $3.60 = $18.00.

In panel (b) the market price is $10; the farm is unprofitable because the price falls below the minimum average total cost, $14. The farm's optimal output choice when producing is indicated by point *A*, corresponding to an output of 3 bushels. The farm's per-unit loss, $14.67 − $10.00 = $4.67, is represented by the vertical distance between *A* and *Y*. The farm's total loss is represented by the shaded rectangle, 3 × $4.67 = $14.00 (adjusted for rounding error).

since *P* is equal to *TR/q* and *ATC* is equal to *TC/q*. The height of the shaded rectangle in panel (a) corresponds to the vertical distance between points *E* and *Z*. It is equal to *P* − *ATC* = $18.00 − $14.40 = $3.60 per bushel. The shaded rectangle has a width equal to the output: *q* = 5 bushels. So the area of that rectangle is equal to Jennifer and Jason's profit: 5 bushels × $3.60 profit per bushel = $18—the same number we calculated in Table 12-1.

What about the situation illustrated in panel (b)? Here the market price of tomatoes is $10 per bushel. Setting price equal to marginal cost leads to a profit-maximizing output of 3 bushels, indicated by point *A*. At this output, Jennifer and Jason have an average total cost of $14.67 per bushel, indicated by point *Y*. At their profit-maximizing output quantity—3 bushels—average total cost exceeds the market price. This means that Jennifer and Jason's farm generates a loss, not a profit.

How much do they lose by producing when the market price is $10? On each bushel they lose $ATC - P = \$14.67 - \$10.00 = \$4.67$, an amount corresponding to the vertical distance between points A and Y. And they would produce 3 bushels, which corresponds to the width of the shaded rectangle. So the total value of the losses is $\$4.67 \times 3 = \$14.00$ (adjusted for rounding error), an amount that corresponds to the area of the shaded rectangle in panel (b).

But how does a producer know, in general, whether or not its business will be profitable? It turns out that the crucial test lies in a comparison of the market price to the producer's *minimum average total cost*. On Jennifer and Jason's farm, minimum average total cost, which is equal to $14, occurs at an output quantity of 4 bushels, indicated by point C. Whenever the market price exceeds minimum average total cost, the producer can find some positive output level for which the average total cost is less than the market price. In other words, the producer can find a level of output at which the firm makes a profit. So with some care, Jennifer and Jason's farm will be profitable whenever the market price exceeds $14. And they will achieve the highest possible profit by producing the quantity at which marginal cost equals the market price.

Conversely, if the market price is less than minimum average total cost, there is no output level at which price exceeds average total cost. As a result, the firm will be unprofitable at any quantity of output. As we saw, at a price of $10—an amount less than minimum average total cost—Jennifer and Jason did indeed lose money. By producing the quantity at which marginal cost equals the market price, Jennifer and Jason did the best they could, but the best that they could do was a loss of $14. Any other quantity would have increased the size of their loss.

The minimum average total cost of a price-taking firm is called its **break-even price,** the price at which it earns zero profit. (Recall that's *economic profit.*) A firm will earn positive profit when the market price is above the break-even price, and it will suffer losses when the market price is below the break-even price. Jennifer and Jason's break-even price of $14 is the price at point C in Figures 12-2 and 12-3.

So the rule for determining whether a producer of a good is profitable (when following the optimal output rule) depends on a comparison of the market price of the good to the producer's break-even price—its minimum average total cost:

- Whenever the market price exceeds minimum average total cost, the producer is profitable (when $MR = P = MC$).

- Whenever the market price equals minimum average total cost, the producer breaks even (when $MR = P = MC$).

- Whenever the market price is less than minimum average total cost, the producer is unprofitable.

> The **break-even price** of a price-taking firm is the market price (at the minimum of the average total cost) at which it earns zero profit.

The Short-Run Production Decision

You might be tempted to say that if a firm is unprofitable because the market price is below its minimum average total cost, it shouldn't produce any output. In the short run, however, this conclusion isn't right. In the short run, sometimes the firm should produce even if price falls below minimum average total cost. The reason is that total cost includes *fixed cost*—cost that does not depend on the amount of output produced and can only be altered in the long run. In the short run, fixed cost must still be paid, regardless of whether or not a firm produces. For example, if Jennifer and Jason have rented a tractor for the year, they have to pay the rent on the tractor regardless of whether they produce any tomatoes. *Since it cannot be changed in the short run, their fixed cost is irrelevant to their decision about whether to produce or shut down in the short run.*

A firm will cease production in the short run if the market price falls below the **shut-down price,** which is equal to minimum average variable cost.

Although fixed cost should play no role in the decision about whether to produce in the short run, other costs—variable costs—do matter. An example of variable costs is the wages of workers who must be hired to help with planting and harvesting. Variable costs can be saved by *not* producing; so they should play a role in determining whether or not to produce in the short run.

Let's turn to Figure 12-4: it shows both the short-run average total cost curve, *ATC,* and the short-run average variable cost curve, *AVC,* drawn from the information in Table 12-3. Recall that the difference between the two curves—the vertical distance between them—represents average fixed cost, the fixed cost per unit of output, *FC/q.* Because the marginal cost curve has a "swoosh" shape—falling at first before rising—the short-run average variable cost curve is U-shaped: the initial fall in marginal cost causes average variable cost to fall as well, before rising marginal cost eventually pulls it up again. The short-run average variable cost curve reaches its minimum value of $10 at point *A,* at an output of 3 bushels.

We are now prepared to fully analyze the optimal production decision in the short run. We need to consider two cases:

- When the market price is below minimum average *variable* cost
- When the market price is greater than or equal to minimum average *variable* cost

When the market price is below minimum average variable cost, the price the firm receives per unit is not covering its variable cost per unit. A firm in this situation should cease production immediately. Why? Because there is no level of output at which the firm's total revenue covers its variable costs—the costs it can avoid by not operating. In this case the firm maximizes its profits by not producing at all—by, in effect, minimizing its losses. It will still incur a fixed cost in the short run, but it will no longer incur any variable cost. This means that the minimum average variable cost is equal to the **shut-down price,** the price at which the firm ceases production in the short run.

When price is greater than minimum average variable cost, however, the firm should produce in the short run. In this case, the firm maximizes profit—or

FIGURE **12-4** **The Short-Run Individual Supply Curve**

When the market price equals or exceeds Jennifer and Jason's *shut-down price* of $10, the minimum average variable cost indicated by point *A,* they will produce the output quantity at which marginal cost is equal to price. So at any price equal to or above the minimum average *variable* cost, the short-run individual supply curve is the firm's marginal cost curve; this corresponds to the upward-sloping segment of the individual supply curve. When market price falls below minimum average variable cost, the firm ceases operation in the short run. This corresponds to the vertical segment of the individual supply curve along the vertical axis.

minimizes loss—by choosing the output quantity at which its marginal cost is equal to the market price. For example, if the market price of tomatoes is $18 per bushel, Jennifer and Jason should produce at point E in Figure 12-4, corresponding to an output of 5 bushels. Note that point C in Figure 12-4 corresponds to the farm's break-even price of $14 per bushel. Since E lies above C, Jennifer and Jason's farm will be profitable; their farm will generate a per-bushel profit of $18.00 – $14.40 = $3.60 when the market price is $18.

But what if the market price lies between the shut-down price and the break-even price—that is, between minimum average *variable* cost and minimum average *total* cost? In the case of Jennifer and Jason's farm, this corresponds to prices anywhere between $10 and $14—say, a market price of $12. At $12, Jennifer and Jason's farm is not profitable; since the market price is below minimum average total cost, the farm is losing the difference between price and average total cost per unit produced. Yet even if it isn't covering its total cost per unit, it is covering its variable cost per unit and some—but not all—of the fixed cost per unit. If a firm in this situation shuts down, it would incur no variable cost but would incur the *full* fixed cost. As a result, shutting down generates an even greater loss than continuing to operate (when $MR = P = MC$).

This means that whenever price lies between minimum average total cost and minimum average variable cost, the firm is better off producing some output in the short run. The reason is that by producing, it can cover its variable cost per unit and at least some of its fixed cost, even though it is incurring a loss. In this case, the firm maximizes profit—that is, minimizes loss—by choosing the quantity of output at which its marginal cost is equal to the market price. So if Jennifer and Jason face a market price of $12 per bushel, their profit-maximizing output is given by point B in Figure 12-4, corresponding to an output of 3.5 bushels.

It's worth noting that the decision to produce when the firm is covering its variable costs but not all of its fixed cost is similar to the decision to ignore *sunk costs*, a concept we studied in Chapter 9. You may recall that a sunk cost is a cost that has already been incurred and cannot be recouped; and because it cannot be changed, it should have no effect on any current decision. In the short-run production decision, fixed cost is, in effect, like a sunk cost—it has been spent, and it can't be recovered in the short run. This comparison also illustrates why variable cost does indeed matter in the short run: it can be avoided by not producing.

And what happens if market price is exactly equal to the shut-down price, minimum average variable cost? In this instance, the firm is indifferent between producing 3 units or 0 units. As we'll see shortly, this is an important point when looking at the behaviour of an industry as a whole. For the sake of clarity, we'll assume that the firm, although indifferent, does indeed produce output when price is equal to the shut-down price.

Putting everything together, we can now draw the **short-run individual supply curve** of Jennifer and Jason's farm, the red line in Figure 12-4; it shows how the profit-maximizing quantity of output in the short run depends on the price. As you can see, the curve is in two segments. The upward-sloping red segment starting at point A shows the short-run profit-maximizing output when market price is equal to or above the shut-down price of $10 per bushel.

As long as the market price is equal to or above the shut-down price, Jennifer and Jason produce the quantity of output at which marginal cost is equal to the market price. That is, at market prices equal to or above the shut-down price, the firm's short-run supply curve corresponds to its marginal cost curve. But at any market price below minimum average variable cost—in this case, $10 per bushel—the firm shuts down and output drops to zero in the short run. This corresponds to the vertical segment of the curve that lies on the vertical axis.

The **short-run individual supply curve** shows how an individual producer's profit-maximizing output quantity depends on the market price, taking fixed cost as given.

Do firms really shut down temporarily without going out of business? Yes. In fact, in some businesses temporary shut-downs are routine. The most common examples are industries in which demand is highly seasonal, like outdoor amusement parks in climates with cold winters. Such parks would have to offer very low prices to entice customers during the colder months—prices so low that the owners would not cover their variable costs (principally wages and electricity). The wiser choice economically is to shut down until warm weather brings enough customers who are willing to pay a higher price.

Changing Fixed Cost

Although fixed cost cannot be altered in the short run, in the long run firms can acquire or get rid of machines, buildings, and so on. As we learned in Chapter 11, in the long run the level of fixed cost is a matter of choice. There we saw that a firm will choose the level of fixed cost that minimizes the average total cost for its desired output quantity. Now we will focus on an even bigger question facing a firm when choosing its fixed cost: whether to incur *any* fixed cost at all by remaining in its current business.

In the long run, a producer can always eliminate fixed cost by selling off its plant and equipment. If it does so, of course, it can't ever produce—it has exited the industry. In contrast, a potential producer can take on some fixed cost by acquiring machines and other resources, which puts it in a position to produce—it can enter the industry. In most perfectly competitive industries the set of producers, although fixed in the short run, changes in the long run as firms enter or exit the industry.

Consider Jennifer and Jason's farm once again. In order to simplify our analysis, we will sidestep the problem of choosing among several possible levels of fixed cost. Instead, we will assume from now on that Jennifer and Jason have only one possible choice of fixed cost if they operate, the amount of $14 that was the basis for the calculations in Tables 12-1, 12-2, and 12-3. (With this assumption, Jennifer and Jason's short-run average total cost curve and long-run average total cost curve are one and the same.) Alternatively, they can choose a fixed cost of zero if they exit the industry.

Suppose that the market price of organic tomatoes is consistently less than $14 over an extended period of time. In that case, Jennifer and Jason never fully cover their fixed cost: their business runs at a persistent loss. In the long run, then, they can do better by closing their business and leaving the industry. In other words, *in the long run* firms will exit an industry if the market price is consistently less than their break-even price—their minimum average total cost.

Conversely, suppose that the price of organic tomatoes is consistently above the break-even price, $14, for an extended period of time. Because their farm is profitable, Jennifer and Jason will remain in the industry and continue producing.

But things won't stop there. The organic tomato industry meets the criterion of *free entry*: there are many potential organic tomato producers because the necessary inputs are easy to obtain. And the cost curves of those potential producers are likely to be similar to those of Jennifer and Jason, since the technology used by other producers is likely to be very similar to that used by Jennifer and Jason. If the price is high enough to generate profits for existing producers, it will also attract some of these potential producers into the industry. So *in the long run* a price in excess of $14 should lead to entry: new producers will come into the organic tomato industry.

As we will see in the next section, exit and entry lead to an important distinction between the *short-run industry supply curve* and the *long-run industry supply curve*.

Summing Up: The Perfectly Competitive Firm's Profitability and Production Conditions

In this chapter, we've studied where the supply curve for a perfectly competitive, price-taking firm comes from. Every perfectly competitive firm makes its production decisions by maximizing profit, and these decisions determine the supply curve. Table 12-4 summarizes the perfectly competitive firm's profitability and production conditions. It also relates them to entry into and exit from the industry.

TABLE 12-4 Summary of the Perfectly Competitive Firm's Profitability and Production Conditions

Profitability condition (minimum *ATC* = break-even price)	Result
P > minimum *ATC*	Firm profitable. Entry into industry in the long run.
P = minimum *ATC*	Firm breaks even. No entry into or exit from industry in the long run.
P < minimum *ATC*	Firm unprofitable. Exit from industry in the long run.

Production condition (minimum *AVC* = shut-down price)	Result
P > minimum *AVC*	Firm produces in the short run. If P < minimum *ATC*, firm covers variable cost and some but not all of fixed cost. If P > minimum *ATC*, firm covers all variable cost and fixed cost.
P = minimum *AVC*	Firm indifferent between producing in the short run or not. Just covers variable cost.
P < minimum *AVC*	Firm shuts down in the short run. Does not cover variable cost.

ECONOMICS ► IN ACTION

PRICES ARE UP ... BUT SO ARE COSTS

According to the U.S. Energy Policy Act of 2005, 28.4 billion litres of alternative fuel, mostly corn-based ethanol, will have been added to the American fuel supply by 2012 in order to reduce gasoline consumption. The unsurprising result of this mandate: the demand for corn skyrocketed, along with the price. In June 2011, a bushel of corn hit a high of US$7.99, nearly quadruple the early January 2005 price of US$2.09.

This sharp rise in the price of corn caught the eye of North American farmers like Ronnie Gerik of Aquilla, Texas, who reduced the size of his cotton crop and increased his corn acreage by 40%. Overall, the U.S. land dedicated to planting corn in 2011 was 9% more than the average over the previous decade. Like Gerik, other farmers substituted corn production for the production of other crops. In 2013, the land dedicated to Canadian corn was 20% more than in the previous decade, and the land dedicated to Canadian barley was down 23% over the prior decade's average planting.

Although this sounds like a sure way to make a profit, Gerik and farmers like him were taking a gamble. Consider the cost of an important input, fertilizer. Corn requires more fertilizer than other crops, and with more farmers planting corn, the increased demand for fertilizer led to a price increase. In 2006 and 2007, fertilizer prices surged to five times their 2005 level; by 2011, they were still three times higher. Moreover, corn is more sensitive to the amount of rainfall than a crop like cotton. So farmers who plant corn in drought-prone places like Texas are

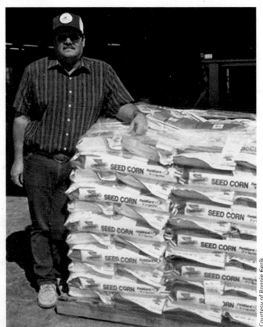

Although Gerik was taking a big gamble when he cut the size of his cotton crop to plant more corn, his decision made good economic sense.

Courtesy of Ronnie Gerik.

increasing their risk of loss. Gerik had to incorporate into his calculations his best guess of what a dry spell would cost him.

Despite all this, what Gerik and other farmers did made complete economic sense. By planting more corn, each one moved up his or her individual short-run supply curve for corn production. And because the individual supply curve is the marginal cost curve, each farmer's costs also went up because of the need to apply more inputs—inputs that are now more expensive to obtain.

So the moral of the story is that farmers will increase the size of their corn fields until the marginal cost of producing corn is approximately equal to the market price of corn, which shouldn't come as a surprise because corn production satisfies all the requirements of a perfectly competitive industry.

● ● ◀

CHECK YOUR UNDERSTANDING 12-2

1. Draw a short-run diagram showing a U-shaped average total cost curve, a U-shaped average variable cost curve, and a "swoosh"-shaped marginal cost curve. On it, indicate the range of output and the range of price for which the following actions are optimal.
   a. The firm shuts down immediately.
   b. The firm operates in the short run despite sustaining a loss.
   c. The firm operates while making a profit.

2. Atlantic Canada has a very active lobster industry, which harvests lobsters during the summer months. During the rest of the year, lobsters can be obtained from other parts of the world but at a much higher price. The region has numerous "lobster shacks," roadside restaurants serving lobster dishes that are open only during the summer. Explain why it is optimal for lobster shacks to operate only during the summer.

Solutions appear at back of book.

The Industry Supply Curve

Why will an increase in the demand for organic tomatoes lead to a large price increase at first but a much smaller increase in the long run? The answer lies in the behaviour of the **industry supply curve**—the relationship between the price and the total output of an industry as a whole. The industry supply curve is what we referred to in earlier chapters as *the* supply curve or the market supply curve. But here we take some extra care to distinguish between the *individual supply curve* of a single firm and the supply curve of the industry as a whole.

As you might guess from the previous section, the industry supply curve must be analyzed in somewhat different ways for the short run and the long run. Let's start with the short run.

The Short-Run Industry Supply Curve

Recall that in the short run the number of producers in an industry is fixed—there is no entry or exit. And you may also remember from Chapter 3 that the industry supply curve is the horizontal sum of the individual supply curves of all producers—you find it by summing the total output across all suppliers at every given price. We will do that exercise here under the assumption that all the producers are alike—an assumption that makes the derivation particularly simple. So let's assume that there are 100 organic tomato farms, each with the same costs as Jennifer and Jason's farm.

Each of these 100 farms will have an individual short-run supply curve like the one in Figure 12-4. At a price below $10, no farms will produce. At a price of more than $10, each farm will produce the quantity of output at which its marginal cost

The **industry supply curve** shows the relationship between the price of a good and the total output supplied by the industry as a whole.

is equal to the market price. As you can see from Figure 12-4, this will lead each farm to produce 4 bushels if the price is $14 per bushel, 5 bushels if the price is $18, and so on. So if there are 100 organic tomato farms and the price of organic tomatoes is $18 per bushel, the industry as a whole will produce 500 bushels, corresponding to 100 farms × 5 bushels per farm, and so on. The result is the **short-run industry supply curve,** shown as S in Figure 12-5. This curve shows the quantity that producers will supply at each price, *taking the number of producers as given.*

The demand curve D in Figure 12-5 crosses the short-run industry supply curve at E_{MKT}, corresponding to a price of $18 and a quantity of 500 bushels. Point E_{MKT} is a **short-run market equilibrium:** the quantity supplied equals the quantity demanded, taking the number of producers as given. But the long run may look quite different, because in the long run farms may enter or exit the industry.

> The **short-run industry supply curve** shows how the quantity supplied by an industry depends on the market price given a fixed number of producers.
>
> There is a **short-run market equilibrium** when the quantity supplied equals the quantity demanded, taking the number of producers as given.

FIGURE 12-5 The Short-Run Market Equilibrium

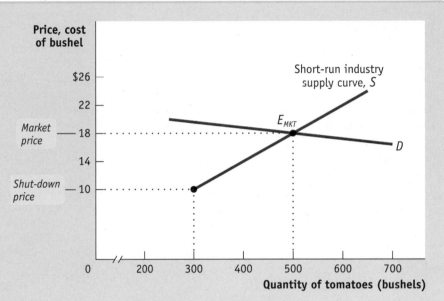

The short-run industry supply curve, S, is the industry supply curve taking the number of producers—here, 100—as given. It is generated by (horizontally) adding together the individual supply curves of the 100 producers. Below the shut-down price of $10, no producer wants to produce in the short run. Above $10, the short-run industry supply curve slopes upward, as each producer increases output as price increases. It intersects the demand curve, D, at point E_{MKT}, the point of short-run market equilibrium, corresponding to a market price of $18 and a quantity of 500 bushels.

The Long-Run Industry Supply Curve

Suppose that in addition to the 100 farms currently in the organic tomato business, there are many other potential producers. Suppose also that each of these potential producers would have the same cost curves as existing producers like Jennifer and Jason if it entered the industry.

In the long run, when will additional producers enter the industry? Whenever existing producers are making a profit—that is, whenever the market price is above the break-even price of $14 per bushel, the minimum average total cost of production. For example, at a price of $18 per bushel, new firms will enter the industry.

What will happen as additional producers enter the industry? Clearly, the quantity supplied at any given price will increase. The short-run industry supply curve will shift to the right. This will, in turn, alter the market equilibrium and result in a lower market price. Existing firms will respond to the lower market price by reducing their output, but the total industry output will increase because of the larger number of firms in the industry.

Figure 12-6 illustrates the effects of this chain of events on an existing firm and on the market; panel (a) shows how the market responds to entry, and panel (b) shows how an individual existing firm responds to entry. (Note that these two graphs have been rescaled in comparison to Figures 12-4 and 12-5 to better illustrate how profit changes in response to price.) In panel (a), S_1 is the initial short-run industry supply curve, based on the existence of 100 producers. The initial

FIGURE   **12-6**   The Long-Run Market Equilibrium

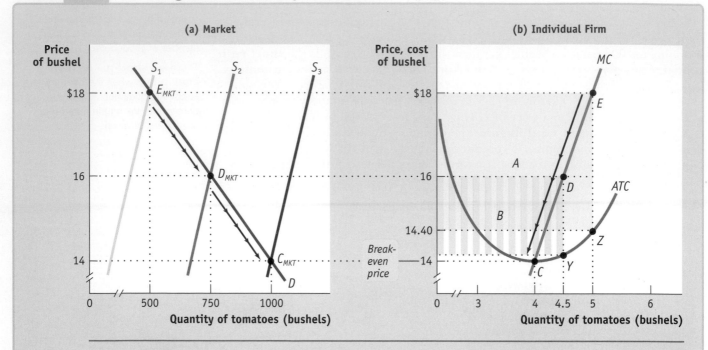

(a) Market

(b) Individual Firm

Point E_{MKT} of panel (a) shows the initial short-run market equilibrium. Each of the 100 existing producers makes an economic profit, illustrated in panel (b) by the green rectangle labelled *A*, the profit of an existing firm. Profits induce entry by additional producers, shifting the short-run industry supply curve outward from S_1 to S_2 in panel (a), resulting in a new short-run equilibrium at point D_{MKT}, at a lower market price of $16 and higher industry output.

Existing firms reduce output and profit falls to the area given by the striped rectangle labelled *B* in panel (b). Entry continues to shift out the short-run industry supply curve, as price falls and industry output increases yet again. Entry ceases at point C_{MKT} on supply curve S_3 in panel (a). Here market price is equal to the break-even price; existing producers make zero economic profits, and there is no incentive for entry or exit. So C_{MKT} is also a long-run market equilibrium.

short-run market equilibrium is at E_{MKT}, with an equilibrium market price of $18 and a quantity of 500 bushels. At this price existing producers are profitable, which is reflected in panel (b): an existing firm makes a total profit represented by the green-shaded rectangle labelled *A* when market price is $18.

In the long run, these profits will induce new producers to enter the industry, shifting the short-run industry supply curve to the right. For example, the short-run industry supply curve when the number of producers has increased to 167 is S_2. Corresponding to this supply curve is a new short-run market equilibrium labelled D_{MKT}, with a market price of $16 and a quantity of 750 bushels. At $16, each firm produces 4.5 bushels, so that industry output is $167 \times 4.5 = 750$ bushels (rounded). From panel (b) you can see the effect of the entry of 67 new producers on an existing firm: the fall in price causes it to reduce its output, and its profit falls to the area represented by the striped rectangle labelled *B*.

Although diminished, the profit of existing firms at D_{MKT} means that entry will continue and the number of firms will continue to rise. If the number of producers rises to 250, the short-run industry supply curve shifts out again to S_3, and the market equilibrium is at C_{MKT}, with a quantity supplied and demanded of 1000 bushels and a market price of $14 per bushel.

Like E_{MKT} and D_{MKT}, C_{MKT} is a short-run equilibrium. But it is also something more. Because the price of $14 is each firm's break-even price, an existing producer makes zero economic profit—neither a profit nor a loss, earning only the opportunity cost of the resources used in production—when producing its profit-maximizing output of 4 bushels. At this price there is no incentive either for potential producers to enter or for existing producers to exit the industry. So C_{MKT} corresponds to a **long-run market equilibrium**—a situation in which quantity supplied equals the quantity demanded given that sufficient time has elapsed for producers to either enter or exit the industry. In a long-run market equilibrium, all existing and potential producers have fully adjusted to their optimal long-run choices; as a result, no producer has an incentive to either enter or exit the industry.

To explore further the significance of the difference between short-run and long-run equilibrium, consider the effect of an increase in demand on an industry with free entry that is initially in long-run equilibrium. Panel (b) in Figure 12-7 shows the market adjustment; panels (a) and (c) show how an existing individual firm behaves during the process.

In panel (b) of Figure 12-7, D_1 is the initial demand curve and S_1 is the initial short-run industry supply curve. Their intersection at point X_{MKT} is both a short-run and a long-run market equilibrium because the equilibrium price of $14 leads to zero economic profit—and therefore neither entry nor exit. It corresponds to point X in panel (a), where an individual existing firm is operating at the minimum of its average total cost curve.

> A market is in **long-run market equilibrium** when the quantity supplied equals the quantity demanded, given that sufficient time has elapsed for entry into and exit from the industry to occur.

FIGURE 12-7 The Effect of an Increase in Demand in the Short Run and the Long Run

Panel (b) shows how an industry adjusts in the short and long run to an increase in demand; panels (a) and (c) show the corresponding adjustments by an existing firm. Initially the market is at point X_{MKT} in panel (b), a short-run and long-run equilibrium at a price of $14 and industry output of Q_X. An existing firm makes zero economic profit, operating at point X in panel (a) at minimum average total cost. Demand increases as D_1 shifts rightward to D_2 in panel (b), raising the market price to $18. Existing firms increase their output, and industry output moves along the short-run industry supply curve S_1 to a short-run equilibrium at Y_{MKT}. Correspondingly, the existing firm in panel (a) moves from point X to point Y. But at a price of $18 existing firms are profitable. As shown in panel (b), in

the long run new entrants arrive and the short-run industry supply curve shifts rightward, from S_1 to S_2. There is a new equilibrium at point Z_{MKT}, at a lower price of $14 and higher industry output of Q_Z. An existing firm responds by moving from Y to Z in panel (c), returning to its initial output level and zero economic profit. Production by new entrants accounts for the total increase in industry output, $Q_Z - Q_X$. Like X_{MKT}, Z_{MKT} is also a short-run and long-run equilibrium: with all firms earning zero economic profit, there is no incentive for any firms to enter or exit the industry. The horizontal line passing through X_{MKT} and Z_{MKT}, LRS, is the long-run industry supply curve: at the break-even price of $14, producers will produce any amount that consumers demand in the long run.

The **long-run industry supply curve** shows how the quantity supplied responds to the price once producers have had time to enter or exit the industry.

Now suppose that the demand curve shifts out for some reason to D_2. As shown in panel (b), in the short run, industry output moves along the short-run industry supply curve S_1 to the new short-run market equilibrium at Y_{MKT}, the intersection of S_1 and D_2. The market price rises to $18 per bushel, and industry output increases from Q_X to Q_Y. This corresponds to an existing firm's movement from X to Y in panel (a) as the firm increases its output in response to the rise in the market price.

But we know that Y_{MKT} is not a long-run equilibrium, because $18 is higher than minimum average total cost, so existing producers are making economic profits. In the longer term, this will lead additional firms to enter the industry. Entry will cause the short-run industry supply curve to shift to the right. In the long run, the short-run industry supply curve will have shifted out to S_2, and the equilibrium will be at Z_{MKT}—with the price falling back to $14 per bushel and industry output increasing yet again, from Q_Y to Q_Z. Like X_{MKT} before the increase in demand, Z_{MKT} is both a short-run and a long-run market equilibrium.

The effect of entry on an existing firm is illustrated in panel (c), in the movement from Y to Z along the firm's individual supply curve. The firm reduces its output in response to the fall in the market price, ultimately arriving back at its original output quantity, corresponding to the minimum of its average total cost curve. In fact, every firm that is now in the industry—the initial set of firms and the new entrants—will operate at the minimum of its average total cost curve, at point Z. This means that the entire increase in industry output, from Q_X to Q_Z, comes from production by new entrants.

The line *LRS* that passes through X_{MKT} and Z_{MKT} in panel (b) is the **long-run industry supply curve.** It shows how the quantity supplied by an industry responds to the price given that producers have had time to enter or exit the industry.

In this particular case, the long-run industry supply curve is horizontal at $14. In other words, in this industry supply is *perfectly elastic* in the long run: given time to enter or exit, producers will supply any quantity that consumers demand at a price of $14. Perfectly elastic long-run supply is actually a good assumption for many industries. In this case we speak of there being *constant costs across the industry*: each firm, regardless of whether it is an incumbent or a new entrant, faces the same cost structure (that is, they each have the same cost curves). Industries that satisfy this condition are industries in which there is a perfectly elastic supply of inputs—industries like agriculture or bakeries.

In other industries, however, even the long-run industry supply curve slopes upward. The usual reason for this is that producers must use some input that is in limited supply (that is, inelastically supplied). As the industry expands, the price of that input is driven up. Consequently, later entrants in the industry find that they have a higher cost structure than early entrants. An example is beachfront resort hotels, which must compete for a limited quantity of prime beachfront property.[2] Industries that behave like this are said to have *increasing costs across the industry*.

It is possible for the long-run industry supply curve to slope downward. This can occur when an industry faces increasing returns to scale, in which average costs fall as output rises. Notice we said that the *industry* faces increasing returns. However, when increasing returns apply at the level of the individual firm, the industry usually ends up dominated by a small number of firms (an *oligopoly*) or a single firm (a *monopoly*). In some cases, the advantages of large scale for an entire industry accrue to all firms in that industry. For example, the costs of new technologies such as solar panels tend to fall as the industry grows because that growth leads to improved knowledge, a larger pool of workers with the right skills, and so on. Such benefits to industry size are known as *external economies*, which we'll learn more about in Chapter 16.

Regardless of whether the long-run industry supply curve is horizontal or sloped, the long-run elasticity of supply is *higher* than the short-run elasticity of

---

[2]In fact, an expanding industry can shift the cost curve of all firms upward. For example, the arrival of more beachfront resorts drives up property values. Higher land values drive up the opportunity cost of all land owners, whether they are recent entrants or one of the first, which shifts everyone's cost curves up.

FIGURE   12-8   Comparing the Short-Run and Long-Run Industry Supply Curves

The long-run industry supply curve may slope upward, but it is always flatter—more elastic—than the short-run industry supply curve. This is because of entry and exit: a higher price attracts new entrants in the long run, resulting in a rise in industry output and a fall in price; a lower price induces existing producers to exit in the long run, generating a fall in industry output and an eventual rise in price.

The long-run industry supply curve is always flatter—more elastic—than the short-run industry supply curve.

supply whenever there is free entry and exit. As shown in Figure 12-8, the long-run industry supply curve is always flatter than the short-run industry supply curve. The reason is entry and exit: a high price caused by an increase in demand attracts entry by new producers, resulting in a rise in industry output and an eventual fall in price; a low price caused by a decrease in demand induces existing firms to exit, leading to a fall in industry output and an eventual increase in price.

The distinction between the short-run industry supply curve and the long-run industry supply curve is very important in practice. We often see a sequence of events like that shown in Figure 12-7: an increase in demand initially leads to a large price increase, but prices return to their initial level once new firms have entered the industry. Or we see the sequence in reverse: a fall in demand reduces prices in the short run, but they return to their initial level as producers exit the industry.

The Cost of Production and Efficiency in Long-Run Equilibrium

Our analysis leads us to three conclusions about the cost of production and efficiency in the long-run equilibrium of a perfectly competitive industry. These results will be important in our discussion in Chapter 13 of how monopoly gives rise to inefficiency.

First, in a perfectly competitive industry in equilibrium, the value of marginal cost is the same for all firms. That's because all firms produce the quantity of output at which marginal cost equals the market price, and as price-takers supplying a standardized product, they all face the same market price.

Second, in a perfectly competitive industry with free entry and exit, each firm will have zero economic profit in long-run equilibrium. Each firm produces the quantity of output that minimizes its average total cost—corresponding to point Z in panel (c) of Figure 12-7. So the total cost of production of the industry's output is minimized in a perfectly competitive industry. (The exception is an industry with increasing costs across the industry. Given a sufficiently high market price, early entrants make positive economic profits, but the last entrants do not. At the long-run equilibrium price, average costs are minimized for later entrants, but not necessarily for the early ones. For early entrants, average costs depend on how much their cost curves have shifted up since the later entrants arrived.)

The third and final conclusion is that the long-run market equilibrium of a perfectly competitive industry is efficient: no mutually beneficial transactions go unexploited. To understand this, we need to recall a fundamental requirement for efficiency from Chapter 4: all consumers who have a willingness to pay greater than or equal to sellers' costs actually get the good. And we also learned that when a market

⚠ PITFALLS

ECONOMIC PROFIT, AGAIN
Some readers may wonder why a firm would want to enter an industry if the market price is only slightly greater than the break-even price. Wouldn't a firm prefer to go into another business that yields a higher profit?

The answer is that here, as always, when we calculate cost, we mean *opportunity cost*—that is, cost that includes the return a firm could get by using its resources elsewhere. And so the profit that we calculate is *economic profit;* if the market price is above the break-even level, no matter how slightly, the firm can earn more in this industry than they could elsewhere.

is efficient (except under certain, well-defined conditions), the market price matches all consumers with a willingness to pay greater than or equal to the market price to all sellers who have a cost of producing the good less than or equal to the market price.

So in the long-run equilibrium of a perfectly competitive industry, production is efficient: costs are minimized and no resources are wasted. In addition, the allocation of goods to consumers is efficient: every consumer willing to pay the cost of producing a unit of the good gets it. Indeed, no mutually beneficial transaction is left unexploited. Moreover, this condition tends to persist over time as the environment changes: the force of competition makes producers responsive to changes in consumers' desires and to changes in technology.

ECONOMICS > IN ACTION

BALEING IN, BAILING OUT

REUTERS/Stringer Shanghai

King Cotton's reign will inevitably end as new producers, seeking to profit from the crop's success, enter the market and bring prices down.

"King Cotton is back," proclaimed a 2010 article in the *Los Angeles Times*, describing a cotton boom that had "turned great swaths of Central California a snowy white during harvest season." Cotton prices were soaring: they more than tripled between early 2010 and early 2011. And farmers responded by planting more cotton.

What was behind the price rise? As we learned in Chapter 3, it was partly caused by temporary factors, notably severe floods in Pakistan that destroyed much of that nation's cotton crop. But there was also a big rise in demand, especially from China, whose burgeoning textile and clothing industries demanded ever more raw cotton to weave into cloth. And all indications were that higher demand was here to stay.

So is cotton farming going to be a highly profitable business from now on? The answer is no, because when an industry becomes highly profitable, it draws in new producers, and that brings prices down. And the cotton industry was following the standard script.

For it wasn't just the Central Valley of California that had turned "snowy white." Farmers around the world were moving into cotton growing. "This summer, cotton will stretch from Queensland through northern NSW [New South Wales] all the way down to the Murrumbidgee valley in southern NSW," declared an Australian report.

And by the summer of 2011 the entry of all these new producers was already having an effect. By the end of July, cotton prices were down 35% from their peak in early 2011. This still left prices high by historical standards, leaving plenty of incentive to expand production. But it was already clear that the cotton boom would eventually reach its limit—and that at some point in the not-too-distant future some of the farmers who had rushed into the industry would leave it again.

▼ Quick Review

- The **industry supply curve** corresponds to the supply curve of earlier chapters. In the short run, the time period over which the number of producers is fixed, the **short-run market equilibrium** is given by the intersection of the **short-run industry supply curve** and the demand curve. In the long run, the time period over which producers can enter or exit the industry, the **long-run market equilibrium** is given by the intersection of the **long-run industry supply curve** and the demand curve. In the long-run market equilibrium, no producer has an incentive to enter or exit the industry.

- The long-run industry supply curve is often horizontal, although it may slope upward when a necessary input is in limited supply. It is always more elastic than the short-run industry supply curve.

- In the long-run market equilibrium of a perfectly competitive industry, each firm produces at the same marginal cost, which is equal to the market price, and the total cost of production of the industry's output is minimized. It is also efficient.

CHECK YOUR UNDERSTANDING 12-3

1. Which of the following events will induce firms to enter an industry? Which will induce firms to exit? When will entry or exit cease? Explain your answer.
   a. A technological advance lowers the fixed cost of production of every firm in the industry.
   b. The wages paid to workers in the industry go up for an extended period of time.
   c. A permanent change in consumer tastes increases demand for the good.
   d. The price of a key input rises due to a long-term shortage of that input.

2. Assume that the egg industry is perfectly competitive and is in long-run equilibrium with a perfectly elastic long-run industry supply curve. Health concerns about cholesterol then lead to a decrease in demand. Construct a figure similar to Figure 12-7, showing the short-run behaviour of the industry and how long-run equilibrium is re-established.

Solutions appear at back of book.

BUSINESS CASE : In Store and Online

Recently in Moncton, New Brunswick, Tri Trang walked into a Future Shop and found the perfect gift for his girlfriend, a $179.99 Garmin GPS system. A year earlier, he would have bought the item right away. Instead, he whipped out his Android phone; using an app that scans bar codes to instantly compare Future Shop's price to those of other retailers, he found the same item on Amazon.ca for $134.98, with no shipping charges. Trang proceeded to buy it from Amazon, right there on the spot.

It doesn't stop there. TheFind, the most popular price comparison site in the United States, will also provide a map to the store with the best price, identify coupon codes and shipping deals, and supply other tools to help users organize their purchases. "Terror" is the word that has been used to describe the reaction of brick-and-mortar retailers.

Before the advent of online price comparisons and smartphones, a retailer could lure customers into its store with enticing specials, and reasonably expect them to buy other, more profitable things, too—with some prompting from salespeople. But those days are disappearing. A recent study by the consulting firm Accenture found that 30% of Canadians use their mobile devices to assist their in-store shopping. According to a survey by GroupM Next, if the in-store and online price difference is close, shoppers will buy the product immediately in-store. But if the price difference is more than $15, most customers simply buy online instead.

Not surprisingly, use of apps like ShopSavvy, RedLaser (from eBay), or Price Check by Amazon (only available in the United States at the time of writing) has increased at an extremely fast clip. In the past few years e-commerce sales have risen by 20% or more per year. It is estimated that Cyber Monday in 2013 was the largest e-commerce day in history, and sales from mobile devices were responsible for between 20 and 25% of all e-commerce sales that day. Retailers are expecting even more shoppers to use their phones to make purchases in the coming years. The Canadian e-commerce market is expected to grow faster than the U.S. market, helping to bring it closer to the traditional ten-to-one U.S.-to-Canada ratio.

According to e-commerce experts, retailers have begun to alter their selling strategies in response. One strategy involves stocking products that manufacturers have slightly modified for the retailer, which allows the retailer to be their exclusive seller. Future Shop and Best Buy have closed stores, switched to smaller outlets, and rented space within their stores for in-store Microsoft mini stores and Sony kiosks. They have even partnered with affiliates to use Futureshop.ca and BestBuy.ca to sell products that they have not traditionally marketed: jewellery, luggage, furniture, children's car seats, and home decor items like paints. In addition, some retailers, when confronted by an in-store customer wielding a lower price on a mobile device, will lower their price to avoid losing the sale (although other stores have responded by asking customers with price comparison apps to leave).

Retailers are clearly frightened. As one analyst said, "Only a couple of retailers can play the lowest-price game. This is going to accelerate the demise of retailers who do not have either competitive pricing or stand-out store experience."

QUESTIONS FOR THOUGHT

1. From the evidence in the case, what can you infer about whether or not the retail market for electronics satisfied the conditions for perfect competition before the advent of mobile-device comparison shopping? What was the most important impediment to competition?

2. What effect will the introduction of price-comparison apps have on competition in the retail market for electronics? On the profitability of brick-and-mortar retailers like Future Shop? What, on average, will be the effect on the consumer surplus of purchasers of these items?

3. Why are some retailers responding by having manufacturers make exclusive versions of products for them? Is this trend likely to increase or diminish?

SUMMARY

1. In a **perfectly competitive market** all producers are **price-taking producers** and all consumers are **price-taking consumers**—no one's actions can influence the market price. Consumers are normally price-takers, but producers often are not. In a **perfectly competitive industry,** all producers are price-takers.

2. There are two necessary conditions for a perfectly competitive industry: there are many producers, none of whom have a large **market share,** and the industry produces a **standardized product** or **commodity**—goods that consumers regard as equivalent (perfect substitutes). A third condition is often satisfied as well: **free entry and exit** into and from the industry.

3. A producer chooses output according to the **optimal output rule:** produce the quantity at which **marginal revenue** equals marginal cost. For a price-taking firm, marginal revenue is equal to price and its **marginal revenue curve** is a horizontal line at the market price. It chooses output according to the **price-taking firm's optimal output rule:** produce the quantity at which price equals marginal cost. However, a firm that produces the optimal quantity may not be profitable.

4. A firm is profitable if total revenue exceeds total cost or, equivalently, if the market price exceeds its **break-even price**—minimum average total cost. If market price exceeds the break-even price, the firm is profitable; if it is less, the firm is unprofitable; if it is equal, the firm breaks even. When profitable, the firm's per-unit profit is $P - ATC$; when unprofitable, its per-unit loss is $ATC - P$.

5. Fixed cost is irrelevant to the firm's optimal short-run production decision, which depends on its **shut-down price**—its minimum average variable cost—and the market price. When the market price is equal to or exceeds the shut-down price, the firm produces the output quantity where marginal cost equals the market price. When the market price falls below the shut-down price, the firm ceases production in the short run. This generates the firm's **short-run individual supply curve.**

6. Fixed cost matters over time. If the market price is below minimum average total cost for an extended period of time, firms will exit the industry in the long run. If above, existing firms are profitable and new firms will enter the industry in the long run.

7. The **industry supply curve** depends on the time period. The **short-run industry supply curve** is the industry supply curve given that the number of firms is fixed. The **short-run market equilibrium** is given by the intersection of the short-run industry supply curve and the demand curve.

8. The **long-run industry supply curve** is the industry supply curve given sufficient time for entry into and exit from the industry. In the **long-run market equilibrium**—given by the intersection of the long-run industry supply curve and the demand curve—no producer has an incentive to enter or exit. The long-run industry supply curve is often horizontal. It may slope upward if there is limited supply of an input, resulting in increasing costs across the industry. It may even slope downward, the case of decreasing costs across the industry. But it is always more elastic (flatter) than the short-run industry supply curve.

9. In the long-run market equilibrium of a competitive industry, profit maximization leads each firm to produce at the same marginal cost, which is equal to market price. Free entry and exit means that each firm earns zero economic profit—producing the output corresponding to its minimum average total cost. So the average total cost of production of an industry's output is minimized. The outcome is efficient because every consumer with a willingness to pay greater than or equal to marginal cost gets the good.

KEY TERMS

PROBLEMS

1. For each of the following, is the business a price-taking producer? Explain your answers.

   a. A cappuccino café in a university town where there are dozens of very similar cappuccino cafés

   b. The makers of Pepsi-Cola

   c. One of many sellers of zucchini at a local farmers' market

2. For each of the following, is the industry perfectly competitive? Referring to market share, standardization of the product, and/or free entry and exit, explain your answers.

   a. the painkiller ibuprofen

   b. Alicia Keys concerts

   c. Sport utility vehicles (SUVs)

3. Kate's Katering provides catered meals, and the catered meals industry is perfectly competitive. Kate's machinery costs $100 per day and is the only fixed input. Her variable cost consists of the wages paid to the cooks and the food ingredients. The variable cost per day associated with each level of output is given in the accompanying table.

Quantity of meals	VC
0	$0
10	200
20	300
30	480
40	700
50	1000

   a. Calculate the total cost, the average variable cost, the average total cost, and the marginal cost for each quantity of output.

   b. What is the break-even price? What is the shut-down price?

   c. Suppose that the price at which Kate can sell catered meals is $21 per meal. In the short run, will Kate earn a profit? In the short run, should she produce or shut down?

   d. Suppose that the price at which Kate can sell catered meals is $17 per meal. In the short run, will Kate earn a profit? In the short run, should she produce or shut down?

   e. Suppose that the price at which Kate can sell catered meals is $13 per meal. In the short run, will Kate earn a profit? In the short run, should she produce or shut down?

4. Bob produces DVD movies for sale, which requires a building and a machine that copies the original movie onto a DVD. Bob rents a building for $30 000 per month and rents a machine for $20 000 a month. Those are his fixed costs. His variable cost per month is given in the accompanying table.

Quantity of DVDs	VC
0	$0
1 000	5 000
2 000	8 000
3 000	9 000
4 000	14 000
5 000	20 000
6 000	33 000
7 000	49 000
8 000	72 000
9 000	99 000
10 000	150 000

   a. Calculate Bob's average variable cost, average total cost, and marginal cost for each quantity of output.

   b. There is free entry into the industry, and anyone who enters will face the same costs as Bob. Suppose that currently the price of a DVD is $25. What will Bob's profit be? Is this a long-run equilibrium? If not, what will the price of DVD movies be in the long run?

5. Consider Bob's DVD company described in Problem 4. Assume that DVD production is a perfectly competitive industry. For each of the following questions, explain your answers.

   a. What is Bob's break-even price? What is his shut-down price?

   b. Suppose the price of a DVD is $2. What should Bob do in the short run?

   c. Suppose the price of a DVD is $7. What is the profit-maximizing quantity of DVDs that Bob should produce? What will his total profit be? Will he produce or shut down in the short run? Will he stay in the industry or exit in the long run?

   d. Suppose instead that the price of DVDs is $20. Now what is the profit-maximizing quantity of DVDs that Bob should produce? What will his total profit be now? Will he produce or shut down in the short run? Will he stay in the industry or exit in the long run?

6. Consider again Bob's DVD company described in Problem 4.

   a. Draw Bob's marginal cost curve.

   b. Over what range of prices will Bob produce no DVDs in the short run?

   c. Draw Bob's individual supply curve.

7. a. A profit-maximizing business incurs an economic loss of $10 000 per year. Its fixed cost is $15 000 per year. Should it produce or shut down in the short run? Should it stay in the industry or exit in the long run?

b. Suppose instead that this business has a fixed cost of $6000 per year. Should it produce or shut down in the short run? Should it stay in the industry or exit in the long run?

8. The first sushi restaurant opens in town. Initially people are very cautious about eating tiny portions of raw fish, as this is a town where large portions of grilled meat have always been popular. Soon, however, an influential health report warns consumers against grilled meat and suggests that they increase their consumption of fish, especially raw fish. The sushi restaurant becomes very popular and the demand for it increases.

a. What will happen to the short-run profit of the sushi restaurant? What will happen to the number of sushi restaurants in town in the long run? Will the first sushi restaurant be able to sustain its short-run profit over the long run? Explain your answers.

b. Local steakhouses suffer from the popularity of sushi and start incurring losses. What will happen to the number of steakhouses in town in the long run? Explain your answer.

9. A perfectly competitive firm has the following short-run total costs:

Quantity	TC
0	$5
1	10
2	13
3	18
4	25
5	34
6	45

Market demand for the firm's product is given by the following market demand schedule:

Price	Quantity demanded
$12	300
10	500
8	800
6	1200
4	1800

a. Calculate this firm's marginal cost and, for all output levels except zero, the firm's average variable cost and average total cost.

b. There are 100 firms in this industry that all have costs identical to those of this firm. Draw the short-run industry supply curve. In the same diagram, draw the market demand curve.

c. What is the market price, and how much profit will each firm make?

10. A new vaccine against a deadly disease has just been discovered. Presently, 55 people die from the disease each year. The new vaccine will save lives, but it is not completely safe. Some recipients of the shots will die from adverse reactions. The projected effects of the inoculation are given in the accompanying table:

Percent of population inoculated	Total deaths due to disease	Total deaths due to inoculation	Marginal benefit of inoculation	Marginal cost of inoculation	"Profit" of inoculation
0	55	0		—	—
10	45	0	—	—	—
20	36	1	—	—	—
30	28	3	—	—	—
40	21	6	—	—	—
50	15	10	—	—	—
60	10	15	—	—	—
70	6	20	—	—	—
80	3	25	—	—	—
90	1	30	—	—	—
100	0	35	—	—	—

a. What are the interpretations of "marginal benefit" and "marginal cost" here? Calculate marginal benefit and marginal cost per each 10% increase in the rate of inoculation. Write your answers in the table.

b. What proportion of the population should optimally be inoculated?

c. What is the interpretation of "profit" here? Calculate the profit for all levels of inoculation.

11. Evaluate each of the following statements. If a statement is true, explain why; if it is false, identify the mistake and try to correct it.

a. A profit-maximizing firm in a perfectly competitive industry should select the output level at which the difference between the market price and marginal cost is greatest.

b. An increase in fixed cost lowers the profit-maximizing quantity of output produced in the short run.

12. The production of agricultural products like wheat is one of the few examples of a perfectly competitive industry. In this question, we analyze results from a study released by the Saskatchewan Ministry of Agriculture about crop production in the province in 2013.

   a. The average variable cost per hectare planted with durum wheat was $376.54 (in the dark brown soil zone). Assuming an expected yield of 101 bushels per hectare, calculate the average variable cost per bushel of durum wheat.

   b. Suppose prior to the 2013 growing season the expected average price of durum wheat in Saskatchewan was $7.20 per bushel. Do you think the average farm would have exited the durum wheat industry in the short run? Explain. Below what price would farms exit the durum wheat industry?

   c. In fact, the average price of durum wheat received by a farmer in Saskatchewan in October 2013 was $6.20 per bushel. At this price would farmers be pleased they did not exit or regret not exiting? Explain.

   d. According to Ministry of Agriculture estimates, a farm with dark brown soil, with an estimated yield of 101 bushels per hectare, would have total costs of production of $530.34 per hectare. Using these figures determine the average cost of production and determine whether the typical farm would be profitable or not.

   e. Suppose you were told that new data from Statistics Canada just arrived and the average durum wheat yield of Saskatchewan farmers was actually 117 bushels per hectare. How does this impact the average variable cost and average total cost figures (both per bushel)? Would the average farmer regret not exiting the industry or be pleased that he or she had remained to produce durum wheat?

   f. The harvested land for durum wheat in Saskatchewan rose from 1 100 000 hectares in 2010 to 1 750 000 hectares in 2013. Using the information on prices and costs here and in parts (a) and (b), explain why this might have happened.

   g. Using the above information, do you think the prices of durum wheat were higher or lower prior to 2013? Why?

(*Note:* Every year the Saskatchewan Ministry of Agriculture prepares cost estimates for various crops for the province's three major soil zones. To access these estimates go to agriculture.gov.sk.ca, and search for "crop planning guide.")

13. The accompanying table presents prices for washing and ironing a man's shirt taken from a survey of dry cleaners in three neighbouring towns.

Dry Cleaner	City	Price
A-1 Cleaners	Savonville	$1.50
Regal Cleaners	Savonville	1.95
Rush Cleaners	Savonville	1.95
Zippy Dry Cleaners	Savonville	1.95
Queen Tailor	Savonville	2.00
Magnolia Wash	Laverham	2.00
Master Cleaners	Savonville	2.00
Tidy Cleaners	Laverham	2.00
Sunny Cleaners	Savonville	2.00
Geddy Clean	Blanchiston	2.10
Rockwell Cleaners	Blanchiston	2.10
Victoria Cleaners	Savonville	2.15
Kim's Fine Cleaners	Savonville	2.25
Gringras Cleaners	Laverham	2.25
Niko the Tailor	Savonville	2.25
Pressed 4 Time	Laverham	2.50
King's Cleaners	Laverham	2.50

   a. What is the average price per shirt washed and ironed in Laverham? In Savonville?

   b. Draw typical marginal cost and average total cost curves for Gingras Cleaners in Laverham, assuming it is a perfectly competitive firm but is making a profit on each shirt in the short run. Mark the short-run equilibrium point and shade the area that corresponds to the profit made by the dry cleaner.

   c. Assume $2.25 is the short-run equilibrium price in Laverham. Draw a typical short-run demand and supply curve for the market. Label the equilibrium point.

   d. Observing profits in the Laverham area, another dry cleaning service, Diamond Cleaners, enters the market. It charges $1.95 per shirt. What is the new average price of washing and ironing a shirt in Laverham? Illustrate the effect of entry on the average Laverham price by a shift of the short-run supply curve, the demand curve, or both.

   e. Assume that Gingras Cleaners now charges the new average price and just breaks even (that is, makes zero economic profit) at this price. Show the likely effect of the entry on your diagram in part (b).

   f. If the dry cleaning industry is perfectly competitive, what does the average difference in price between Laverham and Savonville imply about costs in the two areas?

14. Besides assuming there is a large number of consumers and producers in a perfectly competitive industry, we often also assume:

- Consumers and producers in the market have perfect information about the characteristics of the good sold by every producer and the price charged by each producer.
- A potential producer has access to any necessary resources, to best-practice technology, and to product designs. So there are no barriers to firms wishing to enter this market.
- All producers have the same technology, which results in them all having the same costs of production.

For a perfectly competitive industry with all the usual assumptions, plus the three additional assumptions above, is each of the following statements true, false, or uncertain? Explain why or why not. Highlight which assumptions are key to making your answer what it is.

a. Producers will make goods that are identical in all regards (perfect substitutes).

b. In equilibrium, consumers who are good negotiators are able to buy the product at a lower price than other consumers can.

c. At every point in time, all firms will earn the same level of economic profit.

d. In order to build customer loyalty to their brand, some producers in this market will carefully design their product to serve the needs of their chosen market segment.

e. Prices charged by all producers in the market will be identical.

f. At some points in time, some firms will be more profitable than others. This allows their senior executives to be paid a much high salary than the executives at competing firms.

g. In equilibrium, no producer will be able to sell lower quality goods at the same price, or charge a higher price for goods of the same quality as those being sold by other producers.

h. All firms selling in this market have the power to set their own price independent of what other firms are charging.

15. The extent to which a firm or a person can influence the price of an item by exercising control of its demand, supply, or both is known as *market power*. Under perfect competition all firms and consumers are assumed to have zero market power. Therefore, all market participants must accept the current market price without being able to exercise any control over it. Explain the role played by the following assumptions on the degree of market power possessed by market participants in a perfectly competitive market.

a. There are many producers.

b. There are many consumers.

c. The producers have a standardized product.

d. All producers and consumers possess perfect information.

e. This industry has free entry and exit.

16. This question uses the algebraic method of determining average variable cost from Appendix 11A and the algebraic method of determining equilibrium from Appendix 3A. A firm in a perfectly competitive constant cost industry has total and marginal costs in the short-run given by:

$$TC = 0.5 \times q^2 + 2.5 \times q + 72 \qquad \text{Total Cost}$$
$$MC = q + 2.5 \qquad \text{Marginal Cost}$$

where q is the output per day and TC is the total cost in dollars. The firm has fixed costs of $40 (which is already included in the TC equation above). This TC equation generates minimum average total cost of $14.50 at $q = 12$. This firm generates minimum long run average costs (also at $q = 12$, $LRAC = \$14.50$). (*Hint:* The average total cost curve is at a minimum where it intersects the marginal cost curve (that is, $ATC = MC$). Similarly, the average variable cost curve is at a minimum where $AVC = MC$.)

a. Determine the average variable cost. At what price will the firm shut down in the short run?

b. In the short run, if the firm faces a price of $11.50, how much will the firm produce?

c. In the short run, if the firm faces a price of $20.50, how much profit will the firm earn?

d. In the short run, there are 200 identical firms in the industry. Demand for the output of firms in this industry is given by:

$$P = 32.5 - 0.01 \times Q \qquad \text{Demand Curve}$$

where Q is the total amount sold to consumers. What are the equilibrium price and quantity?

e. Given the demand curve described in part (d), how many firms will there be in this industry in the long run?

f. Suppose in the long run, there is technological change that reduces the long-run minimum average cost of the typical business firm to $8.50 at $q = 8$. Now, how many firms will there be in the industry in the long run?

CHAPTER 13

Monopoly

EVERYBODY MUST GET STONES

Corbis

Marilyn Monroe sang "Diamonds are a Girl's Best Friend" in the 1953 film *Gentlemen Prefer Blondes.*

WHAT YOU WILL LEARN IN THIS CHAPTER

❭ The significance of **monopoly**, where a single **monopolist** is the only producer of a good

❭ How a monopolist determines its profit-maximizing output and price

❭ The difference between monopoly and perfect competition, and the effects of that difference on society's welfare

❭ How policy-makers address the problems posed by monopoly

❭ What **price discrimination** is, and why it is so prevalent when producers have **market power**

A FEW YEARS AGO DE BEERS, THE world's main supplier of diamonds, ran an ad urging men to buy their wives diamond jewellery. "She married you for richer, for poorer," read the ad. "Let her know how it's going."

Crass? Yes. Effective? No question. For generations diamonds have been a symbol of luxury, valued not only for their appearance but also for their rarity.

But geologists will tell you that diamonds aren't all that rare. In fact, according to the *Dow Jones-Irwin Guide to Fine Gems and Jewelry*, diamonds are "more common than any other gem-quality coloured stone. They only seem rarer."

Why do diamonds seem rarer than other gems? Part of the answer is a brilliant marketing campaign. (We'll talk more about marketing and product differentiation in Chapter 15.) But mainly diamonds seem rare because De Beers *makes* them rare: the company controls most of the world's diamond mines (including the Snap Lake Mine in the Northwest Territories and the Victor Mine in Ontario) and limits the quantity of diamonds supplied to the market.

Up to now we have concentrated exclusively on perfectly competitive markets—markets in which the producers are perfect competitors. But De Beers isn't like the producers we've studied so far: it is a *monopolist*, the sole (or almost sole) producer of a good. Monopolists behave differently from producers in perfectly competitive industries: whereas perfect competitors take the price at which they can sell their output as given, monopolists know that their actions affect market prices and take that effect into account when deciding how much to produce. Before we begin our analysis, let's step back and look at *monopoly* and perfect competition as parts of a broader system for classifying markets.

Perfect competition and monopoly are particular types of *market structure*. They are particular categories in a system economists use to classify markets and industries according to two main dimensions. This chapter begins with a brief overview of types of market structure. It will help us here and in subsequent chapters to understand on a deeper level why markets differ and why producers in those markets behave quite differently. ■

Types of Market Structure

In the real world, there is a mind-boggling array of different markets. We observe widely different behaviour patterns by producers across markets: in some markets producers are extremely competitive; in others, they seem somehow to coordinate their actions to avoid competing with one another; and, as we have just described, some markets are monopolies in which there is no competition at all. In order to develop principles and make predictions about markets and how producers will behave in them, economists have developed four principal models of market structure: *perfect competition, monopoly, oligopoly, and monopolistic competition.*

This system of market structures is based on two dimensions:

- The number of producers in the market (one, few, or many)
- Whether the goods offered are identical or *differentiated*

Differentiated goods are goods that are different but considered somewhat substitutable by consumers (think Coke versus Pepsi, or an iPhone versus an Android phone).

Figure 13-1 provides a simple visual summary of the types of market structure classified according to the two dimensions. In *monopoly,* a single producer sells a single, undifferentiated product. In *oligopoly,* a few producers—more than one but not a large number—sell products that may be either identical or differentiated. In *monopolistic competition,* many producers each sell a differentiated product (think of producers of economics textbooks). And finally, as we know, in *perfect competition* many producers each sell an identical product.

You might wonder what determines the number of firms in a market: whether there is one (monopoly), a few (oligopoly), or many (perfect competition and monopolistic competition). We won't answer that question here because it will be covered in detail later in this chapter and in Chapters 14 and 15, which analyze oligopoly and monopolistic competition. We will just briefly note that in the long run it depends on whether there are conditions that make it difficult for new firms to enter the market, such as control of necessary resources or inputs, increasing returns to scale in production, technological superiority, a network externality, or government regulations. When these conditions are present, industries tend to be monopolies or oligopolies; when they are not present, industries tend to be perfectly competitive or monopolistically competitive.

FIGURE   13-1   Types of Market Structure

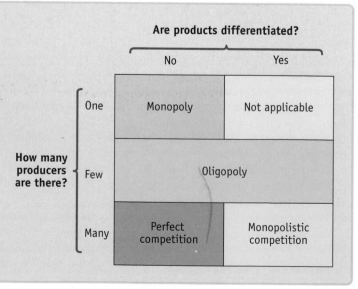

The behaviour of any given firm and the market it occupies are analyzed using one of four models of market structure— monopoly, oligopoly, perfect competition, or monopolistic competition. This system for categorizing market structure is based on two dimensions: (1) whether products are differentiated or identical, and (2) the number of producers in the industry—one, a few, or many.

You might also wonder why some markets have differentiated products but others have identical ones. The answer is that it depends on the nature of the good and consumers' preferences. Some goods—soft drinks, economics textbooks, breakfast cereals—can readily be made into different varieties in the eyes and tastes of consumers. Other goods—hammers, for example—are much less easy to differentiate.

Although this chapter is devoted to monopoly, important aspects of monopoly carry over to oligopoly and monopolistic competition. In the next section, we will define monopoly and review the conditions that make it possible. These same conditions, in less extreme form, also give rise to oligopoly. We then show how a monopolist can increase profit by limiting the quantity supplied to a market—behaviour that also occurs in oligopoly and monopolistic competition. As we'll see, this kind of behaviour is good for the producer but bad for consumers; it also causes inefficiency. An important topic of study will be the ways in which public policy tries to limit the damage. Finally, we turn to one of the surprising effects of monopoly—one that is very often present in oligopoly and monopolistic competition as well: the fact that different consumers often pay different prices for the same good.

> A **monopolist** is a firm that is the only producer of a good that has no close substitutes. An industry controlled by a monopolist is known as a **monopoly**.

The Meaning of Monopoly

The De Beers monopoly of South Africa was created in the 1880s by Cecil Rhodes, a British businessman. By 1880 mines in South Africa already dominated the world's supply of diamonds. There were, however, many mining companies, all competing with each other. During the 1880s Rhodes bought the great majority of those mines and consolidated them into a single company, De Beers. By 1889 De Beers controlled almost all of the world's diamond production.

De Beers, in other words, became a **monopolist.** A producer is a monopolist if it is the sole supplier of a good that has no close substitutes. When a firm is a monopolist, the industry is a **monopoly.**

Monopoly: Our First Departure from Perfect Competition

As we saw in the Chapter 12 section "Defining Perfect Competition," the supply and demand model of a market is not universally valid. Instead, it's a model of perfect competition, which is only one of several different types of market structure. Back in Chapter 12 we learned that a market will be perfectly competitive only if there are many producers, all of whom produce the same good. Monopoly is the most extreme departure from perfect competition.

In practice, true monopolies are hard to find in the modern Canadian economy, partly because of legal obstacles. A contemporary entrepreneur who tried to consolidate all the firms in an industry the way that Rhodes did would soon find himself in court, accused of breaking the Competition Act, Canada's *antitrust* law, which is intended to prevent monopolies from emerging. Oligopoly, a market structure in which there is a small number of large producers, is much more common. In fact, most of the goods you buy, from autos to airline tickets, are supplied by oligopolies, which we will examine in detail in Chapter 14.

Monopolies do, however, play an important role in some sectors of the economy, such as pharmaceuticals. Furthermore, our analysis of monopoly will provide a foundation for our later analysis of other departures from perfect competition, such as oligopoly and monopolistic competition.

What Monopolists Do

Why did Rhodes want to consolidate South African diamond producers into a single company? What difference did it make to the world diamond market?

Market power is the ability of a firm to raise prices.

Figure 13-2 offers a preliminary view of the effects of monopoly. It shows an industry in which the supply curve under perfect competition intersects the demand curve at C, leading to the price P_C and the output Q_C.

Suppose that this industry is consolidated into a monopoly. The monopolist *moves up the demand curve* by reducing quantity supplied to a point like M, at which the quantity produced, Q_M, is lower and the price, P_M, is higher than under perfect competition.

The ability of a monopolist to raise its price above the competitive level by reducing output is known as **market power.** And market power is what monopoly is all about. A wheat farmer who is one of 10 000 wheat farmers has no market power: he or she must sell wheat at the going market price. Your local water utility company, though, does have market power: it can raise prices and still keep many (though not all) of its customers, because they have nowhere else to go. In short, it's a monopolist.

The reason a monopolist reduces output and raises price compared to the perfectly competitive industry levels is to increase profit. Cecil Rhodes consolidated the diamond producers into De Beers because he realized that the whole would be worth more than the sum of its parts—the monopoly would generate more profit than the sum of the profits of the individual competitive firms. As we saw in Chapter 12, under perfect competition economic profits normally vanish in the long run as competitors enter the market. Under monopoly the profits don't go away—a monopolist is able to continue earning economic profits in the long run.

In fact, monopolists are not the only types of firms that possess market power. In the next chapter we will study *oligopolists,* firms that can have market power as well. Under certain conditions, oligopolists can earn positive economic profits in the long run by restricting output like monopolists do.

But why don't profits get competed away? What allows monopolists to be monopolists?

FIGURE 13-2 What a Monopolist Does

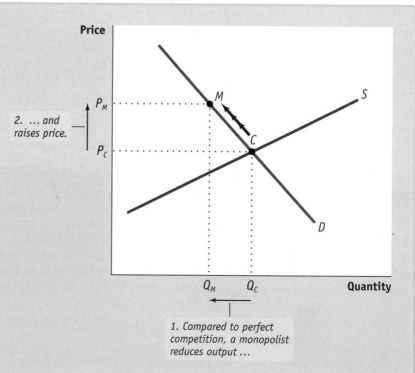

Under perfect competition, the price and quantity are determined by supply and demand. Here, the competitive equilibrium is at C, where the price is P_C and the quantity is Q_C. A monopolist reduces the quantity supplied to Q_M and moves up the demand curve from C to M, raising the price to P_M.

2. ... and raises price.

1. Compared to perfect competition, a monopolist reduces output ...

Why Do Monopolies Exist?

A monopolist making profits will not go unnoticed by others. (Recall that this is "economic profit," revenue over and above the opportunity costs of the firm's resources.) But won't other firms crash the party, grab a piece of the action, and drive down prices and profits in the long run? For a profitable monopoly to persist, something must keep others from going into the same business; that "something" is known as a **barrier to entry.** There are five principal types of barriers to entry: control of a scarce resource or input, increasing returns to scale, technological superiority, a network externality, and a government-created barrier to entry.

1. Control of a Scarce Resource or Input A monopolist that controls a resource or input crucial to an industry can prevent other firms from entering its market. Cecil Rhodes created the De Beers monopoly by establishing control over the mines that produced the great bulk of the world's diamonds.

2. Increasing Returns to Scale Many Canadians have natural gas piped into their homes, for cooking and heating. Invariably, the local gas company is a monopolist. But why don't rival companies compete to provide gas?

In the early nineteenth century, when the gas industry was just starting up, companies did compete for local customers. But this competition didn't last long; soon local gas supply became a monopoly in almost every town because of the large fixed costs involved in providing a town with gas lines. The cost of laying gas lines didn't depend on how much gas a company sold, so a firm with a larger volume of sales had a cost advantage: because it was able to spread the fixed costs over a larger volume, it had lower average total costs than smaller firms.

Local gas supply is an industry in which average total cost falls as output increases. As we learned in Chapter 11, this phenomenon is called *increasing returns to scale*. There we learned that when average total cost falls as output increases, firms tend to grow larger. In an industry characterized by increasing returns to scale, larger companies are more profitable and drive out smaller ones. For the same reason, established companies have a cost advantage over any potential entrant—a potent barrier to entry. So increasing returns to scale can both give rise to and sustain monopoly. For instance, when wet natural gas was discovered in Alberta's Turner Valley in 1914, many investors formed "oil companies" in the region. But according to the Calgary City Directory, the number of "oil mining companies" fell from 226 in 1914 to 21 in 1917. The reduction in the number of firms was due partly to the lower than expected flow of liquid gas from wells and partly to the relatively high cost of extraction.

A monopoly created and sustained by increasing returns to scale is called a **natural monopoly.** The defining characteristic of a natural monopoly is that it possesses increasing returns to scale over the range of output that is relevant for the industry. This is illustrated in Figure 13-3, showing the firm's average total cost curve, *ATC*, and the market demand curve, *D*. Here we can see that the natural monopolist's *ATC* curve declines over the output levels at which price is greater than or equal to average total cost. So the natural monopolist has increasing returns to scale over the entire range of output for which any firm would want to remain in the industry—the range of output at which the firm would at least break even in the long run. The source of this condition is large fixed costs: when large fixed costs are required to operate, a given quantity of output is produced at lower average total cost by one large firm than by two or more smaller firms.

The most visible natural monopolies in the modern economy are local utilities—water, gas, and sometimes electricity. As we'll see later in this chapter, natural monopolies pose a special challenge to public policy.

3. Technological Superiority A firm that maintains a consistent technological advantage over potential competitors can establish itself as a monopolist. For

To earn economic profits, a monopolist must be protected by a **barrier to entry**—something that prevents other firms from entering the industry.

A **natural monopoly** exists when increasing returns to scale provide a large cost advantage to a single firm that produces all of an industry's output.

FIGURE 13-3 Increasing Returns to Scale Create Natural Monopoly

A natural monopoly can arise when fixed costs required to operate are very high. When this occurs, the firm's *ATC* curve declines over the range of output at which price is greater than or equal to average total cost. This gives the firm increasing returns to scale over the entire range of output at which the firm would at least break even in the long run. As a result, a given quantity of output is produced more cheaply by one large firm than by two or more smaller firms.

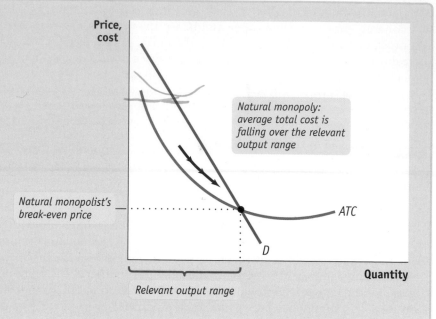

example, from the 1970s through the 1990s the chip manufacturer Intel was able to maintain a consistent advantage over potential competitors in both the design and production of microprocessors, the chips that run computers. But technological superiority is typically not a barrier to entry over the longer term: over time competitors will invest in upgrading their technology to match that of the technology leader. In fact, in the last few years Intel found its technological superiority eroded by a competitor, Advanced Micro Devices (AMD), which now produces chips approximately as fast and as powerful as Intel chips.

We should note, however, that in certain high-tech industries, technological superiority is not a guarantee of success against competitors because of *network externalities*.

4. Network Externality If you were the only person in the world with an Internet connection, what would that connection be worth to you? The answer, of course, is nothing. Your Internet connection is valuable only because other people are also connected. And, in general, the more people who are connected, the more valuable your connection is. This phenomenon, whereby the value of a good or service to an individual is greater when many others use the same good or service, is called a **network externality**—its value derives from enabling its users to participate in a network of other users.

The earliest form of network externalities arose in transportation, where the value of a road or airport increased as the number of people who had access to it rose. But network externalities are especially prevalent in the technology and communications sectors of the economy. The classic case is computer operating systems. Worldwide, most personal computers run on Microsoft Windows. Although many believe that Apple has a superior operating system, the wider use of Windows in the early days of personal computers attracted more software development and technical support, giving it a lasting dominance.

When a network externality exists, the firm with the largest network of customers using its product has an advantage in attracting new customers, one that may allow it to become a monopolist. At a minimum, the dominant firm can charge a higher price and so earn higher profits than competitors. Moreover, a network externality gives an advantage to the firm with the "deepest pockets." Companies with the most money on hand can sell the most goods at a loss with the expectation that doing so will give it the largest customer base.

A **network externality** exists when the value of a good or service to an individual is greater when many other people use the good or service as well.

5. Government-Created Barrier In 1999 the pharmaceutical company Merck Canada Inc. introduced Propecia, a drug effective against baldness. Despite the fact that Propecia was very profitable and other drug companies had the know-how to produce it, no other firms challenged Merck's monopoly. That's because in March 1999 the Canadian government had given Merck a patent for this drug. The patent gave Merck the sole legal right to produce the drug in Canada until the patent expired in 2014. Propecia is an example of a monopoly protected by government-created barriers.

The most important legally created monopolies today arise from *patents* and *copyrights*. A **patent** gives an inventor the sole right to make, use, or sell that invention for a period that in most countries lasts between 16 and 20 years. Patents are given to the creators of new products, such as drugs or devices. In Canada, the Canadian Intellectual Property Office (CIPO), a federal agency under Industry Canada, is responsible for the administration of intellectual property in Canada, including granting and registering patents, trademarks, copyright, and industrial designs. Currently, a Canadian patent grants an inventor the exclusive right to make, use, and sell his or her invention for up to 20 years from the day of filing a patent application. Similarly, a **copyright** gives the creator of a literary

A **patent** gives an inventor a temporary monopoly in the use or sale of an invention.

A **copyright** gives the creator of a literary or artistic work sole rights to profit from that work.

GLOBAL COMPARISON   THE PRICE WE PAY

Although providing cheap patent-protected drugs to patients in poor countries is a new phenomenon, charging different prices to consumers in different countries is not: it's an example of price discrimination.

A monopolist will maximize profits by charging a higher price in the country with a lower price elasticity (the rich country) and a lower price in the country with a higher price elasticity (the poor country). Interestingly, however, drug prices can differ substantially even among countries with comparable income levels. How do we explain this?

The answer is differences in regulation.

This graph compares the prices paid by residents of various wealthy countries for a given basket of drugs. It shows that American consumers pay much more for their drugs than residents of other wealthy countries. And while Canadians only pay 55% of what the Americans pay for drugs, the cost of drugs in Canada is nonetheless higher than in other countries such as France, Spain, and Australia. For example, Spaniards and Australians pay approximately 60% of what Canadians pay for drugs and only about one-third of what Americans pay. The reason: governments in those countries more actively regulate drug prices than Canada and the United States do, helping to keep drug prices affordable for their citizens.

To save money, it's not surprising that Americans travel to Canada and Mexico to purchase their drugs, or buy them from abroad over the Internet.

Yet, American drug-makers contend that higher drug prices are necessary to cover the the high cost of research

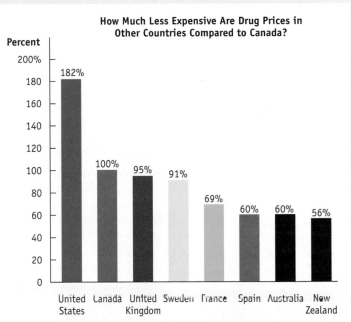

and development, which can run into the tens of millions of dollars over several years for successful drugs. Critics of the drug companies counter that American drug prices are in excess of what is needed for a socially desirable level of drug innovation. Instead, they say that drug companies are too often focused on developing drugs that generate high profits rather than those that improve health or save lives. What's indisputable is that some level of profit is necessary to fund innovation.

Sources: U.S. Energy Information Administration; Natural Resources Canada, 2010.

or artistic work the sole rights to profit from that work, usually for a period equal to the creator's lifetime plus 50 years.

The justification for patents and copyrights is a matter of incentives. If inventors are not protected by patents, they would gain little reward from their efforts: as soon as a valuable invention was made public, others would copy it and sell products based on it. And if inventors could not expect to profit from their inventions, then there would be no incentive to incur the costs of invention in the first place. Likewise for the creators of literary or artistic works. So the law gives a temporary monopoly that encourages invention and creation by imposing temporary property rights.

Patents and copyrights are temporary because the law strikes a compromise. The higher price for the good that holds while the legal protection is in effect compensates inventors for the cost of invention; conversely, the lower price that results once the legal protection lapses and competition emerges benefits consumers and increases economic efficiency.

Because the length of the temporary monopoly cannot be tailored to specific cases, this system is imperfect and leads to some missed opportunities. In some cases there can be significant welfare issues. For example, the violation of drug patents by pharmaceutical companies in poor countries has been a major source of controversy, pitting the needs of poor patients who cannot afford retail drug prices against the interests of drug manufacturers that have incurred high research costs to discover these drugs. To solve this problem, some drug companies and poor countries have negotiated deals in which the patents are honoured but the companies sell their drugs at deeply discounted prices. For example, GlaxoSmithKline, Canada's leading flu vaccine manufacturer, has adopted a policy to not charge the least developed countries more than 25% of the price charged in the developed world for their patented medicines. (This is an example of *price discrimination*, which we'll learn more about later in this chapter.)

ECONOMICS > IN ACTION

NEWLY EMERGING MARKETS: A DIAMOND MONOPOLIST'S BEST FRIEND

When Cecil Rhodes created the De Beers monopoly, it was a particularly opportune moment. The new diamond mines in South Africa dwarfed all previous sources, so almost all of the world's diamond production was concentrated in a few square kilometres.

Until recently, De Beers was able to extend its control of resources even as new mines opened. De Beers either bought out new producers or entered into agreements with local governments that controlled some of the new mines, effectively making them part of the De Beers monopoly. The most remarkable of these was an agreement with the former Soviet Union, which ensured that Russian diamonds would be marketed through De Beers, preserving its ability to control retail prices. De Beers also went so far as to stockpile a year's supply of diamonds in its London vaults so that when demand dropped, newly mined stones would be stored rather than sold, restricting retail supply until demand and prices recovered.

However, over the past few years the De Beers monopoly has been under assault. Government regulators have forced De Beers to loosen its control of the market. For the first time, De Beers has competition: a number of independent companies have begun mining for diamonds in other African countries. In addition, high-quality, inexpensive synthetic dia-

An increase in demand for diamonds in emerging markets has led to increased depletion of the world's diamond mines and higher prices.

monds have become an alternative to real gems, eating into De Beers's profits. So does this mean an end to high diamond prices and De Beers's high profits?

Not really. Although today's De Beers is more of a "near-monopolist" than a true monopolist, it still mines more of the world's supply of diamonds than any other single producer. And it has been benefitting from newly emerging markets. Consumer demand for diamonds has soared in countries like China and India, leading to price increases.

Nevertheless, the economic crisis of 2009 put a serious dent in worldwide demand for diamonds. De Beers responded by cutting 2011 production by 20% (compared to 2008). But affluent Chinese continue to be heavy buyers of diamonds, and De Beers anticipates that Asian demand will accelerate the depletion of the world's existing diamond mines. As a result, diamond analysts predict rough diamond prices to rise by at least 5% per year for the next five years.

In the end, although a diamond monopoly may not be forever, a near-monopoly with rising demand in newly emerging markets may be just as profitable.

CHECK YOUR UNDERSTANDING   13-1

1. Suppose Lamplighter New Brunswick is the only natural gas distributor in the province of New Brunswick. Last winter residents were shocked that the price of natural gas had increased drastically and believed that they were the victims of market power. Explain which of the following pieces of evidence support or contradict that conclusion.
   a. There is a national shortage of natural gas, and Lamplighter New Brunswick could procure only a limited amount.
   b. Last year, Lamplighter New Brunswick and several other competing local natural gas distributing firms merged into a single firm.
   c. The cost to Lamplighter New Brunswick of purchasing natural gas from a natural gas processing plant has gone up significantly.
   d. Recently, some nonlocal firms have begun to offer natural gas to Lamplighter New Brunswick's regular customers at a price much lower than Lamplighter New Brunswick's.
   e. Lamplighter New Brunswick has acquired an exclusive government licence to draw natural gas from the only natural gas pipeline in the province.

2. Suppose the government is considering extending the length of a patent from 20 years to 30 years. How would this change each of the following?
   a. The incentive to invent new products
   b. The length of time during which consumers have to pay higher prices

3. Explain the nature of the network externality in each of the following cases.
   a. A new type of credit card, called Passport
   b. A new type of car engine, which runs on solar cells
   c. A website for trading locally provided goods and services

Solutions appear at back of book.

▼ **Quick Review**

● In a **monopoly,** a single firm uses its **market power** to charge higher prices and produce less output than a competitive industry, generating profits in the short and long run.

● Profits will not persist in the long run unless there is a **barrier to entry** such as control of natural resources, increasing returns to scale, technological superiority, network externalities, or legal restrictions imposed by governments.

● A **natural monopoly** arises when average total cost is declining over the output range relevant for the industry. This creates a barrier to entry because an established monopolist has lower average total cost than an entrant.

● In certain technology and communications sectors of the economy, a **network externality** enables a firm with the largest number of customers to become a **monopolist.**

● **Patents** and **copyrights,** government-created barriers, are a source of temporary monopoly that attempt to balance the need for higher prices as compensation to an inventor for the cost of invention against the increase in consumer surplus from lower prices and greater efficiency.

How a Monopolist Maximizes Profit

As we've suggested, once Cecil Rhodes consolidated the competing diamond producers of South Africa into a single company, the industry's behaviour changed: the quantity supplied fell and the market price rose. In this section, we will learn how a monopolist increases its profit by reducing output. And we will see the crucial role that market demand plays in leading a monopolist to behave differently from a perfectly competitive industry. (Remember that profit here is economic profit, not accounting profit.)

The Monopolist's Demand Curve and Marginal Revenue

In Chapter 12 we derived the firm's optimal output rule: a profit-maximizing firm produces the quantity of output at which the marginal cost of producing the last unit of output equals marginal revenue—the change in total revenue generated by that last unit of output. That is, $MR = MC$ at the profit-maximizing quantity of output. Although the optimal output rule holds for all firms, we will see shortly that its application leads to different profit-maximizing output levels for a monopolist compared to a firm in a perfectly competitive industry—that is, a price-taking firm. The source of that difference lies in the comparison of the demand curve faced by a monopolist to the demand curve faced by an individual perfectly competitive firm.

In addition to the optimal output rule, we also learned in Chapter 12 that even though the market demand curve always slopes downward, each of the firms that make up a perfectly competitive industry faces a *perfectly elastic* demand curve that is horizontal at the market price, like D_C in panel (a) of Figure 13-4. Any attempt by an individual firm in a perfectly competitive industry to charge more than the going market price will cause it to lose all its sales. It can, however, sell as much as it likes at the market price. As we saw in Chapter 12, the marginal revenue of a perfectly competitive producer is simply the market price. As a result, the price-taking firm's optimal output rule is to produce the output level at which the marginal cost of the last unit produced is equal to the market price.

A monopolist, in contrast, is the sole supplier of its good. So its demand curve is simply the market demand curve, which slopes downward, like D_M in panel (b) of Figure 13-4. This downward slope creates a "wedge" between the price of the good and the marginal revenue of the good—the change in revenue generated by producing one more unit.

FIGURE 13-4 **Comparing the Demand Curves of a Perfectly Competitive Producer and a Monopolist**

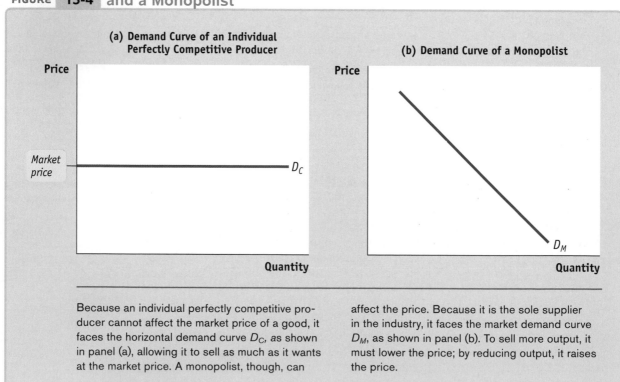

Because an individual perfectly competitive producer cannot affect the market price of a good, it faces the horizontal demand curve D_C, as shown in panel (a), allowing it to sell as much as it wants at the market price. A monopolist, though, can affect the price. Because it is the sole supplier in the industry, it faces the market demand curve D_M, as shown in panel (b). To sell more output, it must lower the price; by reducing output, it raises the price.

Table 13-1 shows this wedge between price and marginal revenue for a monopolist, by calculating the monopolist's total revenue and marginal revenue schedules from its demand schedule.

The first two columns of Table 13-1 show a hypothetical demand schedule for De Beers diamonds. For the sake of simplicity, we assume that all diamonds are exactly alike. And to make the arithmetic easy, we suppose that the number of diamonds sold is far smaller than is actually the case. For instance, at a price of $500 per diamond, we assume that only 10 diamonds are sold. The demand curve implied by this schedule is shown in panel (a) of Figure 13-5.

The third column of Table 13-1 shows De Beers's total revenue from selling each quantity of diamonds—the price per diamond multiplied by the number of diamonds sold. The last column calculates marginal revenue, the change in total revenue from producing and selling another diamond.

Clearly, after the first diamond, the marginal revenue a monopolist receives from selling one more unit is less than the price at which that unit is sold. For example, if De Beers sells 10 diamonds, the price at which the 10th diamond is sold is $500. But the marginal revenue—the change in total revenue in going from 9 to 10 diamonds—is only $50.

Why is the marginal revenue from that 10th diamond less than the price? It is less than the price because an increase in production by a monopolist has two opposing effects on revenue:

- A *quantity effect*. One more unit is sold, increasing total revenue by the price at which the unit is sold.

- A *price effect*. In order to sell an additional unit, the monopolist must cut the market price on *all* units sold. This decreases total revenue.

The quantity effect and the price effect when the monopolist goes from selling 9 diamonds to 10 diamonds are illustrated by the two shaded areas in panel (a) of Figure 13-5. Increasing diamond sales from 9 to 10 means moving down the demand curve from A to B, reducing the price per diamond from $550 to $500. The green-shaded area represents the quantity effect: De Beers sells the 10th diamond at a price of $500. This is offset, however, by the price effect, represented by the orange-shaded area. In order to sell that 10th diamond, De Beers must reduce the price on all its diamonds from $550 to $500. So it loses 9 × $50 = $450 in revenue, the orange-shaded area. As point C indicates, the total effect on revenue of selling one more diamond—the marginal revenue—derived from an increase in diamond sales from 9 to 10 is only $50.

Point C lies on the monopolist's marginal revenue curve, labelled MR in panel (a) of Figure 13-5 and taken from the last column of Table 13-1. The crucial point about the monopolist's marginal revenue curve is that it is always *below* the demand curve. That's because of the price effect: a monopolist's marginal revenue from selling an additional unit is always less than the price the monopolist receives for the previous unit. It is the price effect that creates the wedge between the monopolist's marginal revenue curve and the demand curve: in order to sell an additional diamond, De Beers must cut the market price on all units sold.

In fact, this wedge exists for any firm that possesses market power, such as an oligopolist as well as a monopolist. Having market power means that the firm

TABLE 13-1 Demand, Total Revenue, and Marginal Revenue for the De Beers Monopoly

Price of diamond P	Quantity of diamonds Q	Total revenue TR = P × Q	Marginal revenue MR = ΔTR/ΔQ
$1000	0	$0	
			$950
950	1	950	
			850
900	2	1800	
			750
850	3	2550	
			650
800	4	3200	
			550
750	5	3750	
			450
700	6	4200	
			350
650	7	4550	
			250
600	8	4800	
			150
550	9	4950	
			50
500	10	5000	
			−50
450	11	4950	
			−150
400	12	4800	
			−250
350	13	4550	
			−350
300	14	4200	
			−450
250	15	3750	
			−550
200	16	3200	
			−650
150	17	2550	
			−750
100	18	1800	
			−850
50	19	950	
			−950
0	20	0	

FIGURE 13-5 A Monopolist's Demand, Total Revenue, and Marginal Revenue Curves

Panel (a) shows the monopolist's demand and marginal revenue curves for diamonds from Table 13-1. The marginal revenue curve lies below the demand curve. To see why, consider point *A* on the demand curve, where 9 diamonds are sold at $550 each, generating total revenue of $4950. To sell a 10th diamond, the price on all 10 diamonds must be cut to $500, as shown by point *B*. As a result, total revenue increases by the green area (the quantity effect: +$500) but decreases by the orange area (the price effect: −$450). So the marginal revenue from the 10th diamond is $50 (the difference between the green and orange areas), which is much lower than its price, $500.

Panel (b) shows the monopolist's total revenue curve for diamonds. As output goes from 0 to 10 diamonds, total revenue increases. It reaches its maximum at 10 diamonds—the level at which marginal revenue is equal to 0—and declines thereafter. The quantity effect dominates the price effect when total revenue is rising; the price effect dominates the quantity effect when total revenue is falling.

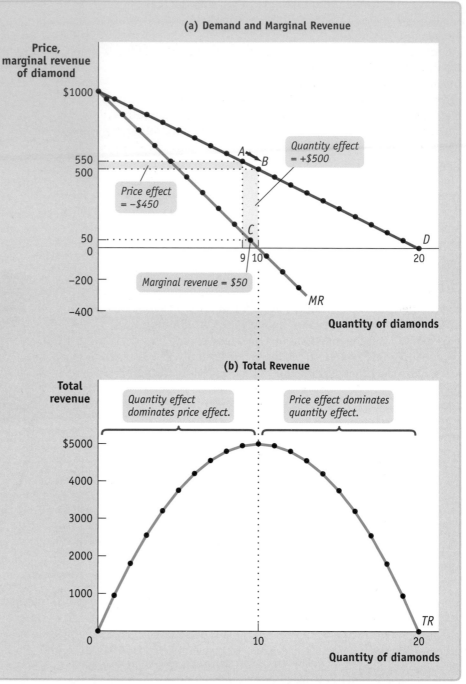

faces a downward-sloping demand curve. As a result, there will always be a price effect from an increase in its output. So for a firm with market power, the marginal revenue curve always lies below its demand curve.

Take a moment to compare the monopolist's marginal revenue curve with the marginal revenue curve for a perfectly competitive firm, one without market power. For such a firm there is no price effect from an increase in output: its marginal revenue curve is simply its horizontal demand curve. So for a perfectly competitive firm, market price and marginal revenue are always equal.

To emphasize how the quantity and price effects offset each other for a firm with market power, De Beers's total revenue curve is shown in panel (b) of Figure 13-5. Notice that it is hill-shaped: as output rises from 0 to 10 diamonds, total revenue increases. This reflects the fact that at *low levels of output, the quantity effect is stronger than the price effect:* as the monopolist sells more, it has to lower the price on only very few units, so the price effect is small. As output rises beyond 10 diamonds, total revenue actually falls. This reflects the fact that *at high levels of output, the price effect is stronger than the quantity effect:* as the monopolist sells more, it now has to lower the price on many units of output, making the price effect very large. Correspondingly, the marginal revenue curve lies below zero at output levels above 10 diamonds. For example, an increase in diamond production from 11 to 12 yields only $400 for the 12th diamond, simultaneously reducing the revenue from diamonds 1 through 11 by $550. As a result, the marginal revenue of the 12th diamond is −$150. Indeed, the monopolist faces an elastic demand when the quantity of diamonds sold is less than 10 and an inelastic demand when the quantity of diamonds sold is greater than 10. Total revenue is maximized when demand is unit-elastic.

The Monopolist's Profit-Maximizing Output and Price

To complete the story of how a monopolist maximizes profit, we now bring in the monopolist's marginal cost. Let's assume that there is no fixed cost of production; we'll also assume that the marginal cost of producing an additional diamond is constant at $200, no matter how many diamonds De Beers produces. Then marginal cost will always equal average total cost, and the marginal cost curve (and the average total cost curve) is a horizontal line at $200, as shown in Figure 13-6.

To maximize profit, the monopolist compares marginal cost with marginal revenue. If marginal revenue exceeds marginal cost, De Beers increases profit by producing more; if marginal revenue is less than marginal cost, De Beers increases

FIGURE 13-6 The Monopolist's Profit-Maximizing Output and Price

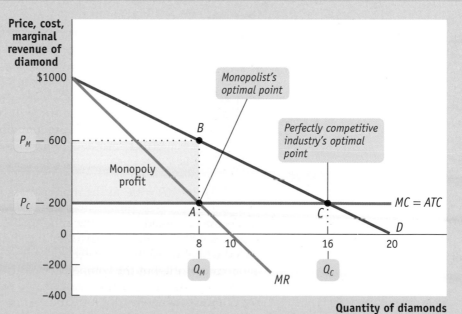

This figure shows the demand, marginal revenue, and marginal cost curves. Marginal cost per diamond is constant at $200, so the marginal cost curve is horizontal at $200. According to the optimal output rule, the profit-maximizing quantity of output for the monopolist is at $MR = MC$, shown by point A, where the marginal cost and marginal revenue curves cross at an output of 8 diamonds. The price De Beers can charge per diamond is found by going to the point on the demand curve directly above point A, which is point B here—a price of $600 per diamond. It makes a profit of $400 × 8 = $3200. A perfectly competitive industry produces the output level at which $P = MC$, given by point C, where the demand curve and marginal cost curves cross. So a competitive industry produces 16 diamonds, sells at a price of $200, and makes zero profit.

profit by producing less. So the monopolist maximizes its profit by using the optimal output rule:

(13-1) $MR = MC$ at the monopolist's profit-maximizing quantity of output

The monopolist's optimal point is shown in Figure 13-6. At *A*, the marginal cost curve, *MC*, crosses the marginal revenue curve, *MR*. The corresponding output level, eight diamonds, is the monopolist's profit-maximizing quantity of output, Q_M. The price at which consumers demand eight diamonds is $600, so the monopolist's price, P_M, is $600—corresponding to point *B*. The average total cost of producing each diamond is $200, so the monopolist earns a profit of $600 − $200 = $400 per diamond, and total profit is 8 × $400 = $3200, as indicated by the shaded area.

Monopoly versus Perfect Competition

When Cecil Rhodes consolidated many independent diamond producers into De Beers, he converted a perfectly competitive industry into a monopoly. We can now use our analysis to see the effects of such a consolidation.

Let's look again at Figure 13-6 and ask how this same market would work if, instead of being a monopoly, the industry were perfectly competitive. We will continue to assume that there is no fixed cost and that marginal cost is constant, so average total cost and marginal cost are equal.

If the diamond industry consists of many perfectly competitive firms, each of those producers takes the market price as given. That is, each producer acts as if its marginal revenue is equal to the market price. So each firm within the industry uses the price-taking firm's optimal output rule:

(13-2) $P = MC$ at the perfectly competitive firm's profit-maximizing quantity of output

In Figure 13-6, this would correspond to producing at *C*, where the price per diamond, P_C, is $200, equal to the marginal cost of production. So the profit-maximizing output of an industry under perfect competition, Q_C, is 16 diamonds.

But does the perfectly competitive industry earn any profits at *C*? No: the price of $200 is equal to the average total cost per diamond. So there are no economic profits for this industry when it produces at the perfectly competitive output level.

We've already seen that once the industry is consolidated into a monopoly, the result is very different. The monopolist's calculation of marginal revenue takes the price effect into account, so that marginal revenue is less than the price. That is,

(13-3) $P > MR = MC$ at the monopolist's profit-maximizing quantity of output

As we've already seen, the monopolist produces less than the competitive industry—8 diamonds rather than 16. The price under monopoly is $600, compared with only $200 under perfect competition. The monopolist earns a positive economic profit, but the competitive industry does not.

So, just as we suggested earlier, we see that compared with a competitive industry, a monopolist does the following:

- Produces a smaller quantity: $Q_M < Q_C$
- Charges a higher price: $P_M > P_C$
- Earns a profit

Monopoly: The General Picture

Figure 13-6 involved specific numbers and assumed that marginal cost was constant, that there was no fixed cost, and, therefore, that the average total cost curve was a horizontal line. Figure 13-7 shows a more general picture of monopoly in action: D is the market demand curve; MR, the marginal revenue curve; MC, the marginal cost curve; and ATC, the average total cost curve. Here we return to the usual assumption that the marginal cost curve has a "swoosh" shape and the average total cost curve is U-shaped.

Applying the optimal output rule, we see that the profit-maximizing level of output is the output at which marginal revenue equals marginal cost, indicated by point A. The profit-maximizing quantity of output is Q_M, and the price charged by the monopolist is P_M. At the profit-maximizing level of output, the monopolist's average total cost is ATC_M, shown by point C.

Recalling how we calculated profit in Equation 12-5, profit is equal to the difference between total revenue and total cost. So we have:

(13-4) $\text{Profit} = TR - TC$
$= (P_M \times Q_M) - (ATC_M \times Q_M)$
$= (P_M - ATC_M) \times Q_M$

Profit is equal to the area of the shaded rectangle in Figure 13-7, with a height of $P_M - ATC_M$ and a width of Q_M.

In Chapter 12 we learned that a perfectly competitive industry can have profits in the *short run but not in the long run.* In the short run, price can exceed average total cost, allowing a perfectly competitive firm to make a profit. But we also know that this cannot persist. In the long run, any profit in a perfectly competitive industry will be competed away as new firms enter the market. In contrast, barriers to entry allow a monopolist to make profits in *both the short run and the long run.*

FIGURE **13-7** The Monopolist's Profit

In this case, the marginal cost curve has a "swoosh" shape and the average total cost curve is U-shaped. The monopolist maximizes profit by producing the level of output at which $MR = MC$, given by point A, generating quantity Q_M. It finds its monopoly price, P_M, from the point on the demand curve directly above point A, point B here. The average total cost of Q_M is shown by point C. Profit is given by the area of the shaded rectangle.

ECONOMICS ▶ IN ACTION

PRIVATIZATION OF NOVA SCOTIA POWER— A GOOD IDEA?

Historically, electric utilities were recognized as natural monopolies. A utility serviced a defined geographical area, owning the plants that generated electricity as well as the transmission lines that delivered it to retail customers. The rates charged customers were managed by the government; set at a level to cover the utility's cost of operation plus a modest return on capital to its shareholders.

Traditionally, public utilities in Canada were corporations owned by the provincial government. However, in the early 1990s the provincial government of Nova Scotia under Premier Donald Cameron decided to privatize the Nova Scotia Power Corporation, the province's electrical utility. This move by Cameron's government caused much controversy. Many believed the sale was driven by the pressure to reduce the province's budget deficits and debt-servicing cost. Cameron's government argued that by privatizing the utility the province could better

City	Average price for residential service (excluding taxes, in ¢ per kWh)
Montreal	6.87
Winnipeg	7.63
Vancouver	8.91
Moncton	11.82
Ottawa	12.39
Toronto	12.48
St. John	12.54
Regina	13.15
Edmonton	13.90
Charlottetown	14.87
Calgary	14.81
Halifax	15.45

Source: Comparison of Electricity Prices in Major North American Cities: Rates in Effect April 1, 2013, Hydro-Quebec.

allocate its limited revenues to other much needed services such as health care and education. Many were skeptical, fearing the sale would create more harm than benefits for Nova Scotians, and some worried that the price of electricity would increase. When the privatization of the Nova Scotia Power Corporation was finalized in 1992 it was the largest private equity transaction in the country's history.

So what happened to the price of electricity in Nova Scotia following the privatization? The privately owned Nova Scotia Power has raised its prices seven times since 2000. These increases in prices have been proposed to finance updates to infrastructure and to cover the cost of investing in renewable energy. However, many perceive these increases as a result of the lack of competition, which allows Nova Scotia Power to exercise its monopoly power to charge consumers higher prices and earn higher profits. The table shows the average price of electricity on April 1, 2013 in cents per kilowatt-hour for selected cities in Canada. It clearly shows that residents in Halifax paid the highest rates (15.45¢/kWh) while residents in Montreal paid the lowest rate (6.87¢/kWh). Not surprisingly, some Nova Scotians have called for the return of a province-owned corporation for electricity.

▼ Quick Review

- The crucial difference between a firm with market power, such as a monopolist, and a firm in a perfectly competitive industry is that perfectly competitive firms are price-takers that face horizontal demand curves, but a firm with market power faces a downward-sloping demand curve.

- Due to the price effect of an increase in output, the marginal revenue curve of a firm with market power always lies below its demand curve. So a profit-maximizing monopolist chooses the output level at which marginal cost is equal to marginal revenue—*not* to price.

- As a result, the monopolist produces less and sells its output at a higher price than a perfectly competitive industry would. It earns profits in the short run and the long run.

CHECK YOUR UNDERSTANDING 13-2

1. Use the accompanying total revenue schedule of Emerald, Inc., a monopoly producer of 10-carat emeralds, to calculate the answers to parts (a) to (d). Then answer part (e).
   a. The demand schedule
   b. The marginal revenue schedule
   c. The quantity effect component of marginal revenue per output level
   d. The price effect component of marginal per output level
   e. What additional information is needed to determine Emerald, Inc.'s profit-maximizing output?

Quantity of emeralds demanded	Total revenue
1	$100
2	186
3	252
4	280
5	250

2. Use Figure 13-6 to show what happens to the following when the marginal cost of diamond production rises from $200 to $400.
   a. Marginal cost curve
   b. Profit-maximizing price and quantity
   c. Profit of the monopolist
   d. Perfectly competitive industry profits

Solutions appear at back of book.

Monopoly and Public Policy

I t's good to be a monopolist, but it's not so good to be a monopolist's customer. A monopolist, by reducing output and raising prices, benefits at the expense of consumers. But buyers and sellers always have conflicting interests. Is the conflict of interest under monopoly any different than it is under perfect competition?

The answer is yes, because monopoly is a source of inefficiency: the losses to consumers from monopoly behaviour are larger than the gains to the monopolist. Because monopoly leads to net losses for the economy, governments often try either to prevent the emergence of monopolies or to limit their effects. In this section, we will see why monopoly leads to inefficiency and examine the policies governments adopt in an attempt to prevent this inefficiency.

Welfare Effects of Monopoly

By restricting output below the level at which marginal cost is equal to the market price, a monopolist increases its profit but hurts consumers. To assess whether this is a net benefit or loss to society, we must compare the monopolist's gain in profit to the loss in consumer surplus. And what we learn is that the loss in consumer surplus is larger than the monopolist's gain. Monopoly causes a net loss for society.

To see why, let's return to the case where the marginal cost curve is horizontal, as shown in the two panels of Figure 13-8. Here the marginal cost curve is MC, the demand curve is D, and, in panel (b), the marginal revenue curve is MR.

Panel (a) shows what happens if this industry is perfectly competitive. Equilibrium output is Q_C; the price of the good, P_C, is equal to marginal cost, and marginal cost is also equal to average total cost because there is no fixed cost and marginal cost is constant. Each firm is earning exactly its average total cost per unit of output, so there is no profit and no producer surplus in this equilibrium. The consumer surplus generated by the market is equal to the area of the blue-shaded triangle CS_C shown in panel (a). Since there is no producer surplus when the industry is perfectly competitive, CS_C also represents the total surplus.

Panel (b) shows the results for the same market, but this time assuming that the industry is a monopoly. The monopolist produces the level of output Q_M, at which marginal cost is equal to marginal revenue, and it charges the price P_M. The industry now earns profit—which is also the producer surplus—equal to the area of the green rectangle, PS_M. Note that this profit is surplus that has been captured from consumers as consumer surplus shrinks to the area of the blue triangle, CS_M.

By comparing panels (a) and (b), we see that in addition to the redistribution of surplus from consumers to the monopolist, another important change has occurred: the sum of profit and consumer surplus—total surplus—is *smaller* under monopoly than under perfect competition. That is, the sum of CS_M and PS_M

FIGURE 13-8 Monopoly Causes Inefficiency

Panel (a) depicts a perfectly competitive industry: output is Q_C, and market price, P_C, is equal to MC. Since price is exactly equal to each producer's average total cost of production per unit, there is no profit and no producer surplus. So total surplus is equal to consumer surplus, the entire shaded area.

Panel (b) depicts the industry under monopoly: the monopolist decreases output to Q_M and charges P_M. Consumer surplus (blue area) has shrunk: a portion of it has been captured as profit (green area), and a portion of it has been lost to deadweight loss (orange area), the value of mutually beneficial transactions that do not occur because of monopoly behaviour. As a result, total surplus falls.

in panel (b) is less than the area CS_C in panel (a). In Chapter 7, we analyzed how taxes generated *deadweight loss* to society. Here we show that monopoly creates a deadweight loss to society equal to the area of the orange triangle, *DWL*. So monopoly produces a net loss for society.

This net loss arises because some mutually beneficial transactions do not occur. There are people for whom an additional unit of the good is worth more than the marginal cost of producing it but who don't consume it because they are not willing to pay P_M.

If you recall our discussion of the deadweight loss from taxes in Chapter 7 you will notice that the deadweight loss from monopoly looks quite similar. Indeed, by driving a wedge between price and marginal cost, monopoly acts much like a tax on consumers and produces the same kind of inefficiency.

So monopoly hurts the welfare of society as a whole and is a source of market failure. Is there anything government policy can do about it?

Preventing Monopoly

Policy toward monopoly depends crucially on whether or not the industry in question is a natural monopoly, one in which increasing returns to scale ensure that a bigger producer has lower average total cost. If the industry is not a natural monopoly, the best policy is to prevent monopoly from arising or break it up if it already exists. Let's focus on that case first, then turn to the more difficult problem of dealing with natural monopoly.

The De Beers monopoly on diamonds didn't have to happen. Diamond production is not a natural monopoly: the industry's costs would be no higher if it consisted of a number of independent, competing producers (as is the case, for example, in gold production).

So if the South African government had been worried about how a monopoly would have affected consumers, it could have blocked Cecil Rhodes in his drive to dominate the industry or broken up his monopoly after the fact. Today, governments often try to prevent monopolies from forming and break up existing ones.

De Beers is a rather unique case: for complicated historical reasons, it was allowed to remain a monopoly. But over the last century, most similar monopolies have been broken up. A noted example of breaking up a monopoly in Canada is Bell Canada. Bell Canada used to be the monopoly provider of certain telephone services in most of Canada east of Manitoba and in the territories. Starting in the 1980s, the federal government began to deregulate the country's telecommunications industry; as new firms were allowed to enter the market Bell Canada gradually lost its monopoly status. The most celebrated example in the United States is Standard Oil, founded by John D. Rockefeller in 1870. By 1878 Standard Oil controlled almost all U.S. oil refining; but in 1911 a court order broke the company into a number of smaller units, including the companies that later became Exxon and Mobil (and more recently merged to become ExxonMobil).

The government policies used to prevent or eliminate monopolies are known as *competition* or *antitrust policy*, which we will discuss in the next chapter.

Dealing with Natural Monopoly

Breaking up a monopoly that isn't natural is clearly a good idea: the gains to consumers outweigh the loss to the producer. But it's not so clear whether a natural monopoly, one in which a large producer has lower average total costs than small producers, should be broken up, because this would raise average total cost. For example, a municipal government that tried to prevent a single company from dominating local gas supply—which, as we've discussed, is almost surely a natural monopoly—would raise the cost of providing gas to its residents.

Yet even in the case of a natural monopoly, a profit-maximizing monopolist acts in a way that causes inefficiency—it charges consumers a price that is higher than marginal cost and, by doing so, prevents some potentially beneficial transactions. Also, it can seem unfair that a firm that has managed to establish a monopoly position earns a large profit at the expense of consumers.

What can public policy do about this? There are two common answers.

Public Ownership In many countries, the preferred answer to the problem of natural monopoly has been **public ownership.** Instead of allowing a private monopolist to control an industry, the government establishes a public agency to provide the good and protect consumers' interests. In Britain, for example, telephone service was provided by the state-owned British Telecom before 1984, and airline travel was provided by the state-owned British Airways before 1987. (These companies still exist, but they have been privatized, competing with other firms in their respective industries.)

In Canada, the government has often assumed control of a monopoly industry by nationalizing it. Publicly owned companies in Canada are called *Crown* corporations. They may be owned by any level of government—federal, provincial, territorial, or municipal government. Federally owned Crown corporations include Canada Post, Atomic Energy of Canada Limited, Via Rail Canada, the Canadian Broadcasting Corporation, and the Bank of Canada. Most electric utilities are Crown corporations at either the provincial level (BC Hydro, Ontario Power Generation, Hydro One, Hydro-Québec, and NB Hydro), territorial level (Northwest Territories Power), or municipal level (Toronto Hydro, EPCOR, ENMAX, London Hydro). In past decades, some governments have privatized some of their Crown corporations, such as Air Canada, Petro Canada, the Canadian National Railway, Potash Corporation of Saskatchewan Inc., and Nova Scotia Power, as discussed in the previous Economics in Action.

The advantage of public ownership, in principle, is that a publicly owned natural monopoly can set prices based on the criterion of efficiency rather than profit maximization as we saw with the Nova Scotia Power Corporation. In a perfectly competitive industry, profit-maximizing behaviour is efficient, because producers produce the quantity at which price is equal to marginal cost; that is why there is no economic argument for public ownership of, say, wheat farms.

Experience suggests, however, that public ownership as a solution to the problem of natural monopoly often works badly in practice. One reason is that publicly owned firms are often less eager than private companies to keep costs down or offer high-quality products. Another is that publicly owned companies all too often end up serving political interests—providing contracts or jobs to people with the right connections. For example, the public U.S. company Amtrak has notoriously provided train service at a loss to destinations that attract few passengers—but that are located in the districts of influential politicians.

Regulation An alternative to operating a natural monopoly as a Crown corporation is to leave the industry in private hands but subject it to regulation. In particular, most local utilities like electricity, land line telephone service, natural gas, and so on are covered by **price regulation** that limits the prices they can charge.

We saw in Chapter 5 that imposing a *price ceiling* on a competitive industry is a recipe for shortages, black markets, and other nasty side effects. Doesn't imposing a limit on the price that, say, a local gas company can charge have the same effects?

Not necessarily: a price ceiling on a monopolist need not create a shortage—in the absence of a price ceiling, a monopolist would charge a price that is higher than its marginal cost of production. So even if forced to charge a lower price—as long as that price is above *MC* and the monopolist at least breaks even on total output—the monopolist still has an incentive to produce the quantity demanded at that price.

Figure 13-9 shows an example of price regulation of a natural monopoly—a highly simplified version of a local gas company. The company faces a demand curve *D*, with an associated marginal revenue curve *MR*. For simplicity, we

In **public ownership** of a monopoly, the good is supplied by the government or by a firm owned by the government.

Price regulation limits the price that a monopolist is allowed to charge.

FIGURE **13-9** Unregulated and Regulated Natural Monopoly

This figure shows the case of a natural monopolist. In panel (a), if the monopolist is allowed to charge P_M, it makes a profit, shown by the green area; consumer surplus is shown by the blue area. If it is regulated and must charge the lower price P_R, output increases from Q_M to Q_R and consumer surplus increases.

Panel (b) shows what happens when the monopolist must charge a price equal to average total cost, the price P_R^*. Output expands to Q_R^*, and consumer surplus is now the entire blue area. The monopolist makes zero profit. This is the greatest total surplus possible when the monopolist is allowed to at least break even, making P_R^* the best regulated price.

assume that the firm's total costs consist of two parts: a fixed cost and variable costs that are incurred at a constant proportion to output. So marginal cost is constant in this case, and the marginal cost curve (which here is also the average variable cost curve) is the horizontal line *MC*. The average total cost curve is the downward-sloping curve *ATC*; it slopes downward because the higher the output, the lower the average fixed cost (the fixed cost per unit of output). Because average total cost slopes downward over the range of output relevant for market demand, this is a natural monopoly.

Panel (a) illustrates a case of natural monopoly without regulation. The unregulated natural monopolist chooses the monopoly output Q_M and charges the price P_M. Since the monopolist receives a price greater than its average total cost, it earns a profit. This profit is exactly equal to the producer surplus in this market, represented by the green-shaded rectangle. Consumer surplus is given by the blue-shaded triangle. Deadweight loss is given by the orange-shaded triangle.

Now suppose that regulators impose a price ceiling on local gas deliveries—one that falls below the monopoly price P_M but above *ATC*, say, at P_R in panel (a). At that price the quantity demanded is Q_R.

Does the company have an incentive to produce that quantity? Yes. If the price at which the monopolist can sell its product is fixed by regulators, the firm's output no longer affects the market price—so it ignores the *MR* curve and is willing to expand output to meet the quantity demanded as long as the price it receives for the next unit is greater than marginal cost and the monopolist at least breaks even on total output. So with price regulation, the monopolist produces more, at a lower price.

Of course, the monopolist will not be willing to produce at all if the imposed price means producing at a loss. That is, the price ceiling has to be set high enough to allow the firm to cover its average total cost. Panel (b) shows a situation in which regulators have pushed the price down as far as possible, at the level where the average total cost curve crosses the demand curve. The practice of regulating the monopoly to set a price equal to its average total cost is called **average cost pricing.** At any lower price the firm loses money. The price here, P^*_R, is the best regulated price: the monopolist is just willing to operate and produces Q^*_R, the quantity demanded at that price. Consumers and society gain as a result.

The welfare effects of this regulation can be seen by comparing the shaded areas in the two panels of Figure 13-9. Consumer surplus is increased by the regulation, with the gains coming from two sources. First, profits are eliminated and added instead to consumer surplus. Second, the larger output and lower price lead to an overall welfare gain—an increase in total surplus. In fact, panel (b) illustrates the largest total surplus possible. An alternative way to look at the welfare effect of this regulation is to look at the change in the deadweight loss. By adopting average cost pricing, the size of deadweight loss falls.

Looking at Figure 13-9, it may seem like the best solution is to force the monopolist to charge a price equal to their marginal cost—another type of price regulation is **marginal cost pricing.** However, when a natural monopolist faces a fixed cost, its average cost will usually be higher than its marginal cost, so marginal cost pricing implies the monopoly will always operate at a loss and it will choose to shut down. In order for marginal cost pricing to work, the government would need to provide a subsidy to the monopolist so that the firm can cover its fixed cost. So even though marginal cost pricing is most efficient for the market, it is seldom used in practice.

Regulating natural monopolies looks terrific: consumers are better off, profits are eliminated, and overall welfare increases. Unfortunately, things are rarely that easy in practice. The main problem is that regulators don't have the information required to set the price exactly at the level at which the demand curve crosses the average total cost curve. Sometimes they set it too low, creating shortages; at other times they set it too high. Also, regulated monopolies, like publicly owned firms, tend to exaggerate their costs to regulators and to provide inferior quality to consumers.

Must Monopoly Be Controlled? Sometimes the cure is worse than the disease. Some economists have argued that the best solution, even in the case of natural monopoly, may be to live with it. The case for doing nothing is that attempts to control monopoly will, one way or another, do more harm than good—for example, by the politicization of pricing, which leads to shortages, or by the creation of opportunities for political corruption.

The following Economics in Action describes the case of wheat, a natural monopoly that has been regulated and deregulated as politicians change their minds about the appropriate policy.

ECONOMICS ▸ IN ACTION

CHANGE WAS BREWING

The Canadian Wheat Board (CWB), one of Canada's biggest exporters and one of the world's largest grain marketing organizations, was once a monopoly for the sale of western wheat and barley destined for export from Canada. The CWB also controlled the domestic sale of wheat and barley. Established by the Canadian Wheat Board Act of 1935, the CWB was an attempt to stabilize income for the wheat farmers in the Prairies. The CWB sells wheat and barley on behalf of its members, which aims at avoiding competition among members so that CWB can command higher return for everyone.

The farmers under the CWB's jurisdiction were required to deliver their crops to the CWB and any selling of their crops via other channels was illegal; for them, the CWB was a *monopsony* (a single buyer). However, it was also a monopoly for anyone buying Canadian wheat and barley. The federal government ended the mandatory use of the CWB in 2012, removing its monopoly power. Now, Canada's

Average cost pricing is a form of price regulation that forces a monopoly to set its price equal to its average total cost.

Marginal cost pricing is a form of price regulation that forces a monopoly to set its price equal to its marginal cost.

western wheat farmers have the option to sell their crops directly in the market or to continue to work with the CWB. By the same token, buyers of Canadian wheat can purchase this grain directly from the producers or through the CWB.

The ending of the monopoly of the Canadian Wheat Board was controversial. Many farmers believe that by handling the delivery of their crops themselves, they can obtain better prices, and have the freedom to deliver their crops to whomever they want and whenever they want. However, supporters of the CWB argue that when the CWB has market power, it is more efficient at marketing Canadian wheat and can negotiate higher prices for its members, freeing farmers to focus on growing crops rather than finding buyers and making their farms more productive. It will still be a few years before we can properly evaluate the effects of the ending of the CWB's monopoly on the market and the general well-being of western wheat farmers.

CHECK YOUR UNDERSTANDING   13-3

1. What policy should the government adopt in the following cases? Explain.
   a. Internet service in Anytown, Prince Edward Island, is provided by cable. Customers feel they are being overcharged, but the cable company claims it must charge prices that let it recover the costs of laying cable.
   b. The only two airlines that currently fly to Yukon need government approval to merge. Other airlines wish to fly to Yukon but need government-allocated landing slots to do so.

2. True or false? Explain your answer.
   a. Society's welfare is lower under monopoly because some consumer surplus is transformed into profit for the monopolist.
   b. A monopolist causes inefficiency because there are consumers who are willing to pay a price greater than or equal to marginal cost but less than the monopoly price.

3. Suppose a monopolist mistakenly believes that its marginal revenue is always equal to the market price. Assuming constant marginal cost and no fixed cost, draw a diagram comparing the level of profit, consumer surplus, total surplus, and deadweight loss for this misguided monopolist compared to a smart monopolist.

Solutions appear at back of book.

Price Discrimination

Up to this point, we have considered only the case of a **single-price monopolist**, one that charges all consumers the same price. As the term suggests, not all monopolists do this. In fact, many if not most monopolists find that they can increase their profits by charging different customers different prices for the same good: they engage in **price discrimination**. There are three degrees of price discriminations: first-degree (also called *perfect price discrimination*), second-degree, and third-degree.

The most striking example of price discrimination many of us encounter regularly involves airline tickets. Although there are a number of Canadian airlines (with Air Canada being the dominant firm), most domestic routes are serviced by only one or two carriers, which, as a result, have market power and can set prices. So any regular airline passenger quickly becomes aware that the question "How much will it cost me to fly there?" rarely has a simple answer.

If you are willing to buy a nonrefundable ticket a month in advance and stay over a Saturday night, a round trip between Toronto and Montreal, for example, may only cost you $250 or less (including taxes, fees, and surcharges). But if you have to go on a business trip tomorrow, which happens to be Tuesday, and come back on Wednesday, the same round trip might cost $550. Yet the business

A **single-price monopolist** offers its product to all consumers at the same price.

Sellers engage in **price discrimination** when they charge different prices to different consumers for the same good.

traveller and the tourist receive the same product—the same cramped seat, the same awful food (if indeed any food is served).

You might object that airlines are not usually monopolists—that in most flight markets the airline industry is an oligopoly. In fact, price discrimination takes place under oligopoly and monopolistic competition as well as monopoly. But it doesn't happen under perfect competition. And once we've seen why monopolists sometimes price-discriminate, we'll be in a good position to understand why it happens in other cases, too.

The Logic of Price Discrimination

To get a preliminary view of why price discrimination might be more profitable than charging all consumers the same price, imagine that Maple Sky offers the only nonstop flights between Toronto and Montreal. Assume that there are no capacity problems—the airline can fly as many planes as the number of passengers warrants. Also assume that there is no fixed cost. The marginal cost to the airline of providing a seat is $225, however many passengers it carries.

Further assume that the airline knows there are two kinds of potential passengers. First, there are business travellers, 2000 of whom want to travel between the destinations each week. Second, there are students, 2000 of whom also want to travel each week.

Will potential passengers take the flight? It depends on the price. The business travellers, it turns out, really need to fly; they will take the plane as long as the price is no more than $550. Since they are flying purely for business, we assume that cutting the price below $550 will not lead to any increase in business travel. The students, however, have less money and more time; if the price goes above $250, they will take the bus. The implied demand curve is shown in Figure 13-10.

So what should the airline do? If it has to charge everyone the same price, its options are limited. It could charge $550; that way it would get as much as possible out of the business travellers but lose the student market. Or it could charge only $250; that way it would get both types of travellers but would make significantly less money from sales to business travellers.

We can quickly calculate the profits from each of these alternatives. If the airline charged $550, it would sell 2000 tickets to the business travellers, earning

FIGURE **13-10** Two Types of Airline Customers

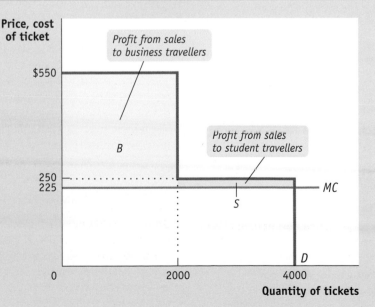

Maple Sky has two types of customers, business travellers willing to pay at most $550 per ticket and students willing to pay at most $250 per ticket. There are 2000 of each kind of customer. Maple Sky has constant marginal cost of $225 per seat. If Maple Sky could charge these two types of customers different prices, it would maximize its profit by charging business travellers $550 and students $250 per ticket. It would capture all of the consumer surplus as profit.

total revenue of 2000 × $550 = $1.1 million and incurring costs of 2000 × $125 = $250 000; so its profit would be $850 000, illustrated by the shaded area *B* in Figure 13-10. If the airline charged only $250, it would sell 4000 tickets to the business travellers and students, receiving revenue of 4000 × $250 = $1 000 000 and incurring costs of 4000 × $225 = $900 000; so its profit would be $100 000. If the airline must charge everyone the same price, charging the higher price and forgoing sales to students is clearly more profitable.

What the airline would really like to do, however, is charge the business travellers the full $550 but offer $250 tickets to the students. That's a lot less than the price paid by business travellers, but it's still above marginal cost; so if the airline could sell those extra 2000 tickets to students, it would make an additional $50 000 in profit. That is, it would make a profit equal to the areas *B* plus *S* in Figure 13-10.

It would be more realistic to suppose that there is some "give" in the demand of each group: at a price below $550, there would be some increase in business travel; and at a price above $250, some students would still purchase tickets. But this, it turns out, does not do away with the argument for price discrimination. The important point is that the two groups of consumers differ in their *sensitivity to price*—that a high price has a larger effect in discouraging purchases by students than by business travellers. As long as different groups of customers respond differently to the price, a monopolist will find that it can capture more consumer surplus and increase its profit by charging them different prices. (Here we have assumed the monopolist can easily distinguish the two groups of customers and reselling from one group to the other is not possible.)

According to Figure 13-10, Maple Sky would maximize its profit by charging different airfares to different groups of travellers and in that figure the demand curve looks like a stepped function. The same logic applies when a firm faces downward sloping demand curves. Figure 13-11 shows how Maple Sky could maximize its profits for two groups of travellers with typical demand curves. When Maple Sky is able to charge different airfares, it will treat the market for student travellers separately from the market for business travellers. In each respective market, Maple Sky chooses the number of tickets sold such that marginal cost is equal to the marginal revenue (setting *MC* = *MR* in each market).

FIGURE **13-11** **Separating Demand for Travellers**

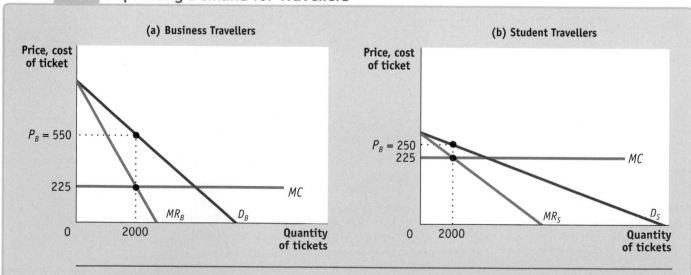

When a company like Maple Sky has two types of customers, business travellers and student travellers, it is worthwhile for them to look at the demand curves for these two types of customers separately in order to

determine prices. If Maple Sky could charge these two groups different prices, it would maximize its profit by equating the marginal revenue in each market to marginal cost.

This is considered *third-degree* price discrimination—monopolist charging different prices in different markets.

You may have noticed that, like the airline industry, attractions such as zoos, science centres, museums, and art galleries often offer different prices to different groups of customers, namely children, students, and seniors. How can these places offer admission discounts to these customers? Usually, seniors and children can be distinguished by their appearance. As for students, colleges and universities issue student ID cards, and student just need to show their valid ID to receive lower prices. Many Canadian schools take part in the International Student Identity Card (ISIC), which grants discounts on a range of activities from shopping at local retail stores to travelling abroad.

Price Discrimination and Elasticity

A more realistic description of the demand that airlines face would not specify particular prices at which different types of travellers would choose to fly. Instead, it would distinguish between the groups on the basis of their sensitivity to the price—their price elasticity of demand.

On many airline routes, the fare you pay depends on the type of traveller you are.

Suppose that a company sells its product to two easily identifiable groups of people—business travellers and students. It just so happens that business travellers are very insensitive to the price: there is a certain amount of the product they just have to have whatever the price, but they cannot be persuaded to buy much more than that no matter how cheap it is. Students, though, are more flexible: offer a good enough price and they will buy quite a lot, but raise the price too high and they will switch to something else. What should the company do?

The answer is the one already suggested by our simplified example: the company should charge business travellers, with their low price elasticity of demand, a higher price than it charges students, with their high price elasticity of demand. To achieve this price difference, several airlines and travel agencies offer discounts to students with valid identification, such as the ISIC card.

The actual situation of the airlines is very much like this hypothetical example. Business travellers typically place a high priority on being at the right place at the right time and are not very sensitive to the price. But nonbusiness travellers are fairly sensitive to the price: faced with a high price, they might take the bus, drive to another airport to get a lower fare, or skip the trip altogether.

So why doesn't an airline simply announce different prices for business and nonbusiness customers? First, this would probably be illegal (the Competition Act places limits on the ability of companies to practise open price discrimination). Second, even if it were legal, it would be a hard policy to enforce: business travellers might be willing to wear casual clothing and claim they were visiting family in Montreal in order to save $300.

So what the airlines do—quite successfully—is impose rules that indirectly charge business and nonbusiness travellers different fares. Business travellers usually travel during the week and want to be home on the weekend; so the round-trip fare is much higher if you don't stay over a Saturday night. The requirement of a weekend stay for a cheap ticket effectively separates business from nonbusiness travellers. Similarly, business travellers often visit several cities in succession rather than make a simple round trip; so round-trip fares are much lower than two one-way fares. Many business trips are scheduled on short notice; so fares are much lower if you book far in advance. Fares are also lower if you purchase a last-minute ticket, taking your chances on whether you actually get a seat—business travellers have to make it to that meeting; people visiting their relatives don't.

Perfect price discrimination takes place when a monopolist charges each consumer his or her willingness to pay—the maximum that the consumer is willing to pay.

Because customers must show their ID at check-in, airlines make sure there are no resales of tickets between the two groups that would undermine their ability to price-discriminate—students can't buy cheap tickets and resell them to business travellers. Look at the rules that govern ticket-pricing, and you will see an ingenious implementation of profit-maximizing price discrimination.

Perfect Price Discrimination

Let's return to the example of business travellers and students travelling between Toronto and Montreal, illustrated in Figure 13-10, and ask what would happen if the airline could distinguish between the two groups of customers in order to charge each a different price.

Clearly, the airline would charge each group its willingness to pay—that is, as we learned in Chapter 4, the maximum that each group is willing to pay. For business travellers, the willingness to pay is $550; for students, it is $250. As we have assumed, the marginal cost is $225 and does not depend on output, making the marginal cost curve a horizontal line. As we noted earlier, we can easily determine the airline's profit: it is the sum of the areas of the rectangle *B* and the rectangle *S*.

In this case, the consumers do not get any consumer surplus! The entire surplus is captured by the monopolist in the form of profit. When a monopolist is able to capture the entire surplus in this way, we say that it achieves **perfect price discrimination** (also called *first-degree price* discrimination).

In general, the greater the number of different prices a monopolist is able to charge, the closer it can get to perfect price discrimination. Figure 13-12 shows a monopolist facing a downward-sloping demand curve, a monopolist who we assume is able to charge different prices to different groups of consumers, with the consumers who are willing to pay the most being charged the most. In panel (a) the monopolist charges two different prices; in panel (b) the monopolist charges three different prices. Two things are apparent:

- The greater the number of prices the monopolist charges, the lower the lowest price—that is, some consumers will pay prices that approach marginal cost.

- The greater the number of prices the monopolist charges, the more money it extracts from consumers.

With a very large number of different prices, the picture would look like panel (c), a case of perfect price discrimination. Here, consumers least willing to buy the good pay marginal cost, and the entire consumer surplus is extracted as profit.

Both our airline example and the example in Figure 13-12 can be used to make another point: a monopolist that can engage in perfect price discrimination doesn't cause any inefficiency! The reason is that the source of inefficiency is eliminated: all potential consumers who are willing to purchase the good at a price equal to or above marginal cost are able to do so. The perfectly price-discriminating monopolist manages to "scoop up" all consumers by offering some of them lower prices than it charges others. The entire surplus is captured by producer surplus, and the deadweight loss is zero.

Perfect price discrimination is almost never possible in practice. At a fundamental level, the inability to achieve perfect price discrimination is a problem of prices as economic signals, a phenomenon we noted in Chapter 4. When prices work as economic signals, they convey the information needed to ensure that all mutually beneficial transactions will indeed occur: the market price signals the seller's cost, and a consumer signals willingness to pay by purchasing the good whenever that willingness to pay is at least as high as the market price.

The problem in reality, however, is that prices are often not perfect signals: a consumer's true willingness to pay can be disguised, as by a business traveller who claims to be a student when buying a ticket in order to obtain a lower

FIGURE 13-12 Price Discrimination

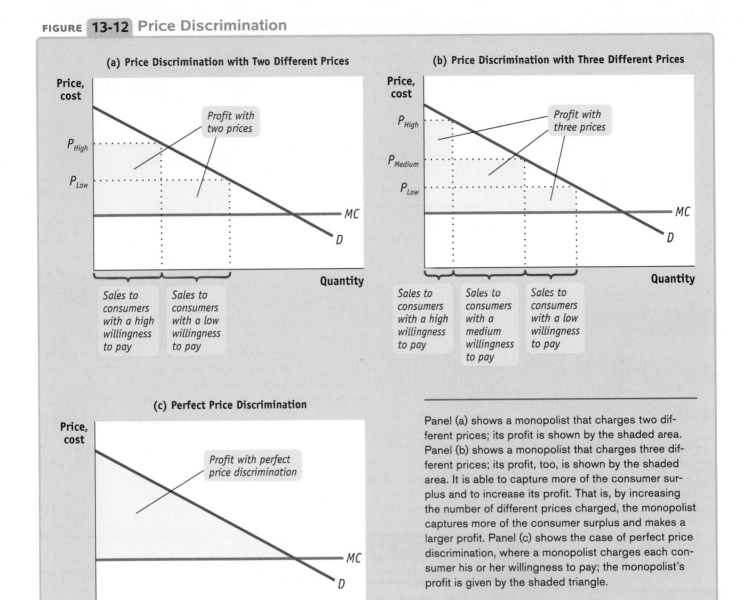

Panel (a) shows a monopolist that charges two different prices; its profit is shown by the shaded area. Panel (b) shows a monopolist that charges three different prices; its profit, too, is shown by the shaded area. It is able to capture more of the consumer surplus and to increase its profit. That is, by increasing the number of different prices charged, the monopolist captures more of the consumer surplus and makes a larger profit. Panel (c) shows the case of perfect price discrimination, where a monopolist charges each consumer his or her willingness to pay; the monopolist's profit is given by the shaded triangle.

fare. When such disguises work, a monopolist cannot achieve perfect price discrimination.

However, monopolists do try to move in the direction of perfect price discrimination through a variety of pricing strategies. Common techniques for price discrimination include the following:

- *Advance purchase restrictions.* Prices are lower for those who purchase well in advance (or in some cases for those who purchase at the last minute). This separates those who are likely to shop for better prices from those who won't.

- *Volume discounts.* Often the price is lower if you buy a large quantity. For a consumer who plans to consume a lot of a good, the cost of the last unit—the marginal cost to the consumer—is considerably less than the average price. This separates those who plan to buy a lot and so are likely to be more sensitive to price from those who don't.

• *Two-part tariffs.* With a two-part tariff, a customer plays a flat fee upfront and then a per-unit fee on each item purchased. So in a discount club like Costco or Sam's Club (which are not monopolists but monopolistic competitors), you pay an annual fee in addition to the cost of the items you purchase. So the cost of the first item you buy is in effect much higher than that of subsequent items, making the two-part tariff behave like a volume discount.

Volume discounts and two-part tariffs are *second-degree* price discriminations. In these cases, the monopolist charges different prices based on the quantity purchased by its customers because the monopolist knows it has different groups of customers but is unable to differentiate them easily. By charging different prices based on the quantity purchased the monopolist is making its customers reveal their own preference by choosing the packages offered.

Our discussion also helps explain why government policies on monopoly typically focus on preventing deadweight losses, rather than preventing price discrimination—unless it causes serious issues of equity. The Competition Bureau, the federal agency responsible for Canada's competition policy, focuses on price discrimination for sales in input or wholesale markets rather than in retail markets. Doing so ensures that firms are charged the same input prices, so no supplier can affect competition at the retail level. Compared to a single-price monopolist, price discrimination—even when it is not perfect—can increase the efficiency of the market. If sales to consumers formerly priced out of the market but now able to purchase the good at a lower price generate enough surplus to offset the loss in surplus to those now facing a higher price and no longer buying the good, then total surplus increases when price discrimination is introduced.

An example of this might be a drug that is disproportionately prescribed to senior citizens, who are often on fixed incomes and so are very sensitive to price. A policy that allows a drug company to charge senior citizens a low price and everyone else a high price may indeed increase total surplus compared to a situation in which everyone is charged the same price. But price discrimination that creates serious concerns about equity is likely to be prohibited—for example, an ambulance service that charges patients based on the severity of their emergency.

ECONOMICS ⟩ IN ACTION

SALES, FACTORY OUTLETS, AND GHOST CITIES

Have you ever wondered why department stores occasionally hold sales, offering their merchandise for considerably less than the usual prices? Or why, driving along Canadian highways, you sometimes encounter clusters of "factory outlet" stores, often a couple of hours' drive from the nearest city?

These familiar features of the economic landscape are actually rather peculiar if you think about them: why should sheets and towels be suddenly cheaper for a week each winter, or raincoats be offered for less in Halton Hills, just west of Toronto, than in Toronto itself? In each case the answer is that the sellers—who are often oligopolists or monopolistic competitors—are engaged in a subtle form of price discrimination.

Why hold regular sales of sheets and towels? Stores are aware that some consumers buy these goods only when they discover that they need them; they are not likely to put a lot of effort into searching for the best price and so have a relatively low price elasticity of demand. So the store wants to charge high prices for customers who come in on an ordinary day. But shop-

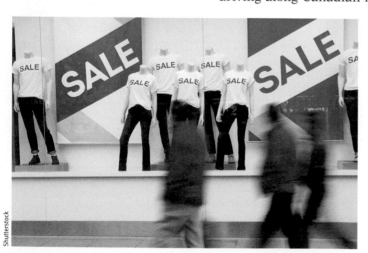

Periodic sales allow stores to price-discriminate between their high-elasticity and low-elasticity customers.

Shutterstock

pers who plan ahead, looking for the lowest price, will wait until there is a sale. By scheduling such sales only now and then, the store is in effect able to price-discriminate between high-elasticity and low-elasticity customers.

An outlet store serves the same purpose: by offering merchandise for low prices, but only at a considerable distance away, a seller is able to establish a separate market for those customers who are willing to make a significant effort to search out lower prices—and who therefore have a relatively high price elasticity of demand.

Finally, let's return to airline tickets to mention one of the truly odd features of their prices. Often a flight from one major destination to another—say, from Vancouver to Montreal—is slightly cheaper than a shorter flight to a smaller city—say, from Vancouver to Ottawa. Again, the reason is a difference in the price elasticity of demand: customers have a choice of many airlines between Vancouver and Montreal, so the demand for any one flight is quite elastic; customers have very little choice in flights to a smaller city, so the demand is much less elastic.

But often there is a flight between two major destinations that makes a stop along the way—say, a flight from Vancouver to Montreal with a stop in Ottawa. In these cases, it is sometimes cheaper to fly to the more distant city than to the city that is a stop along the way. For example, it may be cheaper to purchase a ticket to Montreal and get off in Ottawa than to purchase a ticket to Ottawa! It sounds ridiculous but makes perfect sense given the logic of monopoly pricing.

So why don't passengers simply buy a ticket from Vancouver to Montreal, but get off at Ottawa? Well, some do—but the airlines, understandably, make it difficult for customers to find out about such "ghost cities." In addition, the airline will not allow you to check baggage only part of the way if you have a ticket for the final destination. And airlines refuse to honour tickets for return flights when a passenger has not completed all the legs of the outbound flight. All these restrictions are meant to enforce the separation of markets necessary to allow price discrimination.

CHECK YOUR UNDERSTANDING   13-4

1. True or false? Explain your answer.
   a. A single-price monopolist sells to some customers that a price-discriminating monopolist refuses to.
   b. A price-discriminating monopolist creates more inefficiency than a single-price monopolist because it captures more of the consumer surplus.
   c. Under price discrimination, a customer with highly elastic demand will pay a lower price than a customer with inelastic demand.

2. Which of the following are cases of price discrimination and which are not? In the cases of price discrimination, identify the consumers with high and those with low price elasticity of demand.
   a. Damaged merchandise is marked down.
   b. Restaurants have senior citizen discounts.
   c. Food manufacturers place discount coupons for their merchandise in newspapers.
   d. Airline tickets cost more during the summer peak flying season.

Solutions appear at back of book.

BUSINESS CASE : Macmillan Stares Down Amazon

Chris Ratcliffe/Bloomberg via Getty Images

The normally genteel world of book publishing was anything but in early 2010. War had broken out between Macmillan, a large book publisher, and Amazon.com, the giant Internet book retailer. As one industry insider commented, "everyone thought they were witnessing a knife fight."

In early 2010, Amazon.com dominated the market for ebooks because it owned the best technology platform for distribution at the time: the Kindle, which lets users download books directly from Amazon.com's website. Although some publishers worried that readers' switch from paper books to ebooks would hurt sales, it seemed equally plausible that e-readers would actually increase them. Why? Because e-readers are so convenient to use and ebooks can't be turned into second-hand bargains. Yet book publishers were not at all happy with Amazon's behaviour in the ebook market.

What had spoiled their relationship was Amazon's policy of pricing every ebook at $9.99, a price at which it incurred a loss once it had paid the publisher for the book's copyright. Amazon argued that publishers should welcome its pricing because it would encourage more people to buy ebooks. Publishers, though, worried that the $9.99 price would cut into their sales of printed books. Moreover, Amazon didn't set a higher retail price for ebooks by premium authors, thereby undermining their special status. Perhaps most worrying was the prospect that Amazon would come to permanently dominate the ebook market, becoming the gatekeeper between publishers and readers.

Despite publishers' protests, Amazon refused to budge on its pricing. Matters came to a head in early February 2010, just as Apple was getting ready to launch its iPad, which has an ebook application. After John Sargent, the CEO of Macmillan, was unable to come to an agreement with Amazon, during a tense face-to-face meeting, the retailer removed all Macmillan books—paper and ebooks, even bestsellers—from its website (except for those purchased through third-party sellers).

After a barrage of bad press, Amazon backed down and agreed to allow Macmillan to set the retail price for its books, with Amazon receiving a 30% commission for each book sold, rather than the more common difference between the retail price and the wholesale price. Those terms closely replicated the terms agreed to by the largest publishers and Apple a week earlier.

QUESTIONS FOR THOUGHT

1. What accounts for Amazon's willingness to incur a loss on its ebook sales? Relate its actions to a concept discussed in this chapter.

2. Were publishers right to be fearful of Amazon's pricing policy despite the fact that it probably generated higher ebook sales?

3. How do you think the entry of the Apple iPad into the e-reader market affected the dynamics between publishers and Amazon.com? Why do you think a major publisher like Macmillan was able to force Amazon to retreat from its pricing policy?

SUMMARY

1. There are four main types of market structure based on the number of firms in the industry and product differentiation: perfect competition, monopoly, oligopoly, and monopolistic competition.

2. A **monopolist** is a producer who is the sole supplier of a good without close substitutes. An industry controlled by a monopolist is a **monopoly.**

3. The key difference between a monopoly and a perfectly competitive industry is that a single perfectly competitive firm faces a horizontal demand curve but a monopolist faces a downward-sloping demand curve. This gives the monopolist **market power,** the ability to raise the market price by reducing output compared to a perfectly competitive firm.

4. To persist, a monopoly must be protected by a **barrier to entry.** This can take the form of control of a natural resource or input, increasing returns to scale that give rise to **natural monopoly,** technological superiority, a **network externality,** or government rules that prevent entry by other firms, such as **patents** or **copyrights.**

5. The marginal revenue of a monopolist is composed of a quantity effect (the price received from the additional unit) and a price effect (the reduction in the price at which all units are sold). Because of the price effect, a monopolist's marginal revenue is always less than the market price, and the marginal revenue curve lies below the demand curve.

6. At the monopolist's profit-maximizing output level, marginal cost equals marginal revenue, which is less than market price. At the perfectly competitive firm's profit-maximizing output level, marginal cost equals the market price. So in comparison to perfectly competitive industries, monopolies produce less, charge higher prices, and earn profits in both the short run and the long run.

7. A monopoly creates deadweight losses by charging a price above marginal cost: the loss in consumer surplus exceeds the monopolist's profit. Thus monopolies are a source of market failure and should be prevented or broken up, except in the case of natural monopolies.

8. Natural monopolies can still cause deadweight losses. To limit these losses, governments sometimes impose **public ownership** and at other times impose **price regulation.** A price ceiling on a monopolist, as opposed to a perfectly competitive industry, need not cause shortages and can increase total surplus. **Average cost pricing** is a common method that governments can use to regulate the price charged by the monopolist, while **marginal cost pricing** tends to require subsidies.

9. Not all monopolists are **single-price monopolists.** Monopolists, as well as oligopolists and monopolistic competitors, often engage in **price discrimination** to make higher profits, using various techniques to differentiate consumers based on their sensitivity to price and charging those with less elastic demand higher prices. A monopolist that achieves **perfect price discrimination** (first-degree price discrimination) charges each consumer a price equal to his or her willingness to pay and captures the total surplus in the market. Although perfect price discrimination creates no inefficiency, it is practically impossible to implement. Second-degree price discrimination involves offering volume discounts while the third-degree price discriminatio involves charging different prices in different markets.

KEY TERMS

Monopolist, p. 407
Monopoly, p. 407
Market power, p. 408
Barrier to entry, p. 409
Natural monopoly, p. 409

Network externality, p. 410
Patent, p. 411
Copyright, p. 411
Public ownership, p. 423
Price regulation, p. 423

Average cost pricing, p. 425
Marginal cost pricing, p. 425
Single-price monopolist, p. 426
Price discrimination, p. 426
Perfect price discrimination, p. 430

PROBLEMS

1. Each of the following firms possesses market power. Explain its source.
   a. Merck, the producer of the patented cholesterol-lowering drug Zetia
   b. WaterWorks, a provider of piped water
   c. Chiquita, a supplier of bananas and owner of most banana plantations
   d. The Walt Disney Company, the creators of Mickey Mouse

2. Skyscraper City has a subway system, for which a one-way fare is $1.50. There is pressure on the mayor to reduce the fare by one-third, to $1.00. The mayor is dismayed, thinking that this will mean Skyscraper City is losing one-third of its revenue from sales of subway tickets. The mayor's economic adviser reminds her that she is focusing only on the price effect and ignoring the quantity effect. Explain why the mayor's estimate of a one-third loss of revenue is likely to be an overestimate. Illustrate with a diagram.

3. Consider an industry with the demand curve (*D*) and marginal cost curve (*MC*) shown in the accompanying diagram. There is no fixed cost. If the industry is a single-price monopoly, the monopolist's marginal revenue curve would be *MR*. Answer the following questions by naming the appropriate points or areas.

a. If the industry is perfectly competitive, what will be the total quantity produced? At what price?

b. Which area reflects consumer surplus under perfect competition?

c. If the industry is a single-price monopoly, what quantity will the monopolist produce? Which price will it charge?

d. Which area reflects the single-price monopolist's profit?

e. Which area reflects consumer surplus under single-price monopoly?

f. Which area reflects the deadweight loss to society from single-price monopoly?

g. If the monopolist can price-discriminate perfectly, what quantity will the perfectly price-discriminating monopolist produce?

4. Bob, Bill, Ben, and Brad Baxter have just made a documentary movie about their basketball team. They are thinking about making the movie available for download on the Internet, and they can act as a single-price monopolist if they choose to. Each time the movie is downloaded, their Internet service provider charges them a fee of $4. The Baxter brothers are arguing about which price to charge customers per download. The accompanying table shows the demand schedule for their film.

Price of download	Quantity of downloads demanded
$10	0
8	1
6	3
4	6
2	10
0	15

a. Calculate the total revenue and the marginal revenue per download.

b. Bob is proud of the film and wants as many people as possible to download it. Which price would he choose? How many downloads would be sold?

c. Bill wants as much total revenue as possible. Which price would he choose? How many downloads would be sold?

d. Ben wants to maximize profit. Which price would he choose? How many downloads would be sold?

e. Brad wants to charge the efficient price. Which price would he choose? How many downloads would be sold?

5. Jimmy has a room that overlooks, from some distance, a CFL football stadium. He decides to rent a telescope for $50.00 a week and charge his friends and classmates to use it to peep at the game for 30 seconds. He can act as a single-price monopolist for renting out "peeps." For each person who takes a 30-second peep, it costs Jimmy $0.20 to clean the eyepiece. The accompanying table shows the information Jimmy has gathered about the demand for the service in a given week.

Price of peep	Quantity of peeps demanded
$1.20	0
1.00	100
0.90	150
0.80	200
0.70	250
0.60	300
0.50	350
0.40	400
0.30	450
0.20	500
0.10	550

a. For each price in the table, calculate the total revenue from selling peeps and the marginal revenue per peep.

b. At what quantity will Jimmy's profit be maximized? What price will he charge? What will his total profit be?

c. Jimmy's landlady complains about all the visitors coming into the building and tells Jimmy to stop selling peeps. Jimmy discovers, however, that if he gives the landlady $0.20 for every peep he sells, she will stop complaining. What effect does the $0.20-per-peep bribe have on Jimmy's marginal cost per peep? What is the new profit-maximizing quantity of peeps? What effect does the $0.20-per-peep bribe have on Jimmy's total profit?

6. Suppose that De Beers is a single-price monopolist in the market for diamonds. De Beers has five potential customers: Raquel, Jackie, Joan, Mia, and Sophia. Each of these customers will buy at most one diamond—and only if the price is just equal to, or lower than, her willingness to pay. Raquel's willingness to pay is $400;

Jackie's, $300; Joan's, $200; Mia's, $100; and Sophia's, $0. De Beers's marginal cost per diamond is $100. This leads to the demand schedule for diamonds shown in the accompanying table.

Price of diamond	Quantity of diamonds demanded
$500	0
400	1
300	2
200	3
100	4
0	5

a. Calculate De Beers's total revenue and its marginal revenue. From your calculation, draw the demand curve and the marginal revenue curve.

b. Explain why De Beers faces a downward-sloping demand curve.

c. Explain why the marginal revenue from an additional diamond sale is less than the price of the diamond.

d. Suppose De Beers currently charges $200 for its diamonds. If it lowers the price to $100, how large is the price effect? How large is the quantity effect?

e. Add the marginal cost curve to your diagram from part (a) and determine which quantity maximizes De Beers's profit and which price it will charge.

7. Use the demand schedule for diamonds given in Problem 6. The marginal cost of producing diamonds is constant at $100. There is no fixed cost.

a. If De Beers charges the monopoly price, how large is the individual consumer surplus that each buyer experiences? Calculate total consumer surplus by summing the individual consumer surpluses. How large is producer surplus?

Suppose that upstart Russian and Asian producers enter the market and the market becomes perfectly competitive.

b. What is the perfectly competitive price? What quantity will be sold in this perfectly competitive market?

c. At the competitive price and quantity, how large is the consumer surplus that each buyer experiences? How large is total consumer surplus? How large is producer surplus?

d. Compare your answer to part (c) to your answer to part (a). How large is the deadweight loss associated with monopoly in this case?

8. Use the demand schedule for diamonds given in Problem 6. De Beers is a monopolist, but it can now price-discriminate perfectly among all five of its potential customers. De Beers's marginal cost is constant at $100. There is no fixed cost.

a. If De Beers can price-discriminate perfectly, to which customers will it sell diamonds and at what prices?

b. How large is each individual consumer surplus? How large is total consumer surplus? Calculate producer surplus by summing the producer surplus generated by each sale.

9. Download Records decides to release an album by the group Mary and the Little Lamb. It produces the album with no fixed cost, but the total cost of downloading an album to a CD and paying Mary her royalty is $6 per album. Download Records can act as a single-price monopolist. Its marketing division finds that the demand schedule for the album is as shown in the accompanying table.

Price of album	Quantity of albums demanded
$22	0
20	1000
18	2000
16	3000
14	4000
12	5000
10	6000
8	7000

a. Calculate the total revenue and the marginal revenue per album.

b. The marginal cost of producing each album is constant at $6. To maximize profit, what level of output should Download Records choose, and which price should it charge for each album?

c. Mary renegotiates her contract and now needs to be paid a higher royalty per album. So the marginal cost rises to be constant at $14. To maximize profit, what level of output should Download Records now choose, and which price should it charge for each album?

10. The accompanying diagram illustrates your local electricity company's natural monopoly. The diagram shows the demand curve for kilowatt-hours (kWh) of electricity, the company's marginal revenue (MR) curve, its marginal cost (MC) curve, and its average total cost (ATC) curve. The government wants to regulate the monopolist by imposing a price ceiling.

a. If the government does not regulate this monopolist, which price will it charge? Illustrate the inefficiency this creates by shading the deadweight loss from monopoly.

b. If the government imposes a price ceiling equal to the marginal cost, $0.30, will the monopolist make profits or lose money? Shade the area of profit (or loss) for the monopolist. If the government does impose this price ceiling, do you think the firm will continue to produce in the long run?

c. If the government imposes a price ceiling of $0.50, will the monopolist make a profit, lose money, or break even?

11. The movie theatre in Lafacville serves two kinds of customers: students and professors. There are 900 students and 100 professors in Lafacville. Each student's willingness to pay for a movie ticket is $5. Each professor's willingness to pay for a movie ticket is $10. Each will buy at most one ticket. The movie theatre's marginal cost per ticket is constant at $3, and there is no fixed cost.

a. Suppose the movie theatre cannot price-discriminate and needs to charge students and professors the same price per ticket. If the theatre charges $5, who will buy tickets and what will the theatre's profit be? How large is the consumer surplus?

b. If the movie theatre charges $10, who will buy movie tickets and what will the movie theatre's profit be? How large is consumer surplus?

c. Now suppose that, if it chooses to, the movie theatre can price-discriminate between students and professors by requiring students to show their student ID. If the movie theatre charges students $5 and professors $10, how much profit will the movie theatre make? How large is consumer surplus?

12. A monopolist knows that in order to expand the quantity of output it produces from 8 to 9 units it must lower the price of its output from $2 to $1. Calculate the quantity effect and the price effect. Use these results to calculate the monopolist's marginal revenue of producing the 9th unit. The marginal cost of producing the 9th unit is positive. Is it a good idea for the monopolist to produce the 9th unit?

13. In the United States, the Federal Trade Commission (FTC) is charged with promoting competition and challenging mergers that would likely lead to higher prices. Several years ago, Staples and Office Depot, two of the largest office supply superstores, announced their agreement to merge.

a. Some critics of the merger argued that, in many parts of the country, a merger between the two companies would create a monopoly in the office supply superstore market. Based on the FTC's argument and its mission to challenge mergers that would likely lead to higher prices, do you think it should have allowed the merger?

b. Staples and Office Depot argued that, while they might create a monopoly in the office supply superstore market, the FTC should consider the larger market for all office supplies, which includes many smaller stores that sell office supplies (such as grocery stores and other retailers). In that market, Staples and Office Depot would face competition from many other, smaller stores. If the market for all office supplies is the relevant market that the FTC should consider, would it make the FTC more or less likely to allow the merger?

14. Prior to 1999, the same company that generated electricity in Ontario also distributed it over high-voltage lines. But then the provincial government separated the generation from the distribution of electricity, allowing competition among electricity generators and among electricity distributors.

a. Assume that the market for electricity distribution was and remains a natural monopoly. Use a graph to illustrate the market for electricity distribution if the government sets price equal to average total cost.

b. Assume that deregulation of electricity generation creates a perfectly competitive market. Also assume that electricity generation does not exhibit the characteristics of a natural monopoly. Use a graph to illustrate the cost curves in the long-run equilibrium for an individual firm in this industry.

15. Explain the following situations.

a. Many cellphone service providers give away for free what would otherwise be very expensive cellphones when a service contract is purchased. Why might a company want to do that?

b. In the United Kingdom, the country's competition authority banned the cellphone service provider Vodaphone from offering a plan that gave customers free calls to other Vodaphone customers. Why might Vodaphone have wanted to offer these calls for free? Why might a government want to step in and ban this practice? Why might it not be a good idea for a government to interfere in this way?

16. The market demand for recorders (a simple musical instrument) in Hamelin is given by the following graph. Currently, Pied Piping is the single seller in Hamelin.

Note: Be sure to show your work and do not round your answers.

a. At what level of output and price does Pied Piping maximize its profit? What is the deadweight loss in the market for recorders?

b. In attempt to increase output, the government decides to regulate the industry through an average cost pricing. What are the price charged and quantity sold by the monopolist after the regulation?

c. What is the deadweight loss after the regulation? What is the change in consumer surplus?

17. This question uses the algebraic method to solve problems from Appendix 3A and Appendix 6A. The market of widgets is characterized by a single seller. The market demand and the firm's total cost are given by:

$P = 150 - Q$ Demand Curve
$TC = 475 + 50Q$ Cost Function

where P is the price per widgets and Q is the number of widgets. The firm has fixed costs of $475, and a constant variable cost of production equal to $50 per unit made. The marginal cost is always $50 for another widget.

a. Determine the profit maximizing price and quantity. What are the firm's profit, the consumer surplus, and the deadweight loss?

b. Suppose the government decides to regulate the firm through price regulation. The government is considering either marginal cost pricing or average cost pricing. Calculate the following items under each proposal:

i. Price charged

ii. Quantity produced
iii. Firm's profit
iv. Consumer surplus
v. Deadweight loss

c. You are asked to make a recommendation on which proposal—marginal cost pricing or average cost pricing—the government should adopt. What kind of recommendation would you give? Explain.

18. This question uses the algebraic method to solve problems from Appendix 3A and Appendix 6A. Suppose the Potash Corporation of Saskatchewan (PotashCorp) is the sole producer of the fertilizer potash in the Canadian market. The market demand and PotashCorp's total cost are given by:

$P = 1750 - 6Q$ Demand Curve
$TC = 11\ 400 + 550Q$ Cost Function

where P is the price per tonne of potash and Q is the quantity in tonnes.

Note: Round your answer to two decimal places where needed. Be sure to show your work.

a. Determine the quantity produced and price charged by PotashCrop if it is an unregulated monopoly.

b. Determine the deadweight loss in the market if PotashCorp is an unregulated monopoly.

c. Suppose the federal government decides to regulate the industry to decrease the deadweight loss associated with this monopoly. The new regulation requires PotashCorp to adopt average cost pricing. What will be the price charged by PotashCorp? What is the change in total surplus?

CHAPTER 14

Oligopoly

CAUGHT IN THE ACT

Were Canadian chocolate makers engaging in price-fixing?

WHAT YOU WILL LEARN IN THIS CHAPTER

❭ The meaning of **oligopoly,** and why it occurs

❭ Why **oligopolists** have an incentive to act in ways that reduce their combined profit, and why they can benefit from **collusion**

❭ How our understanding of oligopoly can be enhanced by using **game theory,** especially the concept of the **prisoners' dilemma**

❭ How repeated interactions among oligopolists can help them achieve **tacit collusion**

❭ How oligopoly works in practice, under the legal constraints of **competition, or antitrust, policy**

NESTLÉ, THE SWISS MULTI-national food and beverage company, is arguably the largest food company on the planet. Its list of popular product brands includes many names known around the world, with dozens of them earning more than $1 billion per year in revenue for the company. Most Canadians know the Nestlé name from either their popular bottled water or one of their many chocolate products, including KitKat, Smarties, and Coffee Crisp. In fact, Nestlé Canada is the market leader in Canada's chocolate market, having captured about 16% of Canadian sales.

But on June 6, 2013 everything was certainly not sweet for Nestlé Canada. On that day criminal charges were laid against Nestlé Canada; Robert Leonidas, a former president of Nestlé Canada; Sandra Martinez, a former president of confectionery for Nestlé Canada; Mars Canada; ITWAL Limited

(a national confectionary distributor); and David Glenn Stevens, president and chief executive officer of ITWAL. Those charged, along with Hershey Canada Inc., are alleged to have conspired, agreed, or arranged to set prices of chocolate products, behaviour called *price-fixing*. Executives of each company supposedly met secretly in coffee shops and restaurants and at industry conventions to set prices. It is alleged that from 2002 to 2007 the chief executive of Nestlé Canada took a lead role and even handed envelopes stuffed with pricing information and instructions to competitors.

What the companies were doing was illegal. To understand why it was illegal and why the companies were doing it anyway, we need to examine the issues posed by industries that are neither perfectly competitive nor purely monopolistic. In this chapter we focus on *oligopoly,* a type of market structure

in which there are only a few producers. As we'll see, oligopoly is a very important reality—much more important, in fact, than monopoly and arguably more typical of modern economies than perfect competition.

Although much that we've learned about both perfect competition and monopoly is relevant to oligopoly, oligopoly also raises some entirely new issues. Among other things, firms in an oligopoly are often tempted to engage in the kind of behaviour that got Nestlé and other Canadian chocolate producers and distributors into trouble with the law. Over the past few years, there have been numerous investigations and some convictions for price-fixing in a variety of industries, from insurance to elevators to computer chips.

For example, in 2010, the European Union, which has laws similar to those in Canada, fined 11 airlines $1.11 billion (yes, that's *billion*) for price-fixing of air cargo prices. This price-fixing also resulted in the U.S. Department of Justice imposing more than $1.8 billion in criminal fines against more than 20 airlines, jail terms for four airline executives, and a class action lawsuit settlement cost for airlines of another $500 million. The Canadian Competition Bureau has extracted more than $25 million in fines from 9 airlines for price-fixing and continues to pursue cases against several more.[1]

We will begin by examining what oligopoly is and why it is so important. Then we'll turn to the behaviour of oligopolistic industries. Finally, we'll look at *competition policy* (also called *antitrust policy*), which is primarily concerned with trying to keep oligopolies "well behaved." ∎

---

[1]As a result of charges of price-fixing, the EU fined Air Canada the equivalent of $29.1 million. The U.S. Department of Justice fined Air Canada $7.5 million. But so far, at the time of writing, Air Canada has avoided criminal or class action fines in Canada; it is believed the Canadian Competition Bureau continues to investigate a case against Air Canada.

An **oligopoly** is an industry with only a small number of producers. A producer in such an industry is known as an **oligopolist.**

When no one firm has a monopoly, but producers nonetheless realize that they can affect market prices, an industry is characterized by **imperfect competition.**

The Prevalence of Oligopoly

At the time of the alleged price-fixing, no one company controlled the Canadian chocolate industry, but there were only a few major producers. An industry with only a few sellers is known as an **oligopoly;** a firm in such an industry is known as an **oligopolist.**

Oligopolists obviously compete with one another for sales. But neither Nestlé nor Mars was like a firm in a perfectly competitive industry, which takes the price at which it can sell its product as given. Each of these firms knew that its decision about how much to produce would affect the market price. That is, like monopolists, each of the firms had some *market power*. So the competition in this industry wasn't "perfect."

Economists refer to a situation in which firms compete but also possess market power—which enables them to affect market prices—as **imperfect competition.** As we saw in Chapter 13, there are actually two important forms of imperfect competition: oligopoly and *monopolistic competition*. Of these, oligopoly is probably the more important in practice.

The multibillion dollar chocolate business is not the only oligopoly in Canada. Many other goods and services—some familiar, others not—are supplied by only a few competing sellers, which means the industries in question are oligopolies. For example, most air routes are served by only two or three airlines: in recent years, regularly scheduled shuttle service between Toronto and Calgary or Vancouver has been provided only by Air Canada and WestJet. Three firms—Chiquita, Dole, and Del Monte, which own huge banana plantations in Central America—control 65% of world banana exports. Most cola beverages are sold by Coca-Cola and Pepsi. This list could go on for many pages.

It's important to realize that an oligopoly isn't necessarily made up of large firms. What matters isn't size per se; the question is how many competitors there are. When a small town has only two grocery stores, grocery service there is just as much an oligopoly as air shuttle service between Toronto and Calgary.

Why are oligopolies so prevalent? Essentially, oligopoly is the result of the same factors that sometimes produce monopoly, but in somewhat weaker form. Probably the most important source of oligopoly is the existence of *increasing returns to scale,* which give bigger producers a cost advantage over smaller ones. When these effects are very strong, they lead to monopoly; when they are not that strong, they lead to an industry with a small number of firms. For example, larger grocery stores typically have lower costs than smaller ones. But the advantages of large scale taper off once grocery stores are reasonably large, which is why two or three stores often survive in small towns.

If oligopoly is so common, why has most of this book focused on competition in industries where the number of sellers is very large? And why did we study monopoly, which is relatively uncommon, first? The answer has two parts.

First, much of what we learn from the study of perfectly competitive markets—about costs, entry and exit, and efficiency—remains valid despite the fact that many industries are not perfectly competitive. Second, the analysis of oligopoly turns out to present some puzzles for which there are no easy solutions. It is almost always a good idea—in exams and in life in general—first to deal with the questions you can answer, then to puzzle over the harder ones. We have simply followed the same strategy, developing the relatively clear-cut theories of perfect competition and monopoly first, and only then turning to the puzzles presented by oligopoly.

ECONOMICS ▷ IN ACTION

IS IT AN OLIGOPOLY OR NOT?

In practice, it is not always easy to determine an industry's market structure just by looking at the number of sellers. Many oligopolistic industries contain a number of small "niche" producers, which don't really compete with the major players. For example, the Canadian airline industry includes a number of regional airlines like Air Labrador, which flies propeller planes between Goose Bay and other communities in Labrador, Quebec, and Newfoundland; if you count these carriers, the Canadian airline industry contains nearly a hundred sellers, which doesn't sound like competition among a small group. But there are only a couple of national competitors—Air Canada and WestJet—and on many routes, as we've seen, these are the only competitors.

To get a better picture of market structure, economists often use a measure called the *Herfindahl–Hirschman Index*, or HHI. The HHI for an industry is the square of each firm's market share summed over the firms in the industry. (In Chapter 12 you learned that *market share* is the percentage of sales in the market accounted for by that firm.) For example, if an industry contains only three firms and their market shares are 60%, 25%, and 15%, then the HHI for the industry is:

$$HHI = 60^2 + 25^2 + 15^2 = 4450$$

By squaring each market share, the HHI calculation produces numbers that are much larger when a larger share of an industry output is dominated by fewer firms. So it's a better measure of just how concentrated the industry is. This is confirmed by the data in Table 14-1. Here, the indexes for industries dominated by a small number of firms, like the personal computer operating systems industry or the wide-body aircraft industry, are many times larger than the index for the retail grocery industry, which has numerous firms of approximately equal size.

TABLE 14-1   The HHI for Some Oligopolistic Industries

Industry	HHI	Largest firms
PC operating systems	9182	Microsoft, Linux
Wide-body aircraft	5098	Boeing, Airbus
Diamond mining	2338	De Beers, Alrosa, Rio Tinto
Retail grocers	1819	Loblaws, Sobeys, Metro, Safeway, Costco, Walmart
Automobiles	1432	GM, Ford, Chrysler, Toyota, Honda, Nissan, VW
Movie distributors	1096	Buena Vista, Sony Pictures, 20th Century Fox, Warner Bros., Universal, Paramount, Lionsgate
Internet service providers	908	Bell, Shaw, Rogers, Telus, Cogeco

Sources: Canadian Government; Diamond Facts 2006; www.w3counter.com; Planet retail; ufcw.ca; Autodata; Reuters; cmcrp.org. Data cover 2006–2009.

The HHI is used in the United States by the Justice Department and the Federal Trade Commission, which have the job of enforcing *antitrust policy,* a topic we'll investigate in more detail later in this chapter. Their mission is to try to ensure that there is adequate competition in an industry by prosecuting price-fixing, breaking up economically inefficient monopolies, and disallowing mergers between firms when it's believed that the merger will reduce competition. According to Justice Department guidelines, an HHI below 1500 indicates a strongly competitive market, between 1500 and 2500 indicates a somewhat competitive market, and over 2500 indicates an oligopoly. In an industry with an HHI over 1500, a merger that results in a significant increase in the HHI will receive special scrutiny and is likely to be disallowed.

However, defining an industry can be tricky, so rough rules of thumb are not appropriate for all situations. As a result, while the Canadian Competition Bureau may study changes in the HHI as a sign of changes in the level of competition, it does not employ rule-of-thumb ranges of "good" or "bad" levels for the index. In 2013, the proposed merger between Telus and the much smaller firm Mobilicity was denied by Industry Minister Christian Paradis. This came as no surprise: the Canadian wireless communications market is highly concentrated, with an HHI of about 2900, and the government had promised that the big carriers would not be allowed to buy the new entrants.

Another consideration when deciding whether an industry is an oligopoly is access to the market by external suppliers. For example, in 2009, sugar manufacturing in Ontario had an HHI of 8569, while for all of Canada the HHI was 4936. Both denote a high degree of market concentration, which might imply low levels of competition. But thanks to imports of sugar produced outside of Canada, the degree of competition is actually much higher than the HHI might imply, resulting in Canadian sugar prices actually being below those in the United States and Mexico.

CHECK YOUR UNDERSTANDING 14-1

1. Explain why each of the following industries is an oligopoly, not a perfectly competitive industry.
   a. The world oil industry, where a few countries near the Persian Gulf control much of the world's oil reserves
   b. The microprocessor industry, where two firms, Intel and its bitter rival AMD, dominate the technology
   c. The wide-body passenger jet industry, composed of the American firm Boeing and the European firm Airbus, where production is characterized by extremely large fixed cost
2. The accompanying table shows the Canadian market shares for mobile phone operating systems in April 2014.
   a. Calculate the HHI in this industry.
   b. If Android and BlackBerry were to merge, what would the HHI be?

Mobile operating system	Market share
iOS (Apple)	42%
Android	39
BlackBerry	14
Other	5

Solutions appear at back of book.

Understanding Oligopoly

How much will a firm produce? Up to this point, we have always answered: the quantity that maximizes its profit. Together with its cost curves, the assumption that a firm maximizes profit is enough to determine its output when it is a perfect competitor or a monopolist.

When it comes to oligopoly, however, we run into some difficulties. Indeed, economists often describe the behaviour of oligopolistic firms as a "puzzle."

A Duopoly Example

Let's begin looking at the puzzle of oligopoly with the simplest version, an industry in which there are only two producing firms—a **duopoly**—and each is known as a **duopolist.**

Going back to our opening story, imagine that Nestlé and Mars are the only two producers of chocolate. To make things even simpler, suppose that once a company has incurred the fixed cost needed to produce chocolate, the marginal cost of producing another kilogram is zero. So the companies are concerned only

An oligopoly consisting of only two firms is a **duopoly.** Each firm is known as a **duopolist.**

with the revenue they receive from sales because maximizing revenue results in maximum profit.

Figure 14-1 shows a hypothetical demand schedule for chocolate and the total revenue of the industry at each price–quantity combination.

If this were a perfectly competitive industry, each firm would have an incentive to produce more as long as the market price was above marginal cost. Since the marginal cost is assumed to be zero, this would mean that at equilibrium chocolate would be provided free. Firms would produce until price equals zero (the marginal cost), yielding a total output of 120 million kilograms and zero revenue for both firms.

However, surely the firms would not be that stupid. With only two firms in the industry, each would realize that by producing more, it drives down the market price. So each firm would, like a monopolist, realize that profits would be higher if it and its rival limited their production.

So how much will the two firms produce?

One possibility is that the two companies will engage in **collusion**—they will cooperate to raise their joint profits. The strongest form of collusion is a **cartel,** an arrangement between producers that determines how much each is allowed to produce. The world's most famous cartel is the Organization of Petroleum Exporting Countries, described in Economics in Action later in the chapter. As its name indicates, it's actually an agreement among governments rather than firms. There's a reason this most famous of cartels is an agreement among governments: cartels among firms are illegal in Canada and many other jurisdictions. But let's

Sellers engage in **collusion** when they cooperate to raise their joint profits. A **cartel** is an agreement among several producers to obey output restrictions in order to increase their joint profits.

FIGURE **14-1** Demand Schedule and Curve for Chocolate

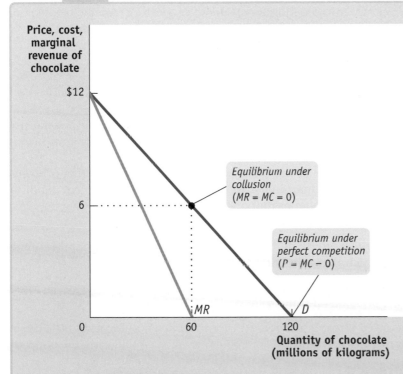

Price of chocolate (per kilogram)	Quantity of chocolate demanded (millions of kilograms)	Total revenue (millions)
$12	0	$0
11	10	110
10	20	200
9	30	270
8	40	320
7	50	350
6	60	360
5	70	350
4	80	320
3	90	270
2	100	200
1	110	110
0	120	0

The rule for maximizing profit is to equate marginal revenue (*MR*) with marginal cost (*MC*). Here, the marginal cost is assumed to be zero. The profit-maximizing level of output under perfect competition is 120 million kilograms with a price of $0. Alternatively, if firms work together and act like a monopoly, they would set the price to $6 per kilogram and produce 60 million kilograms.

ignore the law for a moment (which is, of course, what Nestlé and Mars did in real life—to their own detriment).

So suppose that Nestlé and Mars were to form a cartel and that this cartel decided to act as if it were a monopolist, maximizing total industry profits. It's obvious from Figure 14-1 that in order to maximize the combined profits of the firms, this cartel should set total industry output at 60 million kilograms of chocolate, which would sell at a price of $6 per kilogram, leading to revenue of $360 million, the maximum possible. (Recall that when marginal cost is zero, maximizing revenue results in maximizing profit.) Then the only question would be how much of that 60 million kilograms each firm gets to produce. A "fair" solution might be for each firm to produce 30 million kilograms with revenues for each firm of $180 million.

But even if the two firms agreed on such a deal, they might have a problem: each of the firms would have an incentive to break its word and produce more than the agreed-upon quantity.

Collusion and Competition

Suppose that the presidents of Nestlé and Mars were to agree that each would produce 30 million kilograms of chocolate over the next year. Both would understand that this plan maximizes their combined profits. And both would have an incentive to cheat.

To see why, consider what would happen if Mars honoured its agreement, producing only 30 million kilograms, but Nestlé ignored its promise and produced 40 million kilograms. This increase in total output would drive the price down from $6 to $5 per kilogram, the price at which 70 million kilograms are demanded. The industry's total revenue would fall from $360 million ($6 × 60 million kilograms) to $350 million ($5 × 70 million kilograms). However, Nestlé's revenue would *rise*, from $180 million to $200 million. Since we are assuming a marginal cost of zero, this would mean a $20 million increase in Nestlé's profits.

But Mars's president might make exactly the same calculation. And if both firms were to produce 40 million kilograms of chocolate, the price would drop to $4 per kilogram. So each firm's profits would fall, from $180 million to $160 million.

Why do individual firms have an incentive to produce more than the quantity that maximizes their joint profits? Because neither firm has as strong an incentive to limit its output as a true monopolist would.

Let's go back for a minute to the theory of monopoly. We know that a profit-maximizing monopolist sets marginal cost (which in this case is zero) equal to marginal revenue. But what is marginal revenue? Recall that producing an additional unit of a good has two effects:

1. A positive *quantity* effect: an additional unit is sold, increasing total revenue by the price at which that unit is sold.

2. A negative *price* effect: in order to sell an additional unit, the monopolist must cut the market price on *all* units sold.

The negative price effect is the reason marginal revenue for a monopolist is less than the market price. In the case of oligopoly, when considering the effect of increasing production, a firm is concerned only with the price effect on its *own* units of output, not those of its fellow oligopolists. Both Nestlé and Mars suffer a negative price effect if Nestlé decides to produce extra chocolate and so drives down the price. But Nestlé cares only about the negative price effect on the units it produces, not about the loss to Mars.

This tells us that an individual firm in an oligopolistic industry faces a smaller price effect from an additional unit of output than does a monopolist; therefore, the marginal revenue that such a firm calculates is higher. So it will seem to be profitable for any one company in an oligopoly to increase production, even if that increase reduces the profits of the industry as a whole. But if everyone thinks that way, the result is that everyone earns a lower profit!

Until now, we have been able to analyze producer behaviour by asking what a producer should do to maximize profits. But even if Nestlé and Mars are both trying to maximize profits, what does this predict about their behaviour? Will they engage in collusion, reaching and holding to an agreement that maximizes their combined profits? Or will they engage in **noncooperative behaviour,** with each firm acting in its own self-interest, even though this has the effect of driving down everyone's profits? Both strategies sound like profit maximization. Which will actually describe their behaviour?

Now you see why oligopoly presents a puzzle: there are only a small number of players, making collusion a real possibility. If there were dozens or hundreds of firms, it would be safe to assume they would behave noncooperatively. Yet when there are only a handful of firms in an industry, it's hard to determine whether collusion will actually materialize.

Since collusion is ultimately more profitable than noncooperative behaviour, firms have an incentive to collude if they can. One way to do so is to formalize it—sign an agreement (maybe even make a legal contract) or establish some financial incentives for the companies to set their prices high. But in Canada and many other nations, you can't do that—at least not legally. Companies cannot make a legal contract to keep prices high: not only is the contract unenforceable, but writing it is a one-way ticket to jail. Neither can they sign an informal "gentlemen's agreement," which lacks the force of law but perhaps rests on threats of retaliation—that's illegal, too.

In fact, executives from rival companies rarely meet without lawyers present, who make sure that the conversation does not stray into inappropriate territory. Even hinting at how nice it would be if prices were higher can bring you an unwelcome interview with the Competition Bureau. For example, in 2013 the Competition Bureau announced that Yazaki Corporation, a Japanese supplier of automobile parts, was fined a record $30 million, for participating in a *bid-rigging* cartel involving vehicle parts. Bid-rigging occurs when two or more firms work together to fix their bids for contracts so as to set prices and allocate the market amongst the group. Yazaki pleaded guilty to the charge that they had coordinated bids with competing suppliers for the Canadian operations of Honda and Toyota. Suppliers Furukawa and JTEKT each received $5 million fines. In the United States, Yazaki agreed to pay a US$470 million fine for price-fixing and bid-rigging, the second largest criminal fine to that time. Four U.S.-based Yazaki executives were given prison sentences of 15 months to two years for their roles in this criminal conspiracy.

Sometimes, as we've seen, oligopolistic firms just ignore the rules. But more often they find ways to achieve collusion without a formal agreement, as we'll discuss later in the chapter.

> When firms ignore the effects of their actions on each others' profits, they engage in **noncooperative behaviour.**

ECONOMICS ► IN ACTION

PRICE FIXER TO THE WORLD

The world's largest agricultural products company, Archer Daniels Midland (also known as ADM), has often described itself as "supermarket to the world." Its name is familiar to many North Americans not only because of its important role in the economy but also because of its advertising and sponsorship of U.S. public television programs. But on October 25, 1993, ADM itself was on camera.

On that day executives from ADM and its Japanese competitor Ajinomoto met at the Marriott Hotel in Irvine, California, to discuss the market for lysine, an additive used in animal feed. (How is lysine produced? It's excreted by genetically

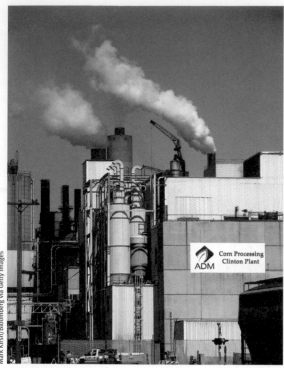

A whistleblower at ADM revealed an international price-fixing cartel.

engineered bacteria.) In this and subsequent meetings, the two companies joined with several other competitors to set targets for the world market price of lysine, the illegal behaviour of price-fixing. Each company agreed to limit its production in order to achieve those targets. Agreeing on specific limits would be their biggest challenge—or so they thought.

Within the first year, the cartel was able to raise lysine prices by 70%. But what the participants in the meeting didn't know was that they had a bigger problem: the FBI had bugged the room and was filming them with a camera hidden in a lamp. As dramatized in the 2009 movie *The Informant*, the FBI had been made aware of this criminal behaviour by Mark Whitacre (portrayed by Matt Damon in the movie), an ADM executive turned whistleblower. Thanks to all the evidence collected, ADM, Japanese firms Ajinomoto and Kyowa Hakko Kogyo, and Korean firms Sewon America Inc. and Cheil Jedang Ltd. all ended up pleading guilty to criminal charges related to this international cartel illegally fixing lysine prices from 1992 to 1996. Fines in the United States were US$105 million (US$70 million from ADM alone). Three former ADM executives were arrested for their role in this criminal conspiracy. In Canada, three of the firms were fined about $20 million ($16 million of that from ADM). North American buyers of lysine launched civil lawsuits to recover damages from the five cartel members. The civil suits were successful, and, when added to the criminal fines, doubled the settlement costs of the firms.

As a result of this sad adventure and other similar accusations, some took to calling ADM the "price fixer to the world."

▼ **Quick Review**

● Some of the key issues in oligopoly can be understood by looking at the simplest case, a **duopoly**—an industry containing only two firms, called **duopolists.**

● By acting as if they were a single monopolist, oligopolists can maximize their combined profits. So there is an incentive to form a **cartel.**

● However, each firm has an incentive to cheat—to produce more than it is supposed to under the cartel agreement. So there are two principal outcomes: successful **collusion** or **noncooperative behaviour** by cheating.

CHECK YOUR UNDERSTANDING 14-2

1. Which of the following factors increase the likelihood that an oligopolist will collude with other firms in the industry? The likelihood that an oligopolist will act noncooperatively and raise output? Explain your answers.
   a. The firm's initial market share is small. (*Hint:* Think about the price effect.)
   b. The firm has a cost advantage over its rivals.
   c. The firm's customers face additional costs when they switch from the use of one firm's product to another firm's product.
   d. The oligopolist has a lot of unused production capacity but knows that its rivals are operating at their maximum production capacity and cannot increase the amount they produce.

Solutions appear at back of book.

Games Oligopolists Play

In our duopoly example and in real life, each oligopolistic firm realizes both that its profit depends on what its competitor does and that its competitor's profit depends on what it does. That is, the two firms are in a situation of **interdependence,** where each firm's decision significantly affects the profit of the other firm (or firms, in the case of more than two).

When a firm's decision significantly affects the profits of other firms in the industry, the firms are in a situation of **interdependence.**

The study of behaviour in situations of interdependence is known as **game theory.**

In effect, the two firms are playing a "game" in which the profit of each player depends not only on its own actions but on those of the other player (or players). In order to understand more fully how oligopolists behave, economists, along with mathematicians, developed the area of study of such games, known as **game theory.** It has many applications, not just to economics but also to military strategy, politics, and other social sciences.

Let's see how game theory helps us understand oligopoly.

Mark Kirsh/Bloomberg via Getty Images

The Prisoners' Dilemma

Game theory deals with any situation in which the reward to any one player—the **payoff**—depends not only on his or her own actions but also on those of other players in the game. In the case of oligopolistic firms, the payoff is simply the firm's profit.

When there are only two players, as in a duopoly, the interdependence between the players can be represented with a **payoff matrix** like that shown in Figure 14-2. Each row corresponds to an action by one player (in this case, Nestlé); each column corresponds to an action by the other (in this case, Mars). For simplicity, let's assume that Nestlé can pick only one of two alternatives: produce 30 million kilograms of chocolate or produce 40 million kilograms. Mars has the same pair of choices.

The matrix contains four boxes, each divided by a diagonal line. Each box shows the payoff to the two firms that results from a pair of choices; the number below the diagonal shows Nestlé's profits, the number above the diagonal shows Mars's profits.

These payoffs show what we concluded from our earlier analysis: the combined profit of the two firms is maximized if they each produce 30 million kilograms. Either firm can, however, increase its own profits by producing 40 million kilograms while the other produces only 30 million kilograms. But if both produce the larger quantity, both will have lower profits than if they had both held their output down.

The particular situation shown here is a version of a famous—and seemingly paradoxical—case of interdependence that appears in many contexts. Known as the **prisoners' dilemma**, it is a type of game in which the payoff matrix implies the following:

- Each player has an incentive, regardless of what the other player does, to cheat—to take an action that benefits it at the other's expense.
- When both players cheat, both are worse off than they would have been if neither had cheated.

The reward received by a player in a game, such as the profit earned by an oligopolist, is that player's **payoff**.

A **payoff matrix** shows how the payoff to each of the participants in a two-player game depends on the actions of both. Such a matrix helps us analyze situations of interdependence.

Prisoners' dilemma is a game based on two premises: (1) Each player has an incentive to choose an action that benefits itself at the other player's expense (2) When both players act in this way, both are worse off than if they had acted cooperatively.

FIGURE **14-2** **A Payoff Matrix**

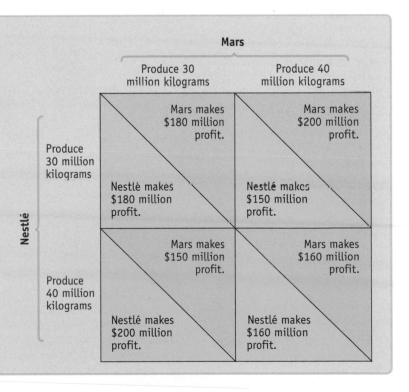

Two firms, Nestlé and Mars, must decide how much chocolate to produce. The profits of the two firms are *interdependent*: each firm's profit depends not only on its own decision but also on the other's decision. Each row represents an action by Nestlé, each column, one by Mars. Both firms will be better off if they both choose the lower output, but it is in each firm's individual interest to choose the higher output.

An action is a **dominant strategy** when it is a player's best action regardless of the action taken by the other player.

The original illustration of the prisoners' dilemma occurred in a fictional story about two accomplices in crime—let's call them Thelma and Louise—who have been caught by the police. The police have enough evidence to put them behind bars for 5 years. They also know that the pair have committed a more serious crime, one that carries a 20-year sentence; unfortunately, they don't have enough evidence to convict the women on that charge. To do so, they would need each of the prisoners to implicate the other in the second crime.

So the police put the miscreants in separate cells and say the following to each: "Here's the deal: if neither of you confesses, you know that we'll send you to jail for 5 years. If you confess and implicate your partner, and she doesn't do the same, we'll reduce your sentence from 5 years to 2. But if your partner confesses and you don't, you'll get the maximum 20 years. And if both of you confess, we'll give you both 15 years."

Figure 14-3 shows the payoffs that face the prisoners, depending on the decision of each to remain silent or to confess. (Usually the payoff matrix reflects the players' payoffs, and higher payoffs are better than lower payoffs. This matrix is an exception in that it shows their costs: a higher number of years in prison is bad, not good!) Let's assume that the prisoners have no way to communicate and that they have not sworn an oath not to harm each other or anything of that sort. So each acts in her own self-interest. What will they do?

The answer is clear: both will confess. Look at it first from Thelma's point of view: she is better off confessing, regardless of what Louise does. If Louise doesn't confess, Thelma's confession reduces her own sentence from 5 years to 2. If Louise *does* confess, Thelma's confession reduces her sentence from 20 to 15 years. Either way, it's clearly in Thelma's interest to confess. And because she faces the same incentives, it's clearly in Louise's interest to confess, too. To confess in this situation is a type of action that economists call a *dominant strategy*. An action is a **dominant strategy** when it is the player's best action regardless of the action taken by the other player.

It's important to note that not all games have a dominant strategy—it depends on the structure of payoffs in the game. But in the case of Thelma and Louise, it

FIGURE 14-3 The Prisoners' Dilemma

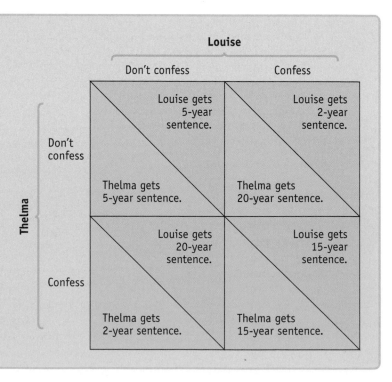

Each of two prisoners, held in separate cells, is offered a deal by the police—a light sentence if she confesses and implicates her accomplice but her accomplice does not do the same, a heavy sentence if she does not confess but her accomplice does, and so on. It is in the joint interest of both prisoners not to confess; it is in each one's individual interest to confess.

is clearly in the interest of the police to structure the payoffs so that confessing is a dominant strategy for each person. So as long as the two prisoners have no way to make an enforceable agreement that neither will confess (something they can't do if they can't communicate, and the police certainly won't allow them to do so because the police want to compel each one to confess), Thelma and Louise will each act in a way that hurts the other.

So if each prisoner acts rationally in her own interest, both will confess. Yet if neither of them had confessed, both would have received a much lighter sentence! In a prisoners' dilemma, each player has a clear incentive to act in a way that hurts the other player—but when both make that choice, it leaves both of them worse off.

When Thelma and Louise both confess, they reach an *equilibrium* of the game. We have used the concept of equilibrium many times in this book; it is an outcome in which no individual or firm has any incentive to change his or her action. In game theory, this kind of equilibrium, in which each player takes the action that is best for her given the actions taken by other players, and vice versa, is known as a **Nash equilibrium,** after the mathematician and Nobel laureate John Nash. (Nash's life was chronicled in the bestselling biography *A Beautiful Mind,* which was made into a movie starring Russell Crowe.) The players in a Nash equilibrium do not take into account the effect of their action on others; in a prisoners' dilemma the Nash equilibrium is also known as a *noncooperative equilibrium.*

Now look back at Figure 14-2: Nestlé and Mars are in the same situation as Thelma and Louise. Each firm is better off producing the higher output, regardless of what the other firm does. Yet if both produce 40 million kilograms, both are worse off than if they had followed their agreement and produced only 30 million kilograms. In both cases, then, the pursuit of individual self-interest—the effort to maximize profits or to minimize jail time—has the perverse effect of hurting both players.

Prisoners' dilemmas appear in many situations. The upcoming For Inquiring Minds describes an example from the days of the Cold War. Clearly, the players in any prisoners' dilemma would be better off if they had some way of enforcing cooperative behaviour—if Thelma and Louise had both sworn to a code of silence or if Nestlé and Mars had signed an enforceable agreement not to produce more than 30 million kilograms of chocolate.

But in Canada an agreement setting the output levels of two oligopolists isn't just unenforceable, it's illegal. So it seems that a noncooperative equilibrium is the only possible outcome. Or is it?

Overcoming the Prisoners' Dilemma: Repeated Interaction and Tacit Collusion

Thelma and Louise in their cells are playing what is known as a *one-shot* game—that is, they play the game with each other only once. They get to choose once and for all whether to confess or hang tough, and that's it. However, most of the games that oligopolists play aren't one-shot; instead, they expect to play the game repeatedly with the same rivals. An oligopolist usually expects to be in business for many years, and it knows that its decision today about whether to cheat is likely to affect the way other firms treat it in the future. So a smart oligopolist doesn't just decide what to do based on the effect on profit in the short run. Instead, it engages in **strategic behaviour,** taking account of the effects of the action it chooses today on the future actions of other players in the game. And under some conditions oligopolists that behave strategically can manage to behave as if they had a formal agreement to collude.

Suppose that Nestlé and Mars expect to be in the chocolate business for many years and therefore expect to play the game of cheat versus collude shown in Figure 14-2 many times. Would they really betray each other time and again?

Probably not. Suppose that Nestlé considers two strategies. In one strategy it always cheats, producing 40 million kilograms of chocolate each year, regardless of

PITFALLS

PLAYING FAIR IN THE PRISONERS' DILEMMA
One common reaction to the prisoners' dilemma is to assert that it isn't really rational for either prisoner to confess. Thelma wouldn't confess because she'd be afraid Louise would beat her up, or Thelma would feel guilty because Louise wouldn't do that to her.

But this kind of answer is, well, cheating—it amounts to changing the payoffs in the payoff matrix. To understand the dilemma, you have to play fair and imagine prisoners who care *only* about the length of their sentences.

Luckily, when it comes to oligopoly, it's a lot easier to believe that the firms care only about their profits. There is no indication that anyone at Nestlé felt either fear of or affection for Mars, or vice versa; it was strictly about business.

A **Nash equilibrium** results when each player in a game chooses the action that maximizes his or her payoff given the actions of other players, ignoring the effects of his or her action on the payoffs received by those other players.

A firm engages in **strategic behaviour** when it attempts to influence the future behaviour of other firms.

A strategy of **tit for tat** involves playing cooperatively at first, then doing whatever the other player did in the previous period.

what Mars does. In the other strategy, it starts with good behaviour, producing only 30 million kilograms in the first year, and watches to see what its rival does. If Mars also keeps its production down, Nestlé will stay cooperative, producing 30 million kilograms again for the next year. But if Mars produces 40 million kilograms, Nestlé will take the gloves off and also produce 40 million kilograms the next year. This latter strategy—start by behaving cooperatively, but thereafter do whatever the other player did in the previous period—is generally known as **tit for tat.**

Tit for tat is a form of strategic behaviour, which we have just defined as behaviour intended to influence the future actions of other players. Tit for tat offers a reward to the other player for cooperative behaviour—if you behave cooperatively, so will I. It also provides a punishment for cheating—if you cheat, don't expect me to be nice in the future.

The payoff to Nestlé of each of these strategies would depend on which strategy Mars chooses. Consider the four possibilities, shown in Figure 14-4:

1. If Nestlé plays tit for tat and so does Mars, both firms will make a profit of $180 million each year.

2. If Nestlé plays always cheat but Mars plays tit for tat, Nestlé makes a profit of $200 million the first year but only $160 million per year thereafter.

3. If Nestlé plays tit for tat but Mars plays always cheat, Nestlé makes a profit of only $150 million in the first year but $160 million per year thereafter.

4. If Nestlé plays always cheat and Mars does the same, both firms will make a profit of $160 million each year.

Which strategy is better? In the first year, Nestlé does better playing always cheat, whatever its rival's strategy: it assures itself that it will get either $200 million or $160 million (which of the two payoffs it actually receives depends on whether Mars plays tit for tat or always cheat). This is better than what it would get in the first year if it played tit for tat: either $180 million or $150 million. But by the second year, a strategy of always cheat gains Nestlé only $160 million per year for the second and all subsequent years, regardless of Mars's actions.

FIGURE 14-4 **How Repeated Interaction Can Support Collusion**

A strategy of tit for tat involves playing cooperatively at first, then following the other player's move. This rewards good behaviour and punishes bad behaviour. If the other player cheats, playing tit for tat will lead to only a short-term loss in comparison to playing always cheat. But if the other player plays tit for tat, also playing tit for tat leads to a long-term gain. So a firm that expects other firms to play tit for tat may well choose to do the same, leading to successful tacit collusion.

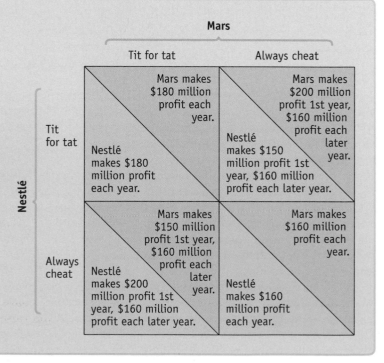

FOR INQUIRING MINDS

PRISONERS OF THE ARMS RACE

Between World War II and the late 1980s, the United States and its allies were locked in a seemingly endless struggle with the Soviet Union that never broke out into open war. During this Cold War, both sides spent huge sums on arms, sums that were a significant drain on the U.S. economy and eventually proved a crippling burden for the Soviet Union, whose underlying economic base was much weaker. Yet neither side was ever able to achieve a decisive military advantage.

As many people pointed out, both sides would have been better off if they had both spent less on arms. Yet the arms race continued for 40 years.

Why? As political scientists were quick to notice, one way to explain the arms race was to suppose that the two sides were locked in a classic prisoners' dilemma. Each government would have liked to achieve decisive military superiority, and each feared military inferiority. But both would have preferred a stalemate with low military spending to one with high spending. However, each

Caught in the prisoners' dilemma: heavy military spending hastened the collapse of the Soviet Union.

TASS/Sovfoto

government rationally chose to engage in high spending. If its rival did not spend heavily, its own high spending would lead to military superiority; not spending heav-

ily would lead to inferiority if the other government continued its arms buildup. Thus, both governments have the incentive to spend heavily on military because this is their best strategy regardless of the other government's action. The countries were trapped in an inferior outcome.

The answer to this trap could have been an agreement not to spend as much; indeed, the two sides tried repeatedly to negotiate limits on some kinds of weapons. But these agreements weren't very effective. In the end the issue was resolved as heavy military spending hastened the collapse of the Soviet Union in 1991.

Unfortunately, the logic of an arms race has not disappeared. A nuclear arms race has developed between Pakistan and India, neighbouring countries with a history of mutual antagonism. In 1998 the two countries confirmed the unrelenting logic of the prisoners' dilemma: both publicly tested their nuclear weapons in a tit-for-tat sequence, each seeking to prove to the other that it could inflict just as much damage as its rival.

Over time, the total amount gained by Nestlé by playing always cheat is less than the amount it would gain by playing tit for tat: for the second and all subsequent years, it would never get any less than $160 million and would get as much as $180 million if Mars played tit for tat as well. Which strategy, always cheat or tit for tat, is more profitable depends on two things: how many years Nestlé expects to play the game and what strategy its rival follows.

If Nestlé expects the chocolate business to end in the near future, it is in effect playing a one-shot game. So it might as well cheat and grab what it can. Even if Nestlé expects to remain in the chocolate business for many years (therefore to find itself repeatedly playing this game with Mars) and, for some reason, expects Mars always to cheat, it should also always cheat. That is, Nestlé should follow the old rule "Do unto others before they do unto you."

But if Nestlé expects to be in the business for a long time and thinks Mars is likely to play tit for tat, it will make more profits over the long run by playing tit for tat, too. It could have made some extra short-term profits by cheating at the beginning, but this would provoke Mars into cheating, too, and would, in the end, mean lower profits.

The lesson of this story is that when oligopolists expect to compete with one another over an extended period of time, each individual firm will often conclude that it is in its own best interest to be helpful to the other firms in the industry. So it will restrict its output in a way that raises the profits of the other firms, expecting them to return the favour. Despite the fact that firms have no way of making an enforceable cooperative agreement to limit output and raise prices (and are in legal jeopardy if they even discuss prices), they manage to act "as if" they had such an agreement. When this happens, we say that firms engage in **tacit collusion.**

When firms limit production and raise prices in a way that raises one another's profits, even though they have not made any formal cooperative agreement, they are engaged in **tacit collusion.**

ECONOMICS > IN ACTION

THE RISE AND FALL AND RISE OF OPEC

It is in OPEC's interest to keep oil prices high and output low.

Call it the cartel that does not need to meet in secret. The Organization of Petroleum Exporting Countries, usually referred to as OPEC, includes 12 national governments (Algeria, Angola, Ecuador, Iran, Iraq, Kuwait, Libya, Nigeria, Qatar, Saudi Arabia, the United Arab Emirates, and Venezuela), and it controls 40% of the world's oil exports and 80% of its proven reserves. Two other oil-exporting countries, Norway and Mexico, are not formally part of the cartel but act as if they were. (Russia, also an important oil exporter, has not yet become part of the club.) Unlike corporations, which are often legally prohibited by governments from reaching agreements about production and prices, national governments can talk about whatever they feel like. OPEC members routinely meet to try to set targets for production.

These nations are not particularly friendly with one another. Indeed, OPEC members Iraq and Iran fought a spectacularly bloody war with each other in the 1980s. And, in 1990, Iraq invaded another member, Kuwait. (A mainly non-OPEC force based in yet another OPEC member, Saudi Arabia, drove the Iraqis out of Kuwait.)

Yet the members of OPEC, whether they like one another or not, are effectively players in a game with repeated interactions. In any given year it is in their combined interest to keep output low and prices high. But it is also in the interest of any one producer to cheat and produce more than the agreed-upon quota—unless that producer believes that its actions will bring future retaliation.

So how successful is the cartel? Well, it's had its ups and downs. Analysts have estimated that of 12 announced quota reductions, OPEC was able to successfully defend its price floor 80% of the time.

Figure 14-5 shows the price of oil in constant dollars (that is, the value of a barrel of oil in terms of other goods) since 1949. OPEC first demonstrated its muscle in 1974: in the aftermath of a war in the Middle East, several OPEC producers limited their output—and they liked the results so much that they decided to continue the practice. Following a second wave of turmoil in the aftermath of Iran's 1979 revolution, prices shot still higher.

By the mid-1980s, however, there was a growing glut of oil on world markets, and cheating by cash-short OPEC members became widespread. The result, in 1985, was that producers who had tried to play by the rules—especially Saudi Arabia, the largest producer—got fed up, and collusion collapsed.

The cartel began to act effectively again at the end of the 1990s, thanks largely to the efforts of Mexico's oil minister to orchestrate output reductions. The cartel's actions helped raise the price of oil from less than $10 a barrel in 1998 to a range of $20 to $30 a barrel in 2003.

Since 2008, OPEC has experienced the steepest roller-coaster ride of oil prices in its history. By 2008, prices had soared to over $145 a barrel. But at the end of 2008, one year into the Great Recession of 2007–2009, the price dropped sharply to $32 a barrel. In response, producers committed to reduce their output by about 5% of global output, with Saudi Arabia, the world's largest exporter, leading with cuts of

FIGURE 14-5 Crude Oil Prices, 1949–2011 (in Constant 2005 U.S. Dollars)

Price of crude oil (per barrel)

- $100
- 80
- 60
- 40
- 20
- 0

Yom Kippur War
Arab oil embargo
Iranian Revolution
Iran–Iraq War
OPEC 10% quota increase
Gulf War
Series of OPEC output cuts
9/11/01
Recession
Rising world demand and Middle East tensions

1949 1960 1970 1980 1990 2000 2011 Year

Source: Energy Information Administration.

20% of its output. By early 2009, prices had begun to rebound. Most recently, OPEC has struggled to contain its success. In 2011 political turmoil in several Middle Eastern countries caused prices to skyrocket again. With other producers unwilling or unable to increase their production, in June 2011 Saudi Arabia increased its output in order to prevent shortages in the global oil market.

CHECK YOUR UNDERSTANDING   14-3

1. Find the Nash equilibrium actions for the following payoff matrix. Which actions maximize the total payoff of Nikita and Margaret? Why is it unlikely that they will choose those actions without some communication?

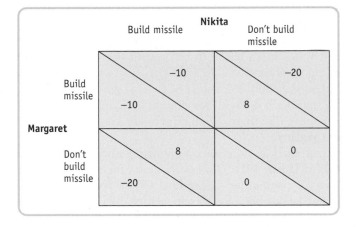

2. Which of the following factors make it more likely that oligopolists will play noncooperatively? Which make it more likely that they will engage in tacit collusion? Explain.
   a. Each oligopolist expects several new firms to enter the market in the future.
   b. It is very difficult for a firm to detect whether another firm has raised output.
   c. The firms have coexisted while maintaining high prices for a long time.

Solutions appear at back of book.

Oligopoly in Practice

In an Economics in Action earlier in the chapter, we described how the five leading manufacturers of lysine were allegedly colluding to significantly raise prices for many years. Collusion is not, fortunately, the norm. But how do oligopolies usually work in practice? The answer depends both on the legal framework that limits what firms can do and on the underlying ability of firms in a given industry to cooperate without formal agreements.

The Legal Framework

To understand oligopoly pricing in practice, we must be familiar with the legal constraints under which oligopolistic firms operate. In North America, oligopoly first became an issue during the second half of the nineteenth century, when the growth of railroads—themselves an oligopolistic industry—created a national market for many goods. Large firms producing oil, steel, and many other products soon emerged. The industrialists quickly realized that profits would be higher if they could limit price competition. So many industries formed cartels—that is, they signed formal agreements to limit production and raise prices. This was perfectly legal until 1889, when the first federal legislation against such cartels (Canada's first competition law) was passed. A similar law in the United States followed in 1890.

Competition or **antitrust policy** consists of efforts undertaken by the government to prevent oligopolistic industries from becoming or behaving like monopolies.

However, although these cartels were legal before 1889, they weren't legally *enforceable*—members of a cartel couldn't ask the courts to force a firm that was violating its agreement to reduce its production. And firms often did violate their agreements, for the reason already suggested by our duopoly example: there is always a temptation for each firm in a cartel to produce more than it is supposed to.

In 1881 clever lawyers at John D. Rockefeller's Standard Oil Company came up with a solution—the so-called trust. In a trust, shareholders of all the major companies in an industry placed their shares in the hands of a board of trustees who controlled the companies. This, in effect, merged the companies into a single firm that could then engage in monopoly pricing. In this way, the Standard Oil Trust established what was essentially an American monopoly of the oil industry, and it was soon followed by trusts in U.S. sugar, whiskey, lead, cottonseed oil, and linseed oil industries.

Eventually there was a public backlash, driven partly by concern about the economic effects of the trust movement, and partly by fear that the owners of the trusts were simply becoming too powerful. The result was the American Sherman Antitrust Act of 1890, which was intended both to prevent the creation of more monopolies and to break up existing ones. At first this law went largely unenforced. But over the decades that followed, the U.S. federal government became increasingly committed to making it difficult for oligopolistic industries either to become monopolies or to behave like them. Such efforts are known to this day as **competition** or **antitrust policy.**

One of the most striking early actions of competition and antitrust policy was the breakup of Standard Oil in 1911. (Its components formed the nuclei of many of today's large U.S. oil companies—Standard Oil of New York became Mobil, Standard Oil of New Jersey became Exxon, which has owned Canada's Imperial Oil since 1898, and so on.) In the 1980s, while Bell Canada was losing its telephone monopoly via government deregulation, a long-running case led to the breakup of Bell Telephone in the United States, which once had a monopoly of both local and long-distance phone service. As we mentioned earlier, the competition and antitrust regulators review proposed mergers between companies in the same industry and will bar mergers that they believe will reduce competition.

Among economically advanced countries, Canada and the United States are unique in their long tradition of competition and antitrust policy. Until recently, other countries did not have policies against price-fixing, and some had even supported the creation of cartels, believing that it would help their own firms against foreign rivals. But the situation has changed radically over the past 25 years, as the EU—a supra national body tasked with enforcing antitrust policy for its member countries—has converged toward North American practices. Today, Canadian, American, and European regulators often target the same firms because price-fixing has "gone global" as international trade has expanded.

During the early 1990s, the United States instituted an amnesty program in which a price-fixer receives a much-reduced penalty if it informs on its co-conspirators. In 2000, the Canadian Competition Bureau introduced its own leniency or amnesty program. In addition, both countries have substantially increased maximum fines levied upon conviction. In the recent amendments to the Competition Act, the maximum monetary fine has been increased to $25 million and the maximum prison sentence has been lengthened to 14 years. These two new policies clearly made informing on your cartel partners a dominant strategy, and it has paid off: in recent years, executives from Belgium, Britain, France, Germany, Italy, Mexico, the Netherlands, South Korea, Switzerland, and the United States, as well as from Canada, have been convicted in courts in Canada and the United States of cartel crimes. As one lawyer commented, "you get a race to the courthouse" as each conspirator seeks to be the first to come clean.

Life has gotten much tougher over the past few years if you want to operate a cartel. So what's an oligopolist to do?

"Frankly, I'm dubious about amalgamated smelting and refining pleading innocent to their anti-trust violation due to insanity."

CONTRASTING APPROACHES TO COMPETITION REGULATION

In the European Union, a competition commission enforces competition and antitrust regulation for the 28 member nations. The commission has the authority to block mergers, force companies to sell subsidiaries, and impose heavy fines if it determines that companies have acted unfairly to inhibit competition. Although companies are able to dispute charges at a hearing once a complaint has been issued, if the commission feels that its own case is convincing, it rules against the firm and levies a penalty. Companies that believe they have been unfairly treated have only limited recourse. Critics complain that the commission acts as prosecutor, judge, and jury.

In contrast, charges of unfair competition in Canada and the United States must be made in court, where lawyers for the Attorney General of Canada (supported by the Competition Bureau) or the United States Federal Trade Commission have to present their evidence to independent judges. Companies employ legions of highly trained and highly paid lawyers to counter the government's case. For Canadian and American regulators, there is no guarantee of success. In fact, judges in many cases have found in favour of companies and against the regulators. Moreover, compa-

nies can appeal unfavourable decisions, so reaching a final verdict can take several years.

Between 2009 and 2011, the average criminal fine imposed by the U.S. Department of Justice (as a percentage of American gross domestic product) was five times larger than the average criminal fine imposed by the Competition Bureau (as a percentage of Canadian GDP). But during the same time period the average criminal fine imposed by the European Union (as a percentage of GDP) was three times larger than the U.S. average. Not surprisingly, companies prefer the North American systems.

Observers, however, criticize both systems for their inadequacies. In the slow-moving, litigious, and expensive North American systems, consumers and rival companies may wait a very long time to secure protection. And companies often prevail, raising questions about how well consumers are protected. But some charge that the EU system gives inadequate protection to companies that are accused. This is a particular concern in high-tech industries, where network externalities are strong and rivals can use complaints of unfair competition to hobble their competitors.

Tacit Collusion and Price Wars

If a real industry were as simple as our chocolate example, it probably wouldn't be necessary for the company presidents to meet or do anything that could land them in jail. Both firms would realize that it was in their mutual interest to restrict output to 30 million kilograms each and that any short-term gains to either firm from producing more would be much less than the later losses as the other firm retaliated. So even without any explicit agreement, the firms would probably achieve the tacit collusion needed to maximize their combined profits.

Real industries are nowhere near that simple. Nonetheless, in most oligopolistic industries, most of the time, the sellers do appear to succeed in keeping prices above their noncooperative level. Tacit collusion, in other words, is the normal state of oligopoly.

Although tacit collusion is common, it rarely allows an industry to push prices all the way up to their monopoly level; collusion is usually far from perfect. (Tacit collusion is illegal in Canada to the extent that an "arrangement" or understanding between firms can be proven, which is not an easy task.) As we discuss next, a variety of factors make it hard for an industry to coordinate on high prices.

Less Concentration In a less concentrated industry, the typical firm will have a smaller market share than in a more concentrated industry. This tilts firms toward noncooperative behaviour because when a smaller firm cheats and increases its output, it gains for itself all of the profit from the higher output. And if its rivals should retaliate by increasing their output, the firm's losses are limited because of its relatively modest market share. A less concentrated industry is often an indication that there are low barriers to entry.

Complex Products and Pricing Schemes In our chocolate example the two firms produce only one product. In reality, however, oligopolists often sell thousands or even tens of thousands of different products. Under these circumstances, keeping track of what other firms are producing and what prices they are charging is difficult. This makes it hard to determine whether a firm is cheating on the tacit agreement.

Differences in Interests In the chocolate example, a tacit agreement for the firms to split the market equally is a natural outcome, probably acceptable to both firms. In real industries, however, firms often differ both in their perceptions about what is fair and in their real interests.

For example, suppose that Mars was a long-established chocolate producer and Nestlé a more recent entrant to the industry. Mars might feel that it deserved to continue producing more than Nestlé, but Nestlé might feel that it was entitled to 50% of the business. (A disagreement along these lines was one of the contentious issues in those meetings the FBI filmed in the lysine price-fixing case.)

Alternatively, suppose that Nestlé's marginal costs were lower than Mars's. Even if they could agree on market shares, they would then disagree about the profit-maximizing level of output.

Bargaining Power of Buyers Often oligopolists sell not to individual consumers but to large buyers—other industrial enterprises, nationwide chains of stores, and so on. These large buyers are in a position to bargain for lower prices from the oligopolists: they can ask for a discount from an oligopolist and warn that they will go to a competitor if they don't get it. An important reason large retailers like Loblaws and Walmart are able to offer lower prices to customers than small retailers is precisely their ability to use their size to extract lower prices from their suppliers.

These difficulties in enforcing tacit collusion have sometimes led companies to defy the law and create illegal cartels. We've already examined the cases of the chocolate industry and the lysine industry. An older, classic example was the U.S. electrical equipment conspiracy of the 1950s, which led to the indictment of and jail sentences for some executives. The industry was one in which tacit collusion was especially difficult because of all the reasons just mentioned. There were many firms—40 companies were indicted. They produced a very complex array of products, often more or less custom-built for particular clients. They differed greatly in size, from giants like General Electric to family firms with only a few dozen employees. And the customers in many cases were large buyers like electrical utilities, which would normally try to force suppliers to compete for their business. Tacit collusion just didn't seem practical—so executives met secretly and illegally for decades to decide who would bid what price for which contract.

Because tacit collusion is often hard to achieve, most oligopolies charge prices that are well below what the same industry would charge if it were controlled by a monopolist—or what they would charge if they were able to collude explicitly. In addition, sometimes collusion breaks down and there is a **price war.** A price war sometimes involves simply a collapse of prices to their noncooperative level. Sometimes they even go *below* that level, as sellers try to put each other out of business or at least punish what they regard as cheating.

Product Differentiation and Price Leadership

Lysine is lysine: there was no question in anyone's mind that ADM and Ajinomoto were producing the same good and that consumers would make their decision about which company's lysine to buy based on the price.

In many oligopolies, however, firms produce products that consumers regard as similar but not identical. A $10 difference in the price won't make many customers switch from a Ford to a Chrysler, or vice versa. Sometimes the differences between products are real, like differences between KitKat and Snickers; sometimes, like differences between brands of vodka (which is supposed to be

A **price war** occurs when tacit collusion breaks down and prices collapse.

tasteless), they exist mainly in the minds of consumers. Either way, the effect is to reduce the intensity of competition among the firms: consumers will not all rush to buy whichever product is cheapest.

As you might imagine, oligopolists welcome the extra market power that comes when consumers think that their product is different from that of competitors. So in many oligopolistic industries, firms make considerable efforts to create the perception that their product is different—that is, they engage in **product differentiation.**

A firm that tries to differentiate its product may do so by altering what it actually produces, adding "extras," or choosing a different design. It may also use advertising and marketing campaigns to create a differentiation in the minds of consumers, even though its product is more or less identical to the products of rivals.

A classic case of how products may be perceived as different even when they are really pretty much the same is over-the-counter medication. For many years there were only three widely sold pain relievers—aspirin, ibuprofen, and acetaminophen. Yet these generic pain relievers were marketed under a number of brand names, each brand using a marketing campaign implying some special superiority (one classic slogan was "contains the pain reliever doctors recommend most"—that is, aspirin).

Whatever the nature of product differentiation, oligopolists producing differentiated products often reach a tacit understanding not to compete on price. For example, during the years when the great majority of cars sold in North America were produced by the Big Three auto companies (General Motors, Ford, and Chrysler), there was an unwritten rule that none of the three companies would try to gain market share by making its cars noticeably cheaper than those of the other two.

But then who would decide on the overall price of cars? The answer was normally General Motors: as the biggest of the three, it would announce its prices for the year first, and the other companies would match it. This pattern of behaviour, in which one company tacitly sets prices for the industry as a whole, is known as **price leadership.** In the years following the dismantling of the U.S. electrical equipment cartel, General Electric became the price leader in its industry.

Interestingly, firms that have a tacit agreement not to compete on price often engage in vigorous **nonprice competition**—adding new features to their products, spending large sums on ads that proclaim the inferiority of their rivals' offerings, and so on.

Perhaps the best way to understand the mix of cooperation and competition in such industries is with a political analogy. During the long Cold War, the United States and the Soviet Union engaged in intense rivalry for global influence. They not only provided financial and military aid to their allies; they sometimes supported forces trying to overthrow governments allied with their rival (as the Soviet Union did in Vietnam in the 1960s and early 1970s, and as the United States did in Afghanistan from 1979 until the collapse of the Soviet Union in 1991). They even sent their own soldiers to support allied governments against rebels (as the United States did in Vietnam and the Soviet Union did in Afghanistan). But they did not get into direct military confrontations with each other; open warfare between the two superpowers was regarded by both as too dangerous—and tacitly avoided.

Price wars aren't as serious as shooting wars, but the principle is the same.

How Important Is Oligopoly?

We have seen that, across industries, oligopoly is far more common than either perfect competition or monopoly. When we try to analyze oligopoly, the economist's usual way of thinking—asking how self-interested individuals would behave, then analyzing their interaction—does not work as well as we might

Product differentiation is an attempt by a firm to convince buyers that its product is different from the products of other firms in the industry.

In **price leadership,** one firm sets its price first, and other firms then follow.

Firms that have a tacit understanding not to compete on price often engage in intense **nonprice competition,** using advertising and other means to try to increase their sales.

hope because we do not know whether rival firms will engage in noncooperative behaviour or manage to engage in some kind of collusion. Given the prevalence of oligopoly, then, is the analysis we developed in earlier chapters, which was based on perfect competition, still useful?

The conclusion of the great majority of economists is yes. For one thing, important parts of the economy are fairly well described by perfect competition. And even though many industries are oligopolistic, in many cases the limits to collusion keep prices relatively close to marginal costs—in other words, the industry behaves "almost" as if it were perfectly competitive.

It is also true that predictions from supply and demand analysis are often valid for oligopolies. For example, in Chapter 5 we saw that price controls will produce shortages. Strictly speaking, this conclusion is certain only for perfectly competitive industries. But in the 1970s, when the U.S. government imposed price controls on the definitely oligopolistic oil industry, the result was indeed to produce shortages and lines at the gas pumps.

So how important is it to take account of oligopoly? Most economists adopt a pragmatic approach. As we have seen in this chapter, the analysis of oligopoly is far more difficult and messy than that of perfect competition; so in situations where they do not expect the complications associated with oligopoly to be crucial, economists prefer to adopt the working assumption of perfectly competitive markets. They always keep in mind the possibility that oligopoly might be important; they recognize that there are important issues, from competition policies to price wars, where trying to understand oligopolistic behaviour is crucial.

We will follow the same approach in the chapters that follow.

ECONOMICS ➤ *IN ACTION*

THE PRICE WARS OF CHRISTMAS

During the last several holiday seasons, the toy aisles of North American retailers have been the scene of cutthroat competition. During the 2011 Christmas shopping season, Target priced the latest Elmo doll at 89 cents less than Walmart (for those with a coupon), and $6 less than Toys "R" Us. So extreme is the price-cutting that since 2003 three U.S. toy retailers—KB Toys, FAO Schwartz, and Zany Brainy—have been forced into bankruptcy. Due to aggressive price-cutting by Walmart, the market share of Toys "R" Us has fallen from first to third.

Canadian retailers, like this one in London, Ontario, offer Black Friday sales to keep customers from travelling to the United States.

What is happening? The turmoil can be traced back to trouble in the toy industry itself as well as to changes in toy retailing. Every year for several years, overall toy sales have fallen a few percentage points as children increasingly turn to video games and the Internet. There have also been new entrants into the toy business: Walmart and Target have expanded their number of stores and have been aggressive price-cutters. The result is much like a story of tacit collusion sustained by repeated interaction run in reverse: because the overall industry is in a state of decline and there are new entrants, the future payoff from collusion is shrinking. The predictable outcome is a price war.

Since toy retailers depend on holiday sales for nearly half of their annual sales, the holidays are a time of particularly intense price-cutting. In the United States, the biggest shopping day of the year has traditionally been the day after Thanksgiving: Black Friday. But in an effort to expand sales and undercut rivals, retailers—particularly Walmart—have now begun their price-cutting earlier in the fall. Now it begins in early November, well before American Thanksgiving. In fact, in 2010, Walmart slashed its toy prices in early November to within a few cents of Target's prices. In response, Target placed about half of its 2000 toys on sale, double the amount in the previous year. Toys "R" Us instead relied on a selection of exclusive toys to avoid direct price competition. The seasonal price-cutting is also spreading into Canada. Competition from cross-border shopping has forced Canadian retailers to offer Black Friday sales in order to keep shoppers in Canada.

With other retailers feeling as if they have no choice but to follow this pattern, we have the phenomenon known as "creeping Christmas": the price wars of Christmas arrive earlier each year.

CHECK YOUR UNDERSTANDING 14-4

1. Which of the following factors are likely to support the conclusion that there is tacit collusion in this industry? Which are not? Explain.
   a. For many years the price in the industry has changed infrequently, and all the firms in the industry charge the same price. The largest firm publishes a catalogue containing a "suggested" retail price. Changes in price coincide with changes in the catalogue.
   b. There has been considerable variation in the market shares of the firms in the industry over time.
   c. Firms in the industry build into their products unnecessary features that make it hard for consumers to switch from one company's products to another company's products.
   d. Firms meet yearly to discuss their annual sales forecasts.
   e. Firms tend to adjust their prices upward at the same times.

Solutions appear at back of book.

BUSINESS CASE : Virgin Atlantic Blows the Whistle ... or Blows It?

The United Kingdom is home to two long-haul airline carriers (carriers that fly between continents): British Airways and its rival, Virgin Atlantic. Although British Airways is the dominant company, with a market share generally between 50% and 100% on routes between London and various American cities, Virgin has been a tenacious competitor.

The rivalry between the two has ranged from relatively peaceable to openly hostile over the years. In the 1990s, British Airways lost a court case alleging it had engaged in "dirty tricks" to drive Virgin out of business. In April 2010, however, British Airways may well have wondered if the tables had been turned.

It all began in mid-July 2004, when oil prices were rising (long-haul airlines are especially vulnerable to oil price hikes). British prosecutors alleged that the two airlines had plotted to levy fuel surcharges on passengers. For the next two years, according to the prosecutors, the rivals had established a cartel through which they coordinated increases in surcharges. British Airways first introduced a £5 ($12) surcharge on long-haul flights when a barrel of oil traded at about $50. It increased the surcharge six times, so that by 2006, when oil was trading at about $75 a barrel, the surcharge was £70 ($145). At the same time, Virgin Atlantic also levied a £70 fee. These surcharges increased within days of each other.

Eventually, three Virgin executives decided to blow the whistle in exchange for immunity from prosecution. British Airways immediately suspended its executives under suspicion and paid fines of nearly $550 million to U.S. and U.K. authorities. And in 2010 four British Airways executives were prosecuted by British authorities for their alleged role in the conspiracy.

The lawyers for the executives argued that although the two airlines had swapped information, this was not proof of a criminal conspiracy. In fact, they argued, Virgin was so fearful of American regulators that it had admitted to criminal behaviour before confirming that it had indeed committed an offense. One of the defense lawyers, Clare Montgomery, argued that because U.S. laws against anti-competitive behaviour are much tougher than those in the United Kingdom, companies may be compelled to blow the whistle to avoid investigation. "It's a race," she said. "If you don't get to them and confess first, you can't get immunity. The only way to protect yourself is to go to the authorities, even if you haven't [done anything]." The result was that the Virgin executives were given immunity in both the United States and the United Kingdom, but the British Airways executives were subject to prosecution (and possible multi-year jail terms) in both countries.

In late 2011 the case came to a shocking end—shocking, that is, for Virgin Atlantic and U.K. authorities. Citing emails that Virgin had finally been forced by the court to turn over, the judge found insufficient evidence that there had ever been a conspiracy between the two airlines. The court was incensed enough to threaten to rescind the immunity granted to the three Virgin executives.

QUESTIONS FOR THOUGHT

1. Explain why Virgin Atlantic and British Airlines might collude in response to increased oil prices. Was the market conducive to collusion or not?

2. How would you determine whether illegal behaviour actually occurred? What might explain these events other than illegal behaviour?

3. Explain the dilemma facing the two airlines as well as their individual executives.

SUMMARY

1. Many industries are **oligopolies**: there are only a few sellers. In particular, a **duopoly** has only two sellers. Oligopolies exist for more or less the same reasons that monopolies exist, but in weaker form. They are characterized by **imperfect competition**: firms compete but possess market power.

2. Predicting the behaviour of **oligopolists** poses something of a puzzle. The firms in an oligopoly could maximize their combined profits by acting as a **cartel**, setting output levels for each firm as if they were a single monopolist; to the extent that firms manage to do this, they engage in **collusion.** But each individual firm has an incentive to produce more than it would in such an arrangement—to engage in **noncooperative behaviour.**

3. The situation of **interdependence,** in which each firm's profit depends noticeably on what other firms do, is the subject of **game theory.** In the case of a game with two players, the **payoff** of each player depends both on its own actions and on the actions of the other; this interdependence can be represented as a **payoff matrix.** Depending on the structure of payoffs in the payoff matrix, a player may have a **dominant strategy**—an action that is always the best regardless of the other player's actions.

4. **Duopolists** face a particular type of game known as a **prisoners' dilemma;** if each acts independently in its own interest, the resulting **Nash equilibrium** will be bad for both. However, firms that expect to play a game repeatedly tend to engage in **strategic behaviour,** trying to influence each other's future actions. A particular strategy that seems to work well in maintaining **tacit collusion** is **tit for tat.**

5. In order to limit the ability of oligopolists to collude and act like monopolists, most governments pursue a **competition** or an **antitrust policy** designed to make collusion more difficult. In practice, however, tacit collusion is widespread.

6. A variety of factors make tacit collusion difficult: large numbers of firms, complex products and pricing, differences in interests, and bargaining power of buyers. When tacit collusion breaks down, there is a **price war.** Oligopolists try to avoid price wars in various ways, such as through **product differentiation** and through **price leadership,** in which one firm sets prices for the industry. Another is through **nonprice competition,** like advertising.

KEY TERMS

Oligopoly, p. 442
Oligopolist, p. 442
Imperfect competition, p. 442
Duopoly, p. 444
Duopolist, p. 444
Collusion, p. 445
Cartel, p. 445
Noncooperative behaviour, p. 447

Interdependence, p. 448
Game theory, p. 448
Payoff, p. 449
Payoff matrix, p. 449
Prisoners' dilemma, p. 449
Dominant strategy, p. 450
Nash equilibrium, p. 451
Strategic behaviour, p. 451

Tit for tat, p. 452
Tacit collusion, p. 453
Competition or antitrust policy, p. 456
Price war, p. 458
Product differentiation, p. 459
Price leadership, p. 459
Nonprice competition, p. 459

PROBLEMS

1. The accompanying table presents recent market share data for the world breakfast cereal market.
   a. Use the data provided to calculate the Herfindahl–Hirschman Index (HHI) for the market.
   b. Based on this HHI, what type of market structure is the world breakfast cereal market?

Company	Market Share
Kellogg's	32.1%
General Mills	10.6
Cereal Partners Worldwide	9.8
PepsiCo (Quaker Oats)	8.6
Ralcorp Holdings (Post)	4.5

Source: Euromonitor 2011.

2. The accompanying table shows the demand schedule for vitamin D. Suppose that the marginal cost of producing vitamin D is zero.

Price of vitamin D (per tonne)	Quantity of vitamin D demanded (tonnes)
$8	0
7	10
6	20
5	30
4	40
3	50
2	60
1	70

a. Assume that BASF is the only producer of vitamin D and acts as a monopolist. It currently produces 40 tonnes of vitamin D at $4 per tonne. If BASF were to produce 10 more tonnes, what would be the price effect for BASF? What would be the quantity effect? Would BASF have an incentive to produce those 10 additional tonnes?

b. Now assume that Roche enters the market by also producing vitamin D and the market is now a duopoly. BASF and Roche agree to produce 40 tonnes of vitamin D in total, 20 tonnes each. BASF cannot be punished for deviating from the agreement with Roche. If BASF, on its own, were to deviate from that agreement and produce 10 more tonnes, what would be the price effect for BASF? What would be the quantity effect for BASF? Would BASF have an incentive to produce those 10 additional tonnes?

3. The market for honey in Winnipeg is controlled by two companies, Busy Bees and Honey Hive. Both companies will ruthlessly eliminate any other company that attempts to enter the Winnipeg honey market. The marginal cost of producing honey is constant and equal to $40 per kilogram. There is no fixed cost. The accompanying table gives the market demand schedule for honey.

Price of honey (per kilogram)	Quantity of honey demanded (kilograms)
$100	1000
90	1500
80	2000
70	2500
60	3000
50	3500
40	4000
30	4500
20	5000
10	5500

a. Suppose Busy Bees and Honey Hive form a cartel. For each of the quantities given in the table, calcu-late the total revenue for their cartel and the marginal revenue for each additional kilogram. How many kilograms of honey would the cartel sell in total and at what price? The two companies share the market equally (each produces half of the total output of the cartel). How much profit does each company make?

b. Beatrice Buzz, the CEO of Busy Bees, breaks the agreement and sells 500 more kilograms of honey than under the cartel agreement. Assuming Honey Hive maintain the agreement, how does this affect the price for honey and the profit earned by each company?

c. Quincy Queen, the CEO of Honey Hive, decides to punish Busy Bees by increasing his sales by 500 kilograms as well. How much profit does each company earn now?

4. In France, the market for bottled water is controlled by two large firms, Perrier and Evian. Each firm has a fixed cost of €1 million and a constant marginal cost of €2 per litre of bottled water (€1 = 1 euro). The following table gives the market demand schedule for bottled water in France.

Price of bottled water (per litre)	Quantity of bottled water demanded (millions of litres)
€10	0
9	1
8	2
7	3
6	4
5	5
4	6
3	7
2	8
1	9

a. Suppose the two firms form a cartel and act as a monopolist. Calculate marginal revenue for the cartel. What will the monopoly price and output be? Assuming the firms divide the output evenly, how much will each produce and what will each firm's profit be?

b. Now suppose Perrier decides to increase production by 1 million litres. Evian doesn't change its production. What will the new market price and output be? What is Perrier's profit? What is Evian's profit?

c. What if Perrier increases production by 3 million litres? Evian doesn't change its production. What would its output and profit be relative to those in part (b)?

d. What do your results tell you about the likelihood of cheating on such agreements?

5. To preserve the North Atlantic fish stocks, it is decided that only two fishing fleets, one from North America (Canada and the United States) and the other from the

European Union (EU), can fish in those waters. The accompanying table shows the market demand schedule per week for fish from these waters. The only costs are fixed costs, so fishing fleets maximize profit by maximizing revenue.

Price of fish (per kilogram)	Quantity of fish demanded (kilograms)
$17	1800
16	2000
15	2100
14	2200
12	2300

a. If both fishing fleets collude, what is the revenue-maximizing output for the North Atlantic fishery? What price will a kilogram of fish sell for?

b. If both fishing fleets collude and share the output equally, what is the revenue to the EU fleet? To the North American fleet?

c. Suppose the EU fleet cheats by expanding its own catch by 100 kilograms per week. The North American fleet doesn't change its catch. What is the revenue to the North American fleet? To the EU fleet?

d. In retaliation for the cheating by the EU fleet, the North American fleet also expands its catch by 100 kilograms per week. What is the revenue to the North American fleet? To the EU fleet?

6. Suppose that the fisheries agreement in Problem 5 breaks down, so that the fleets behave noncooperatively. Assume that North America and the EU each can send out either one or two fleets. The more fleets in the area, the more fish they catch in total but the catch of each fleet decreases. The accompanying matrix shows the profit (in dollars) per week earned by each side.

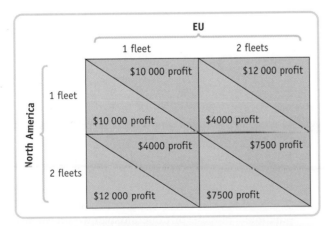

a. What is the Nash equilibrium? Will each side choose to send out one or two fleets?

b. Suppose that the fish stocks are being depleted. Each region considers the future and comes to a tit-for-tat agreement whereby each side will send only one fleet out as long as the other does the same.

If either of them breaks the agreement and sends out a second fleet, the other will also send out two and will continue to do so until its competitor sends out only one fleet. If both play this tit-for-tat strategy, how much profit will each make every week?

7. Maple Sky and North Jet are the only two airlines operating flights between Petiteville and Bigtown. That is, they operate in a duopoly. Each airline can charge either a high price or a low price for a ticket. The accompanying matrix shows their payoffs, in profits per seat (in dollars), for any choice that the two airlines can make.

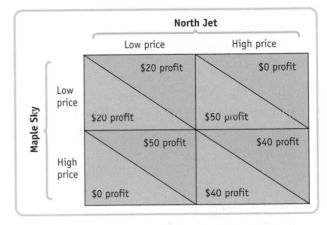

a. Suppose the two airlines play a one-shot game—that is, they interact only once and never again. What will be the Nash equilibrium in this one-shot game?

b. Now suppose the two airlines play this game twice. And suppose each airline can play one of two strategies: it can play either always charge the low price or tit for tat—that is, it starts off charging the high price in the first period, and then in the second period it does whatever the other airline did in the previous period. Write down the payoffs to Maple Sky from the following four possibilities:

   i. Maple Sky plays always charge the low price when North Jet also plays always charge the low price.

   ii. Maple Sky plays always charge the low price when North Jet plays tit for tat.

   iii. Maple Sky plays tit for tat when North Jet plays always charge the low price.

   iv. Maple Sky plays tit for tat when North Jet also plays tit for tat.

8. Suppose that Coke and Pepsi are the only two producers of cola drinks, making them duopolists. Both companies have zero marginal cost and a fixed cost of $100 000.

a. Assume first that consumers regard Coke and Pepsi as perfect substitutes. Currently both are sold for $0.20 per can, and at that price each company sells 4 million cans per day.

   i. How large is Pepsi's profit?

   ii. If Pepsi were to raise its price to $0.30 per can, and Coke does not respond, what would happen to Pepsi's profit?

b. Now suppose that each company advertises to differentiate its product from the other company's. As a result of advertising, Pepsi realizes that if it raises or lowers its price, it will sell less or more of its product, as shown by the demand schedule in the accompanying table.

Price of Pepsi (per can)	Quantity of Pepsi demanded (millions of cans)
$0.10	5
0.20	4
0.30	3
0.40	2
0.50	1

If Pepsi now were to raise its price to $0.30 per can, what would happen to its profit?

c. Comparing your answers from parts (a) and (b), what is the maximum amount Pepsi would be willing to spend on advertising?

9. Second Cup and Starbucks spend huge sums of money each year to advertise their coffee products in an attempt to steal customers from each other. Suppose each year Second Cup and Starbucks have to decide whether or not they want to spend money on advertising. If neither firm advertises, each will earn a profit of $2 million. If they both advertise, each will earn a profit of $1.5 million. If one firm advertises and the other does not, the firm that advertises will earn a profit of $2.8 million and the other firm will earn $1 million.

a. Use a payoff matrix to depict this problem.

b. Suppose Second Cup and Starbucks can write an enforceable contract about what they will do. What is the cooperative solution to this game?

c. What is the Nash equilibrium without an enforceable contract? Explain why this is the likely outcome.

10. Over the last 40 years the Organization of Petroleum Exporting Countries (OPEC) has had varied success in forming and maintaining its cartel agreements. Explain how the following factors may contribute to the difficulty of forming and/or maintaining its price and output agreements.

a. New oil fields are discovered and increased drilling is undertaken in the Gulf of Mexico and the North Sea by nonmembers of OPEC.

b. Crude oil is a product that is differentiated by sulphur content: it costs less to refine low-sulphur crude oil into gasoline. Different OPEC countries possess oil reserves of different sulfur content.

c. Cars powered by hydrogen are developed.

11. Suppose you are an economist working for the Competition Bureau. In each of the following cases you are given the task of determining whether the behaviour warrants an investigation for possible illegal acts or is just an example of tacit collusion. Explain your reasoning.

a. Two companies dominate the industry for industrial lasers. Several people sit on the boards of directors of both companies.

b. Three banks dominate the market for banking in a given country. Their profits have been going up recently as they add new fees for customer transactions. Advertising among the banks is fierce, and new branches are springing up in many locations.

c. The two oil companies that produce most of the petroleum for western Canada have decided to forgo building their own pipelines and to share a common pipeline, the only means of transporting petroleum products to that market.

d. The two major companies that dominate the market for herbal supplements have each created a subsidiary that sells the same product as the parent company in large quantities but with a generic name.

e. The two largest credit card companies, Passport and OmniCard, have required all retailers who accept their cards to agree to limit their use of rival credit cards.

12. Note: This is a challenging question that uses the algebraic method to solve problems from Appendix 3A and Appendix 6A.

The market for widgets is characterized by many buyers but only two producers, A and B. The market demand for widgets is given by:

$$P = 200 - 5Q^d$$

where Q^d = total demand for widgets and $Q^d = q_A + q_B$.

Both producers face the same production cost, which is $20 in fixed cost and a constant variable cost of $5 per widget. In other words, the cost functions for A and B are

$$TC_A = 20 + 5q_A$$
$$TC_B = 20 + 5q_B$$

a. Determine the best response functions for producers A and B.

b. Determine the profit-maximizing levels of output by producers A and B if they both choose the quantity of widgets produced simultaneously. What is the profit for each producer?

c. If both producers collude, what is the equilibrium price and quantity? Determine the industry profit under the collusive outcome.

d. Compare your answers to parts (b) and (c). Which outcome (collusive or noncollusive) would the producers prefer? Explain.

e. Which outcome (collusive or noncollusive) is a more stable outcome? Explain.

CHAPTER 15

Monopolistic Competition and Product Differentiation

FAST-FOOD DIFFERENTIATION

Competing for your tastebuds.

WHAT YOU WILL LEARN IN THIS CHAPTER

A BESTSELLING BOOK TITLED *Fast Food Nation* offered a fascinating if rather negative report on the burgers, pizza, tacos, and fried chicken that make up so much of the modern diet. According to the book, all fast-food chains produce and deliver their food in pretty much the same way. In particular, a lot of the taste of fast food—whatever kind of fast food it is—comes from food additives manufactured across the country.

But each fast-food provider goes to great lengths to convince you that it has something special to offer. As a sign of how well McDonald's carefully cultivates its image, everyone recognizes the McDonald's slogan—"I'm lovin' it!"—and knows what a Big Mac or a Quarter Pounder is. Its rivals Harvey's and Wendy's emphasize their cooking techniques—Harvey's with its "it's a beautiful thing" burger and Wendy's with its "hot and juicy made-to-order old-fashioned hamburger"—to make consumers believe that their burgers are better tasting. A few years ago Wendy's went so far as to mount an advertising claim with a little old lady yelling "Where's the beef?" to highlight its somewhat bigger burgers (compared to those at McDonald's).

So how would you describe the fast-food industry? On the one side, it clearly isn't a monopoly. When you go to a fast-food court, you have a choice among vendors, and there is real competition between the different burger outlets and between the burgers and the fried chicken. On the other side, in a way each vendor *does* possess some aspects of a monopoly: at one point McDonald's had the slogan "Nobody does it like McDonald's." That was literally true—though McDonald's competitors would claim that they did it *better*. In any case, the point is that each fast-food provider offers a product that is *differentiated* from its rivals' products.

In the fast-food industry, many firms compete to satisfy more or less the same demand—the desire of consumers for something tasty but quick. But each firm offers to satisfy that demand with a distinctive, differentiated product—products that consumers typically view as close but not perfect substitutes. When there are many firms offering competing, differentiated products, as there are in the fast-food industry, economists say that the industry is characterized by *monopolistic competition*. This is the

• **The meaning of monopolistic competition**

• **Why oligopolists and monopolistically competitive firms differentiate their products**

• **How prices and profits are determined in monopolistic competition in the short run and the long run**

• **Why monopolistic competition poses a trade-off between lower prices and greater product diversity**

• **The economic significance of advertising and brand names**

fourth and final market structure that we will discuss, after perfect competition, monopoly, and oligopoly.

We'll start by defining monopolistic competition more carefully and explaining its characteristic features. Then we'll explore how firms differentiate their products; this will allow us to analyze how monopolistic competition works. The chapter concludes with a discussion of some ongoing controversies about product differentiation—in particular, the question of why advertising is effective. ■

Monopolistic competition is a market structure in which there are many competing producers in an industry, each producer sells a differentiated product, and there is free entry into and exit from the industry in the long run.

The Meaning of Monopolistic Competition

Leo manages the Wonderful Wok stand in the food court of a big shopping mall. He offers the only Chinese food there, but there are more than a dozen alternatives, from Bodacious Burgers to Pizza Paradise. When deciding what to charge for a meal, Leo knows that he must take those alternatives into account: even people who normally prefer stir-fry won't order a $15 lunch from Leo when they can get a burger, fries, and drink for $6.

But Leo also knows that he won't lose all his business even if his lunches cost a bit more than the alternatives. Chinese food isn't the same thing as burgers or pizza. Some people will really be in the mood for Chinese that day, and they will buy from Leo even if they could dine more cheaply on burgers. Of course, the reverse is also true: even if Chinese is a bit cheaper, some people will choose burgers instead. In other words, Leo does have some market power: he has *some* ability to set his own price.

So how would you describe Leo's situation? He definitely isn't a price-taker, so he isn't in a situation of perfect competition. But you wouldn't exactly call him a monopolist, either. Although he's the only seller of Chinese food in that food court, he does face competition from other food vendors.

Yet it would also be wrong to call him an oligopolist. Oligopoly, remember, involves competition among a small number of interdependent firms in an industry protected by some—albeit limited—barriers to entry and whose profits are highly interdependent. Because their profits are highly interdependent, oligopolists have an incentive to collude, tacitly or explicitly. But in Leo's case there are *lots* of vendors in the shopping mall, too many to make tacit collusion feasible.

Economists describe Leo's situation as one of **monopolistic competition.** Monopolistic competition is particularly common in service industries like restaurants and gas stations, but it also exists in some manufacturing industries. It involves three conditions: large numbers of competing producers, differentiated products, and free entry into and exit from the industry in the long run. In a monopolistically competitive industry, each producer has some ability to set the price of her differentiated product. But exactly how high she can set it is limited by the competition she faces from other existing and potential producers that produce close, but not identical, products.

Large Numbers

In a monopolistically competitive industry, there are many producers. Such an industry does not look either like a monopoly, where the firm faces no competition, or an oligopoly, where each firm has only a few rivals. Instead, each seller has many competitors. For example, there are many vendors in a big food court, many gas stations along a major highway, and many hotels at a popular beach resort.

Differentiated Products

In a monopolistically competitive industry, each producer has a product that consumers view as somewhat distinct from the products of competing firms; at the same time, though, consumers see these competing products as close substitutes. If Leo's food court contained 15 vendors selling exactly the same kind and quality of food, there would be perfect competition: any seller who tried to charge a higher price would have no customers. But suppose that Wonderful Wok is the only Chinese food vendor, Bodacious Burgers is the only hamburger stand, and so on. The result of this differentiation is that each seller has some ability to set his own price: each producer has some—albeit limited—market power.

Free Entry and Exit in the Long Run

In monopolistically competitive industries, new producers, with their own distinct products, can enter the industry freely in the long run. For example, other food vendors would open outlets in the food court if they thought it would be profitable to do so. In addition, firms will exit the industry if they find they are not covering their costs in the long run.

Monopolistic competition, then, differs from the three market structures we have examined so far. It's not the same as perfect competition: firms have some power to set prices. It's not pure monopoly: firms face some competition. And it's not the same as oligopoly: because there are many firms and free entry, the potential for collusion so important in oligopoly no longer exists.

We'll see in a moment how prices, output, and the number of products available are determined in monopolistically competitive industries. But first, let's look a little more closely at what it means to have differentiated products.

Product Differentiation

We pointed out in Chapter 14 that product differentiation often plays an important role in oligopolistic industries. In such industries, product differentiation reduces the intensity of competition between firms when tacit collusion cannot be achieved. Product differentiation plays an even more crucial role in monopolistically competitive industries. Because tacit collusion is virtually impossible when there are many producers, product differentiation is the only way monopolistically competitive firms can acquire some market power.

How do firms in the same industry—such as fast-food vendors, gas stations, or chocolate makers—differentiate their products? Sometimes the difference is mainly in the minds of consumers rather than in the products themselves. We'll discuss the role of advertising and the importance of brand names in achieving this kind of product differentiation later in the chapter. But, in general, firms differentiate their products by—surprise!—actually making them different.

The key to product differentiation is that consumers have different preferences and are willing to pay somewhat more to satisfy those preferences. Each producer can carve out a market niche by producing something that caters to the particular preferences of some group of consumers better than the products of other firms. There are three important forms of product differentiation: differentiation by style or type, differentiation by location, and differentiation by quality.

Differentiation by Style or Type

The sellers in Leo's food court offer different types of fast food: hamburgers, pizza, Chinese food, Mexican food, and so on. Each consumer arrives at the food court with some preference for one or another of these offerings. This preference may depend on the consumer's mood, her diet, or what she has already eaten that day. These preferences will not make consumers indifferent to price: if Wonderful Wok were to charge $15 for an egg roll, everybody would go to Bodacious Burgers or Pizza Paradise instead. But some people will choose a more expensive meal if that type of food is closer to their preference. So the products of the different vendors are substitutes, but they aren't *perfect* substitutes—they are *imperfect substitutes*.

Vendors in a food court aren't the only sellers that differentiate their offerings by type. Clothing stores concentrate on women's or men's clothes, on business attire or sportswear, on trendy or classic styles, and so on. Auto manufacturers offer sedans, minivans, sport-utility vehicles, and sports cars, each type aimed at drivers with different needs and tastes.

Books offer yet another example of differentiation by type and style. Mysteries are differentiated from romances; among mysteries, we can differentiate among hard-boiled detective stories, whodunits, and police procedurals. And no two writers of whodunits are exactly alike: Stieg Larsson and Louise Penny each have their devoted fans.

In fact, product differentiation is characteristic of most consumer goods. As long as people differ in their tastes, producers find it possible and profitable to produce a range of varieties.

Differentiation by Location

Gas stations along a road offer differentiated products. True, the gas may be exactly the same. But the location of the stations is different, and location matters to consumers: it's more convenient to stop for gas near your home, near your workplace, or near wherever you are when the gas gauge gets low.

In fact, many monopolistically competitive industries supply goods differentiated by location. This is especially true in service industries, from dry cleaners to hairdressers, where customers often choose the seller who is closest rather than cheapest.

Differentiation by Quality

Do you have a craving for chocolate? How much are you willing to spend on it? You see, there's chocolate and then there's chocolate: although ordinary chocolate may not be very expensive, gourmet chocolate can cost several dollars per bite.

With chocolate, as with many goods, there is a range of possible qualities. You can get a usable bicycle for less than $100; you can get a much fancier bicycle for 10 times as much. It all depends on how much the additional quality matters to you and how much you will miss the other things you could have purchased with that money.

Because consumers vary in what they are willing to pay for higher quality, producers can differentiate their products by quality—some offering lower-quality, inexpensive products and others offering higher-quality products at a higher price.

Product differentiation, then, can take several forms. Whatever form it takes, however, there are two important features of industries with differentiated products: *competition among sellers* and *value in diversity*.

Competition among sellers means that even though sellers of differentiated products are not offering identical goods, they are to some extent competing for a limited market. If more businesses enter the market, each will find that it sells less quantity at any given price. For example, if a new gas station opens along a road, each of the existing gas stations will sell a bit less.

Value in diversity refers to the gain to consumers from the proliferation of differentiated products. A food court with eight vendors makes consumers happier than one with only six vendors, even if the prices are the same, because some customers will get a meal that is closer to what they had in mind. A road on which there is a gas station every two kilometres is more convenient for drivers than a road where gas stations are 20 kilometres apart. When a product is available in many different qualities, fewer people are forced to pay for more quality than they need or to settle for lower quality than they want. There are, in other words, benefits to consumers from a greater diversity of available products.

As we'll see next, competition among the sellers of differentiated products is the key to understanding how monopolistic competition works.

ECONOMICS ➤ IN ACTION

ANY COLOUR, SO LONG AS IT'S BLACK

The early history of the auto industry offers a classic illustration of the power of product differentiation.

The modern automobile industry was created by Henry Ford, who first introduced assembly-line production. This technique made it possible for him to offer the famous Model T at a far lower price than anyone else was charging for a car; by 1920, Ford dominated the automobile business.

Ford's strategy was to offer just one style of car, which maximized his economies of scale in production but made no concessions to differences in consumers' tastes. He supposedly declared that customers could get the Model T in "any colour, so long as it's black."

This strategy was challenged by Alfred P. Sloan, who had merged a number of smaller automobile companies into General Motors. Sloan's strategy was to offer a range of car types, differentiated by quality and price. Chevrolets were basic cars that directly challenged the Model T, Buicks were bigger and more expensive, and so on up to Cadillacs. And you could get each model in several different colours.

Ford's Model T in basic black.

By the 1930s the verdict was clear: customers preferred a range of styles, and General Motors, not Ford, became the dominant auto manufacturer in North America for the rest of the twentieth century.

▶●●

CHECK YOUR UNDERSTANDING   15-1

1. Each of the following goods and services is a differentiated product. Which are differentiated as a result of monopolistic competition and which are not? Explain your answers.
   a. Ladders
   b. Soft drinks
   c. Department stores
   d. Steel

2. You must determine which of two types of market structure better describes an industry, but you are allowed to ask only one question about the industry. What question should you ask to determine if an industry is:
   a. Perfectly competitive or monopolistically competitive?
   b. A monopoly or monopolistically competitive?

Solutions appear at back of book.

Understanding Monopolistic Competition

Suppose an industry is monopolistically competitive: it consists of many producers, all competing for the same consumers but offering differentiated products. How does such an industry behave?

As the term *monopolistic competition* suggests, this market structure combines some features typical of monopoly with others typical of perfect competition. Because each firm is offering a distinct product, it is in a way like a monopolist: it faces a downward-sloping demand curve and has some market power—the ability within limits to determine the price of its product. However, unlike a pure monopolist, a monopolistically competitive firm does face competition: the amount of its product it can sell depends on the prices and products offered by other firms in the industry.

The same, of course, is true of an oligopoly. In a monopolistically competitive industry, however, there are *many* producers, as opposed to the small number that defines an oligopoly. This means that the "puzzle" of oligopoly—will firms collude or will they behave noncooperatively?—does not arise in the case of monopolistically competitive industries. True, if all the gas stations or all the restaurants in a town could agree—explicitly or tacitly—to raise prices, it would be in their mutual interest to do so. But such collusion is virtually impossible when the number of firms is large and, by implication, there are no barriers to entry. So in situations of monopolistic competition, we can safely assume that firms behave noncooperatively and ignore the potential for collusion.

Monopolistic Competition in the Short Run

We introduced the distinction between short-run and long-run equilibrium back in Chapter 12. The short-run equilibrium of an industry takes the number of firms as given. The long-run equilibrium, by contrast, is reached only after enough time has elapsed for firms to enter or exit the industry. To analyze monopolistic competition, we focus first on the short run and then on how an industry moves from the short run to the long run.

Panels (a) and (b) of Figure 15-1 show two possible situations that a typical firm in a monopolistically competitive industry might face in the short run. In each case, the firm looks like any monopolist: it faces a downward-sloping demand curve, which implies a downward-sloping marginal revenue curve.

FIGURE 15-1 The Monopolistically Competitive Firm in the Short Run

The firm in panel (a) can be profitable for some output quantities: the quantities for which its average total cost curve, *ATC*, lies below its demand curve, D_P. The profit-maximizing output quantity is q_P, the output at which marginal revenue, MR_P, is equal to marginal cost, *MC*. The firm charges price P_P and earns a profit, represented by the area of the green-shaded rectangle. The firm in

panel (b), however, can never be profitable because its average total cost curve lies above its demand curve, D_U, for every output quantity. The best that it can do if it produces at all is to produce quantity q_U and charge price P_U. This generates a loss, indicated by the area of the yellow-shaded rectangle. Any other output quantity results in a greater loss.

We assume that every firm has an upward-sloping marginal cost curve but that it also faces some fixed costs, so that its average total cost curve is U-shaped. This assumption doesn't matter in the short run, but, as we'll see shortly, it is crucial to understanding the long-run equilibrium.

In each case the firm, in order to maximize profit, sets marginal revenue equal to marginal cost. So how do these two figures differ? In panel (a) the firm is profitable; in panel (b) it is unprofitable. (Recall that we are referring always to economic profit, not accounting profit—that is, a profit given that all factors of production are earning their opportunity costs.)

In panel (a) the firm faces the demand curve D_P and the marginal revenue curve MR_P. It produces the profit-maximizing output q_P, the quantity at which marginal revenue is equal to marginal cost, and sells it at the price P_P. This price is above the average total cost at this output, ATC_P. The firm's profit is indicated by the area of the shaded rectangle.

In panel (b) the firm faces the demand curve D_U and the marginal revenue curve MR_U. It chooses the quantity q_U at which marginal revenue is equal to marginal cost. However, in this case the price P_U is *below* the average total cost ATC_U; so at this quantity the firm loses money. Its loss is equal to the area of the shaded rectangle. Since q_U is the profit-maximizing quantity—which means, in this case, the loss-minimizing quantity—there is no way for a firm in this situation to make a profit. We can confirm this by noting that at *any* quantity of output, the average total cost curve in panel (b) lies above the demand curve D_U. Because $ATC > P$ at all quantities of output, this firm always suffers a loss.

As this comparison suggests, the key to whether a firm with market power is profitable or unprofitable in the short run lies in the relationship between its demand curve and its average total cost curve. In panel (a) the demand curve D_P crosses the average total cost curve, meaning that some of the demand curve lies above the average total cost curve. So there are some price–quantity combinations available at which price is higher than average total cost, indicating that the firm can choose a quantity at which it makes positive profit.

In panel (b), by contrast, the demand curve D_U does not cross the average total cost curve—it always lies below it. So the price corresponding to each quantity demanded is always less than the average total cost of producing that quantity. There is no quantity at which the firm can avoid losing money.

These figures, showing firms facing downward-sloping demand curves and their associated marginal revenue curves, look just like ordinary monopoly analysis. The "competition" aspect of monopolistic competition comes into play, however, when we move from the short run to the long run.

Monopolistic Competition in the Long Run

Obviously, an industry in which existing firms are losing money, like the one in panel (b) of Figure 15-1, is not in long-run equilibrium. When existing firms are losing money, some firms will *exit* the industry. The industry will not be in long-run equilibrium until the persistent losses have been eliminated by the exit of some firms.

It may be less obvious that an industry in which existing firms are earning profits, like the one in panel (a) of Figure 15-1, is also not in long-run equilibrium. Given that there is *free entry* into the industry, persistent profits earned by the existing firms will lead to the entry of additional producers. The industry will not be in long-run equilibrium until the persistent profits have been eliminated by the entry of new producers.

How will entry or exit by other firms affect the profits of a typical existing firm? Because the differentiated products offered by firms in a monopolistically competitive industry compete for the same set of customers, entry or exit by other firms will affect the demand curve facing every existing producer. If new gas stations open along a highway, each of the existing gas stations will no longer be

FIGURE **15-2** **Entry and Exit Shift Existing Firm's Demand Curve and Marginal Revenue Curve**

(a) Effects of Entry

(b) Effects of Exit

Entry will occur in the long run when existing firms are profitable. In panel (a), entry causes each existing firm's demand curve and marginal revenue curve to shift to the left. The firm receives a lower price for every unit it sells, and its profit falls. Entry will cease when firms make zero profit. Exit will occur in the long run when existing firms

are unprofitable. In panel (b), exit from the industry shifts each remaining firm's demand curve and marginal revenue curve to the right. The firm receives a higher price for every unit it sells, and profit rises. Exit will cease when the remaining firms make zero profit.

able to sell as much gas as before at any given price. So, as illustrated in panel (a) of Figure 15-2, entry of additional producers into a monopolistically competitive industry will lead to a *leftward* shift of the demand curve and the marginal revenue curve facing a typical existing producer.

Conversely, suppose that some of the gas stations along the highway close. Then each of the remaining stations will be able to sell more gasoline at any given price. So, as illustrated in panel (b), exit of firms from an industry will lead to a *rightward* shift of the demand curve and marginal revenue curve facing a typical remaining producer.

The industry will be in long-run equilibrium when there is neither entry nor exit. This will occur only when every firm earns zero profit. So in the long run, a monopolistically competitive industry will end up in **zero-profit equilibrium,** in which firms just manage to cover their costs at their profit-maximizing output quantities.

We have seen that a firm facing a downward-sloping demand curve will earn positive profits if any part of that demand curve lies above its average total cost curve; it will incur a loss if its demand curve lies everywhere below its average total cost curve. So in zero-profit equilibrium, the firm must be in a borderline position between these two cases; its demand curve must just touch its average total cost curve. That is, it must be just *tangent* to it at the firm's profit-maximizing output quantity—the output quantity at which marginal revenue equals marginal cost.

If this is not the case, the firm operating at its profit-maximizing quantity will find itself making either a profit or loss, as illustrated in the panels of Figure 15-1. But we also know that free entry and exit means that this cannot be a long-run equilibrium. Why? In the case of a profit, new firms will enter the industry, shifting the demand curve of every existing firm leftward until all profits are extinguished. In the case of a loss, some existing firms will exit and

In the long run, a monopolistically competitive industry ends up in **zero-profit equilibrium:** each firm makes zero profit at its profit-maximizing quantity.

FOR INQUIRING MINDS

HITS AND FLOPS

On the face of it, the movie business seems to meet the criteria for monopolistic competition. Movies compete for the same consumers; each movie is different from the others; new companies can and do enter the business. But where's the zero-profit equilibrium? After all, some movies are enormously profitable.

The key is to realize that for every successful blockbuster, there are several flops—and that the movie studios don't know in advance which will be which. (One observer of Hollywood summed up his conclusions as follows: "Nobody knows anything.") And by the time it becomes clear that a movie will be a flop, it's too late to cancel it.

The difference between movie-making and the type of monopolistic competition we model in this chapter is that the fixed costs of making a movie are also *sunk costs*—once they've been incurred, they can't be recovered.

Yet there is still, in a way, a zero-profit equilibrium. If movies on average were highly profitable, more studios would enter the industry and more movies would be made. If movies on average lost money, fewer movies would be made. In fact, as you might expect, the movie industry on average earns just about enough to cover the cost of production—that is, it earns roughly zero economic profit.

This kind of situation—in which firms earn zero profit on average but have a mixture of highly profitable hits and money-losing flops—can be found in other industries characterized by high up-front sunk costs. A notable example is the pharmaceutical industry, where many research projects lead nowhere but a few lead to highly profitable drugs.

---

so shift the demand curve of every remaining firm to the right until all losses are extinguished. All entry and exit ceases only when every existing firm makes zero profit at its profit-maximizing quantity of output.

Figure 15-3 shows a typical monopolistically competitive firm in such a zero-profit equilibrium. The firm produces q_{MC}, the output at which $MR_{MC} = MC$, and charges price P_{MC}. At this price and quantity, represented by point *Z*, the demand curve is just tangent to its average total cost curve. The firm earns zero profit because price, P_{MC}, is equal to average total cost, ATC_{MC}.

The normal long-run condition of a monopolistically competitive industry, then, is that each producer is in the situation shown in Figure 15-3. Each producer acts like a monopolist, facing a downward-sloping demand curve and setting marginal cost equal to marginal revenue so as to maximize profits. But this is just enough to achieve zero economic profit. The producers in the industry are like monopolists without monopoly profits.

FIGURE 15-3 The Long-Run Zero-Profit Equilibrium

If existing firms are profitable, entry will occur and shift each existing firm's demand curve leftward. If existing firms are unprofitable, each remaining firm's demand curve shifts rightward as some firms exit the industry. Entry and exit will cease when every existing firm makes zero profit at its profit-maximizing quantity. So, in long-run zero-profit equilibrium, the demand curve of each firm is tangent to its average total cost curve at its profit-maximizing quantity: at the profit-maximizing quantity, q_{MC}, price, P_{MC}, equals average total cost, ATC_{MC}. A monopolistically competitive firm is like a monopolist without monopoly profits.

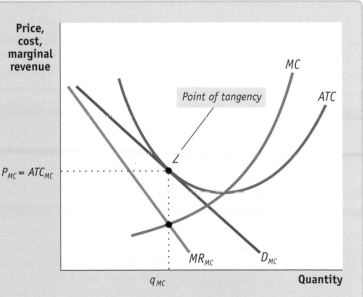

ECONOMICS > IN ACTION

A REALTY CHECK

The vast majority of home sales in Canada are transacted with real estate agents. A homeowner looking to sell hires an agent, who lists the home for sale and shows it to interested buyers. Correspondingly, prospective homebuyers hire their own agents to arrange inspections of available homes. Traditionally, agents were paid, by the seller, a commission equal to a certain percentage of the sale price of the home, which the seller's agent and the buyer's agent would split equally. In Canada, there isn't a set or standard commission percentage; the commission rate a seller pays depends on where the real estate is located. According to the Real Estate Council of Ontario, home sellers can choose from three different commission arrangements: a lump-sum amount, a fixed percentage of the sales price, or a combination of the two. While the commission rate is negotiable, the standard commission rate is 5%. Sellers in Alberta and British Columbia face a two-tiered rate system. For example, sellers in Vancouver pay 7% on the first $100 000 and 3 to 3.5 percent on the remaining balance of the real estate sale price. (Strictly speaking, the commission rate is negotiable between the seller and their agent. We are quoting the usual rates here.)

The real estate brokerage industry is a huge industry; based on an average 5% commission, real estate agents took in more than $8 billion in commission revenue across Canada in 2012. The industry fits the model of monopolistic competition quite well: in any given local market, there are many real estate agents, all competing with one another, but the agents are differentiated by location and personality as well as by the type of home they sell (some focus on condominiums, others on rural homes, and so on). And the industry has free entry.

But for a long time there was one feature that didn't fit the model of monopolistic competition: the standard commission that had not changed over time and was unaffected by the ups and downs of the housing market. For example, in Toronto, where house prices doubled over a period of 12 years, agents received double the compensation on an average transaction as they had 12 years earlier even though the work was no harder.

You may wonder how agents were able to maintain a standard commission. Why didn't new agents enter the market and drive the commission down to the zero-profit level? One tactic used by agents was their control of the Multiple Listing Service, or MLS, which lists nearly all the homes for sale in a community. Traditionally, only sellers who agreed to that fixed rate commission were allowed to list their homes on the MLS.

But protecting standard commissions was always an iffy endeavour because any action by the brokerage industry to fix the commission rate at a given percentage would run afoul of Canada's competition laws. Indeed, changes are coming. In 2010, after an investigation by the Competition Bureau, the Canadian Real Estate Association, which represents all real estate agents in the country and owns MLS and realtor.ca, allowed brokers to post a listing on their sites for a flat fee. The Competition Bureau continues to investigate, negotiate, and litigate with Canada's large realtor bodies in an attempt to get them to change their practices to allow greater entry and competition by other realtors—including those who offer much lower fees.

▼ Quick Review

- Like a monopolist, each firm in a monopolistically competitive industry faces a downward-sloping demand curve and marginal revenue curve. In the short run, it may earn a profit or incur a loss at its profit-maximizing quantity.

- If the typical firm earns positive profit, new firms will enter the industry in the long run, shifting each existing firm's demand curve to the left. If the typical firm incurs a loss, some existing firms will exit the industry in the long run, shifting the demand curve of each remaining firm to the right.

- The long-run equilibrium of a monopolistically competitive industry is a **zero-profit equilibrium** in which firms just break even. The typical firm's demand curve is tangent to its average total cost curve at its profit-maximizing quantity.

CHECK YOUR UNDERSTANDING 15-2

1. Currently a monopolistically competitive industry, composed of firms with U-shaped average total cost curves, is in long-run equilibrium. Describe how the industry adjusts, in both the short and long run, in each of the following situations.
   a. A technological change increases fixed cost for every firm in the industry.
   b. A technological change decreases marginal cost for every firm in the industry.

2. Why, in the long run, is it impossible for firms in a monopolistically competitive industry to create a monopoly by joining together to form a single firm?

Solutions appear at back of book.

Monopolistic Competition versus Perfect Competition

In a way, long-run equilibrium in a monopolistically competitive industry looks a lot like long-run equilibrium in a perfectly competitive industry. In both cases, there are many firms; in both cases, profits have been competed away; in both cases, the price received by every firm is equal to the average total cost of production.

However, the two versions of long-run equilibrium are different—in ways that are economically significant.

Price, Marginal Cost, and Average Total Cost

Figure 15-4 compares the long-run equilibrium of a typical firm in a perfectly competitive industry with that of a typical firm in a monopolistically competitive industry. Panel (a) shows a perfectly competitive firm facing a market price equal to its minimum average total cost; panel (b) reproduces Figure 15-3. Comparing the panels, we see two important differences.

FIGURE   **15-4**   **Comparing Long-Run Equilibrium in Perfect Competition and Monopolistic Competition**

Panel (a) shows the situation of the typical firm in long-run equilibrium in a perfectly competitive industry. The firm operates at the minimum-cost output q_{PC}, sells at the competitive market price P_{PC}, and makes zero profit. It is indifferent to selling another unit of output because P_{PC} is equal to its marginal cost, MC_{PC}. Panel (b) shows the situation of the typical firm in long-run equilibrium

in a monopolistically competitive industry. At q_{MC} it makes zero profit because its price, P_{MC}, just equals average total cost, ATC_{MC}. At q_{MC} the firm would like to sell another unit at price P_{MC} since P_{MC} exceeds marginal cost, MC_{MC}. But it is unwilling to lower price to make more sales. It therefore operates to the left of the minimum-cost output level and has excess capacity.

Firms in a monopolistically competitive industry have **excess capacity:** they produce less than the output at which average total cost is minimized.

First, in the case of the perfectly competitive firm shown in panel (a), the price, P_{PC}, received by the firm at the profit-maximizing quantity, q_{PC}, is equal to the firm's marginal cost of production, MC_{PC}, at that quantity of output. By contrast, at the profit-maximizing quantity chosen by the monopolistically competitive firm in panel (b), q_{MC}, the price, P_{MC}, is *higher* than the marginal cost of production, MC_{MC}.

This difference translates into a difference in the attitude of firms toward consumers. A wheat farmer, who can sell as much wheat as he likes at the going market price, would not get particularly excited if you offered to buy some more wheat at the market price. Since he has no desire to produce more at that price and can sell the wheat to someone else, you are not doing him a favour.

But if you decide to fill up your tank at Jamil's gas station rather than at Katy's, you are doing Jamil a favour. He is not willing to cut his price to get more customers—he's already made the best of that trade-off. But if he gets a few more customers than he expected at the *posted* price, that's good news: an additional sale at the posted price increases his revenue more than it increases his costs because the posted price exceeds marginal cost.

The fact that monopolistic competitors, unlike perfect competitors, want to sell more at the going price is crucial to understanding why they engage in activities like advertising that help increase sales.

The other difference between monopolistic competition and perfect competition that is visible in Figure 15-4 involves the position of each firm on its average total cost curve. In panel (a), the perfectly competitive firm produces at point q_{PC}, at the bottom of the U-shaped *ATC* curve. That is, each firm produces the quantity at which average total cost is minimized—the *minimum-cost output*. As a consequence, the total cost of industry output is also minimized.

Under monopolistic competition, in panel (b), the firm produces at q_{MC}, on the *downward-sloping* part of the U-shaped *ATC* curve: it produces less than the quantity that would minimize average total cost. This failure to produce enough to minimize average total cost is sometimes described as the **excess capacity** issue. The typical vendor in a food court or gas station along a road is not big enough to take maximum advantage of available cost savings. So the total cost of industry output is not minimized in the case of a monopolistically competitive industry.

Some people have argued that, because every monopolistic competitor has excess capacity, monopolistically competitive industries are inefficient. But the issue of efficiency under monopolistic competition turns out to be a subtle one that does not have a clear answer.

Is Monopolistic Competition Inefficient?

A monopolistic competitor, like a monopolist, charges a price that is above marginal cost. As a result, some people who are willing to pay at least as much for an egg roll at Wonderful Wok as it costs to produce it are deterred from doing so. In monopolistic competition, some mutually beneficial transactions go unexploited.

Furthermore, it is often argued that monopolistic competition is subject to a further kind of inefficiency: that the excess capacity of every monopolistic competitor implies *wasteful duplication* because monopolistically competitive industries offer too many varieties. According to this argument, it would be better if there were only two or three vendors in the food court, not six or seven. If there were fewer vendors, they would each have lower average total costs and so could offer food more cheaply.

Is this argument against monopolistic competition right—that it lowers total surplus by causing inefficiency? Not necessarily. It's true that if there were fewer gas stations along a highway, each gas station would sell more gasoline and so would have lower costs per litre. But there is a drawback:

drivers would be inconvenienced because gas stations would be farther apart. The point is that the diversity of products offered in a monopolistically competitive industry is beneficial to consumers. So the higher price consumers pay because of excess capacity is offset to some extent by the value they receive from greater diversity.

There is, in other words, a trade-off: more producers means higher average total costs but also greater product diversity. Does a monopolistically competitive industry arrive at the socially optimal point on this trade-off? Probably not—but it is hard to say whether there are too many firms or too few! Most economists now believe that duplication of effort and excess capacity in monopolistically competitive industries are not important issues in practice.

▷●●

> ### CHECK YOUR UNDERSTANDING   15-3
>
> 1. True or false? Explain your answers.
>   a. Like a firm in a perfectly competitive industry, a firm in a monopolistically competitive industry is willing to sell a good at any price that equals or exceeds marginal cost.
>   b. Suppose there is a monopolistically competitive industry in long-run equilibrium that possesses excess capacity. All the firms in the industry would be better off if they merged into a single firm and produced a single product, but whether consumers are made better off by this is ambiguous.
>   c. Fads and fashions are more likely to arise in monopolistic competition or oligopoly than in monopoly or perfect competition.
>
> Solutions appear at back of book.

> ▼ **Quick Review**
>
> ● In the long-run equilibrium of a monopolistically competitive industry, there are many firms, each earning zero profit.
>
> ● Price exceeds marginal cost, so some mutually beneficial trades are unexploited.
>
> ● Monopolistically competitive firms have **excess capacity** because they do not minimize average total cost. But it is not clear that this is actually a source of inefficiency since consumers gain from product diversity.

Controversies About Product Differentiation

Up to this point, we have assumed that products are differentiated in a way that corresponds to some real desire of consumers. There is real convenience in having a gas station in your neighbourhood; Chinese food and Mexican food are really different from each other.

In the real world, however, some instances of product differentiation can seem puzzling if you think about them. What is the real difference between Crest and Colgate toothpaste? Between Energizer and Duracell batteries? Or a Marriott and a Hilton hotel room? Most people would be hard-pressed to answer any of these questions. Yet the producers of these goods make considerable efforts to convince consumers that their products are different from and better than those of their competitors.

No discussion of product differentiation is complete without spending at least a bit of time on the two related issues—and puzzles—of *advertising* and *brand names*.

The Role of Advertising

Wheat farmers don't advertise their wares on TV, but car dealers do. That's not because farmers are shy and car dealers are outgoing; it's because advertising is worthwhile only in industries in which firms have at least some market power.

The purpose of advertisements is to convince people to buy more of a seller's product at the going price. A perfectly competitive firm, which can sell as much as it likes at the going market price, has no incentive to spend money convincing

"The active ingredient is marketing."

consumers to buy more. Only a firm that has some market power, and that therefore charges a price above marginal cost, can gain from advertising. (Industries that are more or less perfectly competitive, like the milk industry, do advertise—but these ads are sponsored by an association such as a provincial milk marketing board on behalf of the industry, not on behalf of the milk that comes from the cows on a particular farm.)

Given that advertising "works," it's not hard to see why firms with market power would spend money on it. But the big question about advertising is *why* it works. A related question is whether advertising is, from society's point of view, a waste of resources.

Not all advertising poses a puzzle. Much of it is straightforward: it's a way for sellers to inform potential buyers about what they have to offer (or, occasionally, for buyers to inform potential sellers about what they want). Nor is there much controversy about the economic usefulness of ads that provide information: the real estate ad that declares "sunny, charming, 2 br, 1 ba, a/c" tells you things you need to know (even if a few euphemisms are involved— "charming," of course, means "small").

Fortunately, someone is looking out for consumers: providing misleading information in ads violates the Competition Act. For example, in 2012 the Competition Bureau sued Bell Canada, Rogers, Telus, and the Canadian Wireless Telecommunications Association (CWTA) for misleading advertising. The investigation concluded that customers were given the false impression that certain texts and apps were free of charge, but these services were later charged to them. The Competition Bureau sought full refunds for customers and imposed $31 million in penalties ($10 million for each of the telecommunication companies involved and $1 million for the CWTA).

But if ads must be honest, what information is being conveyed when a TV actress proclaims the virtues of one or another toothpaste or a sports hero declares that some company's batteries are better than those inside that pink mechanical rabbit? Surely nobody believes that the sports star is an expert on batteries—or that he chose the company that he personally believes makes the best batteries, as opposed to the company that offered to pay him the most. Yet companies believe, with good reason, that money spent on such promotions increases their sales—and that they would be in big trouble if they stopped advertising but their competitors continued to do so.

Why are consumers influenced by ads that do not really provide any information about the product? One answer is that consumers are not as rational as economists typically assume. Perhaps consumers' judgments, or even their tastes, can be influenced by things that economists think ought to be irrelevant, such as which company has hired the most charismatic celebrity to endorse its product. And there is surely some truth to this. As we learned in Chapter 9, consumer rationality is a useful working assumption; it is not an absolute truth.

However, another answer is that consumer response to advertising is not entirely irrational because ads can serve as indirect "signals" in a world where consumers don't have good information about products. Suppose, to take a common example, that you need to avail yourself of some local service that you don't use regularly—body work on your car, say, or furniture moving. You turn to the Yellow Pages or search online, where you see a number of small listings and several large display, or featured, ads. You know that firms pay extra for the larger ads; still, it may be quite rational to contact one of the firms with a big ad. After all, the big ad probably means that it's a relatively large, successful company—otherwise, the company wouldn't have found it worth spending the money for the larger ad.

The same principle may partly explain why ads feature celebrities. You don't really believe that the supermodel prefers that watch; but the fact that the watch manufacturer is willing and able to pay her fee tells you that it is a major company that is likely to stand behind its product. According to this reasoning, an expensive advertisement serves to establish the quality of a firm's products in the eyes of consumers.

The possibility that it is rational for consumers to respond to advertising also has some bearing on the question of whether advertising is a waste of resources. If ads only work by manipulating the weak-minded, the $14 billion that Canadian businesses spent on advertising (and the $29 billion on marketing-related activities) in 2011 would have been an economic waste—except to the extent that ads sometimes provide entertainment. However, to the extent that advertising conveys important information, it is an economically productive activity after all.

Brand Names

A **brand name** is a name owned by a particular firm that distinguishes its products from those of other firms.

You've been driving all day, and you decide that it's time to find a place to sleep. On your right, you see a sign for the Bates Motel; on your left, you see a sign for a Travelodge, or a Best Western, or some other national chain. Which one do you choose?

Unless they were familiar with the area, most people would head for the chain. In fact, most motels in Canada are members of major chains; the same is true of most fast-food restaurants and many, if not most, stores in shopping malls.

Motel chains and fast-food restaurants are only one aspect of a broader phenomenon: the role of **brand names,** names owned by particular companies that differentiate their products in the minds of consumers. In many cases, a company's brand name is the most important asset it possesses: clearly, Tim Hortons is worth far more than the sum of the coffee and baking equipment the company owns.

In fact, companies often go to considerable lengths to defend their brand names, suing anyone else who uses them without permission. You may talk about blowing your nose on a kleenex or googling a person, but legally only Kleenex can call its facial tissue "Kleenex" and only Google can call its search engine "Google."

As with advertising, with which they are closely linked, the social usefulness of brand names is a source of dispute. Does the preference of consumers for known brands reflect consumer irrationality? Or do brand names convey real information? That is, do brand names create unnecessary market power, or do they serve a real purpose?

As in the case of advertising, the answer is probably some of both. On one side, brand names often do create unjustified market power. Many consumers will pay more for brand-name goods in the supermarket even though consumer experts assure us that the cheaper store brands are equally good. Similarly, many common medicines, like acetylsalicylic acid (ASA, the key ingredient in Aspirin), are cheaper—with no loss of quality—in their generic form.

On the other side, for many products the brand name does convey information. A traveller arriving in a strange town can be sure of what awaits in a Holiday Inn or a Tim Hortons; a tired and hungry traveller may find these standardized products preferable to trying an independent hotel or restaurant that might be better—but might be worse.

In addition, brand names offer some assurance that the seller is engaged in repeated interaction with its customers and so has a reputation to protect. If a traveller eats a bad meal at a restaurant in a tourist trap and vows never to eat there again, the restaurant owner may not care, since the chance is small that the traveller will be in the same area again in the future. But if that traveller eats a bad meal at Tim Hortons and vows never to eat at a Tim Hortons again, that matters to the company. This gives Tim Hortons an incentive to provide consistent quality, thereby assuring travellers that quality controls are in place.

ECONOMICS ▸ IN ACTION

CAN ADVERTISING FOSTER IRRATIONALITY?

Advertising often serves a useful function. Among other things, it can make consumers aware of a wider range of alternatives, which leads to increased competition and lower prices. Indeed, in some cases the courts have viewed industry agreements *not* to advertise as violations of competition law. For example, in 2003 the RE/MAX family of real estate agents was found to be in violation of the Competition Act by prohibiting its agents from advertising and setting their own commission rates. RE/MAX settled the case with the Competition Bureau and agreed to allow its sales associates to set their commission rates independently and to advertise their rates.

Conversely, advertising sometimes creates product differentiation and market power where there is no real difference in the product. Consider, in particular, the spectacularly successful advertising campaign of Absolut vodka.

In *Twenty Ads That Shook the World*, James B. Twitchell puts it this way: "The pull of Absolut's magnetic advertising is curious because the product itself is so bland. Vodka is aquavit, and aquavit is the most unsophisticated of alcohols. ... No taste, no smell. ... In fact, the Swedes, who make the stuff, rarely drink Absolut. They prefer cheaper brands such as Explorer, Renat Brannwinn, or Skane. That's because Absolut can't advertise in Sweden, where alcohol advertising is against the law."

But here's a metaphysical question: if Absolut doesn't really taste any different from other brands, but advertising convinces consumers that they are getting a distinctive product, who are we to say that they aren't? Isn't distinctiveness in the mind of the beholder?

▼ Quick Review

- In industries with product differentiation, firms advertise in order to increase the demand for their products.

- Advertising is not a waste of resources when it gives consumers useful information about products.

- Advertising that simply touts a product is harder to explain. Either consumers are irrational, or expensive advertising communicates that the firm's products are of high quality.

- Some firms create **brand names.** As with advertising, the economic value of brand names can be ambiguous. They convey real information when they assure consumers of the quality of a product.

CHECK YOUR UNDERSTANDING   15-4

1. In which of the following cases is advertising likely to be economically useful? Economically wasteful? Explain your answer.
   a. Advertisements on the benefits of ASA
   b. Advertisements for Bayer Aspirin, which is made with ASA
   c. Advertisements on the benefits of drinking orange juice
   d. Advertisements for Tropicana orange juice
   e. Advertisements that state how long a plumber or an electrician has been in business

2. Some industry analysts have stated that a successful brand name is like a barrier to entry. Explain the reasoning behind this statement.

Solutions appear at back of book.

BUSINESS CASE : Gillette Versus Schick: A Case of Razor Burn?

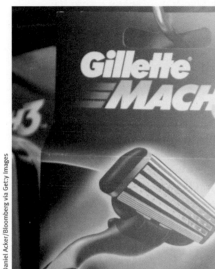

Daniel Acker/Bloomberg via Getty Images

In early 2010, Schick introduced the Hydro system, its latest and most advanced razor, two months before the introduction of Gillette's Pro-Glide, the latest upgrade in its Fusion line. According to reports at the time, Schick and Gillette would jointly spend over $250 million in international advertising for the two systems. It's the latest round in a century-long rivalry between the two razor makers. Despite the rivalry, the razor business has been a profitable one; it has long been one of the priciest and highest profit margin sectors of nonfood packaged goods.

Schick and Gillette clearly hoped that the sophistication and features of their new shavers would appeal to customers. Hydro came with a lubricating gel dispenser and blade guards for smoother shaving, and a five-blade version came with a trimming blade. Schick considered the two versions of Hydro to offer both an upgrade and a value play to its existing product, the four-blade Quattro introduced in 2003. (A *value play* is an item that appeals to customers who are shopping on the basis of price.) And both versions of Hydro were priced below comparable versions of Gillette's five-bladed Fusion and three-bladed Mach razors, as well as the Pro-Glide, which Gillette planned to price at 10 to 15 percent above its existing Fusion line.

This was not the first instance of a competitive razor launch. Back in 2003, Gillette and Schick went head-to-head when Gillette introduced its Mach 3 Turbo (an upgrade to its existing three-blade Mach 3), which delivered battery-powered pulses that Gillette said caused hair follicles to stand up, facilitating a closer shave. In 2003 Schick introduced the Quattro, the world's first four-blade razor, which it called "unlike any other razor."

Gillette is by far the larger company of the two, capturing about 70% of the Canadian razor market. Although Schick has a much smaller market share, many analysts believe it is the leader in innovation. "Schick appears to be grabbing the innovation lead and putting Gillette on the defensive," says William Peoriello, an analyst at investment bank Morgan Stanley. "The roster of new razors from Schick is forcing Gillette to change the pace of its new product launches and appears likely to give Gillette its strongest competition ever."

Some customers, though, are unimpressed with both companies' offerings. In July 2010, the *Wall Street Journal* cited the example of Jeff Hagan, an investment banker, who searches out and stockpiles discontinued versions of Gillette's Mach 3 razors and blades. It also profiled Steven Schimmel, the owner of an upscale pharmacy, who does a brisk business in old-fashioned, double-edge Gillette blades imported from a dealer in India. One disgruntled customer, Nick Meyers, gave up his four-blade Quattro because he got tired of trying to find drug store employees to unlock the blade case when he needed refills. "It's easier to buy uranium," said Meyers. "They're so expensive, they have to keep them locked up, and that's when I realized what a gimmick all of it is."

QUESTIONS FOR THOUGHT

1. What explains the complexity of today's razors and the pace of innovation in their features?

2. Why is the razor business so profitable? What explains the size of the advertising budgets of Schick and Gillette?

3. What explains the reaction of customers like Hagan and Meyers? What dilemma do Schick and Gillette face in their decisions about whether to maintain their older, simpler razor models? What does this indicate about the value of the innovation in razors?

SUMMARY

1. **Monopolistic competition** is a market structure in which there are many competing producers, each producing a differentiated product, and there is free entry and exit in the long run. Product differentiation takes three main forms: by style or type, by location, or by quality. Products of competing sellers are considered imperfect substitutes, and each firm has its own downward-sloping demand curve and marginal revenue curve.

2. Short-run profits will attract entry of new firms in the long run. This reduces the quantity each existing producer sells at any given price and shifts its demand curve to the left. Short-run losses will induce exit by some firms in the long run. This shifts the demand curve of each remaining firm to the right.

3. In the long run, a monopolistically competitive industry is in **zero-profit equilibrium:** at its profit-maximizing quantity, the demand curve for each existing firm is tangent to its average total cost curve. There are zero profits in the industry and no entry or exit.

4. In long-run equilibrium, firms in a monopolistically competitive industry sell at a price greater than marginal cost. They also have **excess capacity** because they produce less than the minimum-cost output; as a result, they have higher costs than firms in a perfectly competitive industry. Whether or not monopolistic competition is inefficient is ambiguous because consumers value the diversity of products that it creates.

5. A monopolistically competitive firm will always prefer to make an additional sale at the going price, so it will engage in advertising to increase demand for its product and enhance its market power. Advertising and **brand names** that provide useful information to consumers are economically valuable. But they are economically wasteful when their only purpose is to create market power. In reality, advertising and brand names are likely to be some of both: economically valuable and economically wasteful.

KEY TERMS

Monopolistic competition, p. 468
Zero-profit equilibrium, p. 474

Excess capacity, p. 478

Brand name, p. 481

PROBLEMS

1. Use the three conditions for monopolistic competition discussed in the chapter to decide which of the following firms are likely to be operating as monopolistic competitors. If they are not monopolistically competitive firms, are they monopolists, oligopolists, or perfectly competitive firms?
   a. A local band that plays for weddings, parties, and so on
   b. Minute Maid, a producer of individual-serving juice boxes
   c. Your local dry cleaner
   d. A farmer who produces soybeans

2. You are thinking of setting up a coffee shop. The market structure for coffee shops is monopolistic competition. There are three Second Cup shops and two other coffee shops very much like Second Cup in your town already. In order for you to have some degree of market power, you may want to differentiate your coffee shop. Thinking about the three different ways in which products can be differentiated, explain how you would decide whether you should copy Second Cup or whether you should sell coffee in a completely different way.

3. The restaurant business in town is a monopolistically competitive industry in long-run equilibrium. One restaurant owner asks for your advice. She tells you that, each night, not all tables in her restaurant are full. She also tells you that she would attract more customers if she lowered the prices on her menu and that doing so would lower her average total cost. Should she lower her prices? Draw a diagram showing the demand curve, marginal revenue curve, marginal cost curve, and average total cost curve for this restaurant to explain your advice. Show in your diagram what would happen to the restaurant owner's profit if she were to lower the price so that she sells the minimum-cost output.

4. The market structure of the local gas station industry is monopolistic competition. Suppose that currently each gas station incurs a loss. Draw a diagram for a typical gas station to show this short-run situation. Then, in a separate diagram, show what will happen to the typical gas station in the long run. Explain your reasoning.

5. The local hairdresser industry has the market structure of monopolistic competition. Your hairdresser boasts that he is making a profit and that if he continues to do so, he will be able to retire in five years. Use a diagram to illustrate your hairdresser's current

situation. Do you expect this to last? In a separate diagram, draw what you expect to happen in the long run. Explain your reasoning.

6. Magnificent Blooms is a florist in a monopolistically competitive industry. It is a successful operation, producing the quantity that minimizes its average total cost and making a profit. The owner also says that at its current level of output, its marginal cost is above marginal revenue. Illustrate the current situation of Magnificent Blooms in a diagram. Answer the following questions by illustrating with a diagram.

   a. In the short run, could Magnificent Blooms increase its profit?

   b. In the long run, could Magnificent Blooms increase its profit?

7. "In the long run, there is no difference between monopolistic competition and perfect competition." Discuss whether this statement is true, false, or ambiguous with respect to the following criteria.

   a. The price charged to consumers

   b. The average total cost of production

   c. The efficiency of the market outcome

   d. The typical firm's profit in the long run

8. "In both the short run and in the long run, the typical firm in monopolistic competition and a monopolist each make a profit." Do you agree with this statement? Explain your reasoning.

9. The market for clothes has the structure of monopolistic competition. What impact will fewer firms in this industry have on you as a consumer? Address the following issues.

   a. Variety of clothes

   b. Differences in quality of service

   c. Price

10. For each of the following situations, decide whether advertising is directly informative about the product or simply an indirect signal of its quality. Explain your reasoning.

    a. Hockey superstar, Hayley Wickenheiser, drinks Gatorade in a TV commercial and claims that she prefers it to any energy drink.

    b. A newspaper ad states, "For sale: 1999 Honda Civic, 250 000 kilometres, new transmission."

    c. McDonald's spends millions of dollars on an advertising campaign that proclaims: "I'm lovin' it."

    d. Subway advertises one of its sandwiches by claiming that it contains 6 grams of fat and fewer than 300 calories.

11. In each of the following cases, explain how the advertisement functions as a signal to a potential buyer. Explain what information the buyer lacks that is being supplied by the advertisement and how the information supplied by the advertisement is likely to affect the buyer's willingness to buy the good.

    a. "Looking for work. Excellent references from previous employers available."

    b. "Electronic equipment for sale. All merchandise carries a one-year, no-questions-asked warranty."

    c. "Car for sale by original owner. All repair and maintenance records available."

12. The accompanying table shows the Herfindahl–Hirschman Index (HHI) for the restaurant, cereal, movie, and laundry detergent industries as well as the advertising expenditures of the top 10 firms in each industry in 2006. Use the information in the table to answer the following questions.

Industry	HHI	Advertising expenditures (millions)
Restaurants	179	$1784
Cereal	2098	732
Movie studios	918	3324
Laundry detergent	2068	132

   a. Which market structure—oligopoly or monopolistic competition—best characterizes each of the industries?

   b. Based on your answer to part (a), which type of market structure has higher advertising expenditures? Use the characteristics of each market structure to explain why this relationship might exist.

13. McDonald's spends millions of dollars each year on legal protection of its brand name, thereby preventing any unauthorized use of it. Explain what information this conveys to you as a consumer about the quality of McDonald's products.

CHAPTER 16

Externalities

WHO'LL STOP THE RAIN?

For many polluters, acid rain was someone else's problem.

> **WHAT YOU WILL LEARN IN THIS CHAPTER**

❯ What **externalities** are and why they can lead to inefficiency and government intervention in the market

❯ The difference among **negative, positive,** and **network externalities**

❯ The importance of the **Coase theorem,** which explains how private individuals can sometimes remedy externalities

❯ Why some government policies to deal with externalities, like **emissions taxes, tradable emissions permits,** or **Pigouvian subsidies,** are efficient and others, like **environmental standards,** are not

❯ What makes network externalities an important feature of high-tech industries

FOR MANY PEOPLE IN EASTERN Canada, there is no better way to relax than to fish in one of the region's thousands of lakes. But in the 1960s, avid fishers noticed something alarming: lakes that had formerly teemed with fish were now almost empty. What had happened?

The answer was acid rain, caused mainly by coal-burning power plants. When coal is burned, it releases sulphur dioxide and nitric oxide into the atmosphere; these gases react with water, producing sulphuric acid and nitric acid. The result: downwind from the industrial heartland of Canada and the United States was rain sometimes as acidic as lemon juice. Acid rain didn't just kill fish; it also damaged trees and crops and in time even began to dissolve limestone buildings.

You'll be glad to hear that the acid rain problem today is much less serious than it was in the 1960s. Power plants have reduced their emissions by switching to low-sulphur coal and installing scrubbers in their smokestacks. But they didn't do this out of the goodness of their hearts; they did it in response to government

policy. Without such government intervention, power companies would have had no incentive to take the environmental effects of their actions into account.

When individuals impose costs on or provide benefits for others, but don't have an economic incentive to take those costs or benefits into account, economists say that *externalities* are generated. You may recall that we briefly noted this phenomenon in Chapters 1 and 4. There we stated that one of the principal sources of market failure is actions that create *side effects* that are not properly taken into account—that is, externalities. In this chapter, we'll examine the economics of externalities, seeing how they can get in the way of economic efficiency and lead to market failure, why they provide a reason for government intervention in markets, and how economic analysis can be used to guide government policy.

Externalities arise from the side effects of actions. First, we'll study the case of pollution, which generates a *negative externality*—a side effect that imposes costs on others. Whenever a

side effect can be directly observed and quantified, it can be regulated: by imposing direct controls on it, by taxing it, or by subsidizing it. As we will see, government intervention in this case should be aimed directly at moving the market to the right quantity of the side effect.

Other activities generate *positive externalities*, a side effect that generates benefits for others—for example, preserving farmland instead of developing it. In this case, government can use subsidies to move the market to the best quantity of the side effect from society's point of view.

In the case of both positive and negative externalities, achieving the best solution takes place at the margin, setting the benefit of doing a little bit more of something equal to the cost of doing that little bit more.

Lastly, we'll return to the case of *network externalities,* a phenomenon we learned about in Chapter 13 that's particularly common in high-tech industries. We'll learn about what creates a network externality and why industries that have them are particularly difficult to regulate. ∎

The **marginal social cost (MSC) of pollution** is the additional cost imposed on society as a whole by an additional unit of pollution.

The **marginal social benefit (MSB) of pollution** is the additional gain to society as a whole from an additional unit of pollution.

The **marginal private cost (MPC) of pollution** is the additional cost imposed on the polluter if the polluter creates another unit of pollution.

The **marginal external cost (MEC) of pollution** is the additional cost imposed on others if the polluter creates another unit of pollution.

The Economics of Pollution

Pollution is a bad thing. Yet most pollution is a side effect of activities that provide us with good things: our air is polluted by power plants generating the electricity that lights our cities, and our rivers are damaged by fertilizer runoff from farms that grow our food. Why shouldn't we accept a certain amount of pollution as the cost of a good life?

Actually, we do. Even highly committed environmentalists don't think that we can or should completely eliminate pollution—even an environmentally conscious society would accept *some* pollution as the cost of producing useful goods and services. What environmentalists argue is that unless there is a strong and effective environmental policy, our society will generate *too much* pollution—too much of a bad thing. And the great majority of economists agree.

To see why, we need a framework that lets us think about how much pollution a society *should* have. We'll then be able to see why a market economy, left to itself, will produce more pollution than it should. We'll start by adopting the simplest framework to study the problem—assuming that the amount of pollution emitted by a polluter is directly observable and controllable.

Costs and Benefits of Pollution

How much pollution should society allow? We learned in Chapter 9 that "how much" decisions always involve comparing the marginal benefit from an additional unit of something with the marginal cost of that additional unit. The same is true of pollution.

The **marginal social cost (MSC) of pollution** is the additional cost imposed on society as a whole by an additional unit of pollution. For example, acid rain damages fisheries, crops, and forests, and each additional tonne of sulphur dioxide released into the atmosphere increases the damage.

The **marginal social benefit (MSB) of pollution**—the additional benefit to society from an additional unit of pollution—may seem like a confusing concept. What's good about pollution? However, avoiding pollution requires using scarce resources that could have been used to produce other goods and services. For example, to reduce the quantity of sulphur dioxide they emit, power companies must either buy expensive low-sulphur coal or install special scrubbers to remove sulphur from their emissions.[1] The more sulphur dioxide they are allowed to emit, the lower these extra costs. Suppose we could calculate how much money the power industry would save if it were allowed to emit an additional tonne of sulphur dioxide. That savings would be the marginal benefit to society of emitting an extra tonne of sulphur dioxide.

The marginal social cost of pollution can be expressed as the sum of two terms ($MSC = MPC + MEC$): **marginal private cost (MPC) of pollution**—the additional cost imposed on the polluter if the polluter creates another unit of pollution—and **marginal external cost (MEC) of pollution**—the

PITFALLS

SO HOW DO YOU MEASURE THE MARGINAL SOCIAL COST OF POLLUTION?

It might be confusing to think of marginal *social* cost—after all, we have up to this point always defined marginal cost as being incurred by an individual or a firm, not society as a whole. But it is easily understandable once we link it to the familiar concept of willingness to pay: the marginal social cost of a unit of pollution is equal to the *sum of the willingness to pay among all members of society* to avoid that unit of pollution. It's the sum because, in general, more than one person is affected by the pollution.

But calculating the true cost to society of pollution—marginal or average—is a difficult matter, requiring a great deal of scientific knowledge, as the upcoming Economics in Action on smoking illustrates. As a result, society often underestimates the true marginal social cost of pollution.

---

[1]Without these methods, the only way to reduce pollution is to either burn less coal for power generation or stop using coal altogether. A reduction in coal burning can be achieved by either using conservation programs to decrease demand (such as mandating the use of energy-efficient appliances and light bulbs) or finding cleaner generation methods (such as water, wind, or solar power).

additional cost imposed on others if the polluter creates another unit of pollution. If, as is often the case, creating another unit of pollution imposes zero additional costs on the polluter (i.e., the pollution only harms others in society), then the marginal social cost is equal to the marginal external cost ($MSC = MEC$, as $MPC = 0$).

Similarly, the marginal social benefit is the sum of two terms ($MSB = MPB + MEB$): **marginal private benefit (MPB) of pollution**—the additional benefit the polluter receives if the polluter creates another unit of pollution—and **marginal external benefit (MEB) of pollution**—the additional benefit others receive if the polluter creates another unit of pollution. If creating another unit of pollution only creates additional benefits for the polluter, the marginal social benefit is equal to the marginal private benefit ($MSB = MPB$, as $MEB = 0$).

Using hypothetical numbers, Figure 16-1 shows how we can determine the **socially optimal quantity of pollution**—the quantity of pollution society would choose if all its costs and benefits were fully accounted for. The upward-sloping marginal social cost curve, MSC, shows how the marginal cost to society of an additional tonne of pollution emissions varies with the quantity of emissions. (An upward slope is likely because nature can often safely handle low levels of pollution but is increasingly harmed as pollution reaches high levels.) The marginal social benefit curve, MSB, is downward sloping because it is progressively harder, and therefore more expensive, to achieve a further reduction in pollution as the total amount of pollution falls—increasingly more expensive technology must be used. As a result, as total pollution falls, the cost savings to a polluter of being allowed to emit one more tonne rises.

PITFALLS

SO HOW DO YOU MEASURE THE MARGINAL SOCIAL BENEFIT OF POLLUTION?
Similar to the problem of measuring the marginal social cost of pollution, the concept of willingness to pay helps us understand the marginal social benefit of pollution in contrast to the marginal benefit to an individual or firm. The marginal social benefit of a unit of pollution is simply equal to the highest willingness to pay for the right to emit that unit measured across all polluters. But unlike the marginal social cost of pollution, the value of the marginal social benefit of pollution is a number likely to be known—to polluters, that is.

The **marginal private benefit (MPB) of pollution** is the additional benefit the polluter receives if the polluter creates another unit of pollution.

The **marginal external benefit (MEB) of pollution** is the additional benefit others receive if the polluter creates another unit of pollution.

The **socially optimal quantity of pollution** is the quantity of pollution that society would choose if all the costs and benefits of pollution were fully accounted for.

FIGURE 16-1 The Socially Optimal Quantity of Pollution

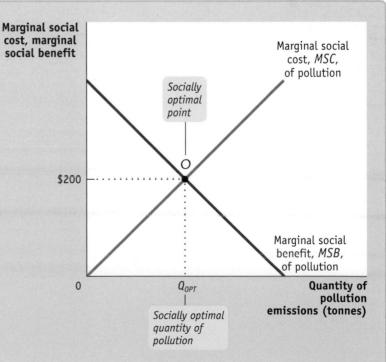

Pollution yields both costs and benefits. Here the MSC curve shows how the marginal cost to society as a whole from emitting one more tonne of pollution emissions depends on the quantity of emissions. The MSB curve shows how the marginal benefit to society as a whole of emitting an additional tonne of pollution emissions depends on the quantity of pollution emissions. The socially optimal quantity of pollution is Q_{OPT}; at that quantity, the marginal social benefit of pollution is equal to the marginal social cost, corresponding to $200.

The socially optimal quantity of pollution in this example isn't zero. It's Q_{OPT}, the quantity corresponding to point O, where MSB crosses MSC. At Q_{OPT}, the marginal social benefit from an additional tonne of emissions and its marginal social cost are equalized at $200.

But will a market economy, left to itself, arrive at the socially optimal quantity of pollution? No, it won't.

Pollution: An External Cost

Pollution yields both benefits and costs to society. But in a market economy without government intervention, those who benefit from pollution—like the owners of power companies—decide how much pollution occurs. They have no incentive to take into account the costs of pollution that they impose on others.

To see why, remember the nature of the benefits and costs from pollution. For polluters, the benefits take the form of monetary savings: by emitting an extra tonne of sulphur dioxide, any given polluter saves the cost of buying expensive, low-sulphur coal or installing pollution-control equipment. So the benefits of pollution accrue directly to the polluters. (This means $MEB = 0$, so $MSB = MPB$).

The costs of pollution, though, fall on people who have no say in the decision about how much pollution takes place: for example, about half of all airborne sulphur dioxide in eastern Canada comes from sources in the United States, especially coal burning power plants in and around the Tennessee Valley. People who fish in Canada do not control the decisions of power plants in Tennessee. (This means $MPC = 0$, so $MSC = MEC > 0$. A competitive market equilibrium will be where $MPB = MPC = 0$, which means too much pollution will be created.)

Figure 16-2 shows the result of this asymmetry between who reaps the benefits and who pays the costs. In a market economy without government intervention to protect the environment, only the benefits of pollution are taken into account in choosing the quantity of pollution. So the quantity of emissions won't be the socially optimal quantity Q_{OPT}; it will be Q_{MKT}, the quantity at which the marginal social benefit of an additional tonne of pollution is zero, but the

FIGURE 16-2 Why a Market Economy Produces Too Much Pollution

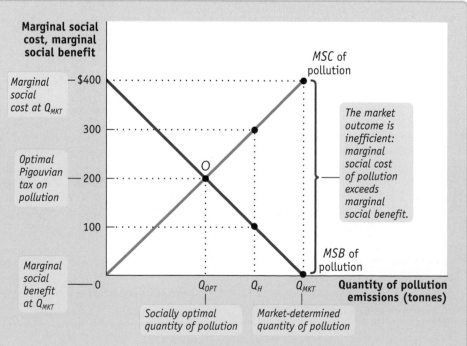

In the absence of government intervention, the quantity of pollution will be Q_{MKT}, the level at which the marginal social benefit of pollution is zero. This is an inefficiently high quantity of pollution: the marginal social cost, $400, greatly exceeds the marginal social benefit, $0. An optimal Pigouvian tax of $200, the value of the marginal social cost of pollution when it equals the marginal social benefit of pollution, can move the market to the socially optimal quantity of pollution, Q_{OPT}. Even halfway between Q_{MKT} and Q_{OPT}, at Q_H, the marginal social cost is three times the marginal social benefit.

FOR INQUIRING MINDS

TALKING, TEXTING, AND DRIVING

Why is that driver in the car in front of us driving so erratically? Could he or she be drunk? Or falling asleep? No, it turns out the driver is talking on a cellphone or maybe texting.

Traffic safety experts take the risks posed by driving while using a cellphone very seriously: A recent study found a six-fold increase in accidents caused by driving while distracted. Drivers engaged in text messaging are twenty-three times more likely to be involved in a crash or near crash event. Of the annual 120 000 traffic accidents in Canada, 30 000 are blamed on distractions such as cellphone use while driving. According to the CBC, cellphone use is the leading cause of fatal collisions in Nova Scotia and Saskatchewan, ahead of speeding and drunk driving. And using hands-free, voice-activated phones to make a call doesn't seem to help much because the main danger is distraction. As one traffic consultant put it, "It's not where your eyes are; it's where your head is."

The Canadian Global Road Safety Committee urges people not to use any phones while driving. In response

"It's not where your eyes are; it's where your head is."

to a growing number of accidents, all Canadian provinces and Yukon have banned the use of all hand-held electronic devices while behind the wheel altogether. Cellphone use while driving is now illegal in many other countries, including Japan and Israel.

Why not leave the decision up to the driver? Because the risk posed by driving while using a cellphone isn't just a

risk to the driver; it's also a safety risk to others—to a driver's passengers, pedestrians, and people in other cars. Even if you decide that the benefit to you of using your cellphone while driving is worth the cost, you aren't taking into account the cost to other people. Driving while using a cellphone, in other words, generates a serious—and sometimes fatal—negative externality.

---

marginal social cost of that additional tonne is much larger—$400. The quantity of pollution in a market economy without government intervention will be higher than its socially optimal quantity. (The Pigouvian tax noted in Figure 16-2 will be explained shortly.)

The reason is that in the absence of government intervention, those who derive the benefits from pollution—in this case, the owners of power plants—don't have to compensate those who bear the costs. So the marginal private cost of pollution to any given polluter is zero: polluters have no incentive to limit the amount of emissions. For example, before the U.S. Clean Air Act of 1970, power plants in the U.S. Midwest used the cheapest type of coal available, despite the fact that cheap coal generated more pollution, and they did nothing to scrub their emissions.

The environmental costs of pollution are the best known and most important example of an **external cost**—an uncompensated cost that an individual or firm imposes on others. There are many other examples of external costs besides pollution. Another important, and certainly very familiar, external cost is traffic congestion—an individual who chooses to drive during rush hour increases congestion and so increases the travel time of other drivers.

We'll see later in this chapter that there are also important examples of **external benefits,** benefits that individuals or firms confer on others without receiving compensation. External costs and benefits are jointly known as **externalities,** with external costs called **negative externalities** and external benefits called **positive externalities.**

As we've already suggested, externalities can lead to individual decisions that are not optimal for society as a whole. Let's take a closer look at why.

An **external cost** is an uncompensated cost that an individual or firm imposes on others.

An **external benefit** is a benefit that an individual or firm confers on others without receiving compensation.

External costs and benefits are known as **externalities.** External costs are **negative externalities,** and external benefits are **positive externalities.**

The Inefficiency of Excess Pollution

We have just shown that in the absence of government action, the quantity of pollution will be *inefficient:* polluters will pollute up to the point at which the marginal social benefit of pollution is zero, as shown by the pollution quantity, Q_{MKT}, in Figure 16-2. Recall that an outcome is efficient if no one could be made better off without making someone else worse off. In Chapter 4 we showed why the market equilibrium quantity in a perfectly competitive market is the efficient quantity of the good, the quantity that maximizes total surplus. Here, we can use a variation of that analysis to show how the presence of a negative externality upsets that result.

Because the marginal social benefit of pollution is zero at Q_{MKT}, reducing the quantity of pollution by one tonne would subtract very little from the total social benefit from pollution. In other words, the benefit to polluters from that last unit of pollution is very low—virtually zero. Meanwhile, the marginal social cost imposed on the rest of society of that last tonne of pollution at Q_{MKT} is quite high—$400. In other words, by reducing the quantity of pollution at Q_{MKT} by one tonne, the total social cost of pollution falls by $400, but total social benefit falls by virtually zero. So total surplus rises by approximately $400 if the quantity of pollution at Q_{MKT} is reduced by one tonne.

If the quantity of pollution is reduced further, there will be more gains in total surplus, though they will be smaller. For example, if the quantity of pollution is Q_H in Figure 16-2, the marginal social benefit of a tonne of pollution is $100, but the marginal social cost is still $300. In other words, reducing the quantity of pollution by one tonne leads to a net gain in total surplus of approximately $300 − $100 = $200. This tells us that Q_H is still an inefficiently high quantity of pollution. Only if the quantity of pollution is reduced to Q_{OPT}, where the marginal social cost and the marginal social benefit of an additional tonne of pollution are both $200, is the outcome efficient.

Externalities and the Competitive Market

Pollution is a by-product of either the manufacture or consumption of goods and services—it is not a product that is directly produced. This implies that another way to study the social welfare impact of pollution is to look at pollution indirectly by investigating the social costs and benefits in the market for the good or service that causes the pollution by its manufacture or consumption.

Figure 16-3 depicts the market for electricity, which we assume is perfectly competitive. The demand curve represents the marginal social benefit of consuming electricity. Since pollution only imposes additional costs on the rest of society, the industry supply curve is the marginal private cost of producing electricity in perfect competition.

The marginal social cost of electricity production is the sum of the marginal private cost of generating the electricity and the marginal external cost of pollution. That means that the gap between *MSC* and *MPC* in the diagram must equal *MEC*. *MSC* gets its upward slope partly from the upward-sloping supply curve—which is also *MPC*—and partly from an increasing marginal external cost of electricity production. *MEC* is increasing because the amount of pollution increases as electricity production increases. As Figure 16-3 shows, increasing the quantity of electricity produced causes the costs related to pollution to rise at a faster rate, even if the amount of pollution created does not rise so quickly. For example, doubling the level of pollution can lead to more than twice as much harm resulting from the pollution.

The perfectly competitive market for electricity is in equilibrium where supply intersects demand at price P_{PC} and quantity Q_{PC}. The resulting consumer surplus is the triangle above P_{PC} (below the demand curve). Likewise, the producer surplus is the triangle below P_{PC} (above the supply curve). But unlike the used books

FIGURE **16-3** Perfect Competition with Externalities

When externalities are created either in production or consumption of a good or service, a perfectly competitive market is inefficient resulting in a deadweight loss. The market for electricity is plagued by a negative externality as the production of electricity often creates significant amounts of harmful pollution. The competitive equilibrium occurs at the intersection between the supply and demand curves. The socially optimal level of output occurs where the marginal social benefit curve intersects the marginal social cost curve. Since the market ignores the negative externality, perfect competition results in too much electricity being produced (and too much pollution) and in electricity being sold at a price that is too low.

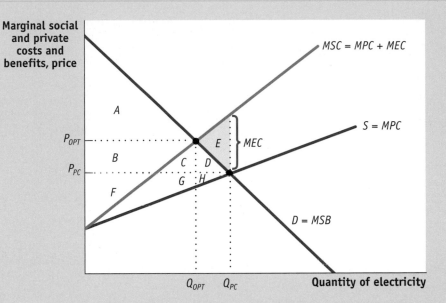

	Perfect Competition Equilibrium	Socially Optimal Production Point
Consumer surplus (*CS*)	$A + B + C + D$	A
Producer surplus (*PS*)	$F + G + H$	$B + C + F + G$
Total external cost (*TEC*)	$C + D + E + G + H$	$C + G$
Total Economic Surplus (Social Welfare = *CS* + *PS* − *TEC*)	$A + B + F − E$	$A + B + F$

we examined in Chapter 4, in this market, the sum of the consumer and producer surplus is not the total benefit to society from the production and consumption of the good—as this sum ignores the impact of pollution. The total external cost imposed by electricity production is the area between *MSC* and the supply curve. The total economic surplus is equal to the sum of consumer surplus and producer surplus minus the total external cost.

The socially optimal level of electricity production occurs where *MSB* intersects *MSC*. Figure 16-3 reveals that the perfectly competitive equilibrium is inefficient; perfect competition is not socially optimal when there are externalities—it results in an overproduction of electricity and added pollution. At the socially optimal level of output, the consumer surplus is the triangle above P_{OPT}, the producer surplus is the area below P_{OPT} but above the supply curve, and the total external cost is the area between *MSC* and the supply curve. Thus the total economic surplus at the socially optimal level is greater than that obtained via perfect competition! The table in Figure 16-3 shows this. Perfect competition results in a deadweight loss equal to the shaded area labelled as *E* in Figure 16-3.

Private Solutions to Externalities

Can the private sector solve the problem of externalities without government intervention? Bear in mind that when an outcome is inefficient, there is potentially a deal that makes people better off. Why don't individuals find a way to make that deal?

According to the **Coase theorem,** even in the presence of externalities an economy can always reach an efficient solution as long as **transaction costs**—the costs to individuals of making a deal—are sufficiently low.

When individuals take external costs or benefits into account, they **internalize the externality.**

In an influential 1960 article, the economist and Nobel laureate Ronald Coase pointed out that in an ideal world the private sector could indeed deal with all externalities. According to the **Coase theorem,** even in the presence of externalities an economy can always reach an efficient solution provided that the costs of making a deal are sufficiently low. The costs of making a deal are known as **transaction costs.**

To get a sense of Coase's argument, imagine two neighbours, Mick and Christina, who both like to barbecue in their backyards on summer afternoons. Mick likes to play golden oldies on his stereo while barbecuing, but this annoys Christina, who can't stand that kind of music.

Who prevails? You might think that it depends on the legal rights involved in the case: if the law says that Mick has the right to play whatever music he wants, Christina just has to suffer; if the law says that Mick needs Christina's consent to play music in his backyard, Mick has to live without his favourite music while barbecuing.

But as Coase pointed out, the outcome need not be determined by legal rights, because Christina and Mick can make a private deal. Even if Mick has the right to play his music, Christina could pay him not to. Even if Mick can't play the music without an okay from Christina, he can offer to pay her to give that okay. These payments allow them to reach an efficient solution, regardless of who has the legal upper hand. If the benefit of the music to Mick exceeds its cost to Christina, the music will go on; if the benefit to Mick is less than the cost to Christina, there will be silence.

The implication of Coase's analysis is that externalities need not lead to inefficiency because individuals have an incentive to make mutually beneficial deals—deals that lead them to take externalities into account when making decisions. When individuals *do* take externalities into account, economists say that they **internalize the externality.** If externalities are fully internalized, the outcome is efficient even without government intervention.

Why can't individuals always internalize externalities? Our barbecue example implicitly assumes the transaction costs are low enough for Mick and Christina to be able to make a deal. In many situations involving externalities, however, transaction costs prevent individuals from making efficient deals. Examples of transaction costs include the following:

- *The costs of communication among the interested parties.* Such costs may be very high if many people are involved.

- *The costs of making legally binding agreements.* Such costs may be high if expensive legal services are required.

- *Costly delays involved in bargaining.* Even if there is a potentially beneficial deal, both sides may hold out in an effort to extract more favourable terms, leading to increased effort and forgone benefit.

In some cases, people do find ways to reduce transaction costs, allowing them to internalize externalities. For example, a house with a junk-filled yard and peeling paint imposes a negative externality on the neighbouring houses, diminishing their value in the eyes of potential house buyers. Some people live in private communities that set rules for home maintenance and behaviour, making bargaining between neighbours unnecessary. But in many cases, transaction costs are too high to make it possible to deal with externalities through private action. For example, tens of millions of people are adversely affected by acid rain. It would be prohibitively expensive to try to make a deal among all those people and all those power companies.

When transaction costs prevent the private sector from dealing with externalities, it is time to look for government solutions. We turn to public policy in the next section.

ECONOMICS ▶ IN ACTION

THANK YOU FOR NOT SMOKING

To some they are known as the "shiver-and-puff people"—the smokers who stand outside their workplaces, even in the depths of winter, to take a cigarette break. Over the past couple of decades, rules against smoking in spaces shared by others have become ever stricter. This is partly a matter of personal dislike—non-smokers really don't like to smell other people's cigarette smoke—but it also reflects concerns over the health risks of second-hand smoke. As Health Canada's warning on many packs says, smoking causes lung cancer, heart disease, and strokes, and may complicate pregnancy. And there's no question that being in the same room as someone who smokes exposes you to at least some health risk.

Second-hand smoke, then, is clearly an example of a negative externality. But how important is it? Putting a dollar-and-cents value on it—that is, measuring the marginal social cost of cigarette smoke—requires not only estimating the health effects but putting a value on these effects. Despite the difficulty, economists have tried. A paper published in 1993 in the *Journal of Economic Perspectives* surveyed the research on the external costs of both cigarette smoking and alcohol consumption.

According to this paper, valuing the health costs of cigarettes depends on whether you count the costs imposed on members of smokers' families, including unborn children, in addition to costs borne by smokers. If you don't, the external costs of second-hand smoke have been estimated at about $0.52 per pack smoked, according to a 2005 study. (This corresponds to the *average* social cost of smoking per pack at the current level of smoking in society.) If you include effects on smokers' families, the number rises considerably—family members who live with smokers are exposed to a lot more smoke. (They are also exposed to the risk of fires, which alone is estimated at $0.09 per pack.) If you include the effects of smoking by pregnant women on their unborn children's future health, the cost is immense—$4.80 per pack, which is more than the pre-tax price charged by cigarette manufacturers.

In 2011, a report issued by Physicians for a Smoke-Free Canada estimated the economic benefit of each smoker who quits: avoiding health care costs of $8553 and $413 000 in benefits from the avoidance of premature deaths—$421 553 in total benefit per smoker who quits. (See source note on copyright page.)

The external costs of second-hand smoke rise considerably when the impact on smokers' families is taken into account.

▼ Quick Review

- The **marginal social cost (*MSC*) of pollution** is equal to the sum of the **marginal private cost (*MPC*) of pollution** and the **marginal external cost (*MEC*) of pollution**: $MSC = MPC + MEC$

- The **marginal social benefit (*MSB*) of pollution** is equal to the sum of the **marginal private benefit (*MPB*) of pollution** and the **marginal external benefit (*MEB*) of pollution**: $MSB = MPB + MEB$

- There are costs as well as benefits to reducing pollution, so the optimal quantity of pollution isn't zero. Instead, the **socially optimal quantity of pollution** is the quantity at which $MSC = MSB$.

- Left to itself, a market economy will typically generate an inefficiently high level of pollution because polluters have no incentive to take into account the costs they impose on others.

- External costs and benefits are known as **externalities.** Pollution is an example of an **external cost,** or **negative externality;** in contrast, some activities can give rise to **external benefits,** or **positive externalities.**

- According to the **Coase theorem,** the private sector can sometimes resolve externalities on its own: if **transaction costs** aren't too high, individuals can reach a deal to **internalize the externality.** When transaction costs are too high, government intervention may be warranted.

CHECK YOUR UNDERSTANDING 16-1

1. Waste water runoff from large poultry farms adversely affects their neighbours. Explain the following:
   a. The nature of the external cost imposed
   b. The outcome in the absence of government intervention or a private deal
   c. The socially optimal outcome

2. According to Yasmin, any student who borrows a book from the university library and fails to return it on time imposes a negative externality on other students. She claims that rather than charging a modest fine for late returns, the library should charge a huge fine so that borrowers will never return a book late. Is Yasmin's economic reasoning correct?

Solutions appear at back of book.

Policies Toward Pollution

Before 1970, there were no rules governing the amount of sulphur dioxide power plants in North America could emit—which is why acid rain got to be such a problem. After 1970, the U.S. Clean Air Act set rules about American sulphur dioxide emissions—and the acidity of rainfall declined significantly. In 1985, Canada passed the Canadian Acid Rain Control Program that set targets to reduce sulphur dioxide emissions in eastern Canada by 50% by 1994. Economists argued, however, that a more flexible system of rules that exploited the effectiveness of markets could achieve lower pollution at less cost. This theory was put into effect with a modified version of the U.S. Clean Air Act in 1990 and the 1991 Canada–U.S. Air Quality Agreement. And guess what? The economists were right!

In this section we'll look at the policies governments use to deal with pollution and at how economic analysis has been used to improve those policies.

Environmental Standards

The most serious external costs in the modern world are surely those associated with actions that damage the environment—air pollution, water pollution, habitat destruction, and so on. Protection of the environment has become a major role of government in all economically advanced nations. Environment Canada is the principal enforcer of environmental policies at the national level, supported by the actions of provincial, territorial, and local governments.

How does a country protect its environment? At present the main policy tools are **environmental standards,** rules that protect the environment by specifying actions by producers and consumers. A familiar example is the law that requires almost all vehicles to have catalytic converters, which reduce the emission of chemicals that can cause smog and lead to health problems. Other rules require communities to treat their sewage or factories to avoid or limit certain kinds of pollution, and so on.

Environmental standards came into widespread use in the 1960s and 1970s, and they have had considerable success in reducing pollution. For example, since the U.S. Clean Air Act in 1970, overall emission of pollutants into the air has fallen by more than a third, even though the U.S. population has grown by a third and the size of its economy has more than doubled. Even in Los Angeles, still famous for its smog, the air has improved dramatically: ozone levels in the South Coast Air Basin exceeded U.S. federal standards on 194 days in 1976; in 2010, on only 7 days. Air pollution levels in Hamilton, Ontario, another city with a long history of smog, have also been trending downward since the mid-1990s.

Despite these successes, economists believe that when regulators can control a polluter's emissions directly, there are more efficient ways than environmental standards to deal with pollution. By using methods grounded in economic analysis, society can achieve a cleaner environment at lower cost. Most current environmental standards are inflexible and don't allow reductions in pollution to be achieved at minimum cost. For example, two power plants—plant A and plant B—might be ordered to reduce pollution by the same percentage, even if their costs of achieving that objective are very different.

How does economic theory suggest that pollution should be directly controlled? There are actually two approaches: taxes and tradable permits. As we'll see, either approach can achieve the efficient outcome at the minimum feasible cost.

Emissions Taxes

One way to deal with pollution directly is to charge polluters an **emissions tax.** Emissions taxes are taxes that depend on the amount of pollution a firm produces. For example, power plants might be charged $200 for every tonne of sulphur dioxide they emit.

Environmental standards are rules that protect the environment by specifying actions by producers and consumers.

An **emissions tax** is a tax that depends on the amount of pollution a firm produces.

Look again at Figure 16-2, which shows that the socially optimal quantity of pollution is Q_{OPT}. At that quantity of pollution, the marginal social benefit and marginal social cost of an additional tonne of emissions are equal at \$200. But in the absence of government intervention, power companies have no incentive to limit pollution to the socially optimal quantity, Q_{OPT}; instead, they will push pollution up to the quantity Q_{MKT}, at which marginal social benefit is zero.

It's now easy to see how an emissions tax can solve the problem. If power companies are required to pay a tax of \$200 per tonne of emissions, they now face a marginal cost of \$200 per tonne and have an incentive to reduce emissions to Q_{OPT}, the socially optimal quantity. This illustrates a general result: an emissions tax equal to the marginal social cost at the socially optimal quantity of pollution induces polluters to internalize the externality—to take into account the true costs to society of their actions.

GLOBAL COMPARISON

ECONOMIC GROWTH AND GREENHOUSE GASES IN SIX COUNTRIES

At first glance, a comparison of the per capita greenhouse gas emissions of various countries, shown in panel (a) of this graph, suggests that Australia, Canada, and the United States are the worst offenders. The average Canadian is responsible for 22.9 tonnes of greenhouse gas emissions (measured in CO_2 equivalents)—the pollution that causes global warming—compared to only 6.9 tonnes for the average Uzbek, 5.5 tonnes for the average Chinese, and 1.7 tonnes for the average Indian.

Such a conclusion, however, ignores an important factor in determining the level of a country's greenhouse gas emissions: its gross domestic product, or GDP—the total value of a country's domestic output. Output typically cannot be produced without more energy, and more energy usage typically results in more pollution. In fact, some have argued that criticizing a country's level of greenhouse gases without taking account of its level of economic development is misguided. It would be equivalent to faulting a country for being at a more advanced stage of economic development.

A more meaningful way to compare pollution across countries is to measure emissions per \$1 million of a country's GDP, as shown in panel (b). On this basis, the

United States, Canada, India, and Australia are now "green" countries, but China and Uzbekistan are not. What explains the reversal once GDP is accounted for? The answer: both economics and government behaviour.

First, there is the issue of economics. Countries that are poor and have begun to industrialize, such as Uzbekistan, often view money spent to reduce pollution as better spent on other things. From their perspective, they are still too poor to afford as clean an environment as wealthy advanced countries. They claim that to impose a wealthy country's environmental standards on them would jeopardize their economic growth.

Second, there is the issue of government behaviour—or more precisely, whether or not a government possesses the tools necessary to effectively control pollution. China is a good illustration of this problem. The Chinese government lacks sufficient regulatory power to enforce its own environmental rules, promote energy conservation, or encourage pollution reduction. To produce \$1 of GDP, China spends three times the world average on energy—far more than Indonesia, for example, which is also a poor country. The case of China illustrates just how important government intervention is in improving society's welfare in the presence of externalities.

Source: World Resources Institute.

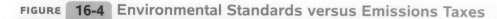

FIGURE 16-4 Environmental Standards versus Emissions Taxes

FIGURE 16-4 Environmental Standards versus Emissions Taxes

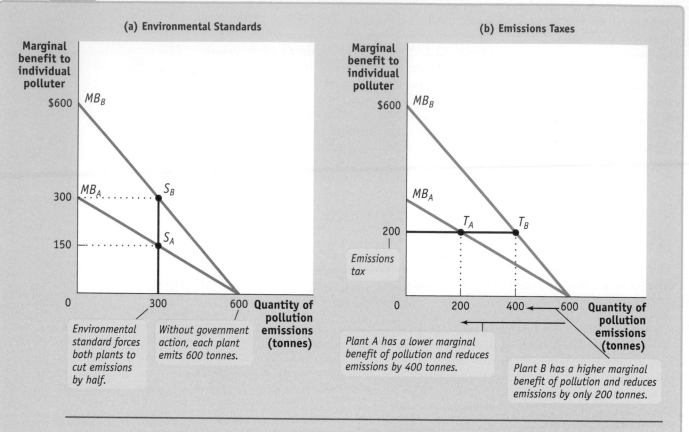

(a) Environmental Standards

Environmental standard forces both plants to cut emissions by half.

Without government action, each plant emits 600 tonnes.

(b) Emissions Taxes

Plant A has a lower marginal benefit of pollution and reduces emissions by 400 tonnes.

Plant B has a higher marginal benefit of pollution and reduces emissions by only 200 tonnes.

In both panels, MB_A shows the marginal benefit of pollution to plant A and MB_B shows the marginal benefit of pollution to plant B. In the absence of government intervention, each plant would emit 600 tonnes. However, the cost of reducing emissions is lower for plant A, as shown by the fact that MB_A lies below MB_B. Panel (a) shows the result of an environmental standard that requires both plants to cut emissions in half; this is inefficient, because it leaves the marginal benefit of pollution higher for plant B than for plant A. Panel (b) shows that an emissions tax achieves the same quantity of overall pollution efficiently: faced with an emissions tax of $200 per tonne, each plant reduces pollution to the point where its marginal benefit is $200.

Why is an emissions tax an efficient way (that is, a cost-minimizing way) to reduce pollution but environmental standards generally are not? Because an emissions tax ensures that the marginal benefit of pollution is equal for all sources of pollution, but an environmental standard does not. Figure 16-4 shows a hypothetical industry consisting of only two plants, plant A and plant B. We'll assume that plant A uses newer technology than plant B and so has a lower cost of reducing pollution. Reflecting this difference in costs, plant A's marginal benefit of pollution curve, MB_A, lies below plant B's marginal benefit of pollution curve, MB_B. Because it is more costly for plant B to reduce its pollution at any output quantity, an additional tonne of pollution is worth more to plant B than to plant A.

In the absence of government action, we know that polluters will pollute until the marginal social benefit of an additional unit of emissions is equal to zero. Recall that the marginal social benefit of pollution is the cost savings, at the margin, to polluters of an additional unit of pollution. As a result, without government intervention each plant will pollute until its own marginal benefit of pollution is equal to zero. This corresponds to an emissions quantity of 600 tonnes each for plants A and B—the quantity of pollution at which MB_A and MB_B are each equal to zero. So although plant A and plant B value a tonne of emissions differently, without government action they will each choose to emit the same amount of pollution.

Now suppose that the government decides that overall pollution from this industry should be cut in half, from 1200 tonnes to 600 tonnes. Panel (a) of Figure 16-4 shows how this might be achieved with an environmental standard that requires each plant to cut its emissions in half, from 600 to 300 tonnes. The standard has the desired effect of reducing overall emissions from 1200 to 600 tonnes but accomplishes it in an inefficient way. As you can see from panel (a), the environmental standard leads plant A to produce at point S_A, where its marginal benefit of pollution is $150, but plant B is now producing at point S_B, where its marginal benefit of pollution is twice as high, $300.

This difference in marginal benefits between the two plants tells us that the same quantity of pollution can be achieved at lower total cost by allowing plant B to pollute more than 300 tonnes but inducing plant A to pollute less. In fact, the efficient way to reduce pollution is to ensure that at the industry-wide outcome, the marginal benefit of pollution is the same for all plants. When each plant values a unit of pollution equally, there is no way to rearrange pollution reduction among the various plants that achieves the socially optimal quantity of pollution at a lower total cost.

We can see from panel (b) how an emissions tax achieves exactly that result. Suppose both plant A and plant B pay an emissions tax of $200 per tonne, so that the marginal cost of an additional tonne of emissions to each plant is now $200 rather than zero. As a result, plant A produces at T_A and plant B produces at T_B. So plant A reduces its pollution more than it would under an inflexible environmental standard, cutting its emissions from 600 to 200 tonnes; meanwhile, plant B reduces its pollution less, going from 600 to 400 tonnes. In the end, total pollution—600 tonnes—is the same as under the environmental standard, but total surplus is higher. That's because the reduction in pollution has been achieved efficiently, allocating most of the reduction to plant A, the plant that can reduce emissions at lower cost.

The term *emissions tax* may convey the misleading impression that taxes are a solution to only one kind of external cost, pollution. In fact, taxes can be used to discourage any activity that generates negative externalities, such as driving during rush hour or operating a noisy bar in a residential area. In general, taxes designed to reduce external costs are known as **Pigouvian taxes,** after the economist A. C. Pigou, who emphasized their usefulness in his classic 1920 book, *The Economics of Welfare*. In our example, the optimal Pigouvian tax is $200; as you can see from Figure 16-2, this corresponds to the marginal social cost of pollution at the socially optimal output quantity, Q_{OPT}.

Are there any problems with emissions taxes? The main concern is that in practice government officials usually aren't sure how high the tax should be set. If they set the tax too low, there will be too little improvement in the environment; if they set it too high, emissions will be reduced by more than is efficient. This uncertainty cannot be eliminated, but the nature of the risks can be changed by using an alternative strategy, issuing tradable emissions permits.

The Pigouvian Tax in the Competitive Market

Rather than levy a tax directly on pollution, it is possible to impose the tax on the production of the good whose production or consumption results in the creation of the pollution. Figure 16-5 below revisits the competitive market for electricity with an optimal Pigouvian tax.

Suppose an excise tax is imposed on electricity producers. This per-unit tax raises the marginal private cost of suppliers by T, effectively shifting the supply curve up. If the tax is set equal to the size of the marginal external cost of electricity at the socially optimal level of output, then the tax results in the socially optimal point being reached. The socially optimal level of electricity (Q_{OPT}) will be

Taxes designed to reduce external costs are known as **Pigouvian taxes.**

FIGURE 16-5 Applying a Pigouvian Tax to Perfect Competition with Externalities

If instead of directly taxing pollution, an excise tax, *T*, is applied on the production of the good causing the pollution, then the optimal per-unit Pigouvian tax on output is equal to its marginal external cost at the socially optimal quantity of output. The tax eliminates the deadweight loss of perfect competition by forcing the market to internalize the costs generated by the externality.

	Optimal Pigouvian Tax	Socially Optimal Production Point
Consumer surplus (*CS*)	A	A
Producer surplus (*PS*)	$H + I$	$B + C + D + E + F + G + H + I$
Tax Revenue ($T \times Q_{OPT}$)	$B + C + D + E + F + G$	0
Total External Cost (*TEC*)	$D + G + I$	$D + G + I$
Total Economic Surplus (Social Welfare = $CS + PS + T \times Q_{OPT} - TEC$)	$A + B + C + E + F + H$	$A + B + C + E + F + H$

produced, consumers will be charged the socially optimal price (P_{OPT}), and firms will receive a price of ($P_{OPT} - T$). Of course, as we discussed in Chapter 7, if the per-unit tax is applied to consumers the same result will occur.

After the tax is applied, the consumer surplus is equal to area A, the producer surplus is equal to the sum of areas *H* and *I*, while the government tax revenue is the rectangle made up of *B*, *C*, *D*, *E*, *F*, and *G*. Since the total external cost is the area between the *MSC* and supply curves it equals the sum of the areas *D*, *G*, and *I*. So with the tax, the total economic surplus is equal to the sum of the areas *A*, *B*, *C*, *E*, *F*, and *H*. The calculations in the table in Figure 16-5 show that this outcome is socially efficient. By charging a per-unit tax on electricity equal to the marginal external cost at the socially optimal level, the market fully internalizes the cost generated by the externality, which eliminates the deadweight loss of perfect competition.

Tradable Emissions Permits

Tradable emissions permits are licences to emit limited quantities of pollutants that can be bought and sold by polluters. They are usually issued to polluting firms according to some formula reflecting their history. For example, each power plant might be issued permits equal to 50% of its emissions before the system went into effect. The more important point, however, is that these permits are *tradable*. Firms with differing costs of reducing pollution can now engage in

Tradable emissions permits are licences to emit limited quantities of pollutants that can be bought and sold by polluters.

mutually beneficial transactions: those that find it easier to reduce pollution will sell some of their permits to those that find it more difficult.

In other words, firms will use transactions in permits to reallocate pollution reduction among themselves, so that in the end those with the lowest cost will reduce their pollution the most, and those with the highest cost will reduce their pollution the least. Assume that the government issues 300 licences each to plant A and plant B, where one licence allows the emission of one tonne of pollution. Under a system of tradable emissions permits, plant A will find it profitable to sell 100 of its 300 government-issued licences to plant B. The effect of a tradable permit system is to create a market in rights to pollute.

Just like emissions taxes, tradable permits provide polluters with an incentive to take the marginal social cost of pollution into account. To see why, suppose that the market price of a permit to emit one tonne of sulphur dioxide is $200. Then every plant has an incentive to limit its emissions of sulphur dioxide to the point where its marginal benefit of emitting another tonne of pollution is $200. This is obvious for plants that buy rights to pollute: if a plant must pay $200 for the right to emit an additional tonne of sulphur dioxide, it faces the same incentives as a plant facing an emissions tax of $200 per tonne.

But it's equally true for plants that have more permits than they plan to use: by *not* emitting a tonne of sulphur dioxide, a plant frees up a permit that it can sell for $200, so the opportunity cost of a tonne of emissions to the plant's owner is $200.

In short, tradable emissions permits have the same cost-minimizing advantage as Pigouvian taxes over environmental standards: either system ensures that those who can reduce pollution most cheaply are the ones who do so. The socially optimal quantity of pollution shown in Figure 16-2 could be efficiently achieved either way: by imposing an emissions tax of $200 per tonne of pollution or by issuing tradable permits to emit Q_{OPT} tonnes of pollution. If regulators choose to issue Q_{OPT} permits, where one permit allows the release of one tonne of emissions, then the equilibrium market price of a permit among polluters will indeed be $200. Why? You can see from Figure 16-2 that at Q_{OPT}, only polluters with a marginal benefit of pollution of $200 or more will buy a permit. And the last polluter who buys—who has a marginal benefit of exactly $200—sets the market price.

It's important to realize that emissions taxes and tradable permits do more than induce polluting industries to reduce their output. Unlike rigid environmental standards, emissions taxes and tradable permits provide incentives to create and use technology that emits less pollution—new technology that lowers the socially optimal level of pollution. The main effect of the permit system for sulphur dioxide has been to change *how* electricity is produced rather than to reduce the nation's electricity output. For example, power companies have shifted to the use of alternative fuels such as low-sulphur coal and natural gas; they have also installed scrubbers that take much of the sulphur dioxide out of a power plant's emissions.

The main problem with tradable emissions permits is the flip-side of the problem with emissions taxes: because it is difficult to determine the optimal quantity of pollution, governments can find themselves either issuing too many permits (that is, they don't reduce pollution enough) or issuing too few (that is, they reduce pollution too much).

Lacking any significant new federal action, in 2008 British Columbia, Manitoba, Ontario, and Quebec, committed to joining the Western Climate Initiative: a tradable permits market in Canada and the United States that seeks to reduce greenhouse gas emissions and the negative externalities they create. After first relying on environmental standards, the U.S. government has turned to a system of tradable permits to control acid rain. And in 2005 the European Union created the largest emissions-trading scheme, with the purpose of controlling emissions of carbon dioxide. The EU scheme is part of a larger global market for the trading of greenhouse gas permits. The upcoming Economics in Action describes these two systems.

Emissions Taxes Versus Tradable Emissions Permits

It turns out that a tax on emissions of greenhouse gases, like the carbon tax in British Columbia, can have the exact same outcome as a system of tradable emissions permit. Figure 16-6 below helps to convey this point.

Suppose we have a product whose production results in the emission of greenhouse gases. Panel (a) of Figure 16-6 shows the impact of a tax on greenhouse gas emissions that is levied on the suppliers of this product. Imposing an excise tax, T, per unit shifts the supply curve up to $(S + T)$ and moves the market equilibrium from A to B. In the new equilibrium, the quantity exchanged has declined (from Q_E to Q_T), the price paid by consumers has increased (from P_E to P_C), and the price received by producers will decline (from P_E to P_P, where $P_P = P_C - T$). The tax revenue is equal to the area shaded in green in Figure 16-6 (Tax revenue = $T \times Q_T$).

Now what if the government decides to impose a system of tradable emissions permits instead? Such a system is described in panel (b) of Figure 16-6: the government creates a volume limit or "cap" on the total quantity of the product that can be supplied. In effect, this makes the supply curve perfectly vertical and shifts it to the left to the new (lower) government imposed upper bound on production. This new supply curve is labelled S_2 in the diagram. In the new equilibrium at B, the quantity exchanged has declined (from Q_E to Q_{Cap}) and the price paid by consumers has increased (from P_E to P_C). If the government issues permits freely, the firms receiving them capture the shaded area as profit since the price earned by firms (P_C) exceeds their cost of production (P_P). Alternatively,

FIGURE 16-6 Comparing Emissions Taxes and Tradable Emissions Permits

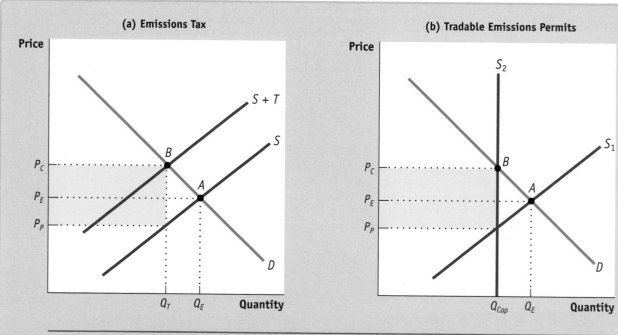

(a) Emissions Tax

(b) Tradable Emissions Permits

As shown in panel (a), a per-unit emissions tax collected from suppliers shifts the supply curve up. This reduces the quantity of the product exchanged, raises the price that consumers pay, lowers the price that suppliers receive, and results in tax revenue for the government (equal to the green-shaded area).

Using a system of tradable emissions permits makes the supply curve perfectly vertical at the government imposed maximum level of output, as shown in panel (b). This reduces the quantity of the product exchanged and raises the price that consumers pay. If the permits are free, the green-shaded area represents profits captured by firms. If permits are sold by the government, this area represents the revenue for the government.

if the government sells the permits, then the green-shaded area is equal to the governments permit revenue and firms earn zero profit.

The lesson is simple. It does not matter whether the government uses an emissions tax or a tradable emissions system; if properly designed both can result in exactly the same outcome for society.

ECONOMICS > IN ACTION

CAP AND TRADE

Unlike the Western Climate Initiative, the tradable emissions permit systems for both acid rain in the United States and greenhouse gases in the European Union are examples of *cap and trade systems:* the government sets a *cap* (a maximum amount of pollutant that can be emitted), issues tradable emissions permits, and enforces a yearly rule that a polluter must hold a number of permits equal to the amount of pollutant emitted. The goal is to set the cap low enough to generate environmental benefits, while giving polluters flexibility in meeting environmental standards and motivating them to adopt new technologies that will lower the cost of reducing pollution.

Starting in the 1980s, the federal government used a cap and trade system to help phase out the consumption of CFCs, methyl bromide, and HCFCs, all of which depleted the ozone layer. But since this successful cap and trade experiment, the federal government has stayed away from introducing either a larger cap and trade system for greenhouse gases or a carbon tax. At the provincial level, Alberta and Ontario have each set up cap and trade systems for nitrogen oxide and sulphur dioxide emitted by large electricity generators. In 2013, Quebec started a cap and trade system for industrial emissions of greenhouse gases. Quebec intends to merge this market with the Western Climate Initiative.

The David Suzuki Foundation recommends companies like Terrapass to individuals and companies looking to manage their carbon emissions.

In 1994 the United States began a cap and trade system for the sulphur dioxide emissions that cause acid rain. Thanks to the system, air pollutants decreased by more than 40% from 1990 to 2008, and 2010 acid rain levels dropped to approximately 50% of their 1980 levels. Economists who have analyzed the sulphur dioxide cap and trade system point to another reason for its success: it would have been 80% more expensive to reduce emissions by this much using a non-marketbased regulatory policy.

The EU cap and trade scheme, covering all 28 member nations of the European Union, is the world's only mandatory trading scheme for greenhouse gases. It is scheduled to achieve a 21% reduction in greenhouse gases by 2020 compared to 2005 levels.

Other countries, like Australia and New Zealand, have adopted less comprehensive trading schemes for greenhouse gases. According to the World Bank, the worldwide market for greenhouse gases—also called *carbon trading*—has grown rapidly, from $11 billion in permits traded in 2005 to $142 billion in 2010. In New Zealand, famous for its sheep and lamb industry, farmers are busy converting grazing land into forests so that they can sell permits beginning in 2015, when companies will be required to pay for their emissions.

Despite all this good news, however, cap and trade systems are not silver bullets for the world's pollution problems. Although they are appropriate for pollution that's geographically dispersed, like sulphur dioxide and greenhouse gases, they don't work for pollution that's localized, like mercury or lead contamination. In addition, the amount of overall reduction in pollution depends on the level of the cap. Under industry pressure, regulators run the risk of issuing too many permits, effectively eliminating the cap. Finally, there must be vigilant monitoring of compliance if the system is to work. Without oversight of how much a polluter is actually emitting, there is no way to know for sure that the rules are being followed.

CHECK YOUR UNDERSTANDING 16-2

1. Some opponents of tradable emissions permits object to them on the grounds that polluters that sell their permits benefit monetarily from their contribution to polluting the environment. Assess this argument.

2. Explain the following.
   a. Why an emissions tax smaller than or greater than the marginal social cost at Q_{OPT} leads to a smaller total surplus compared to the total surplus generated if the emissions tax had been set optimally
   b. Why a system of tradable emissions permits that sets the total quantity of allowable pollution higher or lower than Q_{OPT} leads to a smaller total surplus compared to the total surplus generated if the number of permits had been set optimally

Solutions appear at back of book.

Positive Externalities

Stretching from Niagara Falls through Hamilton and the Greater Toronto Area, the Golden Horseshoe region is probably the most densely populated region in the country, containing a large portion of Canada's industry and about 9 million residents. Yet a drive through this region reveals a surprising feature: farm after farm, growing everything from corn to peaches to the famous Niagara grapes for ice wine. This situation is not an accident: the federal and provincial governments have passed laws that give tax subsidies to farmers who permanently preserve their farmland rather than sell it to developers. These subsidies have helped preserve thousands of hectares of open space.

Why have Canadian citizens raised their own tax burden to subsidize the preservation of farmland? Because they believe that preserved farmland in an already heavily developed area provides external benefits, such as natural beauty, access to fresh food, and the conservation of wild bird populations. In addition, preservation alleviates the external costs that come with more development, such as pressure on roads, water supplies, and municipal services—and, inevitably, more pollution.

In this section we'll explore the topics of external benefits and positive externalities. They are, in many ways, the mirror images of external costs and negative externalities. Left to its own, the market will produce too little of a good (in this case, preserved Ontario farmland) that confers external benefits on others. But society as a whole is better off when policies are adopted that increase the supply of such a good.

Preserved Farmland: An External Benefit

Preserved farmland yields both benefits and costs to society. In the absence of government intervention, the farmer who wants to sell his or her land incurs all

FIGURE   16-7   Why a Market Economy Preserves Too Little Farmland

Without government intervention, the quantity of preserved farmland will be zero, the level at which the marginal social cost of preservation is zero. This is an inefficiently low quantity of preserved farmland: the marginal social benefit is $20 000, but the marginal social cost is zero. An optimal Pigouvian subsidy of $10 000, the value of the marginal social benefit of preservation when it equals the marginal social cost, can move the market to the socially optimal level of preservation, Q_{OPT}.

The market outcome is inefficient: marginal social benefit of farmland preservation exceeds marginal social cost.

MSC of preserved farmland

Marginal social cost, marginal social benefit

Marginal social benefit at Q_{MKT} — $20 000

Optimal Pigouvian subsidy on farmland preservation — 10 000

O

Socially optimal point

MSB of preserved farmland

Marginal social cost at Q_{MKT} — 0

Q_{MKT}

Q_{OPT}

Quantity of preserved farmland (hectares)

Market-determined quantity of preserved farmland

Socially optimal quantity of preserved farmland

the costs of preservation—namely, the forgone profit to be made from selling the farmland to a developer. But the benefits of preserved farmland accrue not to the farmer but to neighbouring residents, who have no right to influence how the farmland is disposed of.[2]

Figure 16-7 illustrates society's problem. The marginal social cost of preserved farmland, shown by *MSC*, is the additional cost imposed on society by an additional hectare of such farmland. This represents the forgone profits that would have accrued to farmers if they had sold their land to developers. The line is upward-sloping because when very few hectares are preserved and there is plenty of land available for development, the profit that could be made from selling a hectare to a developer is small. But as the number of preserved hectares increases and few are left for development, the amount a developer is willing to pay for them, and therefore the forgone profit increases as well.

The *MSB* curve represents the marginal social benefit of preserved farmland. It is the additional benefit that accrues to society—in this case, the farmer's neighbours—when an additional hectare of farmland is preserved. The curve is downward sloping because as more farmland is preserved, the benefit to society of preserving another hectare falls. As Figure 16-7 shows, the socially optimal point, *O*, occurs when the marginal social cost and the marginal social benefit are equalized—here, at a price of $10 000 per hectare. At the socially optimum point, Q_{OPT} hectares of farmland are preserved.

---

[2]In this case, there is no marginal external cost (*MEC* = 0). Therefore, the marginal social cost is entirely the marginal private cost (*MSC = MPC*). Similarly, in the absence of government intervention, since there is no marginal private benefit of preserving farmland (*MPB* = 0), so the marginal social benefit is entirely the marginal external benefit (*MSB = MEB*).

A **Pigouvian subsidy** is a payment designed to encourage activities that yield external benefits.

A **technology spillover** is an external benefit that results when knowledge spreads among individuals and firms.

The market alone will not provide Q_{OPT} hectares of preserved farmland. Instead, in the market outcome no hectares will be preserved; the level of preserved farmland, Q_{MKT}, is equal to zero. That's because farmers will set the marginal social cost of preservation—their forgone profits—at zero and sell all their hectares to developers.[3] Because farmers bear the entire cost of preservation but gain none of the benefits, an inefficiently low quantity of farmland will be preserved in the market outcome.

This is clearly inefficient because at zero hectares preserved, the marginal social benefit of preserving a hectare of farmland is $20 000. So how can the economy be induced to produce Q_{OPT} hectares of preserved farmland, the socially optimal level? The answer is a **Pigouvian subsidy:** a payment designed to encourage activities that yield external benefits. The optimal Pigouvian subsidy, as shown in Figure 16-7, is equal to the marginal social benefit of preserved farmland at the socially optimal level, Q_{OPT}—that is, $10 000 per hectare.

So Canadians are indeed implementing the right policy to raise their social welfare—taxing themselves in order to provide subsidies for farmland preservation.

Positive Externalities in the Modern Economy

In the overall Canadian economy, the most important single source of external benefits is the creation of knowledge. In high-tech industries such as semiconductors, software design, green technology, and bioengineering, innovations by one firm are quickly emulated and improved upon by rival firms. Such spreading of knowledge across individuals and firms is known as a **technology spillover.** In the modern economy, the greatest sources of technology spillovers are major universities and research institutes.

In technologically advanced countries such as Canada, the United States, Japan, the United Kingdom, Germany, France, and Israel, there is an ongoing exchange of people and ideas among private industries, major universities, and research institutes located in close proximity. The dynamic interplay that occurs in these *research clusters* spurs innovation and competition, theoretical advances, and practical applications. (See the Business Case at the end of the chapter for more on research clusters.)

One of Canada's best known and most successful research clusters is located in the so-called Technology Triangle of Kitchener, Waterloo, and Cambridge, anchored by several universities and colleges, the Perimeter Institute, the Institute for Quantum Computing, a number of other research parks and incubators, plus companies such as BlackBerry, OpenText, and Google. Ultimately, these areas of technology spillover increase the economy's productivity and raise living standards.

But research clusters don't appear out of thin air. Except in a few instances in which firms have funded basic research on a long-term basis, research clusters have grown up around major universities. And like farmland preservation, major universities and their research activities are subsidized by government. In fact, government policy-makers in technologically advanced countries have long understood that the external benefits generated by knowledge, stemming from basic education to high-tech research, are key to the economy's growth over time.

---

[3]The competitive market outcome occurs where $MPC = MPB$. Since MPB is zero in the present case, the market outcome is at zero. In the absence of government intervention, no farmland is preserved ($Q_{MKT} = 0$ in Figure 16-7). This is much less than the socially optimal level, which occurs where $MSC = MSB > 0$; society wants some positive quantity of farmland preserved.

ECONOMICS ▶ IN ACTION

THE IMPECCABLE ECONOMIC LOGIC OF EARLY-CHILDHOOD INTERVENTION PROGRAMS

One of the most vexing problems facing any society is how to break what researchers call the "cycle of poverty": children who grow up in disadvantaged socioeconomic circumstances are far more likely to remain trapped in poverty as adults, even after we account for differences in ability. They are more likely to be unemployed or underemployed, to engage in crime, and to suffer chronic health problems.

Early-childhood intervention has offered some hope of breaking the cycle. A 2006 study by the RAND Corporation found that high-quality early-childhood programs that focus on education and health care lead to significant social, intellectual, and financial advantages for kids who would otherwise be at risk of dropping out of high school and of engaging in criminal behaviour. Children in these programs were less likely to engage in such destructive behaviours and more likely to end up with a job and to earn a high salary later in life.

Early-childhood intervention programs focusing on education and health offer many external benefits to society.

Another study by researchers at the University of Toronto in 2003 looked at early-childhood intervention programs from a dollars-and-cents perspective, estimating that a national child-care program launched in Canada could provide annual benefits worth $10.2 billion at a cost of $7.9 billion; a 29% return on investment. A similar U.S. study puts the rate of return in that country as high as $17 per $1 spent!

CHECK YOUR UNDERSTANDING   16-3

1. In 2010-2011, government grants to Canadian universities and colleges totalled almost $20 billion. The federal government channelled another $3 billion in grants and loans to students. Provincial and territorial governments also provided grants and loans to post-secondary students. Explain why this can be an optimal policy to encourage the creation of knowledge.

2. In each of the following cases, determine whether an external cost or an external benefit is imposed and what an appropriate policy response would be.
   a. Trees planted in urban areas improve air quality and lower summer temperatures.
   b. Water-saving toilets reduce the need to pump water from rivers and aquifers. The cost of a litre of water to homeowners is virtually zero.
   c. Old computer monitors contain toxic materials that pollute the environment when improperly disposed of.

Solutions appear at back of book.

> ▼ **Quick Review**
>
> • When there are positive externalities, or external benefits, a market economy, left to itself, will typically produce too little of the good or activity. The socially optimal quantity of the good or activity can be achieved by an optimal **Pigouvian subsidy.**
>
> • The most important example of external benefits in the economy is the creation of knowledge through **technology spillover.**

Network Externalities

In Chapter 13 we explained that a *network externality* exists when the value of a good or service to an individual is greater when a large number of other people also use the good or service. Although network externalities are common in technology-driven sectors of the economy, the phenomenon is considerably more widespread than that.

Unlike positive and negative externalities, network externalities have no inherently favourable or adverse effect on society. What they share, rather, is the existence of an external effect from one person's actions.

Network externalities play a key role both in the modern economy and in a number of policy controversies. Here we will examine more closely where and how network externalities occur and then at some of the regulatory issues they raise.

Types of Network Externalities

For all network externalities, the value of the good or service is derived entirely from its ability to link many people possessing the same good or service. As a result, the marginal benefit of the good or service to any one individual depends on the number of other individuals who use it.

Although most network externalities involve methods of communication—the Internet, telephones, fax machines, and so on—they can exist when other users are not strictly necessary for the use of a good, as long as they enhance its usefulness. For example, in the early days of railroad development, a railroad from Montreal to Winnipeg would have had considerable value all by itself, as would have a railroad from Vancouver to Winnipeg. However, each line was worth more given the existence of the other, because once both were in place, goods could be shipped via Winnipeg between Montreal and Vancouver. In the modern world, a scheduled flight between two airports becomes more valuable if one or both of those airports is a hub with connections to other places.

Even this kind of direct link need not be necessary to create important network externalities. Any way in which other people's consumption of a good or service increases your own marginal benefit from consumption of that good or service can give rise to network effects.

Recall that the classic case of indirect network externalities is computer operating systems and that most personal computers around the world run on Windows by Microsoft.

Why does Windows dominate over other operating systems such as Apple's OSX or Linux? Is a personal computer running Windows useful only to the extent that other people possess the same good? Not in a direct sense; there isn't a literal network issue making Windows the preferred system.

The dominance of Windows is self-reinforcing for at least two indirect reasons. First, it is easier for a Windows user to get help and advice from other computer users than for someone using a less popular system. Second, Windows attracts more attention from software developers, so more programs run on Windows than on any other operating system.

Network externalities in this broad sense occur for many goods and services. Even your choice of a car is influenced by a form of network externalities. Most people would be reluctant to switch to a car that runs on natural gas because fueling the car would be difficult: very few gas stations offer natural gas. And the reason service stations do not offer natural gas is, of course, that few people drive anything other than gasoline-powered cars. Or to take a less drastic example, people who live in small towns are reluctant to drive an unusual imported vehicle: where would they find a mechanic who knows how to fix it? So the circularity that makes one person choose Windows because everyone else uses Windows also applies to non-high-tech goods like cars.

When a good or service is subject to a network externality, it exhibits **positive feedback:** if large numbers of people buy it, other people become more likely to buy it, too. If people *don't* buy the good or service, others become less likely to buy it. So both success and failure tend to be self-reinforcing. This leads to a kind of "chicken-versus-egg problem": if each person places a positive value on a product based on whether another person owns it, how do you get anyone to buy it in the first place? Producers of products that are subject to network externalities are aware of this problem, understanding that of two competing products, it's the one with the largest network—not necessarily the one that's the better product—that

A good is subject to **positive feedback** when success breeds greater success and failure breeds further failure.

will win in the end. That is, the product with the largest network will eventually dominate the market, and competing products will eventually disappear.

One way to gain an advantage at the early stages of this kind of market is to sell the product cheaply, perhaps at a loss, in order to increase the size of the network. So we often see companies introducing new high-technology products at a price well below production costs. For example, during the 1990s, the two main competitors in the market for Internet browser software, Netscape Navigator and Microsoft Internet Explorer, both offered their products for free. And even today, many cellphone companies offer free handsets to attract consumers to their wireless network.

Finally, network externalities present special challenges for antitrust regulators because competition and antitrust laws do not, strictly speaking, forbid monopoly. Rather, they only prohibit "monopolization"—efforts to create a monopoly. If you just happen to end up ruling an industry, that's okay, but if you take actions designed to drive out competition, that's not okay. So we could argue that monopolies in goods with network externalities, because they occur naturally, should not pose legal problems.

Unfortunately, it isn't that simple. Firms investing in new technologies are clearly trying to establish monopoly positions. Furthermore, in the face of positive feedback, firms have an incentive to engage in aggressive strategies to push their goods in order to increase their network size and tip the market in their direction. So what is the dividing line between legal and illegal actions?

At this point, the rules are somewhat in flux. In the Microsoft antitrust case, described in the following Economics in Action, reasonable economists and legal experts disagreed sharply both about whether the company had broken the law by pursuing a monopoly position and about whether the company should be broken up to diminish its ability to tip new markets in its favour.

ECONOMICS ▸ IN ACTION

THE MICROSOFT CASE

In 2000 the U.S. Justice Department took on Microsoft in one of the most watched antitrust cases in history. By that time, Microsoft had become the world's most valuable corporation, and its founder, Bill Gates, was the world's richest man. What the U.S. government sought was nothing less than the breakup of the company.

The case involved almost all of the issues raised by goods with network externalities. Microsoft was, by any reasonable definition, a monopoly: leaving aside the niches of Apple customers and Linux users, just about all personal computers ran the Windows operating system. The key fact sustaining the Windows system was the force of a network externality: people used Windows because other people used Windows.

The U.S. government did not, however, challenge the Windows monopoly itself (although some economists urged it to). Most experts agreed that monopoly per se is a natural thing in such industries and should not be prevented. What the U.S. government claimed, however, was that Microsoft had used its monopoly position in operating systems to give its other products an advantage over competitors. For example, by including Internet Explorer

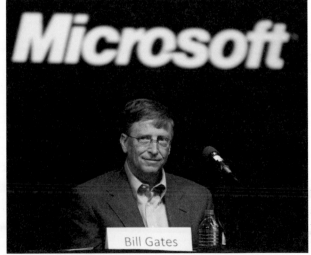

The Microsoft case involved almost all of the issues raised by goods with network externalities.

as part of the Windows system, it was alleged, Microsoft was giving itself an unfair advantage over its rival Netscape in the browser software market.

Why was this considered harmful? The U.S. government argued both that monopolies were being created unnecessarily and that Microsoft was discouraging innovation. Potential innovators in software, the U.S. government claimed, were unwilling to invest large sums out of fear that Microsoft would use its control of the operating system to take away any market competitors might win: Microsoft would produce a competing product that would then be sold as a bundle with the Windows operating system. For its part, Microsoft argued that by setting the precedent that companies would be punished for success, the U.S. government was the real opponent of innovation—innovation that had benefitted customers with lower prices and increasingly sophisticated products.

At first the case went against Microsoft, when a judge ordered the company split in two—into an operating-system company and a company selling the firm's other products. But this judgment was overturned on appeal. In November 2001, the U.S. government reached a settlement with Microsoft in which the company agreed to provide other companies with the technology to develop products that interacted seamlessly with Microsoft's software, thus removing the company's special advantage acquired through bundling its products.

Competitors complained bitterly that this settlement had far too many loopholes and that Microsoft's ability to exploit its monopoly position would remain. And by early 2004, the U.S. government agreed: antitrust lawyers from the Justice Department reported to the judge who negotiated the original settlement that they were increasingly uneasy about the plan's ability to spur competition. However, in mid-2004 an appeals court upheld the 2001 settlement, and in November 2007, Microsoft's obligations under the original settlement expired.

CHECK YOUR UNDERSTANDING 16-4

1. For each of the following goods, explain the nature of the network externality present.
   a. Appliances using a particular voltage, such as 110 volts versus 220 volts
   b. 8½-by-11-inch paper versus 8-by-12½-inch paper
2. Suppose there are two competing companies in an industry that has a network externality. Explain why it is likely that the company able to sustain the largest initial losses will eventually dominate the market.

Solutions appear at back of book.

▼ **Quick Review**

- *Network externalities* arise when the value of a good increases when a large number of other people also use the good. They are prevalent in communications, transportation, and high-technology industries.

- Goods with network externalities exhibit **positive feedback:** success breeds further success, and failure breeds further failure. The good with the largest network eventually dominates the market, and rival goods disappear. As a result, in early stages of the market, firms have an incentive to take aggressive actions, such as lowering price below production cost, to enlarge the size of their good's network.

- Goods with network externalities pose special problems for antitrust regulators because they tend toward monopoly. It can be difficult to distinguish what is a natural growth of the network and what is an illegal monopolization effort by the producer.

BUSINESS CASE : A Tale of Two Research Clusters

Courtesy Silicon Maps

Silicon Valley in California and Route 128 in Massachusetts are the pre-eminent high-tech clusters in the world. Silicon Valley dates back to the early 1930s, when Stanford University encouraged its electrical engineering graduates to stay in the area and start companies.

In the early 1950s Stanford created the Stanford Industrial Park, leasing university land to high-tech companies that worked closely with its engineering school. In the mid-1950s, defense contractors such as Lockheed brought dollars to the area. By the late 1960s, a critical mass of such talent had accumulated. For example, in 1968, eight young engineers left their employer over a disagreement; over the next 20 years, they founded 65 new companies, including Intel Corporation, which later created the microprocessor chip, the brain of personal computers.

This pattern repeated: one researcher estimated that in small and medium-sized firms, 35% of the workforce would, on average, turn over in a year. Silicon Valley became a fertile location for startups, with dozens sprouting every year—everything from firms specializing in hardware and software to network firms like eBay, Facebook, and Google. It also became home to investors who specialize in financing new high-tech companies. Silicon Valley's compact geographical location allowed people to form close social and research bonds even while working for rival firms.

On the other side of the country, a high-tech cluster known as Route 128 lies on a stretch of highway surrounding Boston and Cambridge. It owes its beginnings to the Massachusetts Institute of Technology (MIT), the top engineering university in the world, as well as funding from the U.S. military, NASA, and the National Science Foundation. In the 1950s Route 128 dominated Silicon Valley, with three times the employment.

But early on, Route 128 differed from Silicon Valley in significant ways. Geographically, Route 128 was more spread out than Silicon Valley. Its firms were larger, reflecting the needs of defence contractors during the Cold War. And MIT extended little help to Route 128 firms.

Another major difference between the two clusters lay in how firms were organized. Route 128 firms tended to be "vertically integrated," combining the entire chain of production from research to design to production in the same firm. Silicon Valley firms focused exclusively on research and design, contracting production out to specialized firms that achieved economies of scale. In contrast to the fluidity of employees and ideas across companies in Silicon Valley, Route 128 firms emphasized a commitment to lifetime employment and closely guarded their innovations to remain competitive.

The 1970s and 1980s were harsh for Route 128. Military spending dried up, and it lost its edge in minicomputers when Apollo Computers lost its pre-eminence to an aggressive Silicon Valley firm, Sun Microsystems. By 1980, electronics employment in Silicon Valley was three times that of Route 128. Over time, Route 128 ceded the advantage to Silicon Valley in electronics and networking. Today its niche is in biotechnology, genetics, materials engineering, and finance.

QUESTIONS FOR THOUGHT

1. What positive externalities were common to both Silicon Valley and Route 128? What positive externalities were not common to both? Explain.

2. What factors made Silicon Valley such a fertile place for startups? How did these factors interact with one another? What inhibited startups in Route 128?

3. In hindsight, what could Apollo Computers have done to maintain its advantage in minicomputers? What does this tell you generally about research clusters?

SUMMARY

1. When pollution can be directly observed and controlled, government policies should be geared directly to producing the **socially optimal quantity of pollution,** the quantity at which the **marginal social cost (MSC) of pollution** (the sum of the **marginal external cost (MEC) of pollution** and the **marginal private cost (MPC) of pollution**) is equal to the **marginal social benefit (MSB) of pollution** (the sum of the **marginal external benefit (MEB) of pollution** and the **marginal private benefit (MPB) of pollution**). In the absence of government intervention, a market produces too much pollution because polluters take only their benefit from polluting into account, not the costs imposed on others.

2. The costs to society of pollution are an example of an **external cost;** in some cases, however, economic activities yield **external benefits.** External costs and benefits are jointly known as **externalities,** with external costs called **negative externalities** and external benefits called **positive externalities.**

3. According to the **Coase theorem,** individuals can find a way to **internalize the externality,** making government intervention unnecessary, as long as **transaction costs**—the costs of making a deal—are sufficiently low. However, in many cases transaction costs are too high to permit such deals.

4. Governments often deal with pollution by imposing **environmental standards,** a method, economists argue, that is usually an inefficient way to reduce pollution. Two efficient (cost-minimizing) methods for reducing pollution are **emissions taxes,** a form of **Pigouvian tax,** and **tradable emissions permits.**

The optimal Pigouvian tax on pollution is equal to its marginal social cost at the socially optimal quantity of pollution. If instead of directly taxing the pollution, a tax is applied on the production of the good or service that causes the pollution by its consumption or manufacture, then the optimal Pigouvian tax equals the marginal external cost at the socially optimal quantity. These methods also provide incentives for the creation and adoption of production technologies that cause less pollution.

5. When a good or activity yields external benefits, or positive externalities, such as **technology spillovers,** then an optimal **Pigouvian subsidy** to producers moves the market to the socially optimal quantity of production.

6. Communications, transportation, and high-technology goods are frequently subject to *network externalities,* which arise when the value of the good to an individual is greater when a large number of people use the good. Such goods are likely to be subject to **positive feedback:** if large numbers of people buy the good, other people are more likely to buy it, too. So success breeds greater success and failure breeds failure: the good with the larger network will eventually dominate, and rival goods will disappear. As a result, producers have an incentive to take aggressive action in the early stages of the market to increase the size of their network. Markets with network externalities tend to be monopolies. They are especially challenging for antitrust regulators because it can be hard to differentiate between the natural progression of the network externality and illegal monopolization efforts by producers.

KEY TERMS

Marginal social cost (MSC) of pollution, p. 488
Marginal social benefit (MSB) of pollution, p. 488
Marginal private cost (MPC) of pollution, p. 488
Marginal external cost (MEC) of pollution, p. 488
Marginal private benefit (MPB) of pollution, p. 489

Marginal external benefit (MEB) of pollution, p. 489
Socially optimal quantity of pollution, p. 489
External cost, p. 491
External benefit, p. 491
Externalities, p. 491
Negative externalities, p. 491
Positive externalities, p. 491
Coase theorem, p. 494

Transaction costs, p. 494
Internalize the externality, p. 494
Environmental standards, p. 496
Emissions tax, p. 496
Pigouvian tax, p. 499
Tradable emissions permits, p. 500
Pigouvian subsidy, p. 506
Technology spillover, p. 506
Positive feedback, p. 508

PROBLEMS

1. What type of externality (positive or negative) is present in each of the following examples? Is the marginal social benefit of the activity greater than or equal to the marginal private benefit to the individual? Is the marginal social cost of the activity greater than or equal to the marginal private cost to the individual? Without intervention, will there be too little or too much (relative to what would be socially optimal) of this activity?

   a. Mr. Chau plants lots of colourful flowers in his front yard.

   b. Your next-door neighbour likes to build bonfires in his backyard, and sparks often drift onto your house.

   c. Maija, who lives next to an apple orchard, decides to keep bees to produce honey.

   d. Justine buys a large SUV that consumes a lot of gasoline.

2. The loud music coming from the house next door is a negative externality that can be directly quantified. The accompanying table shows the marginal social benefit and the marginal social cost per decibel (dB, a measure of volume) of music.

Volume of music (dB)	Marginal social benefit of dB	Marginal social cost of dB
90		
	$36	$0
91		
	30	2
92		
	24	4
93		
	18	6
94		
	12	8
95		
	6	10
96		
	0	12
97		

   a. Draw the marginal social benefit curve and the marginal social cost curve. Use your diagram to determine the socially optimal volume of music.

   b. Only the residents of the house benefit from the music, and they bear none of the cost. Which volume of music will they choose?

   c. The city imposes a Pigouvian tax of $3 per decibel above 90 dB of music played. From your diagram, determine the volume of music the residents of the house next door will now choose.

3. Some Canadian dairy farmers are adopting a new technology that allows them to produce their own electricity from methane gas captured from animal wastes. (One cow can produce up to 2 kilowatts a day.) This practice reduces the amount of methane gas released into the atmosphere. In addition to reducing their own utility bills, the farmers are allowed to sell any electricity they produce at favourable rates.

   a. Explain how the ability to earn money from capturing and transforming methane gas behaves like a Pigouvian tax on methane gas pollution and can lead the dairy industry to emit the efficient amount of methane gas pollution.

   b. Suppose some dairy farmers have lower costs of transforming methane into electricity than others. Explain how this system leads to an efficient allocation of emissions reduction among farmers.

4. Voluntary environmental programs have been extremely popular in Canada, the United States, Europe, and Japan. Part of their popularity stems from the fact that these programs do not require legislative authority, which is often hard to obtain. The voluntary Memorandum of Understanding (MOU) between Transport Canada and Canadian airlines in 2005 is an example of such a program. With this agreement, Transport Canada sought to reduce emissions of greenhouse gases. Companies were asked to voluntarily commit to reducing emissions by improving fuel efficiency from their 1990 levels by 24% by 2012. The program actually exceeded its target resulting in a 31% cumulative improvement. In 2012 a new voluntary agreement was signed between these parties that would see fuel efficiency improve by at least 2% per year until 2020.

   For this question assume that fuel efficiency improvements result in an equal percent reduction in greenhouse gas emissions.

   a. As in Figure 16-4, draw marginal benefit curves for pollution generated by two airlines, A and B, in 1990. Assume that without government intervention, each airline emits the same amount of pollution, but that at all levels of pollution less than this amount, airline A's marginal benefit of polluting is less than that of airline B (perhaps due to using a different type of aircraft). Label the vertical axis "Marginal benefit to individual polluter" and the horizontal axis "Quantity of pollution emissions." Mark the quantity of pollution each airline produces without government action.

   b. Do you expect the total quantity of pollution before the program was put in place to have been less than or more than the optimal quantity of pollution? Why?

   c. Suppose the airlines whose marginal benefit curves you depicted in part (a) were participants in this MOU. In a replica of your graph from part (a), mark targeted levels of pollution in 2012 for the two airlines. Which airline was required to reduce emissions more? Was this solution necessarily efficient?

   d. What kind of environmental policy does this MOU most closely resemble? What is the main shortcoming of such a policy? Compare it to two other types of environmental policy discussed in this chapter.

5. According to a report from the Association of Universities and Colleges of Canada, "university graduates will on average earn $1.3 million more during their careers [lifetime earnings] than a high school graduate and $1 million more than a college grad." This indicates that there is a considerable benefit to a graduate from investing in his or her own education. Tuition at Canadian universities in 2011 covered only about 37% of the cost, so the government applies a Pigouvian subsidy to university education. If a Pigouvian subsidy is appropriate, is the externality created by a university education a positive or a negative externality? What does this imply about the differences between the costs and benefits to students compared to social costs and benefits? What are some reasons for the differences?

6. The district municipality of Delta, south of Vancouver, provides free trees planted on municipal property adjacent to the side or front of homeowners' yards when requested.

   a. Using concepts in the chapter, explain why a municipality would provide free trees planted near someone's home.

   b. Draw a diagram similar to Figure 16-7 that shows the marginal social benefit, the marginal social cost, and the optimal Pigouvian subsidy on trees.

7. Fishing for sablefish has been so intensive that sablefish were threatened with extinction. After considering banning such fishing, the Canadian Department of Fisheries and Oceans introduced individual tradable quotas in 1990, each of which entitles its holder to a catch of a certain size. Explain how fishing generates a negative externality and how the quota scheme may overcome the inefficiency created by this externality.

8. The two dry-cleaning companies in Lafacville, Savon Cleaners and Big Green Cleaners, are a major source of air pollution. Together they currently produce 350 units of air pollution, which the town wants to reduce to 200 units. The accompanying table shows the current pollution level produced by each company and each company's marginal cost of reducing its pollution. The marginal cost is constant.

Companies	Initial pollution level (units)	Marginal cost of reducing pollution (per unit)
Savon Cleaners	230	$5
Big Green Cleaners	120	$2

   a. Suppose that Lafacville passes an environmental standards law that limits each company to 100 units of pollution. What would be the total cost to the two companies of each reducing its pollution emissions to 100 units?

Suppose instead that Lafacville issues 100 pollution vouchers to each company, each entitling the company to one unit of pollution, and that these vouchers can be traded.

   b. How much is each pollution voucher worth to Savon Cleaners? To Big Green Cleaners? (That is, how much would each company, at most, be willing to pay for one more voucher?)

   c. Who will sell vouchers and who will buy them? How many vouchers will be traded?

   d. What is the total cost to the two companies of the pollution controls under this voucher system?

9. a. EAuction and EMarketplace are two competing Internet auction sites, where buyers and sellers transact goods. Each auction site earns money by charging sellers for listing their goods. EAuction has decided to eliminate fees for the first transaction for sellers that are new to its site. Explain why this is likely to be a good strategy for EAuction in its competition with EMarketplace.

   b. EMarketplace complained to the Competition Bureau that EAuction's practice of eliminating fees for new sellers was anti-competitive and would lead to monopolization of the Internet auction industry. Is EMarketplace correct? How should the Competition Bureau respond?

   c. EAuction stopped its practice of eliminating fees for new sellers. But since it provided much better technical service than its rival, EMarketplace, buyers and sellers came to prefer EAuction. Eventually, EMarketplace closed down, leaving EAuction as a monopolist. Should the Competition Bureau intervene to break EAuction into two companies? Explain.

   d. EAuction is now a monopolist in the Internet auction industry. It also owns a site that handles payments over the Internet, called PayForIt. It is competing with another Internet payment site, called PayBuddy. EAuction has now stipulated that any transaction on its auction site must use PayForIt, rather than PayBuddy, for the payment. Should the Competition Bureau intervene? Explain.

10. Which of the following are characterized by network externalities? Which are not? Explain.

   a. The choice between installing 110-volt electrical current in structures rather than 220-volt

   b. The choice between purchasing a Toyota versus a Ford

   c. The choice of a printer, where each printer requires its own specific type of ink cartridge

   d. The choice of whether to purchase an iPod Touch or an iPod Nano.

CHAPTER 17

Public Goods and Common Resources

THE GREAT STINK

London's River Thames then ...

... and the same river now, thanks to government intervention.

WHAT YOU WILL LEARN IN THIS CHAPTER

❭ A way to classify goods that predicts whether or not a good is a **private good**—a good that can be efficiently provided by markets

❭ What **public goods** are, and why markets fail to supply them

❭ What **common resources** are, and why they are overused

❭ What **artificially scarce goods** are, and why they are underconsumed

❭ How government intervention in the production and consumption of these types of goods can make society better off

❭ Why finding the right level of government intervention is often difficult

BY THE MIDDLE OF THE NINE-teenth century, London had become the world's largest city, with close to 2.5 million inhabitants. Unfortunately, all those people produced a lot of waste—and there was no place for it to go except into the Thames, the river flowing through the city. Nobody with a working nose could ignore the results. And the river didn't just smell bad—it carried dangerous waterborne diseases like cholera and typhoid. London neighbourhoods close to the Thames had death rates from cholera more than six times greater than the neighbourhoods farthest away. And the great majority of Londoners drew their drinking water from the Thames.

What the city needed, said reformers, was a sewage system that would carry waste away from the river. Yet no private individual was willing to build such a system, and influential people were opposed to the idea that the government should take responsibility for the problem. For example, the magazine *The Economist* weighed in against proposals for a government-built sewage system, declaring that "suffering and evil are nature's admonitions—they cannot be got rid of."

But the hot summer of 1858 brought what came to be known as the Great Stink, which was so bad that one health journal reported "men struck down with the stench." Even the privileged and powerful suffered: Parliament met in a building next to the river. After unsuccessful efforts to stop the smell by covering the windows with chemical-soaked curtains, Parliament finally approved a plan for an immense system of sewers and pumping stations to direct sewage away from the city.

The system, opened in 1865, brought dramatic improvement in the city's quality of life; cholera and typhoid epidemics, which had been regular occurrences, completely disappeared. The Thames was turned from the filthiest to the cleanest metropolitan river in the world, and the sewage system's principal engineer, Sir Joseph Bazalgette, was lauded as having "saved more lives than any single Victorian public official." It was estimated at the time that Bazalgette's sewer system added 20 years to the lifespan of the average Londoner.

The story of the Great Stink and the policy response that followed illustrate two important reasons for government intervention in the economy. London's new sewage system was a clear example of a *public good*—a good that benefits many people, whether or not they have paid for it, and whose benefits to any one individual do not depend on how many others also benefit. As we will see shortly, public goods differ in important ways from the *private goods* we have studied so far—and these differences mean that public goods cannot be efficiently supplied by the market.

In addition, clean water in the Thames is an example of a *common resource*, a good that many people can consume whether or not they have paid for it but whose consumption by each person reduces the amount available to others. Such goods tend to be overused by individuals in a market system unless the government takes action.

In earlier chapters, we saw that markets sometimes fail to deliver efficient levels of production and consumption of a good or activity. We saw how inefficiency can arise from market power, which allows monopolists and colluding oligopolists to charge prices that are higher than marginal cost, thereby preventing mutually beneficial transactions from occurring. We also saw how inefficiency can arise from positive and negative externalities, which cause a divergence between the costs and benefits of an individual's or industry's actions and the costs and benefits of those actions borne by society as a whole.

In this chapter, we will take a somewhat different approach to the question of why markets sometimes fail. Here we focus on how *the characteristics of goods often determine whether markets can deliver them efficiently*. When goods have the "wrong" characteristics, the resulting market failures resemble those associated with externalities or market power. This alternative way of looking at sources of inefficiency deepens our understanding of why markets sometimes don't work well and how government can take actions that increase society's welfare. ■

A good is **excludable** if the supplier of that good can prevent people who do not pay from consuming it.

A good is **rival in consumption** if the same unit of the good cannot be consumed by more than one person at the same time.

A good that is both excludable and rival in consumption is a **private good.**

When a good is **nonexcludable,** the supplier cannot prevent consumption by people who do not pay for it.

A good is **nonrival in consumption** if more than one person can consume the same unit of the good at the same time.

Private Goods—And Others

What's the difference between installing a new bathroom in a house and building a municipal sewage system? What's the difference between growing wheat and fishing in the open ocean?

These aren't trick questions. In each case there is a basic difference in the characteristics of the goods involved. Bathroom fixtures and wheat have the characteristics necessary to allow markets to work efficiently. Public sewage systems and fish in the sea do not.

Let's look at these crucial characteristics and why they matter.

Characteristics of Goods

Goods like bathroom fixtures or wheat have two characteristics that, as we'll soon see, are essential if a good is to be efficiently provided by a market economy.

- They are **excludable:** suppliers and owners of the good can prevent people who don't pay from consuming it.
- They are **rival in consumption:** the same unit of the good cannot be consumed by more than one person at the same time.

When a good is both excludable and rival in consumption, it is called a **private good.** Wheat is an example of a private good. It is *excludable*: the farmer can sell a bushel to one consumer without having to provide wheat to everyone in the county. And it is *rival in consumption*: if I eat bread baked with a farmer's wheat, that wheat cannot be consumed by someone else.

But not all goods possess these two characteristics. Some goods are **nonexcludable**—the supplier cannot prevent consumption of the good by people who do not pay for it. Fire protection is one example: a fire department that puts out fires before they spread protects the whole city, not just people who have made contributions to the Firefighters' Benevolent Fund. An improved environment is another: the city of London couldn't have ended the Great Stink for some residents while leaving the river Thames foul for others.

Nor are all goods rival in consumption. Goods are **nonrival in consumption** if more than one person can consume the same unit of the good at the same time. TV programs are nonrival in consumption: your decision to watch a show does not prevent other people from watching the same show.

Because goods can be either excludable or nonexcludable, rival or nonrival in consumption, there are four types of goods, illustrated by the matrix in Figure 17-1:

FIGURE 17-1 Four Types of Goods

	Rival in consumption	Nonrival in consumption
Excludable	**Private goods** • Wheat • Bathroom fixtures	**Artificially scarce goods** • On-demand movies • Computer software
Nonexcludable	**Common resources** • Clean water • Biodiversity	**Public goods** • Public sanitation • National defense

There are four types of goods. The type of a good depends on (1) whether or not it is excludable—whether a producer can prevent someone from consuming it; and (2) whether or not it is rival in consumption—whether it is impossible for the same unit of a good to be consumed by more than one person at the same time.

- *Private goods,* which are excludable and rival in consumption, like wheat
- *Public goods,* which are nonexcludable and nonrival in consumption, like a public sewer system
- *Common resources,* which are nonexcludable but rival in consumption, like clean water in a river
- *Artificially scarce goods,* which are excludable but nonrival in consumption, like on-demand movies on CinemaNow

There are, of course, many other characteristics that distinguish between types of goods—necessities versus luxuries, normal versus inferior, and so on. Why focus on whether goods are excludable and rival in consumption?

Why Markets Can Supply Only Private Goods Efficiently

As we learned in earlier chapters, markets are typically the best means for a society to deliver goods and services to its members; that is, markets are efficient except in the case of the well-defined problems of market power, externalities, or other instances of market failure. But there is yet another condition that must be met, one rooted in the nature of the good itself: markets cannot supply goods and services efficiently unless they are private goods—excludable and rival in consumption.

To see why excludability is crucial, suppose that a farmer had only two choices: either produce no wheat or provide a bushel of wheat to every resident of the county who wants it, whether or not that resident pays for it. It seems unlikely that anyone would grow wheat under those conditions.

Yet the operator of a municipal sewage system faces pretty much the same problem as our hypothetical farmer. A sewage system makes the whole city cleaner and healthier—but that benefit accrues to all the city's residents, whether or not they pay the system operator. That's why no private entrepreneur came forward with a plan to end London's Great Stink.

The general point is that if a good is nonexcludable, self-interested consumers won't be willing to pay for it—they will take a "free ride" on anyone who *does* pay. So there is a **free-rider problem.** Examples of the free-rider problem are familiar from daily life. One example you may have encountered happens when students are required to do a group project. There is often a tendency of some group members to shirk, relying on others in the group to get the work done. The shirkers *free-ride* on someone else's effort.

Because of the free-rider problem, the forces of self-interest alone do not lead to an efficient level of production for a nonexcludable good. Even though consumers would benefit from increased production of the good, no one individual is willing to pay for more, and so no producer is willing to supply it. The result is that nonexcludable goods suffer from *inefficiently low production* in a market economy. In fact, in the face of the free-rider problem, self-interest may not ensure that any amount of the good—let alone the efficient quantity—is produced.

Goods that are excludable and nonrival in consumption, like on-demand movies, suffer from a different kind of inefficiency. As long as a good is excludable, it is possible to earn a profit by making it available only to those who pay. Therefore, producers are willing to supply an excludable good. But the marginal cost of letting an additional viewer watch an on-demand movie is zero because it is nonrival in consumption. So the efficient price to the consumer is also zero—or, to put it another way, individuals should watch movies up to the point where their marginal benefit is zero.

Goods that are nonexcludable suffer from the **free-rider problem:** many individuals are unwilling to pay for their own consumption and instead will take a "free ride" on anyone who does pay.

 PITFALLS

MARGINAL COST OF WHAT EXACTLY?
In the case of a good that is nonrival in consumption, it's easy to confuse the marginal cost of *producing* a unit of the good with the marginal cost of *allowing* a unit of the good *to be consumed.* For example, CinemaNow incurs a marginal cost in making a movie available to its subscribers that is equal to the cost of the resources it uses to produce and broadcast that movie. However, *once that movie is being broadcast,* no marginal cost is incurred by letting an additional family watch it. In other words, no costly resources are "used up" when one more family consumes a movie that has already been produced and is being broadcast.

This complication does not arise, however, when a good is rival in consumption. In that case, the resources used to produce a unit of the good are "used up" by a person's consumption of it—they are no longer available to satisfy someone else's consumption. So when a good is rival in consumption, the marginal cost to society of allowing an individual to consume a unit is equal to the resource cost of producing that unit—that is, equal to the marginal cost of producing it.

But if CinemaNow actually charges viewers $4, viewers will consume the good only up to the point where their marginal benefit is $4. When consumers must pay a price greater than zero for a good that is nonrival in consumption, the price they pay is higher than the marginal cost of allowing them to consume that good, which is zero. So in a market economy goods that are nonrival in consumption suffer from *inefficiently low consumption*.

Now we can see why private goods are the only goods that can be efficiently produced and consumed in a competitive market. (That is, a private good will be efficiently produced and consumed in a market free of market power, externalities, or other instances of market failure.) Because private goods are excludable, producers can charge for them and so have an incentive to produce them. And because they are also rival in consumption, it is efficient for consumers to pay a positive price—a price equal to the marginal cost of production. If one or both of these characteristics are lacking, a market economy will not lead to efficient production and consumption of the good.

Fortunately for the market system, most goods are private goods. Food, clothing, shelter, and most other desirable things in life are excludable and rival in consumption, so markets can provide us with most things. Yet there are crucial goods that don't meet these criteria—and in most cases, that means that the government must step in.

ECONOMICS ▸ *IN ACTION*

FROM MAYHEM TO RENAISSANCE

Life during the European Middle Ages—from approximately 1100 to 1500—was difficult and dangerous, with high rates of violent crime, banditry, and war casualties. According to researchers, murder rates in Europe in 1200 were 30 to 40 per 100 000 people. But by 1500 the rate had been halved to around 20 per 100 000; today, it is less than 1 per 100 000. What accounts for the sharp decrease in mayhem over the last 900 years?

Think public goods, as the history of medieval Italian city-states illustrates.

Starting around the year 900 in Venice and 1100 in other city-states like Milan and Florence, citizens began to organize and create institutions for protection. In Venice, citizens built a defensive fleet to battle the pirates and other marauders who regularly attacked them. Other city-states built strong defensive walls to encircle their cities and also paid defensive militias. Institutions were created to maintain law and order: cadres of guards, watchmen, and magistrates were hired; courthouses and jails were built.

As a result, trade, commerce, and banking were able to flourish, as well as literacy, numeracy, and the arts. By 1300, the leading cities of Venice, Milan, and Florence had each grown to over 100 000 people. As resources and the standard of living increased, the rate of violent deaths diminished.

For example, the Republic of Venice was known as *La Serenissima*—the most serene one—because of its enlightened governance, overseen by a council of leading citizens. Owing to its stability, diplomatic prowess, and prodigious fleet of vessels, Venice became enormously wealthy in the fifteenth and sixteenth centuries.

Also through stability, high literacy, and numeracy, Florence became the banking centre of Italy. During the fifteenth century it was ruled by the Medici, an immensely wealthy banking family.

Ivy Close Images/Alamy

The emergence of institutions to maintain law and order—public goods—allowed for a move away from the war and brutality that marked the Middle Ages and toward a new era.

And it was the patronage of the Medici to artists such as Leonardo da Vinci and Michelangelo that ushered in the Renaissance.

So Western Europe was able to move from mayhem to Renaissance through the creation of public goods like good governance and defence—goods that benefitted everyone and could not be diminished by any one person's use.

CHECK YOUR UNDERSTANDING   **17-1**

1. Classify each of the following goods according to whether they are excludable and whether they are rival in consumption. What kind of good is each?
   a. Use of a public space such as a park
   b. A cheese burrito
   c. Information from a website that is password-protected
   d. Publicly announced information on the path of an incoming hurricane

2. Which of the goods in Question 1 will be provided by a competitive market? Which will not be? Explain your answer.

Solutions appear at back of book.

Public Goods

A **public good** is the exact opposite of a private good: it is a good that is both nonexcludable and nonrival in consumption. A public sewer system is an example of a public good: you can't keep a river clean without making it clean for everyone who lives near its banks, and my protection from great stinks does not come at my neighbour's expense.

Here are some other examples of public goods:

- *Disease prevention.* When doctors act to stamp out the beginnings of an epidemic before it can spread, they protect people around the world.

- *Scientific research.* More knowledge benefits everyone.

- *National defence.* A strong military protects all citizens.

Because these goods are nonexcludable, they suffer from the free-rider problem, so no private firm would be willing to produce them. And because they are nonrival in consumption, it would be inefficient to charge people for consuming them. As a result, society must find nonmarket methods for providing these goods.

Providing Public Goods

Public goods are provided through a variety of means. The government doesn't always get involved—in many cases a non-governmental solution has been found for the free-rider problem. But these solutions are usually imperfect in some way.

Some public goods are supplied through voluntary contributions. For example, private donations support a considerable amount of scientific research. But private donations are insufficient to finance huge, socially important projects like basic medical research.

Some public goods are supplied by self-interested individuals or firms because those who produce them are able to make money in an indirect way. The classic example is broadcast television, which in Canada is supported entirely by advertising. The downside of such indirect funding is that it skews the nature and quantity of the public goods that are supplied, as well as imposing additional costs on consumers. TV stations show the programs that yield the

A **public good** is both nonexcludable and nonrival in consumption.

On the prowl: a British TV detection van at work.

most advertising revenue (that is, programs best suited for selling prescription drugs, weight-loss programs, antihistamines, and the like to the segment of the population that buys them), which are not necessarily the programs people most want to see. And viewers must also endure many commercials.

Some potentially public goods are deliberately made excludable and therefore subject to charge, like on-demand movies. In the United Kingdom, where most television programming is paid for by a yearly licence fee assessed on every television owner (£145.50 for a colour TV, or about $264 in 2014), television viewing is made artificially excludable by the use of "television detection vans": vans that roam neighbourhoods in an attempt to detect televisions in nonlicensed households and fine them. However, as noted earlier, when suppliers charge a price greater than zero for a nonrival good, consumers will consume an inefficiently low quantity of that good.

In small communities, a high level of social encouragement or pressure can be brought to bear on people to contribute money or time to provide the efficient level of a public good. Volunteer fire departments, which depend both on the volunteered services of the firefighters themselves and on contributions from local residents, are a good example. But as communities grow larger and more anonymous, social pressure is increasingly difficult to apply, compelling larger towns and cities to tax residents to provide salaried firefighters for fire protection services.

As this last example suggests, when these other solutions fail, it is up to the government to provide public goods. Indeed, the most important public goods—the legal system, disease control, national defence, fire protection in large cities, and so on—are provided by government and paid for by taxes. Economic theory tells us that the provision of public goods is one of the crucial roles of government.

How Much of a Public Good Should Be Provided?

In some cases, provision of a public good is an "either–or" decision: London would either have a sewage system—or not. But in most cases, governments must decide not only whether to provide a public good but also *how much* of that public good to provide. For example, street cleaning is a public good—but how often should the streets be cleaned? Once a month? Twice a month? Every other day?

Imagine a city in which there are only two residents, Ted and Alice. Assume that the public good in question is street cleaning and that Ted and Alice truthfully tell the government how much they value a unit of the public good, where a unit is equal to one street cleaning per month. Specifically, each of them tells the government *his or her willingness to pay for another unit of the public good supplied*—an amount that corresponds to that *individual's marginal benefit* of another unit of the public good.

Using this information plus information on the cost of providing the good, the government can use marginal analysis to find the efficient level of providing the public good: the level at which the *marginal social benefit* of the public good is equal to the marginal cost of producing it. Recall from Chapter 16 that the marginal social benefit of a good is the benefit that accrues to society as a whole from the consumption of one additional unit of the good.

But what is the marginal social benefit of another unit of a public good—a unit that generates utility for *all* consumers, not just one consumer, because it is nonexcludable and nonrival in consumption? This question leads us to an important principle: *In the special case of a public good, the marginal social benefit of a unit of the good is equal to the sum of the individual marginal benefits that are enjoyed by all consumers of that unit.* Or to consider it from a slightly different angle, if a consumer could be compelled to pay for a unit before consuming it (the good is made excludable), then the marginal social benefit of a unit is equal to the *sum* of each consumer's willingness to pay for that unit. Using this principle, the marginal social benefit of an additional street cleaning per month is equal to Ted's individual marginal benefit from that additional cleaning *plus* Alice's individual marginal benefit.

Why? Because a public good is nonrival in consumption—Ted's benefit from a cleaner street does not diminish Alice's benefit from that same clean street, and vice versa. Because people can all simultaneously consume the same unit of a public good, the marginal social benefit of an additional unit of that good is the *sum* of the individual marginal benefits of all who enjoy the public good. And the efficient quantity of a public good is the quantity at which the marginal social benefit is equal to the marginal cost of providing it.

Figure 17-2 illustrates the efficient provision of a public good, showing three marginal benefit curves. Panel (a) shows Ted's individual marginal benefit curve from street cleaning, MB_T: he would be willing to pay $25 for the city to clean its streets once a month, an additional $18 to have it done a second time, and so on. Panel (b) shows Alice's individual marginal benefit curve from street cleaning, MB_A. Panel (c) shows the marginal social benefit curve from street cleaning, MSB: it is the vertical sum of Ted's and Alice's individual marginal benefit curves, MB_T and MB_A.

To maximize society's welfare, the government should clean the street up to the level at which the marginal social benefit of an additional cleaning is no longer greater than the marginal cost. Suppose that the marginal cost of street cleaning is $6 per cleaning. Then the city should clean its streets 5 times per month, because the marginal social benefit of going from 4 to 5 cleanings is $8, but going from 5 to 6 cleanings would yield a marginal social benefit of only $2.

Figure 17-2 can help reinforce our understanding of why we cannot rely on individual self-interest to yield provision of an efficient quantity of public goods. Suppose that the city did one fewer street cleaning than the efficient quantity and that either Ted or Alice was asked to pay for the last cleaning. Neither one would be willing to pay for it! Ted would personally gain only the equivalent of $3 in utility from adding one more street cleaning—so he wouldn't be willing to pay the $6 marginal cost of another cleaning. Alice would personally gain the equivalent of $5 in utility—so she wouldn't be willing to pay either. The point is that the marginal social benefit of one more unit of a public good is always greater than the individual marginal benefit to any one individual. That is why no individual is willing to pay for the efficient quantity of the good.

Does this description of the public-good problem, in which the marginal social benefit of an additional unit of the public good is greater than any individual's marginal benefit, sound a bit familiar? It should: we encountered a somewhat similar situation in our discussion of *positive externalities*. Remember that in the case of a positive externality, the marginal social benefit accruing to all consumers of another unit of the good is greater than the price that the producer receives for that unit; as a result, the market produces too little of the good. In the case of a public good, the individual marginal benefit of a consumer plays the same role as the price received by the producer in the case of positive externalities: both cases create insufficient incentive to provide an efficient amount of the good.

The problem of providing public goods is very similar to the problem of dealing with positive externalities; in both cases there is a market failure that calls for government intervention. One basic rationale for the existence of government is that it provides a way for citizens to tax themselves in order to provide public goods—particularly a vital public good like plowing snow.

FIGURE **17-2** A Public Good

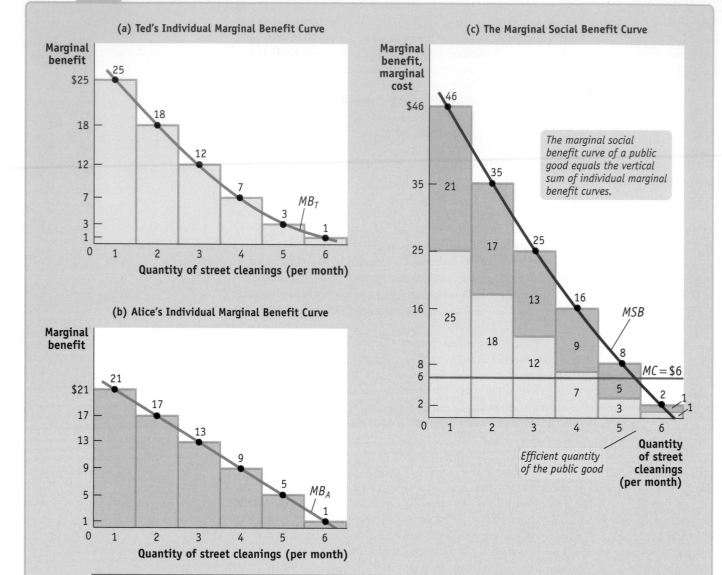

Panel (a) shows Ted's individual marginal benefit curve of street cleanings per month, MB_T, and panel (b) shows Alice's individual marginal benefit curve, MB_A. Panel (c) shows the marginal social benefit of the public good, equal to the sum of the individual marginal benefits to all consumers (in this case, Ted and Alice). The marginal social benefit curve, MSB, is the vertical sum of the individual marginal benefit curves MB_T and MB_A. At a constant marginal cost of $6, there should be 5 street cleanings per month, because the marginal social benefit of going from 4 to 5 cleanings is $8 ($3 for Ted plus $5 for Alice), but the marginal social benefit of going from 5 to 6 cleanings is only $2.

Of course, if society really consisted of only two individuals, they would probably manage to strike a deal to provide the good. But imagine a city with a million residents, each of whose individual marginal benefit from provision of the good is only a tiny fraction of the marginal social benefit. It would be impossible for people to reach a voluntary agreement to pay for the efficient level of street cleaning—the potential for free-riding makes it too difficult to make and enforce an agreement among so many people. But they could and would vote to tax themselves to pay for a citywide sanitation department.

FOR INQUIRING MINDS

VOTING AS A PUBLIC GOOD

It's a sad fact that many Canadians who are eligible to vote don't bother to. As a result, their interests tend to be ignored by politicians. But what's even sadder is that this self-defeating behaviour may be completely rational.

As the economist Mancur Olson pointed out in a famous book titled *The Logic of Collective Action,* voting is a public good, one that suffers from severe free-rider problems.

Imagine that you are one of a million people who would stand to gain the equivalent of $100 each if some plan is passed in a province-wide referendum—say, a plan to improve public schools. And suppose that the opportunity cost of the time it would take you to vote is $10. Will you be sure to go to the polls and vote for the referendum? If you are rational, the answer is no! The reason is that it is very unlikely that your vote will decide the issue, either way. If the measure passes, you benefit, even if you didn't bother to vote—the benefits are non-excludable. If the measure doesn't pass, your vote would not have changed the outcome. Either way, by not voting—by free-riding on those who do vote—you save $10.

Of course, many people do vote out of a sense of civic duty. But because political action is a public good, in general people devote too little effort to defending their own interests.

The result, Olson pointed out, is that when a large group of people share a common political interest, they are likely to exert too little effort promoting their cause and so will be ignored. Conversely, small, well-organized interest groups that act on issues narrowly targeted in their favour tend to have disproportionate power.

Is this a reason to distrust democracy? Winston Churchill said it best: "Democracy is the worst form of government, except for all the other forms that have been tried."

VOTING AS A PUBLIC GOOD: THE GLOBAL PERSPECTIVE

Despite the fact that it can be an entirely rational choice not to vote, many countries consistently achieve astonishingly high turnout rates in their elections by adopting policies that encourage voting. In Belgium, Singapore, and Australia, voting is compulsory; eligible voters are penalized if they fail to do their civic duty by casting their ballots. These penalties are effective at getting out the vote. When Venezuela dropped its mandatory voting requirement, the turnout rate dropped 30%; when the Netherlands did the same, there was a 20% drop-off.

Other countries have policies that reduce the cost of voting; for example, declaring election day a work holiday (giving citizens ample time to cast their ballots), allowing voter registration on election day (eliminating the need for advance planning), and permitting voting by mail (increasing convenience).

This figure shows turnout rates in several countries, measured as the percentage of eligible voters who cast ballots, averaged over elections held between 1945 and 2008. As you can see, Singapore, Australia, and Belgium have the highest voter turnout rates. Canada, however, does not fare well: our voter turnout rate was just above 61%, well below many other countries. In general, the past four decades have seen a decline in voter turnout rates in the major democracies, most dramatically among the youngest voters.

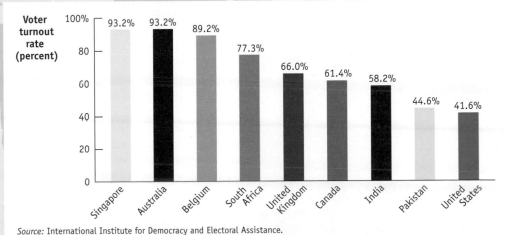

Source: International Institute for Democracy and Electoral Assistance.

Cost-benefit analysis is the estimation and comparison of the social costs and social benefits of providing a public good.

Cost-Benefit Analysis

How do governments decide in practice how much of a public good to provide? Sometimes policy-makers just guess—or do whatever they think will get them re-elected. However, responsible governments try to estimate and compare both the social benefits and the social costs of providing a public good, a process known as **cost-benefit analysis.**

It's straightforward to estimate the cost of supplying a public good. Estimating the benefit is harder. In fact, it is a very difficult problem.

Now you might wonder why governments can't figure out the marginal social benefit of a public good just by asking people their willingness to pay for it (their individual marginal benefit). But it turns out that it's hard to get an honest answer.

This is not a problem with private goods: we can determine how much an individual is willing to pay for one more unit of a private good by looking at his or her actual choices. But because people don't actually pay for public goods, the question of willingness to pay is always hypothetical.

Worse yet, it's a question that people have an incentive not to answer truthfully. People naturally want more rather than less. Because they cannot be made to pay for whatever quantity of the public good they use, people are apt to overstate their true feelings when asked how much they desire a public good. For example, if street cleaning were scheduled according to the stated wishes of homeowners alone, the streets would be cleaned every day—an inefficient level of provision.

So governments must be aware that they cannot simply rely on the public's statements when deciding how much of a public good to provide—if they do, they are likely to provide too much. In contrast, as For Inquiring Minds in the preceding section explains, relying on the public to indicate how much of the public good they want through voting has problems as well—and is likely to lead to too little of the public good being provided.

ECONOMICS ▶ IN ACTION

THE ST. LAWRENCE SEAWAY

The St. Lawrence River plays an important role in the economic development of Canada by connecting the Great Lakes to the Atlantic Ocean. To further promote international trade and to allow larger vessels to get better access to the populated inland market, discussions between Canada and the United States began in the late 1940s on the feasibility of a joint project to build a deeper waterway on the St. Lawrence River. An agreement was reached in 1954, which led to the construction of the St. Lawrence Seaway, a system of locks, canals, and channels that allow ocean-going vessels to navigate from the Atlantic Ocean to the Great Lakes. The Seaway, which officially opened in 1959, cost $470.3 million to build (more than $7 billion in today's dollars). Canada covered about 70% of the cost because most of the locks are located in Canada, and the United States paid the rest.

The opening of this expanded St. Lawrence Seaway had major economic impacts on both countries. By deepening the waterway and allowing large ocean-going vessels access to the Great Lakes, it essentially lowered the freight rates for bulk commodities, which lowered production costs for many industries.

Since its opening, the tonnage of cargo going through the St. Lawrence Seaway has increased significantly from an annual average of 10 million tonnes in the 1950s to 40 million tonnes in recent years. According to the St. Lawrence Seaway Management Corporation, the Seaway moved more than 2.5 billion tonnes

Michael Klinec/Alamy

Major commodities that ship through the Seaway include iron ore, coal, limestone, grains, and cement.

of cargo in the 50 years since it opened, with an estimated value of more than $375 billion. A report on the economic impact of the St. Lawrence Seaway estimated that in 2010 the Seaway generated a total of 98 556 jobs in Canada.[1] The St. Lawrence Seaway is a good example of how the provision of a public good by the government can have a huge positive impact on the economy. If the new locks and canals had not been built in the 1950s, we would still see smaller cargo ships travel along the St. Lawrence River but we would not have the shipping magnitudes and number of jobs created that we have today.

CHECK YOUR UNDERSTANDING 17-2

1. The town of Centreville, population 16, has two types of residents, Homebodies and Revellers. Using the accompanying table, the town must decide how much to spend on its New Year's Eve party. No individual resident expects to directly bear the cost of the party.

   a. Suppose there are 10 Homebodies and 6 Revellers. Determine the marginal social benefit schedule of money spent on the party. What is the efficient level of spending?

   b. Suppose there are 6 Homebodies and 10 Revellers. How do your answers to part (a) change? Explain.

Money spent on party	Individual marginal benefit of additional $1 spent on party	
	Homebody	Reveller
$0		
	$0.05	$0.13
1		
	0.04	0.11
2		
	0.03	0.09
3		
	0.02	0.07
4		

   c. Suppose that the individual marginal benefit schedules are known but no one knows the true proportion of Homebodies versus Revellers. Individuals are asked their preferences. What is the likely outcome if each person assumes that others will pay for any additional amount of the public good? Why is it likely to result in an inefficiently high level of spending? Explain.

Solutions appear at back of book.

▼ **Quick Review**

● A **public good** is both nonexcludable and nonrival in consumption.

● Because most forms of public-good provision by the private sector have serious defects, they are typically provided by the government and paid for with taxes.

● The marginal social benefit of an additional unit of a public good is equal to the sum of each consumer's individual marginal benefit from that unit. At the efficient quantity, the marginal social benefit equals the marginal cost of providing the good.

● No individual has an incentive to pay for providing the efficient quantity of a public good because each individual's marginal benefit is less than the marginal social benefit. This is a primary justification for the existence of government.

● Although governments should rely on **cost-benefit analysis** to determine how much of a public good to supply, doing so is problematic because individuals tend to overstate the good's value to them.

Common Resources

A **common resource** is a good that is nonexcludable but is rival in consumption. An example is the stock of salmon in a limited fishing area, like the fisheries off the coast of British Columbia. Traditionally, anyone who had a boat could go out to sea and catch salmon—salmon in the sea were a nonexcludable good. Yet because the total number of salmon is limited, the salmon that one person catches are no longer available to be caught by someone else. So salmon in the sea are rival in consumption.

Other examples of common resources are clean air and water as well as the diversity of animal and plant species on the planet (biodiversity). In each of these cases the fact that the good, though rival in consumption, is nonexcludable poses a serious problem.

The Problem of Overuse

Because common resources are nonexcludable, individuals cannot be charged for their use. Yet because they are rival in consumption, an individual who

A **common resource** is nonexcludable and rival in consumption: you can't stop me from consuming the good, and more consumption by me means less of the good available for you.

[1] Of these 98 556 jobs, 48 228 were directly created by the St. Lawrence Seaway, 21 947 were induced jobs, and 28 320 were indirect jobs. (*Source:* greatlakes-seaway.com/en/seaway/facts/eco_impact.html)

Common resources left to the market suffer from **overuse:** individuals ignore the fact that their use depletes the amount of the resource remaining for others.

uses a unit depletes the resource by making that unit unavailable to others. As a result, a common resource is subject to **overuse:** an individual will continue to use it until his or her marginal benefit of its use is equal to his or her own individual marginal cost, ignoring the cost that this action inflicts on society as a whole. As we will see shortly, the problem of overuse of a common resource is similar to a problem we studied in Chapter 16: the problem of a good that generates a negative externality, such as pollution-creating electricity generation.

Fishing is a classic example of a common resource. In heavily fished waters, fishing by one person—let's say Eden, in this case—imposes a cost on others by reducing the fish population and making it harder for others to catch fish. But Eden has no personal incentive to take this cost into account, since she cannot be charged for fishing. As a result, from society's point of view, Eden catches too many fish. Traffic congestion is another example of overuse of a common resource. A major highway during rush hour can accommodate only a certain number of vehicles per hour. If Toshiro decides to drive to work alone rather than carpool or work at home, he makes the commute of many other people a bit longer; but he has no incentive to take these consequences into account.

In the case of a common resource, the *marginal social cost* of an individual's use of that resource is higher than his or her *individual marginal cost,* the cost of using an additional unit of the good.

Figure 17-3 illustrates the point. It shows the demand curve for fish, which measures the marginal benefit of fish—the benefit to consumers when an additional unit of fish is caught and consumed. It also shows the supply curve for fish, which measures the marginal cost of production of the fishing industry. We know from Chapter 12 that the industry supply curve is the horizontal sum of each individual fisher's supply curve—equivalent to his or her individual marginal cost curve. The fishing industry supplies the quantity where its marginal cost is equal to the price, the quantity Q_{MKT}. But the efficient outcome is to catch the quantity Q_{OPT}, the quantity of output that equates the marginal benefit to the marginal social cost, not to the fishing industry's marginal cost of production. The market outcome results in overuse of the common resource.

FIGURE   17-3   A Common Resource

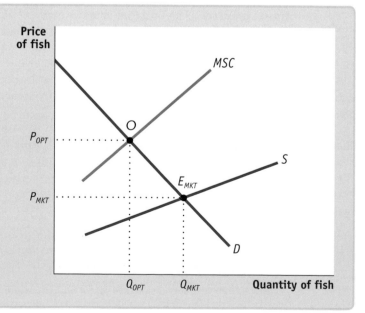

The supply curve S, which shows the marginal cost of production of the fishing industry, is composed of the individual supply curves of the individual fishers. But each fisher's individual marginal cost does not include the cost that his or her actions impose on others: the depletion of the common resource. As a result, the marginal social cost curve, *MSC*, lies above the supply curve; in an unregulated market, the quantity of the common resource used, Q_{MKT}, exceeds the efficient quantity of use, Q_{OPT}.

FOR INQUIRING MINDS

PUTTING A CAP ON BOTTLED WATER

British Columbians are fiercely proud of the pristine beauty and clean environment of their province. But like the rest of Canada, they are somewhat addicted to consuming bottled water. In 2012, retail sales of bottled water reached 2.3 billion litres, generating revenue of $2.3 billion. According to Statistics Canada's 2011 Households and the Environment Survey, about 22% of Canadian households claimed they primarily drank bottled water at home.[2] According to the Canadian Bottled Water Association, more than 95% of bottled water sold in Canada is from a natural source (spring or mineral water), with the remaining originating from a municipal source (i.e., filtered tap water).

Spring water used as drinking water is a valuable commodity; but having private companies extract this valuable resource at little or no cost has Canadians concerned that the bottled water industry is "privatizing" water at the expense of the public. Could companies be overdrawing the groundwater, leaving too little water for future generations? To address these and other concerns, the bottled water industry is subject to both federal and provincial regulations.

The federal government treats bottled water as a food product and regulates bottled water under the *Food and Drugs Act and Regulations*, which set the requirements on quality, composition, and labelling of the product. Provincial

What do water bottlers owe British Columbia for extracting and selling a valuable common resource?

Richard Levine/Alamy

governments are responsible for approving water sources, granting permits, and setting fees, rates of production, watershed protection, and drilling practices. All of these measures are aimed at making the use of this common resource safe and sustainable.

Over the past twenty years many Canadians have petitioned the government to either start imposing royalties for the extraction of groundwater or to raise existing royalty rates—both with the aim of making the extraction of such resources more sustainable. For example, in 2014 the B.C. legislature debated a new Water Sustainability Act intended to modernize and replace the 1909 Water Act. The new act is meant to govern the allocation of water—who gets how much, who gets

to use how much—and to lay out the governments' power to deal with scarcity. Previously, large-scale users of groundwater did not face limits or costs. The act would impose a one-time licence fee of up to $10 000, plus a royalty for each cubic metre of groundwater used. At the time of writing, the B.C. government was consulting stakeholders and citizens as to the appropriate royalties to charge.

To put this into perspective, consider the Nestlé Canada plant in Hope, B.C. that bottles an estimated 320 million litres of groundwater per year. If the groundwater fees are set equal to the 2013 royalty rate of $0.85 per 1000 cubic metres that industrial users are charged for surface water, after the one-time cost of $2000, Nestlé would pay about $272 per year for this water. Not surprisingly, although these fees are better than nothing, many feel that the fees are far too low for some users. The Canadian Bottled Water Association claims that higher fees are not needed for two reasons: first, water is a renewable resource, and second, according to Environment Canada data, the bottled water industry takes less than 0.02% of the fresh water available for taking in Canada. Thus they feel there is no sustainability problem. It seems that advocates on both sides of this debate feel they have a reasonable position and the conviction to hold their ground. Given this, it is unlikely this debate will be easily resolved soon.

As we noted, there is a close parallel between the problem of managing a common resource and the problem posed by negative externalities. In the case of an activity that generates a negative externality, the marginal social cost of production is greater than the industry's marginal cost of production, the difference being the marginal external cost imposed on society. Here, the loss to society arising from a fisher's depletion of the common resource plays the same role as the external cost plays when there is a negative externality. In fact, many negative externalities (such as pollution) can be thought of as involving common resources (such as clean air).

---

[2]According to Health Canada, "bottled water is water which has been packaged in sealed containers for human consumption. The water can come from a variety of sources including springs, aquifers, or municipal supplies and may be treated to make it fit for human consumption." *Source:* hc-sc.gc.ca/fn-an/securit/facts-faits/faqs_bottle_water-eau_embouteillee-eng.php#a1

The Efficient Use and Maintenance of a Common Resource

Because common resources pose problems similar to those created by negative externalities, the solutions are also similar. To ensure efficient use of a common resource, society must find a way of getting individual users of the resource to take into account the costs they impose on other users. This is basically the same principle as that of getting individuals to internalize a negative externality that arises from their actions.

There are three fundamental ways to induce people who use common resources to internalize the costs they impose on others.

- Tax or otherwise regulate the use of the common resource
- Create a system of tradable licences for the right to use the common resource
- Make the common resource excludable and assign property rights to some individuals

Like activities that generate negative externalities, use of a common resource can be reduced to the efficient quantity by imposing a Pigouvian tax. For example, some countries have imposed "congestion charges" on those who drive during rush hour, in effect charging them for use of the common resource of highway space. Likewise, visitors to national and provincial parks must pay a fee, and the number of visitors to any one park is restricted.

A second way to correct the problem of overuse is to create a system of tradable licences for the use of the common resource much like the systems designed to address negative externalities. The policy-maker issues the number of licences that corresponds to the efficient level of use of the good. Making the licences tradable ensures that the right to use the good is allocated efficiently—that is, those who end up using the good (those willing to pay the most for a licence) are those who gain the most from its use.

But when it comes to common resources, often the most natural solution is simply to assign property rights. At a fundamental level, common resources are subject to overuse because *nobody owns them.* The essence of ownership of a good—the *property right* over the good—is that you can limit who can and cannot use the good as well as how much of it can be used. When a good is non-excludable, in a very real sense no one owns it because a property right cannot be enforced—and consequently no one has an incentive to use it efficiently. So one way to correct the problem of overuse is to make the good excludable and assign property rights over it to someone. The good now has an owner who has an incentive to protect the value of the good—to use it efficiently rather than overuse it.

As the upcoming Economics in Action shows, a system of tradable licences, called individual transferable quotas or ITQs, has been a successful strategy in some fisheries.

ECONOMICS ›IN ACTION

A TALE OF TWO FISHERIES

When John Cabot reached Newfoundland in 1497 the seas were so teeming with cod that they impeded the passage of his ship. And for centuries in Newfoundland and Labrador, "cod was king," providing tens of thousands of jobs and feeding the world. But all this came to an end in 1992 when the federal government declared a moratorium on all commercial cod fishing in Atlantic Canada because of overfishing (cod had been overfished almost to the point of extinction). The government hoped that, by shutting down the industry, cod stocks would be able to eventually recover. More than 20 years later, the people of Newfoundland and Labrador are still waiting for the moratorium to be lifted.

Sadly, overfishing is not unique to the cod fishery and because of it the world's oceans are in serious trouble. According to a 2013 report by the International Program on the State of the Oceans, there is an imminent risk of widespread extinctions of multiple species of fish. In Europe, 30% of the fish stocks are in danger of collapse. In the North Sea, 93% of cod are fished before they can breed. And blue-fin tuna, a favourite in Japanese sushi, are in danger of imminent extinction.

Even with a moratorium on cod fishing, the fish is still considered vulnerable.

The decline of fishing stocks has worsened as fishers trawl in deeper waters with their very large nets to catch the remaining fish, unintentionally killing many other marine animals in the process.

The fishing industry is in crisis, too, as fishers' incomes decline and they are compelled to fish for longer periods of time and in more dangerous waters in order to make a living.

But there is hope that individual transferable quotas, or ITQs, may provide a solution to both crises. Under an ITQ scheme, a fisher receives a licence entitling him or her to catch an annual quota within a given fishing ground. The ITQ is given for a long period of time, sometimes indefinitely. Because it is transferable, the owner can sell or lease it.

Researchers who analyzed 121 established ITQ schemes around the world concluded that ITQs can help reverse the collapse of fisheries because each ITQ holder now has a financial interest in the long-term maintenance of his or her particular fishery.

ITQ schemes (also called catch-share schemes) are common in New Zealand, Australia, Iceland, and increasingly in Canada and the United States. Fortunately for Canada's East Coast, thanks to a successful ITQ scheme, there remains a profitable and vibrant lobster fishery that provides direct employment for 30 000 to 35 000 people with annual exports of more than $1 billion. In an attempt to protect the industry, a tradable licence system was established in 1967. To legally set a lobster trap, you must have a licence and only a limited number of licences have been issued. A licence could easily cost more than $200 000 (plus annual government charges). At first Atlantic lobster fishers were skeptical of a system that limited their fishing. But they now support the system because it sustains the value of their licences and protects their livelihood by attempting to limit overfishing. Without a system in place to limit how much lobster can be caught, the Atlantic lobster fishery could have gone the way of the cod fishery.

▼ Quick Review

- A **common resource** is rival in consumption but nonexcludable.

- The problem with common resources is **overuse**: a user depletes the amount of the common resource available to others but does not take this cost into account when deciding how much to use the common resource.

- Like negative externalities, a common resource can be efficiently managed by Pigouvian taxes, by the creation of a system of tradable licences for its use, or by making it excludable and assigning property rights.

CHECK YOUR UNDERSTANDING 17-3

1. Rocky Mountain Forest is Crown land (government-owned) from which private citizens were allowed in the past to harvest as much timber as they wanted free of charge. State in economic terms why this is problematic from society's point of view.

2. You are an advisor to the Minister of Natural Resources and have been instructed to come up with ways to preserve the forest for the general public. Name three different methods you could use to maintain the efficient level of tree harvesting and explain how each would work. For each method, what information would you need to know in order to achieve an efficient outcome?

Solutions appear at back of book.

An **artificially scarce good** is excludable but nonrival in consumption.

Artificially Scarce Goods

An **artificially scarce good** is a good that is excludable but nonrival in consumption. As we've already seen, on-demand movies are a familiar example. The marginal cost to society of allowing an individual to watch the movie is zero, because one person's viewing doesn't interfere with other people's viewing. Yet CinemaNow and companies like it prevent an individual from seeing a movie if he or she hasn't paid. Goods like computer software or audio files, which are valued for the information they embody (and are sometimes called "information goods"), are also artificially scarce.

As we've already seen, markets will supply artificially scarce goods: because they are excludable, the producers can charge people for consuming them.

But artificially scarce goods are nonrival in consumption, which means that the marginal cost of an individual's consumption is zero. So the price that the supplier of an artificially scarce good charges exceeds marginal cost. Because the efficient price is equal to the marginal cost of zero, the good is "artificially scarce," and consumption of the good is inefficiently low. However, unless the producer can somehow earn revenue for producing and selling the good, he or she will be unwilling to produce at all—an outcome that leaves society even worse off than it would otherwise be with positive but inefficiently low consumption.

Figure 17-4 illustrates the loss in total surplus caused by artificial scarcity. The demand curve shows the quantity of on-demand movies watched at any given price. The marginal cost of allowing an additional person to watch the movie is zero, so the efficient quantity of movies viewed is Q_{OPT}. CinemaNow charges a positive price, in this case $4, to unscramble the signal, and as a result only Q_{MKT} on-demand movies will be watched. This leads to a deadweight loss equal to the area of the shaded triangle.

Does this look familiar? Like the problems that arise with public goods and common resources, the problem created by artificially scarce goods is similar to something we have already seen: in this case, it is the problem of *natural monopoly*. A natural monopoly, you will recall, is an industry in which average total cost

FIGURE **17-4** An Artificially Scarce Good

An artificially scarce good is excludable and nonrival in consumption. It is made artificially scarce because producers charge a positive price, but the marginal cost of allowing one more person to consume the good is zero. In this example, the market price of an on-demand movie is $4 and the quantity demanded at that price is Q_{MKT}. But the efficient level of consumption is Q_{OPT}, the quantity demanded when the price is zero. The efficient quantity, Q_{OPT}, exceeds the quantity demanded in an unregulated market, Q_{MKT}. The shaded area represents the loss in total surplus from charging a price of $4.

is above marginal cost for the relevant output range. In order to be willing to produce output, the producer must charge a price at least as high as average total cost—that is, a price above marginal cost. But a price above marginal cost leads to inefficiently low consumption.

ECONOMICS ➤ IN ACTION

BLACKED-OUT GAMES

It's the night of the big game for your local team—a game that is being nationally televised by one of the major networks. So you flip to the local channel that is an affiliate of that network—but the game isn't on. Instead, you get some other show with a message scrolling across the bottom of the screen that this game has been blacked out in your area. What the message probably doesn't say, though you understand quite well, is that this blackout is at the insistence of the team's owners, who don't want people who might have paid for tickets staying home and watching the game on TV instead. It used to be very common for games that failed to sell out their stadium tickets to be blacked out in local broadcast markets.

ONOKY-Photononstop/Alamy

Sports fans have had strong reactions to the artificial scarcity created by blacked-out football games.

So the good in question—watching the game on TV—has been made artificially scarce. Because the game is being broadcast anyway, no scarce resources would be used to make it available in its immediate locality as well. But it isn't available—which means a loss in welfare to those who would have watched the game on TV but are not willing to pay the price, in time and money, to go to the stadium.

Although CFL games on TSN may not air locally, the use of blackouts has become rare in Canada. Owners of NHL teams, for example, no longer feel they need to create artificial scarcity with local TV blackouts—the hockey arenas fill up easily as Canadians love the experience of watching hockey live.

▼ Quick Review

- An **artificially scarce good** is excludable but nonrival in consumption.

- Because the good is nonrival in consumption, the efficient price to consumers is zero. However, because it is excludable, sellers charge a positive price, which leads to inefficiently low consumption.

- The problems of artificially scarce goods are similar to those posed by a natural monopoly.

CHECK YOUR UNDERSTANDING   17-4

1. Xena is a software program produced by Xenoid. Each year Xenoid produces an upgrade that costs $300 000 to produce. It costs nothing to allow customers to download it from the company's website. The demand schedule for the upgrade is shown in the accompanying table.

   a. What is the efficient price to a consumer of this upgrade? Explain your answer.

   b. What is the lowest price at which Xenoid is willing to produce and sell the upgrade? Draw the demand curve and show the loss of total surplus that occurs when Xenoid charges this price compared to the efficient price.

Price of upgrade	Quantity of upgrades demanded
$180	1700
150	2000
120	2300
90	2600
0	3500

Solutions appear at back of book.

BUSINESS CASE • Mauricedale Game Ranch and Hunting Endangered Animals to Save Them

Keren Su/Digital Vision/Getty Images

John Hume's Mauricedale ranch occupies 65 square kilometres in the hot, scrubby grasslands of northeastern South Africa. There he raises endangered species, such as black and white rhinos, and nonendangered species, such as Cape buffalo, antelopes, hippos, giraffes, zebras, and ostriches. From revenues of around $2.5 million per year, the ranch earns a small profit, with about 20% of the revenues coming from trophy hunting and 80% from selling live animals to farmers.

Although he entered this business to earn a profit, Hume sees himself as a conservator of these animals and this land. And he is convinced that in order to protect the black and white rhinos, some amount of legalized hunting of them is necessary. According to Hume, "rhinos are the most incredible animals on earth. I'm desperately sorry for them because they need our help."

The story of one of Hume's male rhinos, named "65," illustrates his point. Hume and his staff knew that 65 was a problem: although too old to breed, he was belligerent enough to kill younger male rhinos. He was part of what wildlife conservationists call the "surplus male problem," a male whose presence inhibits the growth of the herd.

Eventually, Hume obtained permission for the hunting of 65 from CITES (Convention on International Trade in Endangered Species), the international body that regulates the trade and legalized hunting of endangered species. A wealthy hunter paid Hume about $180 000, and the troublesome 65 was quickly dispatched.

Conservationist ranchers like Hume, who advocate regulated hunting of wildlife, point to the experience of Kenya to buttress their case. In 1977, Kenya banned the trophy hunting or ranching of wildlife. Since then, Kenya has lost 60% to 70% of its large wildlife through poaching or conversion of habitat to agriculture. Its herd of black rhinos, once numbered at 20 000, now stands at 600, surviving only in protected areas. In contrast, since regulated hunting of the less endangered white buffalo began in South Africa in 1968, its numbers have risen from 1800 to 19 400.

Many conservationists now agree that the key to recovery for a number of endangered species is legalized hunting on well-regulated game ranches—ranches that are actively engaged in breeding and maintaining the animals.

However, legalized hunting is currently a very controversial policy, strongly opposed by some wildlife advocates. Because establishing a ranch like Mauricedale requires a huge capital investment, many are concerned that smaller, fly-by-night ranches will engage in "canned hunts" with animals—often drugged or sick—obtained from elsewhere. And there is a fear that the high prices paid for trophy hunts will make ranchers too eager to cull animals from their herds. As of the time of writing, those advocating legalized hunting appear to be gaining ground.

QUESTIONS FOR THOUGHT

1. Using the concepts you learned in this chapter, explain the economic incentives behind the huge losses in Kenyan wildlife.

2. Compare the economic incentives facing John Hume with those facing a Kenyan rancher.

3. What regulations should be imposed on a rancher who sells opportunities to trophy hunt? Relate these to the concepts in the chapter.

SUMMARY

1. Goods may be classified according to whether or not they are **excludable** and whether or not they are **rival in consumption.**

2. Free markets can deliver efficient levels of production and consumption for **private goods,** which are both excludable and rival in consumption. When goods are nonexcludable or nonrival in consumption, or both, free markets cannot achieve efficient outcomes.

3. When goods are **nonexcludable,** there is a **free-rider problem:** some consumers will not pay for the good, consuming what others have paid for and leading to inefficiently low production. When goods are **nonrival in consumption,** they should be free, and any positive price leads to inefficiently low consumption.

4. A **public good** is nonexcludable and nonrival in consumption. In most cases a public good must be supplied by the government. The marginal social benefit of a public good is equal to the sum of the individual marginal benefits to each consumer. The efficient quantity of a public good is the quantity at which marginal social benefit equals the marginal cost of providing the good. Like a positive externality, marginal social benefit is greater than any one individual's

marginal benefit, so no individual is willing to provide the efficient quantity.

5. One rationale for the presence of government is that it allows citizens to tax themselves in order to provide public goods. Governments use **cost-benefit analysis** to determine the efficient provision of a public good. Such analysis is difficult, however, because individuals have an incentive to overstate the good's value to them.

6. A **common resource** is rival in consumption but nonexcludable. It is subject to **overuse,** because an individual does not take into account the fact that his or her use depletes the amount available for others. This is similar to the problem of a negative externality: the marginal social cost of an individual's use of a common resource is always higher than his or her individual marginal cost. Pigouvian taxes, the creation of a system of tradable licences, or the assignment of property rights are possible solutions.

7. **Artificially scarce goods** are excludable but nonrival in consumption. Because no marginal cost arises from allowing another individual to consume the good, the efficient price is zero. A positive price compensates the producer for the cost of production but leads to inefficiently low consumption. The problem of an artificially scarce good is similar to that of a natural monopoly.

KEY TERMS

Excludable, p. 516
Rival in consumption, p. 516
Private good, p. 516
Nonexcludable, p. 516

Nonrival in consumption, p. 516
Free-rider problem, p. 517
Public good, p. 519
Cost-benefit analysis, p. 524

Common resource, p. 525
Overuse, p. 526
Artificially scarce good, p. 530

PROBLEMS

1. The government is involved in providing many goods and services. For each of the goods or services listed, determine whether it is rival or nonrival in consumption and whether it is excludable or nonexcludable. What type of good is it? Without government involvement, would the quantity provided be efficient, inefficiently low, or inefficiently high?

   a. Street signs

   b. Via rail service

   c. Regulations limiting pollution

   d. A congested highway without tolls

   e. A lighthouse on the coast

2. An economist gives the following advice to a museum director: "You should introduce 'peak pricing.' At times when the museum has few visitors, you should admit visitors for free. And at times when the museum has many visitors, you should charge a higher admission fee."

   a. When the museum is quiet, is it rival or nonrival in consumption? Is it excludable or nonexcludable? What type of good is the museum at those times? What would be the efficient price to charge visitors during that time, and why?

   b. When the museum is busy, is it rival or nonrival in consumption? Is it excludable or nonexcludable? What type of good is the museum at those times? What would be the efficient price to charge visitors during that time, and why?

3. In many planned communities, various aspects of community living are subject to regulation by a home-owners' association. These rules can regulate house architecture; require snow removal from sidewalks; exclude outdoor equipment, such as backyard swimming pools; require appropriate conduct in shared spaces such as the community clubhouse; and so on. Suppose there has been some conflict in one such

community because some homeowners feel that some of the regulations mentioned above are overly intrusive. You have been called in to mediate. Using what you have learned about public goods and common resources, how would you decide what types of regulations are warranted and what types are not?

4. A residential community has 100 residents who are concerned about security. The accompanying table gives the total cost of hiring a 24-hour security service as well as each individual resident's total benefit.

Quantity of security guards	Total cost	Total individual benefit to each resident
0	$0	$0
1	150	10
2	300	16
3	450	18
4	600	19

a. Explain why the security service is a public good for the residents of the community.

b. Calculate the marginal cost, the individual marginal benefit for each resident, and the marginal social benefit.

c. If an individual resident were to decide about hiring and paying for security guards on his or her own, how many guards would that resident hire?

d. If the residents act together, how many security guards will they hire?

5. The accompanying table shows Tanisha's and Ari's individual marginal benefit of different amounts of street cleanings per month. Suppose that the marginal cost of street cleanings is constant at $9 each.

Quantity of street cleanings per month	Tanisha's individual marginal benefit	Ari's individual marginal benefit
0		
	$10	$8
1		
	6	4
2		
	2	1
3		

a. If Tanisha had to pay for street cleaning on her own, how many street cleanings would there be?

b. Calculate the marginal social benefit of street cleaning. What is the optimal number of street cleanings?

c. Consider the optimal number of street cleanings. The last street cleaning of that number costs $9. Is Tanisha willing to pay for that last cleaning on her own? Is Ari willing to pay for that last cleaning on his own?

6. Anyone with a radio receiver can listen to public radio, which is funded largely by donations.

a. Is public radio excludable or nonexcludable? Is it rival in consumption or nonrival? What type of good is it?

b. Should the government support public radio? Explain your reasoning.

c. In order to finance itself, public radio decides to transmit only to satellite radios, for which users have to pay a fee. What type of good is public radio then? Will the quantity of radio listening be efficient? Why or why not?

7. Your economics professor assigns a group project for the course. Describe the free-rider problem that can lead to a suboptimal outcome for your group. To combat this problem, the instructor asks you to evaluate the contribution of your peers in a confidential report. Will this evaluation have the desired effects?

8. The village of Upper Bigglesworth has a village "commons," a piece of land on which each villager, by law, is free to graze his or her cows. Use of the commons is measured in units of the number of cows grazing on it. Assume that the marginal private cost curve of cow-grazing on the commons is upward-sloping (say due to more time spent herding). There is also a marginal social cost curve of cow grazing on the commons: each additional cow grazed means less grass available for others, and the damage done by overgrazing of the commons increases as the number of cows grazing increases. Finally, assume that the private benefit to the villagers of each additional cow grazing on the commons declines as more cows graze, since each additional cow has less grass to eat than the previous one.

a. Is the commons excludable or nonexcludable? Is it rival in consumption or nonrival? What kind of good is the commons?

b. Draw a diagram showing the marginal social cost, marginal private cost, and the marginal private benefit of cow-grazing on the commons, with the quantity of cows that graze on the commons on the horizontal axis. How does the quantity of cows grazing in the absence of government intervention compare to the efficient quantity? Show both in your diagram.

c. The villagers hire you to tell them how to achieve an efficient use of the commons. You tell them that there are three possibilities: a Pigouvian tax, the assignment of property rights over the commons, and a system of tradable licences for the right to graze a cow. Explain how each one of these options would lead to an efficient use of the commons. In the assignment of property rights, assume that one person is assigned the rights to the commons and the rights to all the cows. Draw a diagram that shows the Pigouvian tax.

9. Prior to 2003, the city of London, England was often one big parking lot. Traffic jams were common, and it could take hours to travel a few kilometres. Each additional commuter contributed to the congestion, which can be measured by the total number of cars on London roads. Although each commuter suffered by spending valuable time in traffic, none of them paid for the inconvenience they caused others. The total cost of travel includes the opportunity cost of time spent in traffic and any fees levied by London authorities.

a. Draw a graph illustrating the overuse of London roads, assuming that there is no fee to enter London in a vehicle and that roads are a common resource. Put the cost of travel on the vertical axis and the quantity of cars on the horizontal axis. Draw typical demand, individual marginal cost (*MC*), and marginal social cost (*MSC*) curves and label the equilibrium point. (*Hint:* The marginal cost takes into account the opportunity cost of spending time on the road for individual drivers but not the inconvenience they cause to others.)

b. In February 2003, the city of London began charging a £5 congestion fee on all vehicles travelling in London. Illustrate the effects of this congestion charge on your graph and label the new equilibrium point. Assume the new equilibrium point is not optimally set (that is, assume that the £5 charge is too low relative to what would be efficient).

c. The congestion fee was raised to £9 in January 2011. Illustrate the new equilibrium point on your graph, assuming the new charge is now optimally set.

10. The accompanying table shows six consumers' willingness to pay (his or her individual marginal benefit) for one MP3 file copy of a Hedley album. The marginal cost of making the file accessible to one additional consumer is constant, at zero.

Consumer	Individual marginal benefit
Adriana	$2
Bhagesh	15
Chizuko	1
Denzel	10
Emma	5
Frank	4

a. What would be the efficient price to charge for a download of the file?

b. All six consumers are able to download the file for free from a file-sharing service, Pantster. Which consumers will download the file? What will be the total consumer surplus to those consumers?

c. Pantster is shut down for copyright law infringement. In order to download the file, consumers now have to pay $4.99 at a commercial music site. Which consumers will download the file? What will be the total consumer surplus to those consumers? How much producer surplus accrues to the commercial music site? What is the total surplus? What is the deadweight loss from the new pricing policy?

11. Butchart Gardens is a very large garden in Victoria, British Columbia, renowned for its beautiful plants. It is so large that it could hold many times more visitors than currently visit it. The garden charges an admission fee of approximately $30. At this price, 1000 people visit the garden each day. If admission were free, 2000 people would visit each day.

a. Are visits to Butchart Gardens excludable or nonexcludable? Are they rival in consumption or nonrival? What type of good is it?

b. In a diagram, illustrate the demand curve for visits to Butchart Gardens. Indicate the situation when Butchart Gardens charges an admission fee of $30. Also indicate the situation when Butchart Gardens charges no admission fee.

c. Illustrate the deadweight loss from charging a $30 admission fee. Explain why charging a $30 admission fee is inefficient.

12. Software has historically been an artificially scarce good—it is nonrival because the cost of replication is negligible once the investment to write the code is made, but software companies make it excludable by charging for user licences. But then open-source software emerged, most of which is free to download and can be modified and maintained by anyone.

a. Discuss the free-rider problem that might exist in the development of open-source software. What effect might this have on quality? Why does this problem not exist for proprietary software, such as the products of a company like Microsoft or Adobe?

b. Some argue that open-source software serves an unsatisfied market demand that proprietary software ignores. Draw a typical diagram that illustrates how proprietary software may be underproduced. Put the price and marginal cost of software on the vertical axis and the quantity of software on the horizontal axis. Draw a typical demand curve and a marginal cost curve (*MC*) that is always equal to zero. Assume that the software company charges a positive price, *P*, for the software. Label the equilibrium point and the efficient point.

13. In developing a vaccine for the SARS virus, a pharmaceutical company incurs a very high fixed cost. The marginal cost of delivering the vaccine to patients, however, is negligible (consider it to be equal to zero). The pharmaceutical company holds the exclusive patent to the vaccine. You are a regulator who must decide what price the pharmaceutical company is allowed to charge.

a. Draw a diagram that shows the price for the vaccine that would arise if the company is unregulated, and label it P_M. What is the efficient price for the vaccine? Show the deadweight loss that arises from the price P_M.

b. On another diagram, show the lowest price that the regulator can enforce that would still induce the pharmaceutical company to develop the vaccine. Label it P^*. Show the deadweight loss that arises from this price. How does it compare to the deadweight loss that arises from the price P_M?

c. Suppose you have accurate information about the pharmaceutical company's fixed cost. How could you use price regulation of the pharmaceutical company, combined with a subsidy to the company, to have the efficient quantity of the vaccine provided at the lowest cost to the government?

The Economics of the Welfare State

FEEDING MORE THAN 800 000

More than 800 000 Canadians turn to food banks every month.

WHAT YOU WILL LEARN IN THIS CHAPTER

❭ What the welfare state is and the rationale for it

❭ What defines poverty, what causes poverty, and the consequences of poverty

❭ How income inequality in Canada has changed over time

❭ How programs like Old Age Security affect poverty and income inequality

❭ The special concerns presented by health care insurance

❭ Why there are political differences and debate over the size of the welfare state

EVERY ONCE IN A WHILE, ESPE-cially around holidays, you have probably heard Food Banks Canada asking for donations and organizing food drive campaigns. Why are food banks calling for such help? Each month, more than 800 000 Canadians seek help from food banks across the country because they face difficulty feeding themselves and their families.

The problem of hunger is not new. It has been around for centuries. The stunning fact is that the number of Canadians getting help from food banks has been rising. According to Food Banks Canada, the average number of people who turned to a food bank rose from 675 735 per month in 2008 to 833 098 in 2013. Unfortunately, in 2013 this rising demand for food bank services forced half of all food banks to cut back on the amount of food provided to each household.

Who seeks help from food banks? According to the Hunger Count 2013 by Food Banks Canada, the people who turned to a food bank came from several different backgrounds including single-parent families, the working poor, individuals on welfare, and Canadians living on fixed income. The following provides a snapshot of those who got help from food banks in 2013:

- 36.4% of those turning to food banks are children and youth
- 4.3% of adults helped are over age 65
- 11.3% of people assisted are Aboriginal
- 50% of households helped receive social assistance (welfare)
- 11.5% have income from current or recent employment

Source: Food Banks Canada.

All levels of government in Canada provide assistance to the less fortunate, either funding charitable organizations or giving direct assistance to those in need. The general consensus is that government should be in charge of providing support to financially troubled families.

It's the same around the world. Modern governments, especially in wealthy countries, devote a large chunk of their budgets to health care, income support for the elderly, aid to the poor, and other programs that reduce economic insecurity and, to some degree, income inequality. The collection of government programs devoted to these tasks is known as the *welfare state.*

We start this chapter by discussing the underlying rationale for welfare state programs. Then we describe and analyze the two main kinds of programs operating in Canada: income support programs, such as support for seniors via Canada/Quebec Pension Plan, Old Age Security, and Guaranteed Income Supplement payments, and health care programs—Canada's largest area of social spending by far. ◼

The **welfare state** is the collection of government programs designed to alleviate economic hardship.

A **government transfer** is a government payment to an individual or a family.

A **social welfare program** is a government program designed to provide payments based on need.

A **social insurance program** is a government program designed to provide protection against unpredictable financial distress.

Poverty, Inequality, and Public Policy

During World War II, a British clergyman gave a speech in which he contrasted the "warfare state" of Nazi Germany, dedicated to conquest, with Britain's "welfare state," dedicated to serving the welfare of its people. Since then, the term **welfare state** has come to refer to the collection of government programs that are designed to alleviate economic hardship. A large share of the government spending of all wealthy countries consists of **government transfers**—payments by the government to individuals and families—that provide financial aid to the poor, assistance to unemployed workers, guaranteed income for the elderly, and assistance in paying medical bills for those with large health care expenses.

The Logic of the Welfare State

There are three major economic rationales for the creation of the welfare state. We'll turn now to a discussion of each.

1. Alleviating Income Inequality Suppose that the Taylor family, which has an income of only $15 000 a year, were to receive a government cheque for $1500. This cheque might allow the Taylors to afford a better place to live, eat a more nutritious diet, or in other ways significantly improve their quality of life. Also suppose that the Fisher family, which has an income of $300 000 a year, were to face an extra tax of $1500. This probably wouldn't make much difference to their quality of life: at worst, they might have to give up a few minor luxuries.

This hypothetical exchange illustrates the first major rationale for the welfare state: *alleviating income inequality*. Because a marginal (or additional) dollar is worth more to a poor person than a rich one, modest transfers from the rich to the poor will do the rich little harm but benefit the poor a lot. So, according to this argument, a government that plays Robin Hood, taking from the rich to give to those in need, does more good than harm. Programs that are designed to provide payments based on need are known as **social welfare programs.**

2. Alleviating Economic Insecurity The second major rationale for the welfare state is *alleviating economic insecurity*. Imagine ten families, each of which can expect an income next year of $50 000 if nothing goes wrong. But suppose the odds are that something *will* go wrong for one of the families, although nobody knows which one. For example, suppose each of the families has a one in ten chance of experiencing a sharp drop in income because one family member is laid off or incurs large medical bills. And assume that this event will produce severe hardship for the family—a family member will have to drop out of school or the family will lose its home. Now suppose there's a government program that provides aid to families in distress, paying for that aid by taxing families that are having a good year. Arguably, this program will make all the families better off, because even families that don't currently receive aid from the program might need it at some point in the future. Each family will therefore feel safer knowing that the government stands ready to help when disaster strikes. Programs designed to provide protection against unpredictable financial distress are known as **social insurance programs.**

These two rationales for the welfare state, alleviating income inequality and alleviating economic insecurity, are closely related to the *ability-to-pay principle* we learned about in Chapter 7. Recall how the ability-to-pay principle is used to justify progressive taxation: it says that people with low incomes, for whom an additional dollar makes a big difference to economic well-being, should pay a smaller fraction of their income in taxes than people with higher incomes, for whom an additional dollar makes much less difference. The same principle suggests that those with very low incomes should actually get money back from the tax system.

3. Reducing Poverty and Providing Access to Health Care The third and final major rationale for the welfare state involves *the social benefits of poverty reduction and access to health care,* especially when applied to children of poor households. Researchers have documented that such children, on average, suffer lifelong disadvantages. As we saw in the Economics in Action in Chapter 16, The Impeccable Economic Logic of Early-Childhood Intervention Programs, children from economically disadvantaged backgrounds, even after adjusting for ability, are more likely to be underemployed or unemployed, engage in crime, and suffer chronic health problems—all of which impose significant social costs. So, according to the evidence, programs that help to alleviate poverty and provide access to health care generate external benefits to society.

More broadly, as the following For Inquiring Minds explains, some political philosophers argue that principles of social justice demand that society take care of the poor and unlucky. Others disagree, arguing that welfare state programs go beyond the proper role of government. To an important extent, the difference between those two philosophical positions defines what we mean in politics by "liberalism" and "conservatism."

But before we get carried away, it's important to realize that things aren't quite that cut and dried. Even conservatives who believe in limited government typically support some welfare state programs. And even economists who support the goals of the welfare state are concerned about the effects of large-scale aid to the poor and unlucky on their incentives to work and save. Like taxes, welfare state programs can create substantial deadweight losses, so their true economic costs can be considerably larger than the direct monetary cost. We'll turn to the costs and benefits of the welfare state later in this chapter. First, however, let's examine the problems the welfare state is supposed to address.

 FOR INQUIRING MINDS

JUSTICE AND THE WELFARE STATE

In 1971 American philosopher John Rawls published *A Theory of Justice,* the most famous attempt to date to develop a theory of economic fairness. He asked readers to imagine deciding economic and social policies behind a "veil of ignorance" about their own identity. That is, suppose you knew you would be a human being but did not know whether you would be rich or poor, healthy or sick, and so on. Rawls argued that the policies that would emerge if people had to make decisions behind the veil of ignorance define what we mean by economic justice. It's sort of a generalized version of the Golden Rule: do unto others as you would have them do unto you if you were in their place.

Rawls further argued that people behind the veil of ignorance would choose policies that placed a high value on the well-being of the worst-off members of society: after all, each of us might be one of those unlucky individuals. As a result, Rawlsian theory is often used as an argument for a generous welfare state.

Three years after Rawls published his book, another American philosopher, Robert Nozick, published *Anarchy, State, and Utopia,* which is often considered the libertarian response. Nozick argued that justice is a matter of rights, not results, and that the government has no right to force people with high incomes to support others with lower incomes. He argued for a minimal government that enforces the law and provides security—the "night watchman state"—and against the welfare state programs that account for so much government spending.

Philosophers, of course, don't run the world. But real-world political debate often contains arguments that clearly reflect either a Rawls-type or a Nozick-type position.

The **poverty line** (or **poverty threshold**) is the annual income below which a family is considered poor.

The **poverty rate** is the percentage of the population with incomes below the poverty threshold.

The Problem of Poverty

Poverty is a social problem that governments around the world try to fight, by assisting the poor and those at risk of becoming poor. Governments in Canada attempt to reduce poverty through the provision of various social welfare and insurance programs such as employment insurance, affordable housing programs, income support, and other programs to alleviate the problems associated with poverty. Together these programs are collectively referred to as social programs.

But what, exactly, do we mean by poverty? Any definition is somewhat arbitrary. In Canada the **poverty line** (or **poverty threshold**) is the minimum level of income considered adequate to purchase the necessities of life. Anyone who falls below the poverty line is considered to be in a state of poverty. Although there is no official definition of the poverty line, Statistics Canada constructs the low income cut-offs (LICOs) to study poverty. The LICOs are income thresholds below which a family will likely devote too large a share of its income to the necessities as compared to the average family. According to the LICOs measures, if a family is expected to spend 20 percentage points more than an average family on necessities (for example, 63% of their income instead of 43%), then that family is considered to be living below the poverty line. Since the LICOs compare individual or family spending to that of the average person or family, they are a *relative measure*. To address issues related to differences in family sizes and the types of communities they live in, Statistics Canada calculates 35 LICOs for 7 different family sizes and 5 different community sizes, using before-tax and after-tax income.

Although the LICOs are the most commonly used criterion to measure poverty in Canada, other measures such as the low-income measure (LIM) are also used, especially for international comparisons. The LIM is defined as 50% of median adjusted household income in which household size is taken into account—a larger household needs more income to meet its needs. The LIM is another relative measure of poverty: households with income below a certain percentage of the median, usually 50%, are deemed poor. If median income declines, then the LIM threshold declines, too.

An *absolute measure*, which defines an amount of money a family or individual needs, is the alternative to a relative measure. The market basket measure (MBM), developed by Human Resources and Skills Development Canada, is an absolute measure of poverty. The MBM is a measure of low income based on the cost of a specific basket of goods and services for a family with two adults aged between 25 and 49 and two children aged between 9 and 13.

The poverty line depends on the size of a family and the size of the community. Using the after-tax LICOs measure, in 2012 the poverty line for a family of four living in a community of at least 500 000 residents was $37 052; if the same family lived in a community of 100 000 to 499 999 people, it was $31 335.

Trends in Poverty Based on conventional wisdom, you might expect that as the economy grows and becomes more prosperous, and as average income rises, the percentage of the population living below the poverty line would decline steadily. Is that the case in Canada? Let's see. Panel (a) of Figure 18-1 shows the **poverty rate**—the percentage of the population below the poverty line—from 1976 to 2011, using the different measures mentioned above. As you can see, the poverty rate fluctuated during that period, and it began to show a declining trend starting in 1996.

Panel (b) shows the poverty rate by age group using the after-tax LICOs. The poverty rate for seniors shows a clear declining trend, dropping from 30% to 5% in recent years. The poverty rate for those who are under 18 was above the overall poverty rate for most of the years during the period and has only dropped slightly below the overall rate in recent years. Unfortunately, the picture for those

FIGURE **18-1** Trends in the Canadian Poverty Rate, 1976–2011

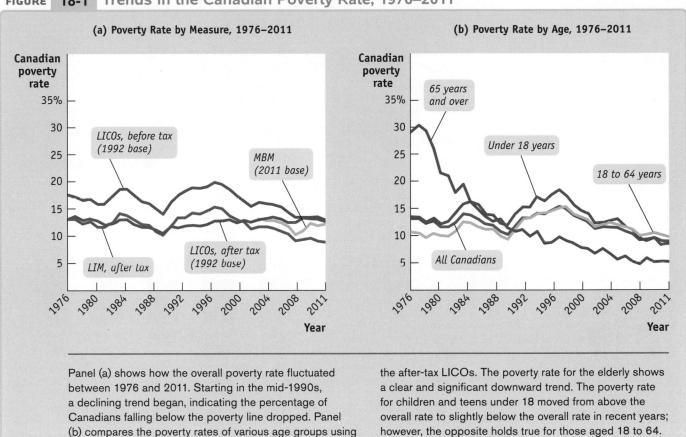

Panel (a) shows how the overall poverty rate fluctuated between 1976 and 2011. Starting in the mid-1990s, a declining trend began, indicating the percentage of Canadians falling below the poverty line dropped. Panel (b) compares the poverty rates of various age groups using the after-tax LICOs. The poverty rate for the elderly shows a clear and significant downward trend. The poverty rate for children and teens under 18 moved from above the overall rate to slightly below the overall rate in recent years; however, the opposite holds true for those aged 18 to 64.

between 18 and 64 was a bit gloomier; their poverty rate moved from below the overall poverty rate in earlier years to just above the overall rate in recent years.

Who Are the Poor? Who are the poor in Canada? Obvious answers are likely to be the single-parent families, families with a female as the primary breadwinner, Aboriginals, and visible minorities. Is this true? Let's take a look of how these groups fare.

In 2011, according to the after-tax LICOs as a measure of poverty, nearly 3 million Canadians were in poverty—about 8.8% of the population, or about one in eleven Canadians. The incidence of poverty was equally split between females (1.5 million) and males (1.46 million). About 1.394 million unattached individuals were considered to be poor in 2011, and 85% of those individuals (about 1.2 million) were under 65.

There is a correlation between family makeup and poverty: families with a woman as the major income earner had a higher chance of living in poverty—about 56% of the poor were families with female breadwinners. Single-parent families had a poverty rate of 19.7%, and almost 90% of these families had single mothers. Although married couples with children were much less likely to be poor, with a poverty rate of 5.1%, about 21% of the poor were in families with children and both parents present.

Based on the 2006 census data and using the LIM to measure poverty, a 2013 report by the Canadian Centre for Policy Alternatives (CCPA) showed that poverty rates among the First Nations were significantly higher than among other ethnic groups in Canada. Even worse, half of the status First Nations children in Canada lived in poverty, compared to a 15% poverty rate for all other children in the country (the average poverty rate for all children in Canada was 17%).

POOR PEOPLE IN RICH COUNTRIES

How does Canada's poverty problem compare with the situation in other wealthy countries? The answer depends, in part, on the definition of poverty.

The figure shows poverty rates in 2000 in five rich countries, under two definitions. One definition, which is widely used in international comparisons, defines someone as poor if that person lives in a household with an income that is less than half his or her country's median income, the low income measure (LIM) defined earlier. This is a *relative* definition of poverty. As the orange bars in the figure show, by this measure Canada was in the middle of the pack compared with other rich nations.

One objection to the relative definition of poverty is that Canada is richer than some other rich countries. Canada has about the same median income as the United Kingdom and a somewhat higher median income than Sweden and Germany. Does Canada still have high poverty when this is taken into account? The purple bars

use a measure of *absolute* poverty, the minimum annual income that is considered adequate. By this definition, Canada has the lowest poverty rate. Thus, depending on the measure of poverty used, Canada's poverty rate may be considered to be high or low.

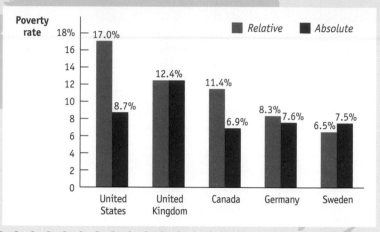

Source: Timothy Smeeding, "Poor People in Rich Nations: The United States in Comparative Perspective," *Journal of Economic Perspectives* 20, no. 1 (2006): 69–90.

Another study by the CCPA showed that race played a role in determining the likelihood of an individual living in poverty.[1] Once again, using the 2006 census data for Ontario, the report found that visible minority families were three times as likely to live under the poverty line as families who did not consider themselves as visible minority (for visible minority families the poverty rate was 18.7%, compared to 6% for non-visible minority families); the findings were similar for individuals.

What really stands out in the data is the number of Canadians moving above or below the poverty line. From 2009 to 2010, the number of individuals remaining below the poverty line was 1.52 million. At the same time, 0.889 million individuals moved out from under the poverty line and 0.78 million individuals fell below it. Individuals without a university degree were more likely to remain poor and to become the poor. Among those who remained poor, about 70% didn't have a post-secondary degree or diploma. For those who moved below the low income line, about two-thirds didn't have a post-secondary degree or diploma. These observations are consistent with the conventional wisdom that the level of education plays an important role in the financial well-being of an individual.

What Causes Poverty? Poverty is often blamed on lack of education, and educational attainment clearly has a strong positive effect on income level—those with more education earn, on average, higher incomes than those with less education. For example, in 1980 male workers with a bachelor's degree earned 32% more than those who had only graduated from high school. Female workers with a bachelor's degree earned 49% more than those who graduated from high school. By 2005, the premium enjoyed by workers with a bachelor's degree had risen to over 45% for males and over 60% for females.

[1]*Source:* Sheila Block, *Ontario's Growing Gap: The Role of Race and Gender,* (Canadian Centre for Policy Alternatives, 2010).

Lack of proficiency in English or French is also a barrier to higher income. For example, immigrants to Alberta with poor English skills are more likely to work for minimum wage in industries like retail and manufacturing, which offer temporary jobs and are more susceptible to economic fluctuations. Even for immigrants who are proficient in English, finding a decent job may not be easy if they lack connections and Canadian experience.

And it's important not to overlook the role of racial and gender discrimination; although less pervasive today than 50 years ago, discrimination still erects formidable barriers to advancement for many Canadians. Visible minorities earn less and are less likely to be employed than whites with comparable levels of education. Studies find that visible minorities and Aboriginals suffer persistent discrimination by employers. Women earn lower incomes than men with similar qualifications.

Canada's poverty rate is near the middle of the pack when compared to other rich countries.

In addition, one important source of poverty that should not be overlooked is bad luck. Many families find themselves impoverished when a wage-earner loses a job or a family member falls seriously ill.

Consequences of Poverty The consequences of poverty are often severe, particularly for children. In 2011, 8.5% of children in Canada lived in poverty; this is using the after-tax LICOs measure (using the after-tax LIM, the child poverty rate was 14.3%).[2] Poverty is often associated with lack of access to a nutritious diet, which can lead to higher risk of suffering health problems, developmental delays, and behavioural problems. Child poverty can also result in lower attainment in education and is more likely to lead to adult poverty when the children grow up. Recent medical studies have shown that children raised in severe poverty tend to suffer from lifelong learning disabilities. As a result, Canadian children growing up in or near poverty don't have an equal chance at the starting line: they tend to be at a disadvantage throughout their lives. Even talented children who come from poor families are unlikely to finish college or university.

To make things worse, the problems of child poverty do not hit the country evenly. Some provinces have higher child poverty rates than others. Table 18-1 shows the provincial child poverty rates in 2011 using the after-tax LICOs. British Columbia and Manitoba had the highest child poverty rates, sitting at 11.3%. The high rate in British Columbia caused lots of concern among advocacy groups who urged the provincial government to take immediate actions to reduce child poverty, with policy recommendations including raising the minimum wage, providing low-cost day care, increasing income assistance payments, and imposing a fairer tax system.

Similarly, some ethnic groups are more likely to live in poverty than others. As mentioned earlier, a report by the Canadian Centre for Policy Alternatives showed that half of First Nations children were living in poverty in 2013. This disturbingly high child poverty rate explains, to some extent, why Aboriginal children were behind non-Aboriginal children in other measures of well-being such as educational attainment and overall health, while dealing with higher rates of substance abuse, suicides, and homelessness. Unfortunately, disadvantages from childhood can carry forward to adulthood, making it more likely that a First Nations person will suffer lifelong poverty.

TABLE 18-1	Provincial Poverty Rates for Canadians under 18, 2011
	Poverty rate, persons under 18
Canada	8.5%
Newfoundland and Labrador	6
Prince Edward Island	4.6
Nova Scotia	8
New Brunswick	6.7
Quebec	7.3
Ontario	8.9
Manitoba	11.3
Saskatchewan	6.2
Alberta	6.8
British Columbia	11.3

Source: Statistics Canada.

[2]Children in single-mother families are more likely to suffer from poverty. The poverty rate for children in families led by a single mother rises to 23% (using the after-tax LICOs) and 39.3% (using the LIM).

Economic Inequality

Canada is a rich country. In 2007, the year prior to the recent recession, the average income for a Canadian household with at least two people was $93 100 (measured in 2011 dollars), far exceeding the poverty line.[3] Even after the 2008–2009 recession, average income rose to $95 000 in 2011. How is it possible, then, that so many Canadians still live in poverty? The answer is that income is unequally distributed, with many households earning much less than the average and others earning much more.

Table 18-2 shows the distribution of pre-tax income in 2011 among Canadian families, as estimated by Statistics Canada. Households are grouped into *quintiles*, each containing 20%, or one-fifth, of the population. The first, or lowest, quintile contains households whose income put them below the 20th percentile in income, the second quintile contains households whose income put them between the 20th and 40th percentiles, and so on.

For each group, Table 18-2 shows three numbers. The second column shows the income ranges that define the group. For example, in 2011, the lowest quintile consisted of households with annual incomes of less than $42 800, the next quintile of households had incomes between $42 800 and $65 300, and so on. The third column shows the average level of family income in each group, families in the highest quintiles had an average income of $202 800, almost seven times the average level of income of families in the lowest quintile. The fourth column shows the percentage of total Canadian income received by each group.

TABLE 18-2 Canada's Income Distribution in 2011

Income group	Income range	Average income	Percent of total income
Lowest quintile	$0 to $42 800	$29 900	6.3%
Second quintile	$42 801 to $65 300	53 900	11.3
Third quintile	$65 301 to $92 700	78 000	16.4
Fourth quintile	$92 701 to $131 900	110 500	23.3
Highest quintile	More than $131 900	202 800	42.7
Mean income = $95 000		**Median income = $77 300**	

Source: Statistics Canada.

Mean versus Median Household Income At the bottom of Table 18-2 are two useful numbers for thinking about the incomes of Canadian households. **Mean household income,** also called average household income, is the total income of all Canadian households divided by the number of households. **Median household income** is the income of a household in the exact middle of the income distribution—the level of income at which half of all households have lower income and half have higher income. It's very important to realize that these two numbers do not measure exactly the same thing.

Economists often illustrate the difference by asking people first to imagine a room containing several dozen more or less ordinary wage-earners, and then to think about what happens to the mean and median incomes of the people in the room if a Bay Street CEO, some of whom earn millions of dollars a year, walks in. The mean income soars, because the CEO's income pulls up the average, but median income hardly rises at all. This example helps explain why economists generally regard median income as a better guide to the economic status of typical families than mean income: mean income is strongly affected by the incomes of a relatively small number of very-high-income Canadian, who are not representative of the population as a whole; median income is not.

What we learn from Table 18-2 is that income in Canada is quite unequally distributed. The average income earned by the poorest fifth of families is less than 40% of the average income earned by families in the middle, and the average

Mean household income is the average income across all households.

Median household income is the income of the household lying at the exact middle of the income distribution.

---

[3]By comparison, using the after-tax LICOs, in 2007 the poverty line for a family of two living in a community with 500 000 or more was $21 851, while for a family of seven (or more) in the same community it was $47 084.

income of the richest fifth is 2.6 times the average income earned by those in the middle. The Economics in Action at the end of this section discusses long-term trends in Canada's income inequality.

The Gini Coefficient It's often convenient to have a single number that summarizes a country's level of income inequality. The **Gini coefficient,** the most widely used measure of inequality, is based on how disparately income is distributed across the quintiles. A country with a perfectly equal distribution of income—that is, one in which the bottom 20% of the population received 20% of the income, the bottom 40% of the population received 40% of the income, and so on—would have a Gini coefficient of 0. At the other extreme, the highest possible value for the Gini coefficient is 1—the level it would attain if all a country's income went to just one person.

One way to get a sense of what Gini coefficients mean in practice is to look at international comparisons. Figure 18-2 shows the most recent estimates of the Gini coefficient for many of the world's countries. Aside from a few countries in Africa, the highest levels of income inequality are found in Latin America, especially Colombia; countries with a high degree of inequality have Gini coefficients close to 0.6. The most equal distributions of income are in Europe, especially in Scandinavia; countries with very equal income distributions, such as Sweden, have Gini coefficients around 0.25. Compared to other wealthy countries, Canada, with a Gini coefficient of 0.365 in 2011 (based on total income for economic families), has high inequality, though it does have the lowest Gini coefficient in all of North and South America.

> The **Gini coefficient** is a number that summarizes a country's level of income inequality based on how unequally income is distributed across quintiles.

FIGURE **18-2** Income Inequality Around the World

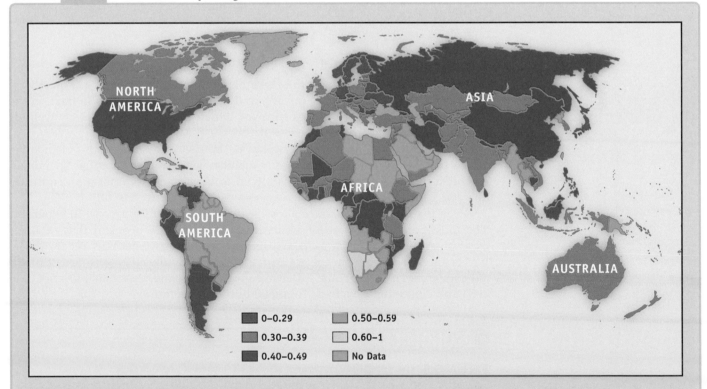

■ 0–0.29	☐ 0.50–0.59
■ 0.30–0.39	☐ 0.60–1
■ 0.40–0.49	■ No Data

The highest levels of income inequality are found in Africa and Latin America. The most equal distributions of income are in Europe, especially in Scandinavia. Compared to other wealthy countries, Canada, with a Gini coefficient of 0.365 in 2011, has high income inequality.

Sources: World Bank, *World Development Indicators* 2010; Statistics Canada.

How serious an issue is income inequality? In a direct sense, high income inequality means that some people don't share in a nation's overall prosperity. Although the poverty rate in Canada has declined somewhat in the past two decades, the Gini coefficient in the country is relatively stable, indicating that income inequality persists. Also, extreme inequality, as found in Latin America, is often associated with political instability because of tension between a wealthy minority and the rest of the population.

It's important to realize, however, that the data shown in Table 18-2 overstate the true degree of inequality in Canada, for several reasons. One is that the data represent a snapshot for a single year, whereas the incomes of many individual families fluctuate over time. That is, many of those near the bottom in any given year are having an unusually bad year and many of those at the top are having an unusually good one. Over time, their incomes will revert to a more normal level. So a table showing average incomes within quintiles over a longer period, such as a decade, would not show as much inequality.

Furthermore, a family's income tends to vary over its life cycle: most people earn considerably less in their early working years than they will later in life, then experience a considerable drop in income when they retire. Consequently, the numbers in Table 18-2, which combine young workers, mature workers, immigrants, and retirees, show more inequality than would a table that compares families of similar ages.

Despite these qualifications, there is a considerable amount of genuine inequality in Canada. In fact, inequality not only persists for long periods of time for individuals, it extends across generations. The children of poor parents are more likely to be poor than the children of affluent parents, and vice versa. Moreover, the fact that families' incomes fluctuate from year to year isn't entirely good news. Measures of inequality in a given year *do* overstate true inequality. But those year-to-year fluctuations are part of a problem that worries even affluent families—economic insecurity.

Economic Insecurity

As we stated earlier, although the rationale for the welfare state rests partly on the social benefits of reducing poverty and inequality, it also rests in part on the benefits of reducing economic insecurity, which afflicts even relatively well-off families.

One form economic insecurity takes is the risk of a sudden loss of income, which usually happens when a family member loses a job and either spends an extended period without work or is forced to take a new job that pays considerably less.

Even if a family doesn't face a loss in income, it can face a surge in expenses. The most common reason for such surges is a medical problem that requires expensive treatment, such as heart disease or cancer. Canadians receive basic health care coverage from the government, which handles a large share of medical expenses. However, some expensive medications and treatments are not covered and could impose a huge financial burden on a family.

ECONOMICS > IN ACTION

TRENDS IN INCOME INEQUALITY IN CANADA

Does inequality tend to rise, fall, or stay the same over time? Let's take a look. Detailed Canadian data on income by quintiles, as shown in Table 18-2, are only available starting in 1976. Panel (a) of Figure 18-3 shows the annual growth rate of average income for economic families, measured in 2011 dollars, for the five quintiles over two periods: from 1980 to 2000 and from 2000 to 2011. There is a clear difference between the two periods. In the first period, there were larger differences in the growth rates of average real income. Canadian households in higher income groups found their real income increasing between 1980 and 2000; however, households in the middle three quintiles experienced the lowest growth rates in that period. People in the lowest quintile experienced the second highest average growth rate of real income of the quintiles, meaning they were gaining on those in the middle three quintiles (the middle class). But this average growth rate of 0.6% per year was only half the growth rate experienced during this period by those in the top quintile, so those at the top were pulling ahead of all those in every other quintile. The good news is that after 2000, average real income within each group grew at about the same rate—around 1% per year—except for those in the lowest quintile that experienced the highest growth rate of average real income of 1.5% per year. So during this period the poorest 20% of families were gaining on the rest of the income distribution—inequality was declining.

Panel (b) of Figure 18-3 shows the share of total income earned by the top 10% of Canadians between 1982 and 2011. Again we can see that inequality in Canada was rising in the 1980s and 1990s when the share of total income earned by the top 10% of Canadians rose from 30% to 35%, but it then stabilized after 2000 (fluctuating around 35%). The average income earned by the top 10% of Canadians, measured in 2011 dollars, rose from $110 509 in 1982 to $147 100 in 2011, with an annual growth rate of 1.05% between 1982 and 2000 and 0.85% between 2000 and 2011. The lower growth rate of real income after 2000 helps explain why the share of total income earned by the top 10% of Canadians had stabilized in later years.

Many believe the persistence of income inequality is caused by rapid technological change. The demand for highly skilled or talented workers increases more rapidly than the demand for other workers, leading to a rise in the wage gap between the highly skilled and other workers. Growing international trade may also have contributed by allowing Canada to import labour-intensive products from low-wage countries rather than making them domestically, reducing the demand for less skilled Canadian workers and depressing their wages. Rising immigration may be yet another source—on average, immigrants earn lower wages than workers born in Canada.

All these explanations, however, fail to account for one key feature: much of the rise in inequality doesn't reflect a rising gap between highly educated workers and those with less education but rather growing differences among highly educated workers themselves. For example, teachers and top business executives

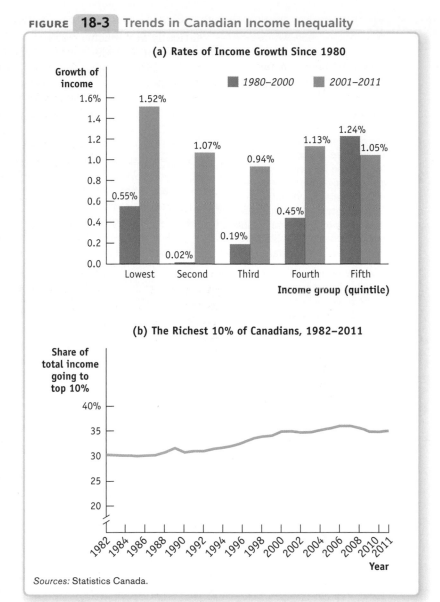

FIGURE 18-3   Trends in Canadian Income Inequality

(a) Rates of Income Growth Since 1980

Sources: Statistics Canada.

have similarly high levels of education, but executive paycheques have risen dramatically and teachers' salaries have not. For some reason, a few "superstars"—a group that includes literal superstars in the entertainment world but also such groups as Bay Street traders and top corporate executives—now earn much higher incomes than was the case a generation ago. It's still unclear what caused this change.

CHECK YOUR UNDERSTANDING 18-1

1. Indicate whether each of the following programs is a social welfare program or a social insurance program.
   a. A pension guarantee program, which provides pensions for retirees if they have lost their employment-based pension due to their employer's bankruptcy
   b. The federal program known as the National Child Benefit Supplement (NCBS), which provides a monthly benefit for low-income families with children.
   c. The federal program known as the Universal Child Care Benefit (UCCB), a monthly payment of $100 paid to all families with children under the age of 6.
   d. The federal flood program, which provides financial help to communities hit by major floods
   e. The Canada Mortgage and Housing Corporation (CMHC), which provides affordable housing to low-income families under the Investment in Affordable Housing (IAH) framework

2. Is the poverty line, as defined by an after-tax LICO, a relative or an absolute measure of poverty? That is, does it define poverty according to how poor someone is relative to others or according to some fixed measure that doesn't change over time? Explain.

3. The accompanying table gives the distribution of income for a very small economy.
   a. What is the mean income? What is the median income? Which measure is more representative of the income of the average person in the economy? Why?
   b. What income range defines the first quintile? The third?

	Income
Sephora	$39 000
Kelly	17 500
Raul	900 000
Vijay	15 000
Oskar	28 000

4. Which of the following statements more accurately reflects the principal source of rising inequality in Canada today?
   a. The salary of the manager of the local branch of Sunrise Bank has risen relative to the salary of the neighbourhood gas station attendant.
   b. The salary of the CEO of Sunrise Bank has risen relative to the salary of the local branch bank manager, who has similar education levels.

Solutions appear at back of book.

The Welfare State in Canada

The welfare state in Canada consists of three huge programs (health care, social security/old age security, and child care benefits) and a number of smaller programs. Table 18-3 shows one useful way to categorize the major welfare state programs in Canada.

The spending on these welfare state programs varies and comes from different levels of governments. For example, in the 2012–2013 fiscal year, governments in Canada spent $40.255 billion on Old Age Security benefits, $12.975 billion on family allowance/children's benefits, and $17.099 billion on Employment Insurance benefits. In 2012, pension benefits payments from the CPP/QPP reached $46.22 billion, bringing total government spending on social benefits to more than $140 billion. Last but not least, the largest component in Canada's welfare state program is the provision of health care services; doctors, hospitals, prescription medicine, and other specialized services, which cost $221.2 billion in 2013 for all levels of government.[4]

Table 18-3 distinguishes between programs that are **means-tested** and those that are not. In means-tested programs, benefits are available only to families or individuals whose income and/or wealth falls below some minimum. Basically, means-tested programs are social welfare programs designed to help only those with low incomes. By contrast, non-means-tested programs provide their benefits to everyone, although, as we'll see, they tend in practice to reduce income inequality.

Table 18-3 also distinguishes between programs that provide monetary transfers that beneficiaries can spend as they choose and those that provide **in-kind benefits,** which are given in the form of goods or services rather than money. The largest in-kind benefits are dominated by federal, provincial, and territorial spending on health care. We'll discuss health care in the next section of this chapter. For now, let's examine the other major programs.

TABLE 18-3	Major Welfare State Programs in Canada	
	Monetary transfers	**In-kind**
Means-tested	Social services	Affordable housing
	National Child Benefit Supplement (NCBS)	Provincial drug plans (for low-income families)
	Old Age Security (OAS)	
	Canada Child Tax Benefit	
Not means-tested	Universal Child Care Benefits (UCCB)	Health care
	Canada/Quebec Pension Plan (CPP/QPP)	
	Employment Insurance (EI)	

Means-Tested Programs

When people speak of welfare, they are often referring to monetary aid to poor families. The main source of such monetary aid in Canada is social services. Social services programs include social assistance, workers' compensation benefits, veterans' benefits, and other social services. These programs are exclusively for low-income families. Some means-tested programs, such as Guaranteed Income Supplement (GIS), National Child Benefit Supplement, Canada Child Tax Benefit, and affordable housing, are designated for specific groups of the population.

Old Age Security (OAS) is a major part of Canada's public pension system. The OAS has two parts: the OAS pension, which is a monthly payment to Canadians who are 65 or above; and the OAS benefits (Guarantee Income Supplement, Allowance, and Allowance for the Survivor, which are additional payments to low-income seniors). At the time of writing, the monthly OAS pension payment was $551.54. Although the OAS pension was originally designed to be paid to all seniors, it now has a clawback feature. This essentially makes it a means-tested program. The clawback raises the marginal effective tax rate by 15 percentage points so that the maximum income to receive the OAS pension in 2014 was $115 716.

Economists use the term **negative income tax** for a program that supplements the earnings of low-income working families. While several countries do have a negative income tax program, Canada does not, though support for the idea is growing across the political spectrum. In the United States the program is known as the Earned Income Tax Credit (EITC). EITC provides additional income to millions of American workers. Under the EITC program, only workers who earn income are eligible for it; over a certain range of incomes, the more a worker earns, the higher the amount of EITC received. That is, the EITC acts as a negative income tax for low-wage workers. In 2010, married couples with two children earning less than $12 550 per year received EITC payments equal to 40% of their earnings. (Payments were slightly lower for single-parent families or workers without children.) The EITC is phased out at higher incomes, disappearing at an income of $45 373 for married couples with two children in 2010.

A **means-tested** program is a program available only to individuals or families whose incomes fall below a certain level.

An **in-kind benefit** is a benefit given in the form of goods or services.

A **negative income tax** is a program that supplements the income of low-income working families.

[4]The federal government provided $40.8 billion in 2012–2013 through the Canada Health and Social Transfer to other levels of government to assist with the provision of health care and other social services by these lower levels of government.

Prime Minister Lester B. Pearson introduced the Canada Pension Plan (CPP) in 1965.

Non-Means-Tested Programs

Non-means-tested programs are available to individuals and families regardless of income. The largest non-means-tested program in Canada is the provision of health care, which will be discussed in detail in the latter part of this chapter. CPP/QPP, a major component of the country's public retirement income system, is also a significant non-means-tested program.

The CPP was established in 1965 by the Pearson government with the goal of providing financial security in the case of retirement, disability, or death. Quebec is the only province to have opted out of the CPP and instead has its own public pension (QPP). CPP/QPP was made mandatory to force workers to save some of their current income for retirement. The goal is to overcome the shortsightedness of workers, especially younger Canadians, who do not save enough money to support themselves after retirement.

CPP/QPP initially had a "pay-as-you-go" structure, similar to how the OAS works. However, in 1997 an agreement among the federal, provincial, and territorial governments raised CPP contributions for both employers and employees and lowered future payouts to ensure CPP/QPP was partially funded and sustainable for at least the next half century. Once CPP/QPP contributors reach the age of 65, they can receive their full (earned) pension. In this way, CPP/QPP is a savings program, unlike OAS, which is financed out of current tax revenue with the aim of bringing the income of elderly Canadians above a threshold income.

Like CPP/QPP, the provision of free (and mandatory) education up to Grade 12 in Canada also helps to alleviate the problem of shortsightedness—in this case, underinvesting in education. As mentioned previously, education plays an important role in an individual's financial well-being. Education not only helps raise people's standard of living—on average the poor tend to have lower levels of education—but higher average levels of education in a country tend to result in fewer social problems and improved health outcomes. Although education can have high returns, households have an incentive to underinvest in it because it takes a long time to see the benefits (see Chapter 16 for the external benefits of education). To reduce the problem of underinvestment in education and to encourage the accumulation of human capital, all levels of government in Canada cooperate to provide free education at elementary and secondary levels and subsidize post-secondary education. The governments are, in effect, making education less expensive to encourage (or force) more people to get educated.

Employment Insurance (EI), although normally a smaller portion of government transfers than social pensions, is another key social insurance program. EI provides qualifying workers who lose their jobs with up to 55% of their insured income up to a yearly maximum insurable amount—$48 600 in 2014—for 14 to 45 weeks, depending on the unemployment rate in the region. (In response to the recession of 2008–2009, the federal government temporarily increased the maximum length by five weeks.) In Canada, both employers and employees are required to pay a payroll tax that finances the operation of EI programs. In 2014 the maximum annual employee premium was $913.63, while employers were required to pay 1.4 times their employees' contributions.

The Effects of the Welfare State on Poverty and Inequality

Because the people who receive government transfers tend to be different from those who are taxed to pay for those transfers, the welfare state in Canada has the effect of redistributing income from some people to others. Each year Statistics Canada computes the amount and share of government transfers provided to the Canadians.

Table 18-4 shows the average total income, average government transfers received, and average income tax paid by families in different income groups in 2011. It is not surprising that there is an inverse relationship between income and average government transfers received. As a household's income rises, it will be less reliant on government assistance, so the amount of government transfers received falls. Given the progressive tax system in Canada, as income rises, tax liabilities also increase because the ability to pay increases.

TABLE **18-4**	Taxes and Transfers by Income, 2011		
Income group	Average total income	Average government transfers	Average income tax
Lowest quintile	$29 900	$15 400	$900
Second quintile	53 900	12 900	4 400
Third quintile	78 000	10 800	9 700
Fourth quintile	110 500	7 700	17 700
Highest quintile	202 800	6 000	44 200

Source: Statistics Canada.

According to Table 18-4, the poorest 20% of Canadian households receive about 30% of the total government transfers and only pay about 1% of the total income tax. On the other hand, the richest 20% of Canadian households receive the smallest share of government transfers and pay more than 57% of the total income tax. This is a clear indication that the design of the welfare state programs and tax system in Canada is aimed at helping the poor and redistributing income from the rich to the poor.

ECONOMICS ▸ IN ACTION

LULA LESSENS INEQUALITY

Brazil was one of the world's most unequal societies in 2002, the year Luiz Inacio Lula da Silva, universally known simply as Lula, was elected president. It was still one of the world's most unequal societies in 2010, when he handed the reins over to Dilma Roussef, his successor. But by 2010 Brazil was less unequal, and poverty was sharply lower. And Brazil's fight against poverty and inequality has become an international role model.

The numbers are striking. Figure 18-4 shows percentage changes in real income for different deciles (tenths) of the Brazilian population from 2001 to 2008. As you can see, there were huge gains for the poorest 10%, and the overall movement was clearly toward greater equality.

How did the Brazilians do it? One key factor was a new program known as *Bolsa Familia* (family grant). This program—modelled on a similar program in Mexico, but carried out on an even larger scale—offers what are known as "conditional cash transfers": payments that are available to poor families provided they meet certain requirements designed to help break the cycle of poverty. In particular, to get their allowances, families must keep their children in school and go for regular medical checkups, and mothers must attend workshops on subjects such as nutrition and disease prevention. The payments go to women rather than men because they are the most likely to spend the money on their families.

| FIGURE **18-4** | Percentage Changes in Real Income for Brazilians, 2001–2008 |

Source: Côrtes Neri, "The decade of falling income inequality and formal employment generation in Brazil," in OECD, *Tackling Inequalities in Brazil, China, India and South Africa: The Role of Labour Market and Social Policies*, (OECD Publishing, 2010).

As of 2010, Bolsa Familia covered 50 million Brazilians, a quarter of the population. The payments don't sound like much by Canadian standards: a monthly stipend of about $13 to poor families for each child age 15 or younger attending school, slightly higher payments for older children still in school, and a basic benefit of about $40 for families in extreme poverty. But Brazil's poor are very poor indeed, and these sums were enough to make a huge difference in their incomes.

The success of Bolsa Familia has led to the establishment of similar programs in many countries, including the United States: a small pilot program along similar lines has been established in New York City.

CHECK YOUR UNDERSTANDING 18-2

1. Explain how the negative income tax avoids the disincentive to work that characterizes social welfare programs that simply give benefits based on low income.

2. According to Table 18-4, what effect does the Canadian welfare state have on the overall poverty rate?

Solutions appear at back of book.

The Economics of Health Care

A large part of the welfare state, in Canada and in other wealthy countries, is devoted to paying for health care. In most wealthy countries, the government pays between 70% and 80% of all medical costs of its citizens and permanent residents. In Canada the public sector picks up 70% of all health care costs—slightly below the OECD average of about 73%—although it is more like 77% when the impact of the tax system is taken into account. The private sector, which covers the remaining 30% of costs in Canada, plays a much larger role in the U.S. health care system, paying 52% of all medical costs.

Figure 18-5 shows who paid for Canadian health care in 2011. Only 14.7% of health care spending was expenses "out of pocket"—that is, paid directly by individuals. Most health care spending, 70.4%, was paid for by the public sector—provincial and territorial governments covered 65.3% of all health care costs and the other 5.1% came from the federal government, municipal governments, and social security spending. Private health insurance covered 11.8% of all health care spending, often for things such as drug and vision care coverage. The final 3.1% of all health care spending is a category called non-consumption. This refers to a mixed bag of private spending on things such as hospital non-patient revenue, capital spending for privately owned facilities, and health research.

Insurance of some form or another paid for the majority of all Canadian health care costs. To understand why, we need to examine the special economics of health care.

FIGURE 18-5 Who Paid for Canadian Health Care in 2011?

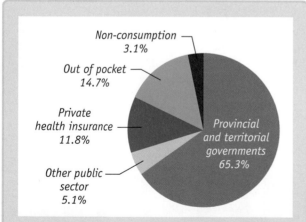

Non-consumption 3.1%
Out of pocket 14.7%
Private health insurance 11.8%
Other public sector 5.1%
Provincial and territorial governments 65.3%

In Canada in 2011, insurance paid for about 80% of health care costs: the sum of 11.8% (private insurance), 65.3% (provincial and territorial governments), and part of the 5.1% (other public sector—mainly spending by social security funds such as workers compensation).

Source: Canadian Institute for Health Information, National Health Expenditure Trends, 1975 to 2013.

The Need for Health Insurance

In 2013, Canadian personal health care expenses were about $6000 per person—11.2% of gross domestic product (above the OECD average of 9.3% of GDP, but well below the United States at 17.7% of GDP). This did not, however, mean that the typical Canadian spent $6000 on medical treatment. In fact, in any given year half the population incurs only minor medical expenses. But a small percentage of the population faces huge medical bills, with 10% of the population typically accounting for almost two-thirds of medical costs.

Is it possible to predict who will have high medical costs? To a limited extent, yes: there are broad patterns to illness. For example, the elderly are more likely to need expensive surgery and/or drugs than the young. But the fact is that anyone can suddenly find himself or herself needing very expensive medical treatment, costing many thousands of dollars in a very short time—far beyond what most families can easily afford. Yet nobody wants to be unable to afford (and obtain) such treatment if it becomes necessary.

Private Health Insurance Market economies have an answer to this problem: health insurance. Under **private health insurance,** each member of a large pool of individuals agrees to pay a fixed amount annually (called a *premium*) into a common fund (or *pool*) that is managed by a private company, which then pays most of the medical expenses of the pool's members. Although members must pay fees even in years in which they don't have large medical expenses, they benefit from the reduction in risk: if they do turn out to have high medical costs, the pool will take care of those expenses.

There are, however, inherent problems with the market for private health insurance. These problems arise from the fact that medical expenses, although basically unpredictable, aren't *completely* unpredictable. That is, people often have some idea whether or not they are likely to face large medical bills over the next few years. This creates a serious problem for private health insurance companies.

Suppose that an insurance company offers a "one-size-fits-all" health care policy, under which customers pay an annual premium equal to the average Canadian's annual medical expenses, plus a bit more to cover the company's operating expenses and a normal rate of profit. In return, the insurance company pays the policyholder's medical bills, whatever they are.

If all potential customers had an equal risk of incurring high medical expenses for the year, this might be a workable business proposition. In reality, however, people often have very different risks of facing high medical expenses—and, crucially, they often know this ahead of time. This reality would quickly undermine any attempt by an insurance company to offer one-size-fits-all health insurance. The policy would be a bad deal for healthy people, who don't face a significant risk of high medical bills: on average, they would pay much more in insurance premiums than the cost of their actual medical bills. But it would be a very good deal for people with chronic, costly conditions, who would on average pay less in premiums than the cost of their care.

As a result, some healthy people are likely to take their chances and go without insurance. This would make the insurance company's average customer less

> Under **private health insurance**, each member of a large pool of individuals pays a fixed amount annually to a private company that agrees to pay most of the medical expenses of the pool's members.

FOR INQUIRING MINDS

A CALIFORNIA DEATH SPIRAL

At the beginning of 2006, 116 000 workers at more than 6000 California small businesses received health coverage from PacAdvantage, a "purchasing pool" that offered employees at member businesses a choice of insurance plans. The idea behind PacAdvantage, which was founded in 1992, was that by banding together, small businesses could get better deals on employee health insurance.

But only a few months later, in August 2006, PacAdvantage announced that it was closing up shop because it could no longer find insurance companies willing to offer plans to its members.

What happened? It was the adverse selection death spiral. PacAdvantage offered the same policies to everyone, regardless of their prior health history. But employees didn't have to get insurance from PacAdvantage—they were free, if they chose, to opt out and buy insurance on their own. And sure enough, healthy workers started to find that they could get lower rates by buying insurance directly for themselves, even though that meant giving up the advantages of bulk purchasing. As a result, PacAdvantage began to lose healthy clients, leaving behind an increasingly sick—and expensive—pool of customers. Premiums had to go up, driving out even more healthy workers, and eventually the whole plan had to shut down.

healthy than the average Canadian. This raises the medical bills the company will have to pay and raises the company's costs per customer. That is, the insurance company would face a problem called *adverse selection*, which is discussed in detail in Chapter 20. Because of adverse selection, a company that offers health insurance to everyone at a price reflecting average medical costs of the general population, and that gives people the freedom to decline coverage, would find itself losing a lot of money.

The insurance company could respond by charging more—raising its premium to reflect the higher-than-average medical bills of its customers. But this would drive off even more healthy people, leaving the company with an even sicker, higher-cost clientele, forcing it to raise the premium even more, driving off even more healthy people, and so on. This phenomenon is known as the *adverse selection death spiral*, which ultimately leads the health insurance company to fail.

This description of the problems with health insurance might lead you to believe that private health insurance can't work. In fact, however, most working Canadians do have some private health insurance that supplements the public coverage available to all. Insurance companies are able, to some extent, to overcome the problem of adverse selection two ways: by carefully *screening* people who apply for coverage and through employment-based health insurance. With screening (which we'll learn more about in Chapter 20), people who are likely to have high medical expenses are charged higher-than-average premiums—or in many cases, refused coverage entirely. The next section explains how employment-based health insurance, a unique feature of the Canadian workplace, also allows private health insurance to work.

Employment-Based Health Insurance For the most part, however, insurance companies overcome adverse selection by selling insurance indirectly, to peoples' employers rather than to individuals. The big advantage of *employment-based health insurance*—insurance that a company provides to its employees—is that these employees are likely to contain a representative mix of healthy and less healthy people, rather than a selected group of people who want insurance because they expect to pay high medical bills. This is especially true if the employer is a large company with thousands or tens of thousands of workers. Employers require their employees to participate in the company health insurance plan because allowing employees to opt out (which healthier ones will be tempted to do) raises the cost of providing insurance for everyone else.

There's another reason employment-based insurance is widespread in Canada: it gets special, favourable tax treatment. Workers pay taxes on their paycheques, but workers who receive health insurance from their employers don't pay taxes on the value of the benefit. Also, employers contributions to these health insurance plans are not a taxable benefit for employees, but are a tax-deductible expense for the employer. So employment-based health insurance is, in effect, subsidized by the Canadian tax system. Economists estimate the value of this subsidy at about $5 billion each year.

In spite of this subsidy, however, many working Canadians don't receive employment-based health insurance. Those who aren't covered include most older Canadians, because relatively few employers offer workers insurance that continues after they retire; the many workers whose employers don't offer coverage (especially part-time workers); and the unemployed.

Government Health Insurance

Canada operates a publicly funded, privately provided, universal, comprehensive, accessible and portable, single-payer, provincially administered national health care system. Let's examine each of these facets in more detail.

Under public health insurance, sometimes called publicly funded health insurance, each member of the public (citizens and permanent residents) qualifies for free access to certain health care services, which are paid for by the government. Canada's public health care system is a **single-payer system** with the government acting as the single insurer and paying the entire cost of all medically insured health care services. Although the public does not directly face any payment, this health care spending is financed through taxes, in some cases including special levies geared toward collecting funding specifically for health care.

Canada's health care system is administered by the provinces and territories according to the constitution. Nevertheless, the federal government plays a key role in the public provision of health care: it sends transfer payments to provinces to help cover health care costs. The *Canada Health Act*, which was unanimously enacted by Parliament in 1984, established five national principles as to how the provision of public health care should operate (otherwise federal transfer payments may be withheld).[5] As described by Parliament these five national principles are:

- *Universality*, meaning the public health care insurance must be provided to all Canadians.
- *Comprehensiveness*, meaning that all medically necessary hospital and doctor services are covered by public health insurance.
- *Accessibility*, meaning that financial or other barriers to the provision of publicly funded health services are discouraged, so that health services are available to all Canadians when they need them.
- *Portability*, meaning that all Canadians are covered under public health care insurance, even when they travel internationally or move within Canada.
- *Public administration*, which requires provincial and territorial health care insurance plans be managed by a public agency on a not-for-profit basis.

According to the federal government, there are two overarching objectives of federal health care policy: (1) to ensure that every Canadian has *timely* access to all medically necessary health services *regardless* of their ability to pay for those services; and (2) to ensure that *no* Canadian suffers *undue* financial hardship as a result of having to pay health care bills.

While publicly funded, Canada's health care is largely provided by private doctors and not-for-profit private hospitals. Provinces and territories determine lists of insured medical services provided by physicians and hospitals and negotiate with the providers of these services to set fee schedules. Should doctors or hospitals attempt to charge additional fees for insured services (sometimes called "user charges," "co-payments," or "extra-billing"), the federal government reserves the right to reduce transfer payments to their jurisdiction by an offsetting amount. This in essence makes such additional user fees illegal, and keeps the system a single-payer model free and accessible to all. The public administration of the system helps keep total costs down, which allows for the affordable provision of good quality health care.

For decades, Canada's health care was privately funded, resulting in access to care based on ability to pay. But in 1947 Saskatchewan introduced Canada's first publicly funded health insurance plan covering hospital services. In 1956 the federal government offered to share the costs with any province setting up a provincially funded health insurance plan. By 1961, all provinces and territories had signed agreements with the federal government and had set up provincial health insurance plans covering hospital care that qualified for federal cost sharing. The public health care system has since evolved into a provincial or territorial provision of many doctor and hospital health care services to all Canadians,

A **single-payer system** is a health care system in which the government is the principal payer of medical bills funded through taxes.

---

[5]This section draws extensively on Chapter 17 of *The Health of Canadians – The Federal Role*, (Standing Senate Committee on Social Affairs, Science and Technology, October 2002), www.parl.gc.ca/Content/SEN/Committee/372/SOCI/rep/repoct02vol6-e.htm.

plus a prescription drug benefit. These drug benefit plans are generally targeted to seniors, recipients of social assistance, and individuals with illnesses or conditions that are associated with high drug costs. All other Canadians have to pay for prescription drugs either out of their own pockets or via private supplemental health insurance. The same goes for any non-insured health care services or medication.

Health Care in Other Countries

Health care is one area in which Canada is very different from the United States. In fact, when it comes to health care the United States is very different from most other wealthy countries in three distinct ways. First, the United States relies much more on private health insurance than any other wealthy country does. Second, they spend much more on health care per person. Third, they're the only wealthy nation in which large numbers of people lack health insurance.

The United States government runs three health insurance programs: Medicare, Medicaid, and military health care. Medicare covers hospitalizations and some other medical costs. It is financed by payroll taxes and is available to all Americans 65 and older, regardless of their income and wealth. Medicaid is a means-tested program for low-income Americans, paid for with federal and state government revenues. Millions of Americans receive health insurance as a consequence of military service. Unlike Medicare and Medicaid, which pay medical bills but don't deliver health care directly, the Veterans Health Administration runs hospitals and clinics throughout the U.S, in a similar system to the British National Health Service.

Table 18-5 shows the breakdown of health insurance coverage across the U.S. population in 2012. A majority of Americans—more than 170 million people—received health insurance through their employers. The majority of those without private insurance were covered by Medicare and Medicaid. (The numbers in Table 18-5 don't add up because some people have more than one form of coverage. For example, many recipients of Medicare also have supplemental coverage either through Medicaid or private policies.)

So the U.S. health care system offers a mix of private insurance, mainly from employers, and public insurance of various forms. Most Americans have health insurance either from private insurance companies or through various forms of government insurance. However, in 2012 almost 48 million Americans, 15.4% of the population, had no health insurance at all.

TABLE 18-5	Number of Americans Covered by Health Insurance, 2012 (millions)
Covered by private health insurance	**198.8**
Employment-based	170.9
Direct purchase	30.6
Covered by government insurance	**101.5**
Medicaid	50.9
Medicare	48.9
Military health care	13.7
Not covered	**48.0**

Source: U.S. Census Bureau.

Table 18-6 compares four wealthy countries: Canada, France, Britain, and the United States. The United States is the only one of the four countries that relies on private health insurance to cover most people; as a result, it's the only one in which private spending on health care is (slightly) larger than public spending on health care.

As previously mentioned, Canadian doctors are generally not employed directly by the government, and hospitals, although they are not-for-profit, are usually privately run. The British system is extended to everyone: a government agency, the British National Health Service, directly employs health care workers and runs hospitals and clinics that are available free of charge to the public. France is somewhere in between the Canadian and British systems. In France, the government acts as a single-payer, providing health insurance to everyone, and French citizens can receive treatment from private doctors and hospitals; but they also have the choice of receiving care from a sizable health care system run directly by the French government.

All three non-U.S. systems provide health insurance to all their citizens; yet all three spend much less on health care per person than the United States. Many Americans assume this must mean that foreign health care is inferior in quality. But many health care experts disagree with the claim. As they point out, Britain, Canada, and France generally match or exceed the United States in terms of many measures of health care provision, such as the number of doctors,

TABLE 18-6 Health Care Systems in Economically Advanced Countries (2011 data unless indicated)

	Government share of health care spending	Health care spending per capita (US$, purchasing power parity)	Life expectancy (total population at birth, years)	Infant mortality (deaths per 1000 live births)
Canada	70.4%	$4522	81.0[1]	4.9[1]
France	76.8	4118	82.2	3.5[2]
Britain	82.8	3405	81.1	4.3
United States	47.8	8508	78.7	6.1

Source: OECD Health Statistics. 2011 data except: (1) 2009 data; (2) 2012 data.

nurses, and hospital beds per 100 000 people. It's true that U.S. medical care includes more advanced technology in some areas and many more expensive surgical procedures. U.S. patients also have shorter waiting times for elective surgery than patients in Canada or Britain. France, however, also has very short waiting times.

Surveys of patients seem to suggest that there are no significant differences in the quality of care received by patients in Canada, Europe, and the United States. And as Table 18-6 shows, the United States does considerably worse than other advanced countries in terms of basic measures such as life expectancy and infant mortality, although their poor performance on these measures may have causes other than the quality of medical care—notably, relatively high levels of poverty and income inequality in the United States.

So why does the United States spend so much more on health care than other wealthy countries do? Some of the disparity is the result of higher doctors' salaries, but most studies suggest that this is a secondary factor. Another possibility is that Americans are getting better care than their counterparts abroad, but statistics don't back up this claim.

However, the most likely explanation is that the U.S. system suffers from serious inefficiencies that other countries manage to avoid. Critics of the U.S. system emphasize the system's reliance on private insurance companies, which expend resources on such activities as marketing and trying to identify and weed out high-risk patients, leading to high operating costs. On average, the operating costs of private health insurers eat up 14% of the premiums clients pay, leaving only 86% to spend on providing health care. By contrast, U.S. Medicare spends only 3% of its funds on operating costs, leaving 97% to spend on health care. In Canada, administration accounted for only 1.7% of public health insurance spending in 2013. A 2007 study by the McKinsey Global Institute found that the United States was spending almost six times as much per person on health care administration as other wealthy countries. Americans also pay higher prices for prescription drugs—or travel to Canada to buy lower priced prescription medication—because in other countries government agencies bargain with pharmaceutical companies to get lower drug prices.

The 2010 U.S. Health Care Reform ("ObamaCare")

However one rates the past performance of the U.S. health care system, by 2009 it was clearly in trouble. The root of the problem was the rising cost of health insurance, both private and public.

An immediate problem was that the cost of private insurance had been rising much faster than incomes. From 1999 to 2009, the average premiums for employment-based health insurance more than doubled, but the wages of the average worker rose only 35%. By 2009, the average cost of insurance for a family of four was almost $14 000.

FIGURE **18-6** Changes in U.S. Health Insurance Status, 2000–2009

In the decade before 2010, the U.S. population grew substantially, but the number of people with employment-based health insurance actually declined. Growth in U.S. public health insurance, mainly Medicaid and the State Children's Health Insurance Program (SCHIP), made up part of the difference. There was also, however, an increase in the number of uninsured.

Source: U.S. Census Bureau.

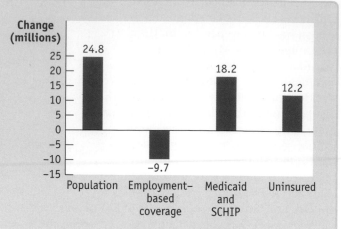

As a result of these rising costs, employment-based health insurance, the centrepiece of the system for Americans under 65, was in decline. Figure 18-6 shows selected changes in the insurance status of Americans between 2000 and 2009. Over that period, while the total American population increased by 25 million, the number of people with employment-based health insurance decreased by almost 10 million. Despite the expansion of Medicaid by 18 million people, by 2009 an additional 12 million people had joined the ranks of the uninsured.

At the same time, as U.S. private health insurance was faltering and the ranks of the uninsured increased, American public health insurance was coming under increasing financial strain. Partly this was because Medicaid and other U.S. government programs covered more people than in the past. Mainly, however, it was because the cost per beneficiary of government health insurance, like the cost per beneficiary of private insurance, had been rising rapidly.

What's behind these rising costs? Figure 18-7 shows overall Canadian and U.S. spending on health care as a percentage of GDP, a measure of the nation's total income, since the 1960s. As you can see, U.S. health spending as a share of income rose about 350% between 1960 and 2011; this increase in spending explains why health insurance became more expensive in the United States. While similar trends can be observed in other countries, in Canada health

FIGURE **18-7** Rising Health Care Costs

Since 1960, U.S. health care spending as a percentage of GDP, a measure of total income, has risen about 350%. While similar trends can be seen in other countries, in Canada health care spending as a percentage of GDP rose just over 200% during this same period. Most analysts believe that the main force behind this trend is medical progress: we spend more on health care because more medical problems are treatable.

Source: OECD Health Statistics 2013.

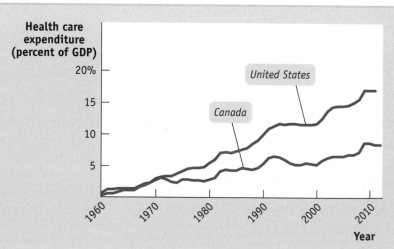

care spending as a percentage of GDP rose by just over 200% during this same period.

The consensus of health experts is that the increase in health spending is a result of medical progress. As medical science progresses, conditions that could not be treated in the past become treatable, but often only at great expense. Both private insurers and government programs feel compelled to cover the new procedures—but this means higher costs, which either have to be passed on in the form of higher insurance premiums or require larger commitments of taxpayer funds.

In the United States, the combination of a rising number of uninsured and rising costs led to many calls for health care reform. And in 2010 the U.S. Congress passed comprehensive health care reform legislation, officially known as the Patient Protection and Affordable Care Act (PPACA, or ACA for short), but often simply referred to as "ObamaCare."

ACA, which took full effect in 2014, is the largest expansion of the American welfare state since the creation of Medicare and Medicaid in 1965. It has two major objectives: covering the uninsured and cost control. Let's look at each in turn.

Covering the Uninsured On the coverage side, ACA was modelled closely on a similar plan that had been introduced in Massachusetts in 2006. To understand the logic of both the Massachusetts plan and ACA, consider the problem facing one major category of uninsured Americans: the many people who seek coverage in the individual insurance market but are turned down because they have pre-existing medical conditions, which insurance companies fear could lead to large future expenses. (Insurance companies have been known to deny coverage for even minor ailments, like allergies or a rash you had in university.) How can insurance be made available to such people?

One answer would be regulations requiring that insurance companies offer the same policies to everyone, regardless of medical history—a rule known as "community rating." But community rating tends to lead to an adverse selection death spiral: healthy individuals don't buy insurance until or unless they get sick, and because only people with health problems are getting coverage, insurance becomes very expensive.

To make community rating work, it's necessary to supplement it with other policies. Both the Massachusetts reform and ACA add two key features. First is the requirement that everyone purchase health insurance—known as the *individual mandate*. This prevents an adverse selection death spiral. Second, U.S. government subsidies make the required insurance affordable for lower- and lower-middle income families.

It's important to realize that this system is like a three-legged stool: all three components must be present in order for it to work. Take away community rating, and those with pre-existing conditions won't get coverage. Take away the individual mandate, and community rating will produce an adverse selection death spiral. And you can't require that people buy insurance without providing subsidies to those with lower incomes.

Will this act, once fully integrated, succeed in covering more or less everyone? The Massachusetts precedent is encouraging on that front: after four years, more than 98% of the state's residents had health insurance and virtually all children were covered. Since the ACA is very similar in structure, it ought to produce similar results.

Cost Control But how does ACA control costs? In itself, the expansion of coverage raises U.S. health care spending, although not by as much as you might think. The uninsured are by and large relatively young, and the young have relatively low health care costs. (The elderly are already covered by Medicare.) The question is whether ACA can succeed in "bending the curve": reducing the rate of growth of health costs over time.

ACA's promise to control costs starts from the premise that the U.S. medical system had skewed incentives that wasted resources. Because most care in the United States is paid for by insurance, neither doctors nor patients have an incentive to worry about costs. In fact, because health care providers are generally paid for each procedure they perform, there's a financial incentive to provide additional care—do more tests and, in some cases, perform more operations—even when there are little or no medical benefits.

The act attempts to correct these skewed incentives in a variety of ways, from stricter oversight of reimbursements, to linking payments to a procedure's medical value, to paying health care providers for improved health outcomes rather than the number of procedures, and by limiting the tax deductibility of employment-based plans. It will be several years before we can determine how well these measures worked, but supporters point out that ACA incorporates virtually every idea for cost control that has been proposed by health care economists and that some of these ideas are likely to be highly successful.

Is Canadian Health Care Spending Sustainable?

The Canadian health care system is a key part of Canada's welfare state. A 2011 Nanos Research poll found that 94% of Canadians were in favour of preserving public health care. In fact, health care is often cited as the biggest issue for voters, beating out issues like taxes, job creation, retirement security, and the environment. But as Figure 18-7 clearly shows, Canadian health care spending as a percentage of total income has been rising. Canadians are right to be concerned about whether the public health care system is sustainable. Can the system survive? In what form? And what, if anything, can Canadians do to help keep the system running?

Between 1960 and 2011 health care costs rose about 350% in the United States and just over 200% in Canada. Canada's public system experienced much smaller cost increases than the United States system with its dependence on for-profit health insurance and health care providers.

But you might ask if this is a fair comparison—what about other industrialized nations? As it turns out, health care costs are rising throughout the developed world. Table 18-7 shows total health care spending as a percentage of total income and the percentage growth of this amount between 1960 and 2011 for a number of major OECD countries. Canada's total health care spending, at 11.2% of total income in 2011, is by no means on the low end for these countries. But at the same time it is not the highest either, nor has it grown any faster than health care costs in these other nations. According to the 2001 Romanov Commission report on the future of health care in Canada, publicly funded health care is both feasible and efficient. The much-publicized problems of Canada's health care system stem from the fact that it is chronically underfunded.

TABLE 18-7 Health Expenditure (1960–2011 data unless indicated)

	Total health expenditure (percent of GDP)	Percent change of health spending		Total health expenditure (percent of GDP)	Percent change of health spending
Australia	8.9%[1]	242%[2]	Ireland	8.9%	244%
Britain	9.4	241	Japan	9.6	325
Canada	11.2	206	Netherlands	11.9	174[4]
Finland	9.0	235	Norway	9.3	322
France	11.6	303	Switzerland	11.0	225
Germany	11.3	189[3]	United States	17.7	345

Source: OECD Health Statistics. 2011 data except: (1) 2009 data; (2) 1960–2009 data; (3) 1970–2011 data; (4) 1972–2011 data.

TABLE 18-8   Health Care Expenditure Shares (by funder and type, 1983 and 2013)

	Public		Private		Total	
	1983	2013	1983	2013	1983	2013
Hospitals	50.5%	38.6%	15.6%	8.6%	42.4%	29.6%
Other institutions	10.7	10.5	11.9	10.8	11.0	10.5
Physicians	19.1	20.9	1.0	0.6	14.8	14.8
Other professionals	2.0	1.3	35.5	30.4	9.8	10.0
Drugs	3.1	8.2	26.8	35.3	8.7	16.3
Capital	4.1	5.3	4.7	3.0	4.2	4.6
Public health	4.8	7.3	0	0	3.6	5.1
Administration	2.3	1.7	2.2	6.2	2.2	3.0
Other health spending	3.4	6.3	2.4	5.1	3.2	5.9
Total	100.0	100.0	100.0	100.0	100.0	100.0
Percent of GDP	**6.4**	**7.9**	**1.9**	**3.3**	**8.3**	**11.2**

Source: Canadian Institute for Health Information, National Health Expenditure Trends, 1975 to 2013.

Table 18-8 attempts to address what exactly is driving health care costs up. This table compares Canadian health care spending in 1983 and 2013. It tabulates spending over major categories and shows the percentage of public, private, and total health care spending in each category. For example, in 1983, 19.1% of public health care spending went to physicians and rose slightly to 20.9% in 2013. In 1983, 1.0% of all private health care spending went to physicians and this share declined to 0.6% of all private health care spending. The table also presents the health care spending as a percentage of GDP, showing that health care costs rose from 8.3% of GDP in 1983 to 11.3% in 2013.

Interestingly, while health care costs now represent a larger share of GDP, the total share spent on hospitals has shrunk. The shares spent on doctors and other professionals have remained stable. What we see instead is that the greatest cost pressures are coming from prescription drugs (both publicly and private funded), public health, and rising administration costs in the private sector.

The reason spending on drugs rose so quickly lies in two related areas. Medical progress offers new drugs for previously untreatable conditions, though often at great expense. Also, the aging population drives up drug costs since older citizens are much more likely to need prescription drugs than younger, healthier patients. This is exactly why some have called on the federal government to take the lead in negotiating with brand name pharmaceutical companies for price concessions, either in return for longer patent protection or through the bulk buying of drugs at the national scale. If this can be achieved, the health care system costs should be more sustainable for the long run. But is this feasible and will it be enough? Sadly, there are no easy answers to these questions.

In 2014, the health care accord that set the funding and health care service delivery agreements between the federal, provincial, and territorial governments expired and was being renegotiated. Unfortunately, at the time of writing, the federal government was ignoring the calls of the provinces and territories to come together and work on a deal, and instead unilaterally announced tens of billions worth of cuts to health care that will come into effect after the next federal election. Supporters of public not-for-profit health care were left scrambling to fight against what they saw as the next big threat to Canadian health care and another push toward the end of a single-payer system with for-profit health care.

ECONOMICS > IN ACTION

TOMMY DOUGLAS, THE GREATEST CANADIAN

Tommy Douglas is one the most prominent Canadians of the past century. In 1935, Douglas was elected to Parliament as a member of the Cooperative Commonwealth Federation (CCF), Canada's first national social democratic party. In 1944, Douglas' CCF won a huge majority in the Saskatchewan provincial election. So Douglas became not only the premier of Saskatchewan (a post he held for 17 years), but also leader of the first socialist government in North America. Douglas introduced many measures geared toward improving the welfare of society. Some of the most lasting measures were in the field of health care services.

Starting in 1944, free medical, hospital, and dental services were introduced for pensioners. Treatment of severe diseases such as cancer, tuberculosis, and STIs was made free for all.

In 1947, Douglas introduced a universal hospitalization insurance plan paid for by the provincial treasury and with a $5 levy per person. In 1959, Douglas announced plans to introduce Medicare: a universal, prepaid, publicly administered medical insurance plan to cover hospital and doctors services, including preventative care. His proposal was aided by Prime Minister Diefenbaker's 1958 promise that the federal government would pay 50% of the cost of any provincial hospital plan. In 1961, after 17 years in the office, he resigned from his position as premier to become the leader of the federal New Democratic Party. The next year, Saskatchewan's Medicare plan came into force on July 1, 1962. Within the next decade, all the provinces had adopted their own provincial plans similar in design to Saskatchewan's Medicare and half paid for by the federal government.

For his contributions as the father of universal health care in Canada and for his other works, Tommy Douglas was voted the greatest Canadian of all time in a CBC survey in 2004.

Kiefer Sutherland unveils a statue of his grandfather Tommy Douglas in Weyburn, Saskatchewan.

▼ Quick Review

- Canada has a universal health care system that is available to all for free. The provincial, territorial, and federal governments operate a **single-payer system,** funding 100% of the costs of all covered medical services.

- In the United States, health insurance satisfies an important need because expensive medical treatment is unaffordable for most families. **Private health insurance** has an inherent problem: the adverse selection death spiral. Screening by insurance companies reduces the problem, and employment-based health insurance, the way most Americans are covered, avoids it altogether.

- The majority of Americans not covered by private insurance are covered by Medicare, which is a non-means-tested single-payer system for those over 65, and Medicaid, which is available based on income.

- Compared to other wealthy countries, the United States depends more heavily on private health insurance, has higher health care spending per person, higher administrative costs, and higher drug prices, but without clear evidence of better health outcomes.

- Health care costs everywhere are increasing rapidly due to scientific progress and an aging population.

CHECK YOUR UNDERSTANDING 18-3

1. Jiro is an international student enrolled in a four-year degree program. He is required to enroll in a health insurance program run by his school.
   a. Explain how Jiro and his parents benefit from this health insurance program even though, given his age, it is unlikely that he will need expensive medical treatment.
   b. Explain how his school's health insurance program avoids the adverse selection death spiral.

2. According to its critics, what accounts for the higher costs of the U.S. health care system compared to those of other wealthy countries?

Solutions appear at back of book.

The Debate over the Welfare State

The goals of the welfare state seem laudable: to help the poor, to protect against severe economic hardship, and to ensure access to essential health care. But good intentions don't always make for good policy. There is an intense debate about how large the welfare state should be, a debate that partly reflects differences in philosophy but also reflects concern about the possibly counterproductive effects on incentives of welfare state programs. Disputes about the size of the welfare state are also one of the defining issues of modern Canadian politics.

Problems with the Welfare State

There are two different arguments against the welfare state. One, which we described earlier in this chapter, is based on philosophical concerns about the proper role of government. As we learned, some political theorists believe that redistributing income is not a legitimate role of government. Rather, they believe that government's role should be limited to maintaining the rule of law, providing public goods, and managing externalities.

The more conventional argument against the welfare state involves the trade-off between efficiency and equity, an issue that we first encountered in Chapter 7. As we explained there, the *ability-to-pay-principle*—the argument that an extra dollar of income matters more to a less well-off individual than to a more well-off individual—implies that the tax system should be progressive, with high-income taxpayers paying a higher fraction of their income in taxes than those with lower incomes.

But this must be balanced against the efficiency costs of high marginal tax rates. Consider an extremely progressive tax system that imposes a marginal rate of 90% on very high incomes. The problem is that such a high marginal rate reduces the incentive to increase a family's income by working hard or making risky investments. As a result, an extremely progressive tax system tends to make society as a whole poorer, which could hurt even those the system was intended to benefit. That's why even economists who strongly favour progressive taxation don't support a return to the extremely progressive system that prevailed in 1948, when the top Canadian marginal income tax rate was 80%. So, the design of the tax system involves a trade-off between equity and efficiency.

A similar trade-off between equity and efficiency implies that there should be a limit to the size of the welfare state. A government that operates a large welfare state requires more revenue than one that restricts itself mainly to provision of public goods such as building highways. A large welfare state requires higher tax revenue and higher marginal tax rates than a smaller welfare state.

Table 18-9 shows "social expenditure," a measure that roughly corresponds to total welfare state spending, as a percentage of GDP in Canada, the United States, Britain, and France. It also compares this with an estimate of the top marginal tax rate faced by an average single wage-earner, including payroll taxes paid by employers and state and local taxes. As you can see, France's large welfare state goes along with a high marginal rate of taxation. As the upcoming Economics in Action explains, some but not all economists believe that this high rate of taxation is a major reason the French work substantially fewer hours per year than North Americans.

TABLE 18-9 Social Expenditure and Marginal Tax Rates

	Social expenditure in 2009 (percent of GDP)	Top marginal tax rate in 2009
Canada	19.2%	49.5%
United States	19.2	34.4
Britain	24.1	38.8
France	32.1	52.0

Source: OECD. Marginal tax rate is defined as a percentage of total labour costs.

One way to hold down the costs of the welfare state is to means-test benefits: make them available only to those who need them. But means-testing benefits creates a different kind of trade-off between equity and efficiency. Consider the following example: Suppose there is some means-tested benefit, worth $2000 per year, that is available only to families with incomes of less than $20 000 per year. Now suppose that a family currently has an income of $19 500 but that one family member is deciding whether to take a new job that will raise the family's income to $20 500. Well, taking that job will actually make the family worse off, because it will gain $1000 in earnings but lose the $2000 government benefit.

This feature of means-tested benefits, which makes a family worse off if it earns more is known as a *notch*. It is a well-known problem with programs that aid the poor and behaves much like a high marginal tax rate on income. Most welfare state programs are designed to avoid a notch by setting a sliding scale for benefits. With a sliding scale, benefits diminish gradually as the recipient's income rises rather than come to an abrupt end.

OCCUPY WALL STREET

In the fall of 2011, Zuccotti Park, a small open space in Manhattan's financial district, was taken over by protestors, part of a movement known as "Occupy Wall Street." The protestors had a number of grievances, but the most pressing were their complaints about Wall Street and its perceived contribution to growing inequality. The Occupy Wall Street takeover and protests inspired similar protests in hundreds of cities in dozens of countries around the entire world, including every province in Canada. "We are the 99 percent!" became the movement's favourite slogan, a reference to the large increase in share of income going to the top 1 percent of the population. Wall Street, they charged, contributed to growing inequality by paying its bankers huge salaries and bonuses, while engaging in overly risky behaviour that led to the U.S. housing boom and bust of 2007–2009 that decimated the global economy. Was this a reasonable charge?

Those who found it unreasonable pointed to the contributions that Wall Street, and the American finance industry in general, have made to the U.S. economy. Compared to other countries, the United States is a leader in financial services and innovation, generating billions annually in revenues, and attracting trillions of dollars of investment from abroad. High salaries on Wall Street, they contend, are simply the rewards to skill and hard work in the competitive market for talent on Wall Street.

What is incontrovertible, however, are the data that show that incomes in the finance industry have contributed to growing inequality in the United States. This is especially clear when you look not at the top percentile of the income distribution, but an even smaller group, the top 0.1 percent—those with a median annual income of US$5.6 million.

Many Occupy protests—like this one in Vancouver—began on October 15, 2011, which was called the Global Day of Action.

Although financial industry people are a minority (18%), within this income elite—consisting also of executives, managers, lawyers, and others—they are greatly overrepresented since only about 6 percent of American workers are employed in finance. So, the protesters were making a valid point: Wall Street salaries are indeed one of the sources of the rapid rise in incomes at the top.

Even so, the combined effect of the major means-tested programs shown in Table 18-3, plus additional means-tested programs such as welfare and housing aid that are offered by provincial, territorial, and municipal governments, is to create very high effective marginal tax rates. For example, a 2013 study by the C.D. Howe Institute found that an Ontario family consisting of two adults and two children that raised its income from $40 000 a year—just above the poverty line in 2012—to $41 000 would lose 68 cents of every additional dollar of income earned to taxes and lost means-tested social benefits.[6]

The Politics of the Welfare State

In 1791, in the early phase of the French Revolution, French citizens convened a congress, the Legislative Assembly, in which representatives were seated according to social class: the upper classes, who pretty much liked the way things were, sat on the right; commoners, who wanted big changes, sat on the left. Ever since, political commentators refer to politicians as being on the "right" (more conservative) or on the "left" (more liberal).

But what do modern politicians on the left and right disagree about? In Canada, besides concerns over the environment and globalization, they mainly disagree about the appropriate size of the welfare state. The debate over the need for a national child care program is a case in point, with support split almost

---

[6]The amount differs among provinces. If the family lived in Quebec they would lose 79 cents of every additional dollar of earned income. In Alberta the family would lose 61 cents and in British Columbia they would only lose 58 cents of every additional dollar of earned income.

entirely according to party lines—Liberals and NDP (on the left) in favour of a national program and Conservatives (on the right) opposed.

You might think that saying that political debate is really about just one thing—how big to make the welfare state—is a huge oversimplification. But anyone can see that most MPs and MPPs vote along party lines. Politicians on the left tend to favour a larger welfare state and those on the right to oppose it. This left–right distinction is central to today's politics. In recent decades, it has become much clearer where the members of the major federal political parties stand on the left–right spectrum.

Can economic analysis help resolve this political conflict? Only up to a point.

Some of the political controversy over the welfare state involves differences in opinion about the trade-offs we have just discussed: if you believe that the disincentive effects of generous benefits and high taxes are very large, you're likely to look less favourably on welfare state programs than if you believe they're fairly small. Economic analysis, by improving our knowledge of the facts, can help resolve some of these differences.

To an important extent, however, differences of opinion on the welfare state reflect differences in values and philosophy. And those are differences economics can't resolve.

ECONOMICS ▸ IN ACTION

FRENCH FAMILY VALUES

France has one of the largest welfare states of any major advanced economy. As we've already described, France has much higher social spending than found in North America as a percentage of total national income, and French citizens face much higher tax rates than North Americans. One argument against a large welfare state is that it has negative effects on efficiency. Does French experience support this argument?

On the face of it, the answer would seem to be a clear yes. French GDP per capita—the total value of the economy's output, divided by the total population—is only about 80% of the Canadian and U.S. levels. This reflects the fact that the French work less: French workers and North American workers have almost exactly the same productivity per hour, but a smaller fraction of the French population is employed, and the average French employee works substantially fewer hours over the course of a year than his or her North American counterpart. Some economists have argued that high tax rates in France explain this difference: the incentives to work are weaker in France than in North America because the government takes away so much of what you earn from an additional hour of work.

A closer examination, however, reveals that the story is more complicated than that. The low level of employment in France is entirely the result of low rates of employment among the young and the old; 80% of French residents of prime working age, 25–54, are employed, exactly the same percentage as in Canada and the United States. So high tax rates don't seem to discourage the French from working in the prime of their lives. But only about 30% of 15- to 24-year-olds are employed in France, compared with more than half of 15- to 24-year-olds in Canada and the United States. And young people in France don't work in part because they don't have to: college education is generally free, and students receive financial support, so French students rarely work while attending school. The French will tell you that that's a virtue of their system, not a problem.

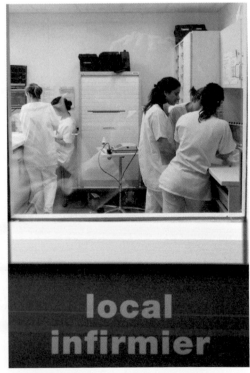

France guarantees health care for all its citizens—a benefit of having one of the largest welfare states in the world.

Shorter working hours also reflect factors besides tax rates. French law requires employers to offer at least a month of paid vacation, but Canadian workers are guaranteed only 10 paid days off. Most U.S. workers get less than two weeks off and have no guaranteed number of paid vacation days. Here, too, the French will tell you that their policy is better than ours because it helps families spend time together.

The aspect of French policy even the French agree is a big problem is that their retirement system allows workers to collect generous pensions even if they retire very early. As a result, only 40% of French residents between the ages of 55 and 64 are employed, compared with more than 60% of North Americans. The cost of supporting all those early retirees is a major burden on the French welfare state—and getting worse as the French population ages.

CHECK YOUR UNDERSTANDING 18-4

1. Explain how each of the following policies creates a disincentive to work or undertake a risky investment.
   a. A high sales tax on consumer items
   b. The complete loss of a housing subsidy when yearly income rises above $25 000

2. Over the past 40 years, has the polarization in the Canadian Parliament increased, decreased, or stayed the same?

Solutions appear at back of book.

▼ **Quick Review**

- Intense debate on the size of the welfare state centres on philosophy and on equity-versus-efficiency concerns. The high marginal tax rates needed to finance an extensive welfare state can reduce the incentive to work. Holding down the cost of the welfare state by means-testing can also cause inefficiency through notches that create high effective marginal tax rates for benefit recipients.

- Politics is often depicted as an opposition between left and right; in modern-day Canada, that division mainly involves disagreement over the appropriate size of the welfare state.

BUSINESS CASE : Welfare State Entrepreneurs

thinkstock

"Wiggo Dalmo is a classic entrepreneurial type: the Working Class Kid Made Good." So began a profile in the January 2011 issue of *Inc.* magazine. Dalmo began as an industrial mechanic who worked for a large company, repairing mining equipment. Eventually, however, he decided to strike out on his own and start his own business. Momek, the company he founded, eventually grew into a $44 million, 150-employee operation that does a variety of contract work on oil rigs and in mines.

You can read stories like this all the time in business magazines. What was unusual about this particular article is that Dalmo and his company are Norwegian—and Norway, like other Scandinavian countries, has a very generous welfare state, supported by high levels of taxation. So what does Dalmo think of that system? He approves, saying that Norway's tax system is "good and fair," and he thinks the system is good for business. In fact, the *Inc.* article was titled, "In Norway, Start-Ups Say Ja to Socialism."

Why? After all, the financial rewards for being a successful entrepreneur are more limited in a country like Norway, with its high taxes. But there are other considerations. For example, a Canadian thinking of leaving a large company to start a new business needs to worry about whether he or she will be able to get supplementary health insurance, whereas a Norwegian in the same position is assured of health care regardless of employment. And the downside of failure is larger in North America, where minimal aid is offered to the unemployed.

Still, is Wiggo Dalmo an exceptional case? Table 18-10 shows the nations with the highest level of entrepreneurial activity, according to a study financed by the U.S. Small Business Administration, which tried to quantify the level of entrepreneurial activity in different nations. Canada and the United States made it into the top 10, but so did Norway. And the list also includes Denmark, New Zealand, Sweden, and Australia—all nations with high taxes and extensive social insurance programs.

The moral is that when comparing how business friendly different welfare state systems really are, you have to think a bit past the obvious question of the level of taxes.

TABLE 18-10

The Top 10 Entrepreneurial Countries

Rank	Country
1	Denmark
2	New Zealand
3	Ireland
4	Puerto Rico
5	Sweden
6	Canada
7	Australia
8	United States
9	Norway
10	Belgium

Source: Zoltan Acs and Laszlo Serb (2011) *The Global Entrepreneurship and Development Index 2010.*

QUESTIONS FOR THOUGHT

1. Why does Norway have to have higher taxes overall than Canada?

2. This case suggests that government-paid health care helps entrepreneurs. How does this relate to the arguments we made for social insurance in the text?

3. How would the incentives of people like Wiggo Dalmo be affected if Norwegian health care was means-tested instead of available to all?

4. Briefly explain how this case influences the care one should use when making international comparisons of competitiveness based on a single indicator such as labour costs (hourly wages) or (highest marginal) personal income tax rates.

SUMMARY

1. The **welfare state** absorbs a large share of government spending in all wealthy countries. **Government transfers** are the payments made by the government to individuals and families. **Social welfare programs** alleviate income inequality by helping those in need; **social insurance programs** alleviate economic insecurity. Welfare state programs also deliver external benefits to society through poverty reduction and improved access to health care, particularly for children.

2. The **poverty line** (or **poverty threshold**) is not officially defined in Canada. The most commonly used criteria to measure poverty in Canada are the low income cut-offs (LICOs), a relative measure. The low-income measure (LIM), another relative measure, and the market basket measure (MBM), an absolute measure, are also used to measure poverty. In Canada, the **poverty rate,** the percentage of the population with an income below the poverty threshold, fluctuates over time. There are various causes of poverty: lack of education, the legacy of discrimination, and bad luck. The consequences of poverty are particularly harmful for children, resulting in more chronic disease, lower lifetime earnings, and higher rates of criminality.

3. **Median household income,** the income of a family at the centre of the income distribution, is a better indicator of the income of the typical household than **mean household income** because it is not distorted by the inclusion of a small number of very wealthy households. The **Gini coefficient,** a number that summarizes a country's level of income inequality based on how unequally income is distributed across quintiles, is used to compare income inequality across countries.

4. Both **means-tested** and non-means-tested programs reduce poverty. The largest means-tested programs in Canada include social services, Old Age Security, the Canada Child Tax Benefit, and the National Child Benefit Supplement. The major **in-kind benefits** program is health care. Some countries also have **negative income tax** programs that supplement the income of the working poor.

5. Canada's health care system is universal (a **single-payer system** paid for by provincial/territorial governments) and guarantees free access to all Canadians for all insured services.

6. Compared to other countries, the United States relies more heavily on **private health insurance** and has substantially higher health care costs per person without clearly providing better care. Throughout the developed world health care costs are rising, largely due to advances in technology. The U.S. Patient Protection and Affordable Care Act (ACA, sometimes called "ObamaCare") was passed in 2010 with the objectives of reducing the number of uninsured Americans and reducing the rate of growth of U.S. health care costs.

7. In the United States, health insurance satisfies an important need because most families cannot afford expensive medical treatment. Private health insurance, unless it is employment-based or carefully screens applicants, has the potential to fall into an adverse selection death spiral. Most Americans are covered by employment-based private health insurance; the majority of the remaining are covered by Medicare (for those over 65) or Medicaid (for those with low incomes). Prior to the ACA coming into effect in 2014 the percentage of Americans who were uninsured had been rising.

8. Debates over the size of the welfare state are based on philosophical and equity-versus-efficiency considerations. Although high marginal tax rates needed to finance an extensive welfare state can reduce the incentive to work, means-testing of programs in order to reduce the cost of the welfare state can also reduce the incentive to work unless carefully designed to avoid notches.

9. Politicians on the left tend to favour a bigger welfare state and those on the right to oppose it. This left–right distinction is central to today's politics. Canada's three major federal political parties have become more polarized in recent decades, with a much clearer distinction than in the past about where their members stand on the left–right spectrum.

KEY TERMS

Welfare state, p. 538
Government transfer, p. 538
Social welfare program p. 538
Social insurance program, p. 538
Poverty line (or poverty threshold), p. 540

Poverty rate, p. 540
Mean household income, p. 544
Median household income, p. 544
Gini coefficient, p. 545
Means-tested, p. 549

In-kind benefit, p. 549
Negative income tax, p. 549
Private health insurance, p. 553
Single-payer system, p. 555

PROBLEMS

1. The accompanying table contains data on the Canadian economy for the years 1980 and 2011. The second column shows the poverty line using the LIM in constant dollars. The third column shows Canada's GDP per capita, a measure of the real standard of living.

Year	Poverty line (in 2011 dollars)	Real GDP per capita (in 2011 dollars)
1980	$18 647	$34 946
2011	22 720	50 105

Source: Statistics Canada.

   a. By what factor has the real poverty line increased from 1980 to 2011? For example, has it doubled? Tripled?

   b. By what factor has real GDP per capita increased from 1980 to 2011? For example, has it doubled? Tripled?

   c. What do your results tell you about how those people classified as "poor" have done economically relative to other Canadian citizens?

2. In the city of Metropolis, there are 100 residents, each of whom lives until age 75. Residents of Metropolis have the following incomes over their lifetime: Through age 14, they earn nothing. From age 15 until age 29, they earn 200 metros (the currency of Metropolis) per year. From age 30 to age 49, they earn 400 metros. From age 50 to age 64, they earn 300 metros. Finally, at age 65 they retire and are paid a pension of 100 metros per year until they die at age 75. Each year, everyone consumes whatever their income is that year (that is, there is no saving and no borrowing). Currently, 20 residents are 10 years old, 20 residents are 20 years old, 20 residents are 40 years old, 20 residents are 60 years old, and 20 residents are 70 years old.

   a. Study the income distribution among all residents of Metropolis. Split the population into quintiles according to their income. How much income does a resident in the lowest quintile have? In the second, third, fourth, and top quintiles? What share of total income of all residents goes to the residents in each quintile? Construct a table showing the share of total income that goes to each quintile. Does this income distribution show inequality?

   b. Now look only at the 20 residents of Metropolis who are currently 40 years old, and study the income distribution among only those residents. Split those 20 residents into quintiles according to their income. How much income does a resident in the lowest quintile have? In the second, third, fourth, and top quintiles? What share of total income of all 40-year-olds goes to the residents in each quintile? Does this income distribution show inequality?

   c. What is the relevance of these examples for assessing data on the distribution of income in any country?

3. The accompanying table presents data from Statistics Canada on median and mean income of male workers for the years 1976 and 2011. The income figures are adjusted to eliminate the effect of inflation.

Year	Median income	Mean income
	(in 2011 dollars)	
1976	$42 400	$47 700
2011	37 100	48 700

Source: Statistics Canada.

   a. By what percentage has median income changed over this period? By what percentage has mean income changed over this period?

   b. Between 1976 and 2011, has the income distribution become less or more unequal? Explain.

4. There are 100 households in the economy of Equalor. Initially, 99 of them have an income of $10 000 each, and one household has an income of $1 010 000.

   a. What is the median income in this economy? What is the mean income?

   Through its social welfare programs, the government of Equalor now redistributes income: it takes $990 000 away from the richest household and distributes it equally among the remaining 99 households.

   b. What is the median income in this economy now? What is the mean income? Has the median income changed? Has the mean income changed? Which indicator (mean or median household income) is a better indicator of the typical Equalorian household's income? Explain.

5. The country of Marxland has the following income tax and social insurance system. Each citizen's income is taxed at an average tax rate of 100%. A social insurance system then provides transfers to each citizen such that each citizen's after-tax income is exactly equal. That is, each citizen gets (through a government transfer payment) an equal share of the income tax revenue. What is the incentive for one individual citizen to work and earn income? What will the total tax revenue in Marxland be? What will be the after-tax income (including the transfer payment) for each citizen? Do you think such a tax system that creates perfect equality will work?

6. The tax system in Taxilvania includes a negative income tax. For all incomes below $10 000, individuals pay an income tax of –40% (that is, they receive a payment of 40% of their income). For any income above the $10 000 threshold, the tax rate on that additional income is

10%. For the first three scenarios below, calculate the amount of income tax to be paid and after-tax income.

a. Lowani earns income of $8000.

b. Midram earns income of $40 000.

c. Hi-Wan earns income of $100 000.

d. Can you find a notch in this tax system? That is, can you find a situation where earning more pre-tax income actually results in less after-tax income?

7. In the city of Notchingham, each worker is paid a wage rate of $10 per hour. Notchingham administers its own unemployment benefit, which is structured as follows: If you are unemployed (that is, if you do not work at all), you get unemployment benefits (a transfer from the government) of $50 per day. As soon as you work for only one hour, the unemployment benefit is completely withdrawn. That is, there is a notch in the benefit system.

a. How much income does an unemployed person have per day? How much daily income does an individual who works four hours per day have? How many hours do you need to work to earn just the same as if you were unemployed?

b. Will anyone ever accept a part-time job that requires working four hours per day, rather than being unemployed?

c. Suppose that Notchingham now changes the way in which the unemployment benefit is withdrawn. For each additional dollar an individual earns, $0.50 of the unemployment benefit is withdrawn. How much daily income does an individual who works four hours per day now have? Is there an incentive now to work four hours per day rather than being unemployed?

8. In a private insurance market, there are two different kinds of people: some who are more likely to require expensive medical treatment and some who are less likely to require medical treatment and who, if they do, require less expensive treatment. One health insurance policy is offered, tailored to the average person's health care needs: the premium is equal to the average person's medical expenses (plus the insurer's expenses and normal profit).

a. Explain why such an insurance policy is unlikely to be feasible.

In an effort to avoid the adverse selection death spiral, a private health insurer offers two health insurance policies: one that is intended for those who are more likely to require expensive treatment (and therefore charges a higher premium) and one that is intended for those who are less likely to require treatment (and therefore charges a lower premium).

b. Could this system overcome the problem created by adverse selection?

c. How do provincial and territorial governments in Canada, the U.S. Veterans Health Administration, and the British National Health Service (NHS) avoid these problems?

CHAPTER 19

Factor Markets and the Distribution of Income

THE VALUE OF A DEGREE

If you have doubts about completing college or university, consider this: factory workers with high school degrees earn much less than post-secondary grads. The present discounted value of the difference in lifetime earnings is more than $1 million.

WHAT YOU WILL LEARN IN THIS CHAPTER

) How factors of production—resources like land, labour, **physical capital**, and **human capital**—are traded in factor markets, determining the **factor distribution of income**

) How the **marginal productivity theory of income distribution** is used to determine factor prices

) About the sources of wage disparities and the role of discrimination

) How labour supply arises from a worker's decision about **time allocation**

DOES HIGHER EDUCATION PAY? Yes, it does: in the modern economy, employers are willing to pay a premium for workers with more education. And the size of that premium has increased over the last few decades. Back in 1980 male workers with a bachelor's degree earned only 32% more than those who had only graduated from high school. By 2005, the premium for a male with a bachelor's degree had risen to over 45%. Females with a bachelor's degree earned 49% more than high school graduates earned in 1980, and this premium had risen to more than 60% in 2005. By 2011, the average employment income of university graduates was 104% higher than the average income of high school graduates and 51% higher than the average income of college graduates. If the gaps observed in 2011 were to persist over a 40-year period of employment, a university graduate would earn $1.4 million more than a high school graduate.[1]

Who decided that the wages of workers with advanced degrees would rise so much compared with those of high school grads? The answer, of course, is that nobody decided it. Wage rates are prices, the prices of different kinds of labour; and they are decided, like other prices, by supply and demand.

Still, there is a qualitative difference between the wage rate of high school grads and the price of used textbooks: the wage rate isn't the price of a *good*, it's the price of a *factor of production*. And although markets for factors of production are in many ways similar to those for goods, there are also some important differences.

In this chapter, we examine *factor markets*, the markets in which the factors of production such as labour, land, and capital are traded. Factor markets, like markets for goods and services, play a crucial role in the economy: they allocate productive resources to producers and help ensure that those resources are used efficiently.

This chapter begins by describing the major factors of production. Then we consider the demand for factors of production, which leads us to a crucial insight: the *marginal productivity theory of income distribution*. We then consider some challenges to the marginal productivity theory. Next, we examine the markets for capital and for land. The chapter concludes with a discussion of the supply of the most important factor, labour. ∎

---

[1]Between 1980 and 2005, the premium paid to males who graduated from college rose from 10% to 17% (compared to the income of male high school graduates). Female college graduates earned 16% more than female high school graduates in 1980; this rose to a 19% premium by 2005. By 2011, the average income of college graduates was 35% above the average earning of high school graduates. (*Source:* Statistics Canada.)

Physical capital—often referred to simply as "capital"—consists of manufactured productive resources such as equipment, buildings, tools, and machines.

Human capital is the improvement in labour created by education and knowledge that is embodied in the workforce.

The Economy's Factors of Production

You may recall that we defined a factor of production in Chapter 2 in the context of the circular-flow diagram: it is any resource that is used by firms to produce goods and services for consumption by households. Factors of production are bought and sold in *factor markets,* and the prices in factor markets are known as *factor prices.*

What are these factors of production, and why do factor prices matter?

The Factors of Production

As we learned in Chapter 2, economists divide factors of production into four principal classes: land, labour, physical capital, and human capital. Land is a resource provided by nature; labour is the work done by human beings.

In Chapter 9 we defined capital: it is the value of the assets that are used by a firm in producing its output. There are two broad types of capital. **Physical capital**—often referred to simply as "capital"—consists of manufactured resources such as equipment, buildings, tools, and machines.

In the modern economy, **human capital,** the improvement in labour created by education and knowledge, and embodied in the workforce, is at least equally significant. The importance of human capital has been greatly increased by the progress of technology, which has made a high level of technical sophistication essential to many jobs—one cause of the increased premium paid for workers with advanced degrees.

Why Factor Prices Matter: The Allocation of Resources

Factor markets and factor prices play a key role in one of the most important processes that must take place in any economy: the allocation of resources among producers.

Consider the exploration, extraction, and processing of petroleum and natural gas in Alberta and Newfoundland and Labrador, part of Canada's booming resource sector. These provinces have a considerable need for workers in the engineering and natural science trades—geoscientists, drillers, welders, construction workers, and so on—to search for new reserves and to construct, repair, and operate drilling and extraction equipment.

What ensured that those needed workers actually came? The factor market: the high demand for workers drove up wages. From 1997 to 2014, the average Canadian hourly wage grew at an annual rate of around 2.7%. But in Alberta and Newfoundland and Labrador, the average hourly wage grew by 3.9% and 3.7%, respectively. The average hourly wage in Alberta went from $0.80 below the national average to the highest in the country. Over time, these higher wages led large numbers of workers with the right skills to move to these provinces to do the work. In other words, the market for a factor of production—energy and construction workers—allocated that factor of production to where it was needed.

In this sense factor markets are similar to goods markets, which allocate goods among consumers. But there are two features that make factor markets special. Unlike in a goods market, demand in a factor market is what we call *derived demand.* That is, demand for the factor is derived from the firm's output choice. The second feature is that factor markets are where most of us get the largest shares of our income (government transfers being the next largest source of income in the economy).

⚠ **PITFALLS**

WHAT IS A FACTOR, ANYWAY?
Imagine a business that produces shirts. The business will make use of workers and machines—that is, of labour and capital. But it will also use other inputs, such as electricity and cloth. Are all of these inputs factors of production? No: labour and capital are factors of production, but cloth and electricity are not.

The key distinction is that a factor of production earns income from the selling of its services over and over again but an input cannot. For example, a worker earns income over time from repeatedly selling his or her efforts; the owner of a machine earns income over time from repeatedly selling the use of that machine.

So a factor of production, such as labour and capital, represents an enduring source of income. An input like electricity or cloth, however, is used up in the production process. Once exhausted, it cannot be a source of future income for its owner.

Factor Incomes and the Distribution of Income

Most Canadian families get most of their income in the form of wages and salaries—that is, they get their income by selling labour. Some people, however, get most of their income from physical capital: when you own stock in a company, what you really own is a share of that company's physical capital. And some people get much of their income from rents earned on land they own.

Obviously, then, the prices of factors of production have a major impact on how the economic "pie" is sliced among different groups. For example, a higher wage rate, other things equal, means that a larger proportion of the total income in the economy goes to people who derive their income from labour, and less goes to those who derive their income from capital or land. Economists refer to how the economic pie is sliced as the "distribution of income." Specifically, factor prices determine the **factor distribution of income**—how the total income of the economy is divided among labour, land, and capital.

As the following Economics in Action explains, the factor distribution of income in Canada has been quite stable over the past few decades. In other times and places, however, large changes have taken place in the factor distribution. One notable example: during the Industrial Revolution, the share of total income earned by land-owners fell sharply, while the share earned by capital owners rose. As explained in the following For Inquiring Minds, this shift had a profound effect on society.

> The **factor distribution of income** is the division of total income among labour, land, and capital.

FOR INQUIRING MINDS

THE FACTOR DISTRIBUTION OF INCOME AND SOCIAL CHANGE IN THE INDUSTRIAL REVOLUTION

Have you read any novels by Jane Austen? How about Charles Dickens? If you've read both, you probably noticed that they seem to be describing quite different societies. Austen's novels, set in England around 1800, describe a world in which the leaders of society are landowning aristocrats. Dickens, writing about 50 years later, describes an England in which businessmen, especially factory owners, are in control.

This literary shift reflects a dramatic transformation in the factor distribution of income. The Industrial Revolution, which took

By altering how people lived and worked, the Industrial Revolution led to huge economic and social changes.

Lewis Hines/Bettmann/Corbis

place between the late eighteenth century and the middle of the nineteenth century, changed England from a mainly agricultural country, in which land earned a fairly substantial share of income, to an urbanized and industrial one, in which land rents were dwarfed by capital income. Recent estimates by the economist Nancy Stokey show that between 1780 and 1850 the share of national income represented by land fell from 20% to 9%, but the share represented by capital rose from 35% to 44%. That shift changed everything—even literature.

(Source note on copyright page.)

ECONOMICS ▸ IN ACTION

THE FACTOR DISTRIBUTION OF INCOME IN CANADA

When we talk about the factor distribution of income, what are we talking about in practice?

In Canada, as in all advanced economies, payments to labour account for most of the economy's total income. Figure 19-1 shows the factor distribution of income in Canada in 2012: in that year, 56% of total income in the economy took the form of "compensation of employees"—a number that includes both wages and benefits, that is, employers' social contributions to programs such as

FIGURE **19-1** Factor Distribution of Income in Canada in 2012

Gross mixed income 12.9%

Gross corporate profits 30.7%

Compensation of employees 56.4%

Source: Statistics Canada.

▼ Quick Review

- Economists usually divide the economy's factors of production into four principal categories: labour, land, **physical capital**, and **human capital**.

- The demand for a factor is a derived demand. Factor prices, which are set in factor markets, determine the **factor distribution of income.** Labour receives the bulk—56% in 2012—of the income in the modern Canadian economy. Although the exact share is not directly measurable, much of what is called compensation of employees is a return to human capital.

health insurance. This number was just slightly below the 58% average value for the previous thirty years.

However, measured wages and benefits don't capture the full income of "labour" because a significant fraction of total income in Canada is "proprietors' income"—the earnings of people who own their own businesses. The "gross mixed income" category includes gross operating income from unincorporated businesses, farms, and rentals. So part of that income should be considered wages these business owners pay themselves. So the true share of labour in the economy is probably a few percentage points higher than the reported "compensation of employees" share.

But much of what we call compensation of employees is really a return on human capital. A surgeon isn't just supplying the services of a pair of ordinary hands (at least the patient hopes not!): that individual is also supplying the result of many years and hundreds of thousands of dollars invested in training and experience. We can't directly measure what fraction of wages is really a payment for education and training, but many economists believe that human capital has become *the* most important factor of production in modern economies.

CHECK YOUR UNDERSTANDING 19-1

1. Suppose that the government places price controls on the market for university professors, imposing a wage that is lower than the market wage. Describe the effect of this policy on the production of university degrees. What sectors of the economy do you think will be adversely affected by this policy? What sectors of the economy might benefit?

Solutions appear at back of book.

Marginal Productivity and Factor Demand

All economic decisions are about comparing costs and benefits—and usually about comparing marginal costs and marginal benefits. This goes both for a consumer, deciding whether to buy another dozen chicken wings, and for a producer, deciding whether to hire an additional worker.

Although there are some important exceptions, most factor markets in the modern Canadian economy are perfectly competitive, meaning that buyers and sellers of a given factor are price-takers. And in a competitive labour market, it's clear how to define an employer's marginal cost of a worker: it is simply the worker's wage rate. But what is the marginal benefit of that worker? To answer that question, we return to a concept first introduced in Chapter 11: the production function, which relates inputs to output. And as in Chapter 12, we will assume throughout this chapter that all producers are price-takers in their output markets—that is, they operate in a perfectly competitive industry.

Value of the Marginal Product

Figure 19-2 reproduces Figures 11-1 and 11-2, which showed the production function for wheat on Alec and Janet's farm. Panel (a) uses the total product curve to show how total wheat production depends on the number of workers employed on the farm; panel (b) shows how the *marginal product* of labour, the increase in out-

FIGURE   **19-2**   The Production Function for Alec and Janet's Farm

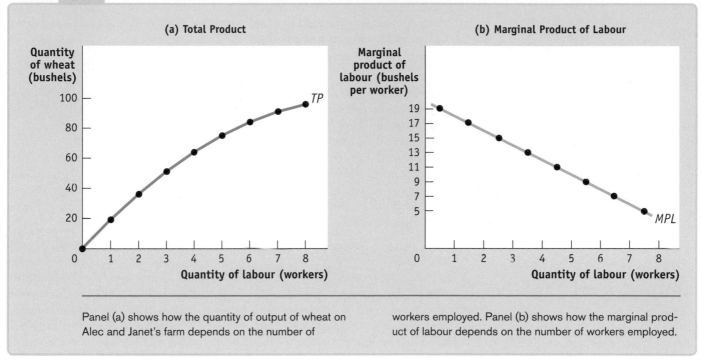

(a) Total Product

(b) Marginal Product of Labour

Panel (a) shows how the quantity of output of wheat on Alec and Janet's farm depends on the number of workers employed. Panel (b) shows how the marginal product of labour depends on the number of workers employed.

put from employing one more worker, depends on the number of workers employed. Table 19-1, which reproduces the table in Figure 11-1, shows the numbers behind the figure.

Assume that Alec and Janet want to maximize their profit, that workers must be paid $200 each, and that wheat sells for $20 per bushel. What is their optimal number of workers? That is, how many workers should they employ to maximize profit?

In Chapters 11 and 12 we showed how to answer this question in several steps. In Chapter 11 we used information from the producer's production function to derive the firm's total cost and its marginal cost. And in Chapter 12 we derived the *price-taking firm's optimal output rule:* a price-taking firm's profit is maximized by producing the quantity of output at which the marginal cost of the last unit produced is equal to the market price. Having determined the optimal quantity of output, we can go back to the production function and find the optimal number of workers—it is simply the number of workers needed to produce the optimal quantity of output.

There is, however, another way to use marginal analysis to find the number of workers that maximizes a producer's profit. We can go directly to the question of what level of employment maximizes profit. This alternative approach is equivalent to the approach we outlined in the preceding paragraph—it's just a different way of looking at the same thing. But it gives us more insight into the demand for factors as opposed to the supply of goods.

To see how this alternative approach works, let's suppose that Alec and Janet are considering whether or not to employ an additional worker. The increase in *cost* from employing that additional worker is the wage rate, *W*. The *marginal benefit* to Alec and Janet from employing that extra worker is the value of the extra

TABLE   **19-1**   Employment and Output for Alec and Janet's Farm

Quantity of labour L (workers)	Quantity of wheat q (bushels)	Marginal product of labour $MPL = \dfrac{\Delta q}{\Delta L}$ (bushels per worker)
0	0	
		19
1	19	
		17
2	36	
		15
3	51	
		13
4	64	
		11
5	75	
		9
6	84	
		7
7	91	
		5
8	96	

The **value of the marginal product** of a factor is the value of the additional output generated by employing one more unit of that factor.

The **value of the marginal product curve** of a factor shows how the value of the marginal product of that factor depends on the quantity of the factor employed.

output that worker can produce. What is this value? It is the marginal product of labour, MPL, multiplied by the price per unit of output, P. This amount—the extra value of output that is generated by employing one more unit of labour—is known as the **value of the marginal product** of labour, or $VMPL$:

(19-1) Value of the marginal product of labour = $VMPL = P \times MPL$

So should Alec and Janet hire that extra worker? The answer is yes if the value of the extra output is more than the cost of the worker—that is, if $VMPL > W$. Otherwise they shouldn't hire that worker.

So the decision to hire labour is a marginal decision, in which the marginal benefit to the producer from hiring an additional worker ($VMPL$) should be compared with the marginal cost to the producer (W). And as with any marginal decision, the optimal choice is where marginal benefit is just equal to marginal cost. That is, to maximize profit Alec and Janet will employ workers up to the point at which, for the last worker employed:

(19-2) $VMPL = W$ at the profit-maximizing level of employment

This rule doesn't apply only to labour; it applies to any factor of production. The value of the marginal product of any factor is its marginal product times the price of the good it produces. The general rule is that *a profit-maximizing price-taking producer employs each factor of production up to the point at which the value of the marginal product of the last unit of the factor employed is equal to that factor's price.*

It's important to realize that this rule doesn't conflict with our analysis in Chapters 11 and 12. There we saw that a profit-maximizing price-taking producer of a good chooses the level of output at which the price of that good is equal to the marginal cost of production. It's just a different way of looking at the same rule. If the level of output is chosen so that price equals marginal cost, then it is also true that at that output level the value of the marginal product of labour will equal the wage rate.[2]

Now let's look more closely at why choosing the level of employment at which the value of the marginal product of the last worker employed is equal to the wage rate works—and at how it helps us understand factor demand.

Value of the Marginal Product and Factor Demand

Table 19-2 calculates the value of the marginal product of labour on Alec and Janet's farm, on the assumption that the price of wheat is $20 per bushel. In Figure 19-3 the horizontal axis shows the number of workers employed; the vertical axis measures the value of the marginal product of labour *and* the wage rate. The curve shown is the **value of the marginal product curve** of labour. This curve, like the marginal product of labour curve, slopes downward because of diminishing returns to labour in production. That is, the value of the marginal product of each worker is less

TABLE 19-2   Value of the Marginal Product of Labour for Alec and Janet's Farm

Quantity of labour L (workers)	Marginal product of labour MPL (bushels per worker)	Value of the marginal product of labour $VMPL = P \times MPL$
0		
	19	$380
1		
	17	340
2		
	15	300
3		
	13	260
4		
	11	220
5		
	9	180
6		
	7	140
7		
	5	100
8		

[2]If a firm is a price-taker, then their marginal revenue equals the price of output ($MR = P$). The marginal revenue of a profit-maximizing firm is equal to its marginal cost ($MR = MC$). Finally, the marginal cost of production is equal to the wage rate divided by the marginal product of labour ($MC = W/MPL$). Combining these expressions together we get $P = MC$, which in turn is $P = W/MPL$. By isolating W we get $W = P \times MPL = VMPL$.

FIGURE **19-3** The Value of the Marginal Product Curve

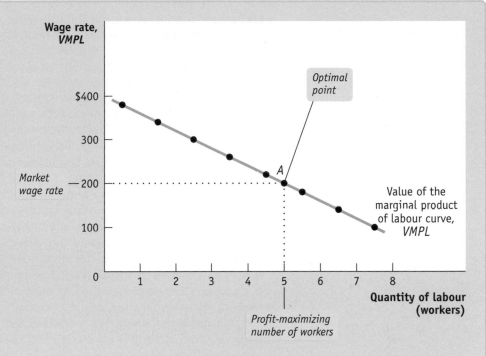

This curve shows how the value of the marginal product of labour depends on the number of workers employed. It slopes downward because of diminishing returns to labour in production. To maximize profit, Alec and Janet choose the level of employment at which the value of the marginal product of labour is equal to the market wage rate. For example, at a wage rate of $200 the profit-maximizing level of employment is 5 workers, shown by point *A*. The value of the marginal product curve of a factor is a profit-maximizing producer's individual demand curve for that factor.

than that of the preceding worker, because the marginal product of each worker is less than that of the preceding worker.

We have just seen that to maximize profit, Alec and Janet must hire workers up to the point at which the wage rate is equal to the value of the marginal product of the last worker employed. Let's use the example to see how this principle really works.

Assume that Alec and Janet currently employ 3 workers and that workers must be paid the market wage rate of $200. Should they employ an additional worker?

Looking at Table 19-2, we see that if Alec and Janet currently employ 3 workers, the value of the marginal product of an additional worker is $260. So if they employ an additional worker, they will increase the value of their production by $260 but increase their cost by only $200, yielding an increased profit of $60. In fact, a producer can always increase total profit by employing one more unit of a factor of production as long as the value of the marginal product produced by that unit exceeds its factor price.

Alternatively, suppose that Alec and Janet employ 8 workers. By reducing the number of workers to 7, they can save $200 in wages. In addition, the value of the marginal product of the last one, the 8th worker, was only $100. So, by reducing employment by one worker, they can increase profit by $200 − $100 = $100. In other words, a producer can always increase total profit by employing one less unit of a factor of production as long as the value of the marginal product produced by that unit is less than the factor price.

Using this method, we can see from Table 19-2 that the profit-maximizing employment level is 5 workers given a wage rate of $200. The value of the marginal product of the 5th worker is $220, so adding the 5th worker results in $20 of additional profit. But Alec and Janet should not hire more than 5 workers: the value of the marginal product of the 6th worker is only $180, $20 less than the cost of that worker. So, to maximize total profit, Alec and Janet should employ workers up to but not beyond the point at which the value of the marginal product of the last worker employed is equal to the wage rate.

Now look again at the value of the marginal product curve in Figure 19-3. To determine the profit-maximizing level of employment, we set the value of the marginal product of labour equal to the price of labour—a wage rate of $200 per worker. This means that the profit-maximizing level of employment is at point *A*, corresponding to an employment level of 5 workers. If the wage rate were higher than $200, we would simply move up the curve and reduce the number of workers employed; if the wage rate were lower than $200, we would move down the curve and increase the number of workers employed.

In this example, Alec and Janet have a small farm in which the potential employment level varies from 0 to 8 workers, and they hire workers up to the point at which the value of the marginal product of the last worker is greater than or equal to the wage rate. (To go beyond this point and hire workers for which the wage exceeds the value of the marginal product would cause Alec and Janet to reduce their level of profit.) Suppose, however, that the firm in question is large and has the potential of hiring many workers. When there are many employees, the value of the marginal product of labour falls only slightly when an additional worker is employed. As a result, there will be some worker whose value of the marginal product almost exactly equals the wage rate. (In keeping with the Alec and Janet example, this means that some worker generates a value of the marginal product of approximately $200.) In this case, the firm maximizes profit by choosing a level of employment at which the value of the marginal product of the last worker hired *equals* (to a very good approximation) the wage rate.

In the interest of simplicity, we will assume from now on that firms use this rule to determine the profit-maximizing level of employment. *This means that the value of the marginal product of labour curve is a profit-maximizing individual producer's labour demand curve.* And, in general, a profit-maximizing producer's value of the marginal product curve for any factor of production is that producer's individual demand curve for that factor of production.

Shifts of the Factor Demand Curve

As in the case of ordinary demand curves, it is important to distinguish between movements along the factor demand curve and shifts of the factor demand curve. What causes factor demand curves to shift? There are three main causes:

1. Changes in prices of goods
2. Changes in supply of other factors
3. Changes in production technology

1. Changes in Prices of Goods Remember that factor demand is derived demand: if the price of the good that is produced with a factor changes, so will the value of the marginal product of the factor. That is, in the case of labour demand, if *P* changes, $VMPL = P \times MPL$ will change at any given level of employment.

Figure 19-4 illustrates the effects of changes in the price of wheat, assuming that $200 is the current wage rate. Panel (a) shows the effect of an *increase* in the price of wheat. This shifts the value of the marginal product of labour curve upward, because *VMPL* rises at any given level of employment. If the wage rate remains unchanged at $200, the optimal point moves from point *A* to point *B:* the profit-maximizing level of employment rises.

Panel (b) shows the effect of a *decrease* in the price of wheat. This shifts the value of the marginal product of labour curve downward. If the wage rate remains unchanged at $200, the optimal point moves from point *A* to point *C:* the profit-maximizing level of employment falls.

2. Changes in Supply of Other Factors Suppose that Alec and Janet acquire more land to cultivate—say, by clearing a woodland on their property. Each worker now produces more wheat because each one has more land to work with. As a result, the marginal product of labour on the farm rises at any given level of

FIGURE **19-4** **Shifts of the Value of the Marginal Product Curve**

Panel (a) shows the effect of an increase in the price of wheat on Alec and Janet's demand for labour. The value of the marginal product of labour curve shifts upward, from $VMPL_1$ to $VMPL_2$. If the market wage rate remains at $200, profit-maximizing employment rises from 5 workers to 8 workers, shown by the movement from point A to point B. Panel (b) shows the effect of a decrease in the price of wheat. The value of the marginal product of labour curve shifts downward, from $VMPL_1$ to $VMPL_3$. At the market wage rate of $200, profit-maximizing employment falls from 5 workers to 2 workers, shown by the movement from point A to point C.

employment. This has the same effect as an increase in the price of wheat, which is illustrated in panel (a) of Figure 19-4: the value of the marginal product of labour curve shifts upward, and at any given wage rate the profit-maximizing level of employment rises. In contrast, suppose Alec and Janet cultivate less land. This leads to a fall in the marginal product of labour at any given employment level. Each worker produces less wheat because each has less land to work with. As a result, the value of the marginal product of labour curve shifts downward—as in panel (b) of Figure 19-4—and the profit-maximizing level of employment falls.

3. Changes in Production Technology In general, the effect of technological progress on the demand for any given factor can go either way: improved technology can either increase or reduce the demand for a given factor of production.

How can technological progress reduce factor demand? Consider horses, which were once an important factor of production. The development of substitutes for horse power, such as automobiles and tractors, greatly reduced the demand for horses.

The usual effect of technological progress, however, is to increase the demand for a given factor by raising its productivity. So despite persistent fears that machinery would reduce the demand for labour, over the long run the Canadian economy has seen both large wage increases and large increases in employment. That's because technological progress has raised labour productivity, and as a result increased the demand for labour.

The Labour Market

We've now seen that each perfectly competitive producer in a perfectly competitive factor market maximizes profit by hiring labour up to the point at which its value of the marginal product is equal to its price—in the case of labour, to the point where *VMPL* = *W*. What does this tell us about labour's share in the factor distribution of income? To answer that question, we need to examine equilibrium in the labour market. From that vantage point we will go on to learn about the markets for land and capital and about how they also influence the factor distribution of income.

Let's start by assuming that the labour market is in equilibrium: at the current market wage rate, the number of workers that producers want to employ is equal to the number of workers willing to work. Thus, all employers pay the *same* wage rate, and *each* employer, whatever he or she is producing, employs labour up to the point at which the value of the marginal product of the last worker hired is equal to the market wage rate.

This situation is illustrated in Figure 19-5, which shows the value of the marginal product curves of two producers—Farmer Jones, who produces wheat, and Farmer Smith, who produces corn. Despite the fact that they produce different products, they compete for the same workers and so must pay the same wage rate, $200. When both farmers maximize profit, both hire labour up to the point at which its value of the marginal product is equal to the wage rate. In the figure, this corresponds to employment of 5 workers by Jones and 7 by Smith.

Figure 19-6 illustrates the labour market as a whole. The *market labour demand curve*, like the market demand curve for a good (shown in Figure 3-5), is the horizontal sum of all the individual labour demand curves of all the producers who hire labour. And recall that each producer's individual labour demand curve is the same as his or her value of the marginal product of labour curve. For now, let's simply assume an upward-sloping labour supply curve; we'll discuss labour supply later in this chapter. Then the equilibrium wage rate is the wage rate at which the quantity of labour supplied is equal to the quantity of labour demanded. In Figure 19-6, this leads to an equilibrium wage rate of *W** and the corresponding equilibrium employment level of *L**. (The equilibrium wage rate is also known as the market wage rate.)

FIGURE 19-5 All Producers Face the Same Wage Rate

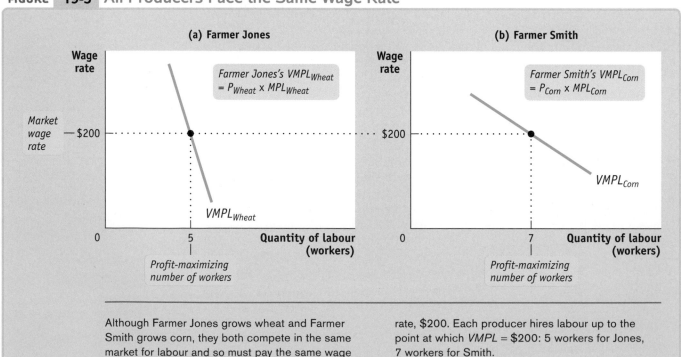

Although Farmer Jones grows wheat and Farmer Smith grows corn, they both compete in the same market for labour and so must pay the same wage rate, $200. Each producer hires labour up to the point at which *VMPL* = $200: 5 workers for Jones, 7 workers for Smith.

FIGURE   **19-6**   Equilibrium in the Labour Market

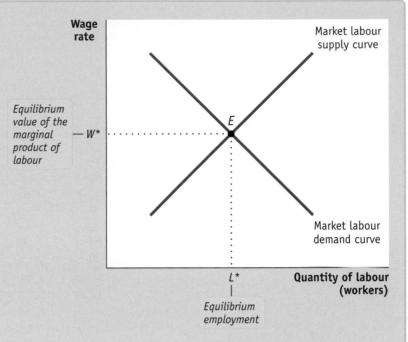

The market labour demand curve is the horizontal sum of the individual labour demand curves of all producers. Here the equilibrium wage rate is W^*, the equilibrium employment level is L^*, and every producer hires labour up to the point at which $VMPL = W^*$. So labour is paid its equilibrium value of the marginal product, the value of the marginal product of the last worker hired in the labour market as a whole.

And as we showed in the examples of the farms of Alec and Janet and of Farmer Jones and Farmer Smith (where the equilibrium wage rate is $200), each farm hires labour up to the point at which the value of the marginal product of labour is equal to the equilibrium wage rate. Therefore, in equilibrium, the value of the marginal product of labour is the same for all employers. So the equilibrium (or market) wage rate is equal to the **equilibrium value of the marginal product** of labour—the additional value produced by the last unit of labour employed in the labour market as a whole. It doesn't matter where that additional unit is employed, since equilibrium $VMPL$ is the same for all producers.

What we have just learned, then, is that the market wage rate is equal to the equilibrium value of the marginal product of labour. And the same is true of each factor of production: in a perfectly competitive market economy, the market price of each factor is equal to its equilibrium value of the marginal product. Let's examine the markets for land and (physical) capital now. (From this point on, we'll refer to physical capital as simply "capital.")

The **equilibrium value of the marginal product** of a factor is the additional value produced by the last unit of that factor employed in the factor market as a whole.

The Markets for Land and Capital

If we maintain the assumption that the markets for both outputs (goods and services) and the factors of production are perfectly competitive, the result that we derived for the labour market also applies to other factors of production. Suppose, for example, that a farmer is considering whether to rent an additional hectare of land for the next year. He or she will compare the cost of renting that hectare with the value of the additional output generated by employing an additional hectare—the value of the marginal product of a hectare of land. To maximize profit, the farmer must employ land up to the point at which the value of the marginal product of a hectare of land is equal to the rental rate per hectare.

What if the farmer already owns the land? We already saw the answer in Chapter 9, which dealt with economic decisions: even if you own land, there is an implicit cost—the opportunity cost—of using it for a given activity, because it could be used for something else, such as renting it out to other farmers at the

FIGURE **19-7** **Equilibria in the Land and Capital Markets**

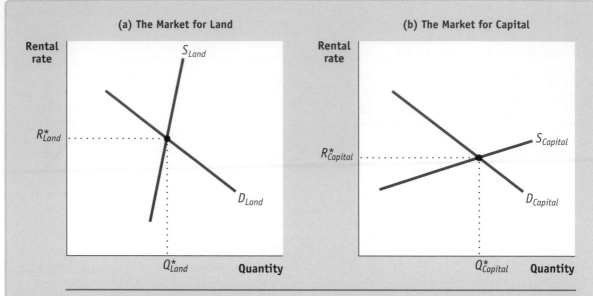

Panel (a) illustrates equilibrium in the rental market for land; panel (b) illustrates equilibrium in the rental market for capital. The supply curve for land is relatively steep, reflecting the high cost of increasing the quantity of productive land. The supply curve for capital, in contrast, is relatively flat, due to the relatively high responsiveness of savings to changes in the rental rate for capital. The equilibrium rental rates for land and capital, as well as the equilibrium quantities transacted, are given by the intersections of the demand and supply curves. In a competitive land market, each unit of land will be paid the equilibrium value of the marginal product of land, R^*_{Land}. Likewise, in a competitive capital market, each unit of capital will be paid the equilibrium value of the marginal product of capital, $R^*_{Capital}$.

The **rental rate** of either land or capital is the cost, explicit or implicit, of using a unit of that asset for a given period of time.

market rental rate. So a profit-maximizing producer employs additional hectares of land up to the point at which the cost of the last hectare employed, explicit or implicit, is equal to the value of the marginal product of that hectare.

The same is true for capital. The explicit or implicit cost of using a unit of land or capital for a set period of time is called its **rental rate.** In general, a unit of land or capital is employed up to the point at which that unit's value of the marginal product is equal to its rental rate over that time period. How are the rental rates for land and capital determined? By the equilibria in the land market and the capital market, of course. Figure 19-7 illustrates those outcomes.

Panel (a) shows the equilibrium in the rental market for land. Summing over the individual demand curves for land of all producers gives us the market demand curve for land. Due to diminishing returns, the demand curve slopes downward, like the demand curve for labour. As we have drawn it, the supply curve of land is relatively steep and therefore relatively inelastic. This reflects the fact that finding new supplies of land for production is typically difficult and expensive—for example, creating new farmland through expensive irrigation. The equilibrium rental rate for land, R^*_{Land}, and the equilibrium quantity of land employed in production, Q^*_{Land}, are given by the intersection of the two curves.

Panel (b) shows the equilibrium in the rental market for capital. In contrast to the supply curve for land, the supply curve for capital is relatively elastic. That's because the supply of capital is relatively responsive to price: capital comes from the savings of investors, and the amount of savings that investors make available is relatively responsive to the rental rate for capital. The equilibrium rental rate for capital, $R^*_{Capital}$, and the equilibrium quantity of capital employed in production, $Q^*_{Capital}$, are given by the intersection of the two curves.

The Marginal Productivity Theory of Income Distribution

So we have learned that when the markets for goods and services and the factor markets are perfectly competitive, a factor of production will be employed up to the point at which its value of the marginal product is equal to its market equilibrium price. That is, it will be paid its equilibrium value of the marginal product. What does this say about the factor distribution of income? It leads us to the **marginal productivity theory of income distribution,** which says that each factor is paid the value of the output generated by the last unit of that factor employed in the factor market as a whole—its equilibrium value of the marginal product.

To understand why the marginal productivity theory of income distribution is important, look back at Figure 19-1, which shows the factor distribution of income in Canada, and ask yourself this question: who or what decided that labour would get 56% of total Canadian income? Why not 90% or 50%?

The answer, according to the marginal productivity theory of income distribution, is that the division of income among the economy's factors of production isn't arbitrary: it is determined by each factor's marginal productivity at the economy's equilibrium. The wage rate earned by *all* workers in the economy is equal to the increase in the value of output generated by the last worker employed in the economy-wide labour market.

Here we have assumed that all workers are of the same ability. (Similarly, we've assumed that all units of land and capital are equally productive.) But in reality workers differ considerably in ability.

Rather than thinking of one labour market for all workers in the economy, we can instead think of different markets for different types of workers, where workers are of equivalent ability within each market. For example, the market for computer programmers is different from the market for pastry chefs. And in the market for computer programmers, all participants are assumed to have equal ability; likewise for the market for pastry chefs. In this scenario, the marginal productivity theory of income distribution still holds. That is, when the labour market for computer programmers is in equilibrium, the wage rate earned by all computer programmers is equal to the market's equilibrium value of the marginal product—the value of the marginal product of the last computer programmer hired in that market.

According to the **marginal productivity theory of income distribution,** every factor of production is paid its equilibrium value of the marginal product.

 PITFALLS

GETTING MARGINAL PRODUCTIVITY THEORY RIGHT

It's important to be careful about what the marginal productivity theory of income distribution says: it says that *all* units of a factor get paid the factor's equilibrium value of the marginal product—the additional value produced by the *last* unit of the factor employed.

The most common source of error is to forget that the relevant value of the marginal product is the equilibrium value, not the value of the marginal products you calculate on the way to equilibrium. In looking at Table 19-2, you might be tempted to think that because the first worker has a value of the marginal product of $380, that worker is paid $380 in equilibrium. Not so: if the equilibrium value of the marginal product in the labour market is equal to $200, then *all* workers receive $200.

ECONOMICS ▸ IN ACTION

HELP WANTED!

Alberta's booming economy, led by the drive to exploit its vast fossil fuel reserves, has created labour shortages in many occupations. Highly skilled machinists are well paid compared to many other workers in the province, earning an average of nearly $68 000 in 2011, excluding benefits. Like most skilled machinists in Canada, Alberta's machinists are very productive: according to Statistics Canada, in 2011 the average worker employed in the province's mining and oil and gas field machinery manufacturing sector generated approximately $144 000 in value added.

Thus there is a $76 000 difference between the salary paid to these skilled machinists and the value added they generate. Does this mean that the marginal productivity theory of income distribution doesn't hold? Doesn't the theory imply that machinists should be paid $144 000, the average value added that each one generates?

The answer is no, for two reasons. First, the $144 000 figure is averaged over *all Albertan machinists currently employed in this sector.* The theory says that machinists will be paid the value of the marginal product of the

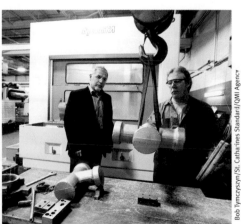

The marginal productivity theory of income distribution holds for skilled machinists.

- In a perfectly competitive market economy, the price of the good multiplied by the marginal product of labour is equal to the **value of the marginal product** of labour: *VMPL* = *P* × *MPL*. A profit-maximizing producer hires labour up to the point at which the value of the marginal product of labour is equal to the wage rate: *VMPL* = *W*. The **value of the marginal product curve** of labour slopes downward due to diminishing returns to labour in production.

- The market demand curve for labour is the horizontal sum of all the individual demand curves of producers in that market. It shifts for three reasons: changes in output price, changes in the supply of other factors, and technological progress.

- As in the case of labour, producers will employ land or capital until the point at which its value of the marginal product is equal to its **rental rate.** According to the **marginal productivity theory of income distribution,** in a perfectly competitive economy each factor of production is paid its **equilibrium value of the marginal product.**

last machinist hired, and due to diminishing returns to labour, that value will be lower than the average over all machinists currently employed. Second, a worker's equilibrium wage rate includes other costs, such as employee benefits, that have to be added to the $68 000 salary. The marginal productivity theory of income distribution says that workers are paid a wage rate, *including all benefits,* equal to the value of the marginal product.

All these additional costs are covered in Alberta's machinery manufacturing sector. The machinists have good benefits and job security, which add to their salaries. Including these benefits, machinists' total compensation will be equal to the value of the marginal product of the last machinist employed.

There is yet another factor that explains the $76 000 gap: there are not enough machinists at the current wage rate. According to the 2011 Alberta Wage and Salary Survey, there was a 10% vacancy rate for industrial engineering and manufacturing technologists and technicians, proving employers would like to hire more. Why don't these companies just raise their wages in order to attract more skilled machinists and technicians? The problem is that the work they do is so specialized that it is hard to hire from the outside, even when these companies raise wages as an inducement. To address this problem, the 2014 federal budget proposed $100 million per year in interest-free loans to students enrolled in apprenticeship programs in skilled trades and $40 million over two years for internship positions in "high-demand fields." The budget also continued to push the Canada Jobs Grant as a means to assist employers train workers for unfilled jobs. In the end, it does appear that the marginal productivity theory of income distribution holds.

● ●◁

CHECK YOUR UNDERSTANDING   19-2

1. In the following cases, state the direction of the shift of the demand curve for labour and what will happen, other things equal, to the market equilibrium wage rate and quantity of labour employed as a result.
   a. Service industries, such as retailing and banking, experience an increase in demand. These industries use relatively more labour than nonservice industries.
   b. Due to overfishing, there is a fall in the amount of fish caught per day by commercial fishers; this decrease affects their demand for workers.

2. Explain the following statement: "When firms in different industries all compete for the same workers, then the value of the marginal product of the last worker hired will be equal across all firms regardless of whether they are in different industries."

Solutions appear at back of book.

Is the Marginal Productivity Theory of Income Distribution Really True?

A lthough the marginal productivity theory of income distribution is a well-established part of economic theory, closely linked to the analysis of markets in general, it is a source of some controversy. There are two main objections to it.

First, in the real world we see large disparities in income between factors of production that, in the eyes of some observers, should receive the same payment. Perhaps the most conspicuous examples in Canada are the large differences in the average wages between women and men and among various racial and ethnic groups. Do these wage differences really reflect differences in marginal productivity, or is something else going on?

Second, many people wrongly believe that the marginal productivity theory of income distribution gives a *moral* justification for the distribution of income, implying that the existing distribution is fair and appropriate. This misconception sometimes leads other people, who believe that the current distribution of income is unfair, to reject marginal productivity theory.

To address these controversies, we'll start by looking at income disparities across gender and ethnic groups. Then we'll ask what factors might account for these disparities and whether these explanations are consistent with the marginal productivity theory of income distribution.

Wage Disparities in Practice

Wage rates in Canada cover a very wide range. In 2014, hundreds of thousands of workers received the legal minimum wage, a rate that varies from $11 per hour in Nunavut and Ontario to $9.95 per hour in Alberta. The average minimum wage worker earns less than $22 000 per year if they are able to get 40 hours of work per week. At the other extreme, the chief executives of two dozen companies were paid more than $10 million, which works out to more than $27 000 per day even if they worked all 365 days of the year. Even leaving out these extremes, there is a huge range of wage rates. Are people really that different in their marginal productivities?

A particular source of concern is the existence of systematic wage differences across gender, ethnicity, and immigration status. Figure 19-8 compares annual median earnings in 2010 of workers age 15 or older classified by gender and ethnicity. As a group, males (averaging across all ethnicities and places of birth) had the highest earnings. Other data show that women (averaging across all ethnicities and places of birth) earned only about 71% as much; treaty Indian workers (male and female combined), only 59% as much; workers who immigrated between 2001 and 2009 (again, male and female combined), only 67% as much; visible minority workers (averaging across places of birth and gender) earned only about 75% as much.

FIGURE 19-8 Median Earnings by Gender, Ethnicity, and Place of Birth, 2010

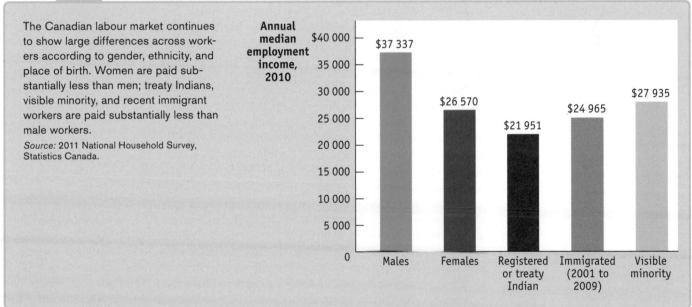

The Canadian labour market continues to show large differences across workers according to gender, ethnicity, and place of birth. Women are paid substantially less than men; treaty Indians, visible minority, and recent immigrant workers are paid substantially less than male workers.

Source: 2011 National Household Survey, Statistics Canada.

We are a nation founded on the belief that every individual is equal before and under the law and has the right to the equal protection and equal benefit of the law without discrimination. So why do workers receive such unequal pay? Let's start with the marginal productivity explanations, and then look at other influences.

Compensating differentials are wage differences across jobs that reflect the fact that some jobs are less pleasant than others.

Marginal Productivity and Wage Inequality

A large part of the observed inequality in wages can be explained by considerations that are consistent with the marginal productivity theory of income distribution. In particular, there are three well-understood sources of wage differences across occupations and individuals.

First is the existence of **compensating differentials:** across different types of jobs, wages are often higher or lower depending on how attractive or unattractive the job is. Workers with unpleasant or dangerous jobs demand a higher wage in comparison to workers with jobs that require the same skill and effort but lack the unpleasant or dangerous qualities. For example, truckers who haul hazardous loads are paid more than truckers who haul non-hazardous loads. But for any *given* job, the marginal productivity theory of income distribution generally holds true. For example, hazardous-load truckers are paid a wage equal to the equilibrium value of the marginal product of the last person employed in the labour market for hazardous-load truckers.

A second reason for wage inequality that is clearly consistent with marginal productivity theory is differences in talent. People differ in their abilities: a higher-ability person, by producing a better product that commands a higher price compared to a lower-ability person, generates a higher value of the marginal product. And these differences in the value of the marginal product translate into differences in earning potential. We all know that this is true in sports: practice is important, but 99.99% (at least) of the population just doesn't have what it takes to skate and score goals like Sidney Crosby or hit tennis balls like Rafael Nadal or Milos Raonic. The same is true, though less obvious, in other fields of endeavour.

A third and very important reason for wage differences is differences in the quantity of *human capital*. Recall that human capital—education and training—is at least as important in the modern economy as physical capital in the form of buildings and machines. Different people "embody" quite different quantities of human capital, and a person with a higher quantity of human capital typically generates a higher value of the marginal product by producing a product that commands a higher price. So differences in human capital account for substantial differences in wages. People with high levels of human capital, such as skilled surgeons or engineers, generally receive high wages.

The most direct way to see the effect of human capital on wages is to look at the relationship between educational levels and earnings. Figure 19-9 shows earnings differentials by gender and four educational levels for people aged 15 or older in 2010. As you can see, regardless of gender, higher education is associated with higher median earnings. For example, in 2010 females without a high school diploma had median earnings 37% less than those with a high school diploma and 59% less than those with a post-secondary degree or diploma below a bachelor's degree—and similar patterns exist for males. Additional data show that specialist physicians and judges—occupations that require many years of formal training—earned median employment income of $126 119 and $228 104, respectively, in 2010.

Because men typically have had more years of education than women, differences in levels of education are part of the explanation for the earnings differences shown in Figure 19-8.

It's also important to realize that formal education is not the only source of human capital; on-the-job training and experience are also very important. This point was highlighted by a 2010 Library of Parliament Background Paper. The study was motivated by concerns over the presence of a male–female earnings gap despite the fact that women have caught up with men in terms of both labour force participation and education attainment. The study showed that the average hourly wage of women between the ages of 25 and 54 was 15% below that of their male counterparts. Indeed, the gender wage gap varies across occupations: the female-to-male earnings ratio ranges from 70% for occupations unique to primary industry to 99% for occupations in art, culture, recreation, and sport.

FIGURE **19-9** Median Earnings by Education and Gender, 2010

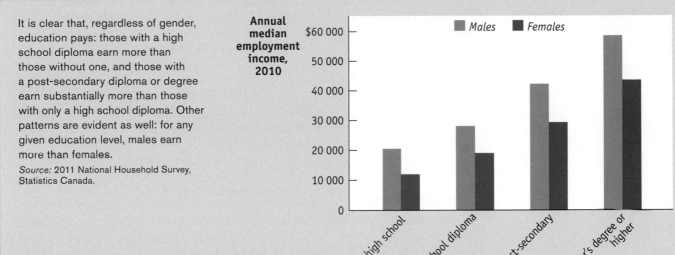

It is clear that, regardless of gender, education pays: those with a high school diploma earn more than those without one, and those with a post-secondary diploma or degree earn substantially more than those with only a high school diploma. Other patterns are evident as well: for any given education level, males earn more than females.

Source: 2011 National Household Survey, Statistics Canada.

Table 19-3 shows the average hourly wage and the female-to-male earnings ratios for selected occupations described in the report. The report suggests that job and demographic characteristics are the contributing factors to these wage gaps. For example, the expectation that women will take on greater household responsibilities related to raising children tends to reduce their working hours and/or lead to interruptions in their participation in the labour market, which has adverse impact on their job experience and the training they receive. The report points out that women represented two-thirds of the workers in 13 of the 20 lowest paid occupations in the country, while men were the majority in only 3 of these 20 occupations. Gender differences in job tenure and experience can partly explain one notable aspect of Figure 19-9: women's median earnings are less than men's median earnings for any given education level.

TABLE **19-3** Average Hourly Wage and the Female-to-Male Earnings Ratio by Occupation, 2008

Occupation	Males ($)	Females ($)	Ratio
Management occupations	36.50	29.11	0.80
Business, finance, and administrative occupations	23.86	20.29	0.85
Natural and applied sciences and related occupations	31.43	27.66	0.88
Health occupations	25.78	25.19	0.98
Occupations in social science, education, government service, and religion	30.68	26.69	0.87
Occupations in art, culture, recreation, and sport	24.14	23.89	0.99
Sales and service occupations	19.72	14.33	0.73
Trades, transport, equipment operators, and related occupations	22.59	16.81	0.74
Occupations unique to primary industry	21.53	14.97	0.70
Occupations unique to processing, manufacturing, and utilities	20.95	14.83	0.71

Source: Julie Cool, *Wage Gap Between Women and Men,* Library of Parliament Background Paper, Publication No. 2010-30-E, (Parliament of Canada, 2010).

Unions are organizations of workers that try to raise wages and improve working conditions for their members by bargaining collectively with employers.

But it's also important to emphasize that earnings differences arising from differences in human capital are not necessarily "fair." A society in which Aboriginal and immigrant children often receive a poor education because they live in underfunded school districts, then go on to earn low wages because they are poorly educated, may have labour markets that are well described by marginal productivity theory (and would be consistent with the earnings differentials across ethnic groups shown in Figure 19-8). Yet many people would still consider the resulting distribution of income unfair.

Still, many observers think that actual wage differentials cannot be entirely explained by compensating differentials, differences in talent, and differences in human capital. They believe that market power, *efficiency wages*, and discrimination also play an important role. We will examine these forces next.

Market Power

The marginal productivity theory of income distribution is based on the assumption that factor markets are perfectly competitive. In such markets we can expect workers to be paid the equilibrium value of their marginal product, regardless of who they are. But how valid is this assumption?

We studied markets that are *not* perfectly competitive in Chapters 13, 14, and 15; now let's touch briefly on the ways in which labour markets may deviate from the competitive assumption.

One undoubted source of differences in wages between otherwise similar workers is the role of **unions**—organizations that try to raise wages and improve working conditions for their members. Labour unions, when they are successful, replace one-on-one wage deals between workers and employers with collective bargaining, in which the employer must negotiate wages with union representatives. Without question, this leads to higher wages for those workers who are represented by unions. In early 2014 the median weekly earnings of union members in Canada were $992.40, compared with $760 for workers not represented by unions—a nearly 34% difference.

Just as workers can sometimes organize to extract higher wages than they would otherwise receive, employers can sometimes organize to pay *lower* wages than would result from competition. For example, health care workers—doctors, nurses, and so on—sometimes argue that provincial health ministries and hospitals are engaged in a collective effort to hold down their wages.

How much does collective action, either by workers or by employers, affect wages in Canada now? Canada's unionization rates have remained relatively stable in the past few decades, falling only from 34% in 1997 to 31.2% in 2013. So unlike the United States, where less than 7% of private sector employees were unionized in 2010, unions in Canada still exert a significant upward effect on wages. In 2013 about 58% of all unionized employees worked in the public sector, balancing the market power governments possesses as employers. However, with deregulation, outsourcing, and globalization, the power of unions has eroded slightly, especially their bargaining power over wages. Nonetheless, they still play an important role in the negotiations of job security, better working conditions, and benefits for their members.

Efficiency Wages

A second source of wage inequality is the phenomenon of *efficiency wages*—a type of incentive scheme used by employers to motivate workers to work hard and to reduce worker turnover. Suppose a worker performs a job that is extremely important—say, serving as a caregiver for the employer's child—but that the employer can observe how well the job is being performed only at infrequent intervals. Then it often makes sense for the employer to pay more than the worker could earn in an alternative job—that is, more than the equilibrium wage. Why?

Because earning a premium makes losing this job and having to take the alternative job quite costly for the worker.

So a worker who happens to be observed performing poorly and is therefore fired is now worse off for having to accept a lower-paying job. The threat of losing a job that pays a premium motivates the worker to perform well and avoid being fired. Likewise, paying a premium also reduces worker turnover—the frequency with which an employee leaves a job voluntarily. Despite the fact that it may take no more effort and skill to be a child's caregiver than to be an office worker, efficiency wages show why it often makes economic sense for a parent to pay a caregiver more than the equilibrium wage of an office worker.

The **efficiency-wage model** explains why we might observe wages offered above their equilibrium level. Like the price floors we studied in Chapter 5—and, in particular, much like the minimum wage—this phenomenon leads to a surplus of labour in labour markets that are characterized by the efficiency-wage model. This surplus of labour translates into unemployment—some workers are actively searching for a high-paying efficiency-wage job but are unable to get one, and other more fortunate but no more deserving workers are able to acquire one.

As a result, two workers with exactly the same profile—the same skills and same job history—may earn unequal wages: the worker who is lucky enough to get an efficiency-wage job earns more than the worker who gets a standard job (or who remains unemployed while searching for a higher-paying job). Efficiency wages are a response to a type of market failure that arises from the fact that some employees don't always perform as well as they should and are able to hide that fact. As a result, employers use nonequilibrium wages in order to motivate their employees, leading to an inefficient outcome.

> According to the **efficiency-wage model,** some employers pay an above-equilibrium wage as an incentive for better performance.

Discrimination

It is a real and ugly fact that throughout history there has been discrimination against workers who are considered to be of the wrong race, ethnicity, gender, or other characteristics. How does this fit into our economic models?

The main insight economic analysis offers is that discrimination is *not* a natural consequence of market competition. On the contrary, market forces tend to work against discrimination. To see why, consider the incentives that would exist if social convention dictated that women be paid, say, 30% less than men with equivalent qualifications and experience. A company whose management was itself unbiased would then be able to reduce its costs by hiring women rather than men—and such companies would have an advantage over other companies that hired men despite their higher cost. The result would be to create an excess demand for female workers, which would tend to drive up their wages.

But if market competition works against discrimination, how is it that so much discrimination has taken place? The answer is twofold. First, when labour markets don't work well, employers may have the ability to discriminate without hurting their profits. For example, market interferences (such as unions or minimum-wage laws) or market failures (such as efficiency wages) can lead to wages that are above their equilibrium levels. In these cases, there are more job applicants than there are jobs, leaving employers free to discriminate among applicants. In 2012, with unemployment over 7%, the Canadian Human Rights Commission, the federal agency tasked with investigating discrimination charges in the federal government and federally regulated industries (e.g., banking, transportation, and communication), reported that the complaints from workers and jobseekers had hit an all-time high, the most logged in the agency's 35-year history.

In research published in the *American Economic Review,* two economists, Marianne Bertrand and Sendhil Mullainathan, documented discrimination in hiring by sending fictitious resumés to prospective employers on a random basis. Applicants with "white-sounding" names such as Emily Walsh were 50% more likely to be contacted than applicants with "African-American-sounding" names

FOR INQUIRING MINDS

THE ECONOMICS OF APARTHEID

The Republic of South Africa is the richest nation in Africa, but it also has a harsh political history. Until the peaceful transition to majority rule in 1994, the country was controlled by its white minority, Afrikaners, who are the descendants of European (mainly Dutch) immigrants. This minority imposed an economic system known as apartheid, which overwhelmingly favoured white interests over those of native Africans and other groups considered "non-white," such as Asians.

The origins of apartheid go back to the early years of the twentieth century, when large numbers of white farmers began moving into South Africa's growing cities. There they discovered, to their horror, that they did not automatically earn higher wages than other races. But they had the right to vote—and non-whites did not. And so the South African government instituted "job-reservation" laws designed to ensure that only whites got jobs that paid well. The

government also set about creating jobs for whites in government owned industries. As Allister Sparks notes in *The Mind of South Africa* (1990), in its efforts to provide high-paying jobs for whites, the country "eventually acquired the largest amount of nationalized industry of any country outside the Communist bloc."

In other words, racial discrimination was possible because it was backed by the power of the government, which prevented markets from following their natural course.

In 1994, in one of the political miracles of modern times, the white regime ceded power and South Africa became a full-fledged democracy. Apartheid was abolished. Unfortunately,

Although abolished, apartheid has left behind a legacy of large racial differences in earnings that will likely persist for many years.

large racial differences in earnings remain. The main reason is that apartheid created huge disparities in human capital, which will persist for many years to come.

such as Lakisha Washington. Also, applicants with white-sounding names and good credentials were much more likely to be contacted than those without such credentials. By contrast, potential employers seemed to ignore the credentials of applicants with African-American-sounding names.

Second, discrimination has sometimes been institutionalized in government policy. This institutionalization of discrimination has made it easier to maintain it against market pressure, and historically it is the form that discrimination has typically taken. For example, in Canada in the late 1800s and early 1900s, Asians faced immigration barriers (including exclusion from entry) and laws restricting the jobs they could have and forcing their wages to be less than what other employees earned. In the United States, African-Americans were barred from attending "whites-only" public schools and universities in many parts of the country and forced to attend inferior schools. Although market competition tends to work against *current* discrimination, it is not a remedy for past discrimination, which typically has had an impact on the education and experience of its victims and thereby reduces their income. The preceding For Inquiring Minds illustrates the way in which government policy enforced discrimination in the world's most famous racist regime, that of the former government of South Africa.

So Does Marginal Productivity Theory Work?

The main conclusion you should draw from this discussion is that the marginal productivity theory of income distribution is not a perfect description of how factor incomes are determined but that it works pretty well. The deviations are important. But, by and large, in a modern economy with well-functioning labour markets, factors of production are paid the equilibrium value of the marginal product—the value of the marginal product of the last unit employed in the market as a whole.

It's important to emphasize, once again, that this does not mean that the factor distribution of income is morally justified.

ECONOMICS ▶ IN ACTION

MARGINAL PRODUCTIVITY AND THE "1%"

In the fall of 2011, there were widespread public demonstrations in the United States, Canada, and a number of other countries against the growing inequality of personal income. American protestors, known as the Occupy Wall Street movement, adopted the slogan "We are the 99%" to emphasize the fact that the incomes of the top 1% of the population had grown much faster than those of most Americans.

One year earlier, the Canadian Centre for Policy Alternatives released a study on income inequality entitled *The Rise of Canada's Richest 1%*. This study found that, between 1977 and 2007, high income Canadians captured an ever-growing share of all income. The richest 10% of all tax filers saw their share of total income rise by one seventh. The top 1% saw their share of income double, the richest 0.1% saw their share almost triple, and the richest 0.01% saw their share of total income more than quintuple. In fact, according to the study "Canada's richest 1%—the 246 000 privileged few whose average income is $405 000 (in 2007)—took in almost a third (32%) of all growth in incomes in the fastest growing decade in this generation, 1997 to 2007." In 2010, the top 1% had a median income that was about seven times the median income of all Canadians.

Why have the richest Canadians and Americans been pulling away from the rest? The short answer is that the causes are a source of considerable dispute and continuing research. One thing is clear, however: this aspect of growing inequality can't be explained simply in terms of the growing demand for highly educated labour. In this chapter's opening story, we pointed out that there has been a growing wage premium for workers with advanced degrees. Yet despite this growing premium, as Figure 19-10 shows, having an advanced degree only increases the *likelihood* of gaining access to the top 1% of all income earners. Having such a degree does not guarantee membership to this group, nor is having such a degree a necessary condition to gain entry to this exclusive club.

This doesn't mean that the top 1% aren't "earning" their incomes. It does show, however, that the explanation for their huge gains is not entirely education.

FIGURE 19-10 The Top 1% by Education, 2010

No high school 3%

High school 10%

Post-secondary below bachelor's degree 20%

University degree 67%

Source: 2011 National Household Survey, Statistics Canada.

▼ Quick Review

- Existing large disparities in wages both among individuals and across groups lead some to question the marginal productivity theory of income distribution.

- **Compensating differentials,** as well as differences in the values of the marginal products of workers that arise from differences in talent, job experience, and human capital, account for some wage disparities.

- Market power, in the form of **unions** or collective action by employers, as well as the **efficiency-wage model,** in which employers pay an above-equilibrium wage to induce better performance, also explain how some wage disparities arise.

- Discrimination has historically been a major factor in wage disparities. Market competition tends to work against discrimination. But discrimination can leave a long-lasting legacy of diminished human capital acquisition.

CHECK YOUR UNDERSTANDING 19-3

1. Assess each of the following statements. Do you think they are true, false, or ambiguous? Explain.
   a. The marginal productivity theory of income distribution is inconsistent with the presence of income disparities associated with gender, ethnicity, or immigration status.
   b. Companies that engage in workplace discrimination but whose competitors do not are likely to have lower profits as a result of their actions.
   c. Workers who are paid less because they have less experience are not the victims of discrimination.

Solutions appear at back of book.

The Supply of Labour

Up to this point we have focused on the demand for factors, which determines the quantities demanded of labour, capital, or land by producers as a function of their factor prices. What about the supply of factors?

In this section we focus exclusively on the supply of labour. We do this for two reasons. First, in the modern Canadian economy, labour is the most important factor of production, accounting for most of factor income. Second, as we'll see,

Decisions about labour supply result from decisions about utility-maximizing **time allocation:** how many hours to spend on different activities.

Leisure is time available for purposes other than earning money to buy marketed goods.

labour supply is the area in which factor markets look most different from markets for goods and services.

Work versus Leisure

In the labour market, the roles of firms and households are the reverse of what they are in markets for goods and services. A good such as wheat is supplied by firms and demanded by households; labour, though, is demanded by firms and supplied by households. How do people decide how much labour to supply?

As a practical matter, most people have limited control over their work hours: either you take a job that involves working a set number of hours per week, or you don't get the job at all. To understand the logic of labour supply, however, it helps to put realism to one side for a bit and imagine an individual who can choose to work as many or as few hours as he or she likes.

Why wouldn't such an individual work as many hours as possible? Because workers are human beings, too, and have other uses for their time. An hour spent on the job is an hour not spent on other, presumably more pleasant, activities. So the decision about how much labour to supply involves making a decision about utility-maximizing **time allocation**—how many hours to spend on different activities.

By working, people earn income that they can use to buy goods. The more hours an individual works, the more goods he or she can afford to buy. But this increased purchasing power comes at the expense of a reduction in **leisure,** the time spent not working. (Leisure doesn't necessarily mean time spent goofing off. It could mean time spent with one's family, pursuing hobbies, exercising, and so on.) And though purchased goods yield utility, so does leisure. Indeed, we can think of leisure itself as a normal good, which most people would like to consume more of as their incomes increase.

How does a rational individual decide how much leisure to consume? By making a marginal comparison, of course. In analyzing consumer choice, we asked how a utility-maximizing consumer uses a marginal *dollar*. In analyzing labour supply, we ask how an individual uses a marginal *hour*.

Consider Clive, an individual who likes both leisure and the goods money can buy. Suppose that his wage rate is $10 per hour. In deciding how many hours he wants to work, he must compare the marginal utility of an additional hour of leisure with the additional utility he gets from $10 worth of goods. If $10 worth of goods adds more to his total utility than an additional hour of leisure, he can increase his total utility by giving up an hour of leisure in order to work an additional hour. If an extra hour of leisure adds more to his total utility than $10 worth of goods, he can increase his total utility by working one fewer hour in order to gain an hour of leisure.

At Clive's optimal labour supply choice, then, his marginal utility of one hour of leisure is equal to the marginal utility he gets from the goods that his hourly wage can purchase. This is very similar to the *optimal consumption rule* we encountered in Chapter 10, except that it is a rule about time rather than money.

Our next step is to ask how Clive's decision about time allocation is affected when his wage rate changes.

Wages and Labour Supply

Suppose that Clive's wage rate doubles, from $10 to $20 per hour. How will he change his time allocation?

You could argue that Clive will work longer hours, because his incentive to work has increased: by giving up an hour of leisure, he can now gain twice as much money as before. But you could equally well argue that he will work less, because he doesn't need to work as many hours to generate the income to pay for the goods he wants.

As these opposing arguments suggest, the quantity of labour Clive supplies can either rise or fall when his wage rate rises. To understand why, let's recall the distinction between *substitution effects* and *income effects* that we learned in Chapter 10 and its appendix. We saw there that a price change affects consumer choice in two ways: by changing the opportunity cost of a good in terms of other goods (the substitution effect) and by making the consumer richer or poorer (the income effect).

Now think about how a rise in Clive's wage rate affects his demand for leisure. The opportunity cost of leisure—the amount of money he gives up by taking an hour off instead of working—rises. That substitution effect gives him an incentive, other things equal, to consume *less* leisure and work *more* hours. Conversely, a higher wage rate makes Clive richer—and this income effect leads him, other things equal, to want to consume *more* leisure and work *fewer* hours, because leisure is a normal good.

So in the case of labour supply, the substitution effect and the income effect work in opposite directions. If the substitution effect is so powerful that it dominates the income effect, an increase in Clive's wage rate leads him to supply *more* hours of labour. If the income effect is so powerful that it dominates the substitution effect, an increase in the wage rate leads him to supply *fewer* hours of labour.

We see, then, that the **individual labour supply curve**—the relationship between the wage rate and the number of hours of labour supplied by an individual worker—does not necessarily slope upward. If the income effect dominates, a higher wage rate will reduce the quantity of labour supplied.

Figure 19-11 illustrates the two possibilities for labour supply. If the substitution effect dominates the income effect, the individual labour supply curve slopes upward; panel (a) shows an increase in the wage rate from $10 to $20 per hour leading to a *rise* in the number of hours worked from 40 to 50. However, if the

> The **individual labour supply curve** shows how the quantity of labour supplied by an individual depends on that individual's wage rate.

FIGURE 19-11 The Individual Labour Supply Curve

When the substitution effect of a wage increase dominates the income effect, the individual labour supply curve slopes upward, as in panel (a). Here a rise in the wage rate from $10 to $20 per hour increases the number of hours worked from 40 to 50. But when the income effect of a wage increase dominates the substitution effect, the individual labour supply curve slopes downward, as in panel (b). Here the same rise in the wage rate reduces the number of hours worked from 40 to 30. The individual labour supply curve shows how the quantity of labour supplied by an individual depends on that individual's wage rate.

FOR INQUIRING MINDS

WHY YOU CAN'T FIND A CAB WHEN IT'S RAINING

Everyone says that you can't find a taxi when you really need one—say, when it's raining. That could be because everyone else is trying to get a taxi at the same time. But according to a study published in the *Quarterly Journal of Economics*, it's more than that: cab drivers actually go home early when it's raining.

The reason is that the hourly wage rate of a taxi driver depends on the weather: when it's raining, drivers get more fares and therefore earn more per hour. But it seems that the income effect of this higher wage rate outweighs the substitution effect.

This behaviour leads the authors of the study to question drivers' rationality. They point out that if taxi drivers thought in terms of the long run, they would realize that rainy days and nice days tend to average out and that their high earnings on a rainy day don't really affect their long-run income very much. Indeed, experienced drivers (who have probably figured this out) are less likely than inexperienced drivers to go home early on a rainy day. But leaving such issues to one side, the study does seem to show clear evidence of a labour supply curve that slopes downward instead of upward, thanks to income effects.

income effect dominates, the quantity of labour supplied goes down when the wage rate increases. Panel (b) shows the same rise in the wage rate leading to a *fall* in the number of hours worked from 40 to 30. (Economists refer to an individual labour supply curve that contains both upward-sloping and downward-sloping segments as a "backward-bending labour supply curve"—a concept that we analyze in detail in Appendix 19A.)

Is a negative response of the quantity of labour supplied to the wage rate a real possibility? Yes: many labour economists believe that income effects on the supply of labour may be somewhat stronger than substitution effects. The most compelling piece of evidence for this belief comes from Canadians' increasing consumption of leisure over the past century. At the end of the nineteenth century, wages adjusted for inflation were only about one-eighth what they are today; the typical workweek was 70 hours, and very few workers retired at age 65. Today the typical workweek is less than 40 hours, and most people retire at age 65 or earlier. So it seems that Canadians have chosen to take advantage of higher wages in part by consuming more leisure.

Shifts of the Labour Supply Curve

Now that we have examined how income and substitution effects shape the individual labour supply curve, we can turn to the market labour supply curve. In any labour market, the market supply curve is the horizontal sum of the individual labour supply curves of all workers in that market. A change in any factor *other than the wage* that alters workers' willingness to supply labour causes a shift of the labour supply curve. A variety of factors can lead to such shifts, including changes in preferences and social norms, changes in population, changes in opportunities, and changes in wealth.

Changes in Preferences and Social Norms Changes in preferences and social norms can lead workers to increase or decrease their willingness to work at any given wage. A striking example of this phenomenon is the large increase in the number of employed women—particularly married employed women—that has occurred in Canada and the United States since the 1960s. Until that time, women who could afford to largely avoided working outside the home. Changes in preferences and norms in post–World War II North America (helped along by the invention of labour-saving home appliances such as washing machines, increasing urbanization of the population, and higher female education levels) have induced large numbers of North American women to join the workforce—a phenomenon often repeated in other countries that experience similar social and technological forces.

Changes in Population Changes in the population size generally lead to shifts of the labour supply curve. A larger population tends to shift the labour supply curve rightward as more workers are available at any given wage; a smaller population tends to shift the labour supply curve leftward. From 1987 to 2013, the Canadian labour force has grown approximately 1.3% per year, largely due to immigration. As a result, from 1987 to 2013 the Canadian labour market had a rightward-shifting labour supply curve. However, while the population continued to grow in the recession years 1992 and 2009, the growth rate of the labour force slowed as workers, disillusioned by bad job prospects, left the labour force. In fact, 1992 was the one year the Canadian labour supply curve did not shift right at all.

Changes in Opportunities At one time, teaching was the only occupation considered suitable for well-educated women. However, as opportunities in other professions opened up to women starting in the 1960s, many women left teaching and potential female teachers chose other careers. This generated a leftward shift of the supply curve for teachers, reflecting a fall in the willingness to work at any given wage and forcing school districts to pay more to maintain an adequate teaching staff. These events illustrate a general result: when superior alternatives arise for workers in another labour market, the supply curve in the original labour market shifts leftward as workers move to the new opportunities. Similarly, when opportunities diminish in one labour market—say, layoffs in the manufacturing industry due to increased foreign competition—the supply in alternative labour markets increases as workers move to these other markets.

GLOBAL COMPARISON

THE OVERWORKED AMERICAN?

Americans today may work less than they did a hundred years ago, but they still work more than workers in any other industrialized country, including Canada.

This figure compares average annual hours worked in the United States with those worked in other industrialized countries. The differences result from a combination of Americans' longer workweeks and shorter vacations. For example, the great majority of full-time American workers put in at least 40 hours per week. Until recently, however, a government mandate limited most French workers to a 35-hour workweek; collective bargaining has achieved a similar reduction in the workweek for many German workers.

In 2011, American workers got, on average, eight paid vacation days, but 23% of American workers got none at all. (Of developed nations, Canadian and Japanese workers are second worst off with a minimum of 10 paid vacation days per year.) In contrast, German workers are guaranteed six weeks of paid vacation a year. Also, American workers use fewer of the vacation days they are entitled to than do workers in other industrialized countries. A 2011 survey found that only 57% of American workers use all the vacation days they are entitled to, compared to 89% in France.

Why do Americans work so much more than others? Unlike their counterparts in other industrialized countries, Americans are not legally entitled to paid vacation days; as a result, the average American worker gets fewer of

them. Moreover, anecdotal evidence suggests that during the recent recession, with its high rates of unemployment, American workers became more reluctant to use the vacation days they were entitled to.

Once again it is good to be a Canadian worker, but perhaps only as compared to Japanese and American workers.

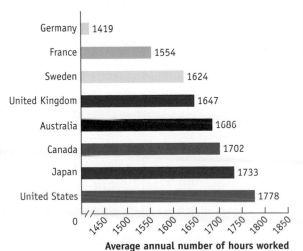

Average annual number of hours worked

Source: OECD (data are from 2010, except French data, which are from 2009).

Changes in Wealth A person whose wealth increases will buy more normal goods, including leisure. So when a class of workers experiences a general rise in their wealth levels—say, due to a stock market boom—the income effect from the wealth increase will shift the labour supply curve associated with those workers leftward as workers consume more leisure and work less. Note that *the income effect caused by a change in wealth shifts the labour supply curve,* but *the income effect from a wage rate increase*—as we discussed in the case of the individual labour supply curve—*is a movement along the labour supply curve.* The following Economics in Action illustrates how such a change in the wealth levels of many families during the late 1990s led to a shift of the market labour supply curve associated with their employable children.

ECONOMICS › IN ACTION

THE DECLINE OF THE SUMMER JOB

keepics/Alamy

While some teenagers want to work and manage to find jobs, the current trend is toward a decline of the summer job due to a steep fall in demand along with falling supply.

Come summertime, teens across the country find themselves facing a recurring annual problem: how do you get a job without lots of experience, and how do you get experience without a job?

Traditionally, landing a job is more challenging for younger Canadians especially if they happen to live in a part of the country with fewer employment opportunities. In recent years, a combination of adverse shifts in both supply and demand has severely diminished summer employment for young workers in Newfoundland and Labrador. In 1977, about 53 000 (or 59%) of Newfoundlanders between the ages of 15 and 24 were employed in the summer workforce. By 2007, that number was about 33 000 (or 52%). In 1977, there were about 116 000 Newfoundlanders between the ages of 15 to 24. Thirty years later, the number was nearly cut in half. Where did all the youth go? A simple answer is that due to the difficult labour market for workers in the 1990s, either Newfoundlanders were having fewer children or families left the province in search of more stable employment opportunities elsewhere (since the declaration of the cod moratorium in 1992, the population of Newfoundland has declined by 12%).

Thus, a fall in supply is one explanation for the 20 000 lost summer jobs. Another explanation for the fall in supply is the substitution effect: increased competition from immigrants and unemployed adults, who are now doing the jobs typically done by teens (like mowing lawns and delivering pizzas), has led to a decline in wages. So some teenagers forgo low-paying summer work to consume leisure or pursue additional study instead.

But it was the deep recession of 2008–2009 that contributed most to the severe fall in youth summer employment in the ensuing years. Youth employment in the summer of 2009 was down by almost 10% in Newfoundland and Labrador versus the previous year and was slow to recover. Thus a long-run trend of falling supply combined with a recession has led to the decline of the summer job and what has long been an important rite of passage for teens.

▼ Quick Review

- The choice of how much labour to supply is a problem of utility-maximizing **time allocation:** a choice between work and **leisure.**

- A rise in the wage rate causes both an income and a substitution effect on an individual's labour supply. The substitution effect of a higher wage rate induces more hours of work supplied, other things equal. This is countered by the income effect: higher income leads to a higher demand for leisure, a normal good. If the income effect dominates, a rise in the wage rate can actually cause the **individual labour supply curve** to slope the "wrong" way: downward.

- The market labour supply curve is the horizontal sum of the individual labour supply curves of all workers in that market. It shifts for four main reasons: changes in preferences and social norms, changes in population, changes in opportunities, and changes in wealth.

CHECK YOUR UNDERSTANDING   19-4

1. Formerly, Clive was free to work as many or as few hours per week as he wanted. But a new law limits the maximum number of hours he can work per week to 35. Explain under what circumstances, if at all, he is made:
   a. Worse off
   b. Equally as well off
   c. Better off

2. Explain in terms of the income and substitution effects how a fall in Clive's wage rate can induce him to work more hours than before.

Solutions appear at back of book.

: # Alta Gracia: Can Fair Trade Work?

David Paul Morris/Bloomberg via Getty Images

The tag on your clothes tells you the country it was made in, but not who made it. In response to concerns about factory conditions around the world, many clothing retailers changed how their goods are produced. Some companies pride themselves on being based entirely in North America: Canada Goose operates factories in Toronto and Winnipeg while American Apparel's clothing is manufactured in Los Angeles. Others, like Roots and Mountain Equipment Co-op, have standards of working conditions that they enforce in factories around the world. But Knights Apparel, a manufacturer with 30 factories worldwide, went further when it created Alta Gracia. The Alta Gracia factory is located in the Dominican Republic, where 120 employees turn out T-shirts and sweats emblazoned with NHL logos and the names of colleges and universities.

Workers at Alta Gracia consider themselves lucky because the company pays what it considers a "living wage"—sufficient to feed and shelter a family of four—and allows workers to join a union. Seamstress Santa Castillo, for example, earns $550 a month, three times the average monthly pay of $160 earned by apparel workers in the Dominican Republic, where a loaf of bread costs more than $1.

Workers at the factory have not always been so fortunate. When the factory was owned by another company, BJ&B, which made baseball caps for Nike and Reebok, workers were paid the prevailing wage and were fired if they complained about working conditions or tried to form a union. Eventually, BJ&B moved its operations to lower-wage Bangladesh, where the minimum wage is 17 cents an hour, compared to 94 cents an hour in the Dominican Republic. In contrast, Alta Gracia pays $3.10 an hour.

Joe Bozich started Knights Apparel in 2000; through scores of deals he has made with universities, his company has surpassed Nike as the number-one supplier to schools in North America. He works closely with the Worker Rights Consortium, a group of 186 universities that press college-logo apparel manufacturers to improve workers' welfare. The consortium is part of the "Fair Trade Movement," an organization dedicated to improving the welfare of workers in developing countries, by raising wages. In 2010, $6.6 billion of Fair Trade–approved goods were sold globally, up 27% from 2009.

Alta Gracia was conceived by Bozich as a model factory to show that an apparel manufacturer could pay its workers a living wage and still succeed. Its production cost for a T-shirt is about $5.30—90 cents, or 20%, higher than if it paid minimum wage. Knights Apparel accepts a lower profit margin so it doesn't have to ask retailers to pay a higher wholesale price for its merchandise.

Some observers, though, are skeptical because Alta Gracia merchandise is sold alongside products made by Nike and Adidas, at approximately the same premium price these well-known brands command. "It's a noble effort, but it is an experiment," says Andrew Jassin, an industry analyst. "There are consumers who really care and will buy this apparel at a premium price, and there are those who say they care, but just want value."

Kellie McElhaney, a professor of corporate social responsibility at the University of California at Berkeley, is less skeptical: "A lot of college students would much rather pay for a brand that shows workers are treated well."

QUESTIONS FOR THOUGHT

1. Use the marginal productivity theory of income distribution to explain how the prevailing wage for apparel workers can fall below a living wage in the Dominican Republic.

2. From the point of view of Knights Apparel, what are the pros and cons of paying the Alta Gracia workers a living wage? What are the pros and cons from the point of view of workers generally?

3. What factors does the success or failure of Alta Gracia depend on? What should Knights Apparel do to improve its chances of success?

SUMMARY

1. Just as there are markets for goods and services, there are markets for factors of production, including labour, land, and both **physical capital** and **human capital.** These markets determine the **factor distribution of income.**

2. Profit-maximizing price-taking producers will employ a factor up to the point at which its price is equal to its **value of the marginal product**—the marginal product of the factor multiplied by the price of the output it produces. The **value of the marginal product curve** is therefore the individual price-taking producer's demand curve for a factor.

3. The market demand curve for labour is the horizontal sum of the individual demand curves of producers in that market. It shifts for three main reasons: changes in output price, changes in the supply of other factors, and technological changes.

4. When a competitive labour market is in equilibrium, the market wage is equal to the **equilibrium value of the marginal product** of labour, the additional value produced by the last worker hired in the labour market as a whole. The same principle applies to other factors of production: the **rental rate** of land or capital is equal to the equilibrium value of the marginal products. This insight leads to the **marginal productivity theory of income distribution,** according to which each factor is paid the value of the marginal product of the last unit of that factor employed in the factor market as a whole.

5. Large disparities in wages raise questions about the validity of the marginal productivity theory of income

distribution. Many disparities can be explained by **compensating differentials** and by differences in talent, job experience, and human capital across workers. Market interference in the forms of **unions** and collective action by employers also creates wage disparities. The **efficiency-wage model,** which arises from a type of market failure, shows how wage disparities can result from employers' attempts to increase worker performance. Free markets tend to diminish discrimination, but discrimination remains a real source of wage disparity, especially through its effects on human captial acquisition. Discrimination is typically maintained either through problems in labour markets or (historically) through institutionalization in government policies.

6. Labour supply is the result of utility-maximizing decisions about **time allocation,** where each worker faces a trade-off between **leisure** and work. An increase in the hourly wage rate tends to increase work hours via the substitution effect but to reduce work hours via the income effect. If the net result is that a worker increases the quantity of labour supplied in response to a higher wage, the **individual labour supply curve** slopes upward. If the net result is that a worker reduces work hours, the individual labour supply curve—unlike supply curves for goods and services—slopes downward.

7. The market labour supply curve is the horizontal sum of the individual labour supply curves of all workers in that market. It shifts for four main reasons: changes in preferences and social norms, changes in population, changes in opportunities, and changes in wealth.

KEY TERMS

Physical capital, p. 572
Human capital, p. 572
Factor distribution of income, p. 573
Value of the marginal product, p. 576
Value of the marginal product curve, p. 576

Equilibrium value of the marginal product, p. 581
Rental rate, p. 582
Marginal productivity theory of income distribution, p. 583
Compensating differentials, p. 588

Unions, p. 588
Efficiency-wage model, p. 589
Time allocation, p. 592
Leisure, p. 592
Individual labour supply curve, p. 593

PROBLEMS

1. In 2012, national income in Canada was $1819.97 billion. In the same year, 17.73 million workers were employed, at an average wage of $45 204 per worker per year (excluding employers' social contributions).
   a. How much direct compensation of employees was paid in Canada in 2012?
   b. Analyze the factor distribution of income. What percentage of national income was received in the form of direct compensation to employees in 2012 (excluding employers' social contributions)? In light

of Figure 19-1, what percentage of national income do employers' social contributions represent?
   c. Suppose that a wave of corporate downsizing leads many Canadians to open their own businesses. What is the effect on the factor distribution of income?
   d. Suppose the supply of labour rises due to an increase in the retirement age. What happens to the percentage of national income received in the form of compensation of employees?

2. Marty's Frozen Yogourt has the production function per day shown in the accompanying table. The equilibrium wage rate for a worker is $80 per day. Each cup of frozen yogourt sells for $2.

Quantity of labour (workers)	Quantity of frozen yogourt (cups)
0	0
1	110
2	200
3	270
4	300
5	320
6	330

a. Calculate the marginal product of labour for each worker and the value of the marginal product of labour per worker.

b. How many workers should Marty employ?

3. Patty's Pizza has the production function per hour shown in the accompanying table. The hourly wage rate for each worker is $10. Each pizza sells for $2.

Quantity of labour (workers)	Quantity of pizza
0	0
1	9
2	15
3	19
4	22
5	24

a. Calculate the marginal product of labour for each worker and the value of the marginal product of labour per worker.

b. Draw the value of the marginal product of labour curve. Use your diagram to determine how many workers Patty should employ.

c. The price of pizza increases to $4. Calculate the value of the marginal product of labour per worker, and draw the new value of the marginal product of labour curve in your diagram. Use your diagram to determine how many workers Patty should employ.

4. The production function for Patty's Pizza is given in the table in Problem 3. The price of pizza is $2, but the hourly wage rate rises from $10 to $15. Use a diagram to determine how Patty's demand for workers responds as a result of this wage rate increase.

5. Patty's Pizza initially had the production function given in the table in Problem 3. A worker's hourly wage rate was $10, and pizza sold for $2. Now Patty buys a new high-tech pizza oven that allows her workers to become twice as productive as before. That is, the first worker produces 18 pizzas per hour instead of 9, and so on.

a. Calculate the new marginal product of labour and the new value of the marginal product of labour.

b. Use a diagram to determine how Patty's hiring decision responds to this increase in the productivity of her workforce.

6. Jameel runs a driver education school. The more driving instructors he hires, the more driving lessons he can sell. But because he owns a limited number of training automobiles, each additional driving instructor adds less to Jameel's output of driving lessons. The accompanying table shows Jameel's production function per day. Each driving lesson can be sold at $35 per hour.

Quantity of labour (driving instructors)	Quantity of driving lessons (hours)
0	0
1	8
2	15
3	21
4	26
5	30
6	33

Determine Jameel's labour demand schedule (his demand schedule for driving instructors) for each of the following daily wage rates for driving instructors: $160, $180, $200, $220, $240, and $260.

7. Dale and Dana work at a self-service gas station and convenience store. Dale opens up every day, and Dana arrives later to help stock the store. They are both paid the current market wage of $9.50 per hour. But Dale feels he should be paid much more because the revenue generated from the gas pumps he turns on every morning is much higher than the revenue generated by the items that Dana stocks. Assess this argument.

8. In 2007 the wage of farmworkers in Mexico was $11 an hour but the wage of immigrant Mexican farmworkers in California was $9 an hour.

a. Assume that the output sells for the same price in the two countries. Does this imply that the marginal product of labour of farmworkers is higher in Mexico or in California? Explain your answer, and illustrate with a diagram that shows the demand and supply curves for labour in the respective markets. In your diagram, assume that the quantity of labour supplied for any given wage rate is the same for Mexican farmworkers as it is for immigrant Mexican farmworkers in California.

b. Now suppose that farmwork in Mexico is more arduous and more dangerous than farmwork in California. As a result, the quantity supplied of labour for any given wage rate is not the same for Mexican farmworkers as it is for immigrant Mexican farmworkers in California. How does this change your answer to part (a)? What concept best accounts for the difference between wage rates for Mexican farmworkers and immigrant Mexican farmworkers in California?

c. Illustrate your answer to part (b) with a diagram. In this diagram, assume that the quantity of labour demanded for any given wage rate is the same for Mexican and Californian employers.

9. Kendra is the owner of Wholesome Farms, a commercial dairy. Kendra employs labour, land, and capital. In her operations, Kendra can substitute between the amount of labour she employs and the amount of capital she employs. That is, to produce the same quantity of output she can use more labour and less land; similarly, to produce the same quantity of output she can use less labour and more land. However, if she uses more land, she must use more of both labour and capital; if she uses less land, she can use less of both labour and capital. Let w^* represent the annual cost of labour in the market, let r_L^* represent the annual cost of a unit of land in the market, and let r_K^* represent the annual cost of a unit of capital in the market.

a. Suppose that Kendra can maximize her profits by employing less labour and more capital than she is now using but the same amount of land. What three conditions must hold for Kendra's operations (involving her value of the marginal product of labour, land, and capital) for this to be true?

b. Kendra believes that she can increase her profits by renting and using more land. What three conditions must hold (involving her value of the marginal product of labour, land, and capital) for this to be true?

10. For each of the following situations in which similar workers are paid different wages, give the most likely explanation for these wage differences.

a. Test pilots for new jet aircraft earn higher wages than airline pilots.

b. College and university graduates usually have higher earnings in their first year on the job than workers without post-secondary degrees have in their first year on the job.

c. Full professors command higher salaries than assistant professors for teaching the same class.

d. Unionized workers are generally better paid than non-unionized workers.

11. Research consistently finds that despite nondiscrimination policies, visible minority workers on average receive lower wages than white workers do. What are the possible reasons for this? Are these reasons consistent with marginal productivity theory?

12. Greta is an enthusiastic amateur gardener and spends a lot of her free time working in her yard. She also has a demanding and well-paid job as a freelance advertising consultant. Because the advertising business is going through a difficult time, the hourly consulting fee Greta can charge falls. Greta decides to spend more time gardening and less time consulting. Explain her decision in terms of income and substitution effects.

13. Wendy works at a fast-food restaurant. When her wage rate was $5 per hour, she worked 30 hours per week. When her wage rate rose to $6 per hour, she decided to work 40 hours. But when her wage rate rose further to $7, she decided to work only 35 hours.

a. Draw Wendy's individual labour supply curve.

b. Is Wendy's behaviour irrational, or can you find a rational explanation? Explain your answer.

14. You are the premier's economic policy adviser. The premier wants to put in place policies that encourage employed people to work more hours at their jobs and that encourage unemployed people to find and take jobs. Assess each of the following policies in terms of reaching that goal. Explain your reasoning in terms of income and substitution effects, and indicate when the impact of the policy may be ambiguous.

a. The provincial income tax rate is lowered, which has the effect of increasing workers' after-tax wage rate.

b. The provincial income tax rate is increased, which has the effect of decreasing workers' after-tax wage rate.

c. The provincial property tax rate is increased, which reduces workers' after-tax income.

15. A study by Employment and Social Development Canada showed that between 1976 and 2010 the average hours worked per week by a Canadian worker fell from 38 hours per week to 36.6 hours per week. Some believe that the fall in weekly working hours is driven by a rise in wage rate.

a. Use the income and substitution effects to describe the labour supply for the average Canadian. Which effect dominates?

b. There has also been an increase in female labour force participation—more women chose to hold jobs rather than exclusively perform household tasks. For the average woman who has newly entered the labour force, which effect dominates?

c. Draw typical individual labour supply curves that illustrate your answers to part (a) and part (b) above.

Indifference Curve Analysis of Labour Supply

In the body of this chapter, we explained why the labour supply curve can slope downward instead of upward: the substitution effect of a higher wage rate, which provides an incentive to work longer hours, can be outweighed by the income effect of a higher wage rate, which may lead individuals to consume more leisure. In this appendix we show how this analysis can be carried out using the *indifference curves* introduced in Appendix 10A.

The Time Allocation Budget Line

L et's return to the example of Clive, who likes leisure but also likes having money to spend. We now assume that Clive has a total of 80 hours per week that he could spend either working or enjoying as leisure time. (The remaining hours in his week, we assume, are taken up with necessary activities, mainly sleeping.) Let's also assume, initially, that his hourly wage rate is $10.

His consumption possibilities are defined by the **time allocation budget line** in Figure 19A-1, a budget line that shows Clive's trade-offs between consumption of leisure and income. Hours of leisure per week are measured on the horizontal axis, and the money he earns from working is measured on the vertical axis.

The horizontal intercept, point X, is at 80 hours: if Clive didn't work at all, he would have 80 hours of leisure per week but would not earn any money. The vertical intercept, point Y, is at $800: if Clive worked all the time, he would earn $800 per week.

Why can we use a budget line to describe Clive's time allocation choice? The budget lines found in Chapter 10 and its appendix represent the trade-offs facing

A **time allocation budget line** shows an individual's trade-off between consumption of leisure and the income that allows consumption of marketed goods.

FIGURE 19A-1 The Time Allocation Budget Line

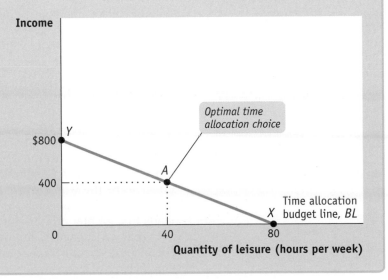

Clive's time allocation budget line shows his trade-off between work, which pays a wage rate of $10 per hour, and leisure. At point X he allocates all his time, 80 hours, to leisure but has no income. At point Y he allocates all his time to work, earning $800, but consumes no leisure. His hourly wage rate of $10, the opportunity cost of an hour of leisure, is equal to minus the slope of the time allocation budget line. We have assumed that point A, at 40 hours of leisure and $400 in income, is Clive's optimal time allocation choice. It obeys the optimal time allocation rule: the additional utility Clive gets from one more hour of leisure must equal the additional utility he gets from the goods he can purchase with one hour's wages.

consumers deciding how to allocate their income among different goods. Here, instead of asking how Clive allocates his income, we ask how he allocates his *time*. But the principles underlying the allocation of income and the allocation of time are the same: each involves allocating a fixed amount of a resource (80 hours of time in this case) with a constant trade-off (Clive must forgo $10 for each additional hour of leisure). So using a budget line is just as appropriate for time allocation as it is for income allocation.

As in the case of ordinary budget lines, opportunity cost plays a key role. The opportunity cost of an hour of leisure is what Clive must forgo by working one less hour—$10 in income. This opportunity cost is, of course, Clive's hourly wage rate and is equal to minus the slope of his time allocation budget line. You can verify this by noting that the slope is equal to minus the vertical intercept, point Y, divided by the horizontal intercept, point X—that is, −$800/(80 hours) = −$10 per hour.

To maximize his utility, Clive must choose the optimal point on the time allocation budget line in Figure 19A-1. In Chapter 10 we saw that a consumer who allocates spending to maximize utility finds the point on the budget line that satisfies the *utility-maximizing principle of marginal analysis:* the marginal utility per dollar spent on two goods must be equal. Although Clive's choice involves allocating time rather than money, the same principles apply.

Since Clive "spends" time rather than money, the counterpart of the utility-maximizing principle of marginal analysis is the **optimal time allocation rule:** the marginal utility Clive gets from the extra money earned from an additional hour spent working must equal the marginal utility of an additional hour of leisure.

The Effect of a Higher Wage Rate

Depending on his tastes, Clive's utility-maximizing choice of hours of leisure and income could lie anywhere on the time allocation budget line in Figure 19A-1. Let's assume that his optimal choice is point A, at which he consumes 40 hours of leisure and earns $400. Now we are ready to link the analysis of time allocation to labour supply.

When Clive chooses a point like A on his time allocation budget line, he is also choosing the quantity of labour he supplies to the labour market. By choosing to consume 40 of his 80 available hours as leisure, he has also chosen to supply the other 40 hours as labour.

Now suppose that Clive's wage rate doubles, from $10 to $20 per hour. The effect of this increase in his wage rate is shown in Figure 19A-2. His time allocation budget line rotates outward: the vertical intercept, which represents the amount he could earn if he devoted all 80 hours to work, shifts upward from point Y to point Z. As a result of the doubling of his wage, Clive would earn $1600 instead of $800 if he devoted all 80 hours to working.

But how will Clive's time allocation actually change? As we saw in the chapter, this depends on the *income effect* and *substitution effect* that we learned about in Chapter 10 and its appendix.

The substitution effect of an increase in the wage rate works as follows. When the wage rate increases, the opportunity cost of an hour of leisure increases; this induces Clive to consume less leisure and work more hours—that is, to substitute hours of work in place of hours of leisure as the wage rate rises. If the substitution effect were the whole story, the individual labour supply curve would look like any ordinary supply curve and would always slope upward—a higher wage rate leads to a greater quantity of labour supplied.

What we learned in our analysis of demand was that for most consumer goods, the income effect isn't very important because most goods account for only a very small share of a consumer's spending. In addition, in the few cases of goods where the income effect is significant—for example, major purchases like housing—it usually reinforces the substitution effect: most goods are normal goods, so when a price increase makes a consumer poorer, he or she buys less of that good.

In the labour/leisure choice, however, the income effect takes on a new significance, for two reasons. First, most people get the great majority of their income from wages. This means that the income effect of a change in the wage rate is *not* small: an increase in the wage rate will generate a significant increase in income. Second, leisure is a normal good: when income rises, other things equal, people tend to consume more leisure and work fewer hours.

So the income effect of a higher wage rate tends to *reduce* the quantity of labour supplied, working in opposition to the substitution effect, which tends to *increase* the quantity of labour supplied. So the net effect of a higher wage rate on the quantity of labour Clive supplies could go either way—depending on his preferences, he might choose to supply more labour, or he might choose to supply less labour. The two panels of Figure 19A-2 illustrate these two outcomes. In each panel, point A represents Clive's initial consumption choice. Panel (a) shows the case in which Clive works more hours in response to a higher wage rate.

FIGURE 19A-2 An Increase in the Wage Rate

The two panels show Clive's initial optimal choice, point A on BL_1, the time allocation budget line corresponding to a wage rate of $10. After his wage rate rises to $20, his budget line rotates out to the new budget line, BL_2: if he spends all his time working, the amount of money he earns rises from $800 to $1600, reflected in the movement from point Y to point Z. This generates two opposing effects: the substitution effect pushes him to consume less leisure and to work more hours; the income effect pushes him to consume more leisure and to work fewer hours. Panel (a) shows the change in time allocation when the substitution effect is stronger: Clive's new optimal choice is point B, representing a decrease in hours of leisure to 30 hours and an increase in hours of labour to 50 hours. In this case the individual labour supply curve slopes upward. Panel (b) shows the change in time allocation when the income effect is stronger: point C is the new optimal choice, representing an increase in hours of leisure to 50 hours and a decrease in hours of labour to 30 hours. Now the individual labour supply curve slopes downward.

(a) The Substitution Effect Dominates

(b) The Income Effect Dominates

FIGURE 19A-3 A Backward-Bending Individual Labour Supply Curve

At lower wage rates, the substitution effect dominates the income effect for this individual. This is illustrated by the movement along the individual labour supply curve from point *A* to point *B*: a rise in the wage rate from W_1 to W_2 leads the quantity of labour supplied to increase from L_1 to L_2. But at higher wage rates, the income effect dominates the substitution effect, shown by the movement from point *B* to point *C*: here, a rise in the wage rate from W_2 to W_3 leads the quantity of labour supplied to decrease from L_2 to L_3.

An increase in the wage rate induces him to move from point *A* to point *B*, where he consumes less leisure than at *A* and therefore works more hours. Here the substitution effect prevails over the income effect. Panel (b) shows the case in which Clive works fewer hours in response to a higher wage rate. Here, he moves from point *A* to point *C*, where he consumes more leisure and works *fewer* hours than at *A*. Here the income effect prevails over the substitution effect.

When the income effect of a higher wage rate is stronger than the substitution effect, the individual labour supply curve, which shows how much labour an individual will supply at any given wage rate will have a segment that slopes the "wrong" way—downward: a higher wage rate leads to a smaller quantity of labour supplied. An example is the segment connecting points *B* and *C* in Figure 19A-3.

Economists believe that the substitution effect usually dominates the income effect in the labour supply decision when an individual's wage rate is low. An individual labour supply curve typically slopes upward for lower wage rates as people work more in response to rising wage rates. But they also believe that many individuals have stronger preferences for leisure and will choose to cut back the number of hours worked as their wage rate continues to rise. For these individuals, the income effect eventually dominates the substitution effect as the wage rate rises, leading their individual labour supply curves to change slope and to "bend backward" at high wage rates. An individual labour supply curve with this feature, called a **backward-bending individual labour supply curve,** is shown in Figure 19A-3. Although an *individual* labour supply curve may bend backward, *market* labour supply curves almost always slope upward over their entire range as higher wage rates draw more new workers into the labour market.

Indifference Curve Analysis

A **backward-bending individual labour supply curve** is an individual labour supply curve that slopes upward at low to moderate wage rates and slopes downward at higher wage rates.

In Appendix 10A, we showed that consumer choice can be represented using the concept of *indifference curves*, which provide a "map" of consumer preferences. If you have covered the appendix, you may find it interesting to learn that indifference curves are also useful for addressing the issue of labour supply. In fact, this is one place where they are particularly helpful.

FIGURE 19A-4 Labour Supply Choice: The Indifference Curve Approach

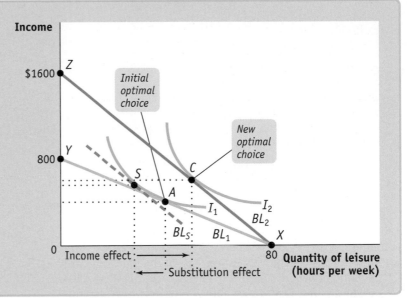

Point A, on BL_1, is Clive's initial optimal choice. After a wage rate increase, his income and utility level increase: his new time allocation budget line is BL_2 and his new optimal choice is point C. This change can be decomposed into the substitution effect, the fall in the hours of leisure from point A to point S, and the income effect, the increase in the number of hours of leisure from point S to point C. As shown here, the income effect dominates the substitution effect: the net result of an increase in the wage rate is an increase in the hours of leisure consumed and a decrease in the hours of labour supplied.

Using indifference curves, Figure 19A-4 shows how an increase in the wage rate can lead to a fall in the quantity of labour supplied. Point A is Clive's initial optimal choice, given an hourly wage rate of $10. It is the same as point A in Figure 19A-2; this time, however, we include an indifference curve to show that it is a point at which the budget line is tangent to the highest possible indifference curve.

Now consider the effect of a rise in the wage rate to $20. Imagine, for a moment, that at the same time Clive was offered a higher wage, he was told that he had to start repaying his student loan and that the good-news/bad-news combination left his utility unchanged. Then he would find himself at point S: on the same indifference curve as at A, but tangent to a steeper budget line, the dashed line BL_S in Figure 19A-4, which is parallel to BL_2. The move from point A to point S is the substitution effect of his wage increase: it leads him to consume less leisure and therefore supply more labour.

But now cancel the repayment on the student loan, and Clive is able to move to a higher indifference curve. His new optimum is at point C, which corresponds to C in panel (b) of Figure 19A-2. The move from point S to point C is the income effect of his wage increase. And we see that this income effect can outweigh the substitution effect: at C he consumes more leisure, and therefore supplies less labour, than he did at A.

PROBLEMS

1. Leandro has 16 hours per day that he can allocate to work or leisure. His job pays a wage rate of $20. Leandro decides to consume 8 hours of leisure. His indifference curves have the usual shape: they slope downward, they do not cross, and they have the characteristic convex shape.

a. Draw Leandro's time allocation budget line for a typical day. Then illustrate the indifference curve at his optimal choice.

Now Leandro's wage rate falls to $10.

b. Draw Leandro's new budget line.

c. Suppose that Leandro now works only 4 hours as a result of his reduced wage rate. Illustrate the indifference curve at his new optimal choice.

d. Leandro's decision to work less as the wage rate falls is the result of a substitution effect and an income effect. In your diagram, show the income effect and the substitution effect from this reduced wage rate. Which effect is stronger?

2. Florence is a highly paid fashion consultant who earns $100 per hour. She has 16 hours per day that she can allocate to work or leisure, and she decides to work for 12 hours.

   a. Draw Florence's time allocation budget line for a typical day, and illustrate the indifference curve at her optimal choice.

   One of Florence's clients is featured on the front page of *Vague*, an influential fashion magazine. As a result, Florence's consulting fee now rises to $500 per hour. Florence decides to work only 10 hours per day.

   b. Draw Florence's new time allocation budget line, and illustrate the indifference curve at her optimal choice.

   c. In your diagram, show the income effect and the substitution effect from this increase in the wage rate. Which effect is stronger?

3. Tamara has 80 hours per week that she can allocate to work or leisure. Her job pays a wage rate of $20 per hour, but Tamara is being taxed on her income in the following way. On the first $400 that Tamara makes, she pays no tax. That is, for the first 20 hours she works, her net wage—what she takes home after taxes—is $20 per hour. On all income above $400,

Tamara pays a 75% tax. That is, for all hours above the first 20 hours, her net wage rate is only $5 per hour. Tamara decides to work 30 hours. Her indifference curves have the usual shape.

   a. Draw Tamara's time allocation budget line for a typical week. Also illustrate the indifference curve at her optimal choice.

   The government changes the tax scheme. Now only the first $100 of income is tax-exempt. That is, for the first 5 hours she works, Tamara's net wage rate is $20 per hour. But the government reduces the tax rate on all other income to 50%. That is, for all hours above the first 5 hours, Tamara's net wage rate is now $10. After these changes, Tamara finds herself exactly equally as well off as before. That is, her new optimal choice is on the same indifference curve as her initial optimal choice.

   b. Draw Tamara's new time allocation budget line on the same diagram. Also illustrate her optimal choice. Bear in mind that she is equally as well off (on the same indifference curve) as before the tax changes occurred.

   c. Will Tamara work more or less than before the changes to the tax scheme? Why?

CHAPTER 20

Uncertainty, Risk, and Private Information

A TOUGH TIME FOR INSURERS

The 2013 flooding in Alberta was the largest insured disaster in Canadian history.

WHAT YOU WILL LEARN IN THIS CHAPTER

❭ That **risk** is a key feature of the economy and that most people are **risk-averse**

❭ Why diminishing marginal utility makes people risk-averse and determines the **premium** they are willing to pay to reduce risk

❭ How risk can be traded—the risk-averse can pay others to assume part of their risk

❭ How exposure to risk can be reduced through **diversification** and **pooling**

❭ The special problems posed by **private information**—when some people know things that other people do not

WORLD INSURERS HAVE FACED tough times in the twenty-first century. The terrorist attacks of September 11, 2001, led to losses of about US$23 billion. A decade later, 2011 was one of the industry's worst ever according to Swiss Reinsurance: economic losses from natural and industrial disasters were US$370 billion worldwide, while insured losses totalled US$116 billion.

According to the Insurance Information Institute, the industry's worst year on record was 2005. That year saw flooding in India, a devastating earthquake in Pakistan, a train derailment in Japan, and three major hurricanes striking the United States. Hurricane Katrina was the single worst natural disaster ever to hit the United States: over 1400 dead, nearly US$50 billion in losses to private insurers, and US$23 billion in losses to the government's National Flood Insurance Program. Moreover, these figures significantly understate the true level of loss because many people were uninsured or underinsured.

For Canadian insurers, 2013 was a record-breaking year. They paid out more than $3 billion for damages due to severe weather. In June massive flooding in Alberta caused an estimated $5 billion in economic damages, about $2 billion of which was insured. The Insurance Bureau of Canada called it the largest insured disaster in Canadian history. On July 6th a train derailment in Lac-Mégantic, Quebec, caused explosions that destroyed most of the downtown and killed 47 people. Insured damages are estimated at $50 million. Two days later, heavy rain in Toronto caused severe flash flooding and resulted in about $940 million in insured damages—Ontario's largest insured natural disaster. Then in December, eastern Canada was hit hard by ice storms resulting in more than $200 million in insured damages.

Anyone who lives in an area threatened by natural disasters knows that uncertainty is a feature of the real world. Up to this point, we have assumed that people make decisions with knowledge of exactly how the future will unfold. (The exception being health insurance decisions, which we discussed in Chapter 19.) In reality, people often make economic decisions, such as whether to build a house in a coastal area, without full knowledge of future events. As the victims of recent catastrophes have learned, making decisions when the future is uncertain carries with it the *risk of loss*.

It is often possible for individuals to use markets to reduce their risk. For example, flood victims who had insurance were able to receive some, if not complete, compensation for their losses. In fact, through insurance and other devices, the modern economy offers many ways for individuals to reduce their exposure to risk.

However, a market economy cannot always solve the problems created by uncertainty. Markets do very well at coping with risk when two conditions hold: when risk can be reasonably well *diversified* and when the probability of loss is equally well known by everyone. Over the past several years, the significant increase in extreme weather events has led many insurers to sharply reduce coverage of weather-related loss: they no longer believe that profits from areas with good weather will offset losses from flood- and tornado-prone areas. But in practice, the second condition is often the more limiting one. Markets run into trouble when some people know things that others do not—a situation that involves what is called *private information*. We'll see that private information can cause inefficiency by preventing mutually beneficial transactions from occurring—especially in insurance markets.

In this chapter we'll examine why most people dislike risk. Then we'll explore how a market economy allows people to reduce risk at a price. Finally, we'll turn to the special problems created for markets by private information. ■

A **random variable** is a variable with an uncertain future value.

The **expected value** of a random variable is the weighted average of all possible values, where the weights on each possible value correspond to the probability of that value occurring.

A **state of the world** is a possible future event.

The Economics of Risk Aversion

In general, people don't like risk and are willing to pay a price to avoid it. Just ask the global insurance industry, which collects more than US$4.6 trillion in premiums every year, including more than $100 billion in Canada alone. But what exactly is risk? And why don't most people like it? To answer these questions, we need to look briefly at the concept of *expected value* and the meaning of uncertainty. Then we can turn to why people dislike *risk*.

Expectations and Uncertainty

The Lee family doesn't know how big its medical bills will be next year. If all goes well, it won't have any medical expenses at all. Let's assume that there's a 50% chance of that happening. But if family members require out-of-country hospitalization or expensive uninsured drugs and time away from paid employment, they will face medical expenses of $10 000. Let's assume that there's also a 50% chance that these high medical expenses will materialize.

In this example—which is designed to illustrate a point, rather than to be realistic—the Lees's medical expenses for the coming year are a **random variable,** a variable that has an uncertain future value. No one can predict with certainty which of its possible values, or outcomes, a random variable will take. But that doesn't mean we can say nothing about the Lees's future medical expenses. On the contrary, an actuary (a person trained in evaluating uncertain future events) could calculate the **expected value** of expenses next year—the weighted average of all possible values, where the weights on each possible value correspond to the probability of that value occurring. In this example, the expected value of the Lees's medical expenses is $(0.5 \times \$0) + (0.5 \times \$10\ 000) = \$5000$.

To derive the general formula for the expected value of a random variable, we imagine that there are a number of different **states of the world,** possible future events. Each state is associated with a different realized value—the value that actually occurs in that state—of the random variable. You don't know which state of the world will actually occur, but you can assign probabilities, one for each state of the world. Let's assume that P_1 is the probability of state 1, P_2 the probability of state 2, and so on. And you know the realized value of the random value in each state of the world: S_1 in state 1, S_2 in state 2, and so on. Let's also assume that there are N possible states. Then the expected value of a random variable is:

(20-1) *Expected value of a random variable*
$$EV = (P_1 \times S_1) + (P_2 \times S_2) + \ldots + (P_N \times S_N)$$

In the case of the Lee family, there are only two possible states of the world, each with a probability of 0.5.

Notice, however, that the Lee family doesn't actually expect to pay $5000 in medical bills next year. That's because in this example there is no state of the world in which the family pays exactly $5000. Either the family pays nothing, or it pays $10 000. So the Lees face considerable uncertainty about their future medical expenses.

But what if the Lee family can buy supplemental health insurance that will cover any medical expenses they face that are not covered by a government health insurance plan, whatever they turn out to be? Suppose, in particular, that the family can pay $5000 up front in return for full coverage of whatever medical expenses actually arise during the coming year. Then the Lees's future medical expenses are no longer uncertain *for them:* in return for $5000—an amount equal to the expected value of the medical expenses—the insurance company assumes all responsibility for paying those medical expenses. Would this be a good deal from the Lees's point of view?

Yes, it would—or at least most families would think so. Most people prefer, other things equal, to reduce **risk**—uncertainty about future outcomes. (We'll focus here on **financial risk,** in which the uncertainty is about monetary outcomes, as opposed to uncertainty about outcomes that can't be assigned a monetary value.) In fact, most people are willing to pay a substantial price to reduce their risk; that's why we have an insurance industry. But before we study the market for insurance, we need to understand why people feel that risk is a bad thing, an attitude that economists call *risk aversion*. The source of risk aversion lies in a concept we first encountered in our analysis of consumer demand, back in Chapter 10: *diminishing marginal utility*.

The Logic of Risk Aversion

To understand how diminishing marginal utility gives rise to risk aversion, we need to look not only at the Lees's medical costs but also at how those costs affect the income the family has left after medical expenses. Let's assume the family knows that it will have an income of $30 000 next year. If the family has no medical expenses, it will be left with all of that income. If its medical expenses are $10 000, its income after medical expenses will be only $20 000. Since we have assumed that there is an equal chance of these two outcomes, the expected value of the Lees's income after medical expenses is (0.5 × $30 000) + (0.5 × $20 000) = $25 000. At times we will simply refer to this as expected income.

But as we'll now see, if the family's utility function has the shape typical of most families', its **expected utility**—the expected value of its total utility given uncertainty about future outcomes—is less than it would be if the family didn't face any risk and knew with certainty that its income after medical expenses would be $25 000.

To see why, we need to look at how total utility depends on income. Panel (a) of Figure 20-1 shows a hypothetical utility function for the Lee family, where total utility depends on income—the amount of money the Lees have available for consumption of goods and services (after they have paid any medical bills). The table within the figure shows how the family's total utility varies over the income range of $20 000 to $30 000. As usual, the utility function slopes upward, because more income leads to higher total utility. Notice as well that the curve gets flatter as we move up and to the right, which reflects diminishing marginal utility.

In Chapter 10 we applied the principle of diminishing marginal utility to individual goods and services: each successive unit of a good or service that a consumer purchases adds less to his or her total utility. The same principle applies to income used for consumption: each successive dollar of income adds less to total utility than the previous dollar. Panel (b) shows how marginal utility varies with income, confirming that marginal utility of income falls as income rises. As we'll see in a moment, diminishing marginal utility is the key to understanding the desire of individuals to reduce risk.

To analyze how a person's utility is affected by risk, economists start from the assumption that individuals facing uncertainty maximize their *expected* utility. We can use the data in Figure 20-1 to calculate the Lee family's expected utility. We'll first do the calculation assuming that the Lees have no supplemental insurance, and then we'll recalculate it assuming that they have purchased supplemental insurance.

Without supplemental insurance, if the Lees are lucky and don't incur any medical expenses, they will have an income of $30 000, generating total utility of 1080 utils. But if they have no supplemental insurance and are unlucky, incurring $10 000 in medical expenses, they will have just $20 000 of their income to spend on consumption and total utility of only 920 utils. So *without supplemental insurance,* the family's expected utility is (0.5 × 1080) + (0.5 × 920) = 1000 utils.

Now let's suppose that an insurance company offers to pay whatever medical expenses the family incurs during the next year in return for a **premium**—a

---

Risk is uncertainty about future outcomes. When the uncertainty is about monetary outcomes, it becomes **financial risk.**

Expected utility is the expected value of an individual's total utility given uncertainty about future outcomes.

A **premium** is a payment to an insurance company in return for the insurance company's promise to pay a claim in certain states of the world.

FIGURE **20-1** The Utility Function and Marginal Utility Curve of a Risk-Averse Family

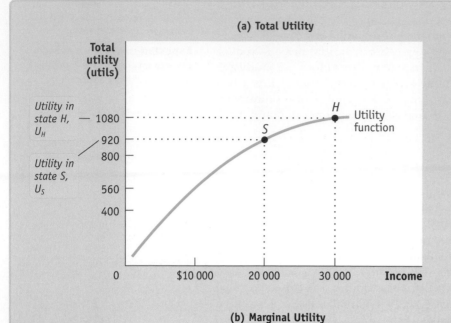

(a) Total Utility

Income	Total utility (utils)
$20 000	920
21 000	945
22 000	968
23 000	989
24 000	1008
25 000	1025
26 000	1040
27 000	1053
28 000	1064
29 000	1073
30 000	1080

(b) Marginal Utility

Panel (a) shows how the total utility of the Lee family depends on its income available for consumption (that is, its income after medical expenses). The curve slopes upward: more income leads to higher total utility. But it gets flatter as we move up it and to the right, reflecting diminishing marginal utility. Panel (b) reflects the negative relationship between income and marginal utility when there is risk aversion: the marginal utility from each additional $1000 of income is lower the higher your income. So the marginal utility of income is higher when the family has high medical expenses (point S) than when it has low medical expenses (point H).

payment to the insurance company—of $5000. Note that the amount of the premium in this case is equal to the expected value of the Lees's medical expenses (not covered by a government health insurance plan)—the expected value of their future claim against the policy. An insurance policy with this feature, for which the premium is equal to the expected value of the claim, has a special name—a **fair insurance policy.**

If the family purchases this fair insurance policy, the expected value of its income available for consumption is the *same* as it would be without insurance: $25 000—that is, $30 000 minus the $5000 premium. But the family's risk has been eliminated: the family has an income available for consumption of $25 000 *for sure*, which means that it receives the utility level associated with an income of $25 000. Reading from the table in Figure 20-1, we see that this utility level is 1025 utils. Or to put it a slightly different way, their expected utility with supplemental insurance is 1 × 1025 = 1025 utils, because with supplemental insurance they will receive a utility of 1025 utils with a probability of 1. And this is higher than the level of expected utility without supplemental insurance—only 1000 utils. So

A **fair insurance policy** is an insurance policy for which the premium is equal to the expected value of the claim.

by eliminating risk through the purchase of a fair insurance policy, the family increases its expected utility even though its expected income hasn't changed.

The calculations for this example are summarized in Table 20-1. This example shows that the Lees, like most people in real life, are **risk-averse:** they will choose to reduce the risk they face when the cost of that reduction leaves the expected value of their income or wealth unchanged. So the Lees, like most people, will be willing to buy fair insurance. Similarly, being risk-averse they will avoid a fair gamble, even if it is free.

Risk-averse individuals will choose to reduce the risk they face when that reduction leaves the expected value of their income or wealth unchanged.

TABLE **20-1**

The Effect of Fair Insurance on the Lee Family's Income Available for Consumption and Expected Utility

	Income in different states of the world		Expected value of income available for consumption	Expected utility
	$0 in extra/supplemental medical expenses (0.5 probability)	$10 000 in extra/supplemental medical expenses (0.5 probability)		
Without supplemental insurance	$30 000	$20 000	(0.5 × $30 000) + (0.5 × $20 000) = $25 000	(0.5 × 1080 utils) + (0.5 × 920 utils) = 1000 utils
With fair supplemental insurance	$25 000	$25 000	(0.5 × $25 000) + (0.5 × $25 000) = $25 000	(0.5 × 1025 utils) + (0.5 × 1025 utils) = 1025 utils

You might think that this result depends on the specific numbers we have chosen. In fact, however, the proposition that the purchase of a fair insurance policy increases expected utility depends on only one assumption: diminishing marginal utility. The reason is that *with diminishing marginal utility, a dollar gained when income is low adds more to utility than a dollar gained when income is high.* That is, having an additional dollar matters more when you are facing hard times than when you are facing good times. And as we will shortly see, a fair insurance policy is desirable because it transfers a dollar from high-income states (where it is valued less) to low-income states (where it is valued more).

But first, let's see how diminishing marginal utility leads to risk aversion by examining expected utility more closely. In the case of the Lee family, there are two states of the world; let's call them H and S, for healthy and sick. In state H the family has no medical expenses; in state S it has $10 000 in medical expenses. Let's use the symbols U_H and U_S to represent the Lee family's total utility in each state. Then the family's expected utility is:

(20-2) Expected utility = (Probability of state H × Total utility in state H) + (Probability of state S × Total utility in state S)
= $(0.5 \times U_H) + (0.5 \times U_S)$

The fair insurance policy *reduces* the family's income available for consumption in state H by $5000, but it *increases* it in state S by the same amount. As we've just seen, we can use the utility function to directly calculate the effects of these changes on expected utility. But as we have also seen in many other contexts, we gain more insight into individual choice by focusing on *marginal* utility.

To use marginal utility to analyze the effects of fair insurance, let's imagine introducing the insurance a bit at a time, say in 5000 small steps. At each of these steps, we reduce income in state H by $1 and simultaneously increase income in state S by $1. At each of these steps, total utility in state H falls by the marginal utility of income in that state but total utility in state S rises by the marginal utility of income in that state.

Now look again at panel (b) of Figure 20-1, which shows how marginal utility varies with income. Point S shows marginal utility when the Lee family's income is

$20 000; point *H* shows marginal utility when income is $30 000. Clearly, marginal utility is higher when income after medical expenses is low. Because of diminishing marginal utility, an additional dollar of income adds more to total utility when the family has low income (point *S*) than when it has high income (point *H*).

This tells us that the gain in expected utility from increasing income in state *S* is larger than the loss in expected utility from reducing income in state *H* by the same amount. So at each step of the process of reducing risk, by transferring $1 of income from state *H* to state *S*, expected utility increases. This is the same as saying that the family is risk-averse; that is, risk aversion is a result of diminishing marginal utility.

Almost everyone is risk-averse, because almost everyone has diminishing marginal utility. But the degree of risk aversion varies among individuals—some people are more risk-averse than others. To illustrate this point, Figure 20-2 compares two individuals, Danny and Mel. We suppose that each of them earns the same income now but is confronted with the possibility of earning either $1000 more or $1000 less.

FIGURE **20-2** **Differences in Risk Aversion**

Danny and Mel have different utility functions. Danny is highly risk-averse: a gain of $1000 in income, which moves him from *N* to *H*$_D$, adds only a few utils to his total utility, but a $1000 fall in income, which moves him from *N* to *L*$_D$, reduces his total utility by a large number of utils. By contrast, Mel gains almost as many utils from a $1000 rise in income (the movement from *N* to *H*$_M$) as he loses from a $1000 fall in income (the movement from *N* to *L*$_M$). This difference—reflected in the differing slopes of the two men's marginal utility curves—means that Danny would be willing to pay much more than Mel for insurance.

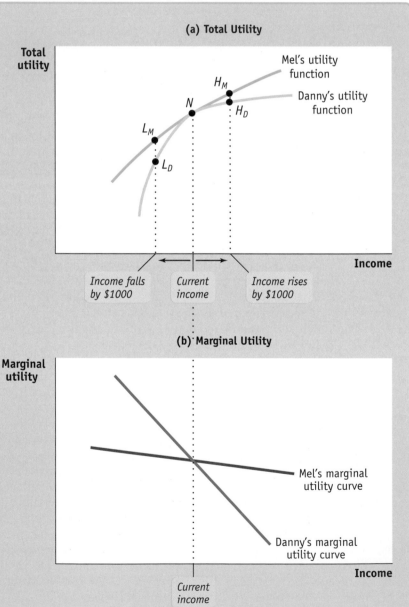

FOR INQUIRING MINDS

THE PARADOX OF GAMBLING

If most people are risk-averse and risk-averse individuals won't take a fair gamble, how come there are about 100 casinos in Canada? And why do Las Vegas, Macau, Monte Carlo, and other places where gambling is legal do so much business?

After all, a casino doesn't even offer gamblers a fair gamble: all the games in any gambling facility are designed so that, on average, the casino makes money. So why would anyone play their games?

You might argue that the gambling industry caters to the minority of people who are actually the opposite of risk-averse: risk-loving. But a glance at the customers of Las Vegas hotels quickly refutes

Gambling: enjoyment or addiction?

that hypothesis: most of them aren't daredevils who also skydive and hang-glide. Instead, most of them are ordinary people who have health and life insurance and who wear seat belts. In other words, they are risk-averse like the rest of us.

So why do people gamble? Presumably because they enjoy the experience.

Also, gambling may be one of those areas where the assumption of rational behaviour goes awry. Psychologists have concluded that gambling can be addictive in ways that are not that different from the addictive effects of drugs. Taking dangerous drugs is irrational; so is excessive gambling. Alas, both happen all the same.

Panel (a) of Figure 20-2 shows how each individual's total utility would be affected by the change in income. Danny would gain very few utils from a rise in income, which moves him from N to H_D, but lose a large number of utils from a fall in income, which moves him from N to L_D. That is, he is highly risk-averse. This is reflected in panel (b) by his steeply declining marginal utility curve. Mel, though, as shown in panel (a), would gain almost as many utils from higher income, which moves him from N to H_M, as he would lose from lower income, which moves him from N to L_M. He is barely risk-averse at all. This is reflected in his marginal utility curve in panel (b), which is almost horizontal. So other things equal, Danny will gain a lot more utility from insurance than Mel will. Someone who is completely insensitive to risk is called **risk-neutral** (and has a linear utility function).

Individuals differ in risk aversion for two main reasons: differences in preferences and differences in initial income or wealth.

- *Differences in preferences.* Other things equal, people simply differ in how much their marginal utility is affected by their level of income. Someone whose marginal utility is relatively unresponsive to changes in income will be much less sensitive to risk. In contrast, someone whose marginal utility depends greatly on changes in income will be much more risk-averse.

- *Differences in initial income or wealth.* The possible loss of $1000 makes a big difference to a family living below the poverty line; it makes very little difference to someone who earns $1 million a year. In general, people with high incomes or high wealth will be less risk-averse.

Differences in risk aversion have an important consequence: they affect how much an individual is willing to pay to avoid risk.

Paying to Avoid Risk

The risk-averse Lee family is clearly better off taking out a fair insurance policy—a policy that leaves their expected income unchanged but eliminates their risk. Unfortunately, real insurance policies are rarely fair: because insurance companies have to cover other costs, such as

A **risk-neutral** person is completely insensitive to risk.

⚠ PITFALLS

BEFORE THE FACT VERSUS AFTER THE FACT

Why is an insurance policy different from a doughnut?

No, it's not a riddle. Although the supply and demand for insurance behave like the supply and demand for any good or service, the payoff is very different. When you buy a doughnut, you know what you're going to get; when you buy insurance, by definition you *don't* know what you're going to get. If you bought car insurance and then didn't have an accident, you got nothing from the policy, except peace of mind, and might wish that you hadn't bothered. But if you did have an accident, you probably would be glad that you bought insurance that covered the cost.

This means we have to be careful in assessing the rationality of insurance purchases (or, for that matter, any decision made in the face of uncertainty). *After the fact*—after the uncertainty has been resolved—such decisions are almost always subject to second-guessing. But that doesn't mean that the decision was wrong *before the fact*, given the information available at the time.

One highly successful Wall Street investor told us that he never looks back—that as long as he believes he made the right decision given what he knew when he made it, he never reproaches himself if things turn out badly. That's the right attitude, and it almost surely contributes to his success.

salaries for salespeople and actuaries, they charge more than they expect to pay in claims. Will the Lee family still want to purchase an "unfair" insurance policy—one for which the premium is larger than the expected claim?

It depends on the size of the premium. Look again at Table 20-1. We know that without supplemental insurance, expected utility is 1000 utils. Also, supplemental insurance costing $5000 raises expected utility to 1025 utils. If the premium were $6000, the Lees would be left with an income of $24 000, which, as you can see from Figure 20-1, would give them a total utility of 1008 utils—which is still higher than their expected utility if they had no supplemental insurance at all. So the Lees would be willing to buy supplemental insurance with a $6000 premium. But they wouldn't be willing to pay $7000, which would reduce their income to $23 000 and their total utility to 989 utils.

This example shows that risk-averse individuals are willing to make deals that reduce their expected income but also reduce their risk: they are willing to pay a premium that exceeds their expected claim. The more risk-averse they are, the higher the premium they are willing to pay. That willingness to pay is what makes the insurance industry possible. In contrast, a risk-neutral person is unwilling to pay anything at all to reduce his or her risk.

ECONOMICS ▸ IN ACTION

WARRANTIES

Many expensive consumer goods—electronic devices, major appliances, cars—come with some form of *warranty*. Typically, the manufacturer guarantees to repair or replace the item if something goes wrong with it during some specified period after purchase—usually six months or one year.

Why do manufacturers offer warranties? Part of the answer is that warranties *signal* to consumers that the goods are of high quality. But mainly warranties are a form of consumer insurance. For many people, the cost of repairing or replacing an expensive item like a refrigerator—or, worse yet, a car—would be a serious burden. If they were obliged to come up with the cash, their consumption of other goods would be restricted; as a result, their marginal utility of income would be higher than if they didn't have to pay for repairs.

So a warranty that covers the cost of repair or replacement increases the consumer's expected utility, even if the cost of the warranty is greater than the expected future claim paid by the manufacturer.

Warranties are a form of consumer insurance.

- The **expected value** of a **random variable** is the weighted average of all possible values, where the weight corresponds to the probability of a given value occurring.

- Uncertainty about **states of the world** entails **risk,** or **financial risk** when there is an uncertain monetary outcome. When faced with uncertainty, consumers choose the option yielding the highest level of **expected utility.**

- Most people are **risk-averse:** they would be willing to purchase a **fair insurance policy** in which the premium is equal to the expected value of the claim.

- Risk aversion arises from diminishing marginal utility. Differences in preferences and in income or wealth lead to differences in risk aversion.

- Depending on the size of the **premium,** a risk-averse person may be willing to purchase an "unfair" insurance policy with a premium larger than the expected claim. The greater your risk aversion, the greater the premium you are willing to pay. A **risk-neutral** person is unwilling to pay any premium to avoid risk.

CHECK YOUR UNDERSTANDING 20-1

1. Compare two families who own homes near the floodplain of the Red River in Manitoba. Which family is likely to be more risk-averse—(i) a family with income of $2 million per year or (ii) a family with income of $60 000 per year? Would either family be willing to buy an "unfair" insurance policy to cover losses to their Manitoba home?

2. Karma's income next year is uncertain: there is a 60% probability she will make $22 000 and a 40% probability she will make $35 000. The accompanying table shows some income and utility levels for Karma.

   a. What is Karma's expected income? Her expected utility?

b. What certain income level, sometimes called the certainty equivalent, leaves her as well off as her uncertain income? What does this imply about Karma's attitudes toward risk? Explain.

c. Would Karma be willing to pay some amount of money greater than zero for an insurance policy that guarantees her an income of $26 000? Explain.

Income	Total utility (utils)
$22 000	850
25 000	1014
26 000	1056
35 000	1260

Solutions appear at back of book.

Buying, Selling, and Reducing Risk

Lloyd's of London is the oldest existing commercial insurance company, and it is an institution with an illustrious past. Originally formed in the eighteenth century to help merchants cope with the risks of commerce, it grew in the heyday of the British Empire into a mainstay of imperial trade.

The basic idea of Lloyd's was simple. In the eighteenth century, shipping goods via sailing vessels was risky: the chance that a ship would sink in a storm or be captured by pirates was fairly high. The merchant who owned the ship and its cargo could easily be ruined financially by such an event. Lloyd's matched shipowners seeking insurance with wealthy investors who promised to compensate a merchant if his ship was lost. In return, the merchant paid the investor a fee in advance; if his ship *didn't* sink, the investor still kept the fee. In effect, the merchant paid a price to relieve himself of risk. By matching people who wanted to purchase insurance with people who wanted to provide it, Lloyd's performed the functions of a market. The fact that British merchants could use Lloyd's to reduce their risk made many more people in Britain willing to undertake merchant trade.

Insurance companies have changed quite a lot from the early days of Lloyd's. They no longer consist of wealthy individuals deciding on insurance deals over port and boiled mutton. But asking why Lloyd's worked to the mutual benefit of merchants and investors is a good way to understand how the market economy as a whole "trades" and thereby transforms risk.

The insurance industry rests on two principles. The first is that trade in risk, like trade in any good or service, can produce mutual gains. In this case, the gains come when people who are less willing to bear risk transfer it to people who are more willing to bear it. The second is that some risk can be made to disappear through *diversification*. Let's consider each principle in turn.

Trading Risk

It may seem a bit strange to talk about "trading" risk. After all, risk is a bad thing—and aren't we supposed to be trading goods and services?

But people often trade away things they don't like to other people who dislike them less. Suppose you have just bought a house for $100 000, the average price for a house in your community. But you have now learned, to your horror, that the building next door is being turned into a nightclub and bar. You want to sell the house immediately and are willing to accept $95 000 for it. But who will now be willing to buy it? The answer: a person who doesn't really mind late-night noise. Such a person might be willing to pay up to $100 000. So there is an opportunity here for a mutually beneficial deal—you are willing to sell for as little as $95 000, and the other person is willing to pay as much as $100 000, so any price in between will benefit both of you.

The key point is that the two parties have different sensitivities to noise, which enables those who most dislike noise, in effect, to pay other people to make their lives quieter. Trading risk works exactly the same way: people who want to reduce the risk they face can pay other people who are less sensitive to risk to take some of their risk away.

The funds that an insurer places at risk when providing insurance are called the insurer's **capital at risk.**

As we saw in the previous section, individual preferences account for some of the variations in people's attitudes toward risk, but differences in income and wealth are probably the principal reason behind different risk sensitivities. Lloyd's made money by matching wealthy investors who were more risk-tolerant with less wealthy and therefore more risk-averse shipowners.

Suppose, staying with our Lloyd's of London story, that a merchant whose ship went down would lose £1000 (this includes the cost of the ship, all its contents, and the lost revenue) and that there was a 10% chance of such a disaster. The expected loss in this case would be 0.10 × £1000 = £100. But the merchant, whose whole livelihood was at stake, might have been willing to pay £150 to be compensated in the amount of £1000 if the ship sank. Meanwhile, a wealthy investor for whom the loss of £1000 was no big deal would have been willing to take this risk for a return only slightly better than the expected loss—say, £110. Clearly, there is room for a mutually beneficial deal here: the merchant pays something less than £150 and more than £110—say, £130—in return for compensation if the ship goes down. In effect, he has paid a less risk-averse individual to bear the burden of his risk. Everyone has been made better off by this transaction.

The funds that an insurer places at risk when providing insurance are called the insurer's **capital at risk.** In our example, the wealthy Lloyd's investor places capital of £1000 at risk in return for a premium of £130. In general, the amount of capital that potential insurers are willing to place at risk depends, other things equal, on the premium offered. If every ship is worth £1000 and has a 10% chance of going down, nobody would offer insurance for less than a £100 premium, equal to the expected claim. In fact, only an investor who isn't risk-averse at all—that is, who is risk-neutral—would be willing to offer a policy at that price, because accepting a £100 premium would leave the insurer's expected income unchanged while increasing his or her risk.

Suppose there is one investor who is risk-neutral; but the next most willing investor is slightly risk-averse and insists on a £105 premium. The next investor, being somewhat more risk-averse, demands a premium of £110, and so on. By varying the premium and asking how many insurers would be willing to provide insurance at that premium, we can trace out a supply curve for insurance, as shown in Figure 20-3. As the premium increases as we move up the supply curve, more risk-averse investors are induced to provide coverage.

FIGURE **20-3** The Supply of Insurance

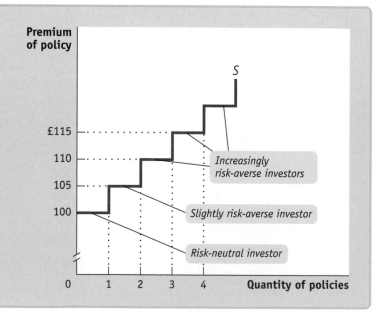

This is the supply of insurance policies to provide £1000 in coverage to a merchant ship that has a 10% chance of being lost. Each investor has £1000 of capital at risk. The lowest possible premium at which a policy is offered is £100, equal to the expected claim, and only a risk-neutral investor is willing to supply this policy. As the premium increases, investors who are more risk-averse are induced to supply policies to the market, increasing the quantity of policies supplied.

FIGURE   **20-4**   The Demand for Insurance

FIGURE   **20-4**   The Demand for Insurance

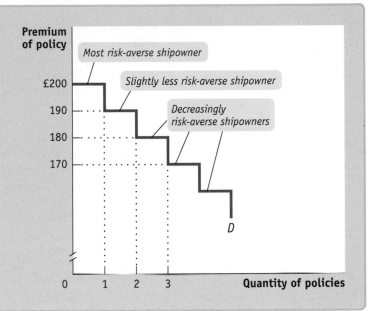

This is the demand for insurance policies for £1000 in coverage of a merchant ship that has a 10% chance of being lost. In this example, the highest premium at which anyone demands a policy is £200, which only the most risk-averse shipowner will desire. As the premium falls, shipowners who are less risk-averse are induced to demand policies, increasing the quantity of policies demanded.

Meanwhile, potential buyers will consider their willingness to pay a given premium, defining the demand curve for insurance. In Figure 20-4, the highest premium that any shipowner is willing to pay is £200. Who's willing to pay this? The most risk-averse shipowner, of course. A slightly less risk-averse shipowner might be willing to pay £190, an even slightly less risk-averse shipowner is willing to pay £180, and so on.

Now imagine a market in which there are thousands of shipowners and potential insurers, so that the supply and demand curves for insurance are smooth lines. In this market, as in markets for ordinary goods and services, there will be an equilibrium price and quantity. Figure 20-5 illustrates such a market equilibrium at a premium of £130, with a total quantity of 5000 policies bought and sold, representing a total capital at risk of £5 000 000.

FIGURE   **20-5**   The Insurance Market

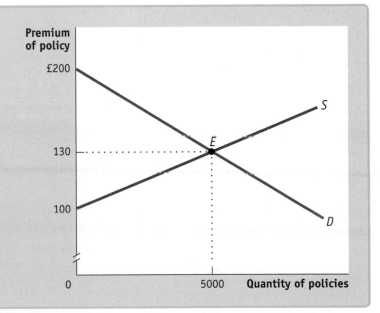

Here we represent the hypothetical market for insuring a merchant ship, where each ship requires £1000 in coverage. The demand curve is made up of shipowners who wish to buy insurance, and the supply curve is made up of wealthy investors who wish to supply insurance. In this example, at a premium of £200, only the most risk-averse shipowners will purchase insurance; at a premium of £100, only risk-neutral investors are willing to supply insurance. The equilibrium is at a premium of £130 with 5000 policies bought and sold. In the absence of *private information*, the insurance market leads to an efficient allocation of risk.

Notice that in this market risk is transferred from the people who most want to get rid of it (the most risk-averse shipowners) to the people least bothered by risk (the least risk-averse investors). So just as markets for goods and services typically produce an efficient allocation of resources, markets for risk also typically lead to an **efficient allocation of risk**—an allocation of risk in which those who are most willing to bear risk are those who end up bearing it. But as in the case of the markets for goods and services, there is an important qualification to this result: there are well-defined cases in which the market for risk fails to achieve efficiency. These arise from the presence of *private information,* an important topic that we will cover in the next section.

The trading of risk between individuals who differ in their degree of risk aversion plays an extremely important role in the economy, but it is not the only way that markets can help people cope with risk. Under some circumstances, markets can perform a sort of magic trick: they can make some (though rarely all) of the risk that individuals face simply disappear.

Making Risk Disappear: The Power of Diversification

In the early days of Lloyd's, British merchant ships traversed the world, trading spices and silk from Asia, tobacco and rum from the New World, and textiles and wool from Britain, among many other goods. Each of the many routes that British ships took had its own unique risks—pirates in the Caribbean, gales in the North Atlantic, typhoons in the Indian Ocean.

In the face of all these risks, how were merchants able to survive? One important way was by reducing their risks by not putting all their eggs in one basket: by sending different ships to different destinations, they could reduce the probability that all their ships would be lost. A strategy of investing in such a way as to reduce the probability of severe losses is known as *diversification.* As we'll now see, diversification can often make some of the economy's risk disappear.

Lloyd's enables its investors to trade risks and diversify.

Let's stay with our shipping example. It was all too likely that a pirate might seize a merchant ship in the Caribbean or that a typhoon might sink another ship in the Indian Ocean. But the key point here is that the various threats to shipping didn't have much to do with each other. So it was considerably less likely that a merchant who had one ship in the Caribbean and another ship in the Indian Ocean in a given year would lose them both, one to a pirate and the other to a typhoon. After all, there was no connection: the actions of cutthroats in the Caribbean had no influence on weather in the Indian Ocean, or vice versa.

Statisticians refer to such events—events that have no connection, so that one is no more likely to happen if the other does than if it does not—as **independent events.** Many unpredictable events are independent of each other. If you toss a coin twice, the probability that it will come up heads on the second toss is the same whether it came up heads or tails on the first toss. If your house burns down today, it does not affect the probability that my house will burn down the same day (unless we live next door to each other or employ the services of the same incompetent electrician).

There is a simple rule for calculating the probability that two independent events will both happen: multiply the probability that one event would happen on its own by the probability that the other event would happen on its own. If you toss a coin once, the probability that it will come up heads is 0.5; if you toss the coin twice, the probability that it will come up heads *both* times is $0.5 \times 0.5 = 0.25$.

But what did it matter to shipowners or Lloyd's investors that ship losses in the Caribbean and ship losses in the Indian Ocean were independent events? The

An **efficient allocation of risk** is an allocation of risk in which those who are most willing to bear risk are those who end up bearing it.

Two possible events are **independent events** if each of them is neither more nor less likely to happen if the other one happens.

answer is that by spreading their investments across different parts of the world, shipowners or Lloyd's investors could make some of the riskiness of the shipping business simply disappear.

Let's suppose that Joseph Moneypenny, Esq., is wealthy enough to outfit two ships—and let's ignore for a moment the possibility of insuring his ships. Should Mr. Moneypenny equip two ships for the Caribbean trade and send them off together? Or should he send one ship to Barbados and one to Calcutta?

Assume that both voyages will be equally profitable if successful, yielding £1000 if the voyage is completed (this payoff includes the cost of the ship, its contents, and the revenue). Also assume that there is a 10% chance both that a ship sent to Barbados will run into a pirate and that a ship sent to Calcutta will be sunk by a typhoon. And if two ships travel to the same destination, we will assume that they share the same fate. So if Mr. Moneypenny were to send both his ships to either destination, he would face a probability of 10% of losing all his investment.

But if Mr. Moneypenny were instead to send one ship to Barbados and one ship to Calcutta, the probability that he would lose both of them would be only $0.1 \times 0.1 = 0.01$, or just 1%. As we will see shortly, his expected payoff would be the same—but the chance of losing it all would be much less. So by engaging in **diversification**—investing in several different things, where the possible losses are independent events—he could make some of his risk disappear.

Table 20-2 summarizes Mr. Moneypenny's options and their possible consequences. If he sends both ships to the same destination, he runs a 10% chance of losing them both. If he sends them to different destinations, there are three possible outcomes. Both ships could arrive safely: because there is a 0.9 probability of either one making it, the probability that both will make it is $0.9 \times 0.9 = 81\%$. Both could be lost—but the probability of that happening is only $0.1 \times 0.1 = 1\%$. Finally, there are two ways that only one ship can arrive. The probability that the first ship arrives and the second ship is lost is $0.9 \times 0.1 = 9\%$. The probability that the first ship is lost but the second ship arrives is $0.1 \times 0.9 = 9\%$. So the probability that only one ship makes it is $9\% + 9\% = 18\%$.

You might think that diversification is a strategy available only to those with a lot of money to begin with. Can Mr. Moneypenny diversify if he is able to afford only one ship? There are ways for even small investors to diversify. Even if Mr. Moneypenny is only wealthy enough to equip one ship, he can enter a partnership with another merchant. They can jointly outfit two ships, agreeing to share the profits equally, and then send those ships to different destinations. That way each faces less risk than if he equips one ship alone.

In the modern economy, diversification is made much easier for investors by the fact that they can easily buy shares in many companies by using the *stock market*. The owner of a **share** in a company is the owner of part of that company—typically a very small part, one-millionth or less. An individual who put all of his or her wealth in shares of a single company would lose all of that wealth if

> An individual can engage in **diversification** by investing in several different things, so that the possible losses are independent events.
>
> A **share** in a company is a partial ownership of that company.

TABLE 20-2   How Diversification Reduces Risk

(a) If both ships sent to the same destination

State	Probability	Payoff	Expected payoff
Both ships arrive	0.9 = 90%	£2000	$(0.9 \times £2000) + (0.1 \times £0) = £1800$
Both ships lost	0.1 = 10%	0	

(b) If one ship sent east, one west

State	Probability	Payoff	Expected payoff
Both ships arrive	$0.9 \times 0.9 = 81\%$	£2000	$(0.81 \times £2000) + (0.01 \times £0) +$
Both ships lost	$0.1 \times 0.1 = 1\%$	0	$(0.18 \times £1000) = £1800$
One ship arrives	$(0.9 \times 0.1) + (0.1 \times 0.9) = 18\%$	1000	

Pooling is a strong form of diversification in which an investor takes a small share of the risk in many independent events. This produces a payoff with very little total overall risk.

the company went bankrupt. But most investors hold shares in many companies, which makes the chance of losing all their investment very small.

In fact, Lloyd's of London wasn't just a way to trade risks; it was also a way for investors to diversify. To see how this worked, let's introduce Lady Penelope Smedley-Smythe, a wealthy aristocrat, who decides to increase her income by placing £1000 of her capital at risk via Lloyd's. She could use that capital to insure just one ship. But more typically she would enter a "syndicate," a group of investors, who would jointly insure a number of ships going to different destinations, agreeing to share the cost if any one of those ships went down. Because it would be much less likely for all the ships insured by the syndicate to sink than for any one of them to go down, Lady Penelope would be at much less risk of losing her entire capital.

In some cases, an investor can make risk almost entirely disappear by taking a small share of the risk in many independent events. This strategy is known as **pooling.** Consider the case of a supplementary health insurance company, which has millions of policyholders, with thousands of them requiring expensive treatment each year. The insurance company can't know whether any given individual will, say, require heart medication. But heart problems for two different individuals are pretty much independent events. And when there are many possible independent events, it is possible, using statistical analysis, to predict with great accuracy *how many* events of a given type will happen. For example, if you toss a coin 1000 times, it will come up heads about 500 times—and it is very unlikely to be more than a percent or two off that figure.

FOR INQUIRING MINDS

THOSE PESKY EMOTIONS

For a small investor (someone investing less than several hundred thousand dollars), financial economists agree that the best strategy for investing in stocks is to buy an index fund.

Why index funds? Because they contain a wide range of stocks that reflect the overall market, they achieve diversification; and they have very low management fees. In addition, financial economists agree that it's a losing strategy to try to "time" the market: to buy when the stock market is low and sell when it's high. Instead, small investors should buy a fixed dollar amount of stocks and other financial assets every year, regardless of the state of the market.

Yet many, if not most, small investors don't follow this advice. Instead, they buy individual stocks or funds that charge high fees. Some spend endless hours in Internet chat rooms chasing the latest hot tip or sifting through data trying to discern patterns in stocks' behaviour. They try to time the market but invariably buy when stocks are high

"Your mother called to remind you to diversify."

and refuse to sell losers before they lose even more. And they fail to diversify, instead concentrating too much money in a few stocks they think are "winners."

So why are human beings so dense when it comes to investing? According to many experts, the culprit is emotion. In his recent book *Your Money and Your Brain*, Jason Zweig states, "the brain is not an optimal tool for making financial decisions." As he explains it, the problem is that the human brain evolved to detect and interpret simple patterns.

(Is there a lion lurking in that bush?) As a consequence, "when it comes to investing, our incorrigible search for patterns leads us to assume that order exists where it often doesn't." In other words, investors fool themselves into believing that they've discovered a lucrative stock market pattern when, in fact, stock market behaviour is largely random.

Not surprisingly, how people make financial decisions is a major topic of study in the area of behavioural economics, a branch of economics that studies why human beings often fail to behave rationally (see Chapter 9 for more on behavioural economics).

So, what's the typical twenty-first-century investor to do? According to Mr. Zweig, there's hope: if you recognize the influence of your emotions, then you can tame them. One test of how well you've evolved from a Cro-Magnon state of mind: are you diversified?

(Source note on copyright page.)

So a company offering fire insurance can predict very accurately how many of its clients' homes will burn down in a given year; a company offering supplementary health insurance can predict very accurately how many of its clients will need heart medication in a given year; a life insurance company can predict how many of its clients will … Well, you get the idea.

When an insurance company is able to take advantage of the predictability that comes from aggregating a large number of independent events, it is said to engage in *pooling of risks*. And this pooling often means that even though insurance companies protect people from risk, the owners of the insurance companies may not themselves face much risk.

Lloyd's of London wasn't just a way for wealthy individuals to get paid for taking on some of the risks of less wealthy merchants. It was also a vehicle for pooling some of those risks. The effect of that pooling was to shift the supply curve in Figure 20-5 rightward: to make investors willing to accept more risk, at a lower price, than would otherwise have been possible.

The Limits of Diversification

Diversification can reduce risk. In some cases it can eliminate it. But these cases are not typical, because there are important limits to diversification. We can see the most important reason for these limits by returning to Lloyd's one more time.

During the period when Lloyd's was creating its legend, there was one important hazard facing British shipping other than pirates or storms: war. Between 1690 and 1815, Britain fought a series of wars, mainly with France (which, among other things, led to the British takeover of New France during the Seven Years' War). Each time, France would sponsor "privateers"—basically pirates with official backing—to raid British ships and thus indirectly damage Britain's war effort.

Whenever war broke out between Britain and France, losses of British merchant ships would suddenly increase. Unfortunately, merchants could not protect themselves against this eventuality by sending ships to different ports: the privateers would prey on British ships anywhere in the world. So the loss of a ship to French privateers in the Caribbean and the loss of another ship to French privateers in the Indian Ocean would *not* be independent events. It would be quite likely that they would happen in the same year.

When an event is more likely to occur if some other event occurs, these two events are said to be **positively correlated.** And like the risk of having a ship seized by French privateers, many financial risks are, alas, positively correlated.

Here are some of the positively correlated financial risks that investors in the modern world face:

- *Severe weather.* Within any given region of Canada, losses due to weather are definitely not independent events. When an ice storm hits Quebec, a lot of Quebec homes will get damaged. To some extent, insurance companies can diversify away this risk by insuring homes in many provinces. But events like El Niño (a recurrent temperature anomaly in the Pacific Ocean that disrupts weather around the world) can cause simultaneous flooding across North America. And as we mentioned in our opening story, over the past several years, there has been a significant increase in extreme weather.

- *Political events.* Modern governments do not, thankfully, license privateers—although submarines served much the same function during World War II. Even today, however, some kinds of political events—say, a war or revolution in a key raw-material-producing area—can damage business around the globe.

- *Business cycles.* The causes of *business cycles,* fluctuations in the output of the economy as a whole, are a subject for macroeconomics. What we can say here is that if one company suffers a decline in business because of a nationwide economic slump, many other companies will also suffer such declines. So these events will be positively correlated.

Two events are **positively correlated** if each event is more likely to occur if the other event also occurs.

When events are positively correlated, the risks they pose cannot be diversified away. An investor can protect herself from the risk that any one company will do badly by investing in many companies; she cannot use the same technique to protect against an economic slump in which *all* companies do badly.

An insurance company can protect itself against the risk of losses from local flooding by insuring houses in many different places; but a global weather pattern that produces floods in many places will defeat this strategy. Not surprisingly, and as we explained in the opening story, insurers pulled back from writing as many weather-related policies when it became clear that extreme weather patterns had become worse. They could no longer be confident that profits from policies written in good weather areas would be sufficient to compensate for losses incurred on policies in flood-, hurricane-, and tornado-prone areas.

So institutions like insurance companies and stock markets usually cannot make risk go away completely. There is usually an irreducible core of risk that cannot be diversified. Markets for risk, however, do accomplish two things: First, they enable the economy to eliminate the risk that can be diversified. Second, they allocate the risk that remains to the people most willing to bear it.

ECONOMICS ➤ IN ACTION

WHEN LLOYD'S ALMOST LLOST IT

At the end of the 1980s, the venerable institution of Lloyd's found itself in severe trouble. Investors who had placed their capital at risk, believing that the risks were small and the return on their investments more or less assured, found themselves required to make large payments to satisfy enormous claims. A number of investors, including members of some very old aristocratic families, found themselves pushed into bankruptcy.

What happened? Part of the answer is that ambitious managers at Lloyd's had persuaded investors to take on risks that were much larger than the investors realized. (Or to put it a different way, the premiums the investors accepted were too small for the true level of risk contained in the policies.)

But the biggest single problem was that many of the events against which Lloyd's had become a major insurer were *not* independent. In the 1970s and 1980s, Lloyd's had become a major provider of corporate liability insurance in the United States: it protected American corporations against the possibility that they might be sued for selling defective or harmful products. Everyone expected such suits to be more or less independent events. Why should one company's legal problems have much to do with another's?

The answer turned out to lie in one word: asbestos. For decades, this fireproofing material had been used in many products, which meant that many companies were responsible for its use. Then it turned out that asbestos can cause severe damage to the lungs, especially in children. The result was a torrent of lawsuits by people who believed they were injured by asbestos and billions of dollars in damage awards—many of them ultimately paid by Lloyd's investors.

DANGER

ASBESTOS
CANCER AND LUNG DISEASE HAZARD

KEEP OUT

AUTHORIZED PERSONNEL ONLY

RESPIRATORS AND PROTECTIVE CLOTHING ARE REQUIRED IN THIS AREA.

The overwhelming number of asbestos claims faced by Lloyd's make it clear that insurance companies cannot completely eliminate risk.

1. Explain how each of the following events would change the equilibrium premium and quantity of insurance in the market, indicating any shifts in the supply and demand curves.
   a. An increase in the number of ships travelling the same trade routes and so facing the same kinds of risks
   b. An increase in the number of trading routes, with the same number of ships travelling a greater variety of routes and so facing different kinds of risk
   c. An increase in the degree of risk aversion among the shipowners in the market
   d. An increase in the degree of risk aversion among the investors in the market
   e. An increase in the risk affecting the economy as a whole
   f. A fall in the wealth levels of investors in the market

Solutions appear at back of book.

▼ **Quick Review**

- Insurance markets exist because there are gains from trade in risk. Except in the case of private information, they lead to an **efficient allocation of risk:** those who are most willing to bear risk place their **capital at risk** to cover the financial losses of those least willing to bear risk.

- When **independent events** are involved, a strategy of **diversification** can substantially reduce risk. Diversification is made easier by the existence of institutions like the stock market, in which people trade **shares** of companies. A form of diversification, relevant especially to insurance companies, is **pooling.**

- When events are **positively correlated,** there is a core of risk that cannot be eliminated, no matter how much individuals diversify.

Private Information: What You Don't Know Can Hurt You

Markets do very well at dealing with diversifiable risk and with risk due to uncertainty: situations in which nobody knows what is going to happen, whose house will be flooded, or who will get sick. However, markets have much more trouble with situations in which *some people know things that other people don't know*—situations of **private information.** As we will see, private information can distort economic decisions and sometimes prevent mutually beneficial economic transactions from taking place. (Sometimes economists use the term *asymmetric information* rather than *private information,* but they are equivalent.)

Why is some information private? The most important reason is that people generally know more about themselves than other people do. For example, you know whether or not you are a careful driver; but unless you have several accidents on your driving record or a spotless record, your auto insurance company does not. You are more likely to have a better estimate than your insurance company of whether or not you will need an expensive medical procedure when you travel outside of Canada. And if you are selling a buyer your used car, you are more likely to be aware of any problems with it than the buyer is.

But why should such differences in who knows what be a problem? It turns out that there are two distinct sources of trouble: *adverse selection,* which arises from having private information about the way things are, and *moral hazard,* which arises from having private information about people's actions.

Adverse Selection: The Economics of Lemons

Suppose that someone offers to sell you an almost brand-new car—purchased just three months ago, with only 3000 kilometres on the odometer and no dents or scratches. Will you be willing to pay almost the same for it as for a new car direct from the dealer?

Probably not, for one main reason: you cannot help but wonder why this car is being sold. Is it because the owner has discovered that something is wrong with it—that it is a "lemon"? Having driven the car for a while, the owner knows more about it than you do—and people are more likely to sell cars that give them trouble.

You might think that the fact that sellers of used cars know more about them than the buyers do represents an advantage to the sellers. But potential buyers know that potential sellers are likely to offer them lemons—they just

Private information is information that some people have but others do not.

Adverse selection occurs when an individual knows more about the way things are than other people do. Private information leads buyers to expect hidden problems in items offered for sale, leading to low prices and the best items being kept off the market.

don't know exactly which car is a lemon. Because potential buyers of a used car know that potential sellers are more likely to sell lemons than good cars, buyers will offer a lower price than they would if they had a guarantee of the car's quality. Worse yet, this poor opinion of used cars tends to be self-reinforcing, precisely because it depresses the prices that buyers offer. Used cars sell at a significant discount because buyers expect a disproportionate share of those cars to be lemons.

Even a used car that is not a lemon would sell only at a large discount because buyers don't know whether it's a lemon or not. But potential sellers who have good cars are unwilling to sell them at a deep discount, except under exceptional circumstances. So good used cars are rarely offered for sale, and used cars that are offered for sale have a strong tendency to be lemons. (This is why people who have a compelling reason to sell a car, such as moving overseas, make a point of revealing that information to potential buyers—as if to say "This car is not a lemon!")

The end result, then, is not only that used cars sell for low prices and that there are a large number of used cars with hidden problems. Equally important, many potentially beneficial transactions—sales of good cars by people who would like to get rid of them to people who would like to buy them—end up being frustrated by the inability of potential sellers to convince potential buyers that their cars are actually worth the higher price being asked. So some mutually beneficial trades between those who want to sell used cars and those who want to buy them go unexploited.

Although economists sometimes refer to situations like this as the "lemons problem" (the issue was introduced in a famous 1970 paper by economist and Nobel laureate George Akerlof entitled "The Market for Lemons"), the more formal name of the problem is **adverse selection.** The reason for the name is obvious: because the potential sellers know more about the quality of what they are selling than the potential buyers, they have an incentive to select the worst things to sell.

Adverse selection does not apply only to used cars. It is a problem for many parts of the economy—notably for insurance companies, and most notably for health insurance companies.

Suppose that a health insurance company were to offer a standard supplementary health policy to everyone with the same premium. The premium would reflect the *average* risk of incurring a medical expense not covered by a provincial health insurance plan. But that would make the policy look very expensive to healthy people, who know that they are less likely than the average person to incur this type of medical expense. So healthy people would be less likely than less healthy people to buy the policy, leaving the health insurance company with exactly the customers it doesn't want: people with a higher-than-average risk of needing supplementary medical care, who would find the premium to be a good deal.

In order to cover its expected losses from this sicker customer pool, the health insurance company is compelled to raise premiums, driving away more of the remaining healthier customers, and so on. Because the insurance company can't determine who is healthy and who is not, it must charge everyone the same premium, thereby discouraging healthy people from purchasing policies and encouraging unhealthy people to buy policies.

As we discussed in Chapter 18, adverse selection can lead to a phenomenon called an *adverse selection death spiral* as the market for supplementary health insurance collapses: insurance companies refuse to offer policies because there is no premium at which the company can cover its losses. Because of the severe adverse selection problems, governments in many advanced countries assume the role of providing health insurance to their citizens. As we saw in Chapter 18, provincial and territorial governments, through their health services insurance plans and drug benefit programs like the Quebec Health Insurance Plan and the Quebec Drug Insurance Fund, now disburse 70% of the total payments for medical care in Canada.

In general, people or firms faced with the problem of adverse selection follow one of several well-established strategies for dealing with it. One strategy is **screening:** using observable information to make inferences about private information. As we discussed in Chapter 18, if you apply for supplementary health insurance, you'll find that the insurance company will demand documentation of your health status in an attempt to "screen out" sicker applicants—people they will refuse to insure or will insure only at very high premiums. Auto insurance companies also provide a very good example of the use of screening to reduce adverse selection. They may not know whether you are a careful driver, but they have statistical data on the accident rates of people who resemble your profile—and use those data in setting premiums. A 19-year-old male who drives a sports car and has already had a fender-bender is likely to pay a very high premium. A 40-year-old female who drives a minivan and has never had an accident is likely to pay much less. In some cases, this may be unfair: some adolescent males are very careful drivers, and some mature women drive minivans as if they were CF-18s. But nobody can deny that the insurance companies are right on average.

Another strategy to counter the problems caused by adverse selection is for people who are good prospects to do something **signalling** their private information—taking some action that wouldn't be worth taking unless they were indeed good prospects. For example, reputable used-car dealers often offer warranties—promises to repair any problems with the cars they sell that arise within a given amount of time. This isn't just a way of insuring their customers against possible expenses; it's a way of credibly showing that they are not selling lemons. As a result, more sales occur and dealers can command higher prices for their used cars when they offer warranties.

Finally, in the face of adverse selection, it can be very valuable to establish a good **reputation:** a used-car dealership will often advertise how long it has been in business to show that it has continued to satisfy its customers. As a result, new customers will be willing to purchase cars and to pay more for that dealer's cars.

Adverse selection can be reduced through **screening:** using observable information about people to make inferences about their private information.

Adverse selection can be diminished by people **signalling** their private information through actions that credibly reveal what they know.

A long-term **reputation** allows an individual to reassure others that he or she isn't concealing adverse private information.

Moral Hazard

In the late 1970s, major North American cities experienced an epidemic of suspicious fires that appeared to be deliberately set. Some of the fires were probably started by teenagers on a lark, others by gang members struggling over turf. But investigators eventually became aware of patterns in a number of the fires. Particular landlords who owned several buildings seemed to have an unusually large number of their buildings burn down. Although it was difficult to prove, police had few doubts that most of these fire-prone landlords were hiring professional arsonists to torch their own properties.

Why burn your own building? These buildings were typically in declining neighbourhoods, where rising crime and middle-class flight had led to a decline in property values. But the insurance policies on the buildings were written to compensate owners based on historical property values, and so would pay the owner of a destroyed building more than the building was worth in the current market. For an unscrupulous landlord who knew the right people, this presented a profitable opportunity.

The arson epidemic became less severe during the 1980s, partly because insurance companies began making it difficult to overinsure properties, and partly because a boom in real estate values made many previously arson-threatened buildings worth more unburned.

Moral hazard occurs when an individual knows more about his or her own actions than other people do. This leads to a distortion of incentives to take care or to exert effort when someone else bears the costs of the lack of care or effort.

A **deductible** in an insurance policy is a sum that the insured individual must pay before being compensated for a claim.

The arson episodes make it clear that it is a bad idea for insurance companies to let customers insure buildings for more than their value—it gives the customers some destructive incentives. You might think, however, that the incentive problem would go away as long as the insurance is no more than 100% of the value of what is being insured.

But, unfortunately, anything close to 100% insurance still distorts incentives—it induces policyholders to behave differently than they would in the absence of insurance. The reason is that preventing fires requires effort and cost on the part of a building's owner. Fire alarms and sprinkler systems have to be kept in good repair, fire safety rules have to be strictly enforced, and so on. All of this takes time and money—time and money that the owner may not find worth spending if the insurance policy will provide close to full compensation for any losses.

Of course, the insurance company could specify in the policy that it won't pay if basic safety precautions have not been taken. But it isn't always easy to tell how careful a building's owner has been—the owner knows, but the insurance company does not.

The point is that the building's owner has private information about his or her own actions, about whether he or she has really taken all appropriate precautions. As a result, the insurance company is likely to face greater claims than if it were able to determine exactly how much effort a building owner exerts to prevent a loss. The problem of distorted incentives arises when an individual has private information about his or her own actions but someone else bears the costs of a lack of care or effort. This is known as **moral hazard.**

To deal with moral hazard, it is necessary to give individuals with private information some personal stake in what happens so they have a reason to exert effort even if others cannot verify that they have done so. Moral hazard is the reason salespeople in many stores receive a commission on sales: it's hard for managers to be sure how hard the salespeople are really working, and if they were paid only a straight salary, they would not have an incentive to exert effort to make those sales. As described in the following Economics in Action, similar logic explains why many stores and restaurants, even if they are part of national chains, are actually franchises, licensed outlets owned by the people who run them.

Insurance companies deal with moral hazard by requiring a **deductible:** they compensate for losses only above a certain amount, so that coverage is always less than 100%. The insurance on your car, for example, may pay for repairs only after the first $500 in loss. This means that a careless driver who gets into a fender-bender will end up paying $500 for repairs even if he is insured, which provides at least some incentive to be careful and reduces moral hazard.

In addition to reducing moral hazard, deductibles provide a partial solution to the problem of adverse selection. Your insurance premium often drops substantially if you are willing to accept a large deductible. This is an attractive option to people who know they are low-risk customers; it is less attractive to people who know they are high-risk—and so are likely to have an accident and end up paying the deductible. By offering a menu of policies with different premiums and deductibles, insurance companies can screen their customers, inducing them to sort themselves out on the basis of their private information.

As the example of deductibles suggests, moral hazard limits the ability of the economy to allocate risks efficiently. You generally can't get full (100%) insurance on your home or car, even though you would like to buy it, and you bear the risk of large deductibles, even though you would prefer not to. The following Economics in Action illustrates how in some cases moral hazard limits the ability of investors to diversify their investments.

ECONOMICS > *IN ACTION*

FRANCHISE OWNERS TRY HARDER

When Canadians go out for a quick meal, they often end up at one of the fast-food chains—McDonald's, Harvey's, Burger King, and so on. Because these are large corporations, most customers probably imagine that the people who serve them are themselves employees of large corporations. But usually they aren't. Most fast-food restaurants—for example, 99.5% of Tim Hortons outlets and 85% of McDonald's outlets—are franchises. That is, some individual has paid the parent company for the right to operate a restaurant selling its product; he or she may look like an arm of a giant company but is in fact a small-business owner.

Becoming a franchisee is not a guarantee of success. You must put up a large amount of money, both to buy the licence

Franchise owners face risk, which motivates them to work harder than salaried managers.

Dave Olecko/Bloomberg via Getty Images

and to set up the restaurant itself (to open a Taco Bell, for example, cost $1.1 million to $1.7 million, excluding land or lease costs, in 2010). And although McDonald's takes care that its franchises are not too close to each other, they often face stiff competition from rival chains and even from a few truly independent restaurants. Becoming a franchise owner, in other words, involves taking on quite a lot of risk.

But why should people be willing to take these risks? Didn't we just learn that it is better to diversify, to spread your wealth among many investments? The logic of diversification would seem to say that it's better for someone with $1.7 million to invest in a wide range of stocks rather than put it all into one Taco Bell. This implies that Taco Bell would find it hard to attract franchisees: nobody would be willing to be a franchisee unless they expected to earn considerably more than they would as a salaried employee with their wealth invested in a diversified portfolio of stocks. So wouldn't it be more profitable for Tim Hortons or Taco Bell simply to hire managers to run their restaurants?

It turns out that it isn't, because the success of a restaurant depends a lot on how hard the manager works, on the effort he or she puts into choosing the right employees, on keeping the place clean and attractive to customers, and so on. Could Tim Hortons get the right level of effort from a salaried manager? Probably not. The problem is moral hazard: the manager knows whether he or she is really putting 100% into the job; but company headquarters, which bears the costs of a poorly run company-owned restaurant, does not. So a salaried manager, who gets a salary even without doing everything possible to make the restaurant a success, does not have the incentive to do that extra bit—an incentive the owner does have because he or she has a substantial personal stake in the success of the restaurant.

In other words, there is a moral hazard problem when a salaried manager runs a Tim Hortons, where the private information is how hard the manager works. Franchising solves this problem. A franchisee, whose wealth is tied up in the business and who stands to profit personally from its success, has every incentive to work extremely hard.

The result is that fast-food chains rely mainly on franchisees to operate their restaurants, even though the contracts with these owner-managers allow the franchisees on average to make much more than it would have cost the companies to employ store managers. The higher earnings of franchisees compensate them for the risk they accept, and the companies are compensated by higher sales that lead to higher licensing fees. In addition, franchisees are forbidden by the licensing agreement with the company from reducing their risk by taking actions such as selling shares of the franchise to outside investors and using the proceeds to diversify. It's an illustration of the fact that moral hazard prevents the elimination of risk through diversification.

CHECK YOUR UNDERSTANDING   20-3

1. Your car insurance premiums are lower if you have had no moving violations for several years. Explain how this feature tends to decrease the potential inefficiency caused by adverse selection.

2. A common feature of home construction contracts is that when it costs more to construct a building than was originally estimated, the contractor must absorb the additional cost. Explain how this feature reduces the problem of moral hazard but also forces the contractor to bear more risk than she would like.

3. True or false? Explain your answer, stating what concept analyzed in this chapter accounts for the feature.

     People with higher deductibles on their auto insurance:
   a. Generally drive more carefully
   b. Pay lower premiums
   c. Generally are wealthier

Solutions appear at back of book.

BUSINESS CASE : The Agony of AIG

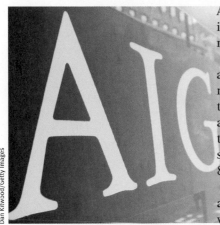

AIG (American International Group) was once the largest insurance company in the United States, known for insuring millions of homes and businesses and managing the pension plans of millions of workers.

But in September 2008, AIG acquired a much more notorious reputation. It was at the epicentre of the crisis sweeping global financial markets because major commercial and investment banks were faced with potentially devastating losses through their transactions with AIG. Fearful that a chaotic bankruptcy of AIG would panic the already distressed financial markets, the U.S. Federal Reserve stepped in and orchestrated the largest corporate bailout in U.S. history, paying a total of US$182 billion to satisfy claims against AIG. In return, American taxpayers became owners of nearly 80% of AIG. The company was essentially nationalized. How did things go so wrong?

AIG's problems originated not in its main lines of business—property insurance and pension management—but in its much smaller Financial Products Division, which sold *credit-default swaps*, or CDS. A CDS is like an insurance policy for an investor who buys a bond. A bond is simply an IOU—a promise to repay on the part of the borrower (the person or company that issued the bond). But any IOU carries with it the possibility that the borrower will default and not pay back the loan. So bond investors who wish to protect themselves against the risk of default purchase a CDS from a company like AIG. Later, if the borrower defaults, bond investors collect an amount equal to their losses from the company that issued the CDS.

During the mid-2000s, Joseph Cassano, the head of AIG's Financial Products Division, sold hundreds of billions of dollars worth of CDSs. They were bought by investors in mortgage-backed securities—bonds created by combining thousands of American home mortgages. As homeowners paid their monthly mortgages, the owners of the mortgage-backed securities received payments of the interest earned and the portion of principal repaid on those mortgages.

For several years AIG earned billions in premiums from selling CDSs, making the Financial Products Division its most profitable department. And there were virtually no costs involved because mortgage defaults were low and the Financial Products Division was based in London, England. Its location meant that AIG was not required to abide by U.S. insurance regulations to set aside capital to cover potential losses—despite the fact that AIG, the parent company, was headquartered in the United States. As Cassano stated in 2007, "It is hard for us … to even see a scenario within any kind of realm of reason that would see us losing $1 in any of those transactions." Cassano was so confident in his strategy and fearful of outside meddling that he prevented AIG's American auditors from inspecting his books, leaving AIG's management and shareholders in the dark about the risks they faced.

Yet the hard-to-see scenario appeared in 2008 in cataclysmic form when the U.S. housing market crashed. As mortgage defaults surged, investors in mortgage-backed securities incurred huge losses and turned to AIG to collect. But with no capital to cover claims, AIG faced bankruptcy until the U.S. government stepped in.

Investment banks, such as Goldman Sachs, had made huge profits by putting together low-quality mortgage-backed securities with high likelihoods of default and then insuring them with AIG. Despite an outcry, Goldman's claims were paid in full by the government because their transaction with AIG was entirely legal.

QUESTIONS FOR THOUGHT

1. Did AIG accurately assess the default risk that it insured? Why or why not?

2. What did AIG assume about the probabilities of defaults by different homeowners in the U.S. housing market? Were they wrong or right?

3. What are the examples of moral hazard in the case? For each example, explain who committed the moral hazard and against whom and identify the source of the private information.

4. Cite an example of adverse selection from the case. What was the source of the private information?

SUMMARY

1. The **expected value** of a **random variable** is the weighted average of all possible values, where the weight corresponds to the probability of a given value occurring.

2. **Risk** is uncertainty about future events or **states of the world.** It is **financial risk** when the uncertainty is about monetary outcomes.

3. Under uncertainty, people maximize **expected utility.** A **risk-averse** person will choose to reduce risk when that reduction leaves the expected value of his or her income or wealth unchanged. In a **fair insurance policy**, the **premium** is equal to the expected value of the claim. A **risk-neutral** person is completely insensitive to risk and therefore unwilling to pay any premium to avoid it.

4. Risk aversion arises from diminishing marginal utility: an additional dollar of income generates higher marginal utility in low-income states than in high-income states. A fair insurance policy increases a risk-averse person's utility because it transfers a dollar from a high-income state (a state when no loss occurs) to a low-income state (a state when a loss occurs).

5. Differences in preferences and income or wealth lead to differences in risk aversion. Depending on the size of the premium, a risk-averse person is willing to purchase "unfair" insurance, a policy for which the premium exceeds the expected value of the claim. The greater your risk aversion, the higher the premium you are willing to pay.

6. There are gains from trade in risk; in the absence of *private information* such trade leads to an **efficient allocation of risk:** those who are most willing to bear risk put their **capital at risk** to cover the losses of those least willing to bear risk.

7. Risk can also be reduced through **diversification,** investing in several different things that correspond to **independent events.** The stock market, where **shares** in companies are traded, offers one way to diversify. Insurance companies can engage in **pooling,** insuring many independent events so as to eliminate almost all risk. But when the underlying events are **positively correlated,** all risk cannot be diversified away.

8. **Private information** can cause inefficiency in the allocation of risk. One problem is **adverse selection,** private information about the way things are. It creates the "lemons problem" in used-car markets, where private information leads buyers to offer low prices, which can cause sellers of high-quality cars to drop out of the market. Adverse selection can be limited in several ways—through **screening** of individuals, through the **signalling** that people use to reveal their private information, and through the building of a **reputation.**

9. A related problem is **moral hazard:** individuals have private information about their actions, which distorts their incentives to exert effort or care when someone else bears the costs of that lack of effort or care. It limits the ability of markets to allocate risk efficiently. Insurance companies try to limit moral hazard by imposing **deductibles,** placing more risk on the insured. Commissions and franchises are also used to reduce moral hazard and help create a more efficient allocation of risk.

KEY TERMS

Random variable, p. 608
Expected value, p. 608
State of the world, p. 608
Risk, p. 609
Financial risk, p. 609
Expected utility, p. 609
Premium, p. 609
Fair insurance policy, p. 610

Risk-averse, p. 611
Risk-neutral, p. 613
Capital at risk, p. 616
Efficient allocation of risk, p. 618
Independent events, p. 618
Diversification, p. 619
Share, p. 619
Pooling, p. 620

Positively correlated, p. 621
Private information, p. 623
Adverse selection, p. 624
Screening, p. 625
Signalling, p. 625
Reputation, p. 625
Moral hazard, p. 626
Deductible, p. 626

PROBLEMS

1. For each of the following situations, calculate the expected value.

   a. Tanisha owns one share of RBC stock, which is currently trading at $80. There is a 50% chance that the share price will rise to $100 and a 50% chance that it will fall to $70. What is the expected value of the future share price?

   b. Sharon buys a ticket in a small lottery. There is a probability of 0.7 that she will win nothing, of 0.2 that she will win $10, and of 0.1 that she will win $50. What is the expected value of Sharon's winnings?

   c. Aaron is a farmer whose rice crop depends on the weather. If the weather is favourable, he will make a profit of $100. If the weather is unfavourable, he will make a profit of –$20 (that is, he will lose money). The weather forecast reports that the probability of weather being favourable is 0.9 and the probability of weather being unfavourable is 0.1. What is the expected value of Aaron's profit?

2. Vicky N. Vestor is considering investing some of her money in a startup company. She currently has income of $4000, and she is considering investing $2000 of that in the company. There is a 0.5 probability that the company will succeed and will pay out $8000 to Vicky (her original investment of $2000 plus $6000 of the company's profits). And there is a 0.5 probability that the company will fail and Vicky will get nothing (and lose her investment). The accompanying table illustrates Vicky's utility function.

Income	Total utility (utils)
$0	0
1 000	50
2 000	85
3 000	115
4 000	140
5 000	163
6 000	183
7 000	200
8 000	215
9 000	229
10 000	241

   a. Calculate Vicky's marginal utility of income for each income level. Is Vicky risk-averse?

   b. Calculate the expected value of Vicky's income if she makes this investment.

   c. Calculate Vicky's expected utility from making the investment.

   d. What is Vicky's utility from not making the investment? Will Vicky therefore invest in the company?

   e. Suppose instead Vicky's utility function is given by, $U(x) = x$, where x is her level of income. Repeat parts (a), (c), and (d). (*Hint:* The slope of the utility function is the change in utility divided by the change in x: 1.)

   f. Suppose instead Vicky's utility function is given by $U(x) = \sqrt{x}$, where x is her level of income (i.e., a square root function of her income). Repeat parts (a), (c), and (d). (*Hint:* The slope of the utility function is the change in utility divided by the change in x: 0.5 divided by $\sqrt{x}$.)

3. Vicky N. Vestor's utility function was given in the table in Problem 2. As in Problem 2, Vicky currently has income of $4000. She is considering investing in a startup company, but the investment now costs $4000 to make. If the company fails, Vicky will get nothing from the company. But if the company succeeds, she will get $10 000 from the company (her original investment of $4000 plus $6000 of the company's profits). Each event has a 0.5 probability of occurring. Will Vicky invest in the company?

4. You have $1000 that you can invest. If you buy Rogers stock, you face the following returns and probabilities from holding the stock for one year: with a probability of 0.2 you will get $1500; with a probability of 0.4 you will get $1100; and with a probability of 0.4 you will get $900. If you put the money into the bank, in one year's time you will get $1100 for certain.

   a. What is the expected value of your earnings from investing in Rogers stock?

   b. Suppose you are risk-averse. Can we say for sure whether you will invest in Rogers stock or put your money into the bank?

5. You have $1000 that you can invest. If you buy Imperial Oil stock, then, in one year's time, with a probability of 0.4 you will get $1600; with a probability of 0.4 you will get $1100; and with a probability of 0.2 you will get $800. If you put the money into the bank, in one year's time you will get $1100 for certain.

   a. What is the expected value of your earnings from investing in Imperial Oil stock?

   b. Suppose you prefer putting your money into the bank to investing it in Imperial Oil stock. What does that tell us about your attitude to risk?

6. Wilbur is an airline pilot who currently has income of $60 000. If he gets sick and loses his flight medical certificate, he loses his job and has only $10 000 income. His probability of staying healthy is 0.6, and his probability of getting sick is 0.4. Wilbur's utility function is given in the accompanying table.

Income	Total utility (utils)
$0	0
10 000	60
20 000	110
30 000	150
40 000	180
50 000	200
60 000	210

a. What is the expected value of Wilbur's income?

b. What is Wilbur's expected utility?

Wilbur thinks about buying "loss-of-licence" insurance that will compensate him if he loses his flight medical certificate.

c. One insurance company offers Wilbur full compensation for his income loss (that is, the insurance company pays Wilbur $50 000 if he loses his flight medical certificate), and it charges a premium of $40 000. That is, regardless of whether he loses his flight medical certificate, Wilbur's income after insurance will be $20 000. What is Wilbur's utility? Will he buy the insurance?

d. What is the highest premium Wilbur would just be willing to pay for full insurance (insurance that completely compensates him for the income loss)?

e. Suppose instead Wilbur's utility function is given by $U(x) = \ln x$, where ln refers to the natural logarithm function on most scientific calculators and x refers to Wilbur's level of income. Repeat parts (b), (c), and (d).

7. In 2012, 1 in approximately every 390 cars in Canada was stolen. Beth owns a car worth $20 000 and is considering purchasing an insurance policy to protect herself from car theft. For the following questions, assume that the chance of car theft is the same in all regions and across all car models.

a. What should the premium for a fair insurance policy have been in 2008 for a policy that replaces Beth's car if it is stolen?

b. Suppose an insurance company charges 0.6% of the car's value for a policy that pays for replacing a stolen car. How much will the policy cost Beth?

c. Will Beth purchase the insurance in part (b) if she is risk-neutral?

d. Discuss a possible moral hazard problem facing Beth's insurance company if she purchases the insurance.

8. Hugh's income is currently $5000. His utility function is shown in the accompanying table.

Income	Total utility (utils)
$0	0
1 000	100
2 000	140
3 000	166
4 000	185
5 000	200
6 000	212
7 000	222
8 000	230
9 000	236
10 000	240

a. Calculate Hugh's marginal utility of income. What is his attitude toward risk?

b. Hugh is thinking about gambling in a casino. With a probability of 0.5 he will lose $3000, and with a probability of 0.5 he will win $5000. What is the expected value of Hugh's income? What is Hugh's expected utility? Will he decide to gamble? (Suppose that he gets no extra utility from going to the casino.)

c. Suppose that the "spread" (how much he can win versus how much he can lose) of the gamble narrows, so that with a probability of 0.5 Hugh will lose $1000, and with a probability of 0.5 he will win $3000. What is the expected value of Hugh's income? What is his expected utility? Is this gamble better for him than the gamble in part (b)? Will he decide to gamble?

9. Eva is risk-averse. Currently she has $50 000 to invest. She faces the following choice: she can invest in the stock of a dot-com company, or she can invest in Telus stock. If she invests in the dot-com company, then with probability 0.5 she will lose $30 000, but with probability 0.5 she will gain $50 000. If she invests in Telus stock, then with probability 0.5 she will lose only $10 000, but with probability 0.5 she will gain only $30 000. Can you tell which investment she will prefer to make?

10. Suppose you have $1000 that you can invest in Ted and Larry's Ice Cream Parlour and/or Ethel's House of Cocoa. The price of a share of stock in either company is $100. The fortunes of each company are closely linked to the weather. When it is warm, the value of Ted and Larry's stock rises to $150 but the value of Ethel's stock falls to $60. When it is cold, the value of Ethel's stock rises to $150 but the value of Ted and Larry's stock falls to $60. There is an equal chance of the weather being warm or cold.

a. If you invest all your money in Ted and Larry's, what is your expected stock value? What if you invest all your money in Ethel's?

b. Suppose you diversify and invest half of your $1000 in each company. How much will your total stock be worth if the weather is warm? What if it is cold?

c. Suppose you are risk-averse. Would you prefer to put all your money in Ted and Larry's, as in part (a)? Or would you prefer to diversify, as in part (b)? Explain your reasoning.

11. Canadian Bond and New Canadian are two portfolios constructed and managed by Mawer Investment Management Ltd. of Calgary. They comprise bonds and debentures (bond-like securities) of Canadian government and corporate issuers and stocks of smaller Canadian companies. The accompanying table shows the expected value of the annual percentage returns associated with these portfolios based on returns from the period 2004 to 2014.

Portfolio	Expected value of return
Mawer Canadian Bond	4.24%
Mawer New Canadian	15.14%

a. Which portfolio would a risk-neutral investor prefer?

b. Jing, a risk-averse investor, chooses to invest in the Canadian Bond portfolio. What can be inferred about the risk of the two portfolios from Jing's choice of investment? Based on the information in the table, would a risk-neutral investor ever choose Canadian Bond?

c. Jing is aware that diversification can reduce risk. She considers a portfolio in which half her investment is in units of the Canadian Bond fund and the other half in New Canadian fund units. What is the expected value of the return for this combined portfolio? Would you expect this combined portfolio to be more risky or less risky than the New Canadian fund portfolio? Why?

12. You are considering buying a second-hand Volkswagen. From reading car magazines, you know that half of all Volkswagens have problems of some kind (they are "lemons") and the other half run just fine (they are "plums"). If you knew that you were getting a plum, you would be willing to pay $10 000 for it: this is how much a plum is worth to you. You would also be willing to buy a lemon, but only if its price was no more than $4000: this is how much a lemon is worth to you. And someone who owns a plum would be willing to sell it at any price above $8000. Someone who owns a lemon would be willing to sell it for any price above $2000.

a. For now, suppose that you can immediately tell whether the car that you are being offered is a lemon or a plum. Suppose someone offers you a plum. Will there be trade?

Now suppose that the seller has private information about the car she is selling: the seller knows whether she has a lemon or a plum. But when the seller offers you a Volkswagen, you do not know whether it is a lemon or a plum. So this is a situation of adverse selection.

b. Since you do not know whether you are being offered a plum or a lemon, you base your decision on the expected value to you of a Volkswagen, assuming you are just as likely to buy a lemon as a plum. Calculate this expected value.

c. Suppose, from driving the car, the seller knows she has a plum. However, you don't know whether this particular car is a lemon or a plum, so the most you are willing to pay is your expected value. Will there be trade?

13. You own a company that produces chairs, and you are thinking about hiring one more employee. Each chair produced gives you revenue of $10. There are two potential employees, Fred Ast and Sylvia Low. Fred is a fast worker who produces ten chairs per day, creating revenue for you of $100. Fred knows that he is fast and so will work for you only if you pay him more than $80 per day. Sylvia is a slow worker who produces only five chairs per day, creating revenue for you of $50. Sylvia knows that she is slow and so will work for you if you pay her more than $40 per day. Although Sylvia knows she is slow and Fred knows he is fast, you do not know who is fast and who is slow. So this is a situation of adverse selection.

a. Since you do not know which type of worker you will get, you think about what the expected value of your revenue will be if you hire one of the two. What is that expected value?

b. Suppose you offered to pay a daily wage equal to the expected revenue you calculated in part (a). Whom would you be able to hire: Fred, or Sylvia, or both, or neither?

c. If you know whether a worker is fast or slow, which one would you prefer to hire and why? Can you devise a compensation scheme to guarantee that you employ only the type of worker you prefer?

14. For each of the following situations, do the following: first describe whether it is a situation of moral hazard or of adverse selection. Then explain what inefficiency can arise from this situation and explain how the proposed solution reduces the inefficiency.

a. When you buy a second-hand car, you do not know whether it is a lemon (low quality) or a plum (high quality), but the seller knows. A solution is for sellers to offer a warranty with the car that pays for repair costs.

b. Some people are prone to see dentists unnecessarily for minor complaints, and health maintenance organizations do not know how urgently you need a dentist. A solution is for insurees to have to make a co-payment of a certain dollar amount (for example, $10) each time they visit a health care provider. All insurees are risk-averse.

c. When airlines sell tickets, they do not know whether a buyer is a business traveller (who is willing to pay a lot for a seat) or a leisure traveller (who has a low willingness to pay). A solution for a profit-maximizing airline is to offer an expensive ticket that is very flexible (it allows date and route changes) and a cheap ticket that is very inflexible (it has to be booked in advance and cannot be changed).

d. A company does not know whether workers on an assembly line work hard or whether they slack off. A solution is to pay the workers "piece rates," that is, pay them according to how much they have produced each day. All workers are risk-averse, but the company is risk-neutral.

e. When making a decision about hiring you, prospective employers do not know whether you are a productive or unproductive worker. A solution is for productive workers to provide potential employers with references from previous employers.

15. Kory owns a house that is worth $300 000. If the house burns down, she loses all $300 000. If the house does not burn down, she loses nothing. Her house burns down with a probability of 0.02. Kory is risk-averse.

a. What would a fair insurance policy cost?

b. Suppose an insurance company offers to insure her fully against the loss from the house burning down, at a premium of $1500. Can you say for sure whether Kory will or will not take the insurance?

c. Suppose an insurance company offers to insure her fully against the loss from the house burning down, at a premium of $6000. Can you say for sure whether Kory will or will not take the insurance?

d. Suppose that an insurance company offers to insure her fully against the loss from the house burning down, at a premium of $9000. Can you say for sure whether Kory will or will not take the insurance?

Solutions to Check Your Understanding Questions

This section offers suggested answers to the "Check Your Understanding" questions found within chapters.

Chapter One

1-1 CHECK YOUR UNDERSTANDING

1. a. This illustrates the concept of opportunity cost. Given that a person can only eat so much at one sitting, having a slice of chocolate cake requires that you forgo eating something else, such as a slice of coconut cream pie.

b. This illustrates the concept that resources are scarce. Even if there were more resources in the world, the total amount of those resources would be limited. As a result, scarcity would still arise. For there to be no scarcity, there would have to be unlimited amounts of everything (including unlimited time in a human life), which is clearly impossible.

c. This illustrates the concept that people usually exploit opportunities to make themselves better off. Students will seek to make themselves better off by signing up for the tutorials of teaching assistants with good reputations and avoiding those teaching assistants with poor reputations. It also illustrates the concept that resources are scarce. If there were unlimited spaces in tutorials with good teaching assistants, they would not fill up.

d. This illustrates the concept of marginal analysis. Your decision about allocating your time is a "how much" decision: how much time spent exercising versus how much time spent studying. You make your decision by comparing the benefit of an additional hour of exercising to its cost, the effect on your grades of one fewer hour spent studying.

2. a. Yes. The increased time spent commuting is a cost you will incur if you accept the new job. That additional time spent commuting—or equivalently, the benefit you would get from spending that time doing something else—is an opportunity cost of the new job.

b. Yes. One of the benefits of the new job is that you will be making $50 000. But if you take the new job, you will have to give up your current job; that is, you have to give up your current salary of $45 000. So $45 000 is one of the opportunity costs of taking the new job.

c. No. A more spacious office is an additional benefit of your new job and does not involve forgoing something else. So it is not an opportunity cost.

1-2 CHECK YOUR UNDERSTANDING

1. a. This illustrates the concept that markets usually lead to efficiency. Any seller who wants to sell a book for at least $30 does indeed sell to someone who is willing to buy a book for $30. As a result, there is no way to change how used textbooks are distributed among buyers and sellers in a way that would make one person better off without making someone else worse off.

b. This illustrates the concept that there are gains from trade. Students trade tutoring services based on their different abilities in academic subjects.

c. This illustrates the concept that when markets don't achieve efficiency, government intervention can improve society's welfare. In this case the market, left alone, will permit bars and nightclubs to impose costs on their neighbours in the form of loud music, costs that the bars and nightclubs have no incentive to take into account. This is an inefficient outcome because society as a whole can be made better off if bars and nightclubs are induced to reduce their noise.

d. This illustrates the concept that resources should be used as efficiently as possible to achieve society's goals. By closing neighbourhood clinics and shifting funds to the main hospital, better health care can be provided at a lower cost.

e. This illustrates the concept that markets move toward equilibrium. Here, because books with the same amount of wear and tear sell for about the same price, no buyer or seller can be made better off by engaging in a different trade than he or she undertook. This means that the market for used textbooks has moved to an equilibrium.

2. a. This does not describe an equilibrium situation. Many students should want to change their behaviour and switch to eating at the restaurants. Therefore, the situation described is not an equilibrium. An equilibrium will be established when students are equally as well off eating at the restaurants as eating at the dining hall—which would happen if, say, prices at the restaurants were higher than at the dining hall.

b. This does describe an equilibrium situation. By changing your behaviour and riding a bicycle, you would not be made better off. Therefore, you have no incentive to change your behaviour.

1-3 CHECK YOUR UNDERSTANDING

1. a. This illustrates the principle that government policies can change spending. The tax cut would increase people's after-tax incomes, leading to higher consumer spending.

b. This illustrates the principle that one person's spending is another person's income. As oil companies increase their spending on labour by hiring more workers, or pay existing workers higher wages, those workers' incomes rise. In turn, these workers increase their consumer spending, which becomes income to restaurants and other consumer businesses.

c. This illustrates the principle that overall spending sometimes gets out of line with the economy's productive capacity. In this case, spending on housing was too high relative to the economy's capacity to create new housing. This first led to a rise in house prices, and then—as a result—to a rise in overall prices, or *inflation*.

Chapter Two

2-1 CHECK YOUR UNDERSTANDING

1. a. False. An increase in the resources available to Bombardier for use in producing CSeries jets and subway trains changes the production possibility frontier by shifting it outward. This is because Bombardier can now produce more CSeries jets and subway trains than before. In the accompanying figure, the line labelled "Bombardier's original *PPF*" represents Bombardier's original production possibility frontier, and the line labelled "Bombardier's new *PPF*" represents the new production possibility frontier that results from an increase in resources available to Bombardier.

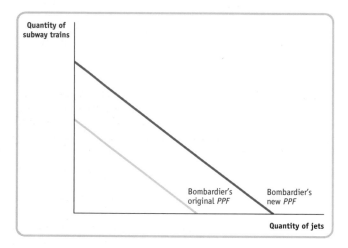

b. True. A technological change that allows Bombardier to build more subway trains for any amount of CSeries jets built results in a change in its production possibility frontier. This is illustrated in the accompanying figure: the new production possibility frontier is represented by the line labelled "Bombardier's new *PPF*," and the original production frontier is represented by the line labelled "Bombardier's original *PPF*." Since the maximum quantity of CSeries jets that Bombardier can build is the same as before, the new production possibility frontier intersects the horizontal axis at the same point as the original frontier. But since the maximum possible quantity of subway trains is now greater than before, the new frontier intersects the vertical axis above the original frontier.

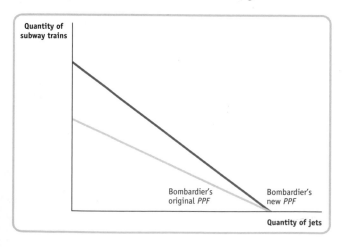

c. False. The production possibility frontier illustrates how much of one good an economy must give up to get more of another good only when resources are used efficiently in production. If an economy is producing inefficiently—that is, inside the frontier—then it does not have to give up a unit of one good in order to get another unit of the other good. Instead, by becoming more efficient in production, this economy can have more of both goods.

2. a. Canada has an absolute advantage in automobile production because it takes fewer Canadians (6) to produce a car in one day than Italians (8). Canada also has an absolute advantage in washing machine production because it takes fewer Canadians (2) to produce a washing machine in one day than Italians (3).

b. In Italy the opportunity cost of a washing machine in terms of an automobile is $3/8$: $3/8$ of a car can be produced with the same number of workers and in the same time it takes to produce 1 washing machine. In Canada the opportunity cost of a washing machine in terms of an automobile is $2/6 = 1/3$: $1/3$ of a car can be produced with the same number of workers and in the same time it takes to produce 1 washing machine. Since $1/3 < 3/8$, Canada has a comparative advantage in the production of washing machines: to produce a washing machine, only $1/3$ of a car must be given up in Canada but $3/8$ of a car must be given up in Italy. This means that Italy has a comparative advantage in automobiles. This can be checked as follows. The opportunity cost of an automobile in terms of a washing machine in Italy is $8/3$, equal to $2\,2/3$: $2\,2/3$ washing machines can be produced with the same number of workers and in the time it takes to produce 1 car in Italy. And the opportunity cost of an automobile in terms of a washing machine in Canada is $6/2$, equal to 3: 3 washing machines can be produced with the same number of workers and in the time it takes to produce 1 car in Canada. Since $2\,2/3 < 3$, Italy has a comparative advantage in producing automobiles.

c. The greatest gains are realized when each country specializes in producing the good for which it has a comparative advantage. Therefore, Canada should specialize in washing machines and Italy should specialize in automobiles.

3. At a trade of 7 Canadian jets for 29 Brazilian subway trains, Brazil gives up less for a jet than it would if it were building the jets itself. Without trade, Brazil gives up 6 subway trains for each jet it produces. With trade, Brazil gives up only $29/7$ subway trains for each jet from Canada. Likewise, Canada gives up less for a subway train than it would if it were producing subway train itself. Without trade, Canada gives up $2/7$ of jet for each subway train. With trade, Canada gives up only $7/29$ of a jet for each subway train from Brazil.

4. An increase in the amount of money spent by households results in an increase in the flow of goods to households. This, in turn, generates an increase in demand for factors of production by firms. So, there is an increase in the number of jobs in the economy.

2-2 CHECK YOUR UNDERSTANDING

1. a. This is a normative statement because it stipulates what should be done. In addition, it may have no "right" answer. That is, should people be prevented from all dangerous personal behaviour if they enjoy that behaviour—like skydiving? Your answer will depend on your point of view.

b. This is a positive statement because it is a description of fact.

2. a. True. Economists often have different value judgments about the desirability of a particular social goal. But despite those differences in value judgments, they will tend to agree that society, once it has decided to pursue a given social goal, should adopt the most efficient policy to achieve that goal. Therefore economists are likely to agree on adopting policy choice B.

b. False. Disagreements between economists are more likely to arise because they base their conclusions on different models or because they have different value judgments about the desirability of the policy.

c. False. Deciding which goals a society should try to achieve is a matter of value judgments, not a question of economic analysis.

Chapter Three

3-1 CHECK YOUR UNDERSTANDING

1. a. The quantity of umbrellas demanded is higher at any given price on a rainy day than on a dry day. This is a rightward *shift of* the demand curve, since at any given price the quantity demanded rises. This implies that any specific quantity can now be sold at a higher price.

b. The quantity of weekend calls demanded rises in response to a price reduction. This is a *movement along* the demand curve for weekend calls.

c. The demand for roses increases the week of Valentine's Day. This is a rightward *shift of* the demand curve.

d. The quantity of gasoline demanded falls in response to a rise in price. This is a *movement along* the demand curve.

3-2 CHECK YOUR UNDERSTANDING

1. a. The quantity of houses supplied rises as a result of an increase in prices. This is a *movement along* the supply curve.

b. The quantity of strawberries supplied is higher at any given price. This is a rightward *shift of* the supply curve.

c. The quantity of labour supplied is lower at any given wage. This is a leftward *shift of* the supply curve compared to the supply curve during school vacation. So, in order to attract workers, fast-food chains have to offer higher wages.

d. The quantity of wheat supplied is higher at any given price. This is a rightward *shift* of the supply curve.

e. The quantity of cabins supplied is higher at any given price. This is a rightward *shift of* the supply curve.

3-3 CHECK YOUR UNDERSTANDING

1. a. The supply curve shifts rightward. At the original equilibrium price of the year before, the quantity of grapes supplied exceeds the quantity demanded. This is a case of surplus. The price of grapes will fall.

b. The demand curve shifts leftward. At the original equilibrium price, the quantity of hotel rooms supplied exceeds the quantity demanded. This is a case of surplus. The rates for hotel rooms will fall.

c. The demand curve for second-hand snowblowers shifts rightward. At the original equilibrium price, the quantity of second-hand snowblowers demanded exceeds the quantity supplied. This is a case of shortage. The equilibrium price of second-hand snowblowers will rise.

3-4 CHECK YOUR UNDERSTANDING

1. a. The market for large cars: this is a rightward shift in demand caused by a decrease in the price of a complement, gasoline. As a result of the shift, the equilibrium price of large cars will rise and the equilibrium quantity of large cars bought and sold will also rise.

b. The market for fresh paper made from recycled stock: this is a rightward shift in supply due to a technological innovation. As a result of this shift, the equilibrium price of fresh paper made from recycled stock will fall and the equilibrium quantity bought and sold will rise.

c. The market for movies at a local movie theatre: this is a leftward shift in demand caused by a fall in the price of a substitute, on-demand films. As a result of this shift, the equilibrium price of movie tickets will fall and the equilibrium number of people who go to the movies will also fall.

2. Upon the announcement of the new chip, the demand curve for computers using the earlier chip shifts leftward, as demand decreases, and the supply curve for these computers shifts rightward, as supply increases.

a. If demand decreases relatively more than supply increases, then the equilibrium quantity falls, as shown here:

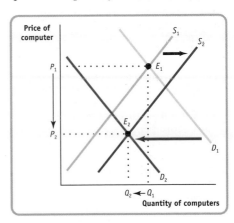

b. If supply increases relatively more than demand decreases, then the equilibrium quantity rises, as shown here:

In both cases, the equilibrium price falls.

Chapter Four
4-1 CHECK YOUR UNDERSTANDING

1. A consumer buys each pepper if the price is less than (or just equal to) the consumer's willingness to pay for that pepper. The demand schedule is constructed by asking how many peppers will be demanded at any given price. The accompanying table illustrates the demand schedule.

Price of pepper	Quantity of peppers demanded	Quantity of peppers demanded by Casey	Quantity of peppers demanded by Josey
$0.90	1	1	0
0.80	2	1	1
0.70	3	2	1
0.60	4	2	2
0.50	5	3	2
0.40	6	3	3
0.30	8	4	4
0.20	8	4	4
0.10	8	4	4
0.00	8	4	4

When the price is $0.40, Casey's consumer surplus from the first pepper is $0.50, from his second pepper $0.30, from his third pepper $0.10, and he does not buy any more peppers. Casey's individual consumer surplus is therefore $0.90. Josey's consumer surplus from her first pepper is $0.40, from her second pepper $0.20, from her third pepper $0.00 (since the price is exactly equal to her willingness to pay, she buys the third pepper but receives no consumer surplus from it), and she does not buy any more peppers. Josey's individual consumer surplus is therefore $0.60. Total consumer surplus at a price of $0.40 is therefore $0.90 + $0.60 = $1.50.

4-2 CHECK YOUR UNDERSTANDING

1. A producer supplies each pepper if the price is greater than (or just equal to) the producer's cost of producing that pepper. The supply schedule is constructed by asking how many peppers will be supplied at any price. The table at top right illustrates the supply schedule.

When the price is $0.70, Cara's producer surplus from the first pepper is $0.60, from her second pepper $0.60, from her third pepper $0.30, from her fourth pepper $0.10, and she does not supply any more peppers. Cara's individual producer surplus is therefore $1.60. Jamie's producer surplus from his first pepper is $0.40, from his second pepper $0.20, from his third pepper $0.00 (since the price is exactly equal to his cost, he sells the third pepper but receives no producer surplus from it), and he does not supply any more peppers. Jamie's individual producer surplus is therefore $0.60. Total producer surplus at a price of $0.70 is therefore $1.60 + $0.60 = $2.20.

Price of pepper	Quantity of peppers supplied	Quantity of peppers supplied by Cara	Quantity of peppers supplied by Jamie
$0.90	8	4	4
0.80	7	4	3
0.70	7	4	3
0.60	6	4	2
0.50	5	3	2
0.40	4	3	1
0.30	3	2	1
0.20	2	2	0
0.10	2	2	0
0.00	0	0	0

4-3 CHECK YOUR UNDERSTANDING

1. The quantity demanded equals the quantity supplied at a price of $0.50, the equilibrium price. At that price, a total quantity of five peppers will be bought and sold. Casey will buy three peppers and receive consumer surplus of $0.40 on his first, $0.20 on his second, and $0.00 on his third pepper. Josey will buy two peppers and receive consumer surplus of $0.30 on her first and $0.10 on her second pepper. Total consumer surplus is therefore $1.00. Cara will supply three peppers and receive producer surplus of $0.40 on her first, $0.40 on her second, and $0.10 on her third pepper. Jamie will supply two peppers and receive producer surplus of $0.20 on his first and $0.00 on his second pepper. Total producer surplus is therefore $1.10. Total surplus in this market is therefore $1.00 + $1.10 = $2.10.

2. a. If Josey consumes one fewer pepper, she loses $0.60 (her willingness to pay for her second pepper); if Casey consumes one more pepper, he gains $0.30 (his willingness to pay for his fourth pepper). This results in an overall loss of consumer surplus of $0.60 − $0.30 = $0.30.

b. Cara's cost of the last pepper she supplied (the third pepper) is $0.40, and Jamie's cost of producing one more (his third pepper) is $0.70. Total producer surplus therefore falls by $0.70 − $0.40 = $0.30.

c. Josey's willingness to pay for her second pepper is $0.60; this is what she would lose if she were to consume one fewer pepper. Cara's cost of producing her third pepper is $0.40; this is what she would save if she were to produce one fewer pepper. If we therefore reduced quantity by one pepper, we would lose $0.60 − $0.40 = $0.20 of total surplus.

3. The new guideline is likely to reduce the total life span of kidney recipients because older recipients (those with small children) are more likely to get a kidney compared to the original guideline. As a result, total surplus is likely to fall. However, this new policy can be justified as an acceptable sacrifice of efficiency for fairness because it's a desirable goal to reduce the chance of a small child losing a parent.

4-4 CHECK YOUR UNDERSTANDING

1. When these rights are separated, someone who owns both the above ground and the mineral rights can sell each of these separately in the market for above ground rights and the market for mineral rights. And each of these markets will achieve efficiency: If the market price for above ground rights is higher than the seller's cost, the seller will sell that right and total surplus increases. If the market price for mineral rights is higher than the seller's cost, the seller will sell that right and total surplus increases. If the two rights, however, cannot be sold separately, a seller can only sell both rights or none at all. Imagine a situation in which the seller values the mineral right highly (that is, has a high cost of selling it) but values the above ground right much less. If the two rights are separate, the owner may sell the above ground right (increasing total surplus) but not the mineral right. If, however, the two rights cannot be sold separately, and the owner values the mineral right sufficiently highly, she may not sell either of the two rights. In this case, surplus could have been created through the sale of the above ground right but goes unrealized because the two rights could not be sold separately.

2. There will be many sellers willing to sell their books but only a few buyers who want to buy books at that price. As a result, only a few transactions will actually occur, and many transactions that would have been mutually beneficial will not take place. This, of course, is inefficient.

3. Markets, alas, do not always lead to efficiency. When there is market failure, the market outcome may be inefficient. This can occur for three main reasons. Markets can fail when, in an attempt to capture more surplus, one party—a monopolist, for instance—prevents mutually beneficial trades from occurring. Markets can also fail when one individual's actions have side effects—externalities—on the welfare of others. Finally, markets can fail when the goods themselves—such as goods about which some relevant information is private—are unsuited for efficient management by markets. And when markets don't achieve efficiency, government intervention can improve society's welfare.

Chapter Five

5-1 CHECK YOUR UNDERSTANDING

1. a. Fewer homeowners are willing to rent out their driveways because the price ceiling has reduced the payment they receive. This is an example of a fall in price leading to a fall in the quantity supplied. It is shown in the accompanying diagram by the movement from point E to point A along the supply curve, a reduction in quantity of 400 parking spaces.

b. The quantity demanded increases by 400 spaces as the price decreases. At a lower price, more fans are willing to drive and rent a parking space. It is shown in the diagram by the movement from point E to point B along the demand curve.

c. Under a price ceiling, the quantity demanded exceeds the quantity supplied; as a result, shortages arise. In this case, there will be a shortage of 800 parking spaces. It is shown by the horizontal distance between points A and B.

d. Price ceilings result in wasted resources. The additional time fans spend to guarantee a parking space is wasted time.

e. Price ceilings lead to inefficient allocation of a good—here, the parking spaces—to consumers.

f. Price ceilings lead to black markets.

2. a. False. By lowering the price that producers receive, a price ceiling leads to a decrease in the quantity supplied.

b. True. A price ceiling leads to a lower quantity supplied than in an efficient, unregulated market. As a result, some people who would have been willing to pay the market price, and so would have gotten the good in an unregulated market, are unable to obtain it when a price ceiling is imposed.

c. True. Those producers who still sell the product now receive less for it and are therefore worse off. Other producers will no longer find it worthwhile to sell the product at all and so will also be made worse off.

3. a. Since the apartment is rented quickly at the same price, there is no change (either gain or loss) in producer surplus. So any change in total surplus comes from changes in consumer surplus. When you are evicted, the amount of consumer surplus you lose is equal to the difference between your willingness to pay for the apartment and the rent-controlled price. When the apartment is rented to someone else at the same price, the amount of consumer surplus the new renter gains is equal to the difference between his or her willingness to pay and the rent-controlled price. So this will be a pure transfer of surplus from one person to another only if both your willingness to pay and the new renter's willingness to pay are the same. Since under rent control apartments are not always allocated to those who have the highest willingness to pay, the new renter's willingness to pay may be either equal to, lower than, or higher than your willingness to pay. If the new renter's willingness to pay is lower than yours, this will create additional deadweight loss: there is some additional consumer surplus that is lost. However, if the new renter's willingness to pay is higher than yours, this will create an increase in total surplus, as the new renter gains more consumer surplus than you lost.

b. This creates deadweight loss: if you were able to give the ticket away, someone else would be able to obtain consumer surplus, equal to his or her willingness to pay for the ticket. You neither gain nor lose any surplus, since you cannot go to the concert whether or not you give the ticket away. If you were able to sell the ticket, the buyer would obtain consumer surplus equal to the difference between his or her willingness to pay for the ticket and the price at which you sell the ticket. In addition, you would obtain producer surplus equal to the difference between the price at which you sell the ticket and your cost of selling the ticket (which, since you won the ticket, is presumably zero). Since the restriction to neither sell nor give away the ticket means that this surplus cannot be obtained by anybody, it creates deadweight loss. If you could give the ticket away, as described above, there would be consumer surplus that accrues to the recipient of the ticket; and if you give the ticket to the person with the highest willingness to pay, there would be no deadweight loss.

c. This creates deadweight loss. If students buy ice cream on campus, they obtain consumer surplus: their willingness to pay must be higher than the price of the ice cream. Your school obtains producer surplus: the price is higher than your school's cost of selling the ice cream. Prohibiting the sale of ice cream on campus means that these two sources of total surplus are lost: there is deadweight loss.

d. Given that your dog values ice cream equally as much as you do, this is a pure transfer of surplus. As you lose consumer surplus, your dog gains equally as much consumer surplus.

5-2 CHECK YOUR UNDERSTANDING

1. a. Some gas station owners will benefit from getting a higher price. Q_F indicates the sales made by these owners. But some will lose; there are those who make sales at the market equilibrium price of P_E but do not make sales at the regulated price of P_F. These missed sales are indicated on the graph by the fall in the quantity demanded along the demand curve, from point E to point A.

b. Those who buy gas at the higher price of P_F will probably receive better service; this is an example of *inefficiently high quality* caused by a price floor as gas station owners compete on quality rather than price. But opponents are correct to claim that consumers are generally worse off—those who buy at P_F would have been happy to buy at P_E, and many who were willing to buy at a price between P_E and P_F are now unwilling to buy. This is indicated on the graph by the fall in the quantity demanded along the demand curve, from point E to point A.

c. Proponents are wrong because consumers and some gas station owners are hurt by the price floor, which creates "missed opportunities"—desirable transactions between consumers and station owners that never take place. The deadweight loss, the amount of total surplus lost because of missed opportunities, is indicated by the shaded area in the accompanying figure. Moreover, the inefficiency of wasted resources arises as consumers spend time and money driving to other provinces or to the United States. The price floor also tempts people to engage in black market activity. With the price floor, only Q_F units are sold. But at prices between P_E and P_F, there are drivers who cumulatively want to buy more than Q_F and owners who are willing to sell to them, a situation likely to lead to illegal activity.

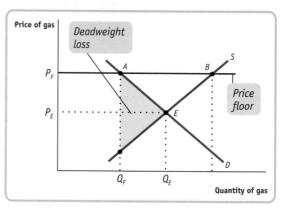

5-3 CHECK YOUR UNDERSTANDING

1. a. The price of a ride is $7 since the quantity demanded at this price is 6 million: $7 is the *demand price* of 6 million rides. This is represented by point A in the accompanying figure.

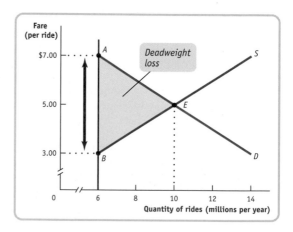

b. At 6 million rides, the supply price is $3 per ride, represented by point *B* in the figure. The wedge between the demand price of $7 per ride and the supply price of $3 per ride is the quota rent per ride, $4. This is represented in the figure above by the vertical distance between points *A* and *B*.

c. The quota discourages 4 million mutually beneficial transactions. The shaded triangle in the figure represents the deadweight loss.

2. At 9 million rides, the demand price is $5.50 per ride, indicated by point *C* in the accompanying figure, and the supply price is $4.50 per ride, indicated by point *D*. The quota rent is the difference between the demand price and the supply price: $1. The deadweight loss is represented by the shaded triangle in the figure. As you can see, the deadweight loss is smaller when the quota is set at 9 million rides than when it is set at 6 million rides.

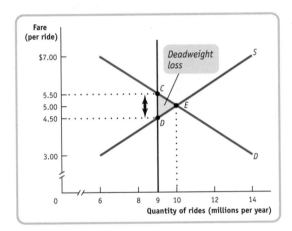

3. The accompanying figure shows a decrease in demand by 4 million rides, represented by a leftward shift of the demand curve from D_1 to D_2: at any given price, the quantity demanded falls by 4 million rides. (For example, at a price of $5, the quantity demanded falls from 10 million to 6 million rides per year.) This eliminates the effect of a quota limit of 8 million rides. At point E_2, the new market equilibrium, the equilibrium quantity is equal to the quota limit; as a result, the quota has no effect on the market.

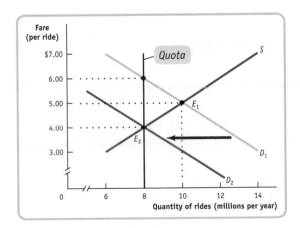

Chapter Six

6-1 CHECK YOUR UNDERSTANDING

1. By the midpoint method, the percentage change in the price of strawberries is

$$\frac{\$1.00 - \$1.50}{(\$1.50 + \$1.00)/2} \times 100 = \frac{\$0.50}{\$1.25} \times 100 = -40\%$$

Similarly, the percentage change in the quantity of strawberries demanded is

$$\frac{200\,000 - 100\,000}{(100\,000 + 200\,000)/2} \times 100 = \frac{100\,000}{150\,000} \times 100 = 67\%$$

Dropping the minus sign, the price elasticity of demand using the midpoint method is 67%/40% = 1.7.

2. By the midpoint method, the percentage change in the quantity of movie tickets demanded in going from 4000 tickets to 5000 tickets is

$$\frac{5000 - 4000}{(4000 + 5000)/2} \times 100 = \frac{1000}{4500} \times 100 = 22\%$$

Since the price elasticity of demand is 1 at the current consumption level, it will take a 22% reduction in the price of movie tickets to generate a 22% increase in quantity demanded.

3. Since price rises, we know that quantity demanded must fall. Given the current price of $0.50, a $0.05 increase in price represents a 10% change, using the method in Equation 6-2. So the price elasticity of demand is

$$\frac{\text{change in quantity demanded}}{10\%} = 1.2$$

so that the percentage change in quantity demanded is 12%. A 12% decrease in quantity demanded represents 100 000 × 0.12, or 12 000 sandwiches.

6-2 CHECK YOUR UNDERSTANDING

1. a. Elastic demand. Consumers are highly responsive to changes in price. For a rise in price, the quantity effect (which tends to reduce total revenue) outweighs the price effect (which tends to increase total revenue). Overall, this leads to a fall in total revenue.

b. Unit-elastic demand. Here the revenue lost to the fall in price is exactly equal to the revenue gained from higher sales. The quantity effect exactly offsets the price effect.

c. Inelastic demand. Consumers are relatively unresponsive to changes in price. For consumers to purchase a given percentage increase in output, the price must fall by an even greater percentage. The price effect of a fall in price (which tends to reduce total revenue) outweighs the quantity effect (which tends to increase total revenue). As a result, total revenue decreases.

d. Inelastic demand. Consumers are relatively unresponsive to price, so a given percentage fall in output is accompanied by an even greater percentage rise in price. The price effect of a rise in price (which tends to increase total revenue) outweighs the quantity effect (which tends to reduce total revenue). As a result, total revenue increases.

2. a. The demand of an accident victim for a blood transfusion is very likely to be perfectly inelastic because there is no substitute and it is necessary for survival. The demand curve will be vertical, at a quantity equal to the needed transfusion quantity.

b. Students' demand for green erasers is likely to be perfectly elastic because there are easily available substitutes: nongreen erasers. The demand curve will be horizontal, at a price equal to that of non-green erasers.

6-3 CHECK YOUR UNDERSTANDING

1. By the midpoint method, the percentage increase in Chelsea's income is

$$\frac{\$18\,000 - \$12\,000}{(\$12\,000 + \$18\,000)/2} \times 100 = \frac{\$6000}{\$15\,000} \times 100 = 40\%$$

Similarly, the percent increase in her consumption of CDs is

$$\frac{40 - 10}{(10 + 40)/2} \times 100 = \frac{30}{25} \times 100 = 120\%$$

So Chelsea's income elasticity of demand for CDs is 120%/40% = 3.

2. Sanjay's consumption of expensive restaurant meals will fall more than 10% because a given percentage change in income (a fall of 10% here) induces a larger percentage change in consumption of an income-elastic good.

3. The cross-price elasticity of demand is 5%/20% = 0.25. Since the cross-price elasticity of demand is positive, the two goods are substitutes.

6-4 CHECK YOUR UNDERSTANDING

1. By the midpoint method, the percentage change in the number of hours of web-design services contracted is

$$\frac{500\,000 - 300\,000}{(300\,000 + 500\,000)/2} \times 100 = \frac{200\,000}{400\,000} \times 100 = 50\%$$

Similarly, the percentage change in the price of web-design services is:

$$\frac{\$150 - \$100}{(\$100 + \$150)/2} \times 100 = \frac{\$50}{\$125} \times 100 = 40\%$$

The price elasticity of supply is 50%/40% = 1.25. So supply is elastic.

2. True. An increase in demand raises price. If the price elasticity of supply of milk is low, then relatively little additional supply will be forthcoming as the price rises. As a result, the price of milk will rise substantially to satisfy the increased demand for milk. If the price elasticity of supply is high, then a relatively large amount of additional supply will be produced as the price rises. As a result, the price of milk will rise only by a little to satisfy the higher demand for milk.

3. False. It is true that long-run price elasticities of supply are generally larger than short-run elasticities of supply. But this means that the short-run supply curves are generally steeper, not flatter, than the long-run supply curves.

4. True. When supply is perfectly elastic, the supply curve is a horizontal line. So a change in demand has no effect on price; it affects only the quantity bought and sold.

Chapter Seven

7-1 CHECK YOUR UNDERSTANDING

1. The following figure shows that, after introduction of the excise tax, the price paid by consumers rises to $1.20; the price received by producers falls to $0.90. Consumers bear $0.20 of the $0.30 tax per kilogram of butter; producers bear $0.10 of the $0.30 tax per kilogram of butter. The tax drives a wedge of $0.30 between the price paid by consumers and the price received by producers. As a result, the quantity of butter bought and sold is now 9 million kilograms.

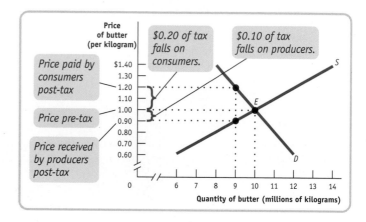

2. The fact that demand is very inelastic means that consumers will reduce their demand for textbooks very little in response to an increase in the price caused by the tax. The fact that supply is somewhat elastic means that suppliers will respond to the fall in the price by reducing supply. As a result, the incidence of the tax will fall heavily on consumers of economics textbooks and very little on publishers, as shown in the accompanying figure.

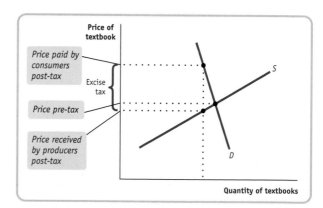

3. True. When a substitute is readily available, demand is elastic. This implies that producers cannot easily pass on the cost of the tax to consumers because consumers will respond to an increased price by switching to the substitute. Furthermore, when producers have difficulty adjusting the amount of the good produced, supply is inelastic. That is, producers cannot easily reduce output in response to a lower price net of tax. So the tax burden will fall more heavily on producers than consumers.

4. The fact that supply is very inelastic means that producers will reduce their supply of bottled water very little in response to the fall in price caused by the tax. Demand, on the other hand, will fall in response to an increase in price because demand is somewhat elastic. As a result, the incidence of the tax will fall heavily on producers of bottled spring water and very little on consumers, as shown in the accompanying figure.

5. True. The lower the elasticity of supply, the more the burden of a tax will fall on producers rather than consumers, other things equal.

7-2 CHECK YOUR UNDERSTANDING

1. a. Without the excise tax, Zhang, Yves, Xavier, and Walter sell, and Ana, Bernice, Chizuko, and Dagmar buy one can of cola each, at $0.40 per can. So the quantity bought and sold is 4.

b. With the excise tax, Zhang and Yves sell, and Ana and Bernice buy one can of cola each. So the quantity bought and sold is 2.

c. Without the excise tax, Ana's individual consumer surplus is $0.70 − $0.40 = $0.30, Bernice's is $0.60 − $0.40 = $0.20, Chizuko's is $0.50 − $0.40 = $0.10, and Dagmar's is $0.40 − $0.40 = $0.00. Total consumer surplus is $0.30 + $0.20 + $0.10 + $0.00 = $0.60. With the tax, Ana's individual consumer surplus is $0.70 − $0.60 = $0.10 and Bernice's is $0.60 − $0.60 = $0.00. Total consumer surplus post-tax is $0.10 + $0.00 = $0.10. So the total consumer surplus lost because of the tax is $0.60 − $0.10 = $0.50.

d. Without the excise tax, Zhang's individual producer surplus is $0.40 − $0.10 = $0.30, Yves's is $0.40 − $0.20 = $0.20, Xavier's is $0.40 − $0.30 = $0.10, and Walter's is $0.40 − $0.40 = $0.00. Total producer surplus is $0.30 + $0.20 + $0.10 + $0.00 = $0.60. With the tax, Zhang's individual producer surplus is $0.20 − $0.10 = $0.10 and Yves's is $0.20 − $0.20 = $0.00. Total producer surplus post-tax is $0.10 + $0.00 = $0.10. So the total producer surplus lost because of the tax is $0.60 − $0.10 = $0.50.

e. With the tax, two cans of cola are sold, so the government tax revenue from this excise tax is 2 × $0.40 = $0.80.

f. Total surplus without the tax is $0.60 + $0.60 = $1.20. With the tax, total surplus is $0.10 + $0.10 = $0.20, and government tax revenue is $0.80. So deadweight loss from this excise tax is $1.20 − ($0.20 + $0.80) = $0.20.

2. a. The demand for gasoline is inelastic because there is no close substitute for gasoline itself and it is difficult for drivers to arrange substitutes for driving, such as taking public transportation. As a result, the deadweight loss from a tax on gasoline would be relatively small, as shown in the accompanying diagram.

b. The demand for milk chocolate bars is elastic because there are close substitutes: dark chocolate bars, milk chocolate kisses, and so on. As a result, the deadweight loss from a tax on milk chocolate bars would be relatively large, as shown in the accompanying diagram.

7-3 CHECK YOUR UNDERSTANDING

1. a. Since drivers are the beneficiaries of highway safety programs, this tax performs well according to the benefits principle. But since the level of the tax does not depend on ability to pay the tax, it does not perform well according to the ability-to-pay principle. Since higher-income car purchasers are likely to spend more on a new car, a tax assessed as a percentage of the purchase price of the car would perform better on the ability-to-pay principle. A $500-per-car tax will cause people to buy fewer new cars, but a percentage-based tax will cause people to buy fewer cars and less expensive cars.

b. This tax does not perform well according to the benefits principle because the payers are nonresidents of the local area, but the beneficiaries are local residents who will enjoy greater government services. But to the extent that people who stay in hotels have higher income compared to those who don't, the tax performs well according to the ability-to-pay principle. It will distort the action of staying in a hotel room in this area, resulting in fewer nights of hotel room stays.

c. This tax performs well according to the benefits principle because local homeowners are the users of local schools. It also performs well according to the ability-to-pay principle because it is assessed as a percentage of home value: higher-income residents, who own more expensive homes, will pay higher taxes. It will distort the action of buying a house in this area versus another area with a lower property tax rate or the action of making changes to a house that increase its assessed value.

d. This tax performs well according to the benefits principle because food consumers are the beneficiaries of government food safety programs. It does not perform well according to the ability-to-pay principle because food is a necessity, and lower-income people will pay approximately as much as higher-income people. This tax will distort the action of buying food, leading people to purchase cheaper varieties of food.

7-4 CHECK YOUR UNDERSTANDING

1. a. The marginal tax rate for someone with income of $5000 is 1%: for each additional $1 in income, $0.01 or 1%, is taxed away. This person pays total tax of $5000 × 1% = $50, which is ($50/$5000) × 100 = 1% of his or her income.

b. The marginal tax rate for someone with income of $20 000 is 2%: for each additional $1 in income, $0.02 or 2%, is taxed away. This person pays total tax of $10 000 × 1% + $10 000 × 2% = $300, which is ($300/$20 000) × 100 = 1.5% of his or her income.

c. Since the high-income taxpayer pays a larger percentage of his or her income than the low-income taxpayer, this tax is progressive.

2. A 1% tax on consumption spending means that a family earning $15 000 and spending $10 000 will pay a tax of 1% × $10 000 = $100, equivalent to 0.67% of its income; ($100/$15 000) × 100 = 0.67%. But a family earning $10 000 and spending $8000 will pay a tax of 1% × $8000 = $80, equivalent to 0.80% of its income; ($80/$10 000) × 100 = 0.80%. So the tax is regressive, since the lower-income family pays a higher percentage of its income in tax than the higher-income family.

3. a. False. Recall that a seller always bears some burden of a tax as long as his or her supply of the good is not perfectly elastic. Since the supply of labour a worker offers is not perfectly elastic, some of the payroll tax will be borne by the worker, and therefore the tax will affect the person's incentive to take a job.

b. False. Under a proportional tax, the percentage of the tax base is the same for everyone. Under a lump-sum tax, the total tax paid is the same for everyone, regardless of their income. A lump-sum tax is regressive.

Chapter Eight

8-1 CHECK YOUR UNDERSTANDING

1. a. To determine comparative advantage, we must compare the two countries' opportunity costs for a given good. Take the opportunity cost of 1 tonne of wheat in terms of bicycles. In China, the opportunity cost of 1 bicycle is 0.01 tonne of wheat; so the opportunity cost of 1 tonne of wheat is 1/0.01 bicycles = 100 bicycles. Canada has the comparative advantage in wheat since its opportunity cost in terms of bicycles is 50, a smaller number. Similarly, the opportunity cost in Canada of 1 bicycle in terms of wheat is 1/50 tonne of wheat = 0.02 tonne of wheat. This is greater than 0.01, the Chinese opportunity cost of 1 bicycle in terms of wheat, implying that China has a comparative advantage in bicycles.

b. Given that Canada can produce 200 000 bicycles if no wheat is produced, it can produce 200 000 bicycles × 0.02 tonne of wheat/bicycle = 4000 tonnes of wheat when no bicycles are produced. Likewise, if China can produce 3000 tonnes of wheat if no bicycles are produced, it can produce 3000 tonnes of wheat × 100 bicycles/tonne of wheat = 300 000 bicycles if no wheat is produced. These points determine the vertical and horizontal intercepts of the Canadian and Chinese production possibility frontiers, as shown in the accompanying diagram.

(a) Canadian Production Possibility Frontier

Quantity of wheat (tonnes)

Canadian production with trade

Slope = −0.02

Canadian consumption with trade

Canadian PPF

Quantity of bicycles

(b) Chinese Production Possibility Frontier

Quantity of wheat (tonnes)

Chinese consumption with trade

Slope = −0.01

Chinese production with trade

China PPF

Quantity of bicycles

c. The diagram shows the production and consumption points of the two countries. Each country is clearly better off with international trade because each now consumes a bundle of the two goods that lies outside its own production possibility frontier, indicating that these bundles were unattainable in autarky.

2. a. According to the Heckscher–Ohlin model, this pattern of trade occurs because Canada has a relatively larger endowment of factors of production, such as human capital and physical capital, that are suited to the production of lumber, but France has a relatively larger endowment of factors of production suited to wine-making, such as vineyards and the human capital of vintners.

b. According to the Heckscher–Ohlin model, this pattern of trade occurs because Canada has a relatively larger endowment of factors of production, such as human and physical capital, that are suited to making machinery, but Brazil has a relatively larger endowment of factors of production suited to shoe-making, such as unskilled labour and leather.

8-2   CHECK YOUR UNDERSTANDING

1. In the accompanying diagram, P_A is the Canadian price of grapes in autarky and P_W is the world price of grapes under international trade. With trade, Canadian consumers pay a price of P_W for grapes and consume quantity Q_D, Canadian grape producers produce quantity Q_S, and the difference, $Q_D - Q_S$, represents imports of Mexican grapes. As a consequence of the strike by truckers, imports are halted, the price paid by Canadian consumers rises to the autarky price, P_A, and Canadian consumption falls to the autarky quantity, Q_A.

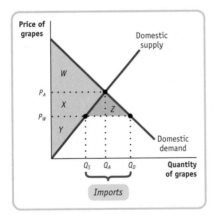

a. Before the strike, Canadian consumers enjoyed consumer surplus equal to areas $W + X + Z$. After the strike, their consumer surplus shrinks to W. So consumers are worse off, losing consumer surplus represented by $X + Z$.

b. Before the strike, Canadian producers had producer surplus equal to the area Y. After the strike, their producer surplus increases to $Y + X$. So Canadian producers are better off, gaining producer surplus represented by X.

c. Canadian total surplus falls as a result of the strike by an amount represented by area Z, the loss in consumer surplus that does not accrue to producers.

2. Mexican grape producers are worse off because they lose sales of exported grapes to Canada, and Mexican grape pickers are worse off because they lose the wages that were associated with the lost sales. The lower demand for Mexican grapes caused by the strike implies that the price Mexican consumers pay

for grapes falls, making them better off. Canadian grape pickers are better off because their wages increase as a result of the increase of $Q_A - Q_S$ in Canadian sales.

8-3   CHECK YOUR UNDERSTANDING

1. a. If the tariff is $2.00, the price paid by domestic consumers for a kilogram of imported butter is $2.00 + $2.00 = $4.00, the same price as a kilogram of domestic butter. Imported butter will no longer have a price advantage over domestic butter, imports will cease, and domestic producers will capture all the feasible sales to domestic consumers, selling amount Q_A in the accompanying figure. But if the tariff is less than $2.00—say, only $1.00—the price paid by domestic consumers for a kilogram of imported butter is $2.00 + $1.00 = $3.00, $1.00 cheaper than a kilogram of domestic butter. Canadian butter producers will gain sales in the amount of $Q_2 - Q_1$ as a result of the $1.00 tariff. But this is smaller than the amount they would have gained under the $2.00 tariff, the amount $Q_A - Q_1$.

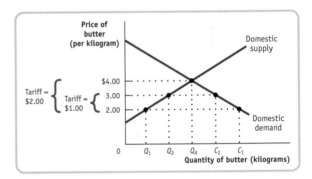

b. As long as the tariff is at least $2.00, increasing it more has no effect. At a tariff of $2.00, all imports are effectively blocked.

2. All imports are effectively blocked at a tariff of $2.00. So such a tariff corresponds to an import quota of 0.

8-4   CHECK YOUR UNDERSTANDING

1. There are many fewer businesses that use steel as an input than there are consumers who buy eggs or clothing. So it will be easier for such businesses to communicate and coordinate among themselves to lobby against tariffs than it will be for consumers. In addition, each business will perceive that the cost of a steel tariff is quite costly to its profits, but an individual consumer is either unaware of or perceives little loss from tariffs on eggs or clothing.

2. Countries are often tempted to protect domestic industries by claiming that an import poses a quality, health, or environmental danger to domestic consumers. A WTO official should examine whether domestic producers are subject to the same stringency in the application of quality, health, or environmental regulations as foreign producers. If they are, then it is more likely that the regulations are for legitimate, non–trade protection purposes; if they are not, then it is more likely that the regulations are intended as trade protection measures.

Chapter Nine

9-1 CHECK YOUR UNDERSTANDING

1. a. Supplies are an explicit cost because they require an outlay of money.

b. If the basement could be used in some other way that generates money, such as renting it to a student, then the implicit cost is that money forgone. Otherwise, the implicit cost is zero.

c. Wages are an explicit cost.

d. By using the van for their business, Karma and Don forgo the money they could have gained by selling it. So use of the van is an implicit cost.

e. Karma's forgone wages from her job are an implicit cost.

2. We need only compare the choice of becoming a machinist to the choice of taking a job in financial services in order to make the right choice. We can discard the choice of acquiring a social work degree because we already know that taking a job in financial services is always superior to it. Now let's compare the remaining two alternatives: becoming a skilled machinist versus immediately taking a job in financial services. As an apprentice machinist, Maria will earn only $30 000 over the first two years, versus $57 000 in financial services. So she has an implicit cost of $30 000 − $57 000 = −$27 000 by becoming a machinist instead of immediately working in financial services. However, two years from now the value of her lifetime earnings as a machinist is $725 000 versus $500 000 in financial services, giving her an accounting profit of $225 000 by choosing to be a machinist. Summing, her economic profit from choosing a career as a machinist over a career in financial services is $225 000 − $27 000 = $198 000. In contrast, her economic profit from choosing the alternative, a career in financial services over a career as a machinist, is −$225 000 + $27 000 = −$198 000. By the principle of "either–or" decision making, Maria should choose to be a machinist because that career has a positive economic profit.

3. You can discard alternative A because both B and C are superior to it. But you must now compare B versus C. You should then choose the alternative—B or C—that carries a positive economic profit.

9-2 CHECK YOUR UNDERSTANDING

1. a. The marginal cost of doing your laundry is any monetary outlays plus the opportunity cost of your time spent doing laundry today—that is, the value you would place on spending time today on your next best alternative activity, like seeing a movie. The marginal benefit is having more clean clothes today to choose from.

b. The marginal cost of changing your oil is the opportunity cost of time spent changing your oil now as well as the explicit cost of the oil change. The marginal benefit is the improvement in your car's performance.

c. The marginal cost is the unpleasant feeling of a burning mouth that you receive from it plus any explicit cost of the jalapeno. The marginal benefit of another jalapeno on your nachos is the pleasant taste that you receive from it.

d. The marginal benefit of hiring another worker in your company is the value of the output that worker produces. The marginal cost is the wage you must pay that worker.

e. The marginal cost is the value lost due to the increased side effects from this additional dose. The marginal benefit of another dose of the drug is the value of the reduction in the patient's disease.

f. The marginal cost is the opportunity cost of your time—what you would have gotten from the next best use of your time. The marginal benefit is the probable increase in your grade.

2. The accompanying table shows Alex's new marginal cost and his new profit. It also reproduces Alex's marginal benefit from Table 9-5.

Years of schooling	Total cost	Marginal cost	Marginal benefit	Profit
0	$0			
		$90 000	$300 000	$210 000
1	90 000			
		30 000	150 000	120 000
2	120 000			
		50 000	90 000	40 000
3	170 000			
		80 000	60 000	−20 000
4	250 000			
		120 000	50 000	−80 000
5	370 000			

Alex's marginal cost is decreasing until he has completed two years of schooling, after which marginal cost increases because of the value of his forgone income. The optimal amount of schooling is still three years. For less than three years of schooling, marginal benefit exceeds marginal cost; for more than three years, marginal cost exceeds marginal benefit.

9-3 CHECK YOUR UNDERSTANDING

1. a. Your sunk cost is $8000 because none of the $8000 spent on the truck is recoverable.

b. Your sunk cost is $4000 because 50% of the $8000 spent on the truck is recoverable.

c. Your sunk cost is $0 because you can fully recover the cost of buying the truck by selling it to another ice-cream vendor.

2. a. This is an invalid argument because the time and money already spent are a sunk cost at this point.

b. This is also an invalid argument because what you should have done two years ago is irrelevant to what you should do now.

c. This is a valid argument because it recognizes that sunk costs are irrelevant to what you should do now.

d. This is a valid argument given that you are concerned about disappointing your parents. But your parents' views are irrational because they do not recognize that the time already spent is a sunk cost.

9-4 CHECK YOUR UNDERSTANDING

1. a. Jenny is exhibiting loss aversion. She has an oversensitivity to loss, leading to an unwillingness to recognize a loss and move on.

b. Dan is doing mental accounting. Dollars from his unexpected overtime earnings are worth less—spent on a weekend getaway—than the dollars earned from his regular hours that he uses to pay down his student loan.

c. Carol may have unrealistic expectations of future behaviour. Even if she does not want to participate in the plan now, she should find a way to commit to participating at a later date.

d. Jeremy is showing signs of status quo bias. He is avoiding making a decision altogether; in other words, he is sticking with the status quo.

2. You would determine whether a decision was rational or irrational by first accurately accounting for all the costs and benefits of the decision. In particular, you must accurately measure all opportunity costs. Then calculate the economic payoff of the decision relative to the next best alternative. If you would still make the same choice after this comparison, then you have made a rational choice. If not, then the choice was irrational.

3. You are being rational in declining the offer because the expected benefits—receiving $10 million with only a 1-in-a-million chance of survival—is less than the expected costs—losing your life.

Chapter Ten
10-1 CHECK YOUR UNDERSTANDING

1. Consuming a unit that generates negative marginal utility leaves the consumer with lower total utility than not consuming that unit at all. A rational consumer, a consumer who maximizes utility, would not do that. For example, from Figure 10-1 you can see that Cassie receives 64 utils if she consumes 8 wings; but if she consumes the 9th wing, she loses a util, netting her a total utility of only 63 utils. So whenever consuming a unit generates negative marginal utility, the consumer is made better off by not consuming that unit, even when that unit is free.

2. Since Marta has diminishing marginal utility of coffee, her first cup of coffee of the day generates the greatest increase in total utility. Her third and last cup of the day generates the least.

3. a. Mabel has increasing marginal utility of exercising since each additional unit consumed brings more additional enjoyment than the previous unit.

b. Mei has constant marginal utility of CDs because each additional unit generates the same additional enjoyment as the previous unit.

c. Dexter has diminishing marginal utility of restaurant meals since the additional utility generated by a good

restaurant meal is less when he consumes lots of them than when he consumed few of them.

10-2 CHECK YOUR UNDERSTANDING

1. a. The accompanying table shows the consumer's consumption possibilities, *A* through *C*. These consumption possibilities are plotted in the accompanying diagram, along with the consumer's budget line, *BL*.

Consumption bundle	Quantity of popcorn (buckets)	Quantity of movie tickets
A	0	2
B	2	1
C	4	0

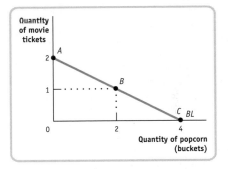

b. The accompanying table shows the consumer's consumption possibilities, *A* through *D*. These consumption possibilities are plotted in the accompanying diagram, along with the consumer's budget line, *BL*.

Consumption bundle	Quantity of underwear (pairs)	Quantity of socks (pairs)
A	0	6
B	1	4
C	2	2
D	3	0

10-3 CHECK YOUR UNDERSTANDING

1. From Table 10-3 you can see that Sammy's marginal utility per dollar from increasing his consumption of wings from 3 kilograms to 4 kilograms and his marginal utility per dollar from increasing his consumption of potatoes from 9 to 10 kilograms are the same, 0.75 utils. But a consumption bundle consisting of 4 kilograms of wings and 10 kilograms of potatoes is not Sammy's optimal consumption bundle because it is not affordable given his income of $20; 4 kilograms of wings and 10 kilograms of potatoes costs $4 × 4 + $2 × 10 = $36, $16 more than Sammy's income. This can be illustrated with Sammy's budget line from Figure 10-3: a bundle of 4 kilograms of wings and 10 kilograms of potatoes is represented by point X in the accompanying diagram, a point that lies outside Sammy's budget line. If you look at the horizontal axis of Figure 10-4, it is quite clear that there is no such thing in Sammy's consumption possibilities as a bundle consisting of 4 kilograms of wings and 10 kilograms of potatoes.

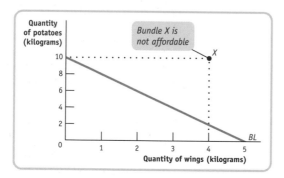

2. Sammy's maximum utility per dollar is generated when he goes from consuming 0 to 1 kilogram of wings (3.75 utils) and as he goes from 0 to 1 kilogram of potatoes (5.75 utils). But this bundle consisting of 1 kilogram of wings and 1 kilogram of potatoes generates only 26.5 utils for him. Instead, Sammy should choose the consumption bundle that satisfies his budget constraint and for which the marginal utility per dollar for both goods is equal.

10-4 CHECK YOUR UNDERSTANDING

1. a. Since spending on orange juice is a small share of Clare's spending, the income effect from a rise in the price of orange juice is insignificant. Only the substitution effect, represented by the substitution of lemonade in place of orange juice, is significant.

b. Since rent is a large share of Delia's expenditures, the increase in rent generates a significant income effect, making Delia feel poorer. Since housing is a normal good for Delia, the income and substitution effects move in the same direction, leading her to reduce her consumption of housing by moving to a smaller apartment.

c. Since a meal ticket is a significant share of the students' living costs, an increase in its price will generate a significant income effect. Because cafeteria meals are an inferior good, the substitution effect (which would induce students to substitute restaurant meals in place of cafeteria meals) and the income effect (which would induce them to eat in the cafeteria more often because they are poorer) move in opposite directions.

2. In order to determine whether any good is a Giffen good, you must first establish whether it is an inferior good. In other words, if students' incomes decrease, other things equal, does the quantity of cafeteria meals

demanded increase? Once you have established that the good is an inferior good, you must then establish that the income effect outweighs the substitution effect. That is, as the price of cafeteria meals rises, other things equal, does the quantity of cafeteria meals demanded increase? Be careful that, in fact, all other things remain equal. But if the quantity of cafeteria meals demanded truly increases in response to a price rise, you really have found a Giffen good.

Chapter Eleven
11-1 CHECK YOUR UNDERSTANDING

1. a. The fixed input is the 10-tonne machine, and the variable input is electricity.

b. As you can see from the declining numbers in the third column of the accompanying table, electricity does indeed exhibit diminishing returns: the marginal product of each additional kilowatt-hour of electricity is less than that of the previous kilowatt-hour.

Quantity of electricity (kilowatt-hours)	Quantity of ice (kilograms)	Marginal product of electricity (kilograms per kilowatt-hour)
0	0	
		1000
1	1000	
		800
2	1800	
		600
3	2400	
		400
4	2800	

c. As you can see from the accompanying table, the average product of the variable input falls as the quantity of variable input used increases.

Quantity of electricity (kilowatt-hours)	Quantity of ice (kilograms)	Average product of the variable input (kilograms per kilowatt-hour)
0	0	
		1000
1	1000	
		900
2	1800	
		800
3	2400	
		700
4	2800	

d. A 50% increase in the size of the fixed input means that Bernie now has a 15-tonne machine. So the fixed input is now the 15-tonne machine. Since it generates a 100% increase in output for any given amount of electricity, the quantity of output and marginal product are now as shown in the accompanying table.

Quantity of electricity (kilowatt-hours)	Quantity of ice (kilograms)	Marginal product of electricity (kilograms per kilowatt-hour)
0	0	
		2000
1	2000	
		1600
2	3600	
		1200
3	4800	
		800
4	5600	

11-2 CHECK YOUR UNDERSTANDING

1. a. As shown in the accompanying table, the marginal cost for each pie is found by multiplying the marginal cost of the previous pie by 1.5. Variable cost for each output level is found by summing the marginal cost for all the pies produced to reach that output level. So, for example, the variable cost of three pies is $1.00 + $1.50 + $2.25 = $4.75. Average fixed cost for Q pies is calculated as $9.00/$Q$ since fixed cost is $9.00. Average variable cost for Q pies is equal to variable cost for the Q pies divided by Q; for example, the average variable cost of five pies is $13.19/5, or approximately $2.64. Finally, average total cost can be calculated in two equivalent ways: as TC/Q or as $AVC + AFC$.

Quantity of pies	Marginal cost of pie	Variable cost	Average fixed cost of pie	Average variable cost of pie	Average total cost of pie
0		$0.00	—	—	—
	$1.00				
1		1.00	$9.00	$1.00	$10.00
	1.50				
2		2.50	4.50	1.25	5.75
	2.25				
3		4.75	3.00	1.58	4.58
	3.38				
4		8.13	2.25	2.03	4.28
	5.06				
5		13.19	1.80	2.64	4.44
	7.59				
6		20.78	1.50	3.46	4.96

b. The spreading effect dominates the diminishing returns effect when average total cost is falling: the fall in *AFC* dominates the rise in *AVC* for pies 1 to 4. The diminishing returns effect dominates when average total cost is rising: the rise in *AVC* dominates the fall in *AFC* for pies 5 and 6.

c. Alicia's minimum-cost output is 4 pies; this generates the lowest average total cost, $4.28. When output is less than 4, the marginal cost of a pie is less than the average total cost of the pies already produced. So making an additional pie lowers average total cost. For example, the marginal cost of pie 3 is $2.25, whereas the average total cost of pies 1 and 2 is $5.75. So making pie 3 lowers average total cost to $4.58, equal to (2 × $5.75 + $2.25)/3. When output is more than 4, the marginal cost of a pie is greater than the average total cost of the pies already produced. Consequently, making an additional pie raises average total cost. So, although the marginal cost of pie 6 is $7.59, the average total cost of pies 1 through 5 is $4.44. Making pie 6 raises average total cost to $4.96, equal to (5 × $4.44 + $7.59)/6.

11-3 CHECK YOUR UNDERSTANDING

1. a. The accompanying table shows the average total cost of producing 12 000, 22 000, and 30 000 units for each of the three choices of fixed cost. For example, if the firm makes choice 1, the total cost of producing 12 000 units of output is $8000 + 12 000 × $1.00 = $20 000. The average total cost of producing 12 000 units of output is therefore $20 000/12 000 = $1.67. The other average total costs are calculated similarly.

	12 000 units	22 000 units	30 000 units
Average total cost from choice 1	$1.67	$1.36	$1.27
Average total cost from choice 2	1.75	1.30	1.15
Average total cost from choice 3	2.25	1.34	1.05

So if the firm wanted to produce 12 000 units, it would make choice 1 because this gives it the lowest average total cost. If it wanted to produce 22 000 units, it would make choice 2. If it wanted to produce 30 000 units, it would make choice 3.

b. Having historically produced 12 000 units, the firm would have adopted choice 1. When producing 12 000 units, the firm would have had an average total cost of $1.67. When output jumps to 22 000 units, the firm cannot alter its choice of fixed cost in the short run, so its average total cost in the short run will be $1.36. In the long run, however, it will adopt choice 2, making its average total cost fall to $1.30.

c. If the firm believes that the increase in demand is temporary, it should not alter its fixed cost from choice 1 because choice 2 generates higher average total cost as soon as output falls back to its original quantity of 12 000 units: $1.75 versus $1.67.

2. a. This firm is likely to experience constant returns to scale. To increase output, the firm must hire more workers, purchase more computers, and pay additional telephone charges. Because these inputs are easily available, their long-run average total cost is unlikely to change as output increases.

b. This firm is likely to experience decreasing returns to scale. As the firm takes on more projects, the costs of communication and coordination required to implement the expertise of the firm's owner are likely to increase.

c. This firm is likely to experience increasing returns to scale. Because diamond mining requires a large initial set-up cost for excavation equipment, long-run average total cost will fall as output increases.

3. The accompanying diagram shows the long-run average total cost curve (*LRATC*) and the short-run average total cost curve corresponding to a long-run output choice of 5 cases of salsa (*ATC*₅). The curve *ATC*₅ shows the short-run average total cost for which the level of fixed cost minimizes average total cost at an output of 5 cases of salsa. This is confirmed by the fact that at 5 cases per day, *ATC*₅ touches *LRATC*, the long-run average total cost curve.

If Selena expects to produce only 4 cases of salsa for a long time, she should change her fixed cost. If she does *not* change her fixed cost and produces 4 cases of salsa, her average total cost in the short run is indicated by point *B* on *ATC*₅; it is no longer on the *LRATC*. If she changes her fixed cost, though, her average total cost could be lower, at point *A*.

Chapter Twelve
12-1 CHECK YOUR UNDERSTANDING

1. a. With only two producers in the world, each producer will represent a sizable share of the market. So the industry will not be perfectly competitive.

b. Because each producer of natural gas from the North Sea has only a small market share of total world supply of natural gas, and since natural gas is a standardized product, the natural gas industry will be perfectly competitive.

c. Because each designer has a distinctive style, high-fashion clothes are not a standardized product. So the industry will not be perfectly competitive.

d. The market described here is the market in each city for tickets to NHL games. Since there are only one or

two teams in each major city, each team will represent a sizable share of the market. So the industry will not be perfectly competitive.

12-2 CHECK YOUR UNDERSTANDING

1. a. The firm should shut down immediately when price is less than minimum average variable cost, the shut-down price. In the accompanying diagram, this is optimal for prices in the range 0 to P_1.

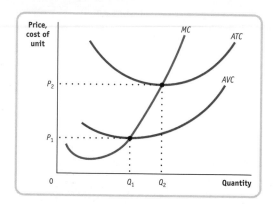

b. When price is greater than minimum average variable cost (the shut-down price) but less than minimum average total cost (the break-even price), the firm should continue to operate in the short run even though it is making a loss. This is optimal for prices in the range P_1 to P_2 and for quantities Q_1 to Q_2.

c. When price exceeds minimum average total cost (the break-even price), the firm makes a profit. This happens for prices in excess of P_2 and results in quantities greater than Q_2.

2. This is an example of a temporary shut-down by a firm when the market price lies below the shut-down price, the minimum average variable cost. In this case, the market price is the price of a lobster meal and variable cost is the variable cost of serving such a meal, such as the cost of the lobster, employee wages, and so on. In this example, however, it is the average variable cost curve rather than the market price that shifts over time, due to seasonal changes in the cost of lobsters. Lobster shacks in Atlantic Canada have relatively low average variable cost during the summer, when cheap lobsters are available. During the rest of the year, their average variable cost is relatively high due to the high cost of imported lobsters. So the lobster shacks are open for business during the summer, when their minimum average variable cost lies below price. But they close during the rest of the year, when price lies below their minimum average variable cost.

12-3 CHECK YOUR UNDERSTANDING

1. a. A fall in the fixed cost of production generates a fall in the average total cost of production and, in the short run, an increase in each firm's profit at the current output level. So in the long run new firms will enter the industry. The increase in supply drives down price and profits. Once profits are driven back to zero, entry will cease.

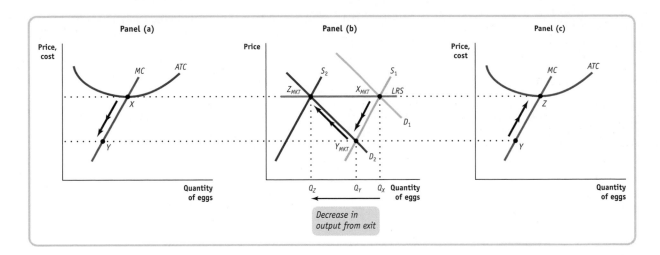

b. An increase in wages generates an increase in the average variable and the average total cost of production at every output level. In the short run, firms incur losses at the current output level, and so in the long run some firms will exit the industry. (If the average variable cost rises sufficiently, some firms may even shut down in the short run.) As firms exit, supply decreases, price rises, and losses are reduced. Exit will cease once losses return to zero.

c. Price will rise as a result of the increased demand, leading to a short-run increase in profits at the current output level. In the long run, firms will enter the industry, generating an increase in supply, a fall in price, and a fall in profits. Once profits are driven back to zero, entry will cease.

d. The shortage of a key input causes that input's price to increase, resulting in an increase in average variable and average total costs for producers. Firms incur losses in the short run, and some firms will exit the industry in the long run. The fall in supply generates an increase in price and decreased losses. Exit will cease when losses have returned to zero.

2. In the above diagram, point X_{MKT} in panel (b), the intersection of S_1 and D_1, represents the long-run industry equilibrium before the change in consumer tastes. When tastes change, demand falls and the industry moves in the short run to point Y_{MKT} in panel (b), at the intersection of the new demand curve D_2 and S_1, the short-run supply curve representing the same number of egg producers as in the original equilibrium at point X_{MKT}. As the market price falls, an individual firm reacts by producing less—as shown in panel (a)—as long as the market price remains above the minimum average variable cost. If market price falls below minimum average variable cost, the firm would shut down immediately. At point Y_{MKT} the price of eggs is below minimum average total cost, creating losses for producers. This leads some firms to exit, which shifts the short-run industry supply curve leftward to S_2. A new long-run equilibrium is established at point Z_{MKT}. As this occurs, the market price rises again, and, as shown in panel (c), each remaining producer reacts by increasing output (here, from point Y

to point Z). All remaining producers again make zero profits. The decrease in the quantity of eggs supplied in the industry comes entirely from the exit of some producers from the industry. The long-run industry supply curve is the curve labelled LRS in panel (b).

Chapter Thirteen

13-1 CHECK YOUR UNDERSTANDING

1. a. This does not support the conclusion. Lamplighter New Brunswick has a limited amount of natural gas, and the price has risen in order to equalize supply and demand.

b. This supports the conclusion because the market for natural gas has become monopolized, and a monopolist will reduce the quantity supplied and raise price to generate profit.

c. This does not support the conclusion. Lamplighter New Brunswick has raised its price to consumers because the price of its input, natural gas, has increased.

d. This supports the conclusion. The fact that other firms have begun to supply natural gas at a lower price implies that Lamplighter New Brunswick must have earned sufficient profits to attract the other firms to New Brunswick.

e. This supports the conclusion. It indicates that Lamplighter New Brunswick enjoys a barrier to entry because it controls access to the only natural gas pipeline.

2. a. Extending the length of a patent increases the length of time during which the inventor can reduce the quantity supplied and increase the market price. Since this increases the period of time during which the inventor can earn economic profits from the invention, it increases the incentive to invent new products.

b. Extending the length of a patent also increases the period of time during which consumers have to pay higher prices. So determining the appropriate length of a patent involves making a trade-off between the desirable incentive for invention and the undesirable high price to consumers.

3. a. When a large number of other people use Passport credit cards, then any one merchant is more likely to accept the card. So the larger the customer base, the more likely a Passport card will be accepted for payment.

b. When a large number of people own a car with a new type of engine, it will be easier to find a knowledgeable mechanic who can repair it.

c. When a large number of people use such a website, the more likely it is that you will be able to find a buyer for something you want to sell or a seller for something you want to buy.

13-2 CHECK YOUR UNDERSTANDING

1. a. The price at each output level is found by dividing the total revenue by the number of emeralds produced; for example, the price when 3 emeralds are produced is $252/3 = $84. The price at the various output levels is then used to construct the demand schedule in the accompanying table.

b. The marginal revenue schedule is found by calculating the change in total revenue as output increases by one unit. For example, the marginal revenue generated by increasing output from 2 to 3 emeralds is ($252 – $186) = $66.

c. The quantity effect component of marginal revenue is the additional revenue generated by selling one more unit of the good at the market price. For example, as shown in the accompanying table, at 3 emeralds, the market price is $84; so when going from 2 to 3 emeralds, the quantity effect is equal to $84.

d. The price effect component of marginal revenue is the decline in total revenue caused by the fall in price when one more unit is sold. For example, as shown in the table, when only 2 emeralds are sold, each emerald sells at a price of $93. However, when Emerald, Inc. sells an additional emerald, the price must fall by $9 to $84. So the price effect component in going from 2 to 3 emeralds is (–$9) × 2 = –$18. That's because 2 emeralds can only be sold at a price of $84 when 3 emeralds in total are sold, although they could have been sold at a price of $93 when only 2 in total were sold.

Quantity of emeralds demanded	Price of emerald	Marginal revenue	Quantity effect component	Price effect component
1	$100			
		$86	$93	–$7
2	93			
		66	84	–18
3	84			
		28	70	–42
4	70			
		–30	50	–80
5	50			

e. In order to determine Emerald, Inc.'s profit-maximizing output level, you must know its marginal cost at each output level. Its profit-maximizing output level is the one at which marginal revenue is equal to marginal cost.

2. As the accompanying diagram shows, the marginal cost curve shifts upward to $400. The profit-maximizing price rises and quantity falls. Profit falls from $3200 to $300 × 6 = $1800. Competitive industry profits, though, are unchanged at zero in the long run.

13-3 CHECK YOUR UNDERSTANDING

1. a. Cable Internet service is a natural monopoly. So the government should intervene only if it believes that price exceeds average total cost, where average total cost is based on the cost of laying the cable. In this case it should impose a price ceiling equal to average total cost. Otherwise, it should do nothing.

b. The government should approve the merger only if it fosters competition by transferring some of the company's landing slots to another, competing airline.

2. a. False. As can be seen from Figure 13-8, panel (b), the inefficiency arises from the fact that some of the consumer surplus is transformed into deadweight loss (the yellow area), not that it is transformed into profit (the green area).

b. True. If a monopolist sold to all customers who have a valuation greater than or equal to marginal cost, all mutually beneficial transactions would occur and there would be no deadweight loss.

3. As shown in the accompanying diagram, a profit-maximizing monopolist produces Q_M, the output level at which $MR = MC$. A monopolist who mistakenly believes that $P = MR$ produces the output level at which $P = MC$ (when, in fact, $P > MR$, and at the true profit-maximizing level of output, $P > MR = MC$). This misguided monopolist will produce the output level Q_C, where the demand curve crosses the marginal cost curve—the same output level produced if the industry were perfectly competitive. It will charge the price P_C, which is equal to marginal cost, and make zero profit. The entire shaded area is equal to the consumer surplus, which is also equal to total surplus in this case (since the monopolist receives zero producer surplus). There is no deadweight loss since every consumer who is willing to pay as much as or more than marginal cost gets the good. A smart monopolist, however, will produce the output level Q_M and charge the price P_M. Profit equals the green area, consumer surplus corresponds to the blue area, and total surplus is equal to the sum of the green and blue areas. The yellow area is the dead-weight loss generated by the monopolist.

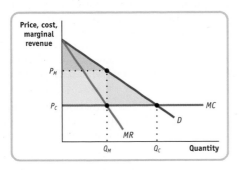

13-4 CHECK YOUR UNDERSTANDING

1. a. False. A price-discriminating monopolist will sell to some customers that a single-price monopolist will refuse to—namely, customers with a high price elasticity of demand who are willing to pay only a relatively low price for the good.

b. False. Although a price-discriminating monopolist does indeed capture more of the consumer surplus, inefficiency is lower: more mutually beneficial transactions occur because the monopolist makes more sales to customers with a low willingness to pay for the good.

c. True. Under price discrimination consumers are charged prices that depend on their price elasticity of demand. A consumer with highly elastic demand will pay a lower price than a consumer with inelastic demand.

2. a. This is not a case of price discrimination because all consumers, regardless of their price elasticities of demand, value the damaged merchandise less than undamaged merchandise. So the price must be lowered to sell the merchandise.

b. This is a case of price discrimination. Senior citizens have a higher price elasticity of demand for restaurant meals (their demand for restaurant meals is more responsive to price changes) than other patrons. Restaurants lower the price to high-elasticity consumers (senior citizens). Consumers with low price elasticity of demand will pay the full price.

c. This is a case of price discrimination. Consumers with a high price elasticity of demand will pay a lower price by collecting and using discount coupons. Consumers with a low price elasticity of demand will not use coupons.

d. This is not a case of price discrimination; it is simply a case of supply and demand.

Chapter Fourteen
14-1 CHECK YOUR UNDERSTANDING

1. a. The world oil industry is an oligopoly because a few countries control a necessary resource for production, oil reserves.

b. The microprocessor industry is an oligopoly because two firms possess superior technology and so dominate industry production.

c. The wide-body passenger jet industry is an oligopoly because there are increasing returns to scale in production.

2. a. The HHI in this industry is $42^2 + 39^2 + 14^2 + 5^2 = 3506$.

b. If Android and BlackBerry were to merge, making their combined market share 39% + 14% = 53%, the HHI in this industry would be $53^2 + 42^2 + 5^2 = 4598$.

14-2 CHECK YOUR UNDERSTANDING

1. a. The firm is likely to act noncooperatively and raise output, which will generate a negative price effect. But because the firm's current market share is small, the negative price effect will fall much more heavily on its rivals' revenues than on its own. At the same time, the firm will benefit from a positive quantity effect.

b. The firm is likely to act noncooperatively and raise output, which will generate a fall in price. Because its rivals have higher costs, they will lose money at the lower price while the firm continues to make profits. So the firm may be able to drive its rivals out of business by increasing its output.

c. The firm is likely to collude. Because it is costly for consumers to switch products, the firm would have to lower its price quite substantially (by increasing quantity a lot) to induce consumers to switch to its product. So increasing output is likely to be unprofitable given the large negative price effect.

d. The firm is likely to act uncooperatively because it knows its rivals cannot increase their output in retaliation.

14-3 CHECK YOUR UNDERSTANDING

1. When Margaret builds a missile, Nikita's payoff from building a missile as well is –10; it is –20 if he does not. The same set of payoffs holds for Margaret when Nikita builds a missile: her payoff is –10 if she builds one as well, –20 if she does not. So it is a Nash equilibrium for both Margaret and Nikita to build missiles, and their total payoff is (–10) + (–10) = –20. But their total payoff is greatest when neither builds a missile: their total payoff is 0 + 0 = 0. But this outcome—the cooperative outcome—is unlikely. If Margaret builds a missile but Nikita does not, Margaret gets a payoff of +8, rather than the 0 she gets if she doesn't build a missile. So Margaret is better off if she builds a missile but Nikita doesn't. Similarly, Nikita is better off if he builds a missile but Margaret doesn't: he gets a payoff of +8, rather than the 0 he gets if he doesn't build a missile. So both players have an incentive to build a missile. Both will build a missile, and each gets a payoff of –10. So unless Nikita and Margaret are able to communicate in some way to enforce cooperation, they will act in their own individual interests and each will build a missile.

2. a. Future entry by several new firms will increase competition and drive down industry profits. As a result, there is less future profit to protect by behaving cooperatively today. So each oligopolist is more likely to behave non-cooperatively today.

b. When it is very difficult for a firm to detect if another firm has raised output, then it is very difficult to enforce cooperation by playing tit for tat. So it is more likely that a firm will behave noncooperatively.

c. When firms have coexisted while maintaining high prices for a long time, each expects cooperation to continue. So the value of behaving cooperatively today is high, and it is likely that firms will engage in tacit collusion.

14-4 CHECK YOUR UNDERSTANDING

1. a. This is likely to be interpreted as evidence of tacit collusion. Firms in the industry are able to tacitly collude by setting their prices according to the published "suggested" price of the largest firm in the industry. This is a form of price leadership.

b. This is not likely to be interpreted as evidence of tacit collusion. Considerable variation in market shares indicates that firms have been competing to capture one anothers' business.

c. This is not likely to be interpreted as evidence of tacit collusion. These features make it more unlikely that consumers will switch products in response to lower prices. So this is a way for firms to avoid any temptation to gain market share by lowering price. This is a form of product differentiation used to avoid direct competition.

d. This is likely to be interpreted as evidence of tacit collusion. In the guise of discussing sales targets, firms can create a cartel by designating quantities to be produced by each firm.

e. This is likely to be interpreted as evidence of tacit collusion. By raising prices together, each firm in the industry is refusing to undercut its rivals by leaving its price unchanged or lowering it. Because it could gain market share by doing so, refusing to do it is evidence of tacit collusion.

Chapter Fifteen
15-1 CHECK YOUR UNDERSTANDING

1. a. Ladders are not differentiated as a result of monopolistic competition. A ladder producer makes different ladders (tall ladders versus short ladders) to satisfy different consumer needs, not to avoid competition with rivals. So two tall ladders made by two different producers will be indistinguishable by consumers.

b. Soft drinks are an example of product differentiation as a result of monopolistic competition. For example, several producers make colas; each is differentiated in terms of taste, which fast-food chains sell it, and so on.

c. Department stores are an example of product differentiation as a result of monopolistic competition. They serve different clienteles that have different price sensitivities and different tastes. They also offer different levels of customer service and are situated in different locations.

d. Steel is not differentiated as a result of monopolistic competition. Different types of steel (beams versus sheets) are made for different purposes, not to distinguish one steel manufacturer's products from another's.

2. a. Perfectly competitive industries and monopolistically competitive industries both have many sellers. So it may be hard to distinguish between them solely in terms of number of firms. And in both market structures, there is free entry into and exit from the industry in the long run. But in a perfectly competitive industry, one standardized product is sold; in a monopolistically competitive industry, products are differentiated. So you should ask whether products are differentiated in the industry.

b. In a monopoly there is only one firm, but a monopolistically competitive industry contains many firms. So you should ask whether or not there is a single firm in the industry.

15-2 CHECK YOUR UNDERSTANDING

1. a. An increase in fixed cost raises average total cost and shifts the average total cost curve upward. In the short run, firms incur losses. In the long run, some will exit the industry, resulting in a rightward shift of the demand curves for those firms that remain in the industry, since each one now serves a larger share of the market. Long-run equilibrium is reestablished when the demand curve for each remaining firm has shifted rightward to the point where it is tangent to the firm's new, higher average total cost curve. At this point each firm's price just equals its average total cost, and each firm makes zero profit.

b. A decrease in marginal cost lowers average total cost and shifts the average total cost curve and the marginal cost curve downward. Because existing firms now make profits, in the long run new entrants are attracted into the industry. In the long run, this results in a leftward shift of each existing firm's demand curve since each firm now has a smaller share of the market. Long-run equilibrium is reestablished when each firm's demand curve has shifted leftward to the point where it is tangent to the new, lower average total cost curve. At this point each firm's price just equals average total cost, and each firm makes zero profit.

2. If all the existing firms in the industry joined together to create a monopoly, they would achieve monopoly profits. But this would induce new firms to create new, differentiated products and then enter the industry and capture some of the monopoly profits. So in the long run it would be impossible to maintain a monopoly. The problem arises from the fact that because free entry means new firms can create new products, there is no barrier to entry that can maintain a monopoly.

15-3 CHECK YOUR UNDERSTANDING

1. a. False. As can be seen from panel (b) of Figure 15-4, a monopolistically competitive firm produces at a point where price exceeds marginal cost—unlike a perfectly competitive firm, which produces where price equals marginal cost (at the point of minimum average total cost). A monopolistically competitive firm will refuse to sell at marginal cost. This would be below average total cost and the firm would incur a loss.

b. True. Firms in a monopolistically competitive industry could achieve higher profits (monopoly profits) if they all joined together and produced a single product. In addition, since the industry possesses excess capacity, producing a larger quantity of output would lower the firm's average total cost. The effect on consumers, however, is ambiguous. They would experience less choice. But if consolidation substantially reduces industry-wide average total cost and therefore substantially increases industry-wide output, consumers may experience lower prices under monopoly.

c. True. Fads and fashions are created and promulgated by advertising, which is found in oligopolies and monopolistically competitive industries but not in monopolies or perfectly competitive industries.

15-4 CHECK YOUR UNDERSTANDING

1. a. This is economically useful because such advertisements are likely to focus on the medical benefits of ASA.

b. This is economically wasteful because such advertisements are likely to focus on promoting Bayer Aspirin versus a rival's ASA product. The two products are medically indistinguishable.

c. This is economically useful because such advertisements are likely to focus on the health and enjoyment benefits of orange juice.

d. This is economically wasteful because such advertisements are likely to focus on promoting Tropicana orange juice versus a rival's product. The two are likely to be indistinguishable by consumers.

e. This is economically useful because the longevity of a business gives a potential customer information about its quality.

2. A successful brand name indicates a desirable attribute, such as quality, to a potential buyer. So, other things equal—such as price—a firm with a successful brand name will achieve higher sales than a rival with a comparable product but without a successful brand name. This is likely to deter new firms from entering an industry in which an existing firm has a successful brand name.

Chapter Sixteen
16-1 CHECK YOUR UNDERSTANDING

1. a. The external cost is the pollution caused by the waste water runoff, an uncompensated cost imposed by the poultry farms on their neighbours.

b. Since poultry farmers do not take the external cost of their actions into account when making decisions about how much waste water to generate, they will create more runoff than is socially optimal in the absence of government intervention or a private deal. They will produce runoff up to the point at which the marginal social benefit of an additional unit of runoff is zero; however, their neighbours experience a high, positive level of marginal social cost of runoff from this output level. So the quantity of waste water runoff is inefficient: reducing runoff by one unit would reduce total social benefit by less than it would reduce total social cost.

c. At the socially optimal quantity of waste water runoff, the marginal social benefit is equal to the marginal social cost. This quantity is lower than the quantity of waste water runoff that would be created in the absence of government intervention or a private deal.

2. Yasmin's reasoning is not correct: allowing some late returns of books is likely to be socially optimal. Although you impose a marginal social cost on others every day that you are late in returning a book, there is some positive marginal social benefit to you of returning a book late—for example, you get a longer period to use it in working on a term paper.

The socially optimal number of days that a book is returned late is the number at which the marginal social benefit equals the marginal social cost. A fine so stiff that it prevents any late returns is likely to result in a situation in which people return books although the marginal social benefit of keeping them another day is greater than the marginal social cost—an inefficient outcome. In that case, allowing an overdue patron another day would increase total social benefit more than it would increase total social cost. So charging a moderate fine that reduces the number of days that books are returned late to the socially optimal number of days is appropriate.

16-2 CHECK YOUR UNDERSTANDING

1. This is a misguided argument. Allowing polluters to sell emissions permits makes polluters face a cost of polluting: the opportunity cost of the permit. If a polluter chooses not to reduce its emissions, it cannot sell its emissions permits. As a result, it forgoes the opportunity of making money from the sale of the permits. So despite the fact that the polluter receives a monetary benefit from selling the permits, the scheme has the desired effect: to make polluters internalize the externality of their actions.

2. a. If the emissions tax is smaller than the marginal social cost at Q_{OPT}, a polluter will face a marginal cost of polluting (equal to the amount of the tax) that is less than the marginal social cost at the socially optimal quantity of pollution. Since a polluter will produce emissions up to the point where the marginal social benefit is equal to its marginal cost, the resulting amount of pollution will be larger than the socially optimal quantity. As a result, there is inefficiency: if the amount of pollution is larger than the socially optimal quantity, the marginal social cost exceeds the marginal social benefit, and society could gain from a reduction in emissions levels.

If the emissions tax is greater than the marginal social cost at Q_{OPT}, a polluter will face a marginal cost of polluting (equal to the amount of the tax) that is greater than the marginal social cost at the socially optimal quantity of pollution. This will lead the polluter to reduce emissions below the socially optimal quantity. This also is inefficient: whenever the marginal social benefit is greater than the marginal social cost, society could benefit from an increase in emissions levels.

b. If the total amount of allowable pollution is set too high, the supply of emissions permits will be high and so the equilibrium price at which permits trade will be low. That is, polluters will face a marginal cost of polluting (the price of a permit) that is "too low"—lower than the marginal social cost at the socially optimal quantity of pollution. As a result, pollution will be greater than the socially optimal quantity. This is inefficient.

If the total level of allowable pollution is set too low, the supply of emissions permits will be low and so the equilibrium price at which permits trade will be high. That is, polluters will face a marginal cost of polluting (the price of a permit) that is "too high"—higher than the marginal social cost at the socially optimal quantity of pollution. As a result, pollution will be lower than the socially optimal quantity. This also is inefficient.

16-3 CHECK YOUR UNDERSTANDING

1. Post secondary education provides external benefits through the creation of knowledge. And government grants and student aid acts like a Pigouvian subsidy on higher education. If the marginal social benefit of higher education is $30 billion, then to obtain an optimal policy provincial and territorial governments need to provide $7 billion in student aid.

2. a. Planting trees imposes an external benefit: the marginal social benefit of planting trees is higher than the marginal benefit to individual tree planters, since many people (not just those who plant the trees) can benefit from the increased air quality and lower summer temperatures. The difference between the marginal social benefit and the marginal benefit to individual tree planters is the marginal external benefit. A Pigouvian subsidy could be placed on each tree planted in urban areas in order to increase the marginal benefit to individual tree planters to the same level as the marginal social benefit.

   b. Water-saving toilets impose an external benefit: the marginal benefit to individual homeowners from replacing a traditional toilet with a water-saving toilet is zero, since water is virtually costless. But the marginal social benefit is large, since fewer rivers and aquifers need to be pumped. The difference between the marginal social benefit and the marginal benefit to individual homeowners is the marginal external benefit. A Pigouvian subsidy on installing water-saving toilets could bring the marginal benefit to individual homeowners in line with the marginal social benefit.

   c. Disposing of old computer monitors imposes an external cost: the marginal cost to those disposing of old computer monitors is lower than the marginal social cost, since environmental pollution is borne by people other than the person disposing of the monitor. The difference between the marginal social cost and the marginal cost to those disposing of old computer monitors is the marginal external cost. A Pigouvian tax on disposing of computer monitors, or a system of tradable permits for their disposal, could raise the marginal cost to those disposing of old computer monitors sufficiently to make it equal to the marginal social cost.

16-4 CHECK YOUR UNDERSTANDING

1. a. The voltage of an appliance must be consistent with the voltage of the electrical outlet it is plugged into. Consumers will want to have 110-volt appliances when houses are wired for 110-volt outlets, and builders will want to install 110-volt outlets when most prospective homeowners use 110-volt appliances. So a network externality arises because a consumer will want to use appliances that operate with the same voltage as the appliances used by most other consumers.

   b. Printers, copy machines, fax machines, and so on are designed for specific paper sizes. Consumers will want to purchase paper of a size that can be used in these machines, and machine manufacturers will want to manufacture their machines for the size of paper that most consumers use. So a network externality arises because a consumer will want to use the size of paper used by most other consumers—namely, 8½-by-11-inch paper rather than 8-by-12½-inch paper.

2. Of the two competing companies, the company able to achieve the higher number of sales is likely to dominate the market. In a market with a network externality, new consumers will base their buying decisions on the number of existing consumers of a specific product. In other words, the more consumers a company can attract initially, the more consumers will choose to buy that company's product; therefore, the good exhibits *positive feedback*. So it is important for a company to make a large number of sales early on. It can do this by pricing its good cheaply and taking a loss on each unit sold. The company that can best afford to subsidize a large number of sales early on is likely to be the winner of this competition.

Chapter Seventeen
17-1 CHECK YOUR UNDERSTANDING

1. a. Use of a public park is nonexcludable, but it may or may not be rival in consumption, depending on the circumstances. For example, if both you and I use the park for jogging, then your use will not prevent my use—use of the park is nonrival in consumption. In this case the public park is a public good. But use of the park is rival in consumption if there are many people trying to use the jogging path at the same time or when my use of the public tennis court prevents your use of the same court. In this case the public park is a common resource.

   b. A cheese burrito is both excludable and rival in consumption. Hence it is a private good.

   c. Information from a password-protected website is excludable but nonrival in consumption (if we assume the website servers are uncongested). So it is an artificially scarce good.

   d. Publicly announced information on the path of an incoming hurricane is nonexcludable and nonrival in consumption. So it is a public good.

2. A private producer will supply only a good that is excludable; otherwise, the producer won't be able to charge a price for it that covers the costs of production. So a private producer would be willing to supply a cheese burrito and information from a password-protected website but unwilling to supply a public park or publicly announced information about an incoming hurricane.

17-2 CHECK YOUR UNDERSTANDING

1. a. With 10 Homebodies and 6 Revellers, the marginal social benefit schedule of money spent on the party is as shown in the accompanying table.

Money spent on party	Marginal social benefit
$0	
	(10 × $0.05) + (6 × $0.13) = $1.28
1	
	(10 × $0.04) + (6 × $0.11) = $1.06
2	
	(10 × $0.03) + (6 × $0.09) = $0.84
3	
	(10 × $0.02) + (6 × $0.07) = $0.62
4	

The efficient spending level is $2, the highest level for which the marginal social benefit is greater than the marginal cost ($1).

b. With 6 Homebodies and 10 Revellers, the marginal social benefit schedule of money spent on the party is as shown in the accompanying table.

Money spent on party	Marginal social benefit
$0	
	(6 × $0.05) + (10 × $0.13) = $1.60
1	
	(6 × $0.04) + (10 × $0.11) = $1.34
2	
	(6 × $0.03) + (10 × $0.09) = $1.08
3	
	(6 × $0.02) + (10 × $0.07) = $0.82
4	

The efficient spending level is now $3, the highest level for which the marginal social benefit is greater than the marginal cost ($1). The efficient level of spending has increased from that in part (a) because with relatively more Revellers than Homebodies, an additional dollar spent on the party generates a higher level of social benefit compared to when there are relatively more Homebodies than Revellers.

c. When the numbers of Homebodies and Revellers are unknown but residents are asked their preferences, Homebodies will pretend to be Revellers to induce a higher level of spending on the public party. That's because a Homebody still receives a positive individual marginal benefit from an additional $1 spent, despite the fact that his or her individual marginal benefit is lower than that of a Reveller for every additional $1. In

this case the "reported" marginal social benefit schedule of money spent on the party will be as shown in the accompanying table.

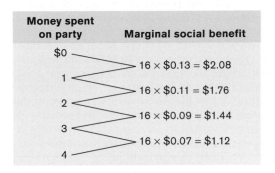

Money spent on party	Marginal social benefit
$0	
	16 × $0.13 = $2.08
1	
	16 × $0.11 = $1.76
2	
	16 × $0.09 = $1.44
3	
	16 × $0.07 = $1.12
4	

As a result, $4 will be spent on the party, the highest level for which the "reported" marginal social benefit is greater than the marginal cost ($1). Regardless of whether there are 10 Homebodies and 6 Revellers, as in part (a), or 6 Homebodies and 10 Revellers, as in part (b), spending $4 in total on the party is clearly inefficient because marginal cost exceeds marginal social benefit at this spending level.

As a further exercise, consider how much Homebodies gain by this misrepresentation. In part (a), the efficient level of spending is $2. So by misrepresenting their preferences, the 10 Homebodies gain, in total, 10 × ($0.03 + $0.02) = $0.50—that is, they gain the marginal individual benefit in going from a spending level of $2 to $4. The 6 Revellers also gain from the misrepresentations of the Homebodies; they gain 6 × ($0.09 + $0.07) = $0.96 in total. This outcome is clearly inefficient—when $4 in total is spent, the marginal cost is $1 but the marginal social benefit of the last $1 spent is only $0.62, indicating that too much money is being spent on the party.

According to part (b), the efficient level of spending is actually $3. The misrepresentation by the 6 Homebodies gains them, in total, 6 × $0.02 = $0.12, but the 10 Revellers gain 10 × $0.07 = $0.70 in total. This outcome is also clearly inefficient—when $4 is spent, marginal social benefit is only $0.12 + $0.70 = $0.82 but marginal cost is $1.

17-3 CHECK YOUR UNDERSTANDING

1. When individuals are allowed to harvest freely, Crown land becomes a common resource, and individuals will overuse it—they will harvest more trees than is efficient. In economic terms, the marginal social cost of harvesting a tree is greater than a private logger's individual marginal cost.

2. The three methods consistent with economic theory are (i) Pigouvian taxes, (ii) a system of tradable licences, and (iii) allocation of property rights.
   i. *Pigouvian taxes.* You would enforce a tax on loggers that equals the difference between the marginal social cost and the individual marginal cost of logging a tree at the socially efficient harvest amount. In order to do this, you must know the marginal social cost schedule and the individual marginal cost schedule.

ii. *System of tradable licences.* You would issue tradable licences, setting the total number of trees harvested equal to the socially efficient harvest number. The market that arises in these licences will allocate the right to log efficiently when loggers differ in their costs of logging: licences will be purchased by those who have a relatively lower cost of logging. The market price of a licence will be equal to the difference between the marginal social cost and the individual marginal cost of logging a tree at the socially efficient harvest amount. In order to implement this level, you need to know the socially efficient harvest amount.

iii. *Allocation of property rights.* Here you would sell or give the forest to a private party. This party will have the right to exclude others from harvesting trees. Harvesting is now a private good—it is excludable and rival in consumption. As a result, there is no longer any divergence between social and private costs, and the private party will harvest the efficient level of trees. You need no additional information to use this method.

17-4 CHECK YOUR UNDERSTANDING

1. a. The efficient price to a consumer is $0, since the marginal cost of allowing a consumer to download it is $0.

b. Xenoid will not produce the software unless it can charge a price that allows it at least to make back the $300 000 cost of producing it. So the lowest price at which Xenoid is willing to produce it is $150. At this price, it makes a total revenue of $150 \times 2000 = $300 000; at any lower price, Xenoid will not cover its cost. The shaded area in the accompanying diagram shows the deadweight loss when Xenoid charges a price of $150.

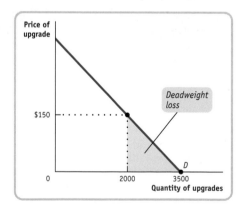

Chapter Eighteen

18-1 CHECK YOUR UNDERSTANDING

1. a. A pension guarantee program is a social insurance program. The possibility of an employer declaring bankruptcy and defaulting on its obligation to pay employee pensions creates insecurity. By providing pension income to those employees, such a program alleviates this source of economic insecurity.

b. The NCBS program is a social welfare program. By providing funding to children in low-income households, it targets its spending specifically to the poor.

c. The UCCB program is not a social welfare program. By providing funding to all families with children, rich or poor, it targets its spending specifically to families with children.

d. The federal flood program is a social insurance program. For many people, the majority of their wealth is tied up in the home they own. The potential for a loss of that wealth creates economic insecurity. By providing assistance to those hit by a major flood, the program alleviates this source of insecurity.

e. The IAH program is a social welfare program. By targeting its support to low-income households, it specifically helps the poor.

2. An after-tax LICO is a relative measure of poverty. The LICOs are income thresholds below which a family is expected to spend too large a share of its income to acquire necessities compared to the average family. The LICOs estimate an income threshold at which families are expected to spend 20 percentage points more than the average family on food, shelter, and clothing. For example, in 2012 using the after-tax LICOs measure the poverty line for a family of four in a community of at least 500 000 residents was $37 052; if this family lived in a community of 100 000 to 499 999 people, it was $31 335. This measure counts about 3 million Canadians as living in poverty, about 1 in eleven people.

3. a. To determine mean (or average) income, we take the total income of all individuals in this economy and divide it by the number of individuals. Mean income is ($39 000 + $17 500 + $900 000 + $15 000 + $28 000)/5 = $999 500/5 = $199 900. To determine median income, look at the accompanying table, which lines up the five individuals in order of their income.

	Income
Vijay	$15 000
Kelly	17 500
Oskar	28 000
Sephora	39 000
Raul	900 000

The median income is the income of the individual in the exact middle of the income distribution: Oskar, with an income of $28 000. So the median income is $28 000.

Median income is more representative of the income of individuals in this economy: almost everyone earns income between $15 000 and $39 000, close to the median income of $28 000. Only Raul is the exception: it is his income that raises the mean income to $199 900, which is not representative of most incomes in this economy.

b. The first quintile is made up of the 20% (or one-fifth) of individuals with the lowest incomes in the economy. Vijay makes up the 20% of individuals with the lowest incomes. His income is $15 000, so that is the average income of the first quintile. Oskar makes up the 20% of individuals with the third-lowest incomes. His income is $28 000, so that is the average income of the third quintile.

4. As the Economics in Action pointed out, much of the rise in inequality reflects growing differences among highly educated workers. That is, workers with similar levels of education earn very dissimilar incomes. As a result, the principal source of rising inequality in Canada today is reflected by statement b: the rise in the bank CEO's salary relative to that of the branch manager.

18-2 CHECK YOUR UNDERSTANDING

1. A negative income tax applies only to those workers who earn income; over a certain range of incomes, the more a worker earns, the higher the credit received. A person who earns no income receives no income tax credit. By contrast, social welfare programs that pay individuals based solely on low income still make those payments even if the individual does not work at all; once the individual earns a certain amount of income, these programs discontinue payments. As a result, such programs contain an incentive not to work and earn income, since earning more than a certain amount makes individuals ineligible for their benefits. The negative income tax, however, provides an incentive to work and earn income because its payments increase the more an individual works.

2. According to the data in Table 18-4, the Canadian welfare state reduces the poverty rate. It does so by sending significantly more transfers to low-income families than it takes via income taxes. Families in the first three quintiles receive more transfer than they pay in income taxes. The poorest 20% of Canadian households receive about 30% of total government transfers and only pay about 1% of the total income tax.

18-3 CHECK YOUR UNDERSTANDING

1. a. The program benefits Jiro and his parents because the pool of all international students contains a representative mix of healthy and less healthy people, rather than a selected group of people who want insurance because they expect to pay high medical bills. In that respect, this insurance is like *employment-based health insurance*. Because no student can opt out, the school can offer health insurance based on the health care costs of its average student. If each student had to buy his or her own health insurance, some students would not be able to obtain any insurance and many would pay more than they do to the school's insurance program.

   b. Since all international students are required to enrol in its health insurance program, even the healthiest students cannot leave the program in an effort to obtain cheaper insurance tailored specifically to healthy people. If this were to happen, the school's insurance program would be left with an adverse selection of less healthy students and so would have to raise premiums, beginning the adverse selection death spiral. But since no student can leave the insurance program, the school's program can continue to

base its premiums on the average student's probability of requiring health care, avoiding the adverse selection death spiral.

2. According to critics, part of the reason the U.S. health care system is so much more expensive than those of other countries is its fragmented nature. Since each of the many insurance companies has significant administrative (overhead) costs—in part because each insurance company incurs marketing costs and exerts significant effort in weeding out high-risk insureds—the system tends to be more expensive than one in which there is only a single medical insurer. Another part of the explanation is that U.S. medical care includes many more expensive treatments than found in other wealthy countries, pays higher physician salaries, and has higher drug prices.

18-4 CHECK YOUR UNDERSTANDING

1. a. Recall one of the principles from Chapter 1: one person's spending is another person's income. A high sales tax on consumer items is the same as a high marginal tax rate on income. As a result, the incentive to earn income by working or by investing in risky projects is reduced, since the payoff, after taxes, is lower.

   b. If you lose a housing subsidy as soon as your income rises above $25 000, your incentive to earn more than $25 000 is reduced. If you earn exactly $25 000, you obtain the housing subsidy; however, as soon as you earn $25 001, you lose the entire subsidy, making you worse off than if you had not earned the additional dollar. The complete withdrawal of the housing subsidy as income rises above $25 000 is what economists refer to as a *notch*.

2. Over the past 40 years, polarization in Canadian politics has increased. Forty years ago, some Conservatives were to the left of some Liberals. Today, the rightmost Liberal and NDP politicians appear to be to the left of the leftmost Conservatives.

Chapter Nineteen

19-1 CHECK YOUR UNDERSTANDING

1. Many university professors will depart for other lines of work if the government imposes a wage that is lower than the market wage. Fewer professors will result in fewer courses taught and therefore fewer university degrees produced. It will adversely affect sectors of the economy that depend directly on universities, such as the local shopkeepers who sell goods and services to students and faculty, university textbook publishers, and so on. It will also adversely affect firms that use the "output" produced by universities: new university graduates. Firms that need to hire new employees with university degrees will be hurt as a smaller supply results in a higher market wage for university graduates. Ultimately, the reduced supply of university-educated workers will result in a lower level of human capital in the entire economy relative to what it would have been without the policy. And this will hurt all sectors of the

economy that depend on human capital. The sectors of the economy that might benefit are firms that compete with universities in the hiring of would-be university professors. For example, accounting firms will find it easier to hire people who would otherwise have been professors of accounting, and publishers will find it easier to hire people who would otherwise have been professors of English (easier in the sense that the firms can recruit would-be professors with a lower wage than before). In addition, workers who already have university degrees will benefit; they will command higher wages as the supply of university-educated workers falls.

19-2 CHECK YOUR UNDERSTANDING

1. a. As the demand for services increases, the price of services will rise. And as the price of the output produced by the industries increases, this shifts the *VMPL* curve upward—that is, the demand for labour rises. This results in an increase in both the equilibrium wage rate and the quantity of labour employed.

b. The fall in the catch per day means that the marginal product of labour in the industry declines. The *VMPL* curve shifts downward, generating a fall in the equilibrium wage rate and the equilibrium quantity of labour employed.

2. When firms from different industries compete for the same workers, then each worker in the various industries will be paid the same equilibrium wage rate, *W*. And since, by the marginal productivity theory of income distribution, $VMPL = P \times MPL = W$ for the last worker hired in equilibrium, the last worker hired in each of these different industries will have the same value of the marginal product of labour.

19-3 CHECK YOUR UNDERSTANDING

1. a. False. Income disparities associated with gender, ethnicity, or immigration status can be explained by the marginal productivity theory of income distribution provided that differences in marginal productivity across people are correlated with gender, ethnicity, or immigration status. One possible source for such correlation is past discrimination. Such discrimination can lower individuals' marginal productivity by, for example, preventing them from acquiring the human capital that would raise their productivity. Another possible source of the correlation is differences in work experience that are associated with gender, ethnicity, or immigration status. For example, in jobs where work experience or length of tenure is important, women may earn lower wages because on average more women than men take child-care-related absences from work.

b. True. Companies that discriminate when their competitors do not are likely to hire less able workers because they discriminate against more able workers who are considered to be of the wrong gender, ethnicity, or other characteristic. And with less able workers, such companies are likely to earn lower profits than their competitors that don't discriminate.

c. Ambiguous. In general, workers who are paid less because they have less experience may or may not be the victims of discrimination. The answer depends on the reason for the lack of experience. If workers have less experience because they are young or have chosen to do something else rather than gain experience, then they are not victims of discrimination if they are paid less. But if workers lack experience because previous job discrimination prevented them from gaining experience, then they are indeed victims of discrimination when they are paid less.

19-4 CHECK YOUR UNDERSTANDING

1. a. Clive is made worse off if, before the new law, he had preferred to work more than 35 hours per week. As a result of the law, he can no longer choose his preferred time allocation; he now consumes fewer goods and more leisure than he would like.

b. Clive's utility is unaffected by the law if, before the law, he had preferred to work 35 or fewer hours per week. The law has not changed his preferred time allocation.

c. Clive can never be made better off by a law that restricts the number of hours he can work. He can only be made worse off (case a) or equally as well off (case b).

2. The substitution effect would induce Clive to work fewer hours and consume more leisure after his wage rate falls—the fall in the wage rate means the price of an hour of leisure falls, leading Clive to consume more leisure. But a fall in his wage rate also generates a fall in Clive's income. The income effect of this is to induce Clive to consume less leisure and therefore work more hours, since he is now poorer and leisure is a normal good. If the income effect dominates the substitution effect, Clive will in the end work more hours than before.

Chapter Twenty
20-1 CHECK YOUR UNDERSTANDING

1. The family with the lower income is likely to be more risk-averse. In general, higher income or wealth results in lower degrees of risk aversion, due to diminishing marginal utility. Both families may be willing to buy an "unfair" insurance policy. Most insurance policies are "unfair" in that the expected claim is less than the premium. The degree to which a family is willing to pay more than an expected claim for insurance depends on the family's degree of risk aversion.

2. a. Karma's expected income is the weighted average of all possible values of her income, weighted by the probabilities with which she earns each possible value of her income. Since she makes $22 000 with a probability of 0.6 and $35 000 with a probability of 0.4, her expected income is $(0.6 \times \$22\,000) + (0.4 \times \$35\,000) = \$13\,200 + \$14\,000 = \$27\,200$. Her expected utility is simply the expected value of the total utilities she will experience. Since with a probability of 0.6 she will experience a total utility of 850 utils (the utility to her from making $22 000), and with a probability of 0.4 she will experience a total utility of 1260 utils (the utility to her from making $35 000), her expected utility is $(0.6 \times 850$ utils$) + (0.4 \times 1260$ utils$) = 510$ utils $+ 504$ utils $= 1014$ utils.

b. If Karma makes $25 000 for certain, she experiences a utility level of 1014 utils. From the answer to part (a), we know that this leaves her equally as well off as when she has a risky expected income of $27 200. Since Karma is indifferent between a risky expected income of $27 200 and a certain income of $25 000, you can conclude that she would prefer a certain income of $27 200 to a risky expected income of $27 200. That is, she would definitely be willing to reduce the risk she faces when this reduction in risk leaves her expected income unchanged. In other words, Karma is risk-averse.

c. Yes. Karma experiences a utility level of 1056 utils when she has a certain income of $26 000. This is higher than the expected utility level of 1014 utils generated by a risky expected income of $27 200. So Karma is willing to pay a premium to guarantee a certain income of $26 000.

20-2 CHECK YOUR UNDERSTANDING

1. a. An increase in the number of ships implies an increase in the quantity of insurance demanded at any given premium. This is a rightward shift of the demand curve, resulting in a rise in both the equilibrium premium and the equilibrium quantity of insurance bought and sold.

b. An increase in the number of trading routes means that investors can diversify more. In other words, they can reduce risk further. At any given premium, there are now more investors willing to supply insurance. This is a rightward shift of the supply curve for insurance, leading to a fall in the equilibrium premium and a rise in the equilibrium quantity of insurance bought and sold.

c. If shipowners in the market become even more risk-averse, they will be willing to pay even higher premiums for insurance. That is, at any given premium, there are now more people willing to buy insurance. This is a rightward shift of the demand curve for insurance, leading to a rise in both the equilibrium premium and the equilibrium quantity of insurance bought and sold.

d. If investors in the market become more risk-averse, they will be less willing to accept risk at any given premium. This is a leftward shift of the supply curve for insurance, leading to a rise in the equilibrium premium and a fall in the equilibrium quantity of insurance bought and sold.

e. As the overall level of risk increases, those willing to buy insurance will be more willing to buy insurance at any given premium; the demand curve for insurance shifts to the right. But since overall risk cannot be diversified away, those ordinarily willing to take on risk will be less willing to do so, leading to a leftward shift in the supply curve for insurance. As a result, the equilibrium premium will rise; the effect on the equilibrium quantity of insurance is uncertain.

f. If the wealth levels of investors fall, investors will become more risk-averse and so less willing to supply insurance at any given premium. This is a leftward shift of the supply curve for insurance, leading to a rise in

the equilibrium premium and a fall in the equilibrium quantity of insurance bought and sold.

20-3 CHECK YOUR UNDERSTANDING

1. The inefficiency caused by adverse selection is that an insurance policy with a premium based on the average risk of all drivers will attract only an adverse selection of bad drivers. Good (that is, safe) drivers will find this insurance premium too expensive and so will remain uninsured. This is inefficient. However, safe drivers are also those drivers who have had fewer moving violations for several years. Lowering premiums for only those drivers allows the insurance company to screen its customers and sell insurance to safe drivers, too. This means that at least some of the good drivers now are also insured, which decreases the inefficiency that arises from adverse selection. In a way, having no moving violations for several years is building a reputation for being a safe driver.

2. The moral hazard problem in home construction arises from private information about what the contractor does: whether she takes care to reduce the cost of construction or allows costs to increase. The home-owner cannot, or can only imperfectly, observe the cost-reduction effort of the contractor. If the contractor were fully reimbursed for all costs incurred during construction, she would have no incentive to reduce costs. Making the contractor responsible for any additional costs above the original estimate means that she now has an incentive to keep costs low. However, this imposes risk on the contractor. For instance, if the weather is bad, home construction will take longer, and will be more costly, than if the weather had been good. Since the contractor pays for any additional costs (such as weather-induced delays) above the original estimate, she now faces risk that she cannot control.

3. a. True. Drivers with higher deductibles have more incentive to take care in their driving, to avoid paying the deductible. This is a moral hazard phenomenon.

b. True. Suppose you know that you are a safe driver. You have a choice of a policy with a high premium but a low deductible or one with a lower premium but a higher deductible. In this case, you would be more likely to choose the cheap policy with the high deductible because you know that you will be unlikely to have to pay the deductible. When there is adverse selection, insurance companies use screening devices such as this to make inferences about people's private information about how skillful they are as drivers.

c. True. The wealthier you are, the less risk-averse you are. If you are less risk averse, you are more willing to bear risk yourself. Having an insurance policy with a high deductible means that you are exposed to more risk: you have to pay more of any insurance claim yourself. This is an implication of how risk aversion changes with a person's income or wealth.

Italicized terms within definitions are key terms that are defined elsewhere in this glossary.

A

ability-to-pay principle the principle of tax fairness by which those with greater ability to pay a tax should pay more tax.

absolute advantage the advantage conferred on an individual or country in an activity if the individual or country can do it better than others. A country with an absolute advantage can produce more output per worker than other countries.

absolute value the value of a number without regard to a plus or minus sign.

accounting profit revenue minus *explicit cost*.

administrative costs (of a tax) the *resources* used (which is a cost) by government to collect the tax, and by taxpayers to pay it, over and above the amount of the tax, as well as to evade it.

adverse selection the case in which an individual knows more about the way things are than other people do. Adverse selection problems can lead to market problems: *private information* leads buyers to expect hidden problems in items offered for sale, leading to low prices and the best items being kept off the market.

antitrust policy legislative and regulatory efforts undertaken by the government to prevent oligopolistic industries from becoming or behaving like *monopolies*; also called *competition policy*.

artificially scarce good a good that is *excludable* but *nonrival in consumption*.

autarky a situation in which a country does not trade with other countries.

average cost an alternative term for *average total cost*; the *total cost* divided by the quantity of output produced.

average cost pricing a form of *price regulation* that forces a *monopoly* to set its price equal to its *average total cost*.

average fixed cost the *fixed cost* per unit of output.

average product the amount of output produced per unit of a particular *input*.

average total cost *total cost* divided by quantity of output produced. Also referred to as *average cost*.

average variable cost the *variable cost* per unit of output.

B

backward-bending individual labour supply curve an *individual labour supply curve* that slopes upward at low to moderate wage rates and slopes downward at higher wage rates.

bar graph a graph that uses bars of varying heights or lengths to show the comparative sizes of different observations of a variable.

barrier to entry something that prevents other firms from entering an industry. Crucial in protecting the profits of a *monopolist*. There are five types of barriers to entry: control over *scarce resources* or *inputs*, increasing returns to scale, technological superiority, *network externalities*, and government-created barriers.

barter the direct exchange of goods or services for other goods or services without the use of money.

benefits principle the principle of tax fairness by which those who benefit from public spending should bear the burden of the tax that pays for that spending.

black market a market in which goods or services are bought and sold illegally, either because it is illegal to sell them at all or because the prices charged are legally prohibited by a *price ceiling* or a *price floor*.

bounded rationality a basis for decision making that leads to a choice that is close to but not exactly the one that leads to the best possible economic outcome; the "good enough" method of decision making.

brand name a name owned by a particular firm that distinguishes its products from those of other firms.

break-even price the market price at which a firm earns zero profits.

budget constraint the limitation that the cost of a consumer's *consumption bundle* cannot exceed the consumer's income.

budget line all the *consumption bundles* available to a consumer who spends all of his or her income.

C

capital the total value of assests owned by an individual or firm—physical assets plus financial assets.

capital at risk funds that an insurer places at *risk* when providing insurance.

cartel an agreement among several producers to obey output restrictions in order to increase their joint profits.

causal relationship the relationship between two variables in which the value taken by one variable directly influences or determines the value taken by the other variable.

circular-flow diagram a diagram that represents the transactions in an *economy* by two kinds of flows around a circle: flows of physical things such as goods or labour in one direction and flows of money to pay for these physical things in the opposite direction.

Coase theorem the proposition that even in the presence of *externalities* an *economy* can always reach an *efficient* solution as long as *transaction costs* are sufficiently low.

collusion cooperation among producers to limit production and raise prices so as to raise one another's profits.

commodity output of different producers regarded by consumers as the same good; also referred to as a *standardized product*.

common resource a *resource* that is *nonexcludable* and *rival in consumption*.

comparative advantage the advantage conferred on an individual or country in producing a good or service if the *opportunity cost* of producing the good or service is lower for that individual or country than for other producers.

compensating differentials wage differences across jobs that reflect the fact that some jobs are less pleasant or more dangerous than others.

competition policy legislative and regulatory efforts undertaken by the government to prevent oligopolistic industries from becoming or behaving like monopolies; also called *antitrust policy*.

competitive market a market in which there are many buyers and sellers of the same good or service, none of whom can influence the price at which the good or service is sold.

complements pairs of goods for which a rise in the price of one good leads to a decrease in the demand for the other good.

constant marginal cost each additional unit costs the same to produce as the previous one.

constant returns to scale long-run *average total cost* is constant as output increases.

consumer surplus a term often used to refer both to *individual consumer surplus* and to *total consumer surplus*.

consumption bundle (of an individual) the collection of all the goods and services consumed by a given individual.

consumption possibilities the set of all *consumption bundles* that can be consumed given a consumer's income and prevailing prices.

copyright the exclusive legal right of the creator of a literary or artistic work to profit from that work; like a *patent*, it is a temporary *monopoly*.

cost (of seller) the lowest price at which a seller is willing to sell a good.

cost-benefit analysis an estimate of the costs and benefits of providing a good. When governments use cost-benefit analysis, they estimate the social costs and social benefits of providing a *public good*.

cross-price elasticity of demand a measure of the effect of the change in the price of one good on the *quantity demanded* of the other; it is equal to the percentage change in the quantity demanded of one good divided by the percentage change in the price of another good.

curve a line on a graph, which may be curved or straight, that depicts a relationship between two *variables*.

D

deadweight loss the loss in *total surplus* that occurs whenever an action or a policy reduces the quantity transacted below the efficient market *equilibrium quantity*.

decreasing marginal benefit each additional unit of an activity yields less benefit than the previous unit.

decreasing marginal cost each additional unit costs less to produce than the previous one.

decreasing returns to scale long-run *average total cost* increases as output increases (also known as diseconomies of scale).

deductible a sum specified in an insurance policy that the insured individual ___ pay before being compensated ___ deductibles reduce *moral*

demand curve a graphical representation of the *demand schedule*, showing the relationship between *quantity demanded* and price.

demand price the price of a given quantity at which consumers will demand that quantity.

demand schedule a list or table showing how much of a good or service consumers will want to buy at different prices.

dependent variable the determined *variable* in a *causal relationship*.

diminishing marginal rate of substitution the principle that the more of one good that is consumed in proportion to another, the less of the second good the consumer is willing to substitute for another unit of the first good.

diminishing returns to an input the effect observed when an increase in the quantity of an *input*, while holding the levels of all other inputs and the production technology fixed, leads to a decline in the *marginal product* of that input.

diversification reducing *risk* by investing in several different things, so that the possible losses are *independent events*.

domestic demand curve a *demand curve* that shows how the quantity of a good demanded by domestic consumers depends on the price of that good.

domestic supply curve a *supply curve* that shows how the quantity of a good supplied by domestic producers depends on the price of that good.

dominant strategy in *game theory*, an action that is a player's best action regardless of the action taken by the other player.

duopolist one of the two firms in a *duopoly*.

duopoly an *oligopoly* consisting of only two firms.

E

economic growth the growing ability of the *economy* to produce goods and services.

economic profit revenue minus the *opportunity cost* of *resources* used; usually less than the *accounting profit*.

economic signal any piece of information that helps people make better economic decisions.

economics the social science that studies the production, distribution, and consumption of goods and services.

economy a system for coordinating society's productive activities.

efficiency-wage model a model in which some employers pay an above-equilibrium wage as an *incentive* for better performance.

efficient description of a market or *economy* that takes all opportunities to make some people better off without making other people worse off.

efficient allocation of risk an allocation of *risk* in which those most willing to bear risk are those who end up bearing it.

elastic demand the case in which the *price elasticity of demand* is greater than 1.

emissions tax a tax that depends on the amount of pollution a firm produces.

environmental standards rules established by a government to protect the environment by specifying actions by producers and consumers.

equilibrium an economic situation in which no individual would be better off doing something different.

equilibrium price the price at which the market is in *equilibrium*, that is, the quantity of a good or service demanded equals the quantity of that good or service supplied; also referred to as the *market-clearing price*.

equilibrium quantity the quantity of a good or service bought and sold at the *equilibrium* (or *market-clearing*) *price*.

equilibrium value of the marginal product the additional value produced by the last unit of a factor employed in the *factor market* as a whole.

equity fairness; everyone gets his or her fair share. Since people can disagree about what is "fair," equity is not as well defined a concept as efficiency.

excess capacity the failure to produce enough to minimize *average total cost*; characteristic of *monopolistically competitive* firms.

excise tax a per unit tax on sales of a good or service.

excludable referring to a good, describes the case in which the supplier can prevent those who do not pay from consuming the good.

expected utility the *expected value* of an individual's total *utility* given uncertainty about future outcomes.

expected value in reference to a *random variable*, the weighted average of all possible values, where the weights on each possible value correspond to the probability of that value occurring.

explicit cost a cost that requires an outlay of money.

exporting industries industries that produce goods and services that are sold abroad.

exports goods and services sold to other countries.

external benefit an uncompensated benefit that an individual or firm confers on others; also known as *positive externality*.

external cost an uncompensated cost that an individual or firm imposes on others; also known as *negative externality*.

externalities *external benefits* and *external costs*.

F

factor distribution of income the division of total income among labour, land, and *capital*.

factor intensity the difference in the ratio of factors used to produce a good in various industries. For example, oil refining is capital-intensive compared to auto seat production because oil refiners use a higher ratio of *capital* to labour than do producers of auto seats.

factor markets markets in which *firms* buy or rent the *resources* they need to produce goods and services.

factors of production the *resources* used to produce goods and services. Labour and *capital* are examples of factors.

fair insurance policy an insurance policy for which the *premium* is equal to the expected value of the claim.

financial risk uncertainty about monetary outcomes.

firm an organization that produces goods and services for sale.

fixed cost a cost that does not depend on the quantity of output produced; the cost of a *fixed input*.

fixed input an *input* whose quantity is fixed for a period of time and cannot be varied (for example, land).

forecast a simple prediction of the future.

free entry and exit describes an industry that potential producers can easily enter or current producers can leave.

free trade *trade* that is unregulated by government *tariffs* or other artificial barriers; the levels of *exports* and *imports* occur naturally, as a result of supply and demand.

free-rider problem problem that results when individuals who have no *incentive* to pay for their own consumption of a good take a "free ride" on anyone who does pay; a problem with goods that are *nonexcludable*.

G

gains from trade gains achieved by dividing tasks and trading; in this way people can get more of what they want through *trade* than they could if they tried to be self-sufficient.

game theory the study of behaviour in situations of *interdependence*. Used to explain the behaviour of an *oligopoly*.

Giffen good the hypothetical *inferior good* for which the *income effect* outweighs the *substitution effect* and the *demand curve* slopes upward.

Gini coefficient a number that summarizes a country's level of income inequality based on how unequally income is distributed across quintiles.

globalization the phenomenon of growing economic linkages among countries.

government transfer a government payment to an individual or a family.

H

Hecksher–Olin model a *model* of international trade in which a country has a *comparative advantage* in a good whose production is intensive in the factors that are abundantly available in that country.

horizontal axis the horizontal number line of a graph along which values of the *x*-variable are measured; also referred to as the *x-axis*.

horizontal intercept the point at which a *curve* hits the *horizontal axis;* it indicates the value of the *x*-variable when the value of the *y*-variable is zero.

household a person or a group of people that share their income.

human capital the improvement in labour created by education and knowledge that is embodied in the workforce.

I

imperfect competition a market structure in which no firm is a *monopolist*, but producers nonetheless have *market power* they can use to affect market prices.

implicit cost a cost that does not require the outlay of money; it is measured by the value, in dollar terms, of forgone benefits.

implicit cost of capital the *opportunity cost* of the use of one's own *capital*— the income earned if the capital had been employed in its next best alternative use.

import quota a legal limit on the quantity of a good that can be imported.

import-competing industries industries that produce goods and services that are also imported.

imports goods and services purchased from other countries.

incentive anything that offers rewards to people who change their behaviour.

incidence (of a tax) a measure of who really pays a tax.

income distribution the way in which total income is divided among the owners of the various factors of production.

income effect the change in the quantity of a good consumed that results from the change in a consumer's purchasing power due to the change in the price of the good.

income elasticity of demand the percentage change in the quantity of a good demanded when a consumer's income changes divided by the percentage change in the consumer's income.

income tax a tax on the income of an individual or family.

income-elastic demand the case in which the *income elasticity of demand* for a good is greater than 1.

income-inelastic demand the case in which the *income elasticity of demand* for a good is positive but less than 1.

increasing marginal cost each additional unit costs more to produce than the previous one.

increasing returns to scale long-run *average total cost* declines as output increases (also referred to as economies of scale).

independent events events for which the occurrence of one does not affect the likelihood of occurrence of any of the others.

independent variable the determining *variable* in a *causal relationship.*

indifference curve a contour line showing all *consumption bundles* that yield the same amount of total *utility* for an individual.

indifference curve map a collection of *indifference curves* for a given individual that represents the individual's entire *utility function*; each curve corresponds to a different total *utility* level.

individual choice the decision by an individual of what to do, which necessarily involves a decision of what not to do.

individual consumer surplus the net gain to an individual buyer from the purchase of a good; equal to the difference between the buyer's *willingness to pay* and the price paid.

individual demand curve a graphical representation of the relationship between *quantity demanded* and price for an individual consumer.

individual labour supply curve a graphical representation showing how the quantity of labour supplied by an individual depends on that individual's wage rate.

individual producer surplus the net gain to an individual seller from selling a good; equal to the difference between the price received and the seller's *cost.*

individual supply curve a graphical representation of the relationship between *quantity supplied* and price for an individual producer.

industry supply curve a graphical representation that shows the relationship between the price of a good and the total output supplied by the industry for that good.

inefficient describes a market or *economy* in which there are missed opportunities: some people could be made better off without making other people worse off.

inefficient allocation to consumers a form of inefficiency in which some people who want the good badly and are willing to pay a high price don't get it, and some who care relatively little ~~about the good and are only willing to~~ ~~pay~~ ~~ce do get it; often a result of~~ ~~ing.~~

inefficient allocation of sales among sellers a form of inefficiency in which sellers who would be willing to sell a good at the lowest price are not always those who actually manage to sell it; often the result of a *price floor.*

inefficiently high quality a form of inefficiency in which sellers offer high-quality goods at a high price even though buyers would prefer a lower quality at a lower price; often the result of a *price floor.*

inefficiently low quality a form of inefficiency in which sellers offer low-quality goods at a low price even though buyers would prefer a higher quality at a higher price; often a result of a *price ceiling.*

inelastic demand the case in which the *price elasticity of demand* is less than 1.

inferior good a good for which a rise in income decreases the demand for the good.

in-kind benefit a benefit given in the form of goods or services.

input a good or service used to produce another good or service.

interaction (of choices) my choices affect your choices, and vice versa; a feature of most economic situations. The results of this interaction are often quite different from what the individuals intend.

interdependence the relationship among firms when their decisions significantly affect one another's profits; characteristic of *oligopolies.*

internalize the externality take into account *external costs* and *external benefits.*

international trade agreements treaties in which a country promises to engage in less *trade protection* against the *exports* of other countries in return for a promise by other countries to do the same for its own exports

invisible hand a phrase used by Adam Smith to refer to the way in which an individual's pursuit of self-interest can lead, without the individual intending it, to good results for society as a whole.

irrational describes a decision maker who chooses an option that leaves him or her worse off than choosing another available option.

L

law of demand the principle that a higher price for a good or service, other things equal, leads people to demand a smaller quantity of that good or service.

leisure the time available for purposes other than earning money to buy marketed goods.

licence the right, conferred by the government or an owner, to supply a good.

linear relationship the relationship between two *variables* in which the *slope* is constant and therefore is depicted on a graph by a *curve* that is a straight line.

long run the time period in which all *inputs* can be varied.

long-run average total cost curve a graphical representation showing the relationship between output and *average total cost* when *fixed cost* has been chosen to minimize average total cost for each level of output.

long-run industry supply curve a graphical representation that shows how *quantity supplied* responds to price once producers have had time to enter or exit the industry.

long-run market equilibrium an economic balance in which, given sufficient time for producers to enter or exit an industry, the *quantity supplied* equals the *quantity demanded.*

loss aversion oversensitivity to loss, leading to unwillingness to recognize a loss and move on.

lump-sum tax a tax that is the same for everyone, regardless of any actions people take.

M

macroeconomics the branch of *economics* that is concerned with the overall ups and downs in the *economy.*

marginal analysis the study of *marginal decisions.*

marginal benefit the additional benefit derived from producing one more unit of a good or service.

marginal benefit curve a graphical representation showing how the benefit from producing one more unit depends on the quantity that has already been produced.

marginal cost the additional cost incurred by producing one more unit of a good or service.

marginal cost curve a graphical representation showing how the cost of producing one more unit depends on the quantity that has already been produced.

marginal cost pricing a form of *price regulation* that forces a *monopoly* to set its price equal to its *marginal cost*.

marginal decision a decision made at the "margin" of an activity to do a bit more or a bit less of that activity.

marginal external benefit (*MEB*) of pollution the additional benefit others receive if the polluter creates another unit of pollution.

marginal external cost (*MEC*) of pollution the additional cost imposed on others if the polluter creates another unit of pollution.

marginal private benefit (*MPB*) of pollution the additional benefit the polluter receives if the polluter creates another unit of pollution.

marginal private cost (*MPC*) of pollution the additional cost imposed on the polluter if the polluter creates another unit of pollution.

marginal product the additional quantity of output produced by using one more unit of a given *input*, holding other inputs and the production technology fixed.

marginal productivity theory of income distribution the proposition that every *factor of production* is paid its *equilibrium value of the marginal product*.

marginal rate of substitution (*MRS*) the ratio of the *marginal utility* of one good to the marginal utility of another.

marginal revenue the change in *total revenue* generated by an additional unit of output.

marginal revenue curve a graphical representation showing how *marginal revenue* varies as output varies.

marginal social benefit (*MSB*) of pollution the additional gain to society as a whole from an additional unit of pollution.

marginal social cost (*MSC*) of pollution the additional cost imposed on society as a whole by an additional unit of pollution.

marginal tax rate the percentage of an increase in income that is taxed away.

marginal utility the change in total *utility* generated by consuming one additional unit of a good or service.

marginal utility curve a graphical representation showing how *marginal utility* depends on the quantity of the good or service consumed.

marginal utility per dollar the additional *utility* gained from spending one more dollar on a good or service.

market-clearing price the price at which the market is in *equilibrium*, that is, the quantity of a good or service demanded equals the quantity of that good or service supplied; also referred to as the *equilibrium price*.

market economy an *economy* in which decisions about production and consumption are made by individual producers and consumers.

market failure the failure of a market to be efficient. This happens when the individual pursuit of self-interest leads to bad results for society as a whole.

market power the ability of a producer to raise prices.

market share the fraction of the total industry output accounted for by a given producer's output.

markets for goods and services markets in which *firms* sell goods and services that they produce to *households*.

maximum the highest point on a *non-linear curve*, where the *slope* changes from positive to negative.

mean household income the average income across all households.

means-tested describes a program in which benefits are available only to individuals or families whose incomes fall below a certain level.

median household income the income of the household lying at the exact middle of the *income distribution*.

mental accounting the habit of mentally assigning dollars to different accounts so that some dollars are worth more than others.

microeconomics the branch of *economics* that studies how people make decisions and how those decisions interact.

midpoint method a technique for calculating the percentage change in which changes in a variable are compared with the average, or midpoint, of the starting and final values.

minimum the lowest point on a *non-linear curve*, where the *slope* changes from negative to positive.

minimum-cost output the quantity of output at which the *average total cost* is lowest—the bottom of the *U-shaped average total cost curve*.

minimum wage a legal floor on the wage rate. The wage rate is the market price of labour.

model a simplified representation of a real situation that is used to better understand real-life situations.

monopolist a firm that is the only producer of a good that has no close substitutes.

monopolistic competition a market structure in which there are many competing producers in an industry, each producer sells a differentiated product, and there is *free entry and exit* into and from the industry in the *long run*.

monopoly an industry controlled by a *monopolist*.

moral hazard the situation that can exist when an individual knows more about his or her own actions than other people do. This leads to a distortion of *incentives* to take care or to expend effort when someone else bears the costs of the lack of care or effort.

movement along the demand curve a change in the *quantity demanded* of a good that results from a change in the price of that good.

movement along the supply curve a change in the *quantity supplied* of a good that results from a change in the price of that good.

N

Nash equilibrium in *game theory*, the *equilibrium* that results when all players choose the action that maximizes their *payoffs* given the actions of other players, ignoring the effect of that action on the *payoffs* of other players; also known as noncooperative equilibrium.

natural monopoly a *monopoly* that exists when *increasing returns to scale* provide a large cost advantage to having all output produced by a single firm.

negative externalities *external costs*.

negative income tax a government program that supplements the income of low-income working families.

negative relationship a relationship between two *variables* in which an increase in the value of one variable is associated with a decrease in the value of the other variable. It is illustrated by a *curve* that slopes downward from left to right.

network externality the increase in the value of a good or service to an individual is greater when a large number of others own or use the same good or service.

noncooperative behaviour actions by firms that ignore the effects of those actions on the profits of other firms.

nonexcludable referring to a good, describes the case in which the supplier cannot prevent those who do not pay from consuming the good.

non-linear curve a curve in which the *slope* is not the same between every pair of points.

non-linear relationship the relationship between two *variables* in which the *slope* is not constant and therefore is depicted on a graph by a *curve* that is not a straight line.

nonprice competition competition in areas other than price to increase sales, such as new product features and advertising; especially engaged in by firms that have a tacit understanding not to compete on price.

nonrival in consumption referring to a good, describes the case in which the same unit can be consumed by more than one person at the same time.

normal good a good for which a rise in income increases the demand for that good—the "normal" case.

normative economics the branch of economic analysis that makes prescriptions about the way the *economy* should work.

North American Free Trade Agreement (NAFTA) a *trade* agreement among the United States, Canada, and Mexico.

O

offshore outsourcing the practice in which businesses hire people in another country to perform various tasks.

oligopolist a firm in an industry with only a small number of producers.

ndustry with only a small oducers.

omitted variable an unobserved *variable* that, through its influence on other variables, creates the erroneous appearance of a direct *causal relationship* among those variables.

opportunity cost the real cost of an item: what you must give up in order to get it.

optimal consumption bundle the *consumption bundle* that maximizes a consumer's total *utility* given that consumer's *budget constraint*.

optimal consumption rule the *optimal consumption bundle* is on the *budget line* and the *marginal utility per dollar* spent on each good in the bundle is equal.

optimal output rule the principle that profit is maximized by producing the quantity of output at which the *marginal revenue* of the last unit produced is equal to its *marginal cost*.

optimal quantity the quantity that generates the highest possible total net profit.

optimal time allocation rule the principle that an individual should allocate time so that the *marginal utility* gained from the income earned from an additional hour worked is equal to the marginal utility of an additional hour of *leisure*.

ordinary goods in a consumer's *utility function*, a pair of goods for which additional units of one good are required to compensate for fewer units of another, and vice versa; and for which the consumer experiences a *diminishing marginal rate of substitution* when substituting one good in place of another.

origin the point where the axes of a two-variable graph meet.

other things equal assumption in the development of a model, the assumption that all relevant factors except the one under study remain unchanged.

overuse the depletion of a *common resource* that occurs when individuals ignore the fact that their use depletes the amount of the resource remaining for others.

P

patent a temporary *monopoly* given by the government to an inventor for the use or sale of an invention.

payoff in *game theory*, the reward received by a player (for example, the profit earned by an *oligopolist*).

payoff matrix in *game theory*, a diagram that shows how the *payoffs* to each of the participants in a two-player game depend on the actions of both; a tool in analyzing *interdependence*.

payroll tax a tax on the earnings an employer pays to an employee.

perfect complements goods a consumer wants to consume in the same ratio, regardless of their *relative price*.

perfect price discrimination the *price discrimination* that results when a *monopolist* charges each consumer the maximum that the consumer is willing to pay.

perfect substitutes goods for which the *indifference curves* are straight lines; the *marginal rate of substitution* of one good in place of another good is constant, regardless of how much of each an individual consumes.

perfectly competitive industry an industry in which all producers are price-takers.

perfectly competitive market a market in which all participants are price-takers.

perfectly elastic demand the case in which any price increase will cause the *quantity demanded* to drop to zero; the *demand curve* is a horizontal line.

perfectly elastic supply the case in which even a tiny increase or reduction in the price will lead to very large changes in the *quantity supplied*, so that the *price elasticity of supply* is infinite; the perfectly elastic *supply curve* is a horizontal line.

perfectly inelastic demand the case in which the *quantity demanded* does not respond at all to changes in the price; the *demand curve* is a vertical line.

perfectly inelastic supply the case in which the *price elasticity of supply* is zero, so that changes in the price of the good have no effect on the *quantity supplied*; the perfectly inelastic *supply curve* is a vertical line.

physical capital manufactured productive resources, such as buildings and machines; often referred to simply as "capital."

pie chart a circular graph that shows how some total is divided among its components, usually expressed in percentages.

Pigouvian subsidy a payment designed to encourage activities that yield *external benefits*.

Pigouvian taxes taxes designed to reduce *external costs.*

pooling a strong form of *diversification* in which an investor takes a small share of the *risk* in many *independent events,* so the *payoff* has very little total overall risk.

positive economics the branch of economic analysis that describes the way the *economy* actually works.

positive externalities *external benefits.*

positive feedback put simply, success breeds success, failure breeds failure; the effect is seen with goods that are subject to *network externalities.*

positive relationship a relationship between two *variables* in which an increase in the value of one variable is associated with an increase in the value of the other variable. It is illustrated by a *curve* that slopes upward from left to right.

positively correlated describes a relationship between events such that each event is more likely to occur if the other event also occurs.

poverty line the annual income below which a family is officially considered poor. Also called the *poverty threshold.*

poverty rate the percentage of the population with incomes below the *poverty line.*

poverty threshold the annual income below which a family is officially considered poor. Also called the *poverty line.*

premium a payment to an insurance company in return for the promise to pay a claim in certain *states of the world.*

price ceiling a maximum price sellers are allowed to charge for a good or service; a form of *price control.*

price controls legal restrictions on how high or low a market price may go.

price discrimination charging different prices to different consumers for the same good.

price elasticity of demand the ratio of the percentage change in the *quantity demanded* to the percentage change in the price as we move along the *demand curve* (using the *absolute value*).

price elasticity of supply a measure of the responsiveness of the quantity of a good supplied to the price of that good; the ratio of the percentage change in the *quantity supplied* to the percentage change in the price as we move along the *supply curve.*

price floor a minimum price buyers are required to pay for a good or service; a form of *price control.*

price leadership a pattern of behaviour in which one firm sets its price and other firms in the industry follow.

price regulation a limitation on the price a *monopolist* is allowed to charge.

price-taking consumer a consumer whose actions have no effect on the market price of the good or service he or she buys.

price-taking firm's optimal output rule the principle that the profit of a price-taking firm is maximized by producing the quantity of output at which the market price is equal to the *marginal cost* of the last unit produced.

price-taking producer a producer whose actions have no effect on the market price of the good or service it sells.

price war a collapse of prices when *tacit collusion* breaks down.

principle of diminishing marginal utility the proposition that each successive unit of a good or service consumed adds less to total *utility* than did the previous unit.

principle of "either–or" decision making the principle that, in a decision between two activities, the one with the positive *economic profit* should be chosen.

prisoner's dilemma a game based on two premises: (1) each player has an *incentive* to choose an action that benefits itself at the other player's expense; and (2) both players are then worse off than if they had acted cooperatively.

private good a good that is both *excludable* and *rival in consumption.*

private health insurance program in which each member of a large pool of individuals pays a fixed amount to a private company that agrees to pay most of the medical expenses of the pool's members.

private information information that some people have but others do not.

producer surplus a term often used to refer both to *individual producer surplus* and to *total producer surplus.*

product differentiation the attempt by firms to convince buyers that their products are different from those of other firms in the industry. If firms can so convince buyers, they can charge a higher price.

production function the relationship between the quantity of *inputs* a firm uses and the quantity of output it produces, for a given state of the production technology.

production possibility frontier a model that illustrates the *trade-offs* facing an *economy* that produces only two goods. It shows the maximum quantity of one good that can be produced for any given quantity produced of the other.

profit-maximizing principle of marginal analysis the proposition that in a profit-maximizing "how much" decision the *optimal quantity* is the largest quantity at which *marginal benefit* is greater than or equal to *marginal cost.*

profits tax a tax on the profits of a firm.

progressive tax a tax that takes a larger share of the income of high-income taxpayers than of low-income taxpayers.

property rights the rights of owners of valuable items, whether *resources* or goods, to use, rent, or dispose of those items as they choose.

property tax a tax on the value of property, such as the value of a home.

proportional tax a tax that is the same percentage of the *tax base* regardless of the taxpayer's income or wealth.

protection an alternative term for *trade protection;* policies that limit *imports.*

public good a good that is both *nonexcludable* and *nonrival in consumption.*

public ownership the case in which goods are supplied by the government or by a firm owned by the government to protect the interests of the consumer in response to *natural monopoly.*

Q

quantity control an upper limit, set by the government, on the quantity of some good that can be bought or sold; also referred to as a *quota.*

quantity demanded the actual amount of a good or service consumers are willing to buy at some specific price.

quantity supplied the actual amount of a good or service producers are willing to sell at some specific price.

quota an upper limit, set by the government, on the quantity of some good that can be bought or sold; also referred to as a *quantity control*.

quota limit the total amount of a good under a *quota* or *quantity control* that can be legally transacted.

quota rent the difference between the *demand price* and the *supply price* at the *quota limit*; this difference, the earnings that accrue to the licence-holder, is equal to the market price of the *licence* when the licence is traded.

R

random variable a *variable* with an uncertain future value.

rational describes a decision maker who chooses the available option that leads to the outcome he or she most prefers.

regressive tax a tax that takes a smaller share of the income of high-income taxpayers than of low-income taxpayers.

relative price the number of units of one good that must be traded in the market to obtain one more unit of another good.

relative price rule at the *optimal consumption bundle*, the *marginal rate of substitution* of one good in place of another is equal to the *relative price*.

rental rate the cost, implicit or explicit, of using a unit of land or *capital* for a given period of time.

reputation a long-term standing in the public regard that serves to reassure others that *private information* is not being concealed; a valuable asset in the face of *adverse selection*.

resource anything, such as land, labour, and *capital*, that can be used to produce something else; includes natural resources (from the physical environment) and human resources (labour, skill, intelligence).

reverse causality the error committed when the true direction of causality between two *variables* is reversed, and the *independent variable* and the *dependent variable* are incorrectly identified.

Ricardian model of international trade a model that analyzes international *trade* under the assumption that *opportunity costs* are constant.

risk uncertainty about future outcomes.

risk-averse describes individuals who choose to reduce *risk* when that reduction leaves the *expected value* of their income or wealth unchanged.

risk-aversion the willingness to sacrifice some economic *payoff* in order to avoid a potential loss.

risk-neutral describes individuals who are completely insensitive to *risk*.

rival in consumption referring to a good, describes the case in which one unit cannot be consumed by more than one person at the same time.

S

sales tax a tax on the value of goods sold.

scarce in short supply; a *resource* is scarce when there is not enough of the resource available to satisfy all the various ways a society wants to use it.

scatter diagram a graph that shows points that correspond to actual observations of the *x*- and *y*-variables; a *curve* is usually fitted to the scatter of points to indicate the trend in the data.

screening using observable information about people to make inferences about their *private information*; a way to reduce *adverse selection*.

share a partial ownership of a company.

shift of the demand curve a change in the *quantity demanded* at any given price, represented graphically by the change of the original *demand curve* to a new position, denoted by a new demand curve.

shift of the supply curve a change in the *quantity supplied* of a good or service at any given price, represented graphically by the change of the original *supply curve* to a new position, denoted by a new supply curve.

short run the time period in which at least one *input* is fixed.

short-run individual supply curve a graphical representation that shows how an individual producer's profit-maximizing output quantity depends on the market price, taking *fixed cost* as given.

short-run industry supply curve a graphical representation that shows how the *quantity supplied* by an industry depends on the market price given a fixed number of producers.

short-run market equilibrium an economic balance that results when the *quantity supplied* equals the *quantity demanded*, taking the number of producers as given.

shortage the insufficiency of a good or service that occurs when the quantity demanded exceeds the quantity supplied; shortages occur when the price is below the *equilibrium price*.

shut-down price the price at which a firm ceases production in the short run because the market price has fallen below the minimum *average variable cost*.

signalling taking some action to establish credibility despite possessing *private information*; a way to reduce *adverse selection*.

single-payer system a health care system in which the government is the principal payer of medical bills funded through taxes.

single-price monopolist a *monopolist* that offers its product to all consumers at the same price.

slope a measure of how steep a line or curve is. The slope of a line is measured by "rise over run"—the change in the *y*-variable between two points on the line divided by the change in the *x*-variable between those same two points.

social insurance program a government program designed to provide protection against unpredictable financial distress.

social welfare program a government program designed to provide payments based on need.

socially optimal quantity of pollution the quantity of pollution that society would choose if all the costs and benefits of pollution were fully accounted for.

specialization the situation in which each person specializes in the task that he or she is good at performing.

standardized product output of different producers regarded by consumers as the same good; also referred to as a *commodity*.

state of the world a possible future event.

status quo bias the tendency to avoid making a decision and sticking with the status quo.

strategic behaviour actions taken by a firm that attempt to influence the future behaviour of other firms.

substitutes pairs of goods for which a rise in the price of one of the goods leads to an increase in the demand for the other good.

substitution effect the change in the quantity of a good consumed as the consumer substitutes other goods that are now relatively cheaper in place of the good that has become relatively more expensive.

sunk cost a cost that has already been incurred and is not recoverable. A sunk cost should be ignored in decisions about future actions.

supply and demand model a model of how a *competitive market* behaves.

supply curve a graphical representation of the *supply schedule*, showing the relationship between *quantity supplied* and price.

supply price the price of a given quantity at which producers will supply that quantity.

supply schedule a list or table showing how much of a good or service producers will supply at different prices.

surplus the excess of a good or service that occurs when the quantity supplied exceeds the quantity demanded; surpluses occur when the price is above the *equilibrium price*.

T

tacit collusion cooperation among producers, without a formal agreement, to limit production and raise prices so as to raise one anothers' profits.

tangency condition on a graph of a consumer's *budget line* and available *indifference curves* of available *consumption bundles*, the point at which an indifference curve and the budget line just touch. When the indifference curves have the typical convex shape, this point determines the *optimal consumption bundle*.

tangent line a straight line that just touches a *non-linear curve* at a particular point; the *slope* of the tangent line is equal to the slope of the non-linear curve at that point.

tariff a tax levied on *imports*.

tax base the measure or value, such as income or property value, that determines how much tax an individual pays.

tax rate the amount of tax people are required to pay per unit of whatever is being taxed.

tax structure specifies how a tax depends on the *tax base*; usually expressed in percentage terms.

technology the technical means for producing goods and services.

technology spillover an *external benefit* that results when knowledge spreads among individuals and firms.

time allocation the decision about how many hours to spend on different activities, which leads to a decision about how much labour to supply.

time allocation budget line an individual's possible *trade-off* between consumption of *leisure* and the income that allows consumption of marketed goods.

time-series graph a two-variable graph that has dates on the *horizontal axis* and values of a *variable* that occurred on those dates on the *vertical axis*.

tit for tat in *game theory*, a strategy that involves playing cooperatively at first, then doing whatever the other player did in the previous period.

total consumer surplus the sum of the *individual consumer surpluses* of all the buyers of a good in a market.

total cost the sum of the *fixed cost* and the *variable cost* of producing a given quantity of output.

total cost curve a graphical representation of the *total cost*, showing how total cost depends on the quantity of output.

total producer surplus the sum of the *individual producer surpluses* of all the sellers of a good in a market.

total product curve a graphical representation of the *production function*, showing how the quantity of output depends on the quantity of the *variable input* for a given quantity of the *fixed input* and production technology.

total revenue the total value of sales of a good or service (the price of the good or service multiplied by the quantity sold).

total surplus the total net gain to consumers and producers from trading in a market; the sum of the *producer surplus* and the *consumer surplus*.

tradable emissions permits *licences* to emit limited quantities of pollutants that can be bought and sold by polluters.

trade the practice, in a *market economy*, in which individuals provide goods and services to others and receive goods and services in return.

trade protection policies that limit *imports*.

trade-off a comparison of costs and benefits of doing something.

trade-off between equity and efficiency the dynamic whereby a well-designed tax system can be made more efficient only by making it less fair, and vice versa.

transaction costs the costs to individuals of making a deal.

truncated cut; in a truncated axis, some of the range of values are omitted, usually to save space or to make changes to a *variable* appear larger.

U

U-shaped average total cost curve a distinctive graphical representation of the relationship between output and *average total cost;* the average total cost curve at first falls when output is low and then rises as output increases.

unions organizations of workers that try to raise wages and improve working conditions for their members by bargaining collectively with employers.

unit-elastic demand the case in which the *price elasticity of demand* is exactly 1.

util a unit of *utility*.

utility (of a consumer) a measure of the satisfaction derived from consumption of goods and services.

utility function (of an individual) the total *utility* generated by an individual's *consumption bundle*.

utility-maximizing principle of marginal analysis the principle that the *marginal utility per dollar* spent must be the same for all goods and services in the *optimal consumption bundle*.

V

value of the marginal product the value of the additional output generated by employing one more unit of a given factor, such as labour.

value of the marginal product curve a graphical representation showing how the *value of the marginal product* of a factor depends on the quantity of the factor employed.

variable a quantity that can take on more than one value.

variable cost a cost that depends on the quantity of output produced; the cost of the least amount of the *variable input* needed to make the quantity of output.

variable input an *input* whose quantity the firm can vary at any time (for example, labour).

vertical axis the vertical number line of a graph along which values of the *y*-variable are measured; also referred to as the *y-axis*.

vertical intercept the point at which a *curve* hits the *vertical axis;* it shows the value of the *y*-variable when the value of the *x*-variable is zero.

W

wasted resources a form of inefficiency in which people expend money, effort, and time to cope with the shortages caused by a *price ceiling*.

wealth tax a tax on the wealth of an individual.

wedge the difference between the *demand price* of the quantity transacted and the *supply price* of the quantity transacted for a good when the supply of the good is legally restricted. Often created by a *quantity control*, or *quota*.

welfare state the collection of government programs designed to alleviate economic hardship.

willingness to pay the maximum price a consumer is prepared to pay for a good.

world price the price at which a good can be bought or sold abroad.

World Trade Organization (WTO) an international organization of member countries that oversees *international trade agreements* and rules on disputes between countries over those agreements.

X

x-axis the horizontal number line of a graph along which values of the *x*-variable are measured; also referred to as the *horizontal axis*.

Y

y-axis the vertical number line of a graph along which values of the *y*-variable are measured; also referred to as the *vertical axis*.

Z

zero-profit equilibrium an economic balance in which each firm makes zero profit at its profit-maximizing quantity.